THE DEVOTIONAL CLASSICS OF C. H. SPURGEON

A BOOK OF DAILY DEVOTIONS CONTAINING
MORNING & EVENING
AND
MORNING & EVENING II
by
C. H Spurgeon

This is Volume I of the Twelve Volume Set Entitled
THE FIFTY GREATEST CHRISTIAN CLASSICS

Published by
Sovereign Grace Publishers, Inc.
P.O. Box 4998
Lafayette, IN 47903

The Devotional Classics of C. H. Spurgeon
contains two books in one volume.
This is Volume 1 of the Twelve Volume Set
Entitled *The Fifty Greatest Christian Classics*

Morning and Evening
is in the public domain.

Morning and Evening II
Copyright © 1990
By Jay P. Green, Sr.

ISBN 978-1-58960-166-6 - Hard Cover Edition

Printed in the United States of America

PUBLISHER'S PREFACE

"I have preached righteousness in the great congregation; lo, I have not kept back my lips, O Lord, You know" — Psalm 40:9.

The first volume of daily devotions by Mr. Spurgeon has delighted and edified countless generations. This second volume has also been selected from his many sermons, or from his justly praised seven-volume set, *The Treasury of David*. It also has met with immediate success, as the Lord has blessed it to many hearts.

In this volume devotions from other famed men of God have been selected, many of these also from Spurgeon's *Treasury of David*. As anyone will know who have had close acquaintance with Mr. Spurgeon's writings, he was an admirer of and lover of all godly men. And this caused him to cherish the great Puritan writers. Because of this he read tens of thousands of pages of their works, and as he did so he would copy out large selections from them. These he might quote copiously in his sermons, and certainly he printed them at length in his work on the Psalms. He also published at least two whole books consisting entirely of sayings of these authors. If the reader of these devotions could but get the pleasure, the joy and the inspiration from them that Mr. Spurgeon derived, then our prayers and his will surely be answered.

Though this volume was finally edited by Jay P. Green, Sr., the credit must go to the one who selected these devotions from Mr. Spurgeon's works: Rebecca Kay Thorpe. She has spent many long hours, with pleasure as well as with much labor, searching through thousands of pages in order to stimulate spiritual growth in the saints who love the Lord enough to meditate on these devotions mornign and evening.

May it please Him through whom we all receive every good and precious gift to bless you as you take these God-honoring thoughts into your heart.

Jay P. Green, Sr. and Rebecca Kay Thorpe
Editors

(Quotations from the Bible are often from *The King James II Version*)

PUBLISHER'S PREFACE

"Blessed is the man who has not walked in the counsel of the ungodly, and has not stood in the way of sinners, and has not sat in the seat of scorners. But his delight is only in the law of Jehovah, and he meditates in His law day and night." — Psalm 1:1, 2

"The delightful study of the Psalms has yielded me boundless profit and ever-growing pleasure. Common gratitude constrains me to communicate to others a portion of the benefit, with the prayer that it may induce them to search further for themselves" (From his preface to the first edition of *The Treasury of David*).

Those comments bare the heart of Charles Haddon Spurgeon, a preacher of righteousness, and to my mind a man after God's own heart. Anyone with only a brief acquaintance with the fruits of his pen must see that this famed but humble soul lived and breathed the Word of God. In a ministry that covered forty years he served his God and Savior Jesus Christ diligently, faithfully, unflinchingly, courageously.

The reader of these daily devotions will quickly discover that Mr. Spurgeon *"did not keep back from declaring to you all the counsel of God"* (Acts 20:27). In his heart he magified the Lord; his heart panted after Him *"as the hart pants after the waterbrooks,"* and so in his devotions he did not forget the teachings of Holy Scripture. These devotions which he has written for the saints of God reflect his own personal devotions. Any sincere lover of God and of His Word should cherish the many brilliant gleams of heavenly light which leap from every page of this volume. And if he bears down on the doctrines of grace which have been hidden from view by an ungodly age, it will soon prove to be a blessing of the highest degree to those who *"seek to know the Lord,"* and to *"grow in grace and knowledge of our Lord and Savior, Jesus Christ"* (2 Peter 3:18).

Morning and Evening has been of great benefit to generations of the children of God, and because of its impact on the hearts of myriads has remained in print for a hundred years. This is the third time that I have had the joy of prresenting an edition to the Christian public. And, God willing, it will not be the last. With love toward all the saints, we pray that as you read these devotions day by day you will find yourselves fervently saying, *'To Him be the glory, both now and to the day of eternity"* (2 Peter 3:18)

Jay P. Green, Sr.,
General Editor

(Quotations from the Bible are often from *The King James II Version.*)

MORNING — January 1

" They ate the fruit of the land of Canaan that year" — Joshua 5:1,

ISRAEL'S WEARY wanderings were all over, and the promised rest was attained. No more moving tents, fiery serpents, fierce Amalekites, and howling wildernesses. They came to the land which flowed with milk and honey, and they ate the old grain of the land. Perhaps this year, beloved Christian reader, this may be your case or mine. Joyful is the prospect, and if faith be in active exercise, it will yield unalloyed delight. To be with Jesus in the rest which remains for the people of God, is a cheering hope indeed, and to expect this glory so soon is double bliss. Unbelief shudders at the Jordan which still rolls between us and the goodly land, but let us rest assured that we have already experienced more ills than death at its worst can cause us. Let us banish every fearful thought, and rejoice with exceeding great joy in the prospect that this year we shall begin to be forever with the Lord.

A part of the host will this year tarry on earth, to do service for their Lord. If this should fall to our lot, there is no reason why the New Year's test should not still be true. *"We who have believed do enter into rest."* The Holy Spirit is the earnest of our inheritance; He gives us *"glory begun below."* In heaven they are secure, and so are we preserved in Christ Jesus; there they triumph over their enemies, and we have victories too. Celestial spirits enjoy communion with their Lord, and this is not denied to us; they rest in His love, and we have perfect peace in Him: they hymn His praise, and it is our privilege to bless Him too. We will this year gather celestial fruits on earthly ground, where faith and hope have made the desert like the garden of the Lord. Man did eat angels' food of old, and why not now? Oh for grace to feed on Jesus, and so to eat of the fruit of the land of Canaan this year!

EVENING

"We will be glad and rejoice in You" — Song of Solomon 1:4

WE WILL BE glad and rejoice in You. We will not open the gates of the year to the dolorous notes of the sackbut, but to the sweet strains of the harp of joy, and the high sounding cymbals of gladness. *"Oh come, let us sing unto the Lord: let us make a joyful noise unto the rock of our salvation."* We, the called and faithful and chosen, we will drive away our griefs, and set up our banners of confidence in the name of God. Let others lament over their troubles, we who have the sweetening tree to cast into Marah's bitter pool, with joy will magnify the Lord. Eternal Spirit, our effectual Comforter, we who are the temples in which You dwell will never cease from adoring and blessing the name of Jesus. We will do it, we are resolved about it, Jesus must have the crown of our heart's delight. We will not dishonor our Bridegroom by mourning in His presence. We are ordained to be the minstrels of the skies, let us rehearse our everlasting anthem before we sing it in the halls of the New Jerusalem.

We will be glad and rejoice: two words with one sense, double joy, blessedness upon blessedness. Need there be any limit to our rejoicing in the Lord, to be camphor and spikenard, calamus and cinnamon even now, and what better fragrance have they in heaven itself? We will be glad and rejoice in You. That last word is the meat in the dish, the kernel of the nut, the soul of the text. What heavens are laid up in Jesus! What rivers of infinite bliss have their source, aye, and every drop of their fulness in Him! Since, 0 sweet Lord Jesus, You are the present portion of Your people, favor us this year with such a sense of Your preciousness, that from its first to its last day we may be glad and rejoice in You. Let January open with joy in the Lord, and December close with gladness in Jesus.

January 2   MORNING

Continue in prayer"— Colossians 4:2

IT IS INTERESTING to remark how large a portion of Sacred Writ is occupied with the subject of prayer, either in furnishing examples, enforcing precepts, or pronouncing promises. We scarcely open the Bible before we read, *"Then began men to call upon the name of the Lord;"* and just as we are about to close the volume, the *Amen* of an earnest supplication meets our ear. Instances are plentiful. Here we find a wrestling Jacob — there a Daniel who prayed three times a day — and a David who with all his heart called upon his God. On the mountain we see Elijah; in the dungeon Paul and Silas. We have multitudes of commands, and myriads of promises. What does this teach us, but the sacred importance and necessity of prayer? We may be certain that whatever God has made prominent in His Word, He intended to be conspicuous in our lives. If He has said much about prayer, it is because He knows we have much need of it. So deep are our necessities, that until we are in heaven we must not cease to pray. Do you lack nothing? Then, I fear you do not know your poverty. Have you no mercy to ask of God? Then, may the Lord's mercy show you your misery!

A prayerless soul is a Christless soul. Prayer is the lisping of the believing infant, the shout of the fighting believer, the requiem of the dying saint falling asleep in Jesus. It is the breath, the watchword, the comfort, the strength, the honor of a Christian. If you be a child of God, you will seek your Father's face, and live in your Father's love. Pray that this year you may be holy, humble, zealous, and patient; have closer communion with Christ, and enter more often into the banqueting-house of His love. Pray that you may be an example and a blessing unto others, and that you may live more to the glory of your Master. The motto for this year must be, *"Continue in prayer."*

EVENING

"Let the people renew their strength" — Isaiah 41:1.

ALL THINGS ON earth need to be renewed. No created thing continues by itself. *"You renew the face of the year,"* was the Psalmist's utterance. Even the trees, which wear not themselves with care, nor shorten their lives with labor, must drink of the rain of heaven and suck from the hidden treasures of the soil. The cedars of Lebanon, which God has planted, only live because day by day they are full of sap fresh drawn from the earth.

Neither can man's life be sustained without renewal from God. As it is necessary to repair the waste of the body by the frequent meal, so we must repair the waste of the soul by feeding upon the Book of God, or by listening to the preached Word, or by the soul-fattening table of the ordinances. How depressed are our graces when means are neglected! What poor starvelings some saints are who live without the diligent use of the Word of God and secret prayer! If our piety can live without God it is not of divine creating; it is but a dream; for if God had begotten it, it would wait upon Him as the flowers wait upon the dew. Without constant restoration we are not ready for the perpetual assaults of hell, or the stern afflictions of heaven, or even for the strifes within. When the whirlwind shall be loosed, woe to the tree that has not sucked up fresh sap, and grasped the rock with many intertwisted roots. When tempests arise, woe to the mariners that have not strengthened their mast, nor cast their anchor, nor sought their haven. If we suffer the good to grow weaker, the evil will surely gather strength and struggle desperately for the mastery over us; and so; perhaps, a painful desolation, and a lamentable disgrace may follow.

Let us draw near to the footstool of divine mercy in humble entreaty, and we shall realize the fulfilment of the promise, *"They that wait on the Lord shall renew their strength."*

MORNING   January 3

"I will give You for a covenant of the people"—Isaiah 49:8.

JESUS CHRIST is Himself the sum and substance of the covenant, and as one of its gifts He is the property of every believer. Believer, can you estimate what you have gotten in Christ? *"In Him dwells all the fulness of the Godhead bodily."* Consider that word *God* and its infinity, and then meditate upon *perfect Man* and all his beauty; for all that Christ, as God and man, ever had, or can have, is yours. Out of pure free favor, all has passed over to you to be your entailed property for ever. Our blessed Jesus, as God, is omniscient, omnipresent, omnipotent. Will it not console you to know that all these great and glorious attributes are altogether yours? Has He power? That power is yours to support and strengthen you, to overcome your enemies, and to preserve you even to the end. Has He love? Well, there is not a drop of love in His heart which is not yours; you may dive into the immense ocean of His love, and you may say of it all, It is mine. Has He justice? It may seem a stern attribute, but even that is yours, for He will by His justice see to it that all which is promised to you in the covenant of grace shall be most certainly secured to you.

And all that He has as perfect Man is yours. As a perfect Man the Father's delight was upon Him. He stood accepted by the Most High. O believer, God's acceptance of Christ is your acceptance; for know you not that the love which the Father set on a perfect Christ, He sets on you now? For all that Christ did is yours. That perfect righteousness which Jesus worked out, when through His stainless life He kept the law and made it honorable, is yours, and is imputed to you. Christ is in the covenant.

My God, I am yours — what a comfort divine! What a blessing to know that the Savior is mine! In the heavenly Lamb thrice happy I am, And my heart it does dance at the sound of His name.

EVENING

"The voice of one crying in the wilderness. Prepare the way of the Lord. Make His paths straight"—Luke 3:4.

THE VOICE CRYING in the wilderness demanded a way for the Lord, a way prepared, and a way prepared in the wilderness. I would be attentive to the Master's proclamation, and give Him a road into my heart, cast up by gracious operations, through the desert of my nature. The four directions in the text must have my serious attention.

Every valley must be exalted. Low and groveling thoughts of God must be given up; doubting and despairing must be removed; and self.seeking and carnal delights must be forsaken. Across these deep valleys a glorious causeway of grace must be raised.

Every mountain and hill shall be laid low. Proud creature-sufficiency, and boastful self-righteousness, must be leveled, to make a highway for the King of kings. Divine fellowship is never vouchsafed to haughty, highminded sinners. The Lord has respect unto the lowly, and visits the contrite in heart, but the lofty are an abomination unto Him. My soul, beseech the Holy Spirit to set you right in this respect.

The crooked shall be made straight. The wavering heart must have a straight path of decision for God and holiness marked out for it. Double-minded men are strangers to the God of truth. My soul, take heed that you be in all things honest and true, as in the sight of the heart-searching God.

The rough places shall be made smooth. Stumbling-blocks of sin must be removed, and thorns and briers of rebellion must be uprooted. So great a visitor must not find miry ways and stony places when He comes to honor His favored ones with His company. Oh that this evening the Lord may find in my heart a highway made ready by His grace, that He may make a triumphal progress through the utmost bounds of my soul, from the beginning of this year even to the end of it.

January 4

MORNING

"Grow in grace and in the knowledge of our Lord and Savior Jesus Christ"—2 Peter 3:18.

"GROW IN GRACE" — not in one grace only, but in all grace. Grow in that root-grace, faith. Believe the promises more firmly than you have done. Let faith increase in fulness, constancy, simplicity. Grow also in love. Ask that your love may become extended, more intense, more practical, influencing every thought, word, and deed. Grow likewise in humility. Seek to lie very low, and know more of your own nothingness. As you grow downward in humility, seek also to grow upward, having nearer approaches to God in prayer and more intimate fellowship with Jesus.

May God the Holy Spirit enable you to *"grow in grace and in the knowledge of our Lord and Savior Jesus Christ."* He who grows not in the knowledge of Jesus, refuses to be blessed. To know Him is life eternal, and to advance in the knowledge of Him is to increase in happiness. He who does not long to know more of Christ, knows nothing of Him yet. Whoever has sipped this wine will thirst for more, for although Christ does satisfy, yet it is such a satisfaction, that the appetite is not cloyed, but whetted. If you know the love of Jesus, as the hart pants for the waterbrooks, so will you pant after deeper draughts of His love. If you do not desire to know Him better, then you love Him not, for love always cries, *"Nearer, nearer."* Absence from Christ is hell; but the presence of Jesus is heaven.

Then do not rest content without an increasing acquaintance with Jesus. Seek to know more of Him, in His divine nature, in His human relationship, in His finished work, in His death, in His resurrection, in His present glorious intercession, and in His future royal advent. Abide hard by the Cross, and search the mystery of His wounds. An increase of love to Jesus, and a more perfect apprehension of His love to us, is one of the best tests of growth in grace.

EVENING

"And Joseph knew his brothers, but they did not know him."— Genesis 42:8

THIS morning our desires went forth for growth in our acquaintance with the Lord Jesus; it may be well tonight to consider a kindred topic, namely, our heavenly Joseph's knowledge of us. This was most blessedly perfect long before we had the slightest knowledge of Him. *"Your eyes saw my embryo, and in Your book* my members LIwere written; the days they were formed, and none was among them" — (Psalm 139:15 LTB). Before we had a being in the world we had a being in His heart. When we were enemies to Him, He knew us, our misery, our madness, and our wickedness. When we wept bitterly in despairing repentance, and viewed Him only as a judge and a ruler, He viewed us as His well-beloved, and His bowels yearned towards us. He never mistook His chosen, but always beheld them as objects of His infinite affection. *"The Lord knows the ones that are His,"* is as true of the prodigals who are feeding swine as of the children who sit at the table.

But, alas! we knew not our royal Brother, and out of this ignorance grew a host of sins. We withheld our hearts from Him, and allowed Him no entrance to our love. We mistrusted Him, and gave no credit to His words. We rebelled against Him, and paid Him no loving homage. The Son of Righteousness shone forth, and we could not see Him. Heaven came down to earth, and earth perceived it not. Let God be praised, those days are over with us; yet even now it is but little that we know of Jesus compared with what He knows of us. We have but begun to study Him, but He knows us altogether. It is a blessed circumstance that the ignorance is not on His side, for then it would be a hopeless case for us. He will not say to us, *"I never knew you,"* but He will confess our names in the day of His appearing, and meanwhile will manifest Himself to us as He does not unto the world.

MORNING   January 5

"And God saw the light that it was good. And God divided between the light and the darkness" — Genesis 1:4.

LIGHT might well be good, since it sprang from that fiat of goodness, *"Let there be light."* We who enjoy it should be more grateful for it than we are, and see more of God in it and by it. Light physical is said by Solomon to be sweet, but gospel light is infinitely more precious, for it reveals eternal things, and ministers to our immortal natures. When the Holy Spirit gives us spiritual light, and opens our eyes to behold the glory of God in the face of Jesus Christ, we behold sin in its true colors, and ourselves in our real position; we see the Most Holy God as He reveals Himself, the plan of mercy as He propounds it, and the world to come as the Word describes it. Spiritual light has many beams and prismatic colors, but whether they be knowledge, joy, holiness, or life, all are divinely good. If the light received be thus good, what must the essential light be, and how glorious must be the place where He reveals Himself! O Lord, since light is so good, give us more of it, and more of Yourself, the true light.

No sooner is there a good thing in the world, than a division is necessary. Light and darkness have no communion; God has divided them, let us not confound them. Sons of light must not have fellowship with deeds, doctrines, or deceits of darkness. The children of the day must be sober, honest, and bold in their Lord's work, leaving the works of darkness to those who shall dwell in it for ever. Our Churches should by discipline divide the light from the darkness, and we should by our distinct separation from the world do the same. In judgment, in action, in hearing, in teaching, in association, we must discern between the precious and the vile, and maintain the great distinction which the Lord made upon the world's first day. Oh Lord Jesus, be our light throughout the whole of this day, for Your light is the light of men.

EVENING
"And God saw the light" — Genesis 1:4.

THIS morning we noticed the goodness of the light, and the Lord's dividing it from the darkness, we now note the special eye which the Lord had for the light. *"God saw the light."* He looked at it with complacency, gazed upon it with pleasure, saw that it *"was good"*. If the Lord has given you light, dear reader, He looks on that light with peculiar interest; for not only is it dear to Him as His own handiwork, but because it is like Himself for *"He is light."* Pleasant it is to the believer to know that God's eye is thus tenderly observant of that work of grace which He has begun. He never loses sight of the treasure which He has placed in our earthen vessels. Sometimes we cannot see the light, but God always sees the light, and that is much better than our seeing it. Better for the judge to see my innocence than for me to think I see it. It is very comfortable for me to know that I am one of God's people. But whether I know it or not, if the Lord knows it, I am still safe.

This is the foundation, *"The Lord knows the ones that are His"* (2 Tim. 2:19). You may be sighing and groaning because of inbred sin, and mourning over your darkness, yet the Lord sees *light* in your heart, for He has put it there, and all the cloudiness and gloom of your soul cannot conceal your light from His gracious eye. You may have sunk low in despondency, and even despair; but if your soul has any longing towards Christ, and if you are seeking to rest in His finished work, God sees the *light.* He not only sees it, but He also preserves it in you. *"I, the Lord, do keep it."* This is a precious thought to those who, after anxious watching and guarding of themselves, feel their own powerlessness to do so. The light thus preserved by His grace, He will one day develop into the splendor of noonday, and the fulness of glory. The light within is the dawn of the eternal day.

January 6   MORNING

"Throwing all your care on Him, because He cares for you" – 1 Peter 5:7.

IT IS a happy way of soothing sorrow when we can feel *"HE cares for me."* Christian! do not dishonor your religion by always wearing a brow of care; come, cast your burden upon your Lord. You are staggering beneath a weight which your Father would not feel. What seems to you a crushing burden, would be to Him but as the small dust of the balance. Nothing is so sweet as to lie passive in God's hands, and to know no will but His.

O child of suffering, be patient; God has not passed you over in His providence. He who is the feeder of sparrows, will also furnish you with what you need. Do not sit down in despair; hope on, hope ever. Take up the arms of faith against a sea of trouble, and your opposition shall yet end your distresses. There is One who cares for you. His eye is fixed on you, His heart beats with pity for your woe, and His omnipotent hand shall yet bring you the needed help. The darkest cloud shall scatter itself in showers of mercy. The blackest gloom shall give place to the morning. He, if you are one of His family, will bind up your wounds, and heal your broken heart. Doubt not His grace because of your tribulation, but believe that He loves you as much in seasons of trouble as in times of happiness.

What a serene and quiet life might you lead if you would leave providing to the God of providence! With a little oil in the cruse, and a handful of meal in the barrel, Elijah outlived the famine, and you will do the same. If God cares for you, why need you care too? Can you trust Him for your soul, and not for your body? He has never refused to bear your burdens, He has never fainted under their weight. Come, then, soul, be done with fretful care, and leave all your concerns in the hand of a gracious God.

EVENING

" Then the hand of the LORD was on me in the evening" – Ezekiel 33:22.

IN THE WAY of judgment this may be the case, and, if so, be it mine to consider the reason of such a visitation, and bear the rod and Him that has appointed it. I am not the only one who is chastened in the night season; let me cheerfully submit to the affliction, and carefully endeavor to be profited by it. But the hand of the Lord may also be felt in another manner, strengthening the soul and lifting the spirit upward towards eternal things. Oh that I may in this sense feel the Lord dealing with me! A sense of the divine presence and indwelling bears the soul towards heaven as upon the wings of eagles. At such times we are full to the brim with spiritual joy, and forget the cares and sorrows of earth; the invisible is near, and the visible loses its power over us. The servant-body waits at the foot of the hill, and the master-spirit worships upon the summit in the presence of the Lord.

Oh that a hallowed season of divine communion may be vouchsafed to me this evening! The Lord knows that I need it very greatly. My graces languish, my corruptions rage, my faith is weak, my devotion is cold; all these are reasons why His healing hand should be laid upon me. His hand can cool the heat of my burning brow, and stay the tumult of my palpitating heart. That glorious right hand which molded the world can new-create my mind; the unwearied hand which bears the earth's pillars up can sustain my spirit. The loving hand which encloses all the saints can cherish me; and the mighty hand which breaks in pieces the enemy can subdue my sins. Why should I not feel that hand touching me this evening? Come, my soul, address your God with the potent plea, that Jesus' hands were pierced for your redemption, and you shall surely feel that same hand upon you which once touched Daniel and set him upon his knees that he might see visions of God.

MORNING January 7

"For me to live is Christ!" — Philippians 1:21.

THE BELIEVER did not always live to Christ. He began to do so when God the Holy Spirit convicted him of sin, and when by grace he was brought to see tahat he dying Savior made a propitiation for his guilt. From the moment of the new and celestial birth the man begins to live to Christ. Jesus is to believers the one pearl of great price, for whom we are willing to part with all that we have. He has so completely won our love, that it beats alone for Him; to His glory we would live, and in defence of His gospel we would die; He is the pattern of our life, and the model after which we would sculpture our character. Paul's words mean more than most men think; they imply that the aim and end of his life was Christ; no, his life itself was Jesus. In the words of an ancient saint, he did eat, and drink and sleep eternal life. Jesus was his very breath, the soul of his soul, the heart of his heart, the life of his life.

Can you say, as a professing Christian, that you live up to this idea? Can you honestly say that for you to live is Christ? Your business, are you doing it for Christ? Is it not done for self-aggrandizement and for family advantage? Do you ask, "Is that a mean reason? For the Christian it is. He professes to live for Christ; how can he live for another object without committing a spiritual adultery? Many there are who carry out this principle in some measure; but who is there that dare say that he has lived wholly for Christ as the apostle did? Yet, this alone is the true life of a Christian. It is its source, its sustenance, its fashion, its end, all gathered up in one word Christ Jesus.

Lord, accept me; I here present myself, praying to live only in You and to You. Let me be as the bullock which stands between the plough and the altar, to work or to be sacrificed; and let my motto be, "Ready for either."

EVENING

" My sister, My spouse" — Song of Solomon 4:1.

OBSERVE THE sweet titles with which the heavenly Solomon with intense affection addresses His bride the church. *"My sister,"* one near to me by ties of nature, partaker of the same sympathies. *"My spouse"*, nearest and dearest, united to me by the tenderest bands of love; my sweet companion, part of my own self. My sister, by my Incarnation, which makes me bone of your bone and flesh of your flesh; my spouse, by heavenly betrothal, in which I have espoused you unto myself in righteousness. My sister, whom I knew of old, and over whom I watched from her earliest infancy; my spouse, taken from among the daughters, embraced by arms of love, and affianced unto me forever. See how true it is that our royal Kinsman is not ashamed of us, for He dwells with manifest delight upon this two-fold relationship.

We have the word *"My"* twice in our version; as if Christ dwelt with rapture on His possession of His Church. *"His delights were with the sons of men,"* because those sons of men were His own chosen ones. He, the Shepherd, sought the sheep, because they were His sheep; He has gone about *"to seek and to save that which was lost,"* because that which was lost was His long before it was lost to itself or lost to Him. The church is the exclusive portion of her Lord; none else may claim a partnership, or pretend to share her love. Jesus, Your church delights to have it so! Let every believing soul drink solace out of these wells. Soul! Christ is near to you in ties of relationship; Christ is dear to you in bonds of marriage union, and you are dear to Him. Behold! He grasps both of your hands with both His own, saying, *"My sister, My spouse."* Mark the two sacred hold fasts by which your Lord gets such a double hold of you that He neither can nor will ever let you go. Be not, beloved, slow to return the hallowed flame of His love.

January 8   MORNING

"The iniquity of the holy things" — Exodus 28:38.

WHAT A VEIL is lifted up by these words, and what a disclosure is made! It will be humbling and profitable for us to pause awhile and see this sad sight. The iniquities of our public worship, its hypocrisy, formality, lukewarmness, irreverence, wandering of heart and forgetfulness of God, what a full measure have we there! Our work for the Lord, its emulation, selfishness, carelessness, slackness, unbelief, what a mass of defilement is there! Our private devotions, their laxity, coldness, neglect, sleepiness, and vanity, what a mountain of dead earth is there!

If we looked more carefully we should find this iniquity to be far greater than appears at first sight. Dr. Payson, writing to his brother, says, "My parish, as well as my heart, very much resembles the garden of the sluggard; and what is worse, I find that very many of my desires for the amelioration of both, proceed either from pride or vanity or indolence. I look at the weeds which overspread my garden, and breathe out an earnest wish that they were eradicated. But why? What prompts the wish? It may be that I may walk out and say to myself, In what fine order is my garden kept! This is pride. Or, it may be that my neighbors may look over the wall and say, How finely your garden flourishes! This is vanity. Or I may wish for the destruction of the weeds, because I am weary of pulling them up. This is indolence." So that even our desires after holiness may be polluted by ill motives. Under the greenest sods worms hide themselves; we need not look long to discover them.

How cheering is the thought, that when the High Priest bore the iniquity of the holy things he wore upon his brow the words, *"HOLINESS TO THE LORD:"* and even so while Jesus bears our sin, He presents before His Father's face not our unholiness, but His own holiness. Oh for grace to view our great High Priest by the eye of faith!

EVENING

"For Your love is better than wine" — Song of Solomon 1:2.

NOTHING GIVES THE believer so much joy as fellowship with Christ. He has enjoyment as others have in the common mercies of life. Life can be glad both in God's gifts and God's works; but in all these separately, yes, and in all of them added together, he does not find such substantial delight as in the matchless person of his Lord Jesus. He has wine which no vineyard on earth ever yielded; he has bread which all the grain fields of Egypt could never bring forth.

Where can such sweetness be found as we have tasted in communion with our Beloved? In our esteem, the joys of earth are little better than husks for swine compared with Jesus, the heavenly manna. We would rather have one mouthful of Christ's love, and a sip of His fellowship, than a whole world full of carnal delights. What is the chaff to the wheat? What is the sparkling paste to the true diamond? What is a dream to the glorious reality? What is time's mirth, in its best trim, compared to our Lord Jesus in His most despised estate? If you know anything of the inner life, you will confess that our highest, purest, and most enduring joys must be the fruit of the tree of life which is in the midst of the Paradise of God. No spring yields such sweet water as that well of God which was dug with the soldier's spear. All earthly bliss is of the earth earthy, but the comforts of Christ's presence are like Himself, heavenly.

We can review our communion with Jesus, and find no regrets of emptiness therein; there are no dregs in this wine, no dead flies in this ointment. The joy of the Lord is solid and enduring. Vanity has not looked upon it, but discretion and prudence testify that it abideth the test of years, and is in time and in eternity worthy to be called *"the only true delight."* For nourishment, consolation, exhilaration, and refreshment, no wine can rival the love of Jesus. Let us drink to the full this evening.

MORNING — January 9

"I will be their God" — Jeremiah 31:33.

CHRISTIAN! HERE IS all you can require. To make you happy you want something that shall satisfy you; and is not this enough? If you can pour this promise into your cup, will you not say, with David, *"My cup runs over; I have more than heart can wish"*? When this is fulfilled, *"I am your God,"* are you not possessor of all things? Desire is insatiable as death, but He who fills all in all can fill it. The capacity of our wishes who can measure? But the immeasurable wealth of God can more than overflow it. I ask you if you are not complete when God is yours? Do you want anything but God? Is not His all-sufficiency enough to satisfy you if all else should fail?

But you want more than quiet satisfaction; you desire rapturous delight. Come, soul, here is music fit for heaven in this portion of yours, for God is the Maker of Heaven. Not all the music blown from sweet instruments, or drawn from living strings, can yield such melody as this sweet promise, *"I will be their God."* Here is a deep sea of bliss, a shoreless ocean of delight; come, bathe your spirit in it; swim an age, and you shall find no shore; dive throughout eternity, and you shall find no bottom. *"I will be their God"* — if this does not make your eyes sparkle, and your heart beat high with bliss, then assuredly your soul is not in a healthy state.

But you desire more than present delights; you crave something concerning which you may exercise hope? What more can you hope for than the fulfilment of this great promise, *"I will be their God"*? This is the masterpiece of all the promises; its enjoyment makes a heaven below, and will make a heaven above. Dwell in the light of your Lord, and let your soul be always ravished with His love. Get out the marrow and fatness which this portion yields you. Live up to your privileges, and rejoice with unspeakable joy.

EVENING

"Serve the LORD with gladness" — Psalm 100:2.

DELIGHT IN DIVINE service is a token of acceptance. Those who serve God with a sad countenance, because they do what is unpleasant to them, are not serving Him at all; they bring the form of homage, but the life is absent. Our God requires no slaves to grace His throne; He is the Lord of the empire of love, and would have His servants dressed in the livery of joy. The angels of God serve Him with songs, not with groans; a murmur or a sigh would be a mutiny in their ranks.

That obedience which is not voluntary is disobedience, for the Lord looks at the heart, and if He sees that we serve Him from force, and not because we love Him, He will reject our offering. Service coupled with cheerfulness is heart service, and therefore true. Take away joyful willingness from the Christian, and you have removed the test of his sincerity. If a man be driven to battle, he is no patriot; but he who marches into the fray with flashing eye and beaming face, singing, *"It is sweet for one's country to die,"* proves himself to be sincere in his patriotism. Cheerfulness is the support of our strength; in the joy of the Lord are we strong. It acts as the remover of difficulties. It is to our service what oil is to the wheels of a railway carriage. Without oil the axle soon grows hot, and accidents occur; and if there be not a holy cheerfulness to oil our wheels, our spirits will be clogged with weariness. The man who is cheerful in his service of God, proves that obedience is his element; he can sing,

> Make me to walk in Your commands,
> It is a delightful road.

Reader, let us put this question: do you serve the Lord with gladness? Let us show to the people of the world, who think our religion to be bondage, that it is to us a delight and joy! Let our gladness proclaim that we serve a good Master.

January 10 MORNING

"Now the crown of righteousness is laid up for me" — 2 Timothy 4:8.

DOUBTING ONE! You have often said, I fear I shall never enter heaven. Fear not! All the people of God shall enter there. I love the quaint saying of a dying man, who exclaimed, I have no fear of going home; I have sent all before me; God's finger is on the latch of my door, and I am ready for Him to enter. But one said, Are you not afraid lest you should miss your inheritance? He said, No, no; there is one crown in heaven which the angel Gabriel could not wear; it will fit no head but mine. There is one throne in heaven which Paul the apostle could not fill; it was made for me, and I shall have it. Oh Christian, what a joyous thought! your portion is secure? *"there remains a rest"* (Hebrews 4:9).

But cannot I forfeit it? No; it is entailed. If I be a child of God I shall not lose it. It is mine as securely as if I were there. Come with me, believer, and let us sit upon the top of Nebo, and view the goodly land, even Canaan. Do you see that little river of death glistening in the sunlight, and across it do you see the pinnacles of the eternal city? Do you mark the pleasant country and all its joyous inhabitants? Know, then, that if you could fly across you would see written upon one of its many mansions, This remains for such a one; preserved for him only. He shall be caught up to dwell forever with God. Poor doubting one, see the fair inheritance; it is yours. If you believe in the Lord Jesus, if you have repented of sin, if you have been renewed in heart, you are one of the Lord's people, and there is a place reserved for you, a crown laid up for you, a harp specially provided for you. No one else shall have your portion, it is reserved in heaven for you, and you shall have it before long, for there shall be no vacant thrones in glory when all the chosen are gathered in.

EVENING

"In my flesh I shall see God" — Job 19:26.

MARK THE SUBJECT of Job's devout anticipation: *"I shall see God."* He does not say, *"I shall see the saints"* — though doubtless that will be untold felicity — but, *"I shall see God."* It is not, I shall see the pearly gates, I shall behold the walls of jasper, I shall gaze upon the crowns of gold, but *"I shall see God."* This is the sum and substance of heaven, this is the joyful hope of all believers. It is their delight to see Him now in the ordinances by faith. They love to behold Him in communion and in prayer; but there in heaven they shall have an open and unclouded vision, and thus seeing *"Him as He is,"* shall be made completely like Him. Likeness to God; what can we wish for more? And a sight of God; what can we desire better?

Some read the passage, *"Yet, I shall see God in my flesh,"* and find here an allusion to Christ, as the *"Word made flesh,"* and that glorious beholding of Him which shall be the splendor of the latter days. Whether so or not it is certain that Christ shall be the object of our eternal vision; nor shall we ever want any joy beyond that of seeing Him. Think not that this will be a narrow sphere for the mind to dwell in. It is but one source of delight, but that source is infinite. All His attributes shall be subjects for contemplation, and as He is infinite under each aspect, there is no fear of exhaustion. His works, His gifts, His love to us, and His glory in all His purposes, and in all His actions, these shall make a theme which will be ever new. The patriarch looked forward to this sight of God as a personal enjoyment. *"Whom my eye shall behold, and not another."* Take realizing views of heaven's bliss; think what it will be to you. Your eyes shall see the King in His beauty. All earthly brightness fades and darkens as we gaze upon it, but here is a brightness which can never dim, a glory which can never fade, *"I shall see God.*

MORNING   January 11

"These have no root" — Luke 8:13.

MY SOUL, EXAMINE yourself this morning by the light of this text. You have received the word with joy; your feelings have been stirred and a lively impression has been made; but, remember, that to receive the word in the ear is one thing, and to receive Jesus into your very soul is quite another; superficial feeling is often joined to inward hardness of heart, and a lively impression of the word is not always a lasting one. In the parable, the seed in one case fell upon ground having a rocky bottom, covered over with a thin layer of earth; when the seed began to take root, its downward growth was hindered by the hard stone, and therefore it spent its strength in pushing its green root aloft as high as it could, but having no inward moisture derived from root nourishment, it withered away.

Is this my case? Have I been making a fair show in the flesh without having a corresponding inner life? Good growth takes place upwards and downward at the same time. Am I rooted in sincere fidelity and love to Jesus? If my heart remains unsoftened and unfertilized by grace, the good seed may germinate for a season, but it must ultimately wither, for it cannot flourish on a rocky, unbroken, unsanctified heart. Let me dread a godliness as rapid in growth and as wanting in endurance as Jonah's gourd; let me count the cost of being a follower of Jesus, above all let me feel the energy of His Holy Spirit, and then I shall possess an abiding and enduring seed in my soul. If my mind remains as obdurate as it was by nature, the sun of trial will scorch, and my hard heart will help to cast the heat the more terribly upon the ill-covered seed, and my religion will soon die, and my despair will be terrible; therefore, Oh heavenly Sower, plow me first, and then cast the truth into me, and let me yield You a bounteous harvest.

EVENING
"I have prayed for you" — Luke 22:32.

HOW ENCOURAGING IS the thought of the Redeemer's never-ceasing intercession for us. When we pray, He pleads for us; and that we are not praying, He is advocating our cause, and by His supplications shielding us from unseen dangers. Notice the word of comfort addressed to Peter: *"Simon, Simon, Satan has desired to have you that he may sift you as wheat; but"* - what? But go and pray for yourself? That would be good advice, but it is not written. Neither does He say, But I will keep you watchful, and so you shall be preserved. That were a great blessing. No, it is, *"But I have prayed for you, that your faith fail not."*

We little know what we owe to our Savior's prayers. When we preach the hill-tops of heaven, and look back upon all the way whereby the Lord our God has led us, how we shall praise Him who, before the eternal throne, undid the mischief which Satan was doing upon earth. How shall we thank Him because He ever held His peace, but day and night pointed to the wounds upon His hands, and carried our names upon His breastplate! Even before Satan had begun to tempt, Jesus had forestalled him and entered a plea in heaven. Mercy outruns malice. Mark, He does not say, Satan has sifted you, and therefore I will pray; but, Satan has desired to have you. He checks Satan even in his very desire, and nips it in the bud. He does not say, But I have desired to pray for you. No, but *"I have prayed for you."* I have done it already; I have gone to court and entered a counterplea even before an accusation is made.

Oh Jesus, what a comfort it is that you have pleaded our cause against our unseen enemies; countermined their mines, and unmasked their ambushes. Here s a matter for joy, gratitude, hope, and confidence.

January 12   MORNING

"You are Christ's"— 1 Corinthians 3:3.

"YOU ARE CHRIST'S." You are His by donation, for the Father gave you to the Son; His by His bloody purchase for He counted down the price for your redemption; His by dedication, for you have consecrated yourself to Him; His by relation, for you are named by His name, and made one of His brethren and joint-heirs. Labor practically to show the world that you are the servant, the friend, the bride of Jesus. When tempted to sin, reply, I cannot do this great wickedness, for I am Christ's. Immortal principles forbid the friend of Christ to sin. When wealth is before you to be won by sin, say that you are Christ's, and touch it not. Are you exposed to difficulties and dangers.? Stand fast in the evil day, remembering that you are Christ's. Are you placed where others are sitting down idly, doing nothing? Rise to the work with all your powers; and when the sweat stands upon your brow, and you are tempted to loiter, cry, No, I cannot stop, for I am Christ's. If I were not purchased by blood, I might be like Issachar, crouching between two burdens; but I am Christ's, and cannot loiter. When the siren song of pleasure would tempt you from the path of right, reply, Your music cannot charm me; I am Christ's.

When the cause of God invites you, give yourself to it; when the poor require you, give your goods and yourself away, for you are Christ's. Never belie your profession. Be you ever one of those whose manners are Christian, whose speech is like the Nazarene, whose conduct and conversation are so redolent of heaven, that all who see you may know that you are the Savior's, recognizing in you His features of love and His countenance of holiness. I am a Roman! was of old a reason for integrity; far more, then, let it be your argument for holiness, I am Christ's!

EVENING

"I have yet to speak on God's behalf"— Job 36:2.

WE OUGHT NOT to court publicity for our virtue, or notoriety for our zeal; but, at the same time, it is a sin to be always seeking to hide that which God has bestowed upon us for the good of others. A Christian is not to be a village in a valley, but *"a city set upon a hill;"* he is not to be a candle under a bushel, but a candle in a candlestick, giving light to all. Retirement may be lovely in its season, and to hide one's self is doubtless modest, but the hiding of Christ in us can never be justified, and the keeping back of truth which is precious to ourselves is a sin against others and an offence against God. If you are of a nervous temperament and of retiring disposition, take care that you do not too much indulge this trembling propensity lest you should be useless to the church. Seek in the name of Him who was not ashamed of you to do some little violence to your feelings, and tell to others what Christ has told to you.

If you can not speak with trumpet tongue, use the still small voice. If the pulpit must not be your tribune, if the press may not carry on its wings your words, yet say with Peter and John, *"Silver and gold have I none; but such as I have give I you."* By Sychar's well talk to the Samaritan woman, if you can not on the mountain preach a sermon; utter the praises of Jesus in the house, if not in the temple; in the field, if not upon the exchange; in the midst of your own household, if you can not in the midst of the great family of man. From the hidden springs within let flowing rivulets of sweet testimony flow forth, giving drink to every passer-by. Hide not your talent; trade with it; and you shall bring in good interest to your Lord and Master. To speak for God will be refreshing to ourselves, cheering to saints, useful to sinners, and honoring to the Savior. Dumb children are an affliction to their parents. Lord, unloose all Your children's tongues.

MORNING   January 13

"Jehoshaphat made ships of Tarshish to go to Ophir for gold. But they did not go, for the ships were broken at Ezion-geber" — 1 Kings 12:48.

SOLOMON'S SHIPS had returned in safety, but Jehoshaphat's vessels never reached the land of gold. Providence prospers one, and frustrates the desires of another, in the same business and at the same spot, yet the Great Ruler is as good and wise at one time as another. May we have grace today, in the remembrance of this text, to bless the Lord for ships broken at Ezion-geber, as well as for vessels freighted with temporal blessings; let us not envy the worldly successful, nor murmur at our losses as though we were singularly and specially tried. Like Jehoshaphat, we may be precious in the Lord's sight, although our schemes end in disappointment.

The secret cause of Jehoshaphat's loss is well worthy of notice, for it is the root of very much of the suffering of the Lord's people; it was his alliance with a sinful family, his fellowship with sinners. In 2 Chron. 20:37, we are told that the Lord sent a prophet to declare, *"Because you have joined yourself with Ahaziah, the Lord has broken your works."* This was a fatherly chastisement, which appears to have been blessed to him; for in the verse which succeeds our morning's text we find him refusing to allow his servants to sail in the same vessels with those of the wicked king. Would to God that Jehoshaphat's experience might be a warning to the rest of the Lord's people, to avoid being unequally yoked together with unbelievers! A life of misery is usually the lot of those who are united in marriage, or in any other way of their own choosing, with the men of the world. Oh for such love to Jesus that we like Him may be holy, harmless, undefiled, and separate from sinners; for if it be not so with us, we may expect to hear it often said, *"The Lord has broken your works."*

EVENING
"And the iron swam" — 2 Kings 6:9.

THE AXE-HEAD seemed hopelessly lost, and as it was borrowed, the honor of the prophetic band was likely to be imperilled, and so the name of their God to be compromised. Contrary to all expectation, the iron was made to mount from the depth of the stream and to swim; for things impossible with man are possible with God. I knew a man in Christ but a few years ago who was called to undertake a work far exceeding his strength. It appeared so difficult as to involve absurdity in the bare idea of attempting it. Yet he was called to it, and his faith rose with the occasion; God honored his faith, unlooked-for aid was sent, and the iron did swim. Another of the Lord's family was in grievous financial straits, he was able to meet all claims, and much more if he could have realized a certain portion of his estate, but he was overtaken with a sudden pressure; he sought for friends in vain, but faith led him to the unfailing Helper, and lo, the trouble was averted, his footsteps were enlarged, and the iron did swim. A third had a sorrowful case of depravity to deal with. He had taught, reproved, warned, invited, and interceded, but all in vain. Old Adam was too strong for young Melancthon, the stubborn spirit would not relent. Then came an agony of prayer, and before long a blessed answer was sent from heaven. The hard heart was broken, the iron did swim.

Beloved reader, what is your desperate case? What heavy matter have you in hand this evening? Bring it here. The God of the prophets lives, and lives to help His saints. He will not suffer you to lack any good thing. Believe in the Lord of hosts! Approach Him pleading the name of Jesus, and the iron shall swim; you too shall see the finger of God working marvels for His people. According to your faith be it unto you, and yet again the iron shall swim.

January 14   MORNING

"Mighty to save" — Isaiah 63:1.

BY THE WORDS *"to save"* we understand the whole of the great work of salvation, from the first holy desire onward to complete sanctification. Indeed, here is all mercy in one word. Christ is not only *"mighty to save"* those who repent, but He is able to make men repent. He will carry those to heaven who believe; but He is, moreover, mighty to give men new hearts and to work faith in them. He is mighty to make the man who hates holiness love it, and to constrain the despiser of His name to bend the knee before Him.

No, this is not all the meaning, for the divine power is equally seen in the after-work. The life of a believer is a series of miracles worked by *"the Mighty God"*. The bush burns, but is not consumed. He is mighty to keep His people holy after He has made them so, and to preserve them in His fear and love until He consummates their spiritual existence in heaven. Christ's might does not lie in making a believer and then leaving him to shift for himself; but He who begins the good work carries it on. He who imparts the first germ of life in the dead soul, prolongs the divine existence, and strengthens it until it bursts asunder every bond of sin, and the soul leaps from earth, perfected in glory.

Believer, here is encouragement. Are you praying for some beloved one? Oh, give not up your prayers, for Christ is *"mighty to save."* You are powerless to reclaim the rebel, but your Lord is Almighty. Lay hold on that mighty arm, and rouse it to put forth its strength. Does your own case trouble you? Fear not, for His strength is sufficient for you. Whether to begin with others, or to carry on the work in you, Jesus is *"mighty to save;"* the best proof of which lies in the fact that He has saved you. What a thousand mercies that you have not found Him mighty to destroy!

EVENING

"Beginning to sink, he cried out, saying, Lord, save me!" — Matthew 14:30.

SINKING TIMES are praying times with the Lord's servants. Peter neglected prayer at starting upon his venturous journey, but when he began to sink his danger made him a suppliant, and his cry though late was not too late. In our hours of bodily pain and mental anguish, we find ourselves as naturally driven to prayer as the wreck is driven upon the shore by the waves. The fox hies to its hole for protection; the bird flies to the wood for shelter; and even so the tried believer hastens to the mercy seat for safety. Heaven's great harbor of refuge is All-prayer; thousands of weather-beaten vessels have found a haven there, and the moment a storm comes on, it is wise for us to make for it with all sail.

Short prayers are long enough. There were but three words in the petition which Peter gasped out, but they were sufficient for his purpose. Not length but strength is desirable. A sense of need is a mighty teacher of brevity. if our prayers had less of the tail feathers of pride and more wing they would be all the better. Verbiage is to devotion as chaff to the wheat. Precious things lie in small compass, and all that is real prayer in many a long address might have been uttered in a petition as short as that of Peter.

Our extremities are the Lord's opportunities. Immediately a keen sense of danger forces an anxious cry from us the ear of Jesus hears, and with Him ear and heart go together, and the hand does not long linger. At the last moment we appeal to our Master, but His swift hand makes up for our delays by instant and effectual action. Are we nearly engulfed by the boisterous waters of affliction? Let us then lift up our souls unto our Savior, and we may rest assured that He will not suffer us to perish. When we can do nothing Jesus can do all things; let us enlist His powerful aid upon our side, and all will be well.

MORNING
January 15
"Do as You have said"— 2 Samuel 7:25.

GOD'S PROMISES were never meant to be thrown aside as waste paper; He intended that they should be used. God's gold is not miser's money, but is minted to be traded with. Nothing pleases our Lord better than to see His promises put in circulation; He loves to see His children bring them up to Him, and say, *Lord, do as You have said.* We glorify God when we plead His promises. Do you think that God will be any the poorer for giving you the riches He has promised? Do you dream that He will be any the less holy for giving holiness to you? Do you imagine He will be any the less pure for washing you from your sins?

He has said *"Come now, and let us reason together, says the Lord: though your sins be as scarlet, they shall be as white as snow; though they be red like crimson, they shall be as wool"* (Isaiah 1:18). Faith lays hold upon the promise of pardon, and it does not delay, saying, This is a precious promise, I wonder if it be true? But it goes straight to the throne with it, and pleads, "Lord, here is the promise, Do as You have said. Our Lord replies, "Be it unto you even as you will." When a Christian grasps a promise, if he does not take it to God, he dishonors Him; but when he hastens to the throne of grace, and cries, Lord, I have nothing to recommend me but this, *You have said it;* then his desire shall be granted.

Our heavenly Banker delights to cash His own notes. Never let the promise rust. Draw the word of promise out of its scabbard, and use it with holy violence. Think not that God will be troubled by your importunity reminding Him of His promises. He loves to hear the loud outcries of needy souls. It is His delight to bestow favors. He is more ready to hear than you are to ask. The sun is not weary of shining, nor the fountain of flowing. It is God's nature to keep His promises; therefore go at once to the throne with *"Do as You have said."*

EVENING
"But I give myself to prayer"— Psalm 109:4.

LYING TONGUES were busy against the reputation of David, but he did not defend himself; he moved the case into a higher court, and pleaded before the great King Himself. Prayer is the safest method of replying to words of hatred. The Psalmist prayed in no coldhearted manner, he gave himself to the exercise. He threw his whole soul and heart into it, straining every sinew and muscle, as Jacob did when wrestling with the Angel. Thus, and thus only, shall any of us speed at the throne of grace. As a shadow has no power because there is no substance in it, even so that supplication, in which a man's proper self is not thoroughly present in agonizing earnestness and vehement desire, is utterly ineffectual, for it lacks that which would give it force. An old divine said, Fervent prayer, like a cannon planted at the gates of heaven, makes them fly open. The common fault with the most of us is our readiness to yield to distractions. Our thoughts go roving here and there, and we make little progress towards our desired end. Like quicksilver our mind will not hold together, but rolls off this way and that. How great an evil this is! It injures us, and what is worse, it insults our God. What would we think of a petitioner, if, while having an audience with a prince, he should be playing with a feather or catching a fly?

Continuance and perseverance are intended in the expression of our text. David did not cry once, and then relapse into silence; his holy clamor was continued till it brought down the blessing. Prayer must not be our chance work, but our daily business, our habit and vocation. As artists give themselves to their models, and poets to their classical pursuits, so must we addict ourselves to prayer. We must be immersed in prayer as in our element, and so pray without ceasing. Lord, teach us so to pray that we may be more and more prevalent in supplication.

January 16

MORNING

"I will help you, says the LORD" — Isaiah 41 14.

THIS MORNING LET us hear the Lord Jesus speak to each one of us: *"I will help you."* It is but a small thing for Me, your God, to help you. Consider what I have done already. What! not help you? Why, I bought you with My blood. What! not help you? I have died for you; and if I have done the greater, will I not do the less? Help you! I made the thing I will ever do for you; I have done more, and will do more. Before the world began I chose you. I made the covenant for you. I laid aside My glory and became a man for you; I gave My life for you; and if I did all this, I will surely help you now. In helping you, I am giving you what I have bought for you already. If you had need of a thousand times as much help, I would give it to you; you require little compared with what I am ready to give. It is much for you to need, but it is nothing for me to bestow. Help you? Fear not! If there were an ant at the door of thy granary asking for help, it would not ruin you to give him a handful of your wheat; and you are nothing but a tiny insect at the door of My all-sufficiency. *"I will help you."*

Oh my soul, is not this enough? Do you need more strength than the omnipotence of the United Trinity? Do you want more wisdom than exists in the Father, more love than displays itself in the Son, or more power than is manifested in the influences of the Spirit? Bring here your empty pitcher! Surely this well will fill it. Haste, gather up your wants, and bring them here: your emptiness, your woes, your needs. Behold, this river of God is full for your supply; what can you desire beside? Go forth, my soul, in this your might. The Eternal God is your helper!

Fear not, I am with you, oh, be not dismayed! I, I am your God, and will still give you aid.

EVENING

"The Messiah shall be cut off, but not for Himself" — Daniel 9:26.

BLESSED BE HIS name, there was no cause of death in Him. Neither original nor actual sin had defiled Him, and therefore death had no claim upon Him. No man could have taken His life from Him justly, for He had done no man wrong, and no man could even have slain Him by force unless He had been pleased to yield Himself to die. But lo, one sins and another suffers. Justice was offended by us, but found its satisfaction in Him. Rivers of tears, mountains of offerings, seas of the blood of bullocks, and hills of frankincense, could not have availed for the removal of sin. But Jesus was cut off for us, and the cause of wrath was cut off at once, for sin was put away for ever. Herein is wisdom, whereby substitution, the sure and speedy way of atonement, was devised! Herein is condescension, which brought Messiah, the Prince, to wear a crown of thorns, and die upon the cross! Herein is love, which led the Redeemer to lay down His life for those who once has been His enemies!

It is not enough, however, to admire the spectacle of the innocent bleeding for the guilty, we must make sure of our interest therein. The special object of the Messiah's death was the salvation of His elect — have we a part and a lot among those for whom He gave His life a ransom? Did the Lord Jesus stand as our representative? Are we healed by His stripes? It will be a terrible thing indeed if we should come short of a portion in His sacrifice; it were better for us that we had never been born. Solemn as the question is, it is a joyful circumstance that it is one which may be answered clearly and without mistake. To all who believe on Him the Lord Jesus is a present Savior, and upon them all the blood of reconciliation has been sprinkled. Let all who trust in the merit of Messiah's death be joyful at every remembrance of Him, and let their holy gratitude lead them to the fullest consecration to His cause.

MORNING   January 17

"And I saw, and behold! A Lamb standing on Mount Zion!" — Revelation 14:1

THE APOSTLE JOHN was privileged to look within the gates of heaven, and in describing what he saw, he begins by saying, *"I looked, and, behold, a Lamb!"* This teaches us that the chief object of contemplation in the heavenly state is *"the Lamb of God, which takes away the sins of the world."* (John 1:29) Nothing else attracted the apostle's attention so much as the person of that Divine Being, who has redeemed us by His blood. He is the theme of the songs of all glorified spirits and holy angels.

Christian, here is joy for you; you have looked, and you have seen the Lamb. Through your tears your eyes have seen the Lamb of God taking away your sins. Rejoice, then. In a little while, when my eyes shall have been wild from tears, you will see the same Lamb exalted on His throne. It is the joy of your heart to hold daily fellowship with Jesus; you shall have the same joy to a higher degree in heaven; you shall enjoy the constant vision of His presence; you shall dwell with Him for ever. *"I looked, and, behold, a Lamb!"* Why, that Lamb is heaven itself; for as good Rutherford says, Heaven and Christ are the same thing; to be with Christ is to be in heaven, and to be in heaven is to be with Christ. That prisoner of the Lord very sweetly writes in one of his glowing letters: Oh my Lord Christ, if I could be in heaven without you, it would be a hell; and if I could be in hell, and have you still, it would be a heaven to me, for you are all the heaven I want.

It is true, is it not, Christian? Does not your soul say so?

> Not all the harps above
> Can make a heavenly place,
> If God His residence remove,
> Or but conceal His face.

All you need to make you blessed, supremely blessed, is *"to be with Christ."*

EVENING

"And one evening David arose from his bed and walked on the roof of the king's house" — 2 Samuel 11:7.

AT THAT HOUR David saw Bathsheba. We are never out of the reach of temptation. Both at home and abroad we are liable to meet with allurements to evil; the morning opens with peril, and the shades of evening find us still in jeopardy. They are well kept whom God keeps, but woe unto those who go forth into the world, or even dare to walk their own house unarmed. Those who think themselves secure are more exposed to danger than any others. The armorbearer of sin is self-confidence.

David should have been engaged in fighting the Lord's battles, instead of which he tarried at Jerusalem, and gave himself up to luxurious repose, for he arose from his bed at eventide. Idleness and luxury are the devil's jackals, and find him abundant prey. In stagnant waters noxious creatures swarm, and neglected soil soon yields a dense tangle of weeds and briars. Oh for the constraining love of Jesus to keep us active and useful! When I see the king of Israel sluggishly leaving his couch at the close of the day, and falling at once into temptation, let me take warning, and set holy watchfulness to guard the door.

Is it possible that the king had mounted his housetop for retirement and devotion? If so, what a caution is given us to count no place, however secret, a sanctuary from sin! While our hearts are so like a tinder-box, and sparks so plentiful, we had need use all diligence in all places to prevent a blaze. Satan can climb housetops, and enter closets, and even if we could shut out that foul fiend, our own corruptions are enough to work our ruin unless grace prevent. Reader, beware of evening temptations. Be not secure. The sun is down but sin is up. We need a watchman for the night as well as a guardian for the day. Oh blessed Spirit, keep us from all evil this night. Amen.

January 18　　　　　　　　MORNING

"So then, there is still a rest to the people of God" — Hebrews 4:9.

HOW DIFFERENT WILL be the state of the believer in heaven from what it is here! Here he is born to toil and suffer weariness, but in the land of the immortal, fatigue is never known. Anxious to serve his Master, he finds his strength unequal to his zeal: his constant cry is, Help me to serve You, Oh my God. If he is thoroughly active, he will have much labor; not too much for his will, but more than enough for his power, so that he will cry out, I am not wearied of the labor, but I am wearied in it.

Ah, Christian, the hot day of weariness lasts not for ever; the sun is nearing the horizon; it shall rise again with a brighter day than you have ever seen, upon a land where they serve God day and night, and yet rest from their labors. Here, rest is but partial, there, it is perfect. Here, the Christian is always unsettled; he feels that he has not yet attained. There, all are at rest; they have attained the summit of the mountain; they have ascended to the bosom of their God. Higher they cannot go.

Ah, toil-worn laborer, only think when you shall rest forever! Can you conceive it? It is a rest eternal; a rest that "remains." Here, my best joys bear "mortal" on their brow; my fair flowers fade; my dainty cups are drained to dregs; my sweetest birds fall before Death's arrows; my most pleasant days are shadowed into nights; and the flood-tides of my bliss subside into ebbs of sorrow. But there everything is immortal; the harp abides unrusted, the crown unwithered, the eye undimmed, the voice unfaltering, the heart unwavering, and the immortal being is wholly absorbed in infinite delight. Happy day! Happy day, when mortality shall be swallowed up of life, and the Eternal Sabbath shall begin.

EVENING

"He explained to them the things about Himself in all the Scriptures" — Luke 24:27.

THE TWO DISCIPLES on the road to Emmaus had a most profitable journey. Their companion and teacher was the best of tutors; their interpreter was One of a thousand, in whom are hidden all the treasures of wisdom and knowledge. The Lord Jesus condescended to become a preacher of the gospel, and He was not ashamed to exercise His calling before an audience of two persons, neither does He now refuse to become the teacher of even one. Let us court the company of so excellent an Instructor, for till He is made unto us wisdom we shall never be wise unto salvation.

This unrivalled Tutor used as His class-book the best of books. Although able to reveal fresh truth, He preferred to expound the old. He knew by His omniscience what was the most instructive way of teaching, and by turning at once to Moses and the prophets, He showed us that the surest road to wisdom is not speculation, reasoning, or reading human books, but meditation upon the Word of God. The readiest way to be spiritually rich in heavenly knowledge is to dig in this mine of diamonds, to gather pearls from this heavenly sea. When Jesus Himself sought to enrich others, He wrought in the quarry of Holy Scripture.

The favored pair were led to consider the best of subjects, for Jesus spoke of Jesus, and explained the things concerning Himself. Here the diamond cut the diamond, and what could be more admirable? The Master of the House unlocked His own doors, conducted the guests to His table, and placed His own dainties upon it. He who hid the treasure in the field Himself guided the searchers to it. Our Lord would naturally discourse upon the sweetest of topics, and He could find none sweeter than His own person and work: with an eye to these we should always search the Word. Oh for grace to study the Bible with Jesus as both our teacher and our lesson!

MORNING   January 19

"I sought Him, but I did not find Him" — Song of Solomon 3:1.

TELL ME WHERE you lost the company of Christ, and I will tell you the most likely place to find Him. Have you lost Christ in the closet by restraining prayer? Then it is there you must seek and find Him. Did you lose Christ by sin? You will find Christ in no other way but by the giving up of the sin, and seeking by the Holy Spirit to mortify the member in which the lust dwells. Did you lose Christ by neglecting the Scriptures? You must find Christ in the Scriptures. It is a true proverb, Look for a thing where you dropped it, it is there. So look for Christ where you lost Him, for He has not gone away. But it is hard work to go back for Christ. Bunyan tells us that the pilgrim found the piece of the road back to the Arbor of Ease, where he lost his roll, the hardest he had ever traveled. Twenty miles onward is easier than to go one mile back for the lost evidence.

Take care, then, when you find your Master, to cling close to Him. But how is it you have lost Him? One would have thought you would never have parted with such a precious friend, whose presence is so sweet, whose words are so comforting, and whose company is so dear to you! How is it that you did not watch him every moment for fear of losing sight of Him? Yet, since you have let Him go, what a mercy that you are seeking Him, even though you mournfully groan, "Oh that I knew where I might find Him!" Go on seeking, for it is dangerous to be without your Lord. Without Christ you are like a sheep without its shepherd; like a tree without water at its roots; like a sere leaf in the tempest, not bound to the tree of life. With your whole heart seek Him, and He will be found of you: only give yourself thoroughly up to the search, and truly you shall yet discover Him to your joy and gladness.

EVENING

"Then He opened their understanding that they might understand the Scriptures" —
Luke 24:45

HE WHOM WE viewed last evening as opening Scripture, we here perceive opening the understanding. In the first work He has many fellow-laborers, but in the second He stands alone; many can bring the Scriptures to the mind, but the Lord alone can prepare the mind to receive the Scriptures. Our Lord Jesus differs from all other teachers; they reach the ear, but He instructs the heart; they deal with the outward letter, but He imparts an inward taste for the truth, by which we perceive its savor and spirit. The most unlearned of men become ripe scholars in the school of grace when the Lord Jesus by His Holy Spirit unfolds the mysteries of the kingdom to them, and grants the divine anointing by which they are enabled to behold the invisible. Happy are we if we have had our understandings cleared and strengthened by the Master!

How many men of profound learning are ignorant of eternal things! They know the killing letter of revelation, but its living spirit they cannot discern; they have a veil upon their hearts which the eyes of carnal reason cannot penetrate. Such was our case a little time ago; we who now see were once utterly blind; truth was to us as beauty in the dark, a thing unnoticed and neglected. Had it not been for the love of Jesus we should have remained to this moment in utter ignorance, for without His gracious opening of our understanding, we could no more have attained to spiritual knowledge than an infant can climb the Pyramids, or an ostrich fly up to the stars. Jesus' College is the only one in which God's truth can be really learned; other schools may teach us what is to be believed, but Christ's alone can show us how to believe it. let us sit at the feet of Jesus, and by earnest prayer call in His blessed aid that our dull wits may grow brighter, and our feeble understandings may receive heavenly things.

January 20   MORNING

"Abel was a keeper of sheep" — Genesis 4:2.

AS A SHEPHERD Abel sanctified his work to the glory of God, and offered a sacrifice of blood upon his altar, and *"the Lord had respect to Abel and his offering."* This early type of our Lord is exceedingly clear and distinct. Like the first streak of light which tinges the east at sunrise, it does not reveal everything, but it clearly manifests the great fact that the sun is coming. As we see Abel, a shepherd and yet a priest, offering a sacrifice of sweet smell unto God, we discern our Lord, who brings before His Father a sacrifice to which Jehovah ever has respect. Abel was hated by his brother, hated without a cause. Even so was the Savior: the natural and carnal man hated the accepted man in whom the Spirit of grace was found, and rested not until His blood had been shed. Abel fell, and sprinkled his altar and sacrifice with his own blood, and therein sets forth the Lord Jesus slain by the enmity of man while service as a priest before the Lord. *"The good Shepherd"* has laid down *"His life for the sheep."* (John 10:11) Let us weep as we view Him slain by the hatred of mankind, staining the horns of His altar with His own blood.

Abel's blood speaks. *"The Lord said unto Cain, The voice of your brother's blood cries unto Me from the ground."* The blood of Jesus has a mighty tongue, and the import of its prevailing cry is not vengeance, but mercy. It is precious beyond all preciousness to stand at the altar of our good Shepherd, there to see Him bleeding as the slaughtered Sacrifice, and then to hear His blood speaking peace to all his flock, peace in our conscience, peace between Jew and Gentile, peace between man and his offended Maker, peace all down the ages of eternity for blood-washed men. Abel is the first shepherd in order of time, but our hearts shall ever place Jesus first in order of excellence. You great Keeper of the sheep, we the people of Your pasture bless You with our whole hearts when we see You slain for us

EVENING

"Turn away my eyes from seeing vanity; in Your way give me life" — Psalm 119:37.

THERE ARE different kinds of vanity. The cap and bells of the fool, the mirth of the world, the dance, the lyre, and the cup of the dissolute, all these men know to be vanities. They wear on their face their proper name and title. Far more treacherous are those equally vain things, the cares of this world and the deceitfulness of riches. A man may follow vanity as truly in the counting-house as in the theatre. If he is spending his life in amassing wealth, he passes his days in a vain show. Unless we follow Christ, and make our God the great object of life, we only differ in appearance from the most frivolous. It is clear that there is much need of the first prayer of our text.

"In Your way give me life" — The Psalmist confesses that he is dull, heavy, lumpy, all but dead. Perhaps, dear reader, you feel the same. We are so sluggish that the best motives cannot quicken us, apart from the Lord Himself. What! Will not the vision of hell quicken me? Shall I think of sinners perishing, and yet not be awakened? Will not heaven quicken me? Can I think of the reward that awaits the righteous, and yet be cold? Will not death quicken me? Can I think of dying, and standing before my God, and yet be slothful in my Master's service? Will not Christ's love constrain me? Can I think of His dear wounds, can I sit at the foot of His cross, and not be stirred with fervency and zeal? It seems so! No mere consideration can quicken us to zeal, but God Himself must do it, hence the cry, *"Give me life."* The Psalmist breathes out his whole soul in vehement pleading: his body and his soul unite in prayer. *"Turn away my eyes,"* says the body: *"Give me life,"* cries the soul. This is a fit prayer for every day. Oh Lord, hear it in my case this night.

MORNING January 21

"And so all Israel shall be saved"— Romans 11:26.

WHEN MOSES SANG at the Red Sea, it was his joy to know that all Israelites were safe. Not a drop of spray fell from that solid wall until the last of God's Israel had safely planted his foot on the other side the flood. That done, immediately the floods dissolved into their proper place again, but not till then. Part of that song was, *"You in Your mercy have led forth the people which You have redeemed."* In the last time, when the elect shall sing the song of Moses, the servant of God, and of the Lamb, it shall be the boast of Jesus, *"Of all whom You have given Me, I have lost none"* (John 17:12). In heaven there shall not be a vacant throne.

> For all the chosen race
> Shall meet around the throne,
> Shall bless the conduct of His grace,
> And make His glories known.

As many as God has chosen, as many as Christ has redeemed, as many as the Spirit has called, as many as believe in Jesus, shall safely cross the dividing sea.

We are not all safely landed yet: Part of the host have crossed the flood, And part are crossing now. The vanguard of the army has already reached the shore. We are marching through the depths; we are at this day following hard after our leader into the heart of the sea. let us be of good cheer: the rear-guard shall soon be where the vanguard already is; the last of the chosen ones shall soon have crossed the sea, and then shall be heard the song of triumph, when all are secure. But oh, if one were absent! Oh, if one of his chosen family should be cast away! It would make an everlasting discord in the song of the redeemed, and cut the strings of the harps of paradise, so that music could never be extorted from them.

EVENING

"He was very thirsty and called on the Lord and said, You have given this great deliverance into the hand of Your servant. And now shall I die for thirst"—Judges 15:18.

SAMSON WAS THIRSTY and ready to die. The difficulty was totally different from any which the hero had met before. Merely to get thirst assuaged is nothing like so great a matter as to be delivered from a thousand Philistines! But when the thirst was upon him, Samson felt that little present difficulty more weighty than the great past difficulty out of which he had so specially been delivered. It is very usual for God's people, when they have enjoyed a great deliverance, to find a little trouble too much for them. Samson slays a thousand Philistines, and piles them up in heaps, and then faints for a little water! Jacob wrestles with God at Peniel, and is allowed to overcome Omnipotence itself, and then goes *"halting on his thigh!"*

Strange that there must be a shrinking of the sinew whenever we win the day. As if the Lord must teach us our littleness, our nothingness in order to keep us within bounds. Samson boasted right loudly when he said, *"I have slain a thousand men."* His boastful throat soon grew hoarse with thirst, and he took himself to prayer. God has many ways of humbling His people. Dear child of God, if after great mercy you are laid very low, your case is not an unusual one. When David had mounted the throne of Israel, he said, *"I am weak today, though anointed king."* You must expect to feel weakest when you are enjoying your greatest triumph.

If God has wrought for you great deliverances in the past, your present difficulty is only like Samson's thirst, and the Lord will not let you faint, nor allow the daughter of the uncircumcised to triumph over you. The road of sorrow is the road to heaven, but there are wells of refreshing water all along the route. So, tried brother, cheer your heart with Samson's words, and rest assured that God will deliver you before long.

January 22   MORNING

"Son of man, what is the vine tree more than any tree, or than a branch which is among the trees of the forest?"— Ezekiel 15:2.

THESE WORDS ARE for the humbling of God's people; they are called God's vine, but what are they by nature more than others? They, by God's goodness, have become fruitful, having been planted in a good soil; the Lord has trained them upon the walls of the sanctuary, and they bring forth fruit to His glory. But what are they without their God? What are they without the continual influence of the Spirit, begetting fruitfulness in them? Oh believer, learn to reject pride, seeing that you have no ground for it. Whatever you are, you have nothing to make you proud. The more you have, the more you are in debt to God; and you should not be proud of that which renders you a debtor. Consider your origin; look back to what you were. Consider what you would have been but for divine grace. Look upon yourself as you are now. Does not your conscience reproach you? Do not your thousand wanderings stand before you, and tell you that you are unworthy to be called His son? And if He has made you anything, are you not taught thereby that it is grace which has made you to differ?

Great believer, you would have been a great sinner if God had not made you to differ. Oh you who are valiant for truth, you would have been as valiant for error if grace had not laid hold upon you. Therefore, be not proud, though you have a large estate, a wide domain of grace, you had not once a single thing to call your own except your sin and misery, Oh strange infatuation, that you, who have borrowed everything, should think of exalting yourself; a poor dependent pensioner upon the bounty of your Savior, one who has a life which dies without fresh streams of life from Jesus, and yet proud! Fie on you, Oh silly heart!

EVENING

"Does Job fear God for nothing?"— Job 1:9.

THIS WAS THE wicked question of Satan concerning that upright man of old, but there are many in the present day concerning whom it might be asked with justice, for they love God after a fashion because He prospers them; but if things went ill with them, they would give up all their boasted faith in God. If they can clearly see that since the time of their supposed conversion the world has gone prosperously with them, then they will love God in their poor carnal way; but if they endure adversity, they rebel against the Lord. Their love is the love of the table, not of the host; a love to the cupboard, not to the master of the house.

As for the true Christian, he expects to have his reward in the next life, and to endure hardness in this. The promise of the old covenant was prosperity, but the promise of the new covenant is adversity. Remember Christ's words: *"Every branch in Me that bears not fruit He takes away, and every branch that bears fruit"* — What? He prunes it, that it may bring forth more fruit. If you bring forth fruit, you will have to endure affliction. Alas! you say, "that is a terrible prospect." But this affliction works out such precious results, that the Christian who is the subject of it must learn to rejoice in tribulations, because as his tribulations abound, so his consolations abound by Christ Jesus.

Rest assured, if you are a child of God, you will be no stranger to the rod. Sooner or later every bar of gold must pass through the fire. Fear not, but rather rejoice that such fruitful times are in store for you, for in them you will be weaned from earth and made fit for heaven; you will be delivered from clinging to the present, and made to long for those eternal things which are so soon to be revealed to you. When you feel that as regards the present you serve God for nothing, you will then rejoice in the infinite reward of the future.

MORNING January 23

"I have lifted up a chosen one out of the people" — Psalm 89:19.

WHY WAS CHRIST chosen out of the people? Speak, my heart, for heart-thoughts are best. Was it not that He might be able to be our brother in the blest tie of kindred blood? Oh, what relationship there is between Christ and the believer! The believer can say, I have a Brother in heaven; I may be poor, but I have a Brother who is rich, and is a King, and will He suffer me to lack while He is on His throne? Oh, No! He loves me; He is my brother. Believer, wear this blessed thought, like a necklace of diamonds, around the neck of your memory; put it, as a golden ring, on the finger of recollection, and use it as the King's own seal, stamping the petitions of your faith with confidence of success. He is a brother born for adversity, treat him as such.

Christ was also chosen out of the people that He might know our wants and sympathize with us. *"He was tempted in all points like as we are, yet without sin."* In all our sorrows we have His sympathy. Temptation, pain, disappointment, weakness, weariness, poverty; He knows them all, for He has felt all. Remember this, Christian, and let it comfort you. However difficult and painful your road, it is marked by the footsteps of your Savior; and even when you reach the dark valley of the shadow of death, and the deep waters of the swelling Jordan, you will find His footprints there. In all places whereever we go, He has been our forerunner; each burden we have to carry, has once been laid on the shoulders of Immanuel.

His way was much rougher and darker than mine; Did Christ, my Lord, suffer, and shall I repine?

Take courage! Royal feet have left a blood-red track upon the road, and consecrated the thorny path forever.

EVENING

"We will remember Your love more than wine" — Song of Solomon 1:4.

JESUS WILL NOT let His people forget His love. If all the love they have enjoyed should be forgotten, He will visit them with fresh love. He says, Do you forget My cross? I will cause you to remember it; for at My table I will manifest Myself anew to you. Do you forget what I did for you in the council-chamber of eternity? I will remind you of it, for you shall need a counsellor, and shall find Me ready at your call. Mothers do not let their children forget them. If the boy has gone to Australia, and does not write home, his mother writes, Has John forgotten his mother? Then there comes back a sweet letter, which proves that the gentle reminder was not in vain. So is it with Jesus, He says to us, *"Remember Me,"* and our response is, *"We will remember Your love."*

We will remember Your love and its matchless history. It is ancient as the glory which You had with the Father before the world was. We remember, Oh Jesus, Your eternal love when You became our Surety, and espoused us as Your betrothed. We remember the love which suggested the sacrifice of Yourself, the love which, until the fulness of time, mused over that sacrifice, and longed for the hour whereof in the volume of the book it was written of You, *"Behold, I come."* We remember Your love, Oh Jesus, as it was manifest to us in Your holy life, from the manger of Bethlehem to the garden of Gethsemane. We track You from the cradle to the grave, for every word and deed of Yours was love. And we rejoice in Your love, which death did not exhaust; Your love which shone resplendent in Your resurrection. We remember that burning fire of love which will never let You hold Your peace until Your chosen ones be all safely housed, until Zion be glorified, and Jerusalem settled on her everlasting foundations of light and love in heaven.

January 24

MORNING

"Surely He will deliver you from the snare of the fowler" — Psalm 91 3.

GOD DELIVERS HIS people from the snare of the fowler in two senses. From, and out of: First, He delivers them from the snare. He does not let them enter it. Secondly, if they should be caught therein, He delivers them out of it. The first promise is the most precious to some; the second is the best to others.

He shall deliver you from the snare." How? Trouble is often the means whereby God delivers us. God knows that our backsliding will soon end in our destruction, and He in mercy sends the rod. We say, Lord, why is this? For we do not know that our trouble has been the means of delivering us from far greater evil. Many have been thus saved from ruin by their sorrows and their crosses; these have frightened the birds from the net. At other times, God keeps His people from the snare of the fowler by giving them great spiritual strength, so that when they are tempted to do evil they say, *"How can I do this great wickedness, and sin against God?"*

But what a blessed thing it is that if the believer shall, in an evil hour, come into the net, yet God will bring him out of it! Oh backslider, be cast down, but do not despair. Wanderer though you have been lost, hear what Your Redeemer says: *"Return, Oh back-sliding children; I will have mercy upon you."* But you say you cannot return, for you are a captive. Then listen to the promise: *"Surely He will deliver you from the snare of the fowler."* You shall yet be brought out of all evil into which you have fallen, and though you shall never cease to repent of your ways, yet He that has loved you will not cast you away; He will receive you, and give you joy and gladness, that the bones which He has broken may rejoice. No bird of paradise shall die in the fowler's net.

EVENING

"But Martha was troubled with so much serving" — Luke 10:40.

HER FAULT WAS not that she served: the condition of a servant well becomes every Christian. *"I serve,"* should be the motto of all the princes of the royal family of heaven. Nor was it her fault that she had "much serving." We cannot do too much. let us do all that we possibly can; let head, and heart, and hands, be engaged in the Master's service. It was no fault of hers that she was busy preparing a feast for the Master. Happy Martha, to have an opportunity of entertaining so blessed a guest; and happy, too, to have the spirit to throw her whole soul so heartily into the engagement. Her fault was that she grew *"troubled with so much serving,"* so that she forgot Him, and only remembered the service. She allowed service to override communion, and so presented one duty stained with the blood of another.

We ought to be Martha and Mary in one: we should do much service, and have much communion at the same time. For this we need great grace. it is easier to serve than to commune. Joshua never grew weary in fighting with the Amalekites; but Moses, on the top of the mountain in prayer, needed two helpers to sustain his hands. The more spiritual the exercise, the sooner we tire in it. The choicest fruits are the hardest to rear: the most heavenly graces are the most difficult to cultivate. Beloved, while we do not neglect external things, which are good enough in themselves, we ought also to see to it that we enjoy living, personal fellowship with Jesus. See to it that sitting at the Savior's feet is not neglected, even though it be under the specious pretext of doing Him service. The first thing for our soul's health, the first thing for His glory, and the first thing for our own usefulness, is to keep ourselves in perpetual communion with the Lord Jesus, and to see that the vital spirituality of our religion is maintained over and above everything else in the world.

MORNING January 25

"I will mention the loving-kindnesses of the LORD and the praises of the LORD, according to all that the LORD has done for us" — Isaiah 63:7.

AND CAN YOU not do this? Are there no mercies which you have experienced? What though you are gloomy now, can you forget that blessed hour when Jesus met you, and said, *"Come unto me"?* Can you not remember that rapturous moment when He snapped your fetters, dashed your chains to the earth, and said, *"I came to break your bonds and set you free"?* Or if the love of your espousals be forgotten, there must surely be some precious milestone along the road of life not quite grown over with moss, on which you can read a happy memorial of His mercy towards you? What, did you never have a sickness like that which you are suffering now, and did He not restore you? Were you never poor before, and did He not supply your wants? Were you never in straits before, and did He not deliver you?

Arise, go to the river of your experience, and pull up a few bulrushes, and plait them into an ark, wherein your infant-faith may float safely on the stream. Forget not what your God has done for you; turn over the book of your remembrance, and consider the days of old. Can you not remember the hill Mizar? Did the Lord never meet with you at Hermon? Have you never climbed the Delectable Mountains? Have you never been helped in time of need? No, I know you have. Go back, then, a little way to the choice mercies of yesterday, and though all may be dark now, light up the lamps of the past, they shall glitter through the darkness, and you shall trust in the Lord till the day break and the shadows flee away. Remember, Oh Lord, Your tender mercies and Your loving-kindnesses, for they have been ever of old.

EVENING

"Do we then do away with Law through faith? Let it not be, Yes, Yes, we establish the Law" — Romans 3:31.

WHEN THE BELIEVER is adopted into the Lord's family, his relationship to old Adam and the law ceases at once; but then he is under a new rule, and a new covenant. Believer, you are God's child; it is your first duty to obey your heavenly Father. A servile spirit you have nothing to do with: you are not a slave, but a child; and now, inasmuch as you are a beloved child, you are bound to obey your Father's faintest wish, the least intimation of His will.

Does He bid you to fulfil a sacred ordinance? It is at your peril that you neglect it, for you will be disobeying your Father. Does He command you to seek the image of Jesus? It is not your joy to do so? Does Jesus tell you, *"Be perfect, even as your Father who is in Heaven is perfect"?* Then not because the law commands, but because your Savior enjoins, you will labor to be perfect in holiness. Does He bid his saints love one another? Do it, not because the law says, *"Love your neighbor,"* but because Jesus says, *"If you love Me, keep My commandments;"* and this is the commandment that He has given unto you, *"that you love one another."* Are you told to distribute to the poor? Do it, not because charity is a burden which you dare not shirk, but because Jesus teaches, *"Give to him that asks of you."* Does the Word say, "Love God with all your heart"? Look at the commandment and reply, Ah, commandment, Christ has fulfilled you already, therefore, I have no need to fulfill you for my salvation. But I rejoice to yield obedience to you because God is my Father now and He has a claim upon me, which I would not dispute.

May the Holy Spirit make your heart obedient to the constraining power of Christ's love, that your prayer may be, *"Make me to go in the path of Your commandments; for in them I delight."* Grace is the mother and nurse of holiness, and not the apologist of sin.

January 26 — MORNING

"Your heavenly Father" — Matthew 6:26.

GOD'S PEOPLE are doubly His children, they are His offspring by creation, and they are His sons by adoption in Christ. Hence they are privileged to call Him, "Our Father who is in heaven." Father! Oh, what a precious word is that, Here is authority: "If I am a Father, where is My honor?" If you are sons, where is your obedience? Here is affection mingled with authority; an authority which does not provoke rebellion; an obedience demanded which is most cheerfully rendered, which would not be withheld even if it might. The obedience which God's children yield to Him must be loving obedience. Do not go about the service of God as slaves to their taskmaster's toil, but run in the way of His commands because it is your Father's way. Yield your bodies as instruments of righteousness, because righteousness is your Father's will, and His will should be the will of His child.

Father! Here is a kingly attribute so sweetly veiled in love that the King's crown is forgotten in the King's face, and His scepter becomes, not a rod of iron, but a silver scepter of mercy. The scepter indeed seems to be forgotten in the tender hand of Him who wields it. Father! Here is honor and love. How great is a father's love to his children! That which friendship cannot do, and mere benevolence will not attempt, a father's heart and hand must do for his sons. They are his offspring, he must bless them; they are his children, he must show himself strong in their defence. If an earthly father watches over his children with unceasing love and care, how much more does our heavenly Father? Abba, Father! He who can say this, has uttered better music than cherubim or seraphim can reach. There is heaven in the depth of that word, Father! There is all I can ask; all my necessities can demand; all my wishes can desire. I have all in all to all eternity when I can say, *"Father."*

EVENING

"And all who heard wondered about these things" — Luke 2: 18.

WE MUST NOT CEASE to wonder at the great marvels of our God. It would be very difficult to draw a line between holy wonder and real worship. For when the soul is overwhelmed with the majesty of God's glory, though it may not express itself in song, or even utter its voice with bowed head in humble prayer, yet it silently adores. Our incarnate God is to be worshipped as the Wonderful One. That God should consider His fallen creature, man, and instead of sweeping him away with the broom of destruction, should Himself undertake to be man's Redeemer, and to pay his ransom price, is, indeed, marvelous!

But to each believer redemption is most marvelous as he views it in relation to himself. It is a miracle of grace indeed, that Jesus should forsake the thrones and royalties above, to suffer ignominiously below for you. let your soul lose itself in wonder, for wonder is in this way a very practical emotion. Holy wonder will lead you to grateful worship and heartfelt thanksgiving. It will cause within you godly watchfulness; you will be afraid to sin against such a love as this. Feeling the presence of the mighty God in the gift of His dear Son, you will pull off your shoes from off your feet, because the place whereon you stand is holy ground. You will be moved at the same time to glorious hope. If Jesus has done such marvelous things on your behalf, you will feel that heaven itself is not too great for your expectation. Who can be astonished at anything, when he has once been astonished at the manger and the Cross? What is there wonderful left after one has seen the Savior?

Dear reader, it may be that from the quietness and solitariness of your life, you are scarcely able to imitate the shepherds of Bethlehem, who told what they had seen and heard, but you can, at least, fill up the circle of the worshippers before the throne, by wondering at what God has done.

MORNING   January 27

"And we all received of His fullness" — John 1:6.

THESE WORDS TELL us that there is a fullness in Christ. There is a fullness of essential Deity, for *"in Him dwells all the fullness of the Godhead."* There is a fullness of perfect manhood, for in Him, bodily, that Godhead was revealed. There is a fullness of atoning efficacy in His blood, for *"the blood of Jesus Christ, His Son, cleanses us from all sin."* There is a fullness of justifying righteousness in His life, for *"there is therefore now no condemnation to those in Christ Jesus."* There is a fullness of divine prevalence in his plea, for *"He is able to save to the uttermost the ones that come to God by Him; since He ever lives to make intercession for them."* There is a fullness of victory in His death. for *"through death He destroyed him that had the power of death, that is the devil."* There is a fullness of efficacy in His resurrection from the dead, for by it *"we are begotten again unto a lively hope."* There is a fullness of triumph in His ascension, for *"when He ascended up on high, He led captivity captive, and received gifts for men."*

There is a fullness of blessings of every sort and shape; a fullness of grace to pardon. of grace to regenerate, of grace to sanctify, of grace to preserve, and of grace to perfect. There is a fullness at all times; a fullness of comfort in affliction; a fullness of guidance in prosperity. A fullness of every divine attribute, of wisdom, of power, of love; a fullness which it were impossible to survey, much less to explore. *"It pleased the Father that in Him should all fullness dwell."*

Oh, what a fullness must this be of which all receive! Fullness, indeed, must there be when the stream is always flowing, and yet the well springs up as free, as rich. as full as ever. Come, believer, and get all your need supplied; ask largely, and you shall receive largely, for this *"fullness"* is inexhaustible, and is treasured up where all the needy may reach it, even in Jesus, Immanuel, God with us.

EVENING

"But Mary treasured all these words keeping them afresh in her heart" — Luke 2:19.

THERE WAS AN exercise, on the part of this blessed woman, of three powers of her being: her memory, she kept all these things; her affections, she kept them in her heart, in her intellect, she pondered them; so that memory. affection, and understanding. were all exercised about the things which she had heard.

Beloved, remember what you have heard of your Lord Jesus, and what He has done for you; make your heart the golden pot of manna to preserve the memorial of the heavenly bread on which you have fed in days gone by. let your memory treasure up everything about Christ which you have either felt, or known, or believed, and then let your fond affections hold Him fast for evermore. Love the person of your Lord! Bring forth the alabaster box of your heart, even though it be broken, and let all the precious ointment of your affection come streaming on His pierced feet. Let your intellect be exercised concerning the Lord Jesus. Meditate upon what you read; stop not at the surface; dive into the depths. Be not as the swallow which touches the brook with her wing, but as the fish which penetrates the lowest wave.

Abide with your Lord: let Him not be to you as a wayfaring man, that tarries for a night, but constrain Him, saying, *"Abide with us, for the day is far spent."* Hold Him, and do not let Him go. The word *"ponder"* means to weigh. Make ready the balances of judgment. Oh, but where are the scales that can weigh the Lord Christ? *"He takes up the isles as a very little thing." "He weighs the mountain in scales."* Who shall take Him up? In what scales shall we weigh Him? Be it so, if your understanding cannot comprehend, let your affections apprehend; and if your spirit cannot compass the Lord Jesus with the grasp of understanding, let it embrace Him in the arms of affection.

January 28   MORNING

"Perfect in Christ Jesus" — Colossians 1:28.

DO YOU NOT feel in your own soul that perfection is not in you? Does not every day teach you that? Every tear which trickles from your eye, weeps *"imperfection;"* every sigh which bursts from your heart, cries *"imperfection;"* every harsh word which proceeds from your lip, mutters *"imperfection."* You have too frequently had a view of your own heart to dream for a moment of any perfection in yourself. But amid this sad consciousness of imperfection, here is comfort for you, you are *"perfect in Christ Jesus."* In God's sight, you are *"complete in Him;"* even now you are *"accepted in the Beloved."*

But there is a second perfection, yet to be realized, which is sure to all the seed. Is it not delightful to look forward to the time when every stain of sin shall be removed from the believer, and he shall be presented faultless before the throne, without spot, or wrinkle, or any such thing? The Church of Christ then will be so pure, that not even the eye of Omniscience will see a spot or blemish in her; so holy and so glorious, that Hart did not go beyond the truth when he said -

    "With my Savior's garments on,
    Holy as the Holy One."

Then shall we know, and taste, and feel the happiness of this vast but short sentence, *"Complete in Christ."* Not till then shall we fully comprehend the heights and depths of the salvation of Jesus.

Does not your heart leap for joy at the thought of it? Black as you are, you shall be white one day; filthy as you are, you shall be clean. Oh, it is a marvelous salvation this! Christ takes a worm and transforms it into an angel; Christ takes a black and deformed thing and makes it clean and matchless in His glory, peerless in His beauty, and fit to be the companion of seraphs. Oh my soul, stand and admire this blessed truth of perfection in Christ.

EVENING

"And the shepherds returned, glorifying and praising God for all those things which they had heard and seen, as it was told them" — Luke 2:20.

WHAT WAS THE subject of their praise? They praised God for what they had heard, for the good tidings of great joy that a Savior was born unto them. Let us copy them; let us also raise a song of thanksgiving that we have heard of Jesus and His salvation. They also praised God for what they had seen. There is the sweetest music, what we have experienced, what we have felt within, what we have made our own, *"the things which we have made touching the King."* It is not enough to hear about Jesus: mere hearing may tune the harp, but the fingers of living faith must create the music. If you have seen Jesus with the God-giving sight of faith, suffer no cobwebs to linger among the harpstrings, but loud to the praise of sovereign grace, awake your psaltery and harp.

One point for which they praised God was the agreement between what they had heard and what they had seen. Observe the last sentence, *"As it was told them."* Have you not found the gospel to be in yourselves just what the Bible said it would be? Jesus said He would give you rest. Have you not enjoyed the sweetest peace in Him? He said you should have joy, and comfort, and life through believing in Him. Have you not received all these? Are not His ways of pleasantness, and His paths of peace? Surely you can say with the queen of Sheba, *"The half has not been told me."* I have found Christ more sweet than His servants ever said He was. I looked upon His likeness as they painted it, but it was a mere daub compared with Himself; for the King in His beauty outshines all imaginable loveliness. Surely what we have *"seen"* keeps pace with, no, far exceeds, what we have *"heard."* Let us, then, glorify and praise God for a Savior so precious, and so satisfying.

MORNING January 29

"The things which are not seen" — 2 Corinthians 4:18.

IN OUR CHRISTIAN pilgrimage it is well, for the most part, to be looking forward. Forward lies the crown, and onward is the goal. Whether it be for hope, for joy, for consolation, or for the inspiring of our love, the future must, after all, be the grand object of the eye of faith. Looking into the future we see sin cast out, the body of sin and death destroyed, the soul made perfect, and fit to be a partaker of the inheritance of the saints in light. Looking further yet, the believer's enlightened eye can see death's river passed, the gloomy stream forded, and the hills of light attained on which stands the celestial city. He sees himself enter within the pearly gates, hailed as more than conqueror, crowned by the hand of Christ, embraced in the arms of Jesus, glorified with Him, and made to sit together with Him on His throne, even as He has overcome and has sat down with the Father on His throne.

The thought of this future may well relieve the darkness of the past and the gloom of the present. The joys of heaven will surely compensate for the sorrows of earth. Hush, my fears! This world is but a narrow span, and you shall soon have passed it. Hush, hush, my doubts! Death is but a narrow stream, and you shall soon have forded it. Time, how short eternity, how long! Death, how brief; immortality, how endless! I think I even now eat of Eshcol's clusters, and sip of the well which is within the gate. The road is so, so short! I shall soon be there.

When the world my heart is rending With its heaviest storm of care, My glad thoughts to heaven ascending, Find a refuge from despair. Faith's bright vision shall sustain me Till life's pilgrimage is past; Fears may vex and troubles pain me, I shall reach my home at last.

EVENING

"And the dove came in to him in the evening" — Genesis 8:11.

BLESSED BE THE LORD for another day of mercy, even though I am now weary with its toils. Unto the preserver of men lift I my song of gratitude. The dove found no rest out of the ark, and therefore returned to it; and my soul has learned yet more fully than ever, this day, that there is no satisfaction to be found in earthly things God alone can give rest to my spirit. As to my business, my possessions, my family, my attainments, these are all well enough in their way, but they cannot fulfil the desires of my immortal nature. *"Return unto your rest, Oh my soul, for the Lord has dealt bountifully with you."*

It was at the still hour, when the gates of the day were closing, that with weary wing the dove came back to the master: Oh Lord, enable me this evening thus to return to Jesus. She could not endure to spend a night hovering over the restless waste, nor can I bear to be even for another hour away from Jesus, the rest of my heart, the home of my spirit. She did not merely alight upon the roof of the ark, she *"came in to him;"* even so would my longing spirit look into the secret of the Lord, pierce to the interior of truth, enter into that which is within the veil, and reach to my Beloved in very deed. To Jesus must I come: short of the nearest and dearest intercourse with Him my panting spirit cannot stay. Blessed Lord Jesus, be with me, reveal Yourself, and abide with me all night, so that when I awake, I may be still with you.

I note that the dove brought in her mouth an olive branch plucked off, the memorial of the past day, and a prophecy of the future. Have I no pleasing record to bring home? No pledge and earnest of loving-kindness yet to come? Yes, my Lord, I present You my grateful acknowledgements for tender mercies which have been new every morning and fresh every evening; and now, I pray You, put forth Your hand and take Your dove into Your bosom.

January 30   MORNING

"And when you hear the sound of marching in the tops of the weeping trees, then you shall strike" — 2 Samuel 5:24.

THE MEMBERS OF Christ's Church should be very prayerful, always seeking the unction of the Holy One to rest upon their hearts, that the kingdom of Christ may come, and that His *"will be done on earth, even as it is in heaven;"* but there are times when God seems especially to favor Zion, such seasons ought to be to them like *"the sound of marching in the tops of the weeping trees."* We ought then to be doubly prayerful, doubly earnest, wrestling more at the throne than we have been accustomed to do. Action should then be prompt and vigorous. The tide is flowing, now let us pull manfully for the shore. Oh for Pentecostal outpourings and Pentecostal labors!

Christian, in yourself there are times *"when you hear the sound of marching in the tops of the weeping trees."* You have a peculiar power in prayer; the Spirit of God gives you joy and gladness; the Scripture is open to you; the promises are applied; you walk in the light of God's countenance; you have peculiar freedom and liberty in devotion, and more closeness of communion with Christ than was your habit. Now, at such joyous periods when you hear the *"sound of marching in the tops of the weeping trees"* is the time to arouse yourself; now is the time to get rid of any evil habit, while God the Spirit helps your infirmities. Spread your sail; but remember what you sometimes sing,

"I can only spread the sail;
You! You! must breathe the auspicious gale."

Only be sure you have the sail up. Do not miss the gale for want of preparation for it. Seek help of God, that you may be more earnest in duty when made more strong in faith; that you may be more constant in prayer when you have more liberty at the throne; that you may be more holy in your conversation while you live more closely with Christ.

EVENING

"In whom we also have been chosen to an inheritance" — Ephesians 1:11.

WHEN JESUS GAVE Himself for us, He gave us all the rights and privileges which went with Himself; so that now, although as eternal God, He has essential rights to which no creature may venture to pretend, yet as Jesus, the Mediator, the federal Head of the covenant of grace, He has no heritage apart from us. All the glorious consequences of His obedience unto death are the joint riches of all who are in Him, and on whose behalf He accomplished the divine will. See, He enters into glory, but not for Himself alone, for it is written, *"where Jesus entered the Forerunner for us"* (Heb. 6:20). Does He stand in the presence of God? *"He appears in the presence of God for us."* (Heb. 9:24).

Consider this, believer. You have no right to heaven in yourself: your right lies in Christ. If you are pardoned, it is through His blood; if you are justified, it is through His righteousness; if you are sanctified, it is because He is made of God unto you sanctification; if you shall be kept from falling, it will be because you are preserved in Christ Jesus; and if you are perfected at the last, it will be because you are complete in Him. Thus Jesus is magnified. For all is in Him and by Him; thus the inheritance is made certain to us for it is obtained in Him; thus each blessing is the sweeter, and even heaven itself the brighter, because it is Jesus our Beloved *"in whom"* we have obtained all.

Where is the man who shall estimate our divine portion? Weigh the riches of Christ in scales, and His treasures in balances, and then think to count the treasures which belong to the saints. Reach the bottom of Christ's sea of joy, and then hope to understand the bliss which God has prepared for them that love Him. Overleap the boundaries of Christ's possessions, and then dream of a limit to the fair inheritance of the elect. *"All things are yours, for you are Christ's and Christ is God's."*

MORNING   January 31

"Jehovah our Righteousness"—Jeremiah 23:6.

IT WILL ALWAYS give a Christian the greatest calm, quiet, ease, and peace, to think of the perfect righteousness of Christ. How often are the saints of God downcast and sad! I do not think they ought to be. I do not think they would if they could always see their perfection in Christ. There are some who are always talking about corruption, and the depravity of the heart, and the innate evil of the soul. This is quite true, but why not go a little further, and remember that we are *"perfect in Christ Jesus."* It is no wonder that those who are dwelling upon their own corruption should wear such downcast looks; but surely if we call to mind that *"Christ is made unto us righteousness,"* we shall be of good cheer. What though distresses afflict me, though Satan assault me, though there may be many things to be experienced before I get to heaven, those are done for me in the covenant of divine grace; there is nothing wanting in my Lord, Christ has done it all.

On the cross He said, *"It is finished!"* And if it be finished, then am I complete in Him, and can rejoice with joy unspeakable and full of glory, *"Not having my own righteousness, which is of the law, but that which is through the faith of Christ, the righteousness which is of God by faith."* You will not find on this side of heaven a holier people than those who receive into their hearts the doctrine of Christ's righteousness. When the believer says, I live on Christ alone; I rest on him solely for salvation; and I believe that, however unworthy, I am still saved in Jesus; then there rises up as a motive of gratitude this thought. Shall I not live to Christ? Shall I not love Him and serve Him, since I am saved by His merits? *"The love of Christ constrains us,"* — *"that they who live should not henceforth live unto themselves, but unto Him who died for them"* (2 Cor. 5:14,15). If saved by imputed righteousness, we shall greatly value imparted righteousness.

EVENING

"Then Ahimaaz ran by the way of the plain and ran past Cushi" — *2 Samuel 18:23.*

RUNNING IS NOT everything, there is much in the way which we select: a swift foot over hill and down dale will not keep pace with a slower traveler upon level ground. How is it with my spiritual journey, am I laboring up the hill of my own works and down into the ravines of my own humiliations and resolutions, or do I run by the plain way of *"Believe and live"?* How blessed is it to wait upon the Lord by faith! The soul runs without weariness, and walks without fainting, in the way of believing. Christ Jesus is the way of life, and He is a plain way, a pleasant way, a way suitable for the tottering feet and feeble knees of trembling sinners: am I found in this way, or am I hunting after another track such as priestcraft or metaphysics may promise me? I read of *"the way of holiness, that the wayfaring man, though a fool, shall not err therein."* Have I been delivered from proud reason and been brought as a little child to rest in Jesus' love and blood? If so, by God's grace, I shall outrun the strongest runner who chooses any other path. This truth I may remember to my profit in my daily cares and needs. It will be my wisest course to go at once to my God, and not to wander in a roundabout manner to this friend and that. He knows my wants and can relieve them, to whom should I repair but to Himself by the direct appeal of prayer, and the plain argument of the promise. Straightforward makes the best runner. I will not parley with the servants, but hasten to their Master.

In reading this passage, it strikes me that if men vie with each other in common matters, and one outruns the other, I ought to be in solemn earnestness so to run that I may obtain. Lord, help me to gird up the loins of my mind, and may I press forward towards the mark for the prize of my high calling of God in Christ Jesus.

February 1 MORNING

"Yea, they shall sing in the ways of the LORD" — Psalm 138:5.

THE TIME WHEN Christians begin to sing in the ways of the Lord is when they first lose their burden at the foot of the Cross. Not even the songs of the angels seem so sweet as the first song of rapture which gushes from the inmost soul of the forgiven child of God. You know how John Bunyan describes it. He says, when poor Pilgrim lost his burden at the Cross, he gave three great leaps, and went on his way singing-
"Blest Cross! blest Sepulchre! blest rather be
The Man that there was put to shame for me!"
Believer, do you recollect the day when your fetters fell off? Do you remember the place when Jesus met you, and said, *"I have loved you with an everlasting love"* (Jer. 31:3); *"I have blotted out as a cloud your transgressions, and as a thick cloud your sins; they shall not be mentioned against you any more for ever"* (Isa. 44:22).

Oh what a sweet season is that when Jesus takes away the pain of sin! When the Lord first pardoned my sin, I was so joyous that I could scarce refrain from dancing. I thought on my road home from the house where I had been set at liberty, that I must tell the stones in the street the story of my deliverance. So full was my soul of joy, that I wanted to tell every snow-flake that was falling from heaven of the wondrous love of Jesus, who had blotted out the sins of one of the chief of rebels. But it is not only at the commencement of the Christian life that believers have reason for song. As long as they live they discover cause to sing in the ways of the Lord, and their experience of His constant loving-kindness leads them to say, *"I will bless the Lord at all times: His praise shall continually be in my mouth."* See to it, brother, that you magnify the Lord this day.
Long as we tread this desert land,
New mercies shall new songs demand.

EVENING

"Your love to me was wonderful" — 2 Samuel 1:6.

COME, DEAR READERS, let each one of us speak for himself of the wonderful love, not of Jonathan, but of Jesus. We will not relate what we have been told, but the things which we have tasted and handled, of the love of Christ. Your love to me, Oh Jesus, was wonderful when I was a stranger wandering far from You, fulfilling the desires of the flesh and of the mind. Your love restrained me from committing the sin which is unto death, and withheld me from self-destruction. Your love held back the axe when Justice said, *"Cut it down! Why does it still waste this ground?"* Your love drew me into the wilderness, stripped me there, and made me feel the guilt of my sin, and the burden of my iniquity. Your love spoke thus comfortably to me when I was sore dismayed, saying, *"Come unto Me, and I will give you rest."* Oh, how matchless Your love when, in a moment, You washed my sins away, and made my polluted soul, which was crimson with the blood of my nativity, and black with the grime of my transgressions, to be white as the driven snow, and pure as the finest wool. How You commended Your love when You whispered in my ears, *"I am Yours and you are Mine."* Kind were those accents when You said, *"The Father Himself loves you."* And sweet the moments, passing sweet, when You declare to me *"the love of the Spirit."*

Never shall my soul forget those chambers of fellowship where You have unveiled Yourself to me. Had Moses his cleft in the rock, where he saw the train, the back parts of his God? We, too, have had our clefts in the rock, where we have seen the full splendors of the Godhead in the person of Christ. Did David remember the tracks of the wild goat, the land of Jordan and the Hermonites? We, too, can remember spots to memory dear, equal to these in blessedness. Precious Lord Jesus, give us a fresh draught of Your wondrous love to begin the month with. Amen.

MORNING February 2

"Without shedding of blood is no remission"— Hebrews 9:22.

THIS IS THE voice of unalterable truth. In none of the Jewish ceremonies were sins, even typically, removed without blood-shedding. In no case, by no means can sin be pardoned without atonement. It is clear, then, that there is no hope for me out of Christ; for there is no other blood-shedding which is worth a thought as an atonement for sin. Am I, then, believing in Him? Is the blood of His atonement truly applied to my soul? All men are on a level as to their need of Him. If we be never so moral, generous, amiable, or patriotic, the rule will not be altered to make an exception for us. Sin will yield to nothing less potent than the blood of Him whom God has set forth as a propitiation. What a blessing that there is the one way of pardon! Why should we seek another?

Persons of merely formal religion cannot understand how we can rejoice that all our sins are forgiven us for Christ's sake. Their works, and prayers, and ceremonies, give them very poor comfort. And well may they be uneasy, for they are neglecting the one great salvation, and endeavoring to get remission without blood. My soul, sit down, and behold the justice of God as bound to punish sin; see that punishment all executed upon your Lord Jesus, and fall down in humble joy, and kiss the dear feet of Him whose blood has made atonement for you. It is in vain when conscience is aroused to fly to feelings and evidences for comfort: this is a habit which we learned in the Egypt of our legal bondage. The only restorative for a guilty conscience is a sight of Jesus suffering on the cross. *"The blood is the life thereof,"* says the Levitical law, and let us rest assured that it is the life of faith and joy and every other holy grace.

Oh! how sweet to view the flowing Of my Savior's precious blood; With divine assurance knowing He has made my peace with God.

EVENING
"And these are ancient things"— 1 Chronicles 4:22.

YET NOT SO ancient as those precious things which are the delight of our souls. Let us for a moment recount them, telling them over as misers count their gold. The sovereign choice of the Father, by which He elected us unto eternal life, before the earth was, is a matter of vast antiquity, since no date can be conceived for it by the mind of man. We were chosen from *"before the foundations of the world"*. Everlasting love went with the choice, for it was not a bare act of divine will by which we were set apart, but the divine affections were concerned. The Father loved us in and from the beginning. Here is a theme for daily contemplation. The eternal purpose to redeem us from our foreseen ruin, to cleanse and sanctify us, and at last to glorify us, was of infinite antiquity, and runs side by side with immutable love and absolute sovereignty.

The covenant is always described as being everlasting, and Jesus, the second party in it, had His goings forth of old; He struck hands in sacred suretyship long before the first of the stars began to shine, and it was in Him that the elect were ordained unto eternal life. Thus in the divine purpose a most blessed covenant union was established between the Son of God and His elect people, which will remain as the foundation of their safety when time shall be no more. Is it not well to be conversant with these ancient things? Is it not shameful that they should be so much neglected and even rejected by the bulk of professors? If they knew more of their own sin, would they not be more ready to adore distinguishing grace? Let us both admire and adore tonight, as we sing:-

> A monument of grace,
> A sinner saved by blood;
> The streams of love I trace
> Up to the Fountain, God;
> And in His sacred bosom see
> Eternal thoughts of love to me.

February 3   MORNING

"So, then, brothers, we are... debtors" — Romans 8:12.

AS GOD'S CREATURES, we are all debtors to Him: to obey Him with all our body, and soul, and strength. Having broken His commandments, as we all have, we are debtors to His justice, and we owe to Him a vast amount which we are not able to pay. But of the Christian it can be said that he does not owe God's justice anything, for Christ has paid the debt His people owed; for this reason the believer owes the more to love. I am a debtor to God's grace and forgiving mercy; but I am no debtor to His justice, for He will never accuse me of a debt already paid. Christ said, *"It is finished!"* and by that He meant, that whatever His people owed was wiped away for ever from the book of remembrance. Christ, to the uttermost, has satisfied divine justice; the account is settled; the handwriting is nailed to the cross; the receipt is given, and we are debtors to God's justice no longer.

But then, because we are not debtors to our Lord in that sense, we become ten times more debtors to God than we should have been otherwise. Christian, pause and ponder for a moment. What a debtor you are to divine sovereignty! How much you owe to His disinterested love, for He gave His own Son that He might die for you. Consider how much you owe to His forgiving grace, that after ten thousand affronts He loves you as infinitely as ever. Consider what you owe to His power; how He has raised you from your death in sin; how He has preserved your spiritual life; how He has kept you from falling; and how, though a thousand enemies have beset your path, you have been able to hold on your way. Consider what you owe to His immutability. Though you have changed a thousand times, He has not changed once. You are as deep in debt as you can be to every attribute of God. To God you owe yourself, and all you have; yield yourself as a living sacrifice, it is but your reasonable service (Romans 12:1-3).

EVENING

"Tell me, You whom my soul loves, where do You feed, where do You lie downn at noon?" — Song of Solomon 1:7.

THESE WORDS EXPRESS the desire of the believer after Christ, and his longing for present communion with Him. Where do You feed Your flock? In Your house? I will go, if I may find You there. In private prayer? Then I will pray without ceasing. In the Word? Then I will read it diligently. In Your ordinances? Then I will walk in them with all my heart. Tell me where You feed, for wherever You stand as the Shepherd, there will I lie down as a sheep; for none but Yourself can supply my need. I cannot be satisfied to be apart from You. My soul hungers and thirsts for the refreshment of Your presence. *"Where do You make Your flock to rest at noon?"* For whether at dawn or noon, my only rest must be where You are and Your beloved flock. My soul's rest must be a grace-given rest, and can only be found in You. Where is the shadow of that rock? Why should I not repose beneath it? *"Why should I be as one that turns aside by the flocks of your companions?"* You have companions; why should I not be one? Satan tells me I am unworthy; but I always was unworthy, and yet You have long loved me; and therefore my unworthiness cannot be a bar to my having fellowship with You now.

It is true I am weak in faith, and prone to fall, but my very feebleness is the reason why I should always be where You feed Your flock, that I may be strengthened, and preserved in safety beside the still waters. Why should I turn aside? There is no reason why I should, but there are a thousand reasons why I should not, for Jesus beckons me to come. If He withdraw Himself a little, it is but to make me prize His presence more. Now that I am grieved and distressed at being away from Him, He will lead me yet again to that sheltered nook where the lambs of His fold are sheltered from the burning sun.

MORNING — February 4

"The love of the LORD" — Hosea 3:1.

BELIEVER, LOOK back through all your experience, and think of the way by which the Lord your God has led you in the wilderness, and how He has fed and clothed you every day, how He has borne with your ill manners, how He has put up with all your murmurings, and all your longings after the flesh-pots of Egypt? How He has opened the rock to supply you, and fed you with manna that came down from heaven! Think of how His grace has been sufficient for you in all your troubles, how His blood has been a pardon to you in all your sins, how His rod and His staff have comforted you. When you have thus looked back upon the love of the Lord, then let faith survey His love in the future, for remember that Christ's covenant and blood have something more in them than the past. He who has loved you and pardoned you, shall never cease to love and pardon. He is Alpha, and He shall be Omega also: He is first, and He shall be last.

Therefore, consider, when you shall pass through the valley of the shadow of death, you need fear no evil, for He is with you. When you shall stand in the cold floods of Jordan, you need not fear, for death cannot separate you from His love. When you shall come into the mysteries of eternity you need not tremble, *"For I am persuaded, that neither death nor life nor angels nor rulers nor powers nor things present nor things to come nor height nor depth nor any other created thing will be able to separate us from the love of God, which is in Christ Jesus, our Lord."*? Now, soul, is not your love refreshed? Does not this make you love Jesus? Does not a flight through illimitable plains of the ether of love inflame your heart and compel you to delight yourself in the Lord your God? Surely as we meditate on *"the love of the Lord,"* our hearts burn within us, and we long to love Him more.

EVENING

"Your refuge from the avenger of blood" Joshua 20:3.

IT IS SAID THAT in the land of Canaan, cities of refuge were so arranged, that any man might reach one of them within half a day at the utmost. Even so the word of our salvation is near to us. Jesus is a present Savior, and the way to Him is short. It is but a simple renunciation of our own merit, and a laying hold of Jesus, to be our all in all. With regard to the roads to the city of refuge, we are told that they were strictly preserved, every river was bridged, and every obstruction removed, so that the man who fled might find an easy passage to the city. Once a year the elders went along the roads and saw to their order, so that nothing might impede the flight of any one, and cause him, through delay, to be overtaken and slain. How graciously do the promises of the gospel remove stumbling blocks from the way! Wherever there were by-roads and turnings, there were fixed up hand-posts, with this inscription upon them: *"To the city of refuge!"*

This is a picture of the road to Christ Jesus. It is no roundabout road of the law; it is no obeying this, that, and the other. It is a straight road: *"Believe, and live."* It is a road so hard, that no self-righteous man can ever tread it, but so easy, that every sinner, who knows himself to be a sinner may by it find his way to heaven. No sooner did the man-slayer reach the outworks of the city than he was safe; it was not necessary for him to pass far within the walls, but the suburbs themselves were sufficient protection. Learn therefore, that if you do but touch the hem of Christ's garment, you shall be made whole; if you do but lay hold upon Him with *"faith as a grain of mustard seed,"* you are safe.

"A little genuine grace ensures
The death of all our sins."

Only waste no time, loiter not by the way, for the avenger of blood is swift of foot; and it may be he is at your heels at this still hour of eventide.

February 5

MORNING

"The Father has sent the Son as Savior of the world" — 1 John 4:14

IT IS A SWEET thought that Jesus Christ did not come forth without His Father's permission, authority, consent, and assistance. He was sent of the Father, that He might be the Savior of men. We are too apt to forget that, while there are distinctions as to the persons in the Trinity, there are no distinctions of honor. We too frequently ascribe the honor of our salvation, or at least the depths of its benevolence, more to Jesus Christ than we do the Father. This is a very great mistake. What if Jesus came? Did not His Father send Him? If He spoke wondrously, did not His Father pour grace into His lips, that He might be an able minister of the new covenant? He who knows the Father, and the Son, and the Holy Ghost as he should know them, never set one before another in his love; he sees them at Bethlehem, at Gethsemane, and on Calvary, all equally engaged in the work of salvation.

Oh Christian, have you put your confidence in the Man Christ Jesus? Have you placed your reliance solely on Him? And are you united with Him? Then believe that you are united unto the God of heaven. Since to the Man Christ Jesus you are brother, and hold closest fellowship, you are linked thereby with God the Eternal, and *"the Ancient of days"* is your Father and your friend. Did you ever consider the depth of love in the heart of Jehovah, when God the Father equipped His Son for the great enterprise of mercy? If not, be this your day's meditation. The Father sent Him! Contemplate that subject. Think how Jesus works what the Father wills. In the wounds of the dying Savior see the love of the great I AM. Let every thought of Jesus be also connected with the Eternal, ever-blessed God, for *"It pleased the Lord to bruise Him; He has put Him to grief."*

EVENING

"At that time Jesus answered" — Matthew 11:25.

THIS IS A SINGULAR way in which to commence a verse: *"At that time Jesus answered."* If you will look at the context you will not perceive that any person had asked Him a question, or that He was in conversation with any human being. Yet it is written, *"Answering at that time, Jesus said, Thank You, Father."* When a man answers, he answers a person who has been speaking to him. Who, then, had spoken to Christ? His Father. Yet there is no record of it; and this should teach us that Jesus had constant fellowship with His Father, and that God spoke into His heart so often, so continually, that it was not a circumstance singular enough to be recorded. It was the habit and life of Jesus to talk with God. Even as Jesus was, in this world, so are we; let us therefore learn the lesson which this simple statement concerning Him teaches us

May we likewise have silent fellowship with the Father, so that often we may answer Him, and though the world knows not to whom we speak, may we be responding to that secret voice unheard of any other ear, which our own ear, opened by the Spirit of God, recognizes with joy. God has spoken to us, let us speak to God — either to set to our seal that God is true and faithful to His promise, or to confess the sin of which the Spirit of God has convinced us, or to acknowledge the mercy which God's providence has given, or to express assent to the great truths which God the Holy Ghost has opened to our understanding. What a privilege is intimate communion with the Father of our spirits! It is a secret hidden from the world, a joy with which even the nearest friend intermeddles not. If we would hear the whispers of God's love, our ear must be purged and fitted to listen to His voice. This very evening may our hearts be in such a state, that when God speaks to us, we, like Jesus, may be prepared at once to answer Him.

MORNING

February 6

"Always praying"—Ephesians 6:18.

WHAT MULTITUDES of prayers we have put up from the first moment when we learned to pray. Our first prayer was a prayer for ourselves; we asked that God would have mercy upon us, and blot out our sin. He heard us. But when He had blotted out our sins like a cloud, then we had more prayers for ourselves. We have had to pray for sanctifying grace, for constraining and restraining grace. We have been led to crave for a fresh assurance of faith, for the comfortable application of the promise, for deliverance in the hour of temptation, for help in the time of duty, and for succor in the day of trial.

We have been compelled to go to God for our souls, as constant beggars asking for everything. Bear witness, children of God, you have never been able to get anything for your souls elsewhere. All the bread your soul has eaten has come down from heaven, and all the water of which it has drunk has flowed from the living rock, Christ Jesus the Lord. Your soul has never grown rich in itself; it has always been a pensioner upon the daily bounty of God. So your prayers have ascended to heaven for a range of spiritual mercies all but infinite. Your wants were innumerable, and therefore the supplies have been infinitely great, and your prayers have been as varied as the mercies have been countless.

Then have you not cause to say, *"I love the Lord, because He has heard the voice of my supplication"*? For as your prayers have been many, so also have been God's answers to them. He has heard you in the day of trouble, has strengthened you, and helped you, even when you dishonored Him by trembling and doubting at the mercy-seat. Remember this, and let it fill your heart with gratitude to God, who has thus graciously heard your poor weak prayers. *"Bless the Lord, Oh my soul, and forget not all His benefits."*

EVENING

"Pray for one another"—James 5:16.

AS AN ENCOURAGEMENT cheerfully to offer intercessory prayer, remember that such prayer is the sweetest God ever hears, for the prayer of Christ is of this character. In all the incense which our Great High Priest now puts into the golden censer, there is not a single grain for Himself. His intercession must be the most acceptable of all supplications. The more like our prayer is to Christ's, the sweeter it will be. So while petitions for ourselves will be accepted, our pleadings for others, having in them more of the fruits of the Spirit, more love, more faith, more brotherly kindness, will be, through the precious merits of Jesus, the sweetest oblation that we can offer to God, the very fat of our sacrifice.

Remember, again, that intercessory prayer is exceedingly prevalent. What wonders it has wrought! The Word of God teems with its marvelous deeds. Believer, you have a mighty engine in your hand, use it well, use it constantly, use it with faith, and you shall surely be a benefactor to your brother. When you have the King's ear, speak to Him for the suffering members of His body. When you are favored to draw very near to His throne, and the King says to you, "Ask, and I will give you what you will," let your petitions be, not for yourself alone, but for the many who need His aid. If you have grace at all, and are not an intercessor, that grace must be small as a grain of mustard seed. You have just enough grace to float your soul clear from the quicksand, but you have no deep floods of grace, or else you would carry in your joyous bark a weighty cargo of the wants of others, and you would bring back from your Lord, for them, rich blessings which but for you they might not have obtained:

Oh, let my hands forget their skill, My tongue be silent, cold, and still, This bounding heart forget to beat, If I forget the mercy-seat!

February 7 MORNING

"Arise and depart!" — Micah 2:10.

THE HOUR IS approaching when the message will come to us, as it comes to all, Arise, and go forth from the home in which you have dwelt, from the city in which you have done your business, from your family, from your friends. Arise, and take your last journey. And what know we of the journey? And what know we of the country to which we are bound? A little we have read thereof, and somewhat has been revealed to us by the Spirit; but how little do we know of the realms of the future! We know that there is a black and stormy river called *"Death."* God bids us cross it, promising to be with us.

And, after death, what comes? What wonder-world will open upon our astonished sight? What scene of glory will be unfolded to our view? No traveler has ever returned to tell. But we know enough of the heavenly land to make us welcome our summons there with joy and gladness. The journey of death may be dark, but we may go forth on it fearlessly, knowing that God is with us as we walk through the gloomy valley, and therefore we need fear no evil. We shall be departing from all we have known and loved here, but we shall be going to our Father's house, to our Father's home, where Jesus is; to that royal *"city which has foundations, whose builder and maker is God."* This shall be our last removal, to dwell for ever with Him we love, in the midst of His people in the presence of God.

Christian, meditate much on heaven, it will help you to press on, and to forget the toil of the way. This vale of tears is but the pathway to the better country: this world of woe is but the stepping-stone to a world of bliss.

Prepare us, Lord, by grace divine, For Your bright courts on high; Then bid our spirits rise, and join The chorus of the sky.

EVENING

"And they heard a great voice out of Heaven saying to them, Come up here!" — Revelation 11:1.

WITHOUT CONSIDERING these words in their prophetical connection, let us regard them as the invitation of our great Forerunner to His sanctified people. In due time there shall be heard *"a great voice from heaven"* to every believer, saying, *"Come up here."* This should be to the saints the subject of joyful anticipation. Instead of dreading the time when we shall leave this world to go unto the Father, we should be panting for the hour of our emancipation. Our song should be,

My heart is with Him on His throne. And ill can brook delay; Each moment listening for the voice, Rise up, and come away. We are not called down to the grave, but up to the skies. Our heaven-born spirits should long for their native air.

Yet should the celestial summons be the object of patient waiting. Our God knows best when to bid us *"Come up here."* We must not wish to antedate the period of our departure. I know that strong love will make us cry,

"Oh Lord of Hosts, the waves divide,
And land us all in heaven;"

but *"patience must have her perfect work"*. God ordains with accurate wisdom the most fitting time for redeemed to abide below. Surely, if there could be regrets in heaven, the saints might mourn that they did not live longer here to do more good. Oh, for more sheaves for my Lord's garner! more jewels for His crown! But how, unless there be more work? True, there is the other side of it, that, living so briefly, our sins are the fewer. But oh! when we are fully serving God, and He is giving us to scatter precious seed, and reap a hundredfold, we would even say it is well for us to abide where we are. Whether our Master shall say "go," or "stay," let us be equally well pleased, so long as He indulges us with His presence.

MORNING February 8

"You shall call His name Jesus"— Matthew 1:21.

WHEN A PERSON is dear, everything connected with him becomes dear for his sake. Thus, so precious is the person of the Lord Jesus in the estimation of all true believers, that everything about Him they consider to be inestimable beyond all price. *"All Your garments smell of myrrh, and aloes, and cassia,"* said David, as if the very vestments of the Savior were so sweetened by His person that he could not but love them. Certain it is, that there is not a spot where that hallowed foot has walked; there is not a word which those blessed lips have uttered, nor a thought which His loving Word has revealed, which is not to us precious beyond all price. And this is true of the names of Christ. They are all sweet in the believer's ear. Whether He be called the Husband of the Church, her Bridegroom, her Friend; whether He be styled the Lamb slain from the foundation of the world, the King, the Prophet, or the Priest — every title of our Master: Shiloh, Emmanuel, Wonderful, the Mighty Counsellor; every name is like the honeycomb dropping with honey, and luscious are the drops that distil from it.

But if there be one name sweeter than another in the believer's ear, it is the name of Jesus. Jesus! It is the name which moves the harps of heaven to melody. Jesus! It is the life of all our joys. If there be one name more charming, more precious than another, it is this name. It is woven into the very warp and woof of our psalmody. Many of our hymns begin with it, and scarcely any, that are good for anything, end without it. It is the sum total of all delights. It is the music with which the bells of heaven ring; a song in a word; an ocean for comprehension, although a drop for brevity: a matchless oratorio in two syllables; a gathering up of the hallelujahs of eternity in five letters.

> Jesus, I love Your charming name,
> It is music to my ear.

EVENING

"He shall save His people from their sins"— Matthew 1:21.

MANY PERSONS, IF they are asked what they understand by salvation, will reply, *"Being saved from hell and taken to heaven."* This is one result of salvation, but it is not one tenth of what is contained in that blessing. It is true our Lord Jesus Christ does redeem all His people from the wrath to come; He saves them from the fearful condemnation which their sins had brought upon them; but His triumph is far more complete than this. He saves His people *"from their sins."* Oh, sweet deliverance from our worst foes! Where Christ works a saving work, He casts Satan from his throne, and will not let him be master any longer. No man is a true Christian if sin reigns in his mortal body. Sin will be in us; it will never be utterly expelled till the spirit enters glory. But it will never have dominion. There will be a striving for dominion, a lusting against the new law and the new spirit which God has implanted but sin will never get the upper hand so as to be absolute monarch of our nature. Christ will be Master of the heart, and sin must be mortified. The Lion of the tribe of Judah shall prevail, and the dragon shall be cast out.

Professor, is sin subdued in you? If your life is unholy your heart is unchanged, and if your heart in unchanged you are an unsaved person. If the Savior has not sanctified you, renewed you, given you a hatred of sin and a love of holiness, He has done nothing in you of a saving character. The grace which does not make a man better than others is a worthless counterfeit. Christ saves His people, not in their sins, but from them: *"Without holiness no man shall see the Lord."*, *"Let every one that names the name of Christ depart from iniquity."* If not saved from sin, how shall we hope to be counted among His people. Lord, save me even now from all evil, and enable me to honor my Savior.

February 9 MORNING

"When David inquired of the LORD"— 2 Samuel 5:23.

WHEN DAVID MADE this inquiry he had just fought the Philistines, and gained a signal victory. The Philistines came up in great hosts, but, by the help of God, David had easily put them to flight. Note, however, that when they came a second time, David did not go up to fight them without inquiring of the Lord. Once he had been victorious, and he might have said, as many have in other cases, I shall be victorious again; I may rest quite sure that if I have conquered once, I shall triumph yet again. Why should I tarry to seek at the Lord's hands? Not so, David. He had gained one battle by the strength of the Lord; he would not venture upon another until he had ensured the same. He inquired, *"Shall I go up against them?"* He waited until God's sign was given.

Learn from David to take no step without God. Christian, if you would know the path of duty, take God for your compass. If you would steer your ship through the dark billows, put the tiller into the hand of the Almighty. Many a rock might be escaped, if we would let our Father take the helm; many a shoal or quicksand we might well avoid, if we would leave to His sovereign will to choose and to command. The Puritan Flavel said, *"As sure as I start to cut my own slice of pie, I cut myself."* This is a great truth. Said another old divine, *"He that goes before the cloud of God's providence goes on a fool's errand."* And so he does. We must mark God's providence leading us; and if providence tarries, tarry till providence comes. He who goes before providence, will be very glad to run back again. *"I will instruct you and teach you in the way which you shall go,"* is God's promise to His people. Let us, then, take all our perplexities to Him, and say, *"Lord, what will you have me to do?"* Leave not your room this morning without inquiring of the Lord.

EVENING

"Lead us not into temptation, but deliver us from evil" — Luke 11:4.

WHAT WE ARE taught to seek or shun in prayer, we should equally pursue or avoid in action. Very earnestly, therefore, should we avoid temptation, seeking to walk so guardedly in the path of obedience, that we may never tempt the devil to tempt us. We are not to enter the thicket in search of the lion. Dearly might we pay for such presumption. This lion may cross our path or leap upon us from the thicket, but we have nothing to do with hunting him. He that meets with him, even though he wins the day, will find it a stern struggle. Let the Christian pray that he may be spared the encounter. Our Savior, who had experience of what temptation meant, thus earnestly admonished His disciples: *"Pray that you enter not into temptation."*

But let us do as we will, we shall be tempted; hence the prayer *"deliver us from evil."* God had one Son without sin; but He has no son without temptation. The natural *"man is born to trouble as the sparks fly upwards"*, and the Christian man is born to temptation just as certainly. We must be always on our watch against Satan, because, like a thief, he gives no intimation of his approach. Believers who have had experience of the ways of Satan, know that there are certain seasons when he will most probably make an attack, just as at certain seasons bleak winds may be expected. Thus the Christian is put on a double guard by fear of danger, and the danger is averted by preparing to meet it. Prevention is better than cure. It is better to be so well armed that the devil will not attack you, than to endure the perils of the fight, even though you come off a conqueror. Pray this evening first that you may not be tempted, and next that if temptation be permitted, you may be delivered from the evil one.

MORNING February 10

"I know how to abound" — Philippians 4:12.

THERE ARE MANY who know *"how to be abased,"* who have not learned *"how to abound."* When they are set upon the top of a pinnacle their heads grow dizzy, and they are ready to fall. The Christian far oftener disgraces his profession in prosperity than in adversity. It is a dangerous thing to be prosperous. The crucible of adversity is a less severe trial to the Christian than the fining-pot of prosperity. Oh, what leanness of soul and neglect of spiritual things have been brought on through the very mercies and bounties of God! Yet this is not a matter of necessity, for the apostle tells us that he knew how to abound. When he had much he knew how to use it. Abundant grace enabled him to bear abundant prosperity. When he had a full sail he was loaded with much ballast, and so floated safely. It needs more than human skill to carry the brimming cup of mortal joy with a steady hand, yet Paul had learned that skill, for he declares, *"In all things I am instructed both to be full and to be hungry."*

It is a divine lesson to know how to be full, for the Israelites were full once, but while the flesh was yet in their mouth, the wrath of God came upon them. Many have asked for mercies that they might satisfy their own hearts' lust. Fullness of bread has often made fullness of blood, and that has brought on wantonness of spirit. When we have much of God's providential mercies, it often happens that we have but little of God's grace, and little gratitude for the bounties we have received. We are full and we forget God: satisfied with earth, we are content to do without heaven. Rest assured it is harder to know how to be full than it is to know how to be hungry, so desperate is the tendency of human nature to pride and forgetfulness of God. Take care that you ask in your prayers that God would teach you *"how to be full."*

> Let not the gifts Your love bestows
> Estrange our hearts from You.

EVENING

"I have blotted out as a thick cloud, your transgressions, and, as a cloud, your sins. Return to Me, for I have redeemed you" — Isaiah 44:22.

ATTENTIVELY observe THE INSTRUCTIVE SIMILITUDE: our sins are like a cloud. As clouds are of many shapes and shades, so are our transgressions. As clouds obscure the light of the sun, and darken the landscape beneath, so do our sins hide from us the light of Jehovah's face, and cause us to sit in the shadow of death. They are earth-born things, and rise from the miry places of our nature; and when so collected that their measure is full, they threaten us with storm and tempest. Alas! that, unlike clouds, our sins yield us no genial showers, but rather threaten to deluge us with a fiery flood of destruction. Oh you black clouds of sin, how can it be fair weather with our souls while you remain?

Let our joyful eye dwell upon THE NOTABLE ACT of divine mercy, *"blotting out."* God Himself appears upon the scene, and in divine benignity, instead of manifesting His anger, reveals His grace: He at once and forever effectually removes the mischief, not by blowing away the cloud, but by blotting it out from existence once for all. Against the justified man no sin remains, the great transaction of the cross has eternally removed His transgressions from him. On Calvary's summit the great deed, by which the sin of all the chosen was for ever put away, was completely and effectually performed.

Practically let us obey THE GRACIOUS COMMAND, *"return unto Me."* Why should pardoned sinners live at a distance from their God? If we have been forgiven all our sins, let no legal fear withhold us from the boldest access to our Lord. Let backslidings be bemoaned, but let us not persevere in them. To the greatest possible nearness of communion with the Lord, let us, in the power of the Holy Spirit, strive mightily to return. Oh Lord, this night restore us!

February 11   MORNING

"And they took note of them, that they had been with Jesus" — *Acts 4:13.*

A CHRISTIAN SHOULD be a striking likeness of Jesus Christ. You have read lives of Christ, beautifully and eloquently written, but the best life of Christ is His living biography, written out in the words and actions of His people. If we were what we profess to be, and what we should be, we should be pictures of Christ; yes, such striking likenesses of Him, that the world would not have to hold us up by the hour together, and say, Well, it seems somewhat of a likeness. But they would, when they once beheld us, exclaim, He has been with Jesus; he has been taught of Him; he is like Him; he has caught the very idea of the holy Man of Nazareth, and he works it out in his life and everyday actions.

A Christian should be like Christ in his boldness. Never blush to own your religion; your profession will never disgrace you: take care you never disgrace that. Be like Jesus, very valiant for your God. Imitate Him in your loving spirit; think kindly, speak kindly, and do kindly, that men may say of you, *"He has been with Jesus."* Imitate Jesus in His holiness. Was He zealous for His Master? So be you; ever go about doing good. Let not time be wasted: it is too precious. Was He self-denying, never looking to His own interest? Be the same. Was He devout? Be you fervent in your prayers. Had He deference to His Father's will? So submit yourselves to Him. Was He patient? So learn to endure.

And best of all, as the highest portraiture of Jesus, try to forgive your enemies, as He did; and let those sublime words of your Master, *"Father, forgive them; for they know not what they do,"* always ring in your ears. Forgive, as you hope to be forgiven. Heap coals of fire on the head of your foe by your kindness to him. Good for evil, remember, is godlike. Be godlike, then; and in all ways and by all means, so live that all may say of you, *"He has been with Jesus."*

EVENING
"You left your first love" — *Revelation 2:4.*

EVER TO BE REMEMBERED is that best and brightest of hours, when first we saw the Lord, lost our burden, received the roll of promise, rejoiced in full salvation, and went on our way in peace. It was spring time in the soul; the winter was past; the mutterings of Sinai's thunders were hushed; the flashings of its lightnings were no more perceived; God was seen as reconciled; the law threatened no vengeance, justice demanded no punishment. Then the flowers appeared in our heart; hope, love, peace, and patience sprung from the sod; the hyacinth of repentance, the snowdrop of pure holiness, the crocus of golden faith, the daffodil of early love, all decked the garden of the soul. The time of the singing of birds was come, and we rejoiced with thanksgiving; we magnified the holy name of our forgiving God, and our resolve was, "Lord, I am Yours, wholly Yours; all I am, and all I have, I would devote to You. You have bought me with Your blood; let me spend myself and be spent in Your service. In life and in death let me be consecrated to You.

How have we kept this resolve? Our espousal love burned with a holy flame of devotedness to Jesus. Is it the same now? Might not Jesus well say to us, *"I have somewhat against you, because you have left your first love"*? Alas! it is but little we have done for our Master's glory. Our winter has lasted all too long. We are as cold as ice when we should feel a summer's glow and bloom with sacred flowers. We give to God pence when He deserves pounds, but He deserves our heart's blood to be coined in the service of His church and of His truth. But shall we continue thus? Oh Lord, after You have so richly blessed us, shall we be ungrateful and become indifferent to Your good cause and work? Oh quicken us that we may return to our first love, and do our first works! Send us a genial spring, Oh Sun of Righteousness.

MORNING   February 12

"For as the sufferings of Christ abound to us, so also our comfort abounds through Christ" — 2 Corinthians 1:5.

HERE IS A BLESSED proportion. The Ruler of Providence bears a pair of scales. In this side He puts His people's trials, and in that He puts their consolations. When the scale of trial is nearly empty, you will always find the scale of consolation in nearly the same condition; and when the scale of trials is full, you will find the scale of consolation just as heavy. When the black clouds gather most, the light is the more brightly revealed to us. When the night lowers and the tempest is coming on, the Heavenly Captain is always closest to His crew. It is a blessed thing, that when we are most cast down, then it is that we are most lifted up by the consolations of the Spirit.

One reason is, because trials make more room for consolation. Great hearts can only be made by great troubles. The spade of trouble digs the reservoir of comfort deeper, and makes more room for consolation. God comes into our heart; He finds it full; He begins to break our comforts and to make it empty; then there is more room for grace. The humbler a man lies, the more comfort he will always have, because he will be more fitted to receive it.

Another reason why we are often most happy in our troubles, is this: then we have the closest dealings with God. When the barn is full, man can live without God: when the purse is bursting with gold, we try to do without so much prayer. But once take our gourds away, and we want our God; once cleanse the idols out of the house, then we are compelled to honor Jehovah. *"Out of the depths have I cried unto you, Oh Lord."* There is no cry so good as that which comes from the bottom of the mountains; no prayer half so hearty as that which comes up from the depths of the soul, through deep trials and afflictions. Hence they bring us to God, and we are happier; for nearness to God is happiness. Come, troubled believer, fret not over your heavy troubles, for they are the heralds of weighty mercies.

EVENING

"He will give you another Comforter, that He may be with you forever" — John 14:16.

THE GREAT FATHER revealed Himself to believers of old before the coming of His Son, and was known to Abraham, Isaac, and Jacob as the God Almighty. Then Jesus came, and the ever-blessed Son in His own proper person, was the delight of His people's eyes. At the time of the Redeemer's ascension, the Holy Spirit became the head of the present dispensation, and His power was gloriously manifested on and after Pentecost. He remains at this hour the present Immanuel God with us, dwelling in and with His people, quickening, guiding, and ruling in their midst.

Is His presence recognized as it ought to be? We cannot control His working; He is most sovereign in all His operations, but are we sufficiently anxious to obtain His help, or sufficiently watchful lest we provoke Him to withdraw His aid? Without Him we can do nothing, but by His almighty energy the most extraordinary results can be produced: everything depends upon His manifesting or concealing His power. Do we always look up to Him both for our inner life and our outward service with the respectful dependence which is fitting? Do we not too often run before His call and act independently of His aid?

Let us humble ourselves this evening for past neglects, and now entreat the heavenly dew to rest upon us, the sacred oil to anoint us, the celestial flame to burn within us. The Holy Ghost is no temporary gift, He abides with the saints. We have but to seek Him aright, and He will be found of us. He is jealous, but He is pitiful; if He leaves in anger, He returns in mercy. Condescending and tender, He does not weary of us, but waits to be gracious still.

Sin has been hammering my heart Unto a hardness, void of love, Let supplant grace to cross his art Drop from above.

February 13 — MORNING

"See what love the Father has given to us, that we should be called the children of God! For this reason, the world does not know us, because it did not know Him. Beloved, now we are children of God" — 1 John 3:1-2.

"BEHOLD, WHAT MANNER of love the Father has bestowed upon us" — Consider who we were, and what we feel ourselves to be even now when corruption is powerful in us, and you will wonder at our adoption. Yet we are called *"the sons of God."* What a high relationship is that of a son, and what privileges it brings! What care and tenderness the son expects from his father, and what love the father feels towards the son! But all that, and more than that, we now have through Christ. As for the temporary drawback of suffering with the elder brother, this we accept as an honor: *"Therefore the world knows us not, because it knew Him not."* We are content to be unknown with Him in His humiliation, for we are to be exalted with Him.

"Beloved, now we are children of God" — That is easy to read, but it is not so easy to feel. How is it with your heart this morning? Are you in the lowest depths of sorrow? Does corruption rise within your spirit, and grace seem like a poor spark trampled under foot? Does your faith almost fail you? Fear not, it is neither your graces nor feelings on which you are to live: you must live simply by faith on Christ. With all these things against us, even in the very depths of our sorrow, wherever we may be; now, as much in the valley as on the mountain, *"Beloved, now we are children of God."* Ah, but, you say, see how I am arrayed! My graces are not bright; my righteousness does not shine with apparent glory. But read the next: *"It does not yet appear what we shall be. But we know that when He shall appear, we shall be like Him."* The Holy Spirit shall purify our minds, and divine power shall refine our bodies, then shall we see Him as He is.

EVENING

"There is therefore now no condemnation" — Romans 8:1.

COME, MY SOUL, think of this. Believing in Jesus, you are actually and effectually cleared from guilt; you are led out of your prison. You are no more in fetters as a bond-slave; you are delivered now from the bondage of the law; you are freed from sin, and can walk at large as a free-man, your Savior's blood has procured your full discharge. You have a right now to approach your Father's throne. No flames of vengeance are there to scare you now; no fiery sword; justice cannot smite the innocent. Your disabilities are taken away: you were once unable to see your Father's face: you can see it now. You could not speak with Him; but now you have access with boldness.

Once there was a fear of hell upon you; but you have no fear of it now, for how can there be punishment for the guiltless? He who believes is not condemned, and cannot be punished. And more than all, the privileges you might have enjoyed, if you had never sinned, are yours now that you are justified. All the blessings which you would have had if you had kept the law, and more, are yours, because Christ has kept it for you. All the love and the acceptance which perfect obedience could have obtained of God, belong to you, because Christ was perfectly obedient on your behalf, and has imputed all His merits to your account, that you might be exceeding rich through Him, who for your sake became exceeding poor. Oh! how great the debt of love and gratitude you owe to your Savior!

> A debtor to mercy alone,
> Of covenant mercy I sing;
> Nor fear with Your righteousness on,
> My person and offerings to bring:
> The terrors of law and of God,
> With me can have nothing to do:
> My Savior's obedience and blood
> Hide all my transgressions from view.

MORNING February 14

"And his allowance was a regular allowance given him from the king, a daily ration for everyday, all the days of his life" – 2 Kings 25:30.

JEHOIACHIN WAS NOT sent away from the king's palace with a store to last him for months, but his provision was given him as a daily pension. Herein he well pictures the happy position of all the Lord's people. A daily portion is all that a man really wants. We do not need tomorrow's supplies; that day has not yet dawned, and its wants are as yet unborn. The thirst which we may suffer in the month of June does not need to be quenched in February, for we do not feel it yet; if we have enough for each day as the days arrive we shall never know want. Sufficient for the day is all that we can enjoy. We cannot eat or drink or wear more than the day's supply of food and raiment; the surplus gives us the care of storing it, and the anxiety of watching against a thief. One staff aids a traveler, but a bundle of staves is a heavy burden. Enough is not only as good as a feast, but is all that the greatest glutton can truly enjoy. This is all that we should expect; a craving for more than this is ungrateful. When our Father does not give us more, we should be content with His daily allowance. Jehoiachin's case is ours, we have a sure portion, a portion given us of the king, a gracious portion, and a perpetual portion. Here is surely ground for thankfulness.

Beloved Christian reader, in matters of grace you need a daily supply. You have no store of strength. Day by day must you seek help from above. It is a very sweet assurance that a daily portion is provided for you. In the word, through the ministry, by meditation, in prayer, and waiting upon God you shall receive renewed strength. In Jesus all needful things are laid up for you. Then enjoy your continual allowance. Never go hungry while the daily bread of grace is on the table of mercy.

EVENING
"She was healed instantly" Luke 8:47.97

ONE OF THE MOST touching and teaching of the Savior's miracles is before us tonight. The woman was very ignorant. She imagined that virtue came out of Christ by a law of necessity, without His knowledge or direct will. Moreover, she was a stranger to the generosity of Jesus' character, or she would not have gone behind to steal the cure which He was so ready to bestow. Misery should always place itself right in the face of mercy. Had she known the love of Jesus' heart, she would have said, I have but to put myself where He can see me. His omniscience will teach Him my case, and His love at once will work my cure. We admire her faith, but we marvel at her ignorance. After she had obtained the cure, she rejoiced with trembling: glad was she that the divine virtue had wrought a marvel in her; but she feared lest Christ should retract the blessing, and put a negative upon the grant of His grace: little did she comprehend the fulness of His love!

We have not so clear a view of Him as we could wish; we know not the heights and depths of His love; but we know of a surety that He is too good to withdraw from a trembling soul the gift which it has been able to obtain. But here is the marvel of it: little as was her knowledge, her faith, because it was real faith, saved her, and saved her at once. There was no tedious delay. Faith's miracle was instantaneous. If we have faith as a grain of mustard seed, salvation is our present and eternal possession. If in the list of the Lord's children we are written as the feeblest of the family, yet, being heirs through faith, no power, human or devilish, can eject us from salvation. if we cannot clasp the Lord in our hands with Simeon, if we dare not lean our heads upon His bosom with John, yet if we can venture in the press behind Him, and touch the hem of His garment, we are made whole. Courage, timid one! your faith has saved you; go in peace. *"Being justified by faith, we have peace with God."*

February 15   MORNING

"To Him be glory both now and to the day of eternity" — 2 Peter 3:18.

HEAVEN WILL be full of the ceaseless praises of Jesus. Eternity! Your unnumbered years shall speed their everlasting course, but forever and forever, *"to Him be glory."* Is He not a *"Priest forever after the order of Melchizedek"*? *"To Him be glory."* Is He not king forever? - King of kings and Lord of lords, the everlasting Father? *"To Him be glory to the day of eternity."* Never shall His praises cease. That which was bought with blood deserves to last while immortality endures. The glory of the cross must never be eclipsed; the lustre of the grave and of the resurrection must never be dimmed. Oh Jesus! You shall be praised forever. Long as immortal spirits live long as the Father's throne endures, forever, forever, unto You shall be glory.

Believer, you are anticipating the time when you shall join the saints above in ascribing all glory to Jesus; but are you glorifying Him now? The apostle's words are, *"To Him be glory both now and forever."* Will you not this day make it your prayer? Lord, help me to glorify You; I am poor, help me to glorify You by contentment; I am sick, help me to give You honor by patience; I have talents, help me to extol You by spending them for You; I have time, Lord, help me to redeem it, that I may serve you; I have a heart to feel, Lord, let that heart feel no love but Yours, and glow with no flame but affection for You; I have a head to think, Lord, help me to think of You and for You; You have put me in this world for something, Lord, show me what that is, and help me to work out my life-purpose: I cannot do much; but as the widow put in her two mites, which were all her living, so, Lord, I cast my time and eternity too into Your treasury; I am all Yours; take me, and enable me to glorify You now, in all that I say, in all that I do, and with all that I have.

EVENING

"By which they have made You glad" — Psalm 45:8.

AND WHO ARE THUS privileged to make the Savior glad? His church, His people. But is it possible? He makes us glad, but how can we make Him glad? By our love. Ah! we think it so cold, so faint; and so, indeed, we must sorrowfully confess it to be, but it is very sweet to Christ. Hear His own eulogy of that love in the golden Song of Solomon: *"How fair is your love, my sister, my spouse! how much better is your love than wine!"* See, loving heart, how He delights in you. When you lean your head on His bosom, you not only receive, but you give Him joy; when you gaze with love upon His all-glorious face, you not only obtain comfort, but impart delight. Our praise, too, gives Him joy, not the song of the lips alone, but the melody of the heart's deep gratitude. Our gifts, too, are very pleasant to Him; He loves to see us lay our time, our talents, our substance upon His altar, not for the value of what we give, but for the sake of the motive from which the gift springs. To Him the lowly offerings of His saints are more acceptable than thousands of gold and silver.

Holiness is like frankincense and myrrh to Him. Forgive your enemy, and you make Christ glad; distribute of your substance to the poor, and He rejoices; be the means of saving souls, and you give Him to see of the travail of His soul; proclaim His gospel, and you are a sweet savor unto Him; go among the ignorant and lift up the cross, and you have given Him honor. It is in your power even now to break the alabaster box, and pour the precious oil of joy upon His head, as did the woman of old, whose memorial is to this day set forth wherever the gospel is preached. Will you be backward then? Will you not perfume your beloved Lord with the myrrh and aloes, and cassia, of your heart's praise? Yes, the ivory palaces shall hear the songs of the saints!

MORNING   February 16

"I have learned to be content in whatever state I am" — Philippians 4:11

THESE WORDS show us that contentment is not a natural propensity of man. Ill weeds grow apace. Covetousness, discontent, and murmuring are as natural to man as thorns are to the soil. We need not sow thistles and brambles; they come up naturally enough, because they are indigenous to earth: and so, we need not teach men to complain; they complain fast enough without any education. But the precious things of the earth must be cultivated. If we would have wheat, we must plough and sow; if we want flowers, there must be the garden, and all the gardener's care.

Now, contentment is one of the flowers of heaven, and if we would have it, it must be cultivated; it will not grow in us by nature; it is the new nature alone that can produce it, and even then we must be specially careful and watchful that we maintain and cultivate the grace which God has sown in us. Paul says, *"I have learned...to be content;"* as much as to say, he did not know how at one time. It cost him some pains to attain to the mystery of that great truth. No doubt he sometimes thought he had learned, and then broke down. And when at last he had attained unto it, and could say, *"I have learned in whatsoever state I am, therewith to be content,"* he was an old, grey-headed man, upon the borders of the grave, a poor prisoner shut up in Nero's dungeon at Rome.

We might well be willing to endure Paul's infirmities, and share the cold dungeon with him, if we too might by any means attain unto his good degree. Do not indulge the notion that you can be contented without learning, or learn without discipline. It is not a power that may be exercised naturally, but a science to be acquired gradually. We know this from experience. Brother, hush that murmur, natural though it be, and continue a diligent pupil in the College of Content.

EVENING
"Your good Spirit" — Nehemiah 9:20.

COMMON, TOO COMMON is the sin of forgetting the Holy Spirit. This is folly and ingratitude. He deserves well at our hands, for He is good, supremely good. As God, He is good essentially. He shares in the threefold ascription of Holy, holy, holy, which ascends to the Triune Jehovah. Unmixed purity, and truth, and grace is He. He is good, benevolently, tenderly bearing with our waywardness, striving with our rebellious wills; quickening us from our death in sin, and then training us for the skies as a loving nurse fosters her child. How generous, forgiving, and tender is this patient Spirit of God

He is good operatively. All His works are good in the most eminent degree: He suggests good thoughts, prompts good actions, reveals good truths, applies good promises, assists in good attainments, and leads to good results. There is no spiritual good in all the world of which He is not the author and sustainer, and heaven itself will owe the perfect character of its redeemed inhabitants to His work.

He is good officially; whether as Comforter, Instructor, Guide, Sanctifier, Quickener, or Intercessor, He fulfils His office well, and each work is fraught with the highest good to the church of God. They who yield to His influences become good, they who obey His impulses do good, they who live under His power receive good.

Let us then act towards so good a Person according to the dictates of gratitude. Let us revere His person, and adore Him as God over all, blessed forever; let us own His power, and our need of Him by waiting upon Him in all our holy enterprises; let us hourly seek His aid, and never grieve Him; and let us speak to His praise whenever occasion occurs. The church will never prosper until more reverently it believes in the Holy Ghost. He is so good and kind, that it is sad indeed that He should be grieved by slights and negligences.

February 17   MORNING

"Isaac lived by the well La-hai-roi" — Genesis 25:11.

HAGAR HAD ONCE found deliverance there and Ishmael had drunk from the water so graciously revealed by the God who lives and sees the sons of men; but this was a merely casual visit, such as worldlings pay to the Lord in times of need, when it serves their turn. They cry to Him in trouble, but forsake Him in prosperity. Isaac dwelled there, and made the well of the living and all-seeing God his constant source of supply. The usual tenor of a man's life, the dwelling of his soul, is the true test of his state. Perhaps the providential visitation experienced by Hagar struck Isaac's mind, and led him to revere the place; its mystical name endeared it to him; his frequent musings by its brim at eventide made him familiar with the well; his meeting Rebekah there had made his spirit feel at home near the spot; but best of all, the fact that he there enjoyed fellowship with the living God, had made him select that hallowed ground for his dwelling.

Let us learn to live in the presence of the living God; let us pray the Holy Spirit that this day, and every other day, we may feel, *"You, God, see me."* May the Lord Jehovah be as a well to us, delightful, comforting, unfailing, springing up unto eternal life'. The bottle of the creature cracks and dries up, but the well of the Creator never fails; happy is the one who dwells at the well, and so has abundant and constant supplies near at hand. The Lord has been a sure helper to others: His name is Shaddai, God All-sufficient; our hearts have often had most delightful intercourse with Him. Through Him our soul has found her glorious Husband, the Lord Jesus; and in Him this day we live, and move, and have our being; let us, then, dwell in closest fellowship with Him. Glorious Lord, constrain us that we may never leave You, but dwell by the well of the living God.

EVENING

"Yet the LORD was there" — Ezekiel 35:10.

EDOM'S PRINCES SAW the whole country left desolate, and counted upon its easy conquest; but there was one great difficulty in their way quite unknown to them: *"The Lord was there;"* and in His presence lay the special security of the chosen land. Whatever may be the machinations and devices of the enemies of God's people, there is still the same effectual barrier to thwart their design. The saints are God's heritage, and He is in the middle of them, and will protect His own. What comfort this assurance yields us in our troubles and spiritual conflicts! We are constantly opposed, and yet perpetually preserved! How often Satan shoots his arrows against our faith, but our faith defies the power of hell's fiery darts; they are not only turned aside, but they are quenched upon its shield, for *"the Lord is there."* Our good works are the subjects of Satan's attacks. A saint never yet had a virtue or a grace which was not the target for hellish bullets: whether it was hope bright and sparkling, or love warm and fervent, or patience all-enduring, or zeal flaming like coals of fire, the old enemy of everything that is good has tried to destroy it. The only reason why anything virtuous or lovely survives in us is this, *"the Lord is there."*

If the Lord is with us through life, we need not fear for our dying confidence; for when we come to die, we shall find that *"the Lord is there;"* Where the billows are most tempestuous, and the water is most chill, we shall feel the bottom, and know that it is good: our feet shall stand upon the Rock of Ages when time is passing away. Beloved, from the first of a Christian's life to the last, the only reason why he does not perish is because *"the Lord is there."* When the God of everlasting love shall change and leave His elect to perish, then may the Church of God be destroyed; but not till then, because it is written, JEHOVAH SHAMMAH, *"the Lord is there."*

MORNING   February 18

"Make me know why You contend with me"—Job 10:2.

PERHAPS, OH TRIED SOUL, the Lord is doing this to develop your graces. There are some of your graces which would never be discovered if it were not for your trials. Do you not know that your faith never looks so grand in summer weather as it does in winter? Love is too often like a glow-worm, showing but little light unless it is in the midst of surrounding darkness. Hope itself is like a star, not to be seen in the sunshine of prosperity, and only to be discovered in the night of adversity. Afflictions are often the black foils in which God sets the jewels of His children's graces, to make them shine the better. It was but a little while ago that on your knees you were saying, Lord, I fear I have no faith: let me know that I have faith. Was not this really, though perhaps unconsciously, praying for trials? For how can you know that you have faith until your faith is exercised? Depend upon it, God often sends us trials that our graces may be discovered, and that we may be certified of their existence.

Besides, it is not merely discovery, real growth in grace is the result of sanctified trials. God often takes away our comforts and our privileges in order to make us better Christians. He trains His soldiers, not in tents of ease and luxury, but by turning them out and causing them to make forced marches and do hard service. He makes them ford through streams, and swim through rivers, and climb mountains, and walk many a long mile with heavy knapsacks of sorrow on their backs. Well, Christian, may not this account for the troubles through which you are passing? Is not the Lord bringing out your graces, and making them grow? Is not this the reason why He is contending with you?

> Trials make the promise sweet;
> Trials give new life to prayer;
> Trials bring me to His feet,
> Lay me low, and keep me there.

EVENING
"Father, I have sinned"—Luke 15:18.

IT IS QUITE certain that those whom Christ has washed in His precious blood need not make a confession of sin, as culprits or criminals, before God the Judge, for Christ has forever taken away all their sins in a legal sense, so that they no longer stand where they can be condemned, but are once for all accepted in the Beloved. But having become children, and offending as children, ought they not every day to go before their heavenly Father and confess their sin, and acknowledge their iniquity in that character? Nature teaches that it is the duty of erring children to make a confession to their earthly father, and the grace of God in the heart teaches us that we, as Christians, owe the same duty to our heavenly Father.

We daily offend, and ought not to rest without daily pardon. For, supposing that my trespasses against my Father are not at once taken to Him to be washed away by the cleansing power of the Lord Jesus, what will be the consequence? If I have not sought forgiveness and been washed from these offenses against my Father, I shall feel at a distance from Him; I shall doubt His love to me; I shall tremble at Him; I shall be afraid to pray to Him: I shall grow like the prodigal, who, although still a child, was yet far off from his father. But if, with a child's sorrow at offending so gracious and loving a Parent, I go to Him and tell Him all, and rest not till I realize that I am forgiven, then I shall feel a holy love to my Father, and shall go through my Christian career, not only as saved, but as one enjoying present peace in God through Jesus Christ my Lord. There is a wide distinction between confessing sin as a culprit, and confessing sin as a child. The Father's bosom is the place for penitent confessions. We have been cleansed once for all, but our feet still need to be washed from the defilement of our daily walk as children of God.

February 19   MORNING

"Thus says the Lord God. I will yet for this be inquired of by the house of Israel to do it for them" — Ezekiel 36:37.

PRAYER IS THE forerunner of mercy. Turn to sacred history, and you will find that scarcely ever did a great mercy come to this world unheralded by supplication. You have found this true in your own personal experience. God has given you many an unsolicited favor, but still great prayer has always been the prelude of great mercy with you. When you first found peace through the blood of the cross, you had been praying much, and earnestly interceding with God that He would remove your doubts, and deliver you from your distresses. Your assurance was the result of prayer. When at any time you have had high and rapturous joys, you have been obliged to look upon them as answers to your prayers. When you have had great deliverances out of sore troubles, and mighty helps in great dangers, you have been able to say, *"I sought the Lord, and He heard me, and delivered me from all my fears."*

Prayer is always the preface to blessing. It goes before the blessing as the blessing's shadow. When the sunlight of God's mercies rises upon our necessities, it casts the shadow of prayer far down upon the plain. Or, to use another illustration, when God piles up a hill of mercies, He Himself shines behind them, and He casts on our spirits the shadow of prayer, so that we may rest certain, if we are much in prayer, our pleadings are the shadows of mercy. Prayer is thus connected with the blessing to show us the value of it. If we had the blessings without asking for them, we should think them common things; but prayer makes our mercies more precious than diamonds. The things we ask for are precious, but we do not realize their preciousness until we have sought for them earnestly.

Prayer makes the darkened cloud withdraw; Prayer climbs the ladder Jacob saw; Gives exercise to faith and love; Brings every blessing from above.

EVENING

"He first found his own brother Simon" John 1:41.

THIS CASE IS AN excellent pattern of all cases where spiritual life is vigorous. As soon as a man has found Christ, he begins to find others. I will not believe that you have tasted of the honey of the gospel if you can eat it all yourself. True grace puts an end to all spiritual monopoly. Andrew first found his own brother Simon, and then others. Relationship has a very strong demand upon our first individual efforts. Andrew, you did well to begin with Simon.

I doubt whether there are not some Christians giving away tracts at other people's houses who would do well to give away a tract at their own; whether there are not some engaged in works of usefulness abroad who are neglecting their special sphere of usefulness at home. You may or you may not be called to evangelize the people in any particular locality, but certainly you are called to see after your own servants, your own kinsfolk and acquaintance. Let your religion begin at home. Many tradesmen export their best commodities. The Christian should not. He should have all his conversation everywhere of the best savor; but let him have a care to put forth the sweetest fruit of spiritual life and testimony in his own family.

When Andrew went to find his brother, he little imagined how eminent Simon would become. Simon Peter was worth ten Andrews so far as we can gather from sacred history, and yet Andrew was instrumental in bringing him to Jesus. You may be very deficient in talent yourself, and yet you may be the means of drawing to Christ one who shall become eminent in grace and service. Ah! dear friend, you little know the possibilities which are in you. You may but speak a word to a child, and in that child there may be slumbering a heart which shall stir the Christian church in years to come. Andrew has only two talents, but he finds Peter. Go and do likewise.

February 20   MORNING

"God, who comforts those who are brought low" — 2 Corinthians 7:6.

AND WHO COMFORTS like Him? Go to some poor, melancholy, distressed child of God; tell him sweet promises, and whisper in his ear choice words of comfort; he is like the deaf adder, he listens not to the voice of the charmer, charm he never so wisely. He is drinking gall and wormwood, and comfort him as you may, it will be only a note or two of mournful resignation that you will get from him; you will bring forth no psalms of praise, no hallelujahs, no joyful sonnets. But let God come to His child, let Him lift up his countenance, and the mourner's eyes glisten with hope. Do you not hear him sing:

> 'Tis paradise, if you are here;
> If you depart, 'tis hell.

You could not have cheered him: but the Lord has done it; *"He is the God of all comfort."* There is no balm in Gilead, but there is balm in God. There is no physician among the creatures, but the Creator is Jehovah-rophi. It is marvelous how one sweet word of God will make whole songs for Christians. One word of God is like a piece of gold, and the Christian is the gold beater, and can hammer that promise out for whole weeks.

So, then, poor Christian, you need not sit down in despair. Go to the Comforter, and ask Him to give you consolation. You are a poor dry well. You have heard it said, that when a pump is dry, you must pour water down it first of all, and then you will get water and so, Christian, when you are dry, go to God, ask Him to shed abroad His joy in your heart, and then your joy shall be full. Do not go to earthly acquaintances, for you will find them Job's comforters after all; but go first and foremost to your *"God, who comforts those who are brought low,"* and you will soon say, *"In the multitude of my thoughts within me Your comforts delight my soul."*

EVENING

"Then Jesus was led up into the wilderness by the Spirit to be tempted by the Devil" — Matthew 4:1.

HOLY CHARACTER does not avert temptation. Jesus was tempted. When Satan tempts us, his sparks fall upon tinder; but in Christ's case, it was like striking sparks on water; yet the enemy continued his evil work. Now, if the devil goes on striking when there is no result, how much more will he do it when he knows what inflammable stuff our hearts are made of! Though you become greatly sanctified by the Holy Spirit, expect that the great dog of hell will bark at you still.

In the haunts of men we expect to be tempted, but even seclusion will not guard us from the same trial. Jesus Christ was led away from human society into the wilderness, and was tested by the devil. Solitude has its charms and its benefits, and may be useful in checking the lust of the eye and the pride of life; but the devil will follow us into the most lovely retreats. Do not suppose that it is only the worldly-minded who have dreadful thoughts and blasphemous temptations, for even spiritual-minded persons endure the same; and in the holiest position we may suffer the darkest temptation.

The utmost consecration of spirit will not insure you against Satanic temptation. Christ was consecrated through and through. It was His meat and drink to do the will of Him that sent Him: and yet He was tested! Your hearts may glow with a seraphic flame of love to Jesus, and yet the devil will try to bring you down to Laodicean lukewarmness. If you will tell me when God permits a Christian to lay aside his armor, I will tell you when Satan has left off temptation. Like the old knights in war time, we must sleep with helmet and breastplate buckled on, for the arch-deceiver will seize our first unguarded hour to make us his prey. The Lord keep us watchful in all seasons, and give us a final escape from the jaw of the lion and the paw of the bear.

February 21 MORNING

"I will never leave you nor ever forsake you" — Hebrews 13:5.

IF WE CAN ONLY grasp these words by faith, we have an all-conquering weapon in our hand. What doubt will not be slain by this two-edged sword? What fear is there which shall not fall smitten with a deadly wound before this arrow from the bow of God's covenant? Will not the distresses of life and the pangs of death; will not the corruptions within, and the snares without; will not the trials from above, and the temptations from beneath, all seem but light afflictions, when we can hide ourselves beneath the bulwark of *"He has said"*? Yes; whether for delight in our quietude, or for strength in our conflict, *"He has said"* must be our daily resort.

And this may teach us the extreme value of searching the Scriptures. There may be a promise in the Word which would exactly fit your case, but you may not know of it, and therefore you miss its comfort. You are like prisoners in a dungeon, and there may be one key in the bunch which would unlock the door, and you might be free, But if you will not look for it, you may remain a prisoner still, though liberty is so near at hand. There may be a potent medicine in the great pharmacopeia of Scripture, and you may yet continue sick unless you will examine and search the Scriptures to discover what *"He has said."*

Should you not be reading the Bible, store your memories richly with the promises of God? You can remember the sayings of great men. You treasure up the verses of renowned poets; ought you not to be profound in your knowledge of the words of God, so that you may be able to quote them readily when you would solve a difficulty, or overthrow a doubt? Since *"He has said"* is the source of all wisdom, and the fountain of all comfort, let it dwell in you richly, as *"A well of water, springing up unto everlasting life."* So shall you grow healthy, strong, and happy in the divine life.

EVENING

"Do you then know what you are reading?" — Acts 8:30.

WE WOULD BE ABLER teachers of others, and less liable to be carried about by every wind of doctrine, if we sought to have a more intelligent understanding of the Word of God. As the Holy Spirit, the Author of the Scriptures, is He who alone can enlighten us rightly to understand them, we should constantly ask His teaching, and His guidance into all truth. When the prophet Daniel would interpret Nebuchadnezzar's dream, what did he do? He set himself to earnest prayer that God would open up the vision. The apostle John, in his vision at Patmos, saw a book sealed with seven seals which none was found worthy to open, or so much as to look upon. The book was afterwards opened by the Lion of the tribe of Judah, who had prevailed to open it; but it is written first: *"I wept much."* The tears of John, which were his liquid prayers, were, so far as he was concerned, the sacred keys by which the folded book was opened.

Therefore if, for your own and others' profiting, you desire to be *"filled with the knowledge of God's will in all wisdom and spiritual understanding,"* remember that prayer is your best means of study: like Daniel, you shall understand the dream, and the interpretation thereof, when you have sought unto God; and like John you shall see the seven seals of precious truth unloosed, after you have wept much. Stones are not broken, except by an earnest use of the hammer; and the stone-breaker must go down on his knees. Use the hammer of diligence, and let the knee of prayer be exercised, and there is not a stony doctrine in revelation which is useful for you to understand, which will not fly into shivers under the exercise of prayer and faith. You may force your way through anything with the leverage of prayer. Thoughts and reasonings are like the steel wedges which give a hold upon truth; but prayer is the lever, the prize which forces open the iron chest of sacred mystery, that we may get the treasure hidden within.

MORNING   February 22

"His bow abode in strength, and the arms of his hands were made strong by the hands of the mighty God of Jacob" — Genesis 49:24.

THAT STRENGTH WHICH God gives to His Josephs is real strength; it is not a boasted valor, a fiction, a thing of which men talk, but which ends in smoke. It is truly divine strength. Why does Joseph stand against temptation? Because God gives him aid. There is nothing that we can do without the power of God. All true strength comes from *"the mighty God of Jacob."* Notice in what a blessedly familiar way God gives this strength to Joseph: *"The arms of his hands were made strong by the hands of the mighty God of Jacob."* Thus God is represented as putting His hands on Joseph's hands, placing His arms on Joseph's arms. Like as a father teaches his children, so the Lord teaches them that fear Him. He puts His arms upon them. Marvelous condescension! God Almighty, Eternal, Omnipotent, stoops from His throne and lays His hand upon the child's hand, stretching His arm upon the arm of Joseph, that he may be made strong!

This strength was also covenant strength, for it is ascribed to *"the mighty God of Jacob."* Now, wherever you read of the God of Jacob in the Bible, you should remember the covenant with Jacob. Christians love to think of God's covenant. All the power, all the grace, all the blessings, all the mercies, all the comforts, all the things we have, flow to us from the well-head, through the covenant. If there were no covenant, then we should fail indeed; for all grace proceeds from it, as light and heat from the sun. No angels ascend or descend, save upon that ladder which Jacob saw, at the top of which stood a covenant God. Christian, it may be that the archers have sorely grieved you, and shot at you, and wounded you, but still your bow abides in strength; be sure, then, to ascribe all the glory to Jacob's God.

EVENING

"The LORD is slow to anger, and great in power" — Nahum 1:3.

JEHOVAH *"is slow to anger."* When mercy comes into the world she drives winged steeds; the axles of her chariot-wheels are red hot with speed. But when wrath goes forth, it toils on with tardy footsteps, for God takes no pleasure in the sinner's death. God's rod of mercy is ever in His hands outstretched; His sword of justice is in its scabbard, held down by that pierced hand of love which bled for the sins of men.

The Lord is slow to anger," because He is GREAT IN POWER. He is truly great in power who has power over himself. When God's power restrains Himself, then it is power indeed: the power that binds omnipotence is omnipotence surpassed. A man who has a strong mind can bear to be insulted long, and only resents the wrong when a sense of right demands his action. The weak mind is irritated at a little: the strong mind bears it like a rock which moves not, though a thousand breakers dash upon it, and cast their pitiful malice in spray upon its summit. God marks His enemies, and yet He moves not Himself, but holds in His anger. If He were less divine that He is, He would long before this have sent forth the whole of His thunders, and emptied the magazines of heaven; He would long before this have blasted the earth with the wondrous fires of its lower regions, and man would have been utterly destroyed. But the greatness of His power brings us mercy.

Dear reader, what is your state this evening? Can you by humble faith look to Jesus, and say, My substitute, You are my rock, my trust? Then, beloved, be not afraid of God's power; for now that you are forgiven and accepted, now that by faith you have fled to Christ for refuge, the power of God need no more terrify you, than the shield and sword of the warrior need terrify those whom he loves. Rather rejoice that He who is *"great in power"* is your Father and Friend.

MORNING February 23
"I will never leave you"—Hebrews 13:5.

NO PROMISE IS OF private interpretation. Whatever God has said to any one saint, He has said to all. When He opens a well for one, it is that all may drink. When He opens a granary-door to give out food, there may be some one starving man who is the occasion of its being opened, but all hungry saints may come and feed too. Whether He gave the word to Abraham or to Moses, matters not, Oh believer; He has given it to you as one of the covenanted seed. There is not a high blessing too lofty for you, nor a wide mercy too extensive for you. Lift up now your eyes to the north and to the south, to the east and to the west, for all this is yours. Climb to Pisgah's top, and view the utmost limit of the divine promise, for the land is all your own. There is not a brook of living water of which you may not drink. If the land flows with milk and honey, eat the honey and drink the milk, for both are yours.

Be bold to believe, for He has said, *"I will never leave you, nor forsake you."* In this promise, God gives to His people everything. *"I will never leave you."* Then no attribute of God can cease to be engaged for us. Is He mighty? He will show Himself strong on the behalf of the ones that trust Him. Is He love? Then with loving-kindness will He have mercy upon us. Whatever attributes may compose the character of Deity, every one of them to its fullest extent shall be engaged on our side. To put everything in one, there is nothing you can want, there is nothing you can ask for, there is nothing you can need in time or in eternity, there is nothing living, nothing dying, there is nothing in this world, nothing in the next world, there is nothing now, nothing at the resurrection.morning, nothing in heaven which is not contained in this text, *"I will never leave you, nor forsake you."*

EVENING
"And come, follow Me, taking up the cross"—Mark 10:21.

YOU HAVE NOT THE making of your own cross, although unbelief is a master carpenter at cross-making. Neither are you permitted to choose your own cross, although self-will would fain be lord and master. But your cross is prepared and appointed for you by divine love, and you are cheerfully to accept it; you are to take up the cross as your chosen badge and burden, and not to stand cavilling at it. This night Jesus bids you submit your shoulder to His easy yoke. Do not kick at it in petulance, or trample on it in vain-glory, or fall under it in despair, or run away from it in fear, but take it up like a true follower of Jesus. Jesus was a cross-bearer; He leads the way in the path of sorrow. Surely you could not desire a better guide! And if He carries a cross, what nobler burden would you desire? The Way of Christ is the way of safety; fear not to tread its thorny paths.

Beloved, the cross is not made of feathers, or lined with velvet, it is heavy and galling to disobedient shoulders. But it is not an iron cross, though your fears have painted it with iron colors, it is a wooden cross, and a man can carry it, for the Man of Sorrows tried the load. Take up your cross, and by the power of the Spirit of God, you will soon be so in love with it, that like Moses, you would not exchange the reproach of Christ for all the treasures of Egypt. Remember that Jesus carried it, and it will smell sweetly; remember that it will soon be followed by the crown, and the thought of the coming weight of glory will greatly lighten the present heaviness of trouble. The Lord help you to bow your spirit in submission to the divine will before you fall asleep this night, that waking with tomorrow's sun, you may go forth to the day's cross with the holy and submissive spirit which becomes a follower of the Crucified.

MORNING   February 24

"And I will cause the shower to come down in its season. There shall be showers of blessing" — Ezekiel 34:26.

HERE IS SOVEREIGN mercy: *"I will give them the shower in its season."* Is it not sovereign, divine mercy? For who can say, *"I will give them showers,"* except God? There is only one voice which can speak to the clouds, and bid them beget the rain. Who sends down the rain upon the earth? Who scatters the showers upon the green herb? Do not I, the Lord? So grace is the gift of God, and is not to be created by man. It is also needed grace. What would the ground do without showers? You may break the clods, you may sow your seeds, but what can you do without the rain? As absolutely needful is the divine blessing. In vain you labor, until God the plenteous shower bestows, and sends salvation down. Then, it is plenteous grace. *"I will send them showers"* — it does not say, *"I will send them drops,"* but *"showers."*

So it is with grace. If God gives a blessing, He usually gives it in such a measure that there is not room enough to receive it. Plenteous grace! Ah! we want plenteous grace to keep us humble, to make us prayerful, to make us holy; plenteous grace to make us zealous, to preserve us through this life, and at last to land us in heaven. We cannot do without saturating showers of grace. Again, it is seasonable grace. *"I will cause the shower to come down in its season."* What is your season this morning? Is it the season of drought? Then that is the season for showers. Is it a season of great heaviness and black clouds? Then that is the season for showers: *"As your days so shall your strength be."*

And here is a varied blessing. *"I will give you showers of blessings."* The word is in the plural. All kinds of blessings God will send. All God's blessings go together, like links in a golden chain. If He gives converting grace, He will also give comforting grace. He will send *"showers of blessings."* Look up today, Oh parched plant, and open your leaves and flowers for a heavenly watering.

EVENING

"O LORD of hosts, how long will You not have mercy on Jerusalem ... And the LORD answered the angel ... with good words and comfortable words" — Zechariah 1:12,13.

WHAT A SWEET answer to an anxious inquiry! This night let us rejoice in it. Oh Zion, there are good things in store for you; your time of travail shall soon be over; your children shall be brought forth; your captivity shall end. Bear patiently the rod for a season, and under the darkness still trust in God, for His love burns towards you. God loves the church with a love too deep for human imagination: He loves her with all His infinite heart.

Therefore let her sons be of good courage; she cannot be far from prosperity to whom God speaks *"Good words and comfortable words."* What these comfortable words are the prophet goes on to tell us: *"I am jealous for Jerusalem and for Zion with a great jealousy."* The Lord loves His church so much that He cannot bear that she should go astray to others; and when she has done so, He cannot endure that she should suffer too much or too heavily. He will not have His enemies afflict her: He is displeased with them because they increase her misery.

When God seems most to leave His church, His heart is warm towards her. History shows us that whenever God uses a rod to chasten His servants, He always breaks it afterwards, as if He loathed the rod which gave His children pain. He feels the smart far more than His people. *"Like as a father pities his children, so the Lord pities them that fear Him."* God has not forgotten us because He smites. His blows are no evidences of lack of love. If this is true of His church collectively, it is of necessity true also of each individual member. You may fear that the Lord has passed you by, but it is not so: He who counts the stars, and calls them by their names, is in no danger of forgetting His own children. He knows your case as thoroughly as if you were the only creature He ever made, or the only saint He ever loved. Approach Him and be at peace.

February 25   MORNING

"The wrath to come"— Matthew 3:7.

IT IS PLEASANT to pass over a country after a storm has spent itself; to smell the freshness of the herbs after the rain has passed away, and to note the drops while they glisten like purest diamonds in the sunlight. That is the position of a Christian. He is going through a land where the storm has spent itself upon His Savior's head, and if there be a few drops of sorrow falling, they distil from clouds of mercy, and Jesus cheers him by the assurance that they are not for his destruction. But how terrible is it to witness the approach of a tempest: to note the forewarnings of the storm; to mark the birds of heaven as they droop their wings; to see the cattle as they lay their heads low in terror; to discern the face of the sky as it grows black, and look to the sun which shines not, and the heavens which are angry and frowning! How terrible to await the dread advance of a hurricane, such as occurs, sometimes, in the tropics, to wait in terrible apprehension till the wind shall rush forth in fury, tearing up trees from their roots, forcing rocks from their pedestals, and hurling down all the dwelling-places of man!

And yet, sinner, this is your present position. No hot drops have as yet fallen, but a shower of fire is coming. No terrible winds howl around you, but God's tempest is gathering its dread artillery. As yet the water-floods are dammed up by mercy, but the flood-gates shall soon be opened: the thunderbolts of God are yet in His storehouse, but lo! the tempest hastens, and how awful shall that moment be when God, robed in vengeance, shall march forth in fury! Where, where, where, Oh sinner, will you hide your head, or where will you flee? Oh that the hand of mercy may now lead you to Christ! He is freely set before you in the gospel: His riven side is the rock of shelter. You know your need of Him; believe in Him, cast yourself upon Him, and then the fury shall be passed over forever.

EVENING

"But Jonah rose up to flee to Tarshish from the presence of the LORD. And he went down to Joppa"— Jonah 1:3.

INSTEAD OF GOING to Nineveh to preach the Word, as God commanded him, Jonah disliked the work, and went down to Joppa to escape from it. There are occasions when God's servants shrink from duty. But what is the consequence? What did Jonah lose by his conduct? He lost the presence and comfortable enjoyment of God's love. When we serve our Lord Jesus as believers should do, our God is with us; and though we have the whole world against us, if we have God with us, what does it matter? But the moment we start back, and seek our own inventions, we are at sea without a pilot. Then may we bitterly lament and groan out, Oh my God, where have You gone? How could I have been so foolish as to shun Your service, and in this way to lose all the bright shining of Your face? This is a price too high. Let me return to my allegiance, that I may rejoice in Your presence.

In the next place, Jonah lost all peace of mind. Sin soon destroys a believer's comfort. It is the poisonous upas tree, from whose leaves distil deadly drops which destroy the life of joy and peace. Jonah lost everything upon which he might have drawn for comfort in any other case. He could not plead the promise of divine protection, for he was not in God's ways. He could not say, Lord, I meet with these difficulties in the discharge of my duty, therefore help me through them. He was reaping his own deeds; he was filled with his own ways. Christian, do not play the Jonah, unless you wish to have all the waves and the billows rolling over your head. You will find in the long run that it is far harder to shun the work and will of God than to at once yield yourself to it. Jonah lost his time, for he had to go to Tarshish after all; It is hard to contend with God; let us yield ourselves at once.

MORNING February 26

"Salvation is of the LORD!" — Jonah 2:9.

SALVATION IS THE work of God. It is He alone who quickens the soul *"dead in trespasses and sins,"* and it is He also who maintains the soul in its spiritual life. He is both *"Alpha and Omega." "Salvation is of the Lord."* If I am prayerful, God makes me prayerful; if I have graces, they are God's gifts to me; if I hold on in a consistent life, it is because He upholds me with His hand. I do nothing whatever towards my own preservation, except what God Himself first does in me. Whatever I have, all my goodness is of the Lord alone. Wherein I sin, that is my own; but wherein I act rightly, that is of God, wholly and completely. If I have repulsed a spiritual enemy, the Lord's strength nerved my arm. Do I live before men a consecrated life? It is not I, but Christ who lives in me. Am I sanctified? I did not cleanse myself: God's Holy Spirit sanctifies me. Am I weaned from the world? I am weaned by God's chastisements sanctified to my good. Do I grow in knowledge? The great Instructor teaches me.

All my jewels were fashioned by heavenly art. I find in God all that I want; but I find in myself nothing but sin and misery. *"He only is my rock and my salvation."* Do I feed on the Word? That Word would be no food for me unless the Lord made it food for my soul, and helped me to feed upon it. Do I live on the manna which comes down from Heaven? What is that manna but Jesus Christ Himself incarnate, whose body and whose blood I eat and drink? Am I continually receiving fresh increase of strength? Where do I gather my might? My help comes from heaven's hills: without Jesus I can do nothing. As a branch cannot bring forth fruit except it abide in the vine, no more can I, except I abide in Him. What Jonah learned in the great deep, let me learn this morning in my closet: *"Salvation is of the Lord."*

EVENING

"Behold, if the leprosy has covered all his flesh, he shall pronounce clean the one that has the plague" — Leviticus 13:13.

STRANGE ENOUGH THIS regulation appears, yet there was wisdom in it, for the throwing out of the disease proved that the constitution was sound. This evening it may be well for us to see the typical teaching of so singular a rule. We, too, are lepers, and may read the law of the leper as applicable to ourselves. When a man sees himself to be altogether lost and ruined, covered all over with the defilement of sin, and in no part free from pollution; when he disclaims all righteousness of his own, and pleads guilty before the Lord, then he is clean through the blood of Jesus, and the grace of God. Hidden, unfelt, unconfessed iniquity is the true leprosy; but when sin is seen and felt, it has received its deathblow, and the Lord looks with eyes of mercy upon the soul afflicted with it.

Nothing is more deadly than self-righteousness, or more hopeful than contrition. We must confess that we are nothing else but sin, for no confession short of this will be the whole truth; and if the Holy Spirit be at work with us, convincing us of sin, there will be no difficulty about making such an acknowledgment. It will spring spontaneously from our lips. What comfort does the text afford to truly awakened sinners: the very circumstance which so grievously discouraged them is here turned into a sign and symptom of a hopeful state! Stripping comes before clothing; digging out the foundation is the first thing in building. And a thorough sense of sin is one of the earliest works of grace in the heart. Oh you poor leprous sinner, utterly destitute of a sound spot, take heart from the text, and come as you are to Jesus,

> For let our debts be what they may, however great or small,
> As soon as we have nothing to pay, our Lord forgives us all.
> 'Tis perfect poverty alone that sets the soul at large:
> While we can call one mite our own, we have no full discharge.

February 27   MORNING

"Because You, O LORD, are my refuge. You have made the Most High your dwelling-place" — Psalm 91:9.

THE ISRAELITES IN the wilderness were continually exposed to change. Whenever the pillar stayed its motion, the tents were pitched; but tomorrow, before the morning sun had risen, the trumpet sounded, the ark was in motion, and the fiery, cloudy pillar was leading the way through the narrow defiles of the mountain, up the hillside, or along the arid waste of the wilderness. They had scarcely time to rest a little before they heard the sound of "Away! this is not your rest; you must still be onward journeying towards Canaan!" They were never long in one place. Even wells and palm trees could not detain them. Yet they had an abiding home in their God, His cloudy pillar was their roof-tree, and its flame by night their household fire. They must go onward from place to place, continually changing, never having time to settle, and to say, "Now we are secure; in this place we shall dwell." "Yet," says Moses, *"though we are always changing, Lord, You have been our dwelling-place throughout all generations."*

The Christian knows no change with regard to God. He may be rich in this world today and poor tomorrow; he may be sickly today and well tomorrow; he may be in happiness today, tomorrow he may be distressed, but there is no change with regard to his relationship to God. If He loved me yesterday, He loves me today. My unmoving mansion of rest is my blessed Lord. Let prospects be blighted; let hopes be blasted; let joy be withered; let mildews destroy everything; I have lost nothing of what I have in God. He is *"my strong habitation to which I can continually resort."* I am a pilgrim in the world, but at home in my God. In the earth I wander, but in God I dwell in a quiet habitation.

EVENING

"Whose goings forth have been from of old, from everlasting" — Micah 5:2.

THE LORD JESUS HAD goings forth for His people as their representative before the throne, long before they appeared upon the stage of time. It was *"from everlasting"* that He signed the compact with His Father, that He would pay blood for blood, suffering for suffering, agony for agony, and death for death, in the behalf of His people. It was *"from everlasting"* that He gave Himself up without a murmuring word; that from the crown of His head to the sole of His foot He might sweat great drops of blood, that He might be spit upon, pierced, mocked, rent asunder, and crushed beneath the pains of death. His goings forth as our Surety were from everlasting.

Pause, my soul, and wonder! You had goings forth in the person of Jesus *"from everlasting."* Not only when you were born into the world did Christ love you, but His delights were with the sons of men before there were any sons of men. Often did He think of them; from everlasting to everlasting He had set His affection upon them. What! my soul, has He been so long about your salvation, and will not He accomplish it? Has He from everlasting been going forth to save me, and will He lose me now? What! has He carried me in His hand, as His precious jewel, and will He now let me slip from between His fingers? Did He choose me before the mountains were brought forth, or the channels of the deep were dug, and will He reject me now?

Impossible! I am sure He would not have loved me so long, if He had not been a changeless Lover. If He could grow weary of me, He would have been tired of me long before now. If He had not loved me with a love as deep as hell, and as strong as death, He would have turned from me long ago. Oh, joy above all joys, to know that I am His everlasting and inalienable inheritance, given to Him by His Father or ever the earth was! Everlasting love shall be the pillow for my head this night.

MORNING   February 28

"My expectation is from Him" – Psalm 62:5.

IT IS THE believer's privilege to use this language. If he is looking for anything from the world, it is a poor *expectation* indeed. But if he looks to God for the supply of his wants, whether in temporal or spiritual blessings, his *expectation* will not be a vain one. Constantly he may draw from the bank of faith, and get his need supplied out of the riches of God's loving-kindness. This I know, I had rather have God for my banker than all the Rothschilds. My Lord never fails to honor His promises; and when we bring them to His throne, He never sends them back unanswered. Therefore I will wait only at His door, for He ever opens it with the hand of munificent grace. At this hour I will try him anew.

But we have *"expectations"* beyond this life. We shall die soon, and then our *"expectation is from Him."* Do we not expect that when we lie upon the bed of sickness He will send angels to carry us to His bosom? We believe that when the pulse is faint, and the heart heaves heavily, some angelic messenger shall stand and look with loving eyes upon us, and whisper, "Sister spirit, come away!" As we approach the heavenly gate, we expect to hear the welcome invitation, *"Come, you blessed of my Father, inherit the kingdom prepared for you from the foundation of the world."* We are expecting harps of gold and crowns of glory; we are hoping soon to be among the multitude of shining ones before the throne; we are looking forward and longing for the time when we shall be like our glorious Lord, for *"We shall see Him as He is."* Then if these be your *"expectations,"* Oh my soul, live for God; live with the desire and resolve to glorify Him from whom comes all your supplies, and of whose grace in your election, redemption, and calling, it is that you have any *"expectation"* of coming glory.

EVENING

"The barrel of meal did not empty, and the jar of oil did not fail, according to the word of the LORD which he spoke by Elijah" – 1 Kings 17:16.

SEE THE Faithfulness of divine love. You observe that this woman had daily necessities. She had herself and her son to feed in a time of famine. Now, in addition, the prophet Elijah was to be fed too. But though the need was threefold, yet the supply of meal wasted not, for she had a constant supply. Each day she made calls upon the barrel, but yet each day it remained the same. You, dear reader, have daily necessities, and because they come so frequently, you are apt to fear that the barrel of meal will one day be empty, and the jar of oil will fail you. Rest assured that, according to the Word of God, this shall not be the case. Each day, though it bring its trouble, shall bring its help. Though you should live to outnumber the years of Methuselah, and though your needs should be as many as the sands of the seashore, yet shall God's grace and mercy last through all your necessities, and you shall never know a real lack.

For three long years, in this widow's days, the heavens never saw a cloud, and the stars never wept a holy tear of dew upon the wicked earth: famine, and desolation, and death, made the land a howling wilderness, but this woman never was hungry, but always joyful in abundance. So shall it be with you. You shall see the sinner's hope perish, for he trusts his native strength. You shall see the proud Pharisee's confidence totter for he builds his hope upon the sand. You shall see even your own schemes blasted and withered, but you yourself shall find that your place of defense shall be the munitions of rocks: *"Your bread shall be given you, and your water shall be sure."* Better have God for your guardian, than the Bank of England for your possession. You might spend the wealth of the Indies, but the infinite riches of God you can never exhaust.

February 29   MORNING

"With loving-kindness I have drawn you"—Jeremiah 31:3.

THE THUNDERS OF the law and the terrors of judgment are all used to bring us to Christ; but the final victory is effected by loving-kindness. The prodigal set out to his father's house from a sense of need; but his father saw him a great way off, and ran to meet him; so that the last steps he took towards his father's house were with the kiss still warm upon his cheek, and the welcome still musical in his ears.

> Law and terrors do but harden
> All the while they work alone;
> But a sense of blood-bought pardon
> Will dissolve a heart of stone.

The Master came one night to the door, and knocked with the iron hand of the law. The door shook and trembled upon its hinges; but the man piled every piece of furniture which he could find against the door, for he said, I will not admit the man. The Master turned away, but by and by He came back, and with His own soft hand, using most that part where the nail had penetrated, He knocked again, Oh, so softly and tenderly. This time the door did not shake, but, strange to say, it opened, and there upon his knees the once unwilling host was found rejoicing to receive his guest, saying, Come in, come in; You have so knocked that my heart is moved for You. I could not think of Your pierced hand leaving its blood-mark on my door, and of You going away houseless, Your head filled with dew, and Your locks with the drops of the night. I yield, I yield, Your love has won my heart.

So in every case: loving-kindness wins the day. What Moses with the tablets of stone could never do, Christ does with His pierced hand. Such is the doctrine of effectual calling. Do I understand it experimentally? Can I say, "He drew me, and I followed on, glad to confess the voice divine?" If so, may He continue to draw me, till at last I shall sit down at the marriage supper of the Lamb.

EVENING

"We have. received...the Spirit which is from God, so that we might know the things given to us by God"—1 Corinthians 2:1.

DEAR READER, have you received the spirit which is of God, worked by the Holy Ghost in your soul? The necessity of the work of the Holy Spirit in the heart may be clearly seen from this fact, that all which has been done by God the Father, and by God the Son, must be ineffectual to us, unless the Spirit shall reveal these things to our souls. What effect does the doctrine of election have upon any man until the Spirit of God enters into him? Election is a dead letter in my consciousness until the Spirit of God calls me out of darkness into marvelous light. Then through my calling, I see my election, and knowing myself to be called of God, I know myself to have been chosen in the eternal purpose.

A covenant was made with the Lord Jesus Christ, by His Father; but what avails that covenant to us until the Holy Spirit brings us its blessings, and opens our hearts to receive them? There hang the blessings on the nail, Christ Jesus. But being short of stature, we cannot reach them; the Spirit of God takes them down and hands them to us, and thus they become actually ours. Covenant blessings in themselves are like the manna in the skies, far out of mortal reach, but the Spirit of God opens the windows of heaven and scatters the living bread around the camp of the spiritual Israel. Christ's finished work is like wine stored in the wine-vat; through unbelief we can neither draw nor drink. The Holy Spirit dips our vessel into this precious wine, and then we drink. But without the Spirit we are as truly dead in sin as though the Father never had elected, and though the Son had never bought us with His blood. The Holy Spirit is absolutely necessary to our well-being. Let us walk lovingly towards Him and tremble at the thought of grieving Him.

MORNING   March 1

"Awake, O north wind; and come, south wind; blow on my garden, so that the spices of it may flow out" — Song of Solomon 4:16.

ANYTHING IS BETTER than the dead calm of indifference. Our souls may wisely desire the north wind of trouble if that alone can be sanctified to the drawing forth of the perfume of our graces. So long as it cannot be said, *"The Lord was not in the wind,"* we will not shrink from the most wintry blast that ever blew upon plants of grace. Did not the spouse in this verse humbly submit herself to the reproofs of her Beloved; only entreating Him to send forth His grace in some form, and making no stipulation as to the peculiar manner in which it should come? Did she not, like ourselves, become so utterly weary of deadness and unholy calm that she sighed for any visitation which would brace her to action? Yet she desires the warm south wind of comfort too, the smiles of divine love, the joy of the Redeemer's presence. These are often mightily effectual to arouse our sluggish life. She desires either one or the other, or both; so that she may but be able to delight her Beloved with the spices of her garden. She cannot endure to be unprofitable, nor can we.

How cheering a thought that Jesus can find comfort in our feeble graces. Can it be? It seems far too good to be true. Well may we court trial or even death itself if we shall thereby be aided to make glad Immanuel's heart. Oh that our heart were crushed to atoms if only by such bruising our sweet Lord Jesus could be glorified. Graces unexercised are as sweet perfumes slumbering in the cups of the flowers; the wisdom of the great Husbandman overrules diverse and opposite causes to produce the one desired result, and makes both affliction and consolation draw forth the grateful odors of faith, love, patience, hope, resignation, joy, and the other fair flowers of the garden. May we know by sweet experience, what this means.

EVENING
"He is precious" — 1 Peter 2:7.

AS ALL THE RIVERS run into the sea, so all delights center in our Beloved. The glances of His eyes outshine the sun; the beauties of His face are fairer than the choicest flowers; no fragrance is like the breath of His mouth. Gems of the mine, and pearls from the sea, are worthless things when measured by His preciousness. Peter tells us that Jesus is precious, but he did not and could not tell us how precious, nor could any of us compute the value of God's unspeakable gift. Words cannot set forth the preciousness of the Lord Jesus to His people, nor fully tell how essential He is to their satisfaction and happiness.

Believer, have you not found in the midst of plenty a sore famine if your Lord has been absent? The sun was shining, but Christ had hidden Himself, and all the world was black to you; or it was night, and since the bright and morning star was gone, no other star could yield you so much as a ray of light. What a howling wilderness is this world without our Lord? If once He hides Himself from us, withered are the flowers of our garden; our pleasant fruits decay; the birds suspend their songs, and a tempest overturns our hopes. All earth's candles cannot make daylight if the Sun of Righteousness be eclipsed. He is the soul of our soul, the light of our light, the life of our life.

Dear reader, what would you do in the world without Him, in the midst of its temptations and its cares? What would you do in the morning without Him, when you wake up and look forward to the day's battle? What would you do at night, when you come home jaded and weary, if there were no door of fellowship between you and Christ? Blessed be His name, He will not suffer us to try our lot without Him, for Jesus never forsakes His own. Yet, let the thought of what life would be without Him enhance His preciousness.

March 2

MORNING

"But all the Israelites went down to the Philistines, each one to sharpen his plow and its blade, and his axe, and his pick" — 1 Samuel 13:20.

WE ARE ENGAGED IN a great war with the Philistines of evil. Every weapon within our reach must be used. Preaching, teaching, praying, giving, all must be brought into action, and talents which have been thought too mean for service, must now be employed. Plow, axe, and pick-axe, may all be useful in slaying Philistines; rough tools may deal hard blows. Killing need not be elegantly done, so long as it is done effectually. Each moment of time, in season or out of season; each fragment of ability, educated or untutored; each opportunity, favorable or unfavorable, must be used, for our foes are many and our force but slender.

Most of our tools want sharpening; we need quickness of perception, tact, energy, promptness, in a word, complete adaptation for the Lord's work. Practical common sense is a very scarce thing among the conductors of Christian enterprises. We might learn from our enemies if we would, and so make the Philistines sharpen our weapons. This morning let us note enough to sharpen our zeal during this day by the aid of the Holy Spirit. See the energy of the Papists, how they compass sea and land to make one proselyte, are they to monopolize all the earnestness? Mark the heathen devotees, what tortures they endure in the service of their idols! Are they alone to exhibit patience and self-sacrifice? Observe the prince of darkness, how persevering in his endeavors, how unabashed in his attempts, how daring in his plans, how thoughtful in his plots, how energetic in all! The devils are united as one man in their infamous rebellion, while we believers in Jesus are divided in our service of God, and scarcely ever work with unanimity. Oh that from Satan's infernal industry we may learn to go about like good Samaritans, seeking whom we may bless!

EVENING

"This grace was given to me (who am less than the least of all the saints,) to preach the gospel of the unsearchable riches of Christ among the Gentiles" — Ephesians 3:8.

THE APOSTLE PAUL felt it a great privilege to be allowed to preach the gospel. He did not look upon his calling as a drudgery, but he entered upon it with intense delight. Yet while Paul was thus thankful for his office, his success in it greatly humbled him. The fuller a vessel becomes, the deeper it sinks in the water. Idlers may indulge a fond conceit of their abilities, because they are untried; but the earnest worker soon learns his own weakness. If you seek humility, try hard work; if you would know your nothingness, attempt some great thing for Jesus. If you would feel how utterly powerless you are apart from the living God, attempt especially the great work of proclaiming the unsearchable riches of Christ, and you will know, as you never knew before, what a weak unworthy thing you are.

Although the apostle thus knew and confessed his weakness, he was never perplexed as to the subject of his ministry. From his first sermon to his last, Paul preached Christ, and nothing but Christ. He lifted up the cross, and extolled the Son of God who bled thereon. Follow his example in all your personal efforts to spread the glad tidings of salvation, and let *"Christ and Him crucified"* be your ever recurring theme. The Christian should be like those lovely spring flowers which, when the sun is shining, open their golden cups, as if saying, "Fill us with your beams!" But when the sun is hidden behind a cloud, they close their cups and droop their heads. So should the Christian feel the sweet influence of Jesus; Jesus must be his sun, and he must be the flower which yields itself to the Sun of Righteousness. Oh! to speak of Christ alone, this is the subject which is both *"seed for the sower, and bread for the eater."* This is the live coal for the lip of the speaker, and the master-key to the heart of the hearer.

MORNING

March 3

"I have chosen you in the furnace of affliction" — Isaiah 48:10.

COMFORT YOURSELF, tried believer, with this thought: God says, *"I have chosen you in the furnace of affliction."* Does not the word come like a soft shower, assuage the fury of the flame? Yes, is it not an asbestos armor, against which the heat has no power? Let affliction come, God has chosen me. Poverty, you may stride in at my door, but God is in the house already, and He has chosen me. Sickness, you may intrude, but I have a balsam ready; God has chosen me. Whatever befalls me in this vale of tears, I know that He has *"chosen"* me.

If, believer, you require still greater comfort, remember that you have the Son of Man with you in the furnace. In that silent chamber of yours, there sits by your side One whom you have not seen, but whom you love. And often when you know it not, He makes all your bed in your affliction, and smoothes your pillow for you. You are in poverty; but in that lonely house of yours the Lord of life and glory is a frequent visitor. He loves to come into these desolate places, that He may visit you. Your friend sticks closely to you. You cannot see Him, but you may feel the pressure of His hands. Do you not hear His voice? Even in the valley of the shadow of death He says, *"Fear not, I am with you; be not dismayed, for I am your God."*

Remember that noble speech of Caesar: "Fear not, you carry Caesar and all his fortune." Fear not, Christian; Jesus is with you. In all your fiery trials, His presence is both your comfort and safety. He will never leave one whom He has chosen for His own. *"Fear not, for I am with you,"* is His sure word of promise to His chosen ones in the *"furnace of affliction."* Will you not, then, take fast hold of Christ, and say:

> Through floods and flames, I, Jesus, lead.
> I'll follow where He goes.

EVENING

"He saw the Spirit of God coming down like a dove" — Matthew 3:16.

AS THE SPIRIT OF God descended upon the Lord Jesus, the head, so He also, in measure, descends upon the members of the mystical body. His descent is to us after the same fashion as that in which it fell upon our Lord. There is often a singular rapidity about it; or ever we are aware, we are impelled onward and heavenward beyond all expectation. Yet is there none of the hurry of earthly haste, for the wings of the dove are as soft as they are swift. Quietness seems essential to many spiritual operations; the Lord is in the still small voice, and like the dew, His grace is distilled in silence. The dove has ever been the chosen type of purity, and the Holy Spirit is holiness itself. Where He comes, everything that is pure and lovely, and of good report, is made to abound, and sin and uncleanness depart.

Peace reigns also where the Holy Dove comes with power; He bears the olive branch which shows that the waters of divine wrath are assuaged. Gentleness is a sure result of the Sacred Dove's transforming power; hearts touched by His benign influence are meek and lowly henceforth and forever. Harmlessness follows, as a matter of course; eagles and ravens may hunt their prey, the turtledove can endure wrong, but cannot inflict it. We must be harmless as doves. The dove is an apt picture of love, the voice of the turtledove is full of affection; and so, the soul visited by the blessed Spirit, abounds in love to God, in love to the brethren, and in love to sinners; and above all, in love to Jesus. The brooding of the Spirit of God upon the face of the deep, first produced order and life, and in our hearts, He causes and fosters new life and light. Blessed Spirit, as You did rest upon our dear Redeemer, even so rest upon us from this time forward and forever.

March 4

MORNING

"My grace is sufficient for you" — 2 Corinthians 12:9.

IF NONE OF GOD'S saints were poor and tried, we should not know half so well the consolations of divine grace. When we find the wanderer who has nowhere to lay his head, who yet can say, "Still will I trust in the Lord"; when we see the pauper starving on bread and water, who still glories in Jesus; when we see the bereaved widow overwhelmed in affliction, and yet having faith in Christ, Oh what honor it reflects on the gospel! God's grace is illustrated and magnified in the poverty and trials of believers. Saints bear up under every discouragement, believing that all things work together for their good, and that out of apparent evils a real blessing shall ultimately spring, that their God will either work a deliverance for them speedily, or most assuredly support them in the trouble, as long as He is pleased to keep them in it. This patience of the saints proves the power of divine grace.

There is a lighthouse out at sea; it is a calm night.

I cannot tell whether the edifice is firm; the tempest must rage about it, and then I shall know whether it will stand. So with the Spirit's work. If it were not on many occasions surrounded with tempestuous waters, we should not know that it was true and strong; if the winds did not blow upon it, we should not know how firm and secure it was. The master-works of God are those men who stand in the midst of difficulties, steadfast, unmovable.

    Calm mid the bewildering cry,
    Confident of victory.

He who would glorify his God must set his account upon meeting with many trials. No man can be illustrious before the Lord unless his conflicts be many. If then, yours be a much-tried path, rejoice in it, because you will the better show forth the all-sufficient grace of God. As for His failing you, never dream of it, hate the thought. The God who has been sufficient until now, should be trusted to the end.

EVENING

"They shall be richly satisfied with the fatness of Your house" — Psalm 36:8.

SHEBA'S QUEEN WAS amazed at the sumptuousness of Solomon's table. She lost all heart when she saw the provision of a single day; and she marveled equally at the company of servants who were feasted at the royal board. But what is this to the hospitalities of the God of grace? Ten thousand thousand of His people are daily fed; hungry and thirsty, they bring large appetites with them to the banquet, but not one of them returns unsatisfied. There is enough for each, enough for all, enough for evermore. Though the host that feed at Jehovah's table is countless as the stars of heaven, yet each one has his portion of meat. Think how much grace one saint requires, so much that nothing but the Infinite could supply his for one day. And yet the Lord spreads His table, not for one, but many saints, not for one day, but for many years; not for many years only, but for generation after generation.

Observe the full feasting spoken of in the text, the guests at mercy's banquet are satisfied, no, more *"abundantly satisfied;"* and that not with ordinary fare, but with fatness, the peculiar fatness of God's own house. And such feasting is guaranteed by a faithful promise to all those children of men who put their trust under the shadow of Jehovah's wings. I once thought if I might but get the broken meat at God's back door of grace I should be satisfied; like the woman who said, *"The dogs eat of the crumbs that fall from the master's table."* But no child of God is ever served with scraps and leavings; like Mephibosheth, they all eat from the king's own table. In matters of grace, we all have Benjamin's mess, we all have ten times more than we could have expected; and though our necessities are great, yet are we often amazed at the marvelous plenty of grace which God gives us experimentally to enjoy.

MORNING   March 5

"So then we should not sleep as the rest do" — *1 Thessalonians 5:6.*

THERE ARE MANY ways of promoting Christian wakefulness. Among the rest, let me strongly advise Christians to converse together concerning the ways of the Lord. Christian and Hopeful, as they journeyed towards the Celestial City, said to themselves, "To prevent drowsiness in this place, let us fall into good discourse." Christian inquired, "Brother, where shall we begin?" And Hopeful answered, "Where God began with us." Then Christian sang this song:
> When saints do sleepy grow, let them come here, And hear
> how these two pilgrims talk together; Yes, let them learn of them, in any wise,
> Thus to keep open their drowsy slumbering eyes.
> Saints' fellowship, it be managed well,
> Keeps them awake, and that in spite of hell.

Christians who isolate themselves and walk alone, are very liable to grow drowsy. Hold Christian company, and you will be kept wakeful by it, and refreshed and encouraged to make quicker progress in the road to heaven.

But as you thus take "sweet counsel" with others in the ways of God, take care that the theme of your conversation is the Lord Jesus. Let the eye of faith be constantly looking unto Him; let your heart be full of Him; let your lips speak of His worth. Friend, live near to the cross, and you will not sleep. Labor to impress yourself with a deep sense of the value of the place to which you are going. If you remember that you are going to heaven, you will not sleep on the road. If you think that hell is behind you, and the devil pursuing you, you will not loiter. Would the manslayer sleep with the avenger of blood behind him, and the city of refuge before him? Christian, will you sleep while the pearly gates are open? The songs of angels waiting for you to join them, a crown of gold ready for your brow. Ah! no; in holy fellowship continue to watch and pray that you enter not into temptation.

EVENING
"Say to my soul, I am your salvation" — *Psalm 35:3.*

WHAT DOES THIS sweet prayer teach me? It shall be my evening's petition; but first let it yield me an instructive meditation. The text informs me first of all that David had his doubts; for why should he pray, *"Say unto my soul, I am your salvation,"* if he were not sometimes exercised with doubts and fears? Let me, then, be of good cheer, for I am not the only saint who has to complain of weakness of faith. If David doubted, I need not conclude that I am no Christian, because I have doubts. The text reminds me that David was not content while he had doubts and fears, but he repaired at once to the mercy-seat to pray for assurance; for he valued it as much fine gold. I too must labor after an abiding sense of my acceptance in the Beloved, and must have no joy when His love is not shed abroad in my soul. When my Bridegroom is gone from me, my soul must and will fast.

I learn also that David knew where to obtain full assurance. He went to his God in prayer, crying, *"Say to my soul, I am your salvation."* I must be much alone with God if I would have a clear sense of Jesus' love. Let my prayers cease, and my eye of faith will grow dim. Much in prayer, much in heaven; slow in prayer, slow in progress. I notice that David would not be satisfied unless his assurance had a divine source. *"Say to my soul."* Lord, do You say it! Nothing short of a divine testimony in the soul will ever content the true Christian. Moreover, David could not rest unless his assurance had a vivid personality about it. *"Say to my soul, I am your salvation."* Lord, if You should say this to all the saints, it would be nothing, unless You should say it to me. Lord, I have sinned; I deserve not Your smile; I scarcely dare to ask it; but Oh! say to my soul, even to my soul, *"I am your salvation."* Let me have a present, personal, infallible, indisputable sense that I am Yours, and that You are mine.

March 6   MORNING

"You need to be born again" — John 3:7.

REGENERATION IS A subject which lies at the very basis of salvation, and we should be very diligent to take heed that we really are *"born again,"* for there are many who fancy they are born again, who are not. Be assured that the name of a Christian is not the nature of a Christian; and that being born in a Christian land, and being recognized as professing the Christian religion is of no avail whatever, unless there be something more added to it — being *"born again"* by the power of the Holy Spirit. To be *"born again,"* is a matter so mysterious, that human words cannot describe it. *"The Spirit breathes where He desires, and you hear the sound of Him, but cannot tell where He comes from, nor where He goes: so is every one that is born of the Spirit"* (John 3:8). Nevertheless, it is a change which is known and felt: known by works of holiness; and felt by a gracious experience.

This great work is supernatural. It is not an operation which a man performs for himself: a new principle is infused, which works in the heart, renews the soul, and affects the entire man. It is not a change of my name, but a re-creation of my nature, so that I am not the man I used to be, but a new man in Christ Jesus. To wash and dress a corpse is a far different thing from making it alive; man can do the one, God alone can do the other. If you have then, been *"born again,"* your acknowledgment will be, "Oh Lord Jesus, the everlasting Father, You are my spiritual Parent; unless Your Spirit had breathed into me the breath of a new, holy, and spiritual life, I had been to this day *"dead in trespasses and sins."* My heavenly life is wholly derived from You, to You I ascribe it. *"My life is hid with Christ in God."* — *"It is no longer I who live, but Christ who lives in me."* May the Lord enable us to be well assured on this vital point, for to be unregenerate is to be unsaved, unpardoned, without God, and without hope.

EVENING

"Before ruin, the heart of man is proud" — Proverbs 18:12.

IT IS AN OLD and common saying, that "coming events cast their shadows before them." The wise man teaches us that a haughty heart is the prophetic prelude of evil. Pride is as safely the sign of destruction as the change of mercury in the weather-glass is the sign of rain; and far more infallibly so than that. When men have ridden the high horse, destruction has always overtaken them. Let David's aching heart show that there is an eclipse of a man's glory when he dotes upon his own greatness (2 Sam. 24:10). See Nebuchadnezzar, the mighty builder of Babylon, creeping on the earth, devouring grass like oxen, until his nails had grown like bird's claws, and his hair like eagle's feathers (Dan. 4:33). Pride made the boaster a beast, as once before it made an angel a devil. God hates high looks, and never fails to bring them down. All the arrows of God are aimed at proud hearts.

Oh Christian, is your heart haughty this evening? For pride can get into the Christian's heart as well as into the sinner's; it can delude him into dreaming that he is *"rich and increased in goods, and has need of nothing."* Are you glorying in your graces or your talents? Are you proud of yourself, that you have had holy frames and sweet experiences? Mark you, reader, there is a destruction coming to you also. Your flaunting poppies of self-conceit will be pulled up by the roots, your mushroom graces will wither in the burning heat, and your self-sufficiency shall become as straw for the dunghill. If we forget to live at the foot of the cross in deepest lowliness of spirit, God will not forget to make us smart under His rod. A destruction will come to you, Oh unduly exalted believer, the destruction of your joys and of your comforts, though there can be no destruction of your soul. Wherefore, *"He that glories, let him glory in the Lord."*

MORNING
March 7

"Have faith in God" — Mark 11:22.

FAITH IS THE foot of the soul by which it can march along the road of the commandments. Love can make the feet move more swiftly; but faith is the foot which carries the soul. Faith is the oil enabling the wheels of holy devotion and of earnest piety to move well; and without faith the wheels are taken from the chariot, and we drag heavily. With faith I can do all things; without faith I shall neither have the inclination nor the power to do anything in the service of God. If you would find the men who serve God the best, you must look for the men of the most faith.

Little faith will save a man, but little faith cannot do great things for God. Poor Little-faith could not have fought Apollyon; it needed Christian to do that. Poor Little-faith could not have slain Giant Despair; it required Great-heart's art to knock that monster down. Little faith will go to heaven most certainly, but it often has to hide itself in a nut-shell, and it frequently loses all but its jewels. Little-faith says, "It is a rough road, beset with sharp thorns, and full of dangers; I am afraid to go"; but Great-faith remembers the promise, "Your shoes shall be iron and brass; as your days, so shall your strength be". And so he boldly ventures. Little-faith stands desponding, mingling her tears with the flood; but great faith sings, *"When you pass through the waters, I will be with you; and through the rivers, they shall not overflow you:"* and she fords the stream at once.

Would you be comfortable and happy? Would you enjoy religion? Would you have the religion of cheerfulness and not that of gloom? Then *"have faith in God."* If you love darkness, and are satisfied to dwell in gloom and misery, then be content with little faith, but if you love the sunshine, and would sing songs of rejoicing, covet earnestly this best gift, *"great faith."*

EVENING

"It is better to trust in the LORD than to trust in man" — Psalm 118:8.

DOUBTLESS THE READER has been tried with the temptation to rely upon the things which are seen, instead of resting alone upon the invisible God. Christians often look to man for help and counsel, and mar the noble simplicity of their reliance upon their God. Does this evening's portion meet the eye of a child of God anxious about temporals, then would we reason with him awhile. You trust in Jesus, and only in Jesus, for your salvation, then why are you troubled? Is it not written, *"Cast your burden upon the Lord"?, "Be careful for nothing, but in everything by prayer and supplication make known your wants unto God."* Cannot you trust God for temporals? "Ah! I wish I could." If you cannot trust God for temporals, how dare you trust Him for spirituals? Can you trust Him for your soul's redemption, and not rely upon Him for a few lesser mercies?

Is not God enough for your need, or is His all-sufficiency too narrow for your wants? Do you want another eye beside that of Him who sees every secret thing? Is His heart faint? Is His arm weary? If so, seek another God; but if He be infinite, omnipotent, faithful, true, and all-wise, why gad about so much to seek another confidence? Why do you rake the earth to find another foundation, when this is strong enough to bear all the weight which you can ever build thereon? Christian, mix not your wine with water, do not alloy your gold of faith with the dross of human confidence. Wait only upon God, and let your expectations be from Him. Covet not Jonah's gourd, but rest in Jonah's God. Let the sandy foundations of terrestrial trust be the choice of fools, but do like one who foresees the storm, build for yourself an abiding place upon the Rock of Ages.

March 8

MORNING

"Through many afflictions we must enter into the kingdom of God" — Acts 14:22.

GOD'S PEOPLE HAVE their trials. It was never designed by God, when He chose His people, that they should be an untried people. They were chosen in the furnace of affliction; they were never chosen to worldly peace and earthly joy. Freedom from sickness and the pains of mortality was never promised them; but when their Lord drew up the charter of privileges, He included chastisements among the things to which they should inevitably be heirs. Trials are a part of our lot; they were predestinated for us in God's solemn decrees, and bequeathed us in Christ's last legacy. So surely as the stars are fashioned by His hands, and their orbits fixed by Him, so surely are our trials allotted to us. He has ordained their season and their place, their intensity and the effect they shall have upon us. Good men must never expect to escape troubles; if they do, they will be disappointed, for none of their predecessors have been without them.

Mark the patience of Job; remember Abraham, for he had his trials, and by his faith under them, he became the *"Father of the faithful."* Note well the biographies of all the patriarchs, prophets, apostles, and martyrs, and you shall discover none of those whom God made vessels of mercy, who were not made to pass through the fire of affliction. It is ordained of old that the cross of trouble should be engraved on every vessel of mercy, as the royal mark whereby the King's vessels of honor are distinguished. But although tribulation is thus the path of God's children, they have the comfort of knowing that their Master has traversed it before them; they have His presence and sympathy to cheer them, His grace to support them, and His example to teach them how to endure. And when they reach *"the kingdom,"* it will more than make amends for the *"much tribulation"* through which they passed to enter it.

EVENING

"She called his name Ben-oni (son of sorrow), but his father called him Benjamin (son of my right hand)" — Genesis 35:18.

TO EVERY MATTER there is a bright as well as a dark side. Rachel was overwhelmed with the sorrow of her own travail and death; Jacob, though weeping the mother's loss, could see the mercy of the child's birth. It is well for us if, while the flesh mourns over trials, our faith triumphs in divine faithfulness. Samson's lion yielded honey, and so will our adversities, if rightly considered. 'The stormy sea feeds multitudes with its fishes; the wild wood blooms with beautiful flowers; the stormy wind sweeps away the pestilence, and the biting frost loosens the soil. Dark clouds distil bright drops, and black earth grows gay flowers.' A vein of good is to be found in every mine of evil. Sad hearts have peculiar skill in discovering the most disadvantageous point of view from which to gaze upon a trial; if there were only one slough in the world, they would soon be up to their necks in it, and if there were only one lion in the desert they would hear it roar.

About us all there is a tinge of this wretched folly, and we are apt, at times, like Jacob, to cry, *"All these things are against me."* Faith's way of walking is to cast all care upon the Lord, and then to anticipate good results from the worst calamities. Like Gideon's men, she does not fret over the broken pitcher, but rejoices that the lamp blazes forth the more. Out of the rough oyster-shell of difficulty she extracts the rare pearl of honor, and from the deep ocean-caves of distress she uplifts the priceless coral of experience. When her flood of prosperity ebbs, she finds treasures hid in the sands; and when her sun of delight goes down, she turns her telescope of hope to the starry promises of heaven. When death itself appears, faith points to the light of resurrection beyond the grave, thus making our dying Ben-oni to be our living Benjamin.

MORNING
March 9

"Yes, He is altogether lovely. This is my Beloved, and this is my Friend, O daughters of Jerusalem" — Song of Solomon 5:16.

THE SUPERLATIVE BEAUTY of Jesus is all-attracting; it is not so much to be admired as to be loved. He is more than pleasant and fair, He is LOVELY. Surely the people of God can fully justify the use of this golden word, for He is the object of their warmest love, a love founded on the intrinsic excellence of His person, the complete perfection of His charms.

Look, Oh disciples of Jesus, to your Master's lips, and say, "Are they not most sweet?" Do not His words cause your hearts to burn within you as He talks with you by the way? You worshippers of Immanuel, look up to His head of much fine gold, and tell me, are not His thoughts precious unto you? Is not your adoration sweetened with affection as you humbly bow before that countenance which is as Lebanon, excellent as the cedars? Is there not a charm in His every feature, and is not His whole person fragrant with such a savor of His good ointments, that therefore the virgins love Him? Is there one member of His glorious body which is not attractive? Is there not one portion of His person which is not a fresh loadstone to our souls, one office which is not a strong cord to bind your heart?

Our love is not as a seal set upon His heart of love alone; it is fastened upon His arm of power also; nor is there a single part of Him upon which it does not fix itself. We anoint His whole person with the sweet spikenard of our fervent love. His whole life we would imitate; His whole character we would transcribe. In all other beings we see some lack, in Him there is all perfection. The best even of His favored saints have had blots upon their garments and wrinkles upon their brows; He is nothing but loveliness. All earthly suns have their spots; the fair world itself has its wilderness; we cannot love the whole of the most lovely thing; but Christ Jesus is gold without alloy, light without darkness, glory without cloud. *"Yes, He is altogether lovely."*

EVENING
"Remain in Me" — John 15:4.

COMMUNION WITH CHRIST is a certain cure for every ill. Whether it be the wormwood of woe, or the cloying surfeit of earthly delight, close fellowship with the Lord Jesus will take bitterness from the one, and satiety from the other. Live near to Jesus, Christian, and it is matter of secondary importance whether you live on the mountain of honor or in the valley of humiliation. Living near to Jesus, you are covered with the wings of God, and underneath you are the everlasting arms. Let nothing keep you from that hallowed intercourse, which is the choice privilege of a soul wedded to THE Well-Beloved. Be not content with an interview now and then, but seek always to retain His company, for only in His presence have you either comfort or safety. Jesus should not be unto us a friend who calls upon us now and then, but one with whom we walk evermore.

You have a difficult road before you. See, oh traveler to heaven, that you go not without your guide. You have to pass through the fiery furnace; enter it not unless, like Shadrach, Meshach, and Abednego, you have the Son of God to be your companion. You have to storm the Jericho of your own corruptions; attempt not the warfare until, like Joshua, you have seen the Captain of the Lord's host, with His sword drawn in His hand. You are to meet the Esau of your many temptations; meet him not until at Jabbok's brook you have laid hold upon the angel, and prevailed. In every case, in every condition, you will need Jesus; but most of all, when the iron gates of death shall open to you. Keep close to your soul's Husband, lean your head upon His bosom, ask to be refreshed with the spiced wine of His pomegranate, and you shall be found of Him at the last, without spot, or wrinkle, or any such thing. Seeing you have lived with Him, and lived in Him here, you shall abide with Him forever.

March 10 MORNING

"And in my blessedness I said, I shall never be moved" — Psalm 30:6.

"MOAB IS SETTLED on his lees, he has not been emptied from vessel to vessel." Give a man wealth; let his ships bring home continually rich freights; let the winds and waves appear to be his servants to bear his vessels across the bosom of the mighty deep; let his lands yield abundantly; let the weather be propitious to his crops; let uninterrupted success attend him; let his stand among men as a successful merchant; let him enjoy continued health; allow him with braced nerve and brilliant eye to march through the world, and live luxuriously; give him the buoyant spirit; let him have the song perpetually on his lips; let his eye be ever sparkling with joy, and the natural consequence of such an easy state to any man, let him be the best Christian who ever breathed — that man will be presumptious. Even David said, *"I shall never be moved;"* and we are not better than David, nor half so good.

Brother, beware of the smooth places of the way; if you are treading them, or if the way be rough, thank God for it. If God should always rock us in the cradle of prosperity; if we were always dandled on the knees of fortune; if we had not some stain on the alabaster pillar; if there were not a few clouds in the sky; if we had not some bitter drops in the wine of this life, we should become intoxicated with pleasure. We should dream "we stand;" and stand we should, but it would be upon a pinnacle; like the man asleep upon the mast, each moment we should be in jeopardy.

We bless God, then, for our afflictions; we thank Him for our changes; we extol His name for losses of property; for we feel that had He not chastened us thus, we might have become too secure. Continued worldly prosperity is a fiery trial.

Afflictions, though they seem severe,
In mercy often are sent.

EVENING

"Man...is of few days and full of trouble" — Job 14:1.

IT MAY BE OF great service to us, before we fall asleep, to remember this mournful fact, for it may lead us to set loose by earthly things. There is nothing very pleasant in the recollection that we are not above the shafts of adversity, but it may humble us and prevent our boasting like the Psalmist in our morning's portion. *"My mountain stands firm: I shall never be moved."* It may stay us from taking too deep root in this soil from which we are so soon to be transplanted into the heavenly garden. Let us remember the frail tenure upon which we hold our temporal mercies. If we would remember that all the trees of earth are marked for the woodman's axe, we should not be so ready to build our nests in them. We should love, but we should love with the love which expects death, and which reckons upon separations. Our dear relations are but loaned to us, and the hour when we must return them to the lender's hand may be even at the door.

The like is certainly true of our worldly goods. Do not riches take to themselves wings and fly away? Our health is equally precarious. Frail flowers of the field, we must not reckon upon blooming forever. There is a time appointed for weakness and sickness, when we shall have to glorify God by suffering, and not by earnest activity. There is no single point in which we can hope to escape from the sharp arrows of affliction; out of our few days there is not one secure from sorrow. Man's life is a cask full of bitter wine; he who looks for joy in it had better seek for honey in an ocean of brine.

Beloved reader, set not your affections upon things of earth; but seek those things which are above, for here the moth devours, and the thief breaks through, but there all joys are perpetual and eternal. The path of trouble is the way home. Lord, make this thought a pillow for many a weary head!

MORNING   March 11

"Sin ... excessively sinful" — Romans 7:13.

BEWARE OF LIGHT thoughts of sin. At the time of conversion, the conscience is so tender, that we are afraid of the slightest sin. Young converts have a holy timidity, a godly fear lest they should offend against God. But alas! very soon the fine bloom upon these first ripe fruits is removed by the rough handling of the surrounding world: the sensitive plant of young piety turns into a willow in after life, too pliant, too easily yielding. It is sadly true, that even a Christian may grow by degrees so callous, that the sin which once startled him does not alarm him in the least. By degrees men gets familiar with sin. The ear in which the cannon has been booming will not notice slight sounds. At first a little sin startles us; but soon we say, "Is it not a little one?" Then there comes another, larger, and then another, until by degrees we begin to regard sin as but a little ill; and then follows an unholy presumption, saying within ourselves, We have not fallen into open sin. True, we tripped a little, but we stood upright in the main. We may have uttered one unholy word, but as for the most of our conversation, it has been consistent.

So we palliate sin; we throw a cloak over it; we call it by dainty names. Christian, beware how you think lightly of sin. Take heed lest you fall by little and little. Sin, a little thing? Is it not a poison? Who knows its deadliness? Sin, a little thing? Do not the little foxes spoil the grapes? Does not the tiny coral insect build a rock which wrecks a navy? Do not little strokes fell lofty oaks? Will not continual drippings wear away stones? Sin, a little thing? It girded the Redeemer's head with thorns, and pierced His heart! It made Him suffer anguish, bitterness, and woe. Could you weigh the least sin in the scales of eternity, you would fly from it as from a serpent, and abhor the least appearance of evil. Look upon all sin as that which crucified the Savior, and you will see it to be *"excessively sinful."* As John Flavel so aptly put it, There are no little sins, because there is no little God to sin against.

EVENING
"You shall be called, Sought out" — Isaiah 62:12.

THE SURPASSING GRACE of God is seen very clearly in that we were not only sought, but sought out. Men seek for a thing which is lost upon the floor of the house, but in such a case there is only seeking, not seeking out. The loss is more perplexing and the search more persevering when a thing is sought out. We were mingled with the mire; we were as when some precious piece of gold falls into the sewer, and men gather out and carefully inspect a mass of abominable filth, and continue to stir and rake, and search among the heap until the treasure is found. Or, to use another figure, we were lost in a labyrinth; we wandered here and there, and when mercy came after us with the gospel, it did not find us at the first coming, it had to search for us and seek us out; for we as lost sheep were so desperately lost, and had wandered into such a strange country, that it did not seem possible that even the Good Shepherd should track our devious roaming. Glory be to unconquerable grace, we were sought out! No gloom could hide us, no filthiness could conceal us, we were found and brought home. Glory be to infinite love, God the Holy Spirit restored us!

The lives of some of God's people, if they could be written, would fill us with holy astonishment. Strange and marvelous are the ways which God used in their case to find His own. Blessed be His name, He never relinquishes the search until the chosen are sought out effectually. They are not a people sought today and cast away tomorrow. Almightiness and wisdom combined will make no failures, they shall be called, *"Sought out!"* That any should be sought out is matchless grace, but that we should be sought out is grace beyond degree! We can find no reason for it but God's own sovereign love, and can only lift up our heart in wonder, and praise the Lord that this night we wear the name of *"Sought out."*

March 12

MORNING

"You shall love your neighbor" — Matthew 5:43.

"LOVE YOUR NEIGHBOR." Perhaps he rolls in riches, and you are poor, and living in your little cot side-by-side with his lordly mansion; you see every day his estates, his fine linen, and his sumptuous banquets. God has given him these gifts, covet not his wealth, and think no hard thoughts concerning him. Be content with your own lot, if you cannot better it, but do not look upon your neighbor, and wish that he were as yourself. Love him, and then you will not envy him.

Perhaps, on the other hand, you are rich, and near you reside the poor. Do not scorn to call them neighbors. Own that you are bound to love them. The world calls them your inferiors. In what are they inferior? They are far more your equals than your inferiors, for *"God has made of one blood all people that dwell upon the face of the earth."* It is your coat which is better than theirs, but you are by no means better than they. They are men, and what are you more than that? Take heed that you love your neighbor even though he be in rags, or sunk in the depths of poverty.

But, perhaps, you say, I cannot love my neighbors, because for all I do they return ingratitude and contempt. So much the more room for the heroism of love. Would you be a leather-bed warrior, instead of bearing the rough fight of love? He who dares the most, shall win the most; and if rough be your path of love, tread it boldly, still loving your neighbors through thick and thin. Heap coals of fire on their heads, and if they be hard to please, seek not to please them, but to please your Master; and remember if they spurn your love, your Master has not spurned it, and your deed is as acceptable to Him as if it had been acceptable to them. Love your neighbor, for in so doing you are following the footsteps of Christ.

EVENING

"To whom do you belong?" — 1 Samuel 30:13.

NO NEUTRALITIES CAN exist in religion. We are either ranked under the banner of Prince Immanuel, to serve and fight His battles, or we are vassals of the black prince, Satan. *"To whom do you belong?"*

Reader, let me assist you in your response. Have you been *"born again"*? If you have, you belong to Christ, but without the new birth you cannot be His. In whom do you trust? Those who believe in Jesus are the sons of God. Whose work are you doing? You are sure to serve your master, for he whom you serve is thereby owned to be your lord. What company do you keep? If you belong to Jesus, you will fraternize with those who wear the livery of the cross. "Birds of a feather flock together." What is your conversation? Is it heavenly or is it earthly? What have you learned of your Master? For servants learn much from their masters to whom they are apprenticed. If you have served your time with Jesus, it will be said of you, as it was of Peter and John, *"They took knowledge of them, that they had been with Jesus."*

We press the question, *"To whom do you belong?"* Answer honestly before you give sleep to your eyes. If you are not Christ's you are in a hard service. Run away from your cruel master! Enter into the service of the Lord of Love, and you shall enjoy a life of blessedness. If you are Christ's, let me advise you to do four things. You belong to Jesus, then obey Him; let His word be your law; let His wish be your will. You belong to the Beloved, then love Him; let your heart embrace Him; let your whole soul be filled with Him. You belong to the Son of God, then trust Him; rest nowhere but on Him. You belong to the King of kings, then be decided for Him. Thus, without your being branded upon the brow, all will know to whom you belong.

MORNING   March 13

"Why do we sit here until we die?" — 2 Kings 7:3.

DEAR READER, THIS little book was mainly intended for the edification of believers, but if you are yet unsaved, our heart yearns over you. And we would fain say a word which may be blessed to you. Open your Bible, and read the story of the lepers, and mark their position, which was much the same as yours. If you remain where you are you must perish; if you go to Jesus you can but die. Nothing ventured, nothing won is the old proverb, and in your case the venture is no great one. If you sit still in sullen despair, no one can pity you when your ruin comes. But if you die with mercy sought, if such a thing were possible, you would be the object of universal sympathy. None escape who refuse to look to Jesus; but you know that some are saved who believe in Him, for certain of your own acquaintances have received mercy: then why not you?

The Ninevites said, *"Who can tell?"* Act upon the same hope, and try the Lord's mercy. To perish is so awful, that if there were but a straw to catch at, the instinct of self-preservation should lead you to stretch out your hand. We have thus been talking to you on your own unbelieving ground, we would now assure you, as from the Lord, that if you seek Him He will be found of you. Jesus casts out none who come unto Him. You shall not perish if you trust Him. On the contrary, you shall find treasure far richer than the poor lepers gathered in Syria's deserted camp. May the Holy Spirit embolden you to go at once, and you shall not believe in vain. When you are saved yourself, publish the good news to others. Hold not your peace; tell the King's household first, and unite with them in fellowship; let the porter of the city, the minister, be informed of your discovery, and then proclaim the good news in every place. The Lord save you before the sun goes down this day.

EVENING

"Then he put out his hand and took her, and pulled her in to him into the ark" —
Genesis 8:9.

WEARIED OUT WITH her wanderings, the dove returns at length to the ark as her only resting place. How heavily she flies, she will drop; she will never reach the ark! But she struggles on. Noah has been looking out for his dove all day long, and is ready to receive her. She has just strength to reach the edge of the ark, she can hardly alight upon it, and is ready to drop, when Noah puts forth his hand and pulls her in unto him. Mark that: *"pulled her in to him."* She did not fly right in herself, but was too fearful, or too weary to do so. She flew as far as she could, and then he put forth his hand and pulled her in to him. This act of mercy was shown to the wandering dove, and she was not scolded for her wanderings. Just as she was, she was pulled into the ark. So you, seeking sinner, with all your sin, will be received.

Only return" — those are God's two gracious words, *"only return."* What! nothing else? No, *"only return."* She had no olive branch in her mouth this time, nothing at all but just herself and her wanderings; but it is *"only return,"* and she does return, and Noah pulls her in. Fly, wanderer; fly fainting one, dove as you are, though you think yourself to be black as the raven with the mire of sin, back, back to the Savior. Every moment you wait does not but increase your misery; your attempts to plume yourself and make yourself fit for Jesus are all vanity. Come to Him just as you are. *"Return, backsliding Israel."* He does not say, *"Return, repenting Israel"* (there is such an invitation doubtless), but *"backsliding one,"* as a backslider with all your backslidings about you, Return, return, return! Jesus is waiting for you! He will stretch forth His hand and *"pull you in"* to Himself, your heart's true home.

March 14

MORNING

"So let him who thinks that he stands be careful lest he fall" — 1 Corinthians 10:12.

IT IS A CURIOUS fact, that there is such a thing as being proud of grace. A man says, "I have great faith, I shall not fall; poor little faith may, but I never shall". Or another says, "I have fervent love, I can stand, there is no danger of my going astray." He who boasts of grace has little grace to boast of. Some who do this imagine that their graces can keep them, knowing not that the stream must flow constantly from the fountain head, or else the brook will soon be dry. If a continuous stream of oil comes not to the lamp, though it burn brightly today, it will smoke tomorrow, and noxious will be its scent. Take heed that you glory not in your graces, but let all your glorying and confidence be in Christ and His strength, for only so can you be kept from falling.

Be much more in prayer. Spend longer time in holy adoration. Read the Scriptures more earnestly and constantly. Watch your lives more carefully. Live nearer to God. Take the best examples for your pattern. Let your conversation be redolent of heaven. Let your hearts be perfumed with affection for men's souls. So live that men may take knowledge of you that you have been with Jesus, and have learned of Him. And when that happy day shall come, when He whom you love shall say, "Come up higher," may it be your happiness to hear Him say, *"You have fought a good fight, you have finished your course, and henceforth there is laid up for you a crown of righteousness which fades not away."* On, Christian, with care and caution! On, with holy fear and trembling! On, with faith and confidence in Jesus alone, and let your constant petition be, *"Uphold me according to Your Word."* He is able, and He alone, *"To keep you from falling, and to present you faultless before the presence of His glory with exceeding joy."*

EVENING

"I will take heed to my ways" — Psalm 39:1.

FELLOW, PILGRIM, SAY not in your heart, I will go here and there, and I shall not sin; for you are never so out of danger of sinning as to boast of security. The road is very miry, it will be hard to pick your path so as not to soil your garments. This is a world of pitch; you will need to watch often, if in handling it you are to keep your hands clean. There is a robber at every turn of the road to rob you of your jewels; there is a temptation in every mercy; there is a snare in every joy; and if you ever reach heaven, it will be a miracle of divine grace to be ascribed entirely to your Father's power. Be on your guard. When a man carries a bomb-shell in his hand, he should mind that he does not go near a candle; and you too must take care that you enter not into temptation. Even your common actions are edged tools; you must mind how you handle them.

There is nothing in this world to foster a Christian's piety, but everything to destroy it. How anxious should you be to look up to God, that He may keep you! Your prayer should be, "Hold me up, and I shall be safe". Having prayed, you must also watch; guarding every thought, word, and action, with holy jealousy. Do not expose yourselves unnecessarily; but if called to exposure, if you are bidden to go where the darts are flying, never venture forth without your shield. For if once the devil finds you without your buckler, he will rejoice that his hour of triumph is come, and will soon make you fall down wounded by his arrows. Though slain you cannot be; wounded you may be. *"Be sober; be vigilant,"* danger may be in an hour when all seems secure to you. Therefore, take heed to your ways, and watch unto prayer. No man ever fell into error through being too watchful. May the Holy Spirit guide us in all our ways, so shall they always please the Lord.

MORNING   March 15

"Be strong in the grace which is in Christ Jesus" — 2 Timothy 2:1.

CHRIST HAS GRACE without measure in Himself, but He has not retained it for Himself. As the reservoir empties itself into the pipes, so has Christ emptied out His grace for His people. *"Of His fulness have all we received, and grace for grace."* He seems only to have in order to dispense to us. He stands like the fountain, always flowing, but only running in order to supply the empty pitchers and the thirsty lips which draw near unto it. Like a tree, He bears sweet fruit, not to hang on boughs, but to be gathered by those who need. Grace, whether its work be to pardon, to cleanse, to preserve, to strengthen, to enlighten, to quicken, or to restore, is ever to be had from Him freely and without price; nor is there one form of the work of grace which He has not bestowed upon His people.

As the blood of the body, though flowing from the heart, belongs equally to every member, so the influences of grace are the inheritance of every saint united to the Lamb; and herein there is a sweet communion between Christ and His Church, inasmuch as they both receive the same grace. Christ is the head upon which the oil is first poured; but the same oil runs to the very skirts of the garments, so that the meanest saint has an unction of the same costly moisture as that which fell upon the head. This is true communion when the sap of grace flows from the stem to the branch, and when it is perceived that the stem itself is sustained by the very nourishment which feeds the branch. As we day by day receive grace from Jesus, and more constantly recognize it as coming from Him, we shall behold Him in communion with us, and enjoy the felicity of communion with Him. Let us make daily use of our riches, and ever repair to Him as to our own Lord in covenant, taking from Him the supply of all we need with as much boldness as men take money from their own purse.

EVENING

"He did it with all his heart and was blessed" — 2 Chronicles 31:21.

THIS IS NO unusual occurrence; it is the general rule of the moral universe that those men prosper who do their work with all their hearts, while those are almost certain to fall who go to their labor leaving half their hearts behind them. God does not give harvests to idle men except harvests of thistles, nor is He pleased to send wealth to those who will not dig in the field to find its hidden treasure. It is universally confessed that if a man would prosper, he must be diligent in business. It is the same in religion as it is in other things. If you would prosper in your work for Jesus, let it be heart work, and let it be done with all your heart; with as much force, energy, heartiness, and earnestness into religion as ever you do into business, for it deserves far more.

The Holy Spirit helps our infirmities, but He does not encourage our idleness; He loves active believers. Who are the most useful men in the Christian church? The men who do what they undertake for God with all their hearts. Who are the most successful Sunday School teachers? The most talented? No, the most zealous; the men whose hearts are on fire, those are the men who see their Lord riding forth prosperously in the majesty of His salvation. Whole-heartedness shows itself in perseverance; there may be failure at first, but the earnest worker will say, "It is the Lord's work, and it must be done; my Lord has bidden me do it, and in His strength I will accomplish it". Christian, are you thus *"with all your heart"* serving your Master? Remember the earnestness of Jesus! Think what heart-work was His! He could say, *"The zeal of Your house has eaten Me up."* When He sweat great drops of blood, it was no light burden He had to carry upon those blessed shoulders; and when He poured out His heart, it was no weak effort He was making for the salvation of His people. Was Jesus in earnest, and are we lukewarm?

March 16

MORNING

"I am a stranger with You" — Psalm 39:12.

YES, OH LORD, with You, but not to You. All my natural alienation from You, Your grace has effectually removed. And now, in fellowship with Yourself, I walk through this sinful world as a pilgrim in a foreign country. You are a stranger in Your own world. Man forgets You, dishonors You, sets up new laws and alien customs, and knows You not. When Your dear Son came unto His own, His own received Him not. He was in the world, and the world was made by Him, and the world knew Him not. Never was foreigner so speckled a bird among the denizens of any land as Your beloved Son among His mother's brethren.

It is no marvel, then, if I who live the life of Jesus, should be unknown and a stranger here below. Lord, I would not be a citizen where Jesus was an alien. His pierced hand has loosened the cords which once bound my soul to earth, and now I find myself a stranger in the land. My speech seems to these Babylonians among whom I dwell an outlandish tongue, my manners are singular, and my actions are strange. A Tartar would be more at home in Cheapside than I could ever be in the haunts of sinners. But here is the sweetness of my lot: I am not a stranger with You. You are my fellow-sufferer, my fellow-pilgrim. Oh, what joy to wander in such blessed society! My heart burns within me by the way when You speak to me, and though I am a sojourner, I am far more blessed than those who sit on thrones, and far more at home than those who dwell in their ceiled houses.

> I can be calm and free from care
> On any shore, since God is there.
> While place we seek, or place we shun,
> The soul finds happiness in none:
> But with a God to guide our way,
> 'Tis equal joy to go or stay.

EVENING

"Keep Your servant back from willful sins" — Psalm 19:13.

SUCH WAS THE prayer of the *"man after God's own heart."* Did holy David need to pray thus? How needful, then, must such a prayer be for us babes in grace! It is as if he said, "Keep me back, or I shall rush headlong over the precipice of sin." Our evil nature, like an ill-tempered horse, is apt to run away. May the grace of God put the bridle upon it, and hold it in, that it rush not into mischief.

What might not the best of us do if it were not for the checks which the Lord sets upon us both in providence and in grace! The psalmist's prayer is directed against the worst form of sin, that which is done with deliberation and wilfulness. Even the holiest need to be "kept back" from the vilest transgressions. It is a solemn thing to find the apostle Paul warning saints against the most loathsome sins. *"So put to death your members which are on the earth; fornication, uncleanness, passion, evil lust and covetousness (which is idolatry)."* What! do saints need warning against such sins as these? Yes, they do. The whitest robes, unless their purity be preserved by divine grace, it will be defiled by the blackest spots.

Experienced Christian, boast not in your experience; you will trip yet if you look away from Him who is able to keep you from falling. You whose love is fervent, whose faith is constant, whose hopes are bright, say not, "We shall never sin", but rather cry, *"Lead us not into temptation."* There is enough tinder in the heart of the best of men to light a fire that shall burn to the lowest hell, unless God shall quench the sparks as they fall. Who would have dreamed that righteous Lot could be found drunken, and committing uncleanness? Hazael said, *"Is Your servant a dog, that he should do this thing?"* and we are very apt to use the same self-righteous question. May infinite wisdom cure us of the madness of self-confidence.

MORNING   March 17

"Remember the poor" — *Galatians 2:10.*

WHY DOES GOD allow so many of His children to be poor? He could make them all rich if He pleased; He could lay bags of gold at their doors; He could send them a large annual income; or He could scatter round their houses abundance of provisions, as once He made the quails lie in heaps round the camp of Israel, and rained bread out of heaven to feed them. There is no necessity that they should be poor, except that He sees it to be best. *"The cattle upon a thousand hills are His."* He could supply them; He could make the richest, the greatest, and the mightiest bring all their power and riches to the feet of His children, for the hearts of all men are in His control. But He does not choose to do so. He allows them to suffer want, He allows them to pine in penury and obscurity.

Why is this? There are many reasons: one is, to give us, who are favored with enough, an opportunity of showing our love to Jesus. We show our love to Christ when we sing of Him and when we pray to Him. But if there were no sons of need in the world we should lose the sweet privilege of evidencing our love, by ministering in alms-giving to His poorer brethren. He has ordained that thus we should prove that our love stands not in word only, but in deed and in truth. If we truly love Christ, we shall care for those who are loved by Him. Those who are dear to Him will be dear to us.

Let us then look upon it not as a duty but as a privilege to relieve the poor of the Lord's flock, remembering the words of the Lord Jesus, *"Inasmuch as you have done it unto one of the least of these my brethren, you have done it unto me."* Surely this assurance is sweet enough, and this motive strong enough to lead us to help others with a willing hand and a loving heart remembering that all we do for His people is graciously accepted by Christ as done to Himself.

EVENING

"Blessed are the peacemakers! For they shall be called the sons of God" — *Matthew 5:9.*

THIS IS THE seventh of the beatitudes; and seven was the number of perfection among the Hebrews. It may be that the Savior placed the peacemaker the seventh upon the list because he most nearly approaches the perfect man in Christ Jesus. He who would have perfect blessedness, so far as it can be enjoyed on earth, must attain to this seventh benediction, and become a peacemaker. There is a significance also in the position of the text. The verse which precedes it speaks of the blessedness of *"the pure in heart: for they shall see God."* It is well to understand that we are to be *"first pure, then peaceable."* Our peaceableness is never to be a compact with sin, or toleration of evil. We must set our faces like flints against everything which is contrary to God and His holiness; purity being in our souls a settled matter, we can go on to peaceableness.

Not less does the verse that follows seem to have been put there on purpose. However peaceable we may be in this world, yet we shall be misrepresented and misunderstood: and no marvel, for even the Prince of Peace, by His very peacefulness, brought fire upon the earth. He Himself, though He loved mankind, and did no ill, was *"despised and rejected of men, a man of sorrows and acquainted with grief."* Lest, therefore, the peaceable in heart should be surprised when they meet with enemies, it is added in the following verse, *"Blessed are they which are persecuted for righteousness sake: for theirs is the kingdom of heaven."* Thus the peacemakers are not only pronounced to be blessed, but they are compassed about with blessings. Lord, give us grace to climb to this seventh beatitude! Purify our minds that we may be *"first pure, then peaceable,"* and fortify our souls, that our peaceableness may not lead us into cowardice and despair, when for Your sake we are persecuted.

March 18

MORNING

"For you are all sons of God through faith in Christ Jesus" — Galatians 3:26.

THE FATHERHOOD OF God is common to all his children. "Ah! Little-faith", you have often said, "Oh that I had the courage of Great-heart, that I could wield his sword and be as valiant as he! But, alas, I stumble at every straw, and a shadow makes me afraid." Listen Little-faith. Great-heart is God's child, and you are God's child too; and Great-heart is not one bit more God's child than you are. Peter and Paul, the highly-favored apostles, were of the family of the Most High; and so are you also; the weak Christian is as much a child of God as the strong one.

> This covenant stands secure,
> Though earth's old pillars bow;
> The strong, the feeble, and the weak,
> Are one in Jesus now.

All the names are in the same family register. One may have more grace than another, but God our heavenly Father has the same tender heart towards all. One may do more mighty works, and may bring more glory to his Father, but he whose name is the least in the kingdom of heaven is as much the child of God as he who stands among the King's mighty men. Let this cheer and comfort us, when we draw near to God and say, *"Our Father."*

Yet, while we are comforted by knowing this, let us not rest contented with weak faith, but ask, like the Apostles, to have it increased. However feeble our faith may be, if it be real faith in Christ, we shall reach heaven at last, but we shall not honor our Master much on our pilgrimage, neither shall we abound in joy and peace. If then you would live to Christ's glory, and be happy in His service, seek to be filled with the spirit of adoption more and more completely, till perfect love shall cast out fear.

EVENING

"As the Father loved Me, I also loved you" — John 15:9.

AS THE FATHER loves the Son, in the same manner Jesus loves His people. What is that divine method? He loved Him without beginning, and thus Jesus loves His members. *"I have loved you with an everlasting love"* (Jer. 31:3). You can trace the beginning of human affection; you can easily find the beginning of your love to Christ, but His love to us is a stream whose source is hidden in eternity. God the Father loves Jesus without any change. Christian, take this for your comfort, that there is no change in Jesus Christ's love to those who rest in Him. Yesterday you were on Tabor's top, and you said, "He loves me"; today you are in the valley of humiliation, but He loves you still the same. On the hill Mizar, and among the Hermons, you heard His voice, which spoke so sweetly with the turtle-notes of love; and now on the sea, or even in the sea, when all His waves and billows go over you, His heart is faithful to His ancient choice.

The Father loves the Son without any end, and thus does the Son love His people. Saint, you need not fear the loosing of the silver cord, for His love for you will never cease. Rest confident that even down to the grave Christ will go with you, and that up again from it He will be your guide to the celestial hills. Moreover, the Father loves the Son without any measure, and the same immeasurable love the Son bestows upon His chosen ones. The whole heart of Christ is dedicated to His people. He *"loved us and gave Himself for us."* His is a love which passes knowledge. Ah! we have indeed an immutable Savior, a precious Savior, one who loves without measure, without change, without beginning, and without end, even as the Father loves Him! There is much food here for those who know how to digest it. May the Holy Ghost lead us into its marrow and fatness!

MORNING   March 19

"Strengthened in faith" — Romans 4:20.

CHRISTIAN, TAKE GOOD care of your faith; for remember faith is the only way whereby you can obtain blessings. If we want blessings from God, nothing can bring them down but faith. Prayer cannot draw down answers from God's throne except it be the earnest prayer of the man who believes. Faith is the angelic messenger between the soul and the Lord Jesus in glory. Let that angel be withdrawn, we can neither send up prayer, nor receive the answers. Faith is the telegraphic wire which links earth and heaven, on which God's messages of love fly so fast, that before we call He answers, and while we are yet speaking He hears us.

But if that telegraphic wire of faith be snapped, how can we receive the promise? Am I in trouble? I can obtain help for trouble by faith. Am I beaten about by the enemy? Then my soul on her dear Refuge leans by faith. But take faith away, in vain I call to God. There is no road between my soul and heaven. In the deepest wintertime faith is a road on which the horses of prayer may travel. Yea, and all the better for the biting frost; but blockade the road, and how can we communicate with the Great King? Faith links me with divinity. Faith clothes me with the power of God. Faith engages on my side the omnipotence of Jehovah. Faith ensures every attribute of God in my defense. It helps me to defy the hosts of hell. It makes me march triumphant over the necks of my enemies.

But without faith how can I receive anything of the Lord? Let him that wavers, who is like a wave of the Sea, not expect that he will receive anything of God! Oh, then, Christian, watch well your faith; for with it you can win all things, however poor you are, but without it you can obtain nothing. *"If you can believe, all things are possible to him that believes."*

EVENING

"And she ate, and was satisfied, and left" — Ruth 2:14.

WHENEVER WE ARE privileged to eat of the bread which Jesus gives, we are, like Ruth, satisfied with the full and sweet repast. When Jesus is the host no guest goes empty from the table. Our head is satisfied with the precious truth which Christ reveals; our heart is content with Jesus, as the altogether lovely object of affection; our hope is satisfied, for whom have we in heaven but Jesus? And our desire is satiated, for what can we wish for more than *"to know Christ and to be found in Him"?* Jesus fills our conscience till it is at perfect peace; our judgment with persuasion of the certainty of His teachings; our memory with recollections of what He has done, and our imagination with the prospects of what He is yet to do. As Ruth was *"satisfied, and left,"* so is it with us. We have had deep draughts; we have thought that we could take in all of Christ; but when we have done our best we have had to leave a vast remainder. We have sat at the table of the Lord's love, and said, "Nothing but the infinite can ever satisfy me; I am such a great sinner that I must have infinite merit to wash my sin away". But we have had our sin removed, and found that there was merit to spare; we have had our hunger relieved at the feast of sacred love, and found that there was a redundance of spiritual meat remaining.

There are certain sweet things in the Word of God which we have not enjoyed yet, and which we are obliged to leave for awhile. For we are like the disciples to whom Jesus said, *"I have yet many things to say unto you, but you cannot bear them now."* Yes, there are graces to which we have not attained; places of fellowship nearer to Christ which we have not reached; and heights of communion which our feet have not climbed. At every banquet of love there are many baskets of fragments left. Let us magnify the liberality of our glorious Boaz.

March 20   MORNING

"My Beloved!" — *Song of Solomon 2:8.*

THIS WAS A golden name which the ancient Church in her most joyous moments was wont to give to the Anointed of the Lord. When the time of the singing of birds was come, and the voice of the turtle was heard in her land, her love-note was sweeter than either, as she sang, *"My Beloved is mine and I am His: He feeds among the lilies."* Ever in her song of songs she calls Him by that delightful name, *"My Beloved!"* Even in the long winter, when idolatry had withered the garden of the Lord, her prophets found space to lay aside the burden of the Lord for a little season, and to say, as Isaiah did, *"Now will I sing to my well-beloved a song of my beloved touching His vineyard."* Though the saints had never seen His face, though as yet He was not made flesh, nor had dwelled among us, nor had man beheld His glory, yet He was the consolation of Israel, the hope and joy of all the chosen, the *"beloved"* of all those who were upright before the Most High.

We, in the summer days of the Church, are also wont to speak of Christ as the best beloved of our soul, and to feel that He is very precious, the *"chiefest"* among ten thousand, and the *"altogether lovely One."* So true is it that the Church loves Jesus, and claims Him as her beloved, that the apostle dares to defy the whole universe to separate her from the love of Christ, and declares that neither persecutions, distress, affliction, peril, or the sword have been able to do it; no, he joyously boasts, *"In all these things we are more than conquerors through Him that loved us."*

    Oh that we knew more of You, You ever precious one!
    My sole possession is Your love;
    In earth beneath, or heaven above,
    I have no other store;
    And though with fervent suit I pray,
    And implore You day by day,
    I ask You nothing more.

EVENING

"Husbands, love your own wives, as Christ also loved the church " — *Ephesians 5:25.*

WHAT A GOLDEN example Christ gives to His disciples! Few masters could venture to say, "If you would practice my teaching, imitate my life". But as the life of Jesus is the exact transcript of perfect virtue, He can point to Himself as the paragon of holiness, as well as the teacher of it. The Christian should take nothing short of Christ for his model. Under no circumstances ought we to be content unless we reflect the grace which was in Him. As a husband, the Christian is to look upon the portrait of Christ Jesus, and he is to paint according to that copy. The true Christian is to be such a husband as Christ was to His church. The love of a husband is special. The Lord Jesus cherishes for the church a peculiar affection, which is set upon her above the rest of mankind: *"I pray for them, I pray not for the world."*

The elect church is the favorite of heaven, the treasure of Christ, the crown of His head, the bracelet of His arm, the breastplate of His heart, the very center and core of His love. A husband should love his wife with a constant love, for thus Jesus loves His church. He does not vary in His affection. He may change in His display of affection, but the affection itself is still the same. A husband should love his wife with an enduring love, for nothing *"shall be able to separate us from the love of God, which is in Christ Jesus our Lord."* A true husband loves his wife with a hearty love, fervent and intense. It is not mere lip-service. Ah! beloved, what more could Christ have done in proof of His love than He has done? Jesus has a delighted love towards His spouse; He prizes her affection, and delights in her with sweet complacence. Believer, you wonder at Jesus' love; you admire it, are you imitating it? In your domestic relationships, is the rule and measure of your love *"even as Christ loved the church"*?

MORNING   March 21

"You will be scattered, each one to his own house. And you will leave Me alone" — John 16:32.

FEW HAD FELLOWSHIP with the sorrows of Gethsemane. The majority of the disciples were not sufficiently advanced in grace to be admitted to behold the mysteries of *"the agony."* Occupied with the Passover feast at their own houses, they represent the many who live upon the letter, but are mere babes as to the spirit of the gospel. To twelve, no, to eleven only was the privilege given to enter Gethsemane and see "this great sight." Out of the eleven, eight were left at a distance; they had fellowship, but not of that intimate sort to which men greatly beloved are admitted. Only three highly favored ones could approach the veil of our Lord's mysterious sorrow. Within that veil even these must not intrude; a stones-cast distance must be left between. He must tread the wine-press alone, and of the people there must be none with Him.

Peter and the two sons of Zebedee, represent the few eminent, experienced saints, who may be written down as "Fathers;" these having done business on great waters, can in some degree measure the huge Atlantic waves of their Redeemer's passion. To some selected spirits it is given, for the good of others, and to strengthen them for future, special, and tremendous conflict, to enter the inner circle and hear the pleadings of the suffering High Priest. These have fellowship with Him in His sufferings, and are made conformable unto His death. Yet even these cannot penetrate the secret places of the Savior's woe. "Your unknown sufferings" is the remarkable expression of the Greek liturgy; there was an inner chamber in our Master's grief, shut out from human knowledge and fellowship. There Jesus is *"left alone."* Here Jesus was more than ever an *"Unspeakable gift"!* Is not Watts right when he sings -

And all the unknown joys He gives,
Were bought with agonies unknown.

EVENING

"Can you bind the chains of the Pleiades or loose the bands of Orion?" — Job 38:31.

IF INCLINED TO boast of our abilities, the grandeur of nature may soon show us how puny we are. We cannot move the least of all the twinkling stars, or quench so much as one of the beams of the morning. We speak of power, but the heavens laugh us to scorn. When the Pleiades shine forth in spring with vernal joy we cannot restrain their influences, and when Orion reigns aloft, and the year is bound in winter's chains, we cannot relax the icy bands. The seasons revolve according to the divine appointment, neither can the whole race of men effect a change therein. Lord, what is man?

In the spiritual, as in the natural world, man's power is limited on all hands. When the Holy Spirit sheds abroad His delights in the soul, none can disturb. All the cunning and malice of men are ineffectual to stay the genial quickening power of the Comforter. When He deigns to visit a church and revive it, the most inveterate enemies cannot resist the good work. They may ridicule it, but they can no more restrain it than they can push back the spring when the Pleiades rule the hour. God wills it, and so it must be. On the other hand, if the Lord in sovereignty, or in justice, bind up a man so that he is in "bondage," who can give him liberty? He alone can remove the winter of spiritual death from an individual or a people. He looses the bands of Orion, and none but He. What a blessing it is that He can do it. Oh that He would perform the wonder tonight.

Lord, end my winter, and let my spring begin. I cannot with all my longings raise my soul out of her death and dullness, but all things are possible with You. I need celestial influences, the clear shining of Your love, the beams of Your grace, the light of Your countenance, these are the Pleiades to me. I suffer much from sin and temptation, these are my wintry signs, my terrible Orion. Lord, work wonders in me, and for me. Amen.

March 22   MORNING

"And going forward a little He fell upon His face praying" — Matthew 26:39.

THERE ARE SEVERAL instructive features in our Savior's prayer in His hour of trial. It was lonely prayer. He withdrew even from His three favored disciples. Believer, be much in solitary prayer, especially in times of trial. Family prayer, social prayer, prayer in the Church, will not suffice, these are very precious, but the best beaten spice will smoke in your censer in your private devotions, where no ear hears but God's.

It was humble prayer. Luke says He knelt, but another evangelist says He *"fell on His face."* Where, then, must be YOUR place, you humble servant of the great Master? What dust and ashes should cover your head! Humility gives us good foot-hold in prayer. There is no hope of prevalence with God unless we abase ourselves that He may exalt us in due time.

It was his prayer. *"Abba, Father."* You will find it a stronghold in the day of trial to plead your adoption. You have no rights as a subject, you have forfeited them by your treason; but nothing can forfeit a child's right to a father's protection. Be not afraid to say, "My Father, hear my cry." Observe that it was persevering prayer. He prayed three times. Cease not until you prevail. Be as the importunate widow, whose continual coming earned what her first supplication could not win. Continue in prayer, and watch in the same with thanksgiving.

Lastly, it was the prayer of resignation. *"Nevertheless, not as I will, but as You will."* Yield, and God yields. Let it be as God wills, and God will determine for the best. Be content to leave your prayer in His hands, who knows when to give, and how to give, and what to give, and what to withhold. So pleading, earnestly, importunately, yet with humility and resignation, you shall surely prevail.

EVENING

"Father I desire that those whom You have given Me may be with Me where I am" — John 17:24.

OH DEATH! WHY do you touch the tree beneath whose spreading branches weariness has rest? Why do you snatch away the excellent of the earth, in whom is all our delight? If you must use your axe, use it upon the trees which yield no fruit; you might be thanked then. But why will you fell the goodly cedars of Lebanon? Oh stay your axe, and spare the righteous. But no, it must not be; death smites the goodliest of our friends; the most generous, the most prayerful, the most holy, the most devoted must die. And why? It is through Jesus' prevailing prayer, *"Father, I will that they also, whom You have given Me, be with Me where I am."* It is that which bears them on eagle's wings to heaven.

Every time a believer mounts from this earth to paradise, it is an answer to Christ's prayer. A good old divine remarks, "Many times Jesus and His people pull against one another in prayer. You bend your knee in prayer and say, 'Father, I will that Your saints be with me where I am'". Christ says, *"Father, I will that they also, whom You have given Me, be with Me where I am."* Thus the disciple is at cross-purposes with his Lord. The soul cannot be in both places; the beloved one cannot be with Christ and with you too.

Now, which pleader shall win the day? If you had your choice; if the King should step from His throne, and say, "Here are two supplicants praying in opposition to one another, which shall be answered?" Oh! I am sure, though it were agony, you would start from your feet, and say, "Jesus, not my will, but Yours be done." You would give up your prayer for your loved one's life, if you could realize the thought that Christ is praying in the opposite direction, *"Father, I will that they also, whom You have given Me, be with Me where I am."* Lord, You shall have them. By faith we let them go.

MORNING March 23

"And His sweat became as great drops of blood falling down to the ground" — Luke 22:44.

THE MENTAL PRESSURE arising from our Lord's struggle with temptation, so forced His frame to an unnatural excitement, that His pores sent forth great drops of blood which fell down to the ground. This proves how tremendous must have been the weight of sin when it was able to crush the Savior so that He distilled great drops of blood! This demonstrates the mighty power of His love. It is a very pretty observation of old Isaac Ambrose that the gum which exudes from the tree without cutting is always the best. This precious camphire-tree yielded most sweet spices when it was wounded under the knotty whips, and when it was pierced by the nails on the cross; but see, it gives forth its best spice when there is no whip, no nail, no wound.

This sets forth the voluntariness of Christ's sufferings, since without a lance the blood flowed freely. No need to put on the leech, or apply the knife; it flows spontaneously. No need for the rulers to cry, "Spring up, O well". Of itself it flows in crimson torrents. If men suffer great pain of mind apparently the blood rushes to the heart. The cheeks are pale; a fainting fit comes on; the blood has gone inward as if to nourish the inner man while passing through its trial. But see our Savior in His agony; He is so utterly oblivious of self, that instead of His agony driving His blood to the heart to nourish Himself, it drives it outward to bedew the earth. The agony of Christ, inasmuch as it pours Him out upon the ground, pictures the fulness of the offering which He made for men.

Do we not perceive how intense must have been the wrestling through which He passed, and will we not hear its voice to us? *"You have not yet resisted unto blood, striving against sin."* Behold the great Apostle and High Priest of our profession, and sweat even to blood rather than yield to the great tempter of your souls.

EVENING

"I tell you that if these should be silent the stones will cry out" — Luke 19:40.

BUT COULD THE stones cry out? Assuredly they could if He who opens the mouth of the dumb should bid them lift up their voice. Certainly if they were to speak, they would have much to testify in praise of Him who created them by the word of His power; they could extol the wisdom and power of their Maker who called them into being. Shall not we speak well of Him who made us anew, and out of stones raised up children unto Abraham? The old rocks could tell of chaos and order, and the handiwork of God in successive stages of creation's drama; and cannot we talk of God's decrees, of God's great work in ancient times, in all that He did for His church in the days of old?

If the stones were to speak, they could tell of their breaker, how he took them from the quarry, and made them fit for the temple. And cannot we tell of our glorious Breaker, who broke our hearts with the hammer of His word, that He might build us into His temple? If the stones should cry out they would magnify their builder, who polished them and fashioned them after the similitude of a palace; and shall not we talk of our Architect and Builder, who has put us in our place in the temple of the living God? If the stones could cry out, they might have a long, long story to tell by way of memorial, for many a time has a great stone been rolled as a memorial before the Lord; and we too can testify of Ebenezers, stones of help, pillars of remembrance.

The broken stones of the law cry out against us, but Christ Himself, who has rolled away the stone from the door of the sepulchre, speaks for us. Stones might well cry out, but we will not let them: we will hush their noise with ours; we will break forth into sacred song, and bless the majesty of the Most High, all our days glorifying Him who is called by Jacob the Shepherd and Stone of Israel.

March 24　　　　　　　　　MORNING

"Having been heard in that He feared God" — Hebrews 5:7.

DID THIS FEAR arise from the infernal suggestion that He was utterly forsaken? There may be sterner trials than this, but surely it is one of the worst to be utterly forsaken? Satan says, "You have a friend nowhere"! Your Father has shut up the bowels of His compassion against You. Not an angel in His courts will stretch out his hand to help You. All heaven is alienated from You; You are left alone. See the companions with whom You have taken sweet counsel, what are they worth? Son of Mary, see there Your brother James, see there Your loved disciple John, and Your bold apostle Peter, how the cowards sleep when You are in Your sufferings! Lo! You have no friend left in heaven or earth. All hell is against You. I have stirred up my infernal den. I have sent my missives throughout all regions summoning every prince of darkness to set upon You this night, and we will spare no arrows, we will use all our infernal might to overwhelm You; and what will You do, You solitary One?

It may be, this was the temptation; we think it was, because the appearance of an angel unto Him strengthening Him removed that fear. He was heard in that He feared; He was no more alone, but heaven was with Him. It may be that this is the reason of His coming three times to His disciples, as Hart puts it:

　　　　Backwards and forwards thrice He ran,
　　　　As if He sought some help from man.

He would see for Himself whether it were really true that all men had forsaken Him. He found them all asleep; but perhaps He gained some faint comfort from the thought that they were sleeping, not from treachery, but from sorrow, the spirit indeed was willing, but the flesh was weak. At any rate He was heard in that He feared. Jesus was heard in His deepest woe; my soul, you shall be heard also.

EVENING

"In that same hour Jesus rejoiced in the Spirit" — Luke 10:21.

THE SAVIOR WAS *"a man of sorrows,"* but every thoughtful mind has discovered the fact that down deep in His innermost soul He carried an inexhaustible treasury of refined and heavenly joy. Of all the human race, there was never a man who had a deeper, purer, or more abiding peace than our Lord Jesus Christ. *"He was anointed with the oil of gladness above His fellows."* His vast benevolence must from the very nature of things, have afforded Him the deepest possible delight, for benevolence is joy. There were a few remarkable seasons when this joy manifested itself. *"At that hour Jesus rejoiced in the spirit, and said, 'I thank You, Oh Father, Lord of heaven and earth.'"* Christ had His songs, though it was night with Him; though His face was marred, and His countenance had lost the lustre of earthly happiness, yet sometimes it was lit up with a matchless splendor of unparalleled satisfaction, as He thought upon the recompense of the reward, and in the midst of the congregation sang His praise unto God.

In this, the Lord Jesus is a blessed picture of His church on earth. At this hour the church expects to walk in sympathy with her Lord along a thorny road; through much tribulation she is forcing her way to the crown. To bear the cross is her office, and to be scorned and counted an alien by her mother's children is her lot; and yet the church has a deep well of joy, of which none can drink but her own children. There are stores of wine, and oil, and corn, hidden in the midst of our Jerusalem, upon which the saints of God are evermore sustained and nurtured. And sometimes, as in our Savior's case, we have our seasons of intense delight, for "There is a river, the streams whereof shall make glad the city of our God." Exiles though we be, we rejoice in our King; yes, in Him we exceedingly rejoice, while in His name we set up our banners.

MORNING — March 25

"Do you betray the Son of man with a kiss?" — Luke 22:48.

"THE KISSES OF an enemy are deceitful." Let me be on my guard when the world puts on a loving face, for it will, if possible, betray me as it did my Master, with a kiss. Whenever a man is about to stab religion, he usually professes very great reverence for it. Let me beware of the sleek-faced hypocrisy which is armor-bearer to heresy and infidelity. Knowing the deceivableness of unrighteousness, let me be wise as a serpent to detect and avoid the designs of the enemy. The young man, void of understanding, was led astray by the kiss of the strange woman; may my soul be so graciously instructed all this day, that "the much fair speech" of the world may have no effect upon me. Holy Spirit, let me not, a poor frail son of man, be betrayed with a kiss!

But what if I should be guilty of the same accursed sin as Judas, that son of perdition? I have been baptized into the name of the Lord Jesus; I am a member of His visible Church; I sit at the communion table. All these are so many kisses of my lips. Am I sincere in them? If not, I am a base traitor. Do I live in the world as carelessly as others do, and yet make a profession of being a follower of Jesus? Then I must expose religion to ridicule, and lead men to speak evil of the holy name by which I am called. Surely if I act thus inconsistently I am a Judas, and it were better for me that I had never been born. Dare I hope that I am clear in this matter? Then, Oh Lord, keep me so. Oh Lord, make me sincere and true. Preserve me from every false way. Never let me betray my Savior. I do love You, Jesus, and though I often grieve You, yet I would desire to abide faithful even unto death. Oh God, forbid that I should be a high-soaring professor, and then fall at last into the lake of fire, because I betrayed my Master with a kiss.

EVENING

"Son of man" — John 3:13.

HOW CONSTANTLY OUR Master used the title, the *"Son of man!"* If He had chosen, He might always have spoken of Himself as the Son of God, the Everlasting Father, the Wonderful, the Counsellor, the Prince of Peace; but behold the lowliness of Jesus! He prefers to call Himself the Son of man. Let us learn a lesson of humility from our Savior; let us never court great titles nor proud degrees. There is here, however, a far sweeter thought. Jesus loved manhood so much, that He delighted to honor it. And since it is a high honor, and indeed, the greatest dignity of manhood, that Jesus is the Son of man, He is wont to display this name, that He may as it were hang royal stars upon the breast of manhood, and show forth the love of God to Abraham's seed. *"Son of man"*. Whenever He said that word, He shed a halo round the head of Adam's children.

Yet there is perhaps a more precious thought still. Jesus Christ called Himself the Son of man to express His oneness and sympathy with His people. He thus reminds us that He is one whom we may approach without fear. As a man, we may take to Him all our griefs and troubles, for He knows them by experience; in that He Himself has suffered as the *"Son of man,"* He is able to succor and comfort us. All hail, You blessed Jesus! inasmuch as You are evermore using the sweet name which acknowledges that You are a brother and a near kinsman, it is to us a dear token of Your grace, Your humility, Your love.

> Oh see how Jesus trusts Himself unto our childish love,
> As though by His free ways with us our earnestness to prove!
> His sacred name a common word on earth He loves to hear;
> There is no majesty in Him which love may not come near.

March 26   MORNING

"Jesus answered ... if it is Me you seek, let these go" — John 18:8.

MARK, MY SOUL, the care which Jesus manifested even in His hour of trial, towards the sheep of His hand! The ruling passion is strong in death. He resigns Himself to the enemy, but He interposes a word of power to set His disciples free. As to Himself, like a sheep before her shearers He is dumb and opened not His mouth, but for His disciples' sake He speaks with Almighty energy. Herein is love, constant, self-forgetting, faithful love.

But is there not far more here than is to be found upon the surface? Have we not the very soul and spirit of the atonement in these words? The Good Shepherd lays down His life for the sheep, and pleads that they must therefore go free. The Surety is bound, and justice demands that those for whom He stands a substitute should go their way. In the midst of Egypt's bondage, that voice rings as a word of power, *"Let these go."* Out of the slavery of sin and Satan the redeemed must come. In every cell of the dungeons of Despair, the sound is echoed, *"Let these go,"* and forth come Despondency and Much-afraid. Satan hears the well-known voice, and lifts his foot from the neck of the fallen; and Death hears it, and the grave opens her gates to let the dead arise.

Their way is one of progress, holiness, triumph, glory, and none shall dare to stay them in it. No lion shall be on their way, neither shall any ravenous beast go up thereon. *"The hind of the morning"* has drawn the cruel hunters upon himself, and now the most timid roes and hinds of the field may graze at perfect peace among the lilies of his loves. The thundercloud has burst over the Cross of Calvary, and the pilgrims of Zion shall never be smitten by the bolts of vengeance. Come, my heart, rejoice in the immunity which your Redeemer has secured you, and bless His name all the day, and every day.

EVENING

"When He comes with the holy angels in the glory of His Father" — Mark 8:38.

IF WE HAVE been partakers with Jesus in His shame, we shall be sharers with Him in the lustre which shall surround Him when He appears again in glory. Are you, beloved one, with Christ Jesus? Does a vital union knit you to Him? Then you are today with Him in His shame; you have taken up His cross, and gone with Him without the camp bearing His reproach; you shall doubtless be with Him when the cross is exchanged for the crown. But judge yourself this evening; for if you are not with Him in the regeneration, neither shall you be with Him when He shall come in His glory. If you start back from the black side of communion, you shall not understand its bright, its happy period, when the King shall come, and all His holy angels with Him. What! are angels with Him? And yet He took not up angels; He took up the seed of Abraham. Are the holy angels with Him?

Come, my soul, if you are indeed His own beloved, you cannot be far from Him. If His friends and His neighbors are called together to see His glory, what think you if you are married to Him? Shall you be distant? Though it be a day of judgment, yet you cannot be far from that heart which, having admitted angels into intimacy, has admitted you into union. Has He not said to you, Oh my soul, *"I will betroth you unto Me in righteousness, and in judgment, and in loving-kindness"?* Have not His own lips said it, *"I am married unto you, and My delight is in you"?* If the angels, who are but friends and neighbors, shall be with Him, it is abundantly certain that His own beloved Hephzibah, in whom is all His delight, shall be near to Him, and sit at His right hand. Here is a morning star of hope for you, of such exceeding brilliance, that it may well light up the darkest and most desolate experience.

MORNING   March 27

"Then all His disciples ran away, forsaking Him" — Matthew 26:56.

HE NEVER DESERTED them, but they in cowardly fear of their lives, fled from Him in the very beginning of His sufferings. This is but one instructive instance of the frailty of all believers if left to themselves; they are but sheep at the best, and they flee when the wolf comes. They had all been warned of the danger, and had promised to die rather than leave their Master; and yet they were seized with sudden panic, and took to their heels. It may be, that I, at the opening of this day, have braced up my mind to bear a trial for the Lord's sake, and I imagine myself to be certain to exhibit perfect fidelity; but let me be very jealous of myself, lest having the same evil heart of unbelief, I should depart from my Lord as the apostles did. It is one thing to promise, and quite another to perform. It would have been to their eternal honor to have stood at Jesus' side right manfully; they fled from honor. May I be kept from imitating them! Where else could they have been so safe as near their Master, who could presently call for twelve legions of angels? They fled from their true safety.

Oh God, let me not play the fool also. Divine grace can make the coward brave. The smoking flax can flame forth like fire on the altar when the Lord wills it. These very apostles who were timid as hares, grew to be bold as lions after the Spirit had descended upon them, and even so the Holy Spirit can make my recreant spirit brave to confess my Lord and witness for His truth.

What anguish must have filled the Savior as He saw His friends so faithless! This was one bitter ingredient in His cup; but that cup is drained dry; let me not put another drop in it. If I forsake my Lord, I shall crucify Him afresh, and put Him to an open shame. Keep me, Oh blessed Spirit, from an end so shameful.

EVENING

"But she said, True, O Lord. But even the little dogs eat of the crumbs, which fall from the table of their masters" — Matthew 5:27.

THIS WOMAN GAINED comfort in her misery by thinking GREAT THOUGHTS OF CHRIST. The Master had talked about the children's bread: Now she argued, Since You are the Master of the table of grace, I know that You are a generous housekeeper, and there is sure to be abundance of bread on Your table; there will be such an abundance for the children that there will be crumbs to throw on the floor for the dogs, and the children will fare none the worse because the dogs are fed. She thought Him one who kept so good a table that all that she needed would only be a crumb in comparison; yet remember, what she wanted was to have the devil cast out of her daughter. It was a very great thing to her, but she had such a high esteem of Christ, that she said, "It is nothing to Him, it is but a crumb for Christ to give".

This is the royal road to comfort. Great thoughts of your sin alone will drive you to despair; but great thoughts of Christ will pilot you into the haven of peace. Say, "My sins are many, but it is nothing to Jesus to take them all away. The weight of my guilt presses me down as a giant's foot would crush a worm, but it is no more than a grain of dust to Him, because He has already borne its curse in His own body on the tree. It will be but a small thing for Him to give me full remission, although it will be an infinite blessing for me to receive it". The woman opens her soul's mouth very wide, expecting great things of Jesus and He fills it with His love.

Dear reader, do the same. She confessed what Christ laid at her door, but she laid fast hold upon Him, and drew arguments even out of His hard words; she believed great things of Him, and she thus overcame Him. SHE WON THE VICTORY BY BELIEVING IN HIM. Her case is an instance of prevailing faith; and if we would conquer like her, we must imitate her tactics.

March 28

MORNING

"Love of Christ which goes beyond our knowledge" — Ephesians 3:19.

THE LOVE OF Christ in its sweetness, its fulness, its greatness, its faithfulness, passes all human comprehension. Where shall language be found which shall describe His matchless, His unparalleled love towards the children of men? It is so vast and boundless that, as the swallow but skims the water, and dives not into its depths, so all descriptive words but touch the surface, while depths immeasurable lie beneath. Well might the poet say:

> Oh love, you fathomless abyss!
> For this love of Christ is indeed measureless and fathomless;
> None can attain unto it.

Before we can have any right idea of the love of Jesus, we must understand His previous glory in its height of majesty and His incarnation upon the earth in all its depths of shame. But who can tell us the majesty of Christ? When He was enthroned in the highest heavens He was very God of very God; by Him were the heavens made, and all the hosts thereof. His own almighty arm upheld the spheres; the praises of cherubim and seraphim perpetually surrounded Him; the full chorus of the hallelujahs of the universe unceasingly flowed to the foot of His throne; He reigned supreme above all His creatures, God over all, blessed forever. Who can tell His height of glory then? And who, on the other hand, can tell how low He descended? To be a man was something, to be a man of sorrows was far more; to bleed, and die, and suffer, these were much for Him who was the Son of God; but to suffer such unparalleled agony, to endure a death of shame and desertion by His Father, this is a depth of condescending love which the most inspired mind must utterly fail to fathom:

Herein is love! and truly it is love that *"passes knowledge."* Oh, let this love fill our hearts with adoring gratitude, and lead us to practical manifestations of its power.

EVENING

"I will receive you with your sweet perfume" — Ezekiel 20:41.

THE MERITS OF our great Redeemer are as sweet savor to the Most High. Whether we speak of the active or passive righteousness of Christ, there is an equal fragrance. There was a sweet savor in His active life by which He honored the law of God, and made every precept to glitter like a precious jewel in the pure setting of His own person. Such, too, was His passive obedience, when He endured with unmurmuring submission, hunger and thirst, cold and nakedness, and at length sweat great drops of blood in Gethsemane, gave His back to the smiters, and His cheeks to them that plucked out the hair, and was fastened to the cruel wood, that He might suffer the wrath of God in our behalf. These two things are sweet before the Most High; and for the sake of His doing and His dying, His substitutionary sufferings and His vicarious obedience, the Lord our God accepts us.

What a preciousness must there be in Him to overcome our want of preciousness! What a sweet savor to put away our ill savor! What a cleansing power in His blood to take away sin such as ours! and what glory in His righteousness to make such unacceptable creatures to be accepted in the Beloved! Mark, believer, how sure and unchanging must be our acceptance, since it is in Him! Take care that you never doubt your acceptance in Jesus. You cannot be accepted without Christ; but when you have received His merit, you cannot be unaccepted. Notwithstanding all your doubts, and fears, and sins, Jehovah's gracious eye never looks upon you in anger. Though He sees sin in you, in yourself, yet when He looks at you through Christ, He sees no sin. You are always accepted in Christ, are always blessed and dear to the Father's heart. Therefore lift up a song, and as you see the smoking incense of the merit of the Savior coming up, this evening, before the sapphire throne, let the incense of your praise go up also.

MORNING   March 29

"Even though He was a Son He learned obedience from the things which He suffered"
— *Hebrews 5:8.*

WE ARE TOLD that the Captain of our salvation was made perfect through suffering, therefore we who are sinful, and who are far from being perfect, must not wonder if we are called to pass through suffering too. Shall the head be crowned with thorns, and shall the other members of the body be rocked upon the dainty lap of ease? Must Christ pass through seas of His own blood to win the crown, and are we to walk to heaven dryshod in silver slippers? No, our Master's experience teaches us that suffering is necessary, and the true-born child of God must not, would not, escape it if he might. But there is one very comforting thought in the fact of Christ's *"being made perfect through suffering"* - it is, that He can have complete sympathy with us. *"He is not an high priest that cannot be touched with the feeling of our infirmities."*

In this sympathy of Christ we find a sustaining power. One of the early martyrs said, "I can bear it all, for Jesus suffered, and He suffers in me now; He sympathizes with me, and this makes me strong". Believer, lay hold of this thought in all times of agony. Let the thought of Jesus strengthen you as you follow in His steps. Find a sweet support in His sympathy; and remember that, to suffer is an honorable thing, to suffer for Christ is glory. The apostles rejoiced that they were counted worthy to do this. Just so far as the Lord shall give us grace to suffer for Christ, to suffer with Christ, just so far does He honor us. The jewels of a Christian are his afflictions. The regalia of the kings whom God has anointed are their troubles, their sorrows, and their griefs. Let us not, therefore, shun being honored. Let us not turn aside from being exalted. Griefs exalt us, and troubles lift us up. *"If we suffer, we shall also reign with Him."*

EVENING

"I called Him, but He gave me no answer" — *Song of Solomon 5:6.*

PRAYER SOMETIMES TARRIES, like a petitioner at the gate, until the King comes forth to fill her bosom with the blessings which she seeks. The Lord, when He has given great faith, has been known to try it by long delayings. He has suffered His servants' voices to echo in their ears as from a brazen sky. They have knocked at the golden gate, but it has remained immovable, as though it were rusted upon its hinges. Like Jeremiah, they have cried, *"You have covered Yourself with a cloud, that our prayer should not pass through."*

Thus have true saints continued long in patient waiting without reply, not because their prayers were not vehement, nor because they were unaccepted, but because it so pleased Him who is a Sovereign, and who gives according to His own pleasure. If it pleases Him to bid our patience exercise itself, shall He not do as He wills with His own? Beggars must not be choosers either as to time, place, or form. But we must be careful not to take delays in prayer for denials: God's long-dated bills will be punctually honored; we must not suffer Satan to shake our confidence in the God of truth by pointing to our unanswered prayers. Unanswered petitions are not unheard. God keeps a file for our prayers; they are not blown away by the wind, they are treasured in the King's archives. This is a registry in the court of heaven wherein every prayer is recorded.

Tried believer, your Lord has a tear-bottle in which the costly drops of sacred grief are put away, and a book in which your holy groanings are numbered. By-and-by, your suit shall prevail. Can you not be content to wait a little? Will not your Lord's time be better than your time? By-and-by He will comfortably appear, to your soul's joy, and make you put away the sackcloth and ashes of long waiting, and put on the scarlet and fine linen of full fruition.

March 30 MORNING

"He was counted among the transgressors" — Isaiah 53:12.

WHY DID JESUS suffer Himself to be enrolled among sinners? This wonderful condescension was justified by many powerful reasons. In such a character He could the better become their advocate. In some trials there is an identification of the counsellor with the client, nor can they be looked upon in the eye of the law as apart from one another. Now, when the sinner is brought to the bar, Jesus appears there Himself. He stands to answer the accusation. He points to His side, His hands, His feet, and challenges Justice to bring anything against the sinners whom He represents; He pleads His blood, and pleads so triumphantly, being numbered with them and having a part with them, that the Judge proclaims, Let them go their way; *"deliver them from going down into the pit, for He has found a ransom."*

Our Lord Jesus was numbered with the transgressors in order that they might feel their hearts drawn towards Him. Who can be afraid of one who is written in the same list with us? Surely we may come boldly to Him, and confess our guilt. He who is numbered with us cannot condemn us. Was He not put down in the transgressor's list that we might be written in the red roll of the saints? He was holy, and written among the holy; we were guilty, and numbered among the guilty. He transfers His name from yonder list to this black indictment, and our names are taken from the indictment and written in the roll of acceptance, for there is a complete transfer made between Jesus and His people. All our estate of misery and sin Jesus has taken; and all that Jesus has comes to us. His righteousness, His blood, and everything that He has He gives us as our dowry. Rejoice, believer, in your union to Him who was numbered among the transgressors; and prove that you are truly saved by being manifestly numbered with those who are new creatures in Him.

EVENING

"Let us search and try out ways and turn again to the LORD" — Lamentations 3:40.

THE SPOUSE WHO fondly loves her absent husband longs for his return; a long protracted separation from her lord is a semi-death to her spirit. So it is with souls who love the Savior much, they must see His face, they cannot bear that He should be away upon the mountains of Bether, and no more hold communion with them. A reproaching glance, an uplifted finger will be grievous to loving children, who fear to offend their tender father, and are only happy in his smile. Beloved, it was so once with you. A text of Scripture, a threatening, a touch of the rod of affliction, and you went to your Father's feet, crying, "Show me wherefore You contend with me? Is it so now"? Are you content to follow Jesus afar off? Can you contemplate suspended communion with Christ without alarm? Can you bear to have your Beloved walking contrary to you, because you walk contrary to Him? Have your sins separated between you and your God, and is your heart at rest? Oh let me affectionately warn you, for it is a grievous thing when we can live contentedly without the present enjoyment of the Savior's face.

Let us labor to feel what an evil thing this is, little love to our own dying Savior, little joy in our precious Jesus, little fellowship with the Beloved! Hold a true Lent in your souls, while you sorrow over your hardness of heart. Do not stop at sorrow! Remember where you first received salvation. Go at once to the cross. There, and there only, can you get your spirit quickened. No matter how hard, how insensible, how dead we may have become, let us go again in all the rags and poverty, and defilement of our natural condition. Let us clasp that cross, let us look into those languid eyes, let us bathe in that fountain filled with blood; this will bring back to us our first love; this will restore the simplicity of our faith, and the tenderness of our heart.

MORNING
March 31

"With His stripes we are healed" — Isaiah 53:5.

PILATE DELIVERED our Lord to be scourged. The Roman scourge was a most dreadful instrument of torture. It was made of the sinews of oxen, and sharp bones were intertwisted here and there among the sinews; so that every time the lash came down these pieces of bone inflicted fearful lacerations, and tore off the flesh from the bone. The Savior was, no doubt, bound to the column, and thus beaten. He had been beaten before; but this of the Roman lictors was probably the most severe of His flagellations. My soul, stand here and weep over His poor stricken body.

Believer in Jesus, can you gaze upon Him without tears, as He stands before you the mirror of agonizing love? He is at once fair as the lily for innocence, and red as the rose with the crimson of His own blood. As we feel the sure and blessed healing which His stripes have wrought in us, does not our heart melt at once with love and grief? If ever we have loved our Lord Jesus, surely we must feel that affection glowing now within our bosoms.

> See how the patient Jesus stands,
> Insulted in His lowest case!
> Sinners have bound the Almighty's hands,
> And spit in their Creator's face.
> With thorns His temples gored and gashed
> Send streams of blood from every part;
> His back's with knotted scourges lashed,
> But sharper scourges tear His heart.

We would fain go to our chambers and weep; but since our business calls us away, we will first pray our Beloved to print the image of His bleeding self upon the tablets of our hearts all the day, and at nightfall we will return to commune with Him, and sorrow that our sin should have cost Him so dear.

EVENING

"And Rizpah the daughter of Aiah took sackcloth and spread it for herself on the rock, from the beginning of harvest until water dropped on them out of the heavens. And she did not allow either the birds of the air to rest on them by day, or the beasts of the field by night" — 2 Samuel 21:10.

IF THE LOVE of a woman to her slain sons could make her prolong her mournful vigil for so long a period, shall we weary of considering the sufferings of our blessed Lord? She drove away the birds of prey, and shall not we chase from our meditations those worldly and sinful thoughts which defile both our minds and the sacred themes upon which we are occupied? Away, birds of evil wing! Leave the sacrifice alone! She bore the heats of summer, the night dews and the rains, unsheltered and alone. Sleep was chased from her weeping eyes; her heart was too full for slumber. Behold how she loved her children!

Shall Rizpah thus endure, and shall we start at the first little inconvenience or trial? Are we such cowards that we cannot bear to suffer with our Lord? She chased away even the wild beasts, with courage unusual in her sex, and will not we be ready to encounter every foe for Jesus' sake? These her children were slain by other hands than hers, and yet she wept and watched. What ought we to do who have by our sins crucified our Lord? Our obligations are boundless, our love should be fervent and our repentance thorough. To watch with Jesus should be our business, to protect His honor our occupation, to abide by His cross our solace. Those ghastly corpses might well have frightened Rizpah, especially by night, but in our Lord, at whose cross-foot we are sitting, there is nothing revolting, but everything attractive. Never was living beauty so enchanting as a dying Savior. Jesus, we will watch with You yet awhile, and do You graciously unveil Yourself to us. Then shall we not sit beneath sackcloth, but in a royal pavilion.

April 1

MORNING

"Let Him kiss me with the kisses of His mouth" — *Song of Solomon 1:2.*

FOR SEVERAL DAYS we have been dwelling upon the Savior's passion, and for some little time to come we shall linger there. In beginning a new month, let us seek the same desires after our Lord as those which glowed in the heart of the elect spouse. See how she leaps at once to Him; there are no prefatory words. She does not even mention His name. She is in the heart of her theme at once, for she speaks of Him who was the only Him in the world to her. How bold is her love! It was much condescension which permitted the weeping penitent to anoint His feet with spikenard; it was rich love which allowed the gentle Mary to sit at His feet and learn of Him. But here, love, strong, fervent love, aspires to higher tokens of regard, and closer signs of fellowship. Esther trembled in the presence of Ahasuerus, but the spouse in joyful liberty of perfect love knows no fear.

If we have received the same free spirit, we also may ask the like. By kisses we suppose to be intended those varied manifestations of affection by which the believer is made to enjoy the love of Jesus. The kiss of reconciliation we enjoyed at our conversion, and it was sweet as honey dropping from the comb. The kiss of acceptance is still warm on our brow, as we know that He has accepted our persons and our works through rich grace. The kiss of daily, present communion, is that which we pant after to be repeated day after day, till it is changed into the kiss of reception, which removes the soul from earth, and the kiss of consummation which fills it with the joy of heaven. Faith is our walk, but fellowship sensibly felt is our rest. Faith is the road, but communion with Jesus is the well from which the pilgrim drinks. Oh lover of our souls, be not strange to us; let the lips of Your blessing meet the lips of our asking: let the lips of Your fulness touch the lips of our need, and straightway the kiss will be effected.

EVENING

"It is time to seek the LORD" — *Hosea 10:12.*

THIS MONTH OF April is said to derive its name from the Latin verb aperio, which signifies to open, because all the buds and blossoms are now opening, and we have arrived at the gates of the flowery year. Reader, if you are yet unsaved, may your heart, in accord with the universal awakening of nature, be opened to receive the Lord. Every blossoming flower warns you that it is time to seek the Lord; be not out of tune with nature, but let your heart bud and bloom with holy desires. Do you tell me that the warm blood of youth leaps in your veins? Then, I entreat you, give your vigor to the Lord.

It was my unspeakable happiness to be called in early youth, and I praise the Lord every day for it. Salvation is priceless, let it come when it may, but oh! an early salvation has a double value in it. Young men and maidens, since you may perish before you reach your prime, *"It is time to seek the Lord."* You who feel the first signs of decay, quicken your pace: that hollow cough, that hectic flush, are warnings which you must not trifle with; with you it is indeed time to seek the Lord. Did I observe a little grey mingled with your once luxuriant tresses? Years are stealing on apace, and death is drawing nearer by hasty marches, let each return of spring arouse you to set your house in order.

Dear reader, if you are now advanced in life, let me entreat and implore you to delay no longer. There is a day of grace for you now; be thankful for that; but it is a limited season and grows shorter every time that clock ticks. Here in this silent chamber, on this first night of another month, I speak to you as best I can by paper and ink, and from my inmost soul, as God's servant, I lay before you this warning, *"It is time to seek the Lord."* Slight not that word, it may be your last call from destruction, the final syllable from the lip of grace.

MORNING April 2

"And He did not answer him even to one word" — Matthew 27:14.

HE HAD NEVER been slow of speech when He could bless the sons of men, but He would not say a single word for Himself. *"Never man spoke like this Man,"* and never man was silent like Him. Was this singular silence the index of His perfect self-sacrifice? Did it show that He would not utter a word to stay the slaughter of His sacred person, which He had dedicated as an offering for us? Had He so entirely surrendered Himself that He would not interfere in His own behalf, even in the minutest degree, but be bound and slain an unstruggling, uncomplaining victim? Was this silence a type of the defenselessness of sin? Nothing can be said in palliation or excuse of human guilt; and, therefore, He who bore its whole weight stood speechless before His judge. Is not patient silence the best reply to a gainsaying world? Calm endurance answers some questions infinitely more conclusively than the loftiest eloquence. The best apologists for Christianity in the early days were its martyrs. The anvil breaks a host of hammers by quietly bearing their blows.

Did not the silent Lamb of God furnish us with a grand example of wisdom? Where every word was occasion for new blasphemy, it was the line of duty to afford no fuel for the flame of sin. The ambiguous and the false, the unworthy and mean, will before long overthrow and confute themselves, and therefore the true can afford to be quiet, and finds silence to be its wisdom. Evidently our Lord, by His silence, furnished a remarkable fulfilment of prophecy. A long defense of Himself would have been contrary to Isaiah's prediction. *"He is led as a lamb to the slaughter, and as a sheep before her shearers is dumb, so He opens not His mouth."* By His quiet He conclusively proved Himself to be the true Lamb of God. As such we salute Him this morning. Be with us, Jesus, and in the silence of our heart, let us hear the voice of Your love.

EVENING

"He shall see His seed. He shall prolong His days, and the pleasure of the LORD shall prosper in His hand" — Isaiah 53:10.

PLEAD FOR THE speedy fulfilment of this promise, all you who love the Lord. It is easy work to pray when we are grounded and bottomed, as to our desires, upon God's own promIse. How can He that gave the word refuse to keep it? Immutable veracity cannot demean itself by a lie, and eternal faithfulness cannot degrade itself by neglect. God must bless His Son, His covenant binds Him to it. That which the Spirit prompts us to ask for Jesus, is that which God decrees to give Him. Whenever you are praying for the kingdom of Christ, let your eyes behold the dawning of the blessed day which draws near, when the Crucified shall receive His coronation in the place where men rejected Him. Courage, you that prayerfully work and toil for Christ with success of the very smallest kind, it shall not be so always; better times are before you. Your eyes cannot see the blissful future; borrow the telescope of faith; wipe the misty breath of your doubts from the glass; look through it and behold the coming glory.

Reader, let us ask, do you make this your constant prayer? Remember that the same Christ who tells us to say, *"Give us this day our daily bread,"* had first given us this petition, *"Hallowed be Your name; Your kingdom come; Your will be done in earth as it is in heaven."* let not your prayers be all concerning your own sins, your own wants, your own imperfections, your own trials, but let them climb the starry ladder, and get up to Christ Himself, and then, as you draw near to the blood-besprinkled mercy-seat, offer this prayer continually, "Lord, extend the kingdom of Your dear Son." Such a petition, fervently presented, will elevate the spirit of all your devotions. Mind that you prove the sincerity of your prayer by laboring to promote the Lord's glory.

April 3

MORNING

"They took Jesus and led Him away" — John 19:16.

HE HAD BEEN all night in agony, He had spent the early morning at the hall of Caiaphas, He had been hurried from Caiaphas to Pilate, from Pilate to Herod, and from Herod back again to Pilate. He had, therefore, but little strength left, and yet neither refreshment nor rest were permitted Him. They were eager for His blood, and therefore led Him out to die, loaded with the cross. Oh grievous procession! Well may Salem's daughters weep. My soul, do you weep also.

What learn we here as we see our blessed Lord let forth? Do we not perceive that truth which was set forth in shadow by the scapegoat? Did not the high-priest bring the scapegoat, and put both his hands upon its head, confessing the sins of the people, that thus those sins might be laid upon the goat, and cease from the people? Then the goat was led away by a fit man into the wilderness, and it carried away the sins of the people, so that if they were sought for they could not be found. Now we see Jesus brought before the priests and rulers, who pronounce Him guilty: God Himself imputes our sins to Him, *"the Lord has laid on Him the iniquity of us all;"*, *"He was made sin for us;"* and, as the substitute for our guilt, bearing our sin upon His shoulders, represented by the cross; we see Him led away by the appointed officers of justice. Beloved, can you feel assured that He carried your sin? As you look at the cross upon His shoulders, does it represent your sin? There is one way by which you can tell whether He carried your sin or not. Have you laid your hand upon His head, confessed your sin, and trusted in Him? Then your sin lies not on you; it has all been transferred by blessed imputation to Christ, and He bears it on His shoulder as a load heavier than the cross.

Let not the picture vanish till you have rejoiced in your own deliverance, and adored the loving Redeemer upon whom your iniquities were laid.

EVENING

"All we like sheep have gone astray; we have turned, each one, to his own way; and the LORD has laid on Him the iniquity of its all — Isaiah 53:6.

HERE IS A confession of sin common to all the elect people of God. They have all fallen, and therefore, in common chorus, they all say, from the first who entered heaven to the last who shall enter there, *"All we like sheep have gone astray."* The confession, while thus unanimous, is also special and particular: *"We have turned, each one, to his own way."* There is a peculiar sinfulness about every one of the individuals; all are sinful, but each one with some special aggravation not found in his fellow. It is the mark of genuine repentance that while it naturally associates itself with other penitents, it also takes up a position of loneliness. *"We have turned, each one, to his own way,"* is a confession that each man had sinned against light peculiar to himself, or sinned with an aggravation which he could not perceive in others. This confession is unreserved; there is not a word to detract from its force, nor a syllable by way of excuse. The confession is a giving up of all pleas of self-righteousness. It is the declaration of men who are consciously guilty, guilty with aggravations, guilty without excuse. They stand with their weapons of rebellion broken in pieces, and cry, *"All we like sheep have gone astray; we have turned, each one, to his own way."* Yet we hear no mournful wailing attending this confession of sin; for the next sentence makes it almost a song. *"The Lord has laid on Him the iniquity of us all."* It is the most grievous sentence of the three, but it overflows with comfort. Strange is it that where misery was concentrated, mercy reigned; where sorrow reached her climax, weary souls find rest. The Savior bruised is the healing of bruised hearts. See how the lowliest penitence gives place to assured confidence through simply gazing at Christ on the cross!

MORNING April 4

"For He made Him who knew no sin to be sin for us, so that we might become the righteousness of God in Him" — 2 Corinthians 5:21.

MOURNING CHRISTIAN! WHY do you weep? Are you mourning over your own corruptions? Look to your perfect Lord, and remember, you are complete in Him; you are in God's sight as perfect as if you have never sinned. No, more than that, the Lord our Righteousness has put a divine garment upon you, so that you have more than the righteousness of man; you have the righteousness of God. Oh you who are mourning by reason of inbred sin and depravity, remember, none of your sins can condemn you. You have learned to hate sin; but you have learned also to know that sin is no longer hanging over your head; it was laid upon Christ's head. Your standing is not in yourself; it is in Christ; your acceptance is not in yourself, but in your Lord; you are as much accepted of God today, with all your sinfulness, as you will be when you stand before His throne, free from all corruption.

Oh, I beseech you, lay hold on this precious thought, perfection in Christ! For you are *"complete in Him."* With your Savior's garment on, you are holy as the Holy One. *"Who is he that condemns? It is Christ that died, yes rather, that is risen again, who is even at the right hand of God, who also makes intercession for us."* Christian, let your heart rejoice, for you are *"accepted in the Beloved"* what have you to fear? let your face ever wear a smile; live near your Master; live in the suburbs of the Celestial City; for soon, when your time has come, you shall rise up where your Jesus sits, and reign at His right hand, even as He has overcome and has sat down at His Father's right hand. All this is true because He made the divine Lord *"who knew no sin to be sin for us, so that we might become the righteousness of God in Him."*

EVENING

"Come, and let us go up the mountain of the LORD" — Isaiah 2:3.

IT IS EXCEEDINGLY beneficial to our souls to mount above this present evil world to something nobler and better. The cares of this world and the deceitfulness of riches are apt to choke everything good within us, and we grow fretful, desponding, perhaps proud and carnal. It is well for us to cut down these thorns and briers, for heavenly seed sown among them is not likely to yield a harvest; and where shall we find a better sickle with which to cut them down than communion with God and the things of the kingdom? In the valleys of Switzerland many of the inhabitants are deformed, and all wear a sickly appearance, for the atmosphere is charged with miasma, and is close and stagnant. But up yonder, on the mountain, you find a hardy race, who breathe the clear fresh air as it blows from the virgin snows of the Alpine summits. It would be well if the dwellers in the valley could frequently leave their abodes among the marshes and the fever mists, and inhale the bracing element upon the hills.

It is to such an exploit of climbing that I invite you this evening. May the Spirit of God assist us to leave the mists of fear and the fevers of anxiety, and all the ills which gather in this valley of earth, and to ascend the mountains of anticipated joy and blessedness. May God the Holy Spirit cut the cords that keep us here below, and assist us to mount! We sit too often like chained eagles fastened to the rock, only that, unlike the eagle, we begin to love our chain, and would, perhaps, if it came really to the test, be loath to have it snapped. May God now grant us grace, if we cannot escape from the chain as to our flesh, yet to do so as to our spirits. And leaving the body, like a servant, at the foot of the hill, may our soul, like Abraham, attain the top of the mountain, there to indulge in communion with the Most High.

April 5   MORNING

"They put the cross on him" — Luke 23:26.

WE SEE IN Simon's carrying the cross a picture of the work of the Church throughout all generations; she is the cross-bearer after Jesus. Mark then, Christian, Jesus does not suffer so as to exclude your suffering. He bears a cross, not that you may escape it, but that you may endure it. Christ exempts you from sin, but not from sorrow. Remember that, and expect to suffer.

But let us comfort ourselves with this thought, that in our case, as in Simon's, it is not our cross, but Christ's cross which we carry. When you are molested for your piety; when your religion brings the trial of cruel mocking upon you, then remember it is not your cross, it is Christ's cross; and how delightful is it to carry the cross of our Lord Jesus!

You carry the cross after Him. You have blessed company; your path is marked with the footprints of your Lord. The mark of His blood-red shoulder is upon that heavy burden. It is His cross, and He goes before you as a shepherd goes before his sheep. Take up your cross daily, and follow Him.

Do not forget, also, that you bear this cross in partnership. It is the opinion of some that Simon only carried one end of the cross, and not the whole of it. That is very possible; Christ may have carried the heavier part, against the transverse beam, and Simon may have borne the lighter end. Certainly it is so with you; you do but carry the light end of the cross, Christ bore the heavier end.

And remember, though Simon had to bear the cross for a very little while, it gave him lasting honor. Even so the cross we carry is only for a little while at most, and then we shall receive the crown, the glory. Surely we should love the cross, and, instead of shrinking from it, count it very dear, when it works out for us "a far more exceeding and eternal weight of glory."

EVENING

"Before honor is humility" — Proverbs 15:33.

HUMILIATION OF SOUL always brings a positive blessing with it. If we empty our hearts of self God will fill them with His love. He who desires close communion with Christ should remember the word of the Lord, *"To this man will I look, even to him that is poor and of a contrite spirit, and trembles at My word."* Stoop if you would climb to heaven. Do we not say of Jesus, *"He descended that He might ascend"?* so must you. You must grow downward, that you may grow upwards; for the sweetest fellowship with heaven is to be had by humble souls, and by them alone. God will deny no blessing to a thoroughly humbled spirit. *"Blessed are the poor in spirit; for theirs is the kingdom of heaven,"* with all its riches and treasures. The whole exchequer of God shall be made over by deed of gift to the soul which is humble enough to be able to receive it without growing proud because of it.

God blesses us all up to the full measure and extremity of what it is right for Him to do. If you do not get a blessing, it is because it is not right for you to have one. If our heavenly Father were to let your unhumbled spirit win a victory in His holy war, you would pilfer the crown for yourself, and meeting with a fresh enemy you would fall a victim; so that you are kept low for your own safety. When a man is sincerely humble, and never ventures to touch so much as a grain of the praise, there is scarcely any limit to what God will do for him. Humility makes us ready to be blessed by the God of all grace, and fits us to deal efficiently with our fellow men. True humility is a flower which will adorn any garden. This is a sauce with which you may season every dish of life, and you will find an improvement in every case. Whether it be prayer or praise, whether it be work or suffering, the genuine salt of humility cannot be used in excess.

MORNING   April 6

"Let us go out to Him outside the camp" — *Hebrews 13:13.*

JESUS, BEARING HIS cross, went forth to suffer outside the gate. The Christian's reason for leaving the camp of the world's sin and religion is not because he loves to be singular, but because Jesus did so; and the disciple must follow his Master. Christ was *"not of the world;"* His life and His testimony were a constant protest against conformity with the world. Never was such overflowing affection for men as you find in Him; but still He was separate from sinners. In like manner Christ's people must *"go out to Him."* They must take their position "outside the camp," as witness-bearers for the truth. They must be prepared to tread the straight and narrow path. They must have bold, unflinching, lion-like hearts, loving Christ first, and His truth next, and Christ and His truth beyond all the world. Jesus would have His people *"go forth outside the camp"* for their own sanctification.

You cannot grow in grace to any high degree while you are conformed to the world. The life of separation may be a path of sorrow, but it is the highway of safety; and though the separated life may cost you many pangs, and make every day a battle, yet it is a happy life after all. No joy can excel that of the soldier of Christ: Jesus reveals Himself so graciously, and gives such sweet refreshment, that the warrior feels more calm and peace in his daily strife that others in their hours of rest. The highway of holiness is the highway of communion. It is thus we shall hope to win the crown if we are enabled by divine grace faithfully to follow Christ *"outside the camp."* The crown of glory will follow the cross of separation. A moment's shame will be well recompensed by eternal honor; a little while of witness-bearing will seem nothing when we are *"forever with the Lord."*

EVENING

"In the name of the LORD I will cut them off!" — *Psalm 118:12.*

OUR LORD JESUS, by His death, did not purchase a right to a part of us only, but to the entire man. He contemplated in His passion the sanctification of us wholly, spirit, soul, and body; that in this triple kingdom He Himself might reign supreme without a rival. It is the business of the newborn nature which God has given to the regenerate to assert the rights of the Lord Jesus Christ. My soul, so far as you are a child of God, you must conquer all the rest of yourself which yet remains unblessed; you must subdue all your powers and passions to the silver scepter of Jesus' gracious reign. And you must never be satisfied till He who is King by purchase becomes also King by gracious coronation, and reigns in you supreme.

Seeing, then, that sin has no right to any part of us, we go about a good and lawful warfare when we seek, in the name of God, to drive it out. Oh my body, you are a member of Christ; shall I tolerate your subjection to the prince of darkness? Oh my soul, Christ has suffered for your sins, and redeemed you with His most precious blood; shall I suffer your memory to become a storehouse of evil, or your passions to be firebrands of iniquity? Shall I surrender my judgment to be perverted by error, or my will to be led in chains of iniquity? No, my soul, you are Christ's, and sin has no right to you.

Be courageous concerning this, Oh Christian! Be not dispirited, as though your spiritual enemies could never be destroyed. You are able to overcome them, not in your own strength, the weakest of them would be too much for you in that; but you can and shall overcome them through the blood of the Lamb. Do not ask, "How shall I dispossess them, for they are greater and mightier than I?" Go to the strong for strength, wait humbly upon God, and the mighty God of Jacob will surely come to the rescue, and you shall sing of victory through His grace.

April 7   MORNING

"O sons of men, how long will you turn My glory into shame?" — Psalm 4:2.

AN INSTRUCTIVE WRITER has made a mournful list of the honors which the blinded people of Israel awarded to their long-expected King. (I) They gave Him a procession of honor, in which Roman legionaries, Jewish priests, men and women, took a part; He Himself bearing His cross. This is the triumph which the world awards to Him who comes to overthrow man's direst foes. Derisive shouts are His only acclamations, and cruel taunts His only paeans of praise. (2) They presented Him with the wine of honor. Instead of a golden cup of generous wine they offered Him the criminal's stupefying death-draught, which He refused because He would preserve an uninjured taste wherewith to taste of death. And afterwards when He cried, *"I thirst,"* they gave Him vinegar mixed with gall, thrust to His mouth upon a sponge. Oh! wretched, detestable inhospitality to the King's Son.

(3) He was provided with a guard of honor, who showed their esteem of Him by gambling over His garments, which they had seized as their booty. Such was the body-guard of the adored of heaven; a quaternion of brutal gamblers. (4) A throne of honor was found for Him upon the bloody tree; no easier place of rest would rebel men yield to their liege Lord. The cross was, in fact, the full expression of the world's feeling towards Him. There, they seemed to say, "You Son of God, this is the manner in which God Himself should be treated, could we reach Him." (5) The title of honor was nominally *"King of the Jews,"* but that the blinded nation distinctly repudiated, and really called Him the king of thieves, by preferring Barabbas, and by placing Jesus in the place of highest shame between two thieves. His glory was thus in all things turned into shame by the sons of men, but it shall yet gladden the eyes of saints and angels, world without end.

EVENING

"Deliver me from the guilt of shedding blood, O God, O God of my salvation, and my tongue shall sing aloud of Your righteousness " — Psalm 51:14.

IN THIS SOLEMN CONFESSION, it is pleasing to observe that David plainly names his sin. He does not call it manslaughter, nor speak of it as an imprudence by which an unfortunate accident occurred to a worthy man, but he calls it by its true name, blood-guiltiness. He did not actually kill the husband of Bathsheba; but still it was planned in David's heart that Uriah should be slain, and he was before the Lord his murderer. Learn in confession to be honest with God. Do not give fair names to foul sins; call them what you will, they will smell no sweeter. What God sees them to be, that do you labor to feel them to be; and with all openness of heart acknowledge their real character. Observe, that David was evidently oppressed with the heinousness of his sin. It is easy to use words, but it is difficult to feel their meaning. The fifty-first Psalm is the photograph of a contrite spirit. Let us seek after the like brokenness of heart; for however excellent our words may be, if our heart is not conscious that our sin deserves Hell, we cannot expect to find forgiveness.

Our text has in it AN EARNEST PRAYER. It is addressed to the God of salvation. It is His prerogative to forgive; it is His very name and office to save those who seek His face. Better still, the text calls Him the God of my salvation. Yes, blessed be His name, while I am yet going to Him through Jesus' blood, I can rejoice in the God of my salvation.

The psalmist ends with A COMMENDABLE VOW: if God will deliver him he will sing; no, more, he will *"sing aloud."* Who can sing in any other style of such a mercy as this! But note the subject of the song: *"YOUR RIGHTEOUSNESS."* We must sing of the finished work of a precious Savior; and he who knows most of forgiving love will sing the loudest.

MORNING April 8

"For if they do these things in the green tree, what may happen in the dry?" — Luke 23:31.

AMONG OTHER INTERPRETATIONS of this suggestive question, the following is full of teaching: "If I, the innocent substitute for sinners, suffer thus, what will be done when the sinner himself — the dry tree — shall fall into the hands of an angry God?" When God saw Jesus in the sinner's place, He did not spare Him; and when He finds the unregenerate without Christ, He will not spare them. Oh sinner, Jesus was led away by His enemies; so shall you be dragged away by fiends to the place appointed for you. Jesus was deserted of God; and if He, who was only by imputation a sinner, was deserted, how much more shall you be?" *"Eloi, Eloi, lama sabachthani?"* what an awful shriek!

But what shall be your cry when you shall cry, "Oh God! Oh God! why have You forsaken me?" And WHAT IF the answer shall come back, "Because you have set at nought all My counsel, and would none of My reproof: I also will laugh at your calamity; I will mock when your fear comes." If God spared not His own Son, how much less will He spare you! What whips of burning wire will be yours when conscience shall smite you with all its terrors? You richest, you merriest, you most self-righteous sinners, who would stand in your place when God shall say, "Awake, Oh sword, against the man that rejected Me; smite him, and let him feel the smart for ever? Jesus was spit upon; sinner, what shame will be yours!"

We cannot sum up in one word all the mass of sorrows which met upon the head of Jesus who died for us, therefore it is impossible for us to tell you what streams, what oceans of grief must roll over your spirit if you die as you now are. You may die so, you may die now. By the agonies of Christ, by His wounds and by His blood, do not bring upon yourselves the wrath to come! Trust in the Son of God, and you shall never die.

EVENING

"I will fear no evil; for You are with me" — Psalm 23:4.

BEHOLD, HOW INDEPENDENT of outward circumstances the Holy Ghost can make the Christian! What a bright light may shine within us when it is all dark without! How firm, how happy, how calm, how peaceful we may be, when the world shakes to and fro, and the pillars of the earth are removed! Even death itself, with all its terrible influences, has no power to suspend the music of a Christian's heart, but rather makes that music become more sweet, more clear, more heavenly, till the last kind act which death can do is to let the earthly strain melt into the heavenly chorus, the temporal joy into the eternal bliss! Let us have confidence, then, in the blessed Spirit's power to comfort us.

Dear reader, are you looking forward to poverty? Fear not; the divine Spirit can give you, in your want, a greater plenty than the rich have in their abundance. You know not what joys may be stored up for you in the cottage around which grace will plant the roses of content. Are you conscious of a growing failure of your bodily powers? Do you expect to suffer long nights of languishing and days of pain? Oh be not sad! That bed may become a throne to you. You little know how every pang that shoots through your body may be a refining fire to consume your dross - a beam of glory to light up the secret parts of your soul. Are the eyes growing dim? Jesus will be your light. Do the ears fail you? Jesus' name will be your soul's best music, and His person your dear delight. Christians can be happier than philosophers when all outward causes of rejoicing are withdrawn. In You, my God, my heart shall triumph, come what may of ills without! By Your power, Oh blessed Spirit, my heart shall be exceeding glad, though all things should fail me here below.

April 9 MORNING

"And a great crowd of the people were following Him, and of women who were beating their breasts and weeping over Him" — Luke 23:27.

AMID THE RABBLE rout which hounded the Redeemer to His doom, there were some gracious souls whose bitter anguish sought vent in wailing and lamentations, fit music to accompany that march of woe. When my soul can, in imagination, see the Savior bearing His cross to Calvary, she joins the godly women and weeps with them; for, indeed, there is true cause for grief, cause lying deeper than those mourning women thought. They bewailed innocence maltreated, goodness persecuted, love bleeding, meekness about to die; but my heart has a deeper and more bitter cause to mourn. My sins were the scourges which lacerated those blessed shoulders, and crowned with thorns those bleeding brows: my sins cried *"Crucify Him! crucify Him!"* and laid the cross upon His gracious shoulders. His being led forth to die is sorrow enough for one eternity: but my having been His murderer, is more, infinitely more, grief than one poor fountain of tears can express.

Why those women loved and wept it were not hard to guess; but they could not have had greater reasons for love and grief than my heart has. Nain's widow saw her son restored, but I myself have been raised to newness of life. Peter's wife's mother was cured of the fever, but I of the greater plague of sin. Out of Magdalene seven devils were cast, but a whole legion out of me. Mary and Martha were favored with visits, but He dwells with me. His mother bore His body, but He is formed in me the hope of glory. In nothing behind the holy women in debt, let me not be behind them in gratitude or sorrow.

> Love and grief my heart dividing,
> With my tears His feet I'll lave -
> Constant still in heart abiding,
> Weep for Him who died to save.

EVENING

"Your gentleness has made me great" — Psalm 18:35.

THE WORDS ARE capable of being translated, *"Your goodness has made me great."* David gratefully ascribed all his greatness not to his own goodness, but to the goodness of God. "Your providence," is another reading; and providence is nothing more than goodness in action. Goodness is the bud of which providence is the flower, or goodness is the seed of which providence is the harvest. Some render it, "Your help," which is but another word for providence; providence being the firm ally of the saints, aiding them in the service of their Lord. Or again, "Your humility has made me great." "Your condescension" may, perhaps, serve as a comprehensive reading, combining the ideas mentioned, including that of humility. It is God's making Himself little which is the cause of our being made great. We are so little, that if God should manifest His greatness without condescension, we should be trampled under His feet; but God, who must stoop to view the skies, and bow to see what angels do, turns His eye yet lower, and looks to the lowly and contrite, and makes them great.

There are yet other readings, as for instance, the Septuagint, which reads, "Your discipline," Your fatherly correction, *"has made me great;"* while the Chaldee paraphrase reads, "Your word has increased me." Still the idea is the same. David ascribes all his own greatness to the condescending goodness of his Father in heaven. May this sentiment be echoed in our hearts this evening while we cast our crowns at Jesus' feet, and cry, *"Your gentleness has made me great."* How marvelous has been our experience of God's gentleness! How gentle have been His corrections! How gentle His forbearance! How gentle His teachings! How gentle His drawings! Meditate upon this theme, Oh believer. let gratitude be awakened; let humility be deepened; let love be quickened before you fall asleep tonight.

April 10

MORNING

"The place called The Skull" — Luke 23:33.

THE HILL OF comfort is the hill of Calvary; the house of consolation is built with the wood of the cross; the temple of heavenly blessing is founded upon the riven rock, riven by the spear which pierced His side. No scene in sacred history ever gladdens the soul like Calvary's tragedy.

> Is it not strange, the darkest hour
> That ever dawned on sinful earth,
> Should touch the heart with softer power,
> For comfort, than an angel's mirth?
> That to the Cross the mourners' eye should turn,

Sooner than where the stars of Bethlehem burn Light springs from the midday-midnight of Golgotha, and every herb of the field blooms sweetly beneath the shadow of the once accursed tree. In that place of thirst, grace has dug a fountain which ever gushes with waters pure as crystal, each drop capable of alleviating the woes of mankind.

You who have had your seasons of conflict, will confess that it was not at Olivet that you ever found comfort, not on the hill of Sinai, nor on Tabor; but Gethsemane, Gabbatha, and Golgotha have been a means of comfort to you. The bitter herbs of Gethsemane have often taken away the bitters of your life; the scourge of Gabbatha has often scourged away your cares, and the groans of Calvary have put all other groans to flight. Thus Calvary yields us comfort rare and rich. We never should have known Christ's love in all its heights and depths if He had not died; nor could we guess the Father's deep affection if He had not given His Son to die. The common mercies we enjoy all sing of love, just as the sea-shell, when we put it to our ears, whispers of the deep sea from where it came; but if we desire to hear the ocean itself, we must not look at everyday blessings, but at the transactions of the crucifixion. He who would know love, let him retire to Calvary and see the Man of sorrows die.

EVENING

"For tonight an angel of God stood by me" — Acts 27:23.

TEMPEST AND LONG darkness, coupled with imminent risk of shipwreck, had brought the crew of the vessel into a sad case; one man alone among them remained perfectly calm, and by His word the rest were reassured. Paul was the only man who had heart enough to say, "Sirs, be of good cheer." There were veteran Roman legionaries on board, and brave old mariners, and yet their poor Jewish prisoner had more spirit than they all. He had a secret Friend who kept his courage up. The Lord Jesus despatched a heavenly messenger to whisper words of consolation in the ear of His faithful servant, therefore he wore a shining countenance and spoke like a man at ease.

If we fear the Lord, we may look for timely interpositions when our case is at its worst. Angels are not kept from us by storms, or hindered by darkness. Seraphs think it no humiliation to visit the poorest of the heavenly family. If angel's visits are few and far between at ordinary times, they shall be frequent in our nights of tempest and tossing. Friends may drop from us when we are under pressure, but our intercourse with the inhabitants of the angelic world shall be more abundant; and in the strength of love-words, brought to us from the throne by the way of Jacob's ladder, we shall be strong to do exploits. Dear reader, is this an hour of distress with you? Then ask for peculiar help. Jesus is the angel of the covenant, and if His presence be now earnestly sought, it will not be denied. What that presence brings in heart-cheer those remember who, like Paul, have had the angel of God standing by them in a night of storm, when anchors would no longer hold, and rocks were near.

> Amid the darkness hush my fear:
> Loud roars the wild tempestuous sea,
> Your presence, Lord, shall comfort me.

April 11　　　　　　　MORNING

"I am poured out like water and all my bones are out of joint" — Psalm 22:14.

DID EARTH OR heaven ever behold a sadder spectacle of woe! In soul and body, our Lord felt Himself to be weak as water poured upon the ground. The placing of the cross in its socket had shaken Him with great violence, had strained all the ligaments, pained every nerve, and more or less dislocated all His bones. Burdened with His own weight, the august Sufferer felt the strain increasing every moment of those six long hours. His sense of faintness and general weakness were overpowering; while to His own consciousness He became nothing but a mass of misery and swooning sickness. When Daniel saw the great vision, he thus describes his sensations, *"There remained no strength in me, for my vigor was turned into corruption, and I retained no strength."* How much more faint must have been our greater Prophet when He saw the dread vision of the wrath of God, and felt it in His own soul!

To us, sensations such as our Lord endured would have been insupportable, and kind unconsciousness would have come to our rescue. But in His case, He was wounded, and felt the sword; He drained the cup and tasted every drop.

> Oh King of Grief! (a title strange, yet true
> To You of all kings only due)
> Oh King of Wounds! how shall I grieve for You,
> Who in all grief prevents me!

As we kneel before our now ascended Savior's throne, let us remember well the way by which He prepared it as a throne of grace for us. Let us in spirit drink of His cup, that we may be strengthened for our hour of heaviness whenever it may come. In His natural body every member suffered, and so must it be in the spiritual; but as out of all His griefs and woes His body came forth uninjured to glory and power, even so shall His mystical body come through the furnace with not so much as the smell of fire upon it.

EVENING

"Look on my affliction and my pain, and forgive all my sins" — Psalm 25:18.

IT IS WELL for us when prayers about our sorrows are linked with pleas concerning our sins; when, being under God's hand, we are not wholly taken up with our pain, that we remember our offenses against God. It is well, also, to take both sorrow and sin to the same place. It was to God that David carried his sorrow: it was to God that David confessed his sin. Observe, then, we must take our sorrows to God. Even your little sorrows you may roll upon God, for He counts the hairs of your head. And your great sorrows you may commit to Him, for He holds the ocean in the hollow of His hand. Go to Him, whatever your present trouble may be, and you shall find Him able and willing to relieve you. But we must take our sins to God too. We must carry them to the cross, that the blood may fall upon them, to purge away their guilt, and to destroy their defiling power.

The special lesson of the text is this: that we are to go to the Lord with sorrows and with sins in the right spirit. Note that all David asks concerning his sorrow is, *"Look on my affliction and my pain,"* but the next petition is vastly more express, definite, decided, plain: *"Forgive all my sins."* Many sufferers would have put it, "Remove my affliction and my pain, and look at my sins." But David does not say so; he cries, "Lord, as for my affliction and my pain, I will not dictate to Your wisdom. Lord, look at them, I will leave them to You, I should be glad to have my pain removed, but do as You will; but as for my sins, Lord, I know what I want with them; I must have them forgiven; I cannot endure to lie under their curse for a moment." A Christian counts sorrow lighter in the scale than sin; he can bear that his troubles should continue, but he cannot support the burden of his transgressions.

MORNING   April 12

"My heart is like wax; it is melted in the midst of my bowels" — *Psalm 22:14.*

OUR BLESSED LORD experienced a terrible sinking and melting of soul. *"The spirit of a man will sustain his infirmity, but a wounded spirit who can bear?"* Deep depression of spirit is the most grievous of all trials; all besides is as nothing. Well might the suffering Savior cry to His God, *"Be not far from me,"* for above all other seasons a man needs his God when his heart is melted within him because of heaviness.

Believer, come near the cross this morning, and humbly adore the King of glory as having once been brought far lower, in mental distress and inward anguish, than any one among us; and mark His fitness to become a faithful High Priest, who can be touched with a feeling of our infirmities. Especially let those of us whose sadness springs directly from the withdrawal of a present sense of our Father's love, enter into near and intimate communion with Jesus. Let us not give way to despair, since through this dark room the Master has passed before us. Our souls may sometimes long and faint, and thirst even to anguish, to behold the light of the Lord's countenance; at such times let us stay ourselves with the sweet fact of the sympathy of our great High Priest. Our drops of sorrow may well be forgotten in the ocean of His griefs; but how high ought our love to rise!

Come in, Oh strong and deep love of Jesus, like the sea at the flood in spring tides, cover all my powers, drown all my sins, wash out all my cares, lift up my earth-bound soul, and float it right up to my Lord's feet, and there let me lie, a poor broken shell, washed up by His love, having no virtue or value; and only venturing to whisper to Him that if He will put His ear to me, He will hear within my heart faint echoes of the vast waves of His own love which have brought me where it is my delight to lie, even at His feet forever.

EVENING

"The king's garden" — *Nehemiah 3:15.*

MENTION OF THE king's garden by Nehemiah brings to mind the paradise which the King of kings prepared for Adam. Sin has utterly ruined that fair abode of all delights, and driven forth the children of men to till the ground, which yields thorns and briers unto them. My soul, remember the fall, for it was your fall. Weep much because the Lord of love was so shamefully ill-treated by the head of the human race, of which you are a member, as undeserving as any. Behold how dragons and demons dwell on this fair earth, which once was a garden of delights.

See yonder another King's garden, which the King waters with His bloody sweat, Gethsemane, whose bitter herbs are sweeter far to renewed souls than even Eden's luscious fruits. There the mischief of the serpent in the first garden was undone: there the curse was lifted from earth, and borne by the woman's promised seed. My soul, think much of the agony and the passion; resort to the garden of the olive-press, and view your great Redeemer rescuing you from your lost estate. This is the garden of gardens indeed, wherein the soul may see the guilt of sin and the power of love, two sights which surpass all others.

Is there no other King's garden? Yes, my heart, you are, or should be such. How do the flowers flourish? Do any choice fruits appear? Does the King walk within, and rest in the bowers of my spirit? Let me see that the plants are trimmed and watered, and the mischievous foxes hunted out. Come, Lord, and let the heavenly wind blow at Your coming, that the spices of Your garden may flow abroad. Nor must I forget the King's garden of the church. Oh Lord, send prosperity unto it. Rebuild her walls, nourish her plants, ripen her fruits, and from the huge wilderness, reclaim the barren waste, and make thereof *"a King's garden."*

April 13   MORNING

"A bundle of myrrh is my Beloved to me" — Song of Solomon 1:13.

MYRRH MAY WELL be chosen as the type of Jesus on account of its preciousness, its perfume, its pleasantness, its healing, preserving, disinfecting qualities, and its connection with sacrifice. But why is He compared to *"a bundle of myrrh"*? First, for plenty. He is not a drop of it, He is a casket full. He is not a sprig or flower of it, but a whole bundle. There is enough in Christ for all my necessities; let me not be slow to avail myself of Him. Our well-beloved is compared to a *"bundle"* again, for variety: for there is in Christ not only the one thing needful, but in *"Him dwells all the fulness of the Godhead bodily,"* everything needful is in Him. Take Jesus in His different characters, and you will see a marvelous variety: Prophet, Priest, King, Husband, Friend, Shepherd. Consider Him in His life, death, resurrection, ascension, second advent; view Him in His virtue, gentleness, courage, self-denial, love, faithfulness, truth, righteousness; everywhere He is a bundle of preciousness.

He is a *"bundle of myrrh"* for preservation, not loose myrrh to be dropped on the floor or trodden on, but myrrh tied up, myrrh to be stored in a casket. We must value Him as our best treasure; we must prize His words and His ordinances; and we must keep our thoughts of Him and knowledge of Him as under lock and key, lest the devil should steal any thing from us. Moreover Jesus is a *"bundle of myrrh"* for specialty. The emblem suggests the idea of distinguishing, discriminating grace. From before the foundation of the world, He was set apart for His people; and He gives forth His perfume only to those who understand how to enter into communion with Him, to have close dealings with Him. Oh! blessed people whom the Lord has admitted into His secrets, and for whom He sets Himself apart. Oh! choice and happy who are thus made to say, *"A bundle of myrrh is my Beloved to me."*

EVENING

"And he shall put his hand on the head of the burnt offering. And it shall be accepted for him to make atonement for him" — Leviticus 1:4.

OUR LORD'S BEING made sin for us is set forth here by the very significant transfer of sin to the bullock, which was made by the elders of the people. The laying on of the hand was not a mere touch of contact, for in some other places of Scripture the original word has the meaning of leaning heavily, as in the expression, *"Your wrath lies hard upon me."* (Psalm 88:7) Surely this is the very essence and nature of faith, which does not only bring us into contact with the great Substitute, but teaches us to lean upon Him with all the burden of our guilt. Jehovah made to meet upon the head of the Substitute all the offenses of His covenant people, but each one of the chosen is brought personally to ratify this solemn covenant act, when by grace he is enabled by faith to lay his hand upon the head of the *"Lamb slain from before the foundation of the world."*

Believer, do you remember that rapturous day when you first realized pardon through Jesus the sin-bearer? Can you not make glad confession, and join with the writer in saying, My soul recalls her day of deliverance with delight. Laden with guilt and full of fears, I saw my Savior as my Substitute, and I laid my hand upon Him. Oh! how timidly at first, but courage grew and confidence was confirmed until I leaned my soul entirely upon Him; and now it is my unceasing joy to know that my sins are no longer imputed to me, but laid on Him, and like the debts of the wounded traveler, Jesus, like the good Samaritan, has said of all my future sinfulness, *"Set that to My account."* Blessed discovery! Eternal solace of a grateful heart!

> My numerous sins transferred to Him,
> Shall never more be found
> Lost in His blood's atoning stream,
> Where ever crime is drowned!

April 14   MORNING

"All who see me laugh me to scorn; they shoot out the lip, they shake the head" — Psalm 22:7.

MOCKERY WAS A great ingredient in our Lord's woe. Judas mocked Him in the garden; the chief priests and scribes laughed Him to scorn; Herod set Him at nought; the servants and the soldiers jeered at Him, and brutally insulted Him; Pilate and his guards ridiculed His royalty; and on the tree all sorts of horrid jests and hideous taunts were hurled at Him. Ridicule is always hard to bear, but when we are in intense pain it is so heartless, so cruel, that it cuts us to the quick. Imagine the Savior crucified, racked with anguish far beyond all mortal capacity. Then picture that motley multitude, all wagging their heads or thrusting out the lip in bitterest contempt of one poor suffering victim!

Surely there must have been something more in the crucified One than they could see, or else such a great and mingled crowd would not unanimously have honored Him with such contempt. Was it not evil confession, in the very moment of its greatest apparent triumph, that after all it could do no more than mock at that victorious goodness which was then reigning on the cross? Oh Jesus, *"despised and rejected of men,"* how could You die for men, even for some of those who treated You so ill? Herein is love amazing, love divine, yes, love beyond degree. We, too, have despised You in the days of our unregeneracy, and even since our new birth we have set the world on high in our hearts, and yet You bled to heal our wounds, and died to give us life. Oh that we could set You on a glorious high throne in all men's hearts! We would ring out Your praises over land and sea till men should as universally adore as once they did unanimously reject.

    Your creatures wrong You, Oh You sovereign God!
    You are not loved, because not understood:

EVENING

"Say to the righteous that it is good; for they shall eat the fruit of their doings" — Isaiah 3:10.

IT IS WELL with the righteous ALWAYS. If it had said, "Say you to the righteous, that it is well with him in his prosperity," we must have been thankful for so great a blessing, for prosperity is an hour of peril, and it is a gift from heaven to be secured from its snares. Or if it had been written, "It is well with him when under persecution," we must have been thankful for so sustaining an assurance, for persecution is hard to bear. But when no time is mentioned, all time is included. God's *"shalls"* must be understood always in their largest sense. From the beginning of the year to the end of the year, from the first gathering of evening shadows until the day-star shines, in all conditions and under all circumstances, it shall be well with the righteous.

It is so well with him that we could not imagine it to be better, for he is well fed, he feeds upon the flesh and blood of Jesus; he is well clothed, he wears the imputed righteousness of Christ; he is well housed, he dwells in God; he is well married, his soul is knit in bonds of marriage union to Christ; he is well provided for, for the Lord is his Shepherd; he is well endowed, for heaven is his inheritance. It is well with the righteous, well upon divine authority; the mouth of God speaks the comforting assurance.

Oh beloved, if God declares that all is well, ten thousand devils may declare it to be ill, but we laugh them all to scorn. Blessed be God for a faith which enables us to believe God when the creatures contradict Him. It is, says the Word, at all times well with you, righteous one. Then, beloved, if you cannot see it, let God's word stand you in stead of sight; yes, believe it on divine authority more confidently than if your eyes and your feelings told it to you. Whom God blesses is blest indeed, and what His lip declares is truth most sure and steadfast.

April 15   MORNING

"My God, my God, why have You forsaken me" — Psalm 22:1.

WE HERE BEHOLD the Savior in the depth of His sorrows. No other place so well shows the griefs of Christ as Calvary, and no other moment at Calvary is so full of agony as that in which His cry rends the air, *"My God, my God, why have You forsaken me?"* At this moment physical weakness was united with acute mental torture from the shame and ignominy through which He had to pass. And to make His grief culminate with emphasis, He suffered spiritual agony surpassing all expression, resulting from the sense of the departure of His Father's presence. This was the black midnight of His horror. Then it was that He descended the abyss of suffering. No man can enter into the full meaning of these words. Some of us think at times that we could cry, *"My God, my God, why have You forsaken me?"* There are seasons when the brightness of our Father's smile is eclipsed by clouds and darkness; but let us remember that God never does really forsake us. It is only a seeming forsaking with us. We grieve at a little withdrawal of our Father's love; but the real turning away of God's face from His Son, who shall calculate how deep the agony which it caused Him?

In our case, our cry is often dictated by unbelief; in His case, it was the utterance of a dreadful fact, for God had really turned away from Him for a season. Oh you poor, distressed soul, who once lived in the sunshine of God's face, but are now in darkness, remember that He has not really forsaken you. God in the clouds is as much our God as when He shines forth in all the lustre of His grace. But since even the thought that He has forsaken us gives us agony, what must the woe of the Savior have been when He exclaimed, *"My God, my God, why have You forsaken me?"*

EVENING

"Lift them up forever" — Psalm 28:9.

GOD'S PEOPLE NEED lifting up. They are very heavy by nature. They have no wings, or, if they have, they are like the dove of old which lay among the pots; and they need divine grace to make them mount on wings covered with silver, and with feathers of yellow gold. By nature sparks fly upward, but the sinful souls of men fall downward. Oh Lord, *"lift them up forever!"* David himself said, *"Unto You, Oh God, do I lift up my soul,"* and he here feels the necessity that other men's souls should be lifted up as well as his own. When you ask this blessing for yourself, forget not to seek it for others also.

There are three ways in which God's people require to be lifted up. They require to be elevated in character. Lift them up, Oh Lord; do not suffer Your people to be like the world's people! The world lies in the wicked one; lift them out of it! The world's people are looking after silver and gold, seeking their own pleasures, and the gratification of their lusts; but, Lord, lift Your people up above all this; keep them from being "muck-rakers," as John Bunyan calls the man who was always scraping after gold! Set their hearts upon their risen Lord and the heavenly heritage! Moreover believers need to be prospered in conflict. In the battle, if they seem to fall, Oh Lord, be pleased to give them the victory. If the foot of the foe is upon their necks for a moment, help them to grasp the sword of the Spirit, and eventually to win the battle. Lord, lift up Your children's spirits in the day of conflict; let them not sit in the dust, mourning forever. Do not allow the adversary to vex them and make them fret. But if they have been, like Hannah, persecuted, let them sing of the mercy of a delivering God.

We may also ask our Lord to lift them up at the last! Lift them up by taking them home; lift their bodies from the tomb, and raise their souls to Your eternal kingdom in glory.

MORNING April 16

"The precious blood of Christ!" — *1 Peter 1:19.*

STANDING AT THE foot of the cross, we see hands, and feet, and side, all distilling crimson streams of precious blood. It is *"precious"* because of its redeeming and atoning efficacy. By it the sins of Christ's people are atoned for; they are redeemed from under the law; they are reconciled to God, made one with Him. Christ's blood is also *"precious"* in its cleansing power; it *"cleanses from all sin."*, *"Though your sins be as scarlet, they shall be as white as snow."* Through Jesus' blood there is not a spot left upon any believer, no wrinkle nor any such thing remains. Oh precious blood, which makes us clean, removing the stains of abundant iniquity, and permitting us to stand accepted in the Beloved, notwithstanding the many ways in which we have rebelled against our God.

The blood of Christ is likewise *"precious"* in its preserving power. We are safe from the destroying angel under the sprinkled blood. Remember it is God's seeing the blood which is the true reason for our being spared. Here is comfort for us when the eye of faith is dim, for God's eye is still the same. The blood of Christ is *"precious"* also in its sanctifying influence. The same blood which justifies by taking away sin, does in its after-action, quicken the new nature and lead it onward to subdue sin and to follow out the commands of God. There is no motive for holiness so great as that which streams from the veins of Jesus. And *"precious,"* unspeakably precious, is this blood, because it has an overcoming power. It is written, *"They overcame through the blood of the Lamb."* How could they do otherwise? He who fights with the precious blood of Jesus, fights with a weapon which cannot know defeat.

The blood of Jesus! Sin dies at its presence, death ceases to be death; heaven's gates are opened. The blood of Jesus! we shall march on, conquering and to conquer, so long as we can trust its power!

EVENING

"And his hands were steady until the going down of the sun" — *Exodus 17:12.*

SO MIGHTY WAS the prayer of Moses, that all depended upon it. The petitions of Moses discomfited the enemy more than the fighting of Joshua. Yet both were needed. So, in the soul's conflict, force and fervor, decision and devotion, valor and vehemence, must join their forces, and all will be well. You must wrestle with your sin, but the major part of the wrestling must be done alone in private with God. Prayer, like Moses', holds up the token of the covenant before the Lord. The rod was the emblem of God's working with Moses, the symbol of God's government in Israel. Learn, Oh pleading saint, to hold up the promise and the oath of God before Him. The Lord cannot deny His own declarations. Hold up the rod of promise, and have what you will.

Moses grew weary, and then his friends assisted him. When at any time your prayer flags, let faith support one hand, and let holy hope uplift the other. Then prayer seating itself upon the stone of Israel, the rock of our salvation, will persevere and prevail. Beware of faintness in devotion; if Moses felt it, who can escape? It is far easier to fight with sin in public, than to pray against it in private. It is remarked that Joshua never grew weary in the fighting, but Moses did grow weary in the praying; the more spiritual an exercise, the more difficult it is for flesh and blood to maintain it. Let us cry, then, for special strength, and may the Spirit of God, who helps our infirmities, as He allowed help to Moses, enable us like him to continue with our hands steady *"until the going down of the sun."* Intermittent supplication avails but little, we must wrestle all night, and hold up our hands, *"until the going down of the sun;"* till the evening of life is over; till we shall come to the rising of a better sun in the land where prayer is swallowed up in praise.

April 17   MORNING

"You have come ... to the blood of sprinkling, speaking better things than that of Abel"
— Hebrews 12:24.

READER, HAVE YOU come to the blood of sprinkling? The question is not whether you have come to a knowledge of doctrine, or an observance of ceremonies, or to a certain form of experience, but have you come to the blood of Jesus? The blood of Jesus is the life of all vital godliness. If you have truly come to Jesus, we know how you came, the Holy Spirit sweetly brought you there. You came to the blood of sprinkling with no merits of your own. Guilty, lost, and helpless, you came to take that blood, and that blood alone, as your everlasting hope. You came to the cross of Christ, with a trembling and an aching heart; and oh! what a precious sound it was to you to hear the voice of the blood of Jesus! The dropping of His blood is as the music of heaven to the penitent sons of earth.

We are full of sin, but the Savior bids us lift our eyes to Him, and as we gaze upon His streaming wounds, each drop of blood, as it falls, cries, *"It is finished"* I have made an end of sin; I have brought in everlasting righteousness. Oh! sweet language of the precious blood of Jesus! If you have come to that blood once, you will come to it constantly. Your life will be *"Looking unto Jesus."* Your whole conduct will be epitomized in this: *"To whom coming."* Not to whom I have come, but to whom I am always coming. If you have ever come to the blood of sprinkling, you will feel your need of coming to it every day. He who does not desire to wash in that every day, has never washed in it at all. The believer ever feels it to be his joy and privilege that there is still a fountain opened. Past experiences are doubtful food for Christians; a present coming to Christ alone can give us joy and comfort. This morning let us sprinkle our door-post fresh with blood, and then feast upon the Lamb, assured that the destroying angel must pass us by.

EVENING

"We want to see Jesus" — John 12:21.

EVERMORE THE WORLDLING's cry is, "Who will show us any good?" He seeks satisfaction in earthly comforts, enjoyments, and riches. But the quickened sinner knows of only one good. "Oh that I knew where I might find HIM!" When he is truly awakened to feel his guilt, if you could pour the gold of India at his feet, he would say, "Take it away: I want to find HIM." It is a blessed thing for a man, when he has brought his desires into a focus, so that they all center in one object. When he has fifty different desires, his heart resembles a pond of stagnant water, spread out into a marsh, breeding miasma and pestilence. But when all his desires are brought into one channel, his heart becomes like a river of pure water, running swiftly to fertilize the fields. Happy is he who has one desire, if that one desire be set on Christ, though it may not yet have been realized. If Jesus be a soul's desire, it is a blessed sign of divine work within. Such a man will never be content with mere ordinances. He will say, I want Christ; I must have Him. Mere ordinances are of no use to me; I want Himself. Do not offer me these; you offer me the empty pitcher, while I am dying of thirst. Give me water, or I die. Jesus is my soul's desire. I would see Jesus!

Is this your condition, my reader, at this moment? Have you but one desire, and is that after Christ? Then you are not far from the kingdom of heaven. Have you but one wish in your heart, and that one wish that you may be washed from all your sins in Jesus' blood? Can you really say, I would give all I have to be a Christian; I would give up everything I have and hope for, if I might but feel that I have an interest in Christ? Then, despite all your fears, be of good cheer, the Lord loves you, and you shall come out into daylight soon, and rejoice in the liberty wherewith Christ makes men free.

MORNING   April 18

"And she set the scarlet line in the window" — *Joshua 2:21.*

RAHAB DEPENDED FOR her preservation upon the promise of the spies, whom she looked upon as the representatives of the God of Israel. Her faith was simple and firm, but it was very obedient. To tie the scarlet line in the window was a very trivial act in itself, but she dared not run the risk of omitting it. Come, my soul, is there not here a lesson for you? Have you been attentive to all your Lord's will, even though some of His commands should seem non-essential? Have you observed in His own way the two ordinances of believers' baptism and the Lord's Supper? These neglected, argue much unloving disobedience in your heart. Be henceforth in all things blameless, even to the tying of a thread, if that be matter of command.

This act of Rahab sets forth a yet more solemn lesson. Have I implicitly trusted in the precious blood of Jesus? Have I tied the scarlet cord, as with a Gordian knot in my window, so that my trust can never be removed? Or can I look out towards the Dead Sea of my sins, or the Jerusalem of my hopes, without seeing the blood, and seeing all things in connection with its blessed power? The passer-by can see a cord of so conspicuous a color, if it hangs from the window; it will be well for me if my life makes the efficacy of the atonement conspicuous to all onlookers. What is there to be ashamed of? Let men or devils gaze if they will, the blood is my boast and my song. My soul, there is One who will see that scarlet line, even when from weakness of faith you cannot see it yourself; Jehovah, the Avenger, will see it and pass over you. Jericho's walls fell flat. Rahab's house was on the wall, and yet it stood unmoved; my nature is built into the wall of humanity, and yet when destruction smites the race, I shall be secure. My soul, tie the scarlet thread in the window afresh, and rest in peace.

EVENING
"And You said, I will surely do you good" — *Genesis 32:12.*

WHEN JACOB WAS on the other side of the brook Jabbok, and Esau was coming with armed men, he earnestly sought God's protection, and as a master reason he pleaded, *"And You said, I will surely do you good."* Oh, the force of that plea! He was holding God to His word: *"You said"*..

The attribute of God's faithfulness is a splendid horn of the altar to lay hold upon; but the promise, which has in it the attribute and something more, is a yet mightier holdfast, *"You said, I will surely do you good."* And has He said, and shall He not do it? *"Let God be true, and every man a liar."* Shall not He be true? Shall He not keep His word? Shall not every word that comes out of His lips stand fast and be fulfilled? Solomon, at the opening of the temple, used this same mighty plea. He pleaded with God to remember the word which He had spoken to his father David, and to bless that place. When a man gives a promissory note, his honor is engaged; he signs his hand, and he must discharge it when the due time comes, or else he loses credit. It shall never be said that God dishonors His bills. The credit of the Most High never was impeached, and never shall be. He is punctual to the moment: He never is before His time, but He never is behind it.

Search God's Word through, and compare it with the experience of God's people, and you shall find the two tally from the first to the last. Many a hoary patriarch has said with Joshua, *"Not one thing has failed of all the good things which the Lord your God spoke concerning you; all have come to pass."* If you have a divine promise, you need not plead it with an "if" you may urge it with certainty. The Lord meant to fulfil the promise, or He would not have given it. God does not give His words merely to quiet us, and to keep us hopeful for awhile with the intention of putting us off at last; but when He speaks, it is because He means to do as He has said.

April 19   MORNING

"And, behold, the veil of the Temple was torn into two from top to bottom!" — Matthew 27:51

NO INSIGNIFICANT MIRACLE was wrought in the tearing of so strong and thick a veil; but it was not intended merely as a display of power. Many lessons were herein taught us. The old law of ordinances was put away, and like a worn-out vesture, torn and laid aside. When Jesus died, the sacrifices were all finished, because all fulfilled in Him, and therefore the place of their presentation was marked with an evident token of decay. That tear also revealed all the hidden things of the old dispensation: the mercy-seat could now be seen, and the glory of God gleamed forth above it. By the death of our Lord Jesus we have a clear revelation of God, for He was *"not as Moses, who put a veil over his face."* Life and immortality are now brought to light, and things which have been hidden since the foundation of the world are manifest in Him.

The annual ceremony of atonement was thus abolished. The atoning blood which was once every year sprinkled within the veil, was now offered once for all by the great High Priest, and therefore the place of the symbolical rite was broken up. No blood of bullocks or of lambs is needed now, for Jesus has entered within the veil with His own blood. Hence access to God is now permitted, and is the privilege of every believer in Christ Jesus. There is no small space laid open through which we may peer at the mercy-seat, but the tear reaches from the top to the bottom. We may come with boldness to the throne of the heavenly grace. Shall we err if we say that the opening of the Holy of Holies in this marvelous manner by our Lord's expiring cry was the type of the opening of the gates of paradise to all the saints by virtue of the Passion? Our bleeding Lord has the key of heaven; He opens and no man shuts; let us enter in with Him into the heavenly places, and sit with Him there till our common enemies shall be made His footstool.

EVENING

"The Amen" — Revelation 3:14.

THE WORD AMEN solemnly confirms that which went before; and Jesus is the great Confirmer; immutable, forever is *"the Amen"* in all His promises. Sinner, I would comfort you with this reflection. Jesus Christ said, *"Come unto me all you that labor and are heavy laden, and I will give you rest."* If you come to Him, He will say *"Amen"* in your soul; His promise shall be true to you. He said in the days of His flesh, *"The bruised reed I will not break."* Oh you poor, broken, bruised heart, if you come to Him, He will say *"Amen"* to you, and that shall be true in your soul as in hundreds of cases in bygone years. Christian, is not this very comforting to you also, that there is not a word which has gone out of the Savior's lips which He has ever retracted? The words of Jesus shall stand when heaven and earth shall pass away. If you get a hold of but half a promise, you shall find it true. Beware of him who is called "Clip-promise," who will destroy much of the comfort of God's word.

Jesus is Yea and Amen in all His offices. He was a Priest to pardon and cleanse one, He is Amen as Priest still. He was a King to rule and reign for His people, and to defend them with His mighty arm, He is an Amen King, the same still. He was a Prophet of old, to foretell good things to come, His lips are most sweet, and drop with honey still. He is an Amen Prophet. He is Amen as to the merit of His blood; He is Amen as to His righteousness. That sacred robe shall remain most fair and glorious when nature shall decay. He is Amen in every single title which He bears; your Husband, never seeking a divorce; your Friend, sticking closer than a brother; your Shepherd, with you in death's dark vale; your Help and your Deliverer; your Castle and your High Tower; the Horn of your strength, your confidence, your joy, your all in all, and your Yea and Amen in all.

MORNING   April 20

"So that through death He might defeat him who has the power of death" — Hebrews 2:14

OH CHILD OF God, death has lost its sting, because the devil's power over it is destroyed. Then cease to fear dying. Ask grace from God the Holy Ghost, that by an intimate knowledge and a firm belief of your Redeemer's death, you may be strengthened for that dread hour. Living near the cross of Calvary you may think of death with pleasure, and welcome it when it comes with intense delight. It is sweet to die in the Lord: it is a covenant-blessing to sleep in Jesus. Death is no longer banishment, it is a return from exile, a going home to the many mansions where the loved ones already dwell. The distance between glorified spirits in heaven and militant saints on earth seems great; but it is not so.

We are not far from home; a moment will bring us there. The sail is spread; the soul is launched upon the deep. How long will be its voyage? How many wearying winds must bear upon the sail before it shall be reefed in the port of peace? How long shall that soul be tossed upon the waves before it comes to that sea which knows no storm? Listen to the answer, *"Absent from the body, present with the Lord."* Yonder ship has just departed, but it is already at its haven. It did but spread its sail and it was there. Like that ship of old, upon the Lake of Galilee, a storm had tossed it, but Jesus said, *"Peace, be still,"* and immediately it came to land. Think not that a long period intervenes between the instant of death and the eternity of glory. When the eyes close of earth they open in heaven. The horses of fire are not an instant on the road.

Then, child of God, what is there for you to fear in death, seeing that through the death of your Lord its curse and sting are destroyed? And now it is but a Jacob's ladder whose foot is in the dark grave, but its top reaches to glory everlasting.

EVENING
"Fight the LORD's battles" — 1 Samuel 18:17.

THE SACRAMENTAL HOST of God's elect is warring still on earth, Jesus Christ being the Captain of their salvation. He has said, *"Lo! I am with you always, even unto the end of the world."* Listen to the shouts of war! Now let the people of God stand fast in their ranks, and let no man's heart fail him. It is true that just now in England the battle is turned against us, and unless the Lord Jesus shall lift His sword, we know not what may become of the church of God in this land; but let us be of good courage, and play the man. There never was a day when Protestantism seemed to tremble more in the scales than now that a fierce effort is making to restore the Romish antichrist to his ancient seat. We greatly want a bold voice and a strong hand to preach and publish the old gospel for which martyrs bled and confessors died. The Savior is, by His Spirit, still on earth; let this cheer us. He is ever in the midst of the fight, and therefore the battle is not doubtful.

And as the conflict rages, what a sweet satisfaction it is to know that the Lord Jesus, in His office as our great Intercessor, is prevalently pleading for His people! Oh anxious gazer, look not so much at the battle below, for there you shall be enshrouded in smoke, and amazed with garments rolled in blood; but lift your eyes yonder where the Savior lives and pleads, for while He intercedes, the cause of God is safe. Let us fight as if it all depended upon us, but let us look up and know that all depends upon Him.

Now, by the lilies of Christian purity, and by the roses of the Savior's atonement, by the roes and by the hinds of the field, we charge you who are lovers of Jesus, to do valiantly in the Holy War, for truth and righteousness, for the kingdom and crown jewels of your Master. Onward! *"for the battle is not yours but God's."*

April 21   MORNING

"I know my Redeemer lives" — Job 19:25.

    THE MARROW OF Job's comfort lies in that little word My, "My Redeemer," and in the fact that the Redeemer lives. Oh! to get hold of a living Christ. We must get a property in Him before we can enjoy Him. What is gold in the mine to me? Men are beggars in Peru, and beg their bread in California. It is gold in my purse which will satisfy my necessities, by purchasing the bread I need. So a Redeemer who does not redeem me, an avenger who will never stand up for my blood, of what avail were such? Rest not content until by faith you can say, "Yes, I cast myself upon my living Lord; and He is mine." It may be you hold Him with a feeble hand; you half think it presumption to say, "He lives as my Redeemer;" yet, remember if you have but faith as a grain of mustard seed, that little faith entities you to say it.
    But there is also another word here, expressive of Job's strong confidence, *"I know."* To say, I hope so, I trust so, is comfortable. And there are thousands in the fold of Jesus who hardly ever get much further. But to reach the essence of consolation you must say, *"I know."* Ifs, buts, and perhapses, are sure murderers of peace and comfort. Doubts are dreary things in times of sorrow. Like wasps that sting the soul! If I have any suspicion that Christ is not mine, then there is vinegar mingled with the gall of death; but if I know that Jesus lives for me, then darkness is not dark: even the night is light about me. Surely if Job, in those ages before the coming and advent of Christ, could say, *"I know,"* we should not speak less positively. God forbid that our positiveness should be presumption. Let us see that our evidences are right, lest we build upon an ungrounded hope, and then let us not be satisfied with the mere foundation, for it is from the upper rooms that we get the widest prospect. A living Redeemer, truly mine, is joy unspeakable.

EVENING

"Who also is at the right hand of God" — Romans 8:34.

    HE WHO WAS once despised and rejected of men, now occupies the honorable position of a beloved and honored Son. The right hand of God is the place of majesty and favor. Our Lord Jesus is His people's representative. When He died for them, they had rest; when He rose again for them, they had liberty; when He sat down at His Father's right hand, they had favor, and honor, and dignity. The raising and elevation of Christ is the elevation, the acceptance, the enshrinement, the glorifying of all His people, for He is their head and representative. This sitting at the right hand of God, then, is to be viewed as the acceptance of the person of the Surety, the reception of the Representative, and therefore, the acceptance of our souls. Oh saint, see in this your sure freedom from condemnation. *"Who is he that condemns?"* Who shall condemn the men who are in Jesus at the right hand of God?
    The right hand is the place of power. Christ at the right hand of God has all power in heaven and in earth. Who shall fight against the people who have such power vested in their Captain? Oh my soul, what can destroy you if Omnipotence be your helper? If the shield of the Almighty cover you, what sword can smite you? Rest secure. If Jesus is your all-prevailing King, and has trodden your enemies beneath His feet; if sin, death, and hell are all vanquished by Him, and you are represented in Him, by no possibility can you be destroyed.

> Jesus' tremendous name puts all our foes to flight:
> Jesus, the meek, the angry Lamb, a Lion is in fight.
> By all hell's host withstood;
> we all hell's host overthrow
> And conquering them, through Jesus' blood
> we still to conquer go.

MORNING
April 22

"A Ruler and a Savior whom God has exalted" — Acts 5:31.

JESUS, OUR LORD, once crucified, dead and buried, now sits upon the throne of glory. The highest place that heaven affords is His by undisputed right. It is sweet to remember that the exaltation of Christ in heaven is a representative exaltation. He is exalted at the Father's right hand, and though as Jehovah He has eminent glories, in which finite creatures cannot share, yet as the Mediator, the honors which Jesus wears in heaven are the heritage of all the saints. It is delightful to reflect how close is Christ's union with His people. We are actually one with Him; we are members of His body; and His exaltation is our exaltation. He will give us to sit upon His throne, even as He has overcome, and is set down with His Father on His throne. He has a crown, and He gives us crowns too; He has a throne, but He is not content with having a throne to Himself, on His right hand there must be His queen, arrayed in *"gold of Ophir."* He cannot be glorified without His bride.

Look up, believer, to Jesus now; let the eye of your faith behold Him with many crowns upon His head; and remember that you will one day be like Him, when you shall see Him as He is. You shall not be so great as He is, you shall not be so divine, but still you shall, in a measure, share the same honors, and enjoy the same happiness and the same dignity which He possesses. Be content to live unknown for a little while, and to walk your weary way through the fields of poverty, or up the hills of affliction; for by-and-by you shall reign with Christ, for He has *"made us kings and priests unto God, and we shall reign for ever and ever."* Oh! wonderful thought for the children of God! We have Christ for our glorious representative in heaven's courts now, and soon He will come and receive us to Himself, to be with Him there, to behold His glory, and to share His joy.

EVENING

"You shall not be afraid because of the terror by night" — Psalm 91:5.

WHAT IS THIS terror? It may be the cry of fire, or the noise of thieves, or fancied appearances, or the shriek of sudden sickness or death. We live in the world of death and sorrow, we may therefore look for ills as well in the night-watches as beneath the glare of the broiling sun. Nor should this alarm us, for be the terror what it may, the promise is that the believer shall not be afraid. Why should he? Let us put it more closely, why should we? God our Father is here, and will be here all through the lonely hours; He is an almighty Watcher, a sleepless Guardian, a faithful Friend. Nothing can happen without His direction, for even hell itself is under His control. Darkness is not dark to Him. He has promised to be a wall of fire around His people, and who can break through such a barrier? Worldlings may well be afraid, for they have an angry God above them, a guilty conscience within them, and a yawning hell beneath them; but we who rest in Jesus are saved from all these through rich mercy. If we give way to foolish fear we shall dishonor our profession, and lead others to doubt the reality of godliness.

We ought to be afraid of being afraid, lest we should vex the Holy Spirit by foolish distrust. Down, then, you dismal foreboding and groundless apprehensions, God has not forgotten to be gracious, nor shut up His tender mercies. It may be night in the soul, but there need be no terror, for the God of love changes not. Children of light may walk in darkness, but they are not therefore cast away, no, they are now enabled to prove their adoption by trusting in their heavenly Father as hypocrites cannot do.

> Though the night be dark and dreary,
> Darkness cannot hide from You;
> You are He, who, never weary,
> Watches where Your people be.

April 23　　　　　　　MORNING

"But in all these things we more than conquer through Him who loved us" — Romans 8:37.

WE GO TO Christ for forgiveness, and then too often look to the law for power to fight our sins. Paul thus rebukes us, *"Oh foolish Galatians, who has bewitched you that you should not obey the truth? This only I desire to learn from you: Did you receive the Spirit by works of the Law? or by the hearing of faith? Are you so foolish? Having begun in the Spirit, are you now made perfect by flesh?"* Take your sins to Christ's cross, for the old man can only be crucified there; we are crucified with Him. The only weapon to fight sin with is the spear which pierced the side of Jesus.

To give an illustration: you want to overcome an angry temper, how do you go to work? It is very possible you have never tried the right way of going to Jesus with it. How did I get salvation? I came to Jesus just as I was, and I trusted Him to save me. I must kill my angry temper in the same way? It is the only way in which I can ever kill it. I must go to the cross with it, and say to Jesus, "Lord, I trust You to deliver me from it." This is the only way to give it a death-blow. Are you covetous? Do you feel the world entangle you? You may struggle against this evil so long as you please, but if it be your besetting sin, you will never be delivered from it in any way but by the blood of Jesus. Take it to Christ. Tell Him, "Lord, I have trusted You, and Your name is Jesus, for You do save Your people from their sins; Lord, this is one of my sins; save me from it!"

Ordinances are nothing without Christ as a means of mortification. Your prayers, and your repentances, and your tears, the whole of them put together, are worth nothing apart from Him. None but Jesus can do helpless sinners good; or helpless saints either. You must be conquerors through Him who has loved you, if conquerors at all. Our laurels must grow among His olives in Gethsemane.

EVENING

"Behold! In the midst of the throne ... a Lamb was standing" — Revelation 5:6.

WHY SHOULD OUR exalted Lord appear in His wounds in glory? The wounds of Jesus are His glories, His jewels, His sacred ornaments. To the eye of the believer, Jesus is passing fair because He is *"white and ruddy;"* white with innocence, and ruddy with His own blood. We see Him as the lily of matchless purity, and as the rose crimsoned with His own gore. Christ is lovely upon Olivet and Tabor, and by the sea, but oh! there never was such a matchless Christ as He that did hang upon the cross. There we behold all His beauties in perfection, all His attributes developed, all His love drawn out, all His character expressed.

Beloved, the wounds of Jesus are far more fair in our eyes than all the splendor and pomp of kings. The thorny crown is more than an imperial diadem. It is true that He bears not now the scepter of reed, but there was a glory in it that never flashed from scepter of gold. Jesus wears the appearance of a slain Lamb as His court dress in which He wooed our souls, and redeemed them by His complete atonement. Nor are these only the ornaments of Christ, they are the trophies of His love and of His victory. He has divided the spoil with the strong. He has redeemed for Himself a great multitude whom no man can number, and these scars are the memorials of the fight. Ah! if Christ thus loves to retain the thought of His sufferings for His people, how precious should His wounds be to us!

> Behold how every wound of His
> A precious balm distills,
> Which heals the scars that sin had made,
> And cures all mortal ills.
> Those wounds are mouths that preach His grace: The ensigns of His love;
> The seals of our expected bliss In paradise above.

MORNING — April 24

"And because of all this we made a sure covenant" — Nehemiah 9:38.

THERE ARE MANY occasions in our experience when we may very rightly, and with benefit, renew our covenant with God. After recovery from sickness when, like Hezekiah, we have had a new term of years added to our life, we may fitly do it. After any deliverance from trouble, when our joys bud forth anew, let us again visit the foot of the cross, and renew our consecration. Especially, let us do this after any sin which has grieved the Holy Spirit, or brought dishonor upon the cause of God; let us then look to that blood which can make us whiter than snow, and again offer ourselves unto the Lord.

We should not only let our troubles confirm our dedication to God, but our prosperity should do the same. If we ever meet with occasions which deserve to be called *"crowning mercies,"* then, surely, if He has crowned us, we ought also to crown our God. Let us bring forth anew all the jewels of the divine regalia which have been stored in the jewel-closet of our heart, and let our God sit upon the throne of our love, arrayed in royal apparel. If we would learn to profit by our prosperity, we should not need so much adversity. If we would gather from a kiss all the good it might confer upon us, we should not so often smart under the rod. Have we lately received some blessing which we little expected? Has the Lord put our feet in a large room? Can we sing of mercies multiplied? Then this is the day to put our hand upon the horns of the altar, and say, "Bind me here, my God; bind me here with cords, even forever."

Inasmuch as we need the fulfillment of new promises from God, let us offer renewed prayers that our old vows may not be dishonored. Let us this morning make with Him a sure covenant, because of the pains of Jesus which for the last month we have been considering with gratitude.

EVENING

"The flowers appear on the earth; the time of the singing of birds has come, and the voice of the turtle-dove is heard in our land" — Song of Solomon 2:12.

SWEET IS THE season of spring, the long and dreary winter helps us to appreciate its genial warmth, and its promise of summer enhances its present delights. After periods of depression of spirit, it is delightful to behold again the light of the Sun of Righteousness; then our slumbering graces rise from their lethargy, like the crocus and the daffodil from their beds of earth; then is our heart made merry with delicious notes of gratitude, far more melodious than the warbling of birds. And the comforting assurance of peace, infinitely more delightful than the turtle's note, is heard within the soul. Now is the time for the soul to seek communion with her Beloved; now must she rise from her native sordidness, and come away from her old associations. If we do not hoist the sail when the breeze is favorable, we shall be blameworthy; times of refreshing ought not to pass over us unimproved.

When Jesus Himself visits us in tenderness, and entreats us to arise, can we be so base as to refuse His request? He has Himself risen that He may draw us after Him; He now by His Holy Spirit has revived us, that we may, in newness of life, ascend into the heavenlies, and hold communion with Himself. Let our wintry state suffice us for coldness and indifference; when the Lord creates a spring within, let our sap flow with vigor, and our branch blossom with high resolve. Oh Lord, if it is not spring time in my chilly heart, I pray You make it so, for I am heartily weary of living at a distance from You. Oh! the long and dreary winter, when will You bring it to an end? Come, Holy Spirit, and renew my soul! Quicken me! restore me, and have mercy upon me! This very night I would earnestly implore the Lord to take pity upon His servant, and send me a happy revival of spiritual life!

April 25   MORNING

"Rise up, My love, My beautiful one and come away" — *Song of Solomon 2:10.*

    LO, I HEAR THE voice of my Beloved! He speaks to me! Fair weather is smiling upon the face of the earth, and He would not have me spiritually asleep while nature is all around me awaking from her winter's rest. He bids me *"Rise up,"* and well He may, for I have long enough been lying among the pots of worldliness. He is risen, I am risen in Him, why then should I cling unto the dust? From lower loves, desires, pursuits, and aspirations, I would rise towards Him. He calls me by the sweet title of *"My love,"* and counts me fair; this is a good argument for my rising. If He has thus exalted me, and thinks me thus comely, how can I linger in the tents of Kedar and find congenial associates among the sons of men? He bids me *"Come away."* Further and further from everything selfish, groveling, worldly, sinful, He calls me; yes, from the outwardly religious world which knows Him not, and has no sympathy with the mystery of the higher life, He calls me. *"Come away"* has no harsh sound in it to my ear, for what is there to hold me in this wilderness of vanity and sin?

    Oh my Lord, would that I could come away, but I am taken among the thorns, and cannot escape from them as I would. I would, if it were possible, have neither eyes, nor ears, nor heart for sin. You call me to Yourself by saying *"Come away,"* and this is a melodious call indeed. To come to You is to come home from exile, to come to land out of the raging storm, to come to rest after long labor, to come to the goal of my desires and the summit of my wishes. But Lord, how can a stone rise, how can a lump of clay come away from the horrible pit? Oh raise me, draw me. Your grace can do it. Send forth Your Holy Spirit to kindle sacred flames of love in my heart, and I will continue to rise until I leave life and time behind me, and indeed come away.

EVENING

"If anyone hears My voice and opens the door, I will come in to him" — *Revelation 3:20.*

    WHAT IS YOUR desire this evening? Is it set upon heavenly things? Do you long to enjoy the high doctrine of eternal love? Do you desire liberty in very close communion with God? Do you aspire to know the heights, and depths, and lengths, and breadths? Then you must draw near to Jesus; you must get a clear sight of Him in His preciousness and completeness; you must view Him in His work, in His offices, in His person. He who understands Christ, receives an anointing from the Holy One, by which He knows all things. Christ is the great master-key of all the chambers of God; there is no treasure-house of God which will not open and yield up all its wealth to the soul that lives near to Jesus.

    Are you saying, "Oh that He would dwell in my bosom? Would that He would make my heart His dwelling-place forever?" Open the door, beloved, and He will come into your souls. He has long been knocking, and all with this object, that He may sup with you, and you with Him. He sups with you because you find the house or the heart, and you with Him because He brings the provision. He could not sup with you if it were not in your heart, you finding the house; nor could you sup with Him, for you have a bare cupboard, if He did not bring the provision with Him. Fling wide, then, the portals of your soul. He will come with that love which you long to feel; He will come with that joy into which you cannot work your poor depressed spirit; He will bring the peace which now you have not. He will come with His flagons of wine and sweet apples of love, and cheer you till you have no other sickness but that of *love overpowering, love divine.*

    Only open the door to Him, drive out His enemies, give Him the keys of your heart, and He will dwell there forever. Oh, wondrous love, that brings such a guest to dwell in such a heart!

MORNING   April 26

"Do, this, in remembrance of Me" — *1 Corinthians 11:24.*

IT SEEMS THEN, that Christians may forget Christ! There could be no need for this loving exhortation, if there were not a fearful supposition that our memories might prove treacherous. Nor is this a bare supposition; it is, alas! too well confirmed in our experience, not as a possibility, but as a lamentable fact. It appears almost impossible that those who have been redeemed by the blood of the dying Lamb, and loved with an everlasting love by the eternal Son of God, should forget that gracious Savior; but, if startling to the ear, it is, alas! too apparent to the eye to allow us to deny the crime.

Forget Him who never forgot us! Forget Him who poured His blood forth for our sins! Forget Him who loved us even to the death! Can it be possible? Yes, it is not only possible, but conscience confesses that it is too sadly a fault with all of us, that we suffer Him to be as a wayfaring man tarrying but for a night. He whom we should make the abiding tenant of our memories is but a visitor therein. The cross where one would think that memory would linger, and unmindfulness would be an unknown intruder, is desecrated by the feet of forgetfulness. Does not your conscience say that this is true? Do you not find yourselves forgetful of Jesus? Some creature steals away your heart, and you are unmindful of Him upon whom your affection ought to be set. Some earthly business engrosses your attention when you should fix your eye steadily upon the cross. It is the incessant turmoil of the world, the constant attraction of earthly things which takes away the soul from Christ. While memory too well preserves a poisonous weed, it suffers the rose of Sharon to wither. Let us charge ourselves to bind a heavenly forget-me-not about our hearts for Jesus our Beloved, and, whatever else we let slip, let us hold fast to Him.

EVENING
"Blessed is he that is alert" — *Revelation 16:15.*

"WE DIE DAILY," said the apostle. This was the life of the early Christians; they went everywhere with their lives in their hands. We are not in this day called to pass through the same fearful persecutions; if we were, the Lord would give us grace to bear the test. But the tests of Christian life, at the present moment, though outwardly not so terrible, are yet more likely to overcome us than even those of the fiery age. We have to bear the sneer of the world that is little; its blandishments, its soft words, its oily speeches, its fawning, its hypocrisy, are far worse. Our danger is lest we grow rich and become proud, lest we give ourselves up to the fashions of this present evil world, and lose our faith. Or if wealth be not the trial, worldly care is quite as mischievous. If we cannot be torn in pieces by the roaring lion, if we may be hugged to death by the bear, the devil little cares which it is, so long as he destroys our love to Christ, and our confidence in Him.

I fear that the Christian church is far more likely to lose her integrity in these soft and silken days than in those rougher times. We must be awake now, for we traverse the enchanted ground, and are most likely to fall asleep to our own undoing, unless our faith in Jesus be a reality, and our love to Jesus a vehement flame. Many in these days of easy profession are likely to prove tares, and not wheat; hypocrites with fair masks on their faces, but not the true-born children of the living God. Christian, do not think that these are times in which you can dispense with watchfulness or with holy ardor; you need these things more than ever, and may God the eternal Spirit display His omnipotence in you, that you may be able to say, in all these softer things, as well as in the rougher, *"We are more than conquerors through Him that loved us."*

April 27   MORNING

"God, our own God" — Psalm 67:6.

IT IS STRANGE how little use we make of the spiritual blessings which God gives us, but it is stranger still how little use we make of God Himself. Though He is *"our own God,"* we apply ourselves but little to Him, and ask but little of Him. How seldom do we ask counsel at the hands of the Lord! How often do we go about our business, without seeking His guidance! In our troubles how constantly do we strive to bear our burdens ourselves, instead of casting them upon the Lord, that He may sustain us! This is not because we may not, for the Lord seems to say, "I am yours, soul, come and make use of Me as you will; you may freely come to My store, and the oftener the more welcome." It is our own fault if we make not free with the riches of our God.

Then, since you have such a friend, and He invites you, draw from Him daily. Never want while you have a God to go to; never fear or faint while you have God to help you. Go to your treasure and take whatever you need; there is all that you can want. Learn the divine skill of making God all things to you. He can supply you with all, or, better still, He can be to you instead of all. Let me urge you, then, to make use of your God. Make use of Him in prayer. Go to Him often, because He is your God. Oh, will you fail to use so great a privilege? Fly to Him, tell Him all your wants. Use Him constantly by faith at all times. If some dark providence has beclouded you, use your God as a sun; if some strong enemy has beset you, find in Jehovah a *"shield,"* for He is a sun and shield to His people. If you have lost your way in the mazes of life, use Him as a guide, for He will direct you. Whatever you are, and wherever you are, remember God is just what you want, and just where you want, and that He can do all you want.

EVENING

"The Lord is King forever and ever" — Psalm 10:16.

JESUS CHRIST IS no despotic claimant of divine right, but He is really and truly the Lord's anointed! *"It has pleased the Father that in Him should all fullness dwell."* God has given to Him all power and all authority. As the Son of man, He is now head over all things to His church, and He reigns over heaven, and earth, and hell, with the keys of life and death at His girdle. Certain princes have delighted to call themselves kings by the popular will, and certainly our Lord Jesus Christ is such in His church. If it could be put to the vote whether He should be King in the church, every believing heart would crown Him. Oh that we could crown Him more gloriously than we do! We would count no expense to be wasted that could glorify Christ. Suffering would be pleasure, and loss would be gain, if thereby we could surround His brow with brighter crowns, and make Him more glorious in the eyes of men and angels.

Yes, He shall reign. Long live the King! All hail to You, King Jesus! Go forth, you virgin souls who love your Lord, bow at His feet, strew His way with the lilies of your love, and the roses of your gratitude: *"Bring forth the royal diadem, and crown Him Lord of all."* Moreover, our Lord Jesus is King in Zion by right of conquest; He has taken and carried by storm the hearts of His people, and has slain their enemies who held them in cruel bondage. In the Red Sea of His own blood, our Redeemer has drowned the Pharaoh of our sins; shall He not be King in Jeshurun? He has delivered us from the iron yoke and heavy curse of the law; shall not the Liberator be crowned? We are His portion, whom He has taken out of the hand of the Amorite with His sword and with His bow; who shall snatch His conquest from His hand? All hail, King Jesus! We gladly own Your gentle sway! Rule in our hearts forever, You lovely Prince of Peace.

MORNING April 28

"Remember the word to Your servant, on which You have caused me to hope" — Psalm 119:49.

WHATEVER YOUR SPECIAL need may be, you may readily find some promise in the Bible suited to it. Are you faint and feeble because your way is rough and you are weary? Here is the promise: *"He gives power to the faint."* When you read such a promise, take it back to the great Promisor, and ask Him to fulfil His own word. Are you seeking after Christ, and thirsting for closer communion with Him? This promise shines like a star upon you: *"Blessed are they that hunger and thirst after righteousness, for they shall be filled."* Take that promise to the throne continually; do not plead anything else, but go to God over and over again with this: *"Lord, You have said it; do as You have said."*

Are you distressed because of sin, and burdened with the heavy load of your iniquities? Listen to these words: *"I, even I, am He that blots out your transgressions, and will no more remember your sins."* You have no merit of your own to plead why He should pardon you, but plead His written engagements and He will perform them. Are you afraid lest you should not be able to hold on to the end, lest, after having thought yourself a child of God, you should prove a castaway? If that is your state, take this word of grace to the throne and plead it: *"The mountains may depart, and the hills may be removed, but the covenant of My love shall not depart from you."*

If you have lost the sweet sense of the Savior's presence, and are seeking Him with a sorrowful heart, remember the promises: *"Return unto Me, and I will return unto you;" "For a small moment have I forsaken you, but with great mercies will I gather you."* Feast your faith upon God's own word, and whatever your fears or wants, repair to the Bank of Faith with your Father's note of hand, saying, *"Remember the word unto Your servant, upon which You have caused me to hope."*

EVENING

"For all the house of Israel have brass foreheads and hard hearts" — Ezekiel 3:7.

ARE THERE NO exceptions? No, not one. Even the favored race are thus described. Are the best so bad? Then what must the worst be? Come, my heart, consider how far you have a share in this universal accusation, and while considering, be ready to take shame unto yourself wherein you may have been guilty. The first charge is impudence, or hardness of forehead, a lack of holy shame, an unhallowed boldness in evil. Before my conversion, I could sin and feel no compunction, hear of my guilt and yet remain unhumbled, and even confess my iniquity and manifest no inward humiliation on account of it. For a sinner to go to God's house and pretend to pray to Him and praise Him argues a brazen-facedness of the worst kind! Alas! since the day of my new birth I have doubted my Lord to His face, murmured unblushingly in His presence, worshipped before Him in a slovenly manner, and sinned without bewailing myself concerning it. If my forehead were not as an adamant, harder than flint, I should have far more holy fear, and a far deeper contrition of spirit. Woe is me, I am one of the impudent house of Israel.

The second charge is hardheartedness, and I must not venture to plead innocent here. Once I had nothing but a heart of stone, and although through grace I now have a new and fleshy heart, much of my former obduracy remains. I am not affected by the death of Jesus as I ought to be; neither am I moved by the ruin of my fellow men, the wickedness of the times, the chastisement of my heavenly Father, and my own failures, as I should be. Oh that my heart would melt at the recital of my Savior's sufferings and death. Would to God I were rid of this nether millstone within me, this hateful body of death. Blessed be the name of the Lord, the disease is not incurable, the Savior's precious blood is the universal solvent, and me, even me, it will effectually soften, till my heart melts as wax before the fire.

April 29   MORNING

"You are my hope in the day of evil" — Jeremiah 17:17.

THE PATH OF the Christian is not always bright with sunshine; he has his seasons of darkness and of storm. True, it is written in God's Word, *"Her ways are ways of pleasantness, and all her paths are peace;"* and it is a great truth, that religion is calculated to give a man happiness below as well as bliss above. But experience tells us that if the course of the just be *"As the shining light that shines more and more unto the perfect day,"* yet sometimes that light is eclipsed. At certain periods clouds cover the believer's sun, and he walks in darkness and sees no light. There are many who have rejoiced in the presence of God for a season; they have basked in the sunshine in the earlier stages of their Christian career; they have walked along the *"green pastures"* by the side of the *"still waters,"* but suddenly they find the glorious sky is clouded; instead of the land of Goshen they have to tread the sandy desert; in the place of sweet waters, they find troubled streams, bitter to their taste, and they say, "Surely, if I were a child of God, this would not happen."

Oh! say not so, you who are walking in darkness. The best of God's saints must drink the wormwood; the dearest of His children must bear the cross. No Christian has enjoyed perpetual prosperity; no believer can always keep his harp from the willows. Perhaps the Lord allotted you at first a smooth and unclouded path, because you were weak and timid. He tempered the wind to the shorn lamb, but now that you are stronger in the spiritual life, you must enter upon the riper and rougher experience of God's full-grown children. We need winds and tempests to exercise our faith, to tear off the rotten bough of self-dependence, and to root us more firmly in Christ. The day of evil reveals to us the value of our glorious hope.

EVENING

"For the LORD takes pleasure in His people" — Psalm 149:4.

HOW COMPREHENSIVE IS the love of Jesus! There is no part of His people's interests which He does not consider, and there is nothing which concerns their welfare which is not important to Him. Not merely does He think of you, believer, as an immortal being, but as a mortal being too. Do not deny it or doubt it: *"The very hairs of your head are all numbered." "The steps of a good man are ordered by the Lord: and he delights in His way."* It were a sad thing for us if this mantle of love did not cover all our concerns, for what mischief might be wrought to us in that part of our business which did not come under our gracious Lord's inspection!

Believer, rest assured that the heart of Jesus cares about your meaner affairs. The breadth of His tender love is such that you may resort to Him in all matters; for in all your afflictions He is afflicted, and like as a father pities his children, so does He pity you. The meanest interests of all His saints are all borne upon the broad bosom of the Son of God. Oh, what a heart is His, that does not merely comprehend the persons of His people, but comprehends also the diverse and innumerable concerns of all those persons! Do you think, Oh Christian, that you can measure the love of Christ? Think of what His love has brought you: justification, adoption, sanctification, eternal life! The riches of His goodness are unsearchable; you shall never be able to tell them out or even conceive them.

Oh, the breadth of the love of Christ! Shall such a love as this have half our hearts? Shall it have a cold love in return? Shall Jesus' marvelous loving-kindness and tender care meet with but faint response and tardy acknowledgement? Oh, my soul, tune your harp to a glad song of thanksgiving! Go to your rest rejoicing, for you are no desolate wanderer, but a beloved child, watched over, cared for, supplied, and defended by your Lord.

MORNING April 30

"And all the children of Israel murmured" — Numbers 14:2.

THERE ARE MURMURERS among Christians now, as there were in the camp of Israel of old. There are those who, when the rod falls, cry out against the afflictive dispensation. They ask, "Why am I thus afflicted? What have I done to be chastened in this manner?" A word with you, Oh murmurer! Why should you murmur against the dispensations of your heavenly Father? Can He treat you more harshly than you deserve? Consider what a rebel you were once, but He has pardoned you! Surely, if He in His wisdom sees fit now to chasten you, you should not complain. After all, are you smitten as harshly as your sins deserve? Consider the corruption which is in your breast, and then will you wonder that there needs so much of the rod to bring it out? Weigh yourself, and discern how much dross is mingled with your gold; and do you think the fire too hot to purge away so much dross as you have? Does not that proud rebellious spirit of yours prove that your heart is not thoroughly sanctified? Are not those murmuring words contrary to the holy submissive nature of God's children? Is not the correction needed?

But if you will murmur against the chastening, take heed, for it will go hard with murmurers. God always chastises His children twice, if they do not bear the first stroke patiently. But know one thing, *"He does not afflict willingly, nor grieve the children of men."* All His corrections are sent in love, to purify you, and to draw you nearer to Himself. Surely it must help you to bear the chastening with resignation if you are able to recognize your Father's hand. For *"whom the Lord loves, He chastens, and scourges every son whom He receives. If you endure chastening, God deals with you as with sons." "Murmur not as some of them also murmured and were destroyed of the destroyer."*

EVENING

"How precious also are Your thoughts to me, Oh God!" — Psalm 139:17.

DIVINE OMNISCIENCE AFFORDS no comfort to the ungodly mind, but to the child of God it overflows with consolation. God is always thinking upon us, never turns aside His mind from us, has us always before His eyes. And this is precisely as we would have it, for it would be dreadful to exist for a moment beyond the observation of our heavenly Father. His thoughts are always tender, loving, wise, prudent, far-reaching, and they bring to us countless benefits; hence it is a choice delight to remember them. The Lord always did think upon His people; hence their election and the covenant of grace by which their salvation is secured. He always will think upon them; hence their final perseverance by which they shall be brought safely to their final rest. In all our wanderings the watchful glance of the Eternal Watcher is evermore fixed upon us; we never roam beyond the Shepherd's eye. In our sorrows He observes us incessantly, and not a pang escapes Him; in our toils He marks all our weariness, and writes in His book all the struggles of His faithful ones. These thoughts of the Lord encompass us in all our paths, and penetrate the innermost region of our being. Not a nerve or tissue, valve or vessel, of our bodily organization is not cared for; all the littles of our little world are thought upon by the great God.

Dear reader, is this precious to you? Then hold to it. Never be led astray by those philosophic fools who preach up an impersonal God, and talk of self-existent, self-governing matter. The Lord lives and thinks upon us, this is a truth far too precious for us to be lightly robbed of it. The notice of a nobleman is valued so highly that he who has it counts his fortune made; but what is it to be thought of by the King of kings! If the Lord thinks upon us, all is well, and we may rejoice evermore.

May 1

MORNING

His cheeks are like a bed of spices — Song of Solomon 5:13.

LO, THE FLOWERY month is come! March winds and April showers have done their work, and the earth is all bedecked with beauty. Come my soul, put on your holiday attire and go forth to gather garlands of heavenly thoughts. You know where to go, for to you the *"beds of spices"* are well known, and you have so often smelled the perfume of the *"sweet flowers,"* that you will go at once to your well-beloved and find all loveliness, all joy in Him. That cheek once so rudely struck with a rod, often wet with tears of sympathy and then defiled with spit; that cheek as it smiles with mercy is as fragrant aromatic to my heart. You did not hide Your face from shame and spitting, Oh Lord Jesus, and therefore I will find my dearest delight in praising You. Those cheeks were furrowed by the plough of grief, and crimsoned with red lines of blood from Your thorn-crowned temples; such marks of love unbounded cannot but charm my soul far more than pillars of perfume. If I may not see the whole of His face I would behold His cheeks, for the least glimpse of Him is exceedingly refreshing to my spiritual sense and yields a variety of delights. In Jesus I find not only fragrance, but a bed of spices; not one flower, but all manner of sweet flowers. He is to me my rose and my lily, my heart's ease and my cluster of camphire. He is with me, it is May all the year round, and my soul goes forth to wash her happy face in the morning-dew of His grace, and to solace herself with the singing of the birds of His promises. Precious Lord Jesus, let me in very deed know the blessedness which dwells in abiding, unbroken fellowship with You. I am a poor worthless one, whose cheek You have deigned to kiss! Oh let me kiss You in return with the kisses of my lips.

EVENING

"I am the rose of Sharon — Song of Solomon 2:1.

WHATEVER THERE MAY be of beauty in the material world, Jesus Christ possesses all that in the spiritual world in a tenfold degree. Among flowers the rose is thought the sweetest, but Jesus is infinitely more beautiful in the garden of the soul than the rose can be in the gardens of earth. He takes the first place as the fairest among ten thousand. He is the sun, and all others are the stars; the heavens and the day are dark in comparison with Him, for the King in His beauty transcends all. *"I am the rose of Sharon."* This was the best and rarest of roses. Jesus is not *"the rose"* alone, He is *"the rose of Sharon,"* just as He calls His righteousness *"gold,"* and then adds, *"the gold of Ophir,"* the best of the best. He is positively lovely, and superlatively the loveliest. There is variety in His charms. The rose is delightful to the eye, and its scent is pleasant and refreshing; so each of the senses of the soul, whether it be the taste or feeling, the hearing, the sight, or the spiritual smell, finds appropriate gratification in Jesus. Even the recollection of His love is sweet. Take *"the rose of Sharon,"* and pull it leaf from leaf, and lay by the leaves in the jar of memory, and you shall find each leaf fragrant long afterwards, filling the house with perfume. Christ satisfied the highest taste of the most educated spirit to the very full. The greatest amateur in perfumes is quite satisfied with the rose: and when the soul has arrived at her highest pitch of true taste, she shall still be content with Christ, no, she shall be the better able to appreciate Him. Heaven itself possesses nothing which excels *"the rose of Sharon."* What emblem can fully set forth His beauty? Human speech and earth-born things fail to tell of Him. Earth's choicest charms commingled, feebly picture His abounding preciousness. Blessed rose, bloom in my heart forever!

MORNING   May 2

I do not pray for You to take them out of the world— John 17:15.

IT IS A SWEET and blessed event which will occur to all believers in God's own time, the going home to be with Jesus. In a few more years the Lord's soldiers, who are now fighting *"the good fight of faith,"* will have done with conflict, and have entered into the joy of their Lord. But although Christ prays that His people may eventually be with Him where He is, He does not ask that they may be taken at once away from this world to heaven. He wishes them to stay here. Yet how frequently does the wearied pilgrim put up the prayer, *"Oh that I had wings like a dove! for then would I fly away and be at rest;"* but Christ does not pray like that, He leaves us in His Father's hands, until, like shocks of corn fully ripe, we shall each be gathered into our Master's garner. Jesus does not plead for our instant removal by death, for to abide in the flesh is needful for others if not profitable for ourselves. He asks that we may be kept from evil, but He never asks for us to be admitted to the inheritance in glory till we are of full age.

Christians often want to die when they have any trouble. Ask them why, and they tell you, "Because we would be with the Lord." We fear it is not so much because they are longing to be with the Lord, as because they desire to get rid of their troubles; else they would feel the same wish to die at other times when not under the pressure of trial. They want to go home, not so much for the Savior's company, as to be at rest. Now it is quite right to desire to depart if we can do it in the same spirit that Paul did, because to be with Christ is far better, but the wish to escape from trouble is a selfish one. Rather let your care and wish be to glorify God by your life here as long as He pleases, even though it be in the midst of toil, and conflict, and suffering, and leave Him to say when *"it is enough."*

EVENING

These all died in faith — Hebrews 11:13.

BEHOLD THE EPITAPH of all those blessed saints who fell asleep before the coming of our Lord! It matters nothing how else they died, whether of old age, or by violent means; this one point, in which they all agree, is the most worthy of record, *"they all died in faith."* In faith they lived; it was their comfort, their guide, their motive and their support. And in the same spiritual grace they died, ending their life-song in the sweet strain in which they had so long continued. They did not die resting in the flesh or upon their own attainments; they made no advance from their first way of acceptance with God, but held to the way of faith to the end. Faith is as precious to die by as to live by.

Dying in faith has distinct reference to the past. They believed the promises which had gone before, and were assured that their sins were blotted out through the mercy of God. Dying in faith has to do with the present. These saints were confident of their acceptance with God, they enjoyed the beams of His love, and rested in His faithfulness. Dying in faith looks into the future. They fell asleep, affirming that the Messiah would surely come, and that when He should in the last days appear upon the earth, they would rise from their graves to behold Him. To them the pains of death were but the birth-pangs of a better state.

Take courage, my soul, as you read this epitaph. Your course, through grace, is one of faith, and sight seldom cheers you. This has also been the pathway of the brightest and the best. Faith was the orbit in which these stars of the first magnitude moved all the time of their shining here; and happy are you that it is yours. Look anew tonight to Jesus, *"the author and finisher of your faith,"* and thank Him for giving you like precious faith with souls now in glory.

May 3   MORNING

You have trouble in the world—John 16:33.

ARE YOU ASKING the reason of this, believer? Look upward to your heavenly Father, and behold Him pure and holy. Do you know that you are one day to be like Him? Will you easily be conformed to His image? Will you not require much refining in the furnace of affliction to purify you? Will it be an easy thing to get rid of your corruptions, and make you perfect even as your Father which is in heaven is perfect?

Next, Christian, turn your eye downward. Do you know what foes you have beneath your feet? You were once a servant of Satan, and no king will willingly lose his subjects. Do you think that Satan will let you alone? No, he will be always at you, for he *"goes about like a roaring lion, seeking whom he may devour."* Expect trouble, therefore, Christian, when you look beneath you.

Then look around you. Where are you? You are in an enemy's country, a stranger and a sojourner. The world is not your friend. If it be, then you are not God's friend, for he who is the friend of the world is the enemy of God. Be assured that you shall find foes everywhere. When you sleep, think that you are resting on the battle-field; when you walk, suspect an ambush in every hedge. As mosquitoes are said to bite strangers more than natives, so will the trials of earth be sharpest to you.

Lastly, look within yourself, into your own heart and observe what is there. Sin and self are still within. Ah! if you had no devil to tempt you, no enemies to fight you, and no world to ensnare you, you would still find in yourself evil enough to be a sore trouble to you, for *"the heart is deceitful above all things, and desperately wicked."* Expect trouble then, but lose not hope on account of it, for God is with you to help and to strengthen you. He has said, *"I will be with you in trouble; I will deliver you and honor you."*

EVENING

A very present help—Psalm 46:1.

COVENANT BLESSINGS are not meant to be looked at only, but to be appropriated. Even our Lord Jesus is given to us for our present use. Believer, you do not make use of Christ as you ought to do. When you are in trouble, why do you not tell Him all your grief? Has He not a sympathizing heart, and can He not comfort and relieve you? No, you are going about to all your friends, save your best Friend, and telling your tale everywhere except into the bosom of your Lord. Are you burdened with this day's sins? Here is a fountain filled with blood: use it, saint, use it. Has a sense of guilt returned upon you? The pardoning grace of Jesus may be proved again and again. Come to Him at once for cleansing. Do you deplore your weakness? He is your strength: why not lean upon Him? Do you feel naked? Come here, soul; put on the robe of Jesus' righteousness. Stand not looking at it, but wear it. Strip off your own righteousness, and your own fears too: put on the fair white linen, for it was meant to wear. Do you feel yourself sick? Pull the night-bell of prayer, and call up the Beloved Physician! He will give the cordial that will revive you. You are poor, but then you have *"a kinsman, a mighty man of wealth."*

What! will you not go to Him, and ask Him to give you of His abundance, when He has given you this promise, that you shall be joint heir with Him, and has made over all that He is and all that He has to be yours? There is nothing Christ dislikes more than for His people to make a show-thing of Him, and not to use Him. He loves to be employed by us. The more burdens we put on His shoulders, the more precious will He be to us.

> Let us be simple with Him, then,
> Not backward, stiff, or cold,
> As though our Bethlehem could be
> What Sinai was of old.

MORNING   May 4

Shall a man make gods to himself and they are no gods? — Jeremiah 16:20.

ONE GREAT BESETTING sin of ancient Israel was idolatry, and the spiritual Israel is vexed with a tendency to the same folly. Remphan's star shines no longer, and the women weep no more for Tammuz, but Mammon still intrudes his golden calf, and the shrines of pride are not forsaken. Self in various forms struggles to subdue the chosen ones under its dominion, and the flesh sets up its altars wherever it can find space for them. Favorite children are often the cause of much sin in believers; the Lord is grieved when He sees us doting upon them above measure; they will live to be as great a curse to us as Absalom was to David, or they will be taken from us to leave our homes desolate. If Christians desire to grow thorns to stuff their sleepless pillows, let them dote upon their dear ones.

It is truly said that *"they are no gods,"* for the objects of our foolish love are very doubtful blessings, the solace which they yield us now is dangerous, and the help which they can give us in the hour of trouble is little indeed. Why, then, are we so bewitched with vanities? We pity the poor heathen who adore a god of stone, and yet worship a god of gold. Where is the vast superiority between a god of flesh and one of wood? The principle, the sin, the folly is the same in either case, only that in ours the crime is more aggravated because we have more light, and sin in the face of it. The heathen bows to a false deity, but the true God he has never known; we commit two evils, inasmuch as we forsake the living God and turn unto idols. May the Lord purge us all from this grievous iniquity!

> The dearest idol I have known,
> Whatever that idol be;
> Help me to tear it from Your throne,
> And worship only Thee.

EVENING

For you have been born again, not of seed which can rot away, but of seed that can never corrupt — 2 Peter 1:23.

PETER MOST earnestly exhorted the scattered saints to love each other "with a pure heart fervently," and he wisely took his argument, not from the law, from nature, or from philosophy, but from that high and divine nature which God has implanted in His people. Just as some judicious tutor of princes might labor to generate and foster in them a kingly spirit and dignified behavior, finding arguments in their position and descent, so, looking upon God's people as heirs of glory, princes of the blood royal, descendants of the King of kings, earth's truest and oldest aristocracy, Peter says to them, See that you love one another, because of your noble birth, being born of incorruptible seed; because of your pedigree, being descended from God, the Creator of all things; and because of your immortal destiny, for you shall never pass away, though the glory of the flesh shall fade, and even its existence shall cease.

It would be well if, in the spirit of humility, we recognized the true dignity of our regenerated nature, and lived up to it. What is a Christian? If you compare him with a king, he adds priestly sanctity to royal dignity. The king's royalty often lies only in his crown, but with a Christian it is infused into his inmost nature. He is as much above his fellows through his new birth, as a man is above the beast that perishes. Surely he ought to carry himself, in all his dealings, as one who is not of the multitude, but chosen out of the world, distinguished by sovereign grace, written among *"the peculiar people"* and who therefore cannot grovel in the dust as others, nor live after the manner of the world's citizens. Let the dignity of your nature, and the brightness of your prospects, believers in Christ, constrain you to cling unto holiness, and to avoid the very appearance of evil.

MORNING

May 5

I will be their God and they shall be My people — 2 Corinthians 6:16.

WHAT A SWEET title: *"My people!"* What a cheering revelation: *"Their God!"* How much of meaning is expressed in those two words, *"My people!"* The whole world is God's; the heaven, even the heaven of heavens is the Lord's, and He reigns among the children of men. But of those whom He has chosen, whom He has purchased to Himself, He says what He says not of others: *"My people."* In this word there is the idea of proprietorship. In a special manner the *"Lord's portion is His people; Jacob is the lot of His inheritance."* All the nations upon earth are His; the whole world is in His power; yet His people, His chosen, are more especially His possession; for He has done more for them than others; He has bought them with His blood; He has brought them near to Himself; He has set His great heart upon them; He has loved them with an everlasting love, a love which many waters cannot quench, and which the revolutions of time shall never suffice in the least degree to diminish.

Dear friends, can you, by faith, see yourselves in that number? Can you look up to heaven and say, *"My Lord and my God;"* mine by that sweet relationship which entitles me to call You Father; mine by that hallowed fellowship which I delight to hold with You when You are pleased to manifest Yourself unto me as You do not unto the world? Can you read the Book of Inspiration, and find there the indentures of your salvation? Can you read your title written in precious blood? Can you, by humble faith, lay hold of Jesus' garments, and say, "My Christ"? If you can, then God says of you, and of others like you, *"My people;"* for, if God is your God, and Christ your Christ, the Lord has a special, peculiar favor to you; you are the object of His choice, accepted in His beloved Son.

EVENING

He who handles a matter wisely shall find good; and whoever trusts in the LORD, Oh how happy is he! — Proverbs 16:20.

WISDOM IS MAN'S true strength; and, under its guidance, he best accomplishes the ends of his being. Wisely handling the matter of life gives to man the richest enjoyment, and presents the noblest occupation for his powers; hence by it he finds good in the fullest sense. Without wisdom, man is as the wild colt, running here and there, wasting strength which might be profitably employed. Wisdom is the compass by which man is to steer across the trackless waste of life. Without it he is a derelict vessel, the sport of winds and waves. A man must be prudent in such a world as this, or he will find no good, but be betrayed into unnumbered ills. The pilgrim will sorely wound his feet among the briers of the wood of life if he does not pick his steps with the utmost caution. He who is in a wilderness infested with robber bands must handle matters wisely if he would journey safely. If, trained by the Great Teacher, we follow where He leads, we shall find good, even while in this dark abode; there are celestial fruits to be gathered this side of Eden's bowers, and songs of paradise to be sung amid the groves of earth.

But where shall this wisdom be found? Many have dreamed of it, but have not possessed it. Where shall we learn it? Let us listen to the voice of the Lord, for He has declared the secret; He has revealed to the sons of men wherein true wisdom lies, and we have it in the text, *"Whoever trusts in the Lord, happy is he."* The true way to handle a matter wisely is to trust in the Lord. This is the sure clue to the most intricate labyrinths of life, follow it and find eternal bliss. He who trusts in the Lord has a diploma for wisdom granted by inspiration; happy is he now, and happier shall he be above. Lord, in this sweet eventide walk with me in the garden, and teach me the wisdom of faith.

MORNING

May 6

"We live in Him" — 1 John 4:13.

DO YOU WANT a house for your soul? Do you ask, "What is the purchase?" It is something less than proud human nature will like to give. It is without money and without price. Ah! you would like to pay a respectable rent! You would love to do something to win Christ? Then you cannot have the house, for it is *"without price."* Will you take my Master's house on a lease for all eternity, with nothing to pay for it, nothing but the ground-rent of loving and serving Him forever? Will you take Jesus and *"dwell in Him?"* See, this house is furnished with all you want; it is filled with riches more than you will spend as long as you live. Here you can have intimate communion with Christ and feast on His love; here are tables well-stored with food for you to live on forever; in it, when weary, you can find rest with Jesus; and from it you can look out and see heaven itself. Will you have the house? Ah! if you are houseless, you will say, I should like to have the house; but may I have it? Yes; there is the key, the key is, "Come to Jesus." But you say, I am too shabby for such a house. Never mind; there are garments inside. If you feel guilty and condemned, come; and though the house is too good for you, Christ will make you good enough for the house by-and-by. He will wash you and cleanse you, and you will yet be able to sing, "We dwell in Him."

Believer: thrice happy are you to have such a dwelling-place! Greatly privileged you are, for you have a strong habitation in which you are ever safe. And *"dwelling in Him,"* you have not only a perfect and secure house, but an everlasting one. When this world shall have melted like a dream, our house shall live, and stand more imperishable than marble, more solid than granite, self-existent as God, for it is God Himself "We dwell in Him."

EVENING

All the days of my warfare will wait — Job 14:14.

A LITTLE STAY on earth will make heaven more heavenly. Nothing makes rest so sweet as toil; nothing renders security so pleasant as exposure to alarms. The bitter cups of earth will give a relish to the new wine which sparkles in the golden bowls of glory. Our battered armor and scarred countenances will render more illustrious our victory above, when we are welcomed to the seats of those who have overcome the world. We should not have full fellowship with Christ if we did not for awhile sojourn below, for He was baptized with a baptism of suffering among men, and we must be baptized with the same if we would share His kingdom. Fellowship with Christ is so honorable that the sorest sorrow is a light price by which to procure it. Another reason for our lingering here is for the good of others. We would not wish to enter heaven till our work is done, and it may be that we are yet ordained to minister light to souls benighted in the wilderness of sin.

Our prolonged stay here is doubtless for God's glory. A tried saint, like a well-cut diamond, glitters much in the King's crown. Nothing reflects so much honor on a workman as a protracted and severe trial of his work, and its triumphant endurance of the ordeal without giving way in any part. We are God's workmanship, in whom He will be glorified by our afflictions. It is for the honor of Jesus that we endure the trial of our faith with sacred joy. Let each man surrender his own longings to the glory of Jesus, and feel, If my lying in the dust would elevate my Lord by so much as an inch, let me still lie among the pots of earth. If to live on earth forever would make my Lord more glorious, it should be my heaven to be shut out of heaven. Our time is fixed and settled by eternal decree. Let us not be anxious about it, but wait with patience till the gates of pearl shall open.

May 7   MORNING

"Great crowds followed Him. And He healed them all" — Matthew 12:15.

WHAT A MASS of hideous sickness must have thrust itself under the eye of Jesus! Yet we read not that He was disgusted, but patiently waited on every case. What a singular variety of evils must have met at His feet! What sickening ulcers and putrefying sores! Yet He was ready for every new shape of the monster evil, and was victor over it in every form. Let the arrow fly from what quarter it might, He quenched its fiery power. The heat of fever, or the cold of dropsy; the lethargy of palsy, or the rage of madness; the filth of leprosy, or the darkness of ophthalmia. All knew the power of His word, and fled at His command. In every corner of the field He was triumphant over evil, and received the homage of delivered captives. He came, He saw, He conquered everywhere. It is even so this morning. Whatever my own case may be, the beloved Physician can heal me; and whatever may be the state of others whom I may remember at this moment in prayer, I may have hope in Jesus that He will be able to heal them of their sins. My child, my friend, my dearest one, I can have hope for each, for all, when I remember the healing power of my Lord; and on my own account, however severe my struggle with sins and infirmities, I may yet be of good cheer. He who on earth walked among the sick, still dispenses His grace, and works wonders among the sons of men: let me go to Him at once in right earnest.

Let me praise Him, this morning, as I remember how He wrought His spiritual cures, which bring Him most renown. It was by taking upon Himself our sicknesses. *"By His stripes we are healed."* The Church on earth is full of souls healed by our beloved Physician; and the inhabitants of heaven itself confess that *"He healed them all."* Come, then, my soul, publish abroad the virtue of His grace, and let it be *"to the Lord for a name, for an everlasting sign which shall not be cut off."*

EVENING
"Jesus said to him, Get up! Take up your bed and walk!" — John 5:8.

LIKE MANY OTHERS, the impotent man had been waiting for a wonder to be wrought, and a sign to be given. Wearily did he watch the pool, but no angel came, or came not for him. Yet, thinking it to be his only chance, he waited still, and knew not that there was One near him whose word could heal him in a moment. Many are in the same plight; they are waiting for some singular emotion, remarkable impression, or celestial vision; they wait in vain and watch for nothing. Even supposing that, in a few cases, remarkable signs are seen, yet these are rare, and no man has a right to look for them in his own case; no man especially who feels his impotency to avail himself of the moving of the water even if it came.

It is a very sad reflection that tens of thousands are now waiting in the use of means, and ordinances, and vows, and resolutions, and have so waited time out of mind, in vain, utterly in vain. Meanwhile these poor souls forget the present Savior, who bids them look unto Him and be saved. He could heal them at once, but they prefer to wait for an angel and a wonder. To trust Him is the sure way to every blessing, and He is worthy of the most implicit confidence; but unbelief makes them prefer the cold porches of Bethesda to the warm bosom of His love. Oh that the Lord may turn His eye upon the multitudes who are in this case tonight; may He forgive the slights which they put upon His divine power, and call them by that sweet constraining voice, to rise from the bed of despair, and in the energy of faith take up their bed and walk. Oh Lord, hear our prayer for all such at this calm hour of sunset, and before the day breaks may they look and live.

Courteous reader, is there anything in this portion for you?

MORNING — May 8

"But he who had been healed did not know who He was"— John 5:13.

YEARS ARE SHORT to the happy and healthy; but thirty-eight years of disease must have dragged a very weary length along the life of the poor impotent man. When Jesus, therefore, healed him by a word, while he lay at the pool of Bethesda, he was delightfully sensible of a change. Even so the sinner who has for weeks and months been paralyzed with despair, and has wearily sighed for salvation, is very conscious of the change when the Lord Jesus speaks the word of power, and gives joy and peace in believing. The evil removed is too great to be removed without our discerning it; the life imparted is too remarkable to be possessed and remain inoperative; and the change wrought is too marvelous not to be perceived.

Yet the poor man was ignorant of the author of his cure; he knew not the sacredness of His person, the offices which He sustained, or the errand which brought Him among men. Much ignorance of Jesus may remain in hearts which yet feel the power of His blood. We must not hastily condemn men for lack of knowledge; but where we can see the faith which saves the soul, we must believe that salvation has been bestowed. The Holy Spirit makes men penitents long before He makes them divines; and he who believes what he knows, shall soon know more clearly what he believes.

Ignorance is, however, an evil; for this poor man was much tantalized by the Pharisees, and was quite unable to cope with them. It is good to be able to answer gainsayers; but we cannot do so if we know not the Lord Jesus clearly and with understanding. The cure of his ignorance, however, soon followed the cure of his infirmity, for he was visited by the Lord in the temple; and after that gracious manifestation, he was found testifying that "it was Jesus who had made him whole." Lord, if You have saved me, show me Yourself, that I may declare You to the sons of men.

EVENING

"Now become one with Him, and be at peace"—Job 22:21.

IF WE WOULD rightly *"become one with Him"* and be at peace, we must know Him as He has revealed Himself, not only in the unity of His essence and subsistence, but also in the plurality of His persons. God said, *"Let us make man in our own image;"* let not man be content until he knows something of the "us" from whom his being was derived.

Endeavor to know the Father; bury your head in His bosom in deep repentance, and confess that you are not worthy to be called His son; receive the kiss of His love; let the ring which is the token of His eternal faithfulness be on your finger; sit at His table and let your heart make merry in His grace.

Then press forward and seek to know much of the Son of God who is the brightness of His Father's glory, and yet in unspeakable condescension of grace became man for our sakes; know Him in the singular complexity of His nature: eternal God, and yet suffering man. Follow Him as He walks the waters with the tread of deity, and as He sits upon the well in the weariness of humanity. Be not satisfied unless you know much of Jesus Christ as your Friend, your Brother, your Husband, your all.

Forget not the Holy Spirit; endeavor to obtain a clear view of His nature and character, His attributes, and His works. Behold that Spirit of the Lord, who first of all moved upon chaos, and brought forth order; who now visits the chaos of your soul, and creates the order of holiness. Behold Him as the Lord and giver of spiritual life, the Illuminator, the Instructor, the Comforter, and the Sanctifier. Behold Him as, like holy unction, He descends upon the head of Jesus, and then afterwards rests upon you who are as the skirts of His garments. Such an intelligent, scriptural, and experimental belief in the Trinity in Unity is yours if you truly know God; and such knowledge brings peace indeed.

May 9

MORNING

"Who has blessed us with every spiritual blessing"— Ephesians 1:3.

ALL THE GOODNESS of the past, the present, and the future, Christ bestows upon His people. in the mysterious ages of the past the Lord Jesus was His Father's first elect, and in His election He gave us an interest, for we were chosen in Him from before the foundation of the world. He had from all eternity the prerogatives of Sonship, as His Father's only-begotten and well-beloved Son, and He has, in the riches of His grace, by adoption and regeneration, elevated us to sonship also, so that to us He has given *"power to become the sons of God."* The eternal covenant, based upon suretyship and confirmed by oath, is ours, for our strong consolation and security. In the everlasting settlements of predestinating wisdom and omnipotent decree, the eye of the Lord Jesus was ever fixed on us; and we may rest assured that in the whole roll of destiny there is not a line which militates against the interests of His redeemed.

The great betrothal of the Prince of Glory is ours, for it is to us that He is affianced, as the sacred nuptials shall before long declare to an assembled universe. The marvelous incarnation of the God of heaven, with all the amazing condescension and humiliation which attended it, is ours. The bloody sweat, the scourge, the cross, are ours forever. Whatever blissful consequences flow from perfect obedience, finished atonement, resurrection, ascension, or intercession, all are ours by His own gift. Upon His breastplate He is now bearing our names; and in His authoritative pleadings at the throne He remembers our persons and pleads our cause. His dominion over principalities and powers, and His absolute majesty in heaven, He employs for the benefit of them who trust in Him. His high estate is as much at our service as was His condition of abasement. He who gave Himself for us in the depths of woe and death, does not withdraw the grant now that He is enthroned in the highest heavens.

EVENING

"Come, my Beloved, let us go forth into the field ... let us see if the vine flowers" — Song of Solomon 7:11-12.

THE CHURCH WAS about to engage in earnest labor, and desired her Lord's company in it. She does not say, I will go, but "let us go." it is blessed working when Jesus is at our side! it is the business of God's people to be trimmers of God's vines. Like our first parents, we are put into the garden of the Lord for usefulness; let us therefore go forth into the field. Observe that the church, when she is in her right mind, in all her many labors desires to enjoy communion with Christ. Some imagine that they cannot serve Christ actively, and yet have fellowship with Him: they are mistaken. Doubtless it is very easy to fritter away our inward life in outward exercises, and come to complain with the spouse, *"They made me keeper of the vineyards; but my own vineyard have I not kept:"* but there is no reason why this should be the case except our own folly and neglect.

Certain is it that a professor may do nothing, and yet grow quite as lifeless in spiritual things as those who are most busy. Mary was not praised for sitting still; but for her sitting at Jesus' feet. Even so, Christians are not to be praised for neglecting duties under the pretense of having secret fellowship with Jesus. It is not sitting, but sitting at Jesus' feet which is commendable. Do not think that activity is in itself an evil; it is a great blessing, and a means of grace to us. Paul called it a grace given to him to be allowed to preach; and every form of Christian service may become a personal blessing to those engaged in it. Those who have most fellowship with Christ are not recluses or hermits, who have much time to spare, but indefatigable laborers who are toiling for Jesus, and who, in their toil, have Him side by side with them, so that they are workers together in God's field. Let us remember then, in anything we have to do for Jesus, that we can do it, and should do it in close communion with Him.

MORNING   May 10

"But now Christ has been raised from among the dead" — 1 Corinthians 15:20.

THE WHOLE SYSTEM of Christianity rests upon the fact that *"Christ has been raised from the dead;"* for, *"If Christ has not been raised, then our preaching is worthless and your faith is also worthless: you are still in your sins."* The divinity of Christ finds its surest proof in His resurrection, since He was *"Declared to be the Son of God with power, according to the spirit of holiness, by the resurrection from the dead."* It would not be unreasonable to doubt His Deity if He had not risen. Moreover, Christ's sovereignty depends upon His resurrection, *"For to this end Christ both died, and rose, and revived, that He might be Lord both of the dead and living."*

Again, our justification, that choice blessing of the covenant, is linked with Christ's triumphant victory over death and the grave; for *"He was delivered for our offenses, and was raised again for our justification."* No, more, our very regeneration is connected with His resurrection, for we are *"Begotten again unto a lively hope by the resurrection of Jesus Christ from the dead."* And most certainly our ultimate resurrection rests here, for, *"If the Spirit of Him that raised up Jesus from the dead dwell in you, He that raised up Christ from the dead shall also quicken your mortal bodies by His Spirit that dwells in you."* If Christ is not risen, then shall we not rise; but if He is risen then they who are asleep in Christ have not perished, but in their flesh shall surely behold their God. Thus, the silver thread of resurrection runs through all the believer's blessings, from his regeneration onwards to his eternal glory, and binds them together. How important then will this glorious fact be in his estimation, and how will he rejoice that beyond a doubt it is established, that *"now Christ has been raised from the dead."*

> The promise is fulfill'd,
> Redemption's work is done,
> Justice with mercy's reconciled,
> For God has raised His Son.

EVENING
"The only-begotten of the Father -full of grace and truth" — John 1:14.

BELIEVER, YOU CAN bear your testimony that Christ is the only begotten of the Father, as well as the first begotten from the dead. You can say, He is divine to me, if He is human to all the world beside. He has done that for me which none but a God could do. He has subdued my stubborn will, melted a heart of adamant, opened gates of brass, and snapped bars of iron. He has turned for me my mourning into laughter, and my desolation into joy; He has led my captivity captive, and made my heart rejoice with joy unspeakable and full of glory. Let others think as they will of Him, to me He must be the only begotten of the Father; blessed be His name. And He is full of grace. Ah! had He not been I should never have been saved. He drew me when I struggled to escape from His grace; and when at last I came all trembling like a condemned culprit to His mercy-seat He said, Your sins which are many are all forgiven you: be of good cheer. And He is full of truth. True have His promises been, not one has failed. I bear witness that never servant had such a master as I have; never brother such a kinsman as He has been to me; never spouse such a husband as Christ has been to my soul; never sinner a better Savior; never mourner a better comforter than Christ has been to my spirit. I want none beside Him. In life He is my life, and in death He shall be the death of death; in poverty Christ is my riches; in sickness He makes my bed; in darkness He is my star, and in brightness He is my sun; He is the manna of the camp in the wilderness, and He shall be the new grain of the host when they come to Canaan. Jesus is to me all grace and no wrath, all truth and no falsehood: and of truth and grace His is full, infinitely full. My soul, this night, bless with all your might 'the only Begotten.

May 11

MORNING

"And lo, I am with you all the days"—Matthew 28:20.

IT IS WELL there is One who is ever the same, and who is ever with us. It is well there is one stable rock amidst the billows of the sea of life. Oh my soul, set not your affections upon rusting, moth-eaten, decaying treasures, but set your heart upon Him who abides forever faithful to you. Build not your house upon the moving quicksand of a deceitful world, but found your hopes upon this rock, which, amid descending rain aid roaring floods, shall stand immovably secure. My soul, I charge you, lay up your treasure in the only secure cabinet; store your jewels where you can never lose them. Put your all in Christ; set all your affections on His person, all your hope in His merit, all your trust in His efficacious blood, all your joy in His presence, and so you may laugh at loss, and defy destruction.

Remember that all the flowers in the world's garden fade by turns, and the day will come when nothing will be left but the black, cold earth. Death's black extinguisher must soon put out your candle. Oh! how sweet to have sunlight when the candle is gone! The dark flood must soon roll between you and all you have; then wed your heart to Him who will never leave you; trust yourself with Him who will go with you through the black and surging current of death's stream, and who will land you safely on the celestial shore and make you sit with Him in heavenly places forever. Go, sorrowing son of affliction, tell your secrets to the Friend who sticks closer than a brother. Trust all your concerns with Him who never can be taken from you, who will never leave you, and who will never let you leave Him, even *"Jesus Christ, the same yesterday, and today, and forever."* *"Lo, I am with you all the days,"* is enough for my soul to live upon, let who will forsake me.

EVENING

"Only be strong and very courageous"—Joshua 1:7.

OUR GOD'S TENDER love for His servants makes Him concerned for the state of their inward feelings. He desires them to be of good courage. Some esteem it a small thing for a believer to be vexed with doubts and fears, but God thinks not so. From this text it is plain that our Master would not have us entangled with fears. He would have us without carefulness, without doubt, without cowardice. Our Master does not think so lightly of our unbelief as we do. When we are depressed we are subject to a grievous malady, not to be trifled with, but to be carried at once to the beloved Physician. The Lord loves not to see our countenance sad. It was a law of Ahasuerus that no one should come into the king's court dressed in mourning. This is not the law of the King of kings, for we may come mourning as we are; but still He would have us put off the spirit of heaviness, and put on the garment of praise, for there is much reason to rejoice.

The Christian man ought to be of a courageous spirit, in order that he may glorify the Lord by enduring trials in an heroic manner. If he be fearful and fainthearted, it will dishonor his God. Besides, what a bad example it is. This disease of doubtfulness and discouragement is an epidemic which soon spreads among the Lord's flock. One downcast believer makes twenty souls sad. Moreover, unless your courage is kept up Satan will be too much for you. Let your spirit be joyful in God your Savior, the joy of the Lord shall be your strength, and no fiend of hell shall make headway against you: but cowardice throws down the banner. Moreover, labor is light to a man of cheerful spirit; and success waits upon cheerfulness. The man who toils, rejoicing in his God, believing with all his heart, has success guaranteed. He who sows in hope shall reap in joy; therefore, dear reader, *"be strong, and very courageous."*

MORNING   May 12

"And will reveal Myself to him" — John 14:21.

THE LORD JESUS gives special revelations of Himself to His people. Even if Scripture did not declare this, there are many of the children of God who could testify the truth of it from their own experience. They have had manifestations of their Lord and Savior Jesus Christ in a peculiar manner, such as no mere reading or hearing could afford. In the biographies of eminent saints, you will find many instances recorded in which Jesus has been pleased, in a very special manner to speak to their souls, and to unfold the wonders of His person; yes, so have their souls been steeped in happiness that they have thought themselves to be in heaven, whereas they were not there, though they were well near on the threshold of it. For when Jesus manifests Himself to His people, it is heaven on earth; it is paradise in embryo; it is bliss begun.

Special manifestations of Christ exercise a holy influence on the believer's heart. One effect will be humility. If a man says, I have had such-and-such spiritual communications, I am a great man, he has never had any communion with Jesus at all; for *"God has respect unto the lowly: but the proud He knows afar off."* He does not need to come near them to know them, and will never give them any visits of love. Another effect will be happiness; for in God's presence there are pleasures forevermore. Holiness will be sure to follow. A man who has no holiness has never had this manifestation. Some men profess a great deal; but we must not believe any one unless we see that his deeds answer to what he says. *"Be not deceived; God is not mocked."* He will not bestow His favors upon the wicked: for while He will not cast away a perfect man, neither will He respect an evil doer. Thus there will be three effects of nearness to Jesus: humility, happiness, and holiness. May God give them to you, Christian!

EVENING

"Do not fear to go down to Egypt, for I will make of you a great nation. I will go down with you into Egypt, and I will also surely bring you up again. And Joseph shall put his hand on your eyes" — Genesis 46:34.

JACOB MUST HAVE shuddered at the thought of leaving the land of his father's sojourning, and dwelling among heathen strangers. It was a new scene, and likely to be a trying one: who shall venture among courtiers of a foreign monarch without anxiety? Yet the way was evidently appointed for him, and therefore he resolved to go.

This is frequently the position of believers now. They are called to perils and temptations altogether untried. At such seasons let them imitate Jacob's example by offering sacrifices of prayer unto God, and seeking His direction; let them not take a step until they have waited upon the Lord for His blessing. Then they will have Jacob's companion to be their friend and helper. How blessed to feel assured that the Lord is with us in all our ways, and condescends to go down into our humiliations and banishments with us! Even beyond the ocean our Father's love beams like the sun in its strength. We cannot hesitate to go where Jehovah promises His presence; even the valley of deathshade grows bright with the radiance of this assurance. Marching onwards with faith in their God, believers shall have Jacob's promise. They shall be brought up again, whether it be from the troubles of life or the chambers of death. Jacob's seed came out of Egypt in due time, and so shall all the faithful pass unscathed through the tribulation of life, and the terror of death.

Let us exercise Jacob's confidence. *"Fear not,"* is the Lord's command and His divine encouragement to those who at His bidding are launching upon new seas; the divine presence and preservation forbid so much as one unbelieving fear. Without our God we should fear to move; but when He bids us go, it would be dangerous to tarry. Reader, go forward and fear not.

May 13

MORNING

"Weeping may endure for a night, but joy comes in the morning" — *Psalm 30:5.*

CHRISTIAN! IF YOU are in a night of trial, think of the morrow; cheer up your heart with the thought of the coming of your Lord. Be patient, for Lo! He comes with clouds descending.

Be patient! The Husbandman waits until He reaps His harvest. Be patient; for you know who has said, *"Behold, I come quickly; and my reward is with Me, to give to every man according as his work shall be."* If you are never so wretched now, remember

> A few more rolling suns, at most,
> Will land you on fair Canaan's coast.

Your head may be crowned with thorny troubles now, but it shall wear a starry crown before long; your hand may be filled with cares; it shall sweep the strings of the harp of heaven soon. Your garments may be soiled with dust now; they shall be white by-and-by. Wait a little longer. Ah! how despicable our troubles and trials will seem when we look back upon them! Looking at them here in the prospect, they seem immense; but when we get to heaven we shall then

> With transporting joys recount,
> The labors of our feet.

Our trials will then seem light and momentary afflictions. Let us go on boldly; if the night be never so dark, the morning comes, which is more than they can say who are shut up in the darkness of hell. Do you know what it is thus to live on the future, to live on expectation, to antedate heaven? Happy believer, to have so sure, so comforting a hope. It may be all dark now, but it will soon be light; it may be all trial now, but it will soon be all happiness. What matters it though *"weeping may endure for a night,"* when *"joy comes in the morning?"*

EVENING

"O LORD, my portion" — *Psalm 119:57.*

LOOK AT YOUR possessions, Oh believer, and compare your portion with the lot of your fellow-men. Some of them have their portion in the field; they are rich, and their harvests yield them a golden increase; but what are harvests compared with your God, who is the God of harvests? What are bursting granaries compared with Him, who is the Husbandman, and feeds you with the bread of heaven? Some have their portion in the city; their wealth is abundant, and flows to them in constant streams, until they become a very reservoir of gold; but what is gold compared with your God? You could not live on it; your spiritual life could not be sustained by it. Put it on a troubled conscience, and could it allay its pangs? Apply it to a desponding heart, and see if it could stay a solitary groan, or give one grief the less?

But you have God, and in Him you have more than gold or riches ever could buy. Some have their portion in that which most men love, applause and fame. But ask yourself, is not your God more to you than that? What if a myriad clarions should be loud in your applause, would this prepare you to pass the Jordan, or cheer you in prospect of judgment? No, there are griefs in life which wealth cannot alleviate; and there is the deep need of a dying hour, for which no riches can provide. But when you have God for your portion, you have more than all else put together. In Him every need is met, whether in life or in death. With God for your portion you are rich indeed, for He will supply your need, comfort your heart, assuage your grief, guide your steps, be with you in the dark valley, and then take you home, to enjoy Him as your portion forever. *"I have enough,"* said Esau; this is the best thing a worldly man can say, but Jacob replies, *"I have all things,"* which is a note too high for carnal minds.

MORNING   May 14

"Joint-heirs with Christ!" — Romans 8:17.

THE BOUNDLESS REALMS of His Father's universe are Christ's by prescriptive right. As *"heir of all things,"* He is the sole proprietor of the vast creation of God, and He has admitted us to claim the whole as ours, by virtue of that deed of joint-heirship which the Lord has ratified with His chosen people. The golden streets of paradise, the pearly gates, the river of life, the transcendent bliss, and the unutterable glory, are, by our blessed Lord, made over to us for our everlasting possession. All that He has He shares with His people. The crown royal He has placed upon the head of His Church, appointing her a kingdom, and calling her sons a royal priesthood, a generation of priests and kings. He uncrowned Himself that we might have a coronation of glory; He would not sit upon His own throne until He had procured a place upon it for all who overcome by His blood.

Crown the head and the whole body shares the honor. Behold here the reward of every Christian conqueror! Christ's throne, crown, scepter, palace, treasure, robes, heritage, are yours. Far superior to the jealousy, selfishness, and greed, which admit of no participation of their advantages, Christ deems His happiness completed by His people sharing it. *"The glory which you gave me have I given them." "These things have I spoken unto you, that My joy might remain in you, and that your joy might be full."* The smiles of His Father are all the sweeter to Him, because His people share them. The honors of His kingdom are more pleasing, because His people appear with Him in glory. More valuable to Him are His conquests, since they have taught His people to overcome. He delights in His throne, because on it there is a place for them. He rejoices in His royal robes, since over them His skirts are spread. He delights the more in His joy, because He calls them to enter into it.

EVENING

"He shall gather the lambs with His arm and carry them in His bosom" — Isaiah 40:1.

WHO IS HE OF whom such gracious words are spoken? He is the Good Shepherd. Why does He carry the lambs in His bosom? Because He has a tender heart, and any weakness at once melts His heart. The sighs, the ignorance, the feebleness of the little ones of His flock draw forth His compassion. It is His office, as a faithful High Priest, to consider the weak. Besides, He purchased them with blood, they are His property; He must and will care for that which cost Him so dear. Then He is responsible for each lamb, bound by covenant engagements not to lose one. Moreover, they are all a part of His glory and reward.

But how may we understand the expression, *"He will carry them"*? Sometimes He carries them by not permitting them to endure much trial. Providence deals tenderly with them. Often they are carried by being filled with an unusual degree of love, so that they bear up and stand fast. Though their knowledge may not be deep, they have great sweetness in what they do know. Frequently He "carries" them by giving them a very simple faith, which takes the promise just as it stands, and in simple belief runs with every trouble straight to Jesus. The simplicity of their faith gives them an unusual degree of confidence, which carries them above the world.

"He carries the lambs in His bosom." Here is boundless affection. Would He put them in His bosom if He did not love them much? Here is tender nearness: so near are they, that they could not possibly be nearer. Here is hallowed familiarity: there are precious love passages between Christ and His weak ones. Here is perfect safety; in His bosom who can hurt them? They must hurt the Shepherd first. Here is perfect rest and sweetest comfort. Surely we are not sufficiently sensible of the infinite tenderness of Jesus!

May 15

MORNING
"Everyone who believes is justified"—Acts 13:39.

THE BELIEVER IN Christ receives a present justification. Faith does not produce this fruit by-and-by, but now. So far as justification is the result of faith, it is given to the soul in the moment when it closes with Christ, and accepts Him as its all in all. Are they who stand before the throne of God justified now? So are we, as truly and as clearly justified as they who walk in white and sing melodious praises to celestial harps. The thief upon the cross was justified the moment that he turned the eye of faith to Jesus; and Paul, the aged, after years of service, was not more justified than was the thief with no service at all.

We are today accepted in the Beloved, today absolved from sin, today acquitted at the bar of God. Oh! soul-transporting thought! There are some clusters of Eshcol's vine which we shall not be able to gather till we enter heaven; but this is a bough which runs over the wall. This is not as the grain of the land, which we can never eat till we cross the Jordan; but this is part of the manna in the wilderness, a portion of our daily nutriment with which God supplies us in our journeying to and fro. We are now, even now, pardoned. Even now are our sins put away; even now we stand in the sight of God accepted, as though we had never been guilty. *"There is therefore now no condemnation to them which are in Christ Jesus."* There is not a sin in the Book of God, even now, against one of His people. Who dares to lay anything to their charge? There is neither speck, nor spot, nor wrinkle, nor any such thing remaining upon any one believer in the matter of justification in the sight of the Judge of all the earth. Let present privilege awaken us to present duty, and now, while life lasts, let us spend and be spent for our sweet Lord Jesus.

EVENING
"Made perfect"—Hebrews 12:23.

REMEMBER THAT THERE are two kinds of perfection which the Christian needs, the perfection of justification in the person of Jesus, and the perfection of sanctification worked in Him by the Holy Spirit. At present, corruption yet remains even in the breasts of the regenerate; experience soon teaches us this. Within us are still lusts and evil imaginations. But I rejoice to know that the day is coming when God shall finish the work which He has begun; and He shall present my soul, not only perfect in Christ, but perfect through the Spirit, without spot or blemish, or any such thing.

Can it be true that this poor sinful heart of mine is to become holy even as God is holy? Can it be that this spirit, which often cries, *"Oh wretched man that I am! Who shall deliver me from the body of this sin and death?"* shall get rid of sin and death, that I shall have no evil things to vex my ears, and no unholy thoughts to disturb my peace? Oh, happy hour! May it be hastened! When I cross the Jordan, the work of sanctification will be finished; but not till that moment shall I even claim perfection in myself. Then my spirit shall have its last baptism in the Holy Spirit's fire. I think I long to die to receive that last and final purification which shall usher me into heaven. Not an angel more pure than I shall be, for I shall be able to say, in a double sense, *"I am clean,"* through Jesus' blood, and through the Spirit's work. Oh, how should we extol the power of the Holy Spirit in thus making us fit to stand before our Father in heaven!

Yet let not the hope of perfection hereafter make us content with imperfection now. If it does this, our hope cannot be genuine; for a good hope is a purifying thing, even now. The work of grace must be abiding in us now or it cannot be perfected then. Let us pray to *"be filled with the Spirit"* that we may bring forth increasingly the fruits of righteousness.

MORNING

May 16

"Who gives us richly all things to enjoy" – 1 Timothy 6:17.

OUR LORD JESUS is ever giving, and does not for a solitary instant withdraw His hand. As long as there is a vessel of grace not yet full to the brim, the oil shall not be stayed. He is a sun ever-shining; He is manna always falling round the camp; He is a rock in the desert, ever sending out streams of life from His smitten side; the rain of His grace is always dropping; the river of His bounty is ever-flowing, and the well-spring of His love is constantly overflowing. As the King can never die, so His grace can never fail.

Daily we pluck His fruit, and daily His branches bend down to our hand with a fresh store of mercy. There are seven feast-days in His weeks, and as many as are the days, so many are the banquets in His years. Who has ever returned from His door unblessed? Who has ever risen from His table unsatisfied, or from His bosom short of paradise? His mercies are new every morning and fresh every evening. Who can know the number of His benefits, or recount the list of His bounties? Every sand which drops from the glass of time is but the tardy follower of a myriad of mercies. The wings of our hours are covered with the silver of His kindness, and with the yellow gold of His affection. The river of time bears from the mountains of eternity the golden sands of His favor. The countless stars are but as the standard bearers of a more innumerable host of blessings. Who can count the dust of the benefits which He bestows on Jacob, or tell the number of the fourth part of His mercies towards Israel? How shall my soul extol Him who daily loads us with benefits, and who crowns us with loving-kindness? Oh that my praise could be as ceaseless as His bounty! Oh miserable tongue, how can you be silent? Wake up I pray you, lest I call you no more my glory, but my shame. *"Awake, psaltery and harp: I myself will awake right early."*

EVENING

"And he said, Thus says the LORD, Make this valley full of ditches. For thus says the LORD, You shall not see wind, nor shall you see rain. Still that valley shall be filled with water, so that you may drink, both you and your cattle and your animals" – 2 Kings 3:16-17.

THE ARMIES OF the three kings were famishing for want of water: God was about to send it, and in these words the prophet announced the coming blessing. Here was a case of human helplessness: not a drop of water could all the valiant men procure from the skies or find in the wells of earth. Thus often the people of the Lord are at their wits' end. They see the vanity of the creature, and learn experimentally where their help is to be found. Still the people were to make a believing preparation for the divine blessing; they were to dig the trenches in which the precious liquid would be held. The church must by her varied agencies, efforts, and prayers, make herself ready to be blessed; she must make the pools, and the Lord will fill them. This must be done in faith, in the full assurance that the blessing is about to descend.

By-and-by there was a singular bestowal of the needed blessing. Not as in Elijah's case did the shower pour from the clouds, but in a silent and mysterious manner the pools were filled. The Lord has His own sovereign modes of action: He is not tied to manner and time as we are, but does as He pleases among the sons of men. It is ours thankfully to receive from Him, and not to dictate to Him. We must also notice the remarkable abundance of the supply; there was enough for the need of all. And so it is in the gospel blessing; all the wants of the congregation and of the entire church shall be met by the divine power in answer to prayer; and above all this, victory shall be speedily given to the armies of the Lord.

What am I doing for Jesus? What trenches am I digging? Oh Lord, make me ready to receive the blessing which You are so willing to bestow.

May 17   MORNING

"To walk himself as He walked" — 1 John 2:6.

WHY SHOULD CHRISTIANS imitate Christ? They should do it for their own sakes. If they desire to be in a healthy state of soul if they would escape the sickness of sin, and enjoy the vigor of growing grace, let Jesus be their model. For their own happiness' sake, if they would drink wine on the lees, well refined; if they would enjoy holy and happy communion with Jesus; if they would be lifted up above the cares and troubles of this world, let them walk even as He walked. There is nothing which can so assist you to walk towards heaven with good speed, as wearing the image of Jesus on your heart to rule all its motions. It is when, by the power of the Holy Spirit, you are enabled to walk with Jesus in His very footsteps, that you are most happy, and most known to be the sons of God. Peter afar off is both unsafe and uneasy.

Next, for religion's sake, strive to be like Jesus. Ah! poor Christianity, you have been sorely shot at by carnal foes, but you have not been wounded one-half so dangerously by your foes as by your friends. Who made those wounds in the fair hand of godliness? The professor who used the dagger of hypocrisy. The man who with pretenses enters the fold, being nothing more than a wolf in sheep's clothing. Such a one worries the flock more than the lion outside. There is no weapon half so deadly as a Judas-kiss. Inconsistent professors injure the gospel more than the sneering critic or the infidel.

But, especially for Christ's own sake, imitate His example. Christian, do you love your Savior? Is His name precious to you? Is His cause dear to you? Would you see the kingdoms of the world become His? Is it your desire that He should be glorified? Are you longing that souls should be won to Him? If so, imitate Jesus; be an *"epistle of Christ, known and read of all men."*

EVENING

"You are My servant, I have chosen you" — Isaiah 41 9.

IF WE HAVE received the grace of God in our hearts, its practical effect has been to make us God's servants. We may be unfaithful servants, we certainly are unprofitable ones, but yet, blessed be His name, we are His servants, wearing His livery, feeding at His table, and obeying His commands. We were once the servants of sin, but He who made us free has now taken us into His family and taught us obedience to His will. We do not serve our Master perfectly, but we would if we could. As we hear God's voice saying unto us, *"You are My servant,"* we can answer with David, *"I am Your servant; You have loosed my bonds."*

But the Lord calls us not only His servants, but His chosen ones: *"I have chosen you."* We have not chosen Him first, but He has chosen us. If we are God's servants, we were not always so; to sovereign grace the change must be ascribed. The eye of sovereignty singled us out, and the voice of unchanging grace declared, *"I have loved you with an everlasting love."* Long before time began or space was created God had written upon His heart the names of His elect people, had predestinated them to be conformed unto the image of His Son, and ordained them heirs of all the fullness of His love, His grace, and His glory.

What comfort is here! Has the Lord loved us so long, and will He yet cast us away? He knew how stiffnecked we should be; He understood that our hearts were evil, and yet He made the choice. Ah! our Savior is no fickle lover. He does not feel enchanted for awhile with some gleams of beauty from His church's eye, and then afterwards cast her off because of her unfaithfulness. No, He married her in old eternity; and it is written of Jehovah, *"He hates putting away."* The eternal choice is a bond upon our gratitude and upon His faithfulness which neither can disown.

MORNING   May 18

"In Him dwells all the fullness of the Godhead bodily. And you are complete in Him" — Colossians 2:9,10.

ALL THE ATTRIBUTES of Christ, as God and man, are at our disposal. All the fullness of the Godhead, whatever that marvelous term may comprehend, is ours to make us complete. He cannot endow us with the attributes of Deity; but He has done all that can be done, for He has made even His divine power and Godhead to serve our salvation. His omnipotence, omniscience, omnipresence, immutability and infallibility, are all combined for our defense. Arise, believer, and behold the Lord Jesus yoking the whole of His divine Godhead to the chariot of salvation! How vast His grace, how firm His faithfulness, how unswerving His immutability, how infinite His power, how limitless His knowledge! All these are by the Lord Jesus made the pillars of the temple of salvation; and all, without diminution of their infinity, are covenanted to us as our perpetual inheritance. The fathomless love of the Savior's heart is every drop of it ours; every sinew in the arm of might, every jewel in the crown of majesty, the immensity of divine knowledge, and the sternness of divine justice, all are ours, and shall be employed for us.

The whole of Christ, in His adorable character as the Son of God, is by Himself made over to us most richly to enjoy. His wisdom is our direction, His knowledge our instruction, His power our protection, His justice our surety, His love our comfort, His mercy our solace, and His immutability our trust. He makes no reserve, but opens the recesses of the Mount of God and bids us dig in its mines for the hidden treasures. "All, all, all are yours," says He, *"be satisfied with favor and full of the goodness of the Lord."* Oh! how sweet thus to behold Jesus, and to call upon Him with the certain confidence that in seeking the interposition of His love or power, we are but asking for that which He has already faithfully promised.

EVENING
"Afterwards" — Hebrews 12:11.

HOW HAPPY ARE tried Christians, afterwards. No calm more deep than that which succeeds a storm. Who has not rejoiced in clear shining after rain? Victorious banquets are for well-exercised soldiers. After killing the lion, we eat the honey; after climbing the Hill Difficulty, we sit down in the arbor to rest. After traversing the Valley of Humiliation, after fighting with Apollyon, the shining One appears, with the healing branch from the tree of life. Our sorrows, like the passing keels of the vessels upon the sea, leave a silver line of holy light behind them *"afterwards."* It is peace, sweet, deep peace, which follows the horrible turmoil which once reigned in our tormented, guilty souls.

See, then, the happy estate of a Christian! He has his best things last, and he therefore in this world receives his worst things first. But even his worst things are *"afterward"* good things, harsh plowings yielding joyful harvests. Even now he grows rich by his losses, he rises by his falls, he lives by dying, and becomes full by being emptied. If, then, his grievous afflictions yield him so much peaceable fruit in this life, what shall be the full vintage of joy *"afterwards"* in heaven? If his dark nights are as bright as the world's days, what shall his days be? If even his starlight is more splendid than the sun, what must his sunlight be? If he can sing in a dungeon, how sweetly will he sing in heaven! If he can praise the Lord in the fires, how will he extol Him before the eternal throne! If evil be good to him now, what will the overflowing goodness of God be to him then? Oh, blessed *"afterward!"* Who would not be a Christian? Who would not bear the present cross for the crown which comes afterwards? But herein is work for patience, for the rest is not for today, nor the triumph for the present, but *"afterward."* Wait, Oh soul, and let patience have her perfect work.

May 19   MORNING

"I have seen servants on horses and princes walking as servants on the earth"—Ecclesiastes 10:7.

UPSTARTS FREQUENTLY usurp the highest places, while the truly great languish in obscurity. This is a riddle in providence whose solution will one day gladden the hearts of the upright; but it is so common a fact, that none of us should murmur if it should fall to our own lot. When our Lord was upon earth, although He is the Prince of the kings of the earth, yet He walked the footpath of weariness and service as the Servant of servants. Then what wonder is it if His followers, who are princes of the blood, should also be looked down upon as inferior and contemptible persons? The world is upside down, and therefore, the first are last and the last first. See how the servile sons of Satan lord it in the earth! What a high horse they ride! How they lift up their horn on high! Haman is in the court, while Mordecai sits in the gate; David wanders on the mountains, while Saul reigns in state; Elijah is complaining in the cave while Jezebel is boasting in the palace. Yet who would wish to take the places of the proud rebels? and who, on the other hand, might not envy the despised saints? When the wheel turns, those who are lowest rise, and the highest sink. Patience, then, believer, eternity will right the wrongs of time.

Let us not fall into the error of letting our passions and carnal appetites ride in triumph, while our nobler powers walk in the dust. Grace must reign as a prince, and make the members of the body instruments of righteousness. The Holy Spirit loves order, and He therefore sets our powers and faculties in due rank and place, giving the highest room to those spiritual faculties which link us with the great King; let us not disturb the divine arrangement, but ask for grace that we may keep under our body and bring it into subjection. We were not new created to allow our passions to rule over us, but that we, as kings, may reign in Christ Jesus over the triple kingdom of our spirit, soul, and body, to the glory of God the Father.

EVENING

"And he begged for his life, that he might die"—1 Kings 19:4.

IT WAS A remarkable thing that the man who was never to die, for whom God had ordained an infinitely better lot, the man who should be carried to heaven in a chariot of fire, and be translated, that he should not see death, should thus pray, "Let me die; I am no better than my fathers." We have here a memorable proof that God does not always answer prayer in kind, though He always does in effect. He gave Elijah something better than that which he asked for, and thus really heard and answered him. Strange was it that the lion-hearted Elijah should be so depressed by Jezebel's threat as to ask to die, and blessedly kind was it on the part of our heavenly Father that He did not take His desponding servant at his word.

There is a limit to the doctrine of the prayer of faith. We are not to expect that God will give us everything we choose to ask for. We know that we sometimes ask, and do not receive, because we ask amiss. If we ask for that which is not promised, if we run counter to the spirit which the Lord would have us cultivate; if we ask contrary to His will, or to the decrees of His providence; if we ask merely for the gratification of our own ease, and without an eye to His glory, we must not expect that we shall receive.

Yet, when we ask in faith, nothing doubting, if we receive not the precise thing asked for, we shall receive an equivalent, and more than an equivalent, for it. As one remarks, If the Lord does not pay in silver, He will in gold; and if He does not pay in gold, He will in diamonds. If He does not give you precisely what you ask for, He will give you that which is tantamount to it, and that which you will greatly rejoice to receive in lieu thereof. Be then, dear reader, much in prayer, and make this evening a season of earnest intercession, but take heed what you ask.

May 20   MORNING

"Marvelous loving-kindness"—*Psalm 17:7.*

WHEN WE GIVE our hearts with our aims, we give well, but we must often plead to a failure in this respect. Not so our Master and our Lord. His favors are always performed with the love of His heart. He does not send to us the cold meat and the broken pieces from the table of His luxury, but He dips our morsel in His own dish, and seasons our provisions with the spices of His fragrant affections. When He puts the golden tokens of His grace into our palms, He accompanies the gift with such a warm pressure of our hand, that the manner of His giving is as precious as the blessing itself. He will come into our houses upon His errands of kindness, and He will not act as some austere visitors do in the poor man's cottage, but He sits by our side, not despising our poverty, nor blaming our weakness.

Beloved, with what smiles does He speak! What golden sentences drop from His gracious lips! What embraces of affection does He bestow upon us! If He had but given us farthings, the way of His giving would have gilded them; but as it is, the costly alms are set in a golden basket by His pleasant carriage. It is impossible to doubt the sincerity of His charity, for there is a bleeding heart stamped upon the face of all His benefactions. He gives liberally and upbraids not. Not one hint that we are burdensome to Him; not one cold look for His poor pensioners; but He rejoices in His mercy, and presses us to His bosom while He is pouring out His life for us. There is a fragrance in His spikenard which nothing but His heart could produce; there is a sweetness in His honey-comb which could not be in it unless the very essence of His soul's affection had been mingled with it. Oh! the rare communion which such singular heartiness effects! May we continually taste and know the blessedness of it!

EVENING

"I drew them with cords of a man, with bands of love"—*Hosea 11:4.*

OUR HEAVENLY FATHER often draws us with the cords of love; but ah! how backward we are to run towards Him! How slowly do we respond to His gentle impulses! He draws us to exercise a more simple faith in Him; but we have not yet attained to Abraham's confidence; we do not leave our worldly cares with God, but, like Martha, we burden ourselves with much serving. Our meager faith brings leanness into our souls; we do not open our mouths wide, though God has promised to fill them. Does He not this evening draw us to trust Him? Can we not hear Him say, "Come, My child, and trust Me. The veil is rent; enter into My presence, and approach boldly to the throne of My grace. I am worthy of your fullest confidence, cast your cares on Me. Shake yourself from the dust of your cares, and put on your beautiful garments of joy." But, alas! though called with tones of love to the blessed exercise of this comforting grace, we will not come.

At another time He draws us to closer communion with Himself. We have been sitting on the doorstep of God's house, and He bids us advance into the banqueting hail and sup with Him, but we decline the honor. There are secret rooms not yet opened to us; Jesus invites us to enter them, but we hold back. Shame on our cold hearts! We are but poor lovers of our sweet Lord Jesus, not fit to be His servants, much less to be His brides, and yet He has exalted us to be bone of His bone and flesh of His flesh, married to Him by a glorious marriage.covenant. Herein is love! But it is love which takes no denial. If we obey not the gentle drawings of His love, He will send affliction to drive us into closer intimacy with Himself. Have us nearer He will. What foolish children we are to refuse those bands of love, and so bring upon our backs that scourge of small cords, which Jesus knows how to use!

May 21

MORNING

"If indeed you have tasted that the Lord is good" — I Peter 2:3.

"IF" — THEN, THIS is not a matter to be taken for granted concerning every one of the human race. *"If:"* — then there is a possibility and a probability that some may not have tasted that the Lord is gracious. *"If:"* — then this is not a general but a special mercy; and it is needful to inquire whether we know the grace of God by inward experience. There is no spiritual favor which may not be a matter for heart-searching.

But while this should be a matter of earnest and prayerful inquiry, no one ought to be content while there is any such thing as an "if" about his having tasted that the Lord is gracious. A jealous and holy distrust of self may give rise to the question even in the believer's heart, but the continuance of such a doubt would be an evil indeed. We must not rest without a desperate struggle to clasp the Savior in the arms of faith, and say, *"I know whom I have believed, and I am persuaded that He is able to keep that which I have committed to Him."* Do not rest, Oh believer, till you have a full assurance of your interest in Jesus. Let nothing satisfy you till, by the infallible witness of the Holy Spirit bearing witness with your spirit, you are certified that you are a child of God. Oh, trifle not here; let no perhaps, peradventure, if, or maybe satisfy your soul. Build on eternal verities, and verily build upon them. Get the sure mercies of David, and surely get them. Let your anchor be cast into that which is within the veil, and see to it that your soul be linked to the anchor by a cable that will not break. Advance beyond these. Abide no more in the wilderness of doubts and fears; cross the Jordan of distrust, and enter the Canaan of peace, where the Canaanite still lingers, but where the land ceases not to flow with milk and honey.

EVENING

"There is grain in Egypt" — Genesis 42:2.

FAMINE PINCHED ALL the nations, and it seemed inevitable that Jacob and his family should suffer great want; but the God of providence, who never forgets the objects of electing love, had stored a granary for His people by giving the Egyptians warning of the scarcity, and leading them to treasure up the grain of the years of plenty. Little did Jacob expect deliverance from Egypt, but there the grain was in store for him.

Believer, though all things are apparently against you, rest assured that God has made a reservation on your behalf; in the roll of your griefs there is a saving clause. Somehow He will deliver you, and somewhere He will provide for you. The quarter from which your rescue shall arise may be a very unexpected one, but help will assuredly come in your extremity, and you shall magnify the name of the Lord. If men do not feed you, ravens shall; and if earth yield not wheat, heaven shall drop with manna. Therefore be of good courage, and rest quietly in the Lord. God can make the sun rise in the west if He pleases, and make the source of distress the channel of delight. The grain in Egypt was all in the hands of the beloved Joseph; he opened or closed the granaries at will. And so the riches of providence are all in the absolute power of our Lord Jesus, who will dispense them liberally to His people. Joseph was abundantly ready to help his own family; and Jesus is unceasing in His faithful care for His brethren.

Our business is to go after the help which is provided for us: we must not sit still in despondency, but arouse ourselves. Prayer will bear us soon into the presence of our royal Brother: once before His throne we have only to ask and have. His stores are not exhausted; there is grain still. His heart is not hard, He will give the grain to us. Lord, forgive our unbelief, and this evening constrain us to draw largely from Your fullness and receive grace for grace.

MORNING   May 22

"And He led them out by the right way" — Psalm 107:7.

CHANGEFUL experience often leads the anxious believer to inquire *"Why is it thus with me?"* I looked for light, but lo, darkness came; for peace, but behold trouble. I said in my heart, my mountain stands firm, I shall never be moved. Lord, you do hide Your face, and I am troubled. It was but yesterday that I could read my title clear; today my evidences are dimmed, and my hopes are clouded. Yesterday I could climb to Pisgah's top, and view the landscape, and rejoice with confidence in my future inheritance; today, my spirit has no hopes, but many fears; no joys, but much distress.

Is this part of God's plan with me? Can this be the way in which God would bring me to heaven? Yes, it is even so. The eclipse of your faith, the darkness of your mind, the fainting of your hope, all these things are but parts of God's method of making you ripe for the great inheritance upon which you shall soon enter. These trials are for the testing and strengthening of your faith; they are waves that wash you further upon the rock; they are winds which bear your ship the more swiftly towards the desired haven. According to David's words, so it might be said of you, *"so He brings them to their desired haven."* By honor and dishonor, by evil report and by good report, by plenty and by poverty, by joy and by distress, by persecution and by peace, by all these things is the life of your soul maintained, and by each of these are you helped on your way. Oh, think not, believer, that your sorrows are out of God's plan; they are necessary parts of it. *"We must, through much tribulation, enter the kingdom."* Learn, then, even to *"count it all joy when you fall into divers temptations."*

> Oh let my trembling soul be still,
> And wait Your wise, Your holy will!
> I cannot, Lord, Your purpose see,
> Yet all is well since ruled by Thee.

EVENING

"Behold, you are beautiful, my Beloved" — Song of Solomon 1:16.

FROM EVERY POINT our Well-beloved is most fair. Our various experiences are meant by our heavenly Father to furnish fresh standpoints from which we may view the loveliness of Jesus. How amiable are our trials when they carry us aloft where we may gain clearer views of Jesus than ordinary life could afford us! We have seen Him from the top of Amana, from the top of Shenir and Hermon, and He has shone upon us as the sun in his strength; but we have seen Him also *"from the lions' dens, from the mountains of the leopards,"* and He has lost none of His loveliness. From the languishing of a sick bed, from the borders of the grave, have we turned our eyes to our soul's spouse, and He has never been otherwise than *"all fair."* Many of His saints have looked upon Him from the gloom of dungeons, and from the red flames of the stake, yet have they never uttered an ill word of Him, but have died extolling His surpassing charms.

Oh, noble and pleasant employment to be forever gazing at our sweet Lord Jesus! Is it not unspeakably delightful to view the Savior in all His offices, and to perceive Him matchless in each, to shift the kaleidoscope, as it were, and to find fresh combinations of peerless graces? In the manger and in eternity, on the cross and on His throne, in the garden and in His kingdom, among thieves or in the midst of cherubim, He is everywhere *"altogether lovely."* Examine carefully every little act of His life, and every trait of His character, and He is as lovely in the minute as in the majestic. Judge Him as you will, you cannot censure; weigh Him as you please, and He will not be found wanting. Eternity shall not discover the shadow of a spot in our Beloved, but rather, as ages revolve, His hidden glories shall shine forth with yet more inconceivable splendor, and His unutterable loveliness shall more and more ravish all celestial minds.

May 23

MORNING

"The LORD will perfect that which concerns me"—Psalm 138:8.

MOST MANIFESTLY THE confidence which the Psalmist here expressed was a divine confidence. He did not say, "I have grace enough to perfect that which concerns me; my faith is so steady that it will not stagger; my love is so warm that it will never grow cold; my resolution is so firm that nothing can move it." No, his dependence was on the Lord alone. If we indulge in any confidence which is not grounded on the Rock of ages, our confidence is worse than a dream, it will fall upon us, and cover us with its ruins, to our sorrow and confusion. All that Nature spins, time will unravel, to the eternal confusion of all who are clothed therein.

The Psalmist was wise, he rested upon nothing short of the Lord's work. It is the Lord who has begun the good work within us; it is He who has carried it on; and if He does not finish it, it never will be complete. If there be one stitch in the celestial garment of our righteousness which we are to insert ourselves, then we are lost; but this is our confidence, the Lord who began will perfect. He has done it all, must do it all, and will do it all. Our confidence must not be in what we have done, nor in what we have resolved to do, but entirely in what the Lord will do.

Unbelief insinuates, saying, You will never be able to stand. Look at the evil of your heart, you can never conquer sin; remember the sinful pleasures and temptations of the world that beset you, you will be certainly allured by them and led astray. Ah! yes, we should indeed perish if left to our own strength. If we had alone to navigate our frail vessels over so rough a sea, we might well give up the voyage in despair; but, thanks be to God, He will perfect that which concerns us, and bring us to the desired haven. We can never be too confident when we confide in Him alone, and never too much concerned to have such a trust.

EVENING

"You have bought Me no sweet cane with money"—Isaiah 43:24.

WORSHIPERS AT the temple were accustomed to bring presents of sweet perfumes to be burned upon the altar of God. But Israel, in the time of her backsliding, became ungenerous, and made but few votive offerings to her Lord. This was an evidence of coldness of heart towards God and His house. Reader, does this never occur with you? Might not the complaint of the text be occasionally, if not frequently, brought against you? Those who are poor in pocket, if rich in faith, will be accepted none the less because their gifts are small; but, poor reader, do you give in fair proportion to the Lord, or is the widow's mite kept back from the sacred treasury?

The rich believer should be thankful for the talent entrusted to him, but should not forget his large responsibility, for where much is given much will be required. But, rich reader, are you mindful of your obligations, and rendering to the Lord according to the benefit received? Jesus gave His blood for us, what shall we give to Him? We are His, and all that we have, for He has purchased us unto Himself. Can we act as if we were our own? Oh for more consecration! And to this end, Oh for more love!

Blessed Jesus, how good it is of You to accept our sweet cane bought with money! Nothing is too costly as a tribute to Your unrivalled love, and yet You do receive with favor the smallest sincere token of affection! You do receive our poor forget-me-nots and love-tokens as though they were intrinsically precious, though indeed they are but as the bunch of wild flowers which the child brings to its mother. Never may we grow niggardly towards You, and from this hour never may we hear You complain of us again for withholding the gifts of our love. We will give You the first fruits of our increase, and pay You tithes of all, and then we will confess "of Your own have we given You."

MORNING

"Blessed be God, who has not turned away my prayer" — Psalm 66:20.

IN LOOKING BACK upon the character of our prayers, if we do it honestly, we shall be filled with wonder that God has ever answered them. There may be some who think their prayers worthy of acceptance, as the Pharisee did. But the true Christian, in a more enlightened retrospect, weeps over his prayers, and if he could retrace his steps he would desire to pray more earnestly. Remember, Christian, how cold your prayers have been. When in your closet you should have wrestled as Jacob did; but instead thereof, your petitions have been faint and few, far removed from that humble, believing, persevering faith, which cries, *"I will not let You go except You bless me."* Yet, wonderful to say, God has heard these cold prayers of yours, and not only heard, but answered them. Reflect also, how infrequent have been your prayers, unless you have been in trouble, and then you have gone often to the mercy-seat: but when deliverance has come, where has been your constant supplication?

Yet, even though you have ceased to pray as once you did, God has not ceased to bless. When you have neglected the mercy-seat, God has not deserted it, but the bright light of the Shekinah has always been visible between the wings of the cherubim. Oh! it is marvelous that the Lord should regard those intermittent spasms of importunity which come and go with our necessities. What a God is He thus to hear the prayers of those who come to Him when they have pressing wants, but neglect Him when they have received a mercy; who approach Him when they are forced to come, but who almost forget to address Him when mercies are plentiful and sorrows are few. Let His gracious kindness in hearing such prayers touch our hearts, so that we may henceforth be found *"Praying always with all prayer and supplication in the Spirit."*

EVENING

"Only keep your conversation worthy of the gospel of Christ" — Philippians 1:27.

THE WORD *"CONVERSATION"* does not merely mean our talk and converse with one another, but the whole course of our life and behavior in the world. The Greek word signifies the actions and the privileges of citizenship: and thus we are commanded to let our actions, as citizens of the New Jerusalem, be such as becomes the gospel of Christ.

What sort of conversation is this? In the first place, the gospel is very simple. So Christians should be simple and plain in their habits. There should be about our manner, our speech, our dress, our whole behavior, that simplicity which is the very soul of beauty. The gospel is pre-eminently true, it is gold without dross; and the Christian's life will be lusterless and valueless without the jewel of truth. The gospel is a very fearless gospel, it boldly proclaims the truth, whether men like it or not; we must be equally faithful and unflinching. But the gospel is also very gentle. Mark this spirit in its Founder: *"a bruised reed He will not break."* Some professors are sharper than a thorn-hedge; such men are not like Jesus. Let us seek to win others by the gentleness of our words and acts. The gospel is very loving. It is the message of the God of love to a lost and fallen race. Christ's last command to His disciples was, *"Love one another."* Oh for more real, hearty union and love to all the saints; for more tender compassion towards the souls of the worst and vilest of men! We must not forget that the gospel of Christ is holy. It never excuses sin: it pardons it, but only through an atonement.

If our life is to resemble the gospel, we must shun, not merely the grosser vices, but everything that would hinder our perfect conformity to Christ. For His sake, for our own sakes, and for the sake of others, we must strive day by day to let our conversation be more in accordance with His gospel.

May 25

MORNING

"Forsake me not, O LORD" — Psalm 38:21.

FREQUENTLY WE PRAY that God would not forsake us in the hour of trial and temptation, but we too much forget that we have need to use this prayer at all times. There is no moment of our life, however holy, in which we can do without His constant upholding. Whether in light or in darkness, in communion or in temptation, we alike need the prayer, *"Forsake me not, Oh Lord." "Hold me up, and I shall be safe."* A little child, while learning to walk, always needs the nurse's aid. The ship left by the pilot drifts at once from her course.

We cannot do without continued aid from above; let it then be your prayer today, "Forsake me not." Father, forsake not Your child, lest he fall by the hand of the enemy. Shepherd, forsake not Your lamb, lest he wander from the safety of the fold. Great Husbandman, forsake not Your plant, lest it wither and die. *"Forsake me not, Oh Lord,"* now; and forsake me not at any moment of my life. Forsake me not in my joys, lest they absorb my heart. Forsake me not in my sorrows, lest I murmur against You. Forsake me not in the day of my repentance, lest I lose the hope of pardon, and fall into despair. And forsake me not in the day of my strongest faith, lest faith degenerate into presumption. Forsake me not, for without You I am weak, but with You I am strong. Forsake me not, for my path is dangerous, and full of snares, and I cannot do without Your guidance. The hen forsakes not her brood, do then evermore cover me with Your feathers, and permit me under Your wings to find my refuge. *"Be not far from me, Oh Lord, for trouble is near, for there is none to help." "Leave me not, neither forsake me, Oh God of my salvation!"*

> Oh ever in our cleansed breast,
> Bid Your Eternal Spirit rest;
> And make our secret soul to be
> A temple pure and worthy Thee.

EVENING

"And rising up that same hour they returned to Jerusalem ... And they told what things happened in the way, and how He was known to them" — Luke 24:33-35.

WHEN THE TWO disciples had reached Emmaus, and were refreshing themselves at the evening meal, the mysterious stranger who had so enchanted them upon the road, took bread and broke it, made Himself known to them, and then vanished out of their sight. They had constrained Him to abide with them, because the day was far spent; but now, although it was much later, their love was a lamp to their feet, yes, wings also. They forgot the darkness, their weariness was all gone, and forthwith they journeyed back the threescore furlongs to tell the gladsome news of a risen Lord, who had appeared to them by the way. They reached the Christians in Jerusalem, and were received by a burst of joyful news before they could tell their own tale. These early Christians were all on fire to speak of Christ's resurrection, and to proclaim what they knew of the Lord; they made common property of their experiences.

This evening let their example impress us deeply. We too must bear witness concerning Jesus. John's account of the sepulchre needed to be lamented by Peter; and Mary could speak of something further still; combined, we have a full testimony from which nothing can be spared. We have each of us peculiar gifts and special manifestations; but the one object God has in view is the perfecting of the whole body of Christ. We must, therefore, bring our spiritual possessions and lay them at the apostle's feet, and make distribution unto all of what God has given to us. Keep back no part of the precious truth, but speak what you know, and testify what you have seen. Let not the toil or darkness, or possible unbelief of your friends, weigh one moment in the scale. Up, and be marching to the place of duty, and there tell what great things God has shown to your soul.

MORNING   May 26

"Cast your burden on the LORD and He will keep you" — Psalm 55:22.

    CARE, EVEN THOUGH exercised upon legitimate objects, if carried to excess, has in it the nature of sin. The precept to avoid anxious care is earnestly inculcated by our Savior, again and again. It is reiterated by the apostles; and it is one which cannot be neglected without involving transgression. For the very essence of anxious care is the imagining that we are wiser than God, and the thrusting ourselves into His place to do for Him that which He has undertaken to do for us. We attempt to think of that which we fancy He will forget; we labor to take upon ourselves our weary burden, as if He were unable or unwilling to take it for us. Now this disobedience to His plain precept, this unbelief in His Word, this presumption in intruding upon His province, is all sinful.

    Yet more than this, anxious care often leads to acts of sin. He who cannot calmly leave his affairs in God's hand, but will carry his own burden, is very likely to be tempted to use wrong means to help himself. This sin leads to a forsaking of God as our counselor, and resorting instead to human wisdom. This is going to the *"broken cistern"* instead of to the *"fountain;"* a sin which was laid against Israel of old. Anxiety makes us doubt God's loving-kindness, and thus our love to Him grows cold, we feel mistrust, and thus grieve the Spirit of God, so that our prayers become hindered, our consistent example marred, and our life one of self-seeking. Thus lack of confidence in God leads us to wander far from Him. But if through simple faith in His promise, we cast each burden as it comes upon Him, and are *"anxious for nothing"* because He undertakes to care for us, it will keep us close to Him, and strengthen us against much temptation. *"You will keep him in perfect peace whose mind is stayed on You, because lie trusts in You."*

EVENING
"Continue in the faith"—Acts 14:22.

    PERSEVERANCE IS THE badge of true saints. The Christian life is not a beginning only in the ways of God, but also a continuance in the same as long as life lasts. It is with a Christian as it was with the great Napoleon: he said, "Conquest has made me what I am, and conquest must maintain me." So, under God, dear brother in the Lord, conquest has made you what you are, and conquest must sustain you. Your motto must be, "Excelsior." He only is a true conqueror, and shall be crowned at the last, who continues till war's trumpet is blown no more.

    Perseverance is, therefore, the target of all our spiritual enemies. The world does not object to your being a Christian for a time, if she can but tempt you to cease your pilgrimage, and settle down to buy and sell with her in Vanity Fair. The flesh will seek to ensnare you, and to prevent your pressing on to glory. It is weary work being a pilgrim; come, give it up. Am I always to be mortified? Am I never to be indulged? Give me at least a furlough from this constant warfare. Satan will make many a fierce attack on your perseverance; it will be the mark for all his arrows. He will strive to hinder you in service; he will insinuate that you are doing no good; and that you want rest. He will endeavor to make you weary of suffering, he will whisper, *"Curse God, and die."* Or he will attack your steadfastness: What is the good of being so zealous? Be quiet like the rest; sleep as do others, and let your lamp go out as the other virgins do. Or he will assail your doctrinal sentiments: Why do you hold to these denominational creeds? Sensible men are getting more liberal; they are removing the old landmarks; fall in with the times. Wear your shield. Christian, therefore, close upon your armor, and cry mightily unto God, that by His Spirit you may endure to the end.

May 27   MORNING

"So Mephibosheth lived in Jerusalem. For he always sat at the king's table. And he was lame in both his feet" — *2 Samuel 9:13.*

MEPHIBOSHETH WAS NO great ornament to a royal table, yet he had a continual place at David's board, because the king could see in his face the features of the beloved Jonathan. Like Mephibosheth, we may cry unto the King of Glory, *"What is Your servant, that You should look upon such a dead dog as I am?"* But still the Lord indulges as with most familiar intercourse with Himself, because He sees in our countenances the remembrance of His dearly-beloved Jesus. The Lord's people are dear for another's sake. Such is the love which the Father bears to His only begotten, that for His sake He raises His lowly brethren from poverty and banishment, to courtly companionship, noble rank, and royal provision. Their deformity shall not rob them of their privileges. Lameness is no bar to sonship; the cripple is as much the heir as if he could run like Asahel. Our right does not limp, though our might may. A king's table is a noble hiding-place for lame legs, and at the gospel feast we learn to glory in infirmities, because the power of Christ rests upon us.

Yet grievous disability may mar the persons of the best-loved saints. Here is one feasted by David, and yet so lame in both his feet that he could not go up with the king when he fled from the city, and was therefore maligned and injured by his servant Ziba. Saints whose faith is weak, and whose knowledge is slender, are great losers; they are exposed to many enemies, and cannot follow the king wheresoever he goes. This disease frequently arises from falls. Bad nursing in their spiritual infancy often causes converts to fall into a despondency from which they never recover, and sin in other cases brings broken bones. Lord, help the lame to leap like an hart, and satisfy all Your people with the bread of Your table!

EVENING

"What is your servant, that you should look on such a dead dog as I am?" — *2 Samuel 9:8.*

IF Mephibosheth was thus humbled by David's kindness, what shall we be in the presence of our gracious Lord? The more grace we have, the less we shall think of ourselves, for grace, like light, reveals our impurity. Eminent saints have scarcely known to what to compare themselves, their sense of unworthiness has been so clear and keen. "I am," says holy Rutherford, "a dry and withered branch, a piece of dead carcass, dry bones, and not able to step over a straw." In another place he writes, "Except as to open outbreakings, I want nothing of what Judas and Cain had."

The meanest objects in nature appear to the humbled mind to have a preference above itself, because they have never contracted sin: a dog may be greedy, fierce, or filthy, but it has no conscience to violate, no Holy Spirit to resist. A dog may be a worthless animal, and yet by a little kindness it is soon won to love its master, and is faithful unto death; but we forget the goodness of the Lord, and follow not at His call. The term *"dead dog"* is the most expressive of all terms of contempt, but it is none too strong to express the self-abhorrence of instructed believers. They do not affect mock modesty, they mean what they say, they have weighed themselves in the balances of the sanctuary, and found out the vanity of their nature. At best, we are but clay, animated dust, mere walking hillocks; but viewed as sinners, we are monsters indeed.

Let it be published in heaven as a wonder, that the Lord Jesus should set His heart's love upon such as we are. Dust and ashes though we be, we must and will *"magnify the exceeding greatness of His grace."* Could not His heart find rest in heaven? Must He needs come to these tents of Kedar for a spouse, and choose a bride upon whom the sun had looked? Oh heavens and earth, break forth into a song, and give all glory to our sweet Lord Jesus.

May 28   MORNING

"Whom He justified, these He also glorified" — Romans 8:30.

HERE IS A precious truth for you, believer. You may be poor, or in suffering, or unknown, but for your encouragement take a review of your "calling" and the consequences that flow from it, and especially that blessed result here spoken of. As surely as you are God's child today, so surely shall all your trials soon be at an end, and you shall be rich to all the intents of bliss. Wait awhile, and that weary head shall wear the crown of glory, and that hand of labor shall grasp the palm-branch of victory. Lament not your troubles, but rather rejoice that before long you will be where *"there shall be neither sorrow, nor crying, neither shall there be any more pain."* The chariots of fire are at your door, and a moment will suffice to bear you to the glorified. The everlasting song is almost on your lip. The portals of heaven stand open for you.

Think not that you can fail of entering into rest. If He has called you, nothing can divide you from His love. Distress cannot sever the bond; the fire of persecution cannot burn the link; the hammer of hell cannot break the chain. You are secure; that voice which called you at first, shall call you yet again from earth to heaven, from death's dark gloom to immortality's unuttered splendors. Rest assured, the heart of Him who has justified you beats with infinite love towards you. You shall soon be with the glorified, where your portion is; you are only waiting here to be made fit for the inheritance, and that done, the wings of angels shall carry you far away, to the mount of peace, and joy, and blessedness, where,

> Far from a world of grief and sin,
> With God eternally shut in.
> You shall rest forever and ever.

EVENING

"I recall this to my mind; therefore I have hope"— Lamentations 3:21.

MEMORY IS frequently the bondslave of despondency. Despairing minds call to remembrance every dark foreboding in the past, and dilate upon every gloomy feature in the present; thus memory, clothed in sackcloth, presents to the mind a cup of mingled gall and wormwood. There is, however, no necessity for this. Wisdom can readily transform memory into an angel of comfort. That same recollection which in its left hand brings so many gloomy omens, may be trained to bear in its right a wealth of hopeful signs. She need not wear a crown of iron, she may encircle her brow with a fillet of gold, all spangled with stars.

Thus it was in Jeremiah's experience. In the previous verse memory had brought him to deep humiliation of soul: *"My soul has them still in remembrance, and is humbled in me;"* and now this same memory restored him to life and comfort. *"I recall this to my mind; therefore I have hope."* Like a two-edged sword, his memory first killed his pride with one edge, and then slew his despair with the other.

As a general principle, if we would exercise our memories more wisely, we might, in our very darkest distress, strike a match which would instantaneously kindle the lamp of comfort. There is no need for God to create a new thing upon the earth in order to restore believers to joy; if they would prayerfully rake the ashes of the past, they would find light for the present; and if they would turn to the book of truth and the throne of grace, their candle would soon shine as before. Be it ours to remember the loving-kindness of the Lord, and to rehearse His deeds of grace. Let us open the volume of recollection which is so richly illuminated with memorials of mercy, and we shall soon be happy. Thus memory may be, as Coleridge calls it, "the bosom-spring of joy," and when the Divine Comforter bends it to His service, it may be chief among earthly comforters.

May 29   MORNING

"You ... hate wickedness" — Psalm 45:7.

"BE YOU ANGRY, and sin not." There can hardly be goodness in a man if he be not angry at sin; he who loves truth must hate every false way. How our Lord Jesus hated it when the temptation came! Thrice it assailed Him in different forms, but ever He met it with, "Get you behind me, Satan." He hated it in others; none the less fervently because He showed His hate oftener in tears of pity than in words of rebuke; yet what language could be more stern, more Elijah-like, than the words, *"Woe unto you, scribes and Pharisees, hypocrites! For you devour widows' houses, and for a pretence make long prayer."* He hated wickedness, so much that He bled to wound it to the heart; He died that it might die; He was buried that He might bury it in His tomb; and He rose that He might forever trample it beneath His feet. Christ is in the Gospel, and that Gospel is opposed to wickedness in every shape. Wickedness arrays itself in fair garments, and imitates the language of holiness; but the precepts of Jesus, like His famous scourge of small cords, chase it out of the temple, and will not tolerate it in the Church.

So, too, in the heart where Jesus reigns, what war there is between Christ and Belial! And when our Redeemer shall come to be our Judge, those thundering words, *"Depart, you cursed,"* which are, indeed, but a prolongation of His life-teaching concerning sin, shall manifest His abhorrence of iniquity. As warm as is His love to sinners, so hot is His hatred of sin; as perfect as is His righteousness, so complete shall be the destruction of every form of wickedness. Oh you glorious champion of right, and destroyer of wrong, *"for this cause has God, even Your God, anointed You with the oil of gladness above Your fellows."*

EVENING

"Cursed before Jehovah is the one who rises up and builds this city of Jericho" — Joshua 6:26.

SINCE HE WAS cursed who rebuilt Jericho, much more the man who labors to restore Popery among us. In our fathers' days the gigantic walls of Popery fell by the power of their faith, the perseverance of their efforts, and the blast of their gospel trumpets; and now there are some who would rebuild that accursed system upon its old foundations.

Oh Lord, be pleased to thwart their unrighteous endeavors, and pull down every stone which they build. It should be a serious business with us to be thoroughly purged of every error which may have a tendency to foster the spirit of Popery, and when we have made a clean sweep at home we should seek in every way to oppose its all too rapid spread abroad in the church and in the world. This last can be done in secret by fervent prayer, and in public by decided testimony. We must warn with judicious boldness those who are inclined towards the errors of Rome; we must instruct the young in gospel truth, and tell them of the black doings of Popery in the olden times. We must aid in spreading the light more thoroughly through the land, for priests, like owls, hate daylight. Are we doing all we can for Jesus and the gospel? If not, our negligence plays into the hands of priestcraft.

What are we doing to spread the Bible, which is the Pope's bane and poison? Are we casting abroad good, sound gospel writings? Luther once said, "The devil hates goose quills," and, doubtless, he has good reason, for ready writers, by the Holy Spirit's blessing, have done his kingdom much damage. If the thousands who will read this short word this night will do all they can to hinder the rebuilding of this accursed Jericho, the Lord's glory shall speed among the sons of men. Reader, what can you do? What will you do?

MORNING

May 30

"Take us the foxes, the little foxes that spoil the vines" — Song of Solomon 2:15

A LITTLE THORN may cause much suffering. A little cloud may hide the sun. *"Little foxes spoil the vines;"* and little sins do mischief to the tender heart. These little sins burrow in the soul, and make it so full of that which is hateful to Christ, that He will hold no comfortable fellowship and communion with us. A great sin cannot destroy a Christian, but a little sin can make him miserable. Jesus will not walk with His people unless they drive out every known sin. He says, *"If you keep My commandments, you shall abide in My love, even as I have kept My Father's commandments and abide in His love."*

Some Christians very seldom enjoy their Savior's presence. How is this? Surely it must be an affliction for a tender child to be separated from his father. Are you a child of God, and yet satisfied to go on without seeing your Father's face? What! you the spouse of Christ, and yet content without His company! Surely, you have fallen into a sad state, for the chaste spouse of Christ mourns like a dove without her mate, when he has left her. Ask, then, the question, what has driven Christ from you? He hides His face behind the wall of your sins. That wall may be built up of little pebbles, as easily as of great stones. The sea is made of drops; the rocks are made of grains: and the sea which divides you from Christ may be filled with the drops of your little sins. And the rock which has well nigh wrecked your barque, may have been made by the daily working of the coral insects of your little sins. If you would live with Christ, and walk with Christ, and see Christ, and have fellowship with Christ, take heed of *"the little foxes that spoil the vines, for our vines have tender grapes."* Jesus invites you to go with Him and take them. He will surely, like Samson, take the foxes at once and easily. Go with Him to the hunting.

EVENING

"So that we no longer should serve sin" — Romans 6:6.

CHRISTIAN, WHAT HAVE you to do with sin? Has it not cost you enough already? Burnt child, will you play with the fire? What! when you have already been between the jaws of the lion, will you step a second time into his den? Have you not had enough of the old serpent? Did he not poison all your veins once, and will you play upon the hole of the asp, and put your hand upon the cockatrice's den a second time? Oh, be not so mad, so foolish! Did sin ever yield you real pleasure? Did you find solid satisfaction in it? If so, go back to your old drudgery, and wear the chain again, if it delight you. But inasmuch as sin did never give you what it promised to bestow, but deluded you with lies, be not a second time snared by the old fowler; be free, and let the remembrance of your ancient bondage forbid you to enter the net again!

It is contrary to the designs of eternal love, which all have an eye to your purity and holiness; therefore run not counter to the purposes of your Lord. Another thought should restrain you from sin. Christians can never sin cheaply; they pay a heavy price for iniquity. Transgression destroys peace of mind, obscures fellowship with Jesus, hinders prayer, brings darkness over the soul; therefore be not the serf and bondman of sin.

There is yet a higher argument: each time you *"serve sin,"* you have *"Crucified the Lord afresh, and put Him to an open shame."* Can you bear that thought? Oh! if you have fallen into any special sin during this day, it may be my Master has sent this admonition this evening, to bring you back before you have backslidden very far. Turn to Jesus anew; He has not forgotten His love to you; His grace is still the same. With weeping and repentance, come to His footstool, and you shall be once more received into His heart; you shall be set upon a rock again, and your goings shall be established.

May 31

MORNING

"The king himself also crossed over the brook Kidron" — 2 Samuel 15:23.

DAVID PASSED THAT gloomy brook when fleeing with his mourning company from his traitor son. The man after God's own heart was not exempt from trouble, no, his life was full of it. He was both the Lord's Anointed, and the Lord's Afflicted. Why then should we expect to escape? At sorrow's gates the noblest of our race have waited with ashes on their heads; why then should we complain as though some strange thing had happened unto us?

The King of kings Himself was not favored with a more cheerful or royal road. He passed over the filthy ditch of Kidron, through which the filth of Jerusalem flowed. God had one Son without sin, but not a single child without the rod. It is a great joy to believe that Jesus has been *"tempted in all points like as we are."* What is our Kidron this morning? Is it a faithless friend, a sad bereavement, a slanderous reproach, a dark foreboding? The King has passed over all these. Is it bodily pain, poverty, persecution, or contempt? Over each of these Kidrons the King has gone before us. *"In all our afflictions He was afflicted."* The idea of strangeness in our trials must be banished at once and forever, for He who is the Head of all saints, knows by experience the grief which we think so peculiar. All the citizens of Zion must be free of the Honorable Company of Mourners, of which the Prince Immanuel is Head and Captain.

Notwithstanding the abasement of David, he yet returned in triumph to his city, and David's Lord arose victorious from the grave; let us then be of good courage, for we also shall win the day. We shall yet with joy draw water out of the wells of salvation, though now for a season we have to pass by the noxious streams of sin and sorrow. Courage, soldiers of the Cross, the King Himself triumphed after going over Kidron, and so shall you.

EVENING

"Who heals all your diseases" — Psalm 103:3.

HUMBLING AS IS the statement, yet the fact is certain, that we are all more or less suffering under the disease of sin. What a comfort to know that we have a great Physician who is both able and willing to heal us! Let us think of Him awhile tonight. His cures are very speedy. There is life in a look at Him; His cures are radical. He strikes at the center of the disease; and hence, His cures are sure and certain. He never fails, and the disease never returns. There is no relapse where Christ heals; no fear that His patients should be merely patched up for a season, He makes new men of them: a new heart also does He give them, and a right spirit does He put within them.

He is well skilled in all diseases. Physicians generally have some specialty. Although they may know a little about almost all our pains and ills, there is usually one disease which they have studied above all others; but Jesus Christ is thoroughly acquainted with the whole of human nature. He is as much at home with one sinner as with another, and never yet did He meet with an out-of-the-way case that was difficult to Him. He has had extraordinary complications of strange diseases to deal with, but He has known exactly with one glance of His eye how to treat the patient. He is the only universal doctor; and the medicine He gives is the only true catholicon, healing in every instance. Whatever our spiritual malady may be, we should apply at once to this Divine Physician. There is no brokenness of heart which Jesus cannot bind up. *"His blood cleanses from all sin."* We have but to think of the myriads who have been delivered from all sorts of diseases through the power and virtue of His touch, and we shall joyfully put ourselves in His hands. We trust Him, and sin dies; we love Him, and grace lives; we wait for Him, and grace is strengthened; we see Him as He is, and grace is perfected forever.

MORNING   June 1

"The evening and the morning were the first day" — Genesis 1:5.

WAS IT SO, EVEN in the beginning? Did light and darkness divide the realm of time in the first day? Then little wonder is it if I have also changes in my circumstances from the sunshine of prosperity to the midnight of adversity. It will not always be the blaze of noon even in my soul concerns. I must expect at seasons to mourn the absence of my former joys, and seek my Beloved in the night. Nor am I alone in this, for all the Lord's beloved ones have had to sing the mingled song of judgment and of mercy, of trial and deliverance, of mourning and of delight. It is one of the arrangements of Divine providence that day and night shall not cease either in the spiritual or natural creation till we reach the land of which it is written, *"there is no night there."* What our heavenly Father ordains is wise and good.

What, then, my soul, is it best for you to do? Learn first to be content with this divine order, and be willing, with Job, to receive what seems to be evil from the hand of the Lord as well as good. Study next, to make the outgoings of the morning and the evening to rejoice. Praise the Lord for the sun of joy when it rises, and for the gloom of evening as it falls. There is beauty both in sunrise and sunset, sing of it, and glorify the Lord. Like the nightingale, pour forth your notes at all hours. Believe that the night is as useful as the day. The dews of grace fall heavily in the night of sorrow. The stars of promise shine forth gloriously amid the darkness of grief. Continue your service under all changes. If in the day your watchword be labor, at night exchange it for watch. Every hour has its duty, continue then in your calling as the Lord's servant until He shall suddenly appear in His glory. My soul, your evening of old age and death is drawing near, dread it not, for it is part of the day; and the Lord has said, *"I will cover him all the day long."*

EVENING

"He will make her a wilderness like Eden" — Isaiah 5:13.

I SEE in vision a howling wilderness, a great and terrible desert, like to the Sahara. I perceive nothing in it to relieve the eye, all around I am wearied with a vision of hot and arid sand, strewn with ten thousand bleaching skeletons of wretched men who have expired in anguish, having lost their way in the pitiless waste. What an appalling sight! How horrible! a sea of sand without a bound, and without an oasis, a cheerless graveyard for a race forlorn! But behold and wonder! Upon a sudden, springing up from the scorching sand I see a plant of renown; and as it grows it buds, the bud expands it is a rose, and at its side a lily bows its modest head; and miracle of miracles! as the fragrance of those flowers is diffused the wilderness is transformed into a fruitful field, and all around it blossoms exceedingly, the glory of Lebanon is given unto it, the excellency of Carmel and Sharon. Call it not Sahara, call it Paradise. Speak not of it any longer as the valley of deathshade, for where the skeletons lay bleaching in the sun, behold a resurrection is proclaimed, and up spring the dead, a mighty army, full of life immortal.

Jesus is that plant of renown, and His presence makes all things new. Nor is the wonder less in each individual's salvation. Yonder I behold you, dear reader, cast out, an infant, not swathed, unwashed, defiled with your own blood, left to be food for beasts of prey. But lo, a jewel has been thrown into your bosom by a divine hand, and for its sake you have been pitied and tended by divine providence, you are washed and cleansed from your defilement, you are adopted into heaven's family, the fair seal of love is upon your forehead, and the ring of faithfulness is on your hand. You are now a prince unto God, though once an orphan, cast away. Oh prize exceedingly the matchless power and grace which changes deserts into gardens, and makes the barren heart to sing for joy.

June 2   MORNING

"For the flesh lusts against the Spirit and the Spirit against the flesh" — Galatians 5:17.

 IN EVERY BELIEVER'S heart there is a constant struggle between the old nature and the new. The old nature is very active. and loses no opportunity of plying all the weapons of its deadly armory against newborn grace; while on the other hand, the new nature is ever on the watch to resist and destroy its enemy. Grace within us will employ prayer, and faith, and hope, and love, to cast out the evil; it takes unto it the *"whole armor of God,"* and wrestles earnestly. These two opposing natures will never cease to struggle so long as we are in this world. The battle of Christian with *"Apollyon"* lasted three hours, but the battle of Christian with himself lasted all the way from the Wicket Gate to the river Jordan. The enemy is so securely entrenched within us that he can never be driven out while we are in this body: but although we are closely beset, and often in sore conflict, we have an Almighty helper, even Jesus, the Captain of our salvation, who is ever with us, and who assures us that we shall eventually come off more than conquerors through Him. With such assistance the new-born nature is more than a match for its foes.

 Are you fighting with the adversary today? Are Satan, the world, and the flesh, all against you? Be not discouraged nor dismayed. Fight on! For God Himself is with you; Jehovah Nissi is your banner, and Jehovah Rophi is the healer of your wounds. Fear not, you shall overcome, for who can defeat Omnipotence? Fight on, *"looking unto Jesus;"* and though long and stern be the conflict, sweet will be the victory, and glorious the promised reward.

> From strength to strength go on;
> Wrestle, and fight, and pray,
> Tread all the powers of darkness down,
> And win the well-fought day.

EVENING
"Good Teacher" — Matthew 19:16.

 IF THE YOUNG MAN in the gospel used this title in speaking to our Lord, how much more fitly may I thus address Him! He is indeed my Master in both senses, a ruling Master and a teaching Master. I delight to run upon His errands, and to sit at His feet. I am both His servant and His disciple, and count it my highest honor to own the double character. If He should ask me why I call Him "good," I should have a ready answer. It is true that *"there is none good but one, that is, God."* but then He is God, and all the goodness of Deity shines forth in Him.

 In my experience, I have found Him good, so good, indeed, that all the good I have has come to me through Him. He was good to me when I was dead in sin, for He raised me by His Spirit's power; He has been good to me in all my needs, trials, struggles, and sorrows. Never could there be a better Master, for His service is freedom, His rule is love. I wish I were one thousand part as good a servant. When He teaches me He is unspeakably good, His doctrine is divine, His manner is condescending, His spirit is gentleness itself. No error mingles with His instruction, pure is the golden truth which He brings forth, and all His teachings lead to goodness, sanctifying as well as edifying the disciple. Angels find Him a good Master and delight to pay their homage at His footstool. The ancient saints proved Him to be a good Master, and each of them rejoiced to sing, *"I am Your servant, Oh Lord!"* My own humble testimony must certainly be to the same effect. I will bear this witness before my friends and neighbors, for possibly they may be led by my testimony to seek my Lord Jesus as their Master. Oh that they would do so! They would never repent so wise a deed. If they would but take His easy yoke, they would found themselves in so royal a service that they would enlist in it forever.

MORNING June 3

"These were the potters and those who lived among plants and hedges. They lived there with the king for his work" — *1 Chronicles 4:23.*

POTTERS WERE NOT the very highest grade of workers, but "the king" needed potters, and therefore they were in royal service, although the material upon which they worked was nothing but clay. We, too, may be engaged in the most menial part of the Lord's work, but it is a great privilege to do anything for "the king;" and therefore we will abide in our calling, hoping that, *"although we have lain among the pots, yet shall we be as the wings of a dove covered with silver and her feathers with yellow gold."*

The text tells us of those who dwell among plants and hedges, having rough, rustic, hedging and ditching work to do. They may have desired to live in the city, amid its life, society, and refinement, but they kept their appointed places, for they also were doing the king's work. The place of our habitation is fixed, and we are not to remove from it out of whim and caprice, but seek to serve the Lord in it, by being a blessing to those among whom we reside. These potters and gardeners had royal company, for they dwelt *"with the king,"* and although among hedges and plants, they dwelt with the king there. No lawful place, or gracious occupation, however mean, can debar us from communion with our divine Lord. In visiting hovels, swarming lodging-houses, workhouses, or jails, we may go with the king. In all works of faith we may count upon Jesus' fellowship. It is when we are in His work that we may reckon upon His smile.

You unknown workers who are occupied for your Lord amid the dirt and wretchedness of the lowest of the low, be of good cheer, for jewels have been found upon dunghills before now, earthen pots have been filled with heavenly treasure, and ill weeds have been transformed into precious flowers. Dwell with the King for His work and when He writes His chronicles your name shall be recorded.

EVENING
"He humbled Himself!" — *Philippians 2:8.*

JESUS IS THE great teacher of lowliness of heart. We need daily to learn of Him. See the Master taking a towel and washing His disciples' feet! Follower of Christ, will you not humble yourself? See Him as the Servant of servants, and surely you cannot be proud!

Is not this sentence the compendium of His biography, *"He humbled Himself"*? Was He not on earth always stripping off first one robe of honor and then another, till, naked, He was fastened to the cross, and there did He not empty out His inmost self, pouring out His life-blood, giving up for all of us, till they laid Him penniless in a borrowed grave? How low was our dear Redeemer brought! How then can we be proud? Stand at the foot of the cross, and count the purple drops by which you have been cleansed; see the thorn-crown; mark His scourged shoulders, still gushing with crimsoned rills; see hands and feet given up to the rough iron, and His whole self to mockery and scorn; see the bitterness, and the pangs, and the throes of inward grief, showing themselves in His outward frame; hear the thrilling shriek, *"My God, my God, why have You forsaken Me?"* And if you do not lie prostrate on the ground before that cross, you have never seen it: if you are not humbled in the presence of Jesus, you do not know Him. You were so lost that nothing could save you but the sacrifice of God's only begotten.

Think of that, and as Jesus stooped for you, bow yourself in lowliness at His feet. A sense of Christ's amazing love to us has a greater tendency to humble us than even a consciousness of our own guilt. May the Lord bring us in contemplation to Calvary, then our position will no longer be that of the pompous man of pride, but we shall take the humble place of one who loves much because much has been forgiven him. Pride cannot live beneath the cross. Let us sit there and learn our lesson, and then rise and carry it into practice.

June 4

MORNING

"The kindness and love of God our Savior" — Titus 3:4.

HOW SWEET IT is to behold the Savior communing with His own beloved people! There can be nothing more delightful than, by the Divine Spirit, to be led into this fertile field of delight. Let the mind for an instant consider the history of the Redeemer's love, and a thousand enchanting acts of affection will suggest themselves, all of which have had for their design the weaving of the heart into Christ, and the intertwining of the thoughts and emotions of the renewed soul with the mind of Jesus. When we meditate upon this amazing love, and behold the all-glorious Kinsman of the Church endowing her with all His ancient wealth, our souls may well faint for joy.

Who is he that can endure such a weight of love? That partial sense of it which the Holy Spirit is sometimes pleased to afford, is more than the soul can contain; how transporting must be a complete view of it! When the soul shall have understanding to discern all the Savior's gifts, wisdom wherewith to estimate them, and time in which to meditate upon them, such as the world to come will afford us, we shall then commune with Jesus in a nearer manner than at present. But who can imagine the sweetness of such fellowship? It must be one of the things which have not entered into the heart of man, but which God has prepared for them that love Him. Oh, to burst open the door of our Joseph's granaries, and see the plenty which he has stored up for us! This will overwhelm us with love. By faith we see, as in a mirror darkly, the reflected image of his unbounded treasures, but when we shall actually see the heavenly things themselves, with our own eyes, how deep will be the stream of fellowship in which our soul shall bathe itself! Till then our loudest sonnets shall be reserved for our loving benefactor, Jesus Christ our Lord, whose love to us is wonderful, passing the love of women.

EVENING

"Received up in glory" — 1 Timothy 3:16.

WE HAVE SEEN our well-beloved Lord in the days of His flesh, humiliated and sore vexed; for He was *"despised and rejected of men, a man of sorrows, and acquainted with grief."* He whose brightness is as the morning, wore the sackcloth of sorrow as His daily dress; shame was His mantle, and reproach was His vesture. Yet now, inasmuch as He has triumphed over all the powers of darkness upon the bloody tree, our faith beholds our King returning with dyed garments from Edom, robed in the splendor of victory. How glorious must He have been in the eyes of seraphs, when a cloud received Him out of mortal sight, and He ascended up to heaven!

Now He wears the glory which He had with God or ever the earth was, and yet another glory above all, that which He has well earned in the fight against sin, death, and hell. As victor He wears the illustrious crown. Hark how the song swells high! It is a new and sweeter song: *"Worthy is the Lamb that was slain, for He has redeemed us unto God by His blood!"* He wears the glory of an Intercessor who can never fail, of a Prince who can never be defeated, of a Conqueror who has vanquished every foe, of a Lord who has the heart's allegiance of every subject. Jesus wears all the glory which the pomp of heaven can bestow upon Him, which ten thousand times ten thousand angels can minister to Him.

You cannot with your utmost stretch of imagination conceive His exceeding greatness; yet there will be a further revelation of it when He shall descend from heaven in great power, with all the holy angels. *"Then shall He sit upon the throne of His glory."* Oh, the splendor of that glory! It will ravish His peoples's hearts. Nor is this the close, for eternity shall sound His praise, *"Your throne, Oh God, is forever and ever!"* Reader, if you would joy in Christ's glory hereafter, He must be glorious in your sight now. Is He so?

MORNING

June 5

"The LORD shut him in" — Genesis 7:16.

NOAH WAS SHUT in away from all the world by the hand of divine love. The door of electing purpose interposes between us and the world which lies in the wicked one. We are not of the world even as our Lord Jesus was not of the world. Into the sin, the gaiety, the pursuits of, the multitude we cannot enter; we cannot play in the streets of Vanity Fair with the children of darkness, for our heavenly Father has shut us in.

Noah was shut in with his God. *"Come into the ark,"* was the Lord's invitation, by which He clearly showed that He Himself intended to dwell in the ark with His servant and his family. Thus all the chosen dwell in God and God in them. Happy people to be enclosed in the same circle which contains God in the Trinity of His persons, Father, Son, and Spirit. Let us never be inattentive to that gracious call, *"Come, my people, enter into your chambers, and shut your doors about you, and hide yourself as it were for a little moment until the indignation be passed over."* (Isa. 26:20)

Noah was so shut in that no evil could reach him. Floods did but lift him heavenward, and winds did but bear him on his way. Outside of the ark all was ruin, but inside all was rest and peace. Without Christ we perish, but in Christ Jesus there is perfect safety.

Noah was so shut in that he could not even desire to come out, and those who are in Christ Jesus are in Him forever. They shall go no more out forever, for eternal faithfulness has shut them in, and infernal malice cannot drag them out. The Prince of the house of David shuts and no man opens; and when once in the last days as Master of the house He shall rise up and shut the door, it will be in vain for mere professors to knock, and cry Lord, Lord open unto us, for that same door which shuts in the wise virgins will shut out the foolish forever. Lord, shut me in by Your grace.

EVENING

"He that does not love never knew God" — 1 John 4:8.

THE DISTINGUISHING mark of a Christian is his confidence in the love of Christ, and the yielding of his affections to Christ in return. First, faith sets her seal upon the mark by enabling the soul to say with the apostle, *"Christ loved me and gave Himself for me."* Then love gives the countersign, and stamps upon the heart gratitude and love to Jesus in return. *"We love Him because He first loved us."*

In those grand old ages, which are the heroic period of the Christian religion, this double mark was clearly to be seen in all believers in Jesus; they were men who knew the love of Christ, and rested upon it as a man leans upon a staff whose trustworthiness he has tried. The love which they felt towards the Lord was not a quiet emotion which they hid within themselves in the secret chamber of their souls, and which they only spoke of in their private assemblies when they met on the first day of the week, and sang hymns in honor of Christ Jesus the crucified. No, it was a passion with them of such a vehement and all-consuming energy, that it was visible in all their actions, spoken in their common talk, and looked out of their eyes even in their commonest glances. Love to Jesus was a flame which fed upon the core and heart of their being; and, therefore, from its own force burned its way into the outer man, and shone there. Zeal for the glory of King Jesus was the seal and mark of all genuine Christians. Because of their dependence upon Christ's love they dared much, and because of their love to Christ they did much, and it is the same now.

The children of God are ruled in their inmost powers by love, the love of Christ constrains them; they rejoice that divine love is set upon them, they feel it shed abroad in their hearts by the Holy Ghost, which is given unto them, and then by force of gratitude they love the Savior with a pure heart, fervently. My reader, do you love Him? Before you sleep give an honest answer to a weighty question!

June 6   MORNING

"Behold, I am vile!" — Job 40:4.

ONE CHEERING WORD, poor lost sinner, for you! You think you must not come to God because you are vile. Now, there is not a saint living on earth but has been made to feel that he is vile. If Job, and Isaiah, and Paul were all obliged to say I am vile, oh, poor sinner, will you be ashamed to join in the same confession? If divine grace does not eradicate all sin from the believer, how do you hope to do it yourself? And if God loves His people while they are yet vile, do you think your vileness will prevent His loving you? Believe on Jesus, you outcast of the world's society! Jesus calls you, and such as you are.

> Not the righteous, not the righteous;
> Sinners, Jesus came to call.

Even now say, You have died for sinners; I am a sinner, Lord Jesus sprinkle Your blood on me. If you will confess your sin you shall find pardon. If, now, with all your heart, you will say, I am vile, wash me, you shall be washed now. If the Holy Spirit shall enable you from your heart to cry

> Just as I am, without one plea,
> But that Thy blood was shed for me
> And that Thou bidd'st me come to Thee,
> Oh Lamb of God, I come!

you shall rise from reading this morning's portion with all your sins pardoned. And though you did wake this morning with every sin that man has ever committed on your head, you shall rest tonight accepted in the Beloved; though once degraded with the rags of sin, you shall be adorned with a robe of righteousness, and appear white as the angels are. For *"now,"* mark it, *"Now is the accepted time."* If you *"believe on Him who justifies the ungodly you are saved."* Oh! may the Holy Spirit give you saving faith in Him who receives the vilest.

EVENING

"Are they Israelites? So am I!" — 2 Corinthians 11:22.

WE HAVE HERE a personal claim, and one that needs proof. The apostle knew that his claim was indisputable, but there are many persons who have no right to the title who yet claim to belong to the Israel of God. If we are with confidence declaring, "So am I also an Israelite," let us only say it after having searched our heart as in the presence of God. But if we can give proof that we are following Jesus, if we can from the heart say, I trust Him wholly, trust Him only, trust Him simply, trust Him now, and trust Him ever, then the position which the saints of God hold belongs to us. Then all their enjoyments are our possessions; we may be the very least in Israel, *"less than the least of all saints,"* yet since the mercies of God belong to the saints as saints, and not as advanced saints, or well-taught saints, we may put in our plea, and say, *"Are they Israelites? so am I;"* therefore the promises are mine, grace is mine, glory will be mine.

The claim, rightfully made, is one which will yield untold comfort. When God's people are rejoicing that they are His, what a happiness if they can say, "So am I!" 'When they speak of being pardoned, and justified, and accepted in the Beloved, how joyful to respond, "Through the grace of God, so am I." But this claim not only has its enjoyments and privileges, but also its conditions and duties. We must share with God's people in cloud as well as in sunshine. When we hear them spoken of with contempt and ridicule for being Christians, we must come boldly forward and say, *"So am I."* When we see them working for Christ, giving their time, their talent, their whole heart to Jesus, we must be able to say, *"So do I."* Oh let us prove our gratitude by our devotion, and live as these who, having claimed a privilege, are willing to take the responsibility connected with it.

MORNING June 7

"You who love the LORD, hate evil" — *Psalm 97:10.*

YOU HAVE GOOD reason to hate evil, for only consider what harm it has already done you. Oh, what a world of mischief sin has brought into your heart! Sin blinded you so that you could not see the beauty of the Savior; it made you deaf so that you could not hear the Redeemer's tender invitations. Sin turned your feet into the way of death, and poured poison into the very fountain of your being; it tainted your heart, and made it *"deceitful above all things, and desperately wicked."* Oh, what a creature you were when evil had done its utmost with you, before divine grace interposed! You were an heir of wrath even as others; you did *"run with the multitude to do evil."*

Such were all of us; but Paul reminds us, *"but you are washed, but you are sanctified, but you are justified in the name of the Lord Jesus, and by the Spirit of our God."* We have good reason, indeed, for hating evil when we look back and trace its deadly workings. Such mischief did evil do us, that our souls would have been lost had not omnipotent love interfered to redeem us. Even now it is an active enemy, ever watching to do us hurt, and to drag us to perdition. Therefore *"hate evil,"* Oh Christians, unless you desire trouble. If you would strew your path with thorns, and plant nettles in your death-pillow, then neglect to *"hate evil;"* but if you would live a happy life, and die a peaceful death, then walk in all the ways of holiness, hating evil, even unto the end. If you truly love your Savior, and would honor Him, then *"hate evil."* We know of no cure for the love of evil in a Christian like abundant intercourse with the Lord Jesus. Dwell much with Him, and it is impossible for you to be at peace with sin.

> Order my footsteps by Your Word,
> And make my heart sincere
> Let sin have no dominion, Lord,
> But keep my conscience clear.

EVENING

"So be fervent" — *Revelation 3:19.*

IF YOU WOULD see souls converted, if you would hear the cry that *"the kingdoms of this world have become the kingdoms of our Lord;"* if you would place crowns upon the head of the Savior, and His throne lifted high, then be filled with zeal. For, under God, the way of the world's conversion must be by the zeal of the church. Every grace shall do exploits, but this shall be first; prudence, knowledge, patience, and courage will follow in their places, but zeal must lead the van. It is not the extent of your knowledge, though that is useful; it is not the extent of your talent, though that is not to be despised; it is your zeal that shall do great exploits.

This zeal is the fruit of the Holy Spirit: it draws its vital force from the continued operations of the Holy Ghost in the soul. If our inner life dwindles, if our heart beats slowly before God, we shall not know zeal. But if all be strong and vigorous within, then we cannot but feel a loving anxiety to see the kingdom of Christ come, and His will done on earth, even as it is in heaven. A deep sense of gratitude will nourish Christian zeal. Looking to the hole of the pit whence we were dug, we find abundant reason why we should spend and be spent for God. And zeal is also stimulated by the thought of the eternal future. It looks with tearful eyes down to the flames of hell, and it cannot slumber: it looks up with anxious gaze to the glories of heaven, and it cannot but arouse itself. It feels that time is short compared with the work to be done, and therefore it devotes all that it has to the cause of its Lord. And it is ever strengthened by the remembrance of Christ's example. He was clothed with zeal as with a cloak. How swift the chariot-wheels of duty went with Him! He knew no loitering by the way. Let us prove that we are His disciples by manifesting the same spirit of zeal.

June 8

MORNING

"For many fell down slain, because the war was of God" — 1 Chronicles 5:22.

WARRIOR, FIGHTING under the banner of the Lord Jesus, observe this verse with holy joy, for as it was in the days of old so is it now, if the war be of God the victory is sure. The sons of Reuben, and the Gadites, and the half tribe of Manasseh could barely muster five and forty thousand fighting men, and yet in their war with the Hagarites, they slew *"man, an hundred thousand," "for they cried to God in the battle, and He was entreated of them, because they put their trust in Him."* The Lord saves not by many nor by few; it is ours to go forth in Jehovah's name if we be but a handful of men, for the Lord of Hosts is with us for our Captain. They did not neglect buckler, and sword, and bow, neither did they place their trust in these weapons; we must use all fitting means, but our confidence must rest in the Lord alone, for He is the sword and the shield of His people.

The great reason of their extraordinary success lay in the fact that *"the war was of God."* Beloved, in fighting with sin without and within, with error doctrinal or practical, with spiritual wickedness in high places or low places, with devils and the devil's allies, you are waging Jehovah's war, and unless He Himself can be worsted, you need not fear defeat. Quail not before superior numbers, shrink not from difficulties or impossibilities, flinch not at wounds or death, smite with the two-edged sword of the Spirit, and the slain shall lie in heaps. The battle is the Lord's and He will deliver His enemies into our hands. With steadfast boot, strong hand, dauntless heart, and flaming zeal, rush to the conflict, and the hosts of evil shall fly like chaff before the gale.

> To him that overcomes,
> A crown of life shall be;
> He with the King of glory
> Shall reign eternally.

EVENING

"You shall see now whether or not My word shall come to pass to you" — Numbers 11:23.

GOD HAD MADE a positive promise to Moses that for the space of a whole month He would feed the vast host in the wilderness with flesh. Moses, being overtaken by a fit of unbelief, looks to the outward means, and is at a loss to know how the promise can be fulfilled. He looked to the creature instead of the Creator. But does the Creator expect the creature to fulfill His promise for Him? No; He who makes the promise ever fulfills it by His own unaided omnipotence. If He speaks, it is done by Himself. His promises do not depend for their fulfillment upon the co-operation of the puny strength of man.

We can at once perceive the mistake which Moses made. And yet how commonly we do the same! God has promised to supply our needs, and we look to the creature to do what God has promised to do; and then, because we perceive the creature to be weak and feeble, we indulge in unbelief. Why look we to that quarter at all? Will you look to the top of the Alps for summer heat? will you journey to the north pole to gather fruits ripened in the sun? Verily, you would act no more foolishly if you did this than when you look to the weak for strength, and to the creature to do the Creator's work.

Let us, then, put the question on the right footing. The ground of faith is not the sufficiency of the visible means for the performance of the promise, but the all-sufficiency of the invisible God, who will most surely do as He has said. If after clearly seeing that the onus lies with the Lord and not with the creature, we dare to indulge in mistrust, the question of God comes home mightily to us: *"Has the Lord's hand waxed short?"* May it happen, too, in His mercy, that with the question there may flash upon our souls that blessed declaration,*"You shall see now whether My word shall come to pass unto you or not."*

MORNING
June 9

"The LORD has done great things for us and we are glad" — Psalm 126:3.

SOME CHRISTIANS ARE sadly prone to look on the dark side of everything, and to dwell more upon what they have gone through than upon what God has done for them. Ask for their impression of the Christian life, and they will describe their continual conflicts, their deep afflictions, their sad adversities, and the sinfulness of their hearts, yet with scarcely any allusion to the mercy and help which God has vouchsafed them. But a Christian whose soul is in a healthy state, will come forward joyously, and say, I will speak, not about myself, but to the honor of my God. He has brought me up out of a horrible pit, and out of the miry clay, and set my feet upon a rock, and established my goings: and He has put a new song in my mouth, even praise unto our God. *"The Lord has done great things for me, whereof I am glad."*

Such an abstract of experience as this is the very best that any child of God can present. It is true that we endure trials, but it is just as true that we are delivered out of them. It is true that we have our corruptions, and mournfully do we know this, but it is quite as true that we have an all-sufficient Savior, who overcomes these corruptions, and delivers us from their dominion. In looking back, it would be wrong to deny that we have been in the Slough of Despond, and have crept along the Valley of Humiliation, but it would be equally wicked to forget that we have been through them safely and profitably; we have not remained in them, thanks to our Almighty Helper and Leader, who has brought us *"out into a wealthy place."* The deeper our troubles, the louder our thanks to God, who has led us through all, and preserved us until now. Our griefs cannot mar the melody of our praise, we reckon them to be the bass part of our life's song, *"He has done great things for us, and we are glad."*

EVENING
"Search the Scriptures" — John 5:39.

THE GREEK WORD here rendered search signifies a strict, close, diligent, curious search, such as men make when they are seeking gold, or hunters when they are in earnest after game. We must not rest content with having given a superficial reading to a chapter or two, but with the candle of the Spirit we must deliberately seek out the hidden meaning of the word.

Holy Scripture requires searching, for much of it can only be learned by careful study. There is milk for babies, but also meat for strong men. The rabbis wisely say that a mountain of matter hangs upon every word, yes, upon every title of Scripture. Tertullian exclaims, I adore the fullness of the Scriptures. No man who merely skims the book of God can profit thereby; we must dig and mine until we obtain the hid treasure. The door of the word only opens to the key of diligence. The Scriptures claim searching. They are the writings of God, bearing the divine stamp and imprimatur: who shall dare to treat them with levity? He who despises them despises the God who wrote them. God forbid that any of us should leave our Bibles to become swift witnesses against us in the great day of account.

The word of God will repay searching. God does not bid us sift a mountain of chaff with here and there a grain of wheat in it, but the Bible is winnowed grain; we have but to open the granary door and find it. Scripture grows upon the student. It is full of surprises. Under the teaching of the Holy Spirit, to the searching eye it glows with splendor of revelation, like a vast temple paved with worked gold, and roofed with rubies, emeralds, and all manner of gems. No merchandise like the merchandise of Scripture truth. Lastly, the Scriptures reveal Jesus: *"They are they which testify of Me."* No more powerful motive can be urged upon Bible readers than this: he who finds Jesus finds life, heaven, all things. Happy he who, searching his Bible, discovers his Savior.

June 10   MORNING

"We live to the Lord" — Romans 14:8.

IF GOD HAD willed it, each of us might have entered heaven at the moment of conversion. It was not absolutely necessary for our preparation for immortality that we should tarry here. It is possible for a man to be taken to heaven, and to be found fit to be a partaker of the inheritance of the saints in light, though he has but just believed in Jesus. It is true that our sanctification is a long and continued process, and we shall not be perfected till we lay aside our bodies and enter within the veil; but nevertheless, had the Lord so willed it, He might have changed us from imperfection to perfection, and have taken us to heaven at once. Why then are we here? Would God keep His children out of paradise a single moment longer than was necessary? Why is the army of the living God still on the battle-field when one charge might give them the victory? Why are His children still wandering here and there through a maze, when a solitary word from His lips would bring them into the center of their hopes in heaven?

The answer is that they are here that they may *"live to the Lord,"* and may bring others to know His love. We remain on earth as sowers to scatter good seed; as plowmen to break up the fallow ground; as heralds publishing salvation. We are here as the *"salt of the earth,"* to be a blessing to the world. We are here to glorify Christ in our daily life. We are here as workers for Him, and as "workers together with Him." Let us see that our life answers its end. Let us live earnest, useful, holy lives, to *"the praise of the glory of His grace."* Meanwhile we long to be with Him, and daily sing:

> My heart is with Him on His throne,
> And ill can brook delay;
> Each moment listening for the voice,
> "Rise up, and come away."

EVENING

"And those Scriptures are they which are witnessing about Me" — John 5:39.

JESUS CHRIST IS the Alpha and Omega of the Bible. He is the constant theme of its sacred pages; from first to last they testify of Him. At the creation we at once discern Him as one of the sacred Trinity; we catch a glimpse of Him in the promise of the woman's seed; we see Him typified in the ark of Noah; we walk with Abraham, as He sees Messiah's day; we dwell in the tents of Isaac and Jacob, feeding upon the gracious promise; we hear the venerable Israel talking of Shiloh; and in the numerous types of the law, we find the Redeemer abundantly foreshadowed. Prophets and kings, priests and preachers, all look one way; they all stand as the cherubs did over the ark, desiring to look within, and to read the mystery of God's great propitiation. Still more manifestly in the New Testament we find our Lord the one pervading subject. It is not an ingot here and there, or dust of gold thinly scattered, but here you stand upon a solid floor of gold; for the whole substance of the New Testament is Jesus crucified, and even its closing sentence is bejewelled with the Redeemer's name.

We should always read Scripture in this light; we should consider the Word to be as a mirror into which Christ looks down from heaven; and then we, looking into it, see His face reflected as in a mirror; darkly, it is true, but still in such a way as to be a blessed preparation for seeing Him as we shall see Him face to face. This volume contains Jesus Christ's letters to us, perfumed by His love. These pages are the garments of our King, and they all smell of myrrh, and aloes, and cassia. Scripture is the royal chariot in which Jesus rides, and it is paved with love for the daughters of Jerusalem. The Scriptures are the swaddling bands of the holy child Jesus; unroll them and you find your Savior. The quintessence of the word of God is Christ.

MORNING — June 11

"We love Him because He first loved us" — 1 John 4:19.

THERE IS NO light in the planet but that which proceeds from the sun; and there is no true love to Jesus in the heart but that which comes from the Lord Jesus Himself. From this overflowing fountain of the infinite love of God, all our love to God must spring. This must ever be a great and certain truth, that we love Him for no other reason than because He first loved us. Our love to Him is the fair offspring of His love to us. Cold admiration, when studying the works of God, anyone may have, but the warmth of love can only be kindled in the heart by God's Spirit. How great the wonder that such as we should ever have been brought to love Jesus at all! How marvelous that when we had rebelled against Him, He should, by a display of such amazing love, seek to draw us back. No! never should we have had a grain of love towards God unless it had been sown in us by the sweet seed of His love to us.

Love, then, has for its parent the love of God poured out in the heart. But after it is thus divinely born, it must be divinely nourished. Love is an exotic; it is not a plant which will flourish naturally in human soil, it must be watered from above. Love to Jesus is a flower of a delicate nature, and if it received no nourishment but that which could be drawn from the rock of our hearts it would soon wither. As love comes from heaven, so it must feed on heavenly bread. It cannot exist in the wilderness unless it be fed by manna from on high. Love must feed on love. The very soul and life of our love to God is His love to us.

> I love Thee, Lord; but all the love is Thine,
> For by Thy love I live,
> I am as nothing, and rejoice to be
> Emptied, and lost, and swallowed up in Thee.

EVENING

"There He broke the arrows of the bow, the shield, and the sword, and the battle" — Psalm 76:3.

OUR REDEEMER'S glorious cry of *"It is finished,"* was the death-knell of all the adversaries of His people, the breaking of *"the arrows of the bow, the shield, and the sword, and the battle."* Behold the hero of Golgotha using His cross as an anvil, and His woes as a hammer, dashing to shivers bundle after bundle of our sins, those poisoned *"arrows of the bow;"* trampling on every indictment, and destroying every accusation. What glorious blows the mighty Breaker gives with a hammer far more ponderous than the fabled weapon of Thor! How the diabolical darts fly to fragments, and the infernal bucklers are broken like potters' vessels! Behold, He draws from its sheath of hellish workmanship the dread sword of Satanic power! He snaps it across His knee, as a man breaks the dry wood of a fagot, and casts it into the fire.

Beloved, no sin of a believer can now be an arrow mortally to wound him; no condemnation can now be a sword to kill him. For the punishment of our sin was borne by Christ, a full atonement was made for all our iniquities by our blessed Substitute and Surety. Who now accuses? Who now condemns? Christ has died, yes rather, has risen again. Jesus has emptied the quivers of hell, has quenched every fiery dart, and broken off the head of every arrow of wrath; the ground is strewn with the splinters and relics of the weapons of hell's warfare, which are only visible to us to remind us of our former danger, and of our great deliverance. Sin has no more dominion over us. Jesus has made an end of it, and put it away forever. Oh you enemy, destructions are come to a perpetual end. Talk of all the wondrous works of the Lord, you who make mention of His name, keep not silence, neither by day, nor when the sun goes to his rest. Bless the Lord, Oh my soul.

June 12   MORNING

"You are weighed in the balances and are found lacking" — Daniel 5:27.

IT IS WELL frequently to weigh ourselves in the scale of God's Word. You will find it a holy exercise to read some Psalm of David, and as you meditate upon each verse, to ask yourself, Can I say this? Have I felt as David felt? Has my heart ever been broken on account of sin, as his was when he penned his penitential Psalms? Has my soul been full of true confidence in the hour of difficulty as his was when he sang of God's mercies in the cave of Adullam, or in the holds of Engedi? Do I take the cup of salvation and call upon the name of the Lord? Then turn to the life of Christ, and as you read, ask yourselves how far you are conformed to His likeness. Endeavor to discover whether you have the meekness, the humility, the lovely spirit which He constantly inculcated and displayed.

Take, then, the epistles, and see whether you can go with the apostle in what he said of his experience. Have you ever cried out as he did: *"Oh wretched man that I am! who shall deliver me from the body of this death"*? Have you ever felt his self-abasement? Have you seemed to yourself the chief of sinners, and less than the least of all saints? Have you known anything of his devotion? Could you join with him and say, *"For me to live is Christ, and to die is gain"*?

If we thus read God's Word as a test of our spiritual condition, we shall have good reason to stop many a time and say, Lord, I feel I have never yet been here, Oh bring me here! give me true penitence, such as this I read of. Give me real faith; give me warmer zeal; inflame me with more fervent love; grant me the grace of meekness; make me more like Jesus. Let me no longer be found wanting when weighed in the balances of the sanctuary, lest I be found wanting in the scales of judgement. *"Judge yourselves that you be not judged."*

EVENING

"Who saved us and called us with a holy calling" — 2 Timothy 1:9.

THE APOSTLE USES the perfect tense and says, *"Who has saved us."* Believers in Christ Jesus are saved. They are not looked upon as persons who are in a hopeful state, and may ultimately be saved, but they are already saved. Salvation is not a blessing to be enjoyed upon the dying bed, and to be sung of in a future state above, but a matter to be obtained, received, promised, and enjoyed now. The Christian is perfectly saved in God's purpose; God has ordained him unto salvation, and that purpose is complete. He is saved also as to the price which has been paid for him: *"It is finished"* was the cry of the Savior before He died. The believer is also perfectly saved in His covenant head, for as he fell in Adam, so he lives in Christ. This complete salvation is accompanied by a holy calling. Those whom the Savior saved upon the cross are in due time effectually called by the power of God the Holy Spirit unto holiness: they leave their sins; they endeavor to be like Christ; they choose holiness, not out of any compulsion, but from the stress of a new nature, which leads them to rejoice in holiness just as naturally as before they delighted in sin.

God neither chose them nor called them because they were holy, but He called them that they might be holy, and holiness is the beauty produced by His workmanship in them. The excellencies which we see in a believer are as much the work of God as the atonement itself. Thus is brought out very sweetly the fullness of the grace of God. Salvation must be of grace, because the Lord is the author of it: and what motive but grace could move Him to save the guilty? Salvation must be of grace, because the Lord works in such a manner that our righteousness is forever excluded. Such is the believer's privilege, a present salvation; such is the evidence that he is called to it, a holy life.

MORNING   June 13

"And whoever will, let him take the water of life freely" — Revelation 22:17.

JESUS SAYS, *"take freely."* He wants no payment or preparation. He seeks no recommendation from our virtuous emotions. If you have no good feelings, if you be but willing, you are invited; therefore come! You have no belief and no repentance, come to Him, and He will give them to you. Come just as you are, and take *"freely," "without money and without price."* He gives Himself to needy ones. The drinking fountains at the corners of our streets are valuable institutions; and we can hardly imagine any one so foolish as to feel for his purse, when he stands before one of them, and to cry, I cannot drink because I have not five pounds in my pocket. However poor the man is, there is the fountain, and just as he is he may drink of it. Thirsty passengers, as they go by, whether they are dressed in fustian or in broadcloth, do not look for any warrant for drinking; its being there is their warrant for taking its water freely. The liberality of some good friends has put the refreshing crystal there and we take it, and ask no questions.

Perhaps the only persons who need go thirsty through the street where there is a drinking fountain, are the fine ladies and gentlemen who are in their carriages. They are very thirsty, but cannot think of being so vulgar as to get out to drink. It would bemean them, they think, to drink at a common drinking fountain: so they ride by with parched lips. Oh, how many there are who are rich in their own supposed good works and cannot therefore come to Christ! I will not be saved, they say, in the same way as the harlot or the swearer. What! go to heaven in the same way as a chimney sweep. Is there no pathway to glory but the path which led the thief there? I will not be saved that way. Such proud boasters must remain without the living water; but, *"And whoever will, let him take the water of life freely."*

EVENING

"Remove far from me vanity and lies" — Proverbs 30:8.   *"Oh my God, be not far from me" — Psalm 38:21.*

HERE WE HAVE two great lessons: what to deprecate and what to supplicate. The happiest state of a Christian is the holiest state. As there is the most heat nearest to the sun, so there is the most happiness nearest to Christ. No Christian enjoys comfort when his eyes are fixed on vanity; he finds no satisfaction unless his soul is quickened in the ways of God. The world may win happiness elsewhere, but he cannot. I do not blame ungodly men for rushing to their pleasures. Why should I? Let them have their fill. That is all they have to enjoy. A converted wife who despaired of her husband was always very kind to him, for she said, I fear that this is the only world in which he will be happy, and therefore I have made up my mind to make him as happy as I can in it.

Christians must seek their delights in a higher sphere than the insipid frivolities or sinful enjoyments of the world. Vain pursuits are dangerous to renewed souls. We have heard of a philosopher who, while he looked up to the stars, fell into a pit; but how deeply do they fall who look down. Their fall is fatal. No Christian is safe when his soul is slothful, and his God is far from him. Every Christian is always safe as to the great matter of his standing in Christ, but he is not safe as regards his experience in holiness, and communion with Jesus in this life. Satan does not often attack a Christian who is living near to God. It is when the Christian departs from his God, becomes spiritually starved, and endeavors to feed on vanities, that the devil discovers his vantage hour. He may sometimes stand foot to foot with the child of God who is active in his Master's service, but the battle is generally short. He who slips as he goes down into the Valley of Humiliation, every time he takes a false step invites Apollyon to assail him. Oh for grace to walk humbly with our God!

June 14   MORNING

"Delight yourself also in the LORD" — Psalm 37:4.

THE TEACHING OF these words must seem very surprising to those who are strangers to vital godliness, but to the sincere believer it is only the inculcation of a recognized truth. The life of the believer is here described as a delight in God, and we are thus certified of the great fact that true religion overflows with happiness and joy. Ungodly persons and mere professors never look upon religion as a joyful thing; to them it is service, duty, or necessity, but never pleasure or delight. If they attend to religion at all, it is either that they may gain thereby, or else because they dare not do otherwise. The thought of delight in religion is so strange to most men, that no two words in their language stand further apart than holiness and delight.

But believers who know Christ, understand that delight and faith are so blessedly united, that the gates of hell cannot prevail to separate them. They who love God with all their hearts, find that His ways are ways of pleasantness, and all His paths are peace. Such joys, such brimful delights, such overflowing blessednesses, do the saints discover in their Lord, that so far from serving Him from custom, they would follow Him though all the world cast out His name as evil. We fear not God because of any compulsion; our faith is no chain, our profession is no bondage, we are not dragged to holiness, nor driven to duty. No, our piety is our pleasure, our hope is our happiness, our duty is our delight.

Delight and true religion are as allied as root and flower; as indivisible as truth and certainty; they are, in fact, two precious jewels glittering side by side in a setting of gold.

> 'Tis when we taste Thy love,
> Our joys divinely grow,
> Unspeakable like those above,
> And heaven begins below.

EVENING

"Oh Lord, to us belongs the shame of our faces ... because we have sinned against You"
— Daniel 9:8.

A DEEP SENSE and clear sight of sin, its heinousness, and the punishment which it deserves, should make us lie low before the throne. We have sinned as Christians. Alas! that it should be so. Favored as we have been, we have yet been ungrateful; privileged beyond most, we have not brought forth fruit in proportion. Who is there, although he may long have been engaged in the Christian warfare, that will not blush when he looks back upon the past? As for our days before we were regenerate, may they be forgiven and forgotten; but since then, though we have not sinned as before, yet we have sinned against light and against love; light which has really penetrated our minds, and love in which we have rejoiced. Oh, the atrocity of the sin of a pardoned soul! An unpardoned sinner sins cheaply compared with the sin of one of God's own elect ones, who has had communion with Christ and leaned his head upon Jesus' bosom.

Look at David! Many will talk of his sin, but I pray you look at his repentance, and hear his broken bones, as each one of them moans out its painful confession! Mark his tears, as they fall upon the ground, and the deep sighs with which he accompanies the softened music of his harp! We have erred: let us, therefore, seek the spirit of penitence. Look, again, at Peter! We speak much of Peter's denying his Master. Remember, also, that it is written, *"He wept bitterly."* We have no denials of our Lord to be lamented with tears? Alas! these sins of ours, before and after conversion, would consign us to the place of inextinguishable fire if it were not for the sovereign mercy which has made us to differ, snatching us like brands from the burning. My soul, bow down under a sense of your natural sinfulness, and worship your God. Admire the grace which saves you, the mercy which spares you the love which pardons you!

MORNING   June 15

"And Sarah said, God has made me laugh, so that all who hear will laugh with me" — Genesis 21:6.

IT WAS FAR above the power of nature, and even contrary to its laws, that the aged Sarah should be honored with a son; and even so it is beyond all ordinary rules that I, a poor, helpless, undone sinner, should find grace to bear about in my soul the indwelling Spirit of the Lord Jesus. I, who once despaired, as well I might, for my nature was as dry, and withered, and barren, and accursed as a howling wilderness, even I have been made to bring forth fruit unto holiness. Well may my mouth be filled with joyous laughter, because of the singular, surprising grace which I have received of the Lord, for I have found Jesus, the promised seed, and He is mine forever. This day will I lift up psalms of triumph unto the Lord who has remembered my low estate, for *"my heart rejoices in the Lord, my horn is exalted in the Lord; my mouth is enlarged over my enemies, because I rejoice in Your salvation."*

I would have all those that hear of my great deliverance from hell, and my most blessed visitation from on high, laugh for joy with me. I would surprise my family with my abundant peace; I would delight my friends with my ever-increasing happiness; I would edify the Church with my grateful confessions; and even impress the world with the cheerfulness of my daily conversation. Bunyan tells us that Mercy laughed in her sleep, and no wonder when she dreamed of Jesus; my joy shall not stop short of hers while my Beloved is the theme of my daily thoughts. The Lord Jesus is a deep sea of joy: my soul shall dive therein, shall be swallowed up in the delights of His society. Sarah looked on her Isaac, and laughed with excess of rapture, and all her friends laughed with her; and you, my soul, look on your Jesus, and bid heaven and earth unite in your joy unspeakable.

EVENING

"He that opens and no one shuts" — Revelation 3:7.

JESUS IS THE keeper of the gates of paradise and before every believing soul He sets an open door, which no man or devil shall be able to close against it. What joy it will be to find that faith in Him is the golden key to the everlasting doors. My soul, do you carry this key in your bosom, or are you trusting to some deceitful pick-lock, which will fail you at last? Hear this parable of the preacher, and remember it. The great King has made a banquet, and He has proclaimed to all the world that none shall enter but those who bring with them the fairest flower that blooms. The spirits of men advance to the gate by thousands, and they bring each one the flower which he esteems the queen of the garden; but in crowds they are driven from the royal presence, and enter not into the festive halls. Some bear in their hand the deadly nightshade of superstition, or the flaunting poppies of Rome, or the hemlock of self-righteousness, but these are not dear to the King, the bearers are shut out of the pearly gates.

My soul, have you gathered the rose of Sharon? Do you wear the lily of the valley in your bosom constantly? If so, when you come up to the gates of heaven you will know its value, for you have only to show this choicest of flowers, and the Porter will open: not for a moment will He deny you admission, for to that rose the Porter opens ever. You shall find your way with the rose of Sharon in your hand up to the throne of God Himself, for heaven itself possesses nothing that excels its radiant beauty, and of all the flowers that bloom in paradise there is none that can rival the lily of the valleys. My soul, get Calvary's blood-red rose into your hand by faith, by love wear it, by communion preserve it, by daily watchfulness make it your all in all, and you shall be blessed beyond all bliss, happy beyond a dream. Jesus, be mine forever, my God, my heaven, my all.

June 16

MORNING

"And I give to them eternal life. And they shall never perish" — *John 10:28.*

THE CHRISTIAN should never think or speak lightly of unbelief. For a child of God to mistrust His love, His truth, His faithfulness, must be greatly displeasing to Him. How can we ever grieve Him by doubting His upholding grace? Christian! it is contrary to every promise of God's precious Word that you should ever be forgotten or left to perish. If it could be so, how could He be true who has said, *"Can a woman forget her sucking child, that she should not have compassion on the son of her womb? Yes, they may forget, yet will I never forget you."*

What were the value of that promise: *"The mountains shall depart, and the hills be removed; but My kindness shall not depart from you, neither shall the covenant of My peace be removed, says the Lord that has mercy on you"*? Where were the truth of Christ's words, *"I give unto My sheep eternal life; and they shall never perish, neither shall any man pluck them out of My hand. My Father, which gave them Me, is greater than all; and no man is able to pluck them out of My Father's hand"*? Where were the doctrines of grace? They would be all disproved if one child of God should perish. Where were the veracity of God, His honor, His power, His grace, His covenant, His oath, if any of those for whom Christ has died, and who have put their trust in Him, should nevertheless be cast away?

Banish those unbelieving fears which so dishonor God. Arise, shake yourself from the dust, and put on your beautiful garments. Remember it is sinful to doubt His Word wherein He has promised you that you shall never perish. Let the eternal life within you express itself in confident rejoicing.

> The gospel bears my spirit up:
> A faithful and unchanging God
> Lays the foundation for my hope,
> In oaths, and promises, and blood.

EVENING

"The LORD is my light and my salvation; whom shall I fear? The LORD is the strength of my life; of whom shall I be afraid?" — *Psalm 27:1.*

"THE LORD IS my light and my salvation." Here is personal interest, *"my light," "my salvation;"* the soul is assured of it, and therefore declares it boldly. Into the soul at the new birth divine light is poured as the precursor of salvation; where there is not enough light to reveal our own darkness and to make us long for the Lord Jesus, there is no evidence of salvation. After conversion our God is our joy, comfort, guide, teacher, and in every sense our light: He is light within, light around, light reflected from us, and light to be revealed to us. Note, it is not said merely that the Lord gives light, but that He is light; nor that He gives salvation, but that He is salvation; he, then, who by faith has laid hold upon God, has all covenant blessings in his possession.

This being made sure as a fact, the argument drawn from it is put in the form of a question, *"Whom shall I fear?"* A question which is its own answer. The powers of darkness are not to be feared, for the Lord, our light, destroys them; and the damnation of hell is not to be dreaded by us, for the Lord is our salvation. This is a very different challenge from that of boastful Goliath, for it rests, not upon the conceited vigor of an arm of flesh, but upon the real power of the omnipotent *"I AM."*

"The Lord is the strength of my life." Here is a third glowing epithet, to show that the writer's hope was fastened with a threefold cord which could not be broken. We may well accumulate terms of praise where the Lord lavishes deeds of grace. Our life derives all its strength from God; and if He deigns to make us strong, we cannot be weakened by all the machinations of the adversary. *"Of whom shall I be afraid?"* The bold question looks into the future as well as the present. *"If God be for us,"* who can be against us, either now or in time to come?

MORNING
June 17
"Help, LORD" — Psalm 12:1.

THE PRAYER ITSELF is remarkable, for it is short, but seasonable, sententious, and suggestive. David mourned the fewness of faithful men, and therefore lifted up his heart in supplication; when the creature failed, he flew to the Creator. He evidently felt his own weakness, or he would not have cried for help; but at the same time he intended honestly to exert himself for the cause of truth, for the word "help" is inapplicable where we ourselves do nothing. There is much of directness, clearness of perception, and distinctness of utterance in this petition of two words; much more, indeed, than in the long rambling expressions of certain professors. The Psalmist runs straightforward to his God, with a well-considered prayer; he knows what he is seeking, and where to seek it. Lord, teach us to pray in the same blessed manner.

The occasions for the use of this prayer are frequent. In providential afflictions how suitable it is for tried believers who find all helpers failing them. Students, in doctrinal difficulties, may often obtain aid by lifting up this cry of *"Help, Lord,"* to the Holy Spirit, the great Teacher. Spiritual warriors in inward conflicts may send to the throne for reinforcements, and this will be a model for their request. Workers in heavenly labor may thus obtain grace in time of need. Seeking sinners, in doubts and alarms, may offer up the same weighty supplication; in fact, in all cases, times, and places, this will serve the turn of needy souls. *"Help, Lord,"* will suit us living and dying, suffering or laboring, rejoicing or sorrowing. In Him our help is found, let us not be slack to cry to Him.

The answer to the prayer is certain, if it be sincerely offered through Jesus. The Lord's character assures us that He will not leave His people; His relationship as Father and Husband guarantee us His aid; His gift of Jesus is a pledge of every good thing; and His sure promise stands, *"Fear not, I will help you."*

EVENING
"Then Israel sang this song, Spring up, O well; Sing to it" — Numbers 21:17.

FAMOUS WAS THE well of Beer in the wilderness, because it was the subject of a promise: *"That is the well whereof the Lord spoke unto Moses. Gather the people together, and I will give them water."* The people needed water, and it was promised by their gracious God. We need fresh supplies of heavenly grace, and in the covenant the Lord has pledged Himself to give all we require. The well next became the cause of a song. Before the water gushed forth, cheerful faith prompted the people to sing; and as they saw the crystal fount bubbling up, the music grew yet more joyous. In like manner, we who believe the promise of God should rejoice in the prospect of divine revivals in our souls, and as we experience them our holy joy should overflow. Are we thirsting? Let us not murmur, but sing. Spiritual thirst is bitter to bear, but we need not bear it. The promise indicates a well; let us be of good heart, and look for it. Moreover, the well was the center of prayer. "Spring up, Oh well." 'What God has engaged to give, we must inquire after, or we manifest that we have neither desire nor faith.

This evening let us ask that the Scripture we have read, and our devotional exercises, may not be an empty formality, but a channel of grace to our souls. Oh that God the Holy Spirit would work in us with all His mighty power, filling us with all the fullness of God. Lastly, the well was the object of effort. *"The nobles of the people dug it with their staves."* The Lord would have us active in obtaining grace. Our staves are ill adapted for digging in the sand, but we must use them to the utmost of our ability. Prayer must not be neglected; the assembling of ourselves together must not be forsaken: ordinances must not be slighted. The Lord will give us His grace most abundantly, but not in a way of idleness. Let us, then, arouse ourselves to seek Him in whom are all our fresh springs.

June 18   MORNING

"Your Redeemer" — Isaiah 54:5.

JESUS, THE REDEEMER, is altogether ours and ours forever. All the offices of Christ are held on our behalf. He is king for us, priest for us, and prophet for us. Whenever we read a new title of the Redeemer, let us appropriate Him as ours under that name as much as under any other. The shepherd's staff, the father's rod, the captain's sword, the priest's miter, the prince's scepter, the Prophet's mantle, all are ours. Jesus has no dignity which He will not employ for our exaltation, and no prerogative which He will not exercise for our defense. His fullness of Godhead is our unfailing, inexhaustible treasure-house.

His manhood also, which He took upon Him for us, is ours in all its perfection. To our gracious Lord communicates the spotless virtue of a stainless character; to us He gives the meritorious efficacy of a devoted life; on us He bestows the reward procured by obedient submission and incessant service. He makes the unsullied garment of His life our covering beauty; the glittering virtues of His character our ornaments and jewels; and the superhuman meekness of His death our boast and glory. He bequeaths us His manger, from which to learn how God came down to man; and His Cross to teach us how man may go up to God. All His thoughts, emotions, actions, utterances, miracles, and intercessions, were for us. He trod the road of sorrow on our behalf, and has made over to us as His heavenly legacy the full results of all the labors of His life. He is now as much ours as heretofore; and He blushes not to acknowledge Himself *"our Lord Jesus Christ,"* though He is the blessed and only Potentate, the King of kings, and Lord of lords. Christ everywhere and every way is our Christ, forever and ever most richly to enjoy. Oh my soul, by the power of the Holy Spirit! call Him this morning, *"your Redeemer."*

EVENING

"I have come into My garden, My sister, My spouse" — Song of Solomon 5:1.

THE HEART OF the believer is Christ's garden. He bought it with His precious blood, and He enters it and claims it as His own. A garden implies separation. It is not the open common; it is not a wilderness; it is walled around, or hedged in. Would that we could see the wall of separation between the church and the world made broader and stronger. It makes one sad to hear Christians saying, "Well, there is no harm in this; there is no harm in that," thus getting as near to the world as possible. Grace is at a low ebb in that soul which can even raise the question of how far it may go in worldly conformity. A garden is a place of beauty, it far surpasses the wild uncultivated lands. The genuine Christian must seek to be more excellent in his life than the best moralist, because Christ's garden ought to produce the best flowers in all the world. Even the best is poor compared with Christ's deservings; let us not put Him off with withering and dwarf plants. The rarest, richest, choicest lilies and roses ought to bloom in the place which Jesus calls His own.

The garden is a place of growth. The saints are not to remain undeveloped, always mere buds and blossoms. We should grow in grace, and in the knowledge of our Lord and Savior Jesus Christ. Growth should be rapid where Jesus is the Husbandman, and the Holy Spirit the dew from above. A garden is a place of retirement. So the Lord Jesus Christ would have us reserve our souls as a place in which He can manifest Himself, as He does not unto the world. Oh that Christians were more retired, that they kept their hearts more closely shut up for Christ! We often worry and trouble ourselves, like Martha, with much serving, so that we have not the room for Christ that Mary had, and do not sit at His feet as we should. The Lord grant the sweet showers of His grace to water His garden this day.

MORNING — June 19

"And they were all filled with the Holy Spirit" — Acts 2:4.

RICH WERE THE blessings of this day if all of us were filled with the Holy Ghost. The consequences of this sacred filling of the soul it would be impossible to overestimate. Life, comfort, light, purity, power, peace; and many other precious blessings are inseparable from the Spirit's benign presence. As sacred oil, He anoints the head of the believer, sets him apart to the priesthood of saints, and gives him grace to execute his office aright. As the only truly purifying water, He cleanses us from the power of sin and sanctifies us unto holiness, working in us to will and to do of the Lord's good pleasure. As the light, He manifested to us at first our lost estate, and now He reveals the Lord Jesus to us and in us, and guides us in the way of righteousness. Enlightened by His pure celestial ray, we are no more darkness but light in the Lord.

As fire, He both purges us from dross, and sets our consecrated nature on a blaze. He is the sacrificial flame by which we are enabled to offer our whole souls as a living sacrifice unto God. As heavenly dew, He removes our barrenness and fertilizes our lives. Oh that He would drop from above upon us at this early hour! Such morning dew would be a sweet commencement for the day. As the dove, with wings of peaceful love He broods over His Church and over the souls of believers, and as a Comforter He dispels the cares and doubts which mar the peace of His beloved. He descends upon the chosen as upon the Lord in Jordan, and bears witness to their sonship by working in them a filial spirit by which they cry, *"Abba, Father.* As the wind, He brings, the breath of life to men; blowing where He desires He performs the quickening operations by which the spiritual creation is animated and sustained. Would to God, that we might feel His presence this day and every day.

EVENING

"My Beloved is mine, and I am His; He feeds among the lilies. Until the day break, and the shadows flee away, turn, my Beloved, and be like a roe or a young hart on the mountains of Bether" — Song of Solomon 2:16, 17.

SURELY IF THERE be a happy verse in the Bible it is this, *"My Beloved is mine, and I am His."* So peaceful, so full of assurance, so overrunning with happiness and contentment is it, that it might well have been written by the same hand which penned the twenty-third Psalm. Yet though the prospect is exceeding fair and lovely, earth cannot show its superior, it is not entirely a sunlit landscape. There is a cloud in the sky which casts a shadow over the scene. Listen, *"Until the day break, and the shadows flee away."*

There is a word, too, about the *"mountains of Bether,"* or, *"the mountains of division,"* and to our love, anything like division is bitterness. Beloved, this may be your present state of mind; you do not doubt your salvation; you know that Christ is yours, but you are not feasting with Him. You understand your vital interest in Him, so that you have no shadow of a doubt of your being His, and of His being yours, but still His left hand is not under your head, nor does His right hand embrace you. A shade of sadness is cast over your heart, perhaps by affliction, certainly by the temporary absence of your Lord, so even while exclaiming, "I am His," you are forced to take to your knees, and to pray, *"Until the day break, and the shadows flee away, turn, my Beloved."*

"Where is He?" asks the soul. And the answer comes, *"He feeds among the lilies."* If we would find Christ, we must get into communion with His people, we must come to the ordinances with His saints. Oh, for an evening glimpse of Him! Oh, to sup with Him tonight!

June 20 — MORNING

"For, lo, I will command, and I will sift the house of Israel among all nations, like grain is shaken in a sieve, yet not a grain shall fall on the earth" — Amos 9:9.

EVERY sifting comes by divine command and permission. Satan must ask leave before he can lay a finger upon Job. No, more, in some sense our siftings are directly the work of heaven, for the text says, *"I will sift the house of Israel."* Satan, like a drudge, may hold the sieve, hoping to destroy the grain; but the overruling hand of the Master is accomplishing the purity of the grain by the very process which the enemy intended to be destructive. Precious, but much sifted grain of the Lord's floor, be comforted by the blessed fact that the Lord directs both flail and sieve to His own glory, and to your eternal profit.

The Lord Jesus will surely use the fan which is in His hand, and will divide the precious from the vile. All are not Israel that are of Israel; the heap on the barn floor is not clean provender, and hence the winnowing process must be performed. In the sieve true weight alone has power. Husks and chaff being devoid of substance must fly before the wind, and only solid grain will remain.

Observe the complete safety of the Lord's wheat; even the least grain has a promise of preservation. God Himself sifts, and therefore it is stern and terrible work; He sifts them in all places, *"among all nations;"* He sifts them in the most effectual manner, *"like as grain is sifted in a sieve;"* and yet for all this, not the smallest, lightest, or most shrivelled grain, is permitted to fall to the ground. Every individual believer is precious in the sight of the Lord; a shepherd would not lose one sheep, nor a jeweler one diamond, nor a mother one child, nor a man one limb of his body, nor will the Lord lose one of His redeemed people. However little we may be, if we are the Lord's, we may rejoice that we are preserved in Christ Jesus.

EVENING

"Immediately they left their nets and followed Him" — Mark 1:18.

WHEN THEY HEARD the call of Jesus, Simon and Andrew obeyed at once without question. If we would always, punctually and with resolute zeal, put in practice what we hear upon the spot, or at the first fit occasion, our attendance at the means of grace, and our reading of good books, could not fail to enrich us spiritually. He will not lose his loaf who has taken care at once to eat it, neither can he be deprived of the benefit of the doctrine who has already acted upon it. Most readers and hearers become moved so far as to purpose to amend; but, alas! the proposal is a blossom which has not been knit, and therefore no fruit comes of it; they wait, they waver, and then they forget, till, like the ponds in nights of frost, when the sun shines by day, they are only thawed in time to be frozen again. That fatal tomorrow is blood-red with the murder of fair resolutions; it is the slaughter-house of the innocents.

We are very concerned that our little book of "Evening Readings" should not be fruitless, and therefore we pray that readers may not be readers only, but doers, of the word. The practice of truth is the most profitable reading of it. Should the reader be impressed with any duty while perusing these pages, let him hasten to fulfil it before the holy glow has departed from his soul, and let him leave his nets, and all that he has, sooner than be found rebellious to the Master's call. Do not give place to the devil by delay! Haste while opportunity and quickening are in happy conjunction. Do not be caught in your own nets, but break the meshes of worldliness, and away where glory calls you. Happy is the writer who shall meet with readers resolved to carry out his teachings; his harvest shall be a hundredfold, and his Master shall have great honor. Would to God that such might be our reward upon these brief meditations and hurried hints. Grant it, Oh Lord, unto your servant!

MORNING June 21

"You are the most beautiful among the sons of men" — Psalm 45:2.

THE ENTIRE PERSON of Jesus is but as one gem, and His life is all along but one impression of the seal. He is altogether complete; not only in His several parts, but as a gracious all-glorious whole. His character is not a mass of fair colors mixed confusedly, nor a heap of precious stones laid carelessly one upon another; He is a picture of beauty and a breastplate of glory. In Him, all the *"things of good repute"* are in their proper places, and assist in adorning each other. Not one feature in His glorious person attracts attention at the expense of others; but He is perfectly and altogether lovely.

Oh, Jesus! Your power, Your grace, Your justice, Your tenderness, Your truth, Your majesty, and Your immutability make up such a man, or rather such a God-man, as neither heaven nor earth has seen elsewhere. Your infancy, Your eternity, Your sufferings, Your triumphs, Your death, and Your immortality, are all woven in one gorgeous tapestry, without seam or rent. You are music without discord; You are many, and yet not divided; You are all things, and yet not diverse. As all the colors blend into one resplendent rainbow, so all the glories of heaven and earth meet in You, and unite so wondrously, that there is none like You in all things; no, if all the virtues of the most excellent were bound in one bundle, they could not rival You. You are the mirror of all perfection. You have been anointed with the holy oil of myrrh and cassia, which Your God has reserved for You alone; and as for Your fragrance, it is as the holy perfume, the like of which none other can ever mingle, even with the art of the apothecary; each spice is fragrant, but the compound is divine.

Oh, sacred symmetry! oh, rare connection Of many perfects, to make one perfection! Oh, heavenly music, where all parts do meet In one sweet strain, to make one perfect sweet!

EVENING

"The foundation of God stands sure" — 2 Timothy 2:19.

THE FOUNDATION UPON which our faith rests is this, that *"God was in Christ reconciling the world unto Himself, not imputing their trespasses unto them."* The great fact on which genuine faith relies is, that *"the Word was made flesh and lived among us,"* and that *"Christ also has suffered for sin, the just for the unjust, that He might bring us to God;" "Who Himself bore our sins in His own body on the tree;" "For the chastisement of our peace was upon Him, and by His stripes we are healed."* In one word, the great pillar of the Christian's hope is substitution. The vicarious sacrifice of Christ for the guilty, Christ being made sin for us that we might be made the righteousness of God in Him, Christ offering up a true and proper expiatory and substitutionary sacrifice in the room, place, and stead of as many as the Father gave Him, who are known to God by name, and are recognized in their own hearts by their trusting in Jesus; this is the cardinal fact of the gospel. If this foundation were removed, what could we do? But it stands firm as the throne of God. We know it; we rest on it; we rejoice in it; and our delight is to hold it, to meditate upon it, and to proclaim it, while we desire to be actuated and moved by gratitude for it in every part of our life and conversation.

In these days a direct attack is made upon the doctrine of the atonement. Men cannot bear substitution. They gnash their teeth at the thought of the Lamb of God bearing the sin of man. But we, who know by experience the preciousness of this truth, will proclaim it in defiance of them confidently and unceasingly. We will neither dilute it nor change it, nor fritter it away in any shape or fashion. It shall still be Christ, a positive substitute, bearing human guilt and suffering in the stead of men. We cannot, dare not, give it up, for it is our life, and despite every controversy we feel that *"Nevertheless the foundation of God stands sure."*

June 22

MORNING

"He shall build the temple of the LORD. And He shall bear the glory" — Zechariah 6:13.

CHRIST HIMSELF is the builder of His spiritual temple, and He has built it on the mountains of His unchangeable affection, His omnipotent grace, and His infallible truthfulness. But as it was in Solomon's temple, so in this; the materials need making ready. There are the "Cedars of Lebanon," but they are not framed for the building; they are not cut down, and shaped and made into those planks of cedar, whose odoriferous beauty shall make glad the courts of the Lord's house in Paradise. There are also the rough stones still in the quarry, they must be hewn thence, and squared. All this is Christ's own work. Each individual believer is being prepared, and polished, and made ready for his place in the temple; but Christ's own hand performs the preparation-work. Afflictions cannot sanctify, excepting as they are used by Him to this end. Our prayers and efforts cannot make us ready for heaven, apart from the hand of Jesus, who fashions our hearts aright.

As in the building of Solomon's temple, *"there was neither hammer, nor axe, nor any tool of iron, heard in the house,"* because all was brought perfectly ready for the exact spot it was to occupy. So is it with the temple which Jesus builds; the making ready is all done on earth. When we reach heaven, there will be no sanctifying us there, no squaring us with affliction, no planing us with suffering. No, we must be made fit here. All that Christ will do beforehand; and when He has done it, we shall be ferried by a loving hand across the stream of death, and brought to the heavenly Jerusalem, to abide as eternal pillars in the temple of our Lord.

> Beneath His eye and care,
> The edifice shall rise,
> Majestic, strong, and fair,
> And shine above the skies.

EVENING

"So that the things which cannot be shaken may remain" — Hebrews 12:27.

WE HAVE MANY things in our possession at the present moment which can be shaken, and it ill becomes a Christian man to set much store by them, for there is nothing stable beneath these rolling skies; change is written upon all things. Yet, we have certain *"things which cannot be shaken,"* and I invite you this evening to think of them, that if the things which can be shaken should all be taken away, you may derive real comfort from the things that cannot be shaken, which will remain.

Whatever your losses have been, or may be, you enjoy present salvation. You are standing at the foot of His cross, trusting alone in the merit of Jesus' precious blood, and no rise or fall of the markets can interfere with your salvation in Him; no breaking of banks, no failures and bankruptcies can touch that. Then you are a child of God this evening. God is your Father. No change of circumstances can ever rob you of that. Although by losses brought to poverty, and stripped bare, you can say, "He is my Father still. In my Father's house are many mansions; therefore will I not be troubled." You have another permanent blessing, namely, the love of Jesus Christ. He who is God and Man loves you with all the strength of His affectionate nature; nothing can affect that. The fig tree may not blossom, and the flocks may cease from the field, it matters not to the man who can sing, *"My Beloved is mine, and I am His."* Our best portion and richest heritage we cannot lose. Whatever troubles come, let us play the man; let us show that we are not such little children as to be cast down by what may happen in this poor fleeting state of time. Our country is Immanuel's land, our hope is above the sky, and, therefore, calm as the summer's ocean; we will see the wreck of everything earthborn, and yet rejoice in the God of our salvation.

MORNING June 23

"Ephraim is a cake not turned" — Hosea 7:8.

A CAKE NOT turned is uncooked on one side; and so Ephraim was, in many respects, untouched by divine grace: though there was some partial obedience, there was very much rebellion left. My soul, I charge you, see whether this be your case. Are you thorough in the things of God? Has grace gone through the very center of your being so as to be felt in its divine operations in all your powers, your actions, your words, and your thoughts? To be sanctified, spirit, soul, and body, should be your aim and prayer; and although sanctification may not be perfect in you anywhere in degree, yet it must be universal in its action; there must not be the appearance of holiness in one place and reigning sin in another, else you, too, will be a cake not turned.

A cake not turned is soon burnt on the side nearest the fire, and although no man can have too much religion, there are some who seem burnt black with bigoted zeal for that part of truth which they have received, or are charred to a cinder with a vain-glorious Pharisaic ostentation of those religious performances which suit their humor. The assumed appearance of superior sanctity frequently accompanies a total absence of all vital godliness. The saint in public is a devil in private. He deals in flour by day and in soot by night. The cake which is burned on one side, is dough on the other.

If it be so with me, Oh Lord, turn me! Turn my unsanctified nature to the fire of Your love and let it feel the sacred glow, and let my burnt side cool a little while I learn my own weakness and want of heat when I am removed from Your heavenly flame. Let me not be found a double-minded man, but one entirely under the powerful influence of reigning grace; for well I know if I am left like a cake unturned, and am not on both sides the subject of Your grace, I must be consumed forever amid everlasting burnings.

EVENING
"Waiting for adoption" — Romans 8:23.

EVEN IN THIS world saints are God's children, but men cannot discover them to be so, except by certain moral characteristics. The adoption is not manifested, the children are not yet openly declared. Among the Romans a man might adopt a child, and keep it private for a long time; but there was a second adoption in public, When the child was brought before the constituted authorities, its former garments were taken off, and the father who took it to be his child gave it raiment suitable to its new condition of life. *"Beloved, now are we the sons of God, and it does not yet appear what we shall be."* We are not yet arrayed in the apparel which befits the royal family of heaven; we are wearing in this flesh and blood just what we wore as the sons of Adam; but we know that *"when He shall appear"* who is the "first-born among many brethren," we shall be like Him, we shall see Him as He is.

Cannot you imagine that a child taken from the lowest ranks of society, and adopted by a Roman senator, would say to himself, "I long for the day when I shall be publicly adopted. Then I shall leave off these plebeian garments, and be robed as becomes my senatorial rank"? Happy in what he has received, for that very reason he groans to get the fullness of what is promised him. So it is with us today. We are waiting till we shall put on our proper garments, and shall be manifested as the children of God. We are young nobles, and have not yet worn our coronets. We are young brides, and the marriage day is not yet come, and by the love our Spouse bears us, we are led to long and sigh for the bridal morning. Our very happiness makes us groan after more; our joy, like a swollen spring, longs to well up like an Iceland geyser, leaping to the skies, and it heaves and groans within our spirit for want of space and room by which to manifest itself to men.

June 24

MORNING

"A certain woman cried out from the crowd to Him, Blessed is the womb that bore You and the breasts which You sucked. But He said., Yes, but rather say, Blessed are those who hear the word of God and keep it" — Luke 11:27-28.

IT IS FONDLY imagined by some that it must have involved very special privileges to have been the mother of our Lord, because they supposed that she had the benefit of looking into His very heart in a way in which we cannot hope to do. There may be an appearance of plausibility in the supposition, but not much. We do not know that Mary knew more than others; what she did know she did well to lay up in her heart; but she does not appear from anything we read in the Evangelists to have been a better instructed believer than any other of Christ's disciples. All that she knew we also may discover.

Do you wonder that we should say so? Here is a text to prove it: *"The secret of the Lord is with them that fear Him, and He will show them His covenant."* Remember the Master's words: *"Henceforth I call you not servants; for the servant knows not what his Lord does: but I have called you friends; for all things that I have heard of my Father I have made known unto you."* So blessedly does this Divine Revealer of secrets tell us His heart, that He keeps back nothing which is profitable to us; His own assurance is, "If it were not so, I would have told you."

Does He not this day manifest Himself unto us as He does not unto the world? It is even so; and therefore we will not ignorantly cry out, *"Blessed is the womb that bore You,"* but we will intelligently bless God that, having heard the Word and kept it, we have first of all as true a communion with the Savior as the Virgin had, and in the second place as true an acquaintance with the secrets of His heart as she can be supposed to have obtained. Happy soul to be thus privileged!

EVENING

"Shadrach, Meshach and Abednego answered and let it be known to you, O king, that we will not serve your gods" — Daniel 3:16-18.

THE NARRATIVE OF the manly courage and marvelous deliverance of the three holy children, or rather champions, is well calculated to excite in the minds of believers firmness and steadfastness in upholding the truth in the teeth of tyranny and in the very jaws of death. Let young Christians especially learn from their example, both in matters of faith in religion, and matters of uprightness in business, never to sacrifice their consciences. Lose all rather than lose your integrity, and when all else is gone, still hold fast a clear conscience as the rarest jewel which can adorn the bosom of a mortal. Be not guided by the will-of-the-wisp of policy, but by the pole-star of divine authority. Follow the right at all hazards. When you see no present advantage, walk by faith and not by sight. Do God the honor to trust Him when it comes to matters of loss for the sake of principle. See whether He will be your debtor! See if He does not even in this life prove His word that *"Godliness, with contentment, is great gain,"* and that they who *"seek first the kingdom of God and His righteousness, shall have all these things added unto them."*

Should it happen that, in the providence of God, you are a loser by conscience, you shall find that if the Lord pays you not back in the silver of earthly prosperity, He will discharge His promise in the gold of spiritual joy. Remember that a man's life consists not in the abundance of that which he possesses. To wear a guileless spirit, to have a heart void of offence, to have the favor and smile of God, is greater riches than the mines of Ophir could yield, or the traffic of Tyre could win. *"Better is a dinner of herbs where love is, than a stalled ox and inward contention with it."* An ounce of hearts-ease is worth a ton of gold.

MORNING   June 25

"Get up into the mountain" — Isaiah 40:9.

OUR KNOWLEDGE OF Christ is somewhat like climbing one of our Welsh mountains. When you are at the base you see but little: the mountain itself appears to be but one-half as high as it really is. Confined in a little valley, you discover scarcely anything but the rippling brooks as they descend into the stream at the foot of the mountain. Climb the first rising knoll, and the valley lengthens and widens beneath your feet. Go higher, and you see the country for four or five miles round, and you are delighted with the widening prospect. Mount still, and the scene enlarges; till at last, when you are on the summit, and look east, west, north, and south, you see almost all England lying before you. Yonder is a forest in some distant county, perhaps two hundred miles away, and here the sea, and there a shining river and the smoking chimneys of a manufacturing town, or the masts of the ships in a busy port. All these things please and delight you, and you say, I could not have imagined that so much could be seen at this elevation.

Now, the Christian life is of the same order. When we first believe in Christ we see but little of Him. The higher we climb the more we discover of His beauties. But who has ever gained the summit? Who has known all the heights and depths of the love of Christ which passes knowledge? Paul, when grown old, sitting grey-haired, shivering in a dungeon in Rome, could say with greater emphasis than we can, *"I know whom I have believed,"* for each experience had been like the climbing of a hill, each trial had been like ascending another summit, and his death seemed like gaining the top of the mountain, from which he could see the whole of the faithfulness and the love of Him to whom he had committed his soul. Get up, dear friend into the high mountain.

EVENING

"But the dove found no rest for the sole of her foot" — Genesis 8:9.

READER, CAN YOU find rest apart from the ark, Christ Jesus? Then be assured that your religion is vain. Are you satisfied with anything short of a conscious knowledge of your union and interest in Christ? Then woe unto you. If you profess to be a Christian, yet find full satisfaction in worldly pleasures and pursuits your profession is false. If your soul can stretch herself at rest, and find the bed long enough, and the coverlet broad enough to cover her in the chambers of sin, then you are a hypocrite, and far enough from any right thoughts of Christ or perception of His preciousness.

But if, on the other hand, you feel that if you could indulge in sin without punishment, yet it would be a punishment of itself; and that if you could have the whole world, and abide in it forever, it would be quite enough misery not to be parted from it; for your God is what your soul craves after. Then be of good courage, you are a child of God. With all your sins and imperfections, take this to your comfort: if your soul has no rest in sin, you are not as the sinner is! If you are still crying after and craving after something better, Christ has not forgotten you, for you have not quite forgotten Him. The believer cannot do without his Lord; words are inadequate to express his thoughts of Him. We cannot live on the sands of the wilderness, we want the manna which drops from on high; our skin bottles of creature confidence cannot yield us a drop of moisture, but we drink of the rock which follows us, and that rock is Christ. When you feed on Him your soul can sing, *"He has satisfied my mouth with good things, so that my youth is renewed like the eagle's,"* but if you have Him not, your bursting wine vat and well-filled barn can give you no sort of satisfaction; rather lament over them in the words of wisdom *"Vanity of vanities, all is vanity!"*

June 26

MORNING

"Have you become like us?" — Isaiah 14:10.

WHAT MUST BE the apostate professor's doom when his naked soul appears before God? How will he bear that voice, *"Depart, you cursed;"* you have rejected Me, and I reject you; you have played the harlot, and departed from Me; I also have banished you forever from My presence, and will not have mercy upon you. What will be this wretch's shame at the last great day when, before assembled multitudes, the apostate shall be unmasked? See the profane, and sinners who never professed religion, lifting themselves up from their beds of fire to point at him. There he is, says one, will he preach the gospel in hell? There he is, says another, he rebuked me for cursing, and was a hypocrite himself! Alas! says another, here comes a psalm-singer, one who was always at his meeting; he is the man who boasted of his being sure of everlasting life; and here he is! No greater eagerness will ever be seen among Satanic tormentors, than in that day when devils drag the hypocrite's soul down to perdition.

Bunyan pictures this with massive but awful grandeur of poetry when he speaks of the back-way to hell. Seven devils bound the wretch with nine cords, and dragged him from the road to heaven, in which he had professed to walk, and thrust him through the back-door into hell. Mind that back-way to hell, professors! *"Examine yourselves, whether you be in the faith."* Look well to your state; see whether you be in Christ or not. It is the easiest thing in the world to give a lenient verdict when one-self is to be tried; but Oh, be just and true here. Be just to all, but be rigorous to yourself. Remember if it be not a rock on which you build, when the house shall fall, great will be the fall of it. Oh may the Lord give you sincerity, constancy, and firmness; and in no day, however evil, may you be led to turn aside.

EVENING

"Having escaped the rottenness that is in the world through lust" — 2 Peter 1:4.

BANISH FOREVER ALL thought of indulging the flesh if you would live in the power of your risen Lord. It were ill that a man who is alive in Christ should dwell in the corruption of sin. *"Why do you seek the living among the dead?"* said the angel to Magdalene. Should the living dwell in the sepulchre? Should divine life be immured in the charnel house of fleshly lust? How can we partake of the cup of the Lord and yet drink the cup of Belial?

Surely, believer, from open lusts and sins you are delivered. Have you also escaped from the more secret and delusive lime-twigs of the Satanic fowler? Have you come forth from the lust of pride? Have you escaped from slothfulness? Have you clean escaped from carnal security? Are you seeking day by day to live above worldliness, the pride of life, and the ensnaring vice of avarice? Remember, it is for this that you have been enriched with the treasures of God. If you be indeed the chosen of God, and beloved by Him, do not suffer all the lavish treasure of grace to be wasted upon you. Follow after holiness; it is the Christian's crown and glory.

An unholy church! It is useless to the world, and of no esteem among men. It is an abomination, hell's laughter, heaven's abhorrence. The worst evils which have ever come upon the world have been brought upon her by an unholy church. Oh Christian, the vows of God are upon you. You are God's priest; act as such. You are God's king; reign over your lusts. You are God's chosen; do not associate with Belial. Heaven is your portion: live like a heavenly spirit, so shall you prove that you have true faith in Jesus, for there cannot be faith in the heart unless there be holiness in the life.

> Lord I desire to live as one
> Who bears a blood-bought name,
> As one who fears but grieving You,
> And knows no other shame.

MORNING   June 27

"Only you shall not go very far away" — Exodus 8:28.

THIS IS A CRAFTY word from the lip of the arch-tyrant Pharaoh. If the poor enslaved Israelites must needs go out of Egypt, then he bargains with them that it shall not be very far away; not too far for them to escape the terror of his arms, and the observation of his spies.

After the same fashion, the world loves not the nonconformity of nonconformity, or the dissidence of dissent, it would have us be more charitable and not carry matters with too severe a hand. Death to the world, and burial with Christ, are experiences which carnal minds treat with ridicule, and hence the ordinance which sets them forth is almost universally neglected, and even condemned. Worldly wisdom recommends the path of compromise, and talks of "moderation." According to this carnal policy, purity is admitted to be very desirable, but we are warned against being too precise; truth is of course to be followed, but error is not to be severely denounced. The world says, Be spiritually minded by all means, but do not deny yourself a little gay society, an occasional ball, and a Christmas visit to a theatre. What's the good of crying down a thing when it is so fashionable, and everybody does it? Multitudes of professors yield to this cunning advice, to their own eternal ruin.

If we would follow the Lord wholly, we must go right away into the wilderness of separation, and leave the Egypt of the carnal world behind us. We must leave its maxims, its pleasures, and its religion too, and go far away to the place where the Lord calls His sanctified ones. When the town is on fire, our house cannot be too far from the flames. When the plague is abroad, a man cannot be too far from its haunts. The further from a viper the better, and the further from worldly conformity the better. To all true believers let the trumpet-call be sounded, *"Come out from among them, and be separate."*

EVENING

"Each one in the calling in which he was called, let him live in this way" — 1 Corinthians 7:20.

SOME PERSONS HAVE the foolish notion that the only way in which they can live for God is by becoming ministers, missionaries, or Bible women. Alas! how many would be shut out from any opportunity of magnifying the Most High if this were the case. Beloved, it is not office, it is earnestness; it is not position, it is grace which will enable us to glorify God. God is most surely glorified in that cobbler's stall, where the godly worker, as he piles the awl, sings of the Savior's love, yes, glorified far more than in many a stall where official religiousness performs its scanty duties. The name of Jesus is glorified by the poor unlearned carter as he drives his horse, and blesses his God, or speaks to his fellow laborer by the roadside, as much as by the popular divine who, throughout the country, like Boanerges, is thundering out the gospel. God is glorified by our serving Him in our proper vocations.

Take care, dear reader, that you do not forsake the path of duty by leaving your occupation, and take care you do not dishonor your profession while in it. Think little of yourselves, but do not think too little of your callings. Every lawful trade may be sanctified by the gospel to noblest ends. Turn to the Bible, and you will find the most menial forms of labor connected either with most daring deeds of faith, or with persons whose lives have been illustrious for holiness. Therefore be not discontented with your calling. Whatever God has made your position, or your work, abide in that, unless you are quite sure that He calls you to something else. Let your first care be to glorify God to the utmost of your power where you are. Fill your present sphere to His praise, and if He needs you in another He will show it to you. This evening lay aside vexatious ambition, and embrace peaceful content.

June 28

MORNING

"Looking to Jesus" — Hebrews 12:2.

IT IS EVER THE Holy Spirit's work to turn our eyes away from self to Jesus; but Satan's work is just the opposite of this, for he is constantly trying to make us regard ourselves instead of Christ. He insinuates, Your sins are too great for pardon; you have no faith; you do not repent enough; you will never be able to continue to the end; you have not the joy of His children; you have such a wavering hold of Jesus. All these are thoughts about self, and we shall never find comfort or assurance by looking within.

But the Holy Spirit turns our eyes entirely away from self: He tells us that we are nothing, but that *"Christ is all in all."* Remember, therefore, it is not your hold of Christ that saves you; it is Christ. It is not your joy in Christ that saves you; it is Christ. It is not even faith in Christ, though that be the instrument, it is Christ's blood and merits. Therefore, look not so much to your hand with which you are grasping Christ, as to Christ. Look not to your hope, but to Jesus, the source of your hope; look not to your faith, but to Jesus, the author and finisher of your faith. We shall never find happiness by looking at our prayers, our doings, or our feelings; it is what Jesus is, not what we are, that gives rest to the soul. If we would at once overcome Satan and have peace with God, it must be by *"looking unto Jesus."*

Keep your eye simply on Him; let His death, His sufferings, His merits, His glories, His intercession, be fresh upon your mind; when you wake in the morning look to Him; when you lie down at night, look to Him. Oh! let not your hopes or fears come between you and Jesus; follow hard after Him, and He will never fail you.

> My hope is built on nothing less
> Than Jesus' blood and righteousness;
> I dare not trust the sweetest frame,
> But wholly lean on Jesus' name.

EVENING

"But Aaron's rod swallowed up their rods" — Exodus 7:12.

THIS INCIDENT IS an instructive emblem of the sure victory of the divine handiwork over all opposition. Whenever a divine principle is cast into the heart, though the devil may fashion a counterfeit, and produce swarms of opponents, as sure as ever God is in the work, it will swallow up all its foes. If God's grace takes possession of a man, the world's magicians may throw down all their rods; and every rod may be as cunning and poisonous as a serpent, but Aaron's rod will swallow up their rods. The sweet attractions of the cross will woo and win the man's heart, and he who lived only for this deceitful earth will now have an eye for the upper spheres, and a wing to mount into celestial heights. When grace has won the day the worldling seeks the world to come.

The same fact is to be observed in the life of the believer. What multitudes of foes has our faith had to meet! Our old sins, the devil threw them down before us, and they turned to serpents. What hosts of them! Ah, but the cross of Jesus destroys them all. Faith in Christ makes short work of all our sins. Then the devil has launched forth another host of serpents in the form of worldly trials, temptations, unbelief; but faith in Jesus is more than a match for them, and overcomes them all. The same absorbing principle shines in the faithful service of God! With an enthusiastic love for Jesus difficulties are surmounted, sacrifices become pleasures, sufferings are honors. But, if religion is thus a consuming passion in the heart, then it follows that there are many persons who profess religion but have it not; for what they have will not bear this test. Examine yourself, my reader, on this point. Aaron's rod proved its heaven-given power. Is your religion doing so? If Christ be anything He must be everything. Oh rest not till love and faith in Jesus be the master passions of your soul!

MORNING   June 29

"God will also bring with Him all those who have died in Jesus" — *1 Thessalonians 4:14.*

LET US NOT imagine that the soul sleeps in insensibility. *"Today shall you be with me in paradise,"* is the whisper of Christ to every dying saint. They sleep in Jesus, but their souls are before the throne of God, praising Him day and night in His temple, singing hallelujahs to Him who washed them from their sins in His blood. The body sleeps in its lonely bed of earth, beneath the coverlet of grass. But what is this sleep? The idea connected with sleep is rest, and that is the thought which the Spirit of God would convey to us. Sleep makes each night a Sabbath for the day. Sleep shuts fast the door of the soul, and bids all intruders tarry for a while, that the life within may enter its summer garden of ease. The toil-worn believer quietly sleeps, as does the weary child when it slumbers on its mother's breast. Oh! happy they who die in the Lord; they rest from their labors, and their works do follow them. Their quiet repose shall never be broken until God shall rouse them to give them their full reward. Guarded by angel watchers, curtained by eternal mysteries, they sleep on, the inheritors of glory, till the fullness of time shall bring the fullness of redemption.

What an awaking shall be theirs! They were laid in their last resting place, weary and worn, but such they shall not rise. They went to their rest with the furrowed brow, and the wasted features, but they wake up in beauty and glory. The shrivelled seed, so destitute of form and comeliness, rises from the dust a beauteous flower. The winter of the grave gives way to the spring of redemption and the summer of glory. Blessed is death, since it, through the divine power, disrobes us of this work-day garment, to clothe us with the wedding garment of incorruption. Blessed are those who *"sleep in Jesus."*

EVENING

"However, in regard to the ambassadors of the princes of Babylon who sent to him to ask about the wonder that was done in the land, God left him in order to test him, so that He might know all in his heart" — *2 Chronicles 32:31.*

HEZEKIAH WAS growing so inwardly great, and priding himself so much upon the favor of God, that self-righteousness crept in, and through his carnal security, the grace of God was for a time, in its more active operations, withdrawn. Here is quite enough to account for his folly with the Babylonians. For if the grace of God should leave the best Christian, there is enough of sin in his heart to make him the worst of transgressors. If left to yourselves, you who are warmest for Christ would cool down like Laodicea into sickening lukewarmness. You who are sound in the faith would be white with the leprosy of false doctrine; you who now walk before the Lord in excellency and integrity would reel to and fro, and stagger with a drunkenness of evil passion. Like the moon, we borrow our light; bright as we are when grace shines on us, we are darkness itself when the Sun of Righteousness withdraws Himself.

Therefore let us cry to God never to leave us. *"Lord, take not Your Holy Spirit from us! Withdraw not from us Your indwelling grace!* Have You not said, *"I the Lord do keep it; I will water it every moment: lest any hurt it, I will keep it night and day"*? Lord, keep us everywhere. Keep us when in the valley, that we murmur not against Your humbling hand; keep us when on the mountain, that we wax not giddy through being lifted up. Keep us in youth, when our passions are strong; keep us in old age, when becoming conceited of our wisdom, we may therefore prove greater fools then the young and giddy; keep us when we come to die, lest, at the very last, we should deny You! Keep us living, keep us dying, keep us laboring, keep us suffering, keep us fighting, keep us resting, keep us everywhere, for everywhere we need You, Oh our God!"

June 30   MORNING

"And the glory which You have given Me, I have given them" — John 17:22.

BEHOLD THE superlative liberality of the Lord Jesus, for He has given us His all. Although a tithe of His possessions would have made a universe of angels rich beyond all thought, yet was He not content until He had given us all that He had. It would have been surprising grace if He had allowed us to eat the crumbs of His bounty beneath the table of His mercy; but He will do nothing by halves, He makes us sit with Him and share the feast. Had He given us some small pension from His royal coffers, we should have had cause to love Him eternally; but no, He will have His bride as rich as Himself, and He will not have a glory or a grace in which she shall not share.

He has not been content with less than making us joint-heirs with Himself, so that we might have equal possessions. He has emptied all His estate into the coffers of the Church, and has all things common with His redeemed. There is not one room in His house the key of which He will withhold from His people. He gives them full liberty to take all that He has to be their own; He loves them to make free with His treasure, and appropriate as much as they can possibly carry. The boundless fullness of His all-sufficiency is as free to the believer as the air he breathes. Christ has put the flagon of His love and grace to the believer's lip, and bidden him drink on forever. For could he drain it, he is welcome to do so, and as he cannot exhaust it, he is bidden to drink abundantly, for it is all his own. What truer proof of fellowship can heaven or earth afford?

> When I stand before the throne
> Dressed in beauty not my own;
> When I see You as You are,
> Love You with unsinning heart;
> Then, Lord, shall I fully know;
> Not till then, how much I owe.

EVENING

"Ah, Lord GOD! You have made the heavens and the earth by Your great power and stretched out arm. There is nothing too hard for You" — Jeremiah 32:17.

AT THE VERY time when the Chaldeans surrounded Jerusalem, and when the sword, famine and pestilence had desolated the land, Jeremiah was commanded by God to purchase a field, and have the deed of transfer legally sealed and witnessed. This was a strange purchase for a rational man to make. Prudence could not justify it, for it was buying with scarcely a probability that the person purchasing could ever enjoy the possession. But it was enough for Jeremiah that his God had bidden him, for well he knew that God will be justified of all His children. He reasoned thus. Ah, Lord God! You can make this plot of ground of use to me; You can rid this land of these oppressors; You can make me yet sit under my vine and my fig tree in the heritage which I have bought; for You did make the heavens and the earth, and nothing is too hard for You.

This gave a majesty to the early saints, that they dared to do at God's command things which carnal reason would condemn. Whether it be a Noah who is to build a ship on dry land, an Abraham who is to offer up his only son, or a Moses who is to despise the treasures of Egypt, or a Joshua who is to besiege Jericho seven days, using no weapons but the blasts of rams' horns, they all act upon God's command, contrary to the dictates of carnal reason. And the Lord gives them a rich reward as the result of their obedient faith. Would to God we had in the religion of these modern times a more potent infusion of this heroic faith in God. If we would venture more upon the naked promise of God, we should enter a world of wonders to which as yet we are strangers. Let Jeremiah's place of confidence be ours; nothing is too hard for the God that created the heavens and the earth.

MORNING July 1

"In summer and in winter it shall be" — *Zechariah 14:8.*

THE STRESS OF living water which flow from Jerusalem are not dried up by the parching heats of sultry midsummer any more than they were frozen by the cold winds of blustering winter. Rejoice, Oh my soul, that you are spared to testify of the faithfulness of the Lord. The seasons change and you change, but your Lord abides evermore the same, and the streams of His love are as deep, as broad and as full as ever. The heats of business cares and scorching trials make me need the cooling influences of the river of His grace. I may go at once and drink to the full from the inexhaustible fountain, for in summer and in winter it pours forth its flood. The upper springs are never scanty, and blessed be the name of the Lord, the nether springs cannot fail either. Elijah found Cherith dried up, but Jehovah was still the same God of providence. Job said his brethren were like deceitful brooks, but he found his God an overflowing river of consolation. The Nile is the great confidence of Egypt, but its floods are variable; our Lord is evermore the same. By turning the course of the Euphrates, Cyrus took the city of Babylon, but no power, human or infernal, can divert the current of divine grace. The tracks of ancient rivers have been found all dry and desolate, but the streams which take their rise on the mountains of divine sovereignty and infinite love shall ever be full to the brim. Generations melt away, but the course of grace is unaltered. The river of God may sing with greater truth then the brook in the poem,

> Men may come, and men may go,
> But I go on forever.

How happy are you, my soul, to be led beside such still waters! never wander to other streams, lest you hear the Lord's rebuke, *"What have you to do in the way of Egypt to drink of the muddy river?"*

EVENING

"And they heard the sound of the LORD God walking in the garden in the cool of the day" — *Genesis 3:8.*

MY SOUL, NOW that the cool of the day has come, retire awhile and hearken to the voice of your God. He is always ready to speak with you when you are prepared to hear. If there be any slowness to commune it is not on His part, but altogether on your own. For He stands at the door and knocks, and if His people will but open He rejoices to enter. But in what state is my heart, which is my Lord's garden? May I venture to hope that it is well trimmed and watered, and is bringing forth fruit fit for Him? If not, He will have much to reprove, but still I pray Him to come unto me, for nothing can so certainly bring my heart into a right condition as the presence of the Sun of Righteousness, who brings healing in His wings.

Come, therefore, Oh Lord, my God, my soul invites You earnestly, and waits for You eagerly. Come to me, Oh Jesus, my well-beloved, and plant fresh flowers in my garden, such as I see blooming in such perfection in Your matchless character! Come, Oh my Father, who is the Husbandman, and deal with me in Your tenderness and prudence! Come, Oh Holy Spirit, and bedew my whole nature, as the herbs are now moistened with the evening dews. Oh that God would speak to me. *"Speak, Lord, for Your servant hears!"* Oh that He would walk with me; I am ready to give up my whole heart and mind to Him, and every other thought is hushed. I am only asking what He delights to give. I am sure that He will condescend to have fellowship with me, for He has given me His Holy Spirit to abide with me forever. Sweet is the cool twilight, when every star seems like the eye of heaven, and the cool wind is as the breath of celestial love. My Father, my elder Brother, my sweet Comforter, speak now in loving-kindness, for You have opened my ear and I am not rebellious.

July 2

MORNING

"For our heart shall rejoice in Him" — *Psalm 33:21.*

BLESSED IS THE fact that Christians can rejoice even in the deepest distress; although trouble may surround them, they still sing; and, like many birds, they sing best in their cages. The waves may roll over them, but their souls soon rise to the surface and see the light of God's countenance; they have a buoyancy about them which keeps their head always above the water, and helps them to sing amid the tempest, "God is with me still." To whom shall the glory be given? Oh! to Jesus; it is all by Jesus. Trouble does not necessarily bring consolation with it to the believer, but the presence of the Son of God in the fiery furnace with him fills his heart with joy. He is sick and suffering, but Jesus visits him and makes his bed for him. He is dying, and the cold chilly waters of Jordan are gathering about him up to the neck, but Jesus puts His arms around him, and cries, Fear not, beloved; to die is to be blessed; the waters of death have their fountain-head in heaven; they are not bitter, they are sweet as nectar, for they flow from the throne of God.

As the departing saint wades through the stream, and the billows gather around him, and heart and flesh fail him, the same voice sounds in his ears, *"Fear not; I am with you; be not dismayed; I am your God."* As he nears the borders of the infinite unknown, and is almost afraid to enter the realm of shades, Jesus says, *"Fear not,"* it is your Father's good pleasure to give you the kingdom. Thus strengthened and consoled, the believer is not afraid to die; no, he is even willing to depart, for since he has seen Jesus as the morning star, he longs to gaze upon Him as the sun in his strength. Truly, the presence of Jesus is all the heaven we desire. He is at once

> The glory of our brightest days;
> The comfort of our nights.

EVENING

"I will cry to You, O LORD; my Rock, do not be deaf to me, lest, if You say nothing to me, I become like those who go down into the pit" — *Psalm 28:1.*

A CRY IS THE natural expression of sorrow, and a suitable utterance when all other modes of appeal fail us; but the cry must be alone directed to the Lord, for to cry to man is to waste our entreaties upon the air. When we consider the readiness of the Lord to hear, and His ability to aid, we shall see good reason for directing all our appeals at once to the God of our salvation. It will be in vain to call to the rocks in the day of judgment, but our Rock attends to our cries.

"Be not silent to me." Mere formalists may be content without answers to their prayers, but genuine supplicants cannot; they are not satisfied with the results of prayer itself in calming the mind and subduing the will. They must go further, and obtain actual replies from heaven, or they cannot rest; and those replies they long to receive at once, they dread even a little of God's silence. God's voice is often so terrible that it shakes the wilderness; but His silence is equally full of awe to an eager supplicant. When God seems to close His ear, we must not therefore close our mouths, but rather cry with more earnestness; for when our note grows shrill with eagerness and grief, He will not long deny us a hearing. What a dreadful case should we be in if the Lord should become forever silent to our prayers? *"Lest, if You be silent to me, I become like them that go down into the pit."* Deprived of the God who answers prayer, we should be in a more pitiable plight than the dead in the grave, and should soon sink to the same level as the lost in hell. We must have answers to prayer: ours is an urgent case of dire necessity; surely the Lord will speak peace to our agitated minds, for He never can find it in His heart to permit His own elect to perish.

MORNING
July 3

"And the evil-appearing and lean-fleshed cows ate up the seven beautiful appearing and fat cows" — Genesis 41:4.

PHARAOH'S DREAM has too often been my waking experience. My days of sloth have ruinously destroyed all that I had achieved in times of zealous industry; my seasons of coldness have frozen all the genial glow of my periods of fervency and enthusiasm; and my fits of worldliness have thrown me back from my advances in the divine life. I had need to beware of lean prayers, lean praises, lean duties, and lean experiences, for these will eat up the fat of my comfort and peace. If I neglect prayer for never so short a time, I lose all the spirituality to which I had attained. If I draw no fresh supplies from heaven, the old grain in my granary is soon consumed by the famine which rages in my soul. When the caterpillars of indifference, the cankerworms of worldliness, and the worms of self-indulgence, lay my heart completely desolate, and make my soul to languish, all my former fruitfulness and growth in grace avails me nothing whatever.

How anxious should I be to have no lean-fleshed days, no ill-favored hours! If every day I journeyed towards the goal of my desires I should soon reach it, but backsliding leaves me still far off from the prize of my high calling, and robs me of the advances which I had so laboriously made. The only way in which all my days can be as the "fat cattle," is to feed them in the right meadow, to spend them with the Lord, in His service, in His company, in His fear, and in His way. Why should not every year be richer than the past, in love, and usefulness, and joy? I am nearer the celestial hills, I have had more experience of my Lord, and should be more like Him. Oh Lord, keep far from me the curse of leanness of soul; let me not have to cry, *"My leanness, my leanness, woe unto me!"* but may I be well-fed an0d nourished in Your house, that I may praise Your name.

EVENING
"If we endure, we shall also reign with Him" — 2 Timothy 2:12.

WE MUST NOT imagine that we are suffering for Christ, and with Christ, if we are not in Christ. Beloved friend, are you trusting to Jesus only? If not, whatever you may have to mourn over on earth, you are not "suffering with Christ," and have no hope of reigning with Him in heaven. Neither are we to conclude that all a Christian's sufferings are sufferings with Christ, for it is essential that he be called by God to suffer. If we are rash and imprudent, and run into positions for which neither providence nor grace has fitted us, we ought to question whether we are not rather sinning than communing with Jesus. If we let passion take the place of judgment, and self-will reign instead of Scriptural authority, we shall fight the Lord's battles with the devil's weapons, and if we cut our own fingers we must not be surprised. Again, in troubles which come upon us as the result of sin, we must not dream that we are suffering with Christ. When Miriam spoke evil of Moses, and the leprosy polluted her, she was not suffering for God. Moreover, suffering which God accepts must have God's glory as its end. If I suffer that I may earn a name, or win applause, I shall get no other reward that than of the Pharisee.

It is requisite also that love to Jesus, and love to His elect, be ever the mainspring of all our patience. We must manifest the Spirit of Christ in meekness, gentleness, and forgiveness. Let us search and see if we truly suffer with Jesus. And if we do thus suffer, what is our *"light affliction"* compared with reigning with Him? Oh it is so blessed to be in the furnace with Christ, and such an honor to stand in the stocks with Him, that if there were no future reward, we might count ourselves happy in present honor; but when the recompense is so eternal, so infinitely more than we had any right to expect, shall we not take up the cross with alacrity, and go on our way rejoicing?

July 4

MORNING

"Sanctify them by Your truth" — John 17:17.

SANCTIFICATION BEGINS in regeneration. The Spirit of God infuses into man that new living principle by which he becomes *"a new creature"* in Christ Jesus. This work which begins in the new birth, is carried on in two ways: mortification, whereby the lusts of the flesh are subdued and kept under; and vivification, by which the life which God has put within us is made to be a well of water springing up unto everlasting life. This is carried on every day in what is called *"perseverance,"* by which the Christian is preserved and continued in a gracious state, and is made to abound in good works unto the praise and glory of God. And it culminates or comes to perfection, in *"glory,"* when the soul, being thoroughly purged, is caught up to dwell with holy beings at the right hand of the Majesty on high.

But while the Spirit of God is thus the author of sanctification, yet there is a visible agency employed which must not be forgotten. *"Sanctify them,"* said Jesus, *"by Your truth: Your word is truth."* The passages of Scripture which prove that the instrument of our sanctification is the Word of God are very many. The Spirit of God brings to our minds the precepts and doctrines of truth, and applies them with power. These are heard in the ear, and being received in the heart, they work in us to will and to do of God's good pleasure. The truth is the sanctifier, and if we do not hear or read the truth, we shall not grow in sanctification. We only progress in sound living as we progress in sound understanding. *"Your word is a lamp unto my feet and a light unto my path."* Do not say of any error, It is a mere matter of opinion. No man indulges an error of judgment, without sooner or later tolerating an error in practice. Hold fast the truth, for by so holding the truth shall you be sanctified by the Spirit of God.

EVENING

"He who has clean hands and a pure heart; who has not lifted up his soul to vanity and has not sworn deceitfully" — Psalm 24:4.

OUTWARD PRACTICAL holiness is a very precious mark of grace. It is to be feared that many professors have perverted the doctrine of justification by faith in such a way as to treat good works with contempt; if so, they will receive everlasting contempt at the last great day. If our hands are not clean, let us wash them in Jesus' precious blood, and so let us lift up pure hands unto God. But *"clean hands"* will not suffice, unless they are connected with *"a pure heart."* True religion is heart-work. We may wash the outside of the cup and the platter as long as we please, but if the inward parts be filthy, we are filthy altogether in the sight of God, for our hearts are more truly ourselves than our hands are; the very life of our being lies in the inner nature, and hence the imperative need of purity within. *"The pure in heart shall see God,"* all others are but blind bats.

The man who is born for heaven *"has not lifted up his soul unto vanity."* All men have their joys, by which their souls are lifted up. The worldling lifts up his soul in carnal delights, which are mere empty vanities; but the saint loves more substantial things; like Jehoshaphat, he is lifted up in the ways of the Lord. He who is content with husks, will be reckoned with the swine. Does the world satisfy you? Then you have your reward and portion in this life; make much of it, for you shall know no other joy.

"Nor sworn deceitfully." The saints are men of honor still. The Christian man's word is his only oath; but that is as good as twenty oaths of other men. False speaking will shut any man out of heaven, for a liar shall not enter into God's house, whatever may be his professions or doings. Reader, does the text before us condemn you, or do you hope to ascend into the hill of the Lord?

MORNING July 5

"called to be saints" — Romans 1:7.

WE ARE VERY apt to regard the apostolic saints as if they were saints in a more special manner than the other children of God. All are saints whom God has called by His grace, and sanctified by His Spirit. But we are apt to look upon the apostles as extraordinary beings, scarcely subject to the same weaknesses and temptations as ourselves. Yet in so doing we are forgetful of this truth, that the nearer a man lives to God the more intensely has he to mourn over his own evil heart. And the more his Master honors him in His service, the more also does the evil of the flesh vex and tease him day by day. The fact is, if we had seen the apostle Paul, we should have thought him remarkably like the rest of the chosen family: and if we had talked with him, we should have said, We find that his experience and ours are much the same. He is more faithful, more holy, and more deeply taught than we are, but he has the selfsame trials to endure. No, in some respects he is more sorely tried than ourselves.

Do not, then, look upon the ancient saints as being exempt either from infirmities or sins; and do not regard them with that mystic reverence which will almost make us idolaters. Their holiness is attainable even by us. We are *"called to be saints"* by that same voice which constrained them to their high vocation. It is a Christian's duty to force his way into the inner circle of saintship. And if these saints were superior to us in their attainments, as they certainly were, let us follow them; let us emulate their ardor and holiness. We have the same light that they had, the same grace is accessible to us, and why should we rest satisfied until we have equaled them in heavenly character? They lived with Jesus, they lived for Jesus, therefore they grew like Jesus. Let us live by the same Spirit as they did, *"looking unto Jesus,"* and our saintship will soon be apparent.

EVENING

"Trust in the LORD forever; for in the LORD JEHOVAH is everlasting strength" — Isaiah 26:4.

SINCE WE have such a God to trust to, let us rest upon Him with all our weight; let us resolutely drive out all unbelief, and endeavor to get rid of doubts and fears, which so much mar our comfort. For there is no excuse for fear where God is the foundation of our trust. A loving parent would be sorely grieved if his child could not trust him; and how ungenerous, how unkind is our conduct when we put so little confidence in our heavenly Father who has never failed us, and who never will. It were well if doubting were banished from the household of God; but it is to be feared that old Unbelief is as nimble nowadays as when the psalmist asked, *"Is mercy clean gone forever? Will He be favorable no more?"* David had not made any very lengthy trial of the mighty sword of the giant Goliath, and yet he said, *"There is none like it."* He had tried it once in the hour of his youthful victory, and it had proved itself to be of the right metal, and therefore he praised it ever afterwards; even so should we speak well of our God, there is none like unto Him in the heaven above or the earth beneath; *"To whom then will you compare Me, or shall I be equal? said the Holy One."*

There is no rock like unto the rock of Jacob, our enemies themselves being judges. So far from suffering doubts to live in our hearts, we will take the whole detestable crew, as Elijah did the prophets of Baal, and slay them over the brook; and for a stream to kill them at, we will select the sacred torrent which wells forth from our Savior's wounded side. We have been in many trials, but we have never yet been cast where we could not find in our God all that we needed. Let us then be encouraged to trust in the Lord forever, assured that His everlasting strength will be, as it has been, our succor and stay.

July 6

MORNING

"But whoever listens to me shall dwell safely and shall be quiet from fear of evil" — Proverbs 1:33.

DIVINE LOVE IS rendered conspicuous when it shines in the midst of judgments. Fair is that lone star which smiles through the rifts of the thunder clouds; bright is the oasis which blooms in the wilderness of sand; so fair and so bright is love in the midst of wrath. When the Israelites provoked the Most High by their continued idolatry, He punished them by withholding both dew and rain, so that their land was visited by a sore famine; but while He did this, He took care that His own chosen ones should be secure. If all other brooks are dry, yet shall there be one reserved for Elijah; and when that fails, God shall still preserve for him a place of sustenance. No, not only so, the Lord had not simply one "Elijah," but He had a remnant according to the election of grace, who were hidden by fifties in a cave, and though the whole land was subject to famine, yet these fifties in the cave were fed, and fed from Ahab's table too by His faithful, God-fearing steward, Obadiah.

Let us from this draw the inference, that come what may, God's people are safe. Let convulsions shake the solid earth, let the skies themselves be rent in twain, yet amid the wreck of worlds the believer shall be as secure as in the calmest hour of rest. If God cannot save His people under heaven, He will save them in heaven. If the world becomes too hot to hold them, then heaven shall be the place of their reception and their safety. Be confident then, when you hear of wars, and rumors of wars. Let no agitation distress you, but be quiet from fear of evil. Whatever comes upon the earth, you, beneath the broad wings of Jehovah, shall be secure. Stay yourself upon His promise; rest in His faithfulness, and bid defiance to the blackest future, for there is nothing in it direful for you. Your sole concern should be to show forth to the world the blessedness of hearkening to the voice of wisdom.

EVENING

"How many are my iniquities and sins?" — Job 13:23.

HAVE YOU EVER really weighed and considered how great the sin of God's people is? Think how heinous is your own transgression, and you will find that not only does a sin here and there tower up like an alp, but that your iniquities are heaped upon each other, as in the old fable of the giants who piled mountain upon mountain. What an aggregate of sin there is in the life of one of the most sanctified of God's children! Attempt to multiply this, the sin of one only, by the multitude of the redeemed, *"a number which no man can number,"* and you will have some conception of the great mass of the guilt of the people for whom Jesus shed His blood.

But we arrive at a more adequate idea of the magnitude of sin by the greatness of the remedy provided. It is the blood of Jesus Christ, God's only and well-beloved Son. God's Son! Angels cast their crowns before Him! All the choral symphonies of heaven surround His glorious throne. *"God over all, blessed forever. Amen."* And yet He takes upon Himself the form of a servant, and is scourged and pierced, bruised and torn, and at last slain; since nothing but the blood of the incarnate Son of God could make atonement for our offenses. No human mind can adequately estimate the infinite value of the divine sacrifice, for great as is the sin of God's people, the atonement which takes it away is immeasurably greater. Therefore, the believer, even when sin rolls like a black flood, and the remembrance of the past is bitter, can yet stand before the blazing throne of the great and holy God, and cry, *"Who is he that condemns? It is Christ that died; yes rather, that has risen again."* While the recollection of his sin fills him with shame arid sorrow, he at the same time makes it a foil to show the uprightness of mercy; guilt is the dark night in which the fair star of divine love shines with serene splendor.

MORNING   July 7

"Brothers, pray for us" — 1 Thessalonians 5:25.

THIS ONE MORNING in the year we reserved to refresh the reader's memory upon the subject of prayer for ministers, and we do most earnestly implore every Christian household to grant the fervent request of the text first uttered by an apostle and now repeated by us. Brothers, our work is solemnly momentous, involving weal or woe to thousands. We treat with souls for God on eternal business, and our word is either a savor of life unto life, or of death unto death. A very heavy responsibility rests upon us, and it will be no small mercy if at the last we be found clear of the blood of all men. As officers in Christ's army, we are the special mark of the enmity of men and devils; they watch for our halting, and labor to take us by the heels. Our sacred calling involves us in temptations from which you are exempt, above all it too often draws us away from our personal enjoyment of truth into a ministerial and official consideration of it.

We meet with many knotty cases, and our wits are at a non plus; we observe very sad backslidings, and our hearts are wounded; we see millions perishing, and our spirits sink. We wish to profit you by our preaching; we desire to be blest to your children; we long to be useful both to saints and sinners; therefore, dear friends, intercede for us with our God. Miserable men are we if we miss the aid of your prayers, but happy are we if we live in your supplications. You do not look to us but to our Master for spiritual blessings, and yet how many times has He given those blessings through His ministers; ask then, again and again, that we may be the earthen vessels into which the Lord may put the treasure of the gospel. We, the whole company of missionaries, ministers, city missionaries, and students, do in the name of Jesus beseech you
    BROTHERS, PRAY FOR US.

EVENING

"And when I passed by you, I said, Live!" — Ezekiel 16:6.

SAVED ONE, CONSIDER gratefully this mandate of mercy. Note that this fiat of God is majestic. In our text, we perceive a sinner with nothing in him but sin, expecting nothing but wrath; but the eternal Lord passes by in His glory; He looks, He pauses, and He pronounces the solitary but royal word, *"Live!"* There speaks a God. Who but He could venture thus to deal with life and dispense it with a single syllable? Again, this fiat is manifold. When He says *"Live,"* it includes many things. Here is judicial life. The sinner is ready to be condemned, but the mighty One says, *"Live,"* and he rises pardoned and absolved. It is spiritual life. We know not Jesus; our eyes could not see Christ, our ears could not hear His voice; Jehovah said, *"Live,"* and we were quickened who were dead in trespasses and sins. Moreover, it includes glory-life, which is the perfection of spiritual life. *"I said unto you, Live:"* and that word rolls on through all the years of time till death comes, and in the midst of the shadows of death, the Lord's voice is still heard, *"Live!"* In the morning of the resurrection it is that self-same voice which is echoed by the arch-angel, *"Live,"* and as holy spirits rise to heaven to be blest for ever in the glory of their God, it is in the power of this same word, *"Live."*

Note again, that it is an irresistible mandate. Saul of Tarsus is on the road to Damascus to arrest the saints of the living God. A voice is heard from heaven and a light is seen above the brightness of the sun, and Saul is crying out, *"Lord, what will You have me to do?"* This mandate is a mandate of free grace. When sinners are saved, it is only and solely because God will do it to magnify His free, unpurchased, unsought grace. Christians, see your position, debtors to grace; show your gratitude by earnest, Christlike lives, and as God has bidden you live, see to it that you live in earnest.

July 8   MORNING

"Please tell me where your great strength lies" — Judges 16:6.

WHERE LIES THE secret strength of faith? It lies in the food it feeds on; for faith studies what the promise is, an emanation of divine grace, an overflowing of the great heart of God. And faith says, My God could not have given this promise, except from love and grace; therefore it is quite certain His Word will be fulfilled. Then faith thinks, Who gave this promise? It considers not so much its greatness, as, Who is the author of it? She remembers that it is God who cannot lie, God omnipotent, God immutable; and therefore concludes that the promise must be fulfilled; and forward she advances in this firm conviction. She remembers, why the promise was given, namely, for God's glory. And she feels perfectly sure that God's glory is safe, that He will never stain His own escutcheon, nor mar the lustre of His own crown; and therefore the promise must and will stand. Then faith also considers the amazing work of Christ as being a clear proof of the Father's intention to fulfil His word. *"He that spared not His own Son, but freely delivered Him up for us all, how shall He not with Him also freely give us all things?"*

Moreover faith looks back upon the past, for her battles have strengthened her, and her victories have given her courage. She remembers that God never has failed her; no, that He never did once fail any of His children. She remembers times of great peril, when deliverance came; hours of awful need, when as her day her strength was found, and she cries, No, I never will be led to think that He can change and leave His servant now. Hitherto the Lord has helped me, and He will help me still. Thus faith views each promise in its connection with the promise-giver, and, because she does so, can with assurance say, *"Surely goodness and mercy shall follow me all the days of my life!"*

EVENING

"Lead me in Your truth, and teach me; for You are the God of my salvation; on You I wait all the day long" — Psalm 25:5.

WHEN THE BELIEVER has begun with trembling feet to walk in the way of the Lord, he asks to be still led onward like a little child upheld by its parent's helping hand, and he craves to be further instructed in the alphabet of truth. Experimental teaching is the burden of this prayer. David knew much, but he felt his ignorance, and desired to be still in the Lord's school: four times over in two verses he applies for a scholarship in the college of grace. It were well for many professors if instead of following their own devices, and cutting out new paths of thought for themselves, they would inquire for the good old ways of God's own truth, and beseech the Holy Ghost to give them sanctified understandings and teachable spirits. *"For you are the God of my salvation."* The Three-One Jehovah is the Author and Perfecter of salvation to His people.

Reader, is He the God of your salvation? Do you find in the Father's election, in the Son's atonement, and in the Spirit's quickening, all the grounds of your eternal hopes? If so, you may use this as an argument for obtaining further blessings; if the Lord has ordained to save you, surely He will not refuse to instruct you in His ways. It is a happy thing when we can address the Lord with the confidence which David here manifests, it gives us great power in prayer, and comfort in trial. *"On You I wait all the day long."* Patience is the fair handmaid and daughter of faith; we cheerfully wait when we are certain that we shall not wait in vain. It is our duty and our privilege to wait upon the Lord in service, in worship, in expectancy, in trust all the days of our life. Our faith will be tried faith, and if it be of the true kind, it will bear continued trial without yielding. We shall not grow weary of waiting upon God if we remember how long and how graciously He once waited for us.

MORNING

July 9

"Forget not all His benefits" — *Psalm 103:2.*

IT IS A DELIGHTFUL and profitable occupation to mark the hand of God in the lives of ancient saints, and to observe His goodness in delivering them, His mercy in pardoning them, and His faithfulness in keeping His covenant with them. But would it not be even more interesting and profitable for us to remark the hand of God in our own lives? Ought we not to look upon our own history as being at least as full of God, as full of His goodness and of His truth, as much a proof of His faithfulness and veracity, as the lives of any of the saints who have gone before? We do our Lord an injustice when we suppose that He worked all His mighty acts, and showed Himself strong for those in the early time, but does not perform wonders or lay bare His arm for the saints who are now upon the earth.

Let us review our own lives. Surely in these we may discover some happy incidents, refreshing to ourselves and glorifying to our God. Have you had no deliverances? Have you passed through no rivers, supported by the divine presence? Have you walked through no fires unharmed? Have you had no manifestations? Have you had no choice favors? The God who gave Solomon the desire of his heart, has He never listened to you and answered your requests? That God of lavish bounty of whom David sang, *"Who satisfies your mouth with good things,"* has He never satiated you with fatness? Have you never been made to lie down in green pastures? Have you never been led by the still waters? Surely the goodness of God has been the same to us as to the saints of old. Let us, then, weave His mercies into a song. Let us take the pure gold of thankfulness, and the jewels of praise and make them into another crown for the head of Jesus. Let our souls give forth music as sweet and as exhilarating as came from David's harp, while we praise the Lord whose mercy endures forever.

EVENING

"And God divided between the light and the darkness" — *Genesis 1:4.*

A BELIEVER HAS TWO principles at work within him. In his natural estate he was subject to one principle only, which was darkness; now light has entered, and the two principles disagree. Mark the apostle Paul's words in the seventh chapter of Romans: *"I find then a law, that, when I would do good, evil is present with me. For I delight in the law of God after the inward man: but I see another law in my members, warring against the law of my mind, and bringing me into captivity to the law of sin, which is in my members."*

How is this state of things occasioned? *"The Lord divided the light from the darkness."* Darkness, by itself, is quiet and undisturbed, but when the Lord sends in light, there is a conflict, for the one is in opposition to the other: a conflict which will never cease till the believer is altogether light in the Lord. If there be a division within the individual Christian, there is certain to be a division without. So soon as the Lord gives to any man light, he proceeds to separate himself from the darkness around; he secedes from a merely worldly religion of outward ceremonial, for nothing short of the gospel of Christ will now satisfy him, and he withdraws himself from worldly society and frivolous amusements, and seeks the company of the saints, for *"We know we have passed from death unto life, because we love the brothers."* The light gathers to itself, and the darkness to itself. What God has divided, let us never try to unite, but as Christ went without the camp, bearing His reproach, so let us come out from the ungodly, and be a peculiar people. He was holy, harmless, undefiled, separate from sinners; and, as He was, so we are to be nonconformists to the world, dissenting from all sin, and distinguished from the rest of mankind by our likeness to our Master.

July 10

MORNING

"But fellow-citizens of the saints" — *Ephesians 2:19.*

WHAT IS MEANT by our being citizens in heaven? It means that we are under heaven's government. Christ the king of heaven reigns in our hearts; our daily prayer is, *"Your will be done on earth as it is in heaven."* The proclamations issued from the throne of glory are freely received by us: the decrees of the Great King we cheerfully obey. Then as citizens of the New Jerusalem, we share heaven's honors. The glory which belongs to beatified saints belongs to us, for we are already sons of God, already princes of the blood imperial; already we wear the spotless robe of Jesus' righteousness; already we have angels for our attendants, saints for our companions, Christ for our Brother, God for our Father and a crown of immortality for our reward. We share the honors of citizenship, for *"we have come to the general assembly and Church of the first-born whose names are written in heaven."*

As citizens, we have confirmed rights to all the property of heaven. Ours are its gates of pearl and walls of chrysolite; ours the azure light of the city that needs no candle nor light of the sun, ours the river of the water of life, and the twelve manner of fruits which grow on the trees planted on the banks thereof; there is nothing in heaven that belongs not to us. *"Things present, or things to come,"* all are ours. Also as citizens of heaven we enjoy its delights. Do they there rejoice over sinners that repent, prodigals that have returned? So do we. Do they chant the glories of triumphant grace? We do the same. Do they cast their crowns at Jesus' feet? Such honors as we have we cast there too. Are they charmed with His smile? It is not less sweet to us who dwell below. Do they look forward, waiting for His second advent? We also look and long for His appearing. If, then, we are thus citizens of heaven, let our walk and actions be consistent with our high dignity.

EVENING

"And the evening and the morning were the first day" — *Genesis 1:5.*

THE EVENING WAS "darkness" and the morning was "light," and yet the two together are called by the name that is given to the light alone! This is somewhat remarkable, but it has an exact analogy in spiritual experience. In every believer there is darkness and light, and yet he is not to be named a sinner because there is sin in him, but he is to be named a saint because he possesses some degree of holiness. This will be a most comforting thought to those who are mourning their infirmities, and who ask, Can I be a child of God while there is so much darkness in me? Yes; for you, like the day, take not your name from the evening, but from the morning: and you are spoken of in the word of God as if you were even now perfectly holy as you will be soon. You are called the child of light, though there is darkness in you still. You are named after what is the predominating quality in the sight of God, which will one day be the only principle remaining.

Observe that the evening comes first. Naturally we are darkness first in order of time, and the gloom is often first in our mournful apprehension, driving us to cry out in deep humiliation, *"God be merciful to me, a sinner."* The place of the morning is second, it dawns when grace overcomes nature. It is a blessed observation of John Bunyan, That which is last, lasts forever. That which is first, yields in due season to the last; but nothing comes after the last. So that though you are naturally darkness, when once you become light in the Lord, there is no evening to follow; *"your sun shall no more go down."* The first day in this life is an evening and a morning; but the second day, when we shall be with God forever, shall be a day with no evening, but one, sacred, high, eternal noon.

MORNING
July 11

"after you have suffered a little while, make you perfect, establish, strengthen, settle you."
— *1 Peter 5:10.*

YOU HAVE SEEN the arch of heaven as it spans the plain: glorious are its colors, and rare its hues. It is beautiful, but, alas, it passes away, and lo, it is not. The fair colors give way to the fleecy clouds, and the sky is no longer brilliant with the tints of heaven. It is not established. How can it be? A glorious show made up of transitory sunbeams and passing rain-drops, how can it abide? The graces of the Christian character must not resemble the rainbow in its transitory beauty, but, on the contrary, must be established, settled, abiding.

Seek, Oh believer, that every good thing you have may be an abiding thing. May your character not be a writing upon the sand, but an inscription upon the rock! May your faith be no "baseless fabric of a vision," but may it be built of material able to endure that awful fire which shall consume the wood, hay, and stubble of the hypocrite. May you be rooted and grounded in love. May your convictions be deep, your love real, your desires earnest. May your whole life be so settled and established, that all the blasts of hell, and all the storms of earth shall never be able to remove you. But notice how this blessing of being *"established in the faith" is gained.*

The apostle's words point us to suffering as the means employed: *"After you have suffered a little while."* It is of no use to hope that we shall be well rooted if no rough winds pass over us. Those old gnarls on the root of the oak tree, and those strange twistings of the branches, all tell of the many storms that have swept over it, and they are also indicators of the depth into which the roots have forced their way. So the Christian is made strong, and firmly rooted by all the trials and storms of life. Shrink not then from the tempestuous winds of trial, but take comfort, believing that by their rough discipline God is fulfilling this benediction to you.

EVENING

"Tell your children of it and your children their children, and their children another generation" — *Joel 1:3.*

IN THIS SIMPLE way, by God's grace, a living testimony for truth is always to be kept alive in the land; the beloved of the Lord are to hand down their witness for the gospel, and the covenant to their heirs, and these again to their next descendants. This is our first duty, we are to begin at the family hearth. He is a bad preacher who does not commence his ministry at home. The heathen are to be sought by all means, and the highways and hedges are to be searched, but home has a prior claim, and woe unto those who reverse the order of the Lord's arrangements. To teach our children is a personal duty; we cannot delegate it to Sunday School teachers, or other friendly aids. These can assist us, but cannot deliver us from the sacred obligation; proxies and sponsors are wicked devices in this case: mothers and fathers must, like Abraham, command their households in the fear of God, and talk with their offspring concerning the wondrous works of the Most High.

Parental teaching is a natural duty; who so fit to look to the child's well-being as those who are the authors of his actual being? To neglect the instruction of our offspring is worse than brutish. Family religion is necessary for the nation, for the family itself, and for the church of God. By a thousand plots Popery is covertly advancing in our land, and one of the most effectual means for resisting its inroads is left almost neglected, namely, the instruction of children in the faith. Would that parents would awaken to a sense of the importance of this matter. It is a pleasant duty to talk of Jesus to our sons and daughters, and the more so because it has often proved to be an accepted work, for God has saved the children through the parents' prayers and admonitions. May every house into which this volume shall come honor the Lord and receive His smile.

July 12   MORNING

"Sanctified by God the Father — Jude 1; Sanctified in Jesus — 1 Corinthians 1:2; Through Sanctification by the Spirit" — 1 Peter 1:2.

MARK THE UNION of the Three Divine Persons in all their gracious acts. How unwisely do those believers talk who make preferences in the Persons of the Trinity; who think of Jesus as if He were the embodiment of everything lovely and gracious, while the Father they regard as severely just, but destitute of kindness. Equally wrong are those who magnify the decree of the Father, and the atonement of the Son, so as to depreciate the work of the Spirit. In deeds of grace none of the Persons of the Trinity act apart from the rest. They are as united in their deeds as in their essence. In their love towards the chosen they are one, and in the actions which flow from that great central source they are still undivided.

Notice this especially in the matter of sanctification. While we may without mistake speak of sanctification as the work of the Spirit, yet we must take heed that we do not view it as if the Father and the Son had no part therein. It is correct to speak of sanctification as the work of the Father, of the Son, and of the Spirit. Still does Jehovah say, *"Let us make man in our own image after our likeness,"* and thus we are *"His workmanship, created in Christ Jesus unto good works, which God has before ordained that we should walk in them."* See the value which God sets upon real holiness, since the Three Persons in the Trinity are represented as co-working to produce a Church without *"spot, or wrinkle, or any such thing."* And you, believer, as the follower of Christ, must also set a high value on holiness, upon purity of life and godliness of conversation. Value the blood of Christ as the foundation of your hope, but never speak disparagingly of the work of the Spirit which is your fitness for the inheritance of the saints in light. This day let us so live as to manifest the work of the Triune God in us.

EVENING
"His heavenly kingdom" 2 Timothy 4:18.

YONDER CITY OF the great King is a place of active service. Ransomed spirits serve Him day and night in His temple. They never cease to fulfil the good pleasure of their King. They always rest, so far as ease and freedom from care is concerned; and never rest, in the sense of indolence or inactivity. Jerusalem the golden is the place of communion with all the people of God. We shall sit with Abraham, Isaac, and Jacob, in eternal fellowship. We shall hold high converse with the noble host of the elect, all reigning with Him who by His love and His potent arm has brought them safely home. We shall not sing solos, but in chorus shall we praise our King.

Heaven is a place of victory realized. Whenever, Christian, you have achieved a victory over your lusts; whenever after hard struggling, you have laid a temptation dead at your feet; you have in that hour a foretaste of the joy that awaits you when the Lord shall shortly tread Satan under your feet, and you shall find yourself more than conqueror through Him who has loved you. Paradise is a place of security. When you enjoy the full assurance of faith, you have the pledge of that glorious security which shall be yours when you are a perfect citizen of the heavenly Jerusalem. Oh my sweet home, Jerusalem, you happy harbor of my soul! Thanks, even now, to Him whose love has taught me to long for You; but louder thanks in eternity, when I shall possess you.

> My soul has tasted of the grapes,
> And now it longs to go
> Where my dear Lord His vineyard keeps
> And all the clusters grow.
> Upon the true and living vine
> My famished soul would feast,
> And banquet on the fruit divine,

MORNING   July 13

"God said to Jonah, Do you do well to be angry" — Jonah 4:9.

ANGER IS NOT always or necessarily sinful, but it has such a tendency to run wild that whenever it displays itself, we should be quick to question its character, with this enquiry, *"Do you do well to be angry?"* It may be that we can answer, "Yes." Very frequently anger is the madman's firebrand, but sometimes it is Elijah's fire from heaven. We do well when we are angry with sin, because of the wrong which it commits against our good and gracious God; or with ourselves because we remain so foolish after so much divine instruction; or with others when the sole cause of anger is the evil which they do. He who is not angry at transgression becomes a partaker in it. Sin is a loathsome and hateful thing, and no renewed heart can patiently endure it. God Himself is angry with the wicked every day, and it is written in His Word, *"You that love the Lord, hate evil."*

Far more frequently it is to be feared that our anger is not commendable or even justifiable, and then we must answer, "No." Why should we be fretful with children, passionate with servants, and wrathful with companions? Is such anger honorable to our Christian profession, or glorifying to God? Is it not the old evil heart seeking to gain dominion, and should we not resist it with all the might of our newborn nature. Many professors give way to temper as though it were useless to attempt resistance; but let the believer remember that he must be a conqueror in every point, or else he cannot be crowned. If we cannot control our tempers, what has grace done for us? Some one told Mr. Jay that grace was often grafted on a crab-stump. Yes, said he, but the fruit will not be crabs. We must not make natural infirmity an excuse for sin, but we must fly to the cross and pray the Lord to crucify our tempers, and renew us in gentleness and meekness after His own image.

EVENING

"When I cry, then my enemies will be turned back. This I know, for God is with me" — Psalm 56:9.

IT IS IMPOSSIBLE for any human speech to express the full meaning of this delightful phrase, *"God is for me."* He was for us before the worlds were made; He was for us, or He would not have given His well-beloved Son; He was for us when He smote the Only-begotten, and laid the full weight of His wrath upon Him. He was for us, though He was against Him; He was for us, when we were ruined in the fall. He loved us notwithstanding all; He was for us, when we were rebels against Him, and with a high hand were bidding Him defiance; He was for us, or He would not have brought us humbly to seek His face. He has been for us in many struggles; we have been summoned to encounter hosts of dangers; we have been assailed by temptations from without and within. How could we have remained unharmed to this hour if He had not been for us?

He is for us, with all the infinity of His being; with all the omnipotence of His love; with all the infallibility of His wisdom; arrayed in all His divine attributes, He is for us, eternally and immutably for us; for us when yonder blue skies shall be rolled up like a worn out vesture; for us throughout eternity. And because He is for us, the voice of prayer will always ensure His help. *"When I cry unto You, then shall my enemies be turned back."* This is no uncertain hope, but a well grounded assurance: *"this I know."* I will direct my prayer unto You, and will look up for the answer, assured that it will come, and that my enemies shall be defeated, *"for God is for me."* Oh believer, how happy you are with the King of kings on Your side! How safe with such a Protector! How sure your cause pleaded by such an Advocate! If God is for you, who can be against you?

July 14

MORNING

"If you lift up your tool on it you have defiled it" — Exodus 20:25.

GOD'S ALTAR WAS to be built of uncut stones, that no trace of human skill or labor might be seen upon it. Human wisdom delights to trim and arrange the doctrines of the cross into a system more artificial and more congenial with the depraved tastes of fallen nature. However, instead of improving the gospel, carnal wisdom pollutes it, until it becomes another gospel, and not the truth of God at all. All alterations and amendments of the Lord's own Word are defilements and pollutions. The proud heart of man is very anxious to have a hand in the justification of the soul before God; preparations for Christ are dreamed of, humblings and repentings are trusted in, good works are cried up, natural ability is much vaunted, and by all means the attempt is made to lift up human tools upon the divine altar. It were well if sinners would remember that so far from perfecting the Savior's work, their carnal confidences only pollute and dishonor it. The Lord alone must be exalted in the work of atonement, and not a single mark of man's chisel or hammer will be endured. There is an inherent blasphemy in seeking to add to what Christ Jesus in His dying moments declared to be finished, or to improve that in which the Lord Jehovah finds perfect satisfaction. Trembling sinner, away with your tools, and fall upon your knees in humble supplications; and accept the Lord Jesus to be the altar of your atonement, and rest in Him alone.

Many professors may take warning from this morning's test as to the doctrines which they believe. There is among Christians far too much inclination to square and reconcile the truths of revelation; this is a form of irreverence and unbelief. Let us strive against it, and receive truth as we find it; rejoicing that the doctrines of the Word are uncut stones, and so are all the more fit to build an altar for the Lord.

EVENING

"As it was dawning. Mary Magdalene. came to see the grave" — Matthew 28:1.

LET US LEARN from Mary Magdalene how to obtain fellowship with the Lord Jesus. Notice how she sought. She sought the Savior very early in the morning. If you can wait for Christ, and be patient in the hope of having fellowship with Him at some distant season, you will never have fellowship at all; for the heart that is fitted for communion is a hungering and a thirsting heart. She sought Him also with very great boldness. Other disciples fled from the sepulchre, for they trembled and were amazed; but Mary, it is said, "stood" at the sepulchre. If you would have Christ with you, seek Him boldly. Let nothing hold you back. Defy the world. Press on where others flee. She sought Christ faithfully; she stood at the sepulchre. Some find it hard to stand by a living Savior, but she stood by One she thought to be dead. Let us seek Christ after this mode, cleaving to the very least thing that has to do with Him, remaining faithful though all others should forsake Him.

Note further, she sought Jesus earnestly, she stood "weeping." Those tear-drops were as spells that led the Savior captive, and made Him come forth and show Himself to her. If you desire Jesus' presence, weep after it! If you cannot be happy unless He come and say to you, *"You are My Beloved,"* you will soon hear His voice. Lastly, she sought the Savior only. What cared she for angels, she turned herself back from them; her search was only for her Lord. If Christ is your one and only love, if your heart has cast out all rivals, you will not long lack the comfort of His presence. Mary Magdalene sought thus because she loved much. Let us arouse ourselves to the same intensity of affection; let our heart, like Mary's, be full of Christ, and our love, like hers, will be satisfied with nothing short of Himself. Oh Lord, reveal Yourself to us this evening!

MORNING July 15

"The fire shall always be burning on the altar. It shall never go out" — *Leviticus 6:13.*

KEEP THE ALTAR of private prayer burning. This is the very life of all piety. The sanctuary and family altars borrow their fires here, therefore let this burn well. Secret devotion is the very essence, evidence, and barometer, of vital and experimental religion.

Burn here the fat of your sacrifices. Let your closet seasons be, if possible, regular, frequent, and undisturbed. Effectual prayer avails much. Have you nothing to pray for? Let us suggest the church, the ministry, your own soul, your children, your relations, your neighbors, your country, and the cause of God and truth throughout the world. Let us examine ourselves on this important matter. Do we engage with lukewarmness in private devotion? Is the fire of devotion burning dimly in our hearts? Do the chariot wheels drag heavily? If so, let us be alarmed at this sign of decay. Let us go with weeping, and ask for the Spirit of grace and of supplications. Let us set apart special seasons for extraordinary prayer. For if this fire should be smothered beneath the ashes of a worldly conformity, it will dim the fire on the family altar, and lessen our influence both in the church and in the world.

The text will also apply to the altar of the heart. This is a golden altar indeed. God loves to see the hearts of His people glowing towards Himself. Let us give to God our hearts, all blazing with love, and seek His grace, that the fire may never be quenched; for it will not burn if the Lord does not keep it burning. Many foes will attempt to extinguish it; but if the unseen hand behind the wall pour thereon the sacred oil, it will blaze higher and higher. Let us use texts of Scripture as fuel for our heart's fire, they are live coals; let us attend sermons, but above all, let us be much alone with Jesus.

EVENING

He first appeared to Mary Magdalene" — *Mark 16:9.*

JESUS FIRST APPEARED to Mary Magdalene, probably not only on account of her great love and persevering seeking, but because, as the context intimates, she had been a special trophy of Christ's delivering power. Learn from this, that the greatness of our sin before conversion should not make us imagine that we may not be specially favored with the very highest grade of fellowship. She was one who had left all to become a constant attendant on the Savior. He was her first, her chief object. Many who were on Christ's side did not take up Christ's cross; she did. She spent her substance in relieving His wants. If we would see much of Christ, let us serve Him. Tell me who they are that sit most often under the banner of His love, and drink deepest draughts from the cup of communion, and I am sure they will be those who give most, who serve best, and who abide closest to the bleeding heart of their dear Lord.

But notice how Christ revealed Himself to this sorrowing one by a word, "Mary." It needed but one word in His voice, and at once she knew Him, and her heart owned allegiance by another word, her heart was too full to say more. That one word would naturally be the most fitting for the occasion. It implies obedience. She said, "Master." There is no state of mind in which this confession of allegiance will be too cold. No, when your spirit glows most with the heavenly fire, then you will say, *"I am Your servant, You have loosed my bonds."* If you can say, "Master," if you feel that His will is your will, then you stand in a happy, holy place. He must have said your name, or else you could not have said, Rabboni. See, then, from all this, how Christ honors those who honor Him, how love draws out, Beloved; how it needs but one word of His to turn our weeping to rejoicing, how His presence makes the heart's sunshine.

July 16

MORNING

"They gathered manna every morning" — *Exodus 16:21.*

LABOR TO MAINTAIN a sense of your entire dependence upon the Lord's good will and pleasure for the continuance of your richest enjoyments. Never try to live on the old manna, nor seek to find help in Egypt. All must come from Jesus, or you are undone forever. Old anointings will not suffice to impart unction to your spirit; your head must have fresh oil poured upon it from the golden horn of the sanctuary, or it will cease from its glory. Today you may be upon the summit of the mount of God, but He who has put you there must keep you there, or you will sink far more speedily than you dream. Your mountain only stands firm when He settles it in its place; if He hide His face, you will soon be troubled. If the Savior should see fit, there is not a window through which you see the light of heaven which He could not darken in an instant. Joshua bade the sun stand still, but Jesus can shroud it in total darkness. He can withdraw the joy of your heart, the light of your eyes, and the strength of your life; in His hand your comforts lie, and at His will they can depart from you. This hourly dependence our Lord is determined that we shall feel and recognize, for He only permits us to pray for "daily bread," and only promises that *"as our days our strength shall be."*

Is it not best for us that it should be so, that we may often repair to His throne, and constantly be reminded of His love? Oh! how rich the grace which supplies us so continually, and does not refrain itself because of our ingratitude! The golden shower never ceases, the cloud of blessing tarries evermore above our habitation. Oh Lord Jesus, we would bow at Your feet, conscious of our utter inability to do anything without You, and in every favor which we are privileged to receive, we would adore Your blessed name and acknowledge Your inexhaustible love.

EVENING

"You shall arise and have mercy on Zion; for the time to pity her, yes, the set time, has come. For Your servants take pleasure in its stores and love its dust" — *Psalm 102:13, 14.*

A SELFISH MAN in trouble is exceedingly hard to comfort, because the springs of his comfort lie entirely within himself, and when he is sad all his springs are dry. But a large-hearted man full of Christian philanthropy, has other springs from which to supply himself with comfort besides those which lie within. He can go to his God first of all, and there find abundant help; and he can discover arguments for consolation in things relating to the world at large, to his country, and, above all, to the church. David in this Psalm was exceedingly sorrowful; he wrote, *"I am like an owl of the desert. I watch, and am as a sparrow alone upon the house top."* The only way in which he could comfort himself was in the reflection that God would arise, and have mercy upon Zion: though He was sad, yet Zion should prosper; however low his own estate, yet Zion would arise.

Christian man! learn to comfort yourself in God's gracious dealing towards the church. That which is so dear to your Master, should it not be dear above all else to you? Though your way be dark, can you not gladden your heart with the triumphs of His cross and the spread of His truth? Our own personal troubles are forgotten while we look, not only upon what God has done, and is doing for Zion, but on the glorious things He will yet do for His church. Try this, Oh believer, whenever you are sad of heart and in heaviness of spirit: forget yourself and your little concerns, and seek the welfare and prosperity of Zion. When you bend your knee in prayer to God, limit not your petition to the narrow circle of your own life, tried though it be, but send out your longing prayers for the church's prosperity, *"Pray for the peace of Jerusalem,"* and your own soul shall be refreshed.

MORNING   July 17

"Knowing, beloved brothers, your election by our God" — I Thessalonians 1:4.

MANY PERSONS WANT to know their election before they look to Christ, but they cannot learn it thus, it is only to be discovered by *"looking unto Jesus."* If you desire to ascertain your own election, assure your heart before God in this way:. Do you feel yourself to be a lost, guilty sinner? Go straightway to the cross of Christ, and tell Jesus so, and tell Him that you have read in the Bible, *"Him that comes unto me, I will in no wise cast out."* Tell Him that He has said, *"This is a faithful saying, and worthy of all acceptation, that Christ Jesus came into the world to save sinners."* Look to Jesus and believe on Him, and you shall make proof of your election directly, for so surely as you believe, you are elect. If you will give yourself wholly up to Christ and trust Him, then you are one of God's chosen ones; but if you stop and say, I want to know first whether I am elect, then you ask you know not what.

Go to Jesus, be you never so guilty, just as you are. Leave all curious inquiry about election alone. Go straight to Christ and hide in His wounds, and you shall know your election. The assurance of the Holy Spirit shall be given to you, so that you shall be able to say, *"I know whom I have believed, and I am persuaded that He is able to keep that which I have committed unto Him."* Christ was at the everlasting council; He can tell you whether you were chosen or not; but you cannot find it out in any other way. Go and put your trust in Him, and His answer will be, *"I have loved you with an everlasting love, therefore with loving-kindness have I drawn you."* There will be no doubt about His having chosen you, when you have chosen Him.

> Sons we are through God's election,
> Who in Jesus Christ believe.

EVENING

"Do not let one of them escape" — 1 Kings 18:40.

WHEN THE PROPHET Elijah had received the answer to his prayer, and the fire from heaven had consumed the sacrifice in the presence of all the people, he called upon the assembled Israelites to take the priests of Baal, and sternly cried, *"Let not one of them escape."* He took them all down to the brook Kishon, and slew them there. So must it be with our sins; they are all doomed, not one must be preserved. Our darling sin must die. Spare it not for its much crying. Strike, though it be as dear as an Isaac. Strike, for God struck at sin when it was laid upon His own Son. With stern unflinching purpose must you condemn to death that sin which was once the idol of your heart.

Do you ask how you are to accomplish this? Jesus will be your power. You have grace to overcome sin given you in the covenant of grace; you have strength to win the victory in the crusade against inward lusts, because Christ Jesus has promised to be with you even unto the end. If you would triumph over darkness, set yourself in the presence of the Sun of Righteousness. There is no place so well adapted for the discovery of sin, and recovery from its power and guilt, as the immediate presence of God. Job never knew how to get rid of sin half so well as he did when his eye of faith rested upon God, and then he abhorred himself, and repented in dust and ashes. The fine gold of the Christian is often becoming dim. We need the sacred fire to consume the dross. Let us fly to our God, He is a consuming fire; He will not consume our spirit, but our sins. let the goodness of God excite us to a sacred jealousy, and to a holy revenge against those iniquities which are hateful in His sight. Go forth to battle with Amalek in His strength, and utterly destroy the accursed crew: let not one of them escape.

July 18   MORNING

"They shall go last with their banners" — Numbers 2:31.

THE CAMP OF Dan brought up the rear when the armies of Israel were on the march. The Danites occupied the last place, but what mattered the position, since they were as truly part of the host as were the first tribes; they followed the same fiery cloudy pillar, they ate of the same manna, drank of the same spiritual rock, and journeyed to the same inheritance. Come, my heart, cheer up, though last and least; it is your privilege to be in the army, and to fare as they fare who lead the van. Some one must be last in honor and esteem, some one must do menial work for Jesus, and why should not I? In a poor village, among an ignorant peasantry; or in a back street, among degraded sinners, I will work on, and "go last with my standard."

The Danites occupied a very useful place. Stragglers have to be picked up upon the march, and lost property has to be gathered from the field. Fiery spirits may dash forward over untrodden paths to learn fresh truth, and win more souls to Jesus; but some of a more conservative spirit may be well engaged in reminding the church of her ancient faith, and restoring her fainting sons. Every position has its duties, and the slowly moving children of God will find their peculiar state one in which they may be eminently a blessing to the whole host.

The rear guard is a place of danger. There are foes behind us as well as before us. Attacks may come from any quarter. We read that Amalek fell upon Israel, and slew some of the last of them. The experienced Christian will find much work for his weapons in aiding those poor doubting, desponding, wavering, souls, who are last in faith, knowledge, and joy. These must not be left unaided, and therefore be it the business of well-taught saints to bear their standards among the last. My soul, do you tenderly watch to help the last this day.

EVENING

"One shall not thrust another. They shall walk each one in his path" — Joel 2:8.

LOCUSTS ALWAYS KEEP their rank, and although their number is legion, they do not crowd upon each other, so as to throw their columns into confusion. This remarkable fact in natural history shows how thoroughly the Lord has infused the spirit of order into His universe, since the smallest animate creatures are as much controlled by it as are the rolling spheres or the seraphic messengers. It would be wise for believers to be ruled by the same influence in all their spiritual life. In their Christian graces no one virtue should usurp the sphere of another, or eat out the vitals of the rest for its own support. Affection must not smother honesty, courage must not elbow weakness out of the field, modesty must not jostle energy, and patience must not slaughter resolution. So also with our duties, one must not interfere with another; public usefulness must not injure private piety; church work must not push family worship into a corner. It is ill to offer God one duty stained with the blood of another. Each thing is beautiful in its season, but not otherwise. It was to the Pharisee that Jesus said, *"This ought you to have done, and not to have left the other undone."*

The same rule applies to our personal position, we must take care to know our place, take it, and keep to it. We must minister as the Spirit has given us ability, and not intrude upon our fellow servant's domain. Our Lord Jesus taught us not to covet the high places, but to be willing to be the least among the brethren. Far from us be an envious, ambitious spirit; let us feel the force of the Master's command, and do as He bids us, keeping rank with the rest of the host. Tonight let us see whether we are keeping *"the unity of the Spirit in the bonds of peace,"* and let our prayer be that, in all the churches of the Lord Jesus, peace and order may prevail.

MORNING July 19

"The LORD our God has shown us His glory" — *Deuteronomy 5:24.*

GOD'S GREAT DESIGN in all His works is the manifestation of His own glory. Any aim less than this were unworthy of Himself. But how shall the glory of God be manifested to such fallen creatures as we are? Man's eye is not single, he has ever a side glance towards his own honor, has too high an estimate of his own powers, and so is not qualified to behold the glory of the Lord. It is clear, then, that self must stand out of the way, that there may be room for God to be exalted. And this is the reason why He often brings His people into straits and difficulties, that, being made conscious of their own folly and weakness, they may be fitted to behold the majesty of God when He comes forth to work their deliverance. He whose life is one even and smooth path, will see but little of the glory of the Lord. For he has few occasions of self-emptying, and hence, but little fitness for being filled with the revelation of God. They who navigate little streams and shallow creeks, know but little of the God of tempests; but they who "do business in great waters," these see His *"wonders in the deep."* Among the huge Atlantic waves of bereavement, poverty, temptation, and reproach, we learn the power of Jehovah, because we feel the littleness of man.

Thank God, then, if you have been led by a rough road: it is this which has given you your experience of God's greatness and loving-kindness. Your troubles have enriched you with a wealth of knowledge to be gained by no other means: your trials have been the cleft of the rock in which Jehovah has set you, as He did His servant Moses, that you might behold His glory as it passed by. Praise God that you have not been left to the darkness and ignorance which continued prosperity might have involved, but that in the great fight of affliction, you have been capacitated for the outshining of His glory in His wonderful dealings with you.

EVENING

"A bruised reed He will not break, and a smoking wick He will not put out" — *Matthew 12:20.*

WHAT IS WEAKER than the bruised reed or the smoking wick? A reed that grows in the fen or marsh, let but the wild duck light upon it, and it snaps; let but the foot of man brush against it, and it is bruised and broken; every wind that flits across the river moves it to and fro. You can conceive of nothing more frail or brittle, or whose existence is more in jeopardy, then a bruised reed. Then look at the smoking wick, what is it? It has a spark within it, it is true, but it is almost smothered; an infant's breath might blow it out; nothing has a more precarious existence than its flame. Weak things are here described, yet Jesus says of them, *"The smoking wick I will not put out; the bruised reed I will not break."*

Some of God's children are made strong to do mighty works for Him; God has His Samsons here and there who can pull up Gaza's gates, and carry them to the top of the hill; He has a few mighties who are lion-like men. But the majority of His people are a timid, trembling race. They are like starlings, frightened at every passer by; a little fearful flock. If temptation comes, they are taken like birds in a snare; if trial threatens, they are ready to faint; their frail skiff is tossed up and down by every wave, they are drifted along like a sea bird on the crest of the billows weak things, without strength, without wisdom, without foresight. Yet, weak as they are, and because they are so weak, they have this promise made specially to them. Herein is grace and graciousness! Herein is love and loving-kindness! How it opens to us the compassion of Jesus so gentle, tender, considerate! We need never shrink back from His touch. We need never fear a harsh word from Him; though He might well chide us for our weakness, He rebukes not. Bruised reeds shall have no blows from Him, and the smoking wick no damping frowns.

July 20

MORNING

"The firstfruit of our inheritance" — Ephesians 1:14.

OH! WHAT ENLIGHTENMENT, what joys, what consolation, what delight of heart is experienced by that man who has learned to feed on Jesus, and on Jesus alone. Yet the realization which we have of Christ's preciousness is, in this life, imperfect at the best. As an old writer says, "Tis but a taste!" We have tasted *"that the Lord is gracious,"* but we do not yet know how good and gracious He is, although what we know of His sweetness makes us long for more. We have enjoyed the first-fruits of the Spirit, and they have set us hungering and thirsting for the fullness of the heavenly vintage. We groan within ourselves, waiting for the adoption. Here we are like Israel in the wilderness, who had but one cluster from Eshcol, there we shall be in the vineyard. Here we see the manna falling small, like coriander seed, but there shall we eat the bread of heaven and the old grain of the kingdom.

We are but beginners now in spiritual education; for although we have learned the first letters of the alphabet, we cannot read words yet, much less can we put sentences together. But as one says, He that has been in heaven but five minutes, knows more than the general assembly of divines on earth. We have many ungratified desires at present, but soon every wish shall be satisfied; and all our powers shall find the sweetest employment in that eternal world of joy. Oh Christian, antedate heaven for a few years. Within a very little time you shall be rid of all your trials and your troubles. Your eyes now suffused with tears shall weep no longer. You shall gaze in ineffable rapture upon the splendor of Him who sits upon the throne. No, more, upon His throne shall you sit. The triumph of His glory shall be shared by you; His crown, His joy, His paradise, these shall be yours, and you shall be co-heir with Him who is the heir of all things.

EVENING

"And now what have you to do in the way of Egypt to drink the waters of Sihor?" — Jeremiah 2:18.

BY SUNDRY MIRACLES, by divers mercies, by strange deliverances Jehovah had proved Himself to be worthy of Israel's trust. Yet they broke down the hedges with which God had enclosed them as a sacred garden; they forsook their own true and living God, and followed after false gods. Constantly did the Lord reprove them for this infatuation, and our text contains one instance of God's expostulating with them, *"What have you to do in the way of Egypt, to drink the waters"* of the muddy river? For so it may be translated. Why do you wander afar and leave your own cool stream from Lebanon? Why do you forsake Jerusalem to turn aside to Noph and to Tahpanhes? Why are you so strangely set on mischief, that you cannot be content with the good and healthful, but would follow after that which is evil and deceitful?

Is there not here a word of expostulation and warning to the Christian? Oh true believer, called by grace and washed in the precious blood of Jesus, you have tasted of better drink than the muddy river of this world's pleasure can give you; you have had fellowship with Christ; you have obtained the joy of seeing Jesus, and leaning your head upon His bosom. Do the trifles, the sins, the honors, the merriment of this earth content you after that? Have you eaten the bread of angels, and can you live on husks? Good Rutherford once said, "I have tasted of Christ's own manna, and it has put my mouth out of taste for the brown bread of this world's joys." I think it should be so with you. If you are wandering after the waters of Egypt, Oh return quickly to the one living fountain: the waters of Sihor may be sweet to the Egyptians, but they will prove only bitterness to you. What have you to do with them? Jesus asks you this question this evening; what will you answer Him?

## MORNING	July 21

"The daughter of Jerusalem has shaken her head at you" — Isaiah 37:22.

REASSURED BY THE Word of the Lord, the poor trembling citizens of Zion grew bold, and shook their heads at Sennacherib's boastful threats. Strong faith enables the servants of God to look with calm contempt upon their most haughty foes. We know that our enemies are attempting impossibilities. They seek to destroy the eternal life, which cannot die while Jesus lives; to overthrow the citadel, against which the gates of hell shall not prevail. They kick against the pricks to their own wounding, and rush upon the bosses of Jehovah's buckler to their own hurt.

We know their weakness. What are they but men? And what is man but a worm? They roar and swell like waves of the sea, foaming out their own shame. When the Lord arises, they shall fly as chaff before the wind, and be consumed as crackling thorns. Their utter powerlessness to do damage to the cause of God and His truth, may make the weakest soldiers in Zion's ranks laugh them to scorn.

Above all, we know that the Most High is with us, and when He dresses Himself in arms, where are His enemies? If He comes forth from His place, the potsherds of the earth will not long contend with their Maker. His rod of iron shall dash them in pieces like a potter's vessel, and their very remembrance shall perish from the earth. Away, then, all fears, the kingdom is safe in the King's hands. Let us shout for joy, for the Lord reigns, and His foes shall be as straw for the dunghill.

> Nor earth, nor hell, with all their crew,
> Against us shall prevail.
> A jest, and by-word, are they grown;
> God is with us, we are His own,
> Our victory cannot fail.

EVENING

"Why do I go mourning" — Psalm 42:9.

CAN YOU ANSWER this, believer? Can you find any reason why you are so often mourning instead of rejoicing? Why yield to gloomy anticipations? Who told you that the night would never end in day? Who told you that the sea of circumstances would ebb out till there should be nothing left but long leagues of the mud of horrible poverty? Who told you that the winter of your discontent would proceed from frost to frost, from snow, and ice, and hail, to deeper snow, and yet more heavy tempest of despair? Do you not know that day follows night, that flood comes after ebb, that spring and summer succeed to winter? Hope then! Hope forever! for God fails you not. Do you not know that your God loves you in the midst of all this? Mountains, when in darkness hidden, are as real as in day, and God's love is as true to you now as it was in your brightest moments. No father chastens always: your Lord hates the rod as much as you do; He only cares to use it for that reason which should make you willing to receive it, namely, that it works your lasting good.

You shall yet climb Jacob's ladder with the angels, and behold Him who sits at the top of it, your covenant God. You shall yet, amidst the splendors of eternity, forget the trials of time, or only remember them to bless the God who led you through them, and worked your lasting good by them. Come, sing in the midst of tribulation. Rejoice even while passing through the furnace. Make the wilderness to blossom like the rose! Cause the desert to ring with your exulting joys, for these light afflictions will soon be over, and then *"forever with the Lord,"* your bliss shall never wane.

> Faint not nor fear, His arms are near,
> He changes not, and you are dear;
> Only believe and you shall see,
> That Christ is all in all to thee.

July 22 MORNING

"I am married to you" — Jeremiah 3:14.

CHRIST JESUS IS joined unto His people in marriage-union. In love He espoused His Church as a chaste virgin, long before she fell under the yoke of bondage. Full of burning affection He toiled, like Jacob for Rachel, until the whole of her purchase-money had been paid. And now, having sought her by His Spirit, and brought her to know and love Him, He awaits the glorious hour when their mutual bliss shall be consummated at the marriage-supper of the Lamb. Not yet has the glorious Bridegroom presented His betrothed, perfected and complete, before the Majesty of heaven; not yet has she actually entered upon the enjoyment of her dignities as His wife and queen: she is as yet a wanderer in a world of woe, a dweller in the tents of Kedar; but she is even now the bride, the spouse of Jesus, dear to His heart, precious in His sight, written on His hands, and united with His person.

On earth He exercises towards her all the affectionate offices of Husband. He makes rich provision for her wants, pays all her debts, allows her to assume His name, and to share in all His wealth. Nor will He ever act otherwise to her. The word divorce He will never mention, for *"He hates putting away."* Death must sever the conjugal tie between the most loving mortals, but it cannot divide the links of this immortal marriage. In heaven they marry not, but are as the angels of God; yet there is this one marvelous exception to the rule, for in Heaven Christ and His church shall celebrate their joyous nuptials. This affinity as it is more lasting, so is it more near than earthly wedlock. Let the love of husband be never so pure and fervent, it is but a faint picture of the flame which burns in the heart of Jesus. Passing all human union is that mystical cleaving unto the Church, for which Christ left His Father, and became one flesh with her.

EVENING

"Behold! The man!" — John 19:5.

IF THERE BE one place where our Lord Jesus most fully becomes the joy and comfort of His people, it is where He plunged deepest into the depths of woe. Come here, gracious souls, and behold the Man in the garden of Gethsemane; behold His heart so brimming with love that He cannot hold it in, so full of sorrow that it must find a vent. Behold the bloody sweat as it distills from every pore of His body, and falls upon the ground. Behold the Man as they drive the nails into His hands and feet. Look up, repenting sinners, and see the sorrowful image of your suffering Lord. Mark Him, as the ruby drops stand on the thorn-crown, and adorn with priceless gems and diadem of the King in the depths of misery. Behold the Man when all His bones are out of joint, and He is poured out like water and brought into the dust of death; God has forsaken Him, and hell compasses Him about. Behold and see, was there ever sorrow like unto His sorrow that is done unto Him!

All you that pass by draw near and look upon this spectacle of grief, unique, unparalleled, a wonder to men and angels, a prodigy unmatched. Behold this Man who had no equal or rival in His agonies! Gaze upon Him, you mourners, for if there be not consolation in a crucified Christ there is no joy in earth or heaven. If in the ransom price of His blood there be not hope, you harps of heaven, there is no joy in you, and the right hand of God shall know no pleasures forevermore. We have only to sit more continually at the foot of the cross to be less troubled with our doubts and woes. We have but to see His sorrows, and we shall be ashamed to mention our sorrows. We have but to gaze into His wounds and heal our own. If we would live aright it must be by the contemplation of His death; if we would rise to dignity, it must be by considering His humiliation and His sorrow.

MORNING   July 23

"Even you were like one of them" — Obadiah 11.

BROTHERLY KINDNESS was due from Edom to Israel in the time of need, but instead the men of Esau made common cause with Israel's foes. Special stress in the sentence before us is laid upon the word you; as when Caesar cried to Brutus, "and you Brutus;" a bad action may be all the worse, because of the person who has committed it. When we sin, who are the chosen favorites of heaven, we sin with an emphasis; ours is a crying offense because we are so peculiarly indulged. If an angel should lay his hand upon us when we are doing evil, he need not use any other rebuke than the question, What, you? What are you doing here? Much forgiven, much delivered, much instructed, much enriched, much blessed, shall we dare to put forth our hand unto evil? God forbid!

A few minutes of confession may be beneficial to you, gentle reader, this morning. Have you never been as the wicked? At an evening party certain men laughed at uncleanness, and the joke was not altogether offensive to your ear, *"even you were like one of them."* When hard things were spoken concerning the ways of God, you were bashfully silent; and so, to onlookers, *"you were like one of them."* When worldlings were bartering in the market, and driving hard bargains, were you not as one of them? When they were pursuing vanity with a hunter's foot, were you not as greedy for gain as they were? Could any difference be discerned between you and them? Is there any difference? Here we come to close quarters. Be honest with your own soul, and make sure that you are a new creature in Christ Jesus; but when this is sure, walk jealously, lest any should again be able to say, *"Even you were like one of them."* You would not desire to share their eternal doom, why then be like them here? Come not into their secret, lest you come into their ruin. Side with the afflicted people of God, and not with the world.

EVENING
"The blood of Jesus Christ His Son cleanses us from all sin" — John 1:7.

CLEANSES, SAYS the text, not shall cleanse. There are multitudes who think that as a dying hope they may look forward to pardon. Oh! how infinitely better to have cleansing now than to depend on the bare possibility of forgiveness when I come to die. Some imagine that a sense of pardon is an attainment only obtainable after many years of Christian experience. But forgiveness of sin is a present thing, a privilege for this day, a joy for this very hour. The moment a sinner trusts Jesus he is fully forgiven. The text, being written in the present tense, also indicates continuance; it was "cleanses" yesterday, it is "cleanses" today, it will be "cleanses" tomorrow: it will be always so with you, Christian, until you cross the river; every hour you may come to this fountain, for it cleanses still. Notice, likewise, the completeness of the cleansing, *"The blood of Jesus Christ His Son cleanses us from ALL sin;"* not only from sin, but *"from ALL sin."*

Reader, I cannot tell you the exceeding sweetness of this word, but I pray God the Holy Ghost to give you a taste of it. Manifold are our sins against God. Whether the bill be little or great, the same receipt can discharge one as the other. The blood of Jesus Christ is as blessed and divine a payment for the transgressions of blaspheming Peter as for the shortcomings of loving John; our iniquity is gone, all gone at once, and all gone forever. Blessed completeness! What a sweet theme to dwell upon as one gives himself to sleep.

> Sins against a holy God;
> Sins against His righteous laws;
> Sins against His love, His blood;
> Sins against His name and cause;
> Sins immense as is the sea
> From them all He cleanses me.

July 24 — MORNING

"Stand still and see the salvation of the LORD" — Exodus 14:13.

THESE WORDS CONTAIN God's command to the believer when he is reduced to great straits and brought into extraordinary difficulties. He cannot retreat; He cannot go forward; He is shut up on the right hand and on the left; what is He now to do? The Master's word to him is, *"Stand still."* It will be well for him if at such times he listens only to his Master's word, for other and evil advisers come with their suggestions.

Despair whispers, Lie down and die; give it all up. But God would have us put on a cheerful courage, and even in our worst times, rejoice in His love and faithfulness. Cowardice says, Retreat; go back to the worldling's way of action; you cannot play the Christian's part, it is too difficult. Relinquish your principles. But, however much Satan may urge this course upon you, you cannot follow it if you are a child of God. His divine fiat has bid you go from strength to strength, and so you shall, and neither death nor hell shall turn you from your course. What, if for a while you are called to stand still, yet this is but to renew your strength for some greater advance in due time. Precipitancy cries, Do something. Stir yourself; to stand still and wait, is sheer idleness. We must be doing something at once, we must do it, so we think; and this instead of looking to the Lord, who will not only do something but will do everything. Presumption boasts, If the sea be before you, march into it and expect a miracle.

But Faith listens neither to Presumption, nor to Despair, nor to Cowardice, nor to Precipitancy, but it hears God say, *"Stand still,"* and immovable as a rock it stands. *"Stand still;"* keep the posture of an upright man, ready for action, expecting further orders, cheerfully and patiently awaiting the directing voice; and it will not be long before God shall say to you, as distinctly as Moses said it to the people of Israel, "Go forward."

EVENING

"His camp is very great" — Joel 2:11.

CONSIDER, MY soul, the mightiness of the Lord who is your glory and defense. He is a man of war, Jehovah is His name. All the forces of heaven are at His beck, legions wait at His door, cherubim and seraphim, watchers and holy ones, principalities and powers, are all attentive to His will. If our eyes were not blinded by the ophthalmia of the flesh, we should see horses of fire and chariots of fire round about the Lord's beloved. The powers of nature are all subject to the absolute control of the Creator: stormy wind and tempest, lightning and rain, and snow, and hail, and the soft dews and cheering sunshine, come and go at His decree. The bands of Orion He looses and binds the sweet influences of the Pleiades. Earth, sea, and air, and the places under the earth, are the barracks for Jehovah's great armies; space is His camping ground, light is His banner, and flame is His sword. When He goes forth to war, famine ravages the land, pestilence smites the nations, hurricane sweeps the sea, tornado shakes the mountains, and earthquake makes the solid world to tremble. As for animate creatures, they all own His dominion, and from the great fish which swallowed the prophet, down to *"all manner of flies,"* which plagued the field of Zoan, all are His servants, and like the palmer-worm, the caterpillar, and the cankerworm, are squadrons of His great army, for His camp is very great.

My soul, see to it that you be at peace with this mighty King, yes, more, be sure to enlist under His banner, for to war against Him is madness, and to serve Him is glory. Jesus, Immanuel, God with us, is ready to receive recruits for the army of the Lord: if I am not already enlisted let me go to Him before I sleep, and beg to be accepted through His merits; and if I be already, as I hope I am, a soldier of the cross, let me be of good courage; for the enemy is powerless compared with my Lord, whose camp is very great.

MORNING
July 25

"And he left his robe in her hand and fled, and got out" — *Genesis 39:12.*

IN CONTENDING WITH certain sins there remains no mode of victory but by flight. The ancient naturalists wrote much of basilisks, whose eyes fascinated their victims and rendered them easy victims; so the mere gaze of wickedness puts us in solemn danger. He who would be safe from acts of evil must haste away from occasions of it. A covenant must be made with our eyes not even to look upon the cause of temptation, for such sins only need a spark to begin with and a blaze follows in an instant. Who would wantonly enter the leper's prison and sleep amid its horrible corruption? He only who desires to be leprous himself would thus court contagion. If the mariner knew how to avoid a storm, he would do anything rather than run the risk of weathering it. Cautious pilots have no desire to try how near the quicksand they can sail, or how often they may touch a rock without springing a leak; their aim is to keep as nearly as possible in the midst of a safe channel.

This day I may be exposed to great peril, let me have the serpent's wisdom to keep out of it and avoid it. The wings of a dove may be of more use to me today than the jaws of a lion. It is true I may be an apparent loser by declining evil company, but I had better leave my cloak than lose my character. It is not needful that I should be rich, but it is imperative upon me to be pure. No ties of friendship, no chains of beauty, no flashings of talent, no shafts of ridicule must turn me from the wise resolve to flee from sin. The devil I am to resist and he will flee from me, but the lusts of the flesh, I must flee, or they will surely overcome me. Oh God of holiness preserve your saints. May the horrible trinity of the world, the flesh, and the devil, never overcome us!

EVENING
"In their affliction, they will seek Me early" — *Hosea 5:15.*

LOSSES AND ADVERSITIES are frequently the means which the great Shepherd uses to fetch home His wandering sheep; like fierce dogs they worry the wanderers back to the fold. There is no making lions tame if they are too well fed; they must be brought down from their great strength, and their stomachs must be lowered, and then they will submit to the tamer's hand; and often have we seen the Christian rendered obedient to the Lord's will by lack of bread and hard labor. When rich and increased in goods many professors carry their heads much too loftily, and speak exceeding boastfully. Like David, they flatter themselves, "My mountain stands fast; I shall never be moved."

When the Christian grows wealthy, is in good repute, has good health, and a happy family, he too often admits Mr. Carnal Security to feast at His table, and then if he be a true child of God there is a rod preparing for him. Wait awhile, and it may be you will see his substance melt away as a dream. There goes a portion of his estate; how soon the acres change hands. That debt, that dishonored bill; how fast his losses roll in, where will they end?

It is a blessed sign of divine life if when these embarrassments occur one after another. Then he begins to be distressed about his backslidings, and takes himself to his God. Blessed are the waves that wash the mariner upon the rock of salvation! Losses in business are often sanctified to our soul's enriching. If the chosen soul will not come to the Lord full-handed, it shall come empty. If God, in His grace, finds no other means of making us honor Him among men, He will cast us into the deep: if we fall to honor Him on the pinnacle of riches, He will bring us into the valley of poverty. Yet faint not, heir of sorrow, when you are thus rebuked, rather recognize the loving hand which chastens, and say, *"I will arise, and go unto my Father."*

July 26   MORNING

"After you have added diligence, fill out your faith with goodness, and your goodness with knowledge, and your knowledge with self-control, and your self-control with patience, and your patience with godliness" — 2 Peter 1:5, 6.

IF YOU WOULD ENJOY the eminent grace of the full assurance of faith, under the blessed Spirit's influence, and assistance, do what the Scripture tells you, *"Give diligence."* Take care that your faith is of the right kind, that it is not a mere belief of doctrine, but a simple faith, depending on Christ, and on Christ alone. Give diligent heed to your courage. Plead with God that He would give you the face of a lion, that you may, with a consciousness of right, go on boldly. Study well the Scriptures, and get knowledge; for a knowledge of doctrine will tend very much to confirm faith. Try to understand God's Word; let it dwell in your heart richly.

When you have done this, *"Add to your knowledge temperance."* Take heed to your body: be temperate without. Take heed to your soul: be temperate within. Get temperance of lip, life, heart, and thought. Add to this, by God's Holy Spirit, patience; ask Him to give you that patience which endures affliction, which, when it is tried, shall come forth as gold. Array yourself with patience, that you may not murmur nor be depressed in your afflictions. When that grace is won, look to godliness. Godliness is something more than religion. Make God's glory your object in life; live in His sight; dwell close to Him; seek for fellowship with Him; and you have "godliness;" and to that add brotherly love. Have a love to all the saints: and add to that a charity, which opens its arms to all men, and loves their souls. When you are adorned with these jewels, and just in proportion as you practice these heavenly virtues, will you come to know by clearest evidence *"your calling and election."* *"Give diligence,"* if you would get assurance, for lukewarmness and doubting very naturally go hand in hand.

EVENING
"So that He may set him with princes" — Psalm 113:8.

OUR SPIRITUAL PRIVILEGES are of the highest order. "Among princes" is the place of select society. *"Truly our fellowship is with the Father, and with His Son Jesus Christ."* Speak of select society, there is none like this! *"We are a chosen generation, a peculiar people, a royal priesthood."* *"We are come unto the general assembly and church of the first-born, whose names are written in heaven."* The saints have courtly audience: princes have admittance to royalty when common people must stand afar off. The child of God has free access to the inner courts of heaven. *"For through Him we both have access by one Spirit unto the Father."* *"Let us come boldly,"* says the apostle, *"to the throne of the heavenly grace."*

Among princes there is abundant wealth, but what is the abundance of princes compared with the riches of believers? for *"all things are yours, and you are Christ's, and Christ is God's."* *"He that spared not His own Son, but delivered Him up for us all, how shall He not with Him also freely give us all things?"* Princes have peculiar power. A prince of heaven's empire has great influence: he wields a scepter in his own domain; he sits upon Jesus' throne, for *"He has made us kings and priests unto God, and we shall reign for ever and ever."* We reign over the united kingdom of time and eternity. Princes, again, have special honor. We may look down upon all earth-born dignity from the eminence upon which grace has placed us. For what is human grandeur to this, *"He has raised us up together, and made us sit together in heavenly places in Christ Jesus"*? We share the honor of Christ, and compared with this, earthly splendors are not worth a thought. Communion with Jesus is a richer gem than ever glittered in imperial diadem. Union with the Lord is a coronet of beauty outshining all the blaze of imperial pump.

MORNING
July 27

"Very great and precious promises" — 2 Peter 1:4.

IF YOU Would know experimentally the preciousness of the promises, and enjoy them in your own heart, meditate much upon them. There are promises which are like grapes in the wine-press; if you will tread them the juice will flow. Thinking over the hallowed words will often be the prelude to their fulfillment. While you are musing upon them, the blessing which you are seeking will insensibly come to you. Many a Christian who has thirsted for the promise has found the favor which it ensured gently distilling into his soul even while he has been considering the divine record; and he has rejoiced that ever he was led to lay the promise near his heart.

But besides meditating upon the promises, seek in your soul to receive them as being the very words of God. Speak to your soul thus, If I were dealing with a man's promise, I should carefully consider the ability and tile character of the man who had covenanted with me. So with the promise of God; my eye must not be so much fixed upon the greatness of the mercy, that may stagger me; as upon the greatness of the promisor, that will cheer me. My soul, it is God, even your God, God that cannot lie, who speaks to you. This word of His which you are now considering is as true as His own existence. He is a God unchangeable. He has not altered the thing which has gone out of His mouth, nor called back one single consolatory sentence. Nor does He lack any power; it is the God that made the heavens and the earth who has spoken thus. Nor can He fail in wisdom as to the time when He will bestow the favors, for He knows when it is best to give and when better to withhold. Therefore, seeing that it is the word of a God so true, so immutable, so powerful, so wise, I will and must believe the promise. If we thus meditate upon the promises, and consider the Promisor, we shall experience their sweetness, and obtain their fulfillment.

EVENING

"Who shall bring any charge against God's elect?" — Romans 8:33.

MOST BLESSED CHALLENGE! How unanswerable it is! Every sin of the elect was laid upon the great Champion of our salvation, and by the atonement carried away. There is no sin in God's book against His people: He sees no sin in Jacob, neither iniquity in Israel; they are justified in Christ forever. When the guilt of sin was taken away, the punishment of sin was removed. For the Christian there is no stroke from God's angry hand; no, not so much as a single frown of punitive justice. The believer may be chastised by his Father, but God the Judge has nothing to say to the Christian, except I have absolved you: you are acquitted. For the Christian there is no penal death in this world, much less any second death. He is completely freed from all the punishment as well as the guilt of sin, and the power of sin is removed too. It may stand in our way, and agitate us with perpetual warfare; but sin is a conquered foe to every soul in union with Jesus.

There is no sin which a Christian cannot overcome if he will only rely upon his God to do it. They who wear the white robe in heaven overcame through the blood of the Lamb, and we may do the same. No lust is too mighty, no besetting sin too strongly entrenched; we can overcome through the power of Christ. Do believe it, Christian, that your sin is a condemned thing. It may kick and struggle, but it is doomed to die. God has written condemnation across its brow. Christ has crucified it, *"nailing it to His cross."* Go now and mortify it, and the Lord help you to live to His praise, for sin with all its guilt, shame, and fear, is gone.

> Here's pardon for transgressions past,
> It matters not how black their cast;
> And, Oh my soul, with wonder view,
> For sins to come here's pardon too.

July 28

MORNING

"So foolish was I and ignorant; I was like a beast before You" — Psalm 73:22.

REMEMBER THIS is the confession of the man after God's own heart; and in telling us his inner life, he writes, *"So foolish was I, and ignorant."* The word foolish, here, means more than it signifies in ordinary language. Asaph, in a former verse of the Psalm, writes, *"I was envious at the foolish when I saw the prosperity of the wicked,"* which shows that the folly he intended had sin in it. He puts himself down as being thus foolish, and adds a word which is to give intensity to it; *"so foolish was I."* How foolish he could not tell. It was a sinful folly, a folly which was not to be excused by frailty, but to be condemned because of its perverseness and wilful ignorance, for he had been envious of the present prosperity of the ungodly, forgetful of the dreadful end awaiting all such.

And are we better than David that we should call ourselves wise? Do we profess that we have attained perfection, or to have been so chastened that the rod has taken all our wilfulness out of us? Ah, this were pride indeed! If the psalmist was foolish, how foolish should we be in our own esteem, if we could but see ourselves! Look back, believer: think of your doubting God when He has been so faithful to you; think of your foolish outcry of "Not so, my Father," when He crossed His hands in affliction to give you the larger blessing; think of the many times when you have read His providences in the dark, misinterpreted His dispensations, and groaned out, *"All these things are against me,"* when they are all working together for your good! Think how often you have chosen sin because of its pleasure, when indeed, that pleasure was a root of bitterness to you! Surely if we know our own heart we must plead guilty to the indictment of a sinful folly; and conscious of this "foolishness," we must make Asaph's consequent resolve our own, *"You shall guide me with Your counsel."*

EVENING

"He went about doing good" — Acts 10:38.

FEW WORDS, BUT yet an exquisite miniature of the Lord Jesus Christ. There are not many touches, but they are the strokes of a master's pencil. Of the Savior and only of the Savior is it true in the fullest, broadest, and most unqualified sense. *"He went about doing good."* From this description it is evident that He did good personally. The evangelists constantly tell us that He touched the leper with His own finger, that He anointed the eyes of the blind, and that in cases where He was asked to speak the word only at a distance, He did not usually comply, but went Himself to the sick bed, and there personally worked the cure. A lesson to us, if we would do good, to do it ourselves. Give alms with your own hand; a kind look, or word, will enhance the value of the gift. Speak to a friend about his soul; your loving appeal will have more influence than a whole library of tracts.

Our Lord's mode of doing good sets forth His incessant activity! He did not only the good which came close to hand, but He "went about" on His errands of mercy. Throughout the whole land of Judea there was scarcely a village or a hamlet which was not gladdened by the sight of Him. How this reproves the creeping, loitering manner, in which many professors serve the Lord. Let us gird up the loins of our mind, and be not weary in well doing.

Does not the text imply that Jesus Christ went out of His way to do good? *"He went about doing good."* He was never deterred by danger of difficulty. He sought out the objects of His gracious intentions. So must we. If old plans will not answer, we must try new ones, for fresh experiments sometimes achieve more than regular methods. Christ's perseverance, and the unity of His purpose, are also hinted at, and the practical application of the subject may be summed up in the words, He has left us an example that we should follow in His steps.

MORNING July 29

"But I am always with You" — Psalm 73:23.

BUT, AS if, notwithstanding all the foolishness and ignorance which Asaph had just been confessing to God, not one atom the less was it true and certain that he was saved and accepted, and that the blessing of being constantly in God's presence was undoubtedly his. Fully conscious of his own lost estate, and of the deceitfulness and vileness of his nature, yet, by a glorious outburst of faith, he sings *"nevertheless I am continually with You."* Believer, you are forced to enter into the confession of Asaph and endeavor in like spirit to say, But, since I belong to Christ I am continually with God! By this is meant continually upon His mind, He is always thinking of me for my good. Continually before His eye; the eye of the Lord never sleeps, but is perpetually watching over my welfare. Continually in His hand, so that none shall be able to pluck me thence. Continually on His heart, worn there as a memorial, even as the high priest bore the names of the twelve tribes upon his heart forever.

You always think of me, Oh God. The heart of Your love continually yearns toward me. You are always making providence work for my good. You have set me as a signet upon Your arm; Your love is strong as death, many waters cannot quench it; neither can the floods drown it. Surprising grace! You see me in Christ, and though in myself abhorred, You behold me as wearing Christ's garments, and washed in His blood, and thus I stand accepted in Your presence. I am thus continually in Your favor: *"continually with You."* Here is comfort for the tried and afflicted soul; vexed with the tempest within; look at the calm without. *"Nevertheless"*

Oh say it in your heart, and take the peace it gives. *"Nevertheless I am continually with You."*

EVENING

"All that the Father gives Me shall come to Me" — John 6:37.

THIS DECLARATION INVOLVES the doctrine of election: there are some whom the Father gave to Christ. It involves the doctrine of effectual calling: these who are given must and shall come; however stoutly they may set themselves against it, yet they shall be brought out of darkness into God's marvelous light. It teaches us the indispensable necessity of faith; for even those who are given to Christ are not saved except they come to Jesus. Even they must come, for there is no other way to heaven but by the door, Christ Jesus. All that the Father gives to our Redeemer must come to Him, therefore none can come to heaven except they come to Christ.

Oh! the power and majesty which rest in the words *"shall come."* He does not say they have power to come, nor they may come if they will, but they *"shall come."* The Lord Jesus does by His messengers, His word, and His Spirit, sweetly and graciously compel men to come in that they may eat of His marriage supper; and this He does, not by any violation of the free agency of man, but by the power of His grace. I may exercise power over another man's will, and yet that other man's will may be perfectly free, because the constraint is exercised in a manner in accordance with the laws of the human mind. Jehovah Jesus knows how to give life and a new heart, then by irresistible arguments addressed to the understanding, by mighty reasons appealing to the affections, and by the mysterious influence of His Holy Spirit operating upon all the powers and passions of the soul, so to subdue the whole man, that whereas he was once rebellious, he yields cheerfully to His government, subdued by sovereign love. But how shall those be known whom God has chosen? By this result: that they do willingly and joyfully accept Christ, and come to Him with simple and unfeigned faith, resting upon Him as all their salvation and all their desire. Reader, have you thus come to Jesus?

July 30   MORNING

"And thinking of this, he broke out into tears" — Mark 14:72.

IT HAS BEEN thought by some that as long as Peter lived, the fountain of his tears began to flow whenever he remembered his denying his Lord. It is not unlikely that it was so, for his sin was very great, and grace in him had afterwards a perfect work. This same experience is common to all the redeemed family according to the degree in which the Spirit of God has removed the natural heart of stone. We, like Peter, remember our boastful promise: *"Though all men shall forsake You, yet will not I."* We eat our own words with the bitter herbs of repentance. When we think of what we vowed we would be, and of what we have been, we may weep whole showers of grief. He thought on his denying his Lord. The place in which he did it, the little cause which led him into such heinous sin, the oaths and blasphemies with which he sought to confirm his falsehood, and the dreadful hardness of heart which drove him to do so again and yet again. Can we, when we are reminded of our sins, and their exceeding sinfulness, remain stolid and stubborn? Will we not make our house a Bochim, and cry unto the Lord for renewed assurances of pardoning love? May we never take a dry-eyed look at sin, lest before long we have a tongue parched in the flames of hell.

Peter also thought upon his Master's look of love. The Lord followed up the cock's warning voice with an admonitory look of sorrow, pity, and love. That glance was never out of Peter's mind so long as he lived. It was far more effectual than ten thousand sermons would have been without the Spirit. The penitent apostle would be sure to weep when he remembered the Savior's full forgiveness, which restored him to his former place. To think that we have offended so kind and good a Lord is more than sufficient reason for being constant weepers. Lord, smite our rocky hearts, and make the waters flow.

EVENING

"Him that comes to Me I will in no way cast out" — John 6:37.

NO LIMIT IS set to the duration of this promise. It does not merely say, "I will not cast out a sinner at his first coming," but, *"I will in no wise cast out."* The original reads, "I will not, not cast out," or "I will never, never cast out." The text means, that Christ will not at first reject a believer; and that as He will not do it at first, so He will not to the last.

But suppose the believer sins after coming? *"If any man sin we have an advocate with the Father, Jesus Christ the righteous."* But suppose that believers backslide? "I will heal their backsliding, I will love them freely: for My anger is turned away from him." But believers may fall under temptation! *"God is faithful, who will not suffer you to be tempted above that you are able; but will with the temptation also make a way to escape, that you may be able to bear it."* But the believer may fall into sin as David did! Yes, but He will *"Purge them with hyssop, and they shall be clean; He will wash them and they shall be whiter than snow;"* *"From all their iniquities will I cleanse them."*

> Once in Christ, in Christ forever,
> Nothing from His love can sever.

"I give unto My sheep," says He, *"eternal life; and they shall never perish, neither shall any man pluck them out of My hand."* What do you say to this, Oh trembling feeble mind? Is not this a precious mercy, that coming to Christ, you do not come to one who will treat you well for a little while, and then send you about your business, but He will receive you and make you His bride, and you shall be His forever? Receive no longer the spirit of bondage again to fear, but the spirit of adoption whereby you shall cry, Abba, Father! Oh! the grace of these words: *"I will in no wise cast out."*

MORNING   July 31

"I in them" — *John 17:23.*

IF SUCH BE THE union which subsists between our souls and the person of our Lord, how deep and broad is the channel of our communion! This is no narrow pipe through which a thread-like stream may wind its way, it is a channel of amazing depth and breadth, along whose glorious length a ponderous volume of living water may roll its floods. Behold He has set before us an open door, let us not be slow to enter. This city of communion has many pearly gates, every several gate is of one pearl, and each gate is thrown open to the uttermost that we may enter, assured of welcome. If there were but one small loophole through which to talk with Jesus, it would be a high privilege to thrust a word of fellowship through the narrow door; how much we are blessed in having so large an entrance!

Had the Lord Jesus been far away from us, with many a stormy sea between, we should have longed to send a messenger to Him to carry Him our loves, and bring us tidings from His Father's house. But see His kindness, He has built His house next door to ours, no, more, He takes lodging with us, and tabernacles in poor humble hearts, that so He may have perpetual intercourse with us. Oh how foolish must we be, if we do not live in habitual communion with Him. When the road is long, and dangerous, and difficult, we need not wonder that friends seldom meet each other, but when they live together, shall Jonathan forget his David? A wife may when her husband is upon a journey, abide many days without holding converse with him, but she could never endure to be separated from him if she knew him to be in one of the rooms of her own house. Why, believer, do you not sit at His banquet of wine? Seek your Lord, for He is near; embrace Him, for He is your Brother. Hold Him fast, for He is your Husband; and press Him to your heart, for He is of your own flesh

EVENING

"And these are the singers. They were employed in that work day and night" — *1 Chronicles 9:33.*

WELL WAS IT so ordered in the temple that the sacred chant never ceased: for evermore did the singers praise the Lord, whose mercy endures forever. As mercy did not cease to rule either by day or by night, so neither did music hush its holy ministry. My heart, there is a lesson sweetly taught to you in the ceaseless song of Zion's temple, you too are a constant debtor, and see to it that your gratitude, like charity, never fails. God's praise is constant in heaven, which is to be your final dwelling-place, learn to practice the eternal hallelujah. Around the earth as the sun scatters his light, his beams awaken grateful believers to tune their morning hymn, so that by the priesthood of the saints perpetual praise is kept up at all hours, they swathe our globe in a mantle of thanksgiving, and girdle it with a golden belt of song.

The Lord always deserves to be praised for what He is in Himself, for His works of creation and providence, for His goodness towards His creatures, and especially for the transcendent act of redemption, and all the marvelous blessing flowing therefrom. It is always beneficial to praise the Lord; it cheers the day and brightens the night; it lightens toil and softens sorrow; and over earthly gladness it sheds a sanctifying radiance which makes it less liable to blind us with its glare. Have we not something to sing about at this moment? Can we not weave a song out of our present joys, or our past deliverances, or our future hopes? Earth yields her summer fruits: the hay is housed, the golden grain invites the sickle, and the sun tarrying long to shine upon a fruitful earth, shortens the interval of shade that we may lengthen the hours of devout worship. By the love of Jesus, let us be stirred up to close the day with a psalm of sanctified gladness.

August 1

MORNING

"Let me now go to the field and glean ears of grain" — Ruth 2:2.

DOWNCAST AND TROUBLED Christian, come and glean today in the broad field of promise. Here are abundance of precious promises, which exactly meet your wants. Take this one: *"He will not break the bruised reed, nor quench the smoking wick."* Does that not suit your case? A reed, helpless, insignificant, and weak; a bruised reed, out of which no music can come; weaker than weakness itself; a reed, and that reed bruised, yet, He will not break you; but on the contrary, will restore and strengthen you. You are like the smoking wick: no light, no warmth, can come from you; but He will not quench you; He will blow with His sweet breath of mercy till He fans you to a flame. Would you glean another ear? *"Come unto Me all you that labor and are heavy laden, and I will give you rest."* What soft words! Your heart is tender, and the Master knows it, and therefore He speaks so gently to you: Will you not obey Him, and come to Him even now?

Take another ear: *"Fear not, worm Jacob, I will help you, says the Lord and your Redeemer, the Holy One of Israel."* How can you fear with such a wonderful assurance as this? You may gather ten thousand such golden ears as these! *"I have blotted out your sins like a cloud, and like a thick cloud your transgressions."* Or this, *"Though your sins be as scarlet, they shall be as white as snow; though they be red like crimson, they shall be as wool."* Or this, *"The Spirit and the Bride say, Come, and let him that is athirst come, and whosoever will let him take the water of life freely."* Our Master's field is very rich; behold the handfuls. See, there they lie before you, poor timid believer! Gather them up, make them your own, for Jesus bids you take them. Be not afraid, only believe! Grasp these sweet promises, thresh them out by meditation and feed on them with joy.

EVENING

"You crown the year with Your goodness" — Psalm 65:11.

ALL THE YEAR round, every hour of every day, God is richly blessing us; both when we sleep and when we wake His mercy waits upon us. The sun may leave us a legacy of darkness, but our God never ceases to shine upon His children with beams of love. Like a river, His loving-kindness is always flowing, with a fullness inexhaustible as His own nature. Like the atmosphere which constantly surrounds the earth, and is always ready to support the life of man, the benevolence of God surrounds all His creatures; in it, as in their element, they live, and move, and have their being. Yet as the sun on summer days gladdens us with beams more warm and bright than at other times, and as rivers are at certain seasons swollen by the rain, and as the atmosphere itself is sometimes fraught with more fresh, more bracing, or more balmy influences than heretofore, so is it with the mercy of God; it has its golden hours; its days of overflow, when the Lord magnifies His grace before the sons of men.

Among the blessings of the nether springs, the joyous days of harvest are a special season of excessive favor. It is the glory of autumn that the ripe gifts of providence are then abundantly bestowed; it is the mellow season of realization, whereas all before was but hope and expectation. Great is the joy of harvest. Happy are the reapers who fill their arms with the liberality of heaven. The Psalmist tells us that the harvest is the crowning of the year. Surely these crowning mercies call for crowning thanksgiving! Let us render it by the inward emotions of gratitude. Let our hearts be warmed; let our spirits remember, meditate, and think upon this goodness of the Lord. Then let us praise Him with our lips, and laud and magnify His name from whose bounty all this goodness flows. Let us glorify God by yielding our gifts to His cause. A practical proof of our gratitude is a special thank offering to the Lord of the harvest.

MORNING August 2

"Who works all things according to the counsel of His own will" — Ephesians 1:11.

OUR BELIEF IN God's wisdom supposes and necessitates that He has a settled purpose and plan in the work of salvation. What would creation have been without His design? Is there a fish in the sea, or a fowl in the air, which was left to chance for its formation? No, in every bone, joint, and muscle, sinew, gland, and blood-vessel, you mark the presence of a God working everything according to the design of infinite wisdom. And shall God be present in creation, ruling over all, and not in grace? Shall the new creation have the fickle genius of free will to preside over it when divine counsel rules the old creation?

Look at Providence! Who does not know that not a sparrow falls to the ground without your Father? Even the hairs of your head are all numbered. God weighs the mountains of our grief in scales, and the hills of our tribulation in balances. And shall there be a God in providence and not in grace? Shall the shell be ordained by wisdom and the kernel be left to blind chance. No; He knows the end from the beginning. He sees in its appointed place, not merely the corner-stone which He has laid in fair colors, in the blood of His dear Son, but He beholds in their ordained position each of the chosen stones taken out of the quarry of nature, and polished by His grace. He sees the whole from corner to cornice, from base to roof, from foundation to pinnacle. He has in His mind a clear knowledge of every stone which shall be laid in its prepared space, and how vast the edifice shall be, and when the top-stone shall be brought forth with shouting of *"Grace! Grace! unto it."* At the last it shall be clearly seen that in every chosen vessel of mercy, Jehovah did as He willed with His own; and that in every part of the work of grace He accomplished His purpose, and glorified His own name.

EVENING
"So she gleaned in the field until the evening" — Ruth 2:17.

LET ME LEARN from Ruth, the gleaner. As she went out to gather the ears of grain, so must I go forth into the fields of prayer, meditation, the ordinances, and hearing the word to gather spiritual food. The gleaner gathers her portion ear by ear; her gains are little by little: so must I be content to search for single truths, if there be no greater plenty of them. Every ear helps to make a bundle, and every gospel lesson assists in making us wise unto salvation. The gleaner keeps her eyes open: if she stumbled among the stubble in a dream, she would have no joy and no load to carry home at eventide. I must be watchful in religious exercises lest they become unprofitable to me; I fear I have lost much already. Oh that I may rightly estimate my opportunities, and glean with greater diligence. The gleaner stoops for all she finds, and so must I. High spirits criticize and object, but lowly minds glean and receive benefit. A humble heart is a great help towards profitably hearing the gospel. The engrafted soul-saving word is not received except with meekness. A stiff back makes a bad gleaner; down, master pride, you are a vile robber, not to be endured for a moment.

What the gleaner gathers she holds; if she dropped one ear to find another, the result of her day's work would be but scant; she is as careful to retain as to obtain, and so at last her gains are great. How often do I forget all that I hear; the second truth pushes the first out of my head, and so my reading and hearing end in much ado about nothing! Do I feel duly the importance of storing up the truth? A hungry belly makes the gleaner wise; if there be no grain in her hand, there will be no bread on her table; she labors under the sense of necessity, and hence her tread is nimble and her grasp is firm. I have even a greater necessity, Lord, help me to feel it, that it may urge me onward to glean in fields which yield so plenteous a reward to diligence.

August 3   MORNING

"Its lamp is the Lamb" — Revelation 21:23.

QUIETLY CONTEMPLATE the Lamb as the light of heaven. Light in Scripture is the emblem of joy. The joy of the saints in heaven is comprised in this: Jesus chose us, loved us, bought us, cleansed us, robed us, kept us, glorified us: we are here entirely through the Lord Jesus. Each one of these thoughts shall be to them like a cluster of the grapes of Eshcol. Light is also the cause of beauty. Nothing of beauty is left when light is gone. Without light no radiance flashes from the sapphire, no peaceful ray proceeds from the pearl; and thus all the beauty of the saints above comes from Jesus. As planets, they reflect the light of the Sun of Righteousness; they live as beams proceeding from the central orb. If He withdrew, they must die; if His glory were veiled, their glory must expire.

Light is also the emblem of knowledge. In heaven our knowledge will be perfect, but the Lord Jesus Himself will be the fountain of it. Dark providences, never understood before, will then be clearly seen, and all that puzzles us now will become plain to us in the light of the Lamb. Oh what unfolding there will be and what glorifying of the God of love! Light also means manifestation. Light manifests. In this world it does not yet appear what we shall be. God's people are a hidden people, but when Christ receives His people into heaven, He will touch them with the wand of His own love, and change them into the image of His manifested glory. They were poor and wretched, but what a transformation! They were stained with sin, but one touch of His finger, and they are bright as the sun, and clear as crystal. Oh! what a manifestation! All this proceeds from the exalted Lamb. Whatever there may be of effulgent splendor, Jesus shall be the center and soul of it all. Oh! to be present and to see Him in His own light, the King of kings, and Lord of lords!

EVENING

"And as He went" — Luke 8:42.

JESUS IS PASSING through the throng to the house of Jairus, to raise the ruler's dead daughter; but He is so profuse in goodness that He works another miracle while upon the road. While yet this rod of Aaron bears the blossom of an unaccomplished wonder, it yields the ripe almonds of a perfect work of mercy. It is enough for us, if we have some one purpose, straightway to go and accomplish it; it were imprudent to expend our energies by the way. Hastening to the rescue of a drowning friend, we cannot afford to exhaust our strength upon another in like danger. It is enough for a tree to yield one sort of fruit, and for a man to fulfil his own peculiar calling. But our Master knows no limit of power or boundary of mission. He is so prolific of grace, that like the sun which shines as it rolls onward in its orbit, His path is radiant with loving-kindness. He is a swift arrow of love, which not only reaches its ordained target, but perfumes the air through which it flies. Virtue is evermore going out of Jesus, as sweet odors exhale from flowers; and it always will be emanating from Him, as water from a sparkling fountain.

What delightful encouragement this truth affords us! if our lord is so ready to heal the sick and bless the needy, then, my soul, be not slow to put yourself in His way, that He may smile on you. Be not slack in asking, if He be so abundant in bestowing. Give earnest heed to His word now, and at all times, that Jesus may speak through it to your heart. Where He is to be found there make your resort, that you may obtain His blessing. When He is present to heal, may He not heal you? But surely He is present even now, for He always comes to hearts which need Him. And do not you need Him? Ah, He knows how much! You Son of David, turn Your eye and look upon the distress which is now before You, and make You suppliant whole.

August 4

MORNING

"But the people who know their God shall be strong" — *Daniel 11:32.*

EVERY BELIEVER understands that to know God is the highest and best form of knowledge; and this spiritual knowledge is a source of strength to the Christian. It strengthens his faith. Believers are constantly spoken of in the Scriptures as being persons who are enlightened and taught of the Lord; they are said to *"have an unction from the Holy One,"* and it is the Spirit's peculiar office to *"guide them into all truth,"* and all this for the increase and the fostering of their faith. Knowledge strengthens love, as well as faith. Knowledge opens the door, and then through that door we see our Savior. Or, to use another similitude, knowledge paints the portrait of Jesus, and when we see that portrait then we love Him, we cannot love a Christ whom we do not know, at least, in some degree. If we know but little of the excellences of Jesus, what He has done for us, and what He is doing now, we cannot love Him much; but the more we know Him, the more we shall love Him.

Knowledge also strengthens hope. How can we hope for a thing if we do not know of its existence? Hope may be the telescope, but till we receive instruction, our ignorance stands in the front of the glass, and we can see nothing whatever; knowledge removes the interposing object, and when we look through the bright optic glass we discern the glory to be revealed, and anticipate it with joyous confidence. Knowledge supplies us reasons for patience. How shall we have patience unless we know something of the sympathy of Christ, and understand the good which is to come out of the correction which our heavenly Father sends us? Nor is there one single grace of the Christian which, under God, will not be fostered and brought to perfection by holy knowledge. How important, then, is it that we should not only *"grow in grace, but in the knowledge of our Lord and Savior Jesus Christ."*

EVENING

"I stuck it with blasting and with mildew and with hail in all the labors of your hands" — *Haggai 2:17.*

HOW DESTRUCTIVE IS the hail to the standing crops, beating out the precious grain upon the ground! How grateful ought we to be when the grain is spared so terrible a ruin! Let us offer unto the Lord thanksgiving. Even more to be dreaded are those mysterious destroyers, smut, bunt, rust, and mildew. These turn the ear into a mass of soot, or render it putrid, or dry up the grain, and all in a manner so beyond all human control that the farmer is compelled to cry, *"This is the finger of God."* Innumerable minute fungi cause the mischief, and were it not for the goodness of God, the rider on the black horse would soon scatter famine over the land. Infinite mercy spares the food of men, but in view of the active agents which are ready to destroy the harvest, right wisely are we taught to pray, *"Give us this day our daily bread."* The curse is abroad; we have constant need of the blessing. When blight and mildew come they are chastisements from heaven, and men must learn to bear the rod, and Him that has appointed it.

Spiritually, mildew is no uncommon evil. When our work is most promising this blight appears. We hoped for many conversions, and lo, a general apathy, an abounding worldliness, or a cruel hardness of heart! There may be no open sin in those for whom we are laboring, but there is a deficiency of sincerity and decision sadly disappointing our desires. We learn from this our dependence upon the Lord, and the need of prayer that no blight may fall upon our work. Spiritual pride or sloth will soon bring upon us the dreadful evil, and only the Lord of the harvest can remove it. Mildew may even attack our own hearts, and shrivel our prayers and religious exercises. May it please the great Husbandman to avert so serious a calamity. Shine, blessed Sun of Righteousness, and drive the blights away.

MORNING August 5

"And we know that all things work together for good to those who love God" — Romans 8:28.

UPON SOME POINTS a believer is absolutely sure. He knows, for instance, that God sits in the stern of the vessel when it rocks most. He believes that an invisible hand is always on the world's tiller, and that wherever providence may drift, Jehovah steers it. That reassuring knowledge prepares him for everything. He looks over the raging waters and sees the spirit of Jesus treading the billows, and he hears a voice saying, *"It is I, be not afraid."* He knows too that God is always wise, and, knowing this, he is confident that there can be no accidents, no mistakes; that nothing can occur which ought not to arise. He can say, "If I should lose all I have, it is better that I should lose than have, if God so wills: the worst calamity is the wisest and the kindest thing that could befall to me if God ordains it." *"We know that all things work together for good to them that love God."*

The Christian does not merely hold this as a theory, but he knows it as a matter of fact. Everything has worked for good as yet; the poisonous drugs mixed in fit proportions have worked the cure; the sharp cuts of the lancet have cleansed out the proud flesh and facilitated the healing. Every event as yet has worked out the most divinely blessed results; and so, believing that God rules all, that He governs wisely, that He brings good out of evil, the believer's heart is assured, and he is enabled calmly to meet each trial as it comes. The believer can in the spirit of true resignation pray, Send me what You will, my God, so long as it comes from You; never came there an ill portion from Your table to any of Your children.

> Say not my soul, From whence can God relive my care?
> Remember that Omnipotence has servants everywhere.
> His method is sublime, His heart profoundly kind,
> God never is before His time, and never is behind.

EVENING

"Shall your brothers go to war and shall you sit here?" — Numbers 32:6.

KINDRED HAS its obligations. The Reubenites and Gadites would have been most unbrotherly if they had claimed the land which had been conquered, and had left the rest of the people to fight for their portions alone. We have received much by means of the efforts and sufferings of the saints in years gone by, and if we do not make some return to the church of Christ by giving her our best energies, we are unworthy to be enrolled in her ranks. Others are combating the errors of the age manfully, or excavating perishing ones from amid the ruins of the fall, and if we fold our hands in idleness we had need be warned, lest the curse of Meroz fall upon us. The Master of the vineyard says, *"Why stand you here all the day idle?"* What is the idler's excuse? Personal service of Jesus becomes all the more the duty of all because it is cheerfully and abundantly rendered by some. The toils of devoted missionaries and fervent ministers shame us if we sit still in indolence. Shrinking from trial is the temptation of those who are at ease in Zion: they would fain escape the cross and yet wear the crown; to them the question for this evening's meditation is very applicable.

If the most precious are tried in the fire, are we to escape the crucible? If the diamond must be vexed upon the wheel, are we to be made perfect without suffering? Who has commanded the wind to cease from blowing because our bark is on the deep? Why and wherefore should we be treated better than our Lord? The Firstborn felt the rod, and why not the younger brother? It is a cowardly pride which would choose a downy pillow and a silken couch for a soldier of the cross. Wiser far is he who, being first resigned to the divine will, grows by the energy of grace to be pleased with it, and so learns to gather lilies at the foot of the crosses Providence puts in his way, and, like Samson, to find honey in the lion.

August 6   MORNING

"Watchman, what of the night?" — Isaiah 21:11.

WHAT ENEMIES ARE abroad? Errors are a numerous horde, and new ones appear every hour: against what heresy am I to be on my guard? Sins creep from their lurking places when the darkness reigns; I must myself mount the watch-tower, and watch unto prayer. Our heavenly Protector foresees all the attacks which are about to be made upon us, and when as yet the evil designed us is but in the desire of Satan, our great Intercessor prays for us that our faith fail not, when we are to be sifted as wheat. Continue Oh gracious Watchman, to forewarn us of our foes, for Zion's sake hold not Your peace.

"Watchman, what of the night?" What weather is coming for the church? Are the clouds lowering, or is it all clear and fair overhead? We must care for the church of God with anxious love; and now that Popery and infidelity are both threatening, let us observe the signs of the times and prepare for conflict.

"Watchman, what of the night?" What stars are visible? What precious promises suit our present case? You sound the alarm, give us the consolation also. Christ, the pole-star, is ever fixed in His place, and all the stars are secure in the right hand of their Lord.

But watchman, when comes the morning? The Bridegroom tarries. Are there no signs of His coming forth as the Sun of Righteousness? Has not the morning star arisen as the pledge of day? When will the day dawn, and the shadows flee away? Oh Jesus, if You come not in person to Your waiting Church this day, yet come in Spirit to my sighing heart, and make it sing for joy.

> Now all the earth is bright and glad
> With the fresh morn;
> But all my heart is cold, and dark and sad:
> Sun of the soul, let me behold Your dawn!
> Come, Jesus, Lord,
> Oh quickly come, according to Your word.

EVENING

"And the whole earth is filled with His glory! Amen and Amen" — Psalm 72:19.

THIS IS A large petition. To intercede for a whole city needs a stretch of faith, and there are times when a prayer for one man is enough to stagger us. But how far-reaching was the psalmist's dying intercession! How comprehensive! How sublime! *"Let the whole earth be filled with His glory."* It does not exempt a single country however crushed by the foot of superstition; it does not exclude a single nation however barbarous. For the cannibal as well as for the civilized, for all climes and races this prayer is uttered; the whole circle of the earth it encompasses, and omits no son of Adam. We must be up and doing for our Master, or we cannot honestly offer such a prayer. The petition is not asked with a sincere heart unless we endeavor, as God shall help us, to extend the kingdom of our Master. Are there not some who neglect both to plead and to labor? Reader, is it your prayer? Turn your eyes to Calvary.

Behold the Lord of Life nailed to a cross, with the thorn-crown about His brow, with bleeding head, and hands, and feet. What! can you look upon this miracle of miracles, the death of the Godman, without feeling within your bosom a marvelous adoration that language never can express? And when you feel the blood applied to your conscience, and know that He has blotted out your sins, you are not a man unless you start from your knees and cry, *"Let the whole earth be filled with His glory; Amen, and Amen."* Can you bow before the Crucified in loving homage, and not wish to see your Monarch master of the world? Shame on you if you can pretend to love your Prince, and desire not to see Him the universal ruler. Your piety is worthless unless it leads you to wish that the same mercy which has been extended to you may bless the whole world. Lord, it is harvest-time, put in Your sickle and reap.

MORNING

August 7

"The upright love You" — Song of Solomon 1:4.

BELIEVERS LOVE JESUS with a deeper affection than they dare to give to any other being. They would sooner lose father and mother than part with Christ. They hold all earthly comforts with a loose hand, but they carry Him fast locked in their bosoms. They voluntarily deny themselves for His sake, but they are not to be driven to deny Him. It is scant love which the fire of persecution can dry up; the true believer's love is a deeper stream than this. Men have labored to divide the faithful from their Master, but their attempts have been fruitless in every age. Neither crowns of honor, nor frowns of anger, have untied this more than Gordian knot. This is no everyday attachment which the world's power may at length dissolve. Neither man nor devil have found a key which opens this lock. Never has the craft of Satan been more at fault than when he has exercised it in seeking to rend apart this union of two divinely welded hearts. It is written, and nothing can blot out the sentence, *"The upright love You."*

The intensity of the love of the upright, however, is not so much to be judged by what it appears as by what the upright long for. It is our daily lament that we cannot love enough. Would that our hearts were capable of holding more, and reaching further. Like Samuel Rutherford, we sigh and cry, "Oh, for as much love as would go round about the earth, and over heaven yes, the heaven of heavens, and ten thousand worlds, that I might let all out upon fair, fair, only fair Christ. Alas! our longest reach is but a span of love, and our affection is but as a drop of a bucket compared with what He deserves. Measure our love by our intentions, and it is high indeed; it is thus, we trust, our Lord does judge of it. Oh, that we could give all the love in all hearts in one great mass, a gathering together of all loves to Him who is altogether lovely!"

EVENING

"Satan held us back" — 1 Thessalonians 2:18.

SINCE THE FIRST hour in which goodness came into conflict with evil, it has never ceased to be true in spiritual experience, that Satan hinders us. From all points of the compass, all along the line of battle, in the vanguard and in the rear, at the dawn of day and in the midnight hour, Satan hinders us. If we toil in the field, he seeks to break the plowshare; if we build the wall, he labors to cast down the stones; if we would serve God in suffering or in conflict; everywhere Satan hinders us. He hinders us when we are first coming to Jesus Christ. Fierce conflicts we had with Satan when we first looked to the cross and lived. Now that we are saved, he endeavors to hinder the completeness of our personal character.

You may be congratulating yourself, saying, "Until now I have walked consistently; no man can challenge my integrity." Beware of boasting, for your virtue will yet be tried; Satan will direct his engines against that very virtue for which you are the most famous. If you have been hitherto a firm believer, your faith will before long be attacked; if you have been meek as Moses, expect to be tempted to speak unadvisedly with your lips. The birds will peck at your ripest fruit, and the wild boar will dash his tusks at your choicest vines. Satan is sure to hinder us when we are earnest in prayer. He checks our importunity, and weakens our faith in order that, if possible, we may miss the blessing. Nor is Satan less vigilant in obstructing Christian effort. There was never a revival of religion without a revival of his opposition. As soon as Ezra and Nehemiah begin to labor, Sanballat and Tobiah are stirred up to hinder them.

What then? We are not alarmed because Satan hinders us, for it is a proof that we are on the Lord's side, and are doing the Lord's work, and in His strength we shall win the victory, and triumph over our adversary.

MORNING   August 8

"They weave the spider's web" — Isaiah 59:5.

SEE THE SPIDER'S web, and behold in it a most suggestive picture of the hypocrite's religion. It is meant to catch his prey. The spider fattens himself on flies, and the Pharisee has his reward. Foolish persons are easily entrapped by the loud professions of pretenders, and even the more judicious cannot always escape. Philip baptized Simon Magus, whose guileful declaration of faith was so soon exploded by the stern rebuke of Peter. Custom, reputation, praise, advancement, and other flies, are the small game which hypocrites take in their nets. A spider's web is a marvel of skill; look at it and admire the cunning hunter's wiles. Is not a deceiver's religion equally wonderful? How does he make so barefaced a lie appear to be a truth? How can he make his tinsel answer so well the purpose of gold? A spider's web comes all from the creature's own bowels. The bee gathers her wax from flowers, the spider sucks no flowers, and yet she spins out her material to any length. Even so hypocrites find their trust and hope within themselves; their anchor was forged on their own anvil, and their cable twisted by their own hands. They lay their own foundation, and hew out the pillars of their own house, disdaining to be debtors to the sovereign grace of God.

But a spider's web is very frail. It is curiously worked, but not manufactured to endure. It is no match for the servant's broom, or the traveler's staff. The hypocrite needs no battery to blow his hope to pieces, a mere puff of wind will do it. Hypocritical cobwebs will soon come down when the broom of destruction begins its purifying work. Which reminds us of one more thought, viz., that such cobwebs are not to be endured in the Lord's house. He will see to it that they and those who spin them shall be destroyed forever. Oh my soul, rest on something better than a spider's web. Be the Lord Jesus your eternal hiding place.

EVENING

"All things are possible to him that believes" — Mark 9:23.

MANY PROFESSED Christians are always doubting and fearing, and they forlornly think that this is the necessary state of believers. This is a mistake, for *"all things are possible to him that believes;"* and it is possible for us to mount into a state in which a doubt or a fear shall be but as a bird of passage flitting across the soul, but never lingering there.

When you read of the high and sweet communions enjoyed by favored saints, you sigh and murmur in the chamber of your heart, "Alas! these are not for me." Oh climber, if you have but faith, you shall yet stand upon the sunny pinnacle of the temple, for *"all things are possible to him that believes."* You hear of exploits which holy men have done for Jesus; what they have enjoyed of Him; how much they have been like Him; how they have been able to endure great persecutions for His sake; and you say, "Ah! as for me, I am but a worm; I can never attain to this." But there is nothing which one saint was, that you may not be. There is no elevation of grace, no attainment of spiritually, no clearness of assurance, no post of duty, which is not open to you if you have but the power to believe.

Lay aside your sackcloth and ashes, and rise to the dignity of your true position; you are little in Israel because you will be so, not because there is any necessity for it. It is not fit that you should grovel in the dust, Oh child of a King. Ascend! The golden throne of assurance is waiting for you! The crown of communion with Jesus is ready to adorn your brow. Wrap yourself in scarlet and fine linen, and fare sumptuously every day; for if you believe, you may eat the fat of kidneys of wheat; your land shall flow with milk and honey, and your soul shall be satisfied as with marrow and fatness. Gather golden sheaves of grace, for they await you in the fields of faith. *"All things are possible to him that believes."*

August 9   MORNING

"The city has no need of the sun or of the moon, that they should shine on it" —
Revelation 21:23.

YONDER IN THE better world, the inhabitants are independent of all creature comforts. They have no need of raiment; their white robes never wear out, neither shall they ever be defiled. They need no medicine to heal diseases, "for the inhabitant shall not say I am sick." They need no sleep to recruit their frames;
they rest not day nor night, but without ceasing praise Him in His temple. They need no social relationship to minister comfort, and whatever happiness they may derive from association with their fellows is not essential to their bliss, for their Lord's society is enough for their largest desires. They need no teachers there; they doubtless commune with one another concerning the things of God, but they do not require this by way of instruction; they shall be all be taught of the Lord. Ours are the alms at the king's gate, but they feast at the table itself.

Here we lean upon the friendly arm, but there they lean upon their Beloved and upon Him alone. Here we must have the help of our companions, but there they find all they want in Christ Jesus. Here we look to the meat which perishes, and to the raiment which decays before the moth, but there they find everything in God. We use the bucket to bring water from the well, but there they drink from the fountain head, and put their lips down to the living water. Here the angels bring us blessings, but we shall want no messengers from heaven then. They shall need no Gabriel there to bring their love-notes from God, for there they shall see Him face to face. Oh! what a blessed time shall that be when we shall have mounted above every second cause and shall rest upon the bare arm of God! 'What a glorious hour when God, and not His creatures; the Lord, and not His works, shall be our daily joy! Our souls shall then have attained the perfection of bliss.

EVENING

"He first appeared to Mary Magdalene, from whom He had thrown out seven demons"
— *Mark 16:9.*

MARY OF MAGDALA was the victim of a fearful evil. She was possessed by not one demon only, but seven. These dreadful inmates caused much pain and pollution to the poor frame in which they had found a lodging. Hers was a hopeless, horrible case. She could not help herself, neither could any human succor avail. But Jesus passed that way, and unsought, and probably even resisted by the poor demoniac, He uttered the word of power, and Mary of Magdala became a trophy of the healing power of Jesus. All the seven demons left her, left her never to return, forcibly ejected by the Lord of all. What a blessed deliverance! What a happy change! From delirium to delight, from despair to peace, from hell to heaven! Straightway she became a constant follower of Jesus, catching His every word, following His devious steps, sharing His toilsome life; and with it all she became His generous helper, first among that band of healed and grateful women who ministered unto Him of their substance.

When Jesus was lifted up in crucifixion, Mary remained the sharer of His shame; we find her first beholding from afar, and then drawing near to the foot of the cross. She could not die on the cross with Jesus, but she stood as near it as she could, and when His blessed body was taken down, she watched to see how and where it was laid. She was the faithful and watchful believer, last at the sepulchre where Jesus slept, first at the grave whence He arose. Her holy fidelity made her a favored beholder of her beloved Rabboni, who deigned to call her by her name, and to make her His messenger of good news to the trembling disciples and Peter. Thus grace found her a demon-possessed, then made her a minister, demons were cast out and she came to behold angels, she was delivered from Satan and united forever to the Lord Jesus. May I also be such a miracle of grace!

MORNING   August 10

"Christ, our life" — *Colossians 3:4.*

PAUL'S MARVELOUSLY rich expression indicates that Christ is the source of our life. *"And He made you live who were once dead in trespasses and sins."* That same voice which brought Lazarus out of the tomb raised us to newness of life. He is now the substance of our spiritual life. It is by His life that we live; He is in us, the hope of glory, the spring of our actions, the central thought which moves every other thought. Christ is the sustenance of our life. What can the Christian feed upon but Jesus' flesh and blood? *"This is the bread which comes down from heaven, that a man may eat thereof, and not die."* Oh wayworn pilgrims in this wilderness of sin, you never get a morsel to satisfy the hunger of your spirits, except you find it in Him! Christ is the solace of our life. All our true joys come from Him; and in times of trouble, His presence is our consolation. There is nothing worth living for but Him; and His loving-kindness is better than life!

Christ is the object of our life. As speeds the ship towards the port, so hastens the believer towards the haven of his Savior's bosom. As flies the arrow to its goal, so flies the Christian towards the perfecting of his fellowship with Christ Jesus. As the soldier fights for his captain, and is crowned in his captain's victory, so the believer contends for Christ, and gets his triumph out of the triumphs of his Master. *"For him to live is Christ."* Christ is the exemplar of our life. Where there is the same life within, there will, there must be, to a great extent, the same developments without; and if we live in near fellowship with the Lord Jesus we shall grow like Him. We shall set Him before us as our Divine copy, and we shall seek to tread in His footsteps, until He shall become the crown of our life in glory. Oh! how safe, how honored, how happy is the Christian, since Christ is our life!

EVENING

"The Son of man has authority on earth to forgive sins" — *Matthew 9:6.*

BEHOLD ONE OF the great Physician's mightiest arts: He has power to forgive sin! While here He lived below, before the ransom had been paid, before the blood had been literally sprinkled on the mercy-seat, He had power to forgive sin. Has He not power to do it now that He has died? What power must dwell in Him who to the utmost farthing has faithfully discharged the debts of His people! He has boundless power now that He has finished transgression and made an end of sin. If you doubt it, see Him rising from the dead! Behold Him in ascending splendor raised to the right hand of God! Hear Him pleading before the eternal Father, pointing to His wounds, urging the merit of His sacred passion! What power to forgive is here! *"He has ascended on high, and received gifts for men."* *"He is exalted on high to give repentance and remission of sins."* The most crimson sins are removed by the crimson of His blood.

At this moment, dear reader, whatever your sinfulness, Christ has power to pardon, power to pardon you, and millions such as you are. A word will speak it. He has nothing more to do to win your pardon; all the atoning work is done. He can, in answer to your tears, forgive your sins today, and make you know it. He can breathe into your soul at this very moment a peace with God which passes all understanding, which shall spring from perfect remission of your manifold iniquities. Do you believe that? I trust you believe it. May you experience now the power of Jesus to forgive sin! Waste no time in applying to the Physician of souls, but hasten to Him with words like these:-

> Jesus! Master! hear my cry;
> Save me, heal me with a word;
> Fainting at Your feet I lie,
> You my whispered plaint have heard.

August 11   MORNING

"Oh that I were as in months past!" — Job 29:2.

NUMBERS OF CHRISTIANS can view the past with pleasure, but regard the present with dissatisfaction; they look back upon the days which they have passed in communing with the Lord as being the sweetest and the best they have ever known, but as to the present, it is clad in a sable garb of gloom and dreariness. Once they lived near to Jesus, but now they feel that they have wandered from Him, and they say, *"Oh that I were as in months past!"* They complain that they have lost their evidences, or that they have not present peace of mind, or that they have no enjoyment in the means of grace, or that conscience is not so tender, or that they have not so much zeal for God's glory.

The causes of this mournful state of things are manifold. It may arise through a comparative neglect of prayer, for a neglected closet is the beginning of all spiritual decline. Or it may be the result of idolatry. The heart has been occupied with something else, more than with God; the affections have been set on the things of earth, instead of the things of heaven. A jealous God will not be content with a divided heart; He must be loved first and best. He will withdraw the sunshine of His presence from a cold, wandering heart. Or the cause may be found in self-confidence and self-righteousness. Pride is busy in the heart, and self is exalted instead of lying low at the foot of the cross.

Christian, if you are not now as you *"were in months past,"* do not rest satisfied with wishing for a return of former happiness, but go at once to seek your Master, and tell Him your sad state. Ask His grace and strength to help you to walk more closely with Him; humble yourself before Him, and He will lift you up, and give you yet again to enjoy the light of His countenance. Do not sit down to sigh and lament; while the beloved Physician lives there is hope, and there is a certainty of recovery for the worst cases.

EVENING

"Everlasting consolation" — 2 Thessalonians 2:16.

CONSOLATION! THERE is music in the word: like David's harp, it charms away the evil spirit of melancholy. It was a distinguished honor to Barnabas to be called *"the son of consolation;"* no, it is one of the illustrious names of a greater than Barnabas, for the Lord Jesus is *"the consolation of Israel."* *"Everlasting consolation;"* here is the cream of all, for the eternity of comfort is the crown and glory of it. What is this *"everlasting consolation"*? It includes a sense of pardoned sin. A Christian man has received in his heart the witness of the Spirit that his iniquities are put away like a cloud, and his transgressions like a thick cloud. If sin be pardoned, is not that an everlasting consolation?

Next, the Lord gives His people an abiding sense of acceptance in Christ. The Christian knows that God looks upon him as standing in union with Jesus. Union to the risen Lord is a consolation of the most abiding order; it is, in fact, everlasting. Let sickness prostrate us, have we not seen hundreds of believers as happy in the weakness of disease as they would have been in the strength of hale and blooming health? Let death's arrows pierce us to the heart, our comfort dies not. For have not our ears full often heard the songs of saints as they have rejoiced because the living love of God was poured out in their hearts in dying moments? Yes, a sense of acceptance in the Beloved is an everlasting consolation.

Moreover, the Christian has a conviction of his security. God has promised to save those who trust in Christ; the Christian does trust in Christ, and he believes that God will be as good as His word, and will save him. He feels that he is safe by virtue of his being bound up with the person and work of Jesus.

MORNING   August 12

"The LORD reigns; let the earth rejoice" — Psalm 97:1.

CAUSES FOR DISQUIETUDE there are none so long as this blessed sentence is true. On earth the Lord's power as readily controls the rage of the wicked as the rage of the sea; His love as easily refreshes the poor with mercy as the earth with showers. Majesty gleams in flashes of fire amid the tempest's horrors, and the glory of the Lord is seen in its grandeur in the fall of empires, and the crash of thrones. In all our conflicts and tribulations, we may behold the hand of the divine King.

> God is God; He sees and hears
> All our troubles, all our tears.
> Soul, forget not, 'mid your pains,
> God o'er all forever reigns.

In hell, evil spirits own, with misery, His undoubted supremacy. When permitted to roam abroad, it is with a chain at their heel; the bit is in the mouth of behemoth, and the hook in the jaws of leviathan. Death's darts are under the Lord's lock, and the grave's prisons have divine power as their warder. The terrible vengeance of the Judge of all the earth makes fiends cower down and tremble, even as dogs in the kennel fear the hunter's whip.

> Fear not death, nor Satan's thrusts,
> God defends who in Him trusts;
> Soul, remember, in your pains,
> God o'er all forever reigns.

In heaven none doubt the sovereignty of the King Eternal, but all fall on their faces to do Him homage. Angels are His courtiers, the redeemed His favorites, and all delight to serve Him day and night. May we soon reach the city of the great King!

> For it is life's long night of sadness
> He will give us peace and gladness.
> Soul, remember, in your pains,
> God o'er all forever reigns.

EVENING

"The bow shall be seen in the cloud" — Genesis 9:14.

THE RAINBOW, THE symbol of the covenant with Noah, is typical of our Lord Jesus, who is the Lord's witness to the people. When may we expect to see the token of the covenant? The rainbow is only to be seen painted upon a cloud. When the sinner's conscience is dark with clouds, when he remembers his past sin, and mourns and laments before God, Jesus Christ is revealed to him as the covenant Rainbow, displaying all the glorious hues of the divine character and betokening peace. To the believer, when his trials and temptations surround him, it is sweet to behold the person of our Lord Jesus Christ, to see Him bleeding, living, rising, and pleading for us. God's rainbow is hung over the cloud of our sins, our sorrows, and our woes, to prophesy deliverance.

Nor does a cloud alone give a rainbow, there must be the crystal drops to reflect the light of the sun. So, our sorrows must not only threaten, but they must really fall upon us. There had been no Christ for us if the vengeance of God had been merely a threatening cloud; punishment must fall in terrible drops upon the Surety. Until there is a real anguish in the sinner's conscience, there is no Christ for him; until the chastisement which he feels becomes grievous, he cannot see Jesus.

But there must also be a sun; for clouds and drops of rain make not rainbows unless the sun shines. Beloved, our God, who is as the sun to us, always shines, but we do not always see Him, clouds hide His face. But no matter what drops may be falling, or what clouds may be threatening, if He does but shine there will be a rainbow at once. It is said that when we see the rainbow the shower is over. Certain it is, that when Christ comes, our troubles remove; when we behold Jesus, our sins vanish, and our doubts and fears subside. When Jesus walks the waters of the sea, how profound the calm!

August 13

MORNING

"The cedars of Lebanon which He has planted" — Psalm 104:16.

LEBANON'S CEDARS are emblematic of the Christian, in that they owe their planting entirely to the Lord. This is quite true of every child of God. He is not man-planted, nor self-planted, but God-planted. The mysterious hand of the divine Spirit dropped the living seed into a heart which He had Himself prepared for its reception. Every true heir of heaven owns the great Husbandman as his planter. Moreover, the cedars of Lebanon are not dependent upon man for their watering; they stand on the lofty rock, not moistened by human irrigation; and yet our heavenly Father supplies them. Thus it is with the Christian who has learned to live by faith. He is independent of man, even in temporal things; for his continued maintenance he looks to the Lord his God, and to Him alone. The dew of heaven is his portion, and the God of heaven is his fountain. Again, the cedars of Lebanon are not protected by any mortal power. They owe nothing to man for their preservation from stormy wind and tempest. They are God's trees, kept and preserved by Him, and by Him alone. It is precisely the same with the Christian. He is not a hot-house plant, sheltered from temptation; he stands in the most exposed position; he has no shelter, no protection, except this, that the broad wings of the eternal God always cover the cedars which He Himself has planted. Like cedars, believers are full of sap, having vitality enough to be ever green, even amid winter's snows. Lastly, the flourishing and majestic condition of the cedar is to the praise of God only. The Lord, even the Lord alone has been everything unto the cedars, and, therefore David very sweetly puts it in one of the psalms, *"Praise the Lord, fruitful trees and all cedars."* In the believer there is nothing that can magnify man; he is planted, nourished, and protected by the Lord's own hand, and to Him let all the glory be ascribed.

EVENING

"And I will remember My covenant" — Genesis 9:15.

NOTE THE FORM of the promise. God does not say, And when you shall look upon the bow, and you shall remember My covenant, then I will not destroy the earth. No, but it is gloriously put, not upon our memory, which is fickle and frail, but upon God's memory, which is infinite and immutable. *"The bow shall be in the cloud; and I will look upon it, that I may remember the everlasting covenant."* Oh! it is not my remembering God, it is God's remembering me which is the ground of my safety; it is not my laying hold of His covenant, but His covenant's laying hold on me. Glory be to God! the whole of the bulwarks of salvation are secured by divine power, and even the minor towers, which we may imagine might have been left to man, are guarded by almighty strength.

Even the remembrance of the covenant is not left to our memories, for we might forget, but our Lord cannot forget the saints whom He has graven on the palms of His hands. It is with us as with Israel in Egypt; the blood was upon the lintel and the two side-posts, but the Lord did not say, *"When you see the blood I will pass over you,"* but *"When I see the blood I will pass over you."* My looking to Jesus brings me joy and peace, but it is God's looking to Jesus which secures my salvation and that of all His elect, since it is impossible for our God to look at Christ, our bleeding Surety, and then to be angry with us for sins already punished in Him. No, it is not left with us even to be saved by remembering the covenant. There is no linsey-woolsey here; not a single thread of the creature mars the fabric. It is not of man, neither by man, but of the Lord alone. We should remember the covenant, and we shall do it, through divine grace. But the hinge of our safety does not hang there; it is God's remembering us, not our remembering Him; and hence the covenant is an everlasting covenant.

MORNING   August 14

"For You, LORD, have made me glad with Your work" — Psalm 92:4.

DO YOU BELIEVE that your sins are forgiven, and that Christ has made a full atonement for them? Then what a joyful Christian you ought to be! How you should live above the common trials and troubles of the world! Since sin is forgiven, can it matter what happens to you now? Luther says, Smite, Lord, smite, for my sin is forgiven; if You have but forgiven me, smite as hard as You will; and in a similar spirit you may say, Send sickness, poverty, losses, crosses, persecution, what You will, You have forgiven me, and my soul is glad. Christian, if you are thus saved, while you are glad, be grateful and loving. Cling to that cross which took your sin away; serve Him who served you. *"I beseech you therefore, by the mercies of God, that you present your bodies a living sacrifice, holy, acceptable unto God, which is your reasonable service."*

Let not your zeal evaporate in some little ebullition of song. Show your love in expressive tokens. Love the brothers of Him who loved you. If there is a Mephibosheth anywhere who is lame or halt, help him for Jonathan's sake. If there is a poor tried believer, weep with him, and bear his cross for the sake of Him who wept for you and carried your sins. Since you are thus forgiven freely for Christ's sake, go and tell to others the joyful news of pardoning mercy. Be not contented with this unspeakable blessing for yourself alone, but publish abroad the story of the cross. Holy gladness and holy boldness will make you a good preacher, and all the world will be a pulpit for you to preach in. Cheerful holiness is the most forcible of sermons, but the Lord must give it to you. Seek it this morning before you go into the world. When it is the Lord's work in which we rejoice, we need not be afraid of being too glad.

EVENING
"I know their sorrows" — Exodus 3:7.

THE CHILD IS cheered as he sings, This my father knows. Shall not we be comforted as we discern that our dear Friend and tender soul-husband knows all about us?

He is the Physician, and if He knows all, there is no need that the patient should know. Hush, you silly, fluttering heart, prying, peeping, and suspecting! What you know not now, you shall know hereafter, and meanwhile Jesus, the beloved Physician, knows your soul in adversities. Why need the patient analyze all the medicine, or estimate all the symptoms? This is the Physician's work, not mine; it is my business to trust, and his to prescribe. If He shall write His prescription in uncouth characters which I cannot read, I will not be uneasy on that account, but rely upon His unfailing skill to make all plain in the result, however mysterious in the working.

He is the Master; and His knowledge is to serve us instead of our own; we are to obey, not to judge: *"The servant knows not what his Lord does."* Shall the architect explain his plans to every hod-carrier on the works? If he knows his own intent, is it not enough? The vessel on the wheel cannot guess to what pattern it shall be conformed, but if the potter understands his art, what matters the ignorance of the clay? My Lord must not be cross-questioned any more by one so ignorant as I am.

He is the Head. All understanding centers there. What judgment has the arm? What comprehension has the foot? All the power to know lies in the head. Why should the member have a brain of its own when the head fulfills for it every intellectual office? Here, then, must the believer rest his comfort in sickness, not that he himself can see the end, but that Jesus knows all. Sweet Lord, be forever eye, and soul, and head for us, and let us be content to know only what You choose to reveal.

August 15   MORNING

"And Isaac went out to meditate in the field at the beginning of the evening" — Genesis 24:63.

VERY ADMIRABLE WAS his occupation. If those who spend so many hours in idle company, light reading, and useless pastimes, could learn wisdom, they would find more profitable society and more interesting engagements in meditation than in the vanities which now have such charms for them. We should all know more, live nearer to God, and grow in grace, if we were more alone. Meditation chews the cud and extracts the real nutriment from the mental food gathered elsewhere. When Jesus is the theme, meditation is sweet indeed. Isaac found Rebekah while engaged in private musings; many others have found their best beloved there.

Very admirable was the choice of place. In the field we have a study hung round with texts for thought. From the cedar to the hyssop, from the soaring eagle down to the chirping grasshopper, from the blue expanse of heaven to a drop of dew, all things are full of teaching, and when the eye is divinely opened, that teaching flashes upon the mind far more vividly than from written books. Our little rooms are neither so healthy, so suggestive, so agreeable, or so inspiring as the fields. Let us count nothing common or unclean, but feel that all created things point to their Maker, and the field will at once be hallowed.

Very admirable was the season. The season of sunset as it draws a veil over the day, befits that repose of the soul when earthborn cares yield to the joys of heavenly communion. The glory of the setting sun excites our wonder, and the solemnity of approaching night awakens our awe. If the business of this day will permit it, it will be well, dear reader, if you can spare an hour to walk in the field at eventide, but if not, the Lord is in the town too, and will meet with you in your chamber or in the crowded street. Let your heart go forth to meet Him.

EVENING
"And I will give you a heart of flesh" — Ezekiel 36:26.

A HEART OF FLESH is known by its tenderness concerning sin. To have indulged a foul imagination, or to have allowed a wild desire to tarry even for a moment, is quite enough to make a heart of flesh grieve before the Lord. The heart of stone calls a great iniquity nothing, but not so the heart of flesh.

> If to the right or left I stray,
> That moment, Lord, reprove;
> And let me weep my life away,
> For having grieved your love.

The heart of flesh is tender of God's will. My Lord Will-be-will is a great blusterer, and it is hard to subject him to God's will; but when the heart of flesh is given, the will quivers like an aspen leaf in every breath of heaven, and bows like an osier in every breeze of God's Spirit. The natural will is cold, hard iron, which is not to be hammered into form, but the renewed will, like molten metal, is soon molded by the hand of grace. In the fleshy heart there is a tenderness of the affections.

The hard heart does not love the Redeemer, but the renewed heart burns with affection towards Him. The hard heart is selfish and coldly demands, Why should I weep for sin? Why should I love the Lord? But the heart of flesh says; *"Lord, You know that I love You;"* help me to love You more! Many are the privileges of this renewed heart; 'Tis here the Spirit dwells, 'tis here that Jesus rests. It is fitted to receive every spiritual blessing, and every blessing comes to it. It is prepared to yield every heavenly fruit to the honor and praise of God, and therefore the Lord delights in it. A tender heart is the best defense against sin, and the best preparation for heaven. A renewed heart stands on its watchtower looking for the coming of the Lord Jesus. Have you this heart of flesh?

MORNING   August 16

"Give to the LORD the glory due to His name" — Psalm 29:2.

GLORY IS the result of His nature and acts. He is glorious in His character, for there is such a store of everything that is holy, and good, and lovely in God, that He must be glorious. The actions which flow from His character are also glorious. But while He intends that they should manifest to His creatures His goodness, and mercy, and justice, He is equally concerned that the glory associated with them should be given only to Himself. Nor is there anything in ourselves in which we may glory; for who makes us to differ from another? And what have we that we did not receive from the God of all grace?

Then how careful ought we to be to walk humbly before the Lord! The moment we glorify ourselves, since there is room for one glory only in the universe, we set ourselves up as rivals to the Most High. Shall the insect of an hour glorify itself against the sun which warmed it into life? Shall the potsherd exalt itself above the man who fashioned it upon the wheel? Shall the dust of the desert strive with the whirlwind? Or the drops of the ocean struggle with the tempest? *"Give unto the Lord, all you righteous, give unto the Lord glory and strength; give unto Him the honor that is due unto His name."* Yet it is, perhaps, one of the hardest struggles of the Christian life to learn this sentence; *"Not unto us, not unto us, but unto Your name be glory."* It is a lesson which God is ever teaching us, and teaching us sometimes by most painful discipline. Let a Christian begin to boast, I can do all things, without adding *"through Christ which strengthens me,"* and before long he will have to groan, I can do nothing, and bemoan himself in the dust. When we do anything for the Lord, and He is pleased to accept of our doings, let us lay our crown at His feet, and exclaim, "Not I, but the grace of God which was with me!"

EVENING

"We ourselves, having the first-fruit of the Spirit!" — Romans 8:23.

PRESENT POSSESSION is declared. At this present moment we have the first-fruits of the Spirit. We have repentance, that gem of the first water; faith, that priceless pearl; hope, the heavenly emerald; and love, the glorious ruby. We are already made *"new creatures in Christ Jesus,"* by the effectual working of God the Holy Spirit. This is called the first-fruit because it comes first. As the wave-sheaf was the first of the harvest, so the spiritual life, and all the graces which adorn that life, are the first operations of the Spirit of God in our souls. The first-fruits were the pledge of the harvest. As soon as the Israelite had plucked the first handful of ripe ears, he looked forward with glad anticipation to the time when the wagon should creak beneath the sheaves. So, brothers, when God gives us things which are pure, lovely, and of good report, as the work of the Holy Spirit, these are to us the prophecies of the coming glory. The first-fruits were always holy to the lord, and our new nature, with all its powers, is a consecrated thing. The new life is not ours that we should ascribe its excellence to our own merit; it is Christ's image and creation, and is ordained for His glory.

But the fast-fruits were not the harvest, and the works of the Spirit in us at this moment are not the consummation; the perfection is yet to come. We must not boast that we have attained, and so reckon the wave-sheaf to be all the produce of the year. We must hunger and thirst after righteousness, and pant for the day of full redemption. Dear reader, this evening open your mouth wide, and God will fill it. Let the blessing in present possession excite in you a sacred avarice for more grace. Groan within yourself for higher degrees of consecration, and your lord will grant them to you, for He is able to do exceeding abundantly above what we ask or even think.

August 17

MORNING

"The mercy of God" — Psalm 52:8.

MEDITATE A LITTLE on this mercy of the Lord. It is tender mercy. With gentle, loving touch, He heals the broken in heart, and binds up their wounds. He is as gracious in the manner of His mercy as in the matter of it. It is great mercy. There is nothing little in God; His mercy is like Himself; it is infinite. You cannot measure it. His mercy is so great that it forgives great sins to great sinners, after great lengths of time, and then gives great favors and great privileges, and raises us up to great enjoyments in the great heaven of the great God. It is undeserved mercy, as indeed all true mercy must be, for deserved mercy is only a misnomer for justice. There was no right on the sinner's part to the kind consideration of the Most High. Had the rebel been doomed at once to eternal fire he would have richly merited the doom, and if delivered from wrath, sovereign love alone has found a cause, for there was none in the sinner himself.

It is rich mercy. Some things are great, but have little efficacy in them, but this mercy is a cordial to your drooping spirits; a golden ointment to your bleeding wounds; a heavenly bandage to your broken bones; a royal chariot for your weary feet; a bosom of love for your trembling heart. It is manifold mercy. As Bunyan says, All the flowers in God's garden are double. There is no single mercy. You may think you have but one mercy, but you shall find it to be a whole cluster of mercies. It is abounding mercy. Millions have received it, yet far from its being exhausted, it is as fresh, as full, and as free as ever. It is unfailing mercy. It will never leave you. If mercy be your friend, mercy will be with you in temptation to keep you from yielding; with you in trouble to prevent you from sinking; with you living to be the light and life of your countenance; and with you dying to be the joy of your soul when earthly comfort is ebbing fast.

EVENING

"This illness is not to death" — John 11:4.

FROM OUR LORD'S words we learn that there is a limit to sickness. Here is a limit within which its ultimate end is restrained, and beyond which it cannot go. Lazarus might pass through death, but death was not to be the ultimatum of his sickness. In all sickness, the Lord says to the waves of pain, *"This far shall you go, but no further."* His fixed purpose is not the destruction, but the instruction of His people. Wisdom hangs up the thermometer at the furnace mouth, and regulates the heat.

The limit is encouragingly comprehensive. The God of providence has limited the time, manner, intensity, repetition, and effects of all our sicknesses; each throb is decreed, each sleepless hour predestinated, each relapse ordained, each depression of spirit foreknown, and each sanctifying result eternally purposed. Nothing great or small escapes the ordaining hand of Him who numbers the hairs of our head.

This limit is wisely adjusted to our strength, to the end designed, and to the grace apportioned. Affliction comes not at haphazard; the weight of every stroke of the rod is accurately measured. He who made no mistakes in balancing the clouds and measuring out the heavens, commits no errors in measuring out the ingredients which compose the medicine of souls. We cannot suffer too much, nor be relieved too late.

The limit is tenderly appointed. The knife of the heavenly Surgeon never cuts deeper than is absolutely necessary. *"He does not afflict willingly, nor grieve the children of men."* A mother's heart cries, Spare my child; but no mother is more compassionate than our gracious God. When we consider how hard-mouthed we are, it is a wonder that we are not driven with a sharper bit. The thought is full of consolation, that He who has fixed the bounds of our habitation, has also fixed the bounds of our tribulation.

MORNING   August 18

"Foreigners have come into the holy places of the LORD's house" — *Jeremiah 51:51.*

ON THIS ACCOUNT the faces of the Lord's people were covered with shame, for it was a terrible thing that men should intrude into the Holy Place reserved for the priests alone. Everywhere about us we see like cause for sorrow. How many ungodly men are now educating with the view of entering into the ministry! What a crying sin is that solemn lie by which our whole population is nominally comprehended in a National Church! How fearful it is that ordinances should be pressed upon the unconverted, and that among the more enlightened churches of our land there should be such laxity of discipline. If the thousands who will read this portion shall all take this matter before the Lord Jesus this day, He will interfere and avert the evil which else will come upon His Church. To adulterate the Church is to pollute a well, to pour water upon fire, to sow a fertile field with stones. May we all have grace to maintain in our own proper way the purity of the Church, as being an assembly of believers, and not a nation, an unsaved community of unconverted men.

Our zeal must, however, begin at home. Let us examine ourselves as to our right to eat at the Lord's table. Let us see to it that we have on our wedding garment, lest we ourselves be intruders in the Lord's sanctuaries. *"Many are called, but few are chosen;"* the way is narrow, and the gate is strait. Oh for grace to come to Jesus aright, with the faith of God's elect. He who smote Uzzah for touching the ark is very jealous of His two ordinances; as a true believer I may approach them freely, as an alien I may not touch them lest I die. Heart searching is the duty of all who are baptized or come to the Lord's table. *"Search me, Oh God, and know my way, try me and know my heart."*

EVENING

"And they gave Him wine mixed with myrrh to drink. But He did not take it" — *Mark 15:23.*

A GOLDEN TRUTH is couched in the fact that the Savior put the cup of wine and myrrh from His lips. On the heights of heaven the Son of God stood of old, and as He looked down upon our globe. He measured the long descent to the utmost depths of human misery; He cast up the sum total of all the agonies which expiation would require, and abated not a jot. He solemnly determined that to offer a sufficient atoning sacrifice He must go the whole way, from the highest to the lowest, from the throne of highest glory to the cross of deepest woe. This cup of myrrh, with its soporific influence, would have stayed Him within a little of the utmost limit of misery, therefore He refused it. He would not stop short of all He had undertaken to suffer for His people.

Ah, how many of us have pined after reliefs to our grief which would have been injurious to us! Reader, did you never pray for a discharge from hard service or suffering with a petulant and wilful eagerness? Providence has taken from you the desire of your eyes with a stroke. Say, Christian, if it had been said, If you so desire it, that loved one of yours shall live, but God will be dishonored, could you have put away the temptation, and said, *"Your will be done"*? Oh, it is sweet to be able to say, My lord, if for other reasons I need not suffer, yet if I can honor You more by suffering, and if the loss of my earthly all will bring You glory, then so let it be. I refuse the comfort, if it comes in the way of Your honor. Oh that we thus walked more in the footsteps of our lord, cheerfully enduring trial for His sake, promptly and willingly putting away the thought of self and comfort when it would interfere with our finishing the work which He has given us to do. Great grace is needed, but great grace is provided.

August 19

MORNING

"And He shall stand and feed in the strength of the LORD" — Micah 5:4.

CHRIST'S REIGN IN His Church is that of a shepherd-king. He has supremacy, but it is the superiority of a wise and tender shepherd over his needy and loving flock. He commands and receives obedience, but it is the willing obedience of the well-cared-for sheep, rendered joyfully to their beloved Shepherd, whose voice they know so well. He rules by the force of love and the energy of goodness.

His reign is practical in its character. It is said, *"He shall stand and feed."* The great Head of the Church is actively engaged in providing for His people. He does not sit down upon the throne in empty state, or hold a scepter without wielding it in government. No, He stands and feeds. The expression feed, in the original, is like an analogous one in the Greek, which means to shepherd, to do everything expected of a shepherd: to guide, to watch, to preserve, to restore, to tend, as well as to feed.

His reign is continual in its duration. It is said, *"He shall stand and feed;"* not "He shall feed now and then, and leave His position;" not, He shall one day grant a revival, and then next day leave His Church to barrenness. His eyes never slumber, and His hands never rest; His heart never ceases to beat with love, and His shoulders are never weary of carrying His people's burdens.

His reign is effectually powerful in its action; *"He shall feed in the strength of Jehovah."* Wherever Christ is, there is God; and whatever Christ does is the act of the Most High. Oh! it is a joyful truth to consider that He who stands today representing the interests of His people is very God of very God, to whom every knee shall bow. Happy are we who belong to such a shepherd, whose humanity communes with us, and whose divinity protects us. Let us worship and bow down before Him as the people of His pasture.

EVENING

"Pull me out of the net that they have laid for me, for You are my strength" — Psalm 31:4.

OUR SPIRITUAL FOES are of the serpent's brood, and seek to ensnare us by subtlety. The prayer before us supposes the possibility of the believer being caught like a bird. So deftly does the fowler do his work, that simple ones are soon surrounded by the net. The text asks that even out of Satan's meshes the captive one may be delivered; this is a proper petition, and one which can be granted: from between the jaws of the lion, and out of the belly of hell, can eternal love rescue the saint. It may need a sharp pull to save a soul from the net of temptation, and a mighty pull to extricate a man from the snares of malicious cunning, but the Lord is equal to every emergency, and the most skillfully placed nets of the hunter shall never be able to hold His chosen ones. Woe unto those who are so clever at net-laying; they who tempt others shall be destroyed themselves.

"For You are my strength." What an inexpressible sweetness is to be found in these few words! How joyfully may we encounter toils, and how cheerfully may we endure sufferings, when we can lay hold upon celestial strength. Divine power will rend asunder all the toils of our enemies, confound their politics, and frustrate their knavish tricks; he is a happy man who has such matchless might engaged upon his side. Our own strength would be of little service when embarrassed in the nets of base cunning, but the Lord's strength is ever available; we have but to invoke it, and we shall find it near at hand. If by faith we are depending alone upon the strength of the mighty God of Israel, we may use our holy reliance as a plea in supplication.

> Lord, evermore Your face we seek:
> Tempted we are, and poor, and weak;
> Keep us with lowly hearts, and meek.
> Let us not fall. Let us not fall.

MORNING   August 20

"The sweet psalmist of Israel" — 2 Samuel 23:1.

AMONG ALL THE saints whose lives are recorded in Holy Writ, David possesses an experience of the most striking, varied, and instructive character. In his history we meet with trials and temptations not to be discovered, as a whole, in other saints of ancient times, and hence he is all the more suggestive a type of our Lord. David knew the trials of all ranks and conditions of men. Kings have their troubles, and David wore a crown. The peasant has his cares, and David handled a shepherd's crook. The wanderer has many hardships, and David abode in the caves of Engedi. The captain has his difficulties, and David found the sons of Zeruiah too hard for him. The psalmist was also tried in his friends, his counselor Ahithophel forsook him, *"He that eats bread with me, has lifted up his heel against me."* His worst foes were they of his own household: his children were his greatest affliction. The temptations of poverty and wealth, of honor and reproach, of health and weakness, all tried their power upon him. He had temptations from without to disturb his peace, and from within to mar his joy. David no sooner escaped from one trial than he fell into another; no sooner emerged from one season of despondency and alarm, than he was again brought into the lowest depths, and all God's waves and billows rolled over him.

It is probably from this cause that David's psalms are so universally the delight of experienced Christians. Whatever our frame of mind, whether ecstasy or depression, David has exactly described our emotions. He was an able master of the human heart, because he had been taught in the best of all schools, the school of heart-felt, personal experience. As we are instructed in the same school, as we grow matured in grace and in years, we increasingly appreciate David's psalms, and find them to be "green pastures." My soul, let David's experience cheer and counsel you this day.

EVENING

"And they fortified Jerusalem to the Broad Wall" — Nehemiah 3:8.

CITIES WELL FORTIFIED have broad walls, and so had Jerusalem in her glory. The New Jerusalem must, in like manner, be surrounded and preserved by a broad wall of nonconformity to the world, and separation from its customs and spirit. The tendency of these days is to break down the holy barrier, and make the distinction between the church and the world merely nominal. Professors are no longer strict and Puritanical, questionable literature is read on all hands, frivolous pastimes are currently indulged, and a general laxity threatens to deprive the Lord's peculiar people of those sacred singularities which separate them from sinners. It will be an ill day for the church and the world when the proposed amalgamation shall be complete, and the sons of God and the daughters of men shall be as one; then shall another deluge of wrath be ushered in. Beloved reader, be it your aim in heart, in word, in dress, in action to maintain the broad wall, remembering that the *"friendship of this world is enmity against God."*

The broad wall afforded a pleasant place of resort for the inhabitants of Jerusalem, from which they could command prospects of the surrounding country. This reminds us of the Lord's exceeding broad commandments, in which we walk at liberty in communion with Jesus, overlooking the scenes of earth, and looking out towards the glories of heaven. Separated from the world, and denying ourselves all ungodliness and fleshly lusts, we are nevertheless not in prison, nor restricted within narrow bounds; no, we walk at liberty, because we keep His precepts. Come, reader, this evening walk with God in His statutes. As friend met friend upon the city wall, so meet your God in the way of holy prayer and meditation. The bulwarks of salvation you have a right to traverse, for you are a freeman of the royal burgh, a citizen of the metropolis of the universe.

August 21　　　　　　　　MORNING

"And he who waters shall also be watered himself" — *Proverbs 11:25.*

WE ARE HERE taught the great lesson, that to get, we must give; that to accumulate, we must scatter; that to make ourselves happy, we must make others happy; and that in order to become spiritually vigorous, we must seek the spiritual good of others. In watering others, we are ourselves watered. How? Our efforts to be useful, bring out our powers for usefulness. We have latent talents and dormant faculties, which are brought to light by exercise. Our strength for labor is hidden even from ourselves, until we venture forth to fight the Lord's battles, or to climb the mountains of difficulty. We do not know what tender sympathies we possess until we try to dry the widow's tears, and soothe the orphan's grief.

We often find in attempting to teach others, that we gain instruction for ourselves. Oh, what gracious lessons some of us have learned at sick beds! We went to teach the Scriptures, we came away blushing that we knew so little of them. In our converse with poor saints, we are taught the way of God more perfectly for ourselves and get a deeper insight into divine truth. So that watering others makes us humble. We discover how much grace there is where we had not looked for it; and how much the poor saint may outstrip us in knowledge.

Our own comfort is also increased by our working for others. We endeavor to cheer them, and the consolation gladdens our own heart. Like the two men in the snow; one chafed the other's limbs to keep him from dying, and in so doing kept his own blood in circulation, and saved his own life. The poor widow of Sarepta gave from her scanty store a supply for the prophet's wants, and from that day she never again knew what want was. Give then, and it shall be given unto you, good measure, pressed down, and running over.

EVENING

"I did not say to the seed of Jacob, Seek me in vain" — *Isaiah 45:19.*

WE MAY GAIN much solace by considering what God has not said. What He has said is inexpressibly full of comfort and delight; what He has not said is scarcely less rich in consolation. It was one of these not saids which preserved the kingdom of Israel in the days of Jeroboam the son of Joash, for "the Lord said not that He would blot out the name of Israel from under heaven." (2 Kings 14:27). In our text we have an assurance that God will answer prayer, because He has not said "unto the seed of Israel, Seek Me in vain." You who write bitter things against yourselves should remember that, let your doubts and fears say what they will, if God has not cut you off from mercy, there is no room for despair: even the voice of conscience is of little weight if it be not seconded by the voice of God.

What God has said, tremble at! But suffer not your vain imaginings to overwhelm you with despondency and sinful despair. Many timid persons have been vexed by the suspicion that there may be something in God's decree which shuts them out from hope, but here is a complete refutation to that troublesome fear, for no true seeker can be decreed to wrath. *"I have not spoken in secret, in a dark place of the earth; I have not said,"* even in the secret of my unsearchable decree, *"Seek Me in vain."* God has clearly revealed that He will hear the prayer of those who call upon Him, and that declaration cannot be contravened. He has so firmly, so truthfully, so righteously spoken, that there can be no room for doubt. He does not reveal His mind in unintelligible words, but He speaks plainly and positively, *"Ask, and you shall receive."* Believe, Oh trembler, this sure truth, that prayer must and shall be heard, and that never, even in the secrets of eternity, has the Lord said unto any living soul, *"Seek Me in vain."*

MORNING   August 22

"I charge you, O daughters of Jerusalem, if you find my Beloved, tell Him that I am sick with love" — Song of Solomon 5:8.

SUCH IS THE language of the believer panting after present fellowship with Jesus, he is sick for his Lord. Gracious souls are never perfectly at ease except they are in a state of nearness to Christ; for when they are away from Him they lose their peace. The nearer to Him, the nearer to the perfect calm of heaven; the nearer to Him, the fuller the heart is, not only of peace, but of life, and vigor, and joy, for these all depend on constant intercourse with Jesus. What the sun is to the day, what the moon is to the night, what the dew is to the flower, such is Jesus Christ to us. What bread is to the hungry, clothing to the naked, the shadow of a great rock to the traveler in a weary land, such is Jesus Christ to us; and, therefore, if we are not consciously one with Him, little marvel if our spirit cries in the words of the Song, *"I charge you, Oh you daughters of Jerusalem, if you find my Beloved, tell Him that I am sick with love."*

This earnest longing after Jesus has a blessing attending it: *"Blessed are they that do hunger and thirst after righteousness;"* and therefore, supremely blessed are they who thirst after the Righteous One. Blessed is that hunger, since it comes from God: if I may not have the full-blown blessedness of being filled, I would seek the same blessedness in its sweet bud-pining in emptiness and eagerness till I am filled with Christ. If I may not feed on Jesus, it shall be next door to heaven to hunger and thirst after Him. There is a holiness about that hunger, since it sparkles among the beatitudes of our Lord. But the blessing involves a promise. Such hungry ones shall be filled with what they are desiring. If Christ thus causes us to long after Himself, He will certainly satisfy those longings; and when He does come to us, as come He will, Oh, how sweet it will be!

EVENING
"The unsearchable riches of Christ" — Ephesians 3:8.

MY MASTER HAS riches beyond the count of arithmetic, the measurement of reason, the dream of imagination, or the eloquence of words. They are unsearchable! You may look, and study, and weigh, but Jesus is a greater Savior than you think Him to be when your thoughts are at the greatest. My Lord is more ready to pardon than you to sin, more able to forgive than you to transgress. My Master is more willing to supply your wants than you are to confess them. Never tolerate low thoughts of my Lord Jesus. When you put the crown on His head, you will only crown Him with silver when He deserves gold. My Master has riches of happiness to bestow upon you now. He can make you to *"lie down in green pastures, and lead you beside still waters."* There is no music like the music of His pipe, when He is the Shepherd and you are the sheep, and you lie down at His feet.

There is no love like His, neither earth nor heaven can match it. To know Christ and to be found in Him, this is life, this is joy, this is marrow and fatness, wine on the lees well refined! My Master does not treat His servants churlishly; He gives to them as a king gives to a king; He gives them two heavens, a heaven below in serving Him here, and a heaven above in delighting in Him forever. His unsearchable riches will be best known in eternity. He will give you on the way to heaven all you need; your place of defense shall be the munitions of rocks, your bread shall be given you, and your waters shall be sure; but it is there, there where you shall hear the song of them that triumph, the shout of them that feast, and shall have a face-to-face view of the glorious and beloved One. The unsearchable riches of Christ! This is the tune for the minstrels of earth, and the song for the harpers of heaven. Lord, teach us more and more of Jesus, and we will tell out the good news to others.

August 23   MORNING

"The voice of weeping shall no more be heard in her" — Isaiah 65:19.

THE GLORIFIED WEEP no more, for all outward causes of grief are gone. There are no broken friendships, nor blighted prospects in heaven. Poverty, famine, peril, persecution, and slander, are unknown there. No pain distresses, no thought of death or bereavement saddens. They weep no more, for they are perfectly sanctified. No *"evil heart of unbelief"* prompts them to depart from the living God; they are without fault before His throne, and are fully conformed to His image. Well may they cease to mourn who have ceased to sin. They weep no more, because all fear of change is past. They know that they are eternally secure. Sin is shut out, and they are shut in. They dwell within a city which shall never be stormed; they bask in a sun which shall never set; they drink of a river which shall never dry; they pluck fruit from a tree which shall never wither. Countless cycles may revolve, but eternity shall not be exhausted, and while eternity endures, their immortality and blessedness shall coexist with it. They are forever with the Lord.

They weep no more, because every desire is fulfilled. They cannot wish for anything which they have not in possession. Eye and ear, heart and hand, judgment, imagination, hope, desire, will, all the faculties, are completely satisfied. Imperfect as our present ideas are of the things which God has prepared for them that love Him, yet we know enough, by the revelation of the Spirit, that the saints above are supremely blessed. The joy of Christ, which is an infinite fullness of delight, is in them. They bathe themselves in the bottomless, shoreless sea of infinite beatitude. That same joyful rest remains for us. It may not be far distant. Before long the weeping willow shall be exchanged for the palm-branch of victory, and sorrow's dewdrops will be transformed into the pearls of everlasting bliss. *"Therefore comfort one another with these words."*

EVENING

"That through faith Christ may dwell in your hearts" — Ephesians 3:17.

BEYOND MEASURE IT is desirable that we, as believers, should have the person of Jesus constantly before us, to inflame our love towards Him, and to increase our knowledge of Him. I would to God that my readers were all entered as diligent scholars in Jesus' college, students of the body of Christ, resolved to attain unto a good degree in the learning of the cross. But to have Jesus ever near, the heart must be full of Him welling up with His love, even to overrunning; hence the apostle prays *"that Christ may dwell in your hearts."* See how near he would have Jesus to be! You cannot get a subject closer to you than to have it in the heart itself. *"That He may dwell;"* not that He may call upon you sometimes, as a casual visitor enters Into a house and tarries for a night, but that He may dwell; that Jesus may become the Lord and Tenant of your inmost being, never more to go out.

Observe the words: that He may *"dwell in your heart,"* that best room of the house of manhood; not in your thoughts alone, but in your affections; not merely in the mind's meditations, but in the heart's emotions. We should pant after love to Christ of a most abiding character, not a love that flames up and then dies out into the darkness of a few embers, but a constant flame, fed by sacred fuel, like the fire upon the altar which never went out. This cannot be accomplished except by faith. Faith must be strong, or love will not be fervent; the root of the flower must be healthy, or we cannot expect the bloom to be sweet. Faith is the lily's root, and love is the lily's bloom. Now, reader, Jesus cannot be in your heart's love except you have a firm hold of Him by your heart's faith; and, therefore, pray that you may always trust Christ in order that you may always love Him. If love be cold, be sure that faith is drooping.

MORNING

August 24

"The breaker has come up before them" — *Micah 2:13.*

INASMUCH AS Jesus has gone before us, things remain not as they would have been had He never passed that way. He has conquered every foe that obstructed the way. Cheer up now you faint-hearted warrior. Not only has Christ traveled the road, but He has slain your enemies. Do you dread sin? He has nailed it to His cross. Do you fear death? He has been the death of Death. Are you afraid of hell? He has barred it against the advent of any of His children; they shall never see the gulf of perdition. Whatever foes may be before the Christian, they are all overcome. There are lions, but their teeth are broken; there are serpents, but their fangs are extracted; there are rivers, but they are bridged or fordable; there are flames, but we wear that matchless garment which renders us invulnerable to fire. The sword that has been forged against us is already blunted; the instruments of war which the enemy is preparing have already lost their point. God has taken away in the person of Christ all the power that anything can have to hurt us.

Well then, the army may safely march on, and you may go joyously along your journey, for all your enemies are conquered beforehand. What shall you do but march on to take the prey? They are beaten, they are vanquished; all you have to do is to divide the spoil. You shall, it is true, often engage in combat; but your fight shall be with a vanquished foe. His head is broken; he may attempt to injure you, but his strength shall not be sufficient for his malicious design. Your victory shall be easy, and your treasure shall be beyond all count.

> Proclaim aloud the Savior's fame,
> Who bears the Breaker's wondrous name;
> Sweet name; and it becomes Him well,
> Who breaks down earth, sin, death, and hell.

EVENING

"If fire breaks out and catches in thorns, so that the stacks of grain, or the standing grain, or the field, is burned up, he who kindled the fire shall surely repay!" — *Exodus 22:6.*

BUT WHAT RESTITUTION can he make who casts abroad the fire-brands of error, or the coals of lasciviousness, and sets men's souls on a blaze with the fire of hell? The guilt is beyond estimate, and the result is irretrievable. If such an offender be forgiven, what grief it will cause him in the retrospect, since he cannot undo the mischief which he has done! An ill example may kindle a flame which years of amended character cannot quench. To burn the food of man is bad enough, but how much worse to destroy the soul! It may be useful to us to reflect how far we may have been guilty in the past, and to inquire whether, even in the present, there may not be evil in us which has a tendency to bring damage to the souls of our relatives, friends, or neighbors.

The fire of strife is a terrible evil when it breaks out in a Christian church. Where converts were multiplied, and God was glorified, jealousy and envy do the devil's work most effectually. Where the golden grain was being housed, to reward the toil of the great Boaz, the fire of enmity comes in and leaves little else but smoke and a heap of blackness. Woe unto those by whom offenses come. May they never come through us, for although we cannot make restitution, we shall certainly be the chief sufferers if we are the chief offenders. Those who feed the fire deserve just censure, but he who first kindles it is most to blame. Discord usually takes first hold upon the thorns; it is nurtured among the hypocrites and base professors in the church, and away it goes among the righteous, blown by the winds of hell, and no one knows where it may end. Oh You Lord and giver of peace, make us peacemakers, and never let us aid and abet the men of strife, or even unintentionally cause the least division among Your people.

August 25   MORNING

"His fruit was sweet to My taste" — Song of Solomon 2:3.

FAITH, IN THE Scripture, is spoken of under the emblem of all the senses. It is sight: *"look unto Me and be saved."* It is hearing: *"Hear, and your soul shall live."* Faith is smelling: *"All your garments smell of myrrh, and aloes, and cassia;" "your name is as ointment poured forth."* Faith is spiritual touch. By this faith the woman came behind and touched the hem of Christ's garment, and by this we handle the things of the good word of life. Faith is equally the spirit's taste. *"How sweet are Your words to my taste! yes, sweeter than honey to my lips." "Except a man eat My flesh,"* says Christ, *"and drink My blood, there is no life in him."*

This *"taste"* is faith in one of its highest operations. One of the first performances of faith is hearing. We hear the voice of God, not with the outward ear alone, but with the inward ear; we hear it as God's Word, and we believe it to be so; that is the "hearing" of faith. Then our mind looks upon the truth as it is presented to us; that is to say, we understand it, we perceive its meaning; that is the seeing of faith. Next we discover its preciousness; we begin to admire it, and find how fragrant it is; that is faith in its smell. Then we appropriate the mercies which are prepared for us in Christ; that is faith in its touch. Hence follow the enjoyments, peace, delight, communion; which are faith in its taste. Any one of these acts of faith is saving. To hear Christ's voice as the sure voice of God in the soul will save us; but that which gives true enjoyment is the aspect of faith wherein Christ, by holy taste, is received into us, and made, by inward and spiritual apprehension of His sweetness and preciousness, to be the food of our souls. It is then we sit *"under His shadow with great delight,"* and find His fruit sweet to our taste.

EVENING

"If you believe from the whole heart it is lawful" — Acts 8:37.

THESE WORDS MAY answer your scruples, devout reader, concerning the ordinances. Perhaps you say, I would be afraid to be baptized; it is such a solemn thing to avow myself to be dead with Christ, and buried with Him. I would not feel at liberty to come to the Master's table; I would be afraid of eating and drinking damnation unto myself, not discerning the Lord's body. Ah! poor trembler, Jesus has given you liberty, be not afraid. If a stranger came to your house, he would stand at the door, or wait in the hall; he would not dream of intruding unbidden into your parlor; he is not at home. But your child makes himself very free about the house; and so is it with the child of God. A stranger may not intrude where a child may venture. When the Holy Spirit has given you to feel the spirit of adoption, you may come to Christian ordinances without fear.

The same rule holds good of the Christian's inward privileges. You think, poor seeker, that you are not allowed to rejoice with *"joy unspeakable and full of glory;"* if you are permitted to get inside Christ's door, or sit at the bottom of His table, you will be well content. Ah! but you shall not have less privileges than the very greatest. God makes no difference in His love to His children. A child is a child to Him; He will not make him a hired servant; but he shall feast upon the fatted calf, and shall have the music and the dancing as much as if he had never gone astray. When Jesus comes into the heart, He issues a general license to be glad in the Lord. No chains are worn in the court of King Jesus. Our admission into full privileges may be gradual, but it is sure. Perhaps our reader is saying, I wish I could enjoy the promises, and walk at liberty in my lord's commands: *"If you believe from the whole heart, it is lawful."* Loose the chains of your neck, Oh captive daughter, for Jesus makes you free.

MORNING   August 26

"He has commanded His covenant forever" — Psalm 111:9.

THE LORD'S PEOPLE delight in the covenant itself. It is an unfailing source of consolation to them so often as the Holy Spirit leads them into its banqueting house and waves its banner of love. They delight to contemplate the antiquity of that covenant, remembering that before the day-star knew its place, or planets ran their round, the interests of the saints were made secure in Christ Jesus. It is peculiarly pleasing to them to remember the sureness of the covenant, while meditating upon *"the sure mercies of David."* They delight to celebrate it as "signed, and sealed, and ratified, in all things ordered well." It often makes their hearts dilate with joy to think of its immutability, as a covenant which neither time nor eternity, life nor death, shall ever be able to violate, a covenant as old as eternity and as everlasting as the Rock of ages.

They rejoice also to feast upon the fullness of this covenant, for they see in it all things provided for them. God is their portion, Christ their companion, the Spirit their Comforter, earth their lodge, and heaven their home. They see in it an inheritance reserved and entailed to every soul possessing an interest in its ancient and eternal deed of gift. Their eyes sparkled when they saw it as a treasure-trove in the Bible; but oh! how their souls were gladdened when they saw in the last will and testament of their divine kinsman, that it was bequeathed to them! More especially it is the pleasure of God's people to contemplate the graciousness of this covenant. They see that the law was made void because it was a covenant of works and depended upon merit, but this they perceive to be enduring because grace is the basis, grace the condition, grace the strain, grace the bulwark, grace the foundation, grace the topstone. The covenant is a treasury of wealth, a granary of food, a fountain of life, a store-house of salvation, a charter of peace, and a haven of joy.

EVENING

And immediately all the crowd was much astonished to see Him. And they ran up to Him and greeted Him" — Mark 9:15.

HOW GREAT THE difference between Moses and Jesus! When the prophet of Horeb had been forty days upon the mountain, he underwent a kind of transfiguration, so that his countenance shone with exceeding brightness, and he put a veil over his face, for the people could not endure to look upon his glory. Not so our Savior. He had been transfigured with a greater glory than that of Moses, and yet, it is not written that the people were blinded by the blaze of His countenance, but rather they were amazed, and running to Him they greeted Him. The glory of the law repels, but the greater glory of Jesus attracts. Though Jesus is holy and just, yet blended with His purity there is so much of truth and grace, that sinners run to Him amazed at His goodness, fascinated by His love; they greet Him, become His disciples, and take Him to be their Lord and Master.

Reader, it may be that just now you are blinded by the dazzling brightness of the law of God. You feel its claims on your conscience, but you cannot keep it in your life. Not that you find fault with the law, on the contrary, it commands your profoundest esteem, still you are in nowise drawn by it to God; you are rather hardened in heart, and are verging towards desperation. Ah, poor heart! turn your eye from Moses, with all his repelling splendor, and look to Jesus, resplendent with milder glories. Behold His flowing wounds and thorn-crowned head! He is the Son of God, and therein He is greater than Moses, but He is the Lord of love, and in this is more tender, though the giver of the law. He bore the wrath of God, and in His death revealed more of God's justice than Sinai on a blaze, but that justice is now vindicated, and henceforth it is the guardian of believers in Jesus. Look, sinner, to the bleeding Savior,

MORNING August 27

"How long will it be before they believe me" — *Numbers 14:11.*

STRIVE WITH ALL diligence to keep out that monster unbelief. It so dishonors Christ, that He will withdraw His visible presence if we insult Him by indulging it. It is true it is a weed, the seeds of which we can never entirely extract from the soil, but we must aim at its root with zeal and perseverance. Among hateful things it is the most to be abhorred. Its injurious nature is so venomous that he that exercises it and he upon whom it is exercised are both hurt thereby.

In your case, Oh believer, it is most wicked, for the mercies of your Lord in the past, increase your guilt in doubting Him now. When you distrust the Lord Jesus, He may well cry out, *"Behold I am pressed under you, as a cart is pressed that is full of sheaves."* This is crowning His head with thorns of the sharpest kind. It is very cruel for a well-beloved wife to mistrust a kind and faithful husband. The sin is needless, foolish, and unwarranted. Jesus has never given the slightest ground for suspicion, and it is hard to be doubted by those to whom our conduct is uniformly affectionate and true. Jesus is the Son of the Highest, and has unbounded wealth; it is shameful to doubt Omnipotence and distrust all-sufficiency. The cattle on a thousand hills will suffice for our most hungry feeding, and the granaries of heaven are not likely to be emptied by our eating. If Christ were only a cistern, we might soon exhaust His fullness, but who can drain a fountain? Myriads of spirits have drawn their supplies from Him, and not one of them has murmured at the scantiness of His resources.

Away, then, with this lying traitor unbelief, for his only errand is to cut the bonds of communion and make us mourn an absent Savior. Bunyan tells us that unbelief has, as many lives as a cat: if so, let us kill one life now, and continue the work till the whole nine are gone. Down with you, you traitor, my heart abhors you.

EVENING

"Into Your hand I commit my spirit; You have redeemed me, O LORD God of truth" — *Psalm 31:5.*

THESE WORDS HAVE been frequently used by holy men in their hour of departure. We may profitably consider them this evening. The object of the faithful man's solicitude in life and death is not his body or his estate, but his spirit; this is his choice treasure. If this be safe, all is well. What is this mortal state compared with the soul? The believer commits his soul to the hand of his God; it came from Him, it is His own, He has before time sustained it, He is able to keep it, and it is most fit that He should receive it. All things are safe in Jehovah's hands; what we entrust to the Lord will be secure, both now and in that day of days towards which we are hastening. It is peaceful living, and glorious dying, to repose in the care of heaven. At all times we should commit our all to Jesus' faithful hand; then, though life may hang on a thread, and adversities may multiply as the sands of the sea, our soul shall dwell at ease, and delight itself in quiet resting places.

"You have redeemed me, Oh LORD God of truth." Redemption is a solid basis for confidence. David had not known Calvary as we have done, but temporal redemption cheered him; and shall not eternal redemption yet more sweetly console us? Past deliverances are strong pleas for present assistance. What the Lord has done He will do again, for He changes not. He is faithful to His promises, and gracious to His saints; He will not turn away from His people.

> Though You slay me I will trust,
> Praise You even from the dust,
> You may chasten and correct,
> But You never can neglect;
> Since the ransom price is paid,
> On Your love my hope is stayed.

MORNING

August 28

"Oil for the light" — Exodus 25:6.

MY SOUL, HOW much you need this, for your lamp will not long continue to burn without it. Your snuff will smoke and become an offense if light be gone, and gone it will be if oil be absent. You have no oil well springing up in your human nature, and therefore you must go to them that sell and buy for yourself, or like the foolish virgins, you will have to cry, *"My lamp is gone out."* Even the consecrated lamps could not give light without oil; though they shone in the tabernacle they needed to be fed, though no rough winds blew upon them they required to be trimmed, and your need is equally as great. Under the most happy circumstances you can not give light for another hour unless fresh oil of grace be given you.

It was not every oil that might be used in the Lord's service; neither the petroleum which exudes so plentifully from the earth, nor the produce of fish, nor that extracted from nuts would be accepted; one oil only was selected, and that the best olive oil. Pretended grace from natural goodness, fancied grace from priestly hands, or imaginary grace from outward ceremonies will never serve the true saint of God; he knows that the Lord would not be pleased with rivers of such oil. He goes to the olive-press of Gethsemane, and draws his supplies from Him who was crushed therein. The oil of gospel grace is pure and free from lees and dregs, and hence the light which is fed thereon is clear and bright. Our churches are the Savior's golden candelabra, and if they are to be lights in this dark world, they must have much holy oil. Let us pray for ourselves, our ministers, and our churches, that they may never lack oil for the light. Truth, holiness, joy, knowledge, love, these are all beams of the sacred light, but we cannot give them forth unless in private we receive oil from God the Holy Spirit.

EVENING

"Rejoice, O unfruitful one" — Isaiah 54:1.

THOUGH WE HAVE brought forth some fruit unto Christ, and have a joyful hope that we are *"plants of His own right hand planting,"* yet there are times when we feel very barren. Prayer is lifeless, love is cold, faith is weak, each grace in the garden of our heart languishes and droops. We are like flowers in the hot sun, requiring the refreshing shower. In such a condition what are we to do? The text is addressed to us in just such a state. *"Sing, Oh barren, break forth and cry aloud."* But what can I sing about? I cannot talk about the present, and even the past looks full of barrenness. Ah! I can sing of Jesus Christ. I can talk of visits which the Redeemer has before time paid to me; or if not of these, I can magnify the great love wherewith He loved His people when He came from the heights of heaven for their redemption. I will go to the cross again. Come, my soul, heavy laden you once were, and you did lose your burden there. Go to Calvary again. Perhaps that very cross which gave you life may give you fruitfulness. What is my barrenness? It is the platform for His fruit-creating power. What is my desolation? It is the black setting for the sapphire of His everlasting love. I will go in poverty, I will go in helplessness, I will go in all my shame and backsliding, I will tell Him that I am still His child, and in confidence in His faithful heart, even I, the barren one, will sing and cry aloud.

Sing, believer, for it will cheer your own heart, and the hearts of other desolate ones. Sing on, for now that you are really ashamed-of being barren, you will be fruitful soon; now that God makes you loath to be without fruit, He will soon cover you with clusters. The experience of our barrenness is painful, but the lord's visitations are delightful. A sense of our own poverty drives us to Christ, and that is where we need to be, for in Him is our fruit found.

MORNING August 29

"Have mercy on me, O God" — Psalm 51:1.

WHEN the great missionary, William Carey, was suffering from a dangerous illness, the inquiry was made, If this sickness should prove fatal, what passage would you select as the text for your funeral sermon? He replied, Oh, I feel that such a poor sinful creature is unworthy to have anything said about him; but if a funeral sermon must be preached, let it be from the words, *"Have mercy upon me, Oh God, according to Your loving-kindness; according to the multitude of Your tender mercies blot out my transgressions."* In the same spirit of humility he directed in his will that the following inscription and nothing more should be cut on his gravestone:

WILLIAM CAREY, BORN AUGUST 17, 1761:
DIED -
A wretched, poor, and helpless worm
On Your kind arms I fall.

Only on the footing of free grace can the most experienced and most honored of the saints approach their God. The best of men are conscious above all others that they are men at the best. Empty boats float high, but heavily laden vessels are low in the water; mere professors can boast, but true children of God cry for mercy upon their unprofitableness. We have need that the Lord should have mercy upon our good works, our prayers, our preachings, our alms-givings, and our holiest things. The blood was not only sprinkled upon the doorposts of Israel's dwelling houses, but upon the sanctuary, the mercy-seat, and the altar, because as sin intrudes into our holiest things, the blood of Jesus is needed to purify them from defilement. If mercy be needed to be exercised towards our duties, what shall be said of our sins? How sweet the remembrance that inexhaustible mercy is waiting to be gracious to us, to restore our backslidings, and make our broken bones rejoice!

EVENING

"All the days of his Nazariteship he shall eat nothing that is made of the vine tree, from the kernels even to the husk" — Numbers 6:4.

NAZARITES HAD TAKEN, among other vows, one which debarred them from the use of wine. In order that they might not violate the obligation, they were forbidden to drink the vinegar of wine or strong liquors. And to make the rule still more clear, they were not to touch the unfermented juice of the grapes, nor even to eat the fruit either fresh or dried. In order, altogether, to secure the integrity of the vow, they were not even allowed anything that had to do with the vine; they were, in fact, to avoid the appearance of evil.

Surely this is a lesson to the Lord's separated ones, teaching them to come away from sin in every form, to avoid not merely its grosser shapes, but even its spirit and similitude. Strict walking is much despised in these days, but rest assured, dear reader, it is both the safest and the happiest. He who yields a point or two to the world is in fearful peril; he who eats the grapes of Sodom will soon drink the wine of Gomorrah. A little crevice in the sea-bank in Holland lets in the sea, and the gap speedily swells till a province is drowned. Worldly conformity, in any degree, is a snare to the soul, and makes it more and more liable to presumptuous sins.

Moreover, as the Nazarite who drank grape juice could not be quite sure whether it might not have endured a degree of fermentation, and consequently could not be clear in heart that his vow was intact, so the yielding, temporizing Christian cannot wear a conscience void of offense, but must feel that the inward monitor is in doubt of him. Things doubtful we need not doubt about; they are wrong to us. Things tempting we must not dally with, but flee from them with speed. Better be sneered at as a Puritan then be despised as a hypocrite. Careful walking may involve much self-denial, but it has pleasures of its own which are more than a sufficient recompense.

MORNING   August 30

"Wait on the LORD" — *Psalm 27:14.*

IT MAY SEEM an easy thing to wait, but it is one of the postures which a Christian soldier learns not without years of teaching. Marching and quick-marching are much easier to God's warriors than standing still. There are hours of perplexity when the most willing spirit, anxiously desires to serve the Lord, knows not what part to take. Then what shall it do? Vex itself by despair? Fly back in cowardice, turn to the right hand in fear, or rush forward in presumption? No, but simply wait. Wait in prayer, however. Call upon God, and spread the case before Him; tell Him your difficulty, and plead His promise of aid. In dilemmas between one duty and another, it is sweet to be humble as a child, and wait with simplicity of soul upon the Lord. It is sure to be well with us when we feel and know our own folly, and are heartily willing to be guided by the will of God. But wait in faith. Express your unwavering confidence in Him; for unfaithful, waiting without trust is but an insult to the Lord. Believe that if He keep you tarrying even till midnight, yet He will come at the right time; the vision shall come and shall not tarry.

Wait in quiet patience, not rebelling because you are under the affliction, but blessing your God for it. Never murmur against the second cause, as the children of Israel did against Moses; never wish you could go back to the world again, but accept the case as it is, and put it as it stands, simply and with your whole heart, without any self-will, into the hand of your covenant God, saying, *"Now, Lord, not my will, but Yours be done."* I know not what to do; I am brought to extremities, but I will wait until You shall cleave the floods, or drive back my foes. I will wait, if You keep me many a day, for my heart is fixed upon You alone, Oh God, and my spirit waits for You in the full conviction that You will yet be *"my joy and my salvation, my refuge and my strong tower."*

EVENING

"Heal me, O Lord, and I shall be healed" — *Jeremiah 17:14. "I have seen his ways and will heal him"* — *Isaiah 57:18.*

IT IS THE sole prerogative of God to remove spiritual disease. Natural disease may be instrumentally healed by men, but even then the honor is to be given to God who gives virtue unto medicine, and bestows power unto the human frame to cast off disease. As for spiritual sicknesses, these remain with the great Physician alone; He claims it as His prerogative, *"I kill and I make alive, I wound and I heal;"* and one of the Lord's choice titles is Jehovah-Rophi, the Lord that heals you. *"I will heal you of your wounds,"* is a promise which could not come from the lip of man, but only from the mouth of the eternal God. On this account the psalmist cried unto the Lord, *"Oh Lord, heal me, for my bones are sore vexed,"* and again, *"Heal my soul, for I have sinned against You."* For this, also, the godly praise the name of the Lord saying, *"He heals all our diseases."* He who made man can restore man; He who was at first the creator of our nature can new create it.

What a transcendent comfort it is that in the person of Jesus *"dwells all the fullness of the Godhead bodily!"* My soul, whatever your disease may be, this great Physician can heal you. If He be God, there can be no limit to His power. Come then with the blind eye of darkened understanding, come with the limping foot of wasted energy, come with the maimed hand of weak faith, the fever of an angry temper, or the ague of shivering despondency, come just as you are, for He who is God can certainly restore you of your plague. None shall restrain the healing virtue which proceeds from Jesus our Lord. Legions of devils have been made to admit the power of the beloved Physician, and never once has He been baffled. All His patients have been cured in the past and shall be in the future, and you shall be one among them, my friend, if you will but rest yourself in Him this night.

August 31 MORNING

"On My arm they shall trust" — Isaiah 51:5.

IN SEASONS OF severe trial, the Christian has nothing on earth that he can trust to, and is therefore compelled to cast himself on his God alone. When his vessel is on its beam-ends, and no human deliverance can avail, he must simply and entirely trust himself to the providence and care of God. Happy storm that wrecks a man on such a rock as this! Oh blessed hurricane that drives the soul to God and God alone! There is no getting at our God sometimes because of the multitude of our friends; but when a man is so poor, so friendless, so helpless that he has nowhere else to turn, he flies into his Father's arms, and is blessedly clasped therein! When he is burdened with troubles so pressing and so peculiar, that he cannot tell them to any but his God, he may be thankful for them; for he will learn more of his Lord then than at any other time.

Oh, tempest-tossed believer, it is a happy trouble that drives you to your Father! Now that you have only your God to trust to, see that you put your full confidence in Him. Dishonor not your lord and Master by unworthy doubts and fears; but be strong in faith, giving glory to God. Show the world that your God is worth ten thousand worlds to you. Show rich men how rich you are in your poverty when the Lord God is your helper. Show the strong man how strong you are in your weakness when underneath you are the everlasting arms. Now is the time for feats of faith and valiant exploits. Be strong and very courageous, and the Lord your God shall certainly, as surely as He built the heavens and the earth, glorify Himself in your weakness, and magnify His might in the midst of your distress. The grandeur of the arch of heaven would be spoiled if the sky were supported by a single visible column, and your faith would lose its glory if it rested on anything discernible by the carnal eye. May the Holy Spirit give you to rest in Jesus this closing day of the month.

EVENING

"If we walk in the light as He is in the light" — 1 John 1:7.

"AS HE IS in the light!" Can we ever attain to this? Shall we ever be able to walk as clearly in the light as He is whom we call *"Our Father,"* of whom it is written, *"God is light, and in Him is no darkness at all"*? Certainly, this is the model which it set before us, for the Savior Himself said, *"Be perfect, even as your Father who is in heaven is perfect;"* and although we may feel that we can never rival the perfection of God, yet we are to seek after it, and never to be satisfied until we attain to it. The youthful artist, as he grasps his early pencil, can hardly hope to equal Raphael or Michelangelo, but still, if he did not have a noble ideal before his mind, he would only attain to something very mean and ordinary.

But what is meant by the expression that the Christian is to walk in light as God is in the light? We conceive it to import likeness, but not degree. We are as truly in the light, we are as heartily in the light, we are as sincerely in the light, as honestly in the light, though we cannot be there in the same measure. I cannot dwell in the sun, it is too bright a place for my residence, but I can walk in the light of the sun; and so, though I cannot attain to that perfection of purity and truth which belongs to the Lord of hosts by nature as the infinitely good, yet I can set the Lord always before me, and strive, by the help of the indwelling Spirit, after conformity to His image. That famous old commentator, John Trapp, says, We may be in the light as God is in the light for quality, but not for equality. We are to have the same light, and are as truly to have it and walk in it as God does, though, as for equality with God in His holiness and purity, that must be left until we cross the Jordan and enter into the perfection of the Most High. Mark that the blessings of sacred fellowship and perfect cleansing are bound up with walking in the light.

MORNING   September 1

"You shall lead me by Your counsel and afterward receive me to glory" — Psalm 73:24.

THE PSALMIST FELT his need of divine guidance. He had just been discovering the foolishness of his own heart, and lest he should be constantly led astray by it, he resolved that God's counsel should henceforth guide him. A sense of our own folly is a great step towards being wise, when it leads us to rely on the wisdom of the Lord. The blind man leans on his friend's arm and reaches home in safety, and so would we give ourselves up implicitly to divine guidance, nothing doubting; assured that though we cannot see, it is always safe to trust the All-seeing God. *"You shall,"* is a blessed expression of confidence. He was sure that the Lord would not decline the condescending task. There is a word for you, Oh believer; rest in it. Be assured that your God will be your counselor and friend; He shall guide you; He will direct all your ways. In His written Word you have this assurance in part fulfilled, for holy Scripture is His counsel to you.

Happy are we to have God's Word always to guide us! What were the mariner without his compass? And what were the Christian without the Bible? This is the unerring chart, the map in which every shoal is described, and all the channels from the quicksand of destruction to the haven of salvation mapped and marked by One who knows all the way. Blessed be You, Oh God, that we may trust You to guide us now, and guide us even to the end!

After this guidance through life, the Psalmist anticipates a divine reception at last: *"and afterward receive me to glory."* What a thought for you, believer! God Himself will receive you to glory; yes, you! Wandering, erring, straying, yet He will bring you safe at last to glory! This is your portion; live on it this day, and if perplexities should surround you, go in the strength of this text straight to the throne.

EVENING
"Trust in Him at all times" — Psalm 62:8.

FAITH IS AS much the rule of temporal as of spiritual life; we ought to have faith in God for our earthly affairs as well as for our heavenly business. It is only as we learn to trust in God for the supply of all our daily need that we shall live above the world. We are not to be idle, that would show we did not trust in God, who works hereto, but in the devil, who is the father of idleness. We are not to be imprudent or rash; that were to trust chance, and not the living God, who is a God of economy and order. Acting in all prudence and uprightness, we are to rely simply and entirely upon the Lord at all times.

Let me commend to you a life of trust in God in temporal things. Trusting in God, you will not be compelled to mourn because you have used sinful means to grow rich. Serve God with integrity, and if you achieve no success, at least no sin will lie upon your conscience. Trusting God, you will not be guilty of self-contradiction. He who trusts in craft, sails this way today, and that way the next, like a vessel tossed about by the ficKle wind; but he that trusts in the Lord is like a vessel propelled by steam, she cuts through the waves, defies the wind, and makes one bright silvery straightforward track to her destined haven. Be you a man with living principles within; never bow to the varying customs of worldly wisdom. Walk in your path of integrity with steadfast steps, and show that you are invincibly strong in the strength which confidence in God alone can confer. Thus you will be delivered from anxious care, you will not be troubled with evil tidings, your heart will be fixed, trusting in the Lord. How pleasant to float along the stream of providence! There is no more blessed way of living than a life of dependence upon a covenant-keeping God. We have no care, for He cares for us; we have no troubles, because we cast our burdens upon the Lord.

September 2   MORNING

"And the mother-in-law of Simon was lying in a fever. And at once they spoke to Him about her — Mark 1:30.

VERY INTERESTING is this little peep into the house of the Apostolic Fisherman. We see at once that household joys and cares are no hindrance to the full exercise of ministry. No, that since they furnish an opportunity for personally witnessing the Lord's gracious work upon one's own flesh and blood, they may even instruct the teacher better than any other earthly discipline. Papists and other sectaries may decry marriage, but true Christianity and household life agree well together. Peter's house was probably a fisherman's hut, but the Lord of Glory entered it, lodged in it, and worked a miracle in it. Should our little book be read this morning in some very humble cottage, let this fact encourage the inmates to seek the company of King Jesus. God is oftener in little huts than in rich palaces. Jesus is looking round your room now, and is waiting to be gracious to you.

Into Simon's house sickness had entered, fever in a deadly form had prostrated his mother-in-law, and as soon as Jesus came they told Him of the sad affliction, and He hastened to the patient's bed. Have you any sickness in the house this morning? You will find Jesus by far the best physician, go to Him at once and tell Him all about the matter. Immediately lay the case before Him. It concerns one of His people, and therefore will not be trivial to Him. Observe, that at once the Savior restored the sick woman; none can heal as He does. We may not make sure that the Lord will at once remove all disease from those we love, but we may know that believing prayer for the sick is far more likely to be followed by restoration than anything else in the world; and where this avails not, we must meekly bow to His will by whom life and death are determined. The tender heart of Jesus waits to hear our griefs, let us pour them into His patient ear.

EVENING

"Unless you see miracles and wonders, you will not believe" — John 4:48.

A CRAVING AFTER marvels was a symptom of the sickly state of men's minds in our Lord's day; they refused solid nourishment, and pined after mere wonder. The gospel which they so greatly needed they would not have; the miracles which Jesus did not always choose to give they eagerly demanded. Many nowadays must see signs and wonders, or they will not believe. Some have said in their heart, "I must feel deep horror of soul, or I never will believe in Jesus." But what if you never should feel it, as probably you never may? Will you go to hell out of spite against God, because He will not treat you like another?

One has said to himself, "If I had a dream, or if I could feel a sudden shock of I know not what, then I would believe." Thus you undeserving mortals dream that my Lord is to be dictated to by you! You are beggars at His gate, asking for mercy, and you must needs draw up rules and regulations as to how He shall give that mercy. Do you think that He will submit to this? My Master is of a generous spirit, but He has a right royal heart, He spurns all dictation, and maintains His sovereignty of action. Why, dear reader, if such be your case, do you crave for signs and wonders? Is not the gospel its own sign and wonder? Is not this a miracle of miracles, that *"God so loved the world that He gave His only begotten Son, that whosoever believes in Him might not perish"*? Surely that precious word, *"whosoever will, let him come and take the water of life freely,"* and that solemn promise, *"Him that comes unto Me, I will in no wise cast out,"* are better than signs and wonders! A truthful Savior ought to be believed. He is truth itself. Why will you ask proof of the veracity of one who cannot lie? The devils themselves declared Him to be the Son of God; will you mistrust Him?

MORNING   September 3

"You whom my soul loves" — Song of Solomon 1:7.

IT IS WELL TO be able, without any if or but, to say of the Lord Jesus, "You whom my soul loves." Many can only say of Jesus that they hope they love Him; they trust they love Him; but only a poor and shallow experience will be content to stay here. No one ought to give any rest to his spirit till he feels quite sure about a matter of such vital importance. We ought not to be satisfied with a superficial hope that Jesus loves us, and with a bare trust that we love Him. The old saints did not generally speak with buts, and ifs, and hopes, and trusts, but they spoke positively and plainly. *"I know whom I have believed,"* says Paul. *"I know that my Redeemer lives,"* says Job. Get positive knowledge of your love of Jesus, and be not satisfied till you can speak of your interest in Him as a reality, which you have made sure by having received the witness of the Holy Spirit, and His seal upon your soul by faith.

True love to Christ is in every case the Holy Spirit's work, and must be worked in the heart by Him. He is the efficient cause of it; but the logical reason why we love Jesus lies in Himself. Why do we love Jesus? Because He first loved us. Why do we love Jesus? Because He *"gave Himself for us."* We have life through His death; we have peace through His blood. Though He was rich, yet for our sakes He became poor. Why do we love Jesus? Because of the excellency of His person. We are filled with a sense of His beauty! an admiration of His charms! a consciousness of His infinite perfection! His greatness, goodness, and loveliness, in one resplendent ray, combine to enchant the soul till it is so ravished that it exclaims, *"Yes, He is altogether lovely."* Blessed love this, a love which binds the heart with chains more soft than silk, and yet more firm than adamant!

EVENING

"The LORD tries the righteous" — Psalm 11:5.

ALL EVENTS ARE under the control of Providence; consequently all the trials of our outward life are traceable at once to the great First Cause. Out of the golden gate of God's ordinance the armies of trial march forth in array, clad in their iron armor, and armed with weapons of war. All providences are doors to trial. Even our mercies, like roses, have their thorns. Men may be drowned in seas of prosperity as well as in rivers of affliction. Our mountains are not too high, and our valleys are not too low for temptations; trials lurk on all roads. Everywhere, above and beneath, we are beset and surrounded with dangers. Yet no shower falls unpermitted from the threatening cloud; every drop has its order before it hastens to the earth.

The trials which come from God are sent to prove and strengthen our graces, and so at once to illustrate the power of divine grace, to test the genuineness of our virtues, and to add to their energy. Our Lord in His infinite wisdom and superabundant love, sets so high a value upon His people's faith that He will not screen them from those trials by which faith is strengthened. You would never have possessed the precious faith which now supports you if the trial of your faith had not been like unto fire. You are a tree that never would have rooted so well if the wind had not rocked you to and fro, and made you take firm hold upon the precious truths of the covenant of grace.

Worldly ease is a great foe to faith; it loosens the joints of holy valor, and snaps the sinews of sacred courage. The balloon never rises until the cords are cut; affliction does this sharp service for believing souls. While the wheat sleeps comfortably in the husk it is useless to man, it must be threshed out of its resting place before its value can be known. Thus it is well that Jehovah tries the righteous, for it causes them to grow rich towards God.

September 4   MORNING

"I desire it! Be clean! — Mark 1:41.

PRIMEVAL DARKNESS HEARD the Almighty fiat, "light be," and straightway light was, and the word of our Creator, the Lord Jesus, is equal in majesty to that ancient word of power. Redemption like Creation has its word of might. Jesus speaks and it is done. Leprosy yielded to no human remedies, but it fled at once at the Lord's *"I desire it."* The disease exhibited no hopeful signs or tokens of recovery, nature contributed nothing to its own healing, but the unaided word effected the entire work on the spot and forever. The sinner is in a plight more miserable than the leper; let him imitate his example and go to Jesus, *"beseeching Him and kneeling down to Him."* Let him exercise what little faith he has, even though it should go no further than *"Lord, if You will, You can make me clean;"* and there need be no doubt as to the result of the application. Jesus heals all who come with spiritual ills, and casts out none.

In reading the narrative in which our morning's text occurs, it is worthy of devout notice that Jesus touched the leper. This unclean person had broken through the regulations of the ceremonial law and pressed into the house, but Jesus so far from chiding him broke through the law Himself in order to meet him. He made an interchange with the leper, for while He cleansed him, He contracted by that touch a Levitical defilement. Even so Jesus Christ was made sin for us, although in Himself He knew no sin, that we might be made the righteousness of God in Him.

Oh that poor sinners would go to Jesus, believing in the power of His blessed substitutionary work, and they would soon learn the power of His gracious touch. That hand which multiplied the loaves, which saved sinking Peter, which upholds afflicted saints, which crowns believers, that same hand will touch every seeking sinner, and in a moment make him clean. The love of Jesus is the source of salvation. He loves, He looks, He touches us, WE LIVE.

EVENING

"You shall have just balances, just weights, a just ephah, and a just hin" — Leviticus 19:36.

WEIGHTS, AND SCALES, and measures were to be all according to the standard of justice. Surely no Christian man will need to be reminded of this in his business, for if righteousness were banished from all the world beside, it should find a shelter in believing hearts. There are, however, other balances which weigh moral and spiritual things, and these often need examining. We will call in the officer tonight.

The balances in which we weigh our own and other men's characters, are they quite accurate? Do we not turn our own ounces of goodness into pounds, and other persons' bushels of excellence into pecks? See to weights and measures here, Christian. The scales in which we measure our trials and troubles, are they according to standard? Paul, who had more to suffer than we have, called his afflictions light, and yet we often consider ours to be heavy; surely something must be amiss with the weights! We must see to this matter, lest we get reported to the court above for unjust dealing. Those weights with which we measure our doctrinal belief, are they quite fair? The doctrines of grace should have the same weight with us as the precepts of the word, no more and no less; but it is to be feared that with many one scale or the other is unfairly weighted.

It is a grand matter to give just measure in truth. Christian, be careful here. Those measures in which we estimate our obligations and responsibilities look rather small. When a rich man gives no more to the cause of God than the poor contribute, is that a just ephah and a just hin? When ministers are half starved, is that honest dealing? When the poor are despised, while ungodly rich men are held in admiration, is that a just balance? Reader, we might lengthen the list, but we prefer to leave it as your evening's work to find out and destroy all unrighteous balances, weights, and measures.

MORNING
September 5

"And not being able to come near Him on account of the crowd they uncovered the roof where He was. And breaking through, they let down the bed on which the paralytic was lying" — Mark 2:4.

FAITH IS FULL of inventions. The house was full, a crowd blocked up the door, but faith found a way of getting at the Lord and placing the palsied man before Him. If we cannot get sinners where Jesus is by ordinary methods we must use extraordinary ones. It seems, according to Luke 5:19, that a tiling had to be removed, which would make dust and cause a measure of danger to those below, but where the case is very urgent we must not mind running some risks and shocking some proprieties. Jesus was there to heal, and therefore fall what might, faith ventured all so that her poor paralyzed charge might have his sins forgiven. Oh that we had more daring faith among us! Cannot we, dear reader, seek it this morning for ourselves and for our fellow-workers, and will we not try today to perform some gallant act for the love of souls and the glory of the Lord.

The world is constantly inventing; genius serves all the purposes of human desire; cannot faith invent too, and reach by some new means the outcasts who lie perishing around us? It was the presence of Jesus which excited victorious courage in the four bearers of the palsied man; is not the Lord among us now? Have we seen His face for ourselves this morning? Have we felt His healing power in our own souls? If so, then through door, through window, or through roof, let us, breaking through all impediments, labor to bring poor souls to Jesus. All means are good and decorous when faith and love are truly set on winning souls. If hunger for souls is not to be hindered in its efforts. Oh Lord, make us quick to suggest methods of reaching Your poor sin-sick ones, and bold to carry them out at all hazards.

EVENING

"There is sorrow on the sea; it cannot be quiet" — Jeremiah 49:23.

LITTLE KNOW WE what sorrow may be upon the sea at this moment. We are safe in our quiet chamber, but far away on the salt sea the hurricane may be cruelly seeking for the lives of men. Hear how the death fiends howl among the cordage; how every timber starts as the waves beat like battering rams upon the vessel! God help you, poor drenched and wearied ones! My prayer goes up to the great Lord of sea and land, that He will make the storm a calm, and bring you to your desired haven! Nor ought I to offer prayer alone, I should try to benefit those hardy men who risk their lives so constantly. Have I ever done anything for them? What can I do? How often does the boisterous sea swallow up the mariner! Thousands of corpses lie where pearls lie deep. There is death-sorrow on the sea, which is echoed in the long wail of widows and orphans. The salt of the sea is in many eyes of mothers and wives. Remorseless billows, you have devoured the love of women, and the stay of households. What a resurrection shall there be from the caverns of the deep when the sea gives up her dead! till then there will be sorrow on the sea.

As if in sympathy with the woes of earth, the sea is forever fretting along a thousand shores, wailing with a sorrowful cry like her own birds, booming with a hollow crash of unrest, raving with uproarious discontent, chafing with hoarse wrath, or jangling with the voices of ten thousand murmuring pebbles. The roar of the sea may be joyous to a rejoicing spirit, but to the son of sorrow the wide, wide ocean is even more forlorn than the wide, wide world. This is not our rest, and the restless billows tell us so. There is a land where there is no more sea; our faces are steadfastly set towards it; we are going to the place of which the Lord has spoken. Till then, we cast our sorrows on the Lord who trod the sea of old, and who makes a way for His people through the depths thereof.

September 6 MORNING

"In the midst of a generation which is crooked and perverted, among whom you shine as lights in the world" — *Philippians 2:15.*

WE USE LIGHTS to make manifest. A Christian man should so shine in his life, that a person could not live with him a week without knowing the gospel. His conversation should be such that all who are about him should clearly perceive whose he is, and whom he serves; and should see the image of Jesus reflected in his daily actions.

Lights are intended for guidance. We are to help those around us who are in the dark. We are to hold forth to them the Word of life. We are to point sinners to the Savior, and the weary to a divine resting-place. Men sometimes read their Bibles, and fail to understand them; we should be ready, like Philip, to instruct the inquirer in the meaning of God's Word, the way of salvation, and the life of godliness.

Lights are also used for warning. On our rocks and shoals a lighthouse is sure to be erected. Christian men should know that there are many false lights shown everywhere in the world, and therefore the right light is needed. The wreckers of Satan are always abroad, tempting the ungodly to sin under the name of pleasure; they hoist the wrong light. Let it be ours to put up the true light upon every dangerous rock, to point out every sin, and tell what it leads to, that so we may be clear of the blood of all men, shining as lights in the world.

Lights also have a very cheering influence, and so have Christians. A Christian ought to be a comforter, with kind words on his lips, and sympathy in his heart; he should carry sunshine wherever he goes, and diffuse happiness around him.

> Gracious Spirit dwell with me;
> I myself would gracious be,
> And with words that help and heal;
> Would Your life in mine reveal,
> And with actions bold and meek
> Would for Christ my Savior speak.

EVENING

"But if you are led by the Spirit, you are not under law" — *Galatians 5:18.*

HE WHO LOOKS at his own character and position from a legal point of view, will not only despair when he comes to the end of his reckoning, but if he be a wise man he will despair at the beginning; for if we are to be judged on the footing of the law, there shall no flesh living be justified. How blessed to know that we dwell in the domains of grace and not of law! When thinking of my state before God the question is not, "Am I perfect in myself before the law?" but, "Am I perfect in Christ Jesus?" That is a very different matter. We need not inquire, Am I without sin naturally? but, Have I been washed in the fountain opened for sin and for uncleanness? It is not, "Am I in myself well pleasing to God?" but it is, "Am I accepted in the Beloved?"

If the Christian views his evidences from the top of Sinai, he will grow alarmed concerning his salvation. It were better far if he read his title by the light of Calvary. "Why," says he, "my faith has unbelief in it, it is not able to save me." Suppose he had considered the object of his faith instead of his faith, then he would have said, "There is no failure in my Savior, and therefore I am safe." He sighs over his hope: Alas! my hope is marred and dimmed by an anxious carefulness about present things; how can I be accepted? Had he regarded the ground of his hope, he would have seen that the promise of God stands sure, and that whatever our doubts may be, the oath and promise never fail. Ah! believer, it is safer always for you to be led of the Spirit into gospel liberty than to wear legal chains. Judge yourself at what Christ is rather than at what you are. Satan will try to mar your peace by reminding you of your sinfulness and imperfections; you can only meet his accusations by faithfully adhering to the gospel and refusing to wear the yoke of bondage.

MORNING — September 7

"I will answer you and show you great and mighty things which you do not know" —
Jeremiah 33:3.

THERE ARE DIFFERENT translations of these words. One version renders it, "I will show you great and fortified things." Another, "Great and reserved things." Now, there are reserved and special things in Christian experience: all the developments of spiritual life are not alike easy of attainment. There are the common frames and feelings of repentance, and faith, and joy, and hope, which are enjoyed by the entire family; but there is an upper realm of rapture, of communion, and conscious union with Christ, which is far from being the common dwelling-place of believers. We have not all the high privilege of John, to lean upon Jesus' bosom; nor of Paul, to be caught up into the third heaven. There are heights in experimental knowledge of the things of God which the eagle's eye of acumen and philosophic thought has never seen. God alone can bear us there; but the chariot in which He takes us up, and the fiery steeds with which that chariot is dragged, are prevailing prayers.

Prevailing prayer is victorious over the God of mercy, *"By his strength he had power with God."* Yes, he had power over the Angel, and prevailed: he wept, and made supplication unto Him: he found Him in Bethel, and *"there He spoke with us."* Prevailing prayer takes the Christian to Carmel, and enables him to cover heaven with clouds of blessing, and earth with floods of mercy. Prevailing prayer bears the Christian aloft to Pisgah, and shows him the inheritance reserved; it elevates us to Tabor and transfigures us, till in the likeness of his Lord, as He is, so are we also in this world. If you would reach to something higher than ordinary groveling experience, look to the Rock that is higher than you, and gaze with the eye of faith through the window of importunate prayer. When you open the window on your side, it will not be bolted on the other.

EVENING

"And twenty-four thrones were around the throne. And I saw twenty-four elders sitting on the thrones, clothed in white robes" — *Revelation 4:4.*

THESE REPRESENTATIVES of the saints in heaven are said to be around the throne. In the passage in Song of Solomon, where Solomon sings of the King sitting at His table, some render it "a round table." From this, some expositors, I think, without straining the text, have said, "There is an equality among the saints." That idea is conveyed by the equal nearness of the twenty-four elders. The condition of glorified spirits in heaven is that of nearness to Christ, clear vision of His glory, constant access to His court, and familiar fellowship with His person. Nor is there any difference in this respect between one saint and another, but all the people of God, apostles, martyrs, ministers, or private and obscure Christians, shall all be seated near the throne, where they shall forever gaze upon their exalted Lord, and be satisfied with His love. They shall all be near to Christ, all ravished with His love, all eating and drinking at the same table with Him, all equally beloved as His favorites and friends even if not all equally rewarded as servants.

Let believers on earth imitate the saints in heaven in their nearness to Christ. Let us on earth be as the elders are in heaven, sitting around the throne. May Christ be the object of our thoughts, the center of our lives. How can we endure to live at such a distance from our Beloved? Lord Jesus, draw us nearer to Yourself! Say unto us, *"Abide in Me, and I in you;"* and permit us to sing, *"His left hand is under my head, and His right hand does embrace me."*

> Oh lift me higher, nearer Thee,
> And as I rise more pure and meet,
> Oh let my soul's humility
> Make me lie lower at Thy feet;
> Less trusting self, the more I prove
> The blessed comfort of Thy love.

September 8

MORNING

"Your fruit is found from Me" — *Hosea 14:8.*

OUR FRUIT IS found from our God as to union. The fruit of the branch is directly traceable to the root. Sever the connection, the branch dies, and no fruit is produced. By virtue of our union with Christ we bring forth fruit. Every bunch of grapes have been first in the root, it has passed through the stem, and flowed through the sap vessels, and fashioned itself externally into fruit, but it was first in the stem; so also every good work was first in Christ, and then is brought forth in us. Oh Christian, prize this precious union to Christ; for it must be the source of all the fruitfulness which you can hope to know. If you were not joined to Jesus Christ, you would be a barren bough indeed.

Our fruit comes from God as to spiritual providence. When the dew-drops fall from heaven, when the cloud looks down from on high, and is about to distil its liquid treasure, when the bright sun swells the berries of the cluster, each heavenly blessing may whisper to the tree and say, *"Your fruit is found from Me."* The fruit owes much to the root; that is essential to fruitfulness; but it owes very much also to external influences. How much we owe to God's grace-providence! For in this He provides us constantly with quickening, teaching, consolation, strength, or whatever else we lack. To this we owe our all of usefulness or virtue.

Our fruit comes from God as to wise husbandry. The gardener's sharp-edged knife promotes the fruitfulness of the tree, by thinning the clusters, and by cutting off superfluous shoots. So is it, Christian, with that pruning which the Lord gives to you. *"My Father is the husbandman. Every branch in Me that bears not fruit He takes away; and every branch that bears fruit He purges it, that it may bring forth more fruit."* Since our God is the author of our spiritual graces, let us give to Him all the glory of our salvation.

EVENING

"The exceeding greatness of His power towards us, who believe according to the working of His mighty strength which He worked in first when He raised Him from among the dead" — *Ephesians 1:19, 20.*

THE RESURRECTION of Christ, as in our salvation, there was put forth nothing short of a divine power. What shall we say of those who think that conversion is worked by the free will of man, and is due to his own disposition? When we shall see the dead rise from the grave by their own power, then may we expect to see ungodly sinners of their own free will turning to Christ. It is not the word preached, nor the word read in itself; all quickening power proceeds from the Holy Spirit. This power was irresistible. All the soldiers and the high priests could not keep the body of Christ in the tomb; Death himself could not hold Jesus in His bonds. Even thus irresistible is the power put forth in the believer when he is raised to newness of life. No sin, no corruption, no devils in hell, nor sinners upon earth, can thwart the hand of God's grace when it intends to convert a man. If God omnipotently says, "You shall," man shall not say, "I will not."

Observe that the power which raised Christ from the dead was glorious. It reflected honor upon God and worked dismay in the hosts of evil. So there is great glory to God in the conversion of every sinner. It was everlasting power. *"Christ being raised from the dead dies no more; death has no more dominion over Him."* So we, being raised from the dead, go not back to our dead works nor to our old corruptions, but we live unto God. *"Because He lives, we live also." "For we are dead, and our life is hid with Christ in God." "Like as Christ was raised up from the dead by the glory of the Father, even so we also should walk in newness of life."* Lastly, in the text mark the union of the new life to Jesus. The same power which raised the Head works life in the members. What a blessing to be quickened together with Christ!

MORNING September 9

"Be separate" — *2 Corinthians 6:17.*

THE CHRISTIAN, WHILE in the world, is not to be of the world. He should be distinguished from it in the great object of his life. To him to live should be Christ. Whether he eats, or drinks, or whatever he does, he should do all to God's glory. You may lay up treasure; but lay it up in heaven, where neither moth nor rust does corrupt, where thieves break not through nor steal. You may strive to be rich; but be it your ambition to be rich in faith, and good works. You may have pleasure; but when you are merry, sing psalms and make melody in your hearts to the Lord.

In your spirit, as well as in your aim, you should differ from the world. Waiting humbly before God, always conscious of His presence, delighting in communion with Him, and seeking to know His will, you will prove that you are of heavenly race. And you should be separate from the world in your actions. If a thing be right, though you lose by it, it must be done; if it be wrong, though you would gain by it, you must scorn the sin for your Master's sake.

You must have no fellowship with the unfruitful works of darkness, but rather reprove them. Walk worthy of your high calling and dignity. Remember, Oh Christian, that you are a son of the King of kings. Therefore, keep yourself unspotted from the world. Soil not the fingers which are soon to sweep celestial strings. Let not these eyes which are soon to see Him in His beauty become instead windows of lust. Let not those feet be defiled in miry places, which are soon to walk the golden streets. Let not those hearts be filled with pride and bitterness which are before long to be filled with heaven, and to overflow with ecstatic joy.

Then rise my soul! and soar away, Above the thoughtless crowd;
Above the pleasures of the gay, And splendors of the proud;
Up where eternal beauties bloom, And pleasures all divine;
Where wealth, that never can consume, And endless glories shine.

EVENING

"Lead Me, O LORD, in Your righteousness because of my enemies, make Your way straight before me" — *Psalm 5:8.*

VERY BITTER IS the enmity of the world against the people of Christ. Men will forgive a thousand faults in others, but they will magnify the most trivial offense in the followers of Jesus. Instead of vainly regretting this, let us turn it to account, and since so many are watching for our halting, let this be a special motive for walking very carefully before God. If we live carelessly, the lynx-eyed world will soon see it, and with its hundred tongues, it will spread the story, exaggerated and emblazoned by the zeal of slander. They will shout triumphantly. Alas! So would we have it! See how these Christians act! They are hypocrites to a man. Thus will much damage be done to the cause of Christ, and much insult offered to His name. The cross of Christ is in itself an offense to the world; let us take heed that we add no offense of our own. It is *"to the Jews a stumbling block"* Let us mind that we put no stumbling blocks where there are enough already. *"To the Greeks it is foolishness?"* Let us not add our folly to give point to the scorn with which the worldly-wise deride the gospel.

How jealous should we be of ourselves! How rigid with our consciences! In the presence of adversaries who will misrepresent our best deeds, and impugn our motives where they cannot censure our actions, how circumspect should we be! Pilgrims travel as suspected persons through Vanity Fair. Not only are we under surveillance, but there are more spies then we can reckon. The espionage is everywhere, at home and abroad. If we fall into the enemies' hands we may sooner expect generosity from a wolf, or mercy from a fiend, then anything like patience with our infirmities from men who spice their infidelity towards God with scandals against His people. Oh Lord, lead us ever, lest our enemies trip us up!

September 10   MORNING

"And He went up into the mountain and called those He wanted. And they went to Him"
— Mark 3:13.

HERE WAS SOVEREIGNTY. Impatient spirits may fret and fume, because they are not called to the highest places in the ministry; but reader be it yours to rejoice that Jesus calls whom He wills. If He shall leave me to be a doorkeeper in His house, I will cheerfully bless Him for His grace in permitting me to do anything in His service. The call of Christ's servants comes from above. Jesus stands on the mountain, evermore above the world in holiness, earnestness, love and power. Those whom He calls must go up the mountain to Him, they must seek to rise to His level by living in constant communion with Him. They may not be able to mount to classic honors, or attain scholastic eminence, but they must like Moses go up into the mount of God and have familiar intercourse with the unseen God, or they will never be fitted to proclaim the gospel of peace.

Jesus went apart to hold high fellowship with the Father, and we must enter into the same divine companionship if we would bless our fellowmen. No wonder that the apostles were clothed with power when they came down fresh from the mountain where Jesus was. This morning we must endeavor to ascend the mount of communion, that there we may be ordained to the life-work for which we are set apart.

Let us not see the face of man today till we have seen Jesus. Time spent with Him is laid out at blessed interest. We too shall cast out devils and work wonders if we go down into the world girded with that divine energy which Christ alone can give. It is of no use going to the Lord's battle till we are armed with heavenly weapons. We must see Jesus, this is essential. At the mercy-seat we will linger till He shall manifest Himself unto us as He does not unto the world, and until we can truthfully say, "We were with Him in the Holy Mount."

EVENING
"Evening wolves" — Habakkuk 1:8.

WHILE PREPARING THE present volume, this particular expression recurred to me so frequently, that in order to be rid of its constant importunity I determined to give a page to it. The evening wolf, infuriated by a day of hunger, was fiercer and more ravenous than he would have been in the morning. May not the furious creature represent our doubts and fears after a day of distraction of mind, losses in business, and perhaps ungenerous taunting from our fellowmen? How our thoughts howl in our ears, *"Where is now your God?"* How voracious and greedy they are, swallowing up all suggestions of comfort, and remaining as hungry as before. Great Shepherd, slay these evening wolves, and bid Your sheep lie down in green pastures, undisturbed by insatiable unbelief. How like are the fiends of hell to evening wolves, for when the flock of Christ are in a cloudy and dark day, and their sun seems going down, they hasten to tear and to devour. They will scarcely attack the Christian in the daylight of faith, but in the gloom of soul conflict they fall upon him. Oh You who has laid down Your life for the sheep, preserve them from the fangs of the wolf.

False teachers who craftily and industriously hunt for the precious life, devouring men by their falsehoods, are as dangerous and detestable as evening wolves. Darkness is their element, deceit is their character, destruction is their end. We are most in danger from them when they wear the sheep's skin. Blessed is he who is kept from them, for thousands are made the prey of grievous wolves that enter within the fold of the church.

What a wonder of grace it is when fierce persecutors are converted, for then the wolf dwells with the lamb, and men of cruel ungovernable dispositions become gentle and teachable. Oh Lord, convert many such; for such we will pray tonight.

MORNING September 11

"Who passing through the valley of weeping make it a fountain; the rain also fills the pools" — Psalm 84:6.

THIS TEACHES US that the comfort obtained by one may often prove serviceable to another; just as wells would be used by the company who came after. We read some book full of consolation, which is like Jonathan's rod, dropping with honey. Ah, we think our brother has been here before us, and dug this well for us as well as for himself. Many a Night of Weeping, Midnight Harmonies, an Eternal Day, A Crook in the Lot, a Comfort for Mourners, has been a well dug by a pilgrim for himself, but has proved quite as useful to others. Especially we notice this in the Psalms, such as that beginning, *"Why are you cast down, Oh my soul?"* Travelers have been delighted to see the footprint of man on a barren shore, and we love to see the waymarks of pilgrims while passing through the vale of tears.

The pilgrims dig the well, but, strange enough, it fills from the top instead of the bottom. We use the means, but the blessing does not spring from the means. We dig a well, but heaven fills it with rain. The horse is prepared against the day of battle, but safety is of the Lord. The means are connected with the end, but they do not of themselves produce it. See here the rain fills the pools, so that the wells become useful as reservoirs for the water; labor is not lost, but yet it does not supersede divine help.

Grace may well be compared to rain for its purity, for its refreshing and vivifying influence, for its coming alone from above, and for the sovereignty with which it is given or withheld. May our readers have showers of blessing, and may the wells they have dug be filled with water! Oh, what are means and ordinances without the smile of heaven! They are as clouds without rain, and pools without water. Oh God of love, open the windows of heaven and pour us out a blessing!

EVENING
"This one receives sinners" — Luke 15:2.

OBSERVE THE CONDESCENSION of this fact. This Man, who towers above all other men, holy, harmless, undefiled, and separate from sinners — this Man receives sinners. This Man, who is no other than the eternal God, before whom angels veil their faces; this Man receives sinners. It needs an angel's tongue to describe such a mighty stoop of love. That any of us should be willing to seek after the lost is nothing wonderful; they are of our own race. But that He, the offended God, against whom the transgression has been committed, should take upon Himself the form of a servant, and bear the sin of many, and should then be willing to receive the vilest of the vile, this is marvelous.

"This one receives sinners" — not, however, that they may remain sinners, but He receives them that He may pardon their sins, justify their persons, cleanse their hearts by His purifying word, preserve their souls by the indwelling of the Holy Spirit, and enable them to serve Him, to show forth His praise, and to have communion with Him. Into His heart's love He receives sinners, takes them from the dunghill, and wears them as jewels in His crown; plucks them as brands from the burning and preserves them as costly monuments of His mercy. None are so precious in Jesus' sight as the sinners for whom He died. When Jesus receives sinners, He has not some out of doors reception place, no casual ward where He charitably entertains them as men do passing beggars, but He opens the golden gates of His royal heart, and receives the sinner right into Himself. Yes, He admits the humble penitent into personal union and makes Him a member of His body, of His flesh, and of His bones. There was never such a reception as this! This fact is still most sure this evening, He is still receiving sinners; would to God sinners would receive Him.

September 12   MORNING

"God is jealous" — Nahum 1:2.

YOUR LORD IS very jealous of your love, Oh believer. Did He choose you? He cannot bear that you should choose another. Did He buy you with His own blood? He cannot endure that you should think that you are your own, or that you belong to this world. He loved you with such a love that He would not stop in heaven without you; He would sooner die than you should perish, and He cannot endure that anything should stand between your heart's love and Himself.

He is very jealous of your trust. He will not permit you to trust in an arm of flesh. He cannot bear that you should hew out broken cisterns, when the overflowing fountain is always free to you. When we lean upon Him, He is glad, but when we transfer our dependence to another, when we rely upon our own wisdom, or the wisdom of a friend; worst of all, when we trust in any works of our own, He is displeased, and will chasten us that He may bring us to Himself.

He is also very jealous of our company. There should be no one with whom we converse so much as with Jesus. To abide in Him only, this is true love; but to commune with the world, to find sufficient solace in our carnal comforts, to prefer even the society of our fellow Christians to secret intercourse with Him, this is grievous to our jealous Lord. He would fain have us abide in Him, and enjoy constant fellowship with Himself; and many of the trials which He sends us are for the purpose of weaning our hearts from the creature, and fixing them more closely upon Himself.

Let this jealousy which should keep us near to Christ be also a comfort to us, for if He loves us so much as to care thus about our love we may be sure that He will suffer nothing to harm us, and will protect us from all our enemies. Oh that we may have grace this day to keep our hearts in sacred chastity for our Beloved alone, with sacred jealousy shutting our eyes to all the fascinations of the world!

EVENING

I will sing of mercy and judgment" — Psalm 101:1.

FAITH TRIUMPHS in trial. When reason is thrust into the inner prison, with her feet made fast in the stocks, faith makes the dungeon walls ring with her merry notes as she cries, *"I will sing of mercy and of judgment. Unto You, Oh Lord, will I sing."* Faith pulls the black mask from the face of trouble, and discovers the angel beneath. Faith looks up at the cloud, and sees that

> 'Tis big with mercy and shall break
> In blessings on her head.

There is a subject for song even in the judgments of God towards us. For, first, the trial is not so heavy as it might have been; next, the trouble is not so severe as we deserved to have it be; and our affliction is not so crushing as the burden which others have to carry.

Faith sees that in her worst sorrow there is nothing penal; there is not a drop of God's wrath in it; it is all sent in love. Faith discerns love gleaming like a jewel on the breast of an angry God. Faith says of her grief, "This is a badge of honor, for the child must feel the rod"; and then she sings of the sweet result of her sorrows, because they work her spiritual good. No, more, says Faith, *"These light afflictions, which are but for a moment, work out for me a far more exceeding and eternal weight of glory."* So Faith rides forth on the black horse, conquering and to conquer, trampling down carnal reason and fleshly sense, and chanting notes of victory amid the thickest of the fray.

> All I meet I find assists me, In my path to heavenly joy;
> Where, though trials now attend me, Trials never more annoy.
> Blest there with a weight of glory, Still the path I'll never forget,
> But, exulting, cry, it led me To my blessed Savior's seat.

MORNING
September 13

"He shall not be afraid of bad news" — Psalm 112:7.

CHRISTIAN, YOU OUGHT not to dread the arrival of evil tidings; because if you are distressed by them, what do you more than other men? Other men have not your God to fly to; they have never proved His faithfulness as you have done, and it is no wonder if they are bowed down with alarm and cowed with fear. But you profess to be of another spirit; you have been begotten again unto a lively hope, and your heart lives in heaven and not on earthly things. Now, if you are seen to be distracted as other men, what is the value of that grace which you profess to have received? Where is the dignity of that new nature which you claim to possess?

Again, if you should be filled with alarm, as others are, you would doubtless be led into the sins so common to others under trying circumstances. The ungodly, when they are overtaken by evil tidings, rebel against God; they murmur, and think that God deals hardly with them. Will you fall into that same sin? Will you provoke the Lord as they do?

Moreover, unconverted men often run to wrong means in order to escape from difficulties, and you will be sure to do the same if your mind yields to the present pressure. Trust in the Lord, and wait patiently for Him. Your wisest course is to do as Moses did at the Red Sea, *"Stand still and see the salvation of God."* For if you give way to fear when you hear of evil tidings, you will be unable to meet the trouble with that calm composure which nerves for duty, and sustains under adversity. How can you glorify God if you play the coward? Saints have often sung God's high praises in the fires, but will your doubting and grieving, as if you had none to help you, magnify the Most High? Then take courage, and relying in sure confidence upon the faithfulness of your covenant God, "let not your heart be troubled, neither let it be afraid."

EVENING
"A people near to Him" — Psalm 148:14.

THE DISPENSATION of the old covenant was that of distance. When God appeared even to His servant Moses, He said, *"Draw not near here, put off your shoes from off your feet;"* And when He manifested Himself upon Mount Sinai, to His own chosen and separated people, one of the first commands was, *"You shall set bounds about the mount."* Both in the sacred worship of the tabernacle and the temple, the thought of distance was always prominent. The mass of the people did not even enter the outer court. Into the inner court none but the priests might dare to intrude; while into the innermost place, or the holy of holies, the high priest entered but once in the year. It was as if the Lord in those early ages would teach man that sin was so utterly loathsome to Him, that He must treat men as lepers put without the camp; and when He came nearest to them, He yet made them feel the width of the separation between a holy God and an impure sinner.

When the gospel came, we were placed on quite another footing. The word "Go" was exchanged for "Come;" distance was made to give place to nearness, and we who before were afar off, were made near by the blood of Jesus Christ. Incarnate Deity has no wall of fire about it. *"Come unto me, all you that labor and are heavy laden, and I will give you rest,"* is the joyful proclamation of God as He appears in human flesh. Not now does He teach the leper his leprosy by setting him at a distance, but by Himself suffering the penalty of His defilement. What a state of safety and privilege is this nearness to God through Jesus! Do you know it by experience? if you know it, are you living in the power of it? Marvelous is this nearness, yet it is to be followed by a dispensation of greater nearness still, when it shall be said, *"The tabernacle of God is with men, and He dwells among them."* Hasten it, Oh Lord.

September 14   MORNING

"Other small ships were also with Him" — Mark 4:36.

JESUS WAS THE Lord King Admiral of the sea that night, and His presence preserved the whole convoy. It is well to sail with Jesus, even though it be in a little ship. When we sail in Christ's company, we may not make sure of fair weather, for great storms may toss the vessel which carries the Lord Himself, and we must not expect to find the sea less boisterous around our little boat. If we go with Jesus we must be content to fare as He fares; and when the waves are rough to Him, they will be rough to us. It is by tempest and tossing that we shall come to land, as He did before us.

When the storm swept over Galilee's dark lake all faces gathered blackness, and all hearts dreaded shipwreck. When all creature help was useless, the slumbering Savior arose, and with a word, transformed the riot of the tempest into the deep quiet of a calm. Then were the little vessels at rest as well as that which carried the Lord. Jesus is the star of the sea; and though there be sorrow upon the sea, when Jesus is on it there is joy too. May our hearts make Jesus their anchor, their rudder, their lighthouse, their life-boat, and their harbor. His Church is the Admirals flagship, let us attend her movements, and cheer her officers with our presence. He Himself is the great attraction; let us follow ever in His wake, mark His signals, steer by His chart, and never fear while He is within hail. Not one ship in the convoy shall suffer wreck; the Great Commodore will steer every bark in safety to the desired haven. By faith we will slip our cable for another day's cruise, and sail forth with Jesus into a sea of tribulation. Winds and waves will not spare us, but they all obey Him; and, therefore, whatever squalls may occur without, faith shall feel a blessed calm within. He is ever in the center of the weather-beaten company; let us rejoice in Him. His vessel has reached the haven, and so shall ours.

EVENING

"I confessed my sin to You, and my iniquity I have not hidden. I said, I will confess my sins to the LORD; and You forgave the iniquity of my sin. Selah" — Psalm 32:5.

DAVID'S GRIEF FOR sin was bitter. Its effects were visible upon his outward frame; *"his bones waxed old; moisture was turned into the drought of summer."* No remedy could he find, until he made a full confession before the throne of the heavenly grace. He tells us that for a time he kept silence, and his heart became more and more filled with grief: like a mountain lake whose outlet is blocked up, his soul was swollen with torrents of sorrow. He fashioned excuses; he endeavored to divert his thoughts, but it was all to no purpose; like a festering sore his anguish gathered, and as he would not use the lancet of confession, his spirit was full of torment, and knew no rest.

At last it came to this, that he must return unto his God in humble penitence, or die outright; so he hastened to the mercy-seat. And there he unrolled the volume of his iniquities before the all-seeing One, acknowledging all the evil of his ways in language such as you read in the fifty-first and other penitential Psalms. Having done this, a work so simple and yet so difficult to pride, he received at once the token of divine forgiveness; the bones which had been broken were made to rejoice, and he came forth from his closet to sing the blessedness of the man whose transgression is forgiven.

See the value of a grace-worked confession of sin! it is to be prized above all price, for in every case where there is a genuine, gracious confession, mercy is freely given, not because the repentance and confession deserve mercy, but for Christ's sake. Blessed be God, there is always healing for the broken heart; the fountain is ever flowing to cleanse us from our sins. Truly, Oh Lord, You are a God *"ready to pardon!"* Therefore will we acknowledge our iniquities.

MORNING   September 15

"Bring him to Me" — *Mark 9:19.*

DESPAIRINGLY THE poor disappointed father turned away from the disciples to their Master. His son was in the worst possible condition, and all means had failed, but the miserable child was soon delivered from the evil one when the parent in faith obeyed the Lord Jesus' word, *"Bring him to Me."* Children are a precious gift from God, but much anxiety comes with them. They may be a great joy or a great bitterness to their parents; they may be filled with the Spirit of God, or possessed with the spirit of evil.

In all cases, the Word of God gives us one recipe for the curing of all their ills, *"Bring him to Me."* Oh for more agonizing prayer on their behalf while they are yet babes! Sin is there, let our prayers begin to attack it. Our cries for our offspring should precede those cries which indicates their actual advent into a world of sin. In the days of their youth we shall see sad tokens of that dumb and deaf spirit which will neither pray aright, nor hear the voice of God in the soul, but Jesus still commands, *"Bring them to Me."* When they are grown up they may wallow in sin and foam with enmity against God; then when our hearts are breaking we should remember the great Physician's words, *"Bring them to Me."* Never must we cease to pray until they cease to breathe. No case is hopeless while Jesus lives.

The Lord sometimes suffers His people to be driven into a corner that they may experimentally know how necessary He is to them. Ungodly children, when they show us our own powerlessness against the depravity of their hearts, drive us to flee to the strong for strength, and this is a great blessing to us. Whatever our morning's need may be, let it like a strong current bear us to the ocean of divine love. Jesus can soon remove our sorrow, He delights to comfort us. Let us hasten to Him while He waits to meet us.

EVENING

"Encourage him" — *Deuteronomy 1:38.*

GOD EMPLOYS HIS people to encourage one another. He did not say to an angel, "Gabriel, My servant Joshua is about to lead My people into Canaan; go, encourage him." God never works needless miracles; if His purposes can be accomplished by ordinary means, He will not use miraculous agency. Gabriel would not have been half so well fitted for the work as Moses. A brother's sympathy is more precious than an angel's embassy. The angel, swift of wing, had better known the Master's bidding than the people's temper. An angel had never experienced the hardness of the road, nor seen the fiery serpents, nor had he led the stiff-necked multitude in the wilderness as Moses had done. We should be glad that God usually works for man by man. It forms a bond of brotherhood, and being mutually dependent on one another, we are fused more completely into one family.

Brothers, take the text as God's message to you. Labor to help others, and especially strive to encourage them. Talk cheerily to the young and anxious inquirer, lovingly try to remove stumbling-blocks out of his way. When you find a spark of grace in the heart, kneel down and blow it into a flame. Leave the young believer to discover the roughness of the road by degrees, but tell him of the strength which dwells in God, of the sureness of the promise, and of the charms of communion with Christ. Aim to comfort the sorrowful, and to animate the desponding. Speak a word in season to him that is weary, and encourage those who are fearful to go on their way with gladness. God encourages you by His promises; Christ encourages you as He points to the heaven He has won for you, and the Spirit encourages you as He works in you to will and to do of His own will and pleasure. Imitate divine wisdom, and encourage others, according to the word of this evening.

September 16 — MORNING

"Partakers of the divine nature" — 2 Peter 14.

TO BE A PARTAKER of the divine nature is not, of course, to become God. That cannot be. The essence of Deity is not to be participated in by the creature. Between the creature and the Creator there must ever be a gulf fixed in respect of essence. But as the first man Adam was made in the image of God, so we, by the renewal of the Holy Spirit, are in a yet diviner sense made in the image of the Most High, and are partakers of the divine nature. We are, by grace, made like God. *"God is love;"* we become love *"He that loves has been born of God."* God is truth; we become true, and we love that which is true: God is good, and He makes us good by His grace, so that we become the pure in heart who shall see God.

Moreover, we become partakers of the divine nature in even a higher sense than this; in fact, in as lofty a sense as can be conceived, short of our being absolutely divine. Do we not become members of the body of the divine person of Christ? Yes, the same blood which flows in the head flows in the hand. And the same life which quickens Christ quickens His people, for *"You are dead, and your life is hid with Christ in God."* No, as if this were not enough, we are married unto Christ. He has betrothed us unto Himself in righteousness and faithfulness, and he who is joined unto the Lord is one spirit. Oh! marvelous mystery! we look into it, but who shall understand it? One with Jesus; so one with Him that the branch is not more one with the vine than we are a part of the Lord, our Savior, and our Redeemer?

While we rejoice in this, let us remember that those who are made partakers of the divine nature will manifest their high and holy relationship in their intercourse with others, and make it evident by their daily walk and conversation that they have escaped the corruption that is in the world though lust. Oh for more divine holiness of life!

EVENING

"Am I like the sea, or a whale, that You set a watch over me?" — Job 7:12.

THIS WAS A strange question for Job to ask of the Lord. He felt himself to be too insignificant to be so strictly watched and chastened, and he hoped that he was not so unruly as to need to be so restrained. The inquiry was natural from one surrounded with such insupportable miseries, but after all, it is capable of a very humbling answer. It is true man is not the sea, but he is even more troublesome and unruly. The sea obediently respects its boundary, and though it be but a belt of sand, it does not overleap the limit. Mighty as it is, it hears the divine hereto, and when most raging with tempest it respects the word; but self-willed man defies heaven and oppresses earth, neither is there any end to his rebellious rage.

The sea, obedient to the moon, ebbs and flows with ceaseless regularity, and thus renders an active as well as a passive obedience. But man, restless beyond his sphere, sleeps within the lines of duty, indolent where he should be active. He will neither come nor go at the divine command, but sullenly prefers to do what he should not, and to leave undone that which is required of him. Every drop in the ocean, every beaded bubble, and every yeasty foam-flake, every shell and pebble, feel the power of law, and yield or move at once. Oh that our nature were but one thousandth part as much conformed to the will of God! We call the sea fickle and false, but how constant it is! Since our fathers' days, and the old time before them, the sea is where it was, beating on the same cliffs to the same tune; we know where to find it, it forsakes not its bed, and changes not in its ceaseless boom; but where is man, vain, fickle man? Can the wise man guess by what folly he will next be seduced from his obedience? We need more watching than the billowy sea, and are far more rebellious. Lord, rule us for Your own glory. Amen.

MORNING September 17

"The freedom with which Christ made us free" — Galatians 5:1.

THIS LIBERTY MAKES us free to heaven's charter, the Bible. Here is a choice passage, believer, *"When you pass through the rivers I will be with you."* You are free to that. Here is another: *"The mountains shall depart, and the hills be removed, but My kindness shall not depart from you;"* you are free to that. You are a welcome guest at the table of the promises. Scripture is a never-failing treasury filled with boundless stores of grace. It is the bank of heaven; you may draw from it as much as you please, without let or hindrance. Come in faith and you are welcome to all covenant blessings. There is not a promise in the Word which shall be withheld. In the depths of tribulations let this freedom comfort you; amidst waves of distress let it cheer you; when sorrows surround you let it be your solace. This is your Father's love-token; you are free to it at all times.

You are also free to the throne of grace. It is the believer's privilege to have access at all times to his heavenly Father. Whatever our desires, our difficulties, our wants, we are at liberty to spread all before Him. It matters not how much we may have sinned, we may ask and expect pardon. It signifies nothing how poor we are, we may plead His promise that He will provide all things needful. We have permission to approach His throne at all times, in midnight's darkest hour, or in noontide's most burning heat. Exercise your right, Oh believer, and live up to your privilege. You are free to all that is treasured up in Christ: wisdom, righteousness, sanctification, and redemption. It matters not what your need is, for there is fullness of supply in Christ, and it is there for you. Oh what a *"freedom"* is yours! It is freedom from condemnation, freedom to the promises, freedom to the throne of grace, and at last freedom to enter heaven!

EVENING
"For this child I was praying" — 1 Samuel 1:27.

DEVOUT SOULS DELIGHT to look upon those mercies which they have obtained in answer to supplication, for they can see God's special love in them. When we can name our blessings Samuel, that is, *"asked of God,"* they will be as dear to us as her child was to Hannah. Peninnah had many children, but they came as common blessings unsought in prayer. Hannah's one heaven-given child was dearer far, because he was the fruit of earnest pleadings. How sweet was that water to Samson which he found at *"the well of him that prayed!"* Quassia cups turn all waters bitter, but the cup of prayer puts a sweetness into the draughts it brings. Did we pray for the conversion of our children? How doubly sweet, when they are saved, to see in them our own petitions fulfilled! Better to rejoice over them as the fruit of our pleadings than as the fruit of our bodies.

Have we sought of the Lord some choice spiritual gift? When it comes to us it will be wrapped up in the gold cloth of God's faithfulness and truth, and so be doubly precious. Have we petitioned for success in the Lord's work? How joyful is the prosperity which comes flying upon the wings of prayer! It is always best to get blessings into our house in the legitimate way, by the door of prayer; then they are blessings indeed, and not temptations. Even when prayer speeds not, the blessings grow all the richer for the delay; the child Jesus was all the more lovely in the eyes of Mary when she found Him after having sought Him sorrowing. That which we win by prayer we should dedicate to God, as Hannah dedicated Samuel. The gift came from heaven, let it go to heaven. Prayer brought it, gratitude sang over it, let devotion consecrate it. Here will be a special occasion for saying, *"Of Your own have I given unto You."* Reader, is prayer your element or your weariness? Which?

September 18   MORNING

"If we live by the Spirit, we should also walk by the Spirit" — Galatians 5:25.

THE TWO MOST important things in our holy religion are the life of faith and the walk of faith. He who shall rightly understand these is not far from being a master in experimental theology, for they are vital points to a Christian. You will never find true faith unattended by true godliness; on the other hand, you will never discover a truly holy life which has not for its root a living faith upon the righteousness of Christ. Woe unto those who seek after the one without the other! There are some who cultivate faith and forget holiness; these may be very high in orthodoxy, but they shall be very deep in condemnation, for they hold the truth in unrighteousness. And there are others who have strained after holiness of life, but have denied the faith, like the Pharisees of old, of whom the Master said, they were *"whitewashed sepulchers."*

We must have faith, for this is the foundation; we must have holiness of life, for this is the superstructure. Of what service is the mere foundation of a building to a man in the day of tempest? Can he hide himself therein? He wants a house to cover him, as well as a foundation for that house. Even so we need the superstructure of spiritual life if we would have comfort in the day of doubt. But seek not a holy life without faith, for that would be to erect a house which can afford no permanent shelter, because it has no foundation on a rock. Let faith and life be put together, and, like the two abutments of an arch, they will make our piety enduring. Like light and heat streaming from the same sun, they are alike full of blessing. Like the two pillars of the temple, they are for glory and for beauty. They are two streams from the fountain of grace; two lamps lit with holy fire; two olive trees watered by heavenly care. Oh Lord, give us this day life within, and it will reveal itself without to your glory.

EVENING

"And they follow Me" — John 10:27.

WE SHOULD FOLLOW our Lord as unhesitatingly as sheep follow their shepherd, for He has a right to lead us wherever He pleases. *"We are not our own, we are bought with a price."* Let us recognize the rights of the redeeming blood. The soldier follows his captain, the servant obeys his master, much more must we follow our Redeemer, to whom we are a purchased possession. We are not true to our profession of being Christians, if we question the bidding of our Leader and Commander. Submission is our duty, cavilling is our folly. Often might our Lord say to us as to Peter, *"What is that to you? Follow Me."* Wherever Jesus may lead us, He goes before us. If we know not where we go, we know with whom we go. With such a companion, who will dread the perils of the road? The journey may be long, but His everlasting arms will carry us to the end. The presence of Jesus is the assurance of eternal salvation, because He lives, we shall live also.

We should follow Christ in simplicity and faith, because the paths in which He leads us all end in glory and immortality. It is true that they may not be smooth paths; they may be covered with sharp flinty trials, but they lead to the *"city which has foundations, whose builder and maker is God."* *"All the paths of the Lord are mercy and truth unto such as keep His covenant."* Let us put full trust in our Leader, since we know that, come prosperity or adversity, sickness or health, popularity or contempt, His purpose shall be worked out, and that purpose shall be pure, unmingled good to every heir of mercy. We shall find it sweet to go up the bleak side of the hill with Christ; and when rain and snow blow into our faces, His dear love will make us far more blest than those who sit at home and warm their hands at the world's fire. To the top of Amana, to the dens of lions, or to the hills of leopards, we will follow our Beloved. Precious Jesus, draw us, and we will run after You.

MORNING — September 19

"Yea, I will rejoice over them to do them good" — Jeremiah 32:41.

HOW HEART-CHEERING to the believer is the delight which God has in His saints! We cannot see any reason in ourselves why the Lord should take pleasure in us; we cannot take delight in ourselves, for we often have to groan, being burdened; conscious of our sinfulness, and deploring our unfaithfulness. And we fear that God's people cannot take much delight in us, for they must perceive so much of our imperfections and our follies, that they may rather lament our infirmities than admire our graces. But we love to dwell upon this transcendent truth, this glorious mystery that as the bridegroom rejoices over the bride, so does the Lord rejoice over us.

We do not read anywhere that God delights in the cloud-capped mountains, or the sparkling stars, but we do read that He delights in the habitable parts of the earth, and that His delights are with the sons of men. We do not find it written that even angels give His soul delight; nor does He say, concerning cherubim and seraphim, *"You shall be called Hephzibah, for the Lord delights in you;"* but He does say all that to poor fallen creatures like ourselves, debased and depraved by sin, but saved, exalted, and glorified by His grace.

In what strong language He expresses His delight in His people! Who could have conceived of the eternal One as bursting forth into a song? Yet it is written, *"He will rejoice over you with joy, He will rest in His love, He will joy over you with singing."* As He looked upon the world He had made, He said, *"It is very good;"* but when He beheld those who are the purchase of Jesus' blood, His own chosen ones, it seemed as if the great heart of the Infinite could restrain itself no longer, but overflowed in divine exclamations of joy. Should not we utter our grateful response to such a marvelous declaration of His love, and sing, *"I will rejoice in the Lord, I will joy in the God of my salvation"*?

EVENING

"Do not take away my soul with sinners" — Psalm 26:9.

FEAR MADE DAVID pray thus, for something whispered, "Perhaps, after all, you may be gathered with the wicked." That fear, although marred by unbelief, springs, in the main, from holy anxiety, arising from the remembrance of past sin. Even the pardoned man will inquire, "What if at the end my sins should be remembered, and I should be left out of the catalogue of the saved?" He remembers his present unfruitfulness, so little grace, so little love, so little holiness, and looking forward to the future, he considers his weakness and the many temptations which beset him, and he fears that he may fall, and become a prey to the enemy. A sense of sin and present evil, and his prevailing corruptions, compel him to pray, in fear and trembling, *"Gather not my soul with sinners"* (Ps. 26:9).

Reader, if you have prayed this prayer, and if your character be rightly described in the Psalm from which it is taken, you need not be afraid that you shall be gathered with sinners. Have you the two virtues which David had, the outward walking in integrity, and the inward trusting in the Lord? Are you resting upon Christ's sacrifice, and can you compass the altar of God with humble hope? If so, rest assured, with the wicked you never shall be gathered, for that calamity is impossible. The gathering at the judgment is like to like. *"Gather you together first the tares, and bind them in bundles to burn them: but gather the wheat into my barn."* If, then, you are like God's people, you shall be with God's people. You cannot be gathered with the wicked, for you are too dearly bought. Redeemed by the blood of Christ, you are His forever, and where He is, there must His people be. You are loved too much to be cast away with reprobates. Shall one dear to Christ perish? Impossible! Hell cannot hold you! Heaven claims you! Trust in your Surety and fear not!

September 20

MORNING

"The sword of the LORD, and of Gideon!" — Judges 7:20.

GIDEON ORDERED HIS men to do two things: covering up a torch in an earthen pitcher, he bade them, at an appointed signal, break the pitcher and let the light shine, and then sound with the trumpet, crying, *"The sword of the Lord, and of Gideon! the sword of the Lord, and of Gideon!"*

This is precisely what all Christians must do. First, you must shine; break the pitcher which conceals your light; throw aside the bushel which has been hiding your candle, and shine. Let your light shine before men; let your good works be such, that when men look upon you, they shall know that you have been with Jesus. Then there must be the sound, the blowing of the trumpet. There must be active exertions for the gathering of sinners by proclaiming Christ crucified. Take the gospel to them; carry it to their door; put it in their way; do not allow them to escape it; blow the trumpet right against their ears.

Remember that the true war-cry of the Church is Gideon's watchword, *"The sword of the Lord, and of Gideon!"* God must do it, it is His own work. But we are not to be idle; instrumentality is to be used: *"The sword of the Lord, and of Gideon!"* If we only cry, *"The sword of the Lord!"* we shall be guilty of an idle presumption; and if we shout, *"The sword of Gideon!"* alone, we shall manifest idolatrous reliance on an arm of flesh: we must blend the two in practical harmony, *"The sword of the Lord, and of Gideon!"* We can do nothing of ourselves, but we can do everything by the help of our God. Let us, therefore, in His name determine to go out personally and serve with our flaming torch of holy example, and with our trumpet tones of earnest declaration and testimony, and God shall be with us, and Midian shall be put to confusion, and the Lord of hosts shall reign forever and ever.

EVENING

"In the evening do not withhold your hand" — Ecclesiastes 11:6.

IN THE EVENING of the day opportunities are plentiful; men return from their labor, and the zealous soul-winner finds time to tell abroad the love of Jesus. Have I no evening work for Jesus? If I have not, let me no longer withhold my hand from a service which requires abundant labor. Sinners are perishing for lack of knowledge; he who loiters may find his skirts crimson with the blood of souls. Jesus gave both His hands to the nails, how can I keep back one of mine from His blessed work? Night and day He toiled and prayed for me, how can I give a single hour to the pampering of my flesh with luxurious ease? Up, idle heart; stretch out your hand to work, or uplift it to pray; heaven and hell are in earnest, let me be so, and this evening sow good seed for the Lord my God.

The evening of life has also its calls. Life is so short that a morning of manhood's vigor, and an evening of decay, make the whole of it. To some it seems long, but a penny is a great sum of money to a poor man. Life is so brief that no man can afford to lose a day. It has been well said that if a great king should bring us a great heap of gold, and bid us take as much as we could count in a day, we should make a long day of it; we should begin early in the morning, and in the evening we should not withhold our hand. But to win souls is far nobler work, how is it that we so soon withdraw from it? Some are spared to a long evening of green old age; if such be my case, let me use such talents as I still retain, and to the last hour serve my blessed and faithful Lord. By His grace I will die in harness, and lay down my charge only when I lay down my body. Age may instruct the young, cheer the faint, and encourage the desponding; if eventide has less of vigorous heat, it should have more of calm wisdom, therefore in the evening I will not withhold my hand.

MORNING — September 21

"Accepted in the Beloved" — Ephesians 1:6.

WHAT A STATE of privilege! It includes our justification before God, but the term acceptance in the Greek means more than that. In signifies that we are the objects of divine complacency, no, even of divine delight. How marvelous that we, worms, mortals, sinners, should be the objects of divine love! But it is only *"in the Beloved."* Some Christians seem to be accepted in their own experience, at least, that is their apprehension. When their spirit is lively, and their hopes bright, they think God accepts them, for they feel so high, so heavenly-minded, so drawn above the earth! But when their souls cleave to the dust, they are the victims of the fear that they are no longer accepted. If they could but see that all their high joys do not exalt them, and all their low despondencies do not really depress them in their Father's sight, but that they stand accepted in One who never alters, in One who is always the beloved of God, always perfect, always *"without spot or wrinkle, or any such thing,"* how much happier they would be, and how much more they would honor the Savior!

Rejoice then, believer, in this: you are accepted *"in the Beloved."* You look within, and you say, "There is nothing acceptable here!" But look at Christ, and see if there is not everything acceptable there. Your sins trouble you; but God has cast your sins behind His back and you are accepted in the Righteous One. You have to fight with corruption, and to wrestle with temptation, but you are already accepted in Him who has overcome the powers of evil. The devil tempts you; be of good cheer, he cannot destroy you, for you are accepted in Him who has broken Satan's head. Know by full assurance your glorious standing. Even glorified souls are not more accepted than you are. They are only accepted in heaven *"in the Beloved,"* and you are even now accepted in Christ after the same manner.

EVENING

"Jesus said to him, If you are able to believe" — Mark 9:23.

A CERTAIN MAN had a demoniac son, who was afflicted with a dumb spirit. The father, having seen the futility of the endeavors of the disciples to heal his child, had little or no faith in Christ, and therefore, when he was bidden to bring his son to Him, he said to Jesus, *"If You can do anything,"* have compassion on us, and help us." Now there was an "if" in the question, but the poor trembling father had put the "if" in the wrong place: Jesus Christ, therefore, without commanding him to retract the "if," kindly puts it in its legitimate position. He seemed to say, There should be no if about My power, nor concerning My willingness; the "if" lies somewhere else." *"If you can believe, all things are possible to him that believes."* The man's trust was strengthened, he offered a humble prayer for an increase of faith, and instantly Jesus spoke the word, and the devil was cast out, with an injunction never to return.

There is a lesson here which we need to learn. We, like this man, often see that there is an "if" somewhere, but we are perpetually blundering by putting it in the wrong place. If Jesus can help me; if He can give me grace to overcome temptation; if He can give me pardon; if He can make me successful? No, if you can believe, He both can and will. You have misplaced your "if." If you can confidently trust, even as all things are possible to Christ, so shall all things be possible to you. Faith stands in God's power, and is robed in God's majesty; it wears the royal apparel, and rides on the King's horse, for it is the grace which the King delights to honor. Girding itself with the glorious might of the all-working Spirit, it becomes, in the omnipotence of God, mighty to do, to dare, and to suffer. All things, without limit, are possible to him that believes. My soul, can you believe your Lord tonight?

September 22　　　　　　MORNING

"Let Israel rejoice in Him" — Psalm 149:2.

 BE GLAD OF heart, Oh believer, but take care that your gladness has it spring in the Lord. You have much cause for gladness in your God, for you can sing with David, *"God, my exceeding joy."* Be glad that the Lord reigns, that Jehovah is King! Rejoice that He sits upon the throne, and rules all things! Every attribute of God should become a fresh ray in the sunlight of our gladness. That He is wise should make us glad, knowing as we do our own foolishness. That He is mighty, should cause us to rejoice who tremble at our weakness. That He is everlasting, should always be a theme of joy when we know that we wither as the grass. That He is unchanging, should perpetually yield us a song, since we change every hour. That He is full of grace, that He is overflowing with it, and that this grace in covenant He has given to us; that it is ours to cleanse us, ours to keep us, ours to sanctify us, ours to perfect us, ours to bring us to glory; all this should tend to make us glad in Him.

 This gladness in God is as a deep river; we have only as yet touched its brink, we know a little of its clear sweet, heavenly streams, but onward the depth is greater, and the current more impetuous in its joy. The Christian feels that he may delight himself not only in what God is, but also in all that God has done in the past. The Psalms show us that God's people in olden times were accustomed to think much of God's actions, and to have a song concerning each of them. So let God's people now rehearse the deeds of the Lord! Let them tell of His mighty acts, and *"sing unto the Lord, for He has triumphed gloriously."* Nor let them ever cease to sing, for as new mercies flow to them day by day, so should their gladness in the Lord's loving acts in providence and in grace show itself in continued thanksgiving. Be glad you children of Zion and rejoice in the Lord your God.

EVENING

"When my heart is faint. Lead me to the Rock that is higher than I" — Psalm 61:2.

 MOST OF US know what it is to be overwhelmed in heart; emptied as when a man wipes a dish and turns it upside down; submerged and thrown on our beam ends like a vessel mastered by the storm. Discoveries of inward corruption will do this, if the Lord permits the great deep of our depravity to become troubled and cast up mire and dirt. Disappointments and heart-breaks will do this when billow after billow rolls over us, and we are like a broken shell hurled to and fro by the surf. Blessed be God, at such seasons we are not without an all-sufficient solace, our God is the harbor of weather-beaten sails, the shelter of forlorn pilgrims.

 Higher than we are is He, His mercy higher than our sins, His love higher than our thoughts. It is pitiful to see men putting their thrust in something lower than themselves; but our confidence is fixed upon an exceeding high and glorious Lord. A Rock He is since He changes not, and a high Rock, because the tempest which overwhelm us roll far beneath at His feet; He is not disturbed by them, but rules them at His will. If we get under the shelter of this lofty Rock we may defy the hurricane; all is calm under the lee of that towering cliff. Alas! such is the confusion in which the troubled mind is often cast, that we need piloting to this divine shelter. Hence the prayer of the text. Oh Lord, our God, by Your Holy Spirit, teach us the way of faith, lead us into Your rest. The wind blows us out to sea, the helm answers not to our puny hand; You, You alone steer us over the bar between yonder sunken rocks, safe into the fair haven. How dependent we are upon You; we need You to bring us to You. To be wisely directed and steered into safety and peace is Your gift, and Yours alone. This night be pleased to deal well with Your servants.

MORNING — September 23

"Just, and the justifier of him who is of the faith of Jesus" — Romans 3:26.

BEING JUSTIFIED BY faith, we have peace with God. Conscience accuses no longer. Judgment now decides for the sinner instead of against him. Memory looks back upon past sins, with deep sorrow for the sin, but yet with no dread of any penalty to come; for Christ has paid the debt of His people to the last jot and tittle, and received the divine receipt; and unless God can be so unjust as to demand double payment for one debt, no soul for whom Jesus died as a substitute can ever be cast into hell.

It seems to be one of the very principles of our enlightened nature to believe that God is just. We feel that it must be so, and this gives us our terror at first; but is it not marvelous that this very same belief that God is just, becomes afterwards the pillar of our confidence and peace! If God be just, I, a sinner, alone and without a substitute, must be punished; but Jesus stands in my stead and is punished for me; and now, if God be just, I, a sinner, standing in Christ, can never be punished. God must change His nature before one soul, for whom Jesus was a substitute, can ever by any possibility suffer the lash of the law. Therefore, Jesus having taken the place of the believer, having rendered a full equivalent to divine wrath for all that His people ought to have suffered as the result of sin, the believer can shout with glorious triumph, *"Who shall lay anything to the charge of God's elect?"* Not God, for He has justified; not Christ, for He has died, *"yes, rather has risen again."*

My hope lives not because I am not a sinner, but because I am a sinner for whom Christ died; my trust is not that I am holy, but that being unholy, He is my righteousness. My faith rests not upon what I am, or shall be, or feel, or know, but in what Christ is, in what He has done, and in what He is now doing for me. On the lion of justice the fair maid of hope rides like a queen.

EVENING

"Who was made to us wisdom from God" — 1 Corinthians 1:30.

MAN'S INTELLECT seeks after rest, and by nature seeks it apart from the Lord Jesus Christ. Men of education are apt, even when converted, to look upon the simplicities of the cross of Christ with an eye too little reverent and loving. They are snared in the old net in which the Grecians were taken, and have a hankering to mix philosophy with revelation. The temptation with a man of refined thought and high education is to depart from the simple truth of Christ crucified, and to invent, as the term is, a more intellectual doctrine. This led the early Christian churches into Gnosticism, and bewitched them with all sorts of heresies. This is the root of Neology, and the other things which in days gone by were so fashionable in Germany, and are now so ensnaring to certain classes of divines. Whoever you are, good reader, and whatever your education may be, if you be the Lord's, be assured you will find no rest in philosophizing divinity. You may receive this dogma of one great thinker, or that dream of another profound reasoner, but what the chaff is to the wheat, that will these be to the pure word of God.

All that reason, when best guided, can find out is but the A B C of truth, and even that lacks certainty, while in Christ Jesus there is treasured up all the fullness of wisdom and knowledge. All attempts on the part of Christians to be content with systems such as Unitarian and Broad-church thinkers would approve of, must fail; true heirs of heaven must come back to the grandly simple reality which makes the plowboy's eye flash with joy, and glads the pious pauper's heart: *"Jesus Christ came into the world to save sinners."* Jesus satisfies the most elevated intellect when He is believingly received, but apart from Him the mind of the regenerate discovers no rest. *"The fear of the Lord is the beginning of knowledge." "A good understanding have all they that do His commandments."*

September 24   MORNING

"For I was ashamed to ask of the king a hand of soldiers and horsemen to help us against the enemy in the way, because we had spoken to the king, saying, The hand of our God is on all those who seek Him for good, but His power and His wrath are against all those who forsake Him" — Ezra 8:22.

A CONVOY ON many accounts would have been desirable for the pilgrim band, but a holy shame-facedness would not allow Ezra to seek one. He feared lest the heathen king should think his professions of faith In God to be mere hypocrisy, or imagine that the God of Israel was not able to preserve His own worshippers. He could not bring his mind to lean on an arm of flesh in a matter so evidently of the Lord, and therefore the caravan set out with no visible protection, guarded by Him who is the sword and shield of His people. It is to be feared that few believers feel this holy jealousy for God; even those who in a measure walk by faith, occasionally mar the lustre of their life by craving aid from man. It is a most blessed thing to have no props and no buttresses, but to stand upright on the Rock of Ages, upheld by the Lord alone. Would any believers seek state endowments for their Church, if they remembered that the Lord is dishonored by their asking Caesar's aid? As if the Lord could not supply the needs of His own cause! Should we run so hastily to friends and relations for assistance, if we remembered that the Lord is magnified by our implicit reliance upon His solitary arm? My soul, wait only upon God.

But one will say, "Are not means to be used?" Assuredly they are; but our fault seldom lies in their neglect. Far more frequently it springs out of foolishly believing in them instead of believing in God. Few run too far in neglecting the creature's arm; but very many sin greatly in making too much of it. Learn, dear reader, to glorify the Lord by leaving means untried, if by using them you would dishonor the name of the Lord.

EVENING
"I sleep, but my heart wakes" — Song of Solomon 5:2.

SEEMING PARADOXES ABOUND IN Christian experience, and here is one: the spouse was asleep, and yet she was awake. He only can read the believer's riddle who has plowed with the heifer of his experience. The two points in this evening's text are; a mournful sleepiness and a hopeful wakefulness.

I sleep. Through sin that dwells in us we may become lax in holy duties, slothful in religious exercises, dull in spiritual joys, and altogether supine and careless. This is a shameful state for one in whom the quickening Spirit dwells; and it is dangerous to the highest degree. Even wise virgins sometimes slumber, but it is high time for all to shake off the bands of sloth. It is to be feared that many believers lose their strength as Samson lost his locks, while sleeping on the lap of carnal security. With a perishing world around us, to sleep is cruel; with eternity so near at hand, it is madness. Yet we are none of us so much awake as we should be; a few thunder-claps would do us all good, and it may be, unless we soon arouse ourselves, we shall have them in the form of war, or pestilence, or personal bereavements and losses. Oh that we may leave forever the couch of fleshly ease, and go forth with flaming torches to meet the coming Bridegroom!

My heart wakes. This is a happy sign. Life is not extinct, though sadly smothered. When our renewed heart struggles against our natural heaviness, we should be grateful to sovereign grace for keeping a little vitality within the body of this death. Jesus will hear our hearts, will help our hearts, will visit our hearts; for the voice of the wakeful heart is really the voice of our Beloved, saying, "Open to me." Holy zeal will surely unbar the door.

> Oh lovely attitude! He stands
> With melting heart and laden hands;
> My soul forsakes her every sin,
> And lets the heavenly stranger in.

MORNING   September 25

"Happy are you, Israel! Who is like you, O people saved by the LORD" — *Deuteronomy 33:29.*

HE WHO AFFIRMS that Christianity makes men miserable, is himself an utter stranger to it. It were strange indeed, if it made us wretched, for see to what a position it exalts us! It makes us sons of God. Do you suppose that God will give all the happiness to His enemies, and reserve all the mourning for His own family? Shall His foes have mirth and joy, and shall His home-born children inherit sorrow and wretchedness? Shall the sinner, who has no part in Christ, call himself rich in happiness, and shall we go mourning as if we were penniless beggars? No, we will rejoice in the Lord always, and glory in our inheritance, for we *"have not received the spirit of bondage again to fear; but we have received the spirit of adoption, whereby we cry, Abba, Father."*

The rod of chastisement must rest upon us in our measure, but it works for us the comfortable fruits of righteousness; and therefore by the aid of the divine Comforter, we, the *"people saved of the Lord,"* will joy in the God of our salvation. We are married unto Christ; and shall our great Bridegroom permit His spouse to linger in constant grief? Our hearts are knit unto Him; we are His members, and though for awhile we may suffer as our Head once suffered, yet we are even now blessed with heavenly blessings in Him. We have the earnest of our inheritance in the comforts of the Spirit, which are neither few nor small. Inheritors of joy forever, we have foretastes of our portion. There are streaks of the light of joy to herald our eternal sun rising. Our riches are beyond the sea; our city with firm foundations lies on the other side the river; gleams of glory from the spirit-world cheer our hearts, and urge us onward. Truly is it said of us, *"Happy are you, Oh Israel; who is like unto you, Oh people saved by the Lord?"*

EVENING

"My Beloved put in his hand by the hole of the door, and my heart was moved for Him" — *Song of Solomon 5:4.*

KNOCKING WAS NOT enough, for my heart was too full of sleep, too cold and ungrateful to arise and open the door, but the touch of His effectual grace has made my soul arouse itself. Oh, the long-suffering of my Beloved, to tarry when He found Himself shut out, and me asleep upon the bed of sloth! Oh, the greatness of His patience, to knock and knock again, and to add His voice to His knocking, beseeching me to open to Him! How could I have refused Him! Base heart, blush and be confounded! But what greatest kindness of all is this, that He becomes His own porter and unbars the door Himself! Thrice blessed is the hand which condescends to lift the latch and turn the key.

Now I see that nothing but my Lord's own power can save such a naughty mass of wickedness as I am; ordinances fail, even the gospel has no effect upon me, till His hand is stretched out. Now, also, I perceive that His hand is good where all else is unsuccessful, He can open when nothing else will. Blessed be His name, I feel His gracious presence even now. Well may my heart move for Him, when I think of all that He has suffered for me, and of my ill return. I have allowed my affections to wander. I have set up rivals. I have grieved Him. Sweetest and dearest of all beloved, I have treated You as an unfaithful wife treats her husband. Oh, my cruel sins, my cruel self! What can I do? Tears are a poor show of my repentance, my whole heart boils with indignation at myself. Wretch that I am, to treat my Lord, my All in All, my exceeding great joy, as though He were a stranger. Jesus, You forgive freely, but this is not enough, prevent my unfaithfulness in the future. Kiss away these tears, and then purge my heart and bind it with sevenfold cords to Yourself, never to wander more.

September 26   MORNING

"The myrtle trees that were in the shade" — Zechariah 1:8.

THE VISION IN this chapter describes the condition of Israel in Zechariah's day; but being interpreted in its aspect towards us, it describes the Church of God as we find it now in the world. The Church is compared to a myrtle grove flourishing in a valley. It is hidden, unobserved, secreted; courting no honor and attracting no observation from the careless gazer. The Church, like her head, has a glory, but it is concealed from carnal eyes, for the time of her breaking forth in all her splendor is not yet come. The idea of tranquil security is also suggested to us; for the myrtle grove in the valley is still and calm, while the storm sweeps over the mountain summits. Tempests spend their force upon the craggy peaks of the Alps, but down yonder where flows the stream which makes glad the city of our God, the myrtles flourish by the still waters, all unshaken by the impetuous wind. How great is the inward tranquility of God's Church! Even when opposed and persecuted, she has a peace which the world gives not, and which, therefore, it cannot take away. The peace of God which passes all understanding keeps the hearts and minds of God's people.

Does not the metaphor forcibly picture the peaceful, perpetual growth of the saints? The myrtle sheds not her leaves, she is always green; and the Church in her worst time still has a blessed verdure of grace about her; no, she has sometimes exhibited most verdure when her winter has been sharpest. She has prospered most when her adversities have been most severe. Hence the text hints at victory. The myrtle is the emblem of peace, and a significant token of triumph. The brows of conquerors were bound with myrtle and with laurel; and is not the Church ever victorious? Is not every Christian more than a conqueror through Him that loved him? Living In peace, do not the saints fall asleep in the arms of victory?

EVENING

"Howl, fir-tree, for the cedar has fallen" — Zechariah 11:2.

WHEN IN THE forest there is heard the crash of a falling oak, it is a sign that the woodman is abroad, and every tree in the whole company may tremble lest tomorrow the sharp edge of the axe should find it out. We are all like trees marked for the axe, and the fall of one should remind us that for every one, whether great as the cedar, or humble as the fir, the appointed hour is stealing on apace. I trust we do not, by often hearing of death, become callous to it. May we never be like the birds in the steeple, which build their nests when the bells are tolling, and sleep quietly when the solemn funeral peals are startling the air. May we regard death as the most weighty of all events, and be sobered by its approach. It ill behooves us to sport while our eternal destiny hangs on a thread. The sword is out of its scabbard; let us not trifle; it is furbished, and the edge is sharp; let us not play with it. He who does not prepare for death is more than an ordinary fool, he is a madman. When the voice of God is heard among the trees of the garden, let fig tree and sycamore, and elm and cedar, alike hear the sound thereof.

Be ready, servant of Christ, for your Master comes on a sudden, when an ungodly world least expects Him. See to it that you be faithful in His work, for the grave shall soon be dug for you. Be ready, parents, see that your children are brought up in the fear of God, for they must soon be orphans. Be ready, men of business, take care that your affairs are correct, and that you serve God with all your hearts, for the days of your terrestrial service will soon be ended, and you will be called to give account for the deeds done in the body, whether they be good or whether they be evil. May we all prepare for the tribunal of the great King with a care which shall be rewarded with the gracious commendation, *"Well done, good and faithful servant."*

MORNING   September 27

"And behold, if the leprosy has covered all his flesh, he shall pronounce him clean that has the plague" — *Leviticus 13:13.*

STRANGE ENOUGH THIS regulation appears, yet there was wisdom in it, for the throwing out of the disease proved that the constitution was sound. This morning it may be well for us to see the typical teaching of so singular a rule. We, too, are lepers, and may read the law of the leper as applicable to ourselves. When a man sees himself to be altogether lost and ruined, covered all over with the defilement of sin, and no part free from pollution; when he disclaims all righteousness of his own, and pleads guilty before the Lord, then is he clean through the blood of Jesus, and the grace of God. Hidden, unfelt, unconfessed iniquity is the true leprosy, but when sin is seen and felt it has received its death blow, and the Lord looks with eyes of mercy upon the soul afflicted with it. Nothing is more deadly than self-righteousness, or more hopeful than contrition. We must confess that we are "nothing else but sin," for no confession short of this will be the whole truth, and if the Holy Spirit be at work with us, convincing us of sin, there will be no difficulty about making such an acknowledgment; it will spring spontaneously from our lips.

What comfort does the text afford to those under a deep sense of sin! Sin mourned and confessed, however black and foul, shall never shut a man out from the Lord Jesus. Whoever comes to Him, He will in no wise cast out. Though dishonest as the thief, though unchaste as the woman who was a sinner, though fierce as Saul of Tarsus, though cruel as Manasseh, though rebellious as the prodigal, the great heart of love will look upon the man who feels himself to have no soundness in him, and will pronounce him clean, when he trusts in Jesus crucified. Come to Him, then, poor heavy-laden sinner,

> Come needy, come guilty,
> Come loathsome and bare;
> You can't come too filthy;
> Come just as you are.

EVENING

"I have found Him whom my soul loves. I held Him and would not let Him go" — *Song of Solomon 3:4.*

DOES CHRIST RECEIVE us when we come to Him, notwithstanding all our past sinfulness? Does He never chide us for having tried all other refuges first? And is there none on earth like Him? Is He the best of all the good, the fairest of all the fair? Oh, then let us praise Him! Daughters of Jerusalem, extol Him with timbrel and harp! Down with your idols, up with the Lord Jesus. Now let the standards of pomp and pride be trampled under foot, but let the cross of Jesus, which the world frowns and scoffs at, be lifted on high. Oh for a throne of ivory for our King Solomon! let Him be set on high forever, and let my soul sit at His footstool, and kiss His feet, and wash them with my tears. Oh, how precious is Christ! How can it be that I have thought so little of Him? How is it I can go abroad for joy or comfort when He is so full, so rich, so satisfying.

Fellow believer, make a covenant with your heart that you will never depart from Him, and ask your Lord to ratify it. Bid Him set you as a signet upon His finger, and as a bracelet upon His arm. Ask Him to bind you about Him, as the bride decks herself with ornaments, and as the bridegroom puts on his jewels. I would live in Christ's heart; in the clefts of that rock my soul would eternally abide. The sparrow has made a house, and the swallow a nest for herself where she may lay her young, even Your altars, Oh Lord of hosts, my King and my God; and so too would I make my nest, my home, in You, and never from You may the soul of Your turtle dove go forth again, but may I nestle close to You, Oh Jesus, my true and only rest.

> When my precious Lord I find,
> All my ardent passions glow;
> Him with cords of love I bind,

September 28   MORNING

"The LORD looks down from Heaven, He beholds all the sons of men" — Psalm 33:13.

PERHAPS NO FIGURE of speech represents God in a more gracious light than when He is spoken of as stooping from His throne, and coming down from heaven to attend to the wants and to behold the woes of mankind. We love Him, who, when Sodom and Gomorrah were full of iniquity, would not destroy those cities until He had made a personal visitation of them. We cannot help pouring out our heart in affection for our Lord who inclines His ear from the highest glory, and puts it to the lip of the dying sinner, whose failing heart longs after reconciliation. How can we but love Him when we know that He numbers the very hairs of our heads, marks our path, and orders our ways?

Especially is this great truth brought near to our heart, when we remember how attentive He is, not merely to the temporal interests of His creatures, but to their spiritual concerns. Though leagues of distance lie between the finite creature and the infinite Creator, yet there are links uniting both. When a tear is wept by you, think not that God does not behold; for, *"Like as a father pities his children, so the Lord pities them that fear Him."* Your sigh is able to move the heart of Jehovah; your whisper can incline His ear unto you; your prayer can stay His hand; your faith can move His arm. Think not that God sits on high taking no account of you. Remember that however poor and needy you are, yet the Lord thinks upon you. For the eyes of the Lord run to and fro throughout the whole earth, to show Himself strong in the behalf of them whose heart is perfect towards Him.

> Oh! then repeat the truth that never tires;
> No God is like the God my soul desires;
> He at whose voice heaven trembles, even He,
> Great as He is, knows how to stoop to me.

EVENING
"Go again seven times" — 1 Kings 18:43.

SUCCESS IS CERTAIN when the Lord has promised it. Although you may have pleaded month after month without evidence of answer, it is not possible that the Lord should be deaf when His people are earnest in a matter which concerns His glory. The prophet on the top of Carmel continued to wrestle with God, and never for a moment gave way to a fear that he should be non-suited in Jehovah's courts. Six times the servant returned, but on each occasion no word was spoken but *"Go again."*

We must not dream of unbelief, but hold to our faith even to seventy times seven. Faith sends expectant hope to look from Carmel's brow, and if nothing is beheld, she sends again and again. So far from being crushed by repeated disappointment, faith is animated to plead more fervently with her God. She is humbled, but not abashed; her groans are deeper, and her sighing more vehement, but she never relaxes her hold or stays her hand. It would be more agreeable to flesh and blood to have a speedy answer, but believing souls have learned to be submissive, and to find it good to wait for as well as upon the Lord. Delayed answers often set the heart searching itself, and so lead to contrition and spiritual reformation; deadly blows are thus struck at our corruption, and the chambers of imagery are cleansed. The great danger is lest men should faint, and miss the blessing.

Reader, do not fall into that sin, but continue in prayer and watching. At last the little cloud was seen, the sure forerunner of torrents of rain, and even so with you, the token for good shall surely be given, and you shall rise as a prevailing prince to enjoy the mercy you have sought. Elijah was a man of like passions with us; his power with God did not lie in his own merits. If his believing prayer availed so much, why not yours? Plead the precious blood with unceasing importunity, and it shall be with you according to your desire.

MORNING   September 29

"Sing out the honor of His name; make His praise glorious" — *Psalm 66:2.*

IT IS NOT left to our own option whether we shall praise God or not. Praise is God's most righteous due, and every Christian, as the recipient of His grace, is bound to praise God from day to day. It is true we have no authoritative rubric for daily praise; we have no commandment prescribing certain hours of song and thanksgiving; but the law written upon the heart teaches us that it is right to praise God; and the unwritten mandate comes to us with as much force as if it had been recorded on the tables of stone, or handed to us from the top of thundering Sinai.

Yes, it is the Christian's duty to praise God. It is not only a pleasurable exercise, but it is the absolute obligation of his life. Think not you who are always mourning, that you are guiltless in this respect, or imagine that you can discharge your duty to your God without songs of praise. You are bound by the bonds of His love to bless His name so long as you live, and His praise should continually be in your mouth, for you are blessed, in order that you may bless Him; *"this people have I formed for Myself, they shall show forth My praise;"* and if you do not praise God, you are not bringing forth the fruit which He, as the Divine Husbandman, has a right to expect at your hands. Let not your harp then hang upon the willows, but take it down, and strive, with a grateful heart, to bring forth its loudest music. Arise and chant His praise. With every morning's dawn, lift up your notes of thanksgiving, and let every setting sun be followed with your song. Girdle the earth with your praises; surround it with an atmosphere of melody, and God Himself will hearken from heaven and accept your music.

> E'en so I love You, and will love,
> And in Your praise will sing,
> Because You are my loving God.
> And my redeeming King.

EVENING
"For a living dog is better than a dead lion" — *Ecclesiastes 9:4.*

LIFE IS A precious thing, and in its humblest form it is superior to death. This truth is eminently certain in spiritual things. It is better to be the least in the kingdom of heaven than the greatest out of it. The lowest degree of grace is superior to the noblest development of unregenerate nature. Where the Holy Spirit implants divine life in the soul, there is a precious deposit which none of the refinements of education can equal. The thief on the cross excels Caesar on his throne; Lazarus among the dogs is better than Cicero among the senators; and the most unlettered Christian is in the sight of God superior to Plato. Life is the badge of nobility in the realm of spiritual things, and men without it are only coarser or finer specimens of the same lifeless material, needing to be quickened, for they are dead in trespasses and sins.

A living, loving, gospel sermon, however unlearned in matter and uncouth in style, is better than the finest discourse devoid of unction and power. A living dog keeps better watch than a dead lion, and is of more service to his master; and so the poorest spiritual preacher is infinitely to be preferred to the exquisite orator who has no wisdom but that of words, no energy but that of sound. The like holds good of our prayers and other religious exercises; if we are quickened in them by the Holy Spirit, they are acceptable to God through Jesus Christ, though we may think them to be worthless things; while our grand performances in which our hearts were absent, like dead lions, are mere carrion in the sight of the living God. Oh for living groans, living signs, living despondencies, rather than lifeless songs and dead calms. Better anything than death. The snarling of the dog of hell will at least keep us awake, but dead faith and dead profession, what greater curses can a man have? Quicken us, quicken us, Oh Lord!

September 30   MORNING

"Sing forth the honor of His name; make His praise glorious" — Psalm 66:2

IT IS NOT left to our own option whether we shall praise God or not. Praise is God's most righteous due, and every Christian, as the recipient of His grace, is bound to praise God from day to day. It is true that we have no authoritative directions for our daily praise; we have no commandment prescribing certain hours of song and thanksgiving. But the law written on the heart teaches us that it is right to praise God. And the unwritten mandate comes to us with as much force as if it had been recorded on the tables of stone, or handed to us from the top of thundering Sinai.

Yes, it is the Christian's duty to praise God. It is not only a pleasurable exercise, ut it is the absolute obligation of his life. Do not think that you are guiltless because you are always mourning; nor imagine that you can discharge your duty to your God without songs of praise. You are bound by the bonds of His love to bless His name so long as your live. And His praise should continually be in your mouth, for you are blessed. *"This people I have formed for Myself; they shall show forth My praise"*

And if you do not praise God, you are not bringing forth the fruit which He. the Divine Husbandman, has a right to expect at your hands. Then to not let your harp hang on the willows, but take it down and with a grateful heart strive to bring forth musical praise from the soul. Arise and chant His praise. With every morning dawn left up your notes of thanksgiving. Let every setting sun be followed with your song. Girdle the earth with your praises; surround it with an atmosphere of melody. Then God Himself will hear from Heaven and accept your music.

EVENING

"A living dog is better than a dead lion" — Eccl. 9:4.

LIFE IS A precious thing, and in its humblest form it is superior to death. This truth is eminently certain in spiritual things. It is better to be the least in the kingdom of Heaven than the greatest out of it. The lowest degree of grace is superior to the noblest development of unregenerate nature. Where the Holy Spirit implants Divine life in the soul, there is a precious deposit which none of the refinements of education can equal. The thief on the cross excels Caesar on his throne. Lazarus among the dogs is better than Cicero among the senators. And the most unlettered Christian is in the sight of God superior to Plato. Life is the badge of nobility in the realm of spiritual things, and men without it are only coarser or finer specimens of the same lifeless material, needing to be enlivened — for they are dead in trespasses and sins.

A living, loving, gospel sermon, however unlearned in matter or uncouth in style, is better than the finest discourse which is devoid of spiritual unction and power. A living dog keeps better watch than a dead lion, and is of more service to his master. And so the poorest spiritual preacher is infinitely to be preferred to the exquisite orator who has no wisdom but that of words; no energy but that of sound. The like holds good of our prayers and other religious exercises. If we are enlivened in them by the Holy Spirit, they are acceptable to God through Jesus Christ, though we may think them to be worthless. Yet our grand performances, if our hearts be absent from them, are like dead lions; they are mere carrion in the sight of the living God. Oh for living groans, living sighs, living dependencies, rather than lifeless songs and dead calms. Better is anything than death. The snarlings of the dog of hell will at least keep us awake, but dead faith and dead profession; what greater curses can a man have?

Oh Lord, quicken us, quicken us!

MORNING   October 1

"Pleasant fruits, new and old, which I have laid up for You, Oh my Beloved" — Song of Solomon 7:13

THE SPOUSE DESIRES to give to Jesus all that she produces. Our heart has *"all manner of pleasant fruits,"* both *"new and old,"* and they are laid up for our Beloved. At this rich autumnal season of fruit, let us survey our stores. We have new fruits. We desire to feel new life, new joy, new gratitude; we wish to make new resolves and carry then out by new labors; our heart blossoms with new prayers, and our soul is pledging herself to new efforts. But we have some old fruits too. There is our first love; a choice fruit that! And Jesus delights in it. There is our first faith; that simple faith by which, having nothing, we became possessors of all things. There is our joy when first we knew the Lord; let us revive it. We have our old remembrances of the promises. How faithful has God been! In sickness, how softly did He make our bed! In deep waters, how placidly did He buoy us up! In the flaming furnace, how graciously did He deliver us. Old fruits, indeed! we have many of them, for His mercies have been more than the hairs of our head. Old sins we must regret, but then we have had repentance which He has given us, by which we have wept our way to the cross, and learned the merit of His blood.

We have fruits, this morning, both new and old; but here is the point: they are all laid up for Jesus. Truly, those are the best and most acceptable services in which Jesus is the solitary aim of the soul, and His glory, without any admixture whatever, the end of all our efforts. Let our many fruits be laid up only for our Beloved; let us display them when He is with us, and not hold them up before the eye of men. Jesus, we will turn the key in our garden door, and none shall enter to rob You of one good fruit from the soil which You have watered with Your bloody sweat. Our all shall be Yours, Yours only, Oh Jesus, our Beloved!

EVENING
"The LORD will give grace and glory" — Psalm 84:11

BOUNTEOUS IS JEHOVAH in His nature; to give is His delight. His gifts are beyond measure precious, and are as freely given as the light of the sun. He gives grace to His elect because He wills it, to His redeemed because of His covenant, to the called because of His promise, to believers because they seek it, to sinners because they need it. He gives grace abundantly, seasonably, constantly, readily, sovereignly; doubly enhancing the value of the blessing by the manner of its bestowal. Grace in all its forms He freely renders to His people: comforting, preserving, sanctifying, directing, instructing, assisting grace, He generously pours into their souls without ceasing, and He always will do so, whatever may occur. Sickness may befall, but the Lord will give grace; poverty may happen to us, but grace will surely be afforded; death must come, but grace will light a candle at the darkest hour. Reader, how blessed it is as years roll around, and the leaves begin again to fall, to enjoy such an unfading promise as this, *"The Lord will give grace."*

The little conjunction "and" in this verse is a diamond rivet binding the present with the future; grace and glory always go together. God has married them, and none can divorce them. The Lord will never deny a soul glory to whom He has freely given to live upon His grace; indeed, glory is nothing more than grace in its Sabbath dress, grace in full bloom, grace like autumn fruit, mellow and perfected. How soon we may have glory none can tell! It may be before this month of October has run out we shall see the Holy City; but be the interval longer or shorter, we shall be glorified before long. Glory, the glory of heaven, the glory of eternity, the glory of Jesus, the glory of the Father, the Lord will surely give to His chosen. Oh, rare promise of a faithful God!

Two golden links of one celestial chain:
Who owns grace shall surely glory gain.

October 2   MORNING

"The hope which is laid up for you in Heaven" — Colossians 1:5.

OUR HOPE IN Christ for the future is the mainspring and the mainstay of our joy here. It will animate our hearts to think often of heaven, for all that we can desire is promised there. Here we are weary and worn, but yonder is the land of rest where the sweat of labor shall no more wet the worker's brow, and fatigue shall be forever banished. To those who are weary and spent, the word "rest" is full of heaven. We are always in the field of battle; we are so tempted within, and so molested by foes without, that we have little or no peace. But in heaven we shall enjoy the victory, when the banner shall be waved aloft in triumph, and the sword shall be sheathed, and we shall hear our Captain say, *"Well done, good and faithful servant."* We have suffered bereavement after bereavement, but we are going to the land of the immortal where graves are unknown things. Here sin is a constant grief to us, but there we shall be perfectly holy, for there shall by no means enter into that kingdom anything which defiles. Hemlock springs not up in the furrows of celestial fields. Oh! is it not joy, that you are not to be in banishment forever, that you are not to dwell eternally in this wilderness, but shall soon inherit Canaan?

Nevertheless let it never be said of us, that we are dreaming about the future and forgetting the present, let the future sanctify the present to highest uses. Through the Spirit of God the hope of heaven is the most potent force for the product of virtue; it is a fountain of joyous effort, it is the corner stone of cheerful holiness. The man who has this hope in him goes about his work with vigor, for the joy of the Lord is his strength. He fights against temptation with ardor, for the hope of the next world repels the fiery darts of the adversary. He can labor without present reward, for he looks for a reward in the world to come.

EVENING
"A man greatly beloved" — Daniel 10:11

CHILD OF GOD, do you hesitate to appropriate this title? Ah! has your unbelief made you forget that you are greatly beloved too? Must you not have been greatly beloved, to have been bought with the precious blood of Christ, as of a lamb without blemish and without spot? When God smote His only begotten Son for you, what was this but being greatly beloved? You lived in sin, and rioted in it, must you not have been greatly beloved for God to have borne so patiently with you? You were called by grace and led to a Savior, and made a child of God and an heir of heaven. All this proves, does it not, a very great and superabounding love? Since that time, whether your path has been rough with troubles, or smooth with mercies, it has been full of proofs that you are a man greatly beloved. If the Lord has chastened you, yet not in anger; if He has made you poor, yet in grace you have been rich. The more unworthy you feel yourself to be, the more evidence have you that nothing but unspeakable love could have led the Lord Jesus to save such a soul as yours. The more demerit you feel, the clearer is the display of the abounding love of God in having chosen you, and called you, and made you an heir of bliss.

Now, if there be such love between God and us let us live in the influence and sweetness of it, and use the privilege of our position. Do not let us approach our Lord as though we were strangers, or as though He were unwilling to hear us; for we are greatly beloved by our loving Father. *"He that spared not His own Son, but delivered Him up for us all, how shall He not with Him also freely give us all things?"* Come boldly, Oh believer, for despite the whisperings of Satan and the doubting of your own heart, you are greatly beloved. Meditate on the exceeding greatness and faithfulness of divine love this evening, and so go to your bed in peace.

MORNING — October 3

"Are they not all ministering spirits sent out in order to serve those who are going to be heirs of salvation?" — Hebrews 1:14.

ANGELS ARE THE unseen attendants of the saints of God; they bear us up in their hands, lest we dash our foot against a stone. Loyalty to their Lord leads them to take a deep interest in the children of His love; they rejoice over the return of the prodigal to his father's house below, and they welcome the advent of the believer to the King's palace above.

In olden times the sons of God were favored with their visible appearance, and at this day, although unseen by us, heaven is still opened, and the angels of God ascend and descent upon the Son of man, that they may visit the heirs of salvation. Seraphim still fly with live coals from off the altar to touch the lips of men greatly beloved. If our eyes could be opened, we should see horses of fire and chariots of fire about the servants of the Lord; for we have come to an innumerable company of angels, who are all watchers and protectors of the seed royal. Spenser's line is no poetic fiction, where he sings:

> How oft do they with golden pinions cleave
> The fitting skies, lie flying pursuivant
> Against foul fiends to aid us militant!

To what dignity are the chosen elevated when the brilliant courtiers of heaven become their willing servitors! Into what communion are we raised since we have intercourse with spotless celestials! How well are we defended since all the twenty thousand chariots of God are armed for our deliverance! To whom do we owe all this? Let the Lord Jesus Christ be forever endeared to us, for through Him we are made to sit in heavenly places far above principalities and powers. He it is whose camp is round about them that fear Him; He is the true Michael whose foot is upon the dragon. All hail, Jesus! You Angel of Jehovah's presence, to You this family offers its morning vows.

EVENING

"He Himself has suffered, having been tempted" — Hebrews 2:18.

IT IS A commonplace thought, and yet it tastes like nectar to the weary heart: Jesus was tempted as I am. You have heard that truth many times; have you grasped it? He was tempted to the very same sins into which we fall. Do not disassociate Jesus from our common manhood. It is a dark room which you are going through, but Jesus went through it before. It is a sharp fight which you are waging, but Jesus has stood foot to foot with the same enemy. Let us be of good cheer, Christ has borne the load before us, and the bloodstained footsteps of the King of glory may be seen along the road which we traverse at this hour. There is something sweeter yet: Jesus was tempted, but Jesus never sinned. Then, my soul, it is not needful for you to sin, for Jesus was a man, and if one man endured these temptations and sinned not, then in His power His members may also cease from sin.

Some beginners in the divine life think that they cannot be tempted without sinning, but they mistake; there is no sin in being tempted, but there is sin in yielding to temptation. Herein is comfort for the sorely tempted ones. There is still more to encourage them if they reflect that the Lord Jesus, though tempted, gloriously triumphed, and as He overcame, so surely shall His followers also. For Jesus is the representative man for His people; the Head has triumphed, and the members share in the victory. Fears are needless, for Christ is with us, armed for our defense. Our place of safety is the bosom of the Savior. Perhaps we are tempted just now, in order to drive us nearer to Him. Blessed be any wind that blows us into the port of our Savior's love! Happy wounds, which make us seek the beloved Physician. You tempted ones, come to your tempted Savior, for He can be touched with a feeling of your infirmities, and will succor every tried and tempted one.

October 4

MORNING

"At evening time it shall be light" — Zechariah 14:7.

OFTENTIMES WE LOOK forward with foreboding to the time of old age, forgetful that at eventide it shall be light. To many saints, old age is the choicest season in their lives. A balmier air fans the mariner's cheek as he nears the shore of immortality, fewer waves ruffle his sea, quiet reigns, deep, still and solemn. From the altar of age the flashes of the fire of youth are gone, but the more real flame of earnest feeling remains. The pilgrims have reached the land Beulah, that happy country, whose days are as the days of heaven upon earth. Angels visit it, celestial gales blow over it, flowers of paradise grow in it, and the air is filled with seraphic music. Some dwell here for years, and others come to it but a few hours before their departure, but it is an Eden on earth. We may well long for the time when we shall recline in its shady groves and be satisfied with hope until the time of fruition comes. The setting sun seems larger than when aloft in the sky, and a splendor of glory tinges all the clouds which surround his going down. Pain breaks not the calm of the sweet twilight of age, for strength made perfect in weakness bears up with patience under it all. Ripe fruits of choice experience are gathered as the rare repast of life's evening, and the soul prepares itself for rest.

The Lord's people shall also enjoy light in the hour of death. Unbelief laments; the shadows fall, the night is coming, existence is ending. "Ah no," cries faith, "the night is far spent, the true day is at hand." Light is come, the light of immortality, the light of a Father's countenance. Gather up your feet in the bed, see the waiting band of spirits! Angels bear you away. Farewell, beloved one, you are gone, you wave your hand. Ah, now it is light. The pearly gates are open, the golden streets shine in the jasper light. We cover our eyes, but you behold the unseen; adieu, brother, you have light at eventide, such as we have not yet.

EVENING

"And if anyone should sin, we have an Advocate with the Father Jesus Christ the righteous" — 1 John 2:1.

"AND IF ANYONE should sin, we have an Advocate." Yes, though we sin; we have Him still. John does not say, If any man sin he has forfeited his advocate, but *"we have an advocate,"* sinners though we are. All the sin that a believer ever did, or can be allowed to commit, cannot destroy his interest in the Lord Jesus Christ as his advocate.

The name here given to our Lord is suggestive. "Jesus." Ah! then He is an advocate such as we need, for Jesus is the name of One whose business and delight it is to save. *"They shall call His name Jesus, for He shall save His people from their sins."* His sweetest name implies His success. Next, it is Jesus Christ, the anointed. This shows His authority to plead. The Christ has a right to plead, for He is the Father's own appointed advocate and elected priest. If He were of our choosing He might fail, but if God has laid help upon One that is mighty, we may safely lay our trouble where God has laid His help. He is Christ, and therefore authorized; He is Christ, and therefore qualified, for the anointing has fully fitted Him for His work. He can plead so as to move the heart of God and prevail. What words of tenderness, what sentences of persuasion will the Anointed use when Ne stands up to plead for me!

One more letter of His name remains, *"Jesus Christ the righteous."* This is not only His character, but His plea. It is His character, and if the Righteous One be my advocate, then my cause is good, or He would not have espoused it. It is His plea, for He meets the charge of unrighteousness against me by the plea that He is righteous. He declares Himself my substitute and puts His obedience to my account. My soul, you have a friend well fitted to be your advocate, He cannot but succeed; leave yourself entirely in His hands.

MORNING   October 5

"And he arose and ate and drank. And he went in the strength of that food forty days and forty nights" — 1 Kings 19:8.

ALL THE STRENGTH supplied to us by our gracious God is meant for service, not for wantonness or boasting. When the prophet Elijah found the cake baked on the coals, and the cruse of water placed at his head, as he lay under the juniper tree, he was no gentleman to be gratified with dainty fare that he might stretch himself at his ease. Far otherwise, he was commissioned to go forty days and forty nights in the strength of it, journeying towards Horeb, the mount of God. When the Master invited the disciples to *"Come and dine"* with Him, after the feast was concluded He said to Peter, *"Feed my sheep;"* further adding, *"Follow me."*

Even thus it is with us; we eat the bread of heaven, that we may expend our strength in the Master's service. We come to the passover, and eat of the paschal lamb with loins girt, and staff in hand, so as to start off at once when we have satisfied our hunger. Some Christians are for living on Christ, but are not so anxious to live for Christ. Earth should be a preparation for heaven; and heaven is the place where saints feast most and work most. They sit down at the table of our Lord, and they serve Him day and night in His temple. They eat of heavenly food and render perfect service.

Believer, in the strength you daily gain from Christ labor for Him. Some of us have yet to learn much concerning the design of our Lord in giving us His grace. We are not to retain the precious grains of truth as the Egyptian mummy held the wheat for ages, without giving it an opportunity to grow; we must sow it and water it. Why does the Lord send down the rain upon the thirsty earth, and give the genial sunshine? Is it not that these may all help the fruits of the earth to yield food for man? Even so the Lord feeds and refreshes our souls that we may afterwards use our renewed strength in the promotion of His glory.

EVENING
"He that believes and is baptized shall be saved" — Mark 16:16.

MR. MACDONALD ASKED the inhabitants of the island of St. Kilda how a man must be saved. An old man replied, "We shall be saved if we repent, and forsake our sins, and turn to God." "Yes," said a middle-aged female, And with a true heart too." A third rejoined, "And with prayer." A fourth added, "It must be the prayer of the heart." "And we must be diligent too in keeping the commandments," said a fifth. Thus, each having contributed his mite, feeling that a very decent creed had been made up, they all looked and listened for the preacher's approbation, but they had aroused his deepest pity. The carnal mind always maps out for itself a way in which self can work and become great, but the Lord's way is quite the reverse.

Believing and being baptized are no matters of merit to be gloried in; they are so simple that boasting is excluded, and free grace bears the palm. It may be that the reader is unsaved; what is the reason? Do you think the way of salvation as laid down in the text to be dubious? How can that be when God has pledged His own word for its certainty? Do you think it too easy? Why, then, do you not attend to it? Its ease leaves those without excuse who neglect it. To believe is simply to trust, to depend, to rely upon Christ Jesus. To be baptized is to submit to the ordinance which our Lord fulfilled at Jordan, to which the converted ones submitted at Pentecost, to which the jailer yielded obedience the very night of his conversion. The outward sign saves not, but it sets forth to us our death, burial, and resurrection with Jesus, and, like the Lord's Supper, is not to be neglected.

Reader, do you believe in Jesus? Then, dear friend, dismiss your fears, you shall be saved. Are you still an unbeliever, then remember there is but one door, and if you will not enter by it you will perish in your sins.

October 6   MORNING

"But whoever may drink of the water which I will give him will never ever thirst" — *John 4:14.*

HE WHO IS A believer in Jesus finds enough in his Lord to satisfy him now, and to content him forevermore. The believer is not the man whose days are weary for want of comfort, and whose nights are long from absence of heart-cheering thought, for he finds in religion such a spring of joy, such a fountain of consolation, that he is content and happy. Put him in a dungeon and he will find good company; place him in a barren wilderness, he will eat the bread of heaven; drive him away from friendship, he will meet the *"friend that sticks closer than a brother."* Blast all his gourds, and he will find shadow beneath the Rock of Ages; sap the foundation of his earthly hopes, but his heart will still be fixed, trusting in the Lord. The heart is as insatiable as the grave till Jesus enters it, and then it is a cup full to overflowing. There is such a fullness in Christ that He alone is the believer's all. The true saint is so completely satisfied with the all-sufficiency of Jesus that he thirsts no more; only for deeper draughts of the living fountain.

In that sweet manner, believer, shall you thirst; it shall not be a thirst of pain, but of loving desire; you will find it a sweet thing to be panting after a fuller enjoyment of Jesus' love. One in days gone by said, "I have been sinking my bucket down into the well full often, but now my thirst after Jesus has become so insatiable, that I long to put the well itself to my lips, and drink right on." Is this the feeling of your heart now, believer? Do you feel that all your desires are satisfied in Jesus, and that you have no want now, but to know more of Him, and to have closer fellowship with Him? Then come continually to the fountain, and take of the water of life freely. Jesus will never think you take too much, but will ever welcome you, saying, "Drink, yes, drink abundantly, Oh beloved."

EVENING

"He had married a Cushite woman" — *Numbers 12:1.*

STRANGE CHOICE OF Moses, but how much more strange the choice of Him who is a prophet like unto Moses, and greater than he! Our Lord, who is fair as the lily, has entered into marriage union with one who confesses herself to be black, because the sun has looked upon her. It is the wonder of angels that the love of Jesus should be set upon poor, lost, guilty men. Each believer must, when filled with a sense of Jesus love, be also overwhelmed with astonishment that such love should be lavished on an object so utterly unworthy of it. Knowing as we do our secret guiltiness, unfaithfulness, and black-heartedness, we are dissolved in grateful admiration of the matchless freeness and sovereignty of grace.

Jesus must have found the cause of His love in His own heart, He could not have found it in us, for it is not there. Even since our conversion we have been black, though grace has made us comely. Holy Rutherford said of himself what we must each subscribe to, saying, "His relation to me is, that I am sick, and He is the Physician of whom I stand in need. Alas! how often I play fast and loose with Christ! He binds, I loose; He builds, I cast down; I quarrel with Christ, and He agrees with me twenty times a day! Most tender and faithful Husband of our souls, pursue Your gracious work of conforming us to Your image, till You shall present even us poor Cushites unto Yourself, without spot, or wrinkle, or any such thing."

Moses met with opposition because of his marriage, and both himself and his spouse were the subjects of an evil eye. Can we wonder if this vain world opposes Jesus and His spouse, and especially when great sinners are converted? For this is ever the Pharisee's ground of objection, *"This one receives sinners."* Still is the old cause of quarrel revived, "Because he had married a Cushite woman."

MORNING   October 7

"Why have You afflicted Your servant?" — Numbers 11:11.

OUR HEAVENLY FATHER sends us frequent troubles to try our faith. If our faith be worth anything, it will stand the test. Gilt is afraid of fire, but gold is not; the paste gem dreads to be touched by the diamond, but the true jewel fears no test. It is a poor faith which can only trust God when friends are true, the body full of health, and the business profitable. But that is true faith which holds by the Lord's faithfulness when friends are gone, when the body is sick, when spirits are depressed, and the light of our Father's countenance is hidden. A faith which can say, in the direst trouble, *"Though He slay me, yet will I trust in Him,"* is heaven-born faith.

The Lord afflicts His servants to glorify Himself, for He is greatly glorified in the graces of His people, which are His own handiwork. When *"tribulation works patience; and patience, experience; and experience, hope,"* the Lord is honored by these growing virtues. We should never know the music of the harp if the strings were left untouched; nor enjoy the juice of the grape if it were not trodden in the wine-press; nor discover the sweet perfume of cinnamon if it were not pressed and beaten; nor feel the warmth of fire if the coals were not utterly consumed. The wisdom and power of the great Workman are discovered by the trials through which His vessels of mercy are permitted to pass.

Present afflictions tend also to heighten future joy. There must be shades in the picture to bring out the beauty of the lights. Could we be so supremely blessed in heaven, if we had not known the curse of sin and the sorrow of earth? Will not peace be sweeter after conflict, and rest more welcome after toil? Will not the remembrance of past sufferings enhance the bliss of the glorified? There are many other comfortable answers to the question with which we opened our brief meditation, let us muse upon it all day long.

EVENING

"Now on whom do you trust" — Isaiah 36:5.

READER, THIS IS an important question. Listen to the Christian's answer, and see if it is yours. *"On whom do you trust?"* The Christian says, I trust in a triune God. I trust the Father, believing that He has chosen me from before the foundations of the world; I trust Him to provide for me in providence, to teach me, to guide me, to correct me if need be, and to bring me home to His own house where the many mansions are. I trust the Son, very God of very God, the man Christ Jesus. I trust in Him to take away all my sins by His own sacrifice, and to adorn me with His perfect righteousness. I trust Him to be my Intercessor, to present my prayers and desires before His Father's throne, and I trust Him to be my Advocate at the last great day, to plead my cause, and to justify me. I trust Him for what He is, for what He has done, and for what He has promised yet to do. And I trust the Holy Spirit; He has begun to save me from my inbred sins; I trust Him to drive them all out; I trust Him to curb my temper, to subdue my will, to enlighten my understanding, to check my passions, to comfort my despondency, to help my weakness, to illuminate my darkness; I trust Hint to dwell in me as my life, to reign in me as my King, to sanctify me wholly, spirit, soul, and body, and then to take me up to dwell with the saints in light forever."

Oh, blessed trust! To trust Him whose power will never be exhausted, whose love will never wane, whose kindness will never change, whose faithfulness will never fail, whose wisdom will never be nonplussed, and whose perfect goodness can never know a diminution! Happy are you, reader, if this trust is yours! So trusting, you shall enjoy sweet peace now, and glory hereafter, and the foundation of your trust shall never be removed.

October 8   MORNING

"Move out into the deep and let down your nets for a haul" — Luke 5:4.

WE LEARN FROM this narrative, the necessity of human agency. The draught of fishes was miraculous, yet neither the fisherman nor his boat, nor his fishing tackle were ignored; but all were used to take the fishes. So in the saving of souls, God works by means; and while the present economy of grace shall stand, God will be pleased by the foolishness of preaching to save them that believe. When God works without instruments, doubtless He is glorified; but He has Himself selected the plan of instrumentality as being that by which He is most magnified in the earth.

Means of themselves are utterly unavailing. *"Master, we have toiled all the night and have taken nothing."* What was the reason of this? Were they not fishermen plying their special calling? Verily, they were no raw hands; they understood the work. Had they gone about the toil unskillfully? No. Had they lacked industry? No, they had toiled. Had they lacked perseverance? No, they had toiled all the night. Was there a deficiency of fish in the sea? Certainly not, for as soon as the Master came, they swam to the net in shoals. What, then, is the reason? Is it not because there is no power in the means of themselves apart front the presence of Jesus? *"Without Him we can do nothing."* But *"through Christ we can do all things."*

Christ's presence confers success. Jesus sat in Peter's boat, and His will, by a mysterious influence, drew the fish to the net. When Jesus is lifted up in His Church, His presence is the Church's power, the shout of a king is in the midst of her. "I, if I be lifted up, will draw all men unto me." Let us go out this morning on our work of soul fishing, looking up in faith, and around us in solemn anxiety. Let us toil till night comes, and we shall not labor in vain, for He who bids us let down the net, will fill it with fishes.

EVENING
"Praying in the Holy Spirit" — Jude 20.

MARK THE GRAND characteristic of true prayer, *"In the Holy Spirit."* The seed of acceptable devotion must come from heaven's storehouse. Only the prayer which comes from God can go to God. We must shoot the Lord's arrows back to Him. That desire which He writes upon our heart will move His heart and bring down a blessing, but the desires of the flesh have no power with Him.

Praying in the Holy Spirit is praying in fervency. Cold prayers ask the Lord not to hear them. Those who do not plead with fervency, plead not at all. As well speak of lukewarm fire as of lukewarm prayer; it is essential that it be red hot. It is praying with perseverance. The true suppliant gathers force as he proceeds, and grows more fervent when God delays to answer. The longer the gate is closed, the more vehemently does he use the knocker, and the longer the angel lingers the more resolved is he that he will never let him go without the blessing. Beautiful in God's sight is tearful, agonizing, unconquerable importunity. It means praying humbly, for the Holy Spirit never puffs us up with pride. It is His office to convince of sin, and so to bow us down in contrition and brokenness of spirit. We shall never sing, *"Glory in the highest,"* except we pray to God out of the depths; we cry, or we shall never behold glory in the highest. It is loving prayer. Prayer should be perfumed with love, saturated with love; love to our fellow saints, and love to Christ. Moreover, it must be a prayer full of faith. A man prevails only as he believes. The Holy Spirit is the author of faith, and strengthens it, so that we pray believing God's promise. Oh that this blessed combination of excellent graces, priceless and sweet as the spices of the merchant, might be fragrant within us because the Holy Spirit is in our hearts! Most blessed Comforter, exert Your mighty power within us, helping our infirmities in prayer.

MORNING
October 9

"Able to keep you from falling" — Jude 24.

IN SOME SENSE the path to heaven is very safe, but in other respects there is no road so dangerous. It is beset with difficulties. One false step, (and how easy it is to take that if grace be absent,) and down we go. What a slippery path is that which some of us have to tread! How many times have we to exclaim with the Psalmist, *"My feet were almost gone; my steps had well nigh slipped."* If we were strong, sure-footed mountaineers, this would not matter so much; but in ourselves, how weak we are! In the best roads we soon falter, in the smoothest paths we quickly stumble. These feeble knees of ours can scarcely support our tottering weight. A straw may throw us, and a pebble can wound us; we are mere children tremblingly taking our first steps in the walk of faith, our heavenly Father holds us by the arms or we should soon be down. Oh, if we are kept from falling, now must we bless the patient power which watches over us day by day! Think, how prone we are to sin, how apt to choose danger, how strong our tendency to cast ourselves down, and these reflections will make us sing more sweetly than we have ever done, *"Glory be to Him, who is able to keep us from falling."*

We have many foes who try to push us down. The road is rough and we are weak, but in addition to this, enemies lurk in ambush, who rush out when we least expect them, and labor to trip us up, or hurl us down the nearest precipice. Only an Almighty arm can preserve us from these unseen foes, who are seeking to destroy us. Such an arm is engaged for our defense. He is faithful that has promised, and He is able to keep us from falling, so that with a deep sense of our utter weakness, we may cherish a firm belief in our perfect safety, and say, with joyful confidence,

> Against me earth and hell combine,
> But on my side is power divine;
> Jesus is all, and He is mine!

EVENING

"But He did not answer her a word" — Matthew 15:23.

GENUINE SEEKERS WHO as yet have not obtained the blessing, may take comfort from the story before us. The Savior did not at once bestow the blessing, even though the woman had great faith in Him. He intended to give it, but He waited awhile. *"But He did not answer her a word."* Were not her prayers good? Never better in the world. Was not her case needy? Sorrowfully needy. Did she not feel her need sufficiently? She felt it overwhelmingly. Was she not earnest enough? She was intensely so. Had she no faith? She had such a high degree of it that even Jesus wondered, and said, *"Oh woman, great is your faith."* See then, although it is true that faith brings peace, yet it does not always bring it instantly.

There may be certain reasons calling for the trial of faith, rather than the reward of faith. Genuine faith may be in the soul like a hidden seed, but as yet it may not have budded and blossomed into joy and peace. A painful silence from the Savior is the grievous trial of many a seeking soul, but heavier still is the affliction of a harsh cutting reply such as this, *"It is not fit to take the children's bread, and to cast it to dogs."* Many in waiting upon the Lord find immediate delight, but this is not the case with all. Some, like the jailer, are in a moment turned from darkness to light, but others are plants of slower growth. A deeper sense of sin may be given to you instead of a sense of pardon, and in such a case you will have need of patience to bear the heavy blow. Ah! poor heart, though Christ beat and bruise you, or even slay you, trust Him. Though He should give you an angry word, believe in the love of His heart. Do not, I beseech you, give up seeking or trusting my Master, because you have not yet obtained the conscious joy which you long for. Cast yourself on Him, and with perseverance depend even where you cannot with rejoicing hope.

October 10   MORNING

"Faultless before the presence of His glory" — Jude 24.

RESOLVE IN YOUR mind that wondrous word *"faultless"*! We are far off from it now; but as our Lord never stops short of perfection in His work of love, we shall reach it one day. The Savior who will keep His people to the end, will also present them at last to Himself, as *"a glorious church, not having spot, or wrinkle, or any such thing, but holy and without blemish."* All the jewels in the Savior's crown are of the first water and without a single flaw. All the maids of honor who attend the Lamb's wife are pure virgins without spot or stain. But how will Jesus make us faultless? He will wash us from our sins in His own blood until, we are white and fair as God's purest angel; and we shall be clothed in His righteousness, that righteousness which makes the saint who wears it positively faultless; yes, perfect in the sight of God.

We shall be unblamable and without reproof even in His eyes. His law will not only have no charge against us, but it will be magnified in us. Moreover, the work of the Holy Spirit within us will be altogether complete. He will make us so perfectly holy, that we shall have no lingering tendency to sin. Judgment, memory, every power and passion shall be emancipated from the thralldom of evil. We shall be holy even as God is holy, and in His presence we shall dwell forever. Saints will not be out of place in heaven, their beauty will be as great as that of the place prepared for them. Oh the rapture of that hour when the everlasting doors shall be lifted up, and we, being made fit for the inheritance, shall dwell with the saints in light. Sin gone, Satan shut out, temptation past forever, and ourselves *"faultless"* before God, this will be heaven indeed! Let us be joyful now as we rehearse the song of eternal praise so soon to roll forth in full chorus from all the blood-washed host; let us copy David's exulting before the ark as a prelude to our ecstasies before the throne.

EVENING

"And I will deliver you out of the hand of the wicked, and I will redeem you out of the hand of the terrible" — Jeremiah 15:21.

NOTE THE GLORIOUS personality of the promise. I will, I will. The Lord Jehovah Himself interposes to deliver and redeem His people. He pledges Himself personally to rescue them. His own arm shall do it, that He may have the glory. Here is not a word said of any effort of our own which may be needed to assist the Lord. Neither our strength nor our weakness is taken into the account, but the lone I, like the sun in the heavens, shines out resplendent in all-sufficiency. Why then do we calculate our forces, and consult with flesh and blood to our grievous wounding? Jehovah has power enough without borrowing from our puny arm. Peace, you unbelieving thoughts, be still, and know that the Lord reigns.

Nor is there a hint concerning secondary means and causes. The Lord says nothing of friends and helpers. He undertakes the work alone, and feels no need of human arms to aid Him. Vain will be all our looking around to companions and relatives. They are broken reeds if we lean upon them; often unwilling when able, and unable when they are willing. Since the promise comes alone from God, it would be well to wait only upon Him; and when we do so, our expectation never fails us.

Who are the wicked that we should fear them? The Lord will utterly consume them; they are to be pitied rather than feared. As for terrible ones, they are only terrors to those who have no God to fly to, for when the Lord is on our side, whom shall we fear? If we run into sin to please the wicked, we have cause to be alarmed, but if we hold fast our integrity, the rage of tyrants shall be overruled for our good. When the fish swallowed Jonah, he found him a morsel which he could not digest; and when the world devours the church, it is glad to be rid of it again. In all times of fiery trial, in patience let us possess our souls.

MORNING
October 11

"Let us lift up our heart with our hands to God in the heavens" — *Lamentations 3:41.*

THE ACT OF prayer teaches us our unworthiness, which is a very salutary lesson for such proud beings as we are. If God gave us favors without constraining us to pray for them we should never know how poor we are, but a true prayer is an inventory of wants, a catalogue of necessities, a revelation of hidden poverty. While it is an application to divine wealth, it is a confession of human emptiness. The most healthy state of a Christian is to be always empty in self and constantly depending upon the Lord for supplies; to be always poor in self and rich in Jesus; weak as water personally, but mighty through God to do great exploits; and hence the use of prayer, because, while it adores God, it lays the creature where it should be, in the very dust.

Prayer is in itself, apart from the answer which it brings, a great benefit to the Christian. As the runner gains strength for the race by daily exercise, so for the great race of life we acquire energy by the hallowed labor of prayer. Prayer plumes the wings of God's young eaglets, that they may learn to mount above the clouds. Prayer girds the loins of God's warriors, and sends them forth to combat with their sinews braced and their muscles firm. An earnest pleader comes out of his closet, even as the sun arises from the chambers of the east, rejoicing like a strong man to run his race. Prayer is that uplifted hand of Moses which routs the Amalekites more than the sword of Joshua; it is the arrow shot from the chamber of the prophet foreboding defeat to the Syrians. Prayer girds human weakness with divine strength, turns human folly into heavenly wisdom, and gives to troubled mortals the peace of God. We know not what prayer cannot do! We thank you, great God, for the mercy-seat, a choice proof of your marvelous loving-kindness. Help us to use it aright throughout this day!

EVENING
"And whom He predestinated, these He also called" — *Romans 8:30.*

IN THE SECOND epistle to Timothy, first chapter, and ninth verse, are these words: *"Who has saved us, and called us with an holy calling."* Now, here is a touchstone by which we may try our calling. It is *"an holy calling, not according to our works, but according to His own purpose and grace."* This calling forbids all trust in our own doings, and conducts us to Christ alone for salvation, but it afterwards purges us from dead works to serve the living and true God. As He that has called you is holy, so must you be holy. If you are living in sin, you are not called, but if you are truly Christ's, you can say, Nothing pains me so much as sin; I desire to be rid of it; Lord, help me to be holy. Is this the panting of your heart? Is this the tenor of your life towards God, and His divine will?

Again, in Philippians, 3:13,14, we are told of *"The high calling of God in Christ Jesus."* Is then your calling a high calling? Has it ennobled your heart, and set it upon heavenly things? Has it elevated your hopes, your tastes, your desires? Has it upraised the constant tenor of your life, so that you spend it with God and for God?

Another test we find in Hebrews 3:1: *"Partakers of the heavenly calling."* Heavenly calling means a call from heaven. If man alone call you; you are uncalled. Is your calling of God? Is it a call to heaven as well as from heaven? Unless you are a stranger here, and heaven your home, you have not been called with a heavenly calling; for those who have been so called, declare that they look for a city which has foundations, whose builder and maker is God, and they themselves are strangers and pilgrims upon the earth. Is your calling thus holy, high, heavenly? Then, beloved, you have been called of God, for such is the calling wherewith God does call His people.

October 12   MORNING

"I will meditate on Your commandments" — *Psalm 119:15.*

THERE ARE TIMES when solitude is better than society, and silence is wiser than speech. We should be better Christians if we were more alone, waiting upon God, and gathering through meditation on His Word spiritual strength for labor in His service. We ought to muse upon the things of God, because we thus get the real nutriment out of them. Truth is something like the cluster of the vine; if we would have wine from it, we must bruise it; we must press and squeeze it many times. The bruisers' feet must come down joyfully upon the bunches, or else the juice will not flow; and they must well tread the grapes, or else much of the precious liquid will be wasted. So we must, by meditation, tread the clusters of truth, if we would get the wine of consolation from it.

Our bodies are not supported by merely taking food into the mouth, but the process which really supplies the muscle, and the nerve, and the sinew, and the bone, is the process of digestion. It is by digestion that the outward food becomes assimilated with the inner life. Our souls are not nourished merely by listening awhile to this, and then to that, and then to the other part of divine truth. Hearing, reading, marking, and learning, all require inwardly digesting to complete their usefulness, and the inward digesting of the truth lies for the most part in meditating upon it. Why is it that some Christians, although they hear many sermons, make but slow advances in the divine life? Because they neglect their closets, and do not thoughtfully meditate on God's Word. They love the wheat, but they do not grind it; they would have the corn, but they will not go forth into the fields to gather it; the fruit hangs upon the tree, but they will not pluck it; the water flows at their feet, but they will not stoop to drink it. From such folly deliver us, Oh Lord, and be this our resolve this morning, *"I will meditate in Your precepts."*

EVENING

"But the Comforter, the Holy Spirit" — *John 14:26.*

THIS AGE IS peculiarly the dispensation of the Holy Spirit, in which Jesus cheers us, not by His personal presence, as He shall do by-and-by, but by the indwelling and constant abiding of the Holy Spirit, who is evermore the Comforter of the church. It is His office to console the hearts of God's people. He convinces of sin; He illuminates and instructs; but still the main part of His work lies in making glad the hearts of the renewed, in confirming the weak, and lifting up all those that be bowed down. He does this by revealing Jesus to them. The Holy Spirit consoles, but Christ is the consolation. If we may use the figure, the Holy Spirit is the Physician, but Jesus is the medicine. He heals the wound, but it is by applying the holy ointment of Christ's name and grace. He takes not of His own things, but of the things of Christ. So if we give to the Holy Spirit the Greek name of Paraclete, as we sometimes do, then our heart confers on our blessed Lord Jesus the title of the Paraclesis. If the one be the Comforter, the other is the Comfort.

Now, with such rich provision for his need, why should the Christian be sad and desponding? The Holy Spirit has graciously engaged to be Your Comforter; do you imagine, Oh you weak and trembling believer, that He will be negligent of His sacred trust? Can you suppose that He has undertaken what He cannot or will not perform? If it be His special work to strengthen you, and to comfort you, do you suppose He has forgotten His business, or that He will fail in the loving office which He sustains towards you? No, think not so hardly of the tender and blessed Spirit whose name is *"the Comforter."* He delights to give the oil of joy for mourning, and the garment of praise for the spirit of heaviness. Trust in Him and He will surely comfort you till the house of mourning is closed forever, and the marriage feast has begun.

MORNING   October 13

"For godly sorrow works repentance" — *2 Corinthians 7:10.*

GENUINE, SPIRITUAL mourning for sin is the work of the Spirit of God. Repentance is too choice a flower to grow in nature's garden. Pearls grow naturally in oysters, but penitence never shows itself in sinners except divine grace works it in them. If you have one particle of real hatred for sin, God must have given it you, for human nature's thorns never produced a single fig. *"That which is born of the flesh is flesh."*

True repentance has a distinct reference to the Savior. When we repent of sin, we must have one eye upon sin and another upon the cross, or it will be better still if we fix both our eyes upon Christ and see our transgressions only, in the light of His love.

True sorrow for sin is eminently practical. No man may say he hates sin, if he lives in it. Repentance makes us see the evil of sin, not merely as a theory, but experimentally, as a burnt child dreads fire. We shall be as much afraid of it, as a man who has lately been stopped and robbed is afraid of the thief upon the highway; and we shall shun it in everything; not in great things only, but in little things, as men shun little vipers as well as great snakes. True mourning for sin will make us very jealous over our tongue, lest it should say a wrong word. We shall be very watchful over our daily actions, lest in anything we offend. And each night we shall close the day with painful confessions of shortcoming, and each morning awaken with anxious prayers, that this day God would hold us up that we may not sin against Him.

Sincere repentance is continual. Believers repent until their dying day. This dropping well is not intermittent. Every other sorrow yields to time, but this dear sorrow grows with our growth, and it is so sweet a bitter, that we thank God we are permitted to enjoy and to suffer it until we enter our eternal rest.

EVENING

"Love is strong as death" — *Song of Solomon 8:6.*

WHOSE LOVE CAN this be which is as mighty as the conqueror of monarchs, the destroyer of the human race? Would it not sound like satire if it were applied to my poor, weak, and scarcely living love to Jesus my Lord? I do love Him, and perhaps by His grace, I could even die for Him, but as for my love in itself, it can scarcely endure a scoffing jest, much less a cruel death. Surely it is my Beloved's love which is here spoken of, the love of Jesus, the matchless lover of souls. His love was indeed stronger than the most terrible death, for it endured the trial of the cross triumphantly. It was a lingering death, but love survived the torment; a shameful death, but love despised the shame; a penal death, but love bore our iniquities; a forsaken, lonely death, from which the eternal Father hid His face, but love endured the curse, and gloried over all. Never such love, never such death. It was a desperate duel, but love bore the palm. What then, my heart? Have you no emotions excited within you at the contemplation of such heavenly affections? Yes, my Lord, I long, I pant to feel Your love flaming like a furnace within me. Come You Yourself and excite the ardor of my spirit.

> For every drop of crimson blood
> Thus shed to make me live
> Oh wherefore, wherefore have not I
> A thousand lives to give?

Why should I despair of loving Jesus with a love as strong as death? He deserves it; I desire it. The martyrs felt such love, and they were but flesh and blood, then why not I? They mourned their weakness, and yet out of weakness were made strong. Grace gave them all their unflinching constancy; there is the same grace for me. Jesus, lover of my soul, shed abroad such love, even Your love in my heart, this evening.

October 14   MORNING

"I also count all things to be but loss because of the excellency of the knowledge of Christ Jesus my Lord" — Philippians 3:8.

SPIRITUAL KNOWLEDGE OF Christ will be a personal knowledge. I cannot know Jesus through another person's acquaintance with Him. No, I must know Him myself; I must know Him on my own account. It will be an intelligent knowledge. I must know Him, not as the visionary dreams of Him, but as the Word reveals Him. I must know His natures, divine and human. I must know His offices, His attributes, His works, His shame, His glory. I must meditate upon Him until I *"comprehend with all saints what is the breadth, and length, and depth, and height; and know the love of Christ, which passes knowledge."*

It will be an affectionate knowledge of Him; indeed, if I know Him at all, I must love Him. An ounce of heart knowledge is worth a ton of head learning. Our knowledge of Him will be a satisfying knowledge. When I know my Savior, my mind will be full to the brim. I shall feel that I have that which my spirit panted after. This is that bread whereof if a man eat he shall never hunger. At the same time it will be an exciting knowledge; the more I know of my Beloved, the more I shall want to know. The higher I climb the loftier will be the summits which invite my eager footsteps. I shall want the more as I get the more. Like the miser's treasure, my gold will make me covet more.

To conclude; this knowledge of Christ Jesus will be a most happy one; in fact, so elevating, that sometimes it will completely bear me up above all trials, and doubts, and sorrows; and it will, while I enjoy it, make me something more than "Man that is born of woman, who is of few days, and full of trouble;" for it will fling about me the immortality of the ever living Savior, and gird me with the golden belt of His eternal joy. Come, my soul, sit at Jesus' feet and learn of Him all this day.

EVENING

"And be not conformed to this world" — Romans 12:2.

IF A CHRISTIAN can by possibility be saved while he conforms to this world, at any rate it must be so as by fire. Such a bare salvation is almost as much to be dreaded as desired. Reader, would you wish to leave this world in the darkness of a desponding death bed, and enter heaven as a shipwrecked mariner climbs the rocks of his native country? Then be worldly; be mixed up with the lovers of Mammon, and refuse to go outside the camp bearing Christ's reproach. But would you have a heaven below as well as a heaven above? Would you comprehend with all saints what are the heights and depths, and know the love of Christ which passes knowledge? Would you receive an abundant entrance into the joy of your Lord? Then come out from among them, and be you separate, and touch not the unclean thing. Would you attain the full assurance of faith? You cannot gain it while you commune with sinners. Would you flame with vehement love? Your love will be damped by the drenching of godless society.

You cannot become a great Christian; you may be a babe in grace, but you never can be a perfect man in Christ Jesus while you yield yourself to the worldly maxims and modes of business of men of the world. It is ill for an heir of heaven to be a great friend with the heirs of hell: *"Do you not know that the friendship of the world is enmity with God? Whoever, then, purposes to be a friend of the world is shown to be an enemy of God"* (James 4:4). It has a bad look when a courtier is too intimate with his king's enemies. Even small inconsistencies are dangerous. Little thorns make great blisters, little moths destroy fine garments, and little frivolities and little rogueries will rob religion of a thousand joys. Oh professor, too little separated from sinners, you know not what you lose by your conformity to the world. It cuts the tendons of your strength, and makes you creep where you ought to run. Then, for your own comfort's sake, and for the sake of your growth in grace, if you be a Christian, be a Christian, and be a marked and distinct one.

MORNING October 15

"But who can endure the day of His coming?" — *Malachi 3:2.*

HIS FIRST COMING was without external pomp or show of power, and yet in truth there were few who could abide its testing might. Herod and all Jerusalem with him were stirred at the news of the wondrous birth. Those who supposed themselves to be waiting for Him, showed the fallacy of their professions by rejecting Him when He came. His life on earth was a winnowing fan, which tried the great heap of religious profession, and few enough could abide the process. But what will His second advent be? What sinner can endure to think of it? *"He shall smite the earth with the rod of His mouth, and with the breath of His lips shall He slay the wicked."* When in His humiliation He did but say to the soldiers, *"I am He,"* they fell backward; what will be the terror of His enemies when He shall more fully reveal Himself as the *"I AM?"*

His death shook earth and darkened heaven, what shall be the dreadful splendor of that day in which as the living Savior, He shall summon the living and dead before Him? Oh that the terrors of the Lord would persuade men to forsake their sins and kiss the Son lest He be angry! Though a lamb, He is yet the lion of the tribe of Judah, tearing the prey in pieces. And though He breaks not the bruised reed, yet will He break His enemies with a rod of iron, and dash them in pieces like a potter's vessel. None of His foes shall bear up before the tempest of His wrath, or hide themselves from the sweeping hail of His indignation; but His beloved blood-washed people look for His appearing with joy, and hope to abide it without fear. To them He sits as a refiner even now, and when He has tried them they shall come forth as gold.

Let us search ourselves this morning and make our calling and election sure, so that the coming of the Lord may cause no dark foreboding in our mind. Oh for grace to cast away all hypocrisy, and to be found of Him sincere and without rebuke in the day of His appearing.

EVENING

"But the firstling of an ass you shall redeem with a lamb. And if you do not redeem it, then you shall break its neck" — *Exodus 34:20.*

EVERY FIRSTBORN creature must be the Lord's, but since the ass was unclean, it could not be presented in sacrifice. What then? Should it be allowed to go free from the universal law? By no means. God admits of no exceptions. The ass is His due, but He will not accept it; He will not abate the claim, but yet He cannot be pleased with the victim. No way of escape remained but redemption; the creature must be saved by the substitution of a lamb in its place; or if not redeemed, it must die. My soul, here is a lesson for you. That unclean animal is yourself; you are justly the property of the Lord who made you and preserves you, but you are so sinful that God will not, cannot, accept you; and it has come to this, the Lamb of God must stand in your stead, or you must die eternally. Let all the world know of your gratitude to that spotless Lamb who has already bled for you, and so redeemed you from the fatal curse of the law.

Must it not sometimes have been a question with the Israelite which should die, the ass or the lamb? Would not the good man pause to estimate and compare? Assuredly there was no comparison between the value of the soul of man and the life of the Lord Jesus, and yet the Lamb dies, and man, the ass, is spared. Believing soul, admire the boundless love of God to you and others of the human race. Worms are bought with the blood of the Son of the Highest! Dust and ashes redeemed with a price far above silver and gold! What a doom had been mine had not plenteous redemption been found! The breaking of the neck of the ass was but a momentary penalty, but who shall measure the wrath to come to which no limit can be imagined? Inestimably dear is the glorious Lamb who has redeemed us from such a doom.

October 16   MORNING

"Jesus said to them, Come and eat" — John 21:12.

IN THESE WORDS the believer is invited to a holy nearness to Jesus. "Come and dine," implies the same table, the same meat; yes, and sometimes it means to sit side by side, and lean our head upon the Savior's bosom. It is being brought into the banqueting-house, where waves the banner of redeeming love. "Come and dine," gives us a vision of union with Jesus, because the only food that we can feast upon when we dine with Jesus is Himself. Oh, what union is this! It is a depth which reason cannot fathom, that we thus feed upon Jesus. *"He that eats My flesh, and drinks My blood, dwells in Me, and I in him."* It is also an invitation to enjoy fellowship with the saints. Christians may differ on a variety of points, but they have all one spiritual appetite; and if we cannot all feel alike, we can all feed alike on the bread of life sent down from heaven. At the table of fellowship with Jesus we are one bread and one cup. As the loving cup goes around we pledge one another heartily therein. Get nearer to Jesus, and you will find yourself linked more and more in spirit to all who are like yourself, supported by the same heavenly manna. If we were more near to Jesus we should be more near to one another.

We likewise see in these words the source of strength for every Christian. To look at Christ is to live, but for strength to serve Him you must "come and dine." We labor under much unnecessary weakness on account of neglecting this precept of the Master. We none of us need to put ourselves on low diet; on the contrary, we should fatten on the marrow and fatness of the gospel that we may accumulate strength therein, and urge every power to its full tension in the Master's service. Thus, then, if you would realize nearness to Jesus, union with Jesus, love to His people and strength from Jesus, "come and dine" with Him by faith.

EVENING
"For with You is the fountain of life" — Psalm 36:9.

THERE ARE TIMES in our spiritual experience when human counsel, or sympathy, or religious ordinances, fail to comfort or help us. Why does our gracious God permit this? Perhaps it is because we have been living too much without Him, and He therefore takes away everything upon which we have been in the habit of depending, that He may drive us to Himself. It is a blessed thing to live at the fountain head. While our skin-bottles are full, we are content, like Hagar and Ishmael, to go into the wilderness. But when those are dry, nothing will serve us but *"You, the God who sees me."*

We are like the prodigal, we feed at the swine-troughs and forget our Father's house. Remember, we can make swine-troughs and husks even out of the forms of religion; they are blessed things, but we may put them in God's place, and then they are of no value. Anything becomes an idol when it keeps us away from God; even the brazen serpent is to be despised as *"Nehushtan,"* if we worship it instead of God. The prodigal was never safer than when he was driven to his father's bosom, because he could find sustenance nowhere else. Our Lord favors us with a famine in the land that it may make us seek after Himself the more. The best position for a Christian is living wholly and directly on God's grace, still abiding where he stood at first, *"Having nothing, and yet possessing all things."*

Let us never for a moment think that our standing is in our sanctification, our mortification, our graces, or our feelings, but know that because Christ offered a full atonement, therefore we are saved; for we are complete in Him. Having nothing of our own to trust to, but resting upon the merits of Jesus; His passion and holy life furnish us with the only sure ground of confidence. Beloved, when we are brought to a thirsting condition, we are sure to turn to the fountain of life with eagerness.

MORNING   October 17

"And David said in his heart, I shall now perish one day by the hand of Saul" — 1 Samuel 27:1

THE THOUGHT OF David's heart at this time was a false thought, because he certainly had no ground for thinking that God's anointing him by Samuel was intended to be left as an empty unmeaning act. On no one occasion had the Lord deserted His servant; he had been placed in perilous positions very often, but not one instance had occurred in which divine interposition had not delivered him. The trials to which he had been exposed had been varied; they had not assumed one form only, but many. Yet in every case He who sent the trial had also graciously ordained a way of escape. David could not put his finger upon any entry in his diary, and say of it, Here is evidence that the Lord will forsake me, For the entire tenor of his past life proved the very reverse. He should have argued from what God had done for him, that God would be his defender still.

But is it not just in the same way that we doubt God's help? Is it not mistrust without a cause? Have we ever had the shadow of a reason to doubt our Father's goodness? Have not His loving-kindnesses been marvelous? Has He once failed to justify our trust? Ah, no! our God has not left us at any time. We have had dark nights, but the star of love has shone forth amid the blackness; we have been in stern conflicts, but over our head He has held aloft the shield of our defense. We have gone through many trials, but never to our detriment, always to our advantage; and the conclusion from our past experience is, that He who has been with us in six troubles, will not forsake us in the seventh. What we have known of our faithful God, proves that He will keep us to the end. Let us not, then, reason contrary to evidence. How can we ever be so ungenerous as to doubt our God? Lord, throw down the Jezebel of our unbelief, and let the dogs devour it.

EVENING
"He shall gather the lambs with His arm" — Isaiah 40:11.

OUR GOOD SHEPHERD has in His flock a variety of experiences, some are strong in the Lord, and others are weak in faith, but He is impartial in His care for all His sheep, and the weakest lamb is as dear to Him as the most advanced of the flock. Lambs are accustomed to lag behind, prone to wander, and apt to grow weary, but from all the danger of these infirmities the Shepherd protects them with His arm of power. He finds new-born souls, like young lambs, ready to perish; He nourishes them till life becomes vigorous. He finds weak minds ready to faint and die; He consoles them and renews their strength. All the little ones He gathers, for it is not the will of our heavenly Father that one of them should perish. What a quick eye He must have to see them all! What a tender heart to care for them all! What a far-reaching and potent arm, to gather them all! In His lifetime on earth He was a great gatherer of the weaker sort, and now that He dwells in heaven, His loving heart yearns towards the meek and contrite, the timid and feeble, and fearful and fainting here below.

How gently did He gather me to Himself, to His truth, to His blood, to His love, to His church! With what effectual grace did He compel me to come to Himself! Since first converted, how frequently has He restored me from my wanderings, and once again folded me within the circle of His everlasting arm! The best of all is, that He does it all Himself personally, not delegating the task of love, but condescending Himself to rescue and preserve His most unworthy servant. How shall I love Him enough or serve Him worthily? I would fain make His name great unto the ends of the earth, but what can my feebleness do for Him? Great Shepherd, add to Your mercies this one other, a heart to love You more truly as I ought.

October 18 MORNING

"And Your paths drop fatness" — Psalm 65:11.

MANY ARE *"the paths of the Lord"* which *"drop fatness,"* but a special one is the path of prayer. No believer, who is much in the closet, will have need to cry, "My leanness, my leanness; woe unto me." Starving souls live at a distance from the mercy-seat, and become like the parched fields in times of drought. Prevalence with God in wrestling prayer is sure to make the believer strong, if not happy. The nearest place to the gate of heaven is the throne of the heavenly grace. Much alone, and you will have much assurance; little alone with Jesus, your religion will be shallow, polluted with many doubts and fears, and not sparkling with the joy of the Lord. Since the soul-enriching path of prayer is open to the very weakest saint; since no high attainments are required; since you are not bidden to come because you are an advanced saint, but freely invited if you be a saint at all; see to it, dear reader, that you are often in the way of private devotion. Be much on your knees, for so Elijah drew the rain upon famished Israel's fields.

There is another special path dropping with fatness to those who walk therein, it is the secret walk of communion. Oh! the delights of fellowship with Jesus! Earth has no words which can set forth the holy calm of a soul leaning on Jesus' bosom. Few Christians understand it. They live in the lowlands and seldom climb to the top of Nebo; they live in the outer court, they enter not the holy place; they take not up the privilege of priesthood. At a distance they see the sacrifice, but they sit not down with the priest to eat thereof, and to enjoy the fat of the burnt offering. But, reader, sit ever under the shadow of Jesus; come up to that palm tree, and take hold of the branches thereof; let your beloved be unto you as the apple.tree among the trees of the wood, and you shall be satisfied as with marrow and fatness. Oh Jesus, visit us with Your salvation!

EVENING

"Behold, to obey is better than sacrifice!" — 1 Samuel 15:22.

SAUL HAD BEEN commanded to slay utterly all the Amalekites and their cattle. Instead of doing so, he preserved the king, and allowed his people to take the best of the oxen and of the sheep. When called to account for this, he declared that he did it with a view of offering sacrifice to God; but Samuel met him at once with the assurance that sacrifices were no excuse for an act of direct rebellion.

The sentence before us is worthy to be printed in letters of gold, and to be hung up before the eyes of the present idolatrous generation, who are very fond of the fineries of will-worship, but utterly neglect the laws of God. Be it ever in your remembrance, that to keep strictly in the path of your Savior's command is better than any outward form of religion; and to hearken to His precept with an attentive ear is better than to bring the fat of rams, or any other precious thing to lay upon His altar. If you are failing to keep the least of Christ's commands to His disciples, I pray you be disobedient no longer. All the pretensions you make of attachment to your Master, and all the devout actions which you may perform, are no recompense for disobedience. *"To obey,"* even in the slightest and smallest thing, *"is better than sacrifice,"* however pompous. Talk not of Gregorian chants, sumptuous robes, incense, and banners. The first thing which God requires of His child is obedience; and though you should give your body to be burned, and all your goods to feed the poor, yet if you do not hearken to the Lord's precepts, all your formalities shall profit you nothing. It is a blessed thing to be teachable as a little child, but it is a much more blessed thing when one has been taught the lesson, to carry it out to the letter. How many adorn their temples and decorate their priests, but refuse to obey the word of the Lord! My soul, come not into their secret.

MORNING   October 19

"Babes in Christ!" — *1 Corinthians 3:1.*

ARE YOU MOURNING, believer, because you are so weak in the divine life; because your faith is so little, your love so feeble? Cheer up, for you have cause for gratitude. Remember that in some things you are equal to the greatest and most full-grown Christian. You are as much bought with blood as he is. You are as much an adopted child of God as any other believer. An infant is as truly a child of its parents as is the full-grown man. You are as completely justified, for your justification is not a thing of degrees; your little faith has made you clean every whit.

You have as much right to the precious things of the covenant as the most advanced believers, for your right to covenant mercies lies not in your growth, but in the covenant itself; and your faith in Jesus is not the measure, but the token of your inheritance in Him. You are as rich as the richest, if not in enjoyment, yet in real possession. The smallest star that gleams is set in heaven; the faintest ray of light has affinity with the great orb of day. In the family register of glory the small and the great are written with the same pen.

You are as dear to your Father's heart as the greatest in the family. Jesus is very tender over you. You are like the smoking wick; a rougher spirit would say, put out that smoking wick, it fills the room with an offensive odor! But the smoking wick He will not quench. You are like a bruised reed; and any less tender hand than that of the Chief Musician would tread upon you or throw you away, but He will never break the bruised reed. Instead of being downcast by reason of what you are, you should triumph in Christ. Am I but little in Israel? Yet in Christ I am made to sit in heavenly places. Am I poor in faith? Still in Jesus I am heir of all things. Though less then nothing I can boast, and vanity confess, yet, if the root of the matter be in me I will rejoice in the Lord, and glory in the God of my salvation.

EVENING

"God my Maker who gives songs in the night" — *Job 35:10.*

ANY MAN CAN sing in the day. When the cup is full, man draws inspiration from it. When wealth rolls in abundance around him, any man can praise the God who gives a plenteous harvest or sends home a loaded argosy. It is easy enough for an Aeolian harp to whisper music when the winds blow; the difficulty is for music to swell forth when no wind is stirring. It is easy to sing when we can read the notes by daylight; but he is skilful who sings when there is not a ray of light to read by; who sings from his heart. No man can make a song in the night of himself; he may attempt it, but he will find that a song in the night must be divinely inspired. Let all things go well, I can weave songs, fashioning them wherever I go out of the flowers that grow upon my path; but put me in a desert, where no green thing grows, and wherewith shall I frame a hymn of praise to God? How shall a mortal man make a crown for the Lord where no jewels are? Let but this voice be clear, and this body full of health, and I can sing God's praise: Silence my tongue, lay me upon the bed of languishing, and how shall I then chant God's high praises, unless He Himself give me the song?

No, it is not in man's power to sing when all is adverse, unless an altar-coal shall touch his lip. It was a divine song, which Habakkuk sang, when in the night he said, *"Although the fig-tree shall not blossom, neither shall fruit be in the vines; the labor of the olive shall fail, and the fields shall yield no food; the flock shall be cut off from the fold, and there shall be no herd in the stalls: yet I will rejoice in the Lord, I will joy in the God of my salvation."* Then, since our Maker gives songs in the night, let us wait upon Him for the music. Oh You chief musician, let us not remain without song because affliction is upon us, but tune our lips to the melody of thanksgiving.

October 20　　　　　　　MORNING

"Grow up into Him in all things" — Ephesians 4:15.

 MANY CHRISTIANS REMAIN stunted and dwarfed in spiritual things, so as to present the same appearance year after year. No up-springing of advanced and refined feeling is manifest in them. They exist but do not *"grow up into Him in all things."* But should we rest content with being in the "green blade," when we might advance to "the ear," and eventually ripen into the "full corn in the ear?" Should we be satisfied to believe in Christ, and to say, "I am safe," without wishing to know in our own experience more of the fullness which is to be found in Him. It should not be so; we should, as good traders in heaven's market, covet to be enriched in the knowledge of Jesus. It is all very well to keep other men's vineyards, but we must not neglect our own spiritual growth and ripening. Why should it always be winter time in our hearts? We must have our seed time, it is true, but Oh for a spring time - yes, a summer season, which shall give promise of an early harvest.

 If we would ripen in grace, we must live near to Jesus, in His presence, ripened by the sunshine of His smiles. We must hold sweet communion with Him. We must leave the distant view of His face and come near, as John did, and pillow our head on His breast; then shall we find ourselves advancing in holiness, in love, in faith, in hope; yes, in every precious gift. The sun rises first on mountain-tops and gilds them with his light, and presents one of the most charming sights to the eye of the traveler. So is it one of the most delightful contemplations in the world to mark the glow of the Spirit's light on the head of some saint, who has risen up in spiritual stature, like Saul, above his fellows, till, like a mighty Alp, snow-capped, he reflects first among the chosen, the beams of the Sun of Righteousness, and bears the sheen of His effulgence high aloft for all to see, and seeing it, to glorify His Father which is in heaven.

EVENING

"Do not keep back" — Isaiah 43:6.

 ALTHOUGH THIS MESSAGE was sent to the south, and referred to the seed of Israel, it may profitably be a summons to ourselves. Backward we are naturally to all good things, and it is a lesson of grace to learn to go forward in the ways of God. Reader, are you unconverted, but do you desire to trust in the Lord Jesus? Then do not keep back. Love invites you, the promises secure you success, the precious blood prepares the way. Let not sins or fears hinder you, but come to Jesus just as you are. Do you long to pray? Would you pour out your heart before the Lord? Do not keep back. The mercy-seat is prepared for such as need mercy; a sinner's cries will prevail with God. You are invited, no, you are commanded to pray, come therefore with boldness to the throne of grace.

 Dear friend, are you already saved? Then do not keep back from union with the Lord's people. Neglect not the ordinances of baptism and the Lord's Supper. You may be of a timid disposition, but you must strive against it, lest it lead you into disobedience. There is a sweet promise made to those who confess Christ; by no means miss it, lest you come under the condemnation of those who deny Him. If you have talents do not keep back from using them. Hoard not your wealth, waste not your time; let not your abilities rust or your influence be unused. Jesus did not keep back, imitate Him by being foremost in self-denials and self-sacrifices. Do not keep back from close communion with God, from boldly appropriating covenant blessings, from advancing in the divine life, from prying into the precious mysteries of the love of Christ. Neither, beloved friend, be guilty of keeping others back by your coldness, harshness, or suspicions. For Jesus' sake go forward yourself, and encourage others to do the like. Hell and the bands of superstition and infidelity are forward to the fight. Oh soldiers of the cross, do not keep back.

MORNING   October 21

"For the love of Christ presses us on every side" — 2 Corinthians 5:14.

HOW MUCH DO you owe unto my Lord? Has He ever done anything for you? Has He forgiven your sins? Has He covered you with a robe of righteousness? Has He set your feet upon a rock? Has He established your goings? Has He prepared heaven for you? Has He prepared you for heaven? Has He written your name in His book of life? Has He given you countless blessings? Has He laid up for you a store of mercies, which eye has not seen nor ear heard? Then do something for Jesus worthy of His love. Give not a mere wordy offering to a dying Redeemer. How will you feel when your Master comes, if you have to confess that you did nothing for Him, but kept your love shut up, like a stagnant pool, neither flowing forth to His poor or to His work. What do men think of a love which never shows itself in action? Why, they say, "Open rebuke is better than secret love." Who will accept a love so weak that it does not actuate you to a single deed of self-denial, of generosity, of heroism, or zeal! Think how He has loved you, and given Himself for you! Do you know the power of that love? Then let it be like a rushing mighty wind to your soul to sweep out the clouds of your worldliness, and clear away the mists of sin.

"For the sake of Christ" be this the tongue of fire that shall sit upon you. *"For the sake of Christ"* be this the divine rapture, the heavenly afflatus to bear you aloft from earth, the divine spirit that shall make you bold as lions and swift as eagles in your Lord's service. Love should give wings to the feet of service, and strength to the arms of labor. Fixed on God with a constancy that is not to be shaken, resolute to honor Him with a determination that is not to be turned aside, and pressing on with an ardor never to be wearied, let us manifest the constraints of love to Jesus. May the divine loadstone draw us heavenward towards itself!

EVENING

"Why are you fearful? And why do doubts come into your heart?" — Luke 24:38.

"WHY WILL YOU SAY, Oh Jacob, and speak, Oh Israel, My way is hidden from the Lord, and my judgment is passed over from my God?" (Isa. 40:27). The Lord cares for all things, and the meanest creatures share in His universal providence, but His particular providence is over His saints. *"The angel of the Lord encamps around about them that fear Him." "Precious shall their blood be in His sight." "Precious in the sight of the Lord is the death of His saints." "We know that all things work together for good to them that love God, to them that are the called according to His purpose."* Let the fact that, while He is the Preserver of all men, He is especially the Savior of the ones that believe, cheer and comfort you. You are His peculiar care; His regal treasure which He guards as the apple of His eye; His vineyard over which He watches day and night. *"The very hairs of your head are all numbered."* Let the thought of His special love to you be a spiritual pain-killer, a dear quietus to your woe: *"I will never leave you, nor forsake you."* God says that as much to you as to any saint of old. "Fear not, I am your shield, and your exceeding great reward."

We lose much consolation by the habit of reading His promises for the whole church, instead of taking them directly home to ourselves. Believer, grasp the divine word with a personal, appropriating faith. Think that you hear Jesus say, *"I have prayed for you that your faith fail not."* Think you see Him walking on the waters of your trouble, for He is there, and He is saying, *"Fear not, it is I; be not afraid."* Oh, those sweet words of Christ! May the Holy Spirit make you feel them as spoken to you; forget others for awhile; accept the voice of Jesus as addressed to you, and say, Jesus whispers consolation; I cannot refuse it; I will sit under His shadow with great delight.

October 22   MORNING

"I will love them freely" — Hosea 14:4.

THIS SENTENCE IS a body of divinity in miniature. He who understands its meaning is a theologian, and he who can dive into its fullness is a true master in Israel. It is a condensation of the glorious message of salvation which was delivered to us in Christ Jesus our Redeemer. The sense hinges upon the word "freely." This is the glorious, the suitable, the divine way by which love streams from heaven to earth; a spontaneous love flowing forth to those who neither deserved it, purchased it, nor sought after it. It is, indeed, the only way in which God can love such as we are.

The text is a death-blow to all sorts of fitness: *"I will love them freely."* Now, if there were any fitness necessary in us, then He would not love us freely, at least, this would be a mitigation and a drawback to the freeness of it. But it stands, "I will love you freely." We complain, Lord, my heart is so hard; but He replies, *"I will love you freely."* But I do not feel my need of Christ as I could wish. He answers, I will not love you because you feel your need; *"I will love you freely."* But I do not feel that softening of spirit which I could desire. Remember, the softening of spirit is not a condition, for there are no conditions; the covenant of grace has no conditionality whatever. Without any fitness we may venture upon the promise of God which was made to us in Christ Jesus, when He said, *"He that believes on Him is not condemned."*

It is blessed to know that the grace of God is free to us at all times, without preparation, without fitness, without money, and without price! *"I will love them freely."* These words invite backsliders to return: indeed, the text was especially written for such: *"I will heal their backsliding; I will love them freely."* Backslider! surely the generosity of the promise will at once break your heart, and you will return, and seek your injured Father's face.

EVENING
"He will take of Mine and will tell it to you" — John 16:15.

THERE ARE TIMES when all the promises and doctrines of the Bible are of no avail, unless a gracious hand shall apply them to us. We are thirsty, but too faint to crawl to the water-brook. When a soldier is wounded in battle it is of little use for him to know that there are those at the hospital who can bind up his wounds, and medicines there to ease all the pains which he now suffers; what he needs is to be carried there, and to have the remedies applied. It is thus with our souls, and to meet this need there is one, even the Spirit of truth, who takes of the things of Jesus, and applies them to us. Think not that Christ has placed His joys on heavenly shelves that we may climb up to them for ourselves, but He draws near, and sheds His peace abroad in our hearts.

Oh Christian, if you are tonight laboring under deep distresses, your Father does not give you promises and then leave you to draw them up from the word like buckets from a well, but the promises He has written in the word He will write anew on your heart. He will manifest His love to you, and by His blessed Spirit, dispel your cares and troubles. Be it known unto you, Oh mourner, that it is God's prerogative to wipe every tear from the eye of His people. The good Samaritan did not say, Here is the wine, and here is the oil for you; he actually poured in the oil and the wine. So Jesus not only gives you the sweet wine of the promise, but holds the golden chalice to your lips, and pours the life-blood into your mouth. The poor, sick, way-worn pilgrim is not merely strengthened to walk, but he is borne on eagles' wings. Glorious gospel! which provides everything for the helpless, which draws near to us when we cannot reach after it. It brings us grace before we seek for grace! Here is as much glory in the giving as in the gift. Happy people who have the Holy Spirit to bring Jesus to them.

MORNING   October 23

"Are you also wishing to go away?" — John 6:67.

MANY HAVE FORSAKEN Christ, and have walked no more with Him; but what reason have you to make a change? Has there been any reason for it in the past? Has not Jesus proved Himself all-sufficient? He appeals to you this morning: "Have I been a wilderness unto you?" When your soul has simply trusted Jesus, have you ever been confounded? Have you not up till now found your Lord to be a compassionate and generous friend to you, and has not simple faith in Him given you all the peace your spirit could desire? Can you so much as dream of a better friend than He has been to you? Then change not the old and tried for new and false.

As for the present, can that compel you to leave Christ? When we are hard beset with this world, or with the severer trials within the Church, we find it a most blessed thing to pillow our head upon the bosom of our Savior. This is the joy we have today that we are saved in Him; and if this joy be satisfying, wherefore should we think of changing? Who barters gold for dross? We will not forswear the sun till we find a better light, nor leave our Lord until a brighter lover shall appear; and, since this can never be, we will hold Him with a grasp immortal, and bind His name as a seal upon our arm.

As for the future, can you suggest anything which can arise that shall render it necessary for you to mutiny, or desert the old flag to serve under another captain? We think not. If life be long, He changes not. If we are poor, what better than to have Christ who can make us rich? When we are sick, what more do we want than Jesus to make our bed in our sickness? When we die, is it not written that *"neither death, nor life, nor things present, nor things to come, shall be able to separate us from the love of God, which is in Christ Jesus our Lord!"* We say with Peter, *"Lord, to whom shall we go?"*

EVENING

"Why do you sleep? Get up and pray, so that you may not enter into temptation" — Luke 22:46.

WHEN IS THE Christian most liable to sleep? Is it not when his temporal circumstances are prosperous? Have you not found it so? When you had daily troubles to take to the throne of grace, were you not more wakeful than you are now? Easy roads make sleepy travelers. Another dangerous time is when all goes pleasantly in spiritual matters. Christian went not to sleep when lions were in the way, or when he was wading through the river, or when fighting with Apollyon, but when he had climbed half way up the Hill Difficulty, and came to a delightful arbor, he sat down, and forthwith fell asleep, to his great sorrow and loss. The enchanted ground is a place of balmy breezes, laden with fragrant odors and soft influences, all tending to lull pilgrims to sleep.

Remember Bunyan's description: "Then they came to an arbor, warm, and promising much refreshing to the weary pilgrims; for it was finely worked above head, beautified with greens, and furnished with benches and settles. It had also in it a soft couch, where the weary might lean. The arbor was called the Slothful's Friend, and was made on purpose to allure, if it might be, some of the pilgrims to take up their rest there when weary." Depend upon it, it is in easy places that men shut their eyes and wander into the dreamy land of forgetfulness. Old Erskine wisely remarked, "I like a roaring devil better than a sleeping devil." There is no temptation half so dangerous as not being tempted. The distressed soul does not sleep; it is after we enter into peaceful confidence and full assurance that we are in danger of slumbering. The disciples fell asleep after they had seen Jesus transfigured on the mountain top. Take heed, joyous Christian, good frames are near neighbors to temptations; be as happy as you will, only be watchful.

October 24   MORNING

"The trees of the LORD are full of sap, the cedars of Lebanon which He has planted" —
Psalm 104:16.

WITHOUT SAP THE tree cannot flourish or even exist. Vitality is essential to a Christian. There must be life - a vital principle infused into us by God the Holy Spirit, or we cannot be trees of the Lord. The mere name of being a Christian is but a dead thing, we must be filled with the spirit of divine life. This life is mysterious. We do not understand the circulation of the sap, by what force it rises, and by what power it descends again. So the life within us is a sacred mystery. Regeneration is worked by the Holy Spirit entering into man and becoming man's life. And this divine life in a believer afterwards feeds upon the flesh and blood of Christ and is thus sustained by divine food, but from where it comes and where it goes who shall explain to us? What a secret thing the sap is! The roots go searching through the soil, but we cannot see them suck out the various gases, or transmute the mineral into the vegetable; this work is done down in the dark.

Our root is Christ Jesus, and our life is hid in Him; this is the secret of the Lord. The radix of the Christian life is as secret as the life itself. How permanently active is the sap in the cedar! In the Christian the divine life is always full of energy; not always in fruit-bearing, but in inward operations. The believer's graces, are not every one of them in constant motion? but his life never ceases to palpitate within. He is not always working for God, but his heart is always living upon Him. As the sap manifests itself in producing the foliage and fruit of the tree, so with a truly healthy Christian, his grace is externally manifested in his walk and conversation. If you talk with him, he cannot help speaking about Jesus. If you notice his actions you will see that he has been with Jesus. He has so much sap within, that it must fill his conduct and conversation with life.

EVENING

"He began to wash the feet of the disciples" — John 13:5.

THE LORD JESUS loves His people so much, that every day He is still doing for them much that is analogous to washing their soiled feet. Their poorest actions He accepts; their deepest sorrow He feels; their slenderest wish He hears, and their every transgression He forgives. He is still their servant as well as their Friend and Master. He not only performs majestic deeds for them, as wearing the miter on His brow, and the precious jewels glittering on His breastplate, and standing up to plead for them, but humbly, patiently, He yet goes about among His people with the basin and the towel.

He does this when He puts away from us day by day our constant infirmities and sins. Last night, when you bowed the knee, you mournfully confessed that much of your conduct was not worthy of your profession; and even tonight, you must mourn afresh that you have fallen again into the selfsame folly and sin from which special grace delivered you long ago; and yet Jesus will have great patience with you; He will hear your confession of sin; He will say, *"I will, be you clean;"* He will again apply the blood of sprinkling, and speak peace to your conscience, and remove every spot.

It is a great act of eternal love when Christ once for all absolves the sinner, and puts him into the family of God; but what condescending patience there is when the Savior with much long-suffering bears the often recurring follies of His wayward disciple; day by day, and hour by hour, washing away the multiplied transgressions of His erring but yet beloved child! To dry up a flood of rebellion is something marvelous, but to endure the constant dropping of repeated offenses, to bear with a perpetual trying of patience, this is divine indeed! While we find comfort and peace in our Lord's daily cleansing, its legitimate influence upon us will be to increase our watchfulness, and quicken our desire for holiness. Is it so?

MORNING   October 25

"For the sake of the truth which lives in us and shall be with us forever" — 2 John 2.

ONCE LET THE truth of God obtain an entrance into the human heart and subdue the whole man unto itself, and no power human or infernal can dislodge it. We entertain it not as a guest but as the master of the house; this is a Christian necessity, he is no Christian who does not thus believe. Those who feel the vital power of the gospel, and know the might of the Holy Spirit as He opens, applies, and seals the Lord's Word, would sooner be torn to pieces than be rent away from the gospel of their salvation. What a thousand mercies are wrapped up in the assurance that the truth will be with us forever; will be our living support, our dying comfort, our rising song, our eternal glory; this is Christian privilege, without it our faith were little worth. Some truths we outgrow and leave behind, for they are but rudiments and lessons for beginners, but we cannot thus deal with Divine truth, for though it is sweet food for babes, it is in the highest sense strong meat for men. The truth that we are sinners is painfully with us to humble and make us watchful; the more blessed truth that whosoever believes on the Lord Jesus shall be saved, abides with us as our hope and joy. Experience, so far from loosening our hold of the doctrines of grace, has knit us to them more and more firmly; our grounds and motives for believing are now more strong, more numerous than ever, and we have reason to expect that it will be so till in death we clasp the Savior in our arms.

Wherever this abiding love of truth can be discovered, we are bound to exercise our love. No narrow circle can contain our gracious sympathies, wide as the election of grace must be our communion of heart. Much of error may be mingled with truth received, let us war with the error but still love the brother for the measure of truth which we see in Him; above all let us love and spread the truth ourselves.

EVENING

"She gleaned in the field after the reapers. And she happened to come upon a part of the field of Boaz, who was of the kindred of Elimelech" — Ruth 2:3.

SHE HAPPENED. Yes, it seemed nothing but an accident, but how divinely was it overruled! Ruth had gone forth with her mother-in-law's blessing, under the care of her mother-in-law's God, to humble but honorable toil, and the providence of God was guiding her every step. Little did she know that amid the sheaves she would find a husband, that he should make her the joint owner of all those broad acres, and that she a poor foreigner should become one of the progenitors of the great Messiah. God is very good to those who trust in Him, and often surprises them with unlooked for blessings. Little do we know what may happen to us tomorrow, but this sweet fact may cheer us, that no good thing shall be withheld. Chance is banished from the faith of Christians, for they see the hand of God in everything. The trivial events of today or tomorrow may involve consequences of the highest importance. Oh Lord, deal as graciously with Your servants as You did with Ruth.

How blessed would it be, if, in wandering in the field of meditation tonight, we should happen to light upon the place where our next Kinsman will reveal Himself to us! Oh Spirit of God, guide us to Him. We would sooner glean in His field than bear away the whole harvest from any other. Oh for the footsteps of His flock, which may conduct us to the green pastures where He dwells! This is a weary world when Jesus is away; we could better do without sun and moon than without Him. But how divinely fair all things become in the glory of His presence! Our souls know the virtue which dwells in Jesus, and can never be content without Him. We will wait in prayer this night until we shall happen to light on a part of the field belonging to Jesus wherein He will manifest Himself to us.

October 26   MORNING

"You looked for much, and behold, little! And when you brought it home, I blew on it. Why, says the LORD of hosts? Because of My house that is ruined, and you, each man of you, runs to his own house" — Haggai 1:9.

CHURLISH SOULS STINT their contributions to the ministry and missionary operations, and call such saving good economy; little do they dream that they are thus impoverishing themselves. Their excuse is that they must care for their own families, and they forget that to neglect the house of God is the sure way to bring ruin upon their own houses. Our God has a method in providence by which He can succeed our endeavors beyond our expectation, or can defeat our plans to our confusion and dismay; by a turn of His hand He can steer our vessel in a profitable channel, or run it aground in poverty and bankruptcy.

It is the teaching of Scripture that the Lord enriches the liberal and leaves the miser to find out that withholding tends to poverty. In a very wide sphere of observation, I have noticed that the most generous Christians of my acquaintance have been always the most happy, and almost invariably the most prosperous. I have seen the liberal giver rise to wealth of which he never dreamed; and I have as often seen the mean, ungenerous churl descend to poverty by the very parsimony by which he thought to rise.

Men trust good stewards with larger and larger sums, and so it frequently is with the Lord; He gives by carloads to those who give by bushels. Where wealth is not bestowed the Lord makes the little much by the contentment which the sanctified heart feels in a portion of which the tithe has been dedicated to the Lord. Selfishness looks first at home, but godliness seeks first the kingdom of God and His righteousness. Yet in the long run selfishness is loss, and godliness is great gain. It needs faith to act towards our God with an open hand, but surely He deserves it of us; and all that we can do is a very poor acknowledgment of our amazing indebtedness to His goodness.

EVENING

"All the rivers run into the sea, yet the sea is not full. To the place from where the rivers come, there they return again" — Ecclesiastes 1:7.

EVERYTHING SUBLUNARY IS on the move, these know nothing of rest. The solid earth is a rolling ball, and the great sun himself a star obediently fulfilling its course around some greater luminary. Tides move the sea, winds stir the airy ocean, friction wears the rock; change and death rule everywhere. The sea is not a miser's storehouse for a wealth of waters, for as by one force the waters flow into it, by another they are lifted from it. Men are born but to die; everything is hurry, worry, and vexation of spirit. Friend of the unchanging Jesus, what a joy it is to reflect upon your changeless heritage; your sea of bliss which will be forever full, since God Himself shall pour eternal rivers of pleasure into it. We seek an abiding city beyond the skies, and we shall not be disappointed.

The passage before us may well teach us gratitude. Father Ocean is a great receiver, but he is a generous distributor. What the rivers bring him he returns to the earth in the form of clouds and rain. That man is out of joint with the universe who takes all, but makes no return. To give to others is but sowing seed for ourselves. He who is so good a steward as to be willing to use his substance for his Lord, shall be entrusted with more. Friend of Jesus, are you rendering to Him according to the benefit received? Much has been given you, what is your fruit? Have you done all? Can you not do more? To be selfish is to be wicked. Suppose the ocean gave up none of its watery treasure, it would bring ruin upon our race. God forbid that any of us should follow the ungenerous and destructive policy of living unto ourselves. Jesus pleased not Himself. All fullness dwells in Him, but of His fullness have we all received. Oh for Jesus' spirit, that henceforth we may live not unto ourselves!

MORNING October 27

"This is a faithful saying" — 2 Timothy 2:11.

PAUL HAS FOUR of these *"faithful sayings."* The first occurs in 1 Timothy 1:15, *"This is a faithful saying, and worthy of all acceptation, that Christ Jesus came into the world to save sinners."* The next is in 1 Timothy 4:6, *"Godliness is profitable unto all things, having the promise of the life that now is, and of that which is to come. This is a faithful saying, and worthy of all acceptation."* The third is in 2 Timothy 2:12, *"It is a faithful saying: If we suffer with Him we shall also reign with Him;"* and the fourth is in Titus 3:3, *"This is a faithful saying, that they who have believed in God might be careful to maintain good works."*

We may trace a connection between these faithful sayings. The first one lays the foundation of our eternal salvation in the free grace of God, as shown to us in the mission of the great Redeemer. The next affirms the double blessedness which we obtain through this salvation, the blessings of the upper and lower springs, of time and of eternity. The third shows one of the duties to which the chosen people are called; we are ordained to suffer for Christ with the promise that *"if we suffer, we shall also reign with Him."* The last sets forth the active form of Christian service, bidding us diligently to maintain good works.

Thus we have the root of salvation in free grace; next, the privileges of that salvation in the life which now is, and in that which is to come; and we have also the two great branches of suffering with Christ and serving with Christ, loaded with the fruits of the Spirit. Treasure up these faithful sayings. Let them be the guides of our life, our comfort, and our instruction. The apostle of the Gentiles proved them to be faithful, they are faithful still, not one word shall fall to the ground; they are worthy of all acceptation, let us accept them now, and prove their faithfulness. Let these four faithful sayings be written on the four corners of My house.

EVENING
"We are all as an unclean thing" — Isaiah 64:6.

THE BELIEVER IS a new creature, he belongs to a holy generation and a peculiar people; the Spirit of God is in him, and in all respects he is far removed from the natural man. But for all that the Christian is a sinner still. He is so from the imperfection of his nature, and will continue so to the end of his earthly life. The black fingers of sin leave smudges upon our fairest robes. Sin mars our repentance, before the great Potter has finished it, upon the wheel. Selfishness defiles our tears, and unbelief tampers with our faith. The best thing we ever did apart from the merit of Jesus only swelled the number of our sins; for when we have been most pure in our own sight, yet, like the heavens, we are not pure in God's sight; and as He charged His angels with folly, much more must He charge us with it, even in our most angelic frames of mind.

The song which thrills to heaven, and seeks to emulate seraphic strains, has human discords in it. The prayer which moves the arm of God is still a bruised and battered prayer, and only moves that arm because the sinless One, the great Mediator, has stepped in to take away the sin of our supplication. The most golden faith or the purest degree of sanctification to which a Christian ever attained on earth, has still so much alloy in it as to be only worthy of the flames, in itself considered. Every time we look in the glass we see a sinner, and had need confess, *"We are all as an unclean thing, and all our righteousness are as filthy rags"* (Isaiah 64:6).

Oh, how precious the blood of Christ to such hearts as ours! How priceless a gift is His perfect holiness hereafter! Even now, though sin dwells in us, its power is broken. It has no dominion; it is a broken-backed snake; we are in bitter conflict with it, but it is with a vanquished foe that we have to deal. Yet a little while and we shall enter victoriously into the city where nothing defiles.

October 28   MORNING

"I chose you out of the world" — John 15:19.

    HERE IS DISTINGUISHING grace and discriminating regard; for some are made the special objects of divine affection. Do not be afraid to dwell upon this high doctrine of election. When your mind is most heavy and depressed, you will find it to be a bottle of richest cordial. Those who doubt the doctrines of grace, or who cast them into the shade, miss the richest clusters of Eshcol; they lose the wines on the lees well refined, the fat things full of marrow. There is no balm in Gilead comparable to it. If the honey in Jonathan's wood when but touched enlightened the eyes, this is honey which will enlighten your heart to love and learn the mysteries of the kingdom of God. Eat, and fear not a surfeit; live upon this choice dainty, and fear not that it will be too delicate a diet. Meat from the King's table will hurt none of His courtiers. Desire to have your mind enlarged, that you may comprehend more and more the eternal, everlasting, discriminating love of God.

    When you have mounted as high as election, tarry on its sister mount, the covenant of grace. Covenant engagements are the munitions of stupendous rock behind which we lie entrenched; covenant engagements with the surety, Christ Jesus, are the quiet resting-places of trembling spirits.

        His oath, His covenant, His blood, Support me in the raging flood;
        When every earthly prop gives way, This still is all my strength and stay.

    If Jesus undertook to bring me to glory, and if the Father promised that He would give me to the Son to be a part of the infinite reward of the travail of His soul; then, my soul, till God Himself shall be unfaithful, till Jesus shall cease to be the truth, you are safe. When David danced before the ark, he told Michal that election made him do so. Come, my soul, exult before the God of grace and leap for joy of heart.

EVENING

"His head is like the finest gold, His locks are bushy and black as a raven" — Song of Solomon 5:11.

    COMPARISONS ALL FAIL to set forth the Lord Jesus, but the spouse uses the best within her reach. By the head of Jesus we may understand His deity, *"for the head of Christ is God;"* and then the ingot of purest gold is the best conceivable metaphor, but all too poor to describe one so precious, so pure, so dear, so glorious. Jesus is not a grain of gold, but a vast globe of it, a priceless mass of treasure such as earth and heaven cannot excel. The creatures are mere iron and clay, they all shall perish like wood, hay, and stubble, but the ever living Head of the creation of God shall shine on forever and ever. In Him is no mixture, nor smallest taint of alloy. He is forever infinitely holy and altogether divine.

    The bushy locks depict His manly vigor. There is nothing effeminate in our Beloved. He is the manliest of men. Bold as a lion, laborious as an ox, swift as an eagle. Every conceivable and inconceivable beauty is to be found in Him, though once He was despised and rejected of men.

        His head the finest gold; With secret sweet perfume,
        His curled locks hang all as black, As any raven's plume.

    The glory of His head is not shorn away, He is eternally crowned with peerless majesty.

    The black hair indicates youthful freshness, for Jesus has the dew of His youth upon Him. Others grow languid with age, but He is forever a Priest as was Melchizedek; others come and go, but He abides as God upon His throne, world without end. We will behold Him tonight and adore Him. Angels are gazing upon Him. Where else is there such a Beloved? Oh for an hour's fellowship with Him! Away, you intruding cares! Jesus draws me, and I run after Him.

MORNING   October 29

"Therefore, pray in this way. Our Father, who is in Heaven," etc. — Matthew 6:9.

THIS PRAYER BEGINS where all true prayer must commence, with the spirit of adoption, *"Our Father."* There is no acceptable prayer until we can say, *"I will arise, and go unto my Father."* This child-like spirit soon perceives the grandeur of the Father *"heaven,"* and ascends to devout adoration, *"Hallowed be Your name."* The child lisping, *"Abba, Father,"* grows into the cherub crying, *"Holy, Holy, Holy."* There is but a step from rapturous worship to the glowing missionary spirit, which is a sure outgrowth of filial love and reverent adoration. *"Your kingdom come, Your will be done on earth as it is in heaven."* Next follows the heartfelt expression of dependence upon God, *"Give us this day our daily bread."*

Being further illuminated by the Spirit, he discovers that he is not only dependent, but sinful, hence he entreats for mercy, *"Forgive us our debts as we forgive our debtors;"* and being pardoned, having the righteousness of Christ imputed, and knowing his acceptance with God, he humbly supplicates for holy perseverance, *"Lead us not into temptation."* The man who is really forgiven, is anxious not to offend again; the possession of justification leads to an anxious desire for sanctification. *"Forgive us our debts,"* that is justification; *"Lead us not into temptation, but deliver us from evil,"* that is sanctification in its negative and positive forms.

As the result of all this, there follows a triumphant ascription of praise, *"Thine is the kingdom, the power, and the glory, forever and ever, Amen."* We rejoice that our King reigns in providence and shall reign in grace, from the river even to the ends of the earth, and of His dominion there shall be no end. Thus from a sense of adoption, up to fellowship with our reigning Lord, this short model of prayer conducts the soul. Lord, teach us thus to pray.

EVENING
"But their eyes were kept from knowing Him" — Luke 24:16.

THE DISCIPLES OUGHT to have known Jesus, they had heard His voice so often, and gazed upon that marred face so frequently, that it is wonderful they did not discover Him. Yet is it not so with you also? You have not seen Jesus lately. You have been to His table, and you have not met Him there. You are in a dark trouble this evening, and though He plainly says, *"It is I, be not afraid,"* yet you cannot discern Him. Alas! our eyes are holden. We know His voice; we have looked into His face; we have leaned our head upon His bosom, and yet, though Christ is very near us, we are saying *"Oh that I knew where I might find Him!"* We should know Jesus, for we have the Scriptures to reflect His image, and yet how possible it is for us to open that precious book and have no glimpse of the Well-beloved!

Dear child of God, are you in that state? Jesus feeds among the lilies of the Word, and you walk among those lilies, and yet you behold Him not. He is accustomed to walk through the glades of Scripture, and to commune with His people, as the Father did with Adam in the Scripture, but cannot see Him, though He is always there. And why do we not see Him? It must be ascribed in our case, as in the disciples', to unbelief. They evidently did not expect to see Jesus, and therefore they did not know Him.

To a great extent in spiritual things we get what we expect of the Lord. Faith alone can bring us to see Jesus. Make it your prayer, "Lord, open my eyes, that I may see my Savior present with me." It is a blessed thing to want to see Him; but Oh! it is better far to gaze upon Him. To those who seek Him He is kind; but to those who find Him, beyond expression is He dear!

October 30   MORNING

"I will give thanks, O LORD" — Psalm 9:1.

    PRAISE SHOULD ALWAYS follow answered prayer; as the mist of earth's gratitude rises when the sun of heaven's love warms the ground. Has the Lord been gracious to you, and inclined His ear to the voice of your supplication? Then praise Him as long as you live. Let the ripe fruit drop upon the fertile soil from which it drew its life. Deny not a song to Him who has answered your prayer and given you the desire of your heart. To be silent over God's mercies is to incur the guilt of ingratitude; it is to act as basely as the nine lepers, who after they had been cured of their leprosy, returned not to give thanks unto the healing Lord. To forget to praise God is to refuse to benefit ourselves; for praise, like prayer, is one great means of promoting the growth of the spiritual life. It helps to remove our burdens, to excite our hope, to increase our faith. It is a healthful and invigorating exercise which quickens the pulse of the believer, and nerves him for fresh enterprises in his Master's service.

    To bless God for mercies received is also the way to benefit our fellow-men; *"the humble shall hear thereof and be glad."* Others who have been in like circumstances shall take comfort if we can say, "Oh! magnify the Lord with me, and let us exalt His name together; this poor man cried, and the Lord heard him." Weak hearts will be strengthened, and drooping saints will be revived as they listen to our "songs of deliverance." Their doubts and fears will be rebuked, as we teach and admonish one another in psalms and hymns and spiritual songs. They too shall "sing in the ways of the Lord," when they hear us magnify His holy name. Praise is the most heavenly of Christian duties. The angels pray not, but they cease not to praise both day and night; and the redeemed; clothed in white robes, with palm-branches in their hands, are never weary of singing the new song, *"Worthy is the Lamb."*

EVENING

"You who dwell in the gardens, the companions listen to your voice; cause me to hear it" — Song of Solomon 8:13.

    MY SWEET LORD Jesus remembers well the garden of Gethsemane, and although He has left that garden, He now dwells in the garden of His church; there He unbosoms Himself to those who keep His blessed company. That voice of love with which He speaks to His beloved is more musical than the harps of heaven. There is a depth of melodious love within it which leaves all human music far behind. Tens of thousands on earth, and millions above, are indulged with its harmonious accents. Some whom I well know, and whom I greatly envy, are at this moment hearkening to the beloved voice. Oh that I were a partaker of their joys! It is true some of these are poor, others bedridden, and some near the gates of death, but Oh my Lord, I would cheerfully starve with them, pine with them, or die with them, if I might but hear Your voice.

    Once I did hear it often, but I have grieved Your Spirit. Return unto me in compassion, and once again say unto me, "I am your salvation." No other voice can content me; I know Your voice, and cannot be deceived by another, let me hear it, I pray You. I know not what You will say, neither do I make any condition, Oh my Beloved, do but let me hear You speak, and if it be a rebuke I will bless You for it. Perhaps to cleanse my dull ear may need an operation very grievous to the flesh, but let it cost what it may I turn not from the one consuming desire, cause me to hear Your voice. Bore my ear afresh; pierce my ear with Your harshest notes, only do not permit me to continue deaf to Your calls. Tonight, Lord, grant Your unworthy one his desire, for I am Yours, and You have bought me with Your blood. You have opened my eye to see You, and the sight has saved me. Lord, open my ear. I have read Your heart, now let me hear Your lips.

MORNING — October 31

"A right spirit within me" — Psalm 51:10.

A BACKSLIDER, IF there be a spark of life left in him will groan after restoration. In this renewal the same exercise of grace is required as at our conversion. We needed repentance then; we certainly need it now. We wanted faith that we might come to Christ at first; only the like grace can bring us to Jesus now. We wanted a word from the Most High, a word from the lip of the loving One, to end our fears then; we shall soon discover, when under a sense of present sin, that we need it now. No man can be renewed without as real and true a manifestation of the Holy Spirit's energy as he felt at first, because the work is as great, and flesh and blood are as much in the way now as ever they were.

Let your personal weakness, Oh Christian, be an argument to make you pray earnestly to your God for help. Remember, David when he felt himself to be powerless, did not fold his arms or close his lips, but he hastened to the mercy-seat with *"renew a right spirit within me."* Let not the doctrine that you, unaided, can do nothing, make you sleep; but let it be a goad in your side to drive you with an awful earnestness to Israel's strong Helper. Oh that you may have grace to plead with God, as though you pleaded for your very life: *"Lord, renew a right spirit within me."* He who sincerely prays to God to do this, will prove his honesty by using the means through which God works. Be much in prayer; live much upon the Word of God; kill the lusts which have driven your Lord from you; be careful to watch over the future uprisings of sin. The Lord has His own appointed ways; sit by the wayside and you will be ready when He passes by. Continue in all those blessed ordinances which will foster and nourish your dying graces; and, knowing that all the power must proceed from Him, cease not to cry, *"Renew a right spirit within me."*

EVENING

"I knew you in the wilderness, in the land of great dryness" — Hosea 13:5.

YES, LORD, YOU did indeed know me in my fallen state, and You did even then choose me for Yourself. When I was loathsome and self-abhorred, You did receive me as Your child, and You did satisfy my craving wants. Blessed forever be Your name for this free, rich, abounding mercy. Since then, my inward experience has often been a wilderness; but You have owned me still as Your beloved, and poured streams of love and grace into me to gladden me, and make me fruitful. Yes, when my outward circumstances have been at the worst, and I have wandered in a land of drought, Your sweet presence has solaced me. Men have not known me when scorn has awaited me, but You have known my soul in adversities, for no affliction dims the lustre of Your love. Most gracious Lord, I magnify You for all Your faithfulness to me in trying circumstances, and I deplore that I should at any time have forgotten You and been exalted in heart, when I have owed all to Your gentleness and love. Have mercy upon Your servant in this thing!

My soul, if Jesus thus acknowledged you in your low estate, be sure that you own both Himself and His cause now that you are in your prosperity. Be not lifted up by your worldly successes so as to be ashamed of the truth or of the poor church with which you have been associated. Follow Jesus into the wilderness; bear the cross with Him when the heat of persecution grows hot. He owned you, Oh my soul, in your poverty and shame; never be so treacherous as to be ashamed of Him. Oh for more shame at the thought of being ashamed of my best Beloved! Jesus, my soul cleaves to You.

> I'll turn to You in days of light,
> As well as nights of care,
> You brightest amid all that's bright!
> You fairest of the fair!

November 1   MORNING

"The church in your house" — Philemon 2.

IS THERE A Church in this house? Are parents, children, friends, servants, all members of it? or are some still unconverted? Let us pause here and let the question go around Am I a member of the Church in this house? How would father's heart leap for joy, and mother's eyes fill with holy tears if from the oldest to the youngest all were saved! let us pray for this great mercy until the Lord shall grant it to us. Probably it had been the dearest object of Philemon's desires to have all his household saved; but it was not at first granted him in its fullness. He had a wicked servant, Onesimus, who, having wronged him, ran away from his service. His master's prayers followed him, and at last, as God would have it, Onesimus was led to hear Paul preach; his heart was changed, and he returned to Philemon, not only to be a faithful servant, but a brother beloved, adding another member to the Church in Philemon's house. Is there an unconverted servant or child absent this morning? Make special supplication that such may, on their return to their home, gladden all hearts with good news of what grace has done! Is there one present? Let him partake in the same earnest entreaty.

If there be such a Church in our house, let us order it well, and let all act as in the sight of God. Let us move in the common affairs of life with studied holiness, diligence, kindness, and integrity. More is expected of a Church than of an ordinary household; family worship must, in such a case, be more devout and hearty; internal love must be more warm and unbroken, and external conduct must be more sanctified and Christlike. We need not fear that the smallness of our number will put us out of the list of Churches, for the Holy Spirit has here enrolled a family-church in the inspired book of remembrance. As a Church let us now draw near to the great head of the one Church universal, and let us beseech Him to give us grace to shine before men to the glory of His name.

EVENING
"And they did not know until the flood came and took all away; so shall be also the coming of the Son of man" — Matthew 24:39.

UNIVERSAL WAS THE doom, neither rich nor poor escaped: the learned and the illiterate, the admired and the abhorred, the religious and the profane, the old and the young. all sank in one common ruin. Some had doubtless ridiculed the patriarch. Where now were their merry jests? Others had threatened him for his zeal which they counted madness. Where now were their boastings and hard speeches? The critic who judged the old man's work is drowned in the same sea which covers his sneering companions. Those who spoke ill of the good man's fidelity to his convictions, but shared not in them, have sunk to rise no more, and the workers who helped to build the wondrous ark are all lost also. The flood swept them all away, and made no single exception. Even so, out of Christ, final destruction is sure to every man of woman born; no rank, possession, or character, shall suffice to save a single soul who has not believed in the Lord Jesus. My soul, behold this wide-spread judgment and tremble at it.

How marvelous the general apathy! they were all eating and drinking, marrying and giving in marriage, till the awful morning dawned. There was not one wise man upon earth out of the ark. Folly duped the whole race, folly as to self-preservation, the most foolish of all follies. Folly in doubting the most true God, the most malignant of fooleries. Strange, my soul, is it not? All men are negligent of their souls till grace gives them reason, then they leave their madness and act like rational beings, but not till then.

All, blessed be God, were safe in the ark, no ruin entered there. From the huge elephant down to the tiny mouse all were safe. The timid hare was equally secure with the courageous lion, the helpless coney as safe as the laborious ox. All are safe in Jesus.

MORNING   November 2

"I am the LORD, I change not" — Malachi 3:6.

IT IS WELL for us that, amidst all the variableness of life, there is One whom change cannot affect; One whose heart can never alter, and on whose brow mutability can make no furrows. All things else have changed; all things are changing. The sun itself grows dim with age; the world is waxing old; the folding up of the worn-out vesture has commenced; the heavens and earth must soon pass away; they shall perish, they shall wax old as does a garment. But there is One who only has immortality, of whose years there is no end, and in whose person there is no change. The delight which the mariner feels, when, after having been tossed about for many a day, he steps again upon the solid shore, is the satisfaction of a Christian when, amidst all the changes of this troublous life, he rests the foot of his faith upon this truth: *"I am the Lord, I change not."*

The stability which the anchor gives the ship when it has at last obtained a hold-fast, is like that which the Christian's hope affords him when it fixes itself upon this glorious truth. With God *"is no variableness, neither shadow of turning."* Whatever His attributes were of old, they are now; His power, His wisdom, His justice, His truth, are alike unchanged. He has ever been the refuge of His people, their stronghold in the day of trouble, and He is their sure helper still. He is unchanged in His love. He has loved His people with *"an everlasting love;"* He loves them now as much as ever He did, and when all earthly things shall have melted in the last conflagration, His love will still wear the dew of its youth. Precious is the assurance that He changes not! The wheel of providence revolves, but its axle is eternal love.

> Death and change are busy ever,
> Man decays, and ages move;
> But His mercy wanes never;
> God is wisdom, God is love.

EVENING

"Horror has taken hold on me because of the wicked who forsake Your law" — Psalm 119:53.

MY SOUL, DO you feel this holy shuddering at the sins of others? For otherwise you lack inward holiness. David's cheeks were wet with rivers of waters because of prevailing unholiness; Jeremiah desired eyes like fountains that he might lament the iniquities of Israel, and Lot was vexed with the conversation of the men of Sodom. Those upon whom the mark was set in Ezekiel's vision, were those who sighed and cried for the abominations of Jerusalem. It cannot but grieve gracious souls to see what pains men take to go to hell. They know the evil of sin experimentally, and they are alarmed to see others flying like moths into its blaze.

Sin makes the righteous shudder, because it violates a holy law, which it is to every man's highest interest to keep; it pulls down the pillars of the commonwealth. Sin in others horrifies a believer, because it puts him in mind of the baseness of his own heart; when he sees a transgressor he cries with the saint mentioned by Bernard, He fell today, and I may fall tomorrow. Sin to a believer is horrible, because it crucified the Savior; he sees in every iniquity the nails and spear. How can a saved soul behold that cursed kill-Christ sin with abhorrence?

Say, my heart, do you sensibly join in all this? It is an awful thing to insult God to His face. The good God deserves better treatment, the great God claims it, the just God will have it, or repay His adversary to His face. An awakened heart trembles at the audacity of sin, and stands alarmed at the contemplation of its punishment. How monstrous a thing is rebellion! How direful a doom is prepared for the ungodly! My soul, never laugh at sin's fooleries, lest you come to smile at sin itself. It is your enemy, and your Lord's enemy; view it with detestation, for so only can you evidence the possession of holiness, without which no man can see the Lord.

November 3   MORNING

"See, he is praying" — Acts 9:11.

    PRAYERS ARE INSTANTLY noticed in heaven. The moment Saul began to pray the Lord heard him. Here is comfort for the distressed but praying soul. Oftentimes a poor broken-hearted one bends his knee, but can only utter his wailing in the language of sighs and tears; yet that groan has made all the harps of heaven thrill with music; that tear has been caught by God and treasured in the lachrymatory of heaven. *"You put my tears into your bottle,"* implies that they are caught as they flow. The suppliant, whose fears prevent his words, will be well understood by the Most High. One may only look up with misty eye; but "prayer is the falling of a tear." Tears are the diamonds of heaven; sighs are a part of the music of Jehovah's court, and are numbered with "the most sublime strains that reach the majesty on high.

    Think not that your prayer, however weak or trembling, will be unregarded. Jacob's ladder is lofty, but our prayers shall lean upon the Angel of the covenant and so climb its starry rounds. Our God not only hears prayer but also loves to hear it. *"He forgets not the cry of the humble."* True, He regards not high looks and lofty words; He cares not for the pomp and pageantry of kings; He listens not to the swell of martial music; He regards not the triumph and pride of man; but wherever there is a heart big with sorrow, or a lip quivering with agony, or a deep groan, or a penitential sigh, the heart of Jehovah is open; He marks it down in the registry of His memory; He puts our prayers, like rose leaves, between the pages of His book of remembrance, and when the volume is opened at last, there shall be a precious fragrance springing up therefrom.

> Faith asks no signal from the skies,
> To show that prayers accepted rise,
> Our Priest is in His holy place,
> And answers from the throne of grace.

EVENING

"Their prayer came up to His holy dwelling-place, to Heaven" — 2 Chronicles 30:27.

    PRAYER IS THE never-failing resort of the Christian in any case, in every plight. When you cannot use your sword, you may take to the weapon of all-prayer. Your powder may be damp, your bow-string may be relaxed, but the weapon of all-prayer need never be out of order. Leviathan laughs at the javelin, but he trembles at prayer. Sword and spear need furbishing, but prayer never rusts, and when we think it most blunt it cuts the best. Prayer is an open door which none can shut. Devils may surround you on all sides, but the way upward is always open, and as long as that road is unobstructed, you will not fall into the enemy's hand. We can never be taken by blockade, mine, or storm, so long as heavenly succors can come down to us by Jacob's ladder to relieve us in the time of our necessities. Prayer is never out of season; in summer and in winter its merchandise is precious. Prayer gains audience with heaven in the dead of night, in the midst of business, in the heat of noonday, in the shades of evening. In every condition, whether of poverty, or sickness, or obscurity, or slander, or doubt, your covenant God will welcome your prayer and answer it from His holy place.

    Nor is prayer ever futile. True prayer is evermore true power. You may not always get what you ask, but you shall always have your real wants supplied. When God does not answer His children according to the letter, He does so according to the spirit. If you ask for coarse meal, will you be angered because He gives you the finest flour? If you seek bodily health, should you complain if instead thereof He makes your sickness turn to the healing of spiritual maladies? is it not better to have the cross sanctified than removed? This evening, my soul, forget not to offer your petition and request, for the Lord is ready to grant you your desires.

MORNING
November 4

"For My strength is made perfect in weakness" — *2 Corinthians 12:9.*

A PRIMARY qualification for serving God with any amount of success, and for doing God's work well and triumphantly, is a sense of our own weakness. When God's warrior marches forth to battle, strong in his own might, when he boasts, "I know that I shall conquer, my own right arm and my conquering sword shall get unto me the victory," defeat is not far distant. God will not go forth with that man who marches in his own strength. He who reckons on victory thus has reckoned wrongly, for *"it is not by might, nor by power, but by my Spirit, says the Lord of hosts."* They who go forth to fight, boasting of their prowess, shall return with their gay banners trailed in the dust, and their armor stained with disgrace.

Those who serve God must serve Him in His own way, and in His strength, or He will never accept their service. That which man does, unaided by divine strength, God can never own. The mere fruits of the earth He casts away; He will only reap that corn, the seed of which was sown from heaven, watered by grace, and ripened by the sun of divine love. God will empty out all that you have before He will put His own into you; He will first clean out your granaries before He will fill them with the finest of the wheat. The river of God is full of water; but not one drop of it flows from earthly springs. God will have no strength used in His battles but the strength which He Himself imparts.

Are you mourning over your own weakness? Take courage, for there must be a consciousness of weakness before the Lord will give you victory. Your emptiness is but the preparation for your being filled, and your casting down is but the making ready for your lifting up.

When I am weak then am I strong,
Grace is my shield and Christ my song.

EVENING
"In Your light we shall see light" — *Psalm 36:9.*

NO LIPS CAN tell the love of Christ to the heart till Jesus Himself shall speak within. Descriptions all fall flat and tame unless the Holy Spirit fills them with life and power; till our Immanuel reveals Himself within, the soul sees Him not. If you would see the sun, would you gather together the common means of illumination, and seek in that way to behold the orb of day? No, the wise man knows that the sun must reveal itself, and only by its own blaze can that mighty lamp be seen. It is so with Christ. *"Blessed are you, Simon Bar-jona,"* said He to Peter, *"for flesh and blood has not revealed this unto you."*

Purify flesh and blood by any educational process you may select, elevate mental faculties to the highest degree of intellectual power, yet none of these can reveal Christ. The Spirit of God must come with power, and overshadow the man with His wings, and then in that mystic holy of holies the Lord Jesus must display Himself to the sanctified eye, as He does not unto the purblind sons of men. Christ must be His own mirror. The great mass of this blear-eyed world can see nothing of the unspeakable glories of Immanuel. He stands before them without form or comeliness, a root out of a dry ground, rejected by the vain and despised by the proud.

Only where the Spirit has touched the eye with His special eye-salve, enlivened the heart with divine life, and educated the soul to a heavenly taste, only there is He understood. *"To you that believe He is precious;"* to you He is the chief corner-stone the Rock of your salvation, your all in all; but to others He is "a stone of stumbling and a rock of offense." Happy are those to whom our Lord manifests Himself, for His promise to such is that He will make His abode with them. Oh Jesus, our Lord, our heart is open, come in, and go out no more forever. Show Yourself to us now Favor us with a glimpse of Your all-conquering charms.

November 5

MORNING

"No weapon that is formed against you shall be blessed" — Isaiah 54:17.

THIS DAY IS notable in English history for two great deliverances worked by God for us. On this day the plot of the Papists to destroy our Houses of Parliament was discovered, 1605.

> While for our princes they prepare
> In caverns deep a burning snare,
> He shot from heaven a piercing ray,
> And the dark treachery brought to day.

And secondly, today is the anniversary of the landing of King William III, at Torbay, by which the hope of Popish ascendancy was quashed, and religious liberty was secured, 1688.

This day ought to be celebrated by the songs of saints. Our Puritan forefathers most devoutly made it a special time of thanksgiving. There is extant a record of the annual sermons preached by Matthew Henry on this day. Our Protestant feeling, and our love of liberty, should make us regard its anniversary with holy gratitude. Let our hearts and lips exclaim, "We have heard with our ears, and our fathers have told us the wondrous things which You did in their day, and in the old time before them." You have made this nation the home of the gospel; and when the foe has risen against her, You have shielded her. Help us to offer repeated songs for repeated deliverances. Grant us more and more a hatred of Antichrist, and hasten on the day of her entire extinction. Till then and ever, we believe the promise, "No weapon that is formed against you shall be blessed." Should it not be laid upon the heart of every lover of the gospel of Jesus on this day to plead for the overturning of false doctrines and the extension of divine truth? Would it not be well to search our own hearts, and turn out any of the Popish lumber of self-righteousness which may lie concealed therein?

EVENING

"Be thankful to Him and bless His name" — Psalm 100:4.

OUR LORD WOULD have all His people rich in high and happy thoughts concerning His blessed person. Jesus is not content that His brothers should think meanly of Him. It is His pleasure that His espoused ones should be delighted with His beauty. We are not to regard Him as a bare necessary, like to bread and water, but as a luxurious delicacy, as a rare and ravishing delight. To this end He has revealed Himself as the *"pearl of great price"* in its peerless beauty, as the *"bundle of myrrh"* in its refreshing fragrance, as the *"rose of Sharon"* in its lasting perfume, as the spotless purity.

As a help to high thoughts of Christ, remember how high the estimation of Christ is beyond the skies, where things are measured by the right standard. Think how God esteems the Only Begotten, His unspeakable gift to us. Consider what the angels think of Him, as they count it their highest honor to veil their faces at His feet. Consider what the blood-washed think of Him, as day without night they sing His well deserved praises. High thoughts of Christ will enable us to act consistently with our relations towards Him. The more loftily we see Christ enthroned, and the more lowly we are when bowing before the foot of the throne, the more truly shall we be prepared to act our part towards Him. Our Lord Jesus desires us to think well of Him, that we may submit cheerfully to His authority. High thoughts of Him increase our love. Love and esteem go together. Therefore, believer, think much of your Master's excellencies. Study Him in His primeval glory, before He took upon Himself your nature! Think of the mighty love which drew Him from His throne to die upon the cross! Admire Him as He conquers all the powers of hell! See Him risen, crowned, glorified! Bow before Him as the Wonderful, the Counsellor, the mighty God, for only thus will your love to Him be what it should.

MORNING November 6

"I will pour water on him who is thirsty" — *Isaiah 44:3.*

WHEN A BELIEVER has fallen into a low, sad state of feeling, he often tries to lift himself out of it by chastening himself with dark and doleful fears. Such is not the way to rise from the dust, but to continue in it. As well chain the eagle's wing to make it mount, as doubt in order to increase our grace. It is not the law, but the gospel which saves the seeking soul at first; and it is not a legal bondage, but gospel liberty which can restore the fainting believer afterwards. Slavish fear brings not back the backslider to God, but the sweet wooing of love allures him to Jesus' bosom.

Are you this morning thirsting for the living God, and unhappy because you cannot find Him to the delight of your heart? Have you lost the joy of your salvation? Is this your prayer, *"Restore unto me the joy of Your salvation"*? Are you conscious also that you are barren, like the dry ground; that you are not bringing forth the fruit unto God which He has a right to expect of you; that you are not so useful in the Church, or in the world, as your heart desires to be? Then here is exactly the promise which you need, *"I will pour water upon him that is thirsty."* You shall receive the grace you so much require, and you shall have it to the utmost reach of your needs. Water refreshes the thirsty; you shall be refreshed; your desires shall be gratified. Water quickens sleeping vegetable life; your life shall be quickened by fresh grace. Water swells the buds and makes the fruits ripen; you shall have fructifying grace: you shall be made fruitful in the ways of God. Whatever good quality there is in divine grace, you shall enjoy it to the full. All the riches of divine grace you shall receive in plenty; you shall be as it were drenched with it. As sometimes the meadows become flooded by the bursting rivers, and the fields are turned into pools, so shall you be; the thirsty land shall be springs of water.

EVENING

"Saying, This is the blood of the covenant which God has commanded to you" — *Hebrews 9:20.*

THERE IS A strange power about the very name of blood, and the sight of it is always affecting. A kind heart cannot bear to see a sparrow bleed, and unless familiarized by use, turns away with horror at the slaughter of a beast. As to the blood of men, it is a consecrated thing; it is murder to shed it in wrath, it is a dreadful crime to squander it in war. Is this solemnity occasioned by the fact that the blood is the life, and the pouring of it forth the token of death? We think so. When we rise to contemplate the blood of the Son of God, our awe is yet more increased, and we shudder as we think of the guilt of sin, and the terrible penalty which the Sin-bearer endured. Blood, always precious, is priceless when it streams from Immanuel's side. The blood of Jesus seals the covenant of grace, and makes it forever sure. Covenants of old were made by sacrifice, and the everlasting covenant was ratified in the same manner. Oh, the delight of being saved upon the sure foundation of divine engagements which cannot be dishonored!

Salvation by the works of the law is a frail and broken vessel whose shipwreck is sure; but the covenant vessel fears no storms, for the blood ensures the whole. The blood of Jesus made His testament valid. Wills are of no power unless the testators die. In this light the soldier's spear is a blessed aid to faith, since it proved our Lord to be really dead. Doubts upon that matter there can be none, and we may boldly appropriate the legacies which He has left for His people. Happy they who see their title to heavenly blessings assured to them by a dying Savior.

But has this blood no voice to us? Does it not bid us sanctify ourselves unto Him by whom we have been redeemed? Does it not call us to newness of life, and incite us to entire consecration to the Lord? Oh that the power of the blood might be known, and felt in us this night!

November 7   MORNING

"Behold, I have carved you on the palms of My hands" — Isaiah 49:16.

NO DOUBT A part of the wonder which is concentrated in the word "*Behold,*" is excited by the unbelieving lamentation of the preceding sentence. Zion said, *"The Lord has forsaken me, and my God has forgotten me."* How amazed the divine mind seems to be at this wicked unbelief! What can be more astounding than the unfounded doubts and fears of God's favored people? The Lord's loving word of rebuke should make us blush; He cries, How can I have forgotten you, "I have carved you on the palms of my hands?" How dare you doubt My constant remembrance, when the Memorial is set upon My very hands? Oh unbelief, how strange a marvel you are! We know not which most to wonder at, the faithfulness of God or the unbelief of His people. He keeps His promise a thousand times, and yet the next trial makes us doubt Him. He never fails; He is never a dry well; He is never as a setting sun, a passing meteor, or a melting vapor. And yet we are as continually vexed with anxieties, molested with suspicious, and disturbed with fears, as if our God were the mirage of the desert.

"Behold," is a word intended to excite admiration. Here, indeed, we have a theme for marveling. Heaven and earth may well be astonished that rebels should obtain so great a nearness to the heart of infinite love as to be written upon the palms of His hands. *"I have carved you."* It does not say, "Your name." The name is there, but that is not all: *"I have carved you."* See the fullness of this! I have graven your person, your image, your case, your circumstances, your sins, your temptations, your weaknesses, your wants, your works; I have carved you, everything about you, all that concerns you; I have put you altogether there. Will you ever say again that your God has forsaken you when He has graven you upon His own palms?

EVENING

"And you shall be witnesses to Me" — Acts 1;8.

IN ORDER TO learn how to discharge your duty as a witness for Christ, look at His example. He is always witnessing; by the well of Samaria, or in the Temple of Jerusalem; by the lake of Gennesaret, or on the mountain's brow. He is witnessing night and day; His mighty prayers are as vocal to God as His daily services. He witnesses under all circumstances; Scribes and Pharisees cannot shut His mouth; even before Pilate He witnesses a good confession. He witnesses so clearly and distinctly that there is no mistake in Him.

Christian, make your life a clear testimony. Be as the brook wherein you may see every stone at the bottom; not as the muddy creek, of which you only see the surface, but clear and transparent, so that your heart's love to God and man may be visible to all. You need not say, "I am true:" be true. Boast not of integrity, but be upright. So shall your testimony be such that men cannot help seeing it. Never, for fear of feeble man, restrain your witness. Your lips have been warmed with a coal from off the altar; let them speak as like heaven-touched lips should do. *"In the morning sow your seed, and in the evening withhold not your hand."* Watch not the clouds, consult not the wind; in season and out of season witness for the Savior. And if it shall come to pass that for Christ's sake and the gospel's you shall endure suffering in any shape, shrink not, but rejoice in the honor thus conferred upon you, that you are counted worthy to suffer with your Lord; and joy also in this, that your sufferings, your losses, and persecutions shall make you a platform, from which the more vigorously and with greater power you shall witness for Christ Jesus. Study your great Exemplar, and be filled with His Spirit. Remember that you need much teaching, much upholding, much grace, and much humility, if your witnessing is to be to your Master's glory.

MORNING November 8

"As you received Christ Jesus the Lord" — *Colossians 2:6.*

THE LIFE OF faith is represented as receiving, an act which implies the very opposite of anything like merit. It is simply the acceptance of a gift. As the earth drinks in the rain, as the sea receives the streams, as night accepts light from the stars, so we, giving nothing, partake freely of the grace of God. The saints are not, by nature, wells, or streams, they are but cisterns into which the living water flows; they are empty vessels into which God pours His salvation. The idea of receiving implies a sense of realization, making the matter a reality. One cannot very well receive a shadow; we receive that which is substantial; so is it in the life of faith, Christ becomes real to us. While we are without faith, Jesus is a mere name to us, a person who lived a long while ago, so long ago that His life is only a history to us now! By an act of faith Jesus becomes a real person in the consciousness of our heart. But receiving also means grasping or getting possession of. The thing which I receive becomes my own; I appropriate to myself that which is given. When I receive Jesus, He becomes my Savior, so mine that neither life nor death shall be able to rob me of Him. All this is to receive Christ, to take Him as God's free gift; to realize Him in my heart, and to appropriate Him as mine.

Salvation may be described as the blind receiving sight, the deaf receiving hearing, the dead receiving life. But we have not only received these blessings, we have received Christ Jesus Himself. It is true that He gave us life from the dead. He gave us pardon of sin; He gave us imputed righteousness. These are all precious things, but we are not content with them; we have received Christ Himself. The Son of God has been poured into us, and we have received Him, and appropriated Him. What a heart-full Jesus must be, for heaven itself cannot contain Him!

EVENING

"The Teacher says, Where is the guest-room where I may eat the passover with My disciples? — *Mark 14:14.*

JERUSALEM AT THE time of the passover was one great inn; each householder had invited his own friends, but no one had invited the Savior, and He had no dwelling of His own. It was by His own supernatural power that He found Himself an upper room in which to keep the feast. It is so even to this day. Jesus is not received among the sons of men, but only where by His supernatural power and grace works to create the heart anew. All doors are open enough to the prince of darkness, but Jesus must clear a way for Himself or lodge in the streets. It was through the mysterious power exerted by our Lord that the householder raised no question, but at once cheerfully and joyfully opened his guest-chamber. Who he was, and what he was, we do not know, but he readily accepted the honor which the Redeemer proposed to confer upon him. In like manner it is still discovered who are the Lord's chosen, and who are not; for when the gospel comes to some, they fight against it, and will not have it, but where men receive it, welcoming it, this is a sure indication that there is a secret work going on in the soul, and that God has chosen them unto eternal life.

Are you willing, dear reader, to receive Christ? Then there is no difficulty in the way; Christ will be your guest; His own power is working with you, making you willing. What an honor to entertain the Son of God! The heaven of heavens cannot contain Him, and yet He condescends to find a house within our hearts! We are not worthy that He should come under our roof, but what an unutterable privilege when He condescends to enter! For then He makes a feast, and causes us to feast with Him upon royal dainties; we sit at a banquet where the viands are immortal, and give immortality to those who feed thereon. Blessed among the sons of Adam is he who entertains the angels' Lord.

November 9   MORNING

"So walk in Him" — Colossians 2:6.

IF WE HAVE received Christ Himself in our inmost hearts, our new life will manifest its intimate acquaintance with Him by a walk of faith in Him. Walking implies action. Our religion is not to be confined to our closet; we must carry out into practical effect that which we believe. If a man walks in Christ, then he so acts as Christ would act; for Christ being in him, his hope, his love, his joy, his life, he is the reflex of the image of Jesus; and men say of that man, "He is like his Master; he lives like Jesus Christ." Walking signifies progress. *"So walk in Him;"* proceed from grace to grace, run forward until you reach the uttermost degree of knowledge that a man can attain concerning our Beloved. Walking implies continuance. There must be a perpetual abiding in Christ. How many Christians think that in the morning and evening they ought to come into the company of Jesus, and may then give their hearts to the world all the day; but this is poor living; we should always be with Him, treading in His steps and doing His will.

Walking also implies habit. When we speak of a man's walk and conversation, we mean his habits, the constant tenor of his life. Now, if we sometimes enjoy Christ, and then forget Him; sometimes call Him ours, and anon lose our hold, that is not a habit; we do not walk in Him. We must keep to Him, cling to Him, never let Him go, but live and have our being in Him. *"As you have received Christ Jesus the Lord, so walk in Him;"* persevere in the same way in which you have begun, and, as at the first Christ Jesus was the trust of your faith, the source of your life, the principle of your action, and the joy of your spirit, so let Him be the same till life's end; the same when you walk through the valley of the shadow of death, and enter into the joy and the rest which remain for the people of God. Oh Holy Spirit, enable us to obey this heavenly precept.

EVENING

"His refuge shall be the strongholds of rocks; bread shall be given him, his waters shall be sure" — Isaiah 33:16.

DO YOU DOUBT, Oh Christian, do you doubt as to whether God will fulfil His promise? Shall the munitions of rock be carried by storm? Shall the storehouses of heaven fail? Do you think that your heavenly Father, though He knows that you have need of food and raiment, will yet forget you? When not a sparrow falls to the ground without your Father, and the very hairs of your head are all numbered, will you mistrust and doubt Him? Perhaps your affliction will continue upon you till you dare to trust your God, and then it shall end. Full many there be who have been tried and sore vexed till at last they have been driven in sheer desperation to exercise faith in God, and the moment of their faith has been the instant of their deliverance; they have seen whether God would keep His promise or not.

Oh, I pray you, doubt Him no longer! Please not Satan, and vex not yourself by indulging any more those hard thoughts of God. Think it not a light matter to doubt Jehovah. Remember, it is a sin; and not a little sin either, but in the highest degree criminal. The angels never doubt Him, nor the devils either: we alone, out of all the beings that God has fashioned, dishonor Him by unbelief, and tarnish His honor by mistrust. Shame upon us for this! Our God does not deserve to be so basely suspected. In our past life we have proved Him to be true and faithful to His word, and with so many instances of His love and of His kindness as we have received, and are daily receiving, at His hands, it is base and inexcusable that we suffer a doubt to sojourn within our heart. May we henceforth wage constant war against doubts of our God, enemies to our peace and to His honor; and with an unstaggering faith believe that what He has promised He will also perform. *"Lord, I believe, help my unbelief."*

MORNING November 10

"The eternal God is your refuge" — Deuteronomy 33:27.

THE WORD REFUGE may be translated mansion, or abiding-place, which gives the thought that God is our abode, our home. There is a fullness and sweetness in the metaphor, for dear to our hearts is our home, although it be the humblest cottage, or the scantiest garret; and dearer far is our blessed God, in whom we live, and move, and have our being. It is at home that we feel safe; we shut the world out and dwell in quiet security. So when we are with our God we *"fear no evil."* He is our shelter and retreat, our abiding refuge. At home, we take our rest; it is there we find repose after the fatigue and toil of the day. And so our hearts find rest in God, when, wearied with life's conflict, we turn to Him, and our soul dwells at ease. At home, also, we let our hearts loose; we are not afraid of being misunderstood, nor of our words being misconstrued. So when we are with God we can commune freely with Him, laying open all our hidden desires. For if the *"secret of the Lord is with them that fear Him,"* the secrets of them that fear Him ought to be, and must be, with their Lord.

Home, too, is the place of our truest and purest happiness; and it is in God that our hearts find their deepest delight. We have joy in Him which far surpasses all other joy. It is also for home that we work and labor. The thought of it gives strength to bear the daily burden, and quickens the fingers to perform the task; and in this sense we may also say that God is our home. Love to Him strengthens us. We think of Him in the person of His dear Son; and a glimpse of the suffering face of the Redeemer constraints us to labor in His cause. We feel that we must work, for we have brothers yet to be saved, and we have our Father's heart to make glad by bringing home His wandering sons; we would fill with holy mirth the sacred family among whom we dwell. Happy are those who have thus the God of Jacob for their refuge!

EVENING

"It is enough that the disciple become like his teacher" — Matthew 10:25.

NO ONE WILL dispute this statement, for it would be unseemly for the servant to be exalted above his Master. When our Lord was on earth, what was the treatment He received? Were His claims acknowledged, His instructions followed, His perfections worshipped, by those whom He came to bless? No; *"He was despised and rejected of men."* Outside the camp was His place; cross-bearing was His occupation. Did the world yield Him solace and rest? *"Foxes have holes, and the birds of the air have nests; but the Son of man has no where to lay His head."* This inhospitable country afforded Him no shelter; it cast Him out and crucified Him. If you are a follower of Jesus, and maintain a consistent, Christ-like walk and conversation, you must expect the same treatment to be the lot of that part of your spiritual life, which, in its outward development, comes under the observation of men. They will treat it as they treated the Savior; they will despise it. Dream not that worldlings will admire you, or that the more holy and the more Christ-like you are, the more peaceably people will act towards you. They prized not the polished gem, how should they value the jewel in the rough? *"If they have called the Master of the house Beelzebub, how much more shall they call them of His household?"*

If we were more like Christ, we should be more hated by His enemies. It would be a sad dishonor to a child of God to be the world's favorite. It is a very ill omen to hear a wicked world clap its hands and shout "Well done" to the Christian man. He may begin to look to his character, and wonder whether he has not been doing wrong, when the unrighteous give him their approval. Let us be true to our Master, and have no friendship with a blind and base world which scorns and rejects Him. Far be it from us to seek a crown of honor where our Lord found a coronet of thorn.

November 11   MORNING

"Underneath are the everlasting arms" — Deuteronomy 33:27.

GOD, THE ETERNAL GOD, is Himself our support at all times, and especially when we are sinking in deep trouble. There are seasons when the Christian sinks very low in humiliation. Under a deep sense of his great sinfulness, he is humbled before God till he scarcely knows how to pray, because he appears, in his own sight, so worthless. Well, child of God, remember that when you are at your worst and lowest, yet *"underneath"* you *"are the everlasting arms."* Sin may drag you ever so low, but Christ's great atonement is still under all. You may have descended into the deeps, but you cannot have fallen so low as *"the uttermost;"* and to the uttermost He saves. Again, the Christian sometimes sinks very deeply in sore trial from without. Every earthly prop is cut away. What then? Still underneath him are *"the everlasting arms."* He cannot fall so deep in distress and affliction but what the covenant grave of an ever-faithful God will still encircle him. The Christian may be sinking under trouble from within through fierce conflict, but even then he cannot be brought so low as to be beyond the reach of the *"everlasting arms."* They are underneath him; and, while thus sustained, all Satan's efforts to harm him avail nothing.

This assurance of support is a comfort to any weary but earnest worker in the service of God. It implies a promise of strength for each day, grace for each need, and power for each duty. And, further, when death comes, the promise shall still hold good. When we stand in the midst of Jordan, we shall be able to say with David, *"I will fear no evil, for You are with me."* We shall descend into the grave, but we shall go no lower, for the eternal arms prevent our further fall. All through life, and at its close, we shall be upheld by the *"everlasting arms,"* arms that neither flag nor lose their strength, for *"the everlasting God faints not, neither is weary."*

EVENING

"He shall choose our inheritance for us" — Psalm 47:4.

BELIEVER, IF YOUR inheritance be a lowly one you should be satisfied with your earthly portion; for you may rest assured that it is the fittest for you. Unerring wisdom ordained your lot, and selected for you the safest and best condition. A ship of large tonnage is to be brought up the river; now, in one part of the stream there is a sandbank; should some one ask, "Why does the captain steer through the deep part of the channel and deviate so much from a straight line?" His answer would be, "Because I should not get my vessel into harbor at all if I did not keep to the deep channel. So, it may be, you would run aground and suffer shipwreck, if your divine Captain did not steer you into the depths of affliction where waves of trouble follow each other in quick succession.

Some plants die if they have too much sunshine. It may be that you are planted where you get but little, you are put there by the loving Husbandman, because only in that situation will you bring forth fruit unto perfection. Remember this, had any other condition been better for you than the one in which you are, divine love would have put you there. You are placed by God in the most suitable circumstances, and if you had the choosing of your lot, you would soon cry, "Lord, choose my inheritance for me, for by my self-will I am pierced through with many sorrows." Be content with such things as you have, since the Lord has ordered all things for your good. Take up your own daily cross; it is the burden best suited for your shoulder, and will prove most effective to make you perfect in every good word and work to the glory of God. Down busy self, and proud impatience, it is not for you to choose, but for the Lord of Love!

> Trials must and will befall,
> But with humble faith to see
> Love inscribed upon them all;
> This is happiness to me.

MORNING — November 12

"The proving of your faith" — 1 Peter 1:7.

FAITH UNTRIED MAY be true faith, but it is sure to be little faith, and it is likely to remain dwarfish so long as it is without trials. Faith never prospers so well as when all things are against her; tempests are her trainers, and lightnings are her illuminators. When a calm reigns on the sea, spread the sails as you will, the ship moves not to its harbor; for on a slumbering ocean the keel sleeps too. Let the winds rush howling forth, and let the waters lift up themselves, then, though the vessel may rock, and her deck may be washed with waves, and her mast may creak under the pressure of the full and swelling sail, it is then that she makes headway towards her desired haven. No flowers wear so lovely a blue as those which grow at the foot of the frozen glacier; no stars gleam so brightly as those which glisten in the polar sky; no water tastes so sweet as that which springs amid the desert sand; and no faith is so precious as that which lives and triumphs in adversity. Tried faith brings experience. You could not have believed your own weakness had you not been compelled to pass through the rivers; and you would never have known God's strength had you not been supported amid the water-floods. Faith increases in solidity, assurance, and intensity, the more it is exercised with tribulation. Faith is precious, and its trial is precious too.

Let not this, however, discourage those who are young in faith. You will have trials enough without seeking them; the full portion will be measured out to you in due season. Meanwhile, if you cannot yet claim the result of long experience, thank God for what grace you have; praise Him for that degree of holy confidence whereunto you have attained. Walk according to that rule, and you shall yet have more and more of the blessing of God, till your faith shall remove mountains and conquer impossibilities.

EVENING

"And in those days Jesus went out into the mountain to pray. And He was spending the night in prayer to God" — Luke 6:12.

IF EVER ONE of woman born might have lived without prayer, it was our spotless, perfect Lord, and yet none was ever so much in supplication as He! Such was His love to His Father, that He loved much to be in communion with Him; such His love for His people, that He desired to be much in intercession for them. The fact of this eminent prayerfulness of Jesus is a lesson for us. He has given us an example that we may follow in His steps. The time He chose was admirable, it was the hour of silence, when the crowd would not disturb Him; the time of inaction, when all but Himself had ceased to labor; and the season when slumber made men forget their woes, and cease their applications to Him for relief. While others found rest in sleep, He refreshed Himself with prayer. The place was also well selected. He was alone where none would intrude, where none could observe; thus was He free from Pharisaic ostentation and vulgar interruption. Those dark and silent hills were a fit oratory for the Son of God. Heaven and earth in midnight stillness heard the groans and sighs of the mysterious Being in whom both worlds were blended.

The continuance of His pleadings is remarkable; the long watches were not too long; the cold wind did not chill His devotions; the grim darkness did not darken His faith, or loneliness check His importunity. We cannot watch with Him one hour, but He watched for us whole nights. The occasion for this prayer is notable; it was after His enemies had been enraged prayer was His refuge and solace; it was before He sent forth the twelve apostles; prayer was the gate of His enterprise, the herald of His new work. Should we not learn from Jesus to resort to special prayer when we are under peculiar trial, or contemplate fresh endeavors for the Master's glory? Lord Jesus, teach us to pray.

November 13 MORNING

"The branch is not able to bear fruit of itself" — John 15:4.

HOW DID YOU begin to bear fruit? It was when you came to Jesus and cast yourselves on His great atonement, and rested on His finished righteousness. Ah! what fruit you had then! Do you remember those early days? Then indeed the vine flourished, the tender grape appeared, the pomegranates budded forth, and the beds of spices gave forth their smell. Have you declined since then? If you have, we charge you to remember that time of love, and repent, and do your first works. Be most in those engagements which you have experimentally proved to draw you nearest to Christ, because it is from Him that all your fruits proceed. Any holy exercise which will bring you to Him will help you to bear fruit.

The sun is, no doubt, a great worker in fruit-creating among the trees of the orchard; and Jesus is still more so among the trees of His garden of grace. When have you been the most fruitless? Has not it been when you have lived farthest from the Lord Jesus Christ, when you have slackened in prayer, when you have departed from the simplicity of your faith, when your graces have engrossed your attention instead of your Lord, when you have said, "My mountain stands firm, I shall never be moved;" and have forgotten where your strength dwells. Has not it been then that your fruit has ceased?

Some of us have been taught that we have nothing out of Christ, by terrible abasement of heart before the Lord. And when we have seen the utter barrenness and death of all creature power, we have cried in anguish, From Him all my fruit must be found, for no fruit can ever come from me. We are taught, by past experience, that the more simply we depend upon the grace of God in Christ, and wait upon the Holy Spirit, the more we shall bring forth fruit unto God. Oh! to trust Jesus for fruit as well as for life.

EVENING

"It is necessary to pray without ceasing" — Luke 18:1.

IF MEN OUGHT always to pray and not to faint, much more Christian men. Jesus has sent His church into the world on the same errand upon which He Himself came, and this mission includes intercession. What if I say that the church is the world's priest? Creation is dumb, but the church is to find a mouth for it. It is the church's high privilege to pray with acceptance. The door of grace is always open for her petitions, and they never return empty-handed. The veil was rent for her, the blood was sprinkled upon the altar for her, God constantly invites her to ask what she wills. Will she refuse the privilege which angels might envy her? Is she not the bride of Christ? May she not go in unto her King at every hour? Shall she allow the precious privilege to be unused? The church always has need for prayer. There are always some in her midst who are declining, or falling into open sin. There are lambs to be prayed for, that they may be carried in Christ's bosom; the strong, lest they grow presumptuous; and the weak, lest they become despairing.

If we kept up prayer-meetings twenty-four hours in the day, all the days in the year, we might never be without a special subject for supplication. Are we ever without the sick and the poor, the afflicted and the wavering? Are we ever without those who seek the conversion of relatives, the reclaiming of backsliders, or the salvation of the depraved? No, with congregations constantly gathering, with ministers always preaching, with millions of sinners lying dead in trespasses and sins; in a country over which the darkness of Romanism is certainly descending; in a world full of idols, cruelties, deviltries, if the church does not pray, how shall she excuse her base neglect of the commission of her loving Lord? Let the church be constant in supplication, let every private believer cast his mite of prayer into the treasury.

MORNING November 14

"I will cut off those who worship and who swear by the LORD and who swear by Malcham" — Zephaniah 1:4,5.

SUCH PERSONS thought themselves safe because they were with both parties; they went with the followers of Jehovah, and bowed at the same time to Malcham. But duplicity is abominable with God, and His soul hates hypocrisy. The idolater who distinctly gives himself to his false god, has one sin less than he who brings his polluted and detestable sacrifice unto the temple of the Lord, while his heart is with the world and the sins thereof. To hold with the hare and run with the hounds, is a dastard's policy. In the common matters of daily life, a double-minded man is despised, but in religion he is loathsome to the last degree. The penalty pronounced in the verse before us is terrible, but it is well deserved; for how should divine justice spare the sinner, who knows the right, approves it, and professes to follow it, and all the while loves the evil, and gives it dominion in his heart?

My soul, search yourself this morning, and see whether you are guilty of double-dealing. You profess to be a follower of Jesus; do you truly love Him? Is your heart right with God? Are you of the family of old Father Honest, or are you a relative of Mr. By-ends? A name to live is of little value if I be indeed dead in trespasses and sins. To have one foot on the land of truth, and another on the sea of falsehood, will involve a terrible fall and a total ruin. Christ will be all or nothing. God fills the whole universe, and hence there is no room for another God. If, then, He reigns in my heart, there will be no space for another reigning power. Do I rest alone on Jesus crucified, and live alone for Him? Is it my desire to do so? Is my heart set upon so doing? If so, blessed be the mighty grace which has led me to salvation; and if not so, Oh Lord, pardon my sad offense, and unite my heart to fear Your name.

EVENING

"And Laban said, It must not be done so in our country, to give the younger before the firstborn" — Genesis 29:26.

WE DO NOT excuse Laban for his dishonesty, but we scruple not to learn from the custom which he quoted as his excuse. There are some things which must be taken in order, and if we would win the second we must secure the first. The second may be the more lovely in our eyes, but the rule of the heavenly country must stand, and the elder must be married first. For instance, many men desire the beautiful and well-favored Rachel of joy and peace in believing, but they must first be wedded to the tender-eyed Leah of repentance. Every one falls in love with happiness, and many would cheerfully serve twice seven years to enjoy it, but according to the rule of the Lord's kingdom, the Leah of real holiness must be beloved of our soul before the Rachel of true happiness can be attained. Heaven stands not first but second, and only by persevering to the end can we win a portion in it. The cross must be carried before the crown can be worn. We must follow our Lord in His humiliation, or we shall never rest with Him in glory.

My soul, what do you say, are you so vain as to hope to break through the heavenly rule? Do you hope for reward without labor, or honor without toil? Dismiss the idle expectation, and be content to take the ill-favored things for the sake of the sweet love of Jesus, which will recompense you for all. In such a spirit, laboring and suffering, you will find bitters grow sweet, and hard things easy. Like Jacob, your years of service will seem unto you but a few days for the love you have to Jesus; and when the dear hour of the wedding feast shall come, all your toils shall be as though they had never been, an hour with Jesus will make up for ages of pain and labor.

> Jesus, to win Yourself so fair,
> Your cross I will with gladness bear:
> Since so the rules of heaven ordain,
> The first I'll wed the next to gain.

November 15   MORNING

"For the LORD'S portion is His people" — *Deuteronomy 32:9.*

HOW ARE THEY His? By His own sovereign choice. He chose them, and set His love upon them. This He did altogether apart from any goodness in them at the time, or any goodness which He foresaw in them. He had mercy on whom He would have mercy and ordained a chosen company unto eternal life; thus, therefore, are they His by His unconstrained election.

They are not only His by choice, but by purchase. He has bought and paid for them to the utmost farthing, hence about His title there can be no dispute. Not with corruptible things, as with silver and gold, but with the precious blood of the Lord Jesus Christ, the Lord's portion has been fully redeemed. There is no mortgage on His estate; no suits can be raised by opposing claimants, the price was paid in open court, and the Church is the Lord's freehold forever. See the blood-mark upon all the chosen, invisible to human eye, but known to Christ, for *"the Lord knows them that are His;"* He forgets none of those whom He has redeemed from among men; He counts the sheep for whom He laid down His life, and remembers well the Church for which He gave Himself.

They are also His by conquest. What a battle He had in us before we would be won! How long He laid siege to our hearts! How often He sent us terms of capitulation! But we barred our gates, and fenced our walls against Him. Do we not remember that glorious hour when He carried our hearts by storm, when He placed His cross against the wall, and scaled our ramparts, planting on our strongholds the blood-red flag of His omnipotent mercy? Yes, we are, indeed, the conquered captives of His omnipotent love. Thus chosen, purchased, and subdued, the rights of our divine possessor are inalienable: we rejoice that we never can be our own; and we desire, day by day, to do His will, and to show forth His glory.

EVENING

"O God, be strong in that which You have worked out for us" — *Psalm 68:28.*

IT IS OUR wisdom, as well as our necessity, to beseech God continually to strengthen that which He has worked in us. It is because of their neglect in this, that many Christians may blame themselves for those trials and afflictions of spirit which arise from unbelief. It is true that Satan seeks to flood the fair garden of the heart and make it a scene of desolation, but it is also true that many Christians leave open the sluice-gates themselves, and let in the dreadful deluge through carelessness and want of prayer to their strong Helper. We often forget that the Author of our faith must be the Preserver of it also. The lamp which was burning in the temple was never allowed to go out, but it had to be daily replenished with fresh oil; in like manner, our faith can only live by being sustained with the oil of grace, and we can only obtain this from God Himself. Foolish virgins we shall prove, if we do not secure the needed sustenance for our lamps. He who built the world upholds it, or it would fall in one tremendous crash; He who made us Christians must maintain us by His Spirit, or our ruin will be speedy and final.

Let us, then, evening by evening, go to our Lord for the grace and strength we need. We have a strong argument to plead, for it is His own work of grace which we ask Him to strengthen that which He has worked out for us. Do you think He will fail to protect and sustain that? Only let your faith take hold of His strength, and all the powers of darkness, led on by the master fiend of hell, cannot cast a cloud or shadow over your joy and peace. Why faint when you may be strong? Why suffer defeat when you may conquer? Oh! take your wavering faith and drooping graces to Him who can revive and replenish them, and earnestly pray, "Strengthen, Oh God, that which You have worked for us."

MORNING   November 16

"The LORD is my portion, says my soul" — Lamentations 3:24.

IT IS NOT, 'The Lord is partly my portion,' nor is it, 'The Lord is in my portion;' but it is that He Himself makes up the sum total of my soul's inheritance. Within the circumference of that circle lies all that we possess or desire. The Lord is my portion. Not His grace merely, nor His love, nor His covenant, but Jehovah Himself. He has chosen us for His portion, and we have chosen Him for ours. It is true that the Lord must first choose our inheritance for us, or else we shall never choose it for ourselves; but if we are really called according to the purpose of electing love, we can sing:

> Lov'd of my God for Him again,
> With love intense I burn;
> Chosen of Him ere time began,
> I choose Him in return.

The Lord is our all-sufficient portion. God fills Himself; and if God is all-sufficient in Himself, He must be all-sufficient for us. It is not easy to satisfy man's desires. When he dreams that he is satisfied, soon he wakes to the perception that there is somewhat yet beyond, and straightway the horse-leech in his heart cries, "Give, give." But all that we can wish for is to be found in our divine portion, so that we ask, *"Whom have I in heaven but You? And there is none upon earth that I desire beside You."* Well may we *"delight ourselves in the Lord"* who makes us to drink of the river of His pleasures. Our faith stretches her wings and mounts like an eagle into the heaven of divine love as to her proper dwelling.place. *"The lines have fallen to us in pleasant places; yes, we have a goodly heritage."* Let us rejoice in the Lord always; let us show to the world that we are a happy and a blessed people, and thus induce them to exclaim, *"We will go with you, for we have heard that God is with you."*

EVENING
"Your eyes shall see the king in his beauty" — Isaiah 33:17.

THE MORE YOU know about Christ the less will you be satisfied with superficial views of Him; and the more deeply you study His transactions in the eternal covenant, His engagements on your behalf as the eternal Surety, and the fullness of His grace which shines in all His offices, the more truly will you see the King in His beauty. Be much in such outlooks. Long more and more to see Jesus.

Meditation and contemplation are often like windows of agate, and gates of carbuncle, through which we behold the Redeemer. Meditation puts the telescope to the eye, and enables us to see Jesus after a better sort than we could have seen Him if we had lived in the days of His flesh. Would that our conversation were more in heaven, and that we were more taken up with the person, the work, the beauty of our incarnate Lord. More meditation, and the beauty of the King would flash upon us with more resplendence. Beloved, it is very probable that we shall have such a sight of our glorious King as we never had before, when we come to die. Many saints in dying have looked up from amidst the stormy waters, and have seen Jesus walking on the waves of the sea, and heard Him say, *"It is I, be not afraid."* Yes, when the tenement begins to shake, and the clay falls away, we see Christ through the rifts, and between the rafters the sunlight of heaven comes streaming in. But if we want to see face to face the *"King in His beauty,"* we must go to heaven for the sight, or the King must come here in person. Oh that He would come on the wings of the wind! He is our Husband, and we are widowed by His absence; He is our Brother dear and fair, and we are lonely without Him. Thick veils and clouds hang between our souls and their true life. When shall the day break and the shadows flee away? Oh, long-expected day, begin!

November 17   MORNING

"To Him be glory forever, amen! — Romans 11:36.

"TO HIM BE *"glory forever."* This should be the single desire of the Christian. All other wishes must be subservient and tributary to this one. The Christian may wish for prosperity in his business, but only so far as it may help him to promote this: *"To Him be glory forever."* He may desire to attain more gifts and more graces, but it should only be that "To Him may be glory forever." You are not acting as you ought to do when you are moved by any other motive than a single eye to your Lord's glory. As a Christian, you are *"of God, and through God,"* then live "to God." Let nothing ever set your heart beating so mightily as love to Him. Let this ambition fire your soul; be this the foundation of every enterprise upon which you enter, and this your sustaining motive whenever your zeal would grow chill; make God your only object. Depend upon it, where self begins sorrow begins; but if God be my supreme delight and only object,

> To me 'tis equal whether love ordain
> My life or death, appoint me ease or pain.

Let your desire for God's glory be a growing desire. You blessed Him in your youth, do not be content with such praises as you gave Him then. Has God prospered you in business? Give Him more as He has given you more. Has God given you experience? Praise Him by stronger faith than you exercised at first. Does your knowledge grow? Then sing more sweetly. Do you enjoy happier times than you once had? Have you been restored from sickness, and has your sorrow been turned into peace and joy? Then give Him more music; put more coals and more sweet frankincense into the censer of your praise. Practically in your life give Him honor, putting the *"Amen"* to this doxology to your great and gracious Lord, by your own individual service and increasing holiness.

EVENING

"He who cuts wood shall be endangered by it" — Ecclesiastes 10:9.

OPPRESSORS MAY GET their will of poor and needy men as easily as they can split logs of wood, but they had better mind, for it is a dangerous business, and a splinter from a tree has often killed the woodman. Jesus is persecuted in every injured saint, and He is mighty to avenge His beloved ones. Success in treading down the poor and needy is a thing to be trembled at: if there be no danger to persecutors here there will be great danger hereafter.

To cut wood is a common everyday business, and yet it has its dangers; so then, reader, there are dangers connected with your calling and daily life which it will be well for you to be aware of. We refer not to hazards by flood and field, or by disease and sudden death, but to perils of a spiritual sort. Your occupation may be as humble as log splitting, and yet the devil can tempt you in it. You may be a domestic servant, a farm laborer, or a mechanic, and you may be greatly screened from temptations to the grosser vices, and yet some secret sin may do you damage. Those who dwell at home, and mingle not with the rough world, may yet be endangered by their very seclusion. Nowhere is he safe who thinks himself so. Pride may enter a poor man's heart; avarice may reign in a cottager's bosom; uncleanness may venture into the quietest home; and anger, and envy, and malice may insinuate themselves into the most rural abode. Even in speaking a few words to a servant we may sin; a little purchase at a shop may be the first link in a chain of temptations; the mere looking out of a window may be the beginning of evil. Oh Lord, how exposed we are! How shall we be secured! To keep ourselves is work too hard for us: only You Yourself are able to preserve us in such a world of evils. Spread Your wings over us, and we, like little chickens, will cower down beneath You, and feel ourselves safe!

MORNING   November 18

"A spring shut up, a fountain sealed" — *Song of Solomon 4:12.*

IN THIS METAPHOR, which has reference to the inner life of a believer, we have very plainly the idea of secrecy. It is *"a spring shut up;"* just as there were springs in the East, over which an edifice was built, so that none could reach them save those who knew the secret entrance; so is the heart of a believer when it is renewed by grace. There is a mysterious life within which no human skill can touch. It is a secret which no other man knows; no, which the very man who is the possessor of it cannot tell to his neighbor. The text includes not only secrecy, but separation. It is not the common spring, of which every passer-by may drink, it is one kept and preserved from all others; it is a fountain bearing a particular mark, a king's royal seal, so that all can perceive that it is not a common fountain, but a fountain owned by a proprietor, and placed specially by itself alone. So is it with the spiritual life. The chosen of God were separated in the eternal decree; they were separated by God in the day of redemption; and they are separated by the possession of a life which others have not; and it is impossible for them to feel at home with the world, or to delight in its pleasures.

There is also the idea of sacredness. The spring shut up is preserved for the use of some special person; and such is the Christian's heart. It is a spring kept for Jesus. Every Christian should feel that he has God's seal upon him and he should be able to say with Paul, *"From henceforth let no man trouble me, for I bear in my body the marks of the Lord Jesus."* Another idea is prominent; it is that of security. Oh! how sure and safe is the inner life of the believer! If all the powers of earth and hell could combine against it, that immortal principle must still exist, for He who gave it pledged His life for its preservation. And who *"is he that shall harm you,"* when God is your protector?

EVENING
"You are from everlasting" — *Psalm 93:2.*

CHRIST IS EVERLASTING. Of Him we may sing with David, *"Your throne, Oh God, is forever and ever."* Rejoice, believer in Jesus Christ, the same yesterday, today, and forever. Jesus always was. The Babe born in Bethlehem was united to the Word, which was in the beginning by whom all things were made. The title by which Christ revealed Himself to John in Patmos was, "Him who is and who was, and who is to come." If He were not God from everlasting, we could not so devoutly love Him; we could not feel that He had any share in the eternal love which is the fountain of all covenant blessings; but since He was from all eternity with the Father, we trace the stream of divine love to Himself equally with His Father and the blessed Spirit.

As our Lord always was, so also He is for evermore. Jesus is not dead; *"He ever lives to make intercession for us."* Resort to Him in all your times of need, for He is waiting to bless you still. Moreover, Jesus our Lord ever shall be. If God should spare your life to fulfil your full day of threescore years and ten, you will find that His cleansing fountain is still opened, and His precious blood has not lost its power; you shall find that the Priest who filled the healing fount with His own blood, lives to purge you from all iniquity. When only your last battle remains to be fought, you shall find that the hand of your conquering Captain has not grown feeble; the living Savior shall cheer the dying saint. When you enter heaven you shall find Him there bearing the dew of His youth; and through eternity the Lord Jesus shall still remain the perennial spring of joy, and life, and glory to His people. Living waters may you draw from this sacred well! Jesus always was, He always is, He always shall be. He is eternal in all His attributes, in all His offices, in all His might, and willingness to bless, comfort, guard, and crown His chosen people.

November 19   MORNING

"But keep back from foolish questions" — Titus 3:9.

OUR DAYS ARE few, and are far better spent in doing good, than in disputing over matters which are, at best, of minor importance. The old schoolmen did a world of mischief by their incessant discussion of subjects of no practical importance; and our Churches suffer much from petty wars over abstruse points and unimportant questions. After everything has been said that can be said, neither party is any the wiser, and therefore the discussion no more promotes knowledge than love, and it is foolish to sow in so barren a field. Questions upon points wherein Scripture is silent; upon mysteries which belong to God alone; upon prophecies of doubtful interpretation; and upon mere modes of observing human ceremonial, are all foolish, and wise men avoid them. Our business is neither to ask nor answer foolish questions, but to avoid them altogether; and if we observe the apostle's precept (Titus 3:8) to be careful to maintain good works, we shall find ourselves far too much occupied with profitable business to take much interest in unworthy, contentious, and needless striving.

There are, however, some questions which are the reverse of foolish, which we must not avoid, but fairly and honestly meet, such as these: Do I believe in the Lord Jesus Christ? Am I renewed in the spirit of my mind? Am I walking not after the flesh, but after the Spirit? Am I growing in grace? Does my conversation adorn the doctrine of God my Savior? Am I looking for the coming of the Lord, and watching as a servant should do who expects his master? What more can I do for Jesus? Such inquiries as these urgently demand our attention; and if we have been at all given to cavilling, let us now turn our critical abilities to a service so much more profitable. Let us be peacemakers, and endeavor to lead others both by our precept and example, to *"keep back from foolish questions."*

EVENING

"Oh that I knew where I might find Him" — Job 23:3.

IN JOB'S UTTERMOST extremity he cried after the Lord. The longing desire of an afflicted child of God is once more to see his Father's face. His first prayer is not, "Oh that I might be healed of the disease which now festers in every part of my body!" Nor is it even, "Oh that I might see my children restored from the jaws of the grave, and my property once more brought from the hand of the spoiler!" But the first and uppermost cry is, *"Oh that I knew where I might find Him,"* who is my God! that I might come even to His seat! God's children run home when the storm comes on. It is the heaven-born instinct of a gracious soul to seek shelter from all ills beneath the wings of Jehovah. He that has made his refuge God, might serve as the title of a true believer.

A hypocrite, when afflicted by God, resents the infliction, and, like a slave, would run from the Master who has scourged him; but not so the true heir of heaven, he kisses the hand which smote him, and seeks shelter from the rod in the bosom of the God who frowned upon him. Job's desire to commune with God was intensified by the failure of all other sources of consolation. The patriarch turned away from his sorry friends, and looked up to the celestial throne, just as a traveler turns from his empty skin bottle, and goes with all speed, to the well. He bids farewell to earthborn hopes, and cries, *"Oh that I knew where I might find my God!"*

Nothing teaches us so much the preciousness of the Creator, as when we learn the emptiness of all besides. Turning away with bitter scorn from earth's hives, where we find no honey, but many sharp stings, we rejoice in Him whose faithful word is sweeter than honey or the honeycomb. In every trouble we should first seek to realize God's presence with us. Only let us enjoy His smile, and we can bear our daily cross with a willing heart for His dear sake.

MORNING November 20

"O LORD, You have spoken for the causes of my soul" — Lamentations 3:58.

OBSERVE HOW positively the prophet speaks. He does not say, I hope, I trust, I sometimes think, that God has pleaded the causes of my soul; but he speaks of it as a matter of fact not to be disputed. *"You have spoken for the causes of my soul."* Let us, by the aid of the gracious Comforter, shake off those doubts and fears which so much mar our peace and comfort. Be this our prayer, that we may have done with the harsh croaking voice of surmise and suspicion, and may be able to speak with the clear, melodious voice of full assurance.

Notice how gratefully the prophet speaks, ascribing all the glory to God alone! You perceive there is not a word concerning himself or his own pleadings. He does not ascribe his deliverance in any measure to any man, much less to his own merit; but it is "You" - *"Oh Lord, You have spoken for the causes of my soul; You have redeemed my life."* A grateful spirit should ever be cultivated by the Christian; and especially after deliverances we should prepare a song for our God. Earth should be a temple filled with the songs of grateful saints, and every day should be a censer smoking with the sweet incense of thanksgiving.

How joyful Jeremiah seems to be while he records the Lord's mercy. How triumphantly he lifts up the strain! He has been in the low dungeon, and is even now no other than the weeping prophet; and yet in the very book which is called "Lamentations," clear as the song of Miriam when she dashed her fingers against the tabret, shrill as the note of Deborah when she met Barak with shouts of victory, we hear the voice of Jeremiah going up to heaven, *"You have spoken for the causes of my soul; You have redeemed my life."* Oh children of God, seek after a vital experience of the Lord's loving-kindness, and when you have it, speak positively of it; sing gratefully; shout triumphantly.

EVENING

"The conies are a feeble folk yet they make their houses in the rocks" — Proverbs 30:26.

CONSCIOUS OF THEIR own natural defenselessness, the conies resort to burrows in the rocks, and are secure from their enemies. My heart, be willing to gather a lesson from these feeble folk. You are as weak and as exposed to peril as the timid coney, be as wise to seek a shelter. My best security is within the munitions of an immutable Jehovah, where His unalterable promises stand like giant walls of rock. It will be well with you, my heart, if you can always hide yourself in the bulwarks of His glorious attributes, all of which are guarantees of safety for those who put their trust in Him. Blessed be the name of the Lord, I have so done, and have found myself like David in Adullam, safe from the cruelty of my enemy. I have not now to find out the blessedness of the man who puts his trust in the Lord, for long ago, when Satan and my sins pursued me, I fled to the cleft of the rock Christ Jesus, and in His riven side I found a delightful resting-place. My heart, run to Him anew tonight, whatever your present grief may be; Jesus feels for you; Jesus consoles you; Jesus will help you.

No monarch in his impregnable fortress is more secure than the coney in his rocky burrow. The master of ten thousand chariots is not one whit better protected than the little dweller in the mountain's cleft. In Jesus the weak are strong, and the defenseless safe; they could not be more strong if they were giants, or more safe if they were in heaven. Faith gives to men on earth the protection of the God of heaven. More they cannot need, and need not wish. The conies cannot build a castle, but they avail themselves of what is there already: I cannot make myself a refuge, but Jesus has provided it, His Father has given it, His Spirit has revealed it, and lo, again tonight I enter it, and am safe from every foe.

November 21

MORNING

"Do not grieve the Holy Spirit" — Ephesians 4:30.

ALL THAT THE believer has must come from Christ, but it comes solely through the channel of the Spirit of all grace. Moreover, as all blessings thus flow to you through the Holy Spirit, so also no good thing can come out of you in holy thought, devout worship, or gracious act, apart from the sanctifying operation of the same Spirit. Even if the good seed be sown in you, yet it lies dormant except He works in you to will and to do of His own good pleasure. Do you desire to speak for Jesus? How can you unless the Holy Spirit touch your tongue? Do you desire to pray? Alas! what dull work it is unless the Spirit makes intercession for you! Do you desire to subdue sin? Would you be holy? Would you imitate your Master? Do you desire to rise to superlative heights of spirituality? Are you wanting to be made like the angels of God, full of zeal and ardor for the Master's cause? You cannot without the Spirit; *"Without Me you can do nothing."* Oh branch of the vine, you can have no fruit without the sap! Oh child of God, you have no life within you apart from the life which God gives you through His Spirit!

Then let us not grieve Him or provoke Him to anger by our sin. Let us not quench Him in one of His faintest motions in our soul; let us foster every suggestion, and be ready to obey every prompting. If the Holy Spirit be indeed so mighty, let us attempt nothing without Him; let us begin no project, and carry on no enterprise, and conclude no transaction, without imploring His blessing. Let us do Him the due homage of feeling our entire weakness apart from Him, and then depending alone upon Him, having this for our prayer, "Open my heart and my whole being to Your incoming, and uphold me with Your free Spirit when I shall have received that Spirit in my inward parts."

EVENING

"Lazarus was one of those at the table with Him" — John 12:2.

HE IS TO be envied. It was well to be Martha and serve, but better to be Lazarus and commune. There are times for each purpose, and each is comely in its season, but none of the trees of the garden yield such clusters as the vine of fellowship. To sit with Jesus, to hear His words, to mark His acts, and receive His smiles, was such a favor as must have made Lazarus as happy as the angels. When it has been our happy lot to feast with our Beloved in His banqueting-hall, we would not have given half a sigh for all the kingdoms of the world, if so much breath could have bought them.

He is to be imitated. It would have been a strange thing if Lazarus had not been at the table where Jesus was, for he had been dead, and Jesus had raised him. For the risen one to be absent when the Lord who gave him life was at his house, would have been ungrateful indeed. We too were once dead, yes, and like Lazarus stinking in the grave of sin; Jesus raised us, and by His life we live. Can we be content to live at a distance from Him? Do we omit to remember Him at His table, where He deigns to feast with His brothers? Oh, this is cruel! It behooves us to repent, and do as He has bidden us, for His least wish should be law to 'us. To have lived without constant intercourse with one of whom the Jews said, *"Behold how He loved him,"* would have been disgraceful to Lazarus, is it excusable in us whom Jesus has loved with an everlasting love? To have been cold to Him who wept over his lifeless corpse, would have argued great brutishness in Lazarus. What does it argue in us over whom the Savior has not only wept, but bled? Come, brothers, who read this portion, let us return unto our heavenly Bridegroom, and ask for His Spirit that we may be on terms of closer intimacy with Him, and henceforth sit at the table with Him.

MORNING   November 22

"Israel served for a wife, and he shepherded for a wife" — *Hosea 12:12.*

JACOB, WHILE expostulating with Laban, thus describes his own toil, *"This twenty years have I been with you. That which was torn of beasts I brought not unto you; I bore the loss of it; of my hand did you require it, whether stolen by day, or stolen by night. Thus I was; in the day the drought consumed me, and the frost by night; and my sleep departed from my eyes."* Even more toilsome than this was the life of our Savior here below. He watched over all His sheep till He gave in as His last account, *"Of all those whom You have given me I have lost none."* His hair was wet with dew, and His locks with the drops of the night. Sleep departed from His eyes, for all night He was in prayer wrestling for His people. One night Peter must be pleaded for; soon, another claims His tearful intercession. No shepherd sitting beneath the cold skies, looking up to the stars, could ever utter such complaints because of the hardness of his toil as Jesus Christ might have brought, if He had chosen to do so, because of the sternness of His service in order to procure His spouse -

> Cold mountains and the midnight air,
> Witnessed the fervor of His prayer;
> The desert His temptations knew,
> His conflict and His victory too.

It is sweet to dwell upon the spiritual parallel of Laban having required all the sheep at Jacob's hand. If they were torn of beasts, Jacob must make it good; if any of them died, he must stand as surety for the whole. Was not the toil of Jesus for His Church the toil of one who was under suretyship obligations to bring every believing one safe to the hand of Him who had committed them to His charge? Look upon toiling Jacob, and you see a representation of Him of whom we read, *"He shall feed His flock like a shepherd."*

EVENING
"The power of His resurrection" — *Philippians 3:10.*

THE DOCTRINE OF a risen Savior is exceedingly precious. The resurrection is the cornerstone of the entire building of Christianity. It is the keystone of the arch of our salvation. It would take a volume to set forth all the streams of living water which flow from this one sacred source, the resurrection of our dear Lord and Savior Jesus Christ; but to know that He has risen, and to have fellowship with Him as such; communing with the risen Savior by possessing a risen life; seeing Him leave the tomb by leaving the tomb of worldliness ourselves — this is even still more precious. The doctrine is the basis of the experience, but as the flower is more lovely than the root, so is the experience of fellowship with the risen Savior more lovely than the doctrine itself.

I would have you believe that Christ rose from the dead so as to sing of it, and derive all the consolation which it is possible for you to extract front this well-ascertained and well-witnessed fact; but I beseech you, rest not contented even there. Though you cannot, like the disciples, see Him visibly, yet I bid you aspire to see Christ Jesus by the eye of faith; and though, like Mary Magdalene, you may not "touch" Him, yet may you be privileged to converse with Him, and to know that He is risen, you yourselves being risen in Him to newness of life.

To know a crucified Savior as having crucified all my sins, is a high degree of knowledge; but to know a risen Savior as having justified me, and to realize that He has bestowed upon me new life, having given me to be a new creature through His own newness of life, this is a noble style of experience: short of it, none ought to rest satisfied. May you both *"know Him, and the power of His resurrection."* Why should souls who are quickened with Jesus, wear the grave.clothes of worldliness and unbelief? Rise, for the Lord is risen.

November 23　　　　　　MORNING

"Fellowship with Him" — *1 John 1:6.*

WHEN WE WERE united by faith to Christ, we were brought into such complete fellowship with Him, that we were made one with Him, and His interests and ours became mutual and identical. We have fellowship with Christ in His love. What He loves we love. He loves the saints; so do we. He loves sinners; so do we. He loves the poor perishing race of man, and works to turn earth's deserts into the garden of the Lord; so do we. We have fellowship with Him in His desires. He desires the glory of God; we also labor for the same. He desires that the saints may be with Him where He is; we desire to be with Him there too. He desires to drive out sin; behold we fight under His banner. He desires that His Father's name may be loved and adored by all His creatures; we pray daily, *"Let Your kingdom come and Your will be done on earth, even as it is in heaven."*

We have fellowship with Christ in His sufferings. We are not nailed to the cross, nor do we die a cruel death, but when He is reproached, we are reproached; and a very sweet thing it is to be blamed for His sake, to be despised for following the Master, to have the world against us. The disciple should not be above His Lord. In our measure we commune with Him in His labors, ministering to men by the word of truth and by deeds of love. Our meat and our drink, like His, is to do the will of Him who has sent us and to finish His work.

We have also fellowship with Christ in His joys. We are happy in His happiness, we rejoice in His exaltation. Have you ever tasted that joy, believer? There is no purer or more thrilling delight to be known this side of heaven than that of having Christ's joy fulfilled in us, that our joy may be full. His glory awaits us to complete our fellowship, for His Church shall sit with Him upon His throne, as His well-beloved bride and queen.

EVENING

"Get up into the mountain" — *Isaiah 40:9.*

EACH BELIEVER should be thirsting for God, for the living God, and longing to climb the hill of the Lord, and see Him face to face. We ought not to rest content in the mists of the valley when the summit of Tabor awaits us. My soul thirsts to drink deep of the cup which is reserved for those who reach the mountain's brow, and bathe their brows in heaven. How pure are the dews of the hills, how fresh is the mountain air, how rich the fare of the dwellers aloft, whose windows look into the New Jerusalem! Many saints are content to live like men in coal mines, who see not the sun; they eat dust like the serpent when they might taste the ambrosial food of angels; they are content to wear the miner's garb when they might put on king's robes; tears mar their faces when they might anoint them with celestial oil. Satisfied I am that many a believer pines in a dungeon when he might walk on the palace roof, and view the goodly land and Lebanon.

Rouse, Oh believer, from your low condition! Cast away your sloth, your lethargy, your coldness, or whatever interferes with your chaste and pure love to Christ, your soul's Husband. Make Him the source, the center, and the circumference of all your soul's range of delight. What enchants you into such folly as to remain in a pit when you may sit on a throne? Live not in the lowlands of bondage now that mountain liberty is conferred upon you. Rest no longer satisfied with your dwarfish attainments, but press forward to things more sublime and heavenly. Aspire to a higher, a nobler, a fuller life. Upward to heaven! Nearer to God!

> When will You come unto me, Lord?
> Oh come, my Lord most dear!
> Come near, come nearer, nearer still,
> I'm blest when You are near.

MORNING   November 24

"But there the glorious LORD will be to us a place of broad rivers and streams" — Isaiah 33:21,

BROAD RIVERS AND streams produce fertility, and abundance in the land. Places near broad rivers are remarkable for the variety of their plants and their plentiful harvests. God is all this to His Church. Having God she has abundance. What can she ask for that He will not give her? What want can she mention which He will not supply? *"In this mountain shall the Lord of Hosts make unto all people a feast of fat things."* Do you want the bread of life? It drops like manna from the sky. Do you want refreshing streams? The rock follows you, and that Rock is Christ. If you suffer any want it is your own fault; if you are straitened you are not straitened in Him, but ill your own heart.

Broad rivers and streams also point to commerce. Our glorious Lord is to us a place of heavenly merchandise. Through our Redeemer we have commerce with the past; the wealth of Calvary, the treasures of the covenant, the riches of the ancient days of election, the stores of eternity, all come to us down the broad stream of our gracious Lord. We have commerce, too, with the future. Through our glorious Lord we have commerce with angels; communion with the bright spirits washed in blood, who sing before the throne; no, better still, we have fellowship with the Infinite One.

Broad rivers and streams are especially intended to set forth the idea of security. Rivers were of old a defense. Oh! beloved, what a defense is God to His Church! The devil cannot cross this broad river of God. How he wishes he could turn the current, but fear not, for God abides immutably the same. Satan may worry, but he cannot destroy us; no galley with oars shall invade our river, neither shall gallant ship pass thereby.

EVENING

"A little sleep, a little slumber, a little folding of the hands to sleep; so shall your poverty come as one who travels; and your need like an armed man" — Proverbs 24:33-34.

THE WORST OF sluggards only ask for a little slumber; they would be indignant if they were accused of thorough idleness. A little folding of the hands to sleep is all they crave, and they have a crowd of reasons to show that this indulgence is a very proper one. Yet by these littles the day ebbs out, and the time for labor is all gone, and the field is grown over with thorns. It is by little procrastinations that men ruin their souls. They have no intention to delay for years; a few months will bring the more convenient season. Tomorrow if you will, they will attend to serious things; but the present hour is so occupied and altogether so unsuitable, that they beg to be excused. Like sands from an hour-glass, time passes, life is wasted by driblets, and seasons of grace lost by little slumbers. Oh, to be wise, to catch the flying hour, to use the moments on the wing!

May the Lord teach us this sacred wisdom, for otherwise a poverty of the worst sort awaits us, eternal poverty which shall want even a drop of water, and beg for it in vain. Like a traveler steadily pursuing his journey, poverty overtakes the slothful, and ruin overthrows the undecided; each hour brings the dreaded pursuer nearer; he pauses not by the way, for he is on his master's business and must not tarry. As an armed man enters with authority and power, so shall want come to the idle, and death to the impenitent, and there will be no escape. Oh that men were wise before it is too late; and would seek diligently unto the Lord Jesus, or before the solemn day shall dawn when it will be too late to plough and to sow, too late to repent and believe. In harvest, it is vain to lament that the seed time was neglected. As yet, faith and holy decision are timely. May we obtain them this night.

November 25 MORNING

"To announce deliverance to the captives' — Luke 4:18.

NONE BUT JESUS can give deliverance to captives. Real liberty comes from Him only. It is a liberty righteously bestowed; for the Son, who is Heir of all things, has a right to make men free. The saints honor the justice of God, which now secures their salvation. It is a liberty which has been dearly purchased. Christ speaks it by His power, but He bought it by His blood. He makes you free, but it is by His own bonds. You go clear, because He bore your burden for you; you are set at liberty, because He has suffered in your stead. But, though dearly purchased, He freely gives it. Jesus asks nothing of us as a preparation for this liberty. He finds us sitting in sackcloth and ashes, and bids us put on the beautiful array of freedom; He saves us just as we are, and all without our help or merit.

When Jesus sets free, the liberty is perpetually entailed; no chains can bind again. Let the Master say to me, Captive, I have delivered you; and it is done forever. Satan may plot to enslave us, but if the Lord be on our side, whom shall we fear? The world, with its temptations, may seek to ensnare us, but mightier is He who is for us than all they who be against us. The machinations of our own deceitful hearts may harass and annoy us, but He who has begun the good work in us will carry it on and perfect it to the end. The foes of God and the enemies of man may gather their hosts together, and come with concentrated fury against us, but if God acquits, who is he that condemns? Not more free is the eagle which mounts to his rocky aerie, and afterwards outsoars the clouds, than the soul which Christ has delivered.

If we are no more under the law, but free from its curse, let our liberty be practically exhibited in our serving God with gratitude and delight. *"I am Your servant, and the son of Your handmaid: You have loosed my bonds." "Lord, what will You have me to do?"*

EVENING

"For He said to Moses, I will show mercy to whom I desire to show mercy, and I will have pity on whom I desire to have pity" — Romans 9:15.

IN THESE WORDS the Lord in the plainest manner claims the right to give or to withhold His mercy according to His own sovereign will. As the prerogative of life and death is vested in the monarch, so the Judge of all the earth has a right to spare or condemn the guilty, as may seem best in His sight. Men by their sins have forfeited all claim upon God; they deserve to perish for their sins. And if they all do so, they have no ground for complaint. If the Lord steps in to save any, He may do so if the ends of justice are not thwarted; but if He judges it best to leave the condemned to suffer the righteous sentence, none may arraign Him at their bar. Foolish and impudent are all those discourses about the rights of men to be all placed on the same footing; ignorant, if not worse, are those contentions against discriminating grace, which are but the rebellions of proud human nature against the crown and scepter of Jehovah. When we are brought to see our own utter ruin and ill desert, and the justice of the divine verdict against sin, we no longer cavil at the truth that the Lord is not bound to save us; we do not murmur if He chooses to save others, as though He were doing us an injury, but feel that if He deigns to look upon us, it will be His own free act of undeserved goodness, for which we shall forever bless His name.

How shall those who are the subjects of divine election sufficiently adore the grace of God? They have no room for boasting, for sovereignty most effectually excludes it. The Lord's will alone is glorified, and the very notion of human merit is cast out to everlasting contempt. There is no more humbling doctrine in Scripture than that of election, none that promote gratitude more, and, consequently, none more sanctifying. Believers should not be afraid of it, but adoringly rejoice in it.

MORNING
November 26

"Whatever your hand finds to do, do it with all your might" — *Ecclesiastes 9:10.*

"WHATEVER YOUR *hand finds to do,"* refers to works that are possible. There are many things which our heart finds to do which we never shall do. It is well it is in our heart; but if we would be eminently useful, we must not be content with forming schemes in our heart, and talking of them; we must practically carry out *"whatever our hand finds to do."* One good deed is more worth than a thousand brilliant theories. Let us not wait for large opportunities, or for a different kind of work, but do just the things we *"find to do"* day by day. We have no other time in which to live. The past is gone; the future has not arrived; we never shall have any time but time present. Then do not wait until your experience has ripened into maturity before you attempt to serve God. Endeavor now to bring forth fruit. Serve God now, but be careful as to the way in which you perform what you find to do, *"do it with all your might."* Do it promptly; do not fritter away your life in thinking of what you intend to do tomorrow as if that could recompense for the idleness of today. No man ever served God by doing things tomorrow. If we honor Christ and are blessed, it is by the things which we do today. Whatever you do for Christ throw your whole soul into it. Do not give Christ a little slurred labor, done as a matter of course now and then; but when you do serve Him, do it with heart, and soul, and strength.

But where is the might of a Christian? It is not in himself, for he is perfect weakness. His might lies in the Lord of Hosts. Then let us seek His help; let us proceed with prayer and faith, and when we have done what our *"hand finds to do"* let us wait upon the Lord for His blessing. What we do thus will be well done, and will not fail in its effect.

EVENING
"They shall rejoice and shall see the plummet in the hand of Zerubbabel" — *Zechariah 4:10.*

SMALL THINGS MARKED the beginning of the work in the hand of Zerubbabel, but none might despise it, for the Lord had raised up one who would persevere until the headstone should be brought forth with shouting. The plummet was in good hands. Here is the comfort of every believer in the Lord Jesus; let the work of grace be ever so small in its beginnings, the plummet is in good hands, a master builder greater than Solomon has undertaken the raising of the heavenly temple, and He will not fail nor be discouraged till the topmost pinnacle shall be raised. If the plummet were in the hand of any merely human being, we might fear for the building, but the pleasure of the Lord shall prosper in Jesus' hand.

The works did not proceed irregularly, and without care, for the master's hand carried a good instrument. Had the walls been hurriedly run up without due superintendence, they might have been out of the perpendicular; but the plummet was used by the chosen overseer. Jesus is evermore watching the erection of His spiritual temple, that it may be built securely and well. We are for haste, but Jesus is for judgment. He will use the plummet, and that which is out of line must come down, every stone of it. Hence the failure of many a flattering work, the overthrow of many a glittering profession. It is not for us to judge the Lord's church, since Jesus has a steady hand, and a true eye, and can use the plummet well. Do we not rejoice to see judgment left to Him?

The plummet was in active use; it was in the builder's hand; a sure indication that he meant to push on the work to completion. Oh Lord Jesus, how would we indeed be glad if we could see You at Your great work. Oh Zion, the beautiful, your walls are still in ruins! Rise, You glorious Builder, and make her desolations to rejoice at Your coming.

November 27   MORNING

"Joshua the high priest standing before the Angel of the LORD" — Zechariah 3:1.

IN JOSHUA THE high priest we see a picture of each and every child of God, who has been made near by the blood of Christ, and has been taught to minister in holy things, and enter into that which is within the veil. Jesus has made us priests and kings unto God, and even here upon earth we exercise the priesthood of consecrated living and hallowed service. But this high priest is said to be *"standing before the angel of the Lord,"* that is standing to minister. This should be the perpetual position of every true believer. Every place is now God's temple, and His people can as truly serve Him in their daily employments as in His house. They are to be always ministering, offering the spiritual sacrifice of prayer and praise, and presenting themselves a *"living sacrifice."*

But notice where it is that Joshua stands to minister, it is before the Angel of Jehovah. It is only through a mediator that we poor defiled ones can ever become priests unto God. I present what I have before the messenger, the Angel of the covenant, the Lord Jesus; and through Him my prayers find acceptance wrapped up in His prayers. My praises become sweet as they are bound up with bundles of myrrh, and aloes, and cassia from Christ's own garden. If I can bring Him nothing but my tears, He will put them with His own tears in His own bottle, for He once wept; if I can bring Him nothing but my groans and sighs, He will accept these as an acceptable sacrifice, for He once was broken in heart, and sighed heavily in spirit. I myself, standing in Him, am accepted in the Beloved; and all my polluted works, though in themselves only objects of divine abhorrence, are so received, that God smells a sweet savor. He is content and I am blessed. See, then, the position of the Christian: *"a priest ... standing ... before the Angel of the Lord."*

EVENING

"The forgiveness of sins, according to the riches of His grace" — Ephesians 1:7.

COULD THERE BE a sweeter word in any language than that word *"forgiveness,"* when it sounds in a guilty sinner's ear, like the silver notes of jubilee to the captive Israelite? Blessed, forever blessed be that dear star of pardon which shines into the condemned cell, and gives the perishing a gleam of hope amid the midnight of despair! Can it be possible that sin, such sin as mine, can be forgiven, forgiven altogether, and forever? Hell is my portion as a sinner, there is no possibility of my escaping from it while sin remains upon me; can the load of guilt be uplifted, the crimson stain removed? Can the adamantine stones of my prison-house ever be loosed from their mortises, or the doors be lifted from their hinges?

Jesus tells me that I may yet be clean. Forever blessed be the revelation of atoning love which not only tells me that pardon is possible, but that it is secured to all who rest in Jesus. I have believed in the appointed propitiation, even Jesus crucified, and therefore my sins are at this moment, and forever, forgiven by virtue of His substitutionary pains and death.

What joy is this! What bliss to be a perfectly pardoned soul! My soul dedicates all her powers to Him who of His own unpurchased love became my surety, and worked out for me redemption through His blood. What riches of grace does free forgiveness exhibit! To forgive at all, to forgive fully, to forgive freely, to forgive forever! Here is a constellation of wonders; and when I think of how great my sins were, how dear were the precious drops which cleansed me from them, and how gracious was the method by which pardon was sealed home to me, I am in a maze of wondering worshipping affection. I bow before the throne which absolves me, I clasp the cross which delivers me, I serve henceforth all my days the Incarnate God, through whom I am this night a pardoned soul.

MORNING   November 28

"For I was very happy when the brothers came and testified of your truth, even as you walk in truth" — 3 John 3.

THE TRUTH WAS in Gaius, and Gaius walked in the truth. If the first had not been the case, the second could never have occurred; and if the second could not be said of him the first would have been a mere pretence. Truth must enter into the soul, penetrate and saturate it, or else it is of no value. Doctrines held as a matter of creed are like bread in the hand, which ministers no nourishment to the frame. But doctrine accepted by the heart is as food digested, which, by assimilation, sustains and builds up the body. In us truth must be a living force, an active energy, an indwelling reality, a part of the woof and warp of our being. If it be in us, we cannot henceforth part with it. A man may lose his garments or his limbs, but his inward parts are vital, and cannot be torn away without absolute loss of life. A Christian can die, but he cannot deny the truth.

Now it is a rule of nature that the inward affects the outward, as light shines from the center of the lantern through the glass; when, therefore, the truth is kindled within, its brightness soon beams forth in the outward life and conversation. It is said that the food of certain worms colors the cocoons of silk which they spin; and just so the nutriment upon which a man's inward nature lives gives a tinge to every word and deed proceeding from him. To walk in the truth, imports a life of integrity, holiness, faithfulness, and simplicity; the natural product of those principles of truth which the gospel teaches, and which the Spirit of God enables us to receive. We may judge of the secrets of the soul by their manifestation in the man's conversation. Be it ours today, Oh gracious Spirit, to be ruled and governed by Your divine authority, so that nothing false or sinful may reign in our hearts, lest it extend its malignant influence to our daily walk among men.

EVENING
"Seeking the welfare of his people" — Esther 10:3.

MORDECAI WAS A true patriot, and therefore, being exalted to the highest position under Ahasuerus, he used his eminence to promote the prosperity of Israel. In this he was a type of Jesus, who, upon His throne of glory, seeks not His own, but spends His power for His people. It were well if every Christian would be a Mordecai to the church, striving according to his ability for its prosperity. Some are placed in stations of affluence and influence, let them honor their Lord in the high places of the earth, and testify for Jesus before great men. Others have what is far better, namely, close fellowship with the King of kings, let them be sure to plead daily for the weak of the Lord's people, the doubting, the tempted, and the comfortless. It will redound to their honor if they make much intercession for those who are in darkness and dare not draw near unto the mercy seat. Instructed believers may serve their Master greatly if they lay out their talents for the general good, and impart their wealth of heavenly learning to others, by teaching them the things of God. The very least in our Israel may at least seek the welfare of his people; and his desire, if he can give no more, shall be acceptable. It is at once the most Christlike and the most happy course for a believer to cease from living to himself. He who blesses others cannot fail to be blessed himself. On the other hand, to seek our own personal greatness is a wicked and unhappy plan of life, its way will be grievous and its end will be fatal.

Here is the place to ask you, my friend, whether you are to the best of your power seeking the wealth of the church in your neighborhood? I trust you are not doing it mischief by bitterness and scandal, nor weakening it by your neglect. Friend, unite with the Lord's poor, bear their cross, do them all the good you can, and you shall not miss your reward.

November 29   MORNING

"You shall not go up and down as a talebearer among your people ... You shall always rebuke your neighbor and not allow sin upon him" — Leviticus 19:16.

    TALE-BEARING EMITS a threefold poison; for it injures the teller, the hearer, and the person concerning whom the tale is told. Whether the report be true or false, we are by this precept of God's Word forbidden to spread it. The reputations of the Lord's people should be very precious in our sight, and we should count it shame to help the devil to dishonor the Church and the name of the Lord. Some tongues need a bridle rather than a spur. Many glory in pulling down their brothers, as if thereby they raised themselves. Noah's wise sons cast a mantle over their father, and he who exposed him earned a fearful curse. We may ourselves one of these dark days need forbearance and silence from our brothers, let us render it cheerfully to those who require it now. Be this our family rule, and our personal bond: speak evil of no man.

    The Holy Spirit, however, permits us to censure sin, and prescribes the way in which we are to do it. It must be done by rebuking our brother to his face, not by railing behind his back. This course is manly, brotherly, Christlike, and under God's blessing will be useful. Does the flesh shrink from it? Then we must lay the greater stress upon our conscience, and keep ourselves to the work, lest by suffering sin upon our friend we become ourselves partakers of it. Hundreds have been saved from gross sins by the timely, wise, affectionate warnings of faithful ministers and brothers. Our Lord Jesus has set us a gracious example of how to deal with erring friends in His warning given to Peter, the prayer with which He preceded it, and the gentle way in which He bore with Peter's boastful denial that he needed such a caution.

EVENING
"Spices for anointing oil" — Exodus 35:8.

    MUCH USE WAS made of this anointing oil under the law, and that which it represents is of primary importance under the gospel. The Holy Spirit, who anoints us for all holy service, is indispensable to us if we would serve the Lord acceptably. Without His aid our religious services are but a vain oblation, and our inward experience is a dead thing. Whenever our ministry is without unction, what miserable stuff it becomes! Nor are the prayers, praises, meditations, and efforts of private Christians one jot superior. A holy anointing is the soul and life of piety, its absence the most grievous of all calamities. To go before the Lord without anointing is as though some common Levite had thrust himself into the priest's office; his ministrations would rather have been sins than services. May we never venture upon hallowed exercises without sacred anointing. They drop upon us from our glorious Head; from His anointing we who are as the skirts of His garments partake of a plenteous unction.

    Choice spices were compounded with rarest art of the apothecary to form the anointing oil, to show forth to us how rich are all the influences of the Holy Spirit. All good things are found in the divine Comforter. Matchless consolation, infallible instruction, immortal quickening, spiritual energy, and divine sanctification all lie compounded with other excellencies in that sacred eye-salve, the heavenly anointing oil of the Holy Spirit. It imparts a delightful fragrance to the character and person of the man upon whom it is poured. Nothing like it can be found in all the treasuries of the rich, or the secrets of the wise. It is not to be imitated. It comes alone from God, and it is freely given, through Jesus Christ, to every waiting soul. Let us seek it, for we may have it, may have it this very evening. Oh Lord, anoint Your servants.

MORNING   November 30

"And Amaziah said to the man of God, But what shall we do for the hundred talents which I have given to the army of Israel? And the man of God answered, The LORD is able to give you much more than this" — 2 Chronicles 25:9.

A VERY IMPORTANT question this seemed to be to the king of Judah, and possibly it is of even more weight with the tried and tempted Christian. To lose money is at no times pleasant, and when principle involves it, the flesh is not always ready to make the sacrifice. Why lose that which may be so usefully employed? May not the truth itself be bought too dear? What shall we do without it? Remember the children, and our small income! All these things and a thousand more would tempt the Christian to put forth his hand to unrighteous gain, or stay himself from carrying out his conscientious convictions, when they involve serious loss. All men cannot view these matters in the light of faith; and even with the followers of Jesus, the doctrine of "we must live" has quite sufficient weight.

"The Lord is able to give you much more than this" is a very satisfactory answer to the anxious question. Our Father holds the purse-strings, and what we lose for His sake He can repay a thousand-fold. It is ours to obey His will, and we may rest assured that He will provide for us. The Lord will be no man's debtor at the last. Saints know that a grain of hearts-ease is of more value than a ton of gold. He who wraps a threadbare coat about a good conscience has gained a spiritual wealth far more desirable than any lie has lost. God's smile and a dungeon are enough for a true heart; His frown and a palace would be hell to a gracious spirit. Let the worst come to the worst, let all the talents go, we have not lost our treasure, for that is above, where Christ sits at the right hand of God. Meanwhile, even now, the Lord makes the meek to inherit the earth, and no good thing does He withhold from them that walk uprightly.

EVENING

"Michael and his angels made war against the dragon. And the dragon and his angels made war" — Revelation 12:7.

WAR ALWAYS WILL rage between the two great sovereignties until one or other be crushed. Peace between good and evil is an impossibility; the very pretense of it would, in fact, be the triumph of the powers of darkness. Michael will always fight; his holy soul is vexed with sin, and will not endure it. Jesus will always be the dragon's foe, and that not in a quiet sense, but actively, vigorously, with full determination to exterminate evil. All His servants, whether angels in heaven or messengers on earth, will and must fight; they are born to be warriors. At the cross they enter into covenant never to make truce with evil; they are a warlike company, firm in defense and fierce in attack. The duty of every soldier in the army of the Lord is daily, with all his heart, and soul, and strength, to fight against the dragon.

The dragon and his angels will not decline the affray; they are incessant in their onslaughts, sparing no weapon, fair or foul. We are foolish to expect to serve God without opposition: the more zealous we are, the more sure are we to be assailed by the myriads of hell. The church may become slothful, but not so her great antagonist; his restless spirit never suffers the war to pause; he hates the woman's seed, and would fain devour the church if he could.

Glory be to God, we know the end of the war. The great dragon shall be cast out and forever destroyed, while Jesus and they who are with Him shall receive the crown. Let us sharpen our swords tonight, and pray the Holy Spirit to nerve our arms for the conflict. Never battle so important, never crown so glorious. Every man to his post, you warriors of the cross, and may the Lord tread Satan under your feet shortly!

December 1   MORNING

"You have made summer and winter" — Psalm 74:17.

MY SOUL BEGIN this wintry month with your God. The cold snows and the piercing winds all remind you that He keeps His covenant with day and night, and tend to assure you that He will also keep that glorious covenant which He has made with you in the person of Christ Jesus. He who is true to His Word in the revolutions of the seasons of this poor sin-polluted world, will not prove unfaithful in His dealings with His own well-beloved Son.

Winter in the soul is by no means a comfortable season, and if it be upon you just now it will be very painful to you: but there is this comfort, namely, that the Lord makes it. He sends the sharp blasts of adversity to nip the buds of expectation: He scatters the hoarfrost like ashes over the once verdant meadows of our joy. He cast forth His ice like morsels freezing the streams of our delight. He does it all, He is the great Winter King, and rules in the realms of frost, and therefore you can not murmur. Losses, crosses, heaviness, sickness, poverty, and a thousand other ills, are of the Lord's sending, and come to us with wise design. Frosts kill noxious insects, and put a bound to raging diseases; they break up the clods, and sweeten the soil. Oh that such good results would always follow our winters of affliction!

How we prize the fire just now! How pleasant is its cheerful glow! Let us in the same manner prize our Lord, who is the constant source of warmth and comfort in every time of trouble. Let us draw near to Him, and in Him find joy and peace in believing. Let us wrap ourselves in the warm garments of His promises, and go forth to labors which suit the season, for it were ill to be as the sluggard who will not plough by reason of the cold; for he shall beg in summer and have nothing.

EVENING

"O that men would praise the LORD for His goodness, and for His wonderful works to the children of men!" — Psalm 107:5.

IF WE COMPLAINED less, and praised more, we should be happier, and God would be more glorified. Let us daily praise God for common mercies; common as we frequently call them, and yet so priceless, that when deprived of them we are ready to perish. Let us bless God for the eyes with which we behold the sun, for the health and strength to walk abroad, for the bread we eat, for the raiment we wear. Let us praise Him that we are not cast out among the hopeless, or confined among the guilty. Let us thank Him for liberty, for friends, for family associations and comforts; let us praise Him, in fact, for everything which we receive from His bounteous hand, for we deserve little, and yet are most plenteously endowed.

But, beloved, the sweetest and the loudest note in our songs of praise should be of redeeming love. God's redeeming acts towards His chosen are forever the favorite themes of their praise. If we know what redemption means, let us not withhold our sonnets of thanksgiving. We have been redeemed from the power of our corruptions, uplifted from the depth of sin in which we were naturally plunged. We have been led to the cross of Christ. Our shackles of guilt have been broken off; we are no longer slaves, but children of the living God, and can antedate the period when we shall be presented before the throne without spot or wrinkle or any such thing. Even now by faith we wave the palm branch and wrap ourselves about with the fair linen which is to be our everlasting array, and shall we not unceasingly give thanks to the Lord our Redeemer? Child of God, can you be silent? Awake, awake, you inheritors of glory, and lead your captivity captive, as you cry with David, *"Bless the Lord, Oh my soul: and all that is within me, bless His holy name."* Let the new month begin with new songs.

MORNING December 2

"You are all fair, My love" — *Song of Solomon 4:7.*

THE LORD'S ADMIRATION of His Church is very wonderful, and His description of her beauty is very glowing. She is not merely fair, but *"all fair."* He views her in Himself, washed in His sin-atoning blood and clothed in His meritorious righteousness, and He considers her to be full of comeliness and beauty. No wonder that such is the case, since it is but His own perfect excellency that He admires; for the holiness, glory, and perfection of His Church are His own glorious garments on the back of His own well-beloved spouse. She is not simply pure, or well-proportioned; she is positively lovely and fair! She has actual merit! Her deformities of sin are removed; but more, she has through her Lord obtained a meritorious righteousness by which an actual beauty is conferred upon her. Believers have a positive righteousness given to them when they become *"accepted in the beloved."* (Eph. 1:6)

Nor is the Church barely lovely, she is superlatively so. Her Lord styles her *"You fairest among women."* She has a real worth and excellence which cannot be rivalled by all the nobility and royalty of the world. If Jesus could exchange His elect bride for all the queens and empresses of earth, or even for the angels in heaven, He would not, for He puts her first and foremost: *"fairest among women."* Like the moon she far outshines the stars. Nor is this an opinion which He is ashamed of, for He invites all men to hear it. He sets a *"behold"* before it, a special note of exclamation, inviting and arresting attention. *"Behold, you are fair, My love; behold you are fair."* (Song of Solomon 4:1) His opinion He publishes abroad even now, and one day from the throne of His glory He will avow the truth of it before the assembled universe. *"Come, you blessed of My Father,"* (Matt. 25:34) will be His solemn affirmation of the loveliness of His elect.

EVENING

"Behold, all is vanity" — *Ecclesiastes 1:14.*

NOTHING CAN SATISFY the entire man but the Lord's love and the Lord's own self. Saints have tried to anchor in other roadsteads, but they have been driven out of such fatal refuges. Solomon, the wisest of men, was permitted to make experiments for us all, and to do for us what we must not dare to do for ourselves. Here is his testimony in his own words: *"So I was great, and increased more than all that were before me in Jerusalem: also my wisdom remained with me. And whatsoever my eyes desired I kept not from them, I withheld not my heart from any joy; for my heart rejoiced in all my labor: and this was my portion of all my labor. Then I looked on all the works that my hands had worked, and on the labor that I had labored to do: and, behold, all was vanity and vexation of spirit, and there was no profit under the sun."* *"Vanity of vanities, all is vanity."* What! the whole of it vanity? Oh favored monarch, is there nothing in all your wealth? Nothing in that wide dominion reaching from the River even to the sea? Nothing in Palmyra's glorious palaces? Nothing in the house of the forest of Lebanon? In all your music and dancing, and wine and luxury, is there nothing? *"Nothing,"* he says, *"but weariness of spirit."* This was his verdict when he had trodden the whole round of pleasure. To embrace our Lord Jesus, to dwell in His love, and be fully assured of union with Him; this is all in all.

Dear reader, you need not try other forms of life in order to see whether they are better than the Christian's: if you roam the world around, you will see no sights like a sight of the Savior's face. If you could have all the comforts of life, if you lost your Savior, you would be wretched; but if you win Christ, then should you rot in a dungeon, you would find it a paradise; should you live in obscurity, or die with famine, you will yet be satisfied with favor and full of the goodness of the Lord.

December 3

MORNING

"Not a blemish is in you" — Song of Solomon 4:7.

HAVING PRONOUNCED His Church positively full of beauty, our Lord confirms His praise by a precious negative, *"Not a blemish is in you."* As if the thought occurred to the Bridegroom that the carping world would insinuate that He has only mentioned her comely parts, and had purposely omitted those features which were deformed or defiled, He sums up all by declaring her universally and entirely fair, and utterly devoid of stain. A spot may soon be removed, and is the very least thing that can disfigure beauty, but even from this little blemish the believer is delivered in his Lord's sight. If He had said there is no hideous scar, no horrible deformity, no deadly ulcer, we might even then have marveled. But when He testifies that she is free from the slightest spot, all these other forms of defilement are included, and the depth of wonder is increased. If He had but promised to remove all spots by-an-by, we should have had eternal reason for joy. But when He speaks of it as already done, who can restrain the most intense emotions of satisfaction and delight? Oh my soul, here is marrow and fatness for you; eat your fill, and be satisfied with royal dainties.

Christ Jesus has no quarrel with His spouse. She often wanders from Him and grieves His Holy Spirit, but He does not allow her faults to affect His love. He sometimes chides, but it is always in the tenderest manner, with the kindest intentions; it is *"my love"* even then. There is no remembrance of our follies, He does not cherish ill thoughts of us, but He pardons and loves as well after the offense as before it. It is well for us it is so, for if Jesus were as mindful of injuries as we are, how could He commune with us? Many a time a believer will put himself out of humor with the Lord for some slight turn in providence, but our precious Husband knows our silly hearts too well to take any offense at our ill manners.

EVENING

"The LORD mighty in battle" — Psalm 24:8.

WELL MAY OUR God be glorious in the eyes of His people, seeing that He has worked such wonders for them, in them and by them. For them, the Lord Jesus upon Calvary routed every foe, breaking all the weapons of the enemy in pieces by His finished work of satisfactory obedience. By His triumphant resurrection and ascension He completely overturned the hopes of hell, leading captivity captive, making a show of our enemies openly, triumphing over them by His cross. Every arrow of guilt which Satan might have shot at us is broken, for who can lay anything to the charge of God's elect? Vain are the sharp swords of infernal malice, and the perpetual battles of the serpent's seed, for in the midst of the church the lame take the prey, and the feeblest warriors are crowned.

The saved may well adore their Lord for His conquests in them, since the arrows of their natural hatred are snapped, and the weapons of their rebellion broken. What victories has grace won in our evil hearts! How glorious is Jesus when the will is subdued, and sin dethroned! As for our remaining corruptions, they shall sustain an equally sure defeat, and every temptation, and doubt, and fear, shall be utterly destroyed. In the Salem of our peaceful hearts, the name of Jesus is great beyond compare; He has won our love, and He shall wear it.

Even thus securely may we look for victories by us. We are more than conquerors through Him that loved us. We shall cast down the powers of darkness which are in the world, by our faith, and zeal, and holiness; we shall win sinners to Jesus, we shall overturn false systems, we shall convert nations, for God is with us, and none shall stand before us. This evening let the Christian warrior chant the war song, and prepare for tomorrow's fight. *"Greater is He that is in us than he that is in the world."*

MORNING   December 4

"I have many people in this city" — *Acts 18:10.*

THIS SHOULD BE a great encouragement to try to do good, since God has among the vilest of the vile, the most reprobate, the most debauched and drunken, an elect people who must be saved. When you take the Word to them, you do so because God has ordained you to be the messenger of life to their souls, and they must receive it, for so the decree of predestination runs. They are as much redeemed by blood as the saints before the eternal throne. They are Christ's property, and yet perhaps they are for a time lovers of the ale-house, and haters of holiness. But if Jesus Christ purchased them He will have them. God is not unfaithful to forget the price which His Son has paid. He will not suffer His substitution to be in any case an ineffectual, dead thing. Tens of thousands of redeemed ones are not regenerated yet, but regenerated they must be; and this is our comfort when we go forth to them with the quickening Word of God.

No, more, these ungodly ones are prayed for by Christ before the throne. *"Neither pray I for these alone,"* says the great Intercessor, *"but for the ones also which shall believe on Me through their word."* Poor, ignorant souls, they know nothing about prayer for themselves, but Jesus prays for them. Their names are on His breastplate, and before long they must bow their stubborn knee, breathing the penitential sigh before the throne of grace. *"The time of figs is not yet."* The predestinated moment has not struck; but, when it comes, they shall obey, for God will have His own; they must, for the Spirit is not to be withstood when He comes forth with fullness of power; they must become the willing servants of the living God. *"My people shall be willing in the day of My power." "He shall justify many." "He shall see of the travail of His soul." "I will divide him a portion with the great, and He shall divide the spoil with the strong."*

EVENING

"We ourselves groan in ourselves, waiting for adoption, the redemption of our body" — *Romans 8:23.*

THIS GROANING IS universal among the saints: to a greater or less extent we all feel it. It is not the groan of murmuring or complaint; it is rather the note of desire than of distress. Having received an earnest, we desire the whole of our portion; we are sighing that our entire manhood, in its trinity of spirit, soul, and body, may be set free from the last vestige of the fall. We long to put off corruption, weakness, and dishonor, and to wrap ourselves in incorruption, in immortality, in glory, in the spiritual body which the Lord Jesus will bestow upon His people. We long for the manifestation of our adoption as the children of God. *"We groan,"* but it is *"within ourselves."* It is not the hypocrite's groan, by which he would make men believe that he is a saint because he is wretched. Our sighs are sacred things, too hallowed for us to tell abroad. We keep our longings to our Lord alone.

Then the apostle says we are *"waiting,"* by which we learn that we are not to be petulant, like Jonah or Elijah, when they said, "Let me die;" nor are we to whimper and sigh for the end of life because we are tired of work, nor wish to escape from our present sufferings till the will of the Lord is done. We are to groan for glorification, but we are to wait patiently for it, knowing that what the Lord appoints is best. Waiting implies being ready. We are to stand at the door expecting the Beloved to open it and take us away to Himself. This groaning is a test. You may judge of a man by what he groans after. Some men groan after wealth; they worship Mammon. Some groan continually under the troubles of life; they are merely impatient. But the man who sighs after God, who is uneasy till he is made like Christ, that is the blessed man. May God help us to groan for the coming of the Lord, and the resurrection which He will bring to us.

December 5   MORNING

"Ask and it shall be given to you" — Matthew 7:7.

WE KNOW OF a place in England still existing, where a dole of bread is served to every passerby who chooses to ask for it. Whoever the traveler may be, he has but to knock at the door of St. Cross Hospital, and there is the dole of bread for him. Jesus Christ so loves sinners that He has built a St. Cross Hospital, so that whenever a sinner is hungry, he has but to knock and have his wants supplied. No, He has done better; He has attached to this Hospital of the Cross a bath; and whenever a soul is black and filthy, it has but to go there and be washed. The fountain is always full, always efficacious. No sinner ever went into it and found that it could not wash away his stains. Sins which were scarlet and crimson have all disappeared, and the sinner has been whiter than snow. As if this were not enough, there is attached to this Hospital of the Cross a wardrobe, and a sinner making application simply as a sinner, may be clothed from head to foot. And if he wishes to be a soldier, he may not merely have a garment for ordinary wear, but armor which shall cover him from the sole of his foot to the crown of his head. If he asks for a sword, he shall have that given to him, and a shield too. Nothing that is good for him shall be denied him. He shall have spending money so long as he lives, and he shall have an eternal heritage of glorious treasure when he enters into the joy of his Lord.

If all these things are to be had by merely knocking at mercy's door, Oh my soul, knock hard this morning, and ask large things of your generous Lord. Leave not the throne of grace till all your wants have been spread before the Lord, and until by faith you have a comfortable prospect that they shall be all supplied. No bashfulness need retard when Jesus invites. No unbelief should hinder when Jesus promises. No cold-heartedness should restrain when such blessings are to be obtained.

EVENING

"And the LORD showed me four carpenters" — Zechariah 1:20.

IN THE VISION described in this chapter, the prophet saw four terrible horns. They were pushing this way and that way, dashing down the strongest and the mightiest; and the prophet asked, *"What are these?"* The answer was, *"These are the horns which have scattered Israel."* He saw before him a representation of those powers which had oppressed the church of God. There were four horns; for the church is attacked from all quarters. Well might the prophet have felt dismayed; but on a sudden there appeared before him four carpenters. He asked, *"What shall these do?"* these are the men whom God has found to break those horns in pieces.

God will always find men for His work, and He will find them at the right time. The prophet did not see the carpenters first, when there was nothing to do, but first the *"horns,"* and then the *"carpenters."* Moreover, the Lord finds enough men. He did not find three carpenters, but four; there were four horns, and there must be four workmen. God finds the right men; not four men with pens to write; not four architects to draw plans; but four carpenters to do rough work.

Rest assured, you who tremble for the ark of God, that when the *"horns"* grow troublesome, the *"carpenters"* will be found. You need not fret concerning the weakness of the church of God at any moment. There may be growing up in obscurity the valiant reformer who will shake the nations: Chrysostoms may come forth from our Ragged Schools, and Augustines from the thickest darkness of London's poverty. The Lord knows where to find His servants. He has in ambush a multitude of mighty men, and at His word they shall start up to the battle; *"for the battle is the Lord's,"* and He shall get to Himself the victory. Let us abide faithful to Christ, and He, in the right time, will raise up for us a defense, whether it be in the day of our personal need, or in the season of peril to His Church.

MORNING   December 6

"Just like the Heavenly One is, so also will be the heavenly ones" — *1 Corinthians 15:48.*

THE HEAD AND members are of one nature, and not like that monstrous image which Nebuchadnezzar saw in his dream. The head was of fine gold, but the belly and thighs were of brass, the legs of iron, and the feet, part of iron and part of clay. Christ's mystical body is no absurd combination of opposites; the members were mortal, and therefore Jesus died; the glorified head is immortal, and therefore the body is immortal too, for thus the record stands, *"Because I live, you shall live also."* As is our loving Head, such is the body, and every member in particular. A chosen Head and chosen members; an accepted Head, and accepted members; a living Head, and living members. If the head be pure gold, all the parts of the body are of pure gold also. Thus is there a double union of nature as a basis for the closest communion.

Pause here, devout reader, and see if you can without ecstatic amazement, contemplate the infinite condescension of the Son of God in thus exalting your wretchedness into blessed union with His glory. You are so mean that in remembrance of your mortality, you may say to corruption, "You are my father," and to the worm, "You are my sister;" and yet in Christ you are so honored that you can say to the Almighty, *"Abba, Father,"* and to the Incarnate God, "You are my brother and my husband." Surely if relationships to ancient and noble families make men think highly of themselves, we have whereof to glory over the heads of them all. Let the poorest and most despised believer lay hold upon this privilege; let not a senseless indolence make him negligent to trace his pedigree, and let him suffer no foolish attachment to present vanities to occupy his thoughts to the exclusion of this glorious, this heavenly honor of union with Christ.

EVENING

"Clothed in a robe reaching to the feet, and tied at the breasts with a golden girdle" — *Revelation 1:13.*

"ONE LIKE UNTO the Son of Man" appeared to John in Patmos, and the beloved disciple marked that he wore a girdle of gold. A girdle, for Jesus never was ungirt while upon earth, but stood always ready for service, and now before the eternal throne He stays not His holy ministry, but as a priest is girt about with *"the curious girdle of the ephod."* Well is it for us that He has not ceased to fulfil His offices of love for us, since this in one of our choicest safeguards that He ever lives to make intercession for us. Jesus is never an idler; His garments are never loose as though His offices were ended; He diligently carries on the cause of His people. A golden girdle, to manifest the superiority of His service, the royalty of His person, the dignity of His state, the glory of His reward. No longer does He cry out of the dust, but He pleads with authority, a King as well as a Priest. Safe enough is our cause in the hands of our enthroned Melchisedek.

Our Lord presents all His people with an example. We must never unbind our girdles. This is not the time for lying down at ease, it is the season of service and warfare. We need to bind the girdle of truth more and more tightly around our loins. It is a golden girdle, and so will be our richest ornament, and we greatly need it, for a heart that is not well braced up with the truth as it is in Jesus, and with the fidelity which is worked of the Spirit, will be easily entangled with the things of this life, and tripped up by the snares of temptation. It is in vain that we possess the Scriptures unless we bind them around us like a girdle, surrounding our entire nature, keeping each part of our character in order, and giving compactness to our whole man. If in heaven Jesus unbinds not the girdle, much less may we upon earth. Stand, therefore, having your loins girt about with truth.

December 7   MORNING

"And God chose the low-born of the world" — *1 Corinthians 1:28.*

WALK THE STREETS by moonlight, if you dare, and you will see sinners then. Watch when the night is dark, and the wind is howling, and the picklock is grating in the door, and you will see sinners then. Go to yonder jail, and walk through the wards, and mark the men with heavy over-hanging brows, men whom you would not like to meet at night, and there are sinners there. Go to the Reformatories, and note those who have betrayed a rampant juvenile depravity, and you will see sinners there. Go across the seas to the place where a man will gnaw a bone upon which is reeking human flesh, and there is a sinner there. Go where you will, you need not ransack earth to find sinners, for they are common enough; you may find them in every lane and street of every city, and town, and village, and hamlet. It is for such that Jesus died. If you will select me the grossest specimen of humanity, if he be but born of women, I will have hope of him yet, because Jesus Christ is come to seek and to save sinners. Electing love has selected some of the worst to be made the best. Pebbles of the brook grace turns into jewels for the crown-royal. Worthless dross He transforms into pure gold. Redeeming love has set apart many of the worst of mankind to be the reward of the Savior's passion. Effectual grace calls forth many of the vilest of the vile to sit at the table of mercy, and therefore let none despair.

Reader, by that love looking out of Jesus' tearful eyes, by that love streaming from those bleeding wounds, by that faithful love, that strong love, that pure, disinterested, and abiding love; by the heart and by the feelings of the Savior's compassion, we adjure you not to turn away as though it were nothing to you; but believe on Him and you shall be saved. Trust your soul with Him and He will bring you to His Father's right hand in glory everlasting.

EVENING

"To all these I have become all things so that by all means I might save some" — *1 Corinthians 9:22.*

PAUL'S GREAT OBJECT was not merely to instruct and to improve, but to save. Anything short of this would have disappointed him; he would have men renewed in heart, forgiven, sanctified, in fact, saved. Have our Christian labors been aimed at anything below this great point? Then let us amend our ways, for of what avail will it be at the last great day to have taught and moralized men if they appear before God unsaved? Blood-red will our skirts be if through life we have sought inferior objects, and forgotten that men needed to be saved.

Paul knew the ruin of man's natural state, and did not try to educate him, but to save him; he saw men sinking to hell, and did not talk of refining them, but of saving from the wrath to come. To compass their salvation, he gave himself up with untiring zeal to telling abroad the gospel, to warning and beseeching men to be reconciled to God. His prayers were importunate and his labors incessant. To save souls was his consuming passion, his ambition, his calling. He became a servant to all men, toiling for his race, feeling a woe within him if he preached not the gospel. He laid aside his preferences to prevent prejudice; he submitted his will in things indifferent, and if men would but receive the gospel, he raised no questions about forms or ceremonies. The gospel was the one all-important business with him. If He might save some he would be content. This was the crown for which he strove, the sole and sufficient reward of all his labors and self-denials.

Dear reader, have you and I lived to win souls at this noble rate? Are we possessed with the same all-absorbing desire? If not, why not? Jesus died for sinners, cannot we live for them? Where is our tenderness? Where our love to Christ, if we seek not His honor in the salvation of men? Oh that the Lord would saturate us through and through with an undying zeal for the souls of men.

MORNING   December 8

"You have a few names also in Sardis which have not made their robes unclean. And they shall walk with Me in white, because they are worthy" — *Revelation 3:4.*

WE MAY UNDERSTAND this to refer to justification. *"They shall walk in white;"* that is, they shall enjoy a constant sense of their own justification by faith; they shall understand that the righteousness of Christ is imputed to them, that they have all been washed and made whiter than the newly-fallen snow.

Again, it refers to joy and gladness; for white robes were holiday dresses among the Jews. They who have not defiled their garments shall have their faces always bright; they shall understand what Solomon meant when he said, *"Go your way, eat your bread with joy, and drink your wine with a merry heart. Let your garments be always white, for God has accepted your works."* He who is accepted of God shall wear white garments of joy and gladness, while he walks in sweet communion with the Lord Jesus. Why so many doubts, so much misery, and mourning? It is because so many believers defile their garments with sin and error, and hence they lose the joy of their salvation, and the comfortable fellowship of the Lord Jesus, they do not here below walk in white.

The promise also refers to walking in white before the throne of God. Those who have not defiled their garments here shall most certainly walk in white up yonder, where the white-robed hosts sing perpetual hallelujahs to the Most High. They shall possess joys inconceivable, happiness beyond a dream, bliss which imagination knows not, blessedness which even the stretch of desire has not reached. The *"undefiled in the way"* shall have all this; not of merit, nor of works, but of grace. They shall walk with Christ in white, for He has made them *"worthy."* In His sweet company they shall drink of the living fountains of Waters.

EVENING
"You, O God have prepared for the poor in Your goodness" — *Psalm 68:10.*

ALL GOD'S GIFTS are prepared gifts laid up in store for wants foreseen. He anticipates our needs, and out of the fullness which He has treasured up in Christ Jesus, He provides of His goodness for the poor. You may trust Him for all the necessities that can occur, for He has infallibly foreknown every one of them. He can say of us in all conditions, "I knew that you would be this and that." A man goes a journey across the desert, and when he has made a day's advance, and pitched his tent, he discovers that he wants many comforts and necessities which he has not brought in his baggage. "Ah!" says he, "I did not foresee this; if I had this journey to go again, I should bring these things with me, so necessary to my comfort." But God has marked with prescient eye all the requirements of His poor wandering children, and when those needs occur, supplies are ready. It is goodness which He has prepared for the poor in heart, goodness and goodness only. *"My grace is sufficient for you." "As your days, so shall your strength be."*

Reader, is your heart heavy this evening? God knew it would be; the comfort which your heart wants is treasured in the sweet assurance of the text. You are poor and needy, but He has thought upon you, and has the exact blessing which you require in store for you. Plead the promise, believe it and obtain its fulfillment. Do you feel that you never were so consciously vile as you are now? Behold, the crimson fountain is open still, with all its former efficacy, to wash your sin away. Never shall you come into such a position that Christ cannot aid you. No pinch shall ever arrive in your spiritual affairs in which Jesus Christ shall not be equal to the emergency, for your history has all been foreknown and provided for in Jesus.

December 9

MORNING

"Therefore the LORD will wait that He may be gracious to you" — Isaiah 30:18.

GOD OFTEN DELAYS in answering prayer. We have several instances of this in sacred Scripture. Jacob did not get the blessing from the angel until near the dawn of day; he had to wrestle all night for it. The poor woman of Syro-phenicia was answered not a word for a long while. Paul besought the Lord thrice that *"the thorn in the flesh"* might be taken from him, and he received no assurance that it should be taken away, but instead thereof a promise that God's grace should be sufficient for him.

If you have been knocking at the gate of mercy, and have received no answer, shall I tell you why the mighty Maker has not opened the door and let you in? Our Father has reasons peculiar to Himself for thus keeping us waiting. Sometimes it is to show His power and His sovereignty, that men may know that Jehovah has a right to give or to withhold. More frequently the delay is for our profit. You are perhaps kept waiting in order that your desires may be more fervent. God knows that delay will quicken and increase desire, and that if He keeps you waiting you will see your necessity more clearly, and will seek more earnestly; and that you will prize the mercy all the more for its long tarrying. There may also be something wrong in you which has need to be removed, before the joy of the Lord is given. Perhaps your views of the Gospel plan are confused, or you may be placing some little reliance on yourself, instead of trusting simply and entirely to the Lord Jesus. Or, God makes you tarry awhile that He may the more fully display the riches of His grace to you at last. Your prayers are all filed in heaven, and if not immediately answered they are certainly not forgotten, but in a little while shall be fulfilled to your delight and satisfaction. Let not despair make you silent, but continue instant in earnest supplication.

EVENING

"And my people shall live in ... quiet resting places" — Isaiah 32:18.

PEACE AND REST belong not to the unregenerate, they are the peculiar possession of the Lord's people, and of them only. The God of Peace gives perfect peace to those whose hearts are stayed upon Him. When man was unfallen, his God gave him the flowery bowers of Eden as his quiet resting places. Alas! How soon sin blighted the fair abode of innocence. in the day of universal wrath when the flood swept away a guilty race, the chosen family were quietly secured in the resting-place of the ark, which floated them from the old condemned world into the new earth of the rainbow and the covenant; herein typifying Jesus, the ark of our salvation. Israel rested safely beneath the blood-besprinkled habitations of Egypt when the destroying angel smote the first-born; and in the wilderness the shadow of the pillar of cloud, and the flowing rock, gave the weary pilgrims sweet repose.

At this hour we rest in the promises of our faithful God, knowing that His words are full of truth and power; we rest in the doctrines of His word, which are consolation itself; we rest in the covenant of His grace, which is a haven of delight. More highly favored are we than David in Adullam, or Jonah beneath his gourd, for none can invade or destroy our shelter. The person of Jesus is the quiet resting-place of His people, and when we draw near to Him in the breaking of bread, in the hearing of the word, the searching of the Scriptures, prayer, or praise, we find any form of approach to Him to be the return of peace to our spirits.

> I hear the words of love, I gaze upon the blood,
> I see the mighty sacrifice, and I have peace with God.
> 'Tis everlasting peace, sure as Jehovah's name,
> 'Tis stable as His steadfast throne, for evermore the same;
> The clouds may go and come, and storms may sweep my sky,
> This blood-sealed friendship changes not, the cross is ever nigh.

MORNING   December 10

"And so we shall always be with the Lord" — 1 Thessalonians 4:17.

EVEN THE SWEETEST visits from Christ, how short they are; and how transitory! One moment our eyes see Him, and we rejoice with joy unspeakable and full of glory, but again a little time and we do not see Him, for our Beloved withdraws Himself from us; like a roe or a young hart He leaps over the mountains of division; He is gone to the land of spices, and feeds no more among the lilies.

> If today He deigns to bless us,
> With a sense of pardoned sin,
> He tomorrow may distress us,
> Make us feel the plague within.

Oh, how sweet the prospect of the time when we shall not behold Him at a distance, but see Him face to face: when He shall not be as a wayfaring man tarrying but for a night, but shall eternally enfold us in the bosom of His glory. We shall not see Him for a little season, but

> Millions of years our wondering eyes,
> Shall over our Savior's beauties rove;
> And myriad ages we will adore,
> The wonders of His love.

In heaven there shall be no interruptions from care or sin; no weeping shall dim our eyes; no earthly business shall distract our happy thoughts; we shall have nothing to hinder us from gazing forever on the Sun of Righteousness with unwearied eyes. Oh, if it be so sweet to see Him now and then, how sweet to gaze on that blessed face for ever, and never have a cloud rolling between, and never have to turn one's eyes away to look on a world of weariness and woe! Blest day, when will you dawn? Rise, Oh unsetting sun! The joys of sense may leave us as soon as they will, for this shall make glorious amends. If to die is but to enter into uninterrupted communion with Jesus, then death is indeed gain, and the black drop is swallowed up in a sea of victory.

EVENING

"Whose heart the Lord opened" — Acts 16:14.

IN LYDIA'S CONVERSION there are many points of interest. It was brought about by providential circumstances. She was a seller of purple, of the city of Thyatira, but just at the right time for hearing Paul we find her at Philippi; providence, which is the handmaid of grace, led her to the right spot. Again, grace was preparing her soul for the blessing; grace preparing for grace. She did not know the Savior, but as a Jewess, she knew many truths which were excellent steppingstones to a knowledge of Jesus. Her conversion took place in the use of the means. On the Sabbath she went when prayer was accustomed to be made, and there prayer was heard. Never neglect the means of grace; God may bless us when we are not in His house, but we have the greater reason to hope that He will when we are in communion with His saints.

Observe the words, *"Whose heart the Lord opened."* She did not open her own heart. Her prayers did not do it; Paul did not do it. The Lord Himself must open the heart, to receive the things which make for our peace. He alone can put the key into the hole of the door and open it, and get admittance for Himself. He is the heart's master as He is the heart's maker.

The first outward evidence of the opened heart was obedience. As soon as Lydia had believed in Jesus, she was baptized. It is a sweet sign of a humble and broken heart, when the child of God is willing to obey a command which is not essential to his salvation, which is not forced upon him by a selfish fear of condemnation, but is a simple act of obedience and of communion with his Master. The next evidence was love, manifesting itself in acts of grateful kindness to the apostles. Love to the saints has ever been a mark of the true convert. Those who do nothing for Christ or His church, give but sorry evidence of an *"opened"* heart. Lord, evermore give me an opened heart.

December 11   MORNING

"He who calls you is faithful, who also will do it" — *1 Thessalonians. 5:24.*

HEAVEN IS A place where we shall never sin; where we shall cease our constant watch against an indefatigable enemy, because there will be no tempter to ensnare our feet. There the wicked cease from troubling, and the weary are at rest. Heaven is the *"undefiled inheritance;"* it is the land of perfect holiness, and therefore of complete security. But do not the saints even on earth sometimes taste the joys of blissful security? The doctrine of God's word is, that all who are in union with the Lamb are safe; that all the righteous shall hold on their way; that those who have committed their souls to the keeping of Christ shall find Him, a faithful and immutable preserver. Sustained by such a doctrine we can enjoy security even on earth; not that high and glorious security which renders us free from every slip, but that holy security which arises from the sure promise of Jesus that none who believe in Him shall ever perish, but shall be with Him where He is. Believer, let us often reflect with joy on the doctrine of the perseverance of the saints, and honor the faithfulness of our God by a holy confidence in Him.

May our God bring home to you a sense of your safety in Christ Jesus! May He assure you that your name is graven on His hand; and whisper in your ear the promise, *"Fear not, I am with you."* Look upon Him, the great Surety of the covenant, as faithful and true, and, therefore, bound and engaged to present you, the weakest of the family, with all the chosen race, before the throne of God; and in such a sweet contemplation you will drink the juice of the spiced wine of the Lord's pomegranate, and taste the dainty fruits of Paradise. You will have an antepast of the enjoyments which ravish the souls of the perfect saints above, if you can believe with unstaggering faith that *"faithful is He that calls you, who also will do it."*

EVENING
"You serve the Lord Christ!" — *Colossians 3:24.*

TO WHAT CHOICE order of officials was this word spoken? To kings who proudly boast a right divine? Ah, no! Too often do they serve themselves or Satan, and forget the God whose sufferance permits them to wear their mimic majesty for their little hour. Speaks then the apostle to those so-called "right reverend fathers in God," the bishops, or "the venerable archdeacons"? No, indeed, Paul knew nothing of these mere inventions of man: Not even to pastors and teachers, or to the wealthy and esteemed among believers, was this word spoken, but to servants, yea, and to slaves. Among the toiling multitudes, the journeyman, the day laborers, the domestic servants, the drudges of the kitchen. The apostle found, as we find still, some of the Lord's chosen, and to them he says, *"Whatsoever you do, do it heartily, as to the Lord, and not unto men; knowing that of the Lord you shall receive the reward of the inheritance: for you serve the Lord Christ."*

This saying ennobles the weary routine of earthly employments, and sheds a halo around the most humble occupations. To wash feet may be servile, but to wash His feet is royal work. To unloose the shoe-lace is poor employ, but to unloose the great Master's shoe is a princely privilege. The shop, the barn, the scullery, and the smithy become temples when men and women do all to the glory of God! Then "divine service" is not a thing of a few hours and a few places, but all life becomes holiness unto the Lord, and every place and thing, as consecrated as the tabernacle and its golden candlestick.

    Teach me, my God and King, in all things You to see;
    And what I do in anything to do it as to Thee.
    All may of You partake, nothing can be so mean
    Which with this tincture, for Your sake, will not grow bright and clean.
    A servant with this clause makes drudgery divine;
    Who sweeps a room, as for Your laws, makes that and the action fine.

MORNING — December 12

"His ways are everlasting" — Habakkuk 3:6.

WHAT HE HAS done at one time, He will do yet again. Man's ways are variable, but God's ways are everlasting. There are many reasons for this most comforting truth. Among them are the following: The Lord's ways are the result of wise deliberation; He orders all things according to the counsel of His own will. Human action is frequently the hasty result of passion, or fear, and is followed by regret and alteration; but nothing can take the Almighty by surprise, or happen otherwise than He has foreseen.

His ways are the outgrowth of an immutable character, and in them the fixed and settled attributes of God are clearly to be seen. Unless the Eternal One Himself can undergo change, His ways, which are Himself in action, must remain forever the same. Is He eternally just, gracious, faithful, wise, tender? Then His ways must ever be distinguished for the same excellences. Beings act according to their nature, when those natures change, their conduct varies also; but since God cannot know the shadow of a turning, His ways will abide everlastingly the same.

Moreover there is no reason from without which could reverse the divine ways, since they are the embodiment of irresistible might. The earth is said, by the prophet, to be cleft with rivers, mountains tremble, the deep lifts up its hands, and sun and moon stand still, when Jehovah marches forth for the salvation of His people. Who can stay His hand, or say unto Him, What do You do? But it is not might alone which gives stability; God's ways are the manifestation of the eternal principles of right, and therefore can never pass away. Wrong breeds decay and involves ruin, but the true and the good have about them a vitality which ages cannot diminish.

This morning let us go to our heavenly Father with confidence, remembering that Jesus Christ is the same yesterday, today, and forever, and in Him the Lord is ever gracious to His people.

EVENING

"They have acted treacherously against the LORD" — Hosea 5:7.

BELIEVER, HERE IS a sorrowful truth! You are the beloved of the Lord, redeemed by blood, called by grace, preserved in Christ Jesus, accepted in the Beloved, on your way to heaven, and yet, "you have acted treacherously" with God, your best friend; treacherously with Jesus, whose you are; treacherously with the Holy Spirit, by whom you have been quickened unto life eternal! How treacherous you have been in the matter of vows and promises. Do you remember the love of your espousals, that happy time, the springtide of your spiritual life? Oh, how closely did you cling to your Master then! saying, "He shall never charge me with indifference; my feet shall never grow slow in the way of His service; I will not suffer my heart to wander after other loves; in Him is every store of unspeakable sweetness. I give all up for my Lord Jesus' sake." Has it been so?

Alas! if conscience speak, it will say, "He who promised so well has performed most ill." Prayer has oftentimes been slurred; it has been short, but not sweet; brief, but not fervent. Communion with Christ has been forgotten. Instead of a heavenly mind, there have been carnal cares, worldly vanities and thoughts of evil. Instead of service, there has been disobedience; instead of fervency, lukewarmness; instead of patience, petulance; instead of faith, confidence in an arm of flesh; and as a soldier of the cross there has been cowardice, disobedience, and desertion, to a very shameful degree. You have acted treacherously. Treachery to Jesus! What words shall be used in denouncing it? Words little avail; let our penitent thoughts execrate the sin which is so surely in us. Treacherous to Your wounds, Oh Jesus! Forgive us, and let us not sin again! How shameful to be treacherous to Him who never forgets us, but who this day stands with our names engraved on His breastplate before the eternal throne.

December 13   MORNING

"without saying how much" — Ezra 7:22.

SALT WAS USED in every offering made by fire unto the Lord, and from its preserving and purifying properties it was the grateful emblem of divine grace in the soul. It is worthy of our attentive regard that, when Artaxerxes gave salt to Ezra the priest, he set no limit to the quantity, and we may be quite certain that when the King of kings distributes grace among His royal priesthood, the supply is not cut short by Him.

Often are we straitened in ourselves, but never in the Lord. He who chooses to gather much manna will find that he may have as much as he desires. There is no such famine in Jerusalem that the citizens should eat their bread by weight and drink their water by measure. Some things in the economy of grace are measured; for instance our vinegar and gall are given us with such exactness that we never have a single drop too much, but of the salt of grace no stint is made, *"Ask what you will and it shall be given unto you."* Parents need to lock up the fruit cupboard, and the sweet jars, but there is no need to keep the salt-box under lock and key, for few children will eat too greedily from that. A man may have too much money, or too much honor, but he cannot have too much grace. When Jeshurun waxed fat in the flesh, he kicked against God, but there is no fear of a man's becoming too full of grace; a plethora of grace is impossible.

More wealth brings more care, but more grace brings more joy. Increased wisdom is increased sorrow, but abundance of the Spirit is fullness of joy. Believer, go to the throne for a large supply of heavenly salt. It will season your afflictions, which are unsavory without salt; it will preserve your heart which corrupts if salt be absent, and it will kill your sins even as salt kills reptiles. You need much; seek much, and have much.

EVENING

"And I will make your windows of agates" — Isaiah 54:12.

THE CHURCH IS most instructively symbolized by a building erected by heavenly power, and designed by divine skill. Such a spiritual house must not be dark, for the Israelites had light in their dwellings; there must therefore be windows to let the light in and to allow the inhabitants to gaze abroad. These windows are precious as agates; the ways in which the church beholds her Lord and heaven, and spiritual truth in general, are to be had in the highest esteem. Agates are not the most transparent of gems, they are but semi-pellucid at the best:

> Our knowledge of that life is small,
> Our eye of faith is dim.

Faith is one of these precious agate windows, but alas! it is often so misty and beclouded, that we see but darkly, and mistake much that we do see. Yet if we cannot gaze through windows of diamonds and know even as we are known, it is a glorious thing to behold the altogether lovely One, even though the glass be hazy as the agate. Experience is another of these dim but precious windows, yielding to us a subdued religious light, in which we see the sufferings of the Man of Sorrows, through our own afflictions. Our weak eyes could not endure windows of transparent glass to let in the Master's glory, but when they are dimmed with weeping, the beams of the Sun of Righteousness are tempered, and shine through the windows of agate with a soft radiance inexpressibly soothing to tempted souls. Sanctification, as it conforms us to our Lord, is another agate window. Only as we become heavenly can we comprehend heavenly things. The pure in heart see a pure God. Those who are like Jesus see Him as He is. Because we are so little like Him, the window is but agate; because we are somewhat like Him, it is agate. We thank God for what we have, and long for more. When shall we see God and Jesus, and heaven and truth, face to face?

MORNING December 14

"They go from strength to strength" — *Psalm 84:7.*

"THEY GO FROM strength to strength." There are various renderings of these words, but all of them contain the idea of progress.

Our own good translation of the authorized version is enough for us this morning. *"They go from strength to strength."* That is, they grow stronger and stronger. Usually, if we are walking, we go from strength to weakness; we start fresh and in good order for our journey, but by-and-by the road is rough, and the sun is hot, we sit down by the wayside, and then again painfully pursue our weary way. But the Christian pilgrim having obtained fresh supplies of grace, is as vigorous after years of toilsome travel and struggle as when he first set out. He may not be quite so elated and buoyant, nor perhaps quite so hot and hasty in his zeal as he once was, but he is much stronger in all that constitutes real power, and travels, if more slowly, far more surely. Some gray-haired veterans have been as firm in their grasp of truth, and as zealous in diffusing it, as they were in their younger day. But, alas, it must be confessed it is often otherwise, for the love of many waxes cold, and iniquity abounds. But this is their own sin and not the fault of the promise which still holds good: *"The youths shall faint and be weary, and the young men shall utterly fall, but they that wait upon the Lord shall renew their strength; they shall mount up with wings as eagles, they shall run and not be weary, and they shall walk and not faint."*

Fretful spirits sit down and trouble themselves about the future. They say, Alas! We go from affliction to affliction. Very true, Oh you of little faith, but then you go from strength to strength also. You shall never find a bundle of affliction which has not bound up in the midst of it sufficient grace. God will give the strength of ripe manhood with the burden allotted to full-grown shoulders.

EVENING
"I have been crucified with Christ" — *Galatians 2:20.*

THE LORD JESUS Christ acted in what He did as a great public representative person, and His dying upon the cross was the virtual dying of all His people. Then all His saints rendered unto justice what was due, and made an expiation to divine vengeance for all their sins. The apostle of the Gentiles delighted to think that as one of Christ's chosen people, he died upon the cross in Christ. He did more than believe this doctrinally, he accepted it confidently, resting his hope upon it. He believed that by virtue of Christ's death, he had satisfied divine justice, and found reconciliation with God. Beloved, what a blessed thing it is when the soul can, as it were, stretch itself upon the cross of Christ, and feel, "I am dead; the law has slain me, and I am therefore free from its power, because in my Surety I have borne the curse, and in the person of my Substitute the whole that the law could do, by way of condemnation, has been executed upon me, for I am crucified with Christ.

But Paul meant even more than this. He not only believed in Christ's death, and trusted in it, but he actually felt its power in himself in causing the crucifixion of his old corrupt nature. When he saw the pleasures of sin, he said, I cannot enjoy these: I am dead to them. Such is the experience of every true Christian. Having received Christ, he is to this world as one who is utterly dead. Yet, while conscious of death to the world, he can, at the same time, exclaim with the apostle, *"Nevertheless I live."* He is fully alive unto God. The Christian's life is a matchless riddle. No worldling can comprehend it; even the believer himself cannot understand it. Dead, yet alive! Crucified with Christ, and yet at the same time risen with Christ in newness of life! Union with the suffering, bleeding, Savior, and death to the world and sin, are soul-cheering things. Oh for more enjoyment of them!

December 15   MORNING

"Orpah kissed her mother-in-law. But Ruth clung to her" — Ruth 1:14.

BOTH OF THEM had an affection for Naomi, and therefore set out with her upon her return to the land of Judah. But the hour of test came; Naomi most unselfishly set before each of them the trials which awaited them, and bade them if they cared for ease and comfort to return to their Moabitish friends. At first both of them declared that they would cast in their lot with the Lord's people; but upon still further consideration Orpah with much grief and a respectful kiss left her mother-in-law, and her people, and her God, and went back to her idolatrous friends, while Ruth with all her heart gave herself up to the God of her mother-in-law.

It is one thing to love the ways of the Lord when all is fair, and quite another to cleave to them under all discouragements and difficulties. The kiss of outward profession is very cheap and easy, but the practical cleaving to the Lord, which must show itself in holy decision for truth and holiness, is not so small a matter. How stands the case with us? Is our heart fixed upon Jesus, is the sacrifice bound with cords to the horns of the altar? Have we counted the cost, and are we solemnly ready to suffer all worldly loss for the Master's sake? The after gain will be an abundant recompense, for Egypt's treasures are not to be compared with the glory to be revealed. Orpah is heard of no more; in glorious ease and idolatrous pleasure her life melts into the gloom of death; but Ruth lives in history and in heaven, for grace has placed her in the noble line from which sprung the King of kings. Blessed among women shall those be who for Christ's sake can renounce all; but forgotten and worse than forgotten shall those be who in the hour of temptation do violence to conscience and turn back unto the world.

Oh that this morning we may not be content with the form of devotion, which may be no better than Orpah's kiss, but may the Holy Spirit work in us a cleaving of our whole heart to, our Lord Jesus.

EVENING

"And lay your foundations with sapphires" — Isaiah 54:11.

NOT ONLY THAT which is seen of the church of God, but that which is unseen, is fair and precious. Foundations are out of sight, and so long as they are firm it is not expected that they should be valuable. But in Jehovah's work everything is of a piece, nothing slurred, nothing mean. The deep foundations of the work of grace are as sapphires for preciousness, no human mind is able to measure their glory. We build upon the covenant of grace, which is firmer than adamant, and as enduring as jewels upon which age spends itself in vain. Sapphire foundations are eternal, and the covenant abides throughout the lifetime of the Almighty. Another foundation is the person of the Lord Jesus, which is clear and spotless, everlasting and beautiful as the sapphire; blending in one the deep blue of earth's ever rolling ocean and the azure of its all embracing sky. Once might our Lord have been likened to the ruby as He stood covered with His own blood, but now we see Him radiant with the soft blue of love, love abounding, deep, eternal. Our eternal hopes are built upon the justice and the faithfulness of God, which are clear and cloudless as the sapphire. We are not saved by a compromise, by mercy defeating justice, or law suspending its operations; no, we defy the eagle's eye to detect a flaw in the groundwork of our confidence; our foundation is of sapphire, and will endure the fire.

The Lord Himself has laid the foundation of His people's hopes. It is matter for grave inquiry whether our hopes are built upon such a basis. Good works and ceremonies are not a foundation of sapphires, but of wood, hay, and stubble; neither are they laid by God, but by our own conceit. Foundations will all be tried before long; woe unto him whose lofty tower shall come down with a crash, because based on a quicksand. He who is built on sapphires may await storm or fire with equanimity, for he shall abide the test.

MORNING   December 16

"Come to Me. — Matthew 11:28.

THE CRY OF the Christian religion is the gentle word, "Come.' The Jewish law harshly said, "Go, take heed unto your steps as to the path in which you shall walk. Break the commandments, and you shall perish; keep them, and you shall live." The law was a dispensation of terror, which drove men before it as with a scourge; the gospel draws with bands of love. Jesus is the good Shepherd going before His sheep, bidding them follow Him, and ever leading them onwards with the sweet word, *"Come."* The law repels, the gospel attracts. The law shows the distance which there is between God and man; the gospel bridges that awful chasm, and brings the sinner across it.

From the first moment of your spiritual life until you are ushered into glory, the language of Christ to you will be, *"Come, come to Me."* As a mother puts out her finger to her little child and woos it to walk by saying, "Come," even so does Jesus. He will always be ahead of you, bidding you follow Him as the soldier follows his captain. He will always go before you to pave your way, and clear your path, and you shall hear His animating voice calling you after Him all through life; while in the solemn hour of death, His sweet words with which He shall usher you into the heavenly world shall be: "Come, you blessed of my Father."

No, further, this is not only Christ's cry to you, but, if you be a believer, this is your cry to Christ: *"Come! come!"* You will be longing for His second advent; you will be saying, *"Come quickly, even so come Lord Jesus."* You will be panting for nearer and closer communion with Him. As His voice to you is *"Come,"* your response to Him will be, "Come, Lord, and abide with me. Come, and occupy alone the throne of my heart; reign there without a rival, and consecrate me entirely to Your service."

EVENING

"Yea, you did not hear; yea, you did not know; yea, from then your ear was not opened"
— Isaiah 48:8.

IT IS PAINFUL to remember that, in a certain degree, this accusation may be laid at the door of believers, who too often are in a measure spiritually insensible. We may well bewail ourselves that we do not hear the voice of God as we ought, *"Yea, you did not hear."* There are gentle motions of the Holy Spirit in the soul which are unheeded by us: there are whisperings of divine command and of heavenly love which are alike unobserved by our leaden intellects.

Alas! We have been carelessly ignorant: *"Yea, you did not know."* There are matters within which we ought to have seen, corruptions which have made headway unnoticed; sweet affections which are being blighted like flowers in the frost, untended by us; glimpses of the divine face which might be perceived if we did not wall up the windows of our soul. But we *"did not know."* As we think of it we are humbled in the deepest self-abasement. How must we adore the grace of God as we learn from the context that all this folly and ignorance, on our part, was foreknown by God, and, notwithstanding that foreknowledge, He yet has been pleased to deal with us in a way of mercy! Admire the marvelous sovereign grace which could have chosen us in the sight of all this! Wonder at the price that was paid for us when Christ knew what we should be! He who hung upon the cross foresaw us as unbelieving, backsliding, cold of heart, indifferent, careless, lax in prayer, and yet He said, *"I am the Lord your God, the Holy One of Israel, your Savior."* Since you were precious in My sight, you have been honorable, and I have loved you: therefore will I give men for you, and people for your life! Oh redemption, how wondrously resplendent do you shine when we think how black we are! Oh Holy Spirit, give us henceforth the hearing ear, the understanding heart!

December 17   MORNING

"I remember you" — Jeremiah 2:2.

LET US NOTE that Christ delights to think upon His Church, and to look upon her beauty. As the bird returns often to its nest, and as the wayfarer hastens to his home, so does the mind continually pursue the object of its choice. We cannot look too often upon that face which we love; we desire always to have our precious things in our sight. It is even so with our Lord Jesus. From all eternity *"His delights were with the sons of men;"* His thoughts rolled onward to the time when His elect should be born into the world; He viewed them in the mirror of His foreknowledge. *"In Your book,"* He says, *"all my members were written, which in continuance were fashioned, when as yet there was none of them."* (Psalm 139:16) When the world was set upon its pillars, He was there, and He set the bounds of the people according to the number of the children of Israel.

Many a time before His incarnation, He descended to this lower earth in the similitude of a man; on the plains of Mamre, (Genesis 18) by the brook of Jabbok, (Genesis 32:24.30) beneath the walls of Jericho, (Joshua 5:13) and in the fiery furnace of Babylon, (Daniel 3:19,25) the Son of Man visited His people. Because His soul delighted in them, He could not rest away from them, for His heart longed after them. Never were they absent from His heart, for He had written their names upon His hands, and graven them upon His side. As the breastplate containing the names of the tribes of Israel was the most brilliant ornament worn by the high priest, so the names of Christ's elect were His most precious jewels, and glittered on His heart. We may often forget to meditate upon the perfections of our Lord, but He never ceases to remember us. Let us chide ourselves for past forgetfulness, and pray for grace ever to bear Him in fondest remembrance. Lord, paint upon the eyeballs of my soul the image of Your Son.

EVENING

"I am the door. if anyone enter in through Me he shall be saved and shall go in and shall go out and shall find pasture" — John 10:9.

JESUS, THE GREAT I AM, is the entrance into the true church, and the way of access to God Himself. He gives to the man who comes to God by Him four choice privileges:

1. He shall be saved. The fugitive manslayer passed through the gate of the city of refuge, and was safe. Noah entered the door of the ark, and was secure. None can be lost who take Jesus as the door of faith to their souls. Entrance through Jesus into peace is the guarantee of entrance by the same door into heaven. Jesus is the only door, an open door, a wide door, a safe door; and blessed is he who rests all his hope of admission to glory upon the crucified Redeemer.

2. He shall go in. He shall be privileged to go in among the divine family, sharing the children's bread, and participating in all their honors and enjoyments. He shall go in to the chambers of communion, to the banquets of love, to the treasures of the covenant, to the storehouses of the promises. He shall go in unto the King of kings in the power of the Holy Spirit, and the secret of the Lord shall be with him.

3. He shall go out. This blessing is much forgotten. We go out into the world to labor and suffer, but what a mercy to go in the name and power of Jesus! We are called to bear witness to the truth, to cheer the disconsolate, to warn the careless, to win souls, and to glorify God; and as the angel said to Gideon, *"Go in this your might,"* even thus the Lord would have us proceed as His messengers in His name and strength.

4. He shall find pasture. He who knows Jesus shall never want. Going in and out shall be alike helpful to him: in fellowship with God he shall grow, and in watering others he shall be watered. Having made Jesus his all, he shall find all in Jesus. His soul shall be as a watered garden, and as a well of water whose waters fail not.

MORNING   December 18

"Tear your heart and not your robes" — Joel 2:13.

GARMENT-TEARING and other outward signs of religious emotion, are easily manifested and are frequently hypocritical; but to feel true repentance is far more difficult, and consequently far less common. Men will attend to the most multiplied and minute ceremonial regulations; for such things are pleasing to the flesh, But true religion is too humbling, too heart-searching, too thorough for the tastes of carnal men; they prefer something more ostentatious, flimsy, and worldly. Outward observances are temporarily comfortable; eye and ear are pleased; self-conceit is fed, and self-righteousness is puffed up; but they are ultimately delusive, for in the article of death, and at the day of judgment, the soul needs something more substantial than ceremonies and rituals to lean upon. Apart from vital godliness all religion is utterly vain; offered without a sincere heart, every form of worship is a solemn sham and an impudent mockery of the majesty of heaven.

Heart-tearing is divinely worked and solemnly felt. It is a secret grief which is personally experienced, not in mere form, but as a deep, soul-moving work of the Holy Spirit upon the inmost heart of each believer. It is not a matter to be merely talked of and believed in, but keenly and sensitively felt in every living child of the living God. It is powerfully humiliating, and completely sin-purging; but then it is sweetly preparative for those gracious consolations which proud unhumbled spirits are unable to receive; and it is distinctly discriminating, for it belongs to the elect of God, and to them alone.

The text commands us to tear our hearts, but they are naturally hard as marble; how, then, can this be done? We must take them to Calvary; a dying Savior's voice tore the rocks once, and it is as powerful now. Oh blessed Spirit, let us hear the death-cries of Jesus, and our hearts shall be torn even as men tear their garments in the day of lamentation.

EVENING

"Be diligent to know the state of your flocks, watch over your herds" — Proverbs 27:23.

EVERY WISE MERCHANT will occasionally hold a stock-taking, when he will cast up his accounts, examine what he has on hand, and ascertain decisively whether his trade is prosperous or declining. Every man who is wise in the kingdom of heaven, will cry, *"Search me, Oh God, and try me;"* and he will frequently set apart special seasons for self-examination, to discover whether things are right between God and his soul. The God whom we worship is a great heart-searcher; and of old His servants knew Him as *"the Lord which searches the heart and tries the reins of the children of men."*

Let me stir you up in His name to make diligent search and solemn trial of your state, lest you come short of the promised rest. That which every wise man does, that which God Himself does with us all, I exhort you to do with yourself this evening. Let the oldest saint look well to the fundamentals of his piety, for grey heads may cover black hearts; and let not the young professor despise the word of warning, for the greenness of youth may be joined to the rottenness of hypocrisy. Every now and then a cedar falls into our midst. The enemy still continues to sow tares among the wheat.

It is not my aim to introduce doubts and fears into your mind; no, verily, but I shall hope the rather that the rough wind of self-examination may help to drive them away. It is not security, but carnal security, which we would kill; not confidence, but fleshly confidence, which we would overthrow; not peace, but false peace, which we would destroy. By the precious blood of Christ, which was not shed to make you a hypocrite, but that sincere souls might show forth His praise, I beseech you, search and look, lest at the last it be said of you, *"Mene, Mene, Tekel: you are weighed in the balances, and are found wanting."*

December 19   MORNING

"The lot is cast into the lap, but the whole ordering of it is from the LORD" — Proverbs 16:33.

IF THE DISPOSAL of the lot is the Lord's, whose is the arrangement of our whole life? If the simple casting of a lot is guided by Him, how much more the events of our entire life; especially when we are told by our blessed Savior: *"The very hairs of your head are all numbered: not a sparrow falls to the ground without your Father."* It would bring a holy calm over your mind, dear friend, if you were always to remember this. It would so relieve your mind from anxiety, that you would be the better able to walk in patience, quiet, and cheerfulness as a Christian should. When one is anxious, he cannot pray with faith; when he is troubled about the world, he cannot serve his Master, his thoughts are serving himself.

If you would *"seek first the kingdom of God and His righteousness,"* all things would then be added unto you. You are meddling with Christ's business, and neglecting your own when you fret about your lot and circumstances. You have been forgetting that it is yours to obey. Be wise and attend to the obeying, and let Christ manage the providing. Come and survey your Father's storehouse, and ask whether He will let you starve while He has laid up so great an abundance in His garner? Look at His heart of mercy; see if that can ever prove unkind! Look at His inscrutable wisdom; see if that will ever be at fault. Above all, look up to Jesus Christ your Intercessor, and ask yourself, while He pleads, can your Father deal ungraciously with you? If He remembers even sparrows, will He forget one of the least of His poor children? *"Cast your burden upon the Lord, and He will sustain you."* He will never suffer the righteous to be moved.

> My soul, rest happy in your low estate,
> Nor hope nor wish to he esteem'd or great;
> To take the impress of the Will Divine;
> Be that your glory, and those riches thine.

EVENING

"And the sea no longer existed" — Revelation 21:1.

SCARCELY COULD WE rejoice at the thought of losing the glorious old ocean: the new heavens and the new earth are none the fairer to our imagination, if, indeed, literally there is to be no great and wide sea, with its gleaming waves and shelly shores. Is not the text to be read as a metaphor, tinged with the prejudice with which the Oriental mind universally regarded the sea in the olden times? A real physical world without a sea it is mournful to imagine, it would be an iron ring without the sapphire which made it precious.

There must be a spiritual meaning here. In the new dispensation there will be no division. The sea separates nations and sunders peoples from each other. To John in Patmos the deep waters were like prison walls, shutting him out from his brothers and his work; there shall be no such barriers in the world to come. Leagues of rolling billows lie between us and many a kinsman whom tonight we prayerfully remember, but in the bright world to which we go there shall be unbroken fellowship for all the redeemed family. In this sense there shall be no more sea.

The sea is the emblem of change; with its ebbs and flows, its glassy smoothness and its mountainous billows, its gentle murmurs and its tumultuous roarings, it is never long the same. Slave of the fickle winds and the changeful moon, its instability is proverbial. In this mortal state we have too much of this; earth is constant only in her inconstancy, but in the heavenly state all mournful change shall be unknown, and with it all fear of storm to wreck our hopes and drown our joys. The sea of glass glows with a glory unbroken by a wave. No tempest howls along the peaceful shores of paradise. Soon shall we reach that happy land where partings, and changes, and storms shall be ended! Jesus will waft us there. Are we in Him or not? This is the grand question.

MORNING   December 20

"Yes, I have loved you with an everlasting love!" — Jeremiah 31:3.

SOMETIMES THE LORD Jesus tells His Church His love thoughts. He does not think it enough behind her back to tell it, but in her very presence He says, *"You are all fair, my love."* It is true, this is not His ordinary method; He is a wise lover, and knows when to keep back the intimation of love and when to let it out; but there are times when He will make no secret of it; times when He will put it beyond all dispute in the souls of His people. (from R. Erskine's Sermons).

The Holy Spirit is often pleased, in a most gracious manner, to witness with our spirits of the love of Jesus. He takes of the things of Christ and reveals them unto us. No voice is heard from the clouds, and no vision is seen in the night, but we have a testimony more sure than either of these. If an angel should fly from heaven and inform the saint personally of the Savior's love to him, the evidence would not be one whit more satisfactory than that which is borne in the heart by the Holy Spirit. Ask those of the Lord's people who have lived the nearest to the gates of heaven, and they will tell you that they have had seasons when the love of Christ towards them has been a fact so clear and sure, that they could no more doubt it than they could question their own existence.

Yes, beloved believer, you and I have had times of refreshing from the presence of the Lord, and then our faith has mounted to the topmost heights of assurance. We have had confidence to lean our heads upon the bosom of our Lord, and we have no more questioned our Master's affection to us than John did when in that blessed posture; no, nor so much: for the dark question, *"Lord, is it I that shall betray you?"* has been put far from us. He has kissed us with the kisses of His mouth, and killed our doubts by the closeness of His embrace. His love has been sweeter than wine to our souls,

EVENING

"Call the workers and pay them their wages" — Matthew 20:8.

GOD IS A good paymaster; He pays His servants while at work as well as when they have done it; and one of His payments is this, an easy conscience. If you have spoken faithfully of Jesus to one person, when you go to bed at night you feel happy in thinking, "I have this day discharged my conscience of that man's blood." There is a great comfort in doing something for Jesus. Oh, what a happiness to place jewels in His crown, and give Him to see of the travail of His soul! There is also very great reward in watching the first buddings of conviction in a soul! To say of that girl in the class, "She is tender of heart, I do hope that there is the Lord's work within." To go home and pray over that boy, who said something in the afternoon which made you think he must know more of divine truth than you had feared! Oh, the joy of hope!

But as for the joy of success! It is unspeakable. This joy, overwhelming as it is, is a hungry thing; you pine for more of it. To be a soul-winner is the happiest thing in the world. With every soul you bring to Christ, you get a new heaven upon earth. But who can conceive the bliss which awaits us above! Oh, how sweet is that sentence, *"Enter into the joy of your Lord!"* Do you know what the joy of Christ is over a saved sinner? This is the very joy which we are to possess in heaven. Yes, when He mounts the throne, you shall mount with Him. When the heavens ring with "Well done, well done," you shall partake in the reward; you have toiled with Him, you have suffered with Him, you shall now reign with Him; you have sown with Him, you shall reap with Him; your face was covered with sweat like His, and your soul was grieved for the sins of men as His soul was, now shall your face be bright with heaven's splendor as is His countenance, and now shall your soul be filled with beatific joys even as His soul is.

December 21 MORNING

"Yet He has made with me an everlasting covenant" — 2 Samuel 23:5.

THIS COVENANT IS divine in its origin. *"He has made with me an everlasting covenant."* Oh, that great word *"He!"* Stop, my soul. God, the everlasting Father, has positively made a covenant with you. Yes, that God who spoke the world into existence by a word; He, stooping from His majesty, takes hold of your hand and makes a covenant with you. Is it not a deed, the stupendous condescension of which might ravish our hearts forever if we could really understand it? *"He has made with me a covenant."* A king has not made a covenant with me; that were somewhat; but the Prince of the kings of the earth, Shaddai, the Lord All-sufficient, the Jehovah of ages, the everlasting Elohim, "He has made with me an everlasting covenant." But notice, it is particular in its application. "Yet has he made with me an everlasting covenant." Here lies the sweetness of it to each believer. It is not so much for me that He made peace for the world; I want to know whether He made peace for me! It is little that He has made a covenant, I want to know whether He has made a covenant with me. Blessed is the assurance that He has made a covenant with me! If God the Holy Spirit gives me assurance of this, then His salvation is mine, His heart is mine, He Himself is mine. He is my God.

This covenant is everlasting in its duration. An everlasting covenant means a covenant which had no beginning, and which shall never, never end. How sweet amidst all the uncertainties of life, to know that *"the foundation of the Lord stands sure,"* and to have God's own promise, *"My covenant will I not break, nor alter the thing that is gone out of My lips."* Like dying David, I will sing of this, even though my house be not so with God as my heart desires.

EVENING

"I also clothed you with embroidered work and made shoes for you of badgers' skin, and I dressed you with fine linen, and I covered you with silk" — Ezekiel 16:10.

SEE WITH WHAT matchless generosity the Lord provides for His people's apparel. They are so arrayed that the divine skill is seen producing an unrivalled embroidered work, in which every attribute takes its part and every divine beauty is revealed. No art like the art displayed in our salvation, no cunning workmanship like that beheld in the righteousness of the saints. Justification has engrossed learned pens in all ages of the church, and will be the theme of admiration in eternity. God has indeed *"curiously worked it."* With all this elaboration there is mingled utility and durability, comparable to our being shod with badgers' skins. The animal here meant is unknown, but its skin covered the tabernacle, and formed one of the finest and strongest leathers known. The righteousness which is of God by faith endures forever, and he who is shod with this divine preparation will tread the desert safely, and may even set his foot upon the lion and the adder.

Purity and dignity of our holy vesture are brought out in the fine linen. When the Lord sanctifies His people, they are clad as priests in pure white; not the snow itself excels them; they are in the eyes of men and angels fair to look upon, and even in the Lord's eyes they are without spot. Meanwhile the royal apparel is delicate and rich as silk. No expense is spared, no beauty withheld, no daintiness denied.

What, then? Is there no inference from this? Surely there is gratitude to be felt and joy to be expressed. Come, my heart, refuse not your evening hallelujah! Tune your pipes! Touch your chords!

> Strangely, my soul, are you arrayed
> By the Great Sacred Three!
> In sweetest harmony of praise
> Let all your powers agree.

MORNING December 22

"I will make you strong" — Isaiah 41:10.

GOD HAS A strong reserve with which to discharge this engagement; for He is able to do all things. Believer, 'till you can drain dry the ocean of omnipotence, 'till you can break into pieces the towering mountains of almighty strength, you never need to fear. Think not that the strength of man shall ever be able to overcome the power of God. While the earth's huge pillars stand, you have enough reason to abide firm in your faith. The same God who directs the earth in its orbit, who feeds the burning furnace of the sun, and trims the lamps of heaven, has promised to supply you with daily strength. While He is able to uphold the universe, dream not that He will prove unable to fulfil His own promises. Remember what He did in the days of old, in the former generations. Remember how He spoke and it was done; how He commanded, and it stood fast. Shall He that created the world grow weary? He hangs the world upon nothing; shall He who does this be unable to support His children? Shall He be unfaithful to His word for want of power? Who is it that restrains the tempest? Does not He ride upon the wings of the wind, and make the clouds His chariots, and hold the ocean in the hollow of His hand? How can He fail you? When He has put such a faithful promise as this on record, will you for a moment indulge the thought that He has outpromised Himself, and gone beyond His power to fulfill? Ah, no! You can doubt no longer.

Oh You who are my God and my strength, I can believe that this promise shall be fulfilled, for the boundless reservoir of Your grace can never be exhausted, and the overflowing storehouse of Your strength can never be emptied by Your friends or rifled by Your enemies.

> Now let the feeble all be strong,
> And make Jehovah's arm their song.

EVENING

"The spot of His children" — Deuteronomy 32:5.

WHAT IS THE secret spot which infallibly betokens the child of God? It were vain presumption to decide this upon our own judgment; but God's word reveals it to us and we may tread surely where we have revelation to be our guide. Now, we are told concerning our Lord, *"to as many as received Him, to them gave He power to become the sons of God, even to as many as believed on His name,"* Then, if I have received Christ Jesus into my heart, I am a child of God. That reception is described in the same verse as believing on the name of Jesus Christ. If, then, I believe on Jesus Christ's name; that is, simply from my heart trust myself with the crucified, but now exalted, Redeemer, I am a member of the family of the Most High. Whatever else I may not have, if I have this, I have the privilege to become a child of God.

Our Lord Jesus puts it in another shape. *"My sheep hear My voice, and I know them, and they follow Me,"* Here is the matter in a nutshell. Christ appears as a shepherd to His own sheep, not to others. As soon as He appears, His own sheep perceive Him; they trust Him, they are prepared to follow Him; He knows them, and they know Him; there is a mutual knowledge; there is a constant connection between them. Thus the one mark, the sure mark, the infallible mark of regeneration and adoption is a hearty faith in the appointed Redeemer.

Reader, are you in doubt, are you uncertain whether you bear the secret mark of God's children? Then let not an hour pass over your head till you have said, *"Search me, Oh God, and know my heart."* Trifle not here, I adjure you! If you must trifle anywhere, let it be about some secondary matter: your health, if you will, or the title deeds of your estate; but about your soul, your never-dying soul and its eternal destinies, I beseech you to be in earnest. Make sure work for eternity.

December 23   MORNING

"Friend, come up higher" — Luke 14:10.

WHEN FIRST THE life of grace begins in the soul, we do indeed draw near to God, but it is with great fear and trembling. The soul conscious of guilt, and humbled thereby, is overawed with the solemnity of its position; it is cast to the earth by a sense of the grandeur of Jehovah, in whose presence it stands. With unfeigned bashfulness it takes the lowest room.

But, in after life, as the Christian grows in grace, although he will never forget the solemnity of his position, and will never lose that holy awe which must encompass a gracious man when he is in the presence of the God who can create or can destroy; yet his fear has all its terror taken out of it; it becomes a holy reverence, and no more an overshadowing dread. He is called up higher, to greater access to God in Christ Jesus. Then the man of God, walking amid the splendors of Deity, and veiling his face like the glorious cherubim, with those twin wings, the blood and righteousness of Jesus Christ, will with reverent and bowed spirit, approach the throne. And seeing there a God of love, of goodness, and of mercy, he will realize rather the covenant character of God than His absolute Deity. He will see in God rather His goodness than His greatness, and more of His love than of His majesty. Then will the soul, bowing still as humbly as before, enjoy a more sacred liberty of intercession. For while prostrate before the glory of the Infinite God, it will be sustained by the refreshing consciousness of being in the presence of boundless mercy and infinite love, and by the realization of acceptance *"in the Beloved."* Thus the believer is bidden to come up higher, and is enabled to exercise the privilege of rejoicing in God, and drawing near to Him in holy confidence, saying, *"Abba, Father."*

> So may we go from strength to strength,
> And daily grow in grace,
> Till in Your image raised at length,
> We see You face to face.

EVENING

"The night also is also Yours" — Psalm 74:16.

YES, LORD, YOU do not abdicate Your throne when the sun goes down, nor do You leave the world all through these long wintry nights to be the prey of evil; Your eyes watch us as the stars, and Your arms surround us as the zodiac belts the sky. The dews of kindly sleep and all the influences of the moon are in Your hand, and the alarms and solemnities of night are equally with You. This is very sweet to me when watching through the midnight hours, or tossing to and fro in anguish. There are precious fruits put forth by the moon as well as by the sun; may my Lord make me a favored partaker in them.

The night of affliction is as much under the arrangement and control of the Lord of Love as the bright summer days when all is bliss. Jesus is in the tempest. His love wraps the night about itself as a mantle, but to the eye of faith the sable robe is scarce a disguise. From the first watch of the night even unto the break of day the eternal Watcher observes His saints, and overrules the shades and dews of midnight for His people's highest good. We believe in no rival deities of good and evil contending for the mastery, but we hear the voice of Jehovah saying, *"I create light and I create darkness; I, the Lord, do all these things."*

Gloomy seasons of religious indifference and social sin are not exempted from the divine purpose. When the altars of truth are defiled, and the ways of God forsaken, the Lord's servants weep with bitter sorrow, but they may not despair, for the darkest eras are governed by the Lord, and shall come to their end at His bidding. What may seem defeat to us may be victory to Him.

> Though enwrapt in gloomy night,
> We perceive no ray of light;
> Since the Lord Himself is here,
> 'Tis not meet that we should fear.

MORNING   December 24

"He became poor for your sake" — *2 Corinthians 8:9.*

THE LORD JESUS Christ was eternally rich, glorious, and exalted; but *"though He was rich, yet He became poor for your sake."* As the rich saint cannot be true in his communion with his poor brothers unless of his substance he ministers to their necessities, so (the same rule holding with the head as between the members), it is impossible that our Divine Lord could have had fellowship with us unless He had imparted to us of His own abounding wealth, and had *"become poor for our sake."* Had He remained upon His throne of glory, and had we continued in the ruins of the fall without receiving His salvation, communion would have been impossible on both sides.

Our position by the fall, apart from the covenant of grace, made it as impossible for fallen man to communicate with God as it is for Belial to be in concord with Christ. In order, therefore that communion might be compassed, it was necessary that the rich kinsman should bestow his estate upon his poor relatives, that the righteous Savior should give to His sinning brothers of His own perfection, and that we, the poor and guilty, should receive of His fullness grace for grace; that thus in giving and receiving, the one might descend from the heights, and the other ascend from the depths, and so be able to embrace each other in true and hearty fellowship. Poverty must be enriched by Him in whom are infinite treasures before it can venture to commune; and guilt must lose itself in imputed and imparted righteousness before the soul can walk in fellowship with purity. Jesus must clothe His people in His own garments, or He cannot admit them into His palace of glory. And He must wash them in His own blood, or else they will be too defiled for the embrace of His fellowship.

Oh believer, herein is love! For your sake the Lord Jesus *"became poor"* that He might lift you up into communion with Himself.

EVENING

"The glory of the LORD shall be revealed, and all flesh shall see it together" — *Isaiah 40:5.*

WE ANTICIPATE THE happy day when the whole world shall be converted to Christ; when the gods of the heathen shall be cast to the moles and the bats; when Romanism shall be exploded, and the crescent of Mohammed shall wane, never again to cast its baleful rays upon the nations. Then kings shall bow down before the Prince of Peace, and all nations shall call the Redeemer blessed. Some despair of this. They look upon the world as a vessel breaking up and going to pieces, never to float again. We know that the world and all that is in it is one day to be burned up, and afterwards we look for new heavens and for a new earth, but we cannot read our Bibles without the conviction that:

> Jesus shall reign where'er the sun
> Does his successive journeys run.

We are not discouraged by the length of His delays; we are not disheartened by the long period which He allots to the church in which to struggle with little seeming success and much apparent defeat. We believe that God will never allow this world, which has once seen Christ's blood shed upon it, to be always the devil's stronghold. Christ came here to deliver this world from the detested sway of the powers of darkness.

What a shout shall that be when men and angels shall unite to cry, *"Hallelujah, hallelujah, for the Lord God Omnipotent reigns!"* What a satisfaction will it be in that day to have had a share in the fight, to have helped to break the arrows of the bow, and to have aided in winning the victory for our Lord! Happy are they who trust themselves with this conquering Lord, and who fight side by side with Him, doing their little in His name and by His strength! How unhappy are those on the side of evil! It is a losing side, and it is a matter wherein to lose is to lose and to be lost forever. On whose side are you?

December 25   MORNING

"Behold, the virgin shall be with child and shall bring forth a son, and they shall call His name Immanuel" — Isaiah 7:14.

LET US TODAY go down to Bethlehem, and in company with wondering shepherds and adoring Magi, let us see Him who was born King of the Jews, for we by faith can claim an interest in Him, and can sing, *"Unto us a child is born, unto us a son is given."* Jesus is Jehovah incarnate, our Lord and our God, and yet our brother and friend; let us adore and admire. Let us notice at the very first glance His miraculous conception. It was a thing unheard of before, and unparalleled since, that a virgin should conceive and bear a Son. The first promise ran thus, *"The seed of the woman,"* not the offspring of the man. Since venturous woman led the way in the sin which brought forth Paradise lost, she, and she alone, ushers in the Regainer of Paradise. Our Savior, although truly man, was as to His human nature the Holy One of God. Let us reverently bow before the holy Child whose innocence is able to restore to manhood its ancient glory; and let us pray that He may be formed in us, the hope of glory.

Fail not to note His humble parentage. His mother has been described simply as "a virgin," not a princess, or prophetess, nor a matron of large estate. True the blood of kings ran in her veins; nor was her mind a weak and untaught one, for she could sing most sweetly a song of praise. But yet how humble was her position, how poor the man to whom she stood affianced, and how miserable the accommodation afforded to the new-born King!

Immanuel, God with us in our nature, in our sorrow, in our lifework, in our punishment, in our grave, and now with us, or rather we with Him, in resurrection, ascension, triumph, and Second Advent splendor.

EVENING

"And when they had gone around the days of their feasting, Job sent and sanctified them And he rose up early in the morning and offered burnt sacrifices according to the number of all of them For Job said, It may be that my sons have sinned and cursed God in their hearts. This Job always did" — Job 1:5.

WHAT THE PATRIARCH did early in the morning, after the family festivities, it will be well for the believer to do for himself before he rests tonight. Amid the cheerfulness of household gatherings it is easy to slide into sinful levities, and to forget our avowed character as Christians. It ought not to be so, but so it is, that our days of feasting are very seldom days of sanctified enjoyment, but too frequently degenerate into unhallowed mirth. There is a way of joy as pure and sanctifying as though one bathed in the rivers of Eden; holy gratitude should be quite as purifying an element as grief. Alas! for our poor hearts, that facts prove that the house of mourning is better than the house of feasting.

Come, believer, in what have you sinned today? Have you been forgetful of your high calling? Have you been even as others in idle words and loose speeches? Then confess the sin, and fly to the sacrifice. The sacrifice sanctifies. The precious blood of the Lamb slain removes the guilt, and purges away the defilement of our sins of ignorance and carelessness. This is the best ending of a Christmas day: to wash anew in the cleansing fountain. Believer, come to this sacrifice continually; if it be so good tonight, it is good every night. To live at the altar is the privilege of the royal priesthood; to them sin, great as it is, is nevertheless no cause for despair, since they draw near yet again to the sin-atoning victim, and their conscience is purged from dead works.

> Gladly I close this festive day,
> Grasping the altar's hallow'd horn;
> My slips and faults are washed away,
> The Lamb has all my trespass borne.

MORNING December 26

"The last Adam" — *1 Corinthians 15:45.*

JESUS IS THE federal head of His elect. As in Adam, every heir of flesh and blood has a personal interest, because he is the covenant head and representative of the race as considered under the law of works; so under the law of grace, every redeemed soul is one with the Lord from heaven, since He is the Last Adam, the Sponsor and Substitute of the elect in the new covenant of love. The apostle Paul declares that Levi was in the loins of Abraham when Melchizedek met him (Heb. 7:4-6): it is a certain truth that the believer was in the loins of Jesus Christ, the Mediator, when in old eternity the covenant settlements of grace were decreed, ratified, and made sure forever. Thus, whatever Christ has done, He has worked for the whole body of His Church. We were crucified in Him and buried with Him, (Read Col. 2:10-13) and to make it still more wonderful, we are risen with Him and even ascended with Him to the seats on high. (Eph. 2:6) It is thus that the Church has fulfilled the law, and is *"accepted in the Beloved."* It is thus that she is regarded with complacency by the just Jehovah, for He views her in Jesus, and does not look upon her as separate from her covenant head. As the Anointed Redeemer of Israel, Christ Jesus has nothing distinct from His Church, but all that He has He holds for her. Adam's righteousness was ours so long as he maintained it, and his sin was ours the moment that he committed it; and in the same manner, all that the Last Adam is or does, is ours as well as His, seeing that He is our representative.

Here is the foundation of the covenant of grace. This gracious system of representation and substitution, which moved Justin Martyr to cry out, "Oh blessed change, Oh sweet permutation!" this is the very groundwork of the gospel of our salvation, and is to be received with strong faith and rapturous joy.

EVENING

"And lo, I am with you all the days" — *Matthew 28:20.*

THE LORD JESUS is in the midst of His church; He walks among the golden candlesticks; His promise is, *"Lo, I am with you all the days."* He is as surely with us now as He was with the disciples at the lake, when they saw coals of fire, and fish laid thereon and bread. Not carnally, but still in real truth, Jesus is with us. And a blessed truth it is, for where Jesus is, love becomes inflamed. Of all the things in the world that can set the heart burning, there is nothing like the presence of Jesus! A glimpse of Him so overcomes us, that we are ready to say, "Turn away Your eyes from me, for they have overcome me." Even the smell of the aloes, and the myrrh, and the cassia, which drop from His perfumed garments, causes the sick and the faint to grow strong. Let there be but a moment's leaning of the head upon that gracious bosom, and a reception of His divine love into our poor cold hearts, and we are cold no longer, but glow like seraphs, equal to every labor, and capable of every suffering, If we know that Jesus is with us, every power will be developed, and every grace will be strengthened, and we shall cast ourselves into the Lord's service with heart, and soul, and strength; therefore is the presence of Christ to be desired above all things.

His presence will be most realized by those who are most like Him. If you desire to see Christ, you must grow in conformity to Him. Bring yourself, by the power of the Spirit, into union with Christ's desires, and motives, and plans of action, and you are likely to be favored with His company. Remember His presence may be had. His promise is as true as ever. He delights to be with us. If He does not come, it is because we hinder Him by our indifference. He will reveal Himself to our earnest prayers, and graciously suffer Himself to be detained by our entreaties, and by our tears, for these are the golden chains which bind Jesus to His people.

December 27

MORNING

"Can the rush grow up without mire?" — Job 8:11.

THE RUSH IS spongy and hollow. Likewise is a hypocrite; there is no substance or stability in him. It is shaken to and fro in every wind just as formalists yield to every influence. For this reason the rush is not broken by the tempest, neither are hypocrites troubled with persecution. I would not willingly be a deceiver or be deceived; perhaps the text for this day may help me to try myself whether I be a hypocrite or not. The rush by nature lives in water, and owes its very existence to the mire and moisture wherein it has taken root; let the mire become dry, and the rush withers very quickly. Its greenness is absolutely dependent upon circumstances, a present abundance of water makes it flourish, and a drought destroys it at once. Is this my case? Do I only serve God when I am in good company, or when religion is profitable and respectable? Do I love the Lord only when temporal comforts are received from His hands? If so I am a base hypocrite, and like the withering rush, I shall perish when death deprives me of outward joys. But can I honestly assert that when bodily comforts have been few, and my surroundings have been rather adverse to grace than at all helpful to it, I have still held fast my integrity? Then have I hope that there is genuine vital godliness in me.

The rush cannot grow without mire, but plants of the Lord's right hand planting can and do flourish even in the year of drought. A godly man often grows best when his worldly circumstances decay. He who follows Christ for His bag is a Judas; they who follow for loaves and fishes are children of the devil. But they who attend Him out of love to Himself are His own beloved ones. Lord, let me find my life in You, and not in the mire of this world's favor or gain.

EVENING

"And the LORD shall always guide you" — Isaiah 58:11.

"THE LORD SHALL guide you." Not an angel, but Jehovah shall guide you. He said He would not go through the wilderness before His people, an angel should go before them to lead them in the way; but Moses said, *"If Your presence go not with me, carry us not up from here."* Christian, God has not left you in your earthly pilgrimage to an angel's guidance: He Himself leads the van. You may not see the cloudy, fiery pillar, but Jehovah will never forsake you. Notice the word shall: *"The Lord shall guide you."* How certain this makes it! How sure it is that God will not forsake us! His precious "shalls and wills" are better than men's oaths. *"I will never leave you, nor forsake you."* Then observe the adverb always. We are not merely to be guided sometimes, but we are to have a perpetual monitor; not occasionally to be left to our own understanding, and so to wander, but we are always to hear the guiding voice of the Great Shepherd. And if we follow close at His heels, we shall not err, but be led by a right way to a city to dwell in.

If you have to change your position in life; if you have to emigrate to distant shores; if it should happen that you are cast into poverty, or uplifted suddenly into a more responsible position than the one you now occupy; if you are thrown among strangers, or cast among foes, yet tremble not, for *"the Lord shall always guide you."* There are no dilemmas out of which you shall not be delivered if you live near to God, and your heart be kept warm with holy love. He goes not amiss who goes in the company of God. Like Enoch, walk with God, and you cannot mistake your road. You have infallible wisdom to direct you, immutable love to comfort you, and eternal power to defend you. "Jehovah," mark the word, *"Jehovah shall always guide you."*

MORNING   December 28

"And the life which I live in the flesh I live by the faith of the Son of God" — *Galatians 2:20.*

WHEN THE LORD in mercy passed by and saw us in our blood, He first of all said, "Live;" and this He did first, because life is one of the absolutely essential things in spiritual matters, and until it be bestowed we are incapable of partaking in the things of the kingdom. Now the life which grace confers upon the saints at the moment of their quickening is none other than the life of Christ, which, like the sap from the stem, runs into us, the branches, and establishes a living connection between our souls and Jesus. Faith is the grace which perceives this union, having proceeded from it as its first-fruit. It is the neck which joins the body of the Church to its all-glorious Head.

Oh Faith! you bond of union with the Lord, Is not this office yours? and your fit name, In the economy of Gospel types, And symbols apposite, the Church's neck; Identifying her in will and work With Him ascended?

Faith lays hold upon the Lord Jesus with a firm and determined grasp. She knows His excellence and worth, and no temptation can induce her to repose her trust elsewhere. And Christ Jesus is so delighted with this heavenly grace, that He never ceases to strengthen and sustain her by the loving embrace and all-sufficient support of His eternal arms. Here, then, is established a living, sensible, and delightful union which casts forth streams of love, confidence, sympathy, complacency, and joy, whereof both the bride and bridegroom love to drink. When the soul can evidently perceive this oneness between itself and Christ, the pulse may be felt as beating for both, and the one blood as flowing through the veins of each. Then is the heart as near Heaven as it can be on earth, and is prepared for the enjoyment of the most sublime and spiritual kind of fellowship.

EVENING
"I did not come to bring peace, but a sword" — *Matthew 10:34.*

THE CHRISTIAN WILL be sure to make enemies. It will be one of his objects to make none; but if to do the right, and to believe the true, should cause him to lose every earthly friend, he will count it but a small loss, since his great Friend in heaven will be yet more friendly, and reveal Himself to him more graciously than ever. Oh you who have taken up His cross, know you not what your Master said? *"I am come to set a man at variance against his father, and the daughter against her mother; and a man's foes shall be they of his own household."* Christ is the great Peacemaker; but before peace, He brings war. Where the light comes, the darkness must retire. Where truth is, the lie must flee; or, if it abides, there must be a stern conflict, for the truth cannot and will not lower its standard, and the lie must be trodden under foot.

If you follow Christ, you shall have all the dogs of the world yelping at your heels. If you would live so as to stand the test of the last tribunal, depend upon it the world will not speak well of you. He who has the friendship of the world is an enemy to God (James 4:4). But if you are true and faithful to the Most High, men will resent your unflinching fidelity, since it is a testimony against their iniquities. Fearless of all consequences, you must do the right. You will need the courage of a lion unhesitatingly to pursue a course which shall turn your best friend into your fiercest foe; but for the love of Jesus you must thus be courageous. For the truth's sake to hazard reputation and affection, is such a deed that to do it constantly you will need a degree of moral principle which only the Spirit of God can work in you. Yet do not turn your back like a coward, but play the man. Follow right manfully in your Master's steps, for He has traversed this rough way before you. Better a brief warfare and eternal rest, than false peace and everlasting torment.

December 29

MORNING

"The LORD has helped us hitherto" — Samuel 7:12.

THE WORD *"HITHERTO"* seems like a hand pointing in the direction of the past. Twenty years or seventy, and yet, "hitherto the Lord has helped!" Through poverty, through wealth, through sickness, through health, at home, abroad, on the land, on the sea, in honor, in dishonor, in perplexity, in joy, in trial, in triumph, in prayer, in temptation, *"hitherto has the Lord helped us!"*

We delight to look down a long avenue of trees. It is delightful to gaze from end to end of the long vista, a sort of verdant temple, with its branching pillars and its arches of leaves even so look down the long aisles of your years, at the green boughs of mercy overhead, and the strong pillars of loving-kindness and faithfulness which bear up your joys. Are there no birds in yonder branches singing? Surely there must be many, and they all sing of mercy received hitherto.

But the word also points forward. For when a man gets up to a certain mark and writes "hitherto," he is not yet at the end, there is still a distance to be traversed. More trials, more joys; more temptations, more triumphs; more prayers, more answers; more toils, more strength; more fights, more victories; and then come sickness, old age, disease, death. Is it over now? No! there is more yet your awakening in Jesus' likeness, thrones, harps, songs, psalms, white raiment, the face of Jesus, the society of saints, the glory of God, the fullness of eternity, the infinity of bliss. Oh be of good courage, believer, and with grateful confidence raise your "Ebenezer," for:

> He who has helped you hitherto
> Will help you all your journey through.

When read in heaven's light how glorious and marvelous a prospect will your "hitherto" unfold to your grateful eye!

EVENING

"What do you think about the Christ?" — Matthew 22:42.

THE GREAT TEST of your soul's health is, *"What do you think of Christ?"* Is He to you *"fairer than the children of men," "the chief among ten thousand," the "altogether lovely One"*? 'Wherever Christ is thus esteemed, all the faculties of the spiritual man exercise themselves with energy. I will judge of your piety by this barometer: does Christ stand high or low with you? If you have thought little of Christ, if you have been content to live without His presence, if you have cared little for His honor, if you have been neglectful of His laws, then I know that your soul is sick; God grant that it may not be sick unto death! But if the first thought of your spirit has been, How can I honor Jesus? If the daily desire of your soul has been, *"Oh that I knew where I might find Him!"* I tell you that you may have a thousand infirmities, and even at times doubt whether you are a child of God at all, and yet I am persuaded, beyond a doubt, that you are safe, since Jesus is great in your esteem.

I care not for your rags, what do you think of His royal apparel? I care not for your wounds, though they bleed in torrents, what do you think of His wounds? Are they like glittering rubies in your esteem? I think none the less of you, though you lie like Lazarus on the dunghill, and the dogs lick you. I judge you not by your poverty; what do you think of the King in His beauty? Has He a glorious high throne in your heart? Would you set Him higher if you could? Would you be willing to die if you could but add another trumpet to the strain which proclaims His praise? Ah! then it is well with you. Whatever you may think of yourself, if Christ be great to you, you shall be with Him before long.

> Though all the world my choice deride,
> Yet Jesus shall my portion be;
> For I am pleased with none beside;
> The fairest of the fair is He.

MORNING   December 30

"Better is the end of a thing than the beginning of it" — Ecclesiastes 7:8.

LOOK AT DAVID'S Lord and Master; see Him as He finished His work on earth. He was despised and rejected of men; a man of sorrows and acquainted with grief. Would you see the end? He sits at His Father's right hand, expecting until His enemies be made His footstool. *"As He is, so are we also in this world."* You must bear the cross, or you shall never wear the crown; you must wade through the mire, or you shall never walk the golden pavement. Cheer up, then, poor Christian. *"Better is the end of a thing than the beginning of it."*

See that creeping worm, how contemptible its appearance! It is the beginning of a thing. Mark that insect with gorgeous wings, playing in the sunbeams, sipping at the flower bells, full of happiness and life; that is the end thereof. That caterpillar is yourself, until you are wrapped up in the chrysalis of death; but when Christ shall appear you shall be like Him, for you shall see Him as He is. Be content to be like Him, a worm and no man, that like Him you may be satisfied when you wake up in His likeness.

That rough-looking diamond is put upon the wheel of the lapidary. He cuts it on all sides. It loses much; much that seemed costly to itself. The king is crowned; the diadem is put upon the monarch's head with trumpet's joyful sound. A glittering ray flashes from that coronet, and it beams from that very diamond which was just now so sorely vexed by the lapidary. You may venture to compare yourself to such a diamond, for you are one of God's people; and this is the time of the cutting process. Let faith and patience have their perfect work, for in the day when the crown shall be set upon the head of the King, Eternal, Immortal, Invisible, one ray of glory shall stream from you. *"They shall be Mine,"* says the Lord, *"in the day when I make up My jewels." "Better is the end of a thing than the beginning of it."*

EVENING

"Do you not know that it will be bitterness in the latter end?" — 2 Samuel 2:26.

IF, OH MY reader! you are merely a professor, and not a possessor, of the faith that is in Christ Jesus, the following lines are a true sketch of your end.

You are a respectable attendant at a place of worship; you go because others go, not because your heart is right with God. This is your beginning. I will suppose that for the next twenty or thirty years you will be spared to go on as you do now, professing religion by an outward attendance upon the means of grace, but having no heart in the matter. Tread softly, for I must show you the deathbed of such a one as yourself. Let us gaze upon him gently. A clammy sweat is on his brow, and he wakes up crying, Oh God, it is hard to die. Did you send for my minister? Yes, he is coming. The minister comes, and you say, "Sir, I fear that I am dying! He says, Have you any hope?" And you say, "I cannot say that I have. I fear to stand before my God; oh! pray for me." The prayer is offered for him with sincere earnestness, and the way of salvation is for the ten-thousandth time put before him; but before you grasp the rope, I see you sink. I may put my finger upon those cold eyelids, for they will never see anything here again.

But where is the man, and where are the man's true eyes? It is written, *"In hell he lifted up his eyes, being in torment."* Ah! why did he not lift up his eyes before? Because he was so accustomed to hear the gospel that his soul slept under it. Alas! if you should lift up your eyes there, how bitter will be your wailings. Let the Savior's own words reveal the woe: *"Father Abraham, send Lazarus, that he may dip the tip of his finger in water, and cool my tongue, for I am tormented in this flame."* There is a frightful meaning in those words. May you never have to spell it out by the red light of Jehovah's wrath!

December 31 — MORNING

"And in the last day, the great one of the feast, Jesus stood and cried, saying, If anyone thirst, let him come to Me and drink" — John 7:37.

PATIENCE HAD HER perfect work in the Lord Jesus, and until the last day of the feast He pleaded with the Jews, even on this last day of the year He pleads with us, and waits to be gracious to us. Admirable indeed is the long-suffering of the Savior in bearing with some of us year after year, notwithstanding our provocations, rebellions, and resistance of His Holy Spirit. Wonder of wonders that we are still in the land of mercy!

Jesus cried, which implies not only the loudness of His voice, but the tenderness of His tones. He entreats us to be reconciled. *"We pray you,"* says the Apostle, *"as though God did beseech you by us."* What earnest, pathetic terms are these! How deep must be the love which makes the Lord cry out to sinners! Surely at the call of such a cry our willing hearts will come.

All is provided that man can need to quench his soul's thirst. To his conscience the atonement brings peace; to his understanding the gospel brings the richest instruction; to his heart the person of Jesus is the noblest object of affection; to the whole man the truth as it is in Jesus supplies the purest nutriment. Thirst is terrible, but Jesus can remove it. Though the soul were utterly famished, Jesus could restore it.

Justification is made most freely, that every thirsty one is welcome. No other distinction is made by that of thirst. Whether it be the thirst of avarice, ambition, pleasure, knowledge, or rest, he who suffers from it is invited. The thirst may be bad in itself, and be no sign of grace, but rather a mark of inordinate sin longing to he gratified with deeper draughts of lust. But it is not goodness in the creature which brings him the invitation, the Lord Jesus sends it freely, and without respect of persons.

The need for a personal relationship is declared most fully. The sinner must come to Jesus, not to works, ordinances, or doctrines, but to a personal Redeemer, who His own self bare our sins in His own body on the tree. The bleeding, dying, rising Savior, is the only star of hope to a sinner. Oh for grace to come now and drink, before the sun sets upon the year's last day!

No waiting or preparation is so much as hinted at. Drinking represents a reception for which no fitness is required. A fool, a thief, a harlot can drink; and so sinfulness of character is no bar to the invitation to believe in Jesus. We want no golden cup, no bejeweled chalice, in which to convey the water to the thirsty; the mouth of poverty is welcome to stoop down and quaff the flowing flood. Blistered, leprous, filthy lips may touch the stream of divine love; they cannot pollute it, but shall themselves be purified. Jesus is the fount of hope. Dear reader, hear the dear Redeemer's loving voice as He cries to each of us, *"If anyone thirst, let him come to Me and drink."*

EVENING — December 31

"The harvest is past, the summer is ended, and we are not saved" — *Jeremiah 8:20.*

NOT SAVED! DEAR reader, is this your mournful plight? Warned of the judgment to come, hidden to escape for your life, and yet at this moment not saved! You know the way of salvation, you read it in the Bible, you hear it from the pulpit, it is explained to you by friends, and yet you neglect it, and therefore are not saved. You will be without excuse when the Lord shall judge the quick and dead. The Holy Spirit has given more or less of blessing upon the word which has been preached in your hearing, and times of refreshing have come from the divine presence, and yet you are without Christ. All these hopeful seasons have come and gone; your summer and your harvest have passed and yet you are not saved. Years have followed one another into eternity, and your last year will soon he here; youth has gone, manhood is going, and yet you are not saved.

Let me ask you: will you ever be saved? Is there any likelihood of it? Already the most propitious seasons have left you unsaved; will other occasions alter your condition? Means have failed with you; the best of means, used perserveringly and with the utmost affection; what more can be done for you? Affliction and prosperity have alike failed to impress you; tears and prayers and tensions have been wasted on your hard heart. Are not the probabilities dead against your ever being saved? Is it not more than likely that you will abide as you are till death forever bars the door of hope? Do you recoil from the supposition? Yet it is a most reasonable one: he who is not washed in so many waters will in all probability go filthy to his end. The convenient time never has come, why should it ever come? It is logical to fear that it never will arrive, and that Felix-like, you will find no convenient season till you are in hell. Oh bethink you of what that hell is, and of the dread probability that you will soon be cast into it!

Reader, suppose you should die unsaved, your doom no words can picture. Write out your dread estate in tears and blood, talk of it with groans and gnashing of teeth; you will be punished with everlasting destruction from the glory of the Lord, and from the glory of His power. A brother's voice would fain startle you into earnestness. Oh be wise, be wise in time, and before another year begins, believe in Jesus, who is able to save to the uttermost. Consecrate these last hours to lonely thought, and if deep repentance be bred in you, it will he well; and if it lead to a humble faith in Jesus, it will be best of all. Oh see to it that this year pass not away, and you an unforgiven spirit. Let not the new year's midnight peals sound upon a joyless spirit! Now, Now, NOW, believe, and live:

"Escape for your life!
Look not behind you,
Neither stay in all the plain;
Escape to the mountain,
Lest you he consumed."

MORNING

AND

EVENING II

A SECOND YEAR OF DAILY DEVOTIONS

By C. H. SPURGEON

WITH SELECTED DEVOTIONS FROM MANY FAMED MEN OF GOD, including Jonathan Edwards, John Calvin, Martin Luther, William Gurnall, Thomas Goodwin, John Owen, Joseph Alleine, John Flavel, Thomas Brooks, John Gill, Thomas Manton, Joseph Caryl and many others

Published by

Sovereign Grace Publishers, Inc.
P.O. Box 4998
Lafayette, IN 47903
Phone: (765) 429-4122
Fax: (765) 429-4142

January 1   MORNING

Because I live, you shall live also — John 14:19.

NOTE CAREFULLY the continuance insisted on in this verse. Continuance is indeed the main element of this promise, *"You shall live."* It means certainly that during our abode in this body we shall live. We shall not be again reduced to our death-state during our sojourn here. Ten thousand attempts will be made to bring us under dominion to the law of sin and death, but this one word baffles all. Your soul may be so assailed that it shall seem as if you could not keep your hold on Christ, but Christ shall keep His hold on you. The incorruptible seed may be crushed, bruised, buried, but the life within it shall not be extinguished, it shall yet arise. *"You shall live"* — when you see all around you ten thousand elements of death, believers, think how grand is this word. No falling from grace for you, no being cast out of the covenant, no being driven from the Father's house and left to perish, *"You shall live."*

Nor is this all. For when the natural death comes, which indeed to us is no longer death, our inner life shall suffer no hurt whatever. It will not even be suspended for a moment. It is not a thing which can be touched by death. The shafts of the last enemy can have no more effect on the spiritual, than a javelin on a cloud. Even in the very crisis, when the soul is separated from the body, no damage shall be done to the spiritual nature. And in the future, when the judgment comes, when the thrones are seen, when the multitudes are gathered, the righteous to the right-hand, the wicked to the left-hand, let what may come forth of terror and of horror, the ones begotten of God shall live. Onward through eternity, whatever may be the changes which yet are to be disclosed, nothing shall affect our God-given life. Like the life of God Himself, eternal and ever-blessed, it shall continue.

EVENING

The wicked shall be turned into Hell, and all the nations that forget God. For the needy shall not always be forgotten, the hope of the poor shall not *perish forever* — Psalm 9:17, 18.

THE JUSTICE which has punished the wicked, and preserved the righteous, remains the same, and so in days to come retribution will surely be meted out. How solemn is the seventeenth verse, especially in its warning to forgetters of God. The moral who are not devout, the honest who are not prayerful, the benevolent who are not believing, the amiable who are not converted — these must all have their portion with the openly wicked in the Hell which is prepared for the Devil and his angels. There are whole nations of such. The forgetters of God are far more numerous than the profane or profligate, and according to the very forceful expression of the Hebrew, the nethermost Hell will be the place into which all of them shall be hurled headlong. Forgetfulness seems a small sin, but it brings eternal wrath on the man who lives and dies in it.

Mercy is ready to her work as ever justice can be. Needy souls fear that they are forgotten. Well, if it is so, let them rejoice that they shall not always be so. Satan tells poor tremblers that their hope shall perish, but they have here Divine assurance that their expectation shall not perish forever. "The Lord's people are a humbled people, afflicted, emptied, sensible of need, driven to a daily attendance on God, daily begging of Him, and living on the hope of what is promised" — such persons may have to wait, but they shall find that they do not wait in vain.

Prayers are the believer's weapons of war. When the battle is too hard for us we call in our great Ally, who, as it were, lies in ambush until faith gives the signal by crying out, "Arise, O Lord!" Although our cause is all but lost, it shall soon be won again if the Almighty only bestirs Himself. He will not allow man to prevail over God, but with swift judgments will confound their gloryings. In the very sight of God the wicked will be punished, and He who is now all tenderness will have no bowels of compassion for them, since they had no tears of repentance while their day of grace endured.

MORNING

Because I live, you shall live also — John 14:19

IT IS TO BE remarked concerning our life in Christ, that it is the removal of the penalty which fell on our race for Adam's sin. *"In the day you eat of it you will surely die,"* was the Lord's threatening to our first parent, who was the representative of the race. He did eat of that fruit, and since God is true, and His word never fails, we may be sure of this, that in that same day Adam died. It is true that he did not cease to exist, but that is quite another thing from dying. The threatening was not that he should ultimately die, but *"In the day you eat of it you will surely die;"* and it is beyond all doubt that the Lord kept His word to the letter. If the first threatening was not carried out we might take liberty to trifle with others. Rest assured, then, that the threat was on the spot fulfilled. The spiritual life departed from Adam. He was no longer as one with God, no more able to live and breathe in the same sphere as the Lord. He fell from his first estate — if he should enter into spiritual life he had need to be born again, even as you and I must be. As he hides himself from his Maker and utters vain excuses before his God, you see that he is dead to the life of God, dead in trespasses and sins. We also, being heirs of wrath even as others, through the Fall are dead, dead in trespasses and sins; and if we ever are to possess spiritual life, it must be said of us, *"And you He has made alive."* We must be as *"as those that are alive from the dead."* The world is the valley of dry bones, and grace raises the chosen into newness of life. The fall brought universal death, in the deep spiritual sense of that word, over all mankind. And Jesus delivers us from the consequences of the Fall by implanting in us a spiritual life.

EVENING

And it came to pass at the end of the four hundred and thirty years, even the same day it came to pass, that all the hosts of the Lord went out from the land of Egypt
— Exodus 12:41

GOD HAD PROMISED Abraham that His people would be in bondage 430 years, and they were not in bondage one day more. As soon as God's bond became due He paid the bill, although it had been drawn up 430 years before. He required no more time to do it in, but He did it at once. Christopher Ness wrote that they had to tarry for the fulfilment of the promise until the night came, for although He fulfilled it the same day, He made them stay to the end of it to prove their faith. Ness was wrong, because Scripture days begin at night: *"The evening and the morning were the second day."* So God did not make them wait, but paid them at once. As soon as the day came, beginning with our night, as the Jewish day does now — as soon as the clock struck — God paid His bond. We have heard of some landlords who come for their rent at twelve o'clock precisely. Well, we admire a man's honesty if he pays him exactly at that minute. God is never behind in fulfilling His promises, not by the ticking of a clock.

Even though His promise seems to tarry, wait for it. You may be mistaken as to the date. If He has promised anything on a certain day, he will not keep you waiting until the morrow. That same day the Lord had promised, the Israelites came out. And so all the Lord's people shall come out of bondage before the appointed time. O you poor distressed heir of Heaven, groaning under sin and seeking rest, but finding none, believe that it is the Lord's will that you should be a little longer where there is a smoking furnace. Wait a little; He is doing you good. Like Jesus, He is speaking hardly to you to try your faith. He is telling you now that you are a dog, because He wants to hear you say, "Truth, Lord, but the dogs eat of the crumbs." He would not keep you waiting if your eagerness did not by it get fresh vigor. He would not keep you crying if He did not mean to make it a sign of better grace to you for the future. So wait, for you shall come out of Egypt and have a joyous rescue in that day when they come with singing to Zion.

January 3 — MORNING

There is joy in the presence of the angels of God over one sinner repenting
— Luke 15:10

BY WHOM was the piece of silver sought? It was sought by its owner personally. Notice, she who lost the money lit a candle and swept the house, seeking diligently till she found it. So, brothers, I have said that the woman represents the Holy Spirit, or rather the church in which the Holy Spirit dwells. Now there never will be a soul found till the Holy Spirit seeks after it. He is the great soul finder. The heart will continue in the dark until He comes with His illuminating power. He is the owner. He possesses it, and He alone can effectually seek after it. The God to whom the soul belongs must seek the soul. But He does it by His church, for souls belong to the church, too; they are sons and daughters of the chosen mother. They are her citizens and treasures. For this reason the church must personally seek after souls. She cannot delegate her work to anybody. The woman did not pay a servant to sweep the house, but she swept it herself. Her eyes were much better than a servant's eyes, for the servant's eyes would only look after somebody else's money. But the mistress would look after her own money, and she would be certain to see it if it were anywhere within sight. When the church of God solemnly feels, "It is our work to look after sinners; we must not delegate it even to the minister, or to the City missionary, or the Bible-woman, but the church must look after the souls of sinners." Then I believe souls will be found and saved. When the church recognizes that these lost souls belong to her, she will be likely to find them. It will be a happy day when every church of God is actively at work for the salvation of sinners. It has been the curse of Christendom that she has ventured to delegate her sacred duties to men called priests, or that she has set apart certain persons to be called the religious, who are to do works of mercy and charity and of evangelization.

EVENING

There is a joy in the presence of the angels of God over one sinner repenting
—Luke 15:10

NOTE THAT THIS seeking became a matter of chief concern with the woman. I do not know what other business she had to do, but I do know that she put it all by to find the piece of money. There was the corn to be ground for the morning meal, perhaps that was done. At any rate, if not so, she left it unprepared. There was a garment to be mended, or water to be drawn, or the fire to be kindled, or the friends and neighbors to converse with — never mind, the mistress forgets everything else; she has lost her piece of money and she must find it at once. So with the church of God, her chief concern should be to seek the perishing sons of men. To bring souls to know Jesus, and to be saved in Him with a great salvation should be the church's longing and concern. She has other things to do. She has her own edification to consider, she has other matters to be attended to in their place, but this first, this evermore and always first. The woman evidently said, "The money is lost; I must find that first." The loss of her piece of silver was so serious a matter that if she sat down to her mending, her hands would miss their nimbleness. Or if any other housework demanded her attention, it would be an irksome task to her, for she was thinking of that piece of coin. If her friend came and talked with her, she would say to herself, "I wish she were gone, for I want to be looking after my lost money." I wish the church of God had such an engrossing love for poor sinners that she would feel everything to be an impertinence which hindered her from soul-saving. As a church we have every now and then a little to do with politics, and a little to do with finance, for we are still in the world. But I love to see in all the churches everything kept in the background compared with soul-saving work. This must be first and foremost.

MORNING

There is joy in the presence of the angels of God over one sinner repenting
— Luke 15:10

THIS WOMAN sought for her piece of silver continuously *"until she found it."* May you and I, as parts of the church of God, look after wandering souls till we find them. We say they discourage us. No doubt that piece of silver did discourage the woman who sought it. We complain that men do not appear inclined to religion. Did the piece of money lend the housewife any help? Was it any assistance to her? She did the seeking; she did it all. And the Holy Spirit through you, my brother, seeks the salvation of the sinner, not expecting the sinner to help Him; for the sinner is averse to being found. What, were you repulsed the other day by one whose spiritual good you longed for? Go again! Were your invitations laughed at? Invite again! Did you become the subject of ridicule through your earnest entreaties? Entreat again! Those are not always the least likely to be saved who at first repel our efforts. A harsh reception is sometimes only an intimation that the heart recognizes the power of truth, although it does not desire at present to yield to it.

Persevere till you find the soul you seek. You who spend so much effort in your Sunday school class, use your candle still, enlighten the child's mind still, sweep the house till you find what you seek. Never give up the child till it is brought to Christ. You dealing with that young man or young woman in your senior class, cease not from your private prayers and from your personal admonitions, till that heart belongs to Jesus. You who preach in the streets, or visit the lodging-houses, or go from door to door with tracts, I charge you all never to give up the pursuit of sinners until they are safely lodged in the hands of Jesus. We must have them saved!

EVENING

In that day a fountain shall be opened to the house of David and to the people of Jerusalem for sin and for uncleanness — Zechariah 13:1.

There is a fountain opened, not a cistern nor a reservoir, but a fountain. A fountain continues to bubble up; it is as full after fifty years as at the first. And so the provision and mercy of God for the forgiveness and the justification of our souls continually flows and overflows. There is a supply so large that when thousands of the sons of Adam come they find that there is enough for their demands. As new generations continue still to come all along the centuries, they shall find that the supply has not in any degree been diminished. For the sin of Adam and Abel the atonement was sufficient, but it shall be equally so for the last repenting sinner. David saw the cleansing flood and washed away his crimson sins. But he left the fountain undefiled, and it is as effectual for you and for me as it was for him. For sinners in the last days the fountain is as full, as cleansing, and as free, as for sinners in the first ages of the world.

Thus I have testified to you that for the great need of men in this double form, there is a divinely appointed and inexhaustible supply. And it is intended for high and low, rich and poor, for the royal and the ragged, the prince and the pauper.

When was this fountain opened? When was this divine and inexhaustible supply revealed to men? The fountain was opened for sin and for uncleanness when the Lord Jesus died. God, the everlasting Word, was made flesh and dwelt among us, and in fulness of time the weight of human sin was laid on Him. In order to put that sin away He must die, for death was the penalty for guilt. Up to the cross He went, suffering unspeakable agonies, and at last He yielded up His soul. And when he did so, sin was put away, and the fountain for the cleansing of sin was effectually opened. We have a Savior who takes away the offense of sin as touching God, and the defilement of sin in human nature.

January 5   MORNING

In that day a fountain shall be opened to the house of David and to the people of Jerusalem for sin and for uncleanness — Zechariah 13:1.

WHEN WE READ that the provision made for the removal of sin and sinfulness is open, we learn that it is personally approachable by us. Certain fanatics in our day will have it that grace comes to us through priests. There is the fountain, but you must not touch a drop of the purifying stream yourself, but that gentleman in white, or black, or blue, or scarlet (as the day of the month or the change of the moon may be) must stand at the fountain head and catch the water as it flows. Then, only after he has practiced on it several manipulations, you may drink from his hand. But you who are unordained must not go to the fountain for yourselves. Ah, my brothers, but we know better than to make gods of men, or saviors of sinners like ourselves. We dispense with priests, for we know that the fountain of salvation is open for us to come personally, and directly, and without any intervention. There is one Mediator between God and man, even the Man Christ Jesus. There is no other mediator. As the dying thief said, *"Lord, remember me,"* so will we turn our eyes to that once crucified Savior sitting in the highest Heaven, and breathe the same prayer. As Stephen looked up directly into Heaven, and found peace even amid that stony shower, so on our dying bed our glance shall be to the Christ in the open Heaven. And we shall find rest in our last hours. Blessed is God, the doctrine of justification by faith is now so openly delcared that priestcraft cannot hold us captives. We, the believers, are truly priests, every one of us; they are mere pretenders.

EVENING

In that day a fountain shall be opened to the house of David and to the people of Jerusalem for sin and for uncleanness — Zechariah 13:1.

THE FOUNTAIN of cleansing is not sealed by any demands in the gospel requiring you to prepare yourself for it before you come. The fountain is open, and if you are filthy, you are welcome to come to it. All that is asked of you is that you believe in Jesus. He gives you this. It is His own work in you. You must also repent and hate the sin which you have committed. He also works this in you, causing you by His Spirit to loathe the sin which you delighted in before. If there had been a sort of purgatorial preparation, a kind of quarantine through which the sinner had to pass before he could be renewed and forgiven, then the fountain would not be completely open. But between you, O sinner, and acceptation before God, there need not be even a step of delay. Believe now, and by believing you shall obtain the perfect pardon and the renewal of your soul.

Nor is there any other real barrier to shut up the fountain from the sinner. Some will say, "Perhaps I am not elected." My friend, read the text; the fountain is open. It is open for all ranks, *"to the house of David and to the people."* The doctrine of election, true though it be, does not make my text a falsehood, nor close the fount of grace on any seeking soul. Can you think of any other doctrine? Does any other truth discourage you? Whatever it is I need only quote the text in order to answer your suspicion: The fountain is open for sin and for uncleanness; who dares say it is shut? If any theologian should say so, I think I would push him into the fountain to make way for the sinner to come. There cannot be anything in theology, nor in nature, nor in Heaven, nor on earth, nor in Hell, which can shut what God declares to be open. If you will to be saved, if you come to Christ, believing in Him, there is nothing to shut up the fountain of life or prevent you from being cleansed and healed. If there is any shutting or forbidding it is your heart that is closed, and your pride which forbids.

MORNING

I have preached righteousness in the great congregation; lo, I have not kept back my lips, O Lord, You know — Psalm 40:9.

THERE ARE some people who, if there is a revival, are so marvelously zealous and earnest that we are ready to clap our hands; then all of a sudden they stop. They were just getting their Sunday school clas into right order, but before there was an opportunity to reap the fruit they suddenly felt it was not precisely what they were called to. That Young Men's Bible Class — yes, that was a happy thought, the pastor was delighted — but, unhappily, some little difficulty occurred that you had not foreseen, and that also has fallen through. So it has been in other cases. Know, then, that those who cannot like the Master look back on a continuous and persevering testimony, these will not be able to speak with a clear conscience as He did.

But although so many classes of those who profess and call themselves Christians will not be able to take a happy retrospect of their lives, yet there are not lacking those who could do so. I have known men of one talent who without any self-righteousness could say, *"I have preached righteousness; I have not kept back my lips, O Lord, You know."* "I have declared Your faithfulness and Your salvation; I have not hidden Your loving-kindness and Your truth." Dear, good men in many a country village, whose names will never be famous, have gathered just a few people together and have preached on, on, and on, for years. And when they come to die in the Lord and rest from their labors, their works will follow them, and the life-service will be as acceptable as the services of many men with ten times the talents and ten times the scope for their exercise. Perhaps the Master will say to them, *"Well done, good and faithful servant,"* with a stronger emphasis than to some who were better known.

EVENING

Whoever believes that Jesus is the Christ has been born of God. And whoever loves Him who brought to birth also loves him that has been born of Him — 1 John 5:1

THE TRUE FAITH is set forth in Scripture by figures. We will mention one or two. It was an eminent type of faith when the Hebrew father in Egypt slew the lamb and caught the warm blood in the basin, then took a bunch of hyssop and dipped it in the blood and marked the two posts of his door, and then struck a red mark across the lintel. That smearing of the door represented faith. The deliverance was wrought by the blood; and the blood availed through the householder's own personally striking of it on his door. Faith does that. It takes of the things of Christ, makes them its own, sprinkles the soul, as it were, with the precious blood, accepts the way of mercy by which the Lord passes over us and exempts His people from destruction. Faith was shown to the Jews in another way. When a beast was offered in sacrifice for sin, the priest, and sometimes the representatives of the tribes, or the individual, laid their hands on the victim in token that they desired their sins to be transferred to it, that it might suffer for them as a type of the great Substitute. Faith lays her hands on Jesus, desiring to receive the benefit of His substitutionary death.

A still more remarkable representation of faith was that of the healing look of the serpent-bitten Israelites. On the great standard in the midst of the camp Moses lifted up a serpent of brass. High overhead above all the tents this serpent gleamed in the sun, and whoever of all the dying host would but look to it was made to live. Looking was a very simple act, but it indicated that the person was obedient to God's command. He looked as he was bidden, and the virtue of healing came from the brazen serpent through a look. Such is faith. It is the simplest thing in the world, but it indicates a great deal more than is seen on its surface:

"There is life for a look at the Crucified One."

January 7   MORNING

In that day a fountain shall be opened to the house of David and to the people of Jerusalem for sin and for uncleanness — Zechariah 13:1.

IF YOU ARE at all like me you will at times feel your inner life to be sadly declining. I am ashamed to confess it, but even when I seek to live nearest to God I still feel an evil heart of unbelief struggling within me. There may come times when you will anxiously inquire, "Can I be a child of God at all? I cannot arouse my feelings toward God; my passions will not stir; even in holy duties I lack the living power; there is the wood, but where is the fire for the burnt-offering? I want to be fervent, zealous, earnest, intense, but I am sluggish, a dolt in the Master's cause." At such times we are apt to say, "I must try to make myself somewhat better than this by some means before I dare hope in God." Then we go off to our own selves and our own works, and we sink in the deep mire where there is no standing.

At such moments it is a happy thing to turn again to Christ and say, "O my Master, unworthy as I am to be Your follower, although the vilest of all those whose names are written on Your roll, yet I still do believe in You. I will cling to Your cross; I will never let go my hope, for You have come to save sinners, even such ones as I am, and on You I will continue to trust." You will find that while this restores your peace, at the same time it excites you to seek after higher degrees of holiness. It is the idea of the worldling that if sin is pardoned so easily men will live in it. But it is not so. To the spiritual mind the great love displayed in the pardon of sin is the very highest motive for overcoming every unhallowed propensity. A sense of blood-bought pardon seals the death-warrant of the most favored sin. We shall ever find our safest mode of battling with sin to be a new resort to the cross. Happy is it for us that the blood cleanses us from all sin; that is, it continues to do so every day.

EVENING

Keep back Your servant also from presumptuous sins; let them not have dominion over me — Psalm 19:13.

THIS EARNEST and humble prayer teaches us that saints may fall into the worst of sins unless restrained by God's grace. So they must watch and pray that they do not enter into temptation. There is a natural proneness to sin in the best of men. All must be held back as a horse is held back by the bit, or they will run away. All sins are great sins, but presumptuous sins are peculiarly dangerous. Every sin has in it the venom of rebellion, and is full of the essential marrow of traitorous rejection of God. But some sins have in them a greater development of rebellion; these wear on their faces more of the brazen pride leading to defiance of the Most High. There are some sins which have a deeper shade of blackness, a more scarlet-dyed hue of criminality than others. Presumptuous sins rank head and foremost in the list of our iniquities. An atonement was provided under Jewish law for every kind of sin, with one exception: *"But the soul that sins presumptuously shall have no atonement. It shall be cut off from the midst of My people"* (Num. 15:30).

Under the Christian dispensation, although in the sacrifice of our blessed Lord there is a great and precious atonement for presumptuous sins which cleanses the sinner, still presumptuous sinners who die without such pardon must expect to receive a double portion of the wrath of God. For this reason David is careful not to come under the reigning power of presumption: *"Then I shall be upright, and I shall be innocent from the great transgression"* (vs. 13b). He shudders at the thought of such sins. Secret sins are stepping-stones to presumptuous sins, easily leading to *the sin that is unto death*. That one who is not willful in his sin is in far better case than the one who tempts the Devil to tempt him. Such a one will be led from bad to worse, and then from the worse to the worst.

MORNING

Whoever believes that Jesus is the Christ has been born of God. And whoever loves Him who brought to birth also loves him that has been born of Him — 1 John 5:1

THE FAITH intended in the text evidently rests on a person — on Jesus. *"Whoever believes that Jesus is the Christ has been born of God."* It is not a belief about a doctrine, nor an opinion, nor a formula, but belief concerning a person. Translate the words, *"Whoever believes that Jesus is the Christ,"* and they stand thus: "Whoever believes the Savior is the Anointed has been born of God." By which it is assuredly not meant, "whoever *professes* to believe that is so," for many do that whose lives prove that they are not regenerate. But it is this, "whoever believes it to be the fact, as truly and in very deed to receive Jesus as God has set Him forth and anointed Him; that one is a regenerate one. What is meant, by *"Jesus is the Christ,"* or *Jesus the Anointed?* First, that He is the Prophet; secondly, that He is the Priest; thirdly, that He is the King of the church — for in all these senses He is the Anointed. I ask myself this question: Do I this day believe that Jesus is the great Prophet anointed of God to reveal to me the way of salvation? Do I accept Him as my teacher and admit that He has the words of eternal life? If I so believe, I will obey His gospel and will possess eternal life. Do I accept Him to be the revealer of God to my soul, the messenger of the covenant, the anointed Prophet of the Most High? But He is also a priest. Now, a priest is ordained from among men to offer sacrifices. Do I firmly believe that Jesus was ordained to offer His one sacrifice for the sins of mankind, by the offering of which sacrifice once for all He has finished atonement and made complete expiation? Do I accept His atonement as an atonement for me, and receive His death as an expiation on which I rest my hope for forgiveness of all my transgressions? Do I in fact believe Jesus to be the one, sole, only propitiating Priest, and accept Him to act as priest for me?

EVENING

I have preached righteousness in the great congregation; lo, I have not kept back my lips, O Lord, You know — Psalm 40:9.

HOW AWFUL to remember that every hour there are hundreds of men and women who are dying without Christ. Turn to the bills of mortality of this one city. Though our sentiments be ever so charitable, let us judge with the utmost liberality, the dreadful fact fill our mind, every knell speaks it to our heart, "They go out of this world unforgiven; they go before thier Maker's bar without a hope!" Our hearts would break with the dread recollection of this if we could not say, *"I have preached righteousness in the great congregation; lo, I have not kept back my lips, O Lord; You know." I have not hidden Your righteousness within my heart; I have declared Your faithfulness and Your salvation. I have not hidden Your loving-kindness and Your truth from the great congregation."*

And how many deaths there are always among our hearers? What comfort can any Christian have of those who knows you, if you die unsaved, unless he is able to appeal to God and say, "Father, I did all I could to teach that soul the way of salvation. I did all I could to persuade him to accept the Christ of God."

Dear friends, whenever you see any of your neighbors, your relatives, your acquaintances die, can you forbear to ask yourselves: Shall their blood be required at my hands? Are your skirts stained? Are there no blood-drops there? Come, look, and say if you can ponder with a clear conscience the fact a sinner is dying in a Christless state without you being able to say, "I have done all I could to bring that soul to Christ?"

January 9 — MORNING

Whoever believes that Jesus is the Christ has been born of God. And whoever loves Him who brought to birth also loves him that has been born of Him — 1 John 5:1.

IF WE ARE BEGOTTEN OF GOD we must love all those who are also born of God. It would be an insult to you if I were to prove that a brother should love his brother. Does not nature herself teach us that? Then those who are born of God ought to love all those of the same household. And who are they? They are all those who have believed that Jesus is the Christ, and are resting their hopes where we rest ours, namely, on Christ the Anointed One of God. We are to love all such. We are to do this because we are of the family. We believe, and so we know we have been begotten of God. Let us act as those who are of the Divine family. Let us count it our privilege that we are received into the household, and rejoice to perform the lovely obligations of our high position. We look around us and see many others who have believed in Jesus Christ; let us love them because they are of the same kindred. "But there are some of them unsound in doctrine; they make gross mistakes as to the Master's ordinances." We are not to love their faults, nor ought we to expect them to love ours. Nevertheless we are to love their persons, for *"whoever believes that Jesus is the Christ has been born of God,"* and therefore he is one of the family. Even as we love the Father who fathered us, we are to love all those that are begotten of Him. First, I love God, and therefore I desire to promote God's truth and to keep God's gospel free from taint. But then I am to love all those whom God has begotten, despite the infirmities and errors I see in them, being also myself compassed about with infirmities.

EVENING

Whoever believes that Jesus is the Christ has been born of God. And whoever loves Him who brought to birth also loves him that has been born of Him — 1 John 5:1.

LIFE IS the reason for love, the common life which is indicated by the common faith in the dear Redeemer is to bind us to each other. Although I would pay every deference to every brother's conscientious judgment, I do not know how I could bring my soul as a child of God to refuse communion at my Master's table to any one who believed that Jesus is the Christ. If he is sincere, I have proof in his doing so, that he is born of God. Has not every child a right to come to the Father's table? In the olden times parents made children go without their meals for punishment. But everyone tells us now that this is cruel and unwise, for it injures the child to deprive it of needed food. There are rods in the Lord's house, and there is no need to keep disobedient children away from the supper. Let them come to the Lord's table, and eat and drink with the Lord Jesus and with all His saints, in the hope that when they become stronger they will throw out the disease which they now labor under and thus come to be obedient to the whole gospel, which says, *"He that believes and is baptized shall be saved."*

Are there any feeble among you? Comfort them. Are there any who want instruction? Bring your knowledge to their help. Are there any in distress? Assist them. Are they backsliding? Restore them. *"Little children, love one another,"* is the rule of Christ's family. May the love of God poured out in our hearts by the Holy Spirit reveal itself by our love to all the saints. And remember, other sheep He has which are not yet of His fold; He must also bring them in. Let us love those who are yet to be brought in, and lovingly go forth to seek them. Whatever form of service God has given us, let us with loving eyes look after our prodigal brothers. Who knows, we may bring into the family some for whom there will be joy in the presence of the angels of God, because the lost one has been found. God bless and comfort you, for Jesus Christ's sake.

But of Him you are in Christ Jesus, who was made to us wisdom from God, and righteousness and sanctification and redemption — 1 Corinthians 1:30.

DIFFERENT TRANSLATORS have read this passage in different ways: *"Of Him you are in Christ Jesus"* — they think it should be *Through Him*, that is, *Through God we are in Christ Jesus*. Are you united to Christ, a stone in that building of which he is both foundation and topstone, a limb of that mystical body of which He is the head? Then you did not get there of yourself. No stone in that wall leaped into its place. No member of that body was its own creator. You came to be in union with Christ through God the Father. You were ordained to this grace by His own purpose, the purpose of the Infinite Jehovah who chose you before the earth was: *"You have not chosen Me, but I have chosen you."* The first cause of your union with Christ lies in the word. And as to the purpose, so to the power of God is your union with Christ to be attributed. He brought you into Christ; you were a stranger, He brought you near. You were an enemy; He reconciled you. You had never come to Christ to seek for mercy if first of all the Spirit of God had not appeared to you to show you your need, and to lead you to cry for the mercy that you needed. Through God's working, as well as through God's decree, you are this day in Christ Jesus. It will do your souls good to think of this very common-place truth. Many days have passed since your conversion, it may be, but do not forget what a high day the day of your new birth was. And do not cease to give glory to that mighty power which brought you out of darkness into marvelous light. You did not convert yourself. If you did you still have need to be converted again. Your regeneration was not of the will of man, nor of blood, nor of birth (John 1:10-12). If it were so, let me tell you the sooner you are rid of it the better. The only true regeneration is of the will of God, and by the working of the Holy Spirit.

EVENING

But of Him you are in Christ Jesus, who was made to us wisdom from God, and righteousness and sanctification and redemption — 1 Corinthians 1:30.

THERE ARE those who will have it that the gospel — the simple gospel — such as might have been preached by John Bunyan or Whitefield, or Wesley, and others, was very well for the many, and for the dark times in which they lived. The great mass of mankind would be helped and improved by it. But according to the wiseacres of this century there is a more progressive theology, far in advance of the evangelism now so generally ridiculed. Men of mind, gentlemen of profound thought, are to teach us doctrines that were unknown to our fathers. We are to go on improving in our knowledge of Divine truth until we leave Peter and Paul and those other old dogmatists far behind. No one knows how wise we are to become. Brothers, our thoughts loathe this. We hate this cant about progress and deep thought. We only wish we could know as much of the Christ as the former preachers did. We are afraid that instead of getting into greater light through the thoughts of men, the speculations and contemplations of the scribes, ancient and modern, and the discoveries of the intellectual and eclectic, have made darkness worse. They have quenched some of the light that was in the world. Again it has been fullfilled: *"I will destroy the wisdom of the wise and will bring to nothing the understanding of the prudent. Where is the wise? Where is the scribe? Where is the disputer of this world? Has not God made foolish the wisdom of this world?"* (1 Cor. 1:19, 20). It is greater wisdom to believe what Christ has said than to believe my deepest thoughts. Although I have thought long on a subject, and turned it over and over, and think I know more of it than another man, yet there is more wisdom in one simple word of Christ than in all my thoughts and ruminatings.

January 11   MORNING   11

But of Him you are in Christ Jesus, who was made to us wisdom from God, and righteousness and sanctification and redemption — 1 Corinthians 1:30.

LET JESUS always be the motive for your sanctification. Is it not a strange thing that some professors should look to Christ alone for pardon and justification, yet run away to Moses when they desire sanctification? For instance, you will hear persons preach this doctrine: "The Christian is to be holy, because if he is not holy he will fall from grace and perish." Do you not hear the crack of the old legal whip in all that? What is that but the yoke of that covenant which none of our fathers were able to bear? It is the bondage of Egypt, not the freedom of the children of God. Christ does not talk so, nor His gospel. Think not to make yourself holy by motives of that kind. They are not right motives for a child of God. How then should we urge the child of God to holiness? Should it not be in this way? "You are God's child. Walk worthy of Him who is your Father." His love to you will never cease. He cannot cast you away. He is faithful and never changes; because of this love Him in return. This is a motive fit for the child of the free woman, and it moves His heart. The child of the bondwoman is driven by the whip, but the child of the free woman is drawn by cords of love: *"The love of Christ constrains us,"* not the fear of Hell; not the fear that God will cast us away. For He cannot do that. It is the joy that we are saved in the Lord with an everlasting salvation that constrains us to cling to Him with all our heart and soul, forever and ever. Rest assured, if motives fetched from the gospel will not kill sin, motives fetched from the law never will. If you cannot be purged at Calvary, you certainly cannot be cleansed at Sinai. If "the water and the blood from the riven side which flowed" are not sufficient to purify you, no blood of bulls and of goats — I mean no argument from the Jewish law, or hope of salvation by your own efforts — will ever furnish motives sufficiently strong to cast out sin.

EVENING

So that, even as it has been written, He that glories, let him glory in the Lord — 1 Corinthians 1:31.

OUR VERY EXISTENCE as Christains, and all that we possess as Christians, we get from God by Jesus Christ. Then let all our glory be to Him. What insanity it is to boast in any but in our Lord Jesus! How foolish are they who are proud of the beauty of their flesh; it is worm's meat at best! How foolish are they who are proud of their wisdom! The wisdom of a man is but folly in a thin disguise. How foolish are they that are vain in their wealth! He must be a poor man who can think much of gold. He must be a beggar indeed who counts a piece of dirt a treasure. They that know Christ always value these things at their right estimate, and that is low indeed. If any glory — and I suppose it is natural for us to glory; there is a boasting bump on all our heads — let us glory in the Lord. And here is a wide field and ample sea-room. Now, put out every stitch of canvas, run up the topgallants, seek as stiff a breeze as you will, there is no fear of running on a lee shore here, or striking a rock, or drifting on a quicksand! O Men, O angels, O cherubim, O seraphim, boast in Jesus Christ! Wisdom, righteousness, sanctification and redemption is He. Because of this you may boast and boast again. You will never exaggerate. You cannot exceed His worth, or reach the tithe of it. You can never go beyond the truth. You do not even reach beyond the skirts of His garments. So glorious is God that all the angels' harps cannot sound forth half His glory. So blessed is Christ that the orchestra of the countless multitudes of the redeemed, although it continue forever and forever its pealing music, can never reach to the majesty of His name or the glory of His work. *"Give to the Lord, O you mighty; give to the Lord glory and strength. Give to the Lord the glory due to His name"* (Ps. 29).

MORNING

January 12

For even Christ our passover is sacrificed for us — 1 Corinthians 5:7

ISRAEL was in Egypt in extreme bondage. The severity of their slavery had continually increased until it was so oppressive that their incessant groans went up to Heaven. God, who avenges His elect, even though they cry day and night to Him, at last determined that He would direct a fearful blow against Egypt's king and nation, and deliver His own people. We can picture the anxieties and the anticipations of Israel, but we can scarcely sympathize with them unless we as Christians have had the same deliverance from spiritual Egypt. Let us go back to the day in our experience when we abode in the land of Egypt, working in the brick-kilns of sin, toiling to make ourselves better and finding it to be of no avail. Let us recall that memorable night, the beginning of months, the commencement of a new life in our spirit, and the beginning of an altogether new era in our soul. The Word of God struck the blow at our sin. He gave us Jesus Christ as our sacrifice. And in that night we went out of Egypt. Though we have passed through the wilderness since then, and have fought the Amalekites, and have trodden on the fiery serpent, and have been scorched by the heat and frozen by the snows, yet we have never since that time gone back to Egypt. Although our hearts may sometimes have desired the leeks, the onions, and the fleshpots of Egypt, yet we have never been brought into slavery since then. Come, let us keep the Passover and think of the night when the Lord delivered us out of Egypt. Let us behold our Savior Jesus as the Paschal Lamb on which we feed. Yes, let us not only look at Him as such, but let us sit down at His table, let us eat of His flesh and drink of His blood, for His flesh is meat indeed, and His blood is drink indeed. In holy solemnity let our hearts approach that ancient supper; let us go back to Egypt's darkness and by holy contemplation behold, instead of the destroying angel, the Angel of the covenant at the head of the feast, *"the Lamb of God who takes away the sins of the world"* (John 1:29).

EVENING

I have set watchmen on your walls, O Jerusalem, who shall never be quiet day or night; you who make mention of the Lord, do not keep silence — Isaiah 62:6

NO WORD has yet been invented which can set forth the perfidy of the man who betrays the cause of Christ and of the gospel; he is the murderer of souls. God has set us to guard His own city, and we must not slumber. Let the other cities go, if they must, but as for You, Salem, city of peace, city of God, if I forget you, let my right hand forget her cunning. If I do not count you beyond my chief joy, let me be in sorrow forever. See to your responsible office, watchmen of God, on the walls of God's own city!

The service is seen to be responsible to the utmost degree when we see that it demands constant care. The Lord says of these watchmen, *"they shall never be quiet day or night."* We are not set to keep the church of God by day only, but amid the dews or frosts of the darkest night we are to maintain our watch. Christians are to be sentries who will not retreat into the barrack-room because of the cold, nor quit the rampart because of the heat. At night watchmen are most required. We are to be instant in season, giving the password at each particular time when the watch reports itself, and thus never holding our peace day or night. We are to be instant out of season; for at such times the enemy is most likely to come. God's watchmen are not taken on by the hour, to watch by turns, but throughout life they are bound to be watchers for souls. We are never off duty. We take a day and a night shift. Our rest is in the Lord's service. Our recreation is in change of occupation. Ours is a life service, and a constant service. Believers raise no discussion with their Lord as to how many hours of the day they shall spend for Him. Our hours are these: *"They shall never be quiet day or night."*

January 13 MORNING 13

And it came to pass at the end of the 430 years, even the same day it came to pass, that all the hosts of the Lord went out from the land of Egypt — Exodus 12:41

ONE AGONIZING SACRIFICE, one death on Calvary, one bloody sweat on Gethsemane, one shriek of, *"It is finished,"* consummated all the work of redemption. O the precious blood of Christ! I love it when I think it saves one sinner. But oh to think of the multitude of sinners that it saves! Beloved, we do not think enough of our Lord Jesus Christ. We have not half such an estimation of His precious person as we ought to have. We do not value His blood at the right price. It is engaged to save thousands on thousands, and myriads of myriads.

Shall the shepherd who gathers the whole flock together and leads them to the pastures lose a single lamb? Perhaps you say, "I am so little." For that very reason you do not lack so much of His power to take care of you. But one says, "I am so great a sinner." Well then, so much the better, for He, *"came to save sinners, of whom I am chief,"* said Paul. And He came to save you. Do not fear, you sons of God. He who brought the Israelites all out in one night can bring you all out, although you are in the worst bondage. Perhaps there is one of you who not only has to make bricks without straw, but has to make twice as many bricks as anyone else, and your taskmaster has a whip and cuts the flesh off of you every time. You have worse bondage than anyone; your slavery is more intense, your oven hotter, your pots harder to make. Very well, I am glad of it. How sweet liberty will be to you, for you shall not be left in Egypt. If you were, what would old Pharaoh say? "He said He would bring them all out, but He has left one." Pharaoh would parade that poor Israelite through the streets; he would take him through Memphis and Thebes, and say, "There is one that God could not deliver. There is one I had so tight in my grasp that He could not get him out." Ah! Master Devil! You shall not say that of one of the Lord's people. They shall all be there, the great and the small. This unworthy hand shall take the hand of the blessed Paul. They shall all be in Heaven, all shall be redeemed; all shall be saved — but all, mark you, through one sacrifice.

EVENING

He shall see His seed — Isaiah 53:10

IF WE ARE thus of a seed, we ought to be united and love each other more and more. Christian people, you ought to have a clannish feeling. "Oh, you mean that the Baptists ought to get together!" — no I do not mean anything of the kind. I mean that the seed of Christ should be of one heart. We ought to recognize that wherever the life and love of Jesus are to be found, there our love goes out. At Christmas time, or at some other time of the year, is very delightful for all the family to meet. Your love to one another gathers warmth, as the glowing coals are drawn together. So may it be in your heart toward all those that belong to Christ. You are of the royal blood of Heaven. You are neither a Guelph nor a Hohenzollern, but you are a Christian. And that is a greater name than all. He has a seed — even He whom, unseen, we adore. My inmost soul glories in the Head of my clan — in Him of the pierced hands and the nailed feet. He who wears for His princely star the lance-mark in His side. Oh, how blessedly bright He is! How transcendently glorious are the nail-prints! We adore Him in the infinite majesty of His unutterable love. We are of His seed, and so we are near akin to Him. Do not think that I am too familiar. I do not go beyond the limit which this word allows me. No, I have scarcely come up to the edge of it. We are truly of the seed of Jesus, even as the Jews are of the seed of Israel — not born after the flesh, for He had none born to Him in that way, but born after the Spirit, wherein His seed is as the stars of heaven. We rejoice with exultation as we read the text, *"He shall see His seed."*

MORNING

The young lions lack and suffer hunger; but they that seek the Lord shall not lack any good thing — Psalm 34:10.

IN THE ENTIRE compass of God's holy word there is not to be found a precious declaration which can excel this in sweetness. For how could God promise to us more than all things? How could even His infinite benevolence stretch the line of His grace farther than it has gone in this verse: *"They that seek the Lord shall not lack any good thing."* There is no reserve here; nothing is kept back. There is no solitary work of exception. There is no clause in this will to strike off the smallest portion of the estate. There is no caveat put in to warn us that there are domains on which we must not intrude. A large field is laid before the children of God; a wide door is opened, and no man can shut it: *" They that seek the Lord shall not lack any good thing."*

The Christian character is beautifully delineated: *"They that seek the Lord."* Notice a promise set in a glorious light by a contrast: *"They shall not lack any good thing."* Young lions lack and suffer hunger, but we will not lack any good thing.

Here is a very short, but very beautiful description of a true Christian. He is said to *"seek the Lord."* — *"They that seek the Lord (Jehovah*, as the original has it) *shall not lack any good thing."* Beloved, if some of us had the drawing up of this description we would have made it too narrow. Some of you might have said, "They that seek the Lord in the established church, within the pale of the state religion, shall not lack any good thing." Others might have said, "They that seek the Lord in the orthodox Calvinistic manner shall not lack any good thing." Others, "They that seek the Lord in the Baptist fashion, or the Methodist, or some other, shall not lack any good thing." But it is not written so, It is, *'They that seek the Lord,"* — that it may take in the Lord's people of all classes and denominations, and all shades of character.

EVENING

They that seek the Lord shall not lack any good thing — Psalm 34:10

WHEN THE Christian has found the Savior, and is justified, does he neglect to seek the Lord? No, he seeks to know more of Him, to understand more of the heights and depths and lengths and breadths of the love of Christ. You who have an assurance a pardoned person, thoroughly justified and complete in Christ, are you not seeking the Lord? You say, "Oh yes, I thirst, I long to know more of Him. I feel that all I have ever known of Him is like the whispering of the sea in the shell, the awful roar of the sea has not yet reached my ears. I have heard the whisperings of Christ in some little mercy, and I have heard His bounties sing of the bottomless, eternal, unchangeable love. I long to plunge into the sea itself, to bathe myself in the broad ocean of His infinite generosity and love to me." No Christian ever fancies that he knows enough of his Master. There is no Christian who has found the Lord who does not desire to be better acquainted with Him. "Lord, I will follow You wherever You go," is the cry of the man who has had his sins forgiven. he sits at the feet of Jesus and looks up to Him, and says, "Master, teach me more. I am a little child. You are a great instructor. I long to love and learn more of You." he is ever seeking the Lord. And in this more advanced state, the promise to him is: *'They that seek the Lord shall not lack any good thing."*

But go further, when the Christian has scarcely ever a shadow of a doubt of his acceptance: He has progressed so far in spiritual life that he has attained to the stature of a perfect man in Christ Jesus. His faith has become so confident that he can read his "title clear to the mansions in the skies." He has climbed the Delectable Mountain; his feet are standing fast on a rock and his goings are established. But even then he is seeking the Lord. In the highest flights of his assurance, on the topmost pinnacle of his faith, there is something yet beyond.

MORNING

When Jesus came to the place, He looked up and saw him, and said to him, Zaccheus, hurry and come down; for today I must stay in your house — Luke 19:5

EFFECTUAL CALLING is a very gracious truth. Zaccheus was a character whom we would suppose the last to be saved. He belonged to a bad city, Jericho, a city which had been cursed. No one would suspect that any one would come out of Jericho to be saved. It does not matter where you are from. You may come from one of the dirtiest streets, one of the worst slums, but if effectual grace calls you, it is an effectual call; it knows no distinction of place. Zaccheus also was of an exceedingly bad trade; he probably cheated the people in order to enrich himself. Indeed, when Christ went into his house, there was a universal murmur that He had gone to be a guest with a man that was a sinner. But grace knows no distinction. It is no respecter of persons. God calls whom He will, and He called this man, worst of the tax-collectors, in the worst of cities, from the worst of trades. Besides, Zaccheus was the least likely to be saved because he was rich. It is true, rich and poor are welcome. No one has the least excuse for despair because of his condition. Yet, it is a fact that, *"not many great men"* after the flesh, *"not many mighty"* are called. But, *"God has chosen the poor of this world, rich in faith."* But grace knows no distinction here. The rich Zaccheus is called from the tree, and is saved. It is one of the greatest instances of God's condescension when Christ looked up to see Zaccheus. For God to look down on His creatures, that is mercy. But for Christ so to humble Himself as to look up to one of His own creatures, that becomes mercy indeed. Many of you have climbed the tree of your own good works, perched yourselves in the branches of your holy actions, and are trusting in the free will of the poor creature, or resting in some worldly maxim. In spite of this, Christ looks up even to proud sinners, and calls them down.

EVENING

But the more they afflicted them, the more they multiplied and grew — Exodus 1:12

THE DARK DAYS of fiendish persecution have witnessed bright deeds of Christian heroism never to be forgotten. How often the riches and ripest fruits of the Spirit have been put forth by the Lord's people when they were most grieved and smitten. Then the saints have been like clusters thrown into the winepress; but who shall bring forth the red wine? Whose but the feet of God's enemies shall tread the grapes? But as they bruise and trample down, they shall crush nothing but husks. The living wine shall flow, and God shall receive the whole of it. These foes work; they think that they can break down our carved work and cast fire into the sanctuary of God. But all the while they burn not the true sanctuary; they burn but the base wooden erection with which man has defaced the living temple. Let them burn; good shall ensue.

If you read *Foxe's Book of Martyrs*, or any of the martyrologies of earlier ages, you will find there patience, self-denial, consecration, confidence in God, and all the finer graces of temper in full bloom, perfuming the air with their fragrance. One is astonished at what our poor, weak humanity has been able to endure for the truth, when made strong by the Spirit of God. Humble and weak, timid women have shown true mettle, waxing valiant, cheering on men of muscle and sinew whose hearts had fainted. We could mention the names of many saints who have endured torment as severe as inquisitors could devise, or relentless executioners could inflict, and yet they have not denied their Lord. This is the patience of the saints, when the martyrs perished in the Roman Amphitheater, and the cruel crowd looked down to watch their agonies as their bones were crushed between the jaws of wild beasts.

Is it not lawful for me to do what I wish with that which is mine? — Matthew 20:15

WE MUST ASSUME one thing is certain, namely, that all blessings are gifts and that we have no claim to them by our own merit. Every considerate mind will grant this. And this being admitted, we shall endeavor to show that He has a right, since they are His own to do what He wills with them — to withhold them wholly if He pleases — to distribute them all if He chooses — to give to some and not to others — to give to none, or to give to all, just as it seems good in His sight.

It is an indisputable fact that God has not, in temporal matters, given to every man alike. He has not distributed to all His creatures the same amount of happiness or the same standing in creation. There is a difference. Mark what a difference there is in men personally. One is born like Saul, head and shoulders taller than the rest. Another lives all his life a Zaccheus, a man of short stature. One has a muscular frame and a share of beauty. Another is weak, far from having any styled comeliness. How many do we find whose eyes have never rejoiced in the sunlight, whose ears have never listened to the charms of music, whose lips have never been moved to sounds intelligible or harmonious. Walk through the earth and you will find people superior to yourself in vigor, health, fashion. Others will be your inferiors in the very same respects. Some are preferred far above their fellows in their outward appearance. Some sink low in the scale and have nothing about them that can make them glory in the flesh. Why has God given to one man beauty, and to another none? To one all his senses, and to another but a portion? Why, in some, has He quickened the sense of apprehension, while others are obliged to bear about them a dull and stubborn body? We reply, let men say what they will, that no answer can be given except this, *"Even so, Father, for so it seemed good in Your sight."*

EVENING

Is it not lawful for me to do what I wish with that which is mine? — Matthew 20:15

THE HOUSEHOLD says, *"Is it not lawful for me to do what I wish with that which is mine?"* So does the God of Heaven and earth ask this same question. There is no attribute of God more comforting to His children than the doctrine of Divine Sovereignty. Under the most adverse circumstances, in the most severe troubles, they believe that Sovereignty has ordained their afflictions, has overruled them, and will sanctify them all. There is nothing for which the children of God ought more earnestly to contend than the dominion of their Master over all creation, the kingship of God over all the works of His own hands, throne of God, and His right to sit on that throne. On the other hand, there is no doctrine more hated by worldlings, no truth of which they have made such a football as the great, most certain doctrine of the Sovereignty of the infinite Jehovah. Men will allow God to be everywhere except on His throne. They will allow Him to be in His workshop to fashion worlds and to make stars. They will allow Him to be in His almonry to dispense His alms and bestow His bounties. They will allow Him to sustain the earth and bear up its pillar; to light the lamps of the heavens, or rule the waves of the ever-moving sea. But when God ascends His throne, His creatures gnash their teeth. When we proclaim an enthroned God, and His right to do as He wills with His own, to dispose of His creatures as he thinks well, without consulting them in the matter, then it is that we are hissed and execrated. Then it is that men turn a deaf ear to us. For God on His throne is not the God they love. They love Him anywhere better than they do when He sits with His sceptre in His hand and His crown on His head. But it is God on the throne that we love to preach. It is God on His throne whom we trust.

January 17　　　　　　　　　MORNING　　　　　　　　　　17

Is it not lawful for me to do what I wish with that which is mine? — Matthew 20:15

GRACE IS not a thing which I use. Grace is something which uses me. But people talk of grace as if it was something they could use, and not as an influence having power over them. Grace is not something which I improve, but which improves me, employs me, works on me. Let people talk as they will about universal grace, it is all nonsense. There is no such thing, nor can there be. The correctly talk of universal blessings, because we see that the natural gifts of God are scattered everywhere, more or less, and men may receive or reject them. However, it is not so with grace. Men cannot take the grace of God and employ it in turning themselves from darkness to light. The light does not come to the darkness and say, use me. The light comes and drives the darkness away. Life does not come to the dead man and say, use me, and be restored to life. But it comes with a power of its own and restores to life. The spiritual influence does not come to the dry bones and say, use this power and clothe yourselves with flesh. It comes and clothes them with flesh, and the work is done. Grace is a thing which comes and exercises an influence on us.

And we say to all of you who gnash your teeth at this doctrine, whether you know it or not, you have a vast deal of enmity toward God in your hearts. Until you can be taught to know this doctrine, there is something which you have not discovered, which makes you opposed to the idea of God absolute, God unbounded, God unfettered, God unchanging, and God having a totally free will (the kind of free will which you are so fond of trying to prove that the creature possesses). I am persuaded that the sovereignty of God must be held by us if we would be in a spiritually healthy state of mind. *"Salvation is of the Lord"* alone. Then give all the glory to His holy name, to whom all glory rightfully belongs.

EVENING

Is it not lawful for me to do what I wish with that which is mine? — Matthew 20:15

MAY HE NOT DO what He will with His own? May He not take back what He has given? The comforts we possess were His before they were ours. There is no joy of the Spirit; there is no exceeding blessed hope, no strong faith, no burning desire, no close fellowship with Christ, which is not the gift of God. we must trace these to Him. When I am in darkness and suffer disappointment, I will look up and say: He gives songs in the night. And when I am made to rejoice, I will say: My mountain shall stand fast forever. The Lord is a sovereign Jehovah. Because of this I lie prostrate at His feet; and if I perish, I will perish there.

But let me say that so far from this doctrine of Divine Sovereignty making you to sit down in sloth, I hope in God it will have a tendency to humble you, and so to lead you to say, "I am unworthy of the least of all Your mercies (Gen. 32:10). I feel that You have a right to do with me as You will. If You crush me, a helpless worm, You will not be dishonored. And I have no right to ask You to have compassion on me, except this, that I want Your mercy. Lord, if You will, You are able to pardon, and You never gave grace to one that wanted it more. Because I am empty, fill me with the bread of Heaven. Because I am naked, clothe me with Your robe. Because I am dead, give me life."

If you press that plea with all your soul and all your mind, although Jehovah is a Sovereign, He will stretch out His sceptre and save, and You shall live to worship Him in the beauty of holiness, loving and adoring His gracious sovereignty. Scripture declares, *"He that believes and is baptized shall be saved, but he that does not believe shall be condemned."* He that believes in Christ alone, and is baptized with water in the name of the Father, the Son, and the Holy Spirit shall be saved. But he who rejects Christ and believes not in Him shall be condemned. That is the sovereign decree and proclamation of Heaven. Bow to it, acknowledge it, obey it, and God bless you.

MORNING

Hold the pattern of sound words which you have heard from me, in faith and love which are in Christ Jesus — 2 Timothy 1:13.

HOLD FAST sound doctrine, for by it you will receive ten thousand blessings. You will receive the blessing of peace in your conscience. Before God I protest that if at any time I ever doubt one of the great things I receive from God, instantly there comes an aching void which the world can never fill, and which I can never get filled until I receive that doctrine again, and believe it with all my heart. When at any time I am cast down and dejected, I always find comfort in reading books which are strong on the doctrines of the faith of the gospel. If I turn to some of them that treat of God's eternal love, revealed to His chosen people in the person of Christ, and if I remember some of the exceeding great and precious promises made to the elect in their covenant Head, my faith at once becomes strong. And then my soul, with wings sublime, mounts upwards toward its God. You cannot tell, beloved, if you have never tasted, how sweet is the peace which the doctrines of grace will give to the soul; there is nothing like them.

The doctrines of grace are God's sweet lullaby, by which He sings His children to sleep, even in storms of conflict or affliction. They are God's sheet anchors, which He casts out to hold our little vessels fast in the midst of tempests. There is a *"peace of God which passes all understanding,"* which accrues to one who is a strong believer, but you know the tendency of the day is to give up old landmarks and to adopt new ones, and to avow anything rather than the old-fashioned divinity. Well, my dear friends, if any of you like to try new doctrines, I warn you that if you are the children of God you will soon be sick enough of those new-fangled notions, those newly invented doctrines which are now continually taught. For the first week you may be pleased with their novelty; you may wonder at their seeming spirituality, or something else which entices you along. But you will not have lived on them long before you will say, "Alas! I have taken in my hands the apples of Sodom. They were fair to look upon, but they are ashes in my mouth." If you would be peaceful, keep fast to the truth, hold fast the pattern of sound words; and so shall *"your peace be like a river, and your righteousness like the waves of the sea."*

EVENING

"YOU SHALL LIVE" — I think I see in that much more than lies on the surface. Whatever is meant by living shall be ours. All the degree of life which is secured in the covenant of grace, believers shall have. Moreover, all your new nature shall live, shall thoroughly live, shall eternally live. By this word it is secured that the eternal life implanted at regeneration shall never die out. As our Lord said, so shall it be: *"Whoever drinks of the water that I shall give him shall never thirst; but the water that I shall give him shall be in him a well of water springing up into everlasting life."* We may be tempted, but we shall not be so led astray as to cease to live in Christ. It may be that we shall decline in grace, a thousand sorrows that it should be so! But we shall not so decline as to become utter apostates, or sons of perdition. *"He that is begotten of God keeps himself, and that evil one does not touch him."* Thus the Redeemer says to you, trembling children of God, *"You shall live;"* you shall never perish, neither shall anyone pluck you out of His hands. May I not view this precious word as referring to all the essential graces which make up the new man? Not even, in part, shall the new man die. *"You shall live,"* applies to all the parts of our new-born nature. If there is any believer here who has not lived to the full extent he might have done, let him lay hold on this promise. For since it secures the preservation of all his new nature, let him have courage to seek a higher degree of spiritual health. Christ says, *"I have come that you might have life, and have it more abundantly."* There is no reason, Christian, why your love to Jesus should not become flaming, ardent, conquering; for it lives, and must ever live.

January 19 — MORNING

O Lord my God, I put my trust in You. Save me from all who pursue me and deliver me, that he not tear my soul like a lion, ripping it to pieces when there is no one to deliver — Psalm 7:1,2.

DAVID APPEARS before God to plead with Him against the Accuser, who had charged him with treason and treachery. The case is here opened with an avowal of confidence in God. Whatever the emergency of our condition we shall never find it amiss to retain our reliance on our God — *"O Lord my God,"* mine by a special covenant, sealed by Jesus' blood, ratified in my own soul by a sense of union to You, *"in You,"* and in You only, *"do I put my trust,"* even now in my sore distress. I shake, but my rock does not move. It is never right to distrust God, and never vain to trust Him. And now, with both Divine relationship and holy trust to strengthen him, David utters the burden of his desire: *"save me from all who pursue me."* His pursuers were very many, and any one of them cruel enough to devour him. For this reason He cries for salvation from them all. We should never think our prayers complete until we ask for preservation from all sin, and all enemies. *"And deliver me,"* extricate me from their snares; acquit me of their accusations; give a true and just deliverance in this trial of my injured character. See how clearly his case is stated. Let us see to it that we know what we would have when we come to the throne of mercy. Pause a little while before you pray, that you may not offer the sacrifice of fools. Get a distinct idea of your need, and then you can pray with the more fluency of fervency.

"That he not tear my soul;" here is a plea of fear co-working with the plea of faith. One of David's foes was mightier than the rest, who had dignity, strength, and ferocity; one *"like a lion."* From this foe he urgently seeks deliverance. Perhaps this was Saul, his royal enemy. But in our case there is one who goes about like a lion, seeking whom he may devour, concerning whom we should ever cry, "Deliver me from the Evil One" (1 Peter 5:8). Notice the vigor of the description: *"ripping it to pieces, when there is no one to deliver."* It is a picture from the shepherd life of David.

EVENING

Yes, He is altogether lovely — Song of Songs 5:16

UNDER ALL ASPECTS, and in all offices and relations, at all times and all seasons, under all circumstances and conditions, anywhere, everywhere, *"He is altogether lovely."* Nor is He in any degree unlovely; the commendation forbids the idea. If He is altogether lovely where could you find room for deformity? When Apelles painted Alexander he laid the monarch's finger on an unsightly scar. But there are no scars to conceal when you portray the face of Immanuel. Of our country we say, "With all her faults we love her still." But we love Jesus, finding no strain put on our heart, for He has not a trace of fault. There is no need of apologies for Jesus, no excuses are required for Him. But what is that I see on His shoulder? It is a hard, rough cross. And if I follow Him I must carry that cross for His sake. Is not that cross unsightly? No! He is *altogether lovely*, cross and all. Whatever it may involve to be a Christian, we count even the reproach of Christ to be greater riches than the treasures of Egypt. The world will honor a half-christ, but a whole Christ it will not acknowledge. The bat's-eyed Socinian says, "I admire the man Christ, but I will not adore Jesus the God." To him the eternal Word is but half-lovely, if lovely at all. Some will have Christ the exemplar, but they will not accept Him as the vicarious sacrifice for sin, the substitute for sinners. Many will have Christ in silver slippers, but they would not listen to the gospel from a poor, gracious Methodist, or think it worthy their while to join the unlettered throng whose devout songs rise from the village green. Alas! How much we see of crosses of gold and ivory, but how little do men love the lowly cross of Jesus!

MORNING

If he will not turn, He will whet His sword. He has bent His bow and made it ready. Yea, He has prepared for him the instruments of death. He will make His arrows hot for the pursuers — Psalm 7:12,13.

THE JUDGE has heard the cause, has cleared the guiltless, has uttered his voice against the persecutors. Let us draw near and learn the results of the great verdict. Yonder is the slandered one; his harp is in hand, hymning the justice of his Lord, rejoicing aloud in his own deliverance. "My defense is of God, who saves the upright heart." Oh, how good to have a true and upright heart! Crooked sinners, with all their craftiness, are foiled by the upright in heart. God defends the right. Filth will not long abide on the pure white garments of the saints. It will be brushed off by Divine providence, to the vexation of the men by whose base hands it was thrown on the godly. When God tries our cause, our sun has risen, and the sun of the wicked is set forever. Like oil, truth is ever above; no power of our enemies can drown it. When the trumpet wakes the dead, we shall refute their slanders; we shall shine in honor when lying lips are put to silence. O believer, do not fear all that your foes can do or say against you, for the tree which God plants cannot be hurt by winds: *"God judges the righteous."* He has not given you up to be condemned by the lips of persecutors. Your enemies cannot sit on God's throne, nor blot out your name from His Book. Let them alone, then, for God will find time for His revenges.

God is angry with the wicked every day." He not only detests sin, but is angry with those who continue to indulge in it. We have not an insensible and stolid God with whom to deal. He can be angry. He is angry today and every day with ungodly and impenitent sinners. The best day that ever dawns on a sinner brings a curse with it. Sinners may have many feast days, but no safe days. There is not an hour in which God's oven is not hot, burning in readiness for the wicked, who shall be as stubble. *"If he will not turn, He will whet His sword."* What blows are those which will be dealt by that long uplifted arm! God's sword has been sharpened on the revolving stone of our daily wickedness. And if we will not repent, it will speedily cut us in pieces.

EVENING

My sheep hear My voice, and I know them. And they follow Me — John 10:27.

CHRIST HAS marked His sheep on their feet, as well as on their ears. They follow Him. They are gently led, not harshly driven. They follow Him as the Captain of their salvation. They trust in the power of His arm to clear the way for them. All their trust is stayed on Him. They lean all their hope on Him. They follow Him as their teacher; they call no man *Rabbi* under the heavens, but Christ alone. He is the infallible source of their creeds. They will not allow their minds to be ruled by conclaves, councils, nor decrees. Has Christ said it? It is enough! If not, it is no more for me than the whistling of the wind. They follow Christ.

Also the sheep of Christ follow Him as their example. They desire to be in this world as He was. It is one of their marks, that to a greater or lesser degree they have a Christ-like spirit. If they could, they would be altogether like their Lord.

They follow Him, too, as their Commander, their Lawgiver, their Prince. *"Whatever He says to you, do it,"* was His mother's wise speech. And it is the wise rule of the children also. Blessed shall they be above many, of whom it shall be said, *"These are they who have not defiled their garments."* These are they who follow the Lamb wherever He goes. Some of His followers are not very scrupulous. They love Him (they say), but it is not for us to judge them. Rather we should place ourselves among them and share in the censure. But happiest of all are they who see the print of that foot that once was pierced with the nail, and put their foot down where He placed His; then again, in the same mark, follow where He trod, until they climb at last to the throne. Keep close to Christ; mind His precepts until the end.

MORNING

I will be glad and rejoice in You. I will sing praise to Your name, O Most High. When my enemies have turned back, they shall fall and perish at Your presence — Psalm 9:2, 3.

GLADNESS and joy are the appropriate spirit in which to praise the goodness of the Lord. Birds extol the Creator in notes of overflowing joy; cattle low forth His praise with tumult; fish leap up in His worship with delight. Moloch may be worshiped with shrieks of pain; Juggernaut may be honored by dying groans and inhuman yells — but He whose name is Love is best pleased with the holy mirth and sanctified gladness of His people. Daily rejoicing is an ornament to the Christian character, and a suitable robe for God's choristers to wear. God loves a cheerful giver, whether it is the gold of his purse, or the gold of his mouth, that he presents on His altar. *"I will sing praise to Your name, O Most High."* Songs are the fitting expressions of inward thankfulness, and it were well if we indulged ourselves and honored our Lord with more of them. The silors give a cheery cry when they weigh anchor; the plowman whistles in the morning as he drives his team; the milkmaid sings her rustic song as she sets about her early task. When soldiers leave friends behind they do not march out to the tune of the Dead March, but to the quick notes of some lively air. A praising spirit would do for us all that their songs and music do for them. If only we could determine to praise the Lord, we would surmount many a difficulty which our low spirits never would have been equal to, and we would do double the work which can be done if the heart be languid in its beating, if we are crushed and trodden down in soul. As the evil spirit in Saul yielded in the old time to the influence of the harp of the son of Jesse, so would the spirit of melancholy often take flight from us if only we would take up the song of praise.

God's presence is evermore sufficient to work the defeat of our most furious foes, and their ruin is so complete when the Lord takes them in hand, that even flight cannot save them — they fall to rise no more when He pursues them. We must be careful, like David, to give all the glory to Him whose presence gives the victory.

EVENING

Because I live, you shall live also — John 14:19

"YOU SHALL LIVE" — then the inbred corruption which rises within us shall not stifle the new creature. Chained as the spirit seems to be to the loathsome and corrupt body of this death, it shall live in spite of its hideous companionship. Besetting sins may be as arrows, and fleshly lusts like drawn swords, yet grace shall not be slain. Neither the fever of hasty passion, nor the palsy of timorousness, nor the leprosy of covetousness, nor any other disease of sin, shall so break forth in the old nature as to destroy the new. Nor shall outward circumstances overthrow the inner life. *"For He shall give His angels charge of You, to keep You in all Your ways. They shall bear You up in their hands, lest You dash Your foot against a stone"* — it was the Devil's word to Jesus, and it is His word to us. If providence cast you into a godless family, where the air you breathe is laden with the miasma of death, yet you shall live. Evil example will not poison your spirit; you shall be kept from giving way to evil. You shall not be decoyed by fair temptation; you shall not be cowed by fierce persecution. Mightier is He that is in you than he which is in the world. Satan will attack you, and his weapons are deadly, but you will foil him at all points. To you it is given to tread on the lion and adder; you shall trample under the young lion and the dragon. If God should allow you to be sorely tried for a while, as He did His servant Job, and if the Devil should have all the world to help him in his attempt to destroy your spiritual life, yet even on the dunghill of poverty, and in the wretchedness of sickness, your spirit shall still maintain its holy life, and you shall prove it so by blessing and magnifying God.

MORNING

Why do You stand far away, O Lord? Why do You hide in times of distress? — Psalm 10:1.

TO THE TEARFUL EYE of the sufferer the Lord seemed to stand still, as if He calmly looked on and did not sympathize with His afflicted one. The Lord appeared to be *"far away,"* no longer *"a very present help in trouble,"* but an inaccessible mountain, into which no man would be able to climb. The presence of God is the joy of His people, but any suspicion of His absence is distracting beyond measure. Let us, then, ever remember that the Lord is near us. The refiner is never far from the mouth of the furnace when his gold is in the fire, and the Son of God is always walking in the midst of the flames when His holy children are cast into them. Yet he who knows the frailty of man will little wonder that when we are sharply exercised, we find it hard to bear the apparent neglect of the Lord when He forbears to work our deliverance.

"Why do You hide in times of distress?" It is not the trouble, but the hiding of our Father's face that cuts us to the quick. When trial and desertion come together, we are in as perilous a plight as Paul, when his ship fell into a place where two seas met (Acts 27:41). It is but little wonder if we are like the vessel which ran aground, and the forepart stuck fast, and remained unmovable, while the hinder part was broken by the violence of the waves. When our sun is eclipsed it is dark indeed. If we need an answer to the question, *"Why do You hide?"* It is to be found in the fact that there is a "needs-be," not only for trial, but for heaviness of heart under trial (1 Peter 1:6). But how could this be the case if the Lord should shine on us while He is afflicting us? Should the parent comfort his child while he is correcting him? Where would be the use of the chastening? A smiling face and a rod are not fit companions. God bares the back that the blow may be felt, for it is only a felt affliction which can become blessed affliction. If we are carried in the arms of God over every stream, where would be the trial, and where the experience which trouble is meant to teach us?

EVENING

And the name of the city from that day shall be, The Lord is there — Ezekiel 48:35

IF THE LORD is among us the first consequence will be the conservation of true doctrine. The true God is not with a lie: He will not give His countenance to falsehood. Those who preach other than according to His word do not abide under His blessing, but are in danger of His curse. If any man speak another gospel (*which is not another, but there are some who trouble us*), God is not with him. Any prosperity which he may enjoy will be blown away as chaff. God is with those who speak the truth faithfully, hold it devoutly, believe it firmly, and live on it as their daily bread. May it always be said of this church, *"The Lord is there,"* and so they are sound in the faith, reverent toward Holy Scripture, zealous for the honor of Christ. Trust-deeds and confessions of faith are useful in their way, even as laws are useful to society. But as laws cannot secure obedience to them, so articles of belief cannot create faith or secure honesty. To men without a conscience they are not worth the paper they are written on. No subscription to articles can keep out the unscrupulous. Wolves leap into the fold even if you carefully watch the door. The fact is, most people say, 'Yes,' that doctrine is in the creed, not to be denied, but you need not preach it. Put it on the shelf as an ornament, and let us hear no more about it. Truth must be written on the heart as well as in the book. If the Lord is among His people, they will cling to the eternal verities and love the doctrine of the cross, not by force of law, but because truth is the life of their souls.

Where God is present, the preservation of purity will be found. The church is nothing if it is not holy. It is worse; it is a den of thieves. Setting the seal of its pestilent example on evil living, it becomes the servant of Satan, and the destroyer of souls.

January 23   MORNING

And the name of the city from that day shall be, The Lord is there — Ezekiel 48:35

    THERE IS a special place where God dwells among men, and that is in His church. He has but one church, chosen by eternal election, redeemed by precious blood, called out by the Holy Spirit, and quickened into newness of life. This as a whole is the dwellingplace of the covenant God. Because God is in this church, therefore the gates of Hell shall not prevail against her. *"The Lord is there"* might be said of the church in all ages. I have seen the crypts and underground chapels of the catacombs; they were glorious places when we remembered that *"the Lord was there"* by His Spirit, with His suffering people. When holy hymn and psalm and solemn prayer went up from the very bowels of the earth, from men hunted to the death by their foes, *the Lord was there.* In those dreary excavations, unvisited by sunlight and wholesome air, God was as he was not in kings' palaces, and is not in the cathedrals of priests. In this land of ours, when a few people met together here and there to hear the gospel and to worship, they made cottages, caves, and hollows in the woods, to be *"holiness to the Lord."* And when crowds met beneath your gospel oaks, or gathered together by the hillside to listen to the pure word of grace, *the Lord was there.* Souls were saved and sanctified. When the Puritans solemn conversed together of the things of God, and held their little conventicles for fear of their foes, *God was there.* On Scotland's bleak moors and mosses, when the covenanters gathered in the darkness and the storm for fear of Claverhouse and his dragoons, *God was there.* Those who wrote in those days tell us that they never knew such seasons in days of peace as they enjoyed among the hills, amid the heather, or by the brookside, for *"the Lord was there."*

EVENING

His mischief shall return on his own head, and his violence shall descend on his own head. I will praise the Lord according to His righteousness, and I will sing praise to the name of the Lord most high — Psalm 7:16, 17.

    COME HERE, make merry with this entrapped hunter, this biter who has bitten himself. Give him no pity, for it will be wasted on such a wretch. He is but rightly and richly rewarded, being paid in his own coin. He cast out evil from his mouth and it has fallen into his bosom. He set fire to his own house with the torch which he lit to burn out a neighbor. He sent out a foul bird, and it has come back to its nest. The rod he lifted on high has smitten his own back. He shot an arrow up, and it has descended *"on his own head."* He hurled a stone at another, and it came back on his own head. Curses are like chickens: they always come home to roost. Ashes fly back in the face of him that throws them. *"As he loved cursing, so let it come to him"* (Psalm 109:17). How often has this been the case in the histories of ancient and modern times. Men have burned their own fingers when they were hoping to brand their neighbor. And if this does not happen now, it will hereafter. The Lord caused dogs to lick the blood of Ahab in Naboth's vineyard. Sooner or later the evil deeds of persecutors have always leaped back into their arms. So it will be in the last great Day. Satan's darts will all be quivered in his own heart; all his followers will reap the harvest which they have sown.

    See the joyful contrast. In this all these Psalms agree. They all exhibit the blessedness of the righteous, and make its colors the more glowing by contrast with the miseries of the wicked. The bright jewel sparkles in a black foil. Praise is the occupation of the godly, their eternal work, and their present pleasure. Singing is the fitting embodiment for praise. Because of this the saints make melody before the Lord most high. The slandered one is now a singer. His harp was unstrung for a very little time, but now we leave him sweeping its harmonious chords, flying on the third Heaven with adoring praise.

MORNING

And the name of the city from that day shall be, The Lord is there — Ezekiel 48:35

WHO IS to keep the church pure? None but God Himself. If *the Lord is there* holiness will abound and fruits of the Spirit will be seen on all sides. But if the Lord is once withdrawn, then flesh and blood will rule, and will tend to corruption, and the church will become a synagogue of formalists. Pray continually that the Lord may dwell in our churches, to maintain us in all holy obedience and purity of life.

Where God is, there is the constant renewal of vitality. A dead church is a reeking Golgotha, a breedingplace of evils, a home of Devils. The tombs may be newly whitewashed, but they are none the less open sepulchres, haunts of unclean spirits. A church all alive is a little Heaven, the resort of angels, the temple of the Holy Spirit. In some of our churches everybody seems to be a little colder than everybody else. The members are holy icicles. A general frost has paralyzed everybody. Though some are colder than others, yet all are below zero. There are no flowing rills of refreshment, but everything is bound hard and fast with the frost of indifference. Oh that the Lord would send forth His wind and melt the glaciers! Oh that the Spirit of God would chase winter out of every heart and church! No human power can keep a church from the frostbite which numbs and kills. Except *the Lord is there,* growth, life, warmth are all impossible. You who make mention of the Lord, keep not silence, give Him no rest; cry day and night to Him, "O Lord, abide with us. Go forth with our armies. Make us to be the living children of the living God."

EVENING

And at the end of the 430 years, even the same day it came to pass, all the hosts of the Lord went out from the land of Egypt — Exodus 12:41.

THE EXODUS of the children of Israel out of Egypt is a type and picture of the going out of all the vessels of mercy from the house of their bondage, and the deliverance of all the lawful captives from the chains of their cruel taskmasters, by sovereign and omnipotent grace, through the Passover of our Lord Jesus Christ.

The land of Egypt is a picture of the house of bondage into which all God's covenant people will be brought on account of their sin. All those whom God means to give an inheritance in Canaan, He will first take down into Egypt. Even Jesus Christ Himself went into Egypt before He appeared publicly as a teacher before the world, so that in His instance, as well as in that of every Christian, the prophecy might be fulfilled: *"Out of Egypt I have called My Son."* Everyone who enjoys the liberty by which Christ makes us free must first feel the galling bondage of sin. Our wrists must be made to smart by the fetters of our iniquity, and our backs to bleed by the lash of the law (the taskmaster that drives us to Jesus Christ). There is no true liberty which is not preceded by true bondage, no deliverance from sin unless we first have groaned and cried to God as did the Israelites when in bondage in Egypt. We must all serve in the brick-kiln. We must all be wearied with toiling among the pots, or else we could never realize that glorious verse: *"Though you have worked among the pots, yet you shall be as the wings of a dove covered with silver, and her feathers with yellow gold"* (Ps. 68).

We must have bondage before liberty. Before resurrection must come death. Before life must come corruption. Before we are brought out of the horrible pit and the miry clay we must be made to exclaim, *"I sink in deep mire, where there is no standing."* Before we can be fetched out of the whale's belly and delivered from our sin, we must be taken down to the bottoms of the mountains, with the weeds wrapped about our heads, shuddering under a deep sense of our own nothingness and fearing that the earth with her bars was about us forever. Taking this as a key, you will see that the deliverance out of Egypt is a beautiful picture of the deliverance of all God's people from the bondage of the law and the slavery of their sins.

MORNING

He shall see His seed — Isaiah 53:10

WE DO NOT read here that the Lord Christ has followers. That would be true, but the text prefers to say He has a seed. We have read in Scrsipture that the Lord Jesus has disciples. That would be distinctly true, but this text does not so read. It says, *"He shall see His seed."* Why His seed? Because everyone who is a true follower or disciple of Christ has been born by a new birth from Him into the position of disciple. There is no knowing Christ except through the new birth. We are naturally sold under sin, and we cannot discern the spiritual and real Christ until we have a spirit created within us by the new birth, of which He said, *"You must be born again."* This is the gate of entrance into discipleship. None can be written in the roll of followers of Christ unless they are also written in the register of the family of God: *"this and that man was born there."* Other men can get disciples for themselves by the means that are usual for such ends, but all the disciples of Christ are produced by miracle. They are all discipled by being newly created. As He looks on them all, Jesus can say, *"Behold, I make all things new."* They all come into the world, of which He is King, by being born into it. There is no other way into the first world but by birth. There is no other way into the second world but by birth. That birth is strictly connected with the pangs of the Savior's passion, *"when You shall make His soul an offering for sin, He shall see His seed."* See, then, the reason why we have the remarkable expression: *"His seed."*

Learn from this that all who truly follow Christ, and are saved by Him, have His life in them. The parent's life is in the child. From the parent that life has been received. It is Christ's life that is in every true believer.

EVENING

I put my trust in the Lord. How can you say to me, Flee like a bird to the mountains? For, behold! The wicked will bend the bow; they will make their arrow ready on the string, so that they may secretly shoot at the upright in heart — Psalm 11:1, 2.

DAVID refuses to retreat from his enemies, exclaiming, *"I put my trust in the Lord. How can you say to me, Flee like a bird to the mountains?"* When Satan cannot overthrow us by presumption, how craftily he seeks to ruin us by distrust! He will employ our dearest friends to argue us out of our confidence, and he will use such plausible logic that unless we once for all assert our immovable trust in Jehovah, Satan will make us like the timid bird which flies to the mountain when danger presents itself. How forcibly the cast is put! *The bow is bent,* the arrow is fitted to the string. " Flee! Flee, you defenseless bird; your safety lies in flight. You enemies will send their shafts into your heart. Hasten, for soon you will be destroyed!" David seems to have felt the force of this advice, for it came home to his soul. Yet he would not yield; he would rather dare the danger than exhibit a distrust in the Lord his God. Doubtless, the perils which encompassed David were great and imminent. It was quite true that his enemies were ready to shoot secretly at him. But what were all these things to the man whose trust is in God alone? He could brave the dangers, escape the enemies, defy the injustice which surrounded him. To the question, "What can the righteous do?" you can counter with this, "What cannot they do?" When prayer engages God on our side, and when faith secures the fulfilment of the promise, what cause can there be for flight, however cruel and mighty our enemies? With a sling and a stone David smote a giant before whom the hosts of Israel were trembling. And the Lord, who delivered him from the uncircumcised Philistine, could surely deliver him from king Saul. There is no such word as impossibility in the language of faith. That martial grace knows how to fight and conquer, but she does not know how to flee.

MORNING

For Pharaoh will say of the children of Israel. They are tangled in the land; the wilderness has shut them in — Exodus 14:3

ISRAEL had completely escaped from Egypt. Not a hoof of their cattle was left behind, nor foot of child or aged man remained in the house of bondage. But even though they were gone, they were not forgotten by the tyrant who had enslaved them. They had been a very useful body of workers, building treasure cities and storehouses for Pharaoh. Compelled to work without wages, they cost the tyrant nothing but the expenditure of the lash. His exactions of forced labor had grown intolerable to the people, but the buildings erected had been a joy to the lord of Egypt. When they were gone, Pharaoh woke to a sense of his loss. His attendants felt the same, so that they cried, *"Why have we done this, that we have let Israel go from serving us?"* Then they resolved to drive them back again, and they thought it easy to do so, for they said, *"They are tangled in the land; the wilderness has shut them in."* They knew that the Israelites had no spirit for war, and they felt sure that they had only to overtake them and hurry them back, like a drove of cattle. They had found them such submissive servants that they expected to fit on them their fetters again, and rivet them forever. Perhaps their God had shot His last arrow, and Egypt might capture His people again without fear of plagues. Men thought this, but the Lord thought otherwise.

Do not I speak at this hour to some who have by the power of the Lord's gracious hand escaped out of the bondage of sin? You have escaped from your old master. With a high hand and an outstretched arm God has brought you forth into liberty. You remember the sprinkling of the blood and the eating of the Paschal Lamb, and you are now on your way to Canaan. But your former master and his friends have not forgotten you. You were once a valuable servant to Satan, and he will not willingly lose you.

EVENING

For Pharaoh will say of the children of Israel, They are tangled in the land; the wilderness has shut them in — Exodus 14:3.

THE GREAT TYRANT has not forgotten you, and he designs in his heart your capture and re-enslavement. He and his are continually looking for opportunities by which they may bring you again into the thraldom of evil, fasten the manacles of habit on your hands, and fit the fetters of despair on your feet. By the grace of God I hope that the Prince of evil and his helpers will be disappointed. But they will leave no stone unturned to effect their purpose. One of their hopes of driving you back is the belief that you are entangled by your circumstances and surroundings. They conceive that you have gotten into serious difficulty through your conversion, and that you cannot find your way out of your perplexity. Now, the enemy says, "I will pursue; I will overtake; I will divide the spoil." The Pharaoh of the infernal regions thinks to drive back the fugitives like a flock of sheep; and, notwithstanding all that God has done for them, he hopes again to bring them under his yoke. If Jehovah has brought you out, His work will never be undone. But the enemy's hope lies in his belief that you are hopelessly entangled by your present environment.

Satan has less hope of getting back those who have escaped from his tyranny for many years. If he can trip them up or worry them, even now, he will take delight in doing it. But he begins to see that the older pilgrims are really the Lord's and cannot fall into his hands. He has greater hope of those who have only lately escaped from his power, they not having proved by the test of experience that the work within them is Divine. He hopes that theirs is only temporary reformation. And if so, he can soon make them slip back into the mire of sin, from which he hopes they only half escaped.

January 27   MORNING

For Pharaoh will say of the children of Israel, They are tangled in the land; the wilderness has shut them in — Exodus 14:3.

WHEN SATAN SAYS, "They are tangled in the land," it is not true; it is only one of the sayings of the father of lies. "They say," says one. Well, what do they say? Let them say it. Their saying will not make it true. A troubled one comes to me and complains of a certain charge which has been made, and he adds as the sharp edge of it all, "Sir, it is not true." Well, then, do not fret about it. One cries out, "They are taking away my character, and I feel keenly because what they say is cruelly false." Friend, do not feel it at all. You ought to feel it if what they say is true. Now, what Pharaoh said was not true, and his speech did not cause the children of Israel to be really entangled in the land. Pharaoh's tongue speaks his wish, but his wish will not be realized. Our adversaries say that our cause is defeated. Is it? They say, "Ah! We have shut him up. The man cannot answer us; we have crushed his faith and argued hs confidence to death." Have you? By the grace of God we stand fast in the once-delivered faith, after all your sophistries and boasts. You say that we are tangled, but we are not. They say, "Show us the way in which you will get out of the wilderness." No, that we cannot do. But, if you will wait a while, the Lord will show you the way by leading us graciously through the divided sea. And it may be He will also drown you in it, as He did the Egyptians when the waters overwhelmed them. Israel could not guess her way, but Israel could wait until God revealed it. Newly-emancipated one, you are shut in with doubts and difficulties suggested by carnal reason. But, I pray you, believe your God. By the blood of the cross, I entreat you, believe the Lord Jesus. By the eternal judgment and the great white throne, believe your God. Then, *"Let God be true, and every man a liar"* (Romans 3:4).

EVENING

For Pharaoh will say of the children of Israel, They are tangled in the land; the wilderness has shut them in — Exodus 14:3.

ALTHOUGH Pharaoh said, *"They are tangled in the land; the wilderness has shut them in,"* yet they had a guide. Look at the surroundings of my text and you will see that they were guided by a pillar of cloud by day, and a pillar of fire by night, so that they had no need to be in any perplexity as to their road. We, too, have a Guide. In providence we are not left without a Leader. And in spiritual things we are not left without the Spirit of God, who will lead us into all truth. Young traveler, you are not turned out alone into a wild wilderness to find a path, for the Good Shepherd goes before you. Follow Him as the sheep follow their shepherd. He never led His flock in the wrong direction yet. Do what He bids you, and you are safe. Do as He did when He was here below; His example is your safe direction. Believe Him and obey Him. Keep to the narrow path. Hold fast your integrity, and never let go your faith. You have a heavenly Guide. You are not left alone, and therefore you cannot be tangled in the land. The wilderness has not shut you in.

Remember, next, that the Lord had appointed a way for these people; there was not only a guide, but a way. But where was that way? Mountains blocked them on either side. They could not turn back, for Pharaoh shut up that route. Where should they go? The reedy Red Sea rolled across their front. Hearken! Their way is across the bottom of that sea, and up from its depths to the other shore. A strange path! "It is no way at all," cries unbelief. Have you never read concerning God, *"Your way is in the sea, and Your path in the great waters, and Your footsteps are not known"*? Tried believer, the Lord will make a way for you where no foot has been before. That which, like the sea, threatens to drown you, shall be a highway for your escape.

MORNING

I have set watchmen on your walls, O Jersualem, who will never be quiet day or night. You who remember Jehovah, do not keep silence — Isaiah 62:6.

OBSERVE WHAT manner of watchmen we ought to be. It is written, *"I have set watchmen."* We are under Divine command. In the old Roman days, when a sentry was placed in his position by his centurion, he never thought of quitting his post. Rocks migh roam, but not the sentinels of the empire. There was found in Pompeii a sentry among the ashes, standing in his place with his javelin in his hand. He had not flinched amid the deadly shower which fell from the volcano and buried the city. His centruion, in the name of the emperor, had set him there, and there he stood. How steadfast and immovable ought those to be, whom the Lord Himself has set in their place in connection with His church! It is Jehovah who says, *"I have set watchmen on your walls."* By a Divine arrangement, and by a sacred command, saints are set in their positions, and they must stand fast. Having done all, they must still stand, for they have received their charge from the King Himself.

These watchmen guarded the city of cities, *"your walls, O Jerusalem."* The legionary who guarded old Rome felt that he would be base indeed if he did not fight for his native city. If we are set to guard the church of God, what shall I say to him who sleeps at his post, or proves a traitor? If you do not throw your whole strength into the guarding of such a cause, what will arouse you? did you not know that the church is purchased by the blood of Christ; that it is God's peculiar heritage? The Lord's portion is His people. O shepherds, watch well the sheep that cost your Lord so dear. *"Feed the flock of God which He has purchased with His own blood."* If we do not guard the truth of God once for all delivered to the saints, we are something worse than traitors.

EVENING

And the name of the city from that day shall be, The Lord is There — Ezekiel 48:35.

WHENEVER it can be said of an assembly, *"the Lord is there,"* unity will be created and fostered. Show me a quarreling church, a church split up into cliques, a church that is divided with personal ambitions, contrary doctrines and opposing schemes, and I am sure that the Lord is *not* there. Where there are envyings, jealousies, suspicions, backbitings, and dislikes, I know that the Holy Dove, who hates confusion, has taken His flight. God is love, and He will only dwell where love reigns. He is the God of peace and will not endure strife. The children of God should be knit together. It would indeed be a shameful sight if children of His family fall out, and chide, and fight. Saints who dwell with God love each other *"with a pure heart, fervently."* Some professors act as if they hated each other — I may not say with a pure heart, but I will say, fervently. Where God is present the church is edified in love, and it grows up like a building fitly framed together, to be a holy temple in the Lord. Oh for this unity!

Where *"the Lord is there,"* happiness is sure to be. What meetings believers have when the Lord is present. It is a prayer-meeting. But when you have said that, you have not fully described it; for it is far more. It is an unusual meeting for prayer, for, God being present, every prayer is spoken into His ear, and all the desires and petitions of the saints are prompted by His Holy Spirit. Why, the very room will seem alight with the glory of the Lord. And whether we are in Heaven or not, we can hardly tell. What happy times we have in preaching the word of the Lord when God's own presence is realized! His paths drop fatness. What joyous seasons we have frequently enjoyed at the communion table! The provision is but bread and wine, but when by faith we perceive the real and spiritual presence of the Lord Jesus Christ in the break of the bread we eat His flesh, and in the fruit of the vine we drink His blood.

MORNING

I have set watchmen on your walls, O Jerusalem, who will never be quiet day or night. You who remember Jehovah, do not keep silence — Isaiah 62:6.

WE ARE to be spokesmen. We are never to hold our peace, but make mention of the Lord. Believers are to speak for God to the people. If you have the ability and the commission, speak to the great congregation. You have both ability and commission, each one of you, to speak to those around you. Always be ready to speak a word in season (1 Peter 3:15). Never run short of a good word for those whom God's providence puts in your way. If there is nobody near to whom you can speak for God, then in your solitude speak to God for your fellow-men. What a blessed thing to be so familiar with God that you have His ear for your friends and neighbors! Plead with Him for the erring, the unbelieving, the profane. Never hold your peace toward God, for in this case speech is more than golden. By prayer you unlock the treasuries of Heaven; keep the golden keey in constant motion. Never cease to pray, since intercession is benediction. If the world is asleep, if the church is asleep, hold not your peace by night. And should the church become active, and the world become a little awakened, redouble your prayer until the world is won. You spokesmen for God and spokesmen to God, never hold your peace day nor night.

Sick saints are espceially set to take the night-watches. While the most of us are blessed with refreshing slumber, these find that sleep forsakes their eyes. They hear the clock's unwearied tick, and listen to the slow striking of the hours. Now let them lift their hearts heavenward on behalf of the Lord's cause and kingdom. Maybe God arouses them to this end, that they may keep the nights safe by their prayers, chasing away ill spirits, and keeping the incense burning on the altar of acceptable intercession. The Lord girdles the globe with intercessions, by His daily and nightly watchers.

EVENING

I have set watchmen on your walls, O Jerusalem, who will never be quiet day or night. You remember Jehovah, do not keep silence — Isaiah 62:6.

TAKE NO REST from prayer. Be always praying. If not always in the act of prayer, be always in the spirit of prayer: *"Pray without ceasing."* Not only reason, but wrestle with God in prayer. Sometimes pray without words, and sometimes with them. Pray alone, and often pray with other believers. There is a special prevalence in the prayer of two or three. *"If two of you shall agree on earth as touching anything that they shall ask, it shall be done for them of My Father who is in Heaven."* Gather in the greater congregation for prayer. *"Forsake not the assembling of yourselves together, as the manner of some is,"* as, I regret to say, the manner of many churches has come to be in these days. The moderns despise the meeting for prayer. And in this they condemn themselves, by owning that they attach little value to their own prayers. Possibly their consciousness of having lost all power with God in prayer is thus betraying itself. Where the prayer-meeting is despised, there may be cleverness in the preacher, but there will be no unction for the hearer. I beseech you, both as individuals and as part of the church, do not restrain prayer, *"Watch and pray."*

Never rest from prayer because you are weary of it. Whenever prayer becomes distasteful, it should be a loud call to pray all the more. No man has such need to pray as the man who does not care to pray. When you can pray, and long to pray, then you will pray. But when you cannot pray, and do not wish to pray, why then you must pray, or evil will come of it. He is on the brink of ruin who forgets the mercy seat. When the heart is apathetic toward prayer, the whole man is sickening for a grievous disease. How can we be weary of prayer? It is essential to life.

By faith Abraham obeyed when he was called to go out to a place which he was going to receive for an inheritance, and went out not understanding where he was going
— Hebrews 11:8.

WE HAVE had to mourn our disobedience with many tears and sighs. But we find joy in yielding ourselves as servants of the Lord, and our deepest desire is to do the Lord's will in all things. Oh, for obedience! It has been supposed by man ill-instructed people that the doctrine of justification by faith is opposed to the teaching of good works, or obedience. There is no truth in the supposition. We preach the obedience of faith. Faith is the fountain, the foundation, the fosterer of obedience. Men do not obey God until they believe Him. We preach faith that men may be brought to obedience. To disbelieve is to disobey. One of the first signs of practical obedience is found in the obedience of the mind, the understanding, and the heart. This is expressed in believing the teaching of Christ, trusting in His work, resting in His salvation. Faith is the morning star of obedience. If we would work God's work, we must believe on Jesus.

We do not give a secondary place to obedience. We look on the obedience of the heart to the will of God as salvation. We regard sanctification, or obedience, as the great design for which the Savior died. He shed His blood that He might cleanse us from dead works and purify to Himself a people zealous for good works. It is for this that we were chosen. We are *"elect unto holiness."* We know nothing of election to continue in sin. It is for this that we have been called *to be saints."* Obedience is the grand object of the work of grace in the hearts of those who are chosen and called to become obedient children, conformed to the image of their Brother, with whom God is well-pleased.

EVENING

By faith Abraham obeyed when he was called to go out to a place which he was going to receive for an inheritance. And he went out without knowing where he was going
— Hebrews 11:8.

THE OBEDIENCE that comes of faith is of a noble sort. The obedience of a slave ranks very little higher than the obedience of a well-trained horse or dog, for it is tuned to the crack of the whip. Obedience not cheerfully given is not the obedience of the heart, and consequently is of little worth before God. If the man obeys because he has no opportunity of doing otherwise, and if, were he free, he would at once become a rebel, there is nothing in his obedience. The obedience of faith springs from a principle within, and not from compulsion without. It is sustained by the mind's most sober reasoning, and the heart's warmest passion. The Christian reasons that he ought to obey his Redeemer, his Father, his God. At the same time, the love of Christ constrains him to do so. So what argument suggests, affection performs. A sense of great obligation, an apprehension of the fitness of obedience, and spiritual renewal of heart, work an obedience which becomes essential to the sanctified soul. Therefore, it is not relaxed in the time of temptation, nor destroyed in the hour of losses and suffering.

Life has no trial which can turn the gracious soul from its passion for obedience. Death itself only enables it to render an obedience which shall be as blissful as it will be complete. Yes, this is a chief ingredient of Heaven: We will see the face of our Lord and serve Him day and night. Meanwhile, the more fully we obey at this present time, the nearer we shall be to Him. May the Holy Spirit work in us to obey by faith, as Abraham.

I preach to you, at this time, obedience, absolute obedience to the Lord God, but I preach the obedience of a child, not the obedience of a slave — the obedience of love, not of terror; the obedience of faith, not of dread.

January 31 MORNING

By faith Abraham obeyed when he was called to go out to a place which he was going to receive for an inheritance. And he went out without knowing where he was going.
—Hebrews 11:8.

OBEDIENCE arises out of a faith which is to us the paramount principle of action. The kind of faith which produces obedience is lord of understanding, a royal faith. The true believer believes in God beyond all his belief in anything else, and everything else. He can say, *"Let God be true, but every man a liar."* His faith in God has become to him the crown of all his believings, the most assured of all his confidences. As gold is to the inferior metals, such is our trust in God to all our other trusts. To the genuine believer the eternal is as much the temporal as the heavens are above the earth. The infinite rolls, like Noah's flood, over the tops of the hills of the present and the finite. To the believer, let a truth be tinctured with the glory of God, and he values it; but if God and eternitey are not there, he will leave these trifles to those who choose them. You must have a paramount faith in God, or else the will of God will not be a paramount rule to you. Only a reigning faith will make us subject to its power, so as to be in all things obedient to the Lord. The chief thought in life with the true believer is, "How can I obey God?" His great anxiety is to do the will of God, or acceptably to suffer that will. And if he can obey, he will make no terms with God, stand on no reservations. He will pray, "Refine me from the dross of rebellion, and let the furnace be as fierce as You will." His choice is neither wealth, nor ease, nor honor, but that he may glorify God in his body, and his spirit, which are the Lord's. Obedience has become as much his rule as self-will is the rule of others. His cry to the Lord is, "By Your command I stay or go. Your will is my will; Your pleasure is my pleasure; Your law is my love." God grant to us a supreme, over-mastering faith, for this is the kind of faith which we must have if we are to lead obedient lives.

EVENING

By faith Abraham obeyed when he was called to go out to a place which he was going to receive for an inheritance. And he went out without knowing where he was going. — Hebrews 11:8.

GENUINE FAITH in God creates a prompt obedience. *"By faith Abraham obeyed when he was called."* There was an immediate response to the command. Delayed obedience is disobedience. I wish some Christians, who put off duty, would remember this. Continued delay of duty is a continuous sin. If I do not obey the Divine command, I sin. And every moment I continue in that condition, I repeat the sin. This is a serious matter. If a certain act is my duty at this hour, and I leave it undone, I have sinned. But it will be equally incumbent on me during the next hour; and if I still refuse, I disobey again; and so on until I do obey. Neglect of a standing command must grow very grievous if it is persisted in for years. In proportion as the conscience becomes callous on the subject, the guilt becomes the more provoking to the Lord. To refuse to do right is a great evil; to continue in the refusal until conscience grows numb on the convenience. I offered to go with him to the brook and baptize him, but he said, "No, believer in the Lord Jesus for forty years, and that he had always seen the ordinance to be Scriptural. I felt grieved that he had so long been disobedient to a known duty, and I proposed to him that he should be baptized at once. He said that there were no conveniences. I offered to go with him to the brook and baptize him, but he said, "No, he who believes shall not make haste." Here was one who had wilfully disobeyed his Lord for as many years as the Israelites in the wilderness, on a matter so easy to perform; yet, after confessing his fault, he was not willing to amend it, but perverted a passage of Scripture to excuse him in further delay. David says, *"I made haste, and delayed not to keep Your commandments."* I give this case as a typical illustration.

MORNING

February 1

My sheep hear My voice and I know them. And they follow Me. — John 10:27.

SHEEP OF CHRIST, you shall be His forever, because you have been His from forever. They are Christ's sheep, because His Father gave them to Him. They were the gift of the Father to Christ. He often speaks of them in this way: *"As many as You have given Me;" "You have given them to Me,"* (John 17:2,9). He says it over and over again. Of old the Father gave His people to Christ. Separating them from among men, He presented them to Him as a gift, committed them into His hand as a trust, and ordained them for Him as the lot of His inheritance. Thus they become a token of the Father's love to His only begotten Son, a proof of the confidence He reposed in Him, and a pledge of the honor that shall be done to Him. Now, I suppose we know how to value a gift for the donor's sake. If presented to us by one whom we love, we set great store by it. If it has been designed to be a love-token, it awakens in our minds many sweet memories. Though the intrinsic worth may be of small account, the associations make it exceedingly precious. We might be content to lose something of far greater value in itself rather than that which is the gift of a friend, the offering of his love.

How weak the words of human passion! But how strong the expressions of Divine ardor. When Jesus speaks to the Father of *"the men whom You gave to Me out of this world,"* He says, *"Yours they were, and You gave them to Me; and those that You have given to Me I have kept."* You sheep of Christ, rest safely. Do not let your soul be disturbed by fear. The Father gave you to His Son, and He will not lightly lose what God Himself has given to Him. The infernal lions shall not rend the meanest lamb that is a love-token from the Father to His best Beloved.

EVENING

My sheep hear My voice and I know them. And they follow Me. — John 10:27.

"MY SHEEP," says Christ. They are His, because, in addition to His choice and to the gift, He has bought them with a price. They had sold themselves for nought; but He has redeemed them — not with corruptible things as with silver and gold, but with His precious blood. A man always esteems that to be exceedingly valuable which he procured with risk, with risk of life and limb. David felt he could not drink the water that the brave warriors who broke through the host of the Philistines brought to him from the well of Bethlehem, because it seemed to him as though it were the blood of the men that went in jeopardy of their lives. And he poured it out before the Lord. It was too precious a draught for him, when men's lives had been hazarded for it. But the good Shepherd not only hazarded His life, but even laid it down for His sheep.

Jacob exceedingly valued one part of his possessions, and he gave it to Joseph. He gave him one portion above his brothers. Now, you may be sure he would give Joseph that which he thought most precious. But why did he give him that particular portion? Because, he says, *"I took it out of the hand of the Amorite with my sword and with my bow."* Now, our blessed Shepherd esteems His sheep because they cost Him His blood. The cost Him His blood — I may say He took them out of the land of the Amorite with His sword and His bow in bloody conflict, where He was victor, but yet was slain. There is not one sheep of all His flock but that he can see the mark of His blood on him. In the face of every saint the Savior sees, as in a mirror, the memorial of His bloody sweat in Gethsemane, and His agonies at Golgotha. *"You are not your own, for you are bought with a price."* That stands as a call to duty, but it is at the same time a consolation, for if He has bought me, He will have me.

February 2   MORNING

My sheep hear My voice and I know them. And they follow Me — John 10:27.

"MY SHEEP HEAR My voice" — the voice of Jesus, His counsel, His command, is clothed with the authority of His own sacred sovereign utterance. When the gospel comes to you as Christ's gospel, with demonstration of the Spirit, the invitation is addressed to you by Him. You can look on it in no other light, so you must accept and receive it. When His princely power comes with it, being mighty to save, He puts saving power into the word, then you hear Christ's voice as a fiat that must be obeyed, as a summons that must be attended to, as a call to which there must be a quick response. O beloved, do not ever rest satisfied with hearing the voice of the preacher. We are only the trumpets of Christ speaking. There is nothing in us. It is only His speaking through us that can do any good. O children of God, some of you do not always listen to Christ's voice in the preaching. While we comment on the word, you make your comments on us. Our style, or our tone, or even our gesture, is enough to absorb (I might rather say, to distract) your thoughts. *"Why do you look so earnestly on us?"* I beseech you, give less heed to the delivery of the servant, and give more care to the message of the Master. Listen warily, if you please; but judge wisely, if you can. See how much pure grain, and how much of Christ, there is in the sermon. Use your sieve; put away all the chaff; take only the good wheat; hear the voice of Christ. It would be well if we could obscure ourselves so that we might manifest Him. I could wish so to preach that you could not see even my little finger, if I might so preach that you could get a full view of Jesus only. O that you could hear His voice drowning ours! This is the mark, the peculiar mark of those who are the peculiar people of Christ: they hear His voice.

EVENING

My sheep hear My voice and I know them. And they follow Me — John 10:27.

I THINK OUR LORD meant here that His sheep, when they hear His voice, know it so well that they can tell it at once from the voice of strangers. The true child of God knows the gospel from the law. It is not by learning catechisms, reading theological books, or listening to endless controversies, that he finds this out. There is an instinct of his regenerate nature far more trustworthy than any lessons he has been taught. The voice of Jesus! Why, there is no music like it! If you had once heard it, you cannot mistake it for another, or another for it. Some are babes in grace; others are of full age, and *by reason of use they have their senses exercised.* But one sense is quickly brought out, the sense of hearing. It is easy to tell the joy-bells of the gospel from the death-knell of the law. For the letter kills, but the Spirit gives life. Moses says, "Do this or die." Christ says, "Believe and live." Recognize each way.

I think, also, that believers are equally shrewd and quick to discriminate between the flesh and the spirit. Let some of the very feeblest of God's people sit down under a fluent ministry, with all the beauties of rhetoric, and let the minister preach up the dignity of human nature, and the sufficiency of man's reason to find out the way of righteousness, and you will hear them say, "It is very clever, but there is no food for me in it." But bring the best and most instructed, most learned Christian man, and set him down under a ministry that is very faulty as to the gift of utterance, and incorrect even in grammar — yet if it is full of Jesus Christ, I know what he will say, "Ah! Never mind the man, never mind the platter on which he brought the meat; it was food to my soul that I fed on with a hearty relish; it was marrow and fatness, for I could hear the voice of Christ in it." I am not going to follow out these tests; but it is certain that the sheep know the voice of Christ, and can easily distinguish it.

My sheep hear My voice and I know them. And they follow Me. — John 10:27.

CHRIST'S SHEEP hear His voice obediently. This is an important proof of discipleship. Indeed, it may serve as a reproof to many. Oh, I wish that you were more careful about this! *"He who has My commandments, and keeps them,"* said Jesus, *"He is the one who loves Me." "He who does not love me does not keep My sayings."* How does it come to pass, then, that there are certain commands of Christ which some Christians will allow to lie in abeyance? They will say, "The Lord commands this, but it is not essential." Unloving spirit, that can think anything unessential that your Bridegroom bids you do. They that love think little things of great moment, especially when they are looked on as tokens of the strength or the tenderness of one's regard. It may not be essential, in order to prove the relation in which a wife stands to her husband, that she should study his tastes, consult his wishes, or attend to his comfort. But will she strive less to please because love, not fear, constrains her? I think not.

And can it be that any of you would harbor such a thought as your negligence implies? Do you really suppose that after the choice of Christ has been fixed on you, and the love of Christ has been plighted to you, you may now be as remiss or careless as you like? No! Stir yourself up, be on the alert, wake at the faintest sound of His voice, keep listening to do His will! However little the precept may appear in the eyes of others, however insignificant as compared with our salvation, yet if the Lord commands it, then His sheep will hear His voice, and they follow Him.

EVENING

Hold the pattern of sound words which you have heard from me, in faith and love which are in Christ Jesus — 2 Timothy 1:13.

"HOLD the pattern of sound words," because it will tend very much to your growth. He holding fast the truth will grow faster than he who is continually shifting from doctrine to doctrine. What a mighty number of spiritual weathercocks are in this world now. We have men who hear a Calvinistic preacher in the morning, and say, "Oh, it is delightful." In the evening they hear an Arminian, and they say, "Oh, it is just as good, and no doubt both are true, though one contradicts the other." The glorious charity of the present day is such that it believes lies to be as good as truth — "lies and truth have met together and kissed each other" — and he who tells truth is called a bigot. Has truth ceased to be honorable in the world? We know better than to profess such unlimited, but false charity. The truth is, we know how to *"hold the pattern of sound words,"* which has been given to us, because in this way we grow.

Changeable people cannot grow much. If you have a tree and plant it in one place today, and tomorrow place it somewhere else, how much bigger will it be in six months? It will be dead, or if it does not die, it will not be very much grown; it will be stunted. So it is with some of you. You plant yourselves there, then you are persuaded that you are not quite right, and you go and plant yourself somewhere else. There are people who are 'anythingarians,' who go dodging about from one denomination to another, and cannot tell what they are. Our opinion of these people is that they believe nothing, are good for nothing, and anybody may have them that likes. We do not consider men worth much unless they have settle principles, and *"hold the pattern of sound words."* You cannot grow unless you hold it fast. How could I know any more of my faith in ten years' time if I allowed it to take ten forms in ten years? I would be but a smatterer in each, knowing nothing thoroughly. But he who has one faith, and knows it to be the faith of God, and holds it fast, how strong he becomes in his faith! Each wind or tempest only confirms him; the fierce winds root the oaks and make them strong.

February 4 — MORNING

Recognize those who labor among you and who are taking the lead of you and warning you; esteem them very highly in love because of their work — 1 Thess. 5:12.

FAITHFUL PREACHERS are among God's best gifts. Cherish them, and be obedient to their admonitions. I have known persons to become offended when a minister is "too personal." But wise men always prize a ministry in proportion as it is personal to themselves. He who never tells me of my faults, nor makes me feel uneasy, is not likely to be the means of good to my soul. What is the use of a dog that never barks? Why have a doctor, and grow angry with him if he points out the source of your disease? Did God send us as His messengers to pander to your taste or flatter your vanity? We seek not your approval if it is not founded on right principles. I have often felt pleased when I have heard people confess, after their conversion, "I came to the Tabernacle, and at the first I could not endure the preaching. I hated the preacher and raged at his doctrine; but I could not help coming again." Just so. Conscience makes men respect the gospel, even when their depravity makes them loathe it. They are held fast by the cords which they would willingly cast from them.

May it often be so, O my unregenerate believers, that while my plain dealing excites your anger, it may nevertheless have a power over you. May every man and woman reading this, whether saved or unsaved, feel that the preaching is the truth of God to his or her soul. Whether it is like or not like, may it become the permanent means of arousing from sleep, and ultimately bringing to Christ every one of you to whom these words shall come. Be sure and attend an arousing ministry, and pray God to make the ministry which you now listen to more and more an arousing ministry to your own soul. Pray for the preacher, for he is in the same danger as yourselves, for he too is compassed with infirmity. The minister soon goes to sleep unless God awakens him.

EVENING

Let us deal wisely with them, lest they multiply, and when there comes a war they also join our enemies and fight against us, and so get out of the land — Exodus 1:10.

THE CHILDREN of this world are wise in their generation. Their policy may be short-sighted and their stratagems crooked, but the world admires the wisdom of their counsels, and makes light of the craftiness of their projects. In their opposition to the Christian church, the men of the world might certainly have been as well able to outwit her by the variety of their maneuvers as to overwhelm her by the force of their numbers, if it were not that there is an unseen One in her midst. He is more than a match for the guile of their hearts and the might of their hosts. Looking back at the early struggles of the Hebrew race to gain a footing among the nations, it is very clear that had the contest been merely between Pharaoh and Israel, the Egyptian king could exercise power and policy enough to defeat the sons of Jacob and reduce them to serfdom. But when a new name is brought in, and the contest appears to be truly between Pharaoh and Jehovah the God of Israel, it is quite another matter, and a far different result may be counted on. There is One behind the curtain that takes Israel's part. He sees through all Pharaoh's plots. Before his thoughts have ripened into plans, they are forestalled. Fast as they are set up, they are upset. For every intrigue, there is a reprisal. So He takes the wise in their own craftiness. The whole history of the long feud between the seed of the woman and the seed of the serpent illustrates the subtlety of the serpent's seed, and the simplicity of the woman's seed. But still more does it bring to light the infinite wisdom of Him who rules the seed of the woman, and who will in the end bruise the serpent's head, and give to His people and the cause they have espoused a complete triumph. Whatever has been done by the enemies in rage or in recklessness, God has always met it calmly and quietly. He has shown Himself ready for every emergency.

MORNING

But the more they afflicted them, the more they multiplied and grew — Exodus 1:12

THE GLORY OF GOD shines forth conspicuously in the use to which He turned the persecutions they endured. The severe treatment they had to bear from the enemy became to them a salutary discipline. This comes of the Lord of Hosts, who is wonderful in counsel, and excellent in working. From that time the children of Israel began to feel a disgust with Egypt. They had settled down very quietly in Goshen, and thought that it was their rest. They had imbibed much of the manners and customs of the Egyptians. We have it on record that they worshiped the gods of Egypt. They seemed greatly to have appreciated what they afterwards called the luxuries of the land — the leeks, the garlics, the onions, the melons, and the cucumbers. They appear to have been almost naturalized to that country. They were little better than Egyptians. Perhaps persons traveling, except by certain tones of language and contour of countenance, would scarcely have known that they were descendants of Ham. But now their masters treat them cruelly, and they loathe the Egyptians. They are scattered up and down throughout the land, and Goshen is no longer dear to them. They are treated like strangers, and they feel they are strangers. Now that they hear from morning until night the taskmaster's oath, and the crack of the cruel whip, and are subjected to incessant toil and bondage, they think far less of Egypt than they used to do. This is what the Lord designed. He never intended that His people Israel should be absorbed into any other family. He never meant them to be other than sojourners on that soil. He had some better thing for them than that they should dwell in that land, and be as the heathen were. God was thus answering one purpose.

EVENING

But the more they afflicted them, the more they multiplied and grew — Exodus 1:12.

WHENEVER there has been a great persecution raised against the Christian church, God has overruled it, as He did in the case of Pharaoh's oppression of the Israelites, by making the aggrieved community more largely to increase. The early persecutions in Judea promoted the spread of the gospel. When after the death of Stephen the disciples were all scattered throughout the regions of Judea and Samaria, except the apostles, the result is thus given: *"Therefore they that were scattered abroad went everywhere preaching the Word."* So, too, when Herod stretched forth his hands to vex certain of the church, and killed James, the brother of John, with the sword, what came of it? Why, Luke tells us in almost the same words that Moses had used: *"The word of God grew and multiplied."* Those terrible and bloody persecutions under the Roman emperor by no means stayed the progress of the gospel. But strangely enough men seemed to press forward for the crown of martyrdom. The church probably never increased at a greater rate than when her foes were most fierce to assail and most resolute to destroy her. It was so in later times. The Reformation in England and throughout Europe never went on so prosperously as when it was most vigorously opposed. You shall find in any individual church that wherever evil men have conspired together, and a storm of opposition has burst forth against the saints, the heart of the Lord has been moved with compassion, and the hand of the Lord has been raised to aid — until we have come to look on opposition as an omen of good, and of persecution for righteousness' sake as a tearful seed-time, quickly to be followed by a harvest of joy. We have looked on our adversaries, even though they seemed like stormy petrels, as being the index of a favorable wind to the food bank of Christ's church.

February 6   MORNING

But the more they afflicted them, the more they multiplied and grew — Exodus 1:12.

PERSECUTION in the church, in whatever form it is sent (even when it does not take the form of burning or imprisonment, but of slander, cruel mockings, jesting, jeering, and venomous spite) helps to keep up the separation between the church and the world. I fear the rich most when they bring gifts. I loathe the world most when it fawns and flatters. When I heard of a lady who had put on Christ by baptism, that the cold shoulder was given her in all the circles in which she moved, do you think that I feel more disposed to console, or to congratulate? It was said that now she had but few invitations to such places and such society as she had previously frequented. Yet I rejoiced and thanked God for it. I was glad of it, for I felt she was farther removed from temptation. When I heard of a young man that, after he joined the church, those in his workshop met him at once with loud laughter and reproached him with bitter scorn, I was thankful, because now he could not take up the same position with themselves. He was a marked man: they who knew him discovered that there was such a thing as Christianity, and such a one was an earnest defender of it. It is no evil to the church, depend on it, to have a great gulf fixed between her and the world. The worst thing that ever could happen for us is to have affinities made between the sons of God and the children of Belial. This brought on the Deluge. And if it could ever be carried out thoroughly again, it would bring judgments terrible to contemplate. It is ill for the worldly ones, since *they that are far from God shall perish.* "But it is a thousand times worse for the professors when they play foul with their profession. For it is written, *"You have destroyed all those who go awhoring from You."* Summary vengeance is their lot. Therefore, *"Come out from among them, and be separate, and touch not the unclean thing; and I will receive you"* (2 Cor. 6:17).

EVENING

But the more they afflicted them, the more they multiplied and grew — Exodus 1:12.

PERSECUTION in the Christian church acts like a winnowing fan to the heaps gathered on the threshing-floor. In these soft and silken days any man may be a Christian professor. Oftentimes it pays well to make a profession of godliness. Men think the better of you. It brings customers to the shop. No one knows how many conveniences may attach to the profession of religion. However, if it is pretence without pretext everlasting destruction awaits such violation of truth, for God will surely avenge hypocrisy. But in the days of persecution it is very inconvenient to profess Christ. To be baptized in water then may involve a baptism in blood. For the soul to burn with zeal for Christ then would probably be followed with the body being burned at the stake. Then a word for Jesus would bring a word of conviction from the judge's mouth, and death close at the heels of that word. At such a time those not loving Christ took themselves to the other side; the cowards and the spies shrunk away: Demas went, and Judas went, and all of that brood went to their own company. Only then the true and the brave, the regenerate, the elect of God, were left. They stood fast and firm, all the stronger for losing such ill company.

In those days the church was like a heap of golden wheat, all winnowed and clean grain, fit for a burnt offering to the Most High, to be offered up as a food offering on His altar. Her martyrs were among her noblest sons, the very glory of the church and of the Lord Jesus Christ. So you see persecution is overruled for this great good. It ought never to be, while there are sinners in this world. It ought never to be that the Christian escapes opposition. I take it that if a man makes an advance in life, comes to a position of fame, he ought to win it, ought to fight for it. Men ought not to be crowned until first of all they have striven for the ministry.

The more they afflicted them, the more they multiplied and grew — Exodus 1:12.

OFTEN IT HAPPENS that the enmity of the world drives the Christian nearer to his God. How many prayers have been offered up as a result of persecution that would never have been offered otherwise, Heaven alone can tell. How many a groan, a sigh, a tear acceptable to God have been forced from the true hearts by their sufferings, God alone knows! Ah, in the soft days, the summer days of peace and prosperity, we are apt to go out after delights. But when winter comes, with its keen and cutting blast, we hurry to our own abode; we cleave to our own hearth; we love to dwell with our own kindred. Even so very frequently, with hearts all chill and cheerless, we have sought the house of our Father and our God, drawn near to His altar, and found a refreshment we wish we might never leave. Why are we so fickle? If we could find aid and solace apart from the Rock, away from the Son, absent from our Lord, our wayward hearts would do so. But when the waters of affliction have covered all the earth, then we fly back to our Noah, our ark, and find rest for the sole of our foot. The friendship of this world is *"enmity to God"* (James 4:4). It rivals God's friendship; it deceives and deludes many hearts. But when the world frowns it is a blessing that makes me seek my Savior's smile. Anything that drives me to my knees is good. Anything that makes me trust in the promise and wait only on God (because my hope is in Him) is healthful to my soul, infuses courage and inspires confidence, and invests it with fresh strength. O brothers, the very glory of the church is to live nearer to God. The more she thinks of her great and glorious Head, and the more she leans on the invisible arm of the Eternal, the more invincible she is. Persecution in driving her to her stronghold is overruled to her help.

EVENING

When Jesus came to the place, He looked up and saw him, and said to him, Zaccheus, hurry and come down; for today I must stay in your house — Luke 19:5.

IT WAS a personal call. Boys were in the tree, as well as Zaccheus, but there was no mistake about the person who was called. *"Zaccheus, hurry and come down —* it was by name. There are other calls mentioned in Scripture, especially, *"Many are called, but few are chosen"* (Matt. 22:14). That is not the effectual call which is intended by the Apostle when he said, *"Whom He called, them He also justified."* All men reject a general call, unless there come after it the personal, particular call which makes us Christians. You will bear me witness that it was a personal call that brought you to the Savior. No doubt it was Scripture which led you to feel that you were the person intended. Perhaps the text was, *"You, God, see me,"* and perhaps the minister seemed to lay stress on the word *"me,"* making you think that God's eye was fixed on you. And before the sermon was concluded you thought that you saw God open the books to your name, and your heart whispered, *"Can any hide himself in secret places that I shall not see him?"* Perhaps you were perched in a window, or packed in the aisle, but you had a solemn conviction that the seromn was preached to you. God does not call His people in crowds, but singly: *"Jesus said to her, Mary! And she turned and said to him, Rabboni, which is to say, Master."* Jesus sees Peter and John fishing by the lake, and He says to them, *"Follow Me."* He sees Matthew sitting at the table at the receipt of custom, and He says to him, *"Rise up and follow Me."* And Matthew did so. When the Holy Spirit comes home to a man, God's arrow goes into his heart. It does not graze his helmet, or make some little mark on his armor, but it penetrates between the joints of the harness, entering the marrow of the soul. Have you felt that personal call? Do you remember when a voice said, *"Rise up, He calls you"*? Can you look back to a time when you said, *"My Lord, my God"*? When you knew the Spirit was striving with you, and you said, Lord, *"I come to You, for I know You call."*

February 8   MORNING

The grass withers, the flower fades, because the Spirit of the Lord blows on it; surely the people is grass — Isaiah 40:7.

MANY PREACHERS of God's gospel have forgotten that the law is the schoolmaster to bring men to Christ. They have sown on the unbroken fallow ground, and have forgotten that the plough must break the clods. We have seen too much of trying to sew without the sharp needle of the Spirit's convincing power. Preachers have labored to make Christ precious to those who think themselves rich, and it has been labor in vain. It is our duty to preach Jesus Christ even to self-righteous sinners, but it is certain that Jesus Christ will never be accepted by them while they hold themselves in high esteem. Only the sick will welcome a physician. It is the work of the Spirit of God to convince men of sin, and until they are convinced of sin, they will never be led to seek the righteousness which is of God by Jesus Christ.

I am persuaded that wherever there is a real work of grace in any soul, it begins with a pulling down: the Holy Spirit does not build on the old foundation. Wood, hay, and stubble will not do for Him to build on. He will come as the fire, and cause a conflagration of all proud nature's Babels. He will break our bow and cut our spear in two, and burn our chariot in the fire.. When every sandy foundation is gone, then, but not until then, He will lay in our souls the great foundation stone, chosen of God and precious. The awakened sinner, when he asks that God would have mercy on him, is much astonished to find that instead of enjoying a speedy peace, his soul is bowed down within him under a sense of Divine wrath. Naturally enough he inquires: "Is this the answer to my prayer? I prayed the Lord to deliver me from sin and self, and is this the way in which He deals with me?" The great Physician will cut with his sharp knife until the corrupt flesh is removed, for only so can a sure healing work be wrought in you.

EVENING

The grass withers, the flower fades, because the Spirit of the Lord blows on it; surely the people is grass — Isaiah 40:7.

THE WITHERING is a withering of what? Of part of the flesh and some portion of its tendencies? No, observe: *"All flesh is as grass; and all the goodliness of it"* — the very choice and pick of it — *"is as the flower of the field,"* and what happens to the grass? Does any of it live? *"The grass withers,"* all of it. The flower, will not that abide? So fair a thing, has not that an immortality? No, it fades; it utterly falls away. So wherever the Spirit of God breathes on the soul of man, there is a withering of everything that is of the flesh, and it is seen that to be carnally minded is death. Of course, we all know and confess that where there is a work of grace, there must be a destruction of our delight in the pleasures of the flesh. When the Spirit of God breathes on us, that which was sweet becomes bitter; that which was bright becomes dim. A man cannot love sin and yet possess the life of God. If he takes pleasure in fleshly joys in which he once delighted, he is still what he was: *"he minds the things of the flesh, and so he is according to flesh"* (Rom. 8:5), and he shall die. The world and its lusts are as beautiful as the meadows in spring to the unregenerate, but to the regenerate soul they are a wilderness, a salt land, and not inhabited. Of those very things in which we once took delight we say, *"Vanity of vanities; all is vanity."* We cry to be delivered from the poisonous joys of earth; we loathe them and wonder that we could once riot in them. Beloved readers, do you know what this kind of withering means? Have you seen the lusts of the flesh, and the pomps and the pleasures of it all fade away before your eyes? It must be so, or the Spirit of God has not visited your soul.

MORNING

The grass withers, the flower fades, because the Spirit of the Lord blows on it; surely the people is grass — Isaiah 40:7.

WHEN THE HOLY SPIRIT has withered our self-righteousness, He has not half completed His work. There is much more to be destroyed yet, and among the rest, away must go our boasted power of resolution. Most people conceive that they can turn to God whenever they resolve to do so. "I am a man of such strength of mind," says one, "that if I made up my mind to be religious, I could do so without difficulty." Another volatile spirit says, "Ah, I believe that one of these days I can correct the errors of the past and commence a new life." Dear readers, the resolutions of the flesh are goodly flowers, but they must all soon fade. When visited by the Spirit of God we find that even when the will is present with us, we do not find how to perform that which we desire to do. And we discover that our will is averse to all that is good, and that by nature we will not come to Christ that we may have life. What poor, frail things resolutions are when seen in the light of God's Spirit!

Still, the man will say, "I believe I have, after all, within myself an enlightened conscience and an intelligence that will guide me correctly. I will use the light of nature. And I do not doubt that if I wander somewhat I will find my way back again." Man, your wisdom, which is the very flower of your nature, is nothing but folly, although you do not know it. Unconverted and unrenewed, you are in the sight of God no wiser than the wild ass's colt. I wish you were in your own esteem humbled as a little child at the feet of Jesus, and made to cry out, "Teach me!"

When the withering wind of the Spirit moves over the carnal mind, it reveals the death of the flesh in all respects, especially in the matter of power toward that which is good. We then learn that word of our Lord: *"Without Me you can do nothing."*

EVENING

O Lord my God, I put my trust in You. Save me from all who pursue me and deliver me that he not tear my soul like a lion, ripping it to pieces when there is no one to deliver — Psalm 7:1, 2.

WHEN the fierce lion had pounced on the defenseless lamb and had made it his prey, he would tear the victim in pieces, break all the bones, and devour all, because no shepherd was near to protect the lamb or rescue it. This is the soul-moving portrait of a saint delivered over to the will of Satan. This will make the bowels of Jehovah yearn. A father cannot be silent when a child is in peril. No, he will not endure the thought of His darling in the jaws of a lion. He will rise up and deliver his persecuted one. Our God is very pitying and He will surely rescue His people from so desperate a destruction. It will be well for us here to remember that this is a description of the danger to which the Psalmist was exposed from slanderous tongues. Surely this is not an overdrawn picture, for the wounds of a sword will heal, but the wounds of the tongue cut deeper than the flesh and are not soon cured. Slander leaves a slur, even it is wholly disproved. Common fame, although notoriously a common liar, has very many believers. Once let an ill word get into men's mouths, and it is not easy to get it fully out again.

The Italians say that good repute is like the cypress; once cut, it never puts forth a leaf again. This is not true if our character is cut by a stranger's hand, but even then it will not soon regain its former verdure. Oh, it is a meanness most detestable to stab a good man in his reputation, but diabolical hatred observed no nobility in its mode of warfare. We must be ready for this trial, for it will surely come on us. If God was slandered in Eden, we shall surely be maligned in this land of sinners. Gird up your loins, you children of the resurrection, for this fiery trial awaits you all.

If we would live without being slandered we must wait until we get to Heaven. Let us be very heedful not to believe the flying rumors which are always harassing gracious men. If there are no believers in lies there will be but a dull market in falsehood, and good men's characters will be safe. Ill-will never spoke well. Sinners have an ill-will to saints, and because of this they surely will not speak well of them.

February 10   MORNING   41

And coming to himself, he said, How many hired servants of my father have more than enough bread, and I am dying with hunger! — Luke 15:17.

IT APPEARS that when the prodigal came to himself he was shut up to two thoughts. Two facts were clear to him: that there was plenty in his father's house, and that he himself was famishing. May the two kindred spiritual facts have absolute power over all your hearts, those of you who are still unsaved. For they are most certainly all important and pressing truths. These are no fancies of one in a dream; no ravings of a maniac; no imaginations of one under fascination. It is most true that there is plenty of all good things in the Father's house, and that the sinner needs them. Nowhere else can grace be found or pardon gained. With God there is plentitude of mercy. Let no one venture to dispute this glorious truth. Equally true is the fact that the sinner without God is perishing. He is perishing now; he will perish everlastingly. All that is worth having in his existence will be utterly destroyed, and he himself shall only remain as a desolation. The owl and the bittern of misery and anguish shall haunt the ruins of his nature forever and forever.

If only we could shut up unconverted men to those two thoughts! Alas! they forget that there is mercy only with God, and fancy that it is to be found somewhere else. And they try to slip away from the humbling fact of their lost estate, and imagine that perhaps there may be some back door of escape; that, after all, they are not so bad as the Scripture declares — or that perchance it shall be right with them at the last, however wrong it may be with them now. Alas! What shall we do with those who wilfully shut their eyes to truths of which the evidence is overwhelming, and the importance overpowering? I earnestly entreat those of you who know how to approach the throne of God in faith, to breathe the prayer that He would now bring into captivity the unconverted heart.

EVENING

And coming to himself, he said, How many hired servants of my father have more than enough bread, and I am dying with hunger! — Luke 15:17.

THE MASTER PROOF that in Christ Jesus there is *"bread enough and to spare,"* is the cross. Will you follow Him to Gethsemane? Can you see the bloody sweat as it falls on the ground in His agony? Can you think of His scourging before Herod and Pilate? Can you trace Him along the Via Dolorosa of Jerusalem? Will your tender hearts endure to see Him nailed to the tree, and lifted up to bleed and die? This is but the shell. As for the inward kernel of His sufferings, no language can describe it, neither can conception peer into it. The everlasting God laid sin on Christ, and where the sin was laid there fell the wrath: *"It pleased God to bruise Him; He has put Him to grief."* Now He that died on the cross was God's only begotten Son. Can you conceive a limit to the merit of such a Savior's death? I know there are some who think it necessary to their system of theology to limit the merit of the blood of Jesus. If my system of theology needed such a limitation, I would cast it to the winds. I cannot, I dare not allow the thought to find a lodging in my mind; it seems so near akin to blasphemy. In Christ's finished work I see an ocean of merit; my plummet finds no bottom, my eye discovers no shore. There must be sufficient efficacy in the blood of Christ, if God had so willed it, to have saved not only all this world, but ten thousand worlds, had they transgressed the Maker's law. Once admit infinity into the matter, and limit is out of the question. Having a Divine person for an offering, it is not consistent to conceive of limited value. Bound and measure are terms inapplicable to the Divine sacrifice. The intent of the Divine purpose fixes the application of the infinite offering, not changes it into a finite work. In the atonement of Christ Jesus there is *"more than enough bread."*

And coming to himself, he said, How many hired servants of my father have more than enough bread, and I am dying with hunger! — Luke 15:17.

IF WE COULD CALL as a witness a weak believer in God, one who is almost unknown in the church, one who sometimes questions whether he is indeed a child of God, one willing to be a hired servant so long as he might belong to God — and if I were to ask him, "Now after all, how has the Lord dealt with you?" What would be his reply? You have many afflictions, many doubts, many fears, but have you any complaints against your Lord? When you have waited on Him for daily grace, has He denied you? When you have been full of troubles, has He refused you comfort? When you have plunged in distress, has He declined to deliver you? The Lord Himself asks, *"Have I been a wilderness to Israel?"* Testify against the Lord, you His people, if you have anything against Him. Hear, O heavens, and give ear, O earth, whoever there is in God's service who has found Him to be a hard taskmaster, let him speak. Among the angels before Jehovah's throne, and among men redeemed on earth, if there is anyone that can say he has been dealt with unjustly, or treated with ungenerous churlishness, let him lift up his voice! But there is not one. Even the Devil himself said, when he spoke of God and of his servant Job, *"Does Job serve God for nothing?"* Of course he did not. God will not allow His servants to serve Him for nothing. He will pay them superabundant wages, and they shall all bear witness that at His table there is *"more than enough bread."* Now if these still enjoy the bread of the Father's house, these who were once great sinners, these who are now only very commonplace saints, surely, sinner, it should encourage you to say, *"I will arise and go to my Father,"* for His hired servants *"have more than enough bread."*

EVENING

Yes, He is altogether lovely — Song of Songs 5:16.

"YES, HE IS ALTOGETHER LOVELY" — remember these words, and know their meaning, and you possess the quintessence of the spouse's portion of the Song of Songs. Now, as in this allegorical song, the bride sums up her witness in these words, so may I say that all the patriarchs, all the prophets, all the apostles, all the confessors, yes. And the entire body of the church have left us no other testimony. They all spoke of Christ, and they all commended Him. Whatever the type, or symbol, or obscure oracle, or open word in which they bore witness, that witness all amounted to this: *"Yes, He is altogether lovely."* Yes, and I will add, that since the canon of inspiration has closed, the testimony of all the saints, on earth and in Heaven, has continued to confirm the declaration made of old. The verdict of each particular saint and of the whole elect host as a body, still is this: *"Yes, He is altogether lovely."* From the sighs and the songs which mingle on the dying beds of saints, and from the songs unmingled with groans, which perpetually peal forth from immortal tongues before the presence of the Most High, I hear this same master note: *"Yes, He is altogether lovely."* If the whole church desired to say with the Apostle, *"Now of the things which we have spoken this is the sum,"* she would not need to wait for a brief and comprehensive summary, for it lies before her in this golden sentence: *"Yes, He is altogether lovely."*

These deep texts show us the shortness of our plumb-line. These ocean verses are so exceeding broad that our skiffs are apt to be driven far out of sight of land, where our timid spirits tremble to spread the sail. If I cannot grasp the ocean in my span, yet may I bathe in it with sweet contentment.

February 12   MORNING

Yes, He is altogether lovely — Song of Songs 5:16.

THE PERSON writing these words evidently feels a great deal more than any language can possibly convey to us. The spouse begins somewhat calmly in her description: *"My Beloved is white and ruddy."* She proceeds with due order, commencing at the head, and proceeding with the different parts of the person of the Beloved. But she warms, she glows, she flames, and at last the heat which had for a while been repressed is like fire within her bones, and she bursts forth in flaming words. And here is the live coal from off the altar of her heart: *"Yes, He is altogether lovely."* It is the utterance of a soul that is altogether overcome with admiration, and therefore feels that in attempting to describe the Well-beloved it has undertaken a task beyond its power. Lost in adoring wonder, the gracious mind desists from description and cries with rapture: *"Yes, He is altogether lovely."* It has often been thus with true saints. They have felt the love of Jesus to be overpowering and inebriating. Believers are not always cool and calm in their thoughts toward their Lord. There are seasons with them when they pass into a state of rapture. Their hearts burn within them; they are in ecstasy; they mount up with wings as eagles; their souls become like the chariots of Amminadib. They feel what they could not tell; they experience what they could not express even though the tongues of men and of angels were perfectly at their command. Favored believers are altogether enraptured with the sight they have of their all-beauteous Lord. It is to be feared that such raptures are not frequent with all Christians, although I should gravely question his saintship, who has never experienced any degree of holy rapture. But there are some saints to whom a state of overwhelming adoration of their Lord has been by no means an unusual thing.

EVENING

Yes, He is altogether lovely — Song of Songs 5:16.

I CANNOT DESCRIBE the King in His beauty, yet I may gaze on Him, since the proverb says, *"A beggar may look at a prince."* Even though I pretend not so to preach from such a heavenly word as that before us, as to spread before you all its marrow and fatness, yet may I gather up a few crumbs which fall from its table. Poor men are glad of crumbs, and crumbs from such a feast are better than loaves from the tables of the world. Better to have a glimpse of Jesus, than to see all the glory of the earth all the days of our life.

This verse has been translated in another way: *"He is all desires;"* and so indeed Jesus is. He was the desire of the ancients. He is still the desire of all nations. To His own people He is their all in all; they are complete in Him; they are filled out of His fullness. He is the delight of His servants, and He fills their expectations to the full. But we will not dispute about translations, for, after all, with such a text, so full of unutterable spiritual sweetness, every man must be his own translator, and into his own soul must the power of the message come, by the enforcement of the Holy Spirit. Such a text as this is very like the manna which fell in the wilderness, of which the rabbis say it tasted after each man's liking. If the flavor in a man's mouth was very sweetness, the angel's food which fell around the camp was luscious as any dainty he had conceived. Whatever he might be, the manna was to him as he was. So shall this text be. To you with low ideas of Christ the words will but glide over your ears and be meaningless. But if your spirit is ravished with the precious love of Jesus, there shall be songs of angels; and more than that, the voice of God's own Spirit will sing to your soul in this short sentence: *"Yes, He is altogether lovely."*

MORNING

Yes, He is altogether lovely — Song of Songs 5:16.

IN JESUS loveliness of all kinds is to be found. If there is anything that is worthy of the love of an immortal spirit, it is to be seen in abundance in the Lord Jesus. Whatever things are true, whatever things are honest, whatever things are just, whatever things are pure, whatever things are lovely, whatever things are of good report; if there is any virtue and if there is any praise, all can be found without measure in Christ Jesus. As all the rivers meet in the sea, so all beauties united in the Redeemer. Take the character of any gracious man, and you will find a measure of loveliness, but it has bounds and mixtures. Peter has many virtues, but he has a few failings. John excels, but in certain points he is deficient. But in this the Lord transcends all His saints, for all human virtues and all Divine are harmoniously blended in Him. He is not this flower or that, but He is the Paradise of perfection. He is not a star here or a constellation there; He is the whole heaven of stars; He is the heaven of heavens, all that is fair and lovely condensed in one.

When the text says again that Jesus *"is altogether lovely,"* it declares that He is lovely in all views of Him. It generally happens that to the noblest building there is an unhappy point of view from which the architecture appears at a disadvantage. The choicest piece of workmanship may not be equally complete in all directions. The best human character is deformed by one flaw, if not with more. But with our Lord all is lovely, regard Him as you will. You will contemplate Him from all points, and will only find new confirmation of the statement that *"He is altogether lovely."*

EVENING

O Lord my God, I put my trust in You. Save me from all who pursue me and deliver me that he not tear my soul like a lion, ripping it to pieces when there is no one to deliver — Psalm 7:1, 2.

WHEN the fierce lion had pounced on the defenseless lamb and had made it his prey, he would tear the victim in pieces, break all the bones, and devour all, because no shepherd was near to protect the lamb or rescue it. This is the soul-moving portrait of a saint delivered over to the will of Satan. This will make the bowels of Jehovah yearn. A father cannot be silent when a child is in peril. No, he will not endure the thought of His darling in the jaws of a lion. He will rise up and deliver his persecuted one. Our God is very pitying and He will surely rescue His people from so desperate a destruction. It will be well for us here to remember that this is a description of the danger to which the Psalmist was exposed from slanderous tongues. Surely this is not an overdrawn picture, for the wounds of a sword will heal, but the wounds of the tongue cut deeper than the flesh and are not soon cured. Slander leaves a slur, even if it is wholly disproved. Common fame, although notoriously a common liar, has very many believers. Once let an ill word get into men's mouths, and it is not easy to get it fully out again.

The Italians say that good repute is like the cypress; once cut, it never puts forth a leaf again. This is not true if our character is cut by a stranger's hand, but even then it will not soon regain its former verdure. Oh, it is a meanness most detestable to stab a good man in his reputation, but diabolical hatred observed no nobility in its mode of warfare. We must be ready for this trial, for it will surely come on us. If God was slandered in Eden, we shall surely be maligned in this land of sinners. Gird up your loins, you children of the resurrection, for this fiery trial awaits you all.

If we would live without being slandered we must wait until we get to Heaven. Let us be very heedful not to believe the flying rumors which are always harassing gracious men. If there are no believers in lies there will be but a dull market in falsehood, and good men's characters will be safe. Ill-will never spoke well. Sinners have an ill-will to saints, and because of this they surely will not speak well of them.

February 14   MORNING

I will cry to You, O Lord. My Rock, do not be deaf to me, lest, if You say nothing to me, I become like those who go down into the pit — Psalm 28:1.

A CRY is the natural expression of sorrow, and is a suitable utterance when all other modes of appeal fail us. But the cry must be directed only to the Lord, for to cry to man is to waste our entreaties. When we consider the readiness of the Lord to hear, and His ability to aid, we shall see good reason for directing all our appeals at once to the God of our salvation and will use language of firm resolve like that in the text, *"I will cry."* The immutable Jehovah is our rock, the immovable foundation of all our hopes and *our refuge in time of trouble*. We are fixed in our determination to flee to Him as our stronghold in every hour of danger. It will be in vain to call to the rocks in the day of judgment, but our Rock attends to our cries.

"Do not be deaf to me." Mere formalists may be content without answers to their prayers, but genuine suppliants cannot. They are not satisfied with the results of prayer itself in calming the mind and subduing the will. They must go further and obtain actual replies from heaven, or they cannot rest. And they long to receive those replies at once, if possible. They dread even a little of God's silence. God's voice is often so terrible that it shakes the wilderness, but His silence is equally full of awe to an eager suppliant. When God seems to close His ear, we must not therefore close our mouths, but rather cry with more earnestness. For when our note grows shrill with eagerness and grief, He will not long deny us a hearing. What a dreadful case would we be in if the Lord would be forever silent to our prayers! This thought suggested itself to David, and he turned it into a plea; by this he teaches us to argue and reason with God in our prayers: *"Lest, if You say nothing to me, I become like those who go down into the pit."* Deprived of the God who answers prayer we would be in a more pitiable plight than the dead in the grave, and would soon sink to the same level as the lost in Hell. We must have answers to prayer. Ours is an urgent case of dire necessity. Surely the Lord will speak peace to our agitated minds, for He never can find it in His heart to allow His own elect to perish.

EVENING

And you know that He was revealed so that He might take away our sins; and in Him there is no sin. Everyone who remains in Him does not sin — 1 John 3:5, 6.

WHAT A MERCY it is that someone was revealed to take away our sins from us! For some of us have been striving a long while to conquer our sins, and we cannot do it. We thought we had driven them out, but they had chariots of iron, and we could not overcome them. They lived in the hill country, and we could not get near them. As often as we defeated them in one battle, they came on us thick and strong, like an army of locusts. When heaps and heaps had been destroyed they seemed as thick as ever. But they shall all be taken away. The time will come when you and I shall stand without spot or blemish before the throne of God. For we are *"without fault before the throne of God"* at this moment, and so shall we be before long.

"Everyone who remains in Him does not sin." This simple verse has been twisted by some who believe in the doctrine of perfection. They have made it declare that it is possible for some to abide in Christ so as not to sin. But you will note that it does not say that *some* that abide in Christ do not sin. It says that *none* who abide in Christ sin. Therefore this passage is not to be applied to a few who attain to what our Arminian friends call the fourth degree — perfection. But it pertains to all believers; it may be said of every soul in Christ, that he does not sin. In reading the Bible we read it simply as we would read another book. We ought not to read it as a preacher does his text, with the intention of making something out of every word. We should read it as we find it written. Now we are sure that cannot mean that he does not sin at all, but it means that he does not sin habitually; he sins not designedly; he does not sin finally, so as to perish.

MORNING

I will praise You, O Lord. For You have lifted me up and have not made my foes to rejoice over me — Psalm 30:1.

"I WILL PRAISE YOU." I will have high and honorable conceptions of You, and give them utterance in my best music. Others may forget You, murmur at You, despise You, blaspheme You, but *"I will praise You."* For I have been favored above all others, I will extol Your name, Your character, Your attributes, Your mercy to me. Your great forbearance to my people. Especially I will speak well of You, *"I will praise You."* O Jehovah, this shall be my cheerful and constant employ. *"For You have lifted me up."* Here is an antithesis, *"I will praise You, for you have lifted me up."* I would render according to the benefit received. The Psalmist's praise was reasonable. He had a reason to give for the praise that was in his heart. He had been drawn up like a prisoner from a dungeon, out of a pit, like Joseph. So he loved his Deliverer. Grace has uplifted us from the pit of Hell, for the ditch of sin, from the Slough of Despond, from the bed of sickness, from the bondage of doubts and fears. Have we no song to offer for all this? How high has our Lord lifted us? Lifted us up into the children's place, to be adopted into the family; lifted us up into union with Christ *"to sit together with Him in the heavenlies."* Lift high the name of our God, for He has lifted us above the stars. *"And have not made my foes to rejoice over me."* This was the judgment which David most feared out of the three evils. He said, let me fall into the hand of the Lord and not into the hand of men. Terrible would be our lot if we were delivered to the will of our enemies. Blessed is the Lord to preserve us from so dire a fate. The Devil and all our spiritual enemies have not been allowed to rejoice over us, for we have been saved from the snare. Our evil companions, who prophesied that we would go back to our old sins, are disappointed. Those who watched for our halting and would willingly say, "Ha! So we would have it!" have watched in vain till now. O happy are they whom the Lord keeps so consistent in character that the lynx eyes of the world can see no real fault in them. Is this our case? Let us ascribe all the glory to Him who has sustained us in our integrity.

EVENING

Eli said to Samuel, Go lie down, and if He calls you, you shall say, Speak, Lord, for your servant hears. So Samuel went to lie down in his place — 1 Samuel 3:9.

WHEN WE HEAR the voice of God we should be deeply impressed by it. Young Samuel gave evidence that he deeply felt the responsibility of hearing the voice of God. We read that *"Samuel lay until morning."* He did not go to sleep, but he did not leave his bed. He lay still, and thought. After hearing that terrible word which made his heart heavy and cause his ears to tingle, like a wise child, he lay still and pondered it in his soul. He did not rush in upon Eli, for the news was hard to tell. Neither did he seek out another confidant. He had been called to be the Lord's prophet; he was conscious of his commission, and he became sober beyond his years. *"He lay until morning."* What thoughts passed through his mind on his lone bed? He had been a child when he went to rest last night, and now he had suddenly become a man with a dread secret entrusted to him. A pressing anxiety was on him as to how he should speak to Eli, and a battle raged within his heart between a fear of grieving God by keeping any of it back. He remained still on his bed, quietly meditating and turning over what he had heard, thinking of what he should do. I would to God that all my readers, young and old, after my message, had a quarter of an hour alone. A night of wakeful thought over it would be better still. I am sure that what is needed with our religious reading is time for private thoughts. We put into the mill more than it grinds. Some people imagine that, if they read so many chapters of the Bible every day, it will be much to their profit. But it is not so if the reading is a mere mechanical exercise. It will be far better to read a tenth as much, and weigh it, and let it take possession of brain and heart. A little food cooked is better for dinner than a great joint still raw.

February 16 — MORNING

Draw me not away with the wicked, and with the workers of iniquity, who speak peace to their neighbors, yet evil is in their hearts. Give to them according to their deeds — Psalm 28:3, 4.

"DRAW ME not away with the wicked." They will be dragged off to Hell like felons drawn away to prison, like logs drawn to a fire, like faggots to the oven. David fears lest he should be bound up in their bundle, drawn to their doom. And the fear is appropriate for every godly man. The best of the wicked are dangerous company in time; in eternity they would make terrible companions. We must avoid them in their pleasures if we would not be with them in their miseries. *"And with the workers of iniquity."* These are overtly sinful and their judgment is sure. Lord, do not make us drink of their cup. Activity is found with the wicked even if it is lacking to the righteous.

"Who speak peace to their neighbors, yet evil is in their hearts:" They have learned the manners of the place to which they are going. The doom of liars is their lot forever, and lying is their converse on the road. Soft words, oily with pretended love, are the deceitful meshes of the infernal net in which Satan catches the precious life. Many of his children are learned in his craft, fishing with their father's nets almost as cunningly as he could do it himself. It is a sure sign of baseness when the tongue and the heart do not ring the same note. Deceitful men are to be dreaded more than wild beasts. Better to be shut up in a pit with asps than to be compelled to live with liars. He crying "peace" too loudly means to sell it if he can get his price. If he were so very peaceful he would not need to say so. Be sure that he means mischief.

When we view the wicked simply as such, and not as our fellow men, our indignation against sin leads us entirely to coincide with the acts of Divine justice which punish evil, and to wish that justice might use her power to restrain by her terrors the cruel and unjust. Ungodly reader, what will be your lot when the Lord deals with you according to your deeds, and weighs out to you His wrath, not only in proportion to what you have actually done, but according to what you would have done if you could?

EVENING

If it is so, our God whom we serve is able to deliver us from the burning fiery furnace. And He will deliver us out of your hand, O king — Daniel 3:17.

THEY AVOWED their faith in the Omnipotent God, knowing that, if He chose, no mighty man of Babylon could ever throw them into that furnace. The furnace itself must die down, and become cool as ice, if God so wills it. They tell the tyrant to his face, enveloped as he was in the flame of his wrath, that God can save them out of the fire. Their God was almighty, and they put their trust in Him.

What is more, they add, *"and He will deliver us out of your hand, O king."* Whether they burned in the fire or not, they were sure they would be delivered. "If we die, we will be out of your reach; but we may not die; we may live beyond your reach. You have asked the question, "Who is that God who shall deliver you out of my hands?" And we answer you, *"Our God is able to deliver us out of your hand, O king."*

If any of you are in great difficulty and trouble, tempted to do wrong, and if you do right, it looks as if you will be great losers and great sufferers. Believe this: God can deliver you. He can prevent your having to suffer what you suppose you may, and if He does not prevent it, He can help you to bear it. And in a short time He can turn all your losses into gains, all your sufferings into happiness. He can make the worst thing that can happen to you to be the very best thing that ever did happen to you. If you are serving God, you are serving an omnipotent Being. And that omnipotent Being will not leave you in the time of difficulty, but He will come to your rescue. Many of us can say with Paul, *"We trust not in ourselves, but in God who raised the dead, who delivered us from so great a death"* (2 Corinthians 1:9).

For His anger is only a moment. In His favor is life. Weeping may endure for a night, but joy comes in the morning — Psalm 30:5.

"FOR HIS anger is only a moment:" David alludes to those dispensations of God's providence which His paternal government orders as chastisement of His erring children, such as the plague which fell on Jerusalem for David's sins. These are but short judgments, and they are removed as soon as real penitence pleads for pardon and presents the great and acceptable sacrifice. What a mercy is this, for if the Lord's wrath smoked for a long time flesh would utterly fail before Him. God puts up His rod with great readiness as soon as its work is done. He is slow to anger and swift to end it. If His temporary and fatherly anger is so severe that it must be short, what must be the terror of eternal wrath exercised by the Judge toward His adversaries? *"In His favor is life."* As soon as the Lord looked favorably on David, the city lived, and the king's heart lived too. We die like withered flowers when the Lord frowns, but His sweet smile revives us as the dews refresh the fields. His favor not only sweetens and cheers life; it is life itself, the very essence of life. Let him who would know life seek the Lord's favor.

"Weeping may endure for a night," but nights are not forever. Even in the dreary winter the Daystar lights his lamp. It seems fit that in our nights the dews of grief should fall. When the Bridegroom's absence makes it dark within, it is needful that the widowed soul should pine for a renewed sight of the Well-beloved. *"But joy comes in the morning:"* When the Sun of Righteousness comes, we wipe our eyes and joy chases out intruding sorrow. Who would not be joyful that knows Jesus? The first beams of morning bring us comfort when Jesus is the day dawn, and all believers know it to be so. Mourning only lasts until morning. When the night is gone the gloom will vanish. This is adduced as a reason for saintly singing and forcible reason it is. Short nights and merry days call for the psaltery and harp.

EVENING

Mary said, My soul magnifies the Lord and my spirit exulted in God my Savior — Luke 1:46, 47

I KNOW that my Savior is a man, and I rejoice in His humanity. But we will contend to the death for this, that He is *more* than a man; He is our Savior. One human being could not redeem another, or give to God a ransom for his brother. An angel's arm could not bear the tremendous load of the disaster of the Fall. But Christ's arm is more than angelic. He whom we magnify as our Savior counted it not robbery to be equal with God. And when He undertook the wondrous task of our redemption, He brought the Godhead with Him to sustain Him in the more than herculean labor. Our trust is in Jesus Christ, very God of very God. We shall never cease not only to believe in Him, but to speak of Him, and rejoice in Him, and sing of Him, as the incarnate Deity. What a frozen religion that is which has not the Godhead of Christ in it! Surely they must be men of a very sanguine and imaginative temperament who can pretend to receive any comfort out of a Christianity which has not the divine Savior as its very center. I would as soon think of going to an iceberg to warm myself, as to a faith of that kind to find comfort. Nobody can ever praise up Christ too much for you and for me. They can never say too much of His wisdom, or His power. Every Divine attribute ascribed to Christ makes us lift up a new song to Him. For whatever He may be to others, He is to us God over all, blessed forever.

I wish that I could sing instead of speaking to you of Him who was with the Father before all worlds began, whose delights even then were with the sons of men in prospect of their creation. I wish that I could tell the wonderful story of how He entered into covenant with God on behalf of His people, and pledged Himself to pay the debts of those His father gave to Him.

February 18   MORNING

See what love the Father has given to us, that we should be called the children of God! For this reason the world does not know us, because it did not know Him — 1 John 3:1

WHAT A HIGH relationship is that of a son to his father! What privileges a son has from his father. What liberties a son may take with his father! And oh what obedience the son owes to his father, and what love the father feels toward the son! But all that, and more than that, we now have through Christ. Behold, you angels! Stop, you seraphs! Here is a thing more wonderful than the jasper walls of Heaven. Behold, universe! Open your eyes, O world!

"Beloved, now are we the sons of God:" That is easy to read, but it is not so easy to feel. How is it with your heart, dear reader? Are you in the lowest depths of sorrow and suffering? Does corruption rise within your spirit, and grace seem like a poor spark trampled under foot? Does your faith almost fail you? Are your graces like a candle well nigh blown out by the wind? Fear not, beloved; it is not your graces, it is not your attitudes, it is not your feelings on which you are to live. You must live simply by naked faith on Christ. With all these things against us, with the foot of the Devil on our neck, and the sword in his hand ready to slay us — beloved now in the very depths of our sorrow, wherever we may be — as much in the valley as on the mountain, as much in the dungeon as in the palace, as much when broken on the wheel of suffering as when exalted on the wings of triumph — *"beloved, now we are the sons of God."*

But you say, "See how I am arrayed! My graces are not bright; my righteousness does not shine with apparent glory." But read the next verse: *"It does not yet appear what we shall be. But we know that when He shall appear, we shall be like Him."* We are not so much like Him now, but we have some more refining to undergo, and death itself is yet to wash us clean, then *"we shall be like Him."*

EVENING

The voice of the Lord is on the waters; the God of glory thunders; the Lord is on many waters — Psalm 29:3.

"THE VOICE of the Lord is on the waters." The thunder is not only poetically but instructively called *the voice of God,* since it peals from on high. It surpasses all other sounds, it inspires awe, it is entirely independent of man. It has been used at times as the grand accompaniment of God's speech to Adam's sons. There is a peculiar terror in a tempest at sea, when deep calls to deep, and the raging sea echoes to the angry sky. No sight is more alarming than the flash of lightning around the mast of the ship; no sound is more calculated to inspire a reverent awe than the roar of the storm. The children of Heaven have often enjoyed the tumult with humble joy peculiar to saints, and even those who do not know God have been forced into unwilling reverence while the storm lasted. *"The God of glory thunders:"* Thunder is no mere electric phenomenon, but is caused by the interposition of God Himself. Even the old heathen spake of Jupiter Tonans; but our modern wise men will have us believe in laws and forces and anything or nothing, just so that they may be rid of God. Electricity of itself can do nothing. It must be called and sent on its errand. And until Almighty God commissions it, its bold of fire is inert and powerless. As well might a rock of granite, or a bar of iron, fly in the midst of the heavens, as the lightning to go without it being sent by the great First Cause. *"The Lord is on many waters:"* Still the Psalmist's ear hears no voice but that of Jehovah, resounding from the multitudinous and dark waters of the upper ocean of clouds, and echoing from the innumerable billows of the storm-tossed sea below. The waters above and beneath the firmament are astonished at the ternal voice. When the Holy Spirit makes the Divine promise to be heard above the many waters of our soul's trouble, then is God as glorious in the spiritual world as in the universe of matter. Above us and beneath us all is the peace of God when He gives us quiet.

MORNING

Eli said to Samuel, Go lie down, and if He calls you, you shall say, Speak, Lord, for your servant hears. So Samuel went to lie down in his place — 1 Samuel 3:9.

GOD, in a renewed manner, speaks to us by His word when His Spirit applies it to us individually. We never truly hear the voice of God in Scripture until the truth is spoken home to each heart and conscience by the Holy Spirit. Revelation must be revealed to each one; otherwise it soon comes to be a veiling of the truth, rather than a discovering of the Lord's mind. The revelation is clear enough in itself, but we have not the opened eye until grace bestows it. If we have not the Spirit of God the letter may actually become a veil to hide the Spirit of Truth. Indeed this should not be, nor is it according to its natural intent and tendency. But our depravity makes it so, turning even light itself into a thing which flings. Do you know what it is to have a text leap out of the Scriptures on you, and carry you away? This special energy and flash of truth is always memorable. How often have the waves of this sea of truth been phosphorescent before my eyes, a sea of glass mingled with fire, of which the spray has dashed over me and set my soul on flame! As surely as the Lord spoke these words to Moses, David, Isaiah, John, or to Paul, so surely does He speak them to our souls by His Spirit.

Moreover, our God has ways of communicating His mind to His children by those of His servants who speak in His name. He directs the thoughts of His ministers and suggests their words, so that they speak to the cases of those led to hear the word of God.

By our own thoughts, also, the Lord communes with us. If we will be still before Him, He will prepare our hearts. In silence we will hear His voice. It would be a strange thing if God could not, and did not, communicate with His own children.

EVENING

"Blessed be the Lord, because He has heard the voice of my prayers. The Lord is my strength and my shield. My heart trusted in Him, and I am helped — Psalm 28:6, 7.

"BLESSED be the Lord:" Saints are full of benedictions. They are a blessed people, and a blessing people. But they give their best blessings, the fat of their sacrifices to their glorious Lord. Our Psalm was prayer up to this point, and now it turns to praise. They who pray well will soon praise well. Prayer and praise are the two lips of the soul; two bells to ring out sweet and acceptable music in the ears of God; two angels to climb Jacob's ladder; two altars smoking with incense; two of Solomon's lilies dropping sweet-smelling myrrh. They are two young does that are twins, feeding on the mountain of myrrh and the hill of frankincense. *"Because He has heard the voice of my prayers:"* Real praise is established on sufficient and constraining reasons. It is not irrational emotion, but rises, like a pure spring, from the deeps of experience. Answered prayers should be acknowledged. Do we not often fail in this duty? Would it not greatly encourage others and strengthen ourselves if we faithfully recorded Divine goodness, if we made a point of extolling it with our tongue? God's mercy is not such an inconsiderable thing that we may safely venture to receive it without so much as thanks. Let us shun ingratitude and live daily in the heavenly atmosphere of thankful love.

Here is David's declaration and confession of faith, coupled with a testimony from his expereience, *"The Lord is my strength."* He employs His power for us, and moreover infuses strength into us in our hour of weakness. By an act of appropriating faith David takes the omnipotence of Jehovah to be his own. Dependence on the invisible God gives great independence of spirit, inspiring us with confidence more than human. *"And my shield:"* In this David found both sword and shield in his God. God preserves His people from unnumbered ills. And sheltered behind his God the Christian warrior is far more safe than the hero when covered with his shield of brass or triple steel. *"My heart trusted in Him, and I am helped:"* Heart work is sure work. Heart trust is never disappointed. Faith must come before help, but help will never be long behind.

February 20   MORNING

And Samuel told him all the things, and hid nothing from him. And he said, It is the Lord; let Him do what seems good to Him — 1 Samuel 3:18.

HAVE WE TOLD what we know? That is a practical point. I speak to quite a number of Christians who have to confess, "No, I am like Samuel in that I fear to tell Eli the vision." You were going to speak to the person who sat in the pew with you the other Sunday, and you almost got a word out, but it died on your lips. For idle words you will have to give an account. Parents, you did mean to pray with your child, but you have not done it yet. What if she dies before you have done so? Good friend, you meant to speak to the man at the next bench in your workshop. You have meant to do it so many times. I had a friend, a dear friend, who now I trust is in Heaven. And there was a man who used to take orders from him for goods, and bring them to him when finished. he was a good and punctual workman, but not a Christian man. Well, my friend intended (for years he intended) to have a quiet conversation with that workman about his soul. One day the goods came in, but a woman brought them. She said, "I am So-and-so's wife. He finished these goods, but he is dead." My friend said that the words were like a bullet to his heart. For he had so often thought of the man, and often said to himself, "I must and I will speak to him the next time he calls," but somehow, when he came into the shop, business was brisk, and he looked over the goods and paid for them as quickly as he could. He never began that conversation. Now the man was beyond the reach of warning or instruction. Do not let it be so with any person with whom you come in contact. Do as Samuel did. Tell the whole of it if they ask you to tell them, or if they do not ask you to tell them. Those who do not ask you are probably those who have the most need of your efforts.

EVENING

That which has born of the flesh is flesh. And that which has been born of the Spirit is spirit — John 3:6.

NOT ONE among us has received the gospel by birthright. We may be children of holy parents, but we are not by this the children of God. To us it is clear that *"that which is born of the flesh is flesh,"* and nothing more. Only *"that which is born of the Spirit is spirit."* Yet we hear of persons whose children do not need conversion. They are spoken of as being free from natural corruption, and born children of God, having a grace within which only needs to be developed. I am sorry to say that my father did not find me such a child. He found out early in my life that I was born in sin, and shaped in iniquity, and that folly was bound up in my heart. Friends and teachers soon perceived in me a natural depravity. And assuredly I have found it in myself. The sad discovery needed no very minute research, for the effect of the evil stared me in the face in my character. This tradition as to our being born with a holy nature is gaining foothold in the professing church, even thought it is contrary to Scripture, and even contrary to the confessions of faith which are still avowedly maintained. Certain preachers hardly dare formulate it as a doctrine. But it is with them a kind of chaotic belief that there may be productions of the flesh which are very superior, which will serve well enough without the new birth of the Spirit. This tacit belief will lead up to the birthright membership, and that is fatal to any Christian community, wherever it comes to be the rule. Without conversion, in certain fellowships, the young people drift into the church as a matter of course. Then the church becomes only a part of the world, with the Christian name affixed to it. May we never in our churches sink into that condition! That religion which is a mere family appendage is of little worth. The true seed as *"born, not of blood, nor of the will of the flesh, nor of the will of man, but of God."*

February 21 — MORNING

Shadrach, Meshach and Abednego answered and said to the king, O Nebuchadnezzar, we are not careful to answer you in this matter — Daniel 3:16.

THEY said, *"We are not careful to answer you in this matter."* The word careful there does not give the meaning. Read it, *"We are not full of care as to how to answer you."* They answered very carefully, but they were not anxious about the answer. It was not a thing that troubled them. They knew what they were going to say. They did not deliberate, nor hesitate, saying, "Nebuchadnezzar, we can answer you at once on that point." They were so calm, so self-controlled; they could talk to him not as a king, but as Nebuchadnezzar. When it came to life-work it was man to man, Shadrach, Meshach, Abednego to Nebuchadnezzar; they had no difficulty in answering him.

They did not judge it theirs to answer at all. I find that it may be read, "Nebuchadnezzar, "We have no need to answer you on this matter" (see in *A Literal Translation of the Bible*—Ed.). It is not for us to answer. You have brought another Person into the quarrel." Let me read the preceding words. Nebuchadnezzar said to them, *"Who is the God that will deliver you out of my hands?"* In effect, the three replied, *"It is not for us to answer you.* There is Another that will do that. You have challenged God, and God will make His own reply." It was bravely spoken. They threw the onus of this matter on God Himself. So may you. If you will do right, it is God's affair to see you through. You have nothing to do with the consequences, except patiently to bear them. The consequences must be with God. You do what is right. Believe in the Lord Jesus Christ, obey Him, and keep the command of the Most High, and then whatever comes of it, it is no blame of yours. That must be left to God.

EVENING

O Lord, You have brought up my soul from the grave; You have kept me alive, so that I should not go down to the pit. Sing to the Lord, O you saints of His, and give thanks at the memory of His holiness — Psalm 30:3, 4.

"O LORD, You have brought up my soul from the grave:" Mark, it is not, "I hope so," but it is, "You have; You have; You have" three times over. David is quite sure, beyond a doubt, that God has done great things for him, of which he is exceedingly glad. He had descended to the brink of the sepulchre, and yet was restored to tell of the forbearance of God. Nor was this all: he acknowledges that nothing but grace had kept him from the lowest hell, and this made him doubly thankful. To be spared from the grave is much, but to be delivered from the pit is more. Thus, there is a growing cause to praise, since both deliverances are alone traceable to the glorious right hand of the Lord, who alone preserves life; He alone is the Redeemer of our souls from Hell.

"Sing to the Lord, O you saints of His." Join my song; assist me to express my gratitude. He felt that he could not praise God enough by himself, and so he would enlist the hearts of others. David would not fill his choir with reprobates, but with saints who could sing from their hearts. He calls to you, you people of God, because you are saints; and if sinners are wickedly silent, let your holiness constrain you to sing. You are His saints, chosen, blood bought, called, and set apart for God, sanctified on purpose that you might offer the daily sacrifice of praise. Abound in this heavenly duty. *"Sing to the Lord."* It is a pleasing exercise and a profitable engagement. Do not need to be stirred up so often to so pleasant a service. *"And give thanks:"* Let your songs be grateful songs, in which the Lord's mercies shall live again in joyful remembrance. The very remembrance of the past should tune our harps, even if present joys are lacking. *"At the memory of His holiness:"* Holiness is an attribute which inspires the deepest awe, and it demands a reverent mind. But still give thanks at the remembrance of it. *"Holy, holy, holy!"* is the song of seraphs and cherubs. Let us join it not dolefully, as though we trembled at the holiness of God, but cheerfully, as humbly rejoicing in it.

February 22 — MORNING

If it is so, our God whom we serve is able to deliver us from the burning fiery furnace. And He will deliver us out of your hand, O king — Daniel 3:17.

LET US WALK in this heroic path. But some will say, "It is too hard. You cannot expect men to love God well enough to die for Him." No, but there was One who loved us well enough to die for us, and to die a thousand deaths in one, that He might save us. If Christ so loved us, we ought so to love Him. One says, "Well, I think it is impossible. I could not bear pain." It is possible, for many have endured it. I remember that one of the martyrs, who was to be burned the following morning, thought that he would try himself: There being a large fire in the cell, he put his foot into it to see whether he could bear to have it burned, but soon shrank back. In doing that he was foolish, for when he went out the next morning to stand on the faggots and burn, he stood like a man and burned bravely to the death, for his Master's sake. The fact was, his Lord did not call him to burn his foot in the stove, and so He did not help him to bear it. But when He called him to give his whole body to the flames, then grace was given.

There is a story of a martyred woman who had a child born to her a few days before she was burned. Being in great pain, she cried aloud. One said to her, "If you cannot bear this, what will you do when you come to burn?" She said, "Now you see the pains of nature which befall a woman, and I have not patience enough to bear them. But by and by you shall see Christ in His members suffering, and you shall see what patience He will have, and what patience He will give to me." It is recorded of her that she seemed as if she had no pain at all when she yielded herself up to Christ. Do not judge by what you are today, what you would be like if you were called into trouble. Grace would be given you. I have no doubt that many of the most timid of those who truly love the Lord would be the very bravest.

EVENING

And He will deliver us out of your hand, O king. But if not, let it be known to you, O king, that we will not serve your gods or worship the golden image which you have set up. — Daniel 3:17, 18.

WE MUST HAVE a deep sense of the Divine law. *"You shall have no other gods before Me. You shall not make to you any graven image, or any likeness of anything that is in Heaven above, or that is in the earth beneath, or that is in the water under the earth. You shall not bow down yourself to them, nor serve them; for I am Jehovah your God, a jealous God"* (Exod. 20:3-5 LTB). No, not to a 'Virgin Mary,' a cross, a crucifix, a picture, an image. Revere no visible object; instead worship God. Put all other things away. For this reason Shadrach, Meshach and Abednego, feeling that God was near, and knowing what the law of God was, they dared not violate the law, but would sooner die.

Above all, to keep us right, we must have a mighty sense of the Divine love. Until we have new hearts we will never obey God. Those hearts must be full of love to Him through Jesus Christ. Then, if you love Him, you will say, "What! Put an image of gold in His place? Never! Join the multitude in worshiping a colossal statue instead of the invisible Jehovah? Never!" With holy indignation you will choose the furnace of fire, than have that purer flame which glows in your heart quenched, or made to burn dimly.

To some of you this must seem very trifling, because you say, "I do not care about religious forms and ceremonies. Let me enjoy myself while I am here; it is all that I ask." Well, you have made your bargain, and a sorry one it is. If this life is all, how ought a person to live? I am sure I cannot tell you. Perhaps the wisest thing of all is, *"Let us eat, and drink, for tomorrow we die."* But there is another world, and a life beyond the grave, and it is sometimes incomparably wise to fling this life away that we may win the life eternal.

MORNING

And Mary said, My soul glorifies the Lord, and my spirit has rejoiced in God my Savior — Luke 1:46, 47.

LET US BLESS God that our religion is not one of gloom. I do not know of any command in Scripture which implies that we should "groan in the Lord always." From the conduct of some people we might almost imagine that they must have altered their New Testament in that particular passage, and so woefully changed the glory of the original verse, *"Rejoice in the Lord always; and again I say, Rejoice."* The first I truly knew of Christ my Master was when I found myself at the foot of His cross, with the great burden that had crushed me effectually removed. I wondered where it could be, and, behold! It was tumbling down into His sepulchre! I have never seen it since, blessed be His name, nor do I ever want to see it again. Well do I remember the leaps I gave for joy when I first found that all my burden of guilt had been borne by Him, and was not buried in the depths of His grave. Whenever I have gone to this well — *"my God, my savior"* — I have never drawn one drop that was not sweet and refreshing. One who truly knows God must be glad in Him. To abide in His house is to be still praising Him. We may exult in Him all the day long. A very notable word is that found in David's mouth: *"God, my exceeding joy."* Other things may give us pleasure. We may be happy in the gifts of God, and in His creatures, but God Himself, the spring of all our joys, is greater than them all. Then, *"Delight yourself also in the Lord."* This is His command, and a loved one. Let no one say that the faith of the Christian is not to be exultant. It is to be a delight. So greatly does God desire us to rejoice in Him, that to the command is added a promise, *'And He will give you the desires of your heart."*

EVENING

For You are my rock and my fortress. For Your name's sake lead me and guide me — Psalm 31:3.

"FOR YOU ARE my rock and my fortress:" Here the tried soul avows yet again its full confidence in God. Faith's repetitions are not vain. The avowal of our reliance on God in times of adversity is a principal method of glorifying Him. Active service is good, but the passive confidence of faith is not one jot less esteemed in the sight of God. The words before us appear to embrace and fasten on the Lord with a grip which is not to be relaxed. The two personal pronouns, like sure nails, lay hold on the faithfulness of the Lord. O for grace to have our heart fixed in firm, unstaggering unbelief in God! The figures of a rock and a fortress may be illustrated to us in these times by the vast fortress of Gibraltar, often besieged by our enemies, but never wrested from us. Ancient strongholds, although far from impregnable by our modes of warfare, were equally important in those more remote ages — when in the mountain fastnesses feeble bands felt themselves to be secure. Note the singular fact that David asked the Lord to be his rock because he was his rock. Learn from it that we may pray to enjoy in experience what we grasp by faith. Faith is the foundation of prayer.

"For Your name's sake lead me and guide me:" The Psalmist argues like a logician with his fors and therefores. "Since I do sincerely trust You," he says, "O my God, be my director." To lead and to guide are two things very like each other, but patient thought will detect different shades of meaning, especially as the last may mean to provide for me. The double word indicates an urgent need — we require double direction, for we are fools, and the way is rough. Lead me as a soldier, guide me as a traveler. Lead me as a babe, guide me as a man. Lead me by Your hand; guide me by Your word. The argument used is one which is fetched from the armory of free grace: Not for my own sake, but for Your name's sake, guide me. Our appeal is not to any fancied virtue in our own name, but to the glorious goodness and graciousness which shine resplendent in the character of Israel's God.

February 24   MORNING   55

He who wins souls is wise — Proverbs 11:30.

THE TEXT does not say, "He who wins sovereigns is wise," although no doubt he who thinks thus may think himself wise; in a groveling sense in these competitive days he may be thought so. But such wisdom is of the earth, and it ends with the earth. There is another world where the currencies of Europe will not be accepted, nor their past possession be any sign of wealth or wisdom. Solomon, in the text before us, awards no crown for wisdom to crafty statesmen, or even to the ablest rulers. He issues no diplomas even to philosophers, poets, or men of wit. He crowns only those who win souls. He does not declare that he who preaches is necessarily wise — and alas! There are multitudes who preach, and gain much applause and eminence, who win no souls, such will find it that it will go hard with them at the last. For in all probability they have run, and the Master has not sent them. He does not say that he who talks about winning souls is wise, since to lay down rules for others is a very simple thing, but to carry them out one's self is far more difficult. He who actually and truly turns men from the error of their ways to God, and so is made the means of saving them from going down to Hell, is a wise man. That is true of him whatever his style of soul-winning may be. He may be a Paul: deeply logical, profound in doctrine, able to command all candid judgments; and if he thus wins souls he is wise. He may be an Apollos: grandly rhetorical, whose lofty genius soars into the very heaven of eloquence; and if he wins souls in that way he is wise, but not otherwise. Or he may be a Cephas: rough and rugged, using uncouth metaphor and stern declamation; but if he wins souls he is no less wise than his polished brother or his argumentative friend, but not else. The great wisdom of soul-winners, according to the text, is proven only by their actual success in really winning souls.

EVENING

He who wins souls is wise — Proverbs 11:30.

HOW DO we win souls, then? Why, the word *win* has a better meaning. It is used in warfare. Warriors win cities and provinces. Now to win a soul is a much more difficult thing than to win a city. Observe the earnest soul-winner at his work: How cautiously he seeks his great Captain's directions, to know when to hang out the white flag to invite the heart to surrender to the sweet love of a Savior who died for sinners. And when, at the proper time, to hang out the black flag of threatening, showing that if grace is not received, judgment will surely follow. And when to unfurl, with dread reluctance, the red flag of terrors of God against stubborn, impenitent souls. The soul-winner has to sit down before a soul as a great captain before a walled town. He must draw his lines, cast up his intrenchments, fix his batteries, etc. He must not advance too fast; he may overdo the fighting. He must not move too slowly, for he may seem not to be in earnest, and may do mischief. Then he must know which gate to attack, how to plant his guns at Ear-gate, and how to discharge them. He must know how to keep the batteries going day and night, with red-hot shot, if perhaps he may make a breach in the walls. At other times he must lay by and cease; then, all of a sudden, he must open up all the batteries with terrific violence, if perhaps he may take the soul by surprise, or cast in a truth when it was not expected, to burst like a shell in the soul and so damage the dominions of sin. The Christian soldier must know how to advance by little and little — to sap that prejudice, to undermine that old enmity, to blow into the air that lust; and at the last to storm the citadel. Our object is to turn the world upside down, so that where sin abounded grace may much more abound. We are aiming at a miracle. I command men in the name of Jesus to repent and believe the gospel, though I know they can do nothing apart from the miraculous infusion of the grace of God.

MORNING

He who wins souls is wise — Proverbs 11:30.

HE WILL SUCCEED best, who keeps closest to soul-saving truth. Now, all truth is not soul-saving, even though all truth may be edifying. He who keeps to the simple story of the cross, who will tell men over and over again that whoever believes in Christ is not condemend, and that to be saved Nothing is needed but a simple trust in the crucified Redeemer — that one whose ministry is much made up of the glorious story of the cross, the sufferings of the sacrificial Lamb, the mercy of God, the willingness of the great Father to receive returning prodigals — in fact, he who cries day after day, *"Behold the Lamb of God who takes away the sin of the world,"* is likely to be a soul-winner. This is especially so if he adds to this much prayer for souls, much anxious desire that men may be brought to Jesus; if he in his private life seeks as much as in his public ministry to be telling out to others of the love of the dear Savior of men.

But I am not talking to ministers, but to you who sit in the pew. Therefore let me turn myself more directly to you. Brothers and sisters, you have different gifts. I hope you use them all. Perhaps some of you, although members of the church, think you have no gifts. But every believer has his gift, and his portion of work. What can you do to win souls? Let me recommend to those who think they can do nothing, this, that they bring others to hear the Word. That is a duty much neglected. Many of you attend places which are not perhaps half-filled. Fill them. Do not grumble at the small congregation, but make it larger. Take somebody with you to the very next sermon, and at once the congregation will be increased. Go up with the prayer that your minister's sermon may be blessed. Thank God that our labors are not in vain in the Lord. I believe that the most of you who have really tried, in the power of the Holy Spirit, by Scriptural teaching and by prayer, to bring others to Jesus, have succeeded.

EVENING

He who wins souls is wise — Proverbs 11:30.

THE SOUL-WINNER must be a master of the art of prayer. You cannot bring souls to God if you do not go to God yourself. You must get your battle-axe and your weapons of war from the armory of sacred communion with Christ. If you are much alone with Jesus you will catch His Spirit. You will be fired with the flame that burned in His breast, and consumed His life. You will weep with the tears that fell on Jerusalem when He saw it perishing. And if you cannot speak so eloquently as He did, yet there shall be about what you say somewhat of the same power which in Him thrilled the hearts and awoke the consciences of men. My dear readers, I am always so anxious lest any of you should begin to lie on your oars, taking things easy in the matters of God's kingdom. If you were all firebrands for Christ, you might set the nation ablaze. If you were all wells of living water, how many thirsty souls might drink and be refreshed!

One more thing you can do. If some of you feel you cannot do much personally, you can always help the Christian colleges. There it is that we find tongues for the dumb. Our young men are called out by God to preach. We give them some little education and training, and then away they go, preaching the Word. And it is often, it must be often, a consolation to some of you to think that if you have not spoken with your own tongue, as you could desire, you have at least spoken by the tongues of others, so that through the word of God has been sounded abroad throughout all this region.

Try after the sermon to talk to strangers. The preacher may have missed the mark, but you need not miss it. You may be able to make the impression deeper by a kind word. If you cannot preach to a hundred, preach to one.

February 26   MORNING

But now in Christ Jesus; you who were at one time far off are made near by the blood of Christ — Ephesians 2:13.

ALL THE ELECT OF GOD are in Christ Jesus by a federal union. He is their head ordained of old to be so from before the foundation of the world. As Adam was the federal head of the race, and as in him all of us fell, so Christ, the second Adam, stands as the head of the chosen people. And in Him they rise again and live. This federal union leads in due time, by the grace of God, to a manifest and vital union of life, and for life, even unto eternal life, of which the visible bond is faith. The soul comes to Jesus and lays hold on Him by an act of faith, because Jesus has already laid hold on that soul by the power of His Spirit, claiming it to be His heritage, since He has bought it with His blood, and His Father has given it to Him as the reward of the travail of His soul. All who are in Christ Jesus in the eternal covenant of grace shall in due time be in Him by the living union of which we now speak — mystical and mysterious, but still most real, most true, and most efficient. Now, beloved, when a soul becomes really in Christ, as the branch is in the vine, and when it draws its nourishment from the stem, as the limb is in the body, and derives all its vitality from the central heart — when a man thus becomes one with Christ, it is clear to the common observer that he must be near to God. For Christ is ever near to God, and those who are one with Him must also be near to God. Jesus is Himself God; here is nearness outdone. As man He is without spot or blemish, and near to God in character. As having finished the work which God had given Him to do, He is near to God in acceptance. As having gone up to Heaven to take the promised crown, He is near to God in person. And since we are one with Him we must be from that very fact near to God, as near to God as Christ Himself is.

EVENING

But now in Christ Jesus; you who were at one time far off are made near by the blood of Christ — Ephesians 2:13.

THE OTHER key-word of the text is *"by the blood of Christ."* If it is asked what power lies in the blood to bring near, it must be answered: First, that the blood is the symbol of the covenant. Always in Scripture when covenants are made, victims are offered, and the victim becomes the place and ground of approach between the two covenanting parties. The blood of our Lord Jesus Christ is expressly called *"the blood of the everlasting covenant,"* for God comes in covenant near to us by the blood of His only begotten Son. Every man whose faith rests on the blood of Jesus slain from before the foundation of the world is in covenant with God. And that covenant becomes to him most sure and certain because it has been ratified by the blood of Jesus Christ, and therefore can never be changed or disannulled.

The blood brings us near in another sense, because it is the taking away of the sin which separated us. When we read the word *blood* as in the text, it means mortal suffering. We are made near by the griefs and agonies of the Redeemer. The shedding of blood indicates pain, loss of energy, health, comfort, happiness. But it goes farther still; the term *blood* signifies death. It is the death of Jesus in which we trust. We glory in His life; we triumph in His resurrection; but the ground of our nearness to God lies in His death. The term *blood* also signifies not a mere expiring, but a painful and ignominious and penal death. A death not brought about by the decay of nature, or the arrows of disease, but caused by the sharp sword of Divine vengeance. The word, in fact, refers directly to the crucifixion of our Lord. We are brought near to God specially and particularly by a crucified Savior pouring out His life's blood for us.

But now in Christ Jesus; you who were at one time far off are made near by the blood of Christ — Ephesians 2:13.

THERE ARE some teachers (and I doubt not very excellent men, too) who seem not to be of Paul's mind when he said, *"God forbid that I should glory, except in the cross of our Lord Jesus Christ,"* and who resolved to know nothing among men *"but Jesus Christ, and Him crucified."* These men are incessantly preaching concerning Christ glorified, a valuable truth, but not the way of a sinner's access to God. Christ's second coming was never intended to take the place of Christ's crucifixion, and yet there have been some who in their zeal for the very great and important truth of the coming glory have allowed the blazing light of the second advent to obscure the milder radiance, and the more healing beams of the first advent, with its bloody sweat, its scourge, and thorn-crown, and ransom price for sinners lost. Let it be never forgotten that while we bless Immanuel, God with us, for His incarnation, and we joyfully perceive that even our Lord's birth in human flesh brought man near to God; while we thank and praise the Man of Sorrows for His divine example, and we see that this is a blessed help to us practically to advance toward our heavenly Father — while we praise and magnify the Lord Jesus for His resurrection and His ascension, and discern in each glorious step fresh rounds of the ladder which leads from earth to Heaven — yet still we are not made nigh to God by the incarnation; we are not made nigh to God by the resurrection, nor by the second advent, but we are made near by the blood of Christ. The first, the grandest, the most essential truth for us to lay hold if and to preach is the fact that Jesus Christ died for our sakes according to the Scriptures. And this is a *faithful saying and worthy of all acceptation, that Christ Jesus came into the world to save sinners,* and He gave Himself up to die for sinners, the Just for the unjust, to bring us to God. God is glorified because Christ was punished for the sin of His people.

EVENING

But now in Christ Jesus; you who were at one time far off are made near by the blood of Christ — Ephesians 2:13.

LOVE HAS its full, but law has its due. On the cross we see sin fully punished and yet fully pardoned. We see justice with her gleaming sword triumphant, and mercy with her silver sceptre regnant in sublimest splendor. Glory be to the wondrous wisdom which discovered the way of blending vengeance with love, make a tender heart to be the mirror of unflinching severity, causing the crystal vase of Jesus' loving nature to be filled with the red wine of righteous wrath.

Beloved, by this you see that we are made near because the blood of Christ has sealed a covenant between us and God, and has forever taken away the sin which separated us from God. Experimentally, we are brought near by the application of the blood to our conscience. We see that sin is pardoned, and we bless the God who has saved us in so admirable a manner. Then we who hated Him before come to love Him; we who had no thought toward Him desire to be like Him. We are experimentally and in our own souls drawn and attracted to God by the blood of Jesus. The great attracting loadstone of the gospel is the doctrine of the cross. To preach the atoning sacrifice of Jesus is the shortest and surest way, under God's Holy Spirit, to draw those that are far off, mentally and spiritually, very near to God.

If we are so near to God, it follows as a very natural exhortation that we should exercise much faith in Him. If I am indeed brought so near to God, why should I be afraid that He will leave me in poverty? Why, my name is on the palms of Jesus' hands. I live in Jesus' heart. And I live, if I am in Christ, under the very eye of God. He will keep me as He keeps the apple of His eye.

Then we shall know, if we follow on to know the Lord, His going forth is prepared as the morning; and He shall come to us as the rain, as the latter and former rain to the earth — Hosea 6:3.

IT IS our solemn conviction that the gifts and calling of God are without repentance; that wherever the Lord bestows spiritual life and salvation He never recalls the gift; that it is not His way to play fast and loose with the sons of men, to give today and to retract tomorrow. We enjoy the doctrine of final perseverance, and we cannot think how anyone can doubt it.

We are persuaded of the immutable love of God toward His children. But mark that the connection of the text leads us to observe the fact that the constancy of God to His people is not occasioned by their constancy to Him. For Ephraim and Judah, of whom this text was written, were the most fickle and inconstant of people. They were as unstable as water toward their God. He accuses them: *"Israel slides back as a backsliding heifer;" "Ephraim is oppressed and broken in judgment because he willingly walked after the commandment"* — that is, the evil commandment of heathen kings. All through the book of Hosea there are exhortations to repentance and returning from backsliding. Then if God remained faithful toward such a people it was not because they remained faithful to Him. Actually wherever there is in any Christian a holy patience and a diligent perseverance, this is the work of God in his soul, and is worked in him by the faithful grace and abiding presence of God. It is not our faithfulness which holds God to His promise, but it is God's faithfulness which holds us near Him. Ah, Lord! If Your love should hang on our poor love, which is as a rusted nail driven into rotten wood, our salvation would soon fail. But when we hang on your faithfulness in Christ Jesus, how safe we are! If one single stone of the entire fabric of our salvation had to be quarried out of our carnal nature, it could never be found, for our whole nature is as a miry place, a quagging bog, in which nothing stable can be discovered. Beloved, although we do not believe, God remains faithful.

EVENING

And we all received of His fulness and grace on top of grace — John 1:16.

IF UP UNTIL NOW we have received out of Christ's fulness, then let us go to Him again. As you have received Christ Jesus the Lord, so walk in Him. I find it my best and safest way, and I recommend it to you all, to live daily in Christ, as when you first trusted Him. If I have ever known Him at all, if He has ever been revealed to me and in me, if He has ever answered my prayers, if He has ever blessed me to your souls and made me the spiritual parent of any that are in the skies, I do know that I had it all from Him. For I never had a grain of anything good of my own, but all my grace has been the free grant of His sovereign will. But the Devil says, "Ah, but you never knew Jesus!" Well, if I never did, I know what to do now. I will go to Jesus at once. If I never did go to Him before, I will hasten to Him now. When I go to Jesus Christ in that way, not as a saint, but as a sinner, not as a preacher, but as a poor, miserable offender, I find my comfort return to me. I would like to be as a baby, always hanging on the breast of Jesus' love. I would like to be always locked up in Christ's battery, never to live on what I had before fed on, but feeding evermore. To this duty I invite you. If you have received, come and receive again. You have not received the whole of Christ's fulness yet. But all that is in Christ is meant to be received. Jesus Christ is like the sun; He is a storehouse of light, but the light is there to be shed abroad. He is like the clouds, a storehouse of waters, but all that is in Him is to descend in showers upon the thirsty souls. There is nothing in Christ but what was meant to be distributed.

And we all received of His fulness, and grace on top of grace — John 1:16.

BELOVED in the Lord, if you and I would receive of the fulness of Christ, it is imperatively necessary that we should have an experience of our own emptiness. All saints receive of Christ, but no vessel can receive beyond the measure of its emptiness. The more full it is, so much the less is its capacity for reception, and the more empty it is, so much the greater the space which can be filled. This is a hard lesson for human nature, for we firmly believe in ourselves. You say, "I am rich and increased in goods, and have need of nothing;" we learn this with our mother tongue. And we repeat it so often that we believe it. Like the Pharisee, we make it our daily boast, *"God, I thank You that I am not as other men are."* The Pharisee would see no chaff in his wheat, whereas grace makes us to be like the publican, who could see no wheat in his chaff. He could only say, *"God, be merciful to me, a sinner."* It is hard going down the ladder of self-knowledge. We give up with great reluctance our flattering opinions of ourselves. We are hard to empty of the notion of our own inherent merit. And if the Lord spills that on the ground, we then hold to the idea of our own inherent strength. What if we have no merit, yet at least we will have some by and by; and we spin out our poor resolves as freely as a spider spins her web, and the fabric is as frail. And if our notion of power is taken from us, we then devote ourselves to our self-justification, by endeavoring to persuade ourselves that we are not responsible; or by wrapping ourselves in despair, we declare that we cannot help ourselves, and wickedly cast our ruin on destiny. Man is hard to be dragged away from the rock of self-justification. Like Theseus in the old mythology, he is glued fast to the great stone of self-conceit which lies hard by the gates of Hell; and a stronger than Hercules is needed to tear him from it; and even such a deliverer must rend him from it, leaving the skin behind.

EVENING

Come and let us return to the Lord. For He has torn, and He will heal us. He has stricken, and He will bind us up — Hosea 6:1.

THE FAITHFULNESS of God to His people does not always show itself in the most pleasing ways. The first verse tells us that God had torn and smitten His people, and the last verse of the former chapter represents the Lord as saying, *"I will go and return to My place."* A father's love does not always reveal itself in kisses and gifts. Love often has to force itself to blows and stripes, and those black love-token which blossom on the rod of chastisement are the true proofs of a father's kindness as the soft blandishment and sweet endearments which at other times He lavishly scatters. Our God does not indulge His people with constant prosperity, lest they drown in the river of worldliness. His beloved are often plunged into troubles: *"Many are the afflictions of the righteous,"* and their troubles are not only outward; the iron enters into their soul also. We who have believed have our deep-sea sorrows, and our downcastings, when every wave and billow goes over us. We smart under dreadful desertions. Some have had to cry with the Master on the cross, *"My God, My God, why have You forsaken Me?"* We know why He has hidden from us, because we have forsaken Him. He has hidden the light of His countenance from us until we could scarcely believe ourselves to be His children at all. We have turned to prayer and found words and even desires fail us when on our knees. We have searched the Scriptures with no consolatory result; every text of Scripture has looked black on us; every promise blockaded its ports against us.

In love and tenderness God often seems to deal hardly with His children. He does not always show His immutable love to His people in the way which they might select. His wine is not sent to us always in golden flagons, nor His apples of love in baskets of gold. Good comes in a chariot of fire, and mercy rides on the pale horse.

March 1   MORNING   61

The heavens declare the glory of God — Psalm 19:1.

THE EMINENT SAINTS of ancient times were watchful observers of the objects and operations of nature. In every event they saw the agency of God. Therefore, they took delight in examining it. For they could not but receive pleasure from witnessing the manifestations of God's wisdom and beneficence. They had not learned, as we have sadly learned in modern times, to interpose unbending laws between the Creator and His works — then by giving inherent power to these laws, to move God away from His creation into an ethereal sphere of repose. Though not extensively held in the church, such a view prevails in many today. The great mass of the community, and even of Christians, are still groping in the darkness, ascribing the operations of the natural world to nature's laws instead of nature's God.

But how different were the feelings of the ancient saints. With the psalmist they could not look up to the heavens without exclaiming, *"The heavens declare the glory of God, and the firmament shows His handiwork."* Casting his eyes on the earth, his full heart cried out, *"O Lord, how manifold are Your works! In wisdom You have made them all; the earth is full of Your riches."* In the eye of the knowledgeable Christian, everything is full of God. It is God who *"sent springs into the valleys."* When the thunderstorm passes, it is *"God's voice in the heavens,"* it is *His lightnings that light the world."* The bellowings and the smoke of the volcano are caused by *"God who looks on the earth, and it trembles. He touches the hills and they smoke."* (Edward Hitchcock, 1867).

EVENING

The heavens declare the glory of God — Psalm 19:1.

These are Thy glorious works, parent of good,
Almighty! Thine this universal frame,
Thus wondrous fair; Thyself how wondrous, then!
Unspeakable, who sitt'st above these heavens
To us invisible, or dimly seen
In these Thy lowest works; yet these declare
Thy goodness beyond thought, and power divine.
— John Milton

How beautiful this dome of sky,
And the vast hills in fluctuation fixed
At Thy command, how awesome! Shall the soul,
Human and rational, report of Thee
Even less than these? Be mute who will, who can
Yet I will praise Thee with impassioned voice.
My lips, that may forget Thee in the crowd,
Cannot forget Thee here, where Thou hast built
For Thine own glory, in the wilderness!
— William Wordsworth

MORNING

The law of the Lord is perfect, converting the soul — Psalm 19:7.

"TO FALLEN MAN the law only convinces of sin, and binds over to death; it is a killing letter. But accompanied by the power of the Spirit the gospel brings life. Again, it is said, *"The law of the Lord is perfect, converting the soul"* — so it seems the law may also be a word of salvation to the creature. I answer: The law there is not meant only that part of the word which we call the covenant of works. There it is put for the whole word, for the whole doctrine of the covenant of life and salvation — as in Psalm 1:2, *"His delight is in the law of the Lord; and in His law he meditates day and night."* And if you take it in the stricter sense, then it converts the soul by accident, as it is joined with the gospel, which is the mystery of life and righteousness, but in itself it is the law of sin and death. Look, as a thing taken simply may be poisonous and deadly in itself, yet if it is mixed with other wholesome medicines it may be of great use, may prove to be an excellent physical ingredient. So with the law; it is of great use as joined with the gospel, efficient to awaken and startle the sinner, to show him his duty, to convince him of sin and judgment; but it is the gospel which properly pulls in the heart — Thomas Manton.

EVENING

Making wise the simple — Psalm 19:7.

THE APOSTLE PAUL in Ephesians 1:8 expresses conversion, and the whole work inherently worked in us, by the making of a man wise. It is usual in the Scriptures, and you may oftentimes meet with it: *"converting the soul"* — *"making wise the simple."* The beginning of conversion, and so all along, the increase of all grace to the end, is expressed by wisdom entering into a man's heart — *"if wisdom enter into your heart"* — and so goes on to do more and more; not only to your head — a man may have all that, and be a fool in the end — but when it enters into the heart and draws all the affections after it, and along with it, *"when knowledge is pleasant to your soul,"* then man is converted. It is when God breaks open a man's heart and makes wisdom fall in, enter in, and make a man wise — Thomas Goodwin.

"sweeter than honey and the honeycomb" — "Love the word written (Ps. 119:97): *"Oh how I love Your law!"* Augustine said, "Lord, let the holy Scriptures be my chaste delight." Chrysostom compares the Scripture to a garden, every truth is a fragrant flower which we should wear in our heart, not in our bosom. David counted the word *'sweeter than honey and the honeycomb.'* There is that in Scripture which may breed delight. It shows us the way to riches (Deut. 28:5; Prov. 3:10;) to long life (Ps. 34:12;) to a kingdom (Heb., 12:28). Well, then, may we count those the sweetest hours which are spent in reading the holy Scriptures. Well may we say with the prophet, *'Your words were found, and I ate them, and they were the joy and rejoicing of my heart'* (Jer. 15:16)" — Thomas Manton.

MORNING

Cleanse me from secret faults — Psalm 19:12.

"IT IS THE DESIRE of a holy person to be cleansed, not only from public sins, but also from private and secret sins. The apostle Paul cries out, *'O wretched man that I am, who shall deliver me from the body of this death?'* (Rom. 7:24). "O blessed apostle, what is it that holds you? What is it that disturbs you? Your life was unblamable before your conversion (you said,) and since your conversion, too (Phil. 3). You have exercised yourself to have always a conscience void of offence toward God and toward men (Acts 24:16). And yet you cry out, *'O wretched man;'* and yet you complain, *'who shall deliver me?'* Truly, brothers, sisters, it was not sin abroad, but sin at home. It was not sin without, but at this time sin within. It was not Paul's sinning with man, but Paul's sinning within Paul. He calls it the *'law of his members warring* (secretly within him) *against the law of his mind.'* It was this that made that holy man cry out and to complain so. It was the private and secret birth of corruption within Paul — the workings of that — that was the cause of his trouble; that was the ground of his exclamation, and of his desires to be delivered. It was Paul that advised the Ephesians *'to put off the former behavior, which had been corrupted according to the deceitful lusts,'* and *'to put on the renewed spirit of the mind'* (Eph. 4:22,23). He intimates that there are sins lurking within us, as well as sins walking about. True Christians must not only sweep the door, but wash the inner rooms. Do not only come off from sins which lie open in the conduct and conversation, but also labor to be cleansed from sins and sinning which remain secret and hidden in the spirit and inward disposition" — Obadiah Sedgwick.

EVENING

Cleanse me from secret faults — Psalm 19:12.

BEWARE of committing sins which it will be necessary to conceal. Guilt is a grim companion, even when the fingers are not bloody red. Secret sins bring fevered eyes and sleepless nights, until men burn out their consciences and become ripe for the pit. Hypocrisy is a hard game to play, for it is one deceiver against many observers. It is a miserable trade which at last will earn as its certain climax a tremendous bankruptcy. Ah, you think you have sinned without discovery. *'Be sure your sin will find you out."* You may find that it will find you out before long, too. Sin, like murder, will come out. Men will even tell tales about themselves that they have experienced in dreams. God has made men to be so wretched in their consciences that they at last feel obliged to stand forth and confess the truth. Secret sinner, if you want the foretaste of condemnation on earth, then continue in your secret sins. For no one is more miserable than the one who sins secretly, and yet tries to preserve a character. The stag followed by hungry open-mouthed hounds is far more happy than one who is pursued by his sins. The bird in the net, laboring to escape, is far more happy than one who has weaved about himself a web of deception, one who labors day by day to escape the consequences of his sins, yet finding the toils of them growing thick into a strong web. One may well pray, *"Cleanse me from secret faults."*

MORNING

But I am a worm, and no man — Psalm 22:6.

"A FISHERMAN, when he casts his hook into the river, does not throw the hook in bare and uncovered. For then he knows the fish will never bite, so he hides the hook within a worm, or some other bait, and biting at the worm the fish is caught by the hook. So Christ, speaking of Himself, says, *'I am a worm, and no man.'* Coming to perform the great work of our redemption, He covered and hid His Godhead within the worm of his human nature. The grand water-serpent, the Devil, thinking to swallow the worm of His humanity, was caught on the hook of His divinity. This hook stuck in his jaws and tore him painfully. By thinking to destroy Christ, he destroyed his own kingdom, and so lost his power forever" — Lancelot Andrewes.

"Christ calls Himself *'a worm'* . . . on account of the opinion that men of the world had of Him. The Jews esteemed Christ as a worm, and treated Him as such. He was loathsome to them and hated by them; every one trampled on Him and trod Him under foot, as men do worms. The Chaldee paraphrase renders it here *a weak worm*; and though Christ is the mighty God, and is also the Son of man, whom God made strong for Himself; yet there was a weakness in His human nature, and he was crucified through it (2 Cor. 13:4). Some have observed that the word here signifies the scarlet worm, or the worm that is in the grain or berry with which scarlet is dyed. And our Lord looked like this scarlet worm when they mocked Him by clothing Him in a scarlet robe. Yes, and when He appeared in His dyed garments, and was red in His apparel, it was as one treading in the wine vat; when His body was covered with blood when He hung on the cross, which was shed to make crimson and scarlet sins as white as snow" — John Gill.

EVENING

This is the generation of those that seek Him, that seek Your face — Psalm 24:6.

"CHRISTIANS MUST BE SEEKERS. This is *'the generation of seekers.'* All mankind, if they ever will come to Heaven, must be a generation of seekers. Heaven is a generation of finders, of possessors, of enjoyers, seekers of God. But here we are a generation of seekers. We lack something, and so we must seek. When we are at our best, we lack the accomplishment of our happiness. It is a state of seeking here, because it is a state of want — we always lack something here. But to come more particularly to this *'seeking the face of God;'* that is, the presence of God. The presence of God here is that presence that He shows *'in the time of need, and in His ordinances.'* He shows a presence in need and necessity; that is, He shows a gracious presence to His children, a gracious face. As when we lack direction, He shows His presence of light to direct us. In weakness He shows us His strength. In trouble and perplexity He will show us His gracious and comfortable presence to comfort us. In perplexity He shows us His presence to set the heart free, answerable to the necessity. So in need God is present with His children, to direct them, to comfort them, to strengthen them" — Richard Sibbes.

MORNING

And the King of Glory will come in — Psalm 24:7.

"YOU THAT are the living temples of the Lord, who have already entertained His sanctifying Spirit within you, do you lift up your hearts in the use of holy ordinances through faith, in joyful desires and assured expectation of Him? Yea, you may abundantly lift up by faith in the use of holy means, you who are the everlasting habitation of an evelasting God, with a joyful and assured welcome of Him. You may invite and undoubtedly entertain the high and mighty Potentate, the Lord Christ, in your souls, and have a glorious manifestation and ravishing operation of His love, His benefits, and His graces. And know, O all you faithful and obedient ones, for your courage and comfort, the quality of your glorious King, the Lord Jesus. The world despises Him, but you honor Him, because He is the Almighty God who has all-sufficient power to preserve and defend His people and His church. Trust in Him and love and serve Him against all the strength and power of men and devils, whoever may malign or oppose themselves against you. Put them to the foil, for we, His Israel, show are His people, have found by experience that if we resist the Devil he and all his servants will flee from us" — George Abbot, 1651.

EVENING

He will teach the meek His way. All the paths of Jehovah are mercy and truth to the keepers of His covenant and His testimonies — Psalm 25:9,10.

MEEK SPIRITS are in high favor with the Father of the meek and lowly Jesus, for He sees in them the image of His only-begotten Son. They know their need of guidance, and are willing to submit their own understandings to the divine will. Trouble puts gentle spirits to their wits' ends, but grace comes to the rescue. This is a rule without an exception. God is good to those that are good. Mercy and faithfulness will abound to those who through mercy are made faithful. Whatever outward appearances may threaten, we should settle it steadfastly in our minds that while grace enables us to obey the Lord's will we do not need to fear that Providence will save us from any real loss. There shall be mercy in every unsavory morsel, faithfulness in every bitter drop. Let not your heart be troubled, obedient one, but rest by faith in the immutable covenant of Jehovah, for it is ordered in all things, and sure. Yet this is not a general truth to be trampled on by swine; it is a pearl only for the neck of the true child. Gracious souls, by faith resting on the finished work of the Lord Jesus, keep the covenant of the Lord. Being sanctified by the Holy Spirit, they walk in *His testimonies*. These will find all things working together for their good. But there is not such promise to the sinner. Keepers of the covenant will be kept by the covenant. Those who follow the Lord's commands will find the Lord's mercy following them.

Because the Father made all fulness pleased to dwell in Him — Colossians 1:19.

"*ALL FULNESS*" is a wide, far-reaching, all-comprehending term, and in its abundant store it offers a source of delight. What joy these words give to us when we remember that our vast necessities demand a fulness, yes, *"all fulness"* before they can be supplied! A little help will be of no use to us, for we are altogether without strength. A limited measure of mercy will only mock our misery. A low degree of grace will never be enough to bring us to Heaven, defiled as we are with sin, beset with dangers, encompassed with infirmities, assailed by temptations, molested with afflictions, and all the while bearing about with us *"the body of this death"* (Rom. 7:24). But *"all fulness"* that will suit us. Here is exactly what our desperate estate demands for its recovery. Had the Savior only put out His finger to help our exertions, or had He only stretched out His hand to perform a measure of salvation's work, while He left us to complete it, our soul would forever have dwelt in darkness. In these words, *"all fulness"* we hear the echo of His death-cry: *'It is finished!'* We are to bring nothing, but to find all in Him; yes, the fulness of all in Him. We are simply to receive out of His fulness grace for grace. We are not asked to contribute nor required to make up deficiencies, for there are none to make up — all, all is laid up in Christ. All that we shall want between this place and Heaven, all we could need between the gates of Hell, where we lay in our blood, to the gates of Heaven, where we shall find welcome admission, is treasured up for us in the Lord Jesus Christ. Did I not say that the two words before us are a noble hymn? Let them, I pray you, lodge in your souls for many days; they will be blessed guests.

EVENING

I have not concealed Your righteousness within my heart. I speak of Your faithfulness and Your salvaton. I have not hidden Your loving-kindness and Your truth from the great congregation — Psalm 40:10.

MANY CHRISTIANS are of a retiring disposition, and their retiring disposition is exemplified somewhat in the same way as that of a soldier who felt unworthy to stand in the front ranks. He felt that it would be too presumptuous a thing for him to be in front where the cannon balls were mowing down men on the right hand and on the left. So he would rather be in the vanguard. I always look on those very modest and retiring people as arrant cowards, and I venture to call them so. I do not ask every man and woman to rush into the front ranks of service, but I do ask every converted man and woman to take some place in the ranks, and to be prepared to make some sacrifice in that position they choose, or think, themselves fit to occupy. But ah! There are some who shrink back from any post that demands toil or vigilance. When they were young their ardor was never kindled, the spirit of enterprise was never stirred within them. Had they shown any mettle then, they might have been lion-hearted now. If they had done something then, their career of usefulness might have been in full vigor now. But alas for the man on whom there is the rest of wasted years. He waits, he doubts, he parleys still, and shelters himself under a fictitious humility. Would God I had more courage myself, but I will tell you one thing, I dare not fold my arms, nor do I dare hold my tongue. It seems to me so awful a thing not to be doing good, and it seems to me so dastardly a thing to shrink back when opportunities lie in one's path. I do wish that some of you would learn to imitate the character of the godly man, "Who holds no parley with unmanly fears. Where duty bids, he confidently steers, faces a thousand dangers at her call; and, trusting in his God, he surmounts them all."

Because the Father made all fulness pleased to dwell in Him — Colossians 1:19.

LET IT BE NOTED HERE, very carefully, that while fulness is treasured up in Christ, it is not said to be treasured up in the doctrines of Christ (although they are full and complete, and we need no other teaching when the Spirit reveals the Son in us). Not is it said to be treasured up in the commands of Christ, although they are amply sufficient for our guidance. But it is said, *"in Him,"* that is, in His person, *"all fulness"* should dwell. In Him, as God incarnate, dwells *"all the fulness of the Godhead bodily"* (Col. 2:9) — not as a myth, a dream, a thought, a fiction, but as a living, real personality. We must lay hold of this. I know that the fulness dwells in Him officially as Prophet, Priest, and King. But the fulness does not lie in the prophetic mantle, nor in the priestly ephod, nor in the royal vesture, but in the Person that wears all these. You must get to the very Christ in your faith, and rest alone in Him, or else you have not reached the treasury in which all fulness is stored up. All fulness is in Him radically. If there is fulness in His work, or His gifts, or His promises, all is derived from His person — this gives weight and value to all. All the promises are yes and amen in Christ Jesus. The merit of His death lies mainly in His person, because He was God who gave Himself for us, and His own self bore our sins in His own body on the tree. The excellence of His person gave fulness to His sacrifice. His power to save at this very day lies in His person, for *"He is able to save to the uttermost those that come to God through Him, ever living to make intercession for them."*

EVENING

Because the Father made all fulness pleased to dwell in Him — Colossians 1:19.

WHY WAS the Father pleased? That is answer enough. He is a sovereign, let Him do as He wills. Ask the reason for election, and you will receive no other answer but this: *"Even so, Father, for so it seemed good in Your sight."* Once, *"it pleased the Father to bruise Him"* (Isa. 53:10), and now the Father was pleased to let all *"fulness dwell in Him."* Sovereignty may answer the question sufficiently, but hearken! I hear justice speak; she cannot be silent. Justice says there was no person in Heaven or under Heaven so fit to contain the fulness of grace, as was Jesus.

There was none so fit to be glorified as the Savior, who *"made Himself of no reputation, and took on Himself the form of a servant, and being found in fashion as a man, humbled Himself, and became obedient to death, even the death of the cross"* (Phil. 2:6-8). It is but justice that the grace which He has brought to us should be treasured up in Him. And while justice speaks, wisdom will not withhold her voice. Wise are You, O Jehovah, to treasure up grace in Christ, for to Him men can come. And coming to Him, as to a living stone, chosen of God and precious, men find Him precious also to their souls. The Lord has laid our help in the right place, for He has laid it on one that is mighty, who is as loving as He is mighty, as ready as He is able to save. And more, in the fitness of things the Father's pleasure is the first point to be considered, for all things ought to be to the good pleasure of God. Is it a great underlying rule of the universe that all things were created for God's pleasure. God is the source and fountain of eternal love, and it is but fitting that He should convey it to us by what channel He may elect.

MORNING

The Lord of hosts is with us; the God of Jacob is our refuge — Psalm 46:7.

WHO CAN STAND AGAINST a people whose people enlist God in their quarrel? We cry to the Lord, and He hears us. He breaks through the ranks of the foe; He gives us triumph in the day of battle. For this reason, terrible as an army with banners are those who wield the weapon of all-prayer.

A true church is bvased upon eternal truth. I do not need to quote to you the old Latin proverb which says that truth is mighty and must prevail. Truth is, and truth shall be. It alone is substance and must outlast the lapse of ages. Lies are soon swollen to their perfection of development, like the bubbles with rainbow hues which children blow. But they are dispersed as easily as they are fashioned; they are children of the hour, while truth is the offspring and heir of eternity. Falsehood dies, pierced through the heart by the arrows of time, but truth, in her impenetrable mail bids defiance to all foes. Men who love the truth are building gold and silver and precious stones. And although their architecture may progress very slowly, it is built for eternity. Ramparts of truth may often be assailed, but they will never be carried by the foe. Establish a power among men of the most ostentatious and apparently stable kind, but rest assured that if untruth is at the root of it, it must perish, sooner or later. Only truth is invincible, eternal, supreme. The fear of the true church and the dread of it falls on the enemy, because they have wit enough left to know that truth has an abiding and indestructible power. It is no aim of ours to please our enemies in our mode of warfare, but the reverse. And if we have discovered a weapon which galls you, O enemy, we will use that same arm more freely than ever.

EVENING

Will he delight himself in the Almighty? Will he always call on God? — Job 27:10.

HERE IS THE QUESTION of constancy. Will he pray constantly? It seems to most men a very difficult thing to praying always, to continue in prayer, to pray without ceasing. Yes, and here again there is a great distinction between the living child of God and the mere pretender. The living child of God soon finds that it is not so much his duty to pray, as his privilege, his joy, a necessity of his being. What moment is there when a Christian is safe without prayer? Where is there a place in which he would find himself secure if he ceased to pray? Just think of it. Every moment of my life I am dependent on the will of God as to whether I shall draw another breath, or not. Nothing stands between me and death but the will of God. An angel's arm could not save me from the grave, if now the Lord willed me to depart. Solemn, then, is the Christian's position. He is ever standing by an open tomb. Should not dying men pray? We are always dying. As life is but a long dying, should it not also be a long praying? Should we not be incessantly acknowledging to God in prayer and praise the continuance of our being, which is due to His grace?

Every moment that we live we are receiving favors and benefits from God. There is never a minute in which we are not recipients of His bounty. We are accustomed to thank God for His mercies as if we thought they came at certain set times; so in truth they do, for they are new every morning. And His mercies soothe us night by night, for His compassion does not fail, but there are mercies streaming on in one incessant flow. We never cease to need; He never ceases to supply. We want constant protection, and He who keeps Israel neither sleeps nor slumbers. He keeps us night and day, that nothing may hurt us.

March 9   MORNING

To open the blind eyes, to bring out the prisoners from the prison, and those who sit in darkness out of the prison house — Isaiah 42:7.

THE WORK OF THE MESSIAH, according to the text, is to bring out the prisoners from the prison. I think this relates to the bondage under which a man lies to his sins. Habits of sin, like iron nets, surround the sinner, and he cannot escape their meshes. The man sins, and imagines that he cannot help sinning. How often do the ungodly tell us that they cannot renounce the world, cannot break off their sins by righteousness, and cannot believe in Jesus? Let all men know that the Savior has come on purpose to remove every bond of sin from the captive, and to set him free from every chain of evil. I have known men to strive against the habit of blasphemy, others against unchaste passions, and many more against a haughty spirit, or an angry temper. And when they have striven manfully, but unsuccessfully, in their own strength, they have been filled with bitter chagrin that they should have been so betrayed by themselves. When a man believes in Jesus his resolve to become a free man is to a great extent accomplished at once. Some sins die the moment we believe in Jesus, and these trouble us no more. Others hang on to us, and these die by slow degrees; but they are overcome so as never again to get the mastery over us. O struggler after mental, moral, spiritual liberty, if you would be free, your only possible freedom is in Christ. If you desire to shake off evil habits, or any other mental bondage, I shall prescribe no remedy to you but this, to commit yourself to Christ the Liberator. Love Him and you will hate sin. Trust Him, and you will no more trust yourself. Submit yourself to the sway fo the incarnate God, and He will break the dragon's head within you, and hurl Satan beneath your feet. Nothing else can do it. Christ must have the glory.

EVENING

To open the blind eyes, to bring out the prisoners from the prison, and those who sit in darkness out of the prison house — Isaiah 42:7.

THE LAST PART of this Divine work is to bring those who sit in darkness out of the prisonhouse. This we will refer to those who are truly emancipated, and yet by reason of despondency sit down in the dark dungeon. We have in our pastoral duties constantly to console persons who are free from their sins, having by Divine grace gotten the mastery over them, but yet they are in sadness. The door is open, the bars are broken, but with strange obstinacy of despondency they remain in the cell of fear, in which there is no necessity for them to continue for a moment. They cannot believe that these good things are true to them. They forgiven? They could believe everybody else to be pardoned but themselves. They made the children of God? No, they could hope for their sisters; they have joy in knowing that their father is a child of God, but as to themselves — can such blessings really fall to the lot of such unworthy ones? We have talked with hundreds of such, and have tried to console them. But we have only learned our own unskilfulness in the art of consolation. They are rich in inventions for self-torture, ingenious in escaping comfort. But, ah! The blessed Master of our souls, whose business it has been, since Adam's fall, to bind up broken hearts, is never foiled. When His eternal Spirit comes to anoint with the oil of joy, He soon gives beauty for ashes. The mournful sentinel of the night-watches must rejoice when the day breaks and the Sun of righteousness shines forth. Although I speak to you in very common-place language, yet the theme is rich. This one thought alone ought to make our hearts dance for joy, to think that the Christ of God undertakes to lift up desponding and despairing spirits into hope and joy once more.

Then Job answered the Lord and said, Behold, I am vile! What shall I answer You? I will lay my hand on my mouth — Job 40:3, 4.

SURELY, if any man had a right to say, "I am not vile," it was Job. According to the testimony of God Himself Job was *"a perfect and an upright man, one that feared God and hated evil."* Yet we find even this eminent saint, when by his nearness to God he had received light enough to discover his own condition, exclaiming, *"Behold, I am vile!"* We are sure that what Job was forced to say, we may also assent to, whether we are God's children or not. And if we are partakers of grace, it becomes a subject of great consideration for us, since even we the regenerated must exclaim, each one for himself, *"Behold, I am vile!"*

It is a doctrine taught us in Holy Writ, that when a man is saved by a Divine grace, he is not wholly cleansed from the corruption of his nature. When we believe in Jesus Christ all our sins are pardoned. Yet the power of sin, although it is weakened and kept under by the dominion of the newborn nature which God infuses into our souls, does not cease. It still tarries in us, and it will do so to our dying day. It is a doctrine held by all the orthodox, that there dwells still in the regenerate the lusts of the flesh, that there still remains in converted ones the evil of the carnal nature. In experimental matters it is very difficult to distinguish concerning sin. It is usual with many writers, especially with hymn writers, to confound the two natures of a Christian. I hold that in every Christian there are two natures, as distinct as were the two natures of the God-man Christ Jesus. There is one nature which cannot sin, because it is born of God — a spiritual nature coming directly from Heaven, as pure and as perfect as its Author, God Himself. And also there is in man that ancient nature which, by the fall of Adam, has become altogether vile, corrupt, sinful, and devilish.

EVENING

Then Job answered the Lord and said, Behold, I am vile! What shall I answer You? I will lay my hand on my mouth — Job 40:3, 4.

EXPERIENCE will tell you that this sin remaining in believers exerts a checking power on every good thing. When you would do good, you have felt that evil was present with you (Rom. 7:21). Just like the chariot, which might go swiftly down the hill, you have had a clog put on your wheels. Like the bird that would mount to the heavens, you have found your sins, like the wires of a cage, preventing your soaring toward the Most High. You have bent your knee to pray, but corruption has distracted your thoughts. You have attempted to sing, but you have felt the hosannahs languish on your tongue. Some insinuation of Satan has taken fire, like a spark to tinder, and almost smothered your soul with its abominable smoke. You would run in your holy duties with all speed, but the sin that so easily besets you entangles your feet; and when you are near your goal it trips you up, to your own dishonor and pain. You will find indwelling sin frequently retarding you the most at times when you are most earnest. When you desire to be most alive to God, you will generally find sin most alive to repel you. The *"evil heart of unbelief"* puts itself in the road, saying, "You shall not come this way." And when the soul says, "I will serve God; I will worship in His temple," the evil heart says, "Bow yourself to false gods, but you shall not approach Jerusalem. I will not allow you to behold the face of the Most High." You have often felt this to be the case. A cold hand has been placed on your hot spirit when you have been full of devotion and prayer. When you have had the wings of a dove, and thought you could flee away and be at rest, a clog has been put on your feet, so that you could not mount.

March 11 — MORNING

Which of them, then, do you say will love him most? And answering Simon said, I suppose that one to whom he forgave the most. And He said to him, You have judged rightly — Luke 7:42, 43.

THERE ARE some who evidently have not had more forgiven than others as to outward sins. On the contrary they have been prudently brought up from childhood, and for many a year they have been foremost in service, and have been special lovers of the Lord. Though by no means great offenders in their unconverted state, these are certainly great saints now; intense in their service, consistent in their character, fervent in their love. How is it that some who shout that they have been snatched from the burning, and according to them were the very chief of sinners, those making a great trumpet-blowing over their own conversion, yet do not love the Lord Jesus half as much as these dear, quiet souls who never went into open sin? The reason is this: Our estimate of sin is, after all, the thing which will create and inflame our love. For if a man thinks sin to be exceedingly sinful, and feels it to be so, he has a deeper sense of his indebtedness than the man who may have committed grosser vices, but has never seen them in their real blackness (as they appear in the light of God's countenance). Too many believers know little of what it is to be amazed and astounded at the heinousness of their transgressions. There was a time, and now is, when if I had inadvertently spoken an untrue word, it cost me more pain to think of what was only a hasty error than it has cost many men to repent of their cursing and swearing. Sorrowfully, I believe that some make a glory of their shame, daring to brag of what they used to be. They stand up and make confession without a tear in their eye, or a blush on their cheek. Such testimony ought never to be heard, for it is a positive creator of evil in the minds of those hearing it.

EVENING

Which of them, then, do you say will love him most? And answering Simon said, I suppose that one to whom he forgave the most. And he said to him, you have judged rightly — Luke 7:42, 43.

IT IS A BLESSED token for good when our work among men is not so much for the sake of sinners as for love of Jesus. When we love the brethren it should be because they belong to Christ. It is sweet to serve the Lord Christ. See how the holy woman offered homage distinctly to our Lord: tears for His travel-stains, hair to wipe His feet, ointment to anoint His flesh. Do your choicest and best for Jesus, for Him personally.

Try to do it most humbly. Stand behind Him. Do not ask anybody to look at you. Do it very quietly. Do it feeling that it is a great honor to be permitted to do the least service for Jesus. Do not dream of saying, "I am somebody. I am doing great things. I do more even than Simon, the Pharisee. Come see my zeal for the Lord of hosts." Jehu talked in that fashion, yet he was good for nothing. Do your personal part without seeking to be seen of men.

Do it self-sacrificingly. Bring your best ointment. Pinch yourself for Christ. Make sacrifices. Go without this or that, to have something with which you can honor Him. Do it patiently. When you serve Him best, still let the tears fall on His feet, mingling with the costly ointment. The tears and the ointment go well together. Mourn your guilt at the same time you rejoice in His grace.

Do it continuously. Christ said, *"This woman, since I came in, has not ceased to kiss My feet."* Do not leave off loving Him and serving Him. Do it on, and on, and on, however much the flesh may ask for rest from service. And do it enthusiastically. See how she kissed His feet; nothing less than this would express her love. Stoop down and kiss and kiss again those blessed feet which traveled so far in love for you.

MORNING

But encourage one another day by day, while it is called Today, so that none of you may be hardened through the deceitfulness of sin — Hebrews 3:13.

SIN IS DECEITFUL in the influence which it carries with it. At first sin cultivates a free and easy bearing. It says to the sinner, "Don't think. Leave consideration to older heads." The guilt one goes on day after day without looking to his way. His happiness lies in carelessness. He hurries downward to destruction, and it is enough for him that the road is easy. With a laugh, a joke, he puts off serious things until tomorrow. He is a free-thinker, and to large extent a free actor. Those near him often find him being too free. Yes, but he is being deceived. By-an-by when conscience wakes up, he will find it so. Out of his own mouth will come the death-warrant of his jollity. In those more serious days what does sin say? "You have provoked the Spirit of God, and there is no mercy for you. Do not listen to the preacher of the gospel; it is impossible for you to be forgiven. Your case is hopeless; you are finally condemned, and there is no changing the verdict. As for the promises of God, they are not for such a sinner as you are; you are given up to despair. Without doubt you will perish everlastingly." This is the opposite pole of sin's deceiving. For though it has changed sides, it is still deceiving. Despair is as much a sin as profanity. For to doubt God is as truly a crime as to take pleasure in uncleanness. In this way sin by any means, by all means, will endeavor to keep men under its tyranny, so as to work their ruin. Let no one think that he cannot be deceived; that one is already deluded by his pride. Let no one dream that he has come to such a state of perfection that he cannot be deluded by sin; that one is even now in imminent peril. We have a cunning enemy, and we have no wit of our own which is able to match the subtlety of the old Serpent, and the deceitfulness of sin.

EVENING

But encourage one another day by day, while it is called Today, so that none of you may be hardened through the deceitfulness of sin — Hebrews 3:13.

THE TEXT SAYS to encourage one another daily. This means, first of all, to hear exhortation from others. Secondly, we must practice exhortation to others. I have known people of this kind, that if a word is spoken to them, however gently, as to a wrong which they are doing, their temper is up in a moment. What are they that they should be spoken to? Dear friend, who are you that you should not be spoken to? Are you such an off-cast and such an outcast that your Christian brothers must give you up? Surely you do not want to bear that character. I have known persons to take offense where we ought to show gratitude. One says, "Oh, I will never hear that man again! He is too personal." What kind of a man would you like to hear? Will you give your ear to one who will please you to your ruin and flatter you to your destruction? Surely, you are not so foolish. Do you choose that kind of doctor who never tells you the truth about your bodily health? Do you trust one who falsely assures you that there is nothing the matter with you at a time when a terrible disease is folding its cruel arms about you? Your doctor would not hurt your feelings, so he washed his hands with invisible soap and gives you a portion of the same. He will send you just a little pill, and will you be all right? He would not have you think of that painful operation which another surgeon has suggested to you. He smirks and smiles, until, after a little while of him and his pills, you say to yourself, I am getting worse and worse. Still he smiles, and smiles; he flatters and soothes me. I will have done with him and his little pills; I will go to one who will examine me honestly and treat me properly. He with the smiles and the soap and the pills may go elsewhere."

March 13   MORNING   73

But encourage one another day by day, while it is called Today, so that none of you may be hardened through the deceitfulness of sin — Hebrews 3:13.

SIN IS DECEITFUL in its object, for the object which it puts before us is not that which is its actual result. We are not tempted to provoke our Maker, or to wilfully cast off the authority of righteousness. We are not invited to do these things for their own sake. No, No! We are moved to do evil under the idea that some present good will come of it. When he yields to sin, the man thinks that he will enjoy an additional pleasure, or shall gain an extra profit, or at least shall avoid a measure of evil, or to escape from something which he dreads. He does wrong for the sake of what he hopes will come of it. In brief, he does evil that good may come. In this way the seeming good is dangled before the short-sighted creature, man, as the bait before the fish. In every case this object is a piece of deceit. Evil does not lead to good, nor does sin promote our real profit. We are fooled if we think so. Yet in most cases the man does not commit the sin with the design of breaking the law of God, defying his Maker, but because he fancies that something is to be gained. And in his judgment he better understands what is good for him even than the Lord God, by whose wisdom he ought to be guided.

Just as in the case of the old serpent, the argument is: God refuses you that which would be for your advantage, and you will be wise to take it. The arch-deceiver insinuated that God knew that if Adam and Eve ate the forbidden fruit their eyes would be opened, and they would be as gods. And, said Satan, God denied them the charming fruit in order to keep them under subjection. Perhaps Milton's idea is right, "See what this fruit has done for me," says the serpent. "I, a mere reptile, am now able to speak and argue like a man. God, take the fruit, and you, as men, will rise to the rank of God."

EVENING

But encourage one another day by day, while it is called Today, so that none of you may be hardened through the deceitfulness of sin — Hebrews 3:13.

THE OBJECT set before us is delusive. The reward of sin may glitter, but it is not gold. Yet it thrusts itself on our erring judgment as gold. This deceitfulness of sin is everywhere present: in the street, the house, in the private room — all come to be enchanted ground unless we dwell in God. Are we not often caused to think just to a little degree that we could make at least a little gain, or do a measure of extra good, if we would quit the straight and narrow way? This is a lie, base as Hell!

Sin is deceitful in the names it wears. It shows great aptitude in changing its titles. It seldom cares for its own true description. Fine words are often used to cover foul deeds. At times we read in the newspapers of gentlemen who have an alias, or possibly a half-a-dozen. In such cases there is always a reason for it. Sin has many names by which it would disguise its real character. In his *Holy War* Mr. Bunyan tells us that Covetousness called himself by the name of Prudent-thrifty; Lasciviousness was named Harmless-mirth; and Anger was known as Good-zeal. Nowadays anger is known as "proper spirit," and infidelity is "advanced theology." Almost every sin has a pretty name to be called by on Sundays, and silver slippers to wear in fine society. The paint brush and the powderbox are much used on the wrinkled countenance of sin, to make it look fair and beautiful. The fig-leaf is not only worn on the man's body, but sin itself puts on the apron. To hide the nakedness of sin is the great desire of Satan. For this way he hopes that even the better sort may fall in love with a 'decent' evil, although they might have shunned an odious transgression. Alas, how sadly prone are men to call things by false names!

But put on the Lord Jesus Christ and do not take thought for the lusts of the flesh —
Romans 13:14.

THIS WE DO when we believe in Him. Then we put on the Lord Jesus Christ as our robe of righteousness. It is a very beautiful picture of what faith does. Faith finds our manhood naked to its shame; it sees that Christ Jesus is the robe of righteousness provided for our need. And at the command of the gospel faith appropriates Him and gets the benefit of Him for it. By faith the soul covers her weakness with His strength, her sin with His atonement, her folly with His wisdom, her failure with His triumphs, her death with His life, her wanderings with His constancy. By faith the soul hides itself within Jesus, until Jesus only is seen, and the man is seen in Him. We take not only His righteousness as being imputed to us, but we take Himself to be really ours; and so His righteousness becomes ours as a matter of fact. *"By the obedience of One shall many be made righteous"* (Romans. 5:19). His righteousness is set to our account; it becomes ours because He is ours. Although long unrighteous in myself, I believe in the testimony of God concerning His Son Jesus Christ, and I am accounted righteous, even as it is written, *"Abraham believed God, and it was counted to him for righteousness"* (Rom. 4:3). The riches of God in Christ Jesus become mine as I take the Lord Jesus Christ to be everything to me.

The apostle is not referring to the imputed righteousness of Christ. The text stands in connection with precepts concerning matters of everyday practical life. And to these it must refer. It is not justification, but sanctification that we have here. Moreover, we cannot be said to put on the imputed righteousness of Christ after we have believed, for that is on us as soon as we believe, and needs no more putting on. The command before us is given to those who have the imputed righteousness of Christ, who are justified and accepted.

EVENING

But put on the Lord Jesus Christ and do not take thought for the lusts of the flesh — Romans 13:14.

IT IS NOT WRITTEN, "Put on this man, or that;' but, *"Put on the Lord Jesus Christ."* The model for a saint is his Savior. We are very apt to select some eminently gracious or useful man to be a pattern for us. A measure of good may result from such a course, but a degree of evil may also come of it. There will always be some fault about the most excellent of our fellow mortals. And, as it is our tendency to caricature virtues until we make them faults, so it is our greater folly to mistake faults for excellences, and to copy them with careful exactness (and generally with abundant exaggeration). By this plan, with the best intentions, we may reach very sad results. Follow Jesus in the way, and you will not go astray. Let your feet go down exactly in His footprints, and you cannot slide. As His grace enables us, let us make it true, that, *"as He was, so are we in this world."* You need not look beyond your Lord for example under any circumstances. Of Him you may inquire as of an unfailing oracle. You need never inquire what is the general custom of those about you: the broad road of the many is no way for you. You may not ask, "What are the rulers of the people doing?" You do not follow the fashion of the great, but the example fo the Greatest-of-all: *"Put on the Lord Jesus Christ"* will then apply to each one of us. If I am a tradesman, I am not to ask myself, "On what principles do other traders conduct their business?" Not so! For what the world may do is no rule for me. If I am a student I should not inquire, "How do others feel toward religion?" Let others do as they will, it is for us to serve the Lord. In every relationship, in the domestic circle, in the literary world, in the sphere of friendship, or in business connections, I am to *"put on the Lord Jesus Christ."*

March 15   MORNING   75

But put on the Lord Jesus Christ and do not take thought for the lusts of the flesh
— Romans 13:14.

WE WANT not only an example, but a motive, an impulse and constraining power to keep us true to that example. We need to put on zeal as a cloak and to be covered with a holy influence which will urge us onward. Let us go to the Lord Jesus for motives. Some fly to Moses; these would drive themselves to duty by the thunders of Sinai. Their design in service is to *earn* eternal life, or to *prevent* the loss of the favor of God. So they come under law and forsake the true way of the believer, which is faith. Not from dread of punishment or hope of hire do believers serve the living God, but we put on Christ. It is the love of Christ that constrains us. Here is the spring of true holiness: *"Sin shall not have dominion over you, for you are not under the law, but under grace"* (Rom. 6:14). A stronger force than law has gripped you; you serve God, not as servants whose sole thought is the wage, but as children whose eye is on the Father and His love. Your motive is gratitude to Him by whose precious blood you are redeemed. He has put on your cause, and therefore you would take up His cause. Do not go to the steep sides of Sinai to find motives for holiness. Hasten to Calvary and find there those sweet herbs of love which shall be the medicine of your soul. *"Put on the Lord Jesus Christ."* Covered with a consciousness of His love, in turn fired with love to Him, you will be strong to be, to do, or to suffer, as the Lord God may appoint.

Need I say, never find a reason for doing right in a desire to win the approval of your fellow men? Do not say, "I must do this or that in order to please my friends." That is a poor life which is sustained by the breath of other men's nostrils. Followers of Jesus will not wear the livery of custom, nor will they stand in awe of human censure.

EVENING

But put on the Lord Jesus Christ and do not take thought for the lusts of the flesh —
Romans 13:14.

FIND IN JESUS your strength. Although you are saved and are made alive by the Holy Spirit, so as to be a living child of the living God, yet you have no strength for heavenly duty, except as you receive it from above. Go to Jesus for power. I charge you, never say, "I shall do the right because I am resolved to do it. I am a man of strong mind; I am determined to resist this evil, and I know I shall not yield. I have made up my mind, and there is no fear of my turning aside." If you rely on yourself in that way, you will soon prove to be a broken reed. Failure follows at the heel of self-confidence.

I charge you, do not rely on what you have acquired in the past. Do not say in your heart, "I am a man of experience, and because of this I can resist the temptation which would crush the younger and greener folk. I have now spent so many years in persistent well-doing that I may reckon myself out of danger. Is it likely that I should ever be led astray?" O sir, it is more than likely! Yea, it is a fact already. The moment that a man declares he cannot fall, that moment he has already fallen from sobriety and humility. Your head must be turned, or else you would not talk of your inward perfection. And when the head has turned, the feet are no longer very safe. Inward conceit is the mother of open sin. Make Christ your strength, and not yourself — not your acquirements or experiences. *"Put on the Lord Jesus Christ"* day by day, and do not make the rags of yesterday to be the clothing of the future. Get grace fresh daily. Say with David, *"all my fresh springs are in You."* Get all your power for holiness and usefulness from Jesus, and from Him alone. "Surely in the Lord have I righteousness and strength." Rely not on resolves, pledges, methods, prayers. But lean on Jesus alone as the strength of your life.

Put on the Lord Jesus Christ and do not take thought for the lusts of the flesh
— Romans 13:14.

THE SACRED TITLES of the Son of God are spread out at length; *"Put on the Lord — Jesus — Christ."* Put Him on as LORD. Call Him your master and Lord, and you will do well. Be His servant in everything. Submit your every faculty, every capacity, every talent, every possession to His government. Submit all that you have and are to Him, and delight to own His superior right and His royal claim to you. Be Christ's man, His servant under bonds to His service forever. Find in this service life and liberty. Let the dominion of your Lord cover the kingdom of your nature.

Then put Him on as JESUS. Jesus means a Savior. In every part be covered by Him in salvation. You, a sinner, hide yourself in Jesus, your Savior, He who shall save you from your sins. He is your sanctifier to drive out sin, your preserver to keep sin from returning. Jesus is your armor against sin. You overcome through His blood. In Him you are defended against every weapon of the enemy. He is your shield, keeping you from all evil. He covers you all over like a complete suit of armor, so that when arrows of temptation fly like a fiery shower, they may be quenched on heavenly mail, and you may stand unharmed amid a shower of deaths.

Put Him on as Jesus, then put Him on as CHRIST. You know that Christ signifies *anointed*. Now, our Lord is anointed a Prophet, Priest and King. And as such we put Him on. What a splendid thing it is to put on Christ as the anointed Prophet, and to accept His teaching as our creed! I believe it. Why? Because He said it. This is argument enough for me. Mine is not to argue, or to doubt, or to criticize. Christ has said it, and I, putting Him on, find in His authority the end of all strife. What Christ declares, I believe. Discussion ends where Christ begins.

EVENING

Put on the Lord Jesus Christ and do not take thought for the lusts of the flesh
— Romans 13:14.

PUT HIM ON ALSO as your Priest. In spite of the fact of your sin, your unworthiness, your defilement, go to the altar of the Lord by Him who as Priest has taken away your sin, clothed you with His merit, and made you acceptable to God. In our great High Priest we enter within the veil. We are in Him. By faith we realize this and so put Him on as our Priest, and lose ourselves in His accepted sacrifice. Our Lord Jesus is also anointed to be King. Oh, put Him on in all His imperial majesty, by yielding your every wish and thought to His sway! Set Him on the throne of your heart. As you have submitted your thought and understanding to His prophetic instruction, submit your action and your practical life to His kingly government. As you put on His priesthood and find atonement in Him, so put on His royalty and find holiness in Him.

I now wish to show the description given in Colossians 3, from the twelfth verse. Let us go to the wardrobe for a minute, there to look over the articles of our outfit: *"Put on therefore, as the elect of God"* — you see everything is to be put on; nothing is to be left on the pegs for the moth to eat, nor in the window to be idly stared at. You put on the whole armor of God. In true religion everything is designed for practical use. We keep no garments in the drawer. We have to put on all that is provided: *"Put on therefore, as the elect of God, holy and beloved, bowels of mercies, kindness."* Here are two choice things: mercy and kindness — silken robes indeed! Have you put them on? I am to be as merciful, as tenderhearted, as kind, as sympathetic, as loving to my fellow men as Christ Himself was. Have I reached this point? Have I ever aimed at it? Who among us has put on these royal gloves?

But put on the Lord Jesus Christ and do not take thought for the lusts of the flesh —
Romans 13:14.

WHAT DOES the apostle say? *"Do not take thought for the lusts of the flesh."* By this he means several things. Give no tolerance to it. Do not say, "Christ has sanctified me so far, but you see I have a bad temper naturally, and you cannot expect it to be wholly removed." Do not make provision for thus sheltering and sparing one of the enemies of your soul. Another may cry, "You know that I always was one to despond a great deal, therefore I can never have much joy in the Lord." Don't make room for your unbelief in this way. If you find a kennel for this dog, you will always lie in it. Another says, "But I was always rather fond of gaiety, and so I must mix up with the world." Well, if you cook a dinner for the Devil, he will take a seat at your table. This is to make provision for the flesh, to fulfil its lusts. Do not do so; slay the Canaanites, break their idols, throw down their altars, fell their groves.

Furthermore, give sin no time. Allow no furlough to your obedience. Do not say to yourself, "At all other times I am exact, but once in a year, at a family meeting, I take a little liberty." Is it liberty to you to sin? I am afraid there is something rotten in your heart. One cries, "Ah! I only allow myself an hour or two occasionally with questionable company. I know it does me harm, but we must all have a little relaxation, and the talk is very amusing, though rather loose." Is evil a relaxation to you? It ought to be worse than slavery. What a trial is foolish talking to a child of God! How can you find pleasure in it? Give no license to the flesh; you cannot tell how far it will go. Keep it always under subjection, and make no space for indulgence — provide no food for it; carve it no rations. Starve it out. If it wants fodder, let it look elsewhere.

EVENING

But put on the Lord Jesus Christ and do not take thought for the lusts of the flesh
— Romans 13:14.

WHEN YOU are allotting your provision to the body, the soul, the spirit, allot nothing to the depraved passions. If the flesh says, "What is for me;" say, "Nothing!." Some people like a little bit of reading for the flesh. As some people like a little bit of what they call "high" meat, so these folk enjoy a portion of tainted doctrine or questionable morality. So they make provision for the flesh, and the flesh feeds on it, giving its lusts a meal. I have known professors to dabble just a little in matters which they would forbid to others. But they think them to be allowable to themselves, if done in secret. They say, "You must not be too exact." But the Apostle says, *"Do not take thought for the lusts of the flesh."* Do not give it a morsel; do not even allow it the crumbs that fall from your table. The flesh is greedy; it never has enough. If you give it some provision, it will steal much more.

"Put on the Lord Jesus Christ," and then you will leave no place for the lusts of the flesh. That which Christ does not cover is naked unto sin. If Christ be my livery, and I wear Him, and so am known to be His avowed servant, then I place myself entirely in His hands always and forever. Then the flesh has no claim whatever on me. If, before I put on Christ, I might make some reserve, and duty did call, yet now that the Lord Jesus Christ is on me, I have done with reserves; I am openly and confessedly my Lord's. The Apostle says, *"Do you not know that as many of you as were baptized into Christ have put on Christ?"* (Gal. 3:27). Being buried with Him, we are dead to the world; we live only unto Him. The Lord brings us up to this mark by His mighty Spirit; and He shall have the glory in it.

MORNING

And about the ninth hour Jesus cried with a loud voice, saying, Eli, Eli, lama sabachthani, that is to say, My God, My God, why have You forsaken Me — Matthew 27:46.

YOU AND I, who are believers in the Lord Jesus Christ, and are resting in Him alone for salvation, let us lean hard. Let us bear with all our weight on our Lord. He will bear the full weight of all our sin and care. As to my sin, I hear its harsh accusings no more when I hear Jesus cry, *"Why have You forsaken Me?"* I know that I deserve the deepest hell at the hand of God's vengeance. But I am not afraid; He will never forsake me. For He hid His face from His Son on my behalf. I shall not suffer for my sin, for Jesus suffered to the full in my stead. Yes, He suffered so far as to cry out, *"My God, My God, why have You forsaken Me?"* Behind this brazen wall of substitution a sinner is safe. These "munitions of rock" guard all believers, and they may rest secure. The rock is cleft for me; I hide in its rifts and no harm can reach me. You have a full atonement, a great sacrifice, glorious vindication of the law. Because of this rest in peace, all you who put your trust in Jesus.

If ever in our lives from now on we should think that God has deserted us, let us learn from our Lord's example how to behave ourselves. If God has left you, do not shut up your Bible. No, open it, as your Lord did, and find a text that will suit your case. If God has left you, or you think it so, do not give over prayer. No, pray as your Lord did, and be more earnest than ever. If you think God has forsaken you, do not give up your faith in Him, but, like your Lord, cry out, *"My God, My God,* again and again. If you have had one anchor before, cast out two anchors now, and double the hold of your faith. If you can not call Jehovah, *"Father,"* as was Christ's habit, yet call Him your *"God."* Let the personal pronouns take their hold: *"My God, My God."* Let nothing drive you from your faith.

EVENING

And about the ninth hour Jesus cried with a loud voice, saying, Eli, Eli, lama sabachthani, that is to say, My God, My God, why have You forsaken Me? — Matthew 27:46.

I WILL BELIEVE that He will be faithful to His Son, and true to the covenant sealed by oaths and blood. he that believes in Jesus has everlasting life: there I cling, like the limpet to the rock. There is but one gate of Heaven. And even if I may not enter it, I will cling to the posts of its door. What am I saying? I shall enter in, for that gate was never shut against a soul that accepted Jesus. And Jesus says, *"He that comes to Me I will in no way cast out."*

Let us abhor the sin which brought such agony on our beloved Lord. What an accursed thing is sin, which crucified the Lord Jesus! Do you laugh at it? Will you go and spend an evening to see a mimic performance of it? Do you roll sin under your tongue as a sweet morsel, and then come to God's house on the Lord's day, thinking to worship Him? Worship Him! Worship Him with sin indulged in your breast? Worship Him with sin loved and pampered in your life? If I had a dear brother who had been murdered, what would you think of me if I valued the knife which had been crimsoned with his blood? — if I made a friend of the murderer, and daily consorted with the assassin who drove the dagger into my brother's heart? Surely I, too, must be an accomplice in the crime! Sin murdered Christ; then will you be a friend to it? Sin pierced the heart of the Incarnate God; c: . you love it? Oh, that there was an abyss as deep as Christ's misery that I might at once hurl this dagger of sin into its depths, from which it might never be brought to light again! Begone, O sin! You are banished from the heart where Jesus reigns. Begone, for you have crucified my Lord, causing Him to cry out, *"My God, My God, why have You forsaken Me."*

March 19   MORNING

But on Mount Zion shall be those who escape, and it shall be holy; and the house of Jacob shall have their own possessions — Obadiah 17.

IF YOU HAVE the power given to you today, by faith, to take the Lord Jesus Christ as yours, and if you now trust in His most precious blood, you need not be afraid that you will be taking possession of what does not belong to you. For every believing soul may know that what he takes by faith was bestowed on him in the covenant of grace from before the foundation of the world. If you believe in Christ, you were chosen of God before the world began. For believers, redemption was specially offered by our Lord on the cross; He bought for them the covenant heritage, and He has made it over to them, so that it shall be theirs forever. You cannot know this before you believe; but faith reveals the Divine choice and gift.

You who now believe were once strangers to such an extraordinary joy as that which comes by faith. You wandered up and down in sin, knowing nothing of what free grace and dying love had done for you. But now you have come to God and have ventured by faith to take possession of what the Lord so freely offers in the gospel. And, behold! it is revealed to you that these things were yours in the purpose of God, even from everlasting. Now it is fulfilled to you: *"the house of Jacob shall have their own possessions."* God gave you all covenant blessings in Christ Jesus, according as He chose you, in Him, from before the foundation of the world. God saw you in Christ as His elect, His beloved, His redeemed, and so for you He prepared a kingdom which you inherit through grace. If you have now the confidence to believe in Christ Jesus, and to say, *"My Beloved is mine, and I am His,"* then you shall know that in grasping gracious blessings, you do but come to your own; you possess your possessions.

EVENING

But on Mount Zion shall be those who escape, and it shall be holy; and the house of Jacob shall have their own possessions — Obadiah 17.

BELOVED friends, many by faith have laid hold on the covenant possessions, but yet they do not to the full possess them. The text leads me to pray that believers may enjoy fully what they have grasped by faith. Christ is mine; but beloved, who among us knows all that is ours in Christ? He is a treasure house which is all ours, but we do not open its doors and take out all its treasures. Our possessions in Christ are very wide, but like Abraham we need to be bidden to lift up our eyes to the north, to the south, to the east, and to the west, that we may form a clearer idea of the goodly land which the Lord our God had given us. We see the blessings of the covenant; but do we feed on them as we might? Do we drink deep into them, and are our souls satisfied by them as with marrow and fatness? I fear we do not by enjoyment possess our possessions. Alas! With many believers times of actual realization and enjoyment are rare. They can talk about the blessing, but they do not habitually rejoice in it themselves. They say, "Oh, yes, it is a very delightful thing to be washed in the blood of the Lamb." But do they enjoy the peace which flows from cleansing? Have they "received the atonement," and with it that peace with God which follows on justification by faith? Do they delight in *"the peace of God which passes all understanding"*?

You know that it is your high privilege to have access to the mercy-seat. But do you use that access and come often and boldly to the throne of grace? Do you avail yourselves of your opportunities? Do you make the utmost use of prayer? In other holy matters, do you really stand where God would have you stand? Are you as rich as Christ has made you? A man may have large possessions, and yet be practically poor, because he is miserly in his expenditure. Is it not so with many a child of God? All things are ours, and yet we live as if nothing were ours.

But on Mount Zion shall be those who escape, and it shall be holy; and the house of Jacob shall have their own possessions — Obadiah 17.

LET OUR PRAYER be that we may use and enjoy to the utmost all that the Lord has given us in His grace, and so possess our possession.

We possess our possessions when we hold firmly what we enjoy. Too many Christians hold their blessings with a feeble hand. They expect where they ought to enjoy, and think where they ought to know. They are never sure, and so they do not *"possess their own possessions."* They are not sufficiently at home with spiritual things to be said to possess them. At times they rise into rapturous joy. But the brother soon came down from that mount; the sister soon quitted that Tabor and made her way to the place of Wailing. Why this fickleness? Some do not stay long enough in the garden of assurance to see a single fruit ripen. They do not possess their possessions.

It is a grand thing when the grace of God enables a man to say, *"I know whom I have believed, and am persuaded that He is able to keep that which I have committed to Him"* (2 Tim. 1:12). When happy feelings vanish, faith remains the same. Be it night or be it day, our soul waits only upon God, for our expectation is from Him. When you have such a grip of the eternal covenant, that if all the devils in Hell were to try to drag it from you, you would defy their efforts, then it is well with you. We know that we have passed from death to life. We know that Christ is ours, and that we are His. We are resting in Him, and are saved in Him with an everlasting salvation. Who shall separate us from the love of God which is in Jesus Christ our Lord? (Rom. 8:35) When we are assured in this, we then really *possess our possessions*: our title deeds are before us, and the inheritance is within sight of our faith.

EVENING

But on Mount Zion shall be those who escape, and it shall be holy; and the house of Jacob shall have their own possessions — Obadiah 17.

WE HAVE POSSESSIONS which we have not yet seen, which we cannot as yet enter upon. We believe in the Second Coming of our Lord from Heaven, and in the glory that shall follow. We believe in the resurrection of the dead, and the eternal bliss of the godly in heaven. We believe that we shall dwell with Christ forever and ever. Can we possess these possessions even now? We cannot now rise from the dead, for we are not yet buried. We cannot yet walk the golden streets, for we have not passed through the gate of pearl. Yet, by the realizations of faith we may make these things to be so near that we may measurably enjoy them even now, and so already *possess our possessions*. For *"He has raised us up together and made us sit together in heavenly places in Christ Jesus"* (Eph. 2:6). Even though we are not actually in Heaven, yet in union with our Lord we are virtually there. We have been buried with Him in baptism, in which also we have risen with Him. We have been raised from spiritual death into newness of life, and we have gone up above all earthly things into the heavenlies, in which we dwell. Yes, beloved, faith has a strange realizing faculty. Imagination can do much in this direction, but faith can do far more. By imagination a man can make fiction appear fact. But faith has nothing to do with fiction; it makes the sure hopes of the future to be the pleasures of the present. Earth can become the vestibule of Heaven. Life here may be the rehearsal for the glory-life above. Even here we may *possess our possessions* by enjoying a period of rest, *"as the days of Heaven upon the earth."* Already we have the earnest of the inheritance in the indwelling of the Holy Spirit, and we have obtained that inheritance in Christ.

March 21 — MORNING

He is precious therefore to you who believe, but to the unbelieving He is the Stone which the builders rejected, which became the Head of the corner — 1 Peter 2:7.

IF YOU CAN personally verify this sentence, it says a great deal for yourself. You need never raise the question as to whether you have the faith of God's elect, and are true believers in Jesus. For if Christ is precious to you, that question is answered once for all by this statement, which covers the whole ground: *"He is precious to you who believe."* The converse of the statement is equally true. You who find Christ precious have true faith in Him. It is important, while looking at this word of the apostle Peter, that we should lay our hands on our hearts and ask: Do I know what this means? Is Jesus more to me than gold, or any other thing that can be desired?

If we can verify this statement, it is not only satisfactory to ourselves, but it is glorifying to our Lord. Certain men are best respected where they are least known. Many a character needs distance to lend enchantment to the view. But our Lord is most precious to those who are best acquainted with Him. Those who are actually trusting Him, and thus putting Him to the test, are those who have the highest opinion of Him. If you would have the best estimate of the Lord Jesus, we refer you to those who have had transactions with Him on the largest scale, to those who cast all their care on Him for time and eternity. Their proof of Him is so satisfactory that He is more and more esteemed every day. He is far more precious to them than when they first heard of Him, and every thought of Him makes Him dearer to their hearts. What a glorious friend is He who is most precious to those who receive most from Him! Usually men feel sadness at an increase of obligation; but in this case, the more we are His debtors, the more we rejoice to be so.

EVENING

He is precious therefore to you who believe, but to the unbelieving He is the Stone which the builders rejected, which became the Head of the corner — 1 Peter 2:7.

TO BELIEVERS the Lord Jesus is evidently very precious, because they would give up all that they have rather than to lose Him. Martyrs and confessors have actually given up all for Jesus times without number; history bears this witness abundantly. Tens of thousands have renounced property, liberty, and life, rather than to deny Christ. To this day we have among us those who dare to go forth into the far countries for His name's sake, not counting their lives dear to them that they might spread abroad His gospel. I hope that we also could part with everything rather than to separate from our Lord. We would, like the holy children, if the chalice lay between apostasy and the fiery furnace, reply, *"We are not careful to answer you in this matter"* (Dan. 3:16). Let all things go, but we must hold fast our Lord.

Could you give up your Savior? Very dear to you are your children, and your wife or husband, and your friends. But if it really came to the point to give these up or the Lord Jesus, I am sure you could not hesitate. It is a desirable thing to be esteemed and respected by one's fellows. But when it comes to this, that for the truth's sake one must be an outcast and become the butt of enmity, there must be no question. Popularity and friendship must at once be sacrificed. Believer, you would far sooner take up your cross and go with Jesus, than take up your crown and go away from Him. Is it not so? We must not speak too confidently, and declare that we would never deny Him; but yet He knows all things, and He knows that we love Him so truly that for His sake we could suffer the loss of all things, and count them but dung, that we might win Christ, and be found in Him. This proves that our Lord is precious, since all else may go to the bottom so long as we can keep our hold on the Well-beloved.

MORNING

He is precious therefore to you who believe, but to the unbelieving He is the Stone which the builders rejected, which became the Head of the corner — 1 Peter 2:7.

"*HE IS PRECIOUS.*" For a thing to be rightly called precious, it should have three qualities: It should be rare; it should have an intrinsic value of its own; and, it should possess useful and important properties. All these three things meet in our adorable Lord and make Him precious to discerning minds. As for rarity: talk not of the rarity of gold, or of gems — He is the only one; He is absolutely unique. Other foundations can no man lay than that which is laid in Him. He is the one sacrifice for sin. Not the infinite God, nor all the wealth of Heaven could supply another like Him. As God and man, He alone combines the two natures in one person: *"There is one Mediator between God and men, the man Christ Jesus."* If we can never find another like Him, after searching all the ages through, we may well call Him precious.

It is also most clear that He is intrinsically valuable. Who shall estimate His worth? If I were to attempt in detail to tell you what He is, I would darken counsel by words without knowledge. Only dwell on the simple fact, that while He is God over all, and thus has the fulness of the Godhead, He is also man, true man of the substance of His mother. So He has all the adaptation of perfect manhood. *"Consider how great this Man was."* Not even Heaven itself can be compared with Christ Jesus. He is incomparably, immeasurably, inconceivably precious. As for useful qualities, where else shall we find such a variety of uses in one place? He is eyes to the blind, ears to the deaf, feet to the lame, healing to the sick, freedom to the slave, joy to the mourner, and life to the dead. Think of His life and how it gives life to the believer! Think of His death and how it redeems from Hell all those who trust in Him! Think of His resurrection and how it justifies believers; and of His Second Coming and how it delights our hearts!

EVENING

He is precious therefore to you who believe, but to the unbelieving He is the Stone which the builders rejected, which became the Head of the corner — 1 Peter 2:7.

IN PROPORTION as you believe with a childlike faith, clear, simple, strong, unbroken, in that proportion will Christ be dearer and dearer to you. I recommend you to keep the door of your mind on the chain in these days. For those tramps and vagrants called doubts are prowling about in every quarter, and they may knock at your door with vile intent. The first thing they say when they are at a good man's door is: "I am an honest doubt." That which so loudly calls itself honest has good need to fabricate for itself a character. The most honest doubt is a great thief. But the most of doubts are as dishonest as common housebreakers. Keep doubt out of your soul, or you will make small progress in the discovery of the preciousness of Christ. Never entertain a thought that is derogatory to Christ's person, or to His atoning sacrifice. Reckon that opinion to be your enemy which is the enemy of the cross of Christ. Do not allow your faith to diminish even in the least degree. Believe in Christ heartily and unsuspectingly.

If you have a doubt as to whether you are a saint, you can have no question that you are a sinner. Come to Christ as a sinner, and put your trust in Him as your Savior. It is wonderful how a renewed confidence in Christ's saving grace will bring back all your joy and delight in Him. Do it at once. *"Before I was aware, my soul make me like the chariots of Amminadab."* When I was dull and dead, suddenly I touched His garment by faith, and my life was renewed in me, even to leaping and rejoicing. God grant you to know the preciousness of Christ by faith; for only to you who believe is He precious. To you that doubt, to you that mistrust, to you that suspect, to you that live in the land of hesitation, He is without form and comeliness.

March 23 — MORNING

Surely I am more like an animal than any man, and I do not have the understanding of a man — Proverbs 30:2.

A SENSE OF INFERIORITY must not keep us from learning. Suppose you have to say, *"I am more like an animal than any man,"* you have so much the more need of being taught the things of God. If you have not the understanding of a man, there is so much more cause that you should go to school to the Holy Spirit until the eye of your understanding shall be enlightened, and *you shall know the truth, and the truth shall set you free.*

Vital truth is simple. A great many things are hard to understand, but that which is essential to salvation is not difficult. To know yourself a sinner, and Christ a Savior, is this a deep mystery? To quit your own self, and your own trusts, simply to rely on the person and work of the Son of God, is this exceedingly difficult to understand? The safest truth is the simplest. Commonly an invention in machinery grows more simple as it nears perfection. And because God's way of salvation is perfect, therefore it is simplicity itself. You can know the gospel, for it is not a tough metaphysical problem, but a revelation which he that runs may read.

If you are staggered by the sublimity of heavenly learning, consider that these things are revealed to babes. Our Lord said, *"I thank You, O Father, Lord of Heaven and earth, because You have hidden these things from the wise and prudent, and have revealed them to babes"* (Matt. 11:25). So if you are more than ever conscious of your spiritual babyhood, be assured that the Lord can and will reveal His truths to you.

Remember, also, that the Holy Spirit is a great Teacher. The best earthly teacher may be able to do very little with such slow scholars as we are; then let us go to our heavenly Teacher, that He may give us of His Spirit, with which we may learn the truth.

EVENING

Surely I am more like an animal than any man, and I do not have the understanding of a man — Proverbs 30:2.

A SENSE OF INFERIORITY must not keep us back from serving God. What if, like Agur, we take the very lowest place. Yet, like him, let us speak on God's behalf. Who knows, he may prophesy by us also. Agur's simple word is called *"the prophecy."* If God shall speak by you, my friend, your thinking so little of yourself will give charm to your speech. If God shall use such as you are, He will have all the glory of it, will He not? When the Lord uses a very clever man, there is always the fear that people will ascribe the success to the human instrument. But when the Lord uses the man who acknowledges himself to be a poor, foolish creature, then the honor is not divided, but all men see that this is the finger of God. The Lord loves to use tools that are not rusted with self-conceit. An axe that boasts itself shall not be used on the thick trees.

God can use inferior persons for grand purposes. He has often done so. Go into His armory and see how He has worked by flies and lice, worms and caterpillars, frogs and serpents. His greatest victories were won by a hammer and a tent-pin, by an ox-goad, by the jawbone of an ass, by a sling and a stone, and such like. His greatest prophets at the first tried to excuse themselves on the ground of unfitness. In the armory of the Lord you will find few swords with golden scabbards, but you will find many unlikely weapons. God uses what no one else would look upon. The Lord can get much glory out of you, my poor desponding friend. So, then, stir up yourself. Although you think yourself quite unworthy, go on in consecration of heart to yield yourself wholly to God, and He will not pass you by.

Surely I am more like an animal than any man, and I do not have the understanding of a man — Proverbs 30:2.

REMEMBER that if, by reason of our inferiority, you and I have to take a back seat, the back seats are still in the house. Our littleness does not alter God's promise. It is the same promise to the small as to the great; to the weak as to the strong. Our deficiency does not alter our God. He is as full of grace and truth as ever. He does not increase because we are enlarged; neither is He diminished because we have declined. My God, as a babe in grace, is the same God as those who have attained to fulness of stature in Christ Jesus. What a blessed God we have! Only to think of Him is hope; to know Him is fruition. "Yes, my own God is He," said David, and he could never have uttered a grander word. *"This God is our God forever and ever,"* is a sentence which might as fairly have been spoken in Heaven as on the lower earth. It has a glory tone about it. Come, you little ones, you backward ones, you foolish ones, dwell on the name of Father, Son and Holy Spirit, with your hearts' delight. The triune God is yours, your Father, your Redeemer, your Comforter: a triple blessing is thus secured to you. Let your triple nature of body, soul and spirit rejoice in this.

This makes no difference to the covenant of grace. Babes in their long clothes, if they are heirs, have quite as sure a right to their inheritance as have those who are of full age. One is as legally protected as one and twenty. The children cannot yet take full possession by reason of their tender years, but the law defies a rogue to rob even an infant heir of his lawful patrimony. Enjoy, therefore, O you little ones, the infinite wealth of the covenant, and do not doubt your title in Christ Jesus! However little you may be, this makes no difference to God's love to you.

EVENING

Surely I am more like an animal than any man, and I do not have the understanding of a man — Proverbs 30:2.

IF YOU FEEL that you are more brutish than anybody else, yet believe in God up to the hilt. Believe in Him and trust Him with all your heart; then feel all the more gratitude that He should have loved so worthless a one as you are. Feel all the more content with that free, rich, sovereign grace which has chosen you and ordained you to eternal life. Glorify God by your very weakness. Glory in your infirmity, because the power of Christ rests on you. Be all the more trustful in God since you have nothing in yourself to rely on. Say, "The great ones may run alone, but I am a babe, and I must be carried in my Father's arms. Because of this I will have the greater faith to match my greater need."

Our deep sense of folly and weakness should also keep us humble before the Lord. Where is the room for boasting? What have we to glory in? We owe all to mercy, and to mercy shall be all the praise!

Lastly, be more tender to others who, like yourself, are feeble. It is wonderful how gracious little ones care for other little ones, sympathize with them, pray for them, and comfort them. I believe that the saying is strictly true, that "the poor help the poor," and I know it is so among the spiritually poor. High and mighty ones cannot help downcast saints. Only those who have been afflicted can console the afflicted. In the East, among the Beouins, in a shepherd's family, the little children, as soon as they can walk, learn to keep the lambs. You see, the little boy who can only go slowly can lead the little lambs admirably; for he and they go well together. The big father would have taken long strides, and so would have tired the little lambs. But his little son can only go at a slow pace, and that pace suits the lambs. The weak lambs are pleased with their little shepherd, who is a lamb like themselves.

March 25 MORNING 85

As You sent Me into the world, I also sent them into the world — John 17:18.

    THERE ARE TWO PETITIONS in our Lord's prayer. First comes the petition: *"Holy Father, keep them."* You cannot serve God unless He preserves you. You will never keep the Lord's flock unless He first shepherds you. The Lord of the vineyard must keep the keepers, or their vineyards will not be kept. The other prayer immediately precedes the text: *"Sanctify them."* You cannot go out into the world as the sent ones of Christ unless you are sanctified. God will use no unholy messenger; you must be consecrated and cleansed, devoted and dedicated to God alone, or else you will not have the first qualification for the Divine mission. Christ's prayer is: *"Sanctify them through Your truth."* The more truth you believe, the more sanctified you will be. The operation of truth on the mind is to separate a man from the world unto the service of God. Just in proportion as truth is given up, worldliness and frivolity are sure to prevail. A church which grows so enlightened as to neglect the doctrines of grace will also fall in love with the vain amusements of the world. It has been so in all past ages, and it is sadly so today. But a church which, in a living way, holds fast the truth once for all delivered to the saints will also separate itself from the ways of the world. In fact, the world and the worldly church will shun it and push it into the place of separation. The more separated we are, after our Master's fashion, the more fit shall we be to do His bidding. Our Lord was evidently more careful as to our commission, which He bases on His own commission, and declares to be as certain and real as His own sending by the Father. He so values this, that He prays, *"Father, keep them,"* and, *"Father, sanctify them."* May those two prayers be heard for us, and then we shall stand with our loins girded, our shoes on our feet, our lamps trimmed, and our lights burning, ready to go forth at the command of the Most High.

EVENING

As You sent Me into the world, I also sent them into the world — John 17:18.

    I ASK YOU TO CONSIDER why our Lord was sent into the world. Our Lord came here with one design: Christ was not sent to teach a correct system of philosophy. He was not Plato, but Jesus; not a sage, but a Savior. He could have solved the problems of the universe, but He did not even allude to them. He was not an Aristotle, ruling the world of human thought; although He could have done so easily had He chosen. Blessed is His name, He came to save from sin. And this no Plato or Aristotle could have done. All the sages and philosophers put together are not worth so much as the little finger of a Christ. Christ entered into no rivalry with the academy. He came on a very different errand. Neither was our Lord sent to be an inventor or a discoverer. All the discoveries that have been made in modern times could have been at once revealed by Him. But that was not His object, and He kept scrupulously to His one design. He could have told us the secret of the Dark Continent, but He was not sent for that end. He could have anticipated all that we have slowly learned, and He could have saved the world the long processes of experiement and observation; but this was not the object of His mission.
    He did not come to be a conqueror. God gave us in Him neither Alexander nor Caesar; the world has always had enough and to spare of such slaughterers. He conquers evil, but not by the sword. Our Lord did not come to be a politician, a reformer of governments, a rectifier of social economics. One came to Him, saying, *"Master, speak to my brother, that he divide the inheritance with me."* You might have supposed that the Lord would have arbitrated that case. But He did not do so, for He said, *"Who made Me a judge or a divider over you?"* He kept to His business.

Jesus took the disciples aside in the highway and said to them, Behold! We are going up to Jerusalem and the Son of man will be betrayed to the chief priests and scribes —
Matthew 20:17, 18.

WHEN our Master took the Twelve apart His conversation was on choice themes. He spoke to them of the Scriptures, *"He took to Him the Twelve, and said to them, Behold, we go up to Jerusalem, and all things that are written by the prophets concerning the Son of man shall be accomplished."* Blessed theme, the Word of the Lord by His prophets and its fulfilment. Have you noticed how our divine Lord delights to speak on the Scriptures? How often He enforces His teaching by *"as the Scripture has said'"*? If He has only two of them, we read, *"Beginning at Moses and all the prophets He expounded to them in all the Scriptures the things concerning Himself"* (Luke 24:27).

Communion with Christ Jesus must be based on the Word of the Lord. If you speak half a word derogatory of holy Scripture your fellowship will evaporate. Men talk about building on Christ, and not on the Scriptures. But they know not what they say, for our Lord continually established His own claims by appealing to Moses and the prophets. They say they are Christo-centric, but I only wish they were. If they take Christ for a center they will inevitably have the Scriptures for a center, too; but these people neither want the one nor the other. They care nothing for the center. They only want to do away with the circumference, that they may roam at their proud wills. Our Lord made the written Word the reason for many of His acts. He did this, and He did not do that because of what the Scriptures had said. He comes not to take away the law and the prophets, not a jot or a tittle does He destroy, so careful is he of the Scriptures. We learn from Him to believe not only in inspired words, but in inspired jots and tittles. Those having been much with Christ always show a profound reverence for the Word.

EVENING

And the multitudes, those going before and those following, were crying out, saying, Hosanna to the Son of David! Blessed is He who comes in the name of the Lord. Hosanna in the highest! — Matthew 21:9.

THIS WAS our Lord's public claiming of authority over Israel. He was the son of David, and so He was by natural right the King of the Jews. If He had taken possession of His own, He would have been sitting on the throne of the chosen dynasty of David by right of birth. Also as the Messiah, the Christ, He was the King of His people Israel. Concerning Him it had been said by the prophet, *"Rejoice greatly, O daughter of Zion; shout, O daughter of Jerusalem. Behold! Your king comes to you. He is just, and having salvation; lowly, and riding on an ass; yea, on a colt the foal of an ass "*(Zech. 9:9). Our Lord Jesus literally came to Zion in this way. As King He rode to His capital and entered His palace. In His priestly royalty the Son of God went to His Father's house, to the temple of sacrifice and sovereignty. Among the tribes of Israel He is seen to be *"One chosen out of the people,"* whom the Lord had given to be a leader and commander for the people. They might afterwards choose Barabbas and cry that they had no king but Caesar, yet Jesus was their King (as Pilate reminded them when he said, *"Shall I crucify your king?"* And also His cross declared it, bearing the legal inscription, *"This is Jesus the King of the Jews."* Before His trial and condemnation He had put in a public claim to the rights and prerogatives of Zion's king, whom God has set on His holy hill. Would to God all fully recognized our Lord's kingdom, yielding to His sway! Oh, that you would bow before Him, and put your trust in Him! Part of His intent in riding through Jerusalem was that we also who dwell in the isles of the sea might know Him and reverence Him as King of kings and Lord of lords.

MORNING

And the multitudes, those going before and those following, were crying out, saying, Hosanna to the Son of David! Blessed is He who comes in the name of the Lord — Matthew 21:9.

WHY THIS PROCESSION? Why these shouts of homage? Our Lord always had a reason, and an excellent one, for all that He arranged or permitted. What did He mean by this? How shall we interpret the scene?

First, it was that He might most openly declare Himself. He had frequently avowed His mission in plain speech. He had told them who He was, and why He came. But they would not hear, so that they dared to say to Him, *"If you are the Christ, tell us plainly."* He had plainly told them times without number. Now He will assure them still more positively of His kingdom by openly riding into the city of Jerusalem in state. Now they shall see that He claims to be the Messiah, sent of God, of whom the prophet said, *"Say to the daughter of Zion, Behold, your salvation comes."* Out of the mouths of babes and sucklings shall His fame be proclaimed. Multitudes shall acknowledge with loud voices that *"He comes in the name of the Lord,"* until the envious Pharisees shall be driven to ask, *"Do you hear what these say?"* You will remember that our Lord rode into Jerusalem as a King, but He was also brought there as the Lamb of God's passover, whose blood must save the people. It was not fit that the Lamb of God should go to the altar without observation, that He who takes away the sin of the world should be led to the temple unobserved. The day was near when He was to be offered up, and all eyes were called to look on Him and know who and what he was. Therefore He permitted this great gathering and this honorable attention to Himself, that He might say to Israel, by deeds as well as by words, "I am He that would come, who of old had said, *"Lo, I come: in the volume of the Book it is written of Me, I delight to do Your will, O my God"* (Heb. 10:9). So unquestionably He manifested Himself to the people. When crucifying Him the rulers knew what He professed to be.

EVENING

And all the people who had come together to see this sight, seeing the things which took place, returned beating their breasts — Luke 23:48.

FAR DIFFERENT was the procession to the gates of Jerusalem from that march of madness which had come out from there. Observe the power that God has over the minds of men! See how he tames the wildest, making the most malicious and proud ones cower at His feet when He but reveals Himself in the wonders of nature! How much more cowed and terrified will they be when He makes bare His arm and comes forth in the judgments of His wrath to deal with them according to their deserts!

This sudden and memorable change in so vast a multitude is the apt representative of two other remarkable mental changes. How like it is to the gracious transformation which a sight of the cross has often worked most blessedly in the hearts of men! Many have come under the sound of the gospel resolved to scoff at it; but they have returned to pray. But the idlest and even the basest motives have brought men under the preaching, but when Jesus has been lifted up they have been savingly drawn to Him. And as a consequence they have smitten on their breasts in repentance, and have gone their way to serve the Savior whom they once had blasphemed. Oh, the power, the melting, conquering, transforming power of that dear cross of Christ! We have but to abide by the preaching of it; we have but constantly to tell abroad the matchless story; then we may expect to see the most remarkable spiritual results. We need despair of no man now that Jesus has died for sinners. With such a hammer as the doctrine of the cross, the most flinty heart will be broken. And with such a fire as the sweet love of Christ, the most mighty iceberg of a heart will be melted.

And about the ninth hour Jesus cried with a loud voice, saying, Eli! Eli, lama sabachthani; that is to say, My God! My God, why have You forsaken Me? — Matthew 27:46.

"ELI! ELI, lama sabachthani" — which words are partly Hebrew, partly Aramaic, *"that is to say, My God! My God, why have You forsaken Me?"* He calls Him His God, not as He was God Himself, but as He was man. As man He was chosen by God to the grace of union to the Son of God; was made and formed by Him; was anointed by Him with the oil of gladness; was supported and upheld by Him in the day of salvation; was raised by Him from the dead and highly exalted by Him at His own right hand. Christ, as man, prayed to Him as His God, believed in Him, loved Him, and obeyed Him as man. And though now God the Father hid His face from Him, yet Christ expressed strong faith and confidence of His interest in Him. When He is said to be *forsaken* of God, the meaning is not that the hypostatical union was dissolved (which was not even by death itself; the fulness of the Godhead still dwelt bodily in Him), nor was He separated from the love of God. He still had the same interest in His Father's heart and favor, both as His Son, and as Mediator, as much as ever. Nor was the principle and habit of joy and comfort lost in His soul, as man, but now He was without a sense of the gracious presence of God; as the Surety of His people He was filled with a sense of Divine wrath, the wrath deserved by the iniquities of the people He now bore on their behalf — the wrath which He must necessarily endure in order to make full satisfaction for them (for one part of the punishment of sin is loss of the Divine presence).

EVENING

And about the ninth hour Jesus cried with a loud voice, saying, Eli! Eli! lama sabachtani; that is to say, My God! My God! Why have You forsaken Me?
— Matthew 27:46.

THE LORD JESUS did not make this expostulation out of ignorance. He knew the reason of it was not out of personal disrespect to Him, or for any sin of His own; but it was because He stood in the law-place and in the stead of sinners. Nor was it out of impatience that he so expressed Himself; for He was entirely resigned to the will of God, and was content to drink the whole of the bitter cup. Nor was it out of despair, for He at the same time strongly claims and asserts His interest in God, and He repeats it.

By this statement He intends to show us that He was bearing all the griefs of His people, even this among the rest, Divine desertion. It was to set forth the bitterness of His sorrows, that not only the sun in the firmament had hidden its face from Him; not only that He was forsaken by His friends and disciples; but even He had been left by (hidden from — Ed.) His God; yet also to express the strength of His faith at such a time. The whole of it evinces the truth of Christ's human nature, that He was in all things made like unto His brethren, that He had a human soul and endured sorrows and sufferings in it, of which this of desertion was not the least. The heinousness of sin may be learned from this, which not only drove the angels out of Heaven, and Adam out of the Garden, but also separates with respect of communion between God and His children — and now even caused Him to hide His face from His own Son all the while He was bearing, and suffering for, the sins of His people. The condescending grace of Christ is seen here, that He, who was the Word that was with God from everlasting, and His only-begotten Son that lay in His bosom, that He should descend from heaven by the assumption of human nature, and be for a while forsaken of God, to bring us near to Him. — *An Exposition of the New Testament*, p. 295, John Gill (London, 1852).

March 29   MORNING

And all the people who had come together to see this sight, seeing the things which took place, returned beating their breasts — Luke 23:48.

IN THAT crowd were many who came together to behold the crucifixion of Jesus in a condition of most furious malice. They had hounded the Savior as dogs pursue a stag; and at last, all made with rage they hemmed Him in for death. Others, willing enough to spend an idle hour, and to gaze on a sensational spectacle, swelled the mob until a vast assembly congregated around the little hill on which the three crosses were raised. Whether of malice or of wantonness unanimously they joined in mockery of the victim hanging on the center cross. Some thrust out the tongue, some wagged their heads, others scoffed and jeered, some taunted Him in words, others in signs, but all alike exulted over the defenceless man who was given as a prey to their teeth. Earth never beheld a scene in which so much unrestrained derision and expressive contempt were poured on one man so unanimously, and for so long a time. It must have been hideous to the last degree to have seen so many grinning faces and mocking eyes, and to have heard so many cruel words and scornful shouts.

The spectacle was too detestable for Heaven to long endure it. Suddenly the sun veiled its face, and for three long hours the ribald crew sat shivering in midday midnight. Meanwhile the earth quaked beneath their feet, the rocks were torn, and the temple in defence of which they were committing the murder of this Just One, had its holy veil torn apart, as if by strong invisible hands. The newness of this, the feeling of horror produced by the darkness and the earth's tremors caused a revulsion of feelings. Gibes and jests, thrustings out of the tongue, cruel mockeries ceased. They went their way solitary and alone to their homes, or in little silent groups, while each being struck with sudden awe went on, beating on their breasts.

EVENING

And all the people who had come together to see this sight, seeing the things which took place, returned beating their breasts — Luke 23:48.

YOU MAY SMITE on your breasts as you look at the cross, and mourn that you should have done so little for your Lord. If anybody could have sketched my future life in the day of my conversion, and could have said, "You will be dull and cold in spiritual things; you will exhibit but little earnestness and little gratitude," I would have said like Hazael *"Is your servant a dog that he should do this great thing?"* I suppose that rightly I read your hearts when I say that most of you are disappointed with your own conduct as compared with your too flattering prophecies of yourselves. What! Am I really pardoned? Am I in very deed washed in that warm stream which gushed from the riven side of Jesus, and yet am I not wholly consecrated to Christ? What! In my body do I bear the marks of the Lord Jesus, and can I live almost without a thought of Him? Am I plucked like a brand from the burning, and do I have but small care to win others from the wrath to come? Has Jesus stooped to win me, and do I not labor to win others for Him? Was He all in earnest about me, and am I only half in earnest about Him? Do I dare waste a minute, dare to trifle away an hour? Do I have an evening to spend in vain gossip and idle frivolities? O my heart, well may I smite you, that at the sight of the death of the dear Lover of my soul I should not be fired by the highest zeal, that I should not be impelled by the most ardent love to a perfect consecration of every power of my nature, every affection of my spirit, every faculty of my whole man? This mournful strain might be pursued to far greater lengths. We might follow up our confessions, still smiting, still accusing, still regretting, still bewailing. We might continue on the bass notes evermore, and yet might we not express sufficient contrition for the shameful manner in which we have treated our blessed Savior.

And all the people who had come together to see this sight, seeing the things which took place, returned beating their breasts — Luke 23:48.

THEY ALL beat on their breasts, but not all from the same cause. They were all afraid, not all from the same reason. The outward manifestations were alike in all, but the grades of difference in feeling were as many as the minds in which they ruled. There were many, no doubt, who were merely moved with a transient emotion. They had seen the death agonies of a remarkable man, and the attendant wonders had persuaded them that He was something more than an ordinary being. So they were afraid. With a kind of indefinite fear, grounded on no very intelligent reasoning, they were alarmed — for God was angry, and He had closed the eye of day on them, and had torn the rocks. And burdened with this indistinct fear they went their way trembling and humbled to their several homes. But perhaps before the morning light had dawned they had forgotten it all, and the next day may have found them greedy for another bloody spectacle, ready to nail another Christ to the cross, if another could be found in the land. Their beating of the breast was not a breaking of the heart. It was like an April shower, a dewdrop of the morning, a hoar-frost that dissolved when the sun had risen. Like a shadow the emotion crossed their minds, and like a shadow it left no trace behind. How often in the teaching of the cross has this been the only result in tens of thousands! Many more have shed tears which have been wiped away, and the reason of their tears has been forgotten. A handkerchief has dried up their emotions. Alas! It is difficult to move men to weep with the story of the cross; but it is even more difficult to make those emotions permanent.

EVENING

And all the people who had come together to see this sight, seeing the things which took place, returned beating their breasts — Luke 23:48.

OTHERS among that great crowd exhibited emotions based on more thoughtful reflection. they saw that they had shared in the murder of an innocent person. They said, "Alas! We see through it all now. That man was no offender. In all that we have heard or seen of Him, He did good, and only good. He always healed the sick, fed the hungry, and raised the dead. There is not a word of all His teaching that is really contrary to the law of God. He was a pure and holy man. We have all been duped. Those priests have egged us on to put to death one whom it were a thousand mercies if we could restore to life again. Our race has killed its benefactor." One says, "Yes, I thrust out my tongue; I found it almost impossible to restrain myself when everybody else was laughing and mocking at His tortures. But I am afraid I have mocked at the innocent, and I tremble lest the darkness which God has sent was His reprobation of my wickedness in oppressing the innocent." Such feelings would abide, but I can suppose that they might not bring men to sincere repentance. For while they might feel sorry that they had oppressed the innocent, yet, perceiving nothing more in Jesus than mere maltreated virtue and suffering manhood, the natural emotion might soon pass away, and the moral and spiritual result might be of no great value.

How frequently we have seen that same description of emotion in our hearers. They have regretted that Christ should have been put to death; they have felt like that old king of France who said, "I wish I had been there with ten thousand of my soldiers; I would have cut their throats rather than that they should have touched Him." But those very feelings have been evidence that they did not feel their share in the guilt as they ought to have done. To them the cross of Jesus was no more a saving spectacle than the death of a common martyr.

March 31   MORNING

And all the people who had come together to see this sight, seeing the things which took place, returned, beating their breasts — Luke 23:48.

BY FAITH we will put ourselves at the foot of the little knoll of Calvary. There we see in the center, between two thieves, the Son of God made flesh, nailed by His hands and feet, dying in an anguish which words cannot portray. Look well, I pray you. Look steadfastly and devoutly, gazing through your tears. It is he who was worshiped by angels, who is now dying for the sons of men. Sit down and watch the death of death's destroyer. First smite your breasts, as you remember that you see in Him your own sins. How great He is! That thorn-crowned head was once crowned with all the royalties of Heaven and earth. He dying there is no common man. He hanging on the cross is the King of kings and Lord of lords. Then see the greatness of your sins, sins that required so great a sacrifice. They must be infinite sins to require an infinite person to lay down His life in order for them to be removed.

You can never compass nor comprehend the greatness of your Lord in His essential character and dignity. Nor can you ever be able to understand the blackness and heinousness of the sin which demanded His life as an atonement. Smite your breast and say, *"God, be merciful to me,"* for I am the greatest of sinners. Look well into the face of Jesus; see how vile they have made Him! They have stained those cheeks with spittle; they have lashed those shoulders with a felon's whip; they have put Him to the death which was only awarded to the meanest Roman slave; they have hung Him between Heaven and earth, as though He were fit for neither; they have stripped Him naked and left Him not a rag to cover Him! See here then, O believer, the shame of your sins. What a shameful thing your sin must have been; what a disgraceful and abominable thing, if Christ must be made such a shame for you.

EVENING

Jesus took the disciples aside in the highway and said to them, Behold! We are going to Jerusalem, and the Son of man will be betrayed to the chief priests and scribes — Matthew 20:17, 18.

NOTE well what our Lord said about His sufferings, *"Behold! We are going to Jerusalem and the Son of man will be betrayed."* Stop there: *"BETRAYED"!* it is as though I heard the deep boom of a death-knell. *"Betrayed"* to die; yes, that is not a word with a sting in it to Him. But *"betrayed"* — that means sold by cruel treachery. It means that one who ate bread with Him lifted up his heel against Him. It means that a familiar acquaintance, with whom He walked to the house of God, sold Him for a paltry bribe. *"Betrayed"* for thirty pieces of silver! What a price for the blood of such a Friend! Hear how He cries, *"If it were an enemy, then I could have borne it"* (Ps. 55:12). It was no stranger, no bloodhound of the Pharisees, who scented Him out in the garden; but *"Judas also, who betrayed Him, knew the place."* Betrayed with a kiss and with a friendly word. Handed over to those seeking His blood, by one who ought to have defended Him to the death. *"Betrayed"!* It is a dreadful word to be set here before the passion, and it throws a lurid light over it all. We read, *"the same night in which He was betrayed He took bread."* This was the bitterest drop in His cup, that He was betrayed. And He is still being betrayed! If the gospel dies here, write on its tomb, *"Betrayed"!* What do we care for infidels? What do we care for those who curse and blaspheme? They cannot hurt the Christ. His wounds are those which He receives in the house of His friends. *"Betrayed"!* O Savior, some of us have been betrayed, but ours was a small sorrow compared with Yours. For You were betrayed into the hands of sinners by one who claimed to be Your friend.

And, behold! There had been a great earthquake. For an angel of the Lord came down out of Heaven and had rolled away the stone from the door — Matthew 28:2.

DEATH'S house was firmly secured by a huge stone. The angel removed it and the living Christ came forth. The massive door was taken away from the grave, not merely opened, but unhinged and flung aside, rolled away. And from this time forth death's ancient prison house is without a door. The saints shall pass in, but they shall not be shut in. They shall tarry there as in an open cavern, but there is nothing to prevent their coming forth from it in due time. As Samson, when he slept in Gaza, and was beset by foes, arose early in the morning and took on his shoulders the gates of Gaza, post and bar. And he carried all away and left the Philistine stronghold open and exposed. So it has been done to the grave by our Master. Having slept out His three days and nights according to the Divine decree, He arose in the greatness of His strength and bore away the iron gates of the sepulcher, tearing every bar from its place. The removal of the imprisoning stone was the outward type of our Lord's having plucked up the gates of the grave, post, bar and all, and so exposing that old fortress of death and Hell, leaving it as a city stormed and taken, and bereft of power from now on.

Remember that our Lord was committed to the grave as a hostage. *"He died for our sins."* Like a debt they were imputed to Him. He discharged the debt of obligation due from us to God. He suffered to the full — the great substitutionary equivalent for our suffering. And then He was confined in the tomb as a hostage until His work should be fully accepted. That acceptance would be denoted by His coming forth from durance vile. That coming forth would become our justification. *"He rose again for our justification."* If He had not fully paid the debt, He would have remained in the grave.

EVENING

And, behold! There had been a great earthquake. For an angel of the Lord came down out of Heaven and had rolled away the stone from the door, and was sitting on it — Matthew 28:2.

THE FIRST thing the angel said was, *"Fear not."* Oh! This is the very genius of our risen Savior's gospel. You who would be saved, you who would follow Christ, you need not fear. Did the earth quake? Fear not. God can preserve you although the earth is burned with fire. Did the angel descend in terrors? Fear not. There are no terrors in Heaven for the child of God who comes to Jesus' cross and trusts his soul to Him who bled on it. Poor women, is it the dark that alarms you? Fear not. God sees and loves you in the dark, and there is nothing in the dark or in the light beyond His control. Are you afraid to come to the tomb? Does a sepulcher alarm you? Fear not. You cannot die. Since Christ has risen, even though you were dead, yet you would live. Oh, the comfort of the gospel! Permit me to say there is nothing in the Bible to make any man fear, and who puts his trust in Jesus. There is nothing in Heaven, nothing on earth, nothing in Hell that need make you fear to trust in Jesus. *"Fear not."* The past you need not fear, it is forgiven you. You need not fear the present, it is provided for; the future is also secured by the living power of Jesus. He says, *"Because I live you shall live also."* Fear? Why that may have been seemly when Christ was dead, but now that He lives there remains no space for it. Do your fear your sins? They are all gone, for Christ would not have risen if He had not put them all away. What is it you fear? If an angel bids you not to fear, why will you fear? If every wound of the risen Savior, and every act of your reigning Lord, consoles you, why are you still dismayed? To be doubting, and fearing, and trembling, now that Jesus has risen is an inconsistent thing in any believer. Jesus is able to aid you in all your temptations, since He ever lives to make intercession for you. He is able to save you to the uttermost.

April 2 MORNING 93

Behold, there had been a great earthquake! For an angel of the Lord came down out of Heaven and had rolled away the stone from the door, and was sitting on it — Matthew 28:2.

NOTE that the angel was a symbolical preacher, with his brow of lightning and his robe of snow. But for whom were the symbols reserved? He did not say a word to the keepers; not a word. He gave them the symbolical gospel. That is to say, he looked on them with a lightning glance; he revealed himself to them in his snow-white garments, and no more. Mark how they quake and tremble! That is the gospel of symbols. Whereever it comes it condemns. It can do no other. Why, the old Mosaic law of symbols, where did it end? How few ever reached its inner meaning! The mass of Israel fell into idolatry, and the symbolic system became death to them. You who delight in symbols, who think it is Christian to make the whole year a kind of practical charade on the life of Christ, who think that all Christianity is to be taught in the kind of dramas men perform in theaters and puppet shows, go your way. For you shall meet no Heaven in that road, no Christ, no life. You shall meet with priests, and formalists, and hypocrites, and will go into the thick woods, and among the dark mountains of destruction, stumbling to your utter ruin. The gospel message is: *"Hear, and your soul shall live"*; *"Incline your ear and come unto Me."* This is the life-giving message, *"Believe in the Lord Jesus Christ, and you shall be saved."* But, O perverse generation, if you look for symbols and signs, you will be deluded with the Devil's gospel and fall prey to the destroyer.

The true gospel is only to be delivered in words. Christ is the Word, and the gospel is a gospel of words and thoughts. It does not appear to the eye; it appeals to the ear, and to the intellect, and to the heart. It is a spiritual thing, and it can only be learned by those whose spirits are awakened to grasp at spiritual truth.

EVENING

We were buried with Him through baptism into death, so that as Christ was raised from among the dead by the glory of the Father, so also we should walk in newness of life — Romans 6:4.

IN ITSELF it was a great marvel. Our Lord was assuredly dead. The Roman guards at the cross took care that no condemned person escaped the death penalty. In our Lord's case His side was pierced with the spear to make sure that no life remained in Him. Joseph begged His body. And He was wrapped in spices and fine linen by loving hands, then laid in the rocky tomb. There lay our Lord in the grave, with a stone rolled at the cave's mouth. And a seal was set on it by those in authority, whose envy made them take double precautions. As when a prince lies slumbering in his pavilion, a watch is posted, so was our Lord's sepulcher watched by a guard of Roman soldiers, so that no man might steal His body. There He lay in the heart of the earth, for a portion of three days and nights. Jesus, the man, was really dead, and in the grave He wore all the marks of decease. A napkin was bound about His head, and the linen clothes enwrapped His limbs. On the morning of the third day it was truly said, *"The Lord has risen,"* for He actually, literally, and in very fact awoke to life, unbound the napkin and laid it by itself, leisurely folded His graveclothes, and when the angel had rolled away the stone from the mouth of the sepulcher, He, the first begotten from the dead, came forth in a material body to live among His disciples for forty days. During the time of His stay His resurrection was established by many infallible proofs. He was seen, and heard, and touched, and handled. One of His disciples put his finger into the print of the nails and thrust his hand into his side. He possessed a real body, for He ate a piece of a broiled fish and of a honeycomb before them all. It was Jesus of Nazareth, and none other than He, who met His disciples at Galilee.

MORNING

Behold, there had been a great earthquake! For an angel of the Lord came down out of Heaven and had rolled away the stone from the door, and was sitting on it.
— Matthew 28:2.

THAT STONE rolled away from the sepulcher, typifying and certifying as it does the resurrection of Jesus Christ, is a foundation stone for Christian faith. The fact of the resurrection is the keystone of Christianity. Disprove the resurrection of our Lord, and our holy faith would be a mere fable. There would be nothing for faith to rest on if He did not also rise again from the tomb — then *"your faith is vain,"* and *"you are yet in your sins,"* while *"they who have fallen asleep in Christ are perished"* (1 Cor. 15:12-16). All the great doctrines of our Divine religion fall apart like an arch falls when the keystone is dislodged. For all our hope hinges on that great fact. If Jesus rose, then this gospel is what it professes to be. If He did not rise from the dead, then all is deceit and delusion. But that Jesus rose from the dead is a fact better established than almost any other fact in history. The witnesses were many. They were men of all classes and conditions. None of them ever confessed himself mistaken or deceptive. They were so persuaded that it was the fact that most of them suffered death for witnessing to it. They had nothing to gain by such a witnessing; they did not rise in power, nor gain honor or wealth. They were truthful, single-minded men who testified what they had seen, and they bore witness to what they had beheld. The resurrection is a fact better attested than any event recorded in any history, whether ancient or modern. Here is the confidence of the saints: Our Lord Jesus Christ, who witnessed a good confession before Pontius Pilate, and was crucified, dead and buried, rose again from the dead; and after forty days He ascended to the throne of God. We rest in Him; we believe in Him. If He had not arisen, we had been of all men most miserable to have followed Him.

EVENING

Behold, there had been a great earthquake! For an angel of the Lord had come down out of Heaven and had rolled away the stone from the door, and was sitting on it.
— Matthew 28:2.

HERE IS rest provided. How leisurely the whole resurrection was effected! Yea, and noiselessly. What an absence of pomp and parade! The angel descended, the stone was rolled away, Christ rose, and then the angel sat down on the stone. He sat there silently, gracefully, breathing defiance to the Jews and to their seal, to the Romans and their spears, to death, to earth, to Hell. He as good as said, "Come, roll that stone back again, enemies of the risen One. All you infernal powers, you who thought to prevail against our ever-living King, roll back that stone again, if you dare, if you can." The angel did not say this in words, but his quiet sitting on the stone meant all this and more. The Master's work is done, and done forever. And this stone, no more to be used; this unhinged door, no more employed to shut in the deathlike house; these signify, *"It is finished"* — finished so as never to be undone; finished so as to last eternally. The resting angel softly whispers to us, "Come here, and rest also." There is no fuller, better, surer, safer rest for the soul than in the fact that the Savior in whom we trust has risen from the dead. Do you soon expect to die? Is the worm at the root? Have you the flush of consumption on your cheek? O come and sit on this stone and consider that death has lost its terror now, for Jesus has risen from the tomb. Come, too, you feeble and trembling ones, and breathe defiance to death and Hell. The angel will vacate his seat for you, and let you sit down in the face of the enemy. Though you are but a humble woman, or a man broken down, languid with long years of weary sickness, yet you may well defy all the hosts of Hell while resting on this precious truth, *"He is not here, but He is risen."*

April 4 — MORNING

We were buried with Him through baptism into death, so that as Christ was raised from among the dead by the glory of the Father, so also we should walk in newness of life — Romans 6:4.

ENTERING on a Christian profession we are met by the ordinance of baptism, which teaches the necessity of purification. In its very form baptism is a washing, and its teaching requires cleansing of the most thorough kind. It is a burial, in which the man is viewed as dead with Christ to sin, and is regarded as rising again as a new man. Baptism sets forth, as in a picture, the union of the believer with the Lord Jesus in His baptism of suffering, and in His death, burial, and resurrection. By submitting to that sacred ordinance we declare that we believe ourselves to be dead with Him, because He endured the death penalty, and dead to the world and to the dominion of sin by His Spirit. We also profess our faith in our Lord's resurrection, and that we ourselves are raised up in union with Him, having come forth through faith into newness of life. It is a very impressive and vivid symbol, but it has not meaning unless we rise to purity of life.

The basis of this confession lies in the union of every believer with Christ Jesus. We are dead with Him, because we are one with Him. We are risen with Him, because we are one with Him. In the purpose of Divine grace every believer is identified with Jesus. Each believer was given to the Lord Jesus from before the foundation of the world, and placed under His covenant headship (2 Thess. 2:13). He suffered as the substitute of each believer; virtually each saved one died in Christ. The believer rose in Christ by virtue of the eternal union which exists between the saint and his Savior. For this reason the believer continues to live, for the Lord said, *"Because I live, you shall live also."* Our destiny is identified with that of our covenant Head. His life is the model of our experience. He makes us to be conformed to His image now, and we shall be like Him.

EVENING

We also wait for a Savior, the Lord Jesus Christ, who will transform our body of humiliation, for it to be conformed to His glorious body — Philippians 3:20, 21.

MANY THOUSANDS of God's people have been denied a quiet slumber in the grave. They were cut off by martyrdom; many sawn apart, or cast to the dogs. Tens of thousands of the precious bodies of the saints have perished by fire, their limbs blown in clouds of smoke to the four winds; their relentless persecutors have even thrown the ashes that remained into rivers. Some of the children of the resurrection were devoured by wild beasts in the Roman amphitheaters; others were left on gibbets for birds of prey. In all sorts of ways the saints' bodies have been hacked and hewn. But what of that? You say, "How can these bodies be refashioned?" By what possibility can the same bodies be raised again? I answer: It needs a miracle to make any of these dry bones to live, and a miracle being granted, impossibility vanishes. He who formed each atom from nothing can gather each particle again from confusion. The omniscient Lord of providence traces each molecule of matter; He knows its position and history. And if it be needful to constitute the identity of the body, to regather each atom, He can do it. It may not be needful at all, and I do not assert that it will be. For there may be a true identity without sameness of material. Even as this my body is the same as that in which I lived twenty years ago, in all probability there is not one grain of the same matter in it. God is then able to cause that the same body which on earth we wear in humiliation, which we call a vile body, shall be fashioned like unto Christ's body.

MORNING

We also wait for a Savior, the Lord Jesus Christ, who will transform our body of humiliation, for it to be conformed to His glorious body — Philippians 3:20, 21.

BELOVED, whatever the body of Jesus may be in His glory, our present body which is now in humiliation is to be conformed to it. Jesus is the standard of man in glory: *"We shall be like Him, for we shall see Him as He is."* Here we dwell in humiliation, but it shall undergo a change, *"in a moment, in the twinkling of an eye, at the last trump; for the trump shall sound, and the dead shall be raised incorruptible, and we shall be changed."* Then we shall come into our glory, and our body being made suitable to the glory state, shall be fitly called the body of glory. We need not curiously pry into the details of the change, nor attempt to define all the differences between the two estates of our body; for, *"it does not yet appear what we shall be,"* and we may be content to leave much to be made known to us hereafter. Yet though we see through a glass darkly, we nevertheless do see something and would not shut our eyes to that little. We know not yet as we are known, but we do know in part, and that part knowledge is precious.

The gates have been ajar at times, and men have looked a while, and have beheld and wondered. Three times, at least, human eyes have seen something of the body of glory. The face of Moses, when he came down from the mount, shone so that those who gathered around him could not look on it, and he had to cover it with a veil. In that lustrous face of the man who had been forty days in high communion with God, you behold some gleams of the brightness of glorified manhood. Our Lord made a yet clearer manifestation of the glorious body when He was transfigured in the presence of the three disciples. When His garments became bright and glistering, whiter than any fuller could make them, then He Himself was all alow with glory, and His disciples saw and marvelled.

EVENING

The king saw there a man not clothed with a wedding garment. And he said to him, Friend, how did you come in here without a wedding garment? — Matthew 22:11,12.

THE WEDDING GARMENT represents anything which is indispensable to a Christian, but which the unrenewed heart is not willing to accept — anything which the Lord ordains to be a necessary attendant of salvation against which selfishness rebels. So it may be said to be Christ's righteousness imputed to us; for, alas! Many nominal Christians kick against the doctrine of justification by the righteousness of the Savior, and set up their own self-righteousness in opposition to it. To be found in Christ, not having our own righteousness which is of the law, but the righteousness which is of God by faith, is a very prominent badge of a real servant of God. To refuse it is to oppose the glory of God, and the name and person and work of His exalted Son.

But we might with equal truth say that the wedding dress is a holy character, the imparted righteousness which the Holy Spirit works in us, and which is equally necessary as a proof of grace. If you question such a statement, remember the dress which adorns the saints in heaven. What is said of it? *"They have washed their robes and made them white in the blood of the Lamb."* Their robes, then, were such as once needed washing; and this could not be said in any sense of the righteousness of the Lord Jesus Christ; that was always perfect and spotless. So it is clear the figure is at times applied to saints in reference to their personal character. Holiness is always present in those who are loyal guests of the great King, for *"without holiness no one shall see the Lord."* Too many pacify themselves with the idea that they possess imputed righteousness, yet are indifferent to the sanctifying work of the Spirit. They refuse to don the garment of obedience; they reject the white linen which is the righteousness of saints. In this they reveal their self-will, enmity to God and non-submission to His Son.

April 6   MORNING   97

The kingdom of Heaven has been compared to a man, a king, who made a wedding feast for his son — Matthew 22:2.

THE GENEROUS method by which God honors Christ is set forth here under the form of a banquet. Matthew Henry describes the objects of a feast with the alliteration of the Puritans: "A feast is for love and for laughter, for fulness and for fellowship." It is even so with the gospel. It is for love: In the gospel, sinner, you are invited to be reconciled to God; you are assured that God forgives your sins, ceases to be angry, and would have you reconciled to Him through His Son. So love is established between God and the soul. Then it is for laughter, happiness and joy. Those coming to God in Christ Jesus, and believe in Him, have their hearts filled with overflowing peace, a calm lake of peace often lifting up itself in waves of joy, clapping their hands in exultation.

It is not to sorrow but to joy that the great King invites His subjects when He glorifies His Son Jesus. It is not that you may be distressed, but that you may be delighted, that He bids you believe in the crucified Savior and live. A feast is for fulness: The hungry famished soul of man is satisfied with the blessings of grace. The gospel fills the whole capacity of our manhood. There is not a faculty of our nature that is not made to feel its need supplied when the soul accepts the provisions of mercy. All our being is satisfied with good things and our youth is renewed: *"For I have satisfied the weary soul, and I have replenished every sorrowful soul."* To crown all, the gospel brings us into fellowship with the Father and His Son Jesus Christ. In Christ Jesus we commune with the sacred Trinity. God is revealed to be our Father with His paternal heart. Jesus reveals Himself to us, and the communion of the Holy Spirit abides with us.

EVENING

They hated Me without a cause — John 15:25.

WAS THERE anything in Christ's doctrine that should have made us hate Him? No! Nothing in His teaching should have excited men's hatred. Take his precepts: Did He not teach us to do to others as we would have them do to us? Was He not also the exponent of everything lovely and honorable, and of good repute? And was not His teaching the very essence of virtue, so that if virtue's self had written it, it could not have written such a perfect code of lovely morals and virtues? Was it the ethical part of His doctrines that men hated? He taught that rich and poor must stand on one level. He taught that His gosepl was not to be confined to one particular nation, but was to be gloriously expansive, so as to cover the world. Perhaps this was one principal reason of their hating Him. But surely there was no justifiable cause for their indignation in this. There was nothing in Christ to lead men to hate Him, but *"they hated Him without a cause."*

It was man's depravity that he should have hated the Savior without a cause. I will not tell you of man's adulteries, fornications, murders, sodomies, etc. I will not tell you of man's wars, and bloodsheds, and cruelties, and rebellions. If I want to tell you man's sin I must tell you that man is a deicide, for he put to death his God; he slew his Savior. And when I have told you that I have given you the essence of all sin, the masterpiece of crime, the very pinnacle and climax of the terrific pyramid of mortal guilt. Man outdid himself when he put his Savior to death, and sin outdid Herod when it slew the Lord of the universe, the lover of the race of man. Never does sin appear so exceedingly sinful as when we see it pointed at the person of Christ, whom it *"hated without a cause"*. In every other case, when man has hated goodness, there have always been extenuating circumstances, but in the case of hatred toward the Savior there was nothing of this.

MORNING

They hated Me without a cause — John 15:25.

IT IS USUALLY understood that the Savior here refers to Psalm 35:19, where David says, speaking of himself immediately, and of the Savior prophetically, *"Do not let those who are my enemies wrongfully rejoice over me, neither let them wink with the eye, those that hate me without a cause."* Our Savior refers to that as being applicable to Himself, and so in effect He really tells us that many of the Psalms are Messianic, referring to the Messiah. So Dr. Hawker did not err when he said he believed the Psalms referred to the Savior, though he carried the truth too far. But it will be a good plan, in reading the Psalms, if we continually look at them as alluding not so much to David, as to the Man of whom David was the type, Jesus Christ, David's Lord.

No being was ever more lovely than the Savior. It would seem almost impossible not to have affection for Him. Certainly at first sight it would seem far more difficult to hate Him than to love Him. And yet, lovable as He was, yes, *"altogether lovely,"* no being so early met with hatred; no one ever endured such a continual persecution as He had to suffer. No sooner is He ushered into the world than Herod's sword is ready to cut Him off, by that dreadful massacre of the babes of Bethlehem. This was but a sad foretaste of the sufferings which Christ would endure, and of the hatred that men would pour on His devoted head. From His first moment to the cross, except for the temporary lull while He was a child, it seemed all the world was in league against Him, and all men sought to destroy Him. In different ways that hatred displayed itself, sometimes in overt deeds (as when they took Him to the brow of the hill to cast Him down headlong — or when they took up stones again to stone Him, because He said that Abraham desired to see this day, and saw it, and was glad). At other times that hatred showed itself in words of slander, such as these: *"He is a drunken man, a winebibber."*

EVENING

We were buried with Him through baptism into death, so that as Christ was raised from among the dead by the glory of the Father, so also we should walk in the newness of life — Romans 6:4.

QUICKENING is a needed part of the process of sanctification. Sanctification, in its operation on our character, consists of three things: First, we die to sin. A wondrous death! By this Jesus strikes at the heart of evil. The death of Christ makes us die to sin. After this comes burial. We are buried with Christ, and of this burial baptism is the type and token. Covered up to be forgotten, we are to sin as a dead shepherd is to his flock. As the sheep pass over the dead shepherd's grave, or even feed on it, and yet he does not regard them — so our old sins and habits come about us, but we, as dead to sin, know them no more. We are buried to them.

To complete our actual sanctification we receive heavenly quickening: *"If we are dead with Christ, we believe that we shall also live with Him."* Yes, we do live in Him, and by Him. Have you been thus dead, buried with Christ in this way? Are you now thus quickened in the likeness of His resurrection? This is your joyful privilege, if you are indeed believers in Christ, joined to the Lord in one spirit.

Being thus quickened you are partakers of a new life. You are not like Lazarus, who, when he was raised from the dead, had the same life restored to him. True, you have that same life about you. Alas, that you should have it! For it will be your burden and plague. But your true life has come to you by your being born again from above: *"This is the record, that God has given to us eternal life, and this life is in His Son. He having the Son has life."* The Holy Spirit has worked in us a higher life than nature's.

count it all joy when you fall into various temptations, knowing that the proving of your faith works patience — James 1:2

THE APOSTLE is supposing a maxim, and building on it, saying that to have our graces, our faith and patience tried and drawn forth to the glory of God, is the greatest blessedness that a Christian may have in this life.

And the reason is this: For grace to approve itself so as to greatly please God, and for one to sincerely desire God's approval, is the greatest privilege a saint can have. And it ought to be of greatest comfort to us. It is our greatest glory, as it is written, *"He that glories, let him glory in the Lord"* (2 Cor. 10:17). For he says next, *"not he that commends himself is approved, but whom the Lord commends."* This is what the Apostle Paul used to comfort himself, and it is what he gloried in, that the Lord approved him. The apostle Peter says, *"The trial of your faith is more precious than gold"* (1 Pet. 1:7), speaking of this trial as being the very instrument by which God tries our graces. It is the fire in which our faith is tried, and it is more precious than gold. And here the apostle James teaches us that these very afflictions and trials are joyous instruments. They are God's refining pot and fire. Your graces are highly valued by God, and that is the reason He tries them, and refines them. Then let us rejoice that we have so much affliction to purify and increase our graces. For once tried and proven, God sets His royal stamp and mark on these proven graces (though it may be secretly in this life, in the next life they will openly appear).

He mentions faith: *"for the trial of your faith,"* as being in the first and chief place as the grace most tried. And it being tried, it sets all the rest to work. It is faith that will be counted for honor and glory at that Day. It is faith by which we overcome: *"This is the victory which we have over the world, even our faith. Who is he that overcomes the world, except the one believing?"* (1 John 5:4, 5).

[Extracted from *Let Patience Have Its Perfect Work*, by Thomas Goodwin.]

EVENING

How long shall your vain thoughts lodge within you — Jeremiah 4:14.

IN THESE WORDS he compares the heart to a house of common resort, one having large rooms to entertain and lodge multitudes of guests. And in this heart, before one's conversion, all the vain, light, wanton, profane, dissolute thoughts that fly up and down the world have free and open access (as your thoughts do, running riot all the day). The unregenerate heart freely gives access to these thoughts, lodging and harboring them, reveling in them day and night, allowing them to defile it. It is for this reasosn that the Lord says to us, *"How long shall your vain thoughts lodge within you?"* Shall they lodge within you while I, and My Spirit, My Son and My train of graces stand knocking, and finding no admittance?

This, your heart, must be washed of all this filthiness: *"Wash your heart from evil"* (Jer. 4:14). It is to be washed, not just swept of the grosser evils. It must be washed and cleansed of these defilements, for they stick closer, and are incorporated and worked into the spirit more, to the hurt of the heart. These vain and unruly guests, these thoughts, must be turned out without any warning. They have stayed far too long, for the Lord says, *"How long?"* — and, *"The time past is enough."* In conversion the soul is not pulled down, but only these ungodly guests are turned out. And though we cannot keep them out — for they will ever be able to enter as long as we are in this house of clay — yet we must not allow them to lodge within us any more.

The conclusion is this: It is not what thoughts are in your heart, or what passes through them, but it is what lodging you give them that makes the difference. If you give them no lodging, you prove your repentance. Many good thoughts and motions may pass as strangers through a bad man's heart. Likewise multitudes of vain thoughts may make a thoroughfare of a believer's heart, disturbing him in good duties, knocking on his heart to interrupt him. These may break in on the heart of a good man, but they will not be allowed to remain there; they will not be fostered or harbored there.

[Extracted from *The Vanity of Thoughts*, by Thomas Goodwin.]

But this Man, after He had offered one sacrifice for sins forever, sat down on the right hand of God — Hebrews 10:12.

AT THE LORD'S table we wish to have no subject for contemplation but our blessed Lord Jesus Christ. Generally we consider Him as the crucified One, *"the Man of sorrows, and acquainted with grief,"* while we have had before us the emblems of His broken body, and of His blood shed for many for the remission of sins. But surely the crucified Savior is not the only appropriate theme, although, perhaps, the most so. It is well to remember how our Savior left us, by what road He traveled through the shadows of death. But it is also quite well to recollect what He is doing while He is away from us; we should remember the high glories to which the crucified Savior has attained. Perhaps this is as much calculated to cheer our spirits to behold Him on His throne, as to consider Him on His cross. We have seen Him on His cross, in some sense; that is to say, the eyes of men saw the crucified Savior. But we have no idea of what His glories are above; they surpass our highest thought. Yet faith can see the Savior exalted on His throne, and surely there is no subject that can keep our expectations alive, or cheer our drooping faith better than to consider that while our Savior is absent, He is on His throne, and that when He has left His church to sorrow for Him, He has not left us comfortless — He has promised to come to us, that while He tarries He is reigning, that while He is absent He is sitting on the Father's throne.

The Apostle shows here the superiority of Christ's sacrifice over that of every other priest: *"Every priest stands daily ministering and offering oftentimes the same sacrifices, which can never take away sins. But this Man, after He had offered one sacrifice for sins, sat down on the right hand of God."* You see the superiority of Christ's sacrifice rests in this, that He finished His work. He did what myriads of scapegoats never did, what hundreds of thousands of lambs never could effect; He perfected our salvation and worked out an entire atonement for the sins of all His chosen ones.

EVENING

We were buried with Him through baptism into death, so that as Christ was raised from among the dead by the glory of the Father, so also we should walk in the newness of life — Romans 6:4.

"NEWNESS of life" — what does it mean? It means this: When we are born again and believe in the Lord Jesus Christ (which takes place at the same time), we receive a life which we never before possessed. We begin to feel, to think, and to act as we never did before. The new life is something foreign to our fallen nature; it is an exotic, a plant of another clime. The carnal mind knows nothing of spiritual things (1 Cor. 2:14). The man who is not born again cannot understand what the new birth means. Spiritual things are spiritually discerned, and the carnal nan is all abroad in reference to them. In your quickening you received a light which had never before shone in your bosom, a life that came not from men, nor by men. It is not a development of something which was hidden in our constitution. It is not the evolution of a principle which really exists, only it is hampered and hindered. No, it is not written, "You He has fostered, who had the germs of dormant life." It is written, *"You He has quickened who were dead in trespasses and sins."* You had no life, you had nothing out of which life could come. Fostered you might have been, but all the fostering possible would only have developed your corrupt nature and caused the evil within to grow at a greater rate. No seeds of eternal life is buried in fallen nature. Eternal life is the gift of God.

This new life is new in its principles. The old life at its very best only said, "I must do right that I may win a reward." Wage earning is the principle of the old legal life when it tries to be obedient. Now you with the new life are moved by gratitude, not by mercenary motive. Now you serve not as a hired servant, but as a loving child. Grace reigns. The love of Christ constrains you.

April 10   MORNING

O Lord, how my adversaries have multiplied! Many are rising up against me. Many are saying to my soul, There is no salvation for him in God — Psalm 3:1, 2.

THE LEGIONS of our sins, the armies of fiends, the crowd of bodily pains, the host of spiritual sorrows, and all the allies of death and Hell set themselves against the Son of man. O how precious to know and believe that He has routed their hosts, trodden them down in His anger! He has removed our adversaries into captivity; He has laid low those rising up against us. The dragon lost his sting when he dashed it into the soul of Jesus.

David complains before his loving God of the worst weapon of his enemies' attack, the bitterest drop of his distresses, saying, *"Many are saying of my soul, There is no salvation for him in God."* Some of his distrustful friends said this sorrowfully, but His enemies exultingly boasted of it; they longed to see their words proved by his destruction. This was the unkindest cut of all, their declaring that his God had forsaken him. Yet David knew in his own conscience that he had given them some ground for their sayings, for he had committed sin against God in the very light of day. Then they flung his crime with Bathsheba in his face, saying, Go up, you bloody man; God has forsaken you and left you. Shimei cursed him and swore at him, for he was bold because of his backers. For multitudes of the men of Belial thought of David in like fashion. No doubt David felt this infernal suggestion to be staggering to his faith. If all the trials which come from Heaven, all the temptations which ascend from Hell, and all the crosses which arise from earth could be mixed and pressed together, they would not make a trial so terrible as that contained in this verse. It is the most bitter of all afflictions to be led to fear that there is no help for us in God. Yet remember our most blessed Savior had to endure this in the deepest degree. He knew full well what it was to walk in darkness and to see no light when He cried, *"My God, My God, why have You forsaken Me?"* This was the curse of the curse. This was the wormwood mingled with the gall. To be deserted of His Father was worse than to be the despised of men.

EVENING

Then I said, Lo, in the roll of the Book it is written of Me. I come to do Your will, O God — Hebrews 10:7.

CHRIST is God's ultimatum. Look for no new revelation, for His *"Lo, I come"* shines on forever. Do not ask, *"Are You He that should come, or do we look for another?"* He has come; look for no other. He came to give what God desires, what God requires, what more would you have? Let Him be all your salvation and all your desire. Let Him be *the desire of all nations."* He is the fulfilment of all the requirements of the human race, as well as the full amount of what God requires.

Note the reference to preceding scriptures. He says, *"Lo, I come: in the volume of the Book it is written of Me."* Preaching from the passage in the Epistle to the Hebrews I might fairly declare that in the whole volume of Holy Scripture much is written of our Lord and prescribed for Him as Messiah. The page of inspiration is fragrant with the name of Jesus. He is the top line of the entire volume; there is a half-allusion to this in the Greek word. He is the headline of contents to every chapter of Scripture. He is of all Scripture the sum. *"In the beginning was the Word."* Everything speaks of Him. The Pentateuch, and the books of the prophets, and the Psalms, and the gospels, and the epistles, all speak of Him. The Pentateuch drips with the prophecies of Christ as a honeycomb overflowing with its honey. Chiefly is He to be found in the head and front of the Book. So early as the opening chapters of the Book of Genesis, when Adam and Eve sinned, and we were lost, behold He is spoken of in the volume of the book in these terms, *"The seed of the woman shall bruise the serpent's head."* So early was it written that the Redeemer would be born in our nature to vanquish our foe.

His name shall endure forever; His name shall be continued as long as the sun, and men shall be blessed in Him; all nations shall call Him blessed — Psalm 72:17.

THERE IS one name that will last when all others have died out. That name is connected with blessing, and only with blessing. Jesus Christ came into the world to bless men. Men, as a race, find in Him a blessing wide as the world. While He was here He blessed, and did not curse. All around Him, both by speech, and act, and glance, and thought He was an incarnate blessing. All that came to Him, unless they wilfully rejected Him, obtained blessings at His hands. The home of His infancy, the friends of His youth, the comrades of His manhood, He blessed. He parted with everything and became poor to bless men. At last He died to bless men. Our Lord's resurrection from the dead brings blessings to mankind. Redemption from the grave, and life eternal, He has won for us. He waited on earth a while, until He ascended, blessing men as He went up. His last attitude below the skies was that of pronouncing a blessing on His disciples.

He is gone into the glory, but He has not ceased to bless our race. The Holy Spirit came among us soon after the ascension, because Jesus had received gifts for men — yes, for the rebellious, too. The wonderful blessings which are comprised in His work, person, and offices of the Holy Spirit, all these come to us through Jesus Christ, the ever-blessed and ever-blessing One. Still He loves to bless. Standing at the helm of all affairs, He guides the tiller of Providence with a view to the blessing of His chosen ones. He spends His time still in interceding for transgressors, that the blessings of God may rest on them.

EVENING

All things are of You, and we have given to You out of Your hand — 1 Chron. 29:14.

YOUR near and dear mercies were first the Lord's before they were yours. The sweetness of mercy is yours, but the sovereign right to dispose of your mercies is the Lord's. Whatever you are, you owe to Him that made you; and whatever you have, you owe to Him that redeemed you (Bernard). You say it is but just and reasonable that men should do with their own as they please. Then is it not just and reasonable that God, who is Lord paramount, should do with His own as He pleases? Do you believe that the great God may do in Heaven what He pleases? And on the seas what He pleases? And in your heart what He pleases? And do you not believe that God may do in your house what He pleases, and do with your mercies what He pleases? *"Behold, He takes away; who can turn Him back?"* (Job 9:12). Who will say to Him, What are You doing? Who dares to question that God who is unquestionable? Where is the king, the peasant, the master, the servant, the husband, the wife, the father, the child that dares say to God, What are you doing? (Isa. 45:9). In matters of arithmetical accounts, set one against ten, ten against a hundred, a hundred against a thousand, a thousand against ten thousand, whatever the odds there is some comparison. But there can be no comparison if a man would set down an infinite number. So set all the kings and powers of the earth in opposition to God; they shall never be able to withstand Him, for He is infinite, and they only finite. Let God but stamp his foot, and He can raise all the world in arms, to own Him, to contend for Him, or to revenge any affronts done to Him. Fire is stronger than water, angels stronger than men, and God stronger than them all. Then who shall say to God, What are You doing, even when He takes their nearest and dearest mercies from them?" — Thomas Brooks, *A Mute Christian Under the Smarting Rod.*

Martha, Martha, you are troubled and anxious about many things, but there is need of only one — Luke 10:41.

CHRIST teaches the Christian when he comes into His school what is the one thing that is necessary. Before, the soul sought after this and that. But now it says, I see that it is not necessary for me to be rich, but it is necessary for me to make my peace with God. It is not necessary that I should live a pleasurable life in this world, but it is absolutely necessary that I should have pardon of my sin. It is not necessary that I should have honor and preferment, but it is necessary that I should have God as my portion, and have my part in Jesus Christ. Other things are pretty fine, and I would be glad if God would give me a fine house, and income, and clothes, and advancement for my wife and children — these are comfortable things, but they are not the necessary things. I may have these, and yet perish forever. But the other is absolutely necessary. And no matter how poor I may be, I may have that which is absolutely necessary. So Christ instructs the soul. Many of you have had some thoughts about this, that it is indeed necessary for you to provide for your souls. But when you come to Christ's school, Christ causes the fear of eternity to fall on you. He causes a real sight of the great things of eternity, and the absolute necessity of those things, that it possess your heart with fear and takes you off from all other things in the world.

When the soul is taken up with the things that are absolutely necessary, it will not be much troubled about other things. What are the things that disquiet us here? They are but by-matters. It is because our hearts are not taken up with the one absolutely necessary thing. Who are the most discontented ones, but idle ones? When the heart of a man has nothing to do except to busy itself with creature-comforts every little thing troubles it. But when the heart is taken up with the weighty things of eternity, with the great things of eternal life, his heart little regards how things fall out here, if he may only have the one thing necessary. — Jeremy Burroughs, *The Rare Jewel of Christian Contentment*, p 36.

EVENING

Whom have I in Heaven but You, and there is none on the earth that I desire beside You — Psalm 73:25.

IF God gave you not only earth, but the heavens, that you should rule over sun, moon, stars, and the highest of the sons of men, it would not be enough to satisfy you, unless you had God Himself. There lies the first mystery of contentment. A Christian comes to contentment not so much by way of addition, as by way of subtraction. It is a way the world has no skill in. One does not become content by adding to what he would have, or what he has, not by adding to his condition. But rather it is by subtracting from his desires, thus making his desires and his circumstances even and equal. A carnal heart knows no way to be contented but to add to his possessions, or his comfort. But contentment comes not in that way. It is all one to a Christian whether he gets up to what he would have, or gets his desires down to what he already has. A heart that has no grace knows no way to get contentment but by adding. But the Christian soon learns that he can be content in whatever state he is in. He desires nothing but Christ, the honoring of His will and name, the doing of His work. Having this he needs nothing else to satisfy him, to give him complete contentment. A soul that is capable of God can be filled with nothing else but God. Nothing but God can fill a soul that is capable of God. Though a gracious heart knows that it is capable of God, and was made for God, carnal hearts think without reference to God. A gracious heart, being enlarged to be capable for God, will enjoy Him. It can be filled by nothing in the world; it must only be filled with God Himself. So, then, whatever God may give to a gracious heart, a heart that is godly, unless He gives Himself with it, it will not do. A godly heart will not only have the mercy, but the God of that mercy as well. If he has the God of mercy, it will little matter what he has of the world. It is not only life that I must have, but the God of my life. It is not riches, but the God of those riches that I must have; not just my preservation, but the God of my preservation (extracted from Jeremy Burroughs, *The Rare Jewel of Christian Contentment*, pages 14-16).

MORNING

We were buried with Him through baptism into death, so that as Christ was raised from among the dead by the glory of the Father, so also we should walk in the newness of life — Romans 6:4.

IN THIS parallel of our history with the story of Christ, in our being spiritually raised from the dead, we have a pre-eminent security for future perfection: *"He that has worked in us for the same thing is God, who also has given to us the earnest of the Spirit"* (2 Cor. 5:5). If He raised us up when we were dead in sin, will He not keep us alive now that we live to Him? If He called us out of our graves when we were under the bondage of death, will He not preserve us now by the life of Him who dies no more? If the life of God has really been infused into us, who shall destroy it? Has not our Master said, *"I give to My sheep eternal life, and they shall never perish, nor shall any man pluck them out of my hand"*? He would not have given us this life unless He had intended to bring it to perfection. As surely as you live by the Father, you live as Jesus does, beyond the range of further death. *"Sin shall not have dominion over you, for you are not under the law, but under grace."* It is written in the covenant, *"I will put My fear in their hearts, that they shall not depart from Me."* The life which is in you springs up to eternal life. You shall surely behold His face whose life is already within your breast. What a blessed thing this is! There is measureless glory in this quickening of souls to God. He might have left us to our corruptions, and have said, "Bury My dead out of My sight. *Depart from Me, you cursed, into everlasting fire prepared for the Devil and his angels."* Instead, in His free love He has come in the person of His dear Son and died for us that we might die in Him. He quickened His Son that we should live in Him.

EVENING

But this Man, after He had offered one sacrifice for sins sat down forever on the right hand of God — Hebrews 10:12.

THE BEST proof that Christ has finished His work is that Christ sits at His Father's right hand. The very fact that Christ is in Heaven, accepted by His Father, proves that His work must be done. As long as an ambassador is at a foreign court, there must be peace; and as long as Jesus Christ our Savior is at His Father's court, there is real peace between His people and His Father. And as He will be there forever, then our peace must be continual. But that peace could not be continual unless the atonement had been wholly made, unless justice had been entirely satisfied. From that very fact it becomes certain that the work of Christ must be done. What! Christ enter into Heaven, sit on His Father's right hand, and the guilt of His people not yet fully rolled away? No, He was the sinner's substitute, and unless He paid the sinner's doom, died the sinner's death, there was no Heaven in view for sinners like you and me. He stood in the sinner's place, and the guilt of all His elect was imputed to Him. God accounted Him as if He were a sinner; and He could not have entered Heaven until He had washed all that sin away in a crimson flood of His precious blood; unless His own righteousness had covered up the sins which He had taken on Himself; unless His own atonement had taken away those sins which had become His by imputation. The fact that the Father allowed Him to ascend up on high, that He permitted Him to enter Heaven; that He said, *"Sit on My right hand,"* proves that He must have perfected His Father's work, and that His Father must have accepted His sacrifice. But He could not have accepted it if it had been imperfect. So, because of this, we prove that the work must have been finished, for God the Father accepted it. This Man had completed it; He was the Author, and He is the Finisher. He was the Alpha, and He is the Omega. Salvation is finished, complete. Otherwise, He would not have ascended up on high, nor would He also sit now at the right hand of God.

April 14   MORNING

For this reason, coming into the world, He says, Sacrifice and offering You did not desire. You prepared a body for Me. — Hebrews 10:5.

HE WHO assumed that body was existent before that body was prepared. He from eternity past dwelt with God: *The Word was in the beginning with God, and the Word was God.* None of us could have said that a body was prepared for us, for we did not have an existence before our bodies were fashioned. From everlasting to everlasting our Lord is God. He came out of eternity into time, the Father bringing Him into the world. Before all worlds were, He was. He came into the world to dwell in His prepared body.

Beloved, the human nature of Christ was taken in order that He might do for us what God desired and required. God desired to see an obedient man, one who would keep His law to the full. And He sees Him in Christ. God desired to see one who would vindicate the eternal justice, and show that sin is no trifle. And our Lord, the eternal Son of God, entering into that prepared body, was ready to do all this by rendering to the law a full recompense for our dishonor of it. An absolutely perfect righteousness He rendered to God. As the second Adam He presents it for all whom He represented. He bowed as a victim beneath Jehovah's sword, that the truth, justice and honor of God might suffer no detriment. His body was prepared for this. Incarnation is a means to atonement. Only a man could vindicate the law, and so the Son of Man became a man. This is a wonderful Being, this God in our nature, *Immanuel.* Think of this; it is a truth fitter for meditation than for sermonizing. The Lord give us to know it well by faith!

EVENING

Then He shall speak to them in His anger, and trouble them in His wrath. Yet I have set My king on My holy mount — Psalm 2:5, 6.

HE HAS already done that which the enemy seeks to prevent. While they are proposing, He has disposed the matter. Jehovah's will is done, and man's will frets and raves in vain. God's Anointed is appointed, and He shall not be disappointed. Look through the ages of infidelity; listen to the high and hard things men have spoken against the Most High; hear the rolling thunder of earth's volleys against the Majesty of Heaven; then think that God is saying all the while: *"Yet I have set My king on My holy mount."* Yet Jesus reigns; yet He sees of the travail of His soul; His kingdom shall yet come when He shall take to Himself His great power and reign from the river to the ends of the earth. Even now He reigns, and our glad lips sound forth the praises of the Prince of Peace. Greater conflicts may here be foretold, but we may be confident that victory will be given to our Lord and King. Glorious triumphs are yet to come. It is Zion's glory and joy that her King is in her, guarding her from foes, and filling her with good things. Jesus sits on the throne of grace, and the throne of power in the midst of His church. In Him is Zion's best safeguard. Let her citizens rejoice and be glad in Him.

The Psalm wears something of a dramatic form, for now another person is introduced as speaking. We have looked into the council-chamber of the wicked, and to the throne of God. And now we behold the Anointed declaring His rights of sovereignty, warning the traitors of their doom.

God has laughed at the counsel and ravings of the wicked, and now Christ the Anointed Himself comes forward as the risen Redeemer, *"declared to be the Son of God with power, according to the spirit of His holiness, by the resurrection from the dead"* (Rom. 1:4). Looking into the angry faces of the rebellious kings, the Anointed One seems to say, "If this does not suffice to make you silent, I will declare the decree." Now this decree is directly in conflict with the device of man, for its tenor is the establishment of the very dominion against which the nations are raving.

MORNING

Lo, I come, in the volume of the Book it is written of Me. I delight to do Your will, O My God; and Your law is within My heart — Psalm 40:7,8.

CHRIST delighted in God. He took an intense delight in glorifying the Father. He came to reveal the Father and to make Him beloved of mankind. He did all things to please God. Also, He took a delight in us. And here, although the object of His love is less, the love itself is heightened by the conspicuous condescension. The Lord Jesus took a deep delight in His people, those whose names were written in His heart and engraved on the palms of His hands. His heart was fixed on their redemption. For this reason He would present Himself a sacrifice on their behalf. Those people whom the Father gave Him from before the foundation of the world lay on His very soul. For them He had a baptism to be baptized with, and He was troubled until it was accomplished. He gave Himself no rest until He had left both joy and rest to ransom His own.

He delighted in His coming among men: *"I delight to do Your will, O My God."* When our Lord was here, He was the most blessed of men. What? But He was *"a man of sorrows."* Yes, none was more afflicted, but yet within Him dwelt a joy of the highest order. To Him it was joy to be in sorrow, honor to be put to shame. Does that lighten our estimate of His self-denial? No, it adds weight to it. Some people fancy that there is no credit in doing a thing unless you are miserable in doing it. But that is the very reverse of true. Obedience which is unwillingly offered and which causes no joy in the soul is not acceptable. We must serve God with our heart, or we do not serve Him at all. Obedience rendered without delight in rendering it is only half-obedience.

EVENING

Arise, O Lord! Save me, O my God! For You have smashed all my enemies on the cheekbone. You have broken the teeth of the ungodly. Salvation belongs to the Lord; Your blessing is on Your people — Psalm 3:7, 8.

HIS ONLY hope is in his God. But that is so strong a confidence that he feels the Lord has only to arise and he is saved. It is enough for the Lord to stand up, then all is well. He compares his enemies to wild beasts, and he declares that God has broken their jaws, so that they could not injure him. Else he alludes to the peculiar temptations to which he was then exposed. They had spoken against him. Then God had smitten them on the cheekbone. They seemed as if they would devour him with their mouths. God has broken their teeth, and let them say what they will, their toothless jaws shall not be able to devour him. Rejoice, O believer, for you have to do with a dragon whose head is broken, with enemies whose teeth are dashed from their jaws!

Search Scripture through, and you must, if you read it with a candid mind, be persuaded that the doctrine of salvation by grace alone is the great doctrine of the word of God, *"Salvation belongs to the Lord."* This is a point concerning which we are daily fighting. Our opponents say, "Salvation belongs to the free will of man; if not to man's merit, yet at least to man's will." We hold and teach that salvation from first to last, in every iota of it, belongs to the Most High God. It is God who chooses His people, calls them by His grace, quickens them by His Spirit, and keeps them by His power. It is not of man, nor by man: *"Not of him that wills, nor of him who runs, but of God who shows mercy."* May we all learn this truth experimentally, for our proud flesh and blood will never permit us to learn it in any other way. In the last sentence the peculiarity and speciality of salvation are plainly stated. God's blessing is not on Egypt, nor on tyre, but is on His chosen, His blood-bought, everlastingly-beloved people. Lift up your hearts and pause; meditate on this doctrine. Divine, discriminating, distinguishing, eternal, infinite, immutable love is a subject for our constant adoration.

April 16 — MORNING

And we know that all things work together for good to those who love God, to those who are the called according to purpose — Romans 8:28.

SEE HERE the wisdom of God, who can make the worst things imaginable turn to the good of the saints. He can by a divine chemistry extract gold out of dross: *"O the depths of the wisdom of God!"* (Rom. 11:33). It is God's great design to set forth the wonder of His wisdom. The Lord made Joseph's prison a step to preferment. There was no way for Jonah to be saved, but by being swallowed up. God allowed the Egyptians to hate Israel (Psalm 106:41), and this was the means of their deliverance. The apostle Paul was bound with a chain, and that chain which bound him was the means of enlarging the gospel (Phil. 1:12). God enriches by impoverishing; He causes the augmentation of grace by the diminution of an estate. When the creature goes further from us, it is tht Christ may come nearer to us. God works strangely. He brings order out of confusion, harmony out of discord. He frequently makes use of unjust men to do that which is just, *"He is wise in heart"* (Job 9:4). He can reap His glory out of the fury of men (Psalm 76:10). Either the wicked shall not do the hurt that they intended, or they shall do the good which they do not intend. God often helps when there is least hope, and He saves His people in that way which they think will destroy them. He made use of the high-priest's malice and the treason of Judas to redeem the world. Through indiscreet passion we are apt to find fault with things that happen — it is as if an illiterate man should censure philosophy, or a blind man find fault with the work in a landscape, *"Vain man would be wise"* (Job 11:12). Silly animals will forever be taxing Providence and calling the wisdom of God to the bar of 'reason', but God's days are *"past finding out"* (Rom. 11:33). They are rather to be admired than fathomed. There is never a providence of God but has either a mercy or a wonder in it. How stupendous and infinite is that wisdom, that makes the most adverse dispensations work for the good of His children — Thomas Watson, *A Divine Cordial*

EVENING

All things work together for those who love God, to those who are the called according to purpose — Romans 8:28.

THE FIRST fruit of love is the musing of the mind on God. He who is in love will have his thoughts ever on the object of his love. He who loves God is ravished and transported with the contemplation of God, *"When I awake, I am still with You"* (Ps. 139:18). Our thoughts are like travelers in the mind. David's thoughts kept Heaven-road, *I am still with You*. God is the treasure, and where the treasure is, there is the heart. By this we may test our love to God. What are our thoughts most upon? Can we say we are ravished with delight when we think on God? Have our thoughts got wings? Do they flee aloft? Do we contemplate Christ and glory? Oh, how far are they from being lovers of God, those who scarcely ever think of God! For *"God is not in all his thoughts"* (Ps. 10:4). A sinner crowds God out of his thoughts. He never thinks of God, unless with horror, as the prisoner thinks of the judge.

The next fruit of love is desire of communion. Love desires familiarity and intercourse, *"My heart and flesh cries out for the living God"* (Ps. 84:2). King David being debarred from the house of God where the tabernacle rested, the visible token of His presence, He breathes after God. In a holy pathos of desire he cries out to the living God. Lovers desire always to be conversing together. If we love God we prize His ordinances, because there we meet with God. He speaks to us in His word, and we speak to Him in prayer. By this let us examine our love to God. Do we desire intimacy of communion with God? Lovers cannot be long away from each other. Such as love God have a holy affection; they do not know how to be away from Him. They can bear the lack of anything but God's presence. They can do without health and friends, but cannot be happy without God, *"Hide not your face from me, lest I be like those going down into the grave."* Lovers have fainting fits. David would faint if he had not God."
— Thomas Watson, *A Divine Cordial*, pages 56, 57.

MORNING

And killed the Prince of life, whom God has raised from the dead, of which we are witnesses — Acts 3:15.

IN THE REALM of life He is Prince, but we are only subjects. He says of His own life, *"I have power to lay it down, and I have power to take it again"* — this is not our case. We pay the debt of nature and die. But our Lord owed no debt ot nature, since He is the Maker of all. He died voluntarily, and of His own accord. You and I may not do this except under the compulsion of obedience to God. He resumed possession of life at His own will, which you and I could not do. He had the right, the authority, the power thus to deal with His own life. If this had not been so, He could not have offered Himself to die in our place and stead. But, having a ower and rulership over His own life, such as we do not have, He could lay down His life for us, and He could take it again. O man! You have not life in your own right; it is loaned to you by Him who is still its owner. You cannnot lay down your life at will, for it is not yours, but God's. Live your appointed time, otherwise you will commit a crime against the majesty of the Life-giver. Our Lord Jesus assumed the life of men, and when He chose He lay it down, for He was still the ever-living God. When He chose He could raise His human body from among the dead and walk again among the sons of men. This He has done, and many witnesses have attested the fact. Let us rejoice that we worship the living God through a living Mediator. How glad are we that we are comforted by the same assurance which sustained the heart of Job, *"I know that My Redeemer lives."* In an hour of great depression of spirit, Luther was seen to write on the table before him these two words, *"He lives!"* When he had so written, he arose and went about his business calmly and quietly, as well he might, since his Almighty Helper lived: *"The Lord is risen indeed."*

EVENING

And killed the Prince of life, whom God has raised from the dead, of which we are witnesses — Acts 3:15.

ON ALL sides He dispenses that everlasting life which He compares to water springing up within a well. They who come under His benign influence live forever, because of their contact with Him. For this is life eternal, to know the Lord Jesus, as sent from God. Beloved, the day will come when our Lord will prove His life-giving power on a grand scale by causing the resurrection of the dead. When He shall come in the glory of the Father, they that are in the grave shall hear the voice of the Son of God, and they that hear shall live. What an Exodus it will be! The slaves of death shall team with the uncountable multitude, and He who called them forth shall be seen to be *"the Prince of life."* Who but He could have released this vast multitude from their long prison? The Roman emperor Theodosius, in a fit of great good humor, set at liberty all persons in prison, or in captivity. And then he sighed and wished that he could release the dead from their graves. Theodosius could not reach the keys of the grave; for these hang at the belt of the *Prince of life*. He shall open the iron gate and bid the myriads to pour forth, as bees from the hive. They sleep together in the dust, but when He calls they shall answer Him. Hear this, O mourner, *"Your brother shall rise again!"* Every man's brother shall rise again; an exceeding great army shall be seen where now we mourn a valley of dry bones. Until that glorious morning nothing pleases our Lord better than to be working spiritual resurrections. He says, *"He who believes in Me, although he were dead, yet he shall live. And whoever lives and believes in Me shall never die. Do you believe this?"* Do you know anything about being quickened from the death in which you lay dead in trespasses and sins?

MORNING

Yes, He is altogether lovely — Song of Songs 5:16.

ARDENT DEVOTION flames from this sentence. It is the language of one who feels that no emotion is too deep when Jesus moves the heart. Do any chide you and say you think too much of your religion? It cannot be! If the zeal of God's house should eat us up until we had no existence except for the Lord's glory, we would not have gone too far. If there is corresponding knowledge to balance it, there cannot be too much of zeal for God. The utterance is that of one whose heart is like a furnace, of which love is the fire. It is the exclamation of one who feels that no language is too strong to commend the Lord. The spouse looked through the Hebrew tongue to find an intense expression, and our translators ransacked the English language for a forcible word, and they put it in the most weighty way: *"He is altogether lovely."* There is no fear of exaggeration when you speak of Christ. Hyperboles are only sober truth when we depict His excellencies. We have heard of a portrait painter who owed his popularity to the fact that he never painted truthfully, but always gave a flattering touch or two. But here is One who would defy such an art, for it is impossible to flatter Jesus. Lay on, you men of eloquence; spare no colors; you shall never depict Him too bravely. Bring forth your harps, your seraphs. Sing aloud, you blood-washed ones. All your praises fall short of the glory which is due to Him.

It is the language of one who feels that no service would be too great to render to the Lord. I wish we felt as the apostles and martyrs and holy men of old did, that Jesus Christ ought to be served at the highest and richest rate. We do little, very little. What if I had said we do next to nothing for our dear Lord and Master nowadays? The love of Christ does not constrain us as it should.

EVENING

You have gone up on high; You have led captivity captive; You have received gifts for men. Yes, for the rebellious also, that the Lord God might dwell among men —
Psalm 68:18.

WHEN WE speak of what Christ has done, we must think much of the doing, but still more of the Doer. We must not forget the Benefactor in the benefits which come to us through Him. Note how David puts it. To him the Lord is first and most prominent. He sees Him; he speaks to Him: *"You have gone up on high; You have led captivity captive; You have received gifts for men."* Three times he addresses Him by that personal pronoun, *"You."* Dwell on the fact that the Son of David came down on earth for our sakes. That Man who lay in the manger, who hung on woman's breast, has gone up on high, into the glory infinite. He who trod the weary ways of Palestine now reigns as a King in His palace. He is now above all the heavens.

Behold your Lord on the cross. Mark the five ghastly wounds, and all the shameful scourging and spitting which men have put upon Him. See how that blessed body, prepared of the Holy Spirit for the indwelling of the Second Person of the adorable Trinity, was evil treated. But there is an end to all this. *"You have gone up on high;"* He who was earth's scorn is now Heaven's wonder. David foresaw: *"You have ascended on high"*, where death cannot touch You; laid in the tomb, wrapped about with burial clothes, embalmed in spices — but *"You have ascended on high."* The Christ that was buried here is now on the throne. The heart which was sorrowful here is palpitating in His bosom now, as full of love and condescension as when He dwelt among men. He has not forgotten us, for He has not forgotten Himself; and we are part and parcel of Himself. He is still mindful of Calvary and Gethsemane. Even when you are dazzled by the superlative splendor of His exalted state, still believe that He is a brother born for adversity.

MORNING

Your own salvation — Philippians 2:12.

CHRIST JESUS bore the wrath of God that we might never bear it. He has made a full atonement to the justice of God for the sins of all believers. Against him that believes there remains no record of guilt. The believer's transgressions are blotted out, for Christ Jesus has finished transgression, made an end of sin, bringing in everlasting righteousness for His chosen. What a comprehensive word is this *"salvation"!* It is triumphant deliverance from the guilt of sin, from its dominion, from its curse, for its punishment, and ultimately from the very existence of it. Salvation is the death of sin, its burial, its annihilation; yes, and the very obliteration of sin's memory. For thus says the Lord, *"their sins and their iniquities will I remember no more"* (Heb. 8:12).

Salvation appears to me to be of the first importance, when I think of what it is in itself, and for this reason I have at the outset set it forth before your eyes. But you may be helped to remember its value if you consider that God the Father thinks highly of salvation. It was on His mind before the earth was. He thinks salvation a lofty business, for He gave His son that He might save rebellious sinners. Jesus Christ, the only Begotten, thinks salvation most important, for He bled, He died to accomplish it. Shall I trifle with that which cost Him His life? If He came from Heaven to earth, shall I be slow to look from earth to Heaven? Shall that which cost the Savior a life of zeal, and a death of agony, be of small account with me? By the bloody sweat of Gethsemane, by wounds of Calvary, I beseech you, be assured that salvation must be worthy of your highest and most anxious thoughts.

EVENING

You have gone up on high; You have led captivity captive; You have received gifts for men. Yes, for the rebellious also, that the Lord God might dwell among men
— Psalm 68:18.

WHAT ARE these great ascension gifts? I answer that the sum of them is the Holy Spirit. Pay adoring attention to the sacred Trinity which is manifested in us. How delightful it is to see the Trinity working out in unity the salvation of men! *"You have gone up on high"*: there is Christ Jesus. *"You have received gifts for men"*: there is the Father, bestowing those gifts. The gift itself is the Holy Spirit. This is the great generous giving of Christ's ascension, which He bestowed on His church at Pentecost. So you have Father, Son, and Holy Spirit blessedly co-working for the benediction of men, the conquest of evil, the establishment of righteousness. O my soul, delight yourself in Father, Son and Holy Spirit. One of the sins of modern theology is keeping these divine Persons in the background, so that they are scarcely mentioned in their several workings and offices. The theology which can feed your souls must be full of Godhead, and yield perpetual praise to Father, Son and Holy Spirit.

Beloved, the gifts here spoken of are those brought by the Holy Spirit. *"The water that I shall give him,"* said Christ, *"shall be in him a well of water springing up into everlasting life."* He said again, *"If any man thirst, let him come to Me and drink."* We read that He *"spoke of the Spirit, which they that believed on Him should receive." "If you then, being evil, know how to give good gifts to your children; how much more shall your heavenly Father give the Holy Spirit to those who ask Him?"* To conquer the world for Christ we need nothing but the Holy Spirit, and in the hour of His personal victory He secured us this boon. If the Holy Spirit is but given we have in Him all the weapons of our holy war. The Holy Spirit, in proportion as He abides in the servants of God, makes them to be precious blessings of Heaven to His people, and they become the champions by whom the world is subdued to the Lord Jesus Christ.

Work out your own salvation — Philippians 2:12.

HAS THE HOLY SPIRIT been pleased to make any one of you earnest about your own salvation? Ask yourself first, *"Am I saved?"* If you are saved this morning, you are the subject of a work within you, as the text says, *"Work out your own salvation, for it is God who works in you both to will and to work, etc."* You cannot work it in, but when God works it in you, you work it out. Have you a work of the Holy Spirit in your soul? Do you feel something more than unaided human nature can attain to? Have you a change worked out in you from above? If so, you are saved. Again, does your salvation rest wholly on Christ? He who hangs anywhere but on the cross, that one hangs on to something which will deceive him. If you stand on Christ, you are on a rock. But if you trust in the merits of Christ in part, and your own merits in part, then you have one foot on a rock but another on the quicksand — then you might as well have both feet on the quicksand, for the result will be the same. You are not saved unless Christ is all in your soul, Alpha and Omega, beginning and ending, first and last.

Again, judge by this: If you are saved, you have turned your back on sin. You have not left off sinning — would God that we could do so — but you have left off loving sin; you do not sin wilfully, but from infirmity. And if you are saved, you are earnestly seeking after God and holiness. You have respect to God; you desire to be like Him; you are longing to be with Him. Your face is toward Heaven. You are a man who journeys to the Equator. You are feeling more and more the warm influence of the heavenly heat and light. Now, if such be your course in life, that *"you do not walk after the flesh, but after the Spirit,* and you bring forth the fruits of holiness, then you are saved. May your answer to that question be given honestly and candidly to your own soul.

EVENING

Work out your own salvation — Philippians 2:12.

"HOW CAN I BE SAVED?" Ah, dear one, I have not need to bring a huge volume, nor a whole armful of folios to you, and to say, "It will take you months and years to understand the plan of salvation." No, the way is plain, the method is simple. You shall be saved within the next moment if you but believe. God's work of salvation is, as far as its commencement and essence is concerned, instantaneous. If you believe that Jesus is the Christ, you have been born of God now. If you do now stand in spirit at the foot of the cross and view the incarnate God suffering, bleeding, dying there, and if as you look at Him your soul consents to have Him for her Savior, and casts herself wholly on Him, you have been born again. How vividly there comes before my memory this evening the moment when I first believed in Jesus! It was the simplest act my mind ever performed, and yet the most wonderful. For the Holy Spirit worked it in me. Simply to have done it with reliance upon myself, and to have done it with confidence in all but Jesus, and to rest in it alone, my undivided confidence in Him, and in what he had done. The sense of the forgiveness of my sin came in that moment, and I was saved. May it all be so with you, my friends, even with you. And it will be if you will but trust in the Lord Jesus.

"Your own salvation" Shall be evidenced by that one simple act of faith. And from this time on you will be kept by the power of God through faith unto salvation. You shall tread the way of holiness until you come to be where Jesus is, in everlasting bliss. Faith is not a grace for old people only, nor for your fathers and mothers only. If your hearts look to Jesus as God and Savior, even if you know but little yet, if you trust in Him, salvation shall be yours.

And you are not your own. You were bought with a price. Then glorify God in your body and in your spirit, which are God's — 1 Corinthians 6:20.

NOTE that the apostle does not trifle with sin when he is exposing it. Like a mighty hunter before the lord, he pursues it with all his might. His hatred to it is intense; he drags it forth to the light; he bids us mark its hideous deformity; he hunts it through all its haunts. He leaves it no breathing time. Argument after argument he hurls on it; he will by no means spare the filthy thing. He who above all others speaks most positively of salvation by grace, and is most clear on the fact that salvation is not by the works of the law, is at the same time most intense earnest for the holiness of Christians, and most zealously denounces those who would say, *"Let us do evil that good may come."*

In this particular instance he sets the sin of fornication in the light of the Holy Spirit; he holds it up, as if the seven-branched lampstand were before it, and lets us see what a filthy thing it is. He tells us that the body is the temple of the Holy Spirit, and so it ought not to be profaned. He declares that bodily unchastity is a sacrilegious desecration of our manhood, a violation of the sacred shrine in which the Spirit takes up its dwelling. Then, as if this were not enough, he seizes the sin and drags it to the foot of the cross. He nails it there hand and foot, that it may die as a criminal; for these are his words, *"You are not your own. You were bought with a price."* The price was the blood of Jesus. He finds no sharper weapon, no keener instrument of destruction than this. The redemption wrought on Calvary by the death of Jesus must be the death of this sin, and of all other sins, wherever the Spirit of God uses it as His sword of execution. Brothers and sisters, it is no slight thing to be holy. A man must not say, *"I have faith,"* and then fall into the sins of an unbeliever. For, after all, our outer life is the test of our inner life.

EVENING

And you are not your own. You were bought with a price. Then glorify God in your body and in your spirit, which are God's — 1 Corinthians 6:20.

YOU WILL NOTICE the text says, *"You were bought with a price."* It is a common classical expression to signify that the purchase was expensive. Of course, the very expression, *"You were bought"* implies a price, but the words *"with a price"* are added as if to show that it was not for nothing that you were purchased. There was a something inestimably precious paid for you. You need scarcely to be reminded that *"you were not redeemed with corruptible things, as silver and gold"; "but with the precious blood of Christ, as of a lamb without blemish and without spot"* (1 Peter 1:19). These words slip over our tongue very glibly, but we may well chide ourselves that we can speak of redemption with dry eyes. That the blood of Christ was shed to buy our souls from death and Hell is a wonder of compassion which fills angels with amazement. And it ought to overwhelm us with adoring love whenever we think of it, glance our eye over the recorded pages, or even to utter the word "redemption."

What does this mean, our being purchased with blood? It signified pain. Have you been racked with pain? Have you suffered acutely? Then at such times you know to some degree what the price was which the Savior paid. His bodily pains were great, hands and feet nailed to the wood, iron breaking through the tenderest nerves. His soul-pains were still greater. His heart was melted like wax; He was very heavy in spirit, His heart broken with reproach, hidden from God and left beneath the thunderclouds of Divine wrath. His soul was exceedingly sorrowful, even unto death. It was pain that bought you. We speak of the drops of blood, but we must not confine our thoughts to the crimson life-floods which distilled from the Savior's veins; we must think of the pangs which He endured, which was the equivalent for what we ought to have suffered, what we ourselves must have suffered for eternity, if we have endured the punishment.

April 22   MORNING   113

And you are not your own. You were bought with a price. Then glorify God in your body and in your spirit, which are God's — 1 Corinthians 6:20.

AS I AM SURE you could not renounce your salvation and cast away your only hope, so I charge you by the living God not to be so inconsistent as to say, "I am redeemed, and yet I will live as I like." As redeemed men and women, let the inevitable consequences follow from that fact, and let it be evident that you are servants of the Lord Jesus.

Remember, too, that this fact is the most important one in all your history. That you were redeemd *"with a price"* is the greatest event in your biography. Even your birth, what was it unless a second birth had also been yours? Might you not say, *"Let the day perish in which I was born, and the night in which it was said"* that you were conceived? Would it not have been to you the direst calamity to be born into the world if you had not been rescued from the wrath which you inherited from your father Adam? You left your father's house, and it was an important step in life. You may have crossed the great wide sea; you may have aspired to high office and obtained it; it is possible you have been very sick; or you may have sunk from affluence to poverty — such events leave their impress on the memory; men cannot forget these great changes in their lives. But all such things shrivel into less than nothing compared with this fact that you were *"bought with a price."* Your connection with Calvary is the most important thing about you. Oh, then, I beseech you, if that is so, then prove it. Remember the just and the righteous proof is by your not being your own, but being consecrated to God. If it is the most important thing in the world to you, that you were *"bought with a price,"* let it exercise the most prominent influence over your entire life. Be a man, or a woman, of most of all be Christ's. You may be a friend, a philanthropist, a patriot — all of these — but most of all be a saint, redeemed by the blood of Christ.

EVENING

And you are not your own. You were bought with a price. Then glorify God in your body and in your spirit, which are God's — 1 Corinthians 6:20.

IF I HAD the power to do it, how I would seek to refresh in your souls a sense of this fact, that you are *"bought with a price."* There, in the midnight hour, amid the olives of Gethsemane, the Son of God, Immanuel, kneels; He groans; He pleads in prayer; He wrestles. See the beady drops stand on His brow, drops of sweat, but not of such sweat as pours from men earning the bread of life — it was the sweat of Him who is procuring life itself for us; it is blood; it is crimson blood, great drops of it falling to the ground. O soul, your Savior speaks to you from out of Gethsemane at this hour, saying, "Here and in this way I bought you with a price." Come and stand. View Him in the agony of the olive garden; understand at what cost He procured your deliverance. Track Him in all His path of shame and sorrow until you see Him on the Pavement. Mark how they bind His hands and fasten Him to the whipping-post. See, they bring the scourges, the cruel Roman whips that tear His flesh!. They plow deep furrows on His blessed body, and the blood gushes forth in streams. And rivulets of blood trickled from His temples, where the crown of thorns pierced them. From beneath the scourges He speaks to you with accents soft and low. And He says, "My child, it is here, in this way, that I bought you with a price."

But see Him on the cross itself when the consummation of all has come. His hands and feet are fountains of blood; His soul is full of anguish even to heartbreak. There, before the soldier pierces His side with a spear, bowing down He whispers to you and to me, "It was here, and in this way, that I bought you with a price." I appeal to you, my beloved ones, to remember that you were *"bought with a price,"* and you *"are not your own."*

MORNING

And you are not your own. You were bought with a price. Then glorify God in your body and in your spirit, which are God's — 1 Corinthians 6:20.

MY BODY is not my own. Then as a Christian I have no right to do anything with it that would defile it. The apostle is mainly arguing against sins of the flesh. He says, *"the body is not for fornication, but for the Lord; and the Lord for the body."* We have no right to commit uncleanness because our bodies are the members of Christ; they are not our own. He would say the same of drunkenness, gluttony, idle sleep, and even of such excessive anxiety after wealth as injures health. We have no right to profane or injure the flesh and blood which are consecrated to God. Every limb of our frame belongs to God; it is His property, for He has bought it *"with a price."* Any honest man will be more concerned about an injury done to another's property placed under his care, than if it were his own. When the son of the prophet was hewing wood with Elisha, you remember how he said, when the axe head flew off into the water, *"Alas! Master, for it was borrowed."* It would be bad enough to lose my own axe, but it is not my own, and so I doubly deplore the accident. I know this would not operate on thievish minds. There are some who, if it was another man's and they had borrowed it, would have no further care about it, "Let the lender get it back, if he can." But we speak to honest men, and with them it is always a strong argument: Your body is Another's; for this reason do it no injury. As for our spirit, too, that is God's. Then how careful we should be of it. I am asked sometimes to read an heretical book. Well, if I believed my reading it would help its refutation, and might be an assistance to others in keeping them out of error, I might do it as a hard matter of duty. But I will not do it unless I see some spiritual good will come from it. I am not going to drag my spirit through a ditch for the sake of having it washed afterwards, for it is not my own.

EVENING

And you are not your own. You were bought with a price. Then glorify God in your body and in your spirit, which are God's — 1 Corinthians 6:20.

OUR BODY AND OUR SPIRIT are God's. Christian, this is certainly a very high honor to you. Your body will rise again from the dead at the first resurrection. Because it is not an ordinary body, it belongs to God. Your spirit is distinguished from the souls of other men. It is God's spirit, and He has set His mark on it, honoring you in doing so. You are God's, because a price has been paid for you. According to some, the price here is an allusion to the dowry that a husband paid for his wife in ancient days. According to the Rabbis there were three ways by which a woman became the wife of a man, and one of these was by the payment of a dowry. This was always held good in Jewish law. The woman was not her own from the moment when the husband had paid to her father or natural guardian the stipulated price for her. Now, at this day, you and I rejoice that Jesus Christ has espoused us to Himself in righteousness before the earth was founded. We rejoice in that language which He uses by the prophet Hosea, *"I will betroth you unto Me forever."* But here is our comfort, the dowry money has been paid; Christ has redeemed us to Himself, and we are Christ's, His forever and ever.

April 24 — MORNING

Keep your heart with all diligence, for out of it are the issues of life — Proverbs 4:23.

MAN originally was of one constant, uniform frame of spirit, held one straight and even course; not one thought or faculty was disordered. His mind had a perfect knowledge for the requirements of God, his will perfectly complied with them, and all his appetites and powers stood in a most obedient subordination.

By his apostasy man has become a most disordered and rebellious creature, opposing his Maker as the First Cause, by self-dependence; as the Chief Good, by self-love; as the Highest Lord, by self-will; and as the Last End, by self-seeking. So he is quite disordered, and all his actions are irregular. But by regeneration the disordered soul is set right. This great change is made by a renovation of the soul after the image of God, in which self-dependence is removed by faith; self-love by the love of God; self-will by subjection and obedience to the will of God and self-seeking by self-denial. The darkened understanding is illuminated, the refractory will is sweetly subdued, and the rebellious appetite is gradually conquered. So the soul which sin had been universally depraved is restored by grace. This being pre-supposed, it will not be difficult to understand what it is to keep the heart. This is nothing but the constant care and diligence of such a renewed one to preserve the soul in that holy frame to which grace has raised it. For though grace has in a great measure rectified the soul, giving it an habitual heavenly temper, yet sin often actually discomposes it again. Even a gracious heart, like a musical instrument (which though it be exactly tuned, a small matter will bring it out of tune again, a gracious heart may be in a desirable frame for one duty, yet dull, dead and disordered when called upon for another. Because of this every duty requires a particular preparation of the heart. Then, to keep the heart is to carefully preserve it from sin, which disorders it; to maintain that spiritual frame which fits it for a life of communion with God. — John Flavel, *Keeping the Heart*, pages 9, 10.

EVENING

Come to Me, all those laboring and being burdened, and I will give you rest — Matthew 11:28.

NOTICE the precept laid down here: *"Come."* It is not *"Learn."* It is not, *"Take My yoke"* — that is in the next verse and is intended for the next stage of experience. In the beginning the word of the Lord is, *"Come to Me," "Come,"* — a simple word, but very full of meaning. To come is to leave one thing and to advance to another. Come, then, you laboring and being burdened; leave your legal labors; leave your self-reliant efforts; leave your sins; leave your presumptions; leave all in which you have trusted before, and come to Jesus. That is, think of Him, advance towards Him, rely on the Savior. Let your contemplations be of Him who bore the load of the sins of His people on the cross of Calvary, where He was made sin for us. Let your minds consider Him who from His cross hurled the enormous mass of His people's transgressions into a bottomless pit, where it was buried forever. Think of Jesus, the Divinely appointed substitute and sacrifice for guilty man. Then, seeing that He is God's own Son, let faith follow your contemplation; rely on Him; trust in Him as having suffered in your place; look to Him for payment of the debt due from you to the wrath of God. This is to come to Jesus. Repentance and faith make up this *"Come"* — the repentance which leaves the place where you now stand, the faith which comes to embrace reliance on Jesus.

Observe that the command to *"come"* is put in the present tense. In the Greek it is intensely present. It might be rendered something like this, "Come here to Me all you who labor and are heavily burdened." It is a "come" which does not mean "Come tomorrow, or next year," but, "come now, at once!" Advance! Flee from your taskmaster now. Weary ones, recline on the promise now, and take your rest. Come now! By an act of instantaneous faith which will bring instantaneous peace, come and rely on Jesus, and He will give you rest. Rest will at once follow your exercise of faith.

MORNING

And I will put My Spirit within you — Ezekiel 36:27.

IT IS NOT merely a spirit, or the spirit, but My Spirit. Now when God's own Spirit comes to reside within our mortal bodies, how near akin we are to the Most High! *"Do you not know that your body is the temple of the Holy Spirit?"* (1 Cor. 6:19). Does this not make a man sublime? Have you never stood in awe of your own selves, O believers? Have you sufficiently contemplated this poor body as being sanctified and dedicated, and elevated into a sacred condition by being set apart to be the temple of the Holy Spirit? In this way we are brought into the closest union with God that we can well conceive of. In this way is the Lord our light and our life, while our spirit is subordinated to the divine Spirit. *"I will put My Spirit within you"* — then God Himself dwells in you. The Spirit of Him that raised up Christ from the dead is in you. With Christ in God your life is hid, and the Spirit seals you, anoints you, and abides in you. By the Spirit we have access to the Father. By the Spirit we are made partakers of the Divine nature and have communion with the thrice holy Lord.

"I will put My Spirit within you" — is it really so, that the Spirit of God who displays the power and energetic force of God, by whom God's word is carried into effect — that the Spirit who of old moved on the face of the waters and brought order and life from chaos and death — can it be so that He will deign to sojourn in men? God in our nature is a very wonderful conception. God in the babe at Bethlehem; God in the carpenter of Nazareth; God in the *"Man of sorrows,"* God in the Crucified One; God in Him who was buried in the tomb — this is all marvelous indeed!

EVENING

Your words were found, and I ate them; and Your word was to me the joy and gladness of my heart; for I am called by Your name, O Lord God of Hosts — Jeremiah 15:16.

A DISTINGUISHING TITLE: *"I am called by Your name, O Lord God of hosts."* This may not appear to some of you a very joyful thing; to Jeremiah it was pre-eminently so. In Jeremiah's day the name of the Lord God of hosts was despised. The God of hosts was the subject of derision among the rabble of Jerusalem, and the weeping prophet of mournful countenance spoiled their mirth, and so was scorned. Now Jeremiah, instead of feeling it a hard thing to be associated with the Lord in this contempt of the wicked, was glad to be so honored. The reproaches of them that reviled the Lord fell on His poor servant, but he was content to have it so.

O you that love Jesus Christ, never shun the scandal of His cross! Count it glory to be despised for His sake. Let fear be far from you. Remember Moses, of whom it is written, *"He esteemed the reproach of Christ to be greater riches than all the treasures of Egypt."* It does not say he esteemed Christ to be greater riches, but that he reckoned the worst thing connected with Christ to be better than the best thing connected with the world. The reproach of Christ he esteemed above Pharaoh's crown. Disciples of Jesus, be willing to bear all the slander the wicked pour out on you for the Lord's sake; for in so doing they help to make you blessed. Through the mire, and through the slough, march side by side with truth, for those who share her pilgrimage shall share her exaltation. Be content to abide with Christ in His humiliation, for only so may you be sure that you shall be with Him in His glory. It was a comfort to Jeremiah that he bore the name of the despised God. It made him the object of very much persecution as well as contempt. The king put him in the dungeon where he was made to eat of the bread of affliction. He was in tribulations often, but he took it all joyfully, for the Lord's sake.

April 26   MORNING

And I will put My Spirit within you — Ezekiel 36:27

THE HOLY SPIRIT comes into us for purification: *"I will put My Spirit within you and cause you to walk in My statutes, and you shall keep My judgments and do them."* When the Spirit comes He infuses a new life, and that new life is a fountain of holiness. The new nature cannot sin, because it has been born of God; *"It is a living and incorruptible seed."* This life produces good fruit, and good fruit only. The Holy Spirit is the life of holiness. At the same time the coming of the Holy Spirit into the soul gives a mortal stab to the power of sin. The old man is not absolutely dead, but it is crucified with Christ. It is under sentence, and before the eye of the law it is dead. But as a man nailed to a cross may linger long, but yet he cannot live, so the power of evil dies hard, but die it must. Sin is an executed criminal. Those nails which fasten it to the cross will hold it fast until nothing remains of it. God the Holy Spirit gives the power of sin its death wound. The old nature struggles in its dying agonies, but it is doomed, and it must die.

But you will never overcome sin by your own power, nor by an energy short of that of the Holy Spirit. Resolves may bind it, as Samson was bound with cords, but sin will snap the cords asunder. The Holy Spirit lays the axe at the root of sin, and it must fall. The Holy Spirit within a man is *"the Spirit of judgment, the Spirit of burning."* Do you know Him in that character? As the Spirit of judgment the Holy Spirit pronounces sentence on sin, and it goes out with the brand of Cain on it. He does more — He delivers sin over to burning. He executes the death penalty on that which He has judged. How many of our sins have we had to burn alive! And it has cost us no pain to do it. Sin must be gotten out of us by fire, if no gentler means will serve; and the Holy Spirit of God is a consuming fire (Heb. 12:29).

EVENING

Keep your heart with all diligence, for out of it are the issues of life — Proverbs 4:23.

THE STABILITY of our souls in the hour of temptation depends on the care we exercise in keeping our hearts. The careless heart is an easy prey to Satan in the hour of temptation. Satan's principal batteries are raised against the heart; if he wins that he wins all, for it commands the whole man. And, alas! How easy a conquest is a neglected heart! It is not more difficult to surprise such a heart than for an enemy to enter a city that is open and unguarded. It is the watchful heart that discovers and suppresses the temptation before it comes to its strength. Some have observed this to be the method in which temptations are ripened and brought to their full strength: First, there is the irritation of the object, or that power it has to provoke our corrupt nature — which is either done by the real presence of the object, or by speculation when the object (though absent) is held out by the imagination before the soul. Next follows the motion of the appetite, which is provoked by the imagination representing it as a sensual good. Next there is a consultation of the mind about the best means of accomplishing it. Next follows the election, or choice of the will. And lastly, the desire, or full engagement of the will to it. All this may be done in a few minutes, for the debates of the soul are quick and soon ended. When it has come that far, the heart is won, and Satan has entered victoriously, displaying his colors on the walls of the heart. But if the heart had been well guarded at first, it would never have come to this; for the temptation would have been stopped in the first or second act. And indeed there it is easily stopped; for it is in the motion of a soul tempted to sin, as in the motion of a stone falling from the brow of a hill — it is easily stopped at first, but once it is set in motion it acquires strength by descending. Because of this it is the greatest wisdom to observe the first motions of the heart, to check and stop sin there. The motions of sin are weakest at first, so a little care and watchfulness may prevent much mischief now. The careless heart is brought within the power of temptation before it knows where it is (like the Syrians brought blindfold into the midst of Samaria) — John Flavel, *Keeping the Heart*.

You have led captivity captive; You have received gifts for men. Yes, for the rebellion, also, that the Lord God might dwell among men — Psalm 68:18.

THE LORD JESUS, by His glorious victory here below has subdued all our adversaries. In His going up on high He has triumphed over them all, exhibiting them as trophies. The imagery alludes to the triumphant return of Roman conquerers: they would pass along the Via Sacra and climb up to the Capitol, dragging at their chariot wheels the vanquished rulers, with their hands bound behind their backs.

All those powers which held you captive have been conquered, vanquished by Christ. Whatever form your spiritual slavery took, you are completely delivered from it, for the Lord Christ has made captives of those who had captured you: *"Sin shall not have dominion over you."* Concerning Satan, our Lord has bruised his head beneath His heel. Death is also overcome and its sting taken away. Death is no more the king of dread: *"the sting of death is sin; and the strength of sin is the law. But thanks be to God who gives us the victory through our Lord Jesus Christ."* Whatever there was or is, all which can oppress our soul and enslave it, the Lord Jesus has subdued and made it captive to Himself. What, then? Why, from now on the power of all our adversaries is broken. Courage, Christians! You can fight your way to Heaven, for the foes disputing your passage have been worsted in the field. they bear on them the proofs of the valor of your Leader. True, the Lord's flock is too feeble to force its way, but *"The Breaker has come up before them, and the King at the head of them."* Easily may the sheep follow where the Shepherd breaks the way. We have but to follow Him, and none of our steps will slide. Move on, O soldiers of Jesus, for your Captain cries, *"Follow Me!"*

EVENING

You have led captivity captive; You have received gifts for men. Yes, for the rebellious also, that the Lord God might dwell among men — Psalm 68:18.

OUR LORD'S work was done. The purpose of His love is secure, or He would not have returned to His rest. The love that brought Him here would have kept Him here if all things necessary for our salvation had not been finished. Our Lord Jesus is not one who rashly commences an enterprise of which He wearies before it is accomplished. He does not give up a work which He has once undertaken; He said, *'I have finished the work which You gave Me to do,"* and then ascended to the Father. All that was required of the Lord Christ for the overthrow of the powers of darkness is performed and endured. All that is needed for the salvation of His redeemed ones is full done. Whatever the design of Christ's death, it will be accomplished to the full. For if He had not secured its accomplishment, He would not have gone back.

Do not believe in a defeated and disappointed Savior, nor in a Divine sacrifice which fails to effect its purpose. Do not believe in an atonement which is admirably wide, but fatally ineffectual. I rejoice to hear my Lord say, *"All that the Father gives to Me shall come to Me."* Whatever was the purpose of the Christ of God in the great transaction of the cross, it must be fully effected. To conceive a failure, even of a partial kind, is scarcely reverent. Jesus has seen to it that in no point shall His work be frustrated. Nothing is left undone of all His covenanted engagements. *'It is finished"* is a description of every item of the Divine labor; because of this He has ascended on high. There are no dropped stitches in the robe of Christ. The love that brought our Lord here would have kept Him here if He had not been absolutely sure that all His work and warfare for our salvation had been accomplished to the full.

April 28   MORNING

But of Him you are in Christ Jesus, who was made to us wisdom from God, and righteousness and sanctification and redemption — 1 Corinthians 1:30.

WE MEET somewhere in the Old Testament with the expression *"salt without prescribing how much"* (Ezra 7:22). Beyond all question the name, person, and work of Jesus are the salt and savor of every true gospel ministry, and we cannot have too much of them. Alas, that in so many ministries there is such a lack of this first spice of the feast, this essence of all soul-satisfying doctrine. We may preach Christ without prescribing how much; the more we extol Him, the better. It would be impossible to sin by excess in preaching Christ crucified. It was an ancient precept, "With all your offerings you shall offer salt." Let it stand as an ordinance of the sanctuary now: "With all your sermonizings and discoursings you shall ever mingle the name of Jesus Christ; you shall ever seek to magnify the alpha and omega of the plan of redemption.

    The Apostle in the first chapter of this epistle was anxious to speak to the Corinthians about their divisions and other serious faults. But he could not confine himself to that unpleasant theme. As naturally as possible his heart bounded over the mountains of division to his Lord and Master. Divisions reminded him of the great uniting One who has made all His people one. Human follies drive us nearer to the infallible Christ who is the wisdom of God. Paul had to write many sharp things to those ancient brothers at Corinth, yet how sweetly did he prevent all bitterness by dipping his pen in the honeyed ink of love to the Lord Jesus, and admiration of His person and work. Let us, dear friends, if we have to preach, preach Christ crucified. If we are private persons, let us in our household life, and in our conversation, make His name to be an ointment poured forth. Let your life be Christ living in you.

EVENING

Do not look at me, because I am black, because the sun has looked on me. My mother's children were angry with me; they made me the keeper of the vineyards; but my own vineyard I have not kept — Song of Songs 1:6.

THE BETTER Christian a man is, the more abashed he always feels; because to him sin is so exceedingly hateful that what sin he sees in himself he loathes himself for it, far more than others do. The ungodly man condones very great sin in himself. Even though he knows it to be there, it does not disturb him. But the Christian, being of another sort, having a love of holiness and a hatred for sin, cannot bear to see the smallest speck of sin on himself. He knows what it is. There are persons living before the public eye, and jealous of popularity, who appear quite indifferent to the good opinion of the ruler in whose kingdom they dwell. There are other persons who are favorites at court, who would lie awake at night tossed to and fro in fear if they thought that something had been reported as disloyal to the ruler. A man who does not fear God will break all His laws with an easy conscience. But one who is the favorite of Heaven, who has been indulged to sit at royal banquets, who knows the eternal love of God to him, such a one cannot bear that there should be any evil way in him that might grieve the Spirit and bring dishonor to the name of Christ (Psalm 139:23, 24). A very little sin, as the world calls it, is a very great sin to a truly awakened Christian. Dear ones, do you know what it is to fret because you have spoken an unadvised word? Do you know what it is to smite on your breast, simply because you were angry? Perhaps you were justly provoked, still you angrily spoke unadvisedly. Have you ever gone to a sleepless bed because in the crush of business you have let fall a word, or have done an action which, on mature deliberation, you could not justify? Does the tear never come from your eye because you are not like your Lord, because you have failed where you hoped to succeed? I would give little for your godliness, if you know nothing of this.

Come to Me, all you that labor and are heavy laden, and I will give you rest —
Matthew 11:28.

WE HAVE OFTEN repeated these memorable words, and they have brought us much comfort. But it is possible that we may never have looked deeply into them, so as to have seen the fulness of their meaning. The works of man will seldom bear close inspection. You can take a highly polished needle, one appearing to be without the slightest inequality on its surface, and when you put it under a microscope it will look like a rough bar of iron. But select what you will from nature, the bark or the leaf of a tree, or the wing or foot of an insect, and you will discover no flaw, magnify it as you will, gaze on it as long as you please. So take the words of man. The first time you hear them they may strike you; you may even hear them again and still admire their sentiment, but soon you will weary of their repetition. The words of Jesus are not so. They never lose their dew; they never become threadbare. You may ring the changes on His words and never exhaust their music. You may consider them by day and by night, but familiarity will never breed contempt for them. You may beat them in the mortar of contemplation, beat on them with the pestle of criticism, yet their perfume will but become the more apparent. Dissect, investigate, and weigh the Master's teaching word by word, and each syllable will repay you. The words of poets and eloquent writers may, as a whole, when heard from afar, sound charming enough, but how few of them bear a near and minute investigation! It is never so with the Divine words of Jesus. You hear them ringing from afar, and they are sweetness itself. Sit and listen to each distinct note of love's perfect peal, and wonderingly you will feel that even angelic harps cannot excel it.

EVENING

And I will put My Spirit within you — Ezekiel 36:27.

THE HOLY SPIRIT is given to lead us into all truth. Truth is like a vast grotto, and the Holy Spirit brings torches and shows us all the splendor of the roof; He makes the passages seem intricate. He knows the way, and He leads us into the deep things of God. He opens up to us one truth after another, by His light and His guidance, and so we are *"taught of the Lord."* He is also our practical guide to Heaven, helping and directing us on the upward journey. I wish Christian people inquired more often of the Holy Spirit as to guidance in their daily life. Do you not know that the Spirit of God dwells in you? You need not always be running to this friend or that to get directions. Wait on the Lord in silence; sit quiet before the oracle of God. Use the judgment God has given you, but when that does not suffice, resort to Him whom Mr. Bunyan calls "the Lord High Secretary," He who lives within, who is infinitely wise, and who can guide you by making you to *"hear a voice behind you saying, This is the way, walk in it."* (Isa. 30:21). The Holy Spirit will guide you in life; He will guide you in death, and on to glory. He will guard you from modern error, and from ancient error, too. He will guide you in a way that you do not know; even through the darkness he will lead you in a way you have not seen. These things He will do to you, and He will not forsake you.

"I will put My Spirit within you — that is, by way of consolation; for His choice name is *"the Comforter."* Our God would not have His children unhappy, therefore He in the third Person of the blessed Trinity has undertaken the office of the Comforter. People of God, who are worried, remember that worry and the Holy Spirit are exceedingly contradictory to one another. *"I will put My Spirit within you"* means that you shall become gentle, peaceful, resigned and acquiescent to the Divine will.

Take My yoke upon you and learn of Me, for I am meek and lowly in heart, and you shall find rest to your souls — Matthew 11:29.

IT LOOKS STRANGE that after having received rest the next verse should begin with, *"Take My yoke upon you."* Having been set free from laboring, shall I become a laborer again? Yes, yes, He says, Take My yoke and begin. But, *"My burden is light."* Burden? Why just now I was heavy laden, and being rid of it, am I now to carry another burden? Yes, actively it is a yoke; passively it is a burden. I am to bear both of these. "But I found rest by getting rid of my yoke and burden!" And you now are to find a further rest by wearing a new yoke, by bearing a new burden. Your old yoke galled, but Christ's yoke is easy. Your old burden was heavy, but Christ's burden is light.

From birth the human soul is under the dominion of Satan; it wears his awful yoke and works for him. It bears his accursed burden, and groans under it. When Jesus sets it free, will it then have a perfect rest? Yes, a rest from, but not a rest in. What is needed now is a new government. The soul must have a sovereign, a ruling principle, a master-motive. And when Jesus has taken that position, rest comes. This further rest is what is spoken of in the twenty-ninth verse.

So our souls are made for activity, and when we are set free from the activities of our self-righteousness, and the slavery of our sin, we must do something. And we shall never rest until we find that something to do. For this reason, in the text you will be pleased to see that there is something about a burden, which is the emblem of enduring. It is in man's mortal nature that he must do, or endure, or else his spirit will stagnate and be far from rest.

EVENING

Take My yoke upon you and learn of Me, for I am meek and lowly in heart, and you shall find rest to your souls — Matthew 11:29.

THE WORD *"meek"* refers to the yoke-bearing, the active labor. If I actively labor for Christ I can only find rest in the labor by possessing the meek spirit of my Lord. For if I go forth to labor for Christ without a meek spirit, then I shall very soon find that there is no rest in it; for then the yoke would gall my shoulder. Somebody will begin objecting that I do not perform my work according to his liking. If I am not meek, then I shall find my proud spirit rising immediately. Then I will be for defending myself; I will be irritated, or I will be discouraged and inclined to do no more because I am not appreciated as I should be. A meek spirit is not apt to be angry; it does not soon take offence. Because of this, if others find fault, the meek spirit will go on working and will not be offended. It will not hear the sharp word, nor will it reply to the severe criticism. If one with a meek spirit should be grieved by some cutting censure, and suffers for even a moment, it is always ready to forgive and to blot out the past, and to go on again.

In working the meek spirit only seeks to do good to others. It denies itself. It never expected to be treated well; nor did it aim at being honored. It never sought itself, but purposed only good to others. The meek spirit bowed its shoulder to the yoke, and it expected to have to continue bowing in order to keep the yoke in the right place for the labor. It did not look to be exalted by yoke-bearing. It is fully contented if it can exalt Christ and do good to His chosen ones. Remember how meek and lowly Jesus was in all His service, and how calmly. Because of this He bore with those who opposed Him? Your labor will become very easy if your spirits are very meek. It is the proud spirit that gets tired of doing good if it finds its labors not appreciated. But the brave, meek spirit finds the yoke to be easy.

And she shall give birth to a son. And you shall call His name Jesus; for He shall save His people from their sins — Matthew 1:21.

THE NAME JESUS is particularly rich and suggestive to the mind of the Hebrew scholar. It comes from a root signifying amplitude, spaciousness; and from this it comes to mean a setting at large, a setting free, a delivering. And its common use among us has come to be used of our Savior. There are two words in the name Jesus. The one is a contraction of the word *"Jehovah,"* the other is the word which I have just now explained to you as ultimately coming to mean *"salvation."* Taken to pieces, the word Jesus means Jehovah-Salvation. You have the glorious essense and nature of Christ revealed to you as Jehovah, *"I AM THAT I AM,"* and then you have in the second part of His name His great work for you in setting you at large and delivering you from all the distress from your sins. Think, beloved fellow-Christian, of the amplitude, the spaciousness, the breadth, the abundance, the boundless all-sufficiency laid up in the person of the Lord Jesus.

"It pleased the Father that in Him should all fulness dwell" (Col. 1:19). You have not contracted Christ; you have no narrow Savior. Oh, the infinity of His love, the abundance of His grace, the exceeding greatness of the riches of His love toward us! There are no words in any language that can bring out sufficiently the unlimited, the infinite extent of the riches of the glory of Christ Jesus, our Lord. The word which lies at the root of this name *Jesus* (or *Joshua*), has sometimes the meaning of riches; and who can tell what a wealth of grace and glory are laid up in our Immanuel? Another form of the same word signifies "a cry." *"Hear the voice of my cry, my King and my God."* (Ps. 5:2) — so salvation, riches, and a cry are all derived from the same root, and all find their answer in our Jesus, our Joshua, our Christ.

EVENING

Jesus Christ, the same yesterday, and today, and forever — Hebrews 13:8.

IMMUTABILITY is ascribed to Christ. He was evermore to His people what He is now, for He was the same yesterday. Distinctions have been drawn by certain very 'wise' men (measured by their own estimate of themselves), between the people of God who lived before the coming of Christ, and those who lived afterwards. We have even heard it asserted that those who lived before the coming of Christ do not belong to the church of God. We never know what we will hear next. Perhaps it is a mercy that these absurdities are revealed one at a time, in order that we may be able to endure their stupidity without dying of amazement. Why, every child of God in every age and place stands on the same footing. The Lord has not some children best beloved, some second-rate offspring, and others whom He hardly cares about. Those who saw Christ's day before it came differed in what they knew, and perhaps in the same measure a difference as to what they enjoyed in meditating on Christ while on earth. But they were all washed in the same blood, all redeemed with the same ransom price and made members of the same body. Israel in the covenant of grace is not natural Israel, but all believers in all ages. Before the first advent all the types and shadows all pointed one way, to Christ. And to Him all the saints looked with hope. Those who lived before Christ were not saved with a different salvation to that which shall come to us. They exercised faith as we must; their faith struggled as ours struggles; their faith obtained its reward as ours shall. As like as a man's face to that which he sees in a mirror is the spiritual life of David to the spiritual life of the believer now. Take the book of Psalms in your hand, and forgetting for now that you have the representation of the life of one of the old time, then you might suppose that David wrote only yesterday.

May 2 — MORNING

Jesus Christ, the same yesterday, and today, and forever — Hebrews 13:8

JESUS CHRIST is the same now as He was in times gone by, for the text says, *"the same yesterday, and today."* He is the same today as He was from eternity. Before all worlds He planned our salvation; He entered into covenant with His Father to undertake it. His delights were with the sons of men in prospect, and now today He is as steadfast to that covenant as ever. He will not lose those who were then given to Him, nor will He fail nor be discouraged until every stipulation of that covenant shall be fulfilled. Whatever was in the heart of Christ before the stars began to shine, that same infinite love is there today. Jesus is the same today as He was when He was here on earth. There is much comfort in this thought. When He tabernacled among men, He was willing to save. *"Come to Me, all you that labor and are heavy laden,"* was the burden of His cry. He is still calling to the weary and heavy laden to come to Him. In the days of His flesh He would not curse the woman taken in adultery, nor would He reject the publicans and sinners who gathered to hear Him. He is pitiful to sinners still, and says to them yet, *"Neither do I condemn you; go, and sin no more."* That delightful sentence which so graciously fell from His lips, *"Your sins, which are many, are forgiven you,"* is still His favorite utterance in human hearts.

O do not think that Christ in Heaven has become distant and reserved, so that you may not approach Him. Such as He was here, a Lamb, gentle and meek, a man to whom men drew near without a moment's hesitation, such is He now. Come boldly to Him, you the lowliest and guiltiest ones; come near to Him with broken hearts and weeping eyes. Even though He is King and Priest, surrounded with unknown splendor, yet still He retains the same loving heart, and the same generous sympathies toward the sons of men. He is still the same in His ability as well as in His willingness to save.

EVENING

Jesus Christ, the same yesterday, and today, and forever — Hebrews 13:8.

THE EVIDENT claim of Christ on us is that we should be steadfast in the faith. Notice the ninth verse: *"Do not be carried about with different and strange doctrines."* There is nothing new in theology, only that which is false. All that is true is old (but I do not say that all that is old is true). Some speak of developments as though we had not the whole Christian religion discovered yet. The religion of Paul is the religion of every man who is taught of the Holy Spirit. We ought not, then, to indulge for a moment the idea that something has been discovered which may correct the teaching of Christ. No new philosopy or discovery of science has risen up to correct the declared testimony of our Redeemer. Let us hold fast that which we have received and never depart from *"the truth once delivered to the saints"* by Christ Himself.

If Jesus is immutable, unchangeable, He has an evident claim to our most solemn worship. Immutability can be the attribute of none but God. Whoever can be said to be *"the same yesterday, and today, and forever,"* must be Divine. Ever, then, believer, bring your adoration to Jesus. At the feet of Him that was crucified cast down your crown. Give royal and Divine honors to Him who stooped to the ignominy of crucifixion. Let no one stop you from glorying in, from boasting of the Son of God made man for you. Worship Him as God over all, blessed forever.

He claims of us that we should trust Him. If He is always the same, here is a Rock that cannot be moved. Build on it. Here is an anchorage; cast your anchor of hope into it and hold fast in time of storm. If Christ were variable, He would not be worthy of our confidence. Since He is evermore unchanged, rest on Him without fear.

Your words were found, and I ate them; and Your word was to me the joy and gladness of my heart; for I am called by Your name, O Lord God of hosts —Jeremiah 15:16

OUR TEXT testifies to an eager reception. It is not "I did hear them," for that he might have done and yet have perished. Herod heard John gladly, and yet became his murderer. He does not say, "I did learn them by heart" — hundreds have committed chapters to memory, and were rather wearied than benefited by it. The Scribes fought over jots and tittles of the law, but were blind leaders of the blind. It is not, "Your words were found, and I repeated them," for that he might have done as a parrot repeats language it has been taught. Nor is it even, "Your words were found, and I remembered them" —for though it is an excellent thing to store truth in the memory, yet the blessed effect of the Divine words comes rather to those who ponder them in their hearts. What is meant by eating God's words? The phrase signifies more than any other word could express. It implies an eager study: *"I ate them."* I could not have too much of them, could not enter too thoroughly into their consideration. He who loves the Savior desires to grow in the grace and knowledge of Him. He cannot read or hear too much or too often concerning his great Redeemer. He turns to the holy page with every new delight. He seeks the blessing of the man who meditates in God's law, both day and night. It is pleasing to notice the sharp-set, spiritual appetite of a new convert. He hungers and thirsts after righteousness; he will hear a sermon without fatigue, although he may have to stand in an uncomfortable position. And when one discourse is over, he is ready for another. Oh that we all had our first appetites back again! Some professors grow very squeamish and proudly delicate; they cannot feed on heavenly truth because they see defects in the style of the preacher, or in the manner of the service.

EVENING

Your words were found, and I ate them; and Your word was to me the joy and gladness of my heart; for I am called by Your name, O Lord God of hosts —Jeremiah 15:16.

WHEN we find God's truth, we delight to meditate, contemplate and consider. We let it dwell in our hearts richly until at last its sustaining, upbuilding, nourishing influence is felt. And we grow by it. It is not a hasty swallowing of the word which is blessed to us, but a deliberate eating of it. Our inward life acts on the truth, and the truth acts on our life. We become one with the truth, and the truth one with us. I would to God we were all more given to feeding and lying down in the green pastures of God's word. The sheep fattens as it chews the cud in peace, and so do we.

Establishment in the gospel is the result of meditation. Nothing is more desirable at this present time than that all believers should more constantly study and weigh the word of God. Neglect in this matter has weakened, is weakening, and will weaken the church. Now we lack not merely persons who have been aroused by solemn exhortation, led to give their hearts to Christ under the influence of deep emotion, but Christians well instructed in the things which are truly believed by us, rooted and grounded in gospel doctrines. Many professing Christians think very lightly of Scriptural knowledge, especially of an experimental acquaintance with Divine truth. Few have studied the doctrines of grace so as to be able to give *"a reason for the hope"* that is in them. Too often converts are made by excitement; then when the excitement is gone they grow cold. Some of them go back to the world and prove that they were never taught of God, but others linger on in a half-starved condition because soul-sustaining truth is hidden from them. The one who knows the truth, and feels the truth has made him free, is the one who will continue to be free at all hazards.

May 4 MORNING

Your words were found, and I ate them; and Your word was to me the joy and gladness of my heart; for I am called by Your name, O Lord God of hosts —Jeremiah 15:16.

THE TEXT tells us of happy consequences. He who has spiritually found God's word, and consequently feeds on it, is the happy man. But in order to get joy from God's word we must receive it universally. Jeremiah first speaks of God's *"words,"* then he changes the number and speaks of God's *"word."* We are not only to receive parts of the gospel, but the whole of it, and then it will afford us great joy. That one's heart is right with God who can honestly say that all the testimonies of God are dear to him. But one may say, "that is impossible; parts of the Bible are full of terrible denunciations; how can they afford us joy?" In this way: If God appoints that sin should be punished, we are not to rebel against His righteous ordinance, nor to close our minds to the consideration of Divine justice. God's judgments are right, and what is right we must rejoice in. Moreover, by the threatenings of the word many are led to forsake their sin, and thus the warning itself is a means of grace. To tenderhearted Jeremiah I have no doubt it was a trial to say, *"Your city will be destroyed, and your women and your children will be slain."* But when he considered that some might be led to repentance, he would with tearful vehemence deal out the thunder of the Lord.

But God's word is not all threatening. How much of it consists of exceeding great and precious promises! Grace drops from it like honey from the comb. How would even Jeremiah brush away the falling tear, while that face usually so clouded, would beam as the sun when he spoke of the Messiah? Surely, if there is anything in the whole range of truth which can make our hearts leap for joy, it is the part of it which touches on the lovely person and finished work of our adorable Redeemer, to whom be honor and glory forever. Receive the whole of God's word. Hold the truth in its entirety and harmony, and then as a matter of certainty it will become to you the joy and rejoicing of your spirit.

EVENING

Yes, He is altogether lovely — Song of Songs 5:16.

THE LORD JESUS *"is altogether lovely."* Here is very sweet instruction. Then if I want to be lovely, I must be like Him. The model for me as a Christian is Christ. Have you ever noticed how badly boys write at the bottom of their copy-book pages? There is the copy at the top; and in the first line they look at that; in the second line, they copy their own imitation; in the third line they copy their imitation of their imitation, and so on till the writing grows worse and worse. Now the apostles followed Christ; the first fathers imitated the apostles; the next fathers copied the first fathers. And so the standard of holiness fell dreadfully. And now we are too apt to follow the very lees and dregs of Christianity, and we think if we are about as good as our poor, imperfect ministers or leaders in the church, that we shall do well and deserve praise.

But now cover up the mere copies and imitations and live by the first line. Copy Jesus, for *"He is altogether lovely."* If you write by the first line, you will write by the truest and best model in the world. We want to have Christ's zeal, but we must balance it with His prudence and discretion. We must seek to have Christ's love to God, and we must feel His love to men, His forgiveness and lowliness, His utter unselfishness. His entire consecration to His Father's business. Oh that we had all this! For depend on it whatever other pattern we select, we have made a mistake; we are not following the true classic model of the Christian artist. Our master model is the *"altogether lovely"* One. How sweet it is to think of our Lord in the double aspect as our Exemplar and our Savior!

Do not look at me, because I am black, because the sun has looked on me. My mother's children were angry with me; they made me the keeper of the vineyards; but my own vineyard I have not kept — Song of Songs 1:6.

THE FAIREST CHRISTIANS are the most shamefaced with regard to themselves. The person who says, *"Do not look upon me, because I am black,"* is described by some one else in the eighth verse as the *"fairest among women."* Others, who thought her the fairest of the fair, spoke no less than the truth when they affirmed it. But in her own esteem she felt herself to be so little fair, so much uncomely, that she begged them not even to look on her. Why is it that the best Christians depreciate themselves the most?

Is it not because they are most accustomed to look within? They keep their books in a better condition than those of mere professors, those who think themselves to be "rich and increased in goods," when they are in fact bankrupt. The Christian in his right state tests himself to see where he is in the faith. He values too much his own soul to go on blindly. He knows that Heedless and Toobold are always bad pilots, so he sets Caution and Self-examination at the helm. He cries to God, *"Search me, and know my heart."* He is accustomed to examine his actions and his motives, to pass his words and his thoughts in review. He does not live the life of one who goes recklessly on; he stops and considers his ways; he looks well to the state of everything within him, in order *"to have a conscience void of offence toward God and toward men."* Solomon says, *"The wise man looks to the state of his flocks and his herds;"* and it is no marvel if any one suffers loss who neglects the counsel. But he also says, *"Keep your heart with all diligence, for out of it are the issues of life"* — and it is quite certain that he who fails in this exercise is liable to every kind of moral disorder.

EVENING

Your own salvation — Philippians 2:12.

I SHALL STEADFASTLY ASSERT that nothing so much concerns any one of you as salvation. Your health, by all means. Let the physician be brought if you are sick; care well for diet and exercise; obey all sanitary laws. Look wisely to your constitution and its peculiarities. But after all, what does it matter if you have a healthy body, if you have a perishing soul? Wealth, yes, if you must have it — although you shall find it an empty thing if you set your heart on it. Prosperity in this world, earn it if you can do so fairly. But, *"What shall it profit a man, if he shall gain the whole world, and lose his own soul?"* A golden coffin will be a poor compensation for a condemned soul. To be cast away from God's presence, can that misery be assuaged by mountains of treasure? Can the bitterness of the second death be sweetened by the thought that the wretch was once a millionaire, and that his wealth could affect the politics of nations? No! There is nothing in health or wealth to compare with salvation.

Nor can honor and reputation bear a comparison with it. Truly they are but trinkets — and yet for all that they have a strange fascination for the sons of men. Oh, sirs, if every harpstring in the world should resound your glories, and every trumpet should proclaim your fame, what would it matter if a louder voice should say, *"Depart from Me, cursed ones, into everlasting fire prepared for the Devil and his angels"?* Salvation! Salvation! Nothing on earth can match it, for the merchandise of it is better than silver, and the gain of it than fine gold. The possession of the whole universe would be no equivalent to a lost soul for the awful damage it has sustained and must sustain forever.

May 6   MORNING

So I will bless You while I live; I will lift up my hands in Your name — Psalm 63:4.

HOW MANY a thing have we taken in hand, as we say, which we expected to find an agreeable task, an interest in life, a something towards filling up that unconfessed 'aching void' which is often most real when least acknowledged. And after a while we have found it change under our hands into irksome travail, involving perpetual vexation of spirit!. The thing may have been of the earth and for the world, and then no wonder it failed to satisfy even the instinct of work which comes natural to many of us. Or it may have been right enough in itself, something for the good of others so far as we understood their good, and unselfish in all but unraveled motive, and yet we found it full of tangled vexations because the hands that held it were not simply consecrated to God. Well, if so, let us bring these soiled and tangle-making hands to the Lord. Let us lift up our heart with our hands to Him, asking Him to clear and cleanse them.

If He says, What is in your hand? Let us examine honestly whether it is something which He can use for His glory, or not. If not, do not let us hesitate an instant about dropping it. It may be something we do not like to part with, but the Lord is able to give you much more than this. And the first glimpse of *the excellency of the knowledge of Christ Jesus our Lord* will enable us to count those things loss which were before considered gain to us.

But if it is something which He can use, He will make us do ever so much more with it than before. Moses little thought what the Lord was going to make him do with that rod in his hand. The first thing he had to do with it was to throw it on the ground and observe it pass through a startling change. After this he was to take it up again. Then it was the rod of God in his hand (Ex. 4:20), with which he would do signs, and by which God Himself would do *marvelous things* (Psalm 78:12).

EVENING

Fill your hand today for Jehovah (Exodus 32:29 LTB).

IF WE LOOK at any Old Testament text about consecration, we will see that the marginal reading is *"fill the hand."* But if our hands are full of other things, they cannot be filled with *"the things that are Jesus Christ's"* — there must be an emptying before there can be any true filling. So if we are sorrowfully seeing that our hands have not been kept for Jesus, let us humbly begin at the beginning and ask Him to empty them thoroughly, that He may fill them completely.

For they must be emptied. Either we come to our Lord willingly about it, allowing Him to unclasp their hold, gladly dropping the glittering weights they have been carrying; or in love He will force them open and force out the earthly things which are keeping them from having their rightful use for Him. There is only one other alternative, a terrible one: to be let alone until the day comes when not a gentle Master, but a relentless king of terrors shall empty the trembling hands as our feet follow him out of the busy world into the dark valley, for *"it is certain that we can carry nothing out."*

Yet the emptying and the filling are not all that has to be considered. Before the hands of the priests could be filled with the emblems of consecration, they had to be laid on the emblem of atonement (Lev. 8:14, etc.). That came first. So the transference of guilt to our Substitute, typified by that Levitical act, must precede the dedication of ourselves to God. The blood of our Holy Substitute as shed to make reconciliation for us. Without it we cannot offer anything acceptable to God. (The above two devotions are from *Kept for the Master's Use,* Frances Havergal.)

And I will also take some of them for priests and for Levites, says the Lord
— Isaiah 66:21.

THINK of the compass of this great promise. Evidently a high honor is here conferred. The connection leads us to see that not only a great promise but likewise a great privilege is implied in this. What is this privilege? It is that we shall be priests and Levites. Now the priests or Levites were persons set apart to be God's peculiar property. When the firstborn were spared in Egypt, God claimed the firstborn. They were to be the Lord's. Although all Israel belonged to God, yet the tribe of Levi was especially selected and particularly appointed to do the service of the tabernacle of the congregation. And of this tribe of Levi, chief among them the house of Aaron was chosen to minister in the sanctuary as priests.

So, now, glory be to God, He takes out of all nations a people that are to be peculiarly His own — His own by election, as He chose them — His own by redemption, as He bought them — His own by endowment through the regeneration and sanctifying working of God the Holy Spirit. *"They shall be Mine, says the Lord of hosts, in that day when I make up my jewels* (Mal. 3:17). His own now, and after time forever. Being thus set apart as the Lord's property, the priests and Levites lived only for Divine service. While others were engaged with their trade or husbandry the Levites were attending to the Lord's business, doing those things which He had given them as a charge, to His glory, and for the benefit of His people. It was in sacred things that they were occupied. So it is now; it is the duty of everyone to serve the Lord. But, alas! Man is not so inclined. Because of this God takes to Himself a people out of all nations, and kindreds, and tongues.

EVENING

And I will also take some of them for priests and for Levites, says the Lord
— Isaiah 66:21.

PRIESTS AND LEVITES had two works to do: something to do toward God for men — and something to do toward men for God. They were engaged to do something toward God for men: And so they offered the sacrifices that were brought to the door of the tabernacle, whether according to the general ordinances, or to any special vows. Spiritually minded, they were much engaged in intercession for the rest of Israel. So in this day there is a people who offer to God acceptable prayer and praise, and in answer to their prayer unnumbered blessings come down on the sons of men. Surely, there are some of you who have power with God in prayer. You are the King's remembrancers; you make mention of His name. You do not keep silence, but cry to God even for Sodom. And even more hopefully you cry to God for Jerusalem. Your prayer does not cease, and God's grace and favor always follow it. In this sense God is constantly taking out, even from among the vilest of the vile, a people whom He makes to be priests and Levites for men toward Himself.

Another part of the priestly office in speaking for God to the people: *"For the priest's lips should keep knowledge."* As for the Levites, they were as ushers in the schools and tutors in the families of Israel. Among the Levites were found those scribes who became the instructors of the people, the copyists of the law, and the expounders of its statutes and ordinances. There were ministers who opened up the knotty points of the old covenant, who expounded the word (as Ezra did). So not all of us in the same degree, but all of us in a measure, are to be teachers of God's revealed truth, even as He has taught us. And He has in this place, and throughout the world, taken out a certain company whom He has made to speak as His mouth to the sons of men.

May 8   MORNING

And I will also take some of them for priests and for Levites, says the Lord
— Isaiah 66:21.

OBSERVE that according to the text men have nothing to do with the selection; for here it is said, *"I will take some of them,"* — not "their parents shall bring them up to it;" — not, "those shall be sought out who are most fit and proper men on account of some natural bent and bias, or gift and talent;" — but, *"I will take."* God's priesthood in the world is a priesthood of His own choosing, of His own setting apart, of His own anointing: *"He has made us kings and priests to God."* The believing church is a royal priesthood, not of man, neither by man, nor of the will of man, nor of blood, nor of birth (John 1:13); it is of God's own choosing. This sacred and consecrated band of priests and Levites, and all that serve God effectually and acceptably are men whom He has Himself chosen to the work. He has done it, and only His own will has been consulted in the matter. In their case, it appears from the text that whatever was unfit in their character has been overcome by Divine grace. If God takes them for Levites, He makes them Levites. If He chooses them for priests, He makes them priests. So, glory be to His name, when He chose you, my dear one, when He chose you to be His servants, to be His priests and His Levites, He gave the grace that you lacked. He found in you no natural fitness, no suitability, but a fitness for sin, a suitability to go astray, to become a brand for the burning. But if there is a fitness in you to serve Him on earth and in Heaven, it is His grace that has given it to you. It is His grace speaking in all its wondrous majesty: *"I will take some of them for priests and for Levites"* — in this He has effected in you the great transformation, making in you all things new, and so qualifying you to become the servants of the Most High.

EVENING

And I will also take some of them for priests and for Levites, says the Lord
— Isaiah 66:21.

ANOTHER REASON why the Lord takes the vilest ones to make them the saintliest is that He might openly triumph over Satan. How must the Devil feel defeat when such a man as Paul is taken from persecuting to preaching! Surely, it makes Satan bite his chains and gnash his teeth when he loses his slaves so easily. Just when he has trained them and has gotten them into fine condition to do his mischief, in comes Divine grace and arrests them, giving them new hearts. You know none ever do the Devil so much mischief as those who once did him service. They know the ins and outs of his castle, where to attack it. They understand so well his devices and tactics, and so they become all the more powerful adversaries of Satan when they are converted.

All Heaven rings with rapture when a great sinner is saved. Yea, and all Hell howls with dismay when one of the arch-host bows down to kiss the feet of Christ, to receive the mercy of God. Glory be to God when He takes those that would have been deepest damned, and sets them highest among the saved on earth to be priests and Levites to Him. By these means also He secures another end. He encourages poor penitents, for when he was a sinner under the sense of sin, and meets a brother in Christ who was like himself once, but is now living near to God, he is much encouraged. Why, he thinks to himself, "Is this how God receives sinners when they turn to Him? Perhaps He will receive me." And if he gets into conversation with one of those whom God has made a priest or a Levite, he says, "Tell me what the Lord has done for your soul." And this saved one, being of like passions, and having had like experience, delights to describe to his questioner the works and the ways of God with hardened sinners and chief offenders.

MORNING

Then was our mouth filled with laughter — Psalm 126:2.

We must earnestly endeavor to learn this practice, or at the least to attain to some knowledge of it. And we must raise up ourselves with this consideration, that the gospel is nothing else but laughter and joy. This joy properly pertains to captives, to those that feel the captivity of sin and death; to those tender hearts terrified with the feeling of the wrath and judgment of God. These are the disciples in whose hearts should be planted laughter and joy, and that by the authority of the Holy Spirit, which this verse sets forth. This people was in Zion, and, after the outward show of the kingdom and priesthood, mightily flourished. But if a man consider them according to the spirit, he will see them to be in miserable captivity, that their tongue is full of heaviness and mourning, because their heart is terrified with the sense of sin and death. This is Moses' tongue or Moses' mouth, full of wormwood and of the bitterness of death. With it he designs to kill none but those who are too lively and too full of security. But those who feel their captivity shall have their mouths filled with laughter and joy; that is, redemption and deliverance from sin and deaths will be preached to them. This is the sense and meaning of the Holy Spirit, that the mouth of such will be filled with laughter; that is, their mouth will show forth nothing else but gladness through the inestimable consolations of the gospel, with voices of triumph and victory by Christ, overcoming Satan, destroying death, and taking away sins. This was first spoken to the Jews; for this laughter was first offered to that people, they then having the promises. Now he turns to the Gentiles, whom he calls to the partaking of this laughter — Martin Luther.

EVENING

that I may know how frail I am (Heb. *that I may know how lacking I am*) — Psalm 39:4.

GOD DELAYS and puts off His people many times so that He may make a fuller discovery of themselves to themselves. Few Christians see themselves and understand themselves. By delays God reveals much of a man's sinful self to his religious self, much of his worser part to his better part, much of his ignoble part to his most noble part. When the fire is put under the pot, then the scum appears. When God puts His child in the fire of affliction, Oh, how does the scum of pride, the scum of murmuring, the scum of quarreling, the scum of distrust, the scum of impatience, the scum of despair, reveal itself in the heart of the poor creature. When God shuts the door on His people, Oh what cause they have to cry out. But cry out to God, not out of proud self, of worldly self, of carnal self, of foolish self, etc. God's delays are as a looking glass in which God gives His people opportunity to see their faults. Oh what baseness, what vileness, what wretchedness, what wickedness God often reveals by delays in the hearts of men! Surely, one who has often and long put off the motions of the Spirit, the directions of His word and the offers of His grace cannot complain if God delays for a time in granting His mercy of communion and satisfaction. If God serves you as you have often served Him, you have no reason to complain. — Thomas Brooks, *The Mute Christian Under the Smarting Rod*, p. 109.

MORNING

My sheep hear My voice, and I know them, and they follow Me — John 10:27.

CHRISTIANS are here compared to sheep. It is not a very flattering comparison, but then we do not wish to be flattered (nor would our Lord deem it good to flatter us). While far from flattering, it is yet eminently consoling, for of all creatures there are not any more compassed about with infirmity than sheep. In this frailty of their nature they are a fit emblem of ourselves — at least of those of us who have believed in Jesus and have become His disciples. Let others boast how strong they are. If there are strong ones anywhere, certainly we confess we are weak. We have proved our weakness, and day by day we lament it. Confessing our weakness, yet we do not repine at it. For, as the apostle Paul said, so we also find: that *when we are weak then we are strong*, because God's power is perfected in weakness (2 Cor. 12:9). Sheep have many wants; they are very helpless, quite unable to provide for themselves. Except for the shepherd's care they would soon perish.

This is our case also. Our spiritual needs are numerous and pressing. Yet we cannot supply any of them. We are travelers through a wilderness that yields us neither food nor water. Unless our bread drop down from Heaven, and our water flow out of the living Rock, we must die. We keenly feel our weakness and our need. Still we have no cause to murmur, since the Lord knows our poor estate and aids us with the tenderest care. Sheep, too, are silly creatures. In this respect we are also very sheepish. We meekly own it to Him who is ready to shepherd us. We say with David, *"O God, You know my foolishness."* And He says to us, as He said to David, *"I will instruct you and teach you in the way which you shall go."* If Christ were not our wisdom we would soon fall a prey to the destroyer. Every grain of true wisdom that we possess we have received from Him.

EVENING

My sheep hear My voice, and I know them, and they follow Me — John 10:27.

SHEEP OF CHRIST, you shall be His forever, because you have been His from everlasting. The sheep of Christ are His because His Father gave them to Him (John 17:6). They were the gift of the Father to Christ. He often speaks of them in this way, *"As many as You have given Me." "You have given them to Me."* Over and over again He says it. Before the foundation of the world the Father gave His people to Christ. Separating them from among men, He gave them as a gift, committing them into His hand as a trust, ordaining them to Him as the lot of His inheritance. So they become a token of the Father's love to His only-begotten Son, a proof of the confidence He reposed in Him, and a pledge of the honor that shall be done to Him. Now it is for the donor's sake that we value a gift. If presented to us by one whom we love, we set great store by it. If it has been designed as a love-token, it awakens in our minds many sweet memories. Although the intrinsic worth may be of small account, the associations make it exceedingly precious. We might be content to lose something of far greater value in itself, rather than that which is the gift of one whom we love.

How weak are the words of human passion! But how strong are the expressions of Divine ardor. When Jesus speaks to the Father of *"the men whom You gave me out of the world,"* He says, *"They were Yours, and You gave them to Me; and those that You gave to Me I have kept."* You sheep of Christ, rest safely. Do not let your soul be disturbed with fear. The Father gave you to His Son, and He will not lightly lose what God Himself has given to Him. The infernal lions of evil shall not tear the meanest lamb that has been given as a love-token from the Father to His best Beloved.

Restore to me the joy of Your salvation, and uphold me with a willing spirit — Psalm 51:12.

IT IS no small comfort to a man that has lost his receipt for a debt paid when he remembers that the man he deals with is a good and just man, though his discharge of the debt is not presently found. That God with whom you have to deal is very gracious. What you have lost He is ready to restore — I mean the evidence of your grace. David begged this, and he obtained it. Yea, faith says, if it were true, that which you fear, that your grace was never true, then there is mercy enough in God's heart to pardon all your former hypocrisy if you but come in the sincerity of your heart. And so faith persuades the soul by an act of adventure to cast itself on God in Christ. Faith says, Will you not expect to find as much mercy at God's hands as you can look for at a man's hands? It is not beyond the line of created mercy to forgive many unkindnesses, much falseness and unfaithfulness, if an humble, sincere acknowledgment is made of the same. The world is not so bad but it abounds with parents who can do that much for their children, and masters for their servants. And is it too hard for God to do that which even a creature can do? So faith vindicates God's name. And so long as we have not lost sight of the merciful heart of God our head will be kept above water, though we may lack the evidence of our own grace. — William Gurnall, *A Christian in Complete Armor.*

"uphold me with a willing spirit" — I am tempted to think that I am now an established Christian, that I have overcome this or that lust so long that I have gotten into the habit of the opposite grace, so that there is no fear. I may even venture very near the temptation, nearer than other men. This is a lie of Satan. I might as well speak of gunpowder getting by habit a power to resist fire. As long as the Spirit dwells in my heart, He deadens me to sin, so that if lawfully called through temptation I may reckon on God to carry me through. But when the Spirit leaves me, I am like dry gunpowder. Oh, for a sense of this! — Robert M. McCheyne (From *The Treasury of David, p 471*)

EVENING

Search me, O God, and know my heart; try me, and know my thoughts, and see if any wicked way is in me, and lead me in the way everlasting — Psalm 139:23, 24.

DAVID is no accomplice with traitors. He has disowned them in set form, and now he appeals to God that he does not harbor a trace of fellowship with them. He will have God himself search him, and search him thoroughly, till every point of his being is known and read, and understood. For he is sure that even by such an investigation there will be found in him no complicity with wicked men. He challenges the fullest investigation, the innermost search. He had need be a true man who can put himself deliberately into such a crucible. Yet we may each one desire such searching. For it would be a terrible calamity to us for sin to remain in our hearts unknown and undiscovered. *"Try me, and know my thoughts."* Exercise any and every test on me. By fire and by water let me be examined. Do not only read the desires of my heart, but the fugitive thoughts of my head. Know with all-penetrating knowledge all that is or has been in the chambers of my mind. What a mercy that there is One who can know us to perfection. He is intimately at home with us. He is graciously inclined toward us and is willing to bend His omniscience to serve the end of our sanctification. Let us pray, as David did, and let us be honest, as he was. We cannot hide our sin; salvation lies the other way, in a plain discovery of evil, and in effectual severance from it.

(Above is from *The Treasury of David,* C. H. Spurgeon, pp. 229, 230

May 12   MORNING

Where the birds make their nests; as for the stork, the fir trees are her house; the high hills are a refuge for the wild goats and the rocks for the conies —Psalm 104:17, 18.

    WE SHALL FIND that for all parts of the spiritual universe God has provided suitable forms of divine life. Think that out for a moment. Each age has its saints. The first age had its holy men, men who walked with God. And when the golden age had gone, and men everywhere had polluted themselves, God had His Noah. In after days, when men had again multiplied on the face of the earth, the sin abounded, but there was Job in the land of Uz, and Abraham and Isaac and Jacob dwelling in tents in the land which had been given to them by promise. On whatever period of the world's history you choose to place your finger you may rest assured that as God is there, so there also is some form of the divine life extant. Some of God's twice-born creatures are to be found even in the most barren ages.

    If you come to a period like that of Ahab, when a lonely Elijah bitterly complains, *"I, I only am left, and they seek my life to destroy it,"* you shall hear a still small voice that says, *"Yet I have reserved to Myself seven thousand men that have not bowed the knee to Baal."* God has still His elect remnant in the most wicked times, to whom He has given a banner, because of the truth. When the light was almost gone from Israel, and formalism had eclipsed the sun of Judaism, there were still a Simeon and an Anna waiting for the coming of the Messiah. Times of fearful persecution, when to mention the name of Christ was to sentence yourself to death, have not been devoid of saints, but rather in the hottest times of oppression God has brought forth heroes equal to the emergency. The fiercer the trial, the stronger the men. The church of God has lived and flourished amid the flames, and has seemed to feed on the flames that threatened to devour her. As on the crags, where it appears impossible for life to exist, God places wild goats, so on the high crags of persecution He upholds men whose feet are like hind's feet, and who glory as they tread on their high places.

EVENING

For now we see through a mirror, darkly; but then face to face — 1 Corinthians 13:12.

    WE KNOW there is a church of God. We know that the Lord has a people whom He has chosen from before the foundation of the world. We believe that these are scattered up and down throughout the lands. We know this church, we know its glory; it is moved with one life, quickened with one Spirit, redeemed with one blood. We believe in this church, and we feel attachment to it for the sake of Jesus Christ, who has married the church as the Bride. But, oh, when we shall get to Heaven, how much more we shall know of the church, and how we shall see her face to face, and not *"through a mirror, darkly."* There we shall know something more of the numbers of the chosen than we do now; it may be to our intense surprise. There we shall find some among the company of God's elect whom we in our bitterness of spirit had condemned. And there we shall miss some whom we had conceived to be perfectly secure. We shall know better then who are the Lord's, and who are not. Here all our processes of discernment fail us. Judas comes in with the apostles, and Demas takes his part among the saints. But there we shall know the righteous, for we shall see them. There will be one flock and one Shepherd, and He who on the throne reigns forever more shall be glorified. We shall understand then what the history of the church has been in all the past, and why it has been so strange a history of conflict and conquest. Probably we shall know more of the history of the church in the future. From that higher elevation and brighter atmosphere we shall understand better what are the Lord's designs concerning His people in the latter day, and what glory shall redound to His own name from His redeemed ones.

MORNING

Where the birds make their nests; as for the stork, the fir trees are her house. The high hills are a refuge for the wild goats, and the rocks for the conies — Psalm 104:17, 18.

EACH CREATURE has its appropriate place. Birds with their nests for the cedars of Lebanon, storks for the fir trees, wild goats for the high hills, and conies for the rocks. Each of these creatures looks most beautiful in their native home. Go into the Zoological Gardens and see the poor animals there under artificial conditions, and you can little guess what they are like at home. A lion in a cage is a very different creature from a lion in the wilderness. The stork looks wretched in his wire pen, and you would hardly know him as the same creature if you saw him on the housetops or on the fir trees. Each creature looks best in its own place.

Take that truth and use it for yourself. Each one has a position providentially appointed to him or her. The position ordained for each Christian is that in which he looks best; it is the best for him and he is the best for it. And if you could change position, and shift to another, you would not be half as happy, nor half as useful, nor half so much as yourself. Put the stork on the high hills, put the wild goat on the fir trees — what monstrosities! Take a man working with his hands twenty years, though always a spiritually-minded man, and make him Lord Mayor of London, and you would spoil him altogether. Take a good hearer and set him to preaching, and he would make a sorry appearance. A man out of place is not seen to advantage; you then see the wrong side of him, the gracious side is hidden. The position in which God has placed me is the best for me. Let me remember this when I feel like grumbling and complaining. Perhaps you may at times repine, thinking that if you were in a different position you could glorify God more. Beware of such insinuating discontentment. God knows best.

EVENING

Where the birds make their nests; as for the stork, the fir trees are her house. The high hills are a refuge for the wild goats, and the rocks for the conies — Psalm 104:17, 18.

EACH CREATURE has its appropriate place as to individuality of character. Each constitution is meant, under the power of grace, to be suitable for a man's position. I might wish to be of a different temperament than what I am. But in wiser moments I would not wish to alter anything in myself but that which is sinful. Martin Luther at times might have wished that he had been as gentle as Melancthon, but then we might have had no Reformation. Melancthon at times might have wished that he had been as energetic as Luther, but then Luther might have lacked his most tender comforter. It might seem that Peter would have been improved if he had not been so rough, and John if he had been somewhat more firm. But after all it must be recognized that when God makes Peter, he is best as Peter; and when He makes John, he is best as John. It is very foolish when Peter wants to be John, and when John pines to be Peter.

Dear ones, the practical matter is this, that you must be yourselves in your religion. Never attempt to counterfeit another's virtues, nor try to square your experience according to another's feelings. Never try to mold your character so that you may look as if you were like some other good person. No, ask the Lord, who made a new creature of you, to make you come out as He meant it, with whatever grace He meant to be prominent in you. If you were meant to be a hero that rushes into the thick of the battle, then let courage be developed. If He designed you to lie in the hospital to suffer and pray, then let patience have its perfect work. But ask the Lord to mold you after His own mind, that as He finds a stork for a certain fir tree, and a fir tree for a stork, so He will find a place for you, and put you in a place He intended you to be.

May 14   MORNING

You give, they gather; You open your hand, they are filled with good —Psalm 104:28

The work of God in providing for His creatures is stupendous. It is done with ease only because He is infinite. It is every way our sweetest consolation that the personal God is still at work in the world.

The general principle of the text is that God gives to His creatures, and His creatures gather. That applies to our own case as men and women. For it is as true of us as it is of the fish of the sea. First, we have only to gather, for God gives. In temporal things God gives us day by day our daily bread; our business is simply to gather it. In spiritual things the principle is most emphatically true, for we only have to gather what He has freely given to us. The natural man thinks that he has to earn Divine favor, that he has to purchase the blessing of Heaven. He is in grave error; the soul is fashioned so that it only has to receive that which Jesus freely gives. Secondly, we can only gather what God gives. However eager we may be, that is the end of the matter. The diligent bird can gather no more than the Lord has provided for it. Nor can the most avaricious and covetous man do so: *"It is vain for you to rise up early and to sit up late, to eat the bread of carefulness; for so He gives His beloved sleep."* Thirdly, God feeds the innumerable creepers, but each creature collects the food provided for itself. The huge sea-animal receives his vast provision, but he must go plowing through the boundless sea to gather up his supply. There are fish that must leap up to catch their food; swallows must hawk for their food; young lions must hunt for their prey. Fourthly, we know certainly that we may gather what God gives. We have Divine permission to enjoy freely what the Lord grants to us. Lastly, God will always give us something to gather, for it is written, *"The Lord will provide,"* in spiritual things as well as in natural things.

EVENING

O give thanks to the Lord; call on His name; make known His deeds among the people; sing to Him; sing psalms to Him; talk of His wondrous works —Psalm 105:1

JEHOVAH is the Author of all our benefits; then let Him have all our gratitude, *"Call on His name."* Proclaim His titles; fill the world with His renown, *"Make known His deeds among the people,"* (*"among the nations"*). Let the heathen hear of our God, that they may forsake their idols and learn to worship Him.

"Sing to Him" — Bring your best thoughts and express them in the best language to the sweetest sounds. Take care that your singing is *"to Him,"* not simply the making of music to delight the ears of you or others. Singing is a delightful exercise; therefore do not waste it on trifles, or that which is worse than trifles. Emulate the nightingale, almost rival the angels in your praise, that your hearts may be renewed in a way that will bring floods of melody from your heart, then pour it out to your Maker's and your Redeemer's feet.

"Talk of His wondrous works." Men love to speak of marvels, and others are generally glad to hear marvelous things. Surely the believer in the living God has before him the most amazing series of wonders ever heard, or to be imagined. His themes are inexhaustible, and they are such as should hold men spellbound. We ought to have more of this talk. No one should be blamed for being a Mr. Talkative if the marvelous works of God are his constant theme. You saints know something by experience of His marvelous loving-kindness; talk of it. In this way, by all of us dwelling on this blessed subject, all His wondrous works will be published. One cannot do it; ten thousand times ten thousand cannot, but if all speak to the Lord's honor and glory, they will at least come nearer to accomplishing it. Obedience to this verse will give every sanctified tongue some work to do. Make yours praise God to all near you.

Christ is all, and in all — Colossians 3:11.

THE APOSTLE is arguing for holiness. He is earnestly contending against sin and for the maintenance of Christian graces. But he does not, as some preachers of the gospel try to do, resort to reasons inconsistent with the gospel of free grace. He did not bring forward a single legal argument. He did not say, "Do this, and you will merit reward." He knows that he is writing to believers, those not under the Law, but under grace. So he uses arguments taken from grace, those suitable to the character and condition of *"the elect of God, holy and beloved."* He feeds the flame of their love with suitable fuel; he fans their zeal with appropriate motivation.

In this chapter he begins by reminding the saints that they have risen with Christ. If they indeed have risen with Him, he argues that they then leave the grave of iniquity and the grave-clothes of their sins behind them, that they should act as ones who are endowed with superior life, and act as if sin indeed is death and corruption. He then goes on to declare that the believer's life is in Christ, *"for you are dead, and your life is hidden with Christ in God."* He infers holiness from this also. Shall those who have Christ for their life defile themselves with guilt? If the Holy One of Israel is in them as their life, their life should be filled with everything that is virtuous and good. And then he brings the third argument, that in the Christian church Christ is the only distinguishing mark. In the new birth we are created in the image of Jesus, the second Adam; and in consequence all the distinctions that pertain to the old creation are rendered valueless: *"there is neither Greek nor Jew, circumcision nor uncircumcision, Barbarian, Scythian, bond nor free — for "Christ is all, and in all."*

EVENING
Christ is all, and in all — Colossians 3:11.

WHATEVER TRIALS you may see, Christ is all in all to meet them. Are you poor? Even so He will make you rich in your poverty by His consoling presence. Are you sick? He will make your bed in your sickness, then your sick-bed will be much better than your walks while in health. Are you persecuted? If it is for His sake, then you may even leap for joy. Are you oppressed? Remember how He also was oppressed, afflicted and persecuted, then you will have fellowship with Him in His sufferings. Amid all the vicissitudes of this present life Christ is all that the believer needs to bear him up under them; yea, and bear him through them. No wave can sink the one who clings to Christ as his life-buoy; for by this such a one swims to glory.

So, too, within us Christ is all. If you look to the chambers of your inner nature, you will see all manner of deficiencies and deformities. Then you may well be filled with dismay. But when you see Christ there your heart will be comforted. For He will both destroy the works of the Devil, and perfect that which He has begun in you. You are a sinner, but your heart rests on its Savior. You are burdened with this body of sin and death, but behold your Savior has formed in you the hope of glory: *"Who will deliver me from this body of death? I thank God through Jesus Christ our Lord."* By nature you were an heir of wrath, even as others; but now you are born into the second Adam's household, and because of this you are beloved of the Most High, a joint-heir with Christ. Is Christ in your heart? Then everything that is there that would cause you sorrow may also suggest to you a topic for joy. The saint is grieved to think that he has sin to confess, but he is glad to think that he is able to confess sin. The saint is vexed that he should have so much infirmity, yet he glories in infirmity because the power of Christ rests on him. We are grieved day by day to observe our wanderings, but we also rejoice to see how closely the Good Shepherd follows and leads us, restoring our souls.

May 16   MORNING

Christ is all, and in all — Colossians 3:11.

    CHRIST IS ALL by way of national distinction, subject for glorying, and ground for custom. In the new creation there is no difference between Jew and Gentile; neither barbarian simplicity nor Greek cultivation are anything. As long as we are in the flesh perhaps we will set some store by nationality. Like Paul, we may somewhat glory that we were born free. But surely in spiritual matters the less of this the better. In the Christian church we are cosmopolitan; we are citizens of the New Jerusalem only. Be glad, if you will, of what nationality you are, but not with the same joy which should fill you when you remember that you are a Christian. When you meet another who fears God, you do not want him to think of you as an Englishman, or an American, or a Frenchman, but as a Christian. For we are no longer strangers and foreigners, but fellow-citizens. If anyone is a Christian, though a foreigner to us after the flesh, that one is yet in spirit ten thousand times more allied to you than if he were an unbeliever and of the same nationality, or origin.

    It is to be deplored greatly whenever the convulsions of nations drag Christian men into opposition to one another. One part of the body of Christ should not be at war with another, and in good conscience cannot be. It is a shameful thing to allow our earthly nationality to dominate over our heavenly citizenship. Let the earthly queens and presidents be in their places, but let King Jesus be Lord of all. We are above all things subjects of His imperial highness, the Prince of Peace. No one comes into the church as a Jew, or as a Gentile. Nor does anyone remain there as a Greek or a Scythian, whatever he may have been before. When one becomes a Christian, then Christ is all. Earthly distinctions of rank, if they still exist, as they must while we are in this world, are brought to a minimum within the church. They are then almost obliterated, and what remains should be sanctified to sacred ends.

EVENING

Christ is all, and in all — Colossians 3:11.

    THERE ARE SOME who think that Christ is all in only some things; they have not yet seen the full teaching of the text. They say, "He is all in justification; He pardons all our sins and covers us with His righteousness; but as to our sanctification surely we are to effect that ourselves. As to our final perseverance, that must depend wholly on our own watchfulness. Are we not in jeopardy still? Are there not some points which depend on our own virtue and goodness?" Beloved, God forbid that I should say a word against the most earnest watchfulness, the most diligent endeavors. But I beg you not to place them in the wrong position. Do not speak as though the ultimate salvation of the believer were based on such shifting sand. We are saved in Christ. We are complete in Him. We are sanctified in Him, *"And of God He is made to us wisdom, righteousness, sanctification, and redemption."* Christ is all, not only in justification, but also in sanctification. He is all, not only in the first steps of faith, but in the last: *"He is Alpha and Omega; He is the beginning and the end, says the Lord."*

    There is no point between the gates of Hell and the gates of Heaven where a believer shall have to say, "Christ fails me here, and I must rely on my own endeavors." From the dunghill of our corruption up to the throne of our perfection there is no point left to hazard, or set aside for us to supply. Our salvation has Christ to begin with, Christ to go on with, and Christ to finish with — and that in all points, at all times, for every person that ever was or shall be saved. There is no point in which the creature comes in to claim merit, or to bring strength, or to make up for that which is lacking. The saints are *"perfect in Christ Jesus."* He said, *"It is finished!"* and surely it IS finished.

MORNING

We love Him because He first loved us — 1 John 4:19.

GET THIS THOUGHT into your head: "God loves me, not merely bears with me; He thinks of me, feeds me, but also He loves me." Oh, it is a very sweet thing to feel that we have the love of another, and there is much sweetness in being loved by another. But to think that it is God that loves you, this must be infinitely better! Who is it that is here said to love you? It is God, the Maker of Heaven and earth, the Almighty. The all-sufficient One, does He love me? Yes, even He. If all men and all angels, all living creatures loved me, it were nothing to this: He who is the Infinite One loves me!

And who is it that He loves? ME! The text says, *"us,"* — We love Him because He first loved US." But this is a personal point: He loves me, an insignificant nobody, full of sin, one deserving to go to Hell. Though I love Him so little in return, God loves ME. Beloved believer, does this not melt you? Does this not fire your soul? If you really are a believer, it must. And how much did He love you? He loved you so much that He gave up His only-begotten Son for you, to be nailed to a tree and made to bleed and die. And what will come of it? Why, because He loved you and forgave you, you are on your way to Heaven. Within a few years, months, or even days, you will see His face and will sing His praises. He loved you before you were born; yea, *"from everlasting,"* before a star began to shine. And He has never ceased to love you, not even in the days when you in your sin cursed Him. He will love you when your knees tremble, and when your hair is gray with age. *"Even to the hoar hairs"* He will bear up and uphold His servant. And He will love you when the world is on a blaze. Believer, He will love you forever and ever.

EVENING

As soon as Zion travailed, she brought forth her children — Isaiah 66:8.

A SOUL-WINNER throws himself into what he says. We must ram ourselves into our cannons; we must fire ourselves at our hearers. When we do this, then by God's grace their hearts are often carried by storm. Do any of you desire your children's conversions? Agonize for them. Many a parent who has been privileged to see his child walking in the truth will tell you that before that blessing came many hours had been spent in prayer and in earnest pleading with God. Only then did the Lord visit the child and renew his soul. I have heard of a young man, grown but left under the parental roof. Through evil influences this one had been enticed into holding sceptical views. His father and mother were both earnest Christians, and it almost broke their hearts to see their son so opposed to the Redeemer. Once they induced him to go with them to hear a celebrated minister. He went with them only to please them, and for no higher motive. The sermon was on the glories of Heaven. It was a very extraordinary sermon, calculated to make every Christian in the audience to leap for joy. The young man was much impressed with the eloquence of the preacher, but nothing more. He gave him credit for superior oratorical ability, and was interested in the sermon, but he felt none of its power. He looked at his father and mother during the sermon, and he was surprised to see them weeping. He could not imagine why these good Christian people should sit and weep under a sermon which was so jubilant in its strain. Reaching home he said, "Father, it was a capital sermon, but I could not understand what made you and mother sit there and cry." His father said, "My son, I certainly had no reason to weep concerning myself, nor for your mother, but I could not help thinking all through the sermon about you. For, alas! I had no hope that you would be a partaker of those bright joys which await the righteous. It breaks my heart to think that you will be shut out of Heaven." That so touched the young man's heart that he was led to seek the God of his father, and before long he was rejoicing in the God and Savior worshiped by his parents.

May 18   MORNING

As soon as Zion travailed, she brought forth her children — Isaiah 66:8.

GOD'S WORKS are not tied to time. The more spiritual a force, the less it lies within the chains of time. Electricity has a greater likeness to the spiritual than the grosser forms of materialism, because it is so inconceivably rapid, and thus all but annihilates time. The influences of the Spirit of God are a force most spiritual, and far more quick than anything beneath the sun. No sooner do we agonize in soul than the Holy Spirit can, if He so pleased, convert the person for whom we are pleading. While we are yet speaking, He hears. Yea, before we call, He answers.

There are those who calculate the progress of a church by arithmetic. I have heard of arithmetical sermons in which there have been ingenious calculations as to how many missionaries it would take to convert the world, and how much cash would be demanded. There is no room in this for the application of mathematics. Spiritual forces cannot be calculated by arithmetic. A truth which is calculated to strike the mind of one man today may readily enough produce a like effect on a million minds tomorrow. The preaching which moves one heart needs not be altered to cause it to tell on ten thousand. With God's Spirit our present instrumentalities will be enough to win the souls. Without the Spirit, ten thousand times as much apparent force would be only so much weakness. The spread of truth is not reckonable by time. In such matters God's messengers are flames of fire. The Spirit of God is able to operate on the minds of men instantaneously, as was seen in the case of the conversion of the apostle Paul. Between now and tomorrow morning He could excite holy thoughts in all the minds of all the thousands of millions of the sons of Adam. Oh for the travail that would produce immediate results.

EVENING

The people sitting in darkness have seen a great Light! And Light has sprung up to those sitting in the region and shadow of death — Matthew 4:16.

SOME SOULS are in greater darkness than others. It appears from the text that it was so in Christ's days; it certainly is so now. Divine sovereignty runs through all God's dealings. He does not even distribute the privilege of hearing the gospel to all alike, for some lands are yet untrodden by the missionary's foot. Here on every corner the gospel is preached to us. Some, from the very circumstances of their birth and parentage, have never attended the worship of God. Others, even before they had the discretion to choose, were carried in their parents' arms to the place where prayer is customarily made. God distributes His grace and privileges as He wills.

In this text those persons who were more deplorably circumstanced than others are described first as being in darkness (by which is meant ignorance). The Gallileans were notoriously ignorant. Few teachers of the law had been among them; they did not even know the letter of the law. So there are many now to whom the gospel, even in its theory, is a thing scarcely known. They may have gone to places of worship in this country from their youth up, and yet never have heard the gospel. For the gospel is a rare thing in some churches. In many you hear philosophy, you hear ceremonialism, you hear sacramentarianism cried up. But the blessed truth, *"Believe and live,"* is kept in the background, so that men may come to full age, and even to old age, and yet the plan of salvation by the righteousness of Jesus Christ may be an unknown thing to them. They sit in the darkness of ignorance.

The consequence is this, that another darkness follows, the darkness of error. Men who do not know the truth, since they must have some faith, seek out many inventions. If they are not taught of God, they soon become instructed by Satan.

MORNING

The people sitting in darkness have seen a great Light! And Light has sprung up to those sitting in the region and shadow of death — Matthew 4:16.

IT IS A consolation to sad hearts, that many promises are made to such characters, even to those who are most dark. How precious is that word, *"Come to Me, all you that labor and are heavy laden, and I will give you rest."* Is that not made for you who are burdened and laboring sinners? What do you say to that gracious word, *"When the poor and needy seek water, and there is none, and their tongue fails for thirst, I the Lord will hear them, I the God of Jacob will not forsake them"*? Is there no light in that word of love, *"Let the wicked forsake his way, and the unrighteous man his thoughts; and let him return to the Lord, and He will have mercy on him; and to our God, for He will abundantly pardon"*? Is there no music in this passage, *"Who is a God like You that pardons iniquity, and passes by the transgression of the remnant of His heritage? He does not retain His anger forever, because He delights in mercy. He will turn again; He will have compassion on us; He will subdue our iniquities; yea, You will cast all their sins into the depths of the sea"*?

I recollect when my soul was stayed for weeks on that one short word, *"Whoever CALLS on the Lord shall be saved."* I knew I did call on His name, and therefore I hoped to see His salvation. Many have laid hold and rested themselves on this faithful saying, *"He who comes to Me, I will in no way cast out."* He will receive any person in all the world that comes, be he or she ever so defiled. That also is a rich word, *"He is able to save them to the uttermost who come to God by Him, since He ever lives to make intercession for them."* What a word was that of our Master when He commanded His disciples to commence their labors among His murderers, among hypocritical Pharisees and proud Herodians. Then see that great sinners, so far from being excluded, are just those to whom the good news is to be published.

EVENING

Remember me, O Lord, with the favor which You bear to your people — Psalm 106:4

INSIGNIFICANT as I am, do not forget me, Lord. Think of me with kindness, even as You think of Your own elect. I cannot ask more, nor would I seek less. Treat me as the least of Your saints, and I will be content. It should be enough for us if we fare as the rest of the family. If even Balaam desired no more than to die the death of the righteous, we may be content both to live as they live, and to die as they die. This feeling would prevent our wishing to escape trial, persecution and chastisement. This has been the lot of other saints; why should we escape them? At the same time we pray to have their sweets as well as their bitters. We would have the Lord's smiles, too; we would dwell where they dwell, rejoice as they rejoice, weep when they weep.

"O visit me with Your salvation." Bring it home to me. Come to my house and to my heart, and give me the salvation which You have prepared, which You alone are able to give. We sometimes hear of a man's dying by the visitation of God, but here is the Psalmist who knows that he can only live by the visitation of God. Jesus said to Zaccheus, *"This day salvation has come to this house,"* and that was the case because He Himself had come there. There is no salvation apart from the Lord, and He must visit us with it or we shall never obtain it. All of us are too sick to visit our Great Physician, and for this reason He visits us. O that our great Bishop would hold a visitation of all the churches, and there give His benediction on all His flock. Sometimes the second prayer of this verse seems to be too great for us, for we feel that we are not worthy that the Lord should come under our roof. You say, Visit me, Lord. Can it be? Do I dare to ask for it? And yet I must, for You alone can bring me salvation. Because of this, Lord, I entreat You to come to me and abide with me forever.

May 20 MORNING

Oh that I were as in month's past, as in the days when God watched over me, when His lamp shone on my head, when I walked through darkness by His light — Job 29:2.

BE REMINDED that these regrets are not inevitable. It is not absolutely necessary that a Christian should ever feel them, or should be compelled to express them. It has grown to be a tradition among us, that every Christian must backslide in a measure, and that growth in grace cannot be sustained without a break. It is regarded by many as a sort of law of nature, that our first love must grow cold and our early zeal must necessarity decline. Do not believe it for a moment! *"The path of the just is as the shining light which shines more and more to the perfect day"* — and just is as the shining light which shines more and more to the perfect day" — and if we were watchful and careful to live near to God, there is no reason at all why our spiritual life should not continuously make progress both in strength and beauty.

There is no inherent necessity in the Divine life itself compelling it to decline. For it is written, *"It shall be in him a well of water springing up into everlasting life,"* and, *"out of his belly shall flow rivers of living water."* Grace is a living and incorruptible seed that lives and abides forever. There is nowhere impressed on the Divine life a law of pining and decay. If we do falter and faint in the onward path, it is our sin; and it is doubly sinful to forge excuses for it. It is not to be laid on the back of some mysterious necessity of the new nature that it should be so, but it is to be brought as a charge against ourselves. Nor do outward circumstances ever furnish a justification to us if we decline in grace. When deprived of the joys of Christian fellowship and denied the comforts of the means of grace, believers have nevertheless been known to attain to a high degree of likeness to Jesus Christ.

EVENING

From where do wars and fightings among you come? Is it not from this, from your lusts warring in your members? — James 4:1.

IT IS UNMORTIFIED LUST which is the sting of every trouble, which makes every sweet bitter, and every bitter more bitter. Unmortified sin adds weight to every burden; it puts gall to our wormwood and adds chain to chain; it makes the bed uneasy, the room a prison, relaxations troublesome, and everything vexatious to the soul.

Philosophy may hide a sin, but it cannot quench it (Lactantius). A black patch may cover some deformities in nature, but it does not cure them. Neither will flagellations, vows, resolutions, nor an imaginary purgatory cleanse the fretting leprosy of sin. In the strength of Christ, and in the power of the Spirit, set upon the mortifying of every lust. Oh hug none, indulge none, hide none, but resolvedly set upon the ruin of all through Christ. Remember, one leak will sink a ship, one wound will strike even a Goliath dead, one Delilah will do more mischief than a host of Philistines — one broken wheel spoils all the clock; one bleeding vein will let out all the vitals; one fly will spoil a rich ointment. By eating one apple Adam lost Paradise; one lick of honey endangered Jonathan's life; one Jonah raised a violent storm. So one unmortified lust will be able to raise strange and strong storms and tempests in your soul in the days of affliction. If you would have a blessed calm and quietness of spirit even under sharp trial, then set thoroughly on the work of mortification. Gideon had seventy sons, but one bastard; but that bastard destroyed all his seventy sons. Christian, you know what a world of mischief one unmortified lust can do. Then let nothing satisfy you but the life-blood of all your lusts — Thomas Brooks, *The Mute Christian Under the Rod*, pp. 114, 115.

MORNING

Oh that I were as in month's past, as in the days when God watched over me, when His lamp shone on my head, when I walked through darkness by His light —Job 29:2

VERY OFTEN our regrets about the past are not wise. It is impossible to draw a fair comparison between the various stages of Christian experience so as to give a judicious preference to one about another. Consider the seasons of the year. There are many persons who, in the midst of the beauties of spring, say, "Ah, but how fitful is the weather! These March winds and April showers come and go by such fits and starts that nothing is to be depended on. Give me the safer glories of summer." Yet when they feel the heat of summer, wiping the sweat from their brows they say, "After all, we much more admire the freshness, verdure and vivacity of spring. The snowdrop and the crocus coming forth as the advance guard of the army of flowers have a superior charm about them." It is idle to compare spring and summer. They differ, each having its beauties.

Whoever will claim precedence for any season will have me for an opponent. They are all beautiful in their season; each excels after its kind. Even so it is wrong to compare the early zeal of the young Christian with the mature and mellow experience of the older believer. Each is beautiful according to its time. You, dear young friend, with your intense zeal are to be commended and imitated. But let not your fire arise merely from novelty; be strong and earnest; like a new born river you are swift in current, but not yet deep nor broad. And you, my more advanced friend, you may be much tried and buffeted; it is not easy to hold on your way under great inward struggles and severe depressions. But your deeper sense of weakness, your firmer grasp of truth, your more intense fellowship with the Lord Jesus in His sufferings, are all lovely in the eyes of the Lord your God.

EVENING

Oh that I were as in month's past, as in the days when God watched over me, when His lamp shone on my head, when I walked through darkness by His light —Job 29:2, 3.

ARE THERE NOT many among us who once walked humbly with God, and near to Him, who have fallen into a sense of carnal security? Have these not taken it for granted that all is well, that they may settle on their lees? How little of heart-searching and self-examination are practiced in these days! How little inquiry is made as to whether the root of the matter is really in us! Woe to those who take their safety for granted, who sit down in God's house and say, *"The temple of the Lord, the temple of the Lord are we."* Woe to those that are at ease in Zion! Of all our enemies, the one most to be dreaded is presumption. To be secure in Christ is a blessing; but to be secure in ourselves is a curse. Where carnal security reigns, the Spirit of God withdraws. He is with the humble and contrite (Isa. 57:15). But He is not with the proud and self-sufficient. Are we all clear in this respect? Do not many of God's people also need to bemoan their worldliness? Once Christ was all in all with you. Is it so now? Once you despised the world, condemning its pleasures and its frowns. But now are not the chains of worldly custom on you? Are not many of you enslaved by fashion, eaten up by frivolity? Do not some of you run as greedily as worldlings after the questionable enjoyments of this present life? Ought these things to be so? Can they remain so and yet your souls enjoy the Lord's smile? *"You cannot serve God and mammon." "If anyone loves the world, the love of the Father is not in him"* (1 John 2:15). You cannot be Christ's disciples and be in fellowship with the ungodly. *"Come out from among them; be separate; touch not the unclean thing;"* then you shall know right joyfully that the Lord is a Father to you, and that you are His sons and daughters. Have you gone out to Jesus, outside the camp, and do you abide there with Him? (Heb. 13:13).

But one thing is needful — Luke 10:42

WE HAVE no difficulty whatever in deciding what that one thing needful is. We are not allowed to say that it is the Savior, for He is not a thing. We are not permitted to say that it is attention to our own salvation, for, although that would be true, it is not mentioned in the context. The one thing needful evidently is that which Mary chose, that good part which would not be taken away from her. Very clearly this was to sit at the feet of Jesus to hear His word. If anything is plain at all in Holy Scripture, it is most clear that this is the one thing needful, to sit at the feet of Jesus and hear His word. This and nothing less, this and nothing more.

The mere posture of sitting down and listening to the Savior's word was nothing in itself; it was that which it indicated — in Mary's case it indicated a readiness to believe what the Savior taught, to accept and to obey; yea, to delight in the precepts which fell from His lips. And this is the one thing needful. He who has it has a spirit of grace and life. To sit at the feet of Jesus implies submission. Such a one is no longer resisting His power, for he has cast down the weapons of his rebellion and has come humbly to acknowledge the Redeemer as Lord and King in his soul. This is needful, absolutely needful. For no rebel can enter the kingdom of Heaven with the weapons of rebellion in his hands. We cannot know Christ while we resist Christ. We must be reconciled to His gentle sway, confessing that He is Lord, to the glory of God the Father.

To sit at the feet of Jesus implies faith as well as submission. Mary believed in what Jesus said, and for this reason she sat there to be taught by Him. It is absolutely necessary that we have faith in the Lord Jesus Christ, in His power as God and man, in His death as being expiatory, in His crucifixion as being a sacrifice for our sins.

EVENING

But one thing is needful — Luke 10:42.

IT MAY BE you are a very hard-worker. You have very little rest during the week. In order to bring up your family comfortably you strain every nerve. You live economically and work diligently. From morning to night your thought is: "How shall I fill these many mouths? How shall I bring them up properly? And this is very right. I wish all would be equally thoughtful and economical, that there were fewer foolish spendthrifts wasting their substance. The spendthrifts become paupers, loafing on the charity of others the moment there is a frost in their earnings. Industry is to be commended, but at the same time, is that all there is? Were you made only to be a machine, working at this and that most of your waking hours? Do you think your God made you for that and that only? Is this the chief end of man, merely to earn so much a week in order to make ends meet? Is that all immortal men were made to be and do?

As a person with a soul, capable of thought and judgment, and not a mere animal like a dog, nor a machine like an engine, can you stand up and look at yourself and say, "I believe I am perfectly fulfilling my destiny"? Pause amidst your labor and apply your wisdom. There is a higher bread to be earned, and there is a higher life to be considered. The Lord says, *"Do not labor for the food that perishes,"* that is to say, not for that first and foremost, *"but for that which endures to eternal life."* But one thing is needful, to *"grow in grace and in the knowledge of the Lord Jesus Christ"* by sitting at His feet to learn true wisdom. God has made man that he may glorify Him.

MORNING

But one thing is needful — Luke 10:42.

EVEN TO THOSE of you who can honestly declare that Christ is your sole confidence, it is possible for you to forget the necessity of sitting at His feet. You are looking to His precious blood alone for your salvation, and His name is sweet to you, and you desire in all things to be conformed to His will. So far it is well with you, for in this you have a measure of sitting at His feet. But so had Martha: she loved her Lord, and she knew His word, and she was a saved soul, for *"Jesus loved Mary and Martha."* But you have not perhaps so much of this needful thing as Mary had, and as you ought to have. You have been very busy this week and have drifted from your moorings. Perhaps you have not lived with your Lord in conscious fellowship, being full of care and empty of prayer. You may not have committed your sorrows to your loving Friend; you blundered on in duty without asking His guidance or assistance; you have not maintained the communion of your spirit with the Well-beloved. If such has been the case with you, stop whatever you have been laudably engaged in, even teaching and preaching, and say to yourself: " To me, as a worker, the one thing needful is to keep near my Lord; I must not allow the watering of others to occupy me so as to neglect my own heart. Else I may have to say 'woe is me,' they made me keeper in the vineyards, but my own vineyard I have not kept.' To the saints, as well as to others, the one thing needful is to sit at the feet of Jesus. We are to be always learners and lovers of Jesus. Departure from Him, and independence from Him should never be once named among you, not even for a moment.

EVENING

Look to Me, and be saved, all the ends of the earth; for I am God, there is no other — Isaiah 45:22.

OF ALL BEINGS those whom God has made the objects of His grace are perhaps the most apt to forget this cardinal truth, that He is God, that beside Him there is no other. How did the church in Canaan forget it, when they bowed to other gods! So He brought against them mighty kings and rulers and afflicted them greatly. How did Israel forget it! So He carried them away into captivity. And what Israel did in Canaan, and afterward in Babylon, that we do now. We also too often forget that He is God, and there is no other. Does not the Christian know this great fact? Have you not done this yourself at times? In certain times prosperity has come, soft gales have blown his ship along to anywhere a wild wish steered, and the thought comes, "Now I have peace, now I have happiness; now the object I wished for is in my grasp. Now I can say, Sit down, soul, and *take your rest, Eat, drink and be merry.*" It may be these things seem to content you, and you make them your God for blessings and happiness. But surely you have seen our God dash such goblets to the earth, spilling the sweet wine and filling it up with gall. And as He has given it to us He has said: "Drink it; you have thought to find a God on earth, but drain the cup and you will know its bitterness." And when we have drunk it, it was nauseating to us, and we have cried out, "Ah, God, I will drink no more from such things. You are God, and there is no other God for me." How often we have devised our schemes for the future without asking God's permission. You may have said, as James mentions, *"Today or tomorrow we will go into this city, and we will trade and make a profit"* (James 4:13). But did you know that there certainly would be a tomorrow. For many, long before tomorrow came, they were unable to buy and sell, for death had claimed them. God teaches His people every day, by sickness, by affliction, by depression of spirits, by the forsakings of God, by the loss of the Spirit for a season, by the lacking of the joys of His countenance, that He alone is God, and there is no other God besides Him.

May 24 — MORNING

The Lord reigns; He is clothed in majesty — Psalm 93:1.

JEHOVAH reigns. Whatever opposition may arise, His throne is unmoved. He has reigned, He does reign, and He will reign forever and ever. Whatever turmoil and rebellion there may be beneath the clouds, the eternal King sits above all in supreme serenity. Everywhere He is the true Master; let his foes rage as they may. All things are ordered according to His eternal purposes, and His will is done. He sits on His throne clothed in majesty. What can give greater joy to a loyal subject than a sight of the king in his beauty? Let us whisper this in the ears of the desponding, publish it in the face of the foe: *"The Lord reigns; He is clothed with majesty."* His is not the semblance, but the reality of sovereignty. In nature, in providence, and in salvation the Lord is infinite in majesty. Happy are the people among whom the Lord appears in all the glory of His grace, conquering their enemies, subduing all things to Himself. At such times He is seen to be reigning, to be clothed with majesty.

"The Lord is clothed with strength" — His garments of glory are not His only array; He wears strength also as His girdle. He is always strong, but sometimes He displays His power in a special manner. He is always essentially majestic, but there are seasons when He reveals His glory, wearing His majesty and showing Himself in it. May the Lord appear in our day manifesting majesty and might in saving sinners, in slaying errors, and in bringing honor and glory to His name.

EVENING

The Lord reigns — Psalm 93:1.

JEHOVAH REIGNS, these words are to us as *"a light that shines in a dark place until the day dawn and the Daystar arise in our hearts."* So long as such words are left to us, all that threatens us from without is only like the noise of a breaking wave. The unspeakable comfort conveyed in this assurance is ever tested in the experience of God's people. There is no truth more precious to the heart of the Christian than that *"The Lord reigns."* The conviction of this must carry us far above all cares and fears. A personal God, a living God, a God who reigns over the armies of Heaven and among the inhabitants of the earth, this God in three Persons reigns over all. Faith in this great truth causes us to ascend the heights, where removed from the turmoil of men we gain a comprehensive and clear view of the earth and its concerns. Could any be so foolish as to exchange the assurance which those two words *"Jehovah reigns"* convey for all the combined wisdom and power of this world? Received into the heart they are the solution of every difficulty, the end of all perplexity. In every real trial there is but this one final and full comfort, *Jehovah reigns.* What does it matter what men think, whether they be for you or against you, whether with you or forsaking you, if God reigns? Who would speak of prospects, of wealth, of power, or even the defections of friends on whose sympathy and help we counted? *JEHOVAH REIGNS!* There is light in those words across every path, if I follow Christ, walking in the narrow way. If I am on the Lord's side, in the Lord's way, nothing else matters. My God holds the hearts of all men at his disposal. He directs all events, from the least to the greatest. Whatever I want from men, I will pray my God, He who reigns over them.

MORNING

So then we should not sleep as the rest also, but we should watch and be calm — 1 Thessalonians 5:6.

SLEEP IS a state of inaction. No daily bread is earned by a sleeper. The man stretched on his couch will neither write books, nor till ground, nor do anything else. His hands hang down, his pulse beats; there is life, but he is dead as to activity. Oh, beloved, is this not the state of too many of you. How many Christians are inactive! Once it was their delight to instruct the young, but now that is given up. Once they attended every prayer meeting, but not now. Once they were hewers of wood and drawers of water for the faithful, but alas! they are asleep now. Is this not all too true universally? Are not the churches asleep? Where are ministers that truly preach? We have men that read their manuscripts, who talk essays, but is that preaching? We have those that can amuse an audience for twenty minutes. Is that preaching? Where are the men that preach their hearts out, who express their souls in every sentence? Where are those who make it a calling, not a profession, the breath of their bodies, the marrow of their bones, the delight of their spirits? Where are the Whitefields and Wesleys now? Are they not gone? Rowland Hill preached every day, sometimes three times a day. He was not afraid of preaching everywhere, at all times, the unsearchable riches of Christ.

Brothers, sisters, the church slumbers. It is not merely that the pulpit is a sentry-box with the sentinel fast asleep. The pews are asleep, too. How often are the prayer meetings universally neglected? Look and you will see a small band of people assembled around the pastor. Looking at them, is it any wonder his heart is heavy? Where is the spirit of prayer, where is the life of devotion? Is it not almost extinct? Are not our churches *"fallen, fallen, fallen"* from their high estate? May God awaken us!

EVENING

My soul refused to be comforted — Psalm 77:2.

THE TEXT might very fittingly describe individuals who, although free from outward trial or bereavement, are subject to deep depression of spirits. There are times with the brightest-eyed Christians when they can hardly brush away the tears. Strong faith and joyous hope at times subside into a fearfulness which is scarcely able to keep the spark of hope and faith alive in the soul. It seems that the more rejoicing a man does at one time, the more sorrowful he will be at others. They who mount highest often descend lowest. There are cold-blooded persons who neither rejoice with joy unspeakable nor groan with anguish unutterable. But others are of a more excitable temperament, capable of lofty delights and also liable to horrible sinkings of heart. Just because these have gazed in ecstacy within the gates of pearl, they are too apt to make a descent to the land of deathshade, and to seem to stand shivering on the brink of Hell.

In these times of gloom, when the soul is well nigh overwhelmed, it is our duty to grasp the promise, to rejoice in the Lord. But it is not easy to do. The duty is indisputable, but the fulfilment of it is difficult. The star of promise and the candle of experience seem to be in vain for us at such times. The darkness which may be felt seems to smother all cheering lights. Barnabas the son of consolation would be hard put to cheer the victims of depression when their fits are on them. The oil of joy is poured out in vain for those heads on which the dust and ashes of melancholy are heaped. At such times, unhappy ones, you must wisely consider taking a rest from your labor. "O despairing souls, you see that others whose conditions have been as bad have obtained mercy. God has turned their hell into a Heaven; He pacified their raging consciences, quieted their distracted souls, wiped all tears from their eyes. He has been a well-spring of life to their hearts. Be not discouraged, O despairing souls, but look up at the mercy-seat" — Thomas Brooks.

MORNING

Let him that glories glory in this, that he understands and knows Me" —
Jeremiah 9:24.

TO UNDERSTAND God does not barely note our having received some natural or metaphysical notions of God, and the truths that are in Him. (1.) It notes an approving of Him; therefore an approving or liking of the things that are excellent: *"That your love may abound more and more in knowledge, and in all judgment, that you may approve the things that are excellent"* (Phil. 1:9, 10). (2.) The knowing of God as a reconciled God; a God, and a God to me; One good, and good to me; One wise, and wise for me; my Lord and my God. To know God in Christ, reconciled through Christ, propitious through Christ, this is saving knowledge. To know and not possess, to see and not eat, to know an angry God, a wrathful God, a God lost — what is that to you? To know goodness, mercy, loving-kindness, compassion, all-sufficiency, and to have the heart say, What is this to you, since none of it is yours; condemned ones know these things and yet die. (3.) To understand Him and know Him is to love Him. As *"those that know Your name will trust in You"* (Ps. 9:10), so those that know Him will love Him, and fear Him, and rejoice in Him, and bless His name. The devils know and yet hate God, know and condemn God, know and flee from God, know and yet blaspheme and curse God, and they tremble because of it.

But especially this knowledge of God is a transforming and fructifying power. Beholding the glory of the Lord, we are changed into the same image (2 Cor. 3:18). Therefore, *"Be not conformed to this present world, but be transformed by the renewing of your minds"* (Rom. 12:2.)

EVENING

Be not conformed to this present world, but be transformed by the renewing of your minds — Romans 12:2.

BY THE RENEWING of your minds, the renovation of the mind, works upon the whole soul giving new light to the new creature. Old things pass away, all things become new, when the mind is savingly enlightened. God known in the soul is God united in the soul. Christ revealed in the heart is Christ formed on the heart. This is no other than the light of life. The knowledge of God spirits and animates every grace and duty. As the same soul sees in the eye, hears in the ear, tastes in the palate, so the same grace which is light in the mind is also in the heart love, holy desire, holy fear, holy joy. All the organs of sense are inseparable. The eye feels and sees, the ear feels and hears, the palate feels and tastes. So knowledge is involved in every grace. Faith knows and believes, charity knows and loves, temperance knows and abstains, patience knows and suffers, humility knows and stoops, repentance knows and mourns, obedience knows and does, compassion knows and pities, hope knows and expects, confidence knows and rejoices. Because of this we believe, and love, and obey, and hope, and rejoice — it is because we know and understand God.

(The above is condensed from *Heaven Opened*, Richard Alleine)

MORNING

Out of darkness Light shall shine, Who shone in our hearts to give the brightness of the knowledge of the glory of God in the face of Jesus Christ — 2 Corinthians 4:6.

DAYLIGHT is not that light we receive by reflection from the moon and stars, at second-hand; when the sun has risen and comes in among us, then it is day. When the Sun of Righteousness has risen in the heart, there is the light of life. God is light, and God dwells in this light. And where God dwells, every unclean thing vanishes. Can darkness dwell with the sun? Can death dwell with life? No! So much of a measure of the manifestation of God in us, so far is sin necessarily vanished. If Christ is not formed in your heart, if the love, the humility, the meekness, the patience, the compassion, the holiness of the Lord Jesus is not begotten in you, whatever you know, you know nothing as you ought to know. If you have all knowledge and do not have love (also if you have all knowledge and do not have humility, meekness, holiness, you are nothing,) you are but as sounding brass, or a tinkling cymbal (1 Cor. 13). Doubting Christian, do you complain of and bewail your ignorance, and do you fear that you do not know God? Look upwards where His glory dwells. Lift up your eyes and see. Or if you cannot see, lift up your heart for eyes and seek Him: Lord, where do You dwell? Let me see Your face; show me Your glory; pity me and let my blind eyes be opened; let my dumb tongue be loosed to speak forth Your praise. Yea, look upward and if you do not yet see your God, then look inward. Can you see His face in your soul? Can you see His image on your heart? Can you behold in this mirror the glory of the Lord, and find then yourself changed into His image? Comfort your heart. However short-sighted you seem to be, however dim your candle burns, however weak you are in the knowledge of God, realize this, that you have seen God, and you have seen His face in peace. That God who commanded the light to shine out of darkness has shined into your heart, and He has given you the knowledge of His glory in the face of Jesus Christ.

(Condensed from *Heaven opened*, Richard Alleine)

EVENING

Because this is the covenant which I will covenant with the house of Israel after those days, says the Lord, giving My laws into their mind, and I will write them on their hearts, and I will be their God, and they will be My people — Hebrews 8:10.

I GIVE MY SON to you in a marriage covenant forever. I make Him over to you as wisdom, for your illumination; righteousness, for your justification; sanctification, for the curing of your corruptions, redemption, for your deliverance from your enemies. I bestow Him on you with all His fullness, all His merits, all His graces. He is yours in all His offices. He is anointed as your Prophet. Are you ignorant, He will teach you. He will be eyesalve to you. I have sent Him to preach the gospel to the poor, *"to set at liberty those that are bruised."* I have established Him by My oath as your Priest forever. If you have any sin, He will be your Advocate; He will expiate your guilt and make the atonement. Have you any sacrifice, any service to offer? Then bring it to Him, and you will receive an answer of peace.

Present your petitions by His hand; I will accept Him. Having such a High Priest over the house of God, you may come with boldness. I have set Him as your King. He shall rule you; He shall defend you. He is the King of righteousness, and the King of peace for you. I will set up His standard for you. I will set up His throne in you. HE shall reign in righteousness and rule in judgment. And He will be a hiding-place, be a covert from the tempest for you, a great Rock in a weary land. He will hear your causes, judge your enemies, and He will reign until He has put all of them under His feet; yea, and under your feet, too. All your enemies will be as ashes under you, and you shall tread on them. Yea, I will undo the ones who afflict you, all who despise you; they shall bow down at your feet. And you shall go out and see the carcases of all who have trespassed against me, for their worm shall not die, nor shall their fire be quenched.

(Condensed from a chapter in *Heaven Opened*, by Joseph Alleine)

May 28   MORNING

But sanctify the Lord God in your hearts, and always be ready to give an answer to everyone asking you a reason concerning the hope in you, with meekness and fear, having a good conscience — 1 Peter 3:15, 16.

OH HOW HIGHLY we are to be concerned that our conscience be tender, and yet how little care is taken of it! What has become of the authority of conscience, when your thoughts and your passions, when your eyes and your ears and your appetite and your tongue are left unbridled and unconquered? When every servant is set up to be master, to bear rule in you, where is your conscience? When your soul is no better kept, what poverty and leanness is growing on it, whate a starveling it is both in grace and peace, eaten out with lust, evaporated into vanity, sunk into sensuality, your spirit even transubstantiated into perishing flesh, ready to die away, because you have not had a tender conscience. If you have not better kept your covenant with God, when you have not performed the duties you have vowed, when your hours of prayer are so short, your sabbaths such wintry, cold days, where has your conscience been? When your God is so shamefully neglected, never hears from you even when you havea nothing else to do; yea, when your corn, your cattle, your pleasures, your friends (even those you vowed to renounce), are invited into your heart to steal it away from Heaven, then where is your conscience? When you lie asleep and allow God's enemies to sow tares in your field; when you are being a busy-body in other men's affairs, while your own vineyard is not being kept; when both your heart and your house are so much out of order, where is your conscience? When you leave your wife and your children and your servants to do all that is right in their own eyes; when you take care more for your possessions than for your sons and daughters, ready to die for lack of instruction, where is your conscience? And if you have no conscience, then where is your covenant? And if you have no covenant, then where is your God and your peace?

EVENING

Therefore, brothers, I call on you through the compassions of God to present your bodies a living sacrifice, holy, pleasing to God, which is your reasonable service — Romans 12:1.

ADD TO YOUR COVENANT your sacrifice. God has made a covenant with His saints, and He expects His saints to make a covenant with Him by sacrifice. Sacrifices are seals of the covenant. God's part was sealed with blood, the blood of His beloved Son; ours must be sealed with the blood of our sins. We sacrifice ourselves by alienation, by dedication, and by offerings.

1. Alienation: we must give up ourselves from ourselves: *"You are not your own; you are bought with a price"* (1 Cor. 6:20). You must say, then, "True, Lord, I am not my own."

2. Dedication: the passing over of ourselves to the Lord: *"Now you have consecrated your hand to Jehovah, come near and bring sacrifices"* (2 Chr. 29:31). We are His by purchase, but He expects that we will also be His by donation. We are His by conquest, but He expects us to be His by consent also. Though He may challenge us as His right, yet the most acceptable claim is when He has us by gift. When our hearts say, "I am Yours, Lord,' His heart will answer, Soul, you are Mine.

3. By Offerings: the offering up of ourselves to Him, fully surrendering ourselves. To offer ourselves, we must in a spiritual sense slay ourselves, be mortified, be crucified with Christ, and so be offered up as a sacrifice to Him. Why are we required to offer up ourselves as a living sacrifice? It is because we are not ever truly alive until we are dead: *"You are dead, and your life is hid with Christ in God"* (Col. 3:3). When our flesh is dead, our spirit is life (Romans 8:10). *"What you sow is not made alive until it dies"* (1 Cor. 15:36). It is only the mortified Christian that is a living sacrifice.

(The above devotions are from *Heaven Opened*, by Richard Alleine)

MORNING

My soul refused to be comforted — Psalm 77:2

MANY cast their doubts into the shape of foolish inferences drawn from the doctrine of predestination. I do not find that the doctrine of predestination impresses people in the way of sadness except in the way of religion. Everybody believes that there is a predestination about the casting of lots, and yet the spirit of gambling is rife everywhere. Men in crowds subscribe to the public lotteries, which to our shame are still tolerated. They know that only two or three can win a large prize, yet away goes the money, and nobody stands at the door and says, "I shall not invest my money because if I ams to get a prize I shall get a prize, and if I am not to win a prize I shall not do so." Men are not such fools when they come to things of common life as they are when they deal with religion. This predestination sticks in the way of many as a huge stumbling-block when they come to the things of God. The fact is, there is nothing in predestination to stumble a man. The evil lies in what he chooses to make of it. When a man wants to find excuses for not believing in Christ, he can always discover one somewhere or other. For this cause so many run to this predestination doctrine, because it happens to be a handle place of resort. God has a people whom He will save, a chosen and special people, redeemed by the blood of Christ. But tshere is no more in that doctrine to deny the other grand truth that whoever believes in Jesus Christ is not condemned, than there is in the fact that Ethiopia is in Africa, to contradict the doctrine that ed, than there is in the fact that Ethiopia is in Africa, to contradict the dictrine that Hindustan is in Asia. They are two truths which stand together; even though it may not always be easy for us to reconcile them, it would be even harder to make them disagree.

EVENING

Zealous of good works — Titus 2:14.

GOOD WORKS are the witnesses or testimony to other people of the truth of what we believe. Every Christian was sent into the world to be a preacher. And like the other creatures God has made, we should always be preaching about our Lord. Does not the whole world preache God? When they shine, do not the stars look down from the heavens and say there is a God? Assuredly they do. And a new-born creature — the new man created in Christ — must preach Jesus Christ everywhere he goes. This is the use of good works. He will preach, not always with his mouth, but with his life. The use of good works is that they are a Christian sermon. A sermon is not always what a man says, but what he does. You who practice Christianity are preaching. It is not preaching and practicing, but practicing is preaching.

The sermon that is preached by the mouth is soon forgotten, but what we preach by our lives is never forgotten. There is nothing like faithful practice and holy living, if we would preach to the world. The reason why Christianity does not advance with a mightier stride is simply this, that professors are largely a disgrace to religion. Many of those joined to the churches have no more godliness than those out of it. If I preached such a contradictory sermon on a Sunday as some of you have preached the most part of your lives, you would go out and say, " We will not go back until he can be a little more consistent with himself." There is a difference in the very tone of voice of some peole when they are in the chapel engaged in prayer, and when they are in the workshop. You would hardly think them the same persons. Professors, take heed that your inconsistences not blot out your evidence, and some of you should be found manifesting not only inconsistency but a most fearful consistency. For living in sin and iniquity, you are being consistent with yourselves in hypocrisy, a consistent hypocrite.

MORNING

My soul refused to be comforted — Psalm 77:2.

IT IS UNRREASONABLE to be sad when you might rejoice. It is unreasonable to be wretched when mercy provides every cause for making you hapy. Why are you sad, and why is your countenance fallen? If there were no Savior, no Holy Spirit, no Father willing to forgive, you might then go your way and put and end to your existence in despair. But while all this grace is ready for you, why not take it? One would think that you were like Tantalus, placed up to his neck in water, which, when he tried to drink of it, receded from his lips. But you are in no such condition. Instead of water flowing away from you, grace is rippling up to your lips; it is inviting you but to open your mouth and receive it.

While it is unreasonable to continue such a persistence, it is also most weakening to you. Every hour that you continue sad you spoil the possibilities of your getting out of that sadness. You are dissolving the strength even of your bodily frame. And, as for your soul, the pillars of it are being shaken.

And, mark you, it is most dangerous, too. For it may be that God, who gives you light, when He sees you shut your eyes again, will say, "Let the sun be darkened and the moon be turned into blood. The creature I made for light rejects it, and no light shall ever come to it from now on, even forever." The King who kills the fatlings and makes ready the feast, then brings you to the table, if he sees you still refuse to partake, he may swear in His wrath that you shall not eat of His supper. I have known parents, when their children cried for nothing, take care to give them something to cry about. And it may be if you are miserable when there is no cause for it, you may have cause for it — cause that will never end.

EVENING

Zealous of good works — Titus 2:14.

THERE ARE Christian men and Christian women who forget what God has written in His word — and it is as true now as it ever was — that Christians should array themselves with modesty. It would be a good thing, perhaps, if we went back to Wesley's rule, to come out from the world in the matter of our apparel, to dress as plainly and neatly as the Quakers. But, alas! They have sadly gone from their primitive simplicity. At times I must depart a little from what we call the high things of the gospel, for really the children of God cannot now be told by outward appearance from the children of the Devil — and they really out to be easily distinguished. There should be some distinction between the one and the other. Although religion allows distinction of rank and dress, yet everything in the Bible cries out against our arraying ourselves in finery, making ourselves proud by the goodliness of our apparel.

Some will say, "I wish you would leave that subject alone." Of course you do, because it aplies to yourself. But we let nothing alone which we believe to be in the Scriptures. While I would not spare any man's soul, honesty to every man's conscience and honesty to myself demands that I should always speak of that which I see to be an evil breaking out in the churches. We should always yake care that in everything we do to keep as near as possible to the written word. If you want ornaments, here they are in the Scriptures. Here are jewels, rings, dresses, and all kinds of ornament. Men and women, you may dress yourselves until you shine like angels. How can you do it? By dressing yourselves out in benevolence, in love to the saints, in honesty and integrity, in uprightness, in godliness, in brotherly-kindness, in charity. These are the ornaments which angels themselves admire, and which even the world will admire. For people must give admiration to the man or woman who is arrayed in the jewels of a holy life and godly conversation. I beseech you to *"adorn the doctrine of God our Savior in all things."*

I came to hurl fire into the earth, and what if I desire it already to be kindled?
— Luke 12:49.

THERE IS no test like fire. That piece of jewelry may seem to be gold, the color an exact imitation; you could scarcely tell that it was not the genuine metal. Yes, but the melting pot will prove all. Put it into the crucible, and you will soon see. So it is in ths world; there are a thousand things that glitter, things that draw admirers, things advocated in the name of philanthropy or philosophy. But it is wonderful how different the schemes of politicians and the devises of wise men appear when they are once put into the refining pot of the gospel of Jesus Christ. Despotic rulers and kings are very shrewd in trying to keep the gospel out of their dominions. For if they have anything crooked in the statute book, the gospel is sure to reveal it. If there is anything rotten in the foundations of government, there is nothing like a preached gospel to discover and unveil it.

What is the reason today that we enjoy such precious liberties? These liberties are such as are not excelled by any people under the heavens. And what has been our groundwork for freedom, but this, that the gospel is preached among us? Evermore, like fire, it is testing and trying everything in our institutions, and that which is not right is sure in the end to give way. Much which now stands, but is not according to the Master's will is marked to be consumed. Thank God it is so. For we shall all be better for the overthrow of injustice and wrong. The gospel proves all things; it is the great ultimate test of right and wrong. O how the gospel tests a man's heart! A man thinks he has something good in him, wrapping himself in the robes of his own righteousness. But when the gospel comes, he then finds that he is naked, and poor, and miserable.

EVENING

I came to hurl fire into the earth, and what if I desire it already to be kindled?
— Luke 12:49.

DO YOU believe that if Jesus Christ came into this world He would call nine-tenths of our modern religion the Christian which He preached? Is it even a little like His own zeal? Many who think it to be all the faith that Christianity requires is to put on your best things on Sunday, go to your place of worship with your Bible or hymn or prayer book, and there to sit decorously and look at other people's bonnets and dresses, and then come home again. Others think it s sufficient to listen to the sermon discreetly, perhaps making a few observations on the discourse, perhaps making none, because there is not enough in the sermon to be a peg to hang a remark on. The religion of many professors is nothing more than that; it is hardly that.

Do you not know of people who believe in the articles of the faith? They do not doubt them because they never think of them! They have packed them away in an iron safe, with their title deeds, which they fell so sure about that they do not care to read them. They are orthodox, but they feel no power in their own souls produced by these truths, and no depression because the truth convinces them of sin. They have no exhilaration because the truth is showing them their safety in Christ. Many, getting a supposed saving faith, get no farther. They think they are saved, and seems to be all they care about. Their neighbors may be condemned, but what do they care? They may be scarcely a person on their street attending a place of worship, but what business is that of theirs? They belong to the denomination of Canin, saying, *"Am I my brothers' keeper?"* Such persons are denying the faith. The selfishness which reigns supreme in them is as antichristian as covetousness, adultery, or murder. For the spirit of Christian is unselfishness and love to others, care of other's souls, a devotedness to the increase of the Master's kingdom.

MORNING

Ane he brought him to Jesus — John 1:42.

ANDREW is the picture of what all disciples of Christ should be. This first successful Christian missionary was himself a sincere follower of Jesus. Is it needful to make that observation? Will it ever be needless while so many make a profession of a faith which they do not possess? While so many will wantonly thrust themselves into the offices of Christ's church, having no concern for the glory of His kingdom, and no part or lot in it, it will be always needful to repeat that warning: *"To the wicked God says, What have you to do to declare My statutes?"* Men who have never seen the beauties of Emmanuel are not fit persons to describe them to others. An experimental acquaintance with vital godliness is the first necessity for a useful worker for Jesus. That preacher is accursed who does not know Christ for himself. In infinite sovereignty God may make him the means of blessing to others, but every moment he remains in the pulpit he is an impostor. Every time he preaches he is a mocker of God. Woe to him when his Master calls him to his dread account! You unconverted young people who enter on the work of Sabbath school instruction, undertaking to teach others what you do not know yourselves, you place yourselves in a position of unusual solemnity and of extraordinary peril. Extraordinary peril, I say, because you do by the fact of being a teacher profess to know. You will be judged by your profession, and I fear will be condemned out of your own mouths. You know only the theory of religion. Of what use is that while you are strangers to its power? How can you lead others along a way which you yourself refuse to tread? Besides, I have noticed that persons who become active in church work before they have first believed in Christ are very apt to remain without faith, resting content with the general repute which they have gained.

EVENING

And he brought him to Jesus — John 1:42.

ANDREW was a disciple, a new disciple; yea, I might add, he was a commonplace disciple, a man of average capacity. He wa not at all the brilliant character that his brother Simon Peter turned out to be. Throughout the life of Jesus Christ Andrew's name occurs. But no notable incident is connected with it. Although in after life he no doubt became a most useful apostle, and according to tradition sealed his life's ministry by deaton on a cross, yet as to talent at the first Andrew was an ordinary believer. He was one of that common standard, nothing remarkable. Yet Andrew became a useful minister, and so it is clear that servants of Jesus Christ are not to excuse themselves from endeavoring to extend the boundaries of His kingdom by saying, "I have no remarkable talent, no singular ability." I very much disagree with those who decry ministers of slender gifts, sneering at them, as though they ought not to occupy the pulpit at all. After all, are we as servants of God to be measured by mere oratorical ability? Is this after the fashion of Paul? For he renounced the wisdom of words that the faith of the disciples should not stand in the wisdom of men, and not in the power of God? If you could blot out from the Christian church all the minor stars, leaving nothing but those of the first magnitude, the darkness of this poor world would be increased manyfold. How often the eminent preachers, those delightig the churches, are bought into the church by those of lesser degree, even as Simon Peter was brought to Jesus by Andrew! Who shall say that the church would ever has possessed a Peter if she had closed the mouth of Andrew? And who shall put their finger on the brother or sister of inferior talent, and say, "These must hold their peace"?

MORNING

And he brought him to Jesus — John 1:42.

MANY may be brought to Christ through your example. Believe me, there is no preaching in this world like the preaching of a holy life. At times it shames me and weakens me in my testimony for my Master when I stand here and recollect that some professors of religion are a disgrace not only to their religion, but even to common morality. It makes me feel I must speak with bated breath and trembling knees, remembering the damnable hypocrisy of those thrusting themselves into a church of God while their abominable sins are bringing disgreace on the cause of God and eternal destruction on themselves. In proportion as a church is holy, in that proportion will its testimony for Christ be powerful. Oh, that the saints were immaculate, that our testimony would be like fire among the stubble, like the flaming firebrand in the midst of the sheaves of corn! Were the saints of God less like the world, more disinterested, more prayerful, more godlike, then the tramp of the armies of Zion would shake the nations, and the day of victory of Christ would surely dawn. Freely might the church barter her most golden-mouthed preacher if she but received in exchange men of apostolic lives and spirits. I would be content that the pulpit be empty if all the members of the church would preach Jesus by their patience in suffering, by their endurance in temptation, by exhibiting in the household those graces which adorn the gospel of Jesus Christ. Oh, so live in God's fear and by the Spirit's power that they seeing you may ask, "From where has this one this holiness?" Then they may follow you and be led by you to Jesus Christ to learn the secret by which men live to God. You can bring sinners to Christ by your example. Our object should be to bring men to Jesus through intercession, instruction, example, and by occasionally giving a word of importunate entreaty.

EVENING

Be glad in the Lord, and rejoice, you righteous ones; and shout for joy, all you that are upright in heart — Psalm 32:11.

HAPPINESS is not only our privilege, but our duty. Truly we serve a generous God, since He makes it a part of our obedience to be joyful. How sinful are our rebellious murmurings! How nature does it seem that a man blessed with forgiveness should be glad! We read of one who died at the foot of the scaffold, being overjoyed at the receipt of his monarch's pardon. And shall we receive the free pardon of the King of kigns and the Lord of lords, and yet pine away in inexcusable sorrow?

"*In the lord,*" is the directory by which gladness is preserved from levity. We are not to be glad in sin, or to find comfort in wine and oil, but in ou God is to be the garden of our soul's delight. That there is a God, and such a God, and that He is ours, ours forever, our Father and our reconciled Lord, is matter enough for a never-ending Psalm of rapturous joy. God has clothed His choristers in white garments of holiness; then do not restrain your joyful voice, but sing aloud and shout as those who find great spoil.

Our happiness hould be demonstrative. A lack of love often represses the noble flame of joy. Too many Christians whisper their praises when a hearty outburst of song would be far more natural. It is to be feared that the church of the present day, through a crafing for excessive propriety, is growing too artificial, and by this the cries of inquirers and believers would be silenced if they were heard in our assemblies. This may be better than boistrous fanaticism, but there is as much danger in the one direction as the other. For our part we are touched to the heart by a little sacred excess, when godly ones overleap in their joy the narrow bounds of decorum we do not eye them with a sneering heart. Note how the pardoned are represented here as upright, righteous, without guile. You may have many faults and yet be saved, but a false heart is everywhere the damning mark.

On account of this let every godly one pray to You, at a time of finding; surely when great floods come, they will not reach him — Psalm 32:6.

IF THE PSALMIST means that on account of God's mercy others would become hopeful, his witness is true. Remarkable answers to prayer very much quicken the prayerfulness of other godly persons. Where one finds a golden nugget, others will feel inclined to dig. The benefit of our experience to others should reconcile us to it. No doubt the case of David has led thousands to seek the Lord with hopeful courage. Without such an instance to cheer them, they might have died in despair. Perhaps the Psalmist meant for this favor, or something like it, would be sought by all godly souls. Here again we can confirm his testimony, for all will draw near to God in the same manner as he did when godliness rules their heart.

The mercy seat is the way to Heaven for all who shall ever come there. But there is a set time for prayer, beyond which it will be unavailing. It is between the time of sin and the day of punishment that mercy rules the hour. Then God may be found. But when the sentence has gone forth, pleading will be useless. For the Lord will not be found by a condemned soul. O dear one, do not slight the accepted time; waste not the day of salvation. The godly pray while the Lord has promised to answer. The ungodly postpone their petitions until the Master has shut the door; then their knockings are too late. What a blessing to be led to seek the Lord before the great floods leap forth from their lairs. For then the faithful will be safe. The floods will come, and the waves rage; whirlpools and waterspouts will be on every hand — but the praying ones will be safe, most surely secured from evry ill. David was probably most familiar with those great land floods which fill up with rushing torrents the beds of rivers, but which at other times are almost dry. These overflowing waters often did great damage, as in the case of the Kishon, sufficient to sweep away whole armies. From sudden and overwhelming disasters thus set forth in metaphor, the true suppliant will certainly be held secure. He who is saved from sin has no need to fear anything else.

EVENING

But one thing is needful — Luke 10:42.

I AM GLAD it says *"one thing,"* because a division of ends and objects is always weakening. A man cannot follow two things well. Our life flood suffices not to fill two streams or three. There is only enough water, as it were, in our life's brook to turn one wheel. It is a great pity when a one fritters away energies by being "everything by turns, and nothing long" — trying all things, and mastering none. Oh, soul, it is well for you that there is only one thing in this world that is absolutely necessary. Then give your whole soul to that. If other things are necessary in a secondary place, *"Seek first the kingdom of God and His righteousness, and all these will be added to you."*

One thing is needful, and this is well arranged, for we cannot follow two things. If Christ is one of these, we cannot follow another. Is it not written, *"No man can serve two mastes; either he will hate the one and love the other, or cling to the one and despise the other. You cannot serve God and mammon."* Not only would it be very weakening to you to attempt to serve both, but it is absolutely impossible that you should do so. Jesus Christ is a monopolizer of human hearts. He will never accept a portion of us. He bought us altogether, and He will have the whole of our personality. Christ must be everything, or He will be nothing. That one loving anything as well as Christ cannot be said to love Christ. Nor does such a one trust Him who trusts in anything besides. Christ must reign alone. *"Jesus only"* must be the motto of our spirits. It is well for us, then, that only *"one thing is needful,"* for only one thing is possible. It is an unspeakable mercy that the one thing needful is a very simple one.

Blessed is he who looks upon the poor; the Lord will deliver him in time of trouble — Psalm 41:1.

THIS IS the third Psalm opening with a benediction, and there is a growth in it beyond the first two. To search the Word of God comes first, pardoned sin is second. Now the forgiven sinner brings forth fruit to God for the good of others. The word used is as emphatic as in the former cases, and so is the blessing which follows it. The poor intended are those poor in substance, weak in bodily strength, despised in repute, and desponding in spirit. These are those avoided and frequently scorned. The worldly proverb bequeathes the hindmost to one who has no mercy. The sick and the sorry are poor company, and the world deserts them. Such as have been made partakers of Divine grace receive a more tender nature and are not hardened against their own flesh and blood. They undertake the cause of the down-trodden and turn their minds to the promotion of their welfare. They do not toss a penny and go on their way, but inquire into their sorrows, study the best ways for their relief, and come to their rescue.

Such as these have the mark of the Divine favor plainly on them and are as surely the sheep of the Lord's pasture as if they wore a brand on their foreheads. They are not said to have considered the poor in times past, but they still do. Stale benevolence argues present stinginess. First and foremost, far above all others in tender compassion for the needy is our Lord Jesus, who so remembered our low estate, that although He was rich, for our sakes He became poor. All His attributes were charged with the task of our uplifting. He weighed our case and came in the fulness of wisdom to execute the wonderful work of mercy by which we are redeemed from our destruction. Our wretchedness excited His pity; our misery moved His mercy; thrice blessed is He for His attentive care and wise action toward us. He still considers us; His mercy is always in the present tense, and so let our praises be.

EVENING

When I remember these things I pour out my soul in me. For I had gone with the multitude; I went with them to the house of God, with joyful voice and praise — Psalm 42:4.

WHEN HE continually thought about his woes, his heart melted into water and was poured out on itself. God hidden, and foes raging, a pair of evils enough to bring down the stoutest heart! Yet let no reflections so gloomy engross us, since the result is of no value. Merely to turn the soul on itself, to empty it from itself into itself is useless. How much better to pour out the heart before the Lord! The prisoner's treadwheel might sooner land him in the skies than mere inward questioning raise us nearer to consolation.

Painful reflections were awakened by the memory of past joys. He had mingled in the pious throng; their numbers had helped to give him exhilaration and to awaken holy delight. Their company had been a charm to him as he ascended the hill of Zion with them. Gently proceeding with holy ease, in comely procession, with frequent strains of song, he and the people of Jehovah had marched in reverent ranks up to the shrine of sacrifice, the abode of peace and holiness. Now far away, the holy man pictures the sacred scene and dwells on the details of that pious march. The festive noise is in his ears, and the solemn dance before his eyes. Perhaps he alludes to the removal of the ark and the glorious gatherings of the tribes on that grand holy day. How changed was his present place! For Zion, a wilderness; for the priests in white linen, soldiers in garments of war. For the song was the sneer of blasphemy; for the festivity, lamentation; for the joy in the Lord, a mournful dirge over His absence. When in a foreign land, like David we have said, "Ziona, Ziona, our holy and beautiful house, when shall I see you again? The church of the living God, when shall I hear your Psalms and holy prayers, and again behold the Lord in the midst of His people?" David appears to have a peculiarly tender remembrance of the singing of the pilgrims; it is assuredly the most delightful part of worship, that which comes nearest to the adoration of Heaven.

June 5   MORNING

Why are you cast down, O my soul? Why do you moan within me? Hope in God; for I shall yet praise Him for the help of His face — Psalm 42:5.

AS THOUGH he were two men, the Psalmist talks to himself. His faith reasons with his fears; his hope argues with his sorrows. These present troubles, will they last forever? The rejoicings of my foes, are they more than empty talk? My absence from the solemn feasts, is that a perpetual exile? Why this deep depression, this faithless fainting, this melancholy? David chides David out of the dumps, and in this he is an example for all desponding ones. To search out the cause of our sorrow is often the best surgery for grief. Self-ignorance is not bliss; in this case it is misery. The mist of ignorance magnifies the causes of our alarm. A clearer view will make monsters dwindle into tribles. Why is my quiet gone? If I cannot keep a public Sabbath, yet why do I deny my soul an indoor Sabbath? Why am I agitated like a troubled sea, and why do my thoughts make a noise like a tumultuous multitude? The causes are not enough to justify such utter yielding to despondency. Up, my heart! What ails you? Play the man, and your castings down will turn to liftings up, your uneasiness to calm.

If every evil is let loose from Pandora's box, yet there is hope at the bottom. This is the grace that swims even while the waves roar and are troubled. God is unchangeable, therefore His grace is the ground for unshaken hope. If everything is dark, yet the day will come; meanwhile hope carries stars in her eyes. Her lamps are not dependent on oil from without; her light is fed by the secret visitations from God that sustain the spirit, *"for I shall yet praise Him."* My sighs will yet give place to songs, my mournful ditties shall yet be exchanged for triumphal paeans. A loss of the present sense of God's love is not a loss of that love itself. The jewel is there, although it does not gleam on our breast. Hope knows her title is good, even when she cannot read it clearly. She expects the promised boon, though present providence stands before her empty.

EVENING

I came to hurl fire into the earth, and what if I desire it already to be kindled? — Luke 12:49.

WHEN the fire of conversion has kindled the fire of persecution, it proves its own infinite energy by subjecting even persecution to itself. That famous master in Israel and servant of God, the Swiss divine Farel, was converted to God by the sight of a martyr burned in one of the streets of Paris. The wonderful demeanor of the saint as he stood in the midst of the fire to die made an impression on Farel's youthful spirit, a spirit never afterwards shaken off. It has often been through opposition that the church has made her greatest advances. This is partly the reason that our Lord said, *"What if I desire that it already be kindled?"* It is as if our Lord meant, "What does My kingdom care if opposition comes?" — let it come; it will be a fruitful thing to the church of God; the sooner it comes, the better. We might almost say today, if there could be a return to the persecutions of the past, if it were not for the sin which would be caused by it, "What do we care if the flames are already kindled?"

The Christian who is slandered and opposed can afford to smile with a sacred contempt at all that can be done against the gospel of Christ. It was during the persecution which raged against the saints at Jerusalem that the church obtained one of the greatest pillars that have ever strengthened and adorned her — I mean the apostle Paul. Breathing out threatenings against the people of God, he is on his road to Damascus, but the blaze of heavenly fire blinds him, strikes him to the ground, and afterwards he becomes a chosen vessel to carry, like an uplifted cresset, that very fire throughout the nations of the earth. I look for recruits to the truth of God from the ranks of our enemies. Do not despair; the brightest preacher of Christ may yet be fashioned out of the wretched raw material he now is.

Let those who love Your salvation say without ending, Let God be magnified
— Psalm 70:4.

THE CLAUSE which we have selected for our text also follows immediately after another which may be looked on as a stepping stone to it. Before we can love God's salvation, we must be seekers after it — so we read, *"Let all who seek You rejoice and be glad in You."* There is a duty peculiar to seekers, let them see to it. Then follows a further obligation peculiar to those who have found what they sought. Let joy and rejoicing be first realized by the seeker through his perceiving personally the grace of God, and then let us go on to a further stage. The fresh convert has his business mainly within. It will be well with that one if his heart can sincerely be glad in the Lord. When believers are young and feeble they are not fit for the battle yet. So let them tarry at home awhile, and under their vine and fig tree enjoy the sweet fruits of the gospel, none making them afraid. We do not send our children to hard service. We wait until their limbs are developed, then we appoint them their share in life's labors. Let the newly-called ones be carried like lambs in the Savior's bosom, borne as on eagles' wings. But when they have advanced beyond the earliest stage, when they are persuaded that Christ is theirs, that they have been adopted into the family of God, then let them cheerfully accept active service. Let it not be now the main concern with them to possess a joyous experience on their own account, but let them studiously seek the good of their fellow creatures, and the glory of God. Strong men have strength given them that they may bear burdens and perform labors; light is this burden, and blessed is this labor. Let them *"say without ending, Let God be magnified."*

EVENING

Deep calls to deep at the noise of Your water-spouts; all Your waves and Your billows have gone over me — Psalm 42:7.

YOUR SEVERE dealings with me seem to excite all creation to attack me. Heaven and earth and hell call to each other, stirring each other up in dreadful conspiracy against my peace. As in a water-spout, the deeps above and below clasp hands, so it seemed to David that Heaven and earth united to create a tempest around him. His woes were unceasing, and overwhelming. Billow followed billow, one sea echoed the roaring of another. Bodily pain aroused mental fear. Satan with his suggestions chimed in with mistrustful forebodings; outward tribulation thundered in awful harmony with inward anguish. His soul seemed drowned as in a universal deluge of trouble, over whose waves the providence of God moved as a watery pillar, in dreadful majesty inspiring the utmost terror. As for the afflicted one, he was like a lonely bark around which the fury of a storm is bursting; or like a mariner floating on a mast, almost every moment submerged.

David thought that every trouble in the world had met in him. But he exaggerated, for *all* the breaking waves of Jehovah have passed over none but the Lord Jesus. There are griefs to which He makes His children strangers for His love's sake. Sorrow naturally states its case forcibly. The mercy is that the Lord after all has not dealt with us according to our fears. Yet what a plight to be in! Massive waves sweeping in ceaseless succession over one's head, water-spouts coming nearer and nearer, all the ocean roaring around the weary swimmer. Most of the heirs of Heaven can realize the description, having experienced the same. This is a deep experience unknown to babes in grace. It is common to such as do business on great waters of affliction. To such it is some comfort to remember that the waves and billows are the Lord's. They are all sent and directed by Him, achieving His designs. The child of God knowing this is the more resigned.

June 7 MORNING 159

Judge me, O God, and plead my cause against an ungodly nation. O deliver me from the deceitful and unjust man — Psalm 43:1.

OTHERS are unable to understand my motives, and unwilling to give me a just verdict. My heart is clear as to it intent, therefore I bring my case before You, content that You will impartially weigh my character and right my wrongs. If You will judge, Your acceptance of my conduct will be enough for me. I can laugh at human misrepresentation if my conscience knows that You are on my side. You are the only One I care for. Besides, Your verdict will not sleep, but You will see practical justice done to Your slandered servant. One such advocate as the Lord will more than suffice to answer a nation of brawling accusers. When people are ungodly no wonder that they are unjust. Those who are not true to God Himself cannot be expected to deal rightly with His people. Hating the King, they will not love His subjects. Popular opinion weighs with many, but Divine opinion is far more weighty with the gracious few. One good word from God outweighs ten thousand railing speeches of men. He bears a brazen shield before him, he who relies in all things on his God. The arrows of calumny fall harmlessly from such a buckler.

Deceit and injustice are boon companions. A fawner will not fear to slander. From two such devils none can deliver us but God. His wisdom can outwit the craft of the vilest serpent; His power can overmatch the most raging lion. Whether this was Doeg or Ahithophel is no matter; such double-distilled villains are plentiful. The only way of dealing with them is to refer the matter to the righteous Judge of all. If we try to fight them with their own weapons, we shall suffer more serious injury from ourselves than from them. O child of God, leave your enemies in better hands, remembering that vengeance belongs not to you, but to the Lord. Turn to Him in prayer, crying, *"O deliver me,"* and before long you will publish abroad the remembrance of His salvation.

EVENING

And he brought him to Jesus — John 1:42.

EARNESTNESS often gives prudence, putting a man in possession of tact, if not of talent. Andrew used what ability he had. If he had been as some young men are, he would have said, "I would like to serve God. O how I would like to preach! And I would want a large congregation." Well, there is a pulpit in every street in London, a most wide and effectual door for preaching in this great city beneath God's blue sky. But this young zealot would prefer an easier berth than the open air. And because he is not invited to the largest pulpits, he does nothing. How much better it would be if he, like Andrew, began to use his ability among those accessible to him, and from that stepped to something else, and from that to something else, advancing year by year! If Andrew had not been the means of converting his brother, the probabilities are that he never would have been an apostle. Christ had some reason in the choice of His apostles to their office, and perhaps the ground of His choice of Andrew as an apostle was this, that he was an earnest man. He was always speaking privately to individuals. Now you young men, if you become diligent in tract distribution, diligent in the Sunday school, then you are likely men to be made into ministers. But if you stop and do nothing until you can do everything, you will ever remain useless, an impediment to the church instead of being a help. Dear sisters in Jesus Christ, you must not dream that you are in such a position that you can do nothing at all. That would be such a mistake in providence as God cannot commit. You must have some talent entrusted to you; He has given you something to do which no one else can do. Then find out what your sphere is, then occupy it.

MORNING

Let those who love Your salvation say without ending, Let God be magnified
— Psalm 70:4.

I AM SURE you delight in the plan of salvation. What is that plan? It is summed up in a single word: substitution. Sin was not pardoned absolutely, else Justice would have been dishonored. But upon His agreement, sin was transferred from the guilty to the Innocent One, *"The Lord has laid on Him the iniquity of us all."* When our iniquity was found on the innocent Lamb of God, He was *"smitten of God and afflicted,"* as if He had been the sinner rather than us. He was made to suffer for transgressions not His own, as if they had been His own. And in this way mercy and justice met together, righteousness and grace kissed each other.

But, alas! There are many who fight against this plan. I rejoice that I am surrounded by warm hearts who love it and would die for it. I know no other gospel; let this tongue be dumb rather than it should ever preach any other. Substitution is the very marrow of the whole Bible, the soul of salvation, the essence of the gospel. Our sermons should be saturated with it, for it is the life-blood of a gospel ministry. We must daily show how God the Judge can be both *"just, and the Justifier of him that believes."* Let us declare that God has made the Redeemer a sacrifice for sin, judging Him to be sin for us, Him who knew no sin, that we might be made the righteousness of God in Him. Our testimony must be that *"He was made a curse for us;"* that *"He His own self bore our sins in His own body on the tree;"* that *"He was once offered to bear the sins of many;"* that *"He was numbered with the transgressors, and He bore the sins of many."* Never speak about this with bated breath, that you not be found unfaithful to your charge. And why should we not joyfully proclaim this doctrine? It is the grandest, noblest, most Divine doctrine under Heaven!

EVENING

You are He, my King, O God; command deliverances for Jacob; by You we will push our enemies; through Your name we will trample those rising against us —
Psalm 44:4,5

KNOWING WELL Your power and grace, my heart is glad to own You as my sovereign prince. Who among the mighty are so illustrious as You? To whom, then, should I yield homage, or turn for aid? God of my fathers, You are my soul's monarch and liege Lord, *"Command victories for Jacob."* To whom should a people look but to their king? It is he who by virtue of his office fights their battles for them. In the case of our King, how easy it is for Him to scatter all our foes! O Lord the King of kings, with what ease can You rescue Your people. A word of Yours can do it. Give but the command and Your persecuted people shall be free. Jacob's long life was crowded with trials and deliverances, and his descendants are here called by his name, as if to typify the similarity of their experience to that of their great forefather. He who would win the blessings of Israel must share the sorrows of Jacob. This fourth verse contains a personal declaration and an intercessory prayer. Those who make sure of their personal interest in God pray best. Those having the fullest assurance that the Lord is their God should be foremost to plead for the rest of the faithful family in trials.

The fight was very close, bows were of no avail, and swords failed to be of service. It came to daggers drawn, to hand-to-hand wrestling, pushing and tugging, Jacob's God was renewing in the seed of Jacob their father's wrestling. And how did faith fare then? Could faith stand foot to foot with her foe and hold her own? Yes, truly, she came forth victorious from the encounter, for she is great at a close push; she overthrows all her adversaries, the Lord being her helper. The Lord's name served instead of weapons, and it enabled those who used it to leap on their foes and with joy valiantly crush them. In union and communion with God the saints work wonders. If God is for us, who can be against us? (Romans 8:31)

MORNING

Now You will let Your servant go in peace, Lord, according to Your word. For my eyes have seen Your salvation — Luke 2:29,30.

EVERY BELIEVER may be assured of ultimately departing in peace. This is no privilege peculiar to Simeon. It is common to all the saints, since the grounds on which this privilege rests are not monopolized by Simeon — they belong to all of us.

Note that all the saints have seen God's salvation. Because of this they should all depart in peace. It is true that we cannot, like Simeon, take the infant Christ into our arms. But He is *"formed in us, the hope of glory."* We cannot look on Him with these mortal eyes, but we have seen Him with those the immortal eyes of faith, which death cannot dim; the eyes of our own spirit have been opened by God the Holy Spirit. A sight of Christ with the natural eye is not saving, for thousands saw Him and yet cried, *"Crucify! Crucify Him!"* After all, even in Simeon's case, it was the spiritual eye that saw, the eye of faith beheld the Christ of God. There were others in the temple who saw the babe, the priest performing the circumcision, and other officials gathered around the group. But I do not know if any of them saw God's salvation. They saw the little child that was brought there by its parents, but they saw nothing remarkable in Him. Perhaps it was Simeon and Anna alone who saw with the inward eye the real Anointed of God revealed as a feeble infant. Even though you and I miss the outward sight of Christ, we do not need to regret it — it is a secondary privilege. If with the inner sight we have seen the Incarnate God and have accepted Him as our savlation, We, too, are blessed. Abraham saw Christ's day before it dawned, and now after it has passed, we see it, and with faithful Abraham we are glad. We have looked and are enlightened.

EVENING

Now you will let Your servant go in peace, Lord, according to Your word. For my eyes have seen Your salvation — Luke 2:29,30.

FOR A MOMENT attentively review the words of this aged saint. Every believer shall in death depart in the same sense as Simeon did. The word here used is suggestive and encouraging: it may be applied either to escape from confinement, or to deliverance from toil. The Christian in his present state is like a bird in a cage — his body imprisons his soul. It is true that our spirit ranges Heaven and earth, laughing at the limits of matter, space and time. But for all that, the flesh is a poor scabbard unworthy of the glittering soul; it is a mean cottage unfit for a princely spirit, a clog, a burden, and a fetter. When we would watch and pray, we find full often that the spirit is willing, but the flesh is weak; *"we that are in this body do groan."* The fact is, we are caged birds, but the day comes when the great Master shall open the cage door and release His prisoners. We do not need to dread the act of unfastening the door, for it will give to our soul the liberty for which it yearns. And then with the wings of a dove covered with silver our soul will soar into its native air, singing all the way, with a rapture beyond imagination.

Simeon looked on dying as a mode of being let loose — a deliverance of our vile imprisonment, an escape from captivity, a release from bondage. The like redemption shall be dealt to us. How often does my soul feel like an unhatched chick shut up within a narrow shell, in darkness and discomfort! The life within labors hard to chip away and break the shell, to know a little more of the great universe of truth, and to see in clearer light the infinite of Divine love. Oh, happy day, when the shell shall be broken, when the soul shall be complete in the image of Christ, when it shall enter into the freedom for which she is preparing! We look for that, and we shall certainly have it.

Now You will let Your servant go in peace, Lord, according to Your word. For my eyes have seen Your salvation — Luke 2:29,30.

SOME BELIEVERS are conscious of a special readiness to depart in peace. When do they feel this? First, when their graces are vigorous. All the graces are in all Christians, but they are not all there in the same proportion; nor are they at all times in the same degree of strength. In certain believers faith is strong and active. When faith becomes *"the evidence of things not seen,"* and *"the substance of things hoped for,"* then the soul is sure to say, *"Now You will let Your servant go in peace, Lord."* Faith brings graces, the clusters of flowers into the desert of life, making us long for the land that flows with milk and honey. When the old Gauls had drunk of the wines of Italy, they said, "Let us cross the Alps and take possession of the vineyards which yield such generous draughts." So, when faith makes us realize the joys of Heaven, then it is that our soul stands waiting on the wing, watchig for the signal to depart to the glory land.

The same is true of the grace of hope, for hope peers into the things invisible. She brings near to us the golden gates of the Eternal City. Like Moses, our hope climbs to the top of a spiritual Pisgah to behold the Canaan of the true Israel. Moses had a delightful vision of the promised land, seeing it all from Dan to Beersheba. So also hope drinks in the charming prospect of our Promised Land, and then exclaims exultingly, *"Now You will let Your servant go in peace, Lord."* Heaven realized and anticipated by hope renders the thought of departure most precious to the heart. And this also is the effect of the grace of love on us. Love puts the heart, like a sacrifice, on the altar. And then she fetches heavenly fire to kindle it.

EVENING

Let those who love Your salvation say without ending, Let God be magnified — Psalm 70:4.

WE LOVE God's salvation because it is so complete. Nothing remains unfinished which is necessary to remove sin from the believer and give him righteousness before God. As far as atonement for sin is concerned, the expiation is most gloriously complete. Remember that remarkable expression of the Apostle, where he describes the priests as continually standing at the altar, offering sacrifices year by year, and even day by day, because atonement by such means could never be finished. Such sacrifices could never take away sin. Therefore they must be perpetually offered; the priest must always stand at the altar. But the Apostle says, *"This Man, after He had offered one sacrifice for sin forever, sat down at the right hand of God,"* because the work was accomplished forever. Jesus has performed what the Aaronic priesthood in long succession had failed to do. Even though streams of blood might flow from bullocks and goats, and although incense might smoke until the pile of it was high as Lebanon, what was there in all this to make propitiation for sin? This work was but to shadow the real expiation to be offered by Christ. It was a picture, but the substance itself was not there. But when our Divine Lord went up to Calvary and gave up His body, His soul, His spirit as a sacrifice for sin, on the cross, He finished transgression, made an end of sin for all His chosen people, bringing in everlasting righteousness. In this we have strong consolation; these are unchangeable things in which it is impossible for God to lie; His word and oath are our immovable security. By the atonement we are infalliby, effectually, eternally saved, for He has become the *"Author of salvation to all those who obey Him."* How we love this salvation! Our inmost heart rejoices in it.

MORNING

But one thing is needful — Luke 10:42.

IN ORDER to enter Heaven it is necessary that our nature should become like the nature of Christ. This earth is for those who bear the image of the first Adam. But the new heaven and the new earth are for those who bear the image of the Second Adam. And this must be wrought in us by regeneration, and developed in us by acquaintance with Him. By sitting at His feet and beholding Him, we become changed into the same image, going from glory to glory even as by the Spirit of the Lord. If we reject the Lord Jesus as our trust, teacher, and example, we have no new life; we are not new creatures in Christ and therefore can never be admitted within the holy gates. For there only those who are fashioned after His likeness are permitted to dwell. Then we must sit at His feet; it is absolutely necessary. Without it our whole life will be a complete failure. We may make money, but we will lose our souls. We may gain honor, but we will have come short of the glory of God. We may enjoy pleasure, but we will forfeit the pleasures which are at God's right hand forever. We may have served our country, but we shall have rendered no service to our God—for we cannot serve God if we will not obey Christ: *"He who does not honor the Son does not honor the Father who has sent Him."* To the one who does not submit his life to Jesus, this life is a blank, a long rebellion. Then the life forever for such a one will be darkness and confusion, in a land of sorrow, and of weeping, and of wailing, and of gnashing of teeth, in a land of despair, where no star shall ever shine, where no sun will ever rise. Woe! Woe! Woe to the Godless, Christless spirit that passes across the river of death without a hope. Woe eternally to the soul that will not sit at the feet of Jesus! He will be trodden beneath the feet of Jesus in His anger; he will be crushed in His hot displeasure. May God grant that such will never be your portion.

EVENING

Now You will let Your servant go in peace, Lord, according to Your word. For my eyes have seen Your salvation — Luke 2:29,30.

SAINTS feel most their readiness to go when their communion with Christ is near and sweet. When Christ hides Himself we are afraid to talk of dying, or of Heaven. But when He only shows Himself through the lattices, and we can see those eyes which are *"as the eyes of doves by the rivers of waters, washed with milk and fitly set,"* when our own soul melts even at that hazy sight of Him, Oh then we desire to be at home with Him. Our soul then cries out for the day when her eyes will see the King in His beauty, in that beautiful New Jerusalem. Have you never felt this heavenly homesickness? Have you never pined for the home-bringing? Surely, when your heart has been full of the Bridegroom's beauty, when your soul has been ravished with His dear and precious love, then you have said, *"When shall the day break and the shadows flee away? Why are His chariots so long in coming?"* As with love sickness for your precious Savior, you have swooned, thirsting to see Him as He is, and to be like Him. The world is black, while Christ is fair. It is a poor heap of ashes, while He is altogether lovely to us. When a precious Christ is manifested to our spirits, it is then we feel that we could see Jesus and die. Samuel Rutherford wrote, "Black sun, black moon, black stars, but inconceivable bright and glorious is the Lord Jesus." How often did that devout man write words of this sort: "Oh, if I had to swim through seven hells to reach Him, if He would but say to me, like Peter, 'Come to me,' I would go to Him not only on the sea, but on the boiling floods of hell, if I might but reach Him and come to Him." These are his own words, "I profess to you that I have no rest, I have no ease, still I be over head and ears in love's ocean."

MORNING

But one thing is needful — Luke 10:42.

A WORD ABOUT the church of God in this country at the present time: She, too, is as Martha, cumbered with much serving. If the church would be more like Mary, and sit at the feet of Jesus, it would become her wisdom and her strength. Just now we need revival. Oh that God would send it! Oh for a mighty flood of spiritual influences, such influences that would bear the stranded churches right out into a sea of usefulness. But how can we get revival? When we commune with Christ, brothers and sisters, then we shall have it. When the saints habitually sit at the feet of Jesus they will be revived. Then, of necessity, the revival will spread from them, and then the hearts of sinners will be touched.

There is great talk now-a-days of church union. The walls of various churches are to be broken down, and the denominations are to be blended. Do not think of it in such a fashion. The only union possible, or desirable, is that we all unite to sit at Jesus' feet. It is not allowable that we concede one truth and you another. That is not natural charity; it is but common treason to Christ. We have no right to yield an atom of the truth of God under the pretence of love. Truth is no property of ours; we are only God's stewards. Then it behoves us to be faithful to all His truth. Neither one church nor another has any right to change its testimony one jot, if it is true. To alter the statute book of Christ is blasphemy. True union will come when all the churches learn of Christ, for Christ does not teach two things opposed to each other. There are not two baptisms in the Bible. We shall not find two sets of dogmas diametrically opposite to each other. If we give up the various things that are of man, each of us holding fast only that which is of God, then we shall be united in principle and in doctrine, and *"One Lord, one faith, one baptism"* will once again be emblazoned on the banners of the church of God.

EVENING

Not unto us, O Jehovah, not unto us, but unto Your name give glory — Psalm 115:1.

THERE are many sweet and precious texts of Scripture which are so endeared, having become habituated to us, and we to them, that one cannot but think we must carry them with us to Heaven, and that they will form not only the theme of our song, but a portion of our blessedness and joy even in that happy home. But if there is one text which more especially belongs to all, which must break forth from *every* redeemed one as he enters Heaven, it is the first verse of this psalm. I am sure that not one of the Lord's chosen ones on earth, as he reviews the way by which he has been led, as he sees such thorough evidence and conviction that his weakness is made perfect in the Lord's strength, but must from the very ground of his heart cry out, *"Not unto us, O Jehovah, not unto us, but unto Your name"* be the praise and the glory. And if we could see Heaven opened, and hear its glad and glorious hallelujahs — if we could see the innumerable company of angels and its band of glorified saints as they cast their crowns before the throne, we would hear it from every lip, *"Not unto us, O Jehovah, not unto us, but unto Your name give glory, for Your mercy and for Your truth's sake."* Why should this not be as gladly and as gratefully the angels' song as the song of the redeemed? They stand not in their own power. They kept not their first estate through any inherent strength of their own. Like their feebler brothers of the human race they are also *"kept by the power of God"*. Even our blessed Lord, as on that night of sorrow He sung this hymn of praise, even He could truly say in that nature in which He was to suffer for our sins, *"Not unto us"* — not unto man be ascribed the glory of this great salvation which I am now with My own blood to purchase, but *"unto Your name"* and Your love be the praise given. — abridged from Barton Bouchier.

To appoint to those who mourn in Zion, to give to them beauty for ashes, the oil of joy instead of mourning, the mantle of praise instead of the spirit of infirmity, so that one calls them trees of righteousness, the planting of Jehovah, in order to beautify Himself — Isaiah 61:3.

WHERE THERE is joy imparted and unction given from the Holy Spirit, instead of despondency, men will say, "It is God's work; it is a tree that God has planted. It could not grow like that if anybody else had planted it. This man is a man of God's making, his joy is a joy of God's giving." In the case of some of us we were under such sadness of heart before conversion, through a sense of sin, that when we did find peace everybody noticed the change in us, and they said to one another, "Who has made this man so happy, for he was just now most heavy and depressed?" And when we told them where we lost our burden, they said, "Ah, there is something in Christianity after all." *"Then they said among the heathen, The Lord has done great things for them."*

Remember poor Christian in *Pilgrim's Progress*. Mark what heavy sighs he heaved, what tears fell from his eyes, what a wretched man he was when he wrung his hands and said, "The city in which I dwell is to be burned up with fire from Heaven, and I shall be consumed in it. And, besides, I am myself undone by reason of a burden that lies hard on me. Oh that I could get rid of it." Do you remember John Bunyan's description of how he got rid of the burden? He stood at the foot of the cross, and there was a sepulcher nearby. And as he stood and looked, and saw One hanging on the tree, suddenly the bands that bound his burden cracked, and the load rolled away into the sepulcher. And when he looked for it, it could not be found. He gave three leaps for joy. Oh then live such a happy life that you may compel the most wicked man to ask where you learned the art of living.

EVENING

In order to beautify Himself — Isaiah 61:3.

THAT IS THE END of it all, that is the great result we drive at, and that is the object even of God Himself, *"in order to glorify Himself"*. For when men see the cheerful Christian and perceive that this is God's work, then they must own the power of God. Not always do they do this with their hearts, as they should, but still they are obliged to confess that *"this is the finger of God."* Meanwhile, the saints, being comforted by your example, will praise and bless God, and all the church will lift up a song to the Most High. Come, my brothers and sisters, are any of you down-hearted; are you almost beneath your enemy's foot? Here is a word for you, "Do not rejoice over me, O my enemy; even though I fall, yet I shall rise again." Are any of you in deep trouble, very deep trouble? Another word for you, then, *"When you pass through the waters I will be with you; and through the rivers, they shall not overflow you. When you walk through the fire, you shall not be burned, nor shall the flame kindle on you."* Are you pressed with labors and afflictions? *"As your days, so shall your strength be." All things work together for good to those that love God, to those that are called according to His purpose."* Are you persecuted? Here is a note of encouragement for you, *"Blessed are you when men shall revile you and persecute you, and shall say all manner of evil against you falsely, for My sake. Rejoice and be exceeding glad, for great is your reward in Heaven. For so they persecuted My prophets which were before you."*

Whatever your circumstances are, *"Rejoice in the Lord always, and again I say, Rejoice."* Think what Jesus has given you. Your sins are pardoned for the sake of His name. Your Heaven is made secure to you, and all that is needed to bring you there. You have grace in your hearts, and glory awaits you.

MORNING

When you awake, it will talk with you — Proverbs 6:22.

LET US take care how we trifle with the Bible which is so instinct with life. Might not many of you remember your faults this day if we were to ask you whether you are habitual students of Holy Writ? I believe you are readers of the Bible, but are you searchers? For the promise is not to those who merely read, but to those who delight in the Law of the Lord, who meditate in it day and night. Are you sitting at the feet of Jesus, using His Word as your school book? If not, remember this, that even though you may be saved, you are lacking very much of the blessing which you might enjoy otherwise. Have you been backsliding? Refresh your soul by meditating in the Divine statutes. Then with David you will say, *"Your word has quickened me."*

Are you faint and weary? Go and talk with this living Book. It will give you back your energy. Then you shall mount up again, as with wings of eagles. But are you unconverted? Then I would urge upon you unconverted people great reverence for Scripture, an intimate acquaintance with its contents, and a frequent perusal of its pages. For it has happened myriads of times that those studying the Word of Life have been brought to life by the life-giving Word. *'The entrace of Your word gives life."* Like Elijah and the dead child, the Word has stretched itself on them, and their dead souls were made to live. One of the likeliest places in which to find Christ is in the garden of the Scriptures. For He delights to walk there. In olden times the blind men were accustomed to sit by the wayside begging, so that, if Jesus passed by they might cry out to Him. So I would have you sit down by the wayside of the Holy Scriptures. Hear its promises; listen to its gracious words. They are the footsteps of the Savior. And when you hear them, may you be led to cry out, *"Son of David, have mercy on me "!*

EVENING

When you awake, it will talk with you — Proverbs 6:22.

SCRIPTURE is influential. Solomon says, *"When you awake, it will talk with you;"* and he follows that with the remark that it keeps a man from the strange woman, and from other sins which he goes on to mention. When the Word of God talks with us, it influences us. All talk influences us, more or less. There is more done in this world for good or bad by talk than there is by preaching. Indeed, the preacher preaches best when he talks. There is no oratory in the world that is equal to simple talk, which is the model of eloquence. All a rhetorician's action and verbiage is so much rubbish. Simply talking is the most efficient way of preaching, a man permitting his heart to run over at his lips into other men's hearts. Now the Scriptures, as it talks with us, influences us in many, many ways.

It soothes our sorrows; it encourages us. Many a warrior has been ready to steal away from God's battle, but the Word has laid its hand on him, saying, "Stand on your feet; do not be discouraged; be of good cheer and I will strengthen you; I will help you. Yes, I will uphold you with the right hand of My righteousness." We have read of brave saints , but we little know how often they would have been arrant cowards if the good Word had not come to strengthen them. Then they went back to be stronger than lions and swifter than eagles.

While this Book soothes and cheers, it also has a wonderful elevating power. Did you never feel it put fresh life-blood into you? You have thought, "How can I continue to live at such a dying rate; I must gain something nobler? Read that part of the Word which tells of the agonies of your Master, Read of the glories of Heaven which this Book reveals. Then you will feel that you can run the race with quickened speed.

I also taught Ephraim to go, taking them by their arms. But they did not know that I healed them — Hosea 11:3.

WE COME upon the blessing of holy rearing and education: *"I also taught Ephraim to go, taking them by their arms."* As they who teach little children to walk, supporting their tottering footsteps, instructing them how to put one foot before the other until they are able at last to run alone, so here. Calvin says it means, "I have led him on foot. As a child who cannot yet walk with a firm foot is, by degrees, accustomed to do so, and the nurse, or the father, or the mother who leads him, has a regard for his infancy — so also God led Israel, as much as his feet could bear." And if this mercy and condescension of God, in thus comparing Himself to a woman with her baby, were not sufficient, in addition to this He becomes a physician, too, granting healing. He says, *"I have healed them."* They had not only weakness that needed to be supported, and ignorance that needed to be tutored; but in addition they had sickness and infirmity that needed healing. He who had carried them as Shaddai — the Lord All-sufficient — became to them Jehovah Rophi — the Lord that heals them.

Who shall tell how much we all owe to heavenly pharmacy? Our diseases are deep-seated and most dangerous. How happy are we in having an omnipotent Physician whose word alone is more than a match for all our maladies. Surely we have a sickness for every day in the year, but the Beloved Physician has a remedy for every complaint. Glory be to Him who forgives all our iniquities and heals all our diseases.

As if this were not enough, we find Him drawing them on in the paths of obedience and holiness — not with ropes and chains that would compel against their will, overhauling them roughly — but with forces suited for minds and hearts: *"I drew them with cords of a man, with bands of love."* In this way the gracious Spirit of God works in us to will and to do of His own good pleasure: *"The love of Christ constrains us . . . that if One died for all, then all died . . . that the living ones may live no more to themselves, but to the One having died for them, and having been raised"* (2 Cor. 5)

EVENING

I also taught Ephraim to go, taking them by their arms. But they did not know that I healed them — Hosea 11:3.

DO WE remember how tottering our first steps were? We limped very sadly. Our walking was comparable to the seeing of the man to whom men looked like trees. Our state of mind was a mixture of light and darkness. We cried, *"Lord, I believe; help my unbelief."* There were only one or two promises in God's word which I could get any hold on when I first came to Him. My soul was stayed a little while on that word, *"Whoever calls on the name of the Lord will be saved."* I could grasp only that. Some can get consolation from nothing but that sweet word, *"He who comes to Me I will in no way cast out."* They could believe only a little. They reached as far as hoping and trusting, intermittently mixed up with a world of doubting and fearing; but they could not stir any further. Very delightful to the Christian pastor it is to see a young convert begin to take the first step or two. We have seen them fall down with doubts and fears, but we have been so pleased that they could walk even a little in the way of faith, that they could believe even a portion of the Word of God. What a mercy it is that the Lord reveals to us His own truth by slow degrees! We ought never to expect our young converts to understand the doctrine of election, or to be able to split hairs in orthodoxy. It is vain to overload them with such a precious truth as union with Christ, or so deep a doctrine as predestination. Do they know Christ as their Savior, and themselves as sinners? Well, then, do not try to make a child race; it will never walk if you do so. Do not try to teach the baby gymnastics. First let it totter on and tremble forward a little way. The Savior said, *"I have many things to say to you, but you cannot bear them now."*

MORNING

I also taught Ephraim to go, taking them by their arms. But they did not know that I healed them — Hosea 11:3.

THE LORD has dealt with us as children. For instance, He has not chided us for our many mistakes. If the nurse were to scold the child for not walking as she does; if she were to be angry with it because it is not as strong as she is, then the poor thing might be long before it came to walk at all. God sometimes does with His people as Apelles did with Alexander when he painted him — he did not draw the scar on Alexander's face, but placed his finger over it. Note how the Holy Spirit describes Sarah. There was not much good in what Sarah said on that day when she lied, but she called her husband, Lord. The Holy Spirit lights on that, mentioning it to her honor (1 Peter 3:6). He has often accepted our poor service, giving us sweetly to feel that it was so, although now we look back on it and wonder how it could have been accepted at all.

Many of us who preach the gospel had God's blessings on our early preaching. Our knowledge was dreadfully scant, and our ability slender. We wonder how God could have blessed us, but He did. If He were to let us know how badly we do His work even now we would despair and do no more. But in His great mercy He allows the light to shine on the brighter spots; He lets us see what His Spirit is doing. Then we take courage and go on, learning to walk after all. With all our tremblings and tumblings, and fallings down, we do at length learn to stand upright, and even to run in His ways.

Dear brothers and sisters, do you not feel that God has had great patience with you? Do you not wonder that He has endured you? Could you have had so much patience with another as God has had with you? You can hardly run alone, and yet you are persuaded that His patience will hold out until there is no more need of it.

EVENING

I also taught Ephraim to go, taking them by their arms. But they did not know that I healed them — Hosea 11:3.

WHY IS IT that mothers take so much pains in teaching their children to walk? It is because these are their own offspring. And the reason why the Lord has been so patient with us, and will continue to be so, is because we are His children, still and always His children. Ah, there is wondrous power in that — still His children. Sitting at a table once I heard a mother speaking at length about her son. She said a very great deal about him. Then someone sitting near me said, "I wish that good woman would be quiet." But I said, "What is the matter? May she not speak of her son?" He said, "Why he has been deported. He was as bad a fellow as ever lived, and yet she always sees something wonderful in him." So some time later when I had gained her acquaintance with her I ventured to say something to her about this son. I remember her remark, "If there is nobody else to speak up for him, then his mother will." Just so. She loved him so that if she could not be altogether blind to his faults, yet she would also see all that was hopeful in him.

Our blessed God does not bring into the foreground what we are, but emphasizes what He means to make us: *"Their sins and iniquities I will remember no more, forever."* He puts our sin away; He sees us as we shall be when we shall bear the image of the heavenly, when we shall be like our Lord. For the sake of Christ, beholding our shield and looking on the face of His Anointed, God loves us and goes on to instruct us. If it seems at times as if He felt He must surely give us up, then His love rushes to the rescue; then it comes to this: *"How shall I make you as Admah? How shall I set you as Zeboim? My heart is turned within Me; My repentings are kindled together"* (Hosea 11:8). He returns to us with such a word as this: *"I betrothed you to Me in righteousness, and in mercy, and in judgment, and in compassions"* (Hosea 2:19).

MORNING

So then we should not sleep, as the rest do, but we should watch and be sober
— 1 Thessalonians 5:6.

THERE IS OUR LORD, our great Exemplar, before us now. Behold Him in Gethsemane! Imagination readily sees Him amid the olives. It might be said that His whole life on earth was pictured in that agony in the garden — for in a sense it was all an agony. It was all a sweating, not such as distills from those who purchase the staff of life by the sweat of their face, but such as He must feel who purchased life itself with the agony of His heart. Seen throughout the whole of His ministry the Savior appears to me as one on his knees pleading. As a man He agonized before God, laying out His life for the sons of men.

But is it harsh to say that the sleeping disciples are a fit emblem of our own usual lives? As compared, rather as contrasted, with our Master, I fear it is so. Where is our zeal for God? Where is our compassion for men? Do we ever feel the weight of souls as we ought to feel it? Do we ever melt in the presence of the terrors of God which we know to be coming on others? Have we realized the passing away of an immortal spirit to the judgment bar of God? Have we felt pangs and throes of sympathy when we have remembered that multitudes of our fellow creatures have received as their eternal sentence those words, *"Depart you cursed ones into everlasting fire in Hell, prepared for the Devil and his angels"*? Why, if these thoughts really possessed us, we should scarcely sleep. If they became as real to us as they were to Him, then we would wrestle with God for souls as He did; we would become willing to lay down our lives, if by any means we might save some. By the eye of faith I can see at this moment Jesus pleading at the mercy-seat, saying, *"For Zion's sake I will not hold My peace, and for Jerusalem's sake I will not rest."* And yet around Him we all lie asleep, without any self-denying activity; yea, almost without prayer, missing our many opportunities.

EVENING

So then we should not sleep, as the rest do — but we should watch and be sober
— 1 Thessalonians 5:6.

LET US NOT SLEEP, as did that ancient hero Samson. While he slept he lost his locks, his strength, and by and by he also lost his liberty, his eyes, and ultimately his life. With respect to ourselves in our slumbering, Samson is the sad picture of many professors of Christianity. We are about to sketch a portrait of one whom we knew years ago. He was *"strong in the Lord, and in the power of His might."* Picturing this man — and it is not fancy portrait, for we have seen many such men — when the Spirit of the Lord came upon him, he did mighty things. We looked on and wondered; yea, we envied him, saying, "Would God that we had an hour of such strength as has fallen on this man." He was the leader among the weak; he often infused courage into faint hearts. But where is he now? All our Israel knew him, for his name was a tower of strength. Our enemies knew him, too, for he was a valiant man in battle. Where is this hero now? We hear little of him now in the fields of service where he once glorified God and smote the enemies of Israel. We do not meet him now at the prayer meeting, or in the Sunday School, or at the evangelistic station. We hear nothing of his seeking for souls. Surely, he has gone to sleep. He thinks that he has much spiritual goods laid up for many years, and he is now taking his rest. He has had his share of labor, and the time has now come for him to take a little ease — so he says. It is our loss, and his peril, that he has allowed himself to fall into such a drowsy condition. O that we could stir him! Alas! Carnal security is always a Delilah. It gives us many a dainty kiss, lulling us into tranquil slumbers, causing us to imagine that it is God's own peace.

MORNING

And I will settle you as in your old estates, and will do better than at your beginnings. And you shall know that I am the Lord — Ezekiel 36:11.

LET US LOOK BACK. Some of us have been converted to God for a good number of years now. And all the while we have enjoyed spiritual life. Others are young beginners, but their present enjoyment will assist them to answer this question: What is there so good about those first days? We read of our first love as *"the love of our espousals"*; and we all know that there was something especially charming about those first hours when forgiving love was so precious to us, and we rejoiced in the Lord.

One choice enjoyment was our vivid sense of pardon. We knew that we were forgiven. We had not a shadow of a doubt of it. We were so recently sinful, now being washed from our stains, we saw the change. It would not have been possible then for Satan to make us doubt it. When we stood at the cross and said, "Thus my sins were washed away," then things went well with us. When substitution was a novelty to us, and when we seemed to hear a voice like that of the angels before the throne, singing, *"There is therefore no condemnation to those who are in Christ Jesus,"* then we all knew that we had looked to Jesus, for we felt that we could look nowhere else. We were newly-cleansed sinners, and we knew it to be so. Oh, that blessed period! Our earthly comforts were forgotten in the greater sweetness; our earthly sorrows ceased to matter, because our guilt was gone. Taken out of the bonds of iniquity, our hearts danced at the very sound of the redeeming Name. We sang, "I am forgiven! I am forgiven!" We wanted to tell the angels this strange wonder of almighty love. That was one of the good things at your beginning.

EVENING

And I will settle you as in your old estates, and will do better than at your beginnings. And you shall know that I am the Lord — Ezekiel 36:11.

IN WHAT RESPECTS can our future be better than that which is behind? Faith can go on and be stronger. By the grace of God it will be firmer, more robust. At first it shoots up like the lily, very beautiful, but fragile. Afterwards faith is like the oak with great roots that grip the soil, with rugged branches that defy the winds. Faith in the young beginner is apt to be cast down, doubts and fears breaking in. But if we grow in grace, then we become rooted and grounded. These days it is fashionable to sneer at the doctrines of Scripture. No one is thought to be sensible who believes any strong doctrine. The younger believer is apt to be staggered. But it would take a great many of the critics and divines of the present day, with all their skepticism, to shake some of us. We have tasted, and have handled, and have lived on these things, being established in them by the Scriptures. We are not going to be moved from the hope of our calling. Even though all the wiseacres in the world should dip their pens in tenfold darkness, and write it down as if it were proven that there was no such thing as light, yet we have seen it with our eyes of faith, and we will live in it. We are not to be moved from the eternal verities. This is something better than early faith, is it not? Go on, then, and obtain it.

Again, God gives to His people, as they advance, much more knowledge. At first they enjoy what they know, but they hardly know what they enjoy. As we grow in grace we know more. We are surprised to see that what we thought to be one blessing is actually fifty blessings in one. We learn the art of dissecting truth, taking it apart to see the different veins of Divine thought that run through it. And then we see with delight the blessings conveyed to us by the person and sacrifice of our exalted God and Savior, Jesus Christ. Surely, if years and experience make us to know more, then our present is better than our beginnings.

So let us keep the feast, not with old leaven, nor with leaven of malice and of evil, but with unleavened bread of sincerity and truth — 1 Corinthians 5:8.

SINCERITY keeps up the soul's credit at the throne of grace, so that no sinful infirmity can hinder its welcome with God. It is the regarding of iniquity in the heart, not the having of it, that stops God's ear from hearing our prayer. This is a temptation not a few have found some work to get over — whether such as they who see so many sinful failings in themselves, may take the boldness to pray — or they think it may be presumption to expect God to hear their prayers. In some this prevails so far as to cause some to forbear praying, because they cannot pray as they would. It is like those poor people who will keep away from the congregation because they have not clothes to come in as they desire. But those turning away from the duty of prayer must study the promises of God — for they are the only ground for prayer, and they are our chief plea in prayer. The promises of God are accommodated and fitted to the lowest degree of grace. It is as a picture in a room; it is there for all to look on it. So the promises of the gospel-covenant smile on all that sincerely look to God in Christ. Note that it is not said, *"If you have faith like a cedar,"* but, *"If you have faith as a grain of mustard-seed."* Neither is justifying faith beneath miraculous faith in its own sphere of activity. The least faith on Christ, if sincere, as truly removes the mountainous guilt of sin from the soul, as the strongest faith. So all the saints are said to have *"like precious faith"* (2 Pet. 1:1). Sarah's faith is little seen in the story in Genesis, yet she obtains a rare, honorable mention in Hebrews, where God owns her for a believer as well as Abraham with his stronger faith; also she is mentioned favorably by Peter (1 Pet. 3:6). What love is expressed in that promise: *"Blessed are the ones who hunger and thirst after righteousness"* (Matt. 5:6)! —Note, it is not, "Blessed are the ones who are holy." All saints thirst after righteousness, even to the least newly born babe in Christ.

EVENING

So let us keep the feast, not with old leaven, nor with leaven of malice and of evil, but with unleavened bread of sincerity and truth — 1 Corinthians 5:8.

WHY IS THIS grace of sincerity so delightful to God, even captivating Him in love to the soul where He finds it? Sincerity makes the soul willing. When it is clogged with so many infirmities, as to disable it from the full performance of its duty, yet then the soul stands on tip-toe to go after it. Like a hawk, as soon as it sees her game, the soul launches forth after sincerity, inwardly pricked and provoked by a strong desire to fulfill its love by doing its duty. A perfect heart and a willing mind are joined together. It is David's counsel to his son Solomon, to *"serve God with a perfect heart and a willing mind"* (1 Chr. 28:9). A false heart is a shifting heart. It puts off its work as long as it dares. And it is not worthy of thanks when a duty is performed because of a threatening rod. Yet hypocrites are like tops that go no longer than they are whipped. The sincere soul is ready and forward; it does not lack will to do a duty when it lacks skill and strength to do it. It is said that *"the Levites were more upright in heart to sanctify themselves than the priests"* (2 Chr. 29:34). How did that appear? In this, that they were more forward and willing to work. No sooner did the word come out of Hezekiah's mouth concerning a reformation, than presently the Levites rose up to sanctify themselves. The sincere heart is uniform to the will of God. If God says, *"Seek My face,"* it will rebound with, *"Lord, I will seek Your face."*
(The above condensed from *The Christian in Complete Armor*, William Gurnall.)

MORNING

Jesus said to them, Why do you cause trouble to the woman? For she has done a good work towards Me — Matthew 26:10.

OBSERVE ESPECIALLY that her good work was a good work upon the Lord Jesus. It was of no immediate benefit to anybody else, nor was it meant to be. *"This ointment might have been sold for much and given to the poor"* — so Judas and the other disciples said. The five hundred denarii, or whatever the cost, might have been spent on bread, and so it would have fed many poor people. But she expended it on Jesus, fully meaning that all of it should be used in His honor. Poor or no poor, she thought only of Him. The ointment might have been used for certain purposes at festivals, or in other ways, and so have been more or less beneficial to a number of persons. But on this occasion the benefit was for the Lord alone, and so the woman meant it to be. Because it did not seem practical or philanthropic to them, people called it a *waste*. But is anything done for Jesus wasted? It might rather seem as if all would be wasted which was not given to Him.

This box of precious ointment was all for Him. Other persons in the room might smell the sweet, precious perfume, but that was not what the grateful woman aimed at. She intended all the sweetness for Jesus; it was a good work towards Him. The woman's thought was that she would honor the Lord; her only intent was to show her reverence for Him. If He would be pleased with her deed, then she would be perfectly content, although no one else might be gratified. Her first and last thoughts were for the Lord Jesus Himself.

EVENING

Jesus said to them, Why do you cause trouble to the woman? For she has done a good work towards Me. — Matthew 26:10.

THE GOOD WORK which she performed was a most appropriate one, far beyond her own thought. Love is ever wise. Jesus was her King. He had ridden through the streets of Jerusalem in triumph. The multitude had strewn the branches in the way. They had saluted Him with hosannas. They had done much by way of coronation. But they had not anointed Him. Why this omission? If no one else will do it, she will anoint Him. Her hands will bring out the perfumed nard and will pour the precious unguent on the King of Israel. He was a priest, too — especially a pardoning priest for her. She recognized His sacred priesthood. But the oil that fell on Aaron's head never, literally, had fallen on the head of Jesus. Therefore she must needs anoint Him plenteously, until the oil not only ran to the skirts of His garment, but filled all the house where they were sitting. As King and as Priest she will take care that He is not without a costly anointing. Moreover, it was customary to anoint travelers for their refreshment at the end of a long journey, at the time they came into the house. The host on this occasion had neglected this act of courtesy. It was most suitable that when this great Lord, whose path had been weary and woeful, who had at length nearly ended His years of travel in this thorny wilderness, He should receive refreshment from the woman's hospitable hand. Weary and worn He was, and she would willingly anoint Him with the oil of gladness. Although others had rejected Him, she anointed His head. She owned Him as the noblest guest earth ever entertained. In all this her good deed was fit and seasonable.

Our Lord then said — and here I am free from any charge of following my fancy — that she did this for His burial. Whether this woman with some prophetic spirit resting on her saw further into our Lord's words than His disciples did, we do not know. We do know that the Lord said that this woman's deed would be spoken of as a memorial of her. And so it has been done for these many centuries. Such is the Lord's memory of our good deeds.

MORNING

They shall not hunger any more, nor shall they thirst any more, nor shall the sun ever fall on them, or any heat — Revelation 7:16.

IN HEAVEN no need is unsatisfied and no desire ungratified. There can be nothing needed for their bodies, for they are as the angels of God. Children of poverty, your scarcity of bread will soon be ended, then your care will end in plenty. The worst hunger is that of the heart, and this will be unknown above. There is a ravenous hunger, fierce as that of a wolf, which possesses some men. All the world cannot satisfy the greed of such men. A thousand worlds would scarce be a mouthful for these lusters. Now, in Heaven there are no sinful or selfish desires. The ravening of covetousness, or of ambition, does not enter the sacred gate of the New Jerusalem. In glory there are no desires which should not be. And the desires which should be are all so tempered and so fulfilled that they can never become the cause of sorrow or of pain; *"they shall not hunger any more."* Even the saints need love, fellowship and rest. They have all these in union to God, in the communion of saints, and in the rest of Jesus. The unrenewed man cursed to be always thirsting. But can Christ slake such a thirst, even now. For He says, *"whoever may drink of the water which I will give him will never ever thirst."* Be sure then that from the golden cup of glory we shall drink that which will quench all thirst forever. In all the golden streets of Heaven there is not a single person who is desiring what he may not have, or wanting what he cannot obtain — or even wishing for that which he has not to his hand. O happy state! The mouths of the glorified saints will be satisfied with good things; they will be filled with all the fullness of God. And as there is in Heaven a supply for every need, so there is the removal of every ill. So the Spirit says of them, *"nor shall the sun ever fall on them, or any heat."*

EVENING

They shall not hunger any more, nor shall they thirst any more, nor shall the sun ever fall on them, or any heat — Revelation 7:16.

WE ARE such poor creatures that excess even of things good in themselves soon becomes evil to us. If you have ever seen the sun shining in the clear blue heavens, you would not wonder that I love the sun. Life, joy and health stream from it in lands where it is enough to bask in its beams. But too much of the sun overpowers us. Its warmth makes men faint; its stroke destroys men. Too great a blessing may prove too heavy a cargo for the ship of life. So we need guarding from dangers which at first sight may look to be without peril. In the beatific state in Heaven, if our bodies of flesh and blood were still to be our dwelling-place, then we could not live under the celestial conditions. Even here too much of spiritual joy may prostrate a man, casting him into a swoon. Seemingly we would like to die for such a disease, yet it is possible for a sickness to come on one to whom heavenly things are revealed in great measure, and enjoyed with special vividness. One of the saints is said to have cried out in an agony of delight, "Hold, Lord, hold! Remember I am but an earthen vessel; I can contain no more!" The Lord has to limit His revelations to us who are on earth still. Some who have looked imprudently at the sun for long have been blinded by it. The very sunlight of Divine revelation, favor and fellowship could readily prove too much for our feeble vision, heart and brain. For this reason, in the glorious state flesh and blood shall be removed. The raised body will be strengthened so as to endure that glorious light which issues forth from the throne of our God and Savior. As for us, as we now are, we might well cry, "Who among us shall dwell with the devouring fire?" But when the redemption of the body has occurred, when the soul has been strengthened with all might, then we shall be able to be at home with our God, although He is a consuming fire.

And He will lead them to living fountains of waters. And God will wipe away every tear from their eyes — Revelation 7:17.

HEAVEN is to know the substance and the secret of the Divine life. There we shall drink of the living water, although we hold no cup. This teaching is precious, but it is far better to know the thing about which the teaching speaks. It is a salver of silver, but the blessing itself is the apple of gold. Blessed are they that are always fed on the substance of the truth, the verity of verities, the essence of essential things.

"He will lead them to living fountains of waters." There the eternal source is unveiled. Those there not only receive mercy, but they see how it comes, and where it flows. They not only drink, but they drink with their eye on the glorious Well-head. Did you ever see a boy lie down on a hot day, being thirsty, putting his mouth down on the top of the water at the brim of the well? Oh how sweetly he draws up the cool refreshment! He has no fear that he will drink the well dry. How pleasant it is to take from an inexhaustible source! That which we drink is all the sweeter because of the measureless remainder. Enough is not enough. But when we have God for our all in all, then we are content. When I am near to God I dwell in the overflowing of His love. I feel like the cattle on a burning summer's day when they take to the brook which ripples around them up to their knees, and there they stand, filled, cooled, and sweetly refreshed.

O my God, in You I feel that I have not only all that I can contain, but all that contains me. In You I live and move with perfect contentment. Such is Heaven! We shall have bliss within and bliss around us. We shall drink at the Source; and we shall dwell by the Well-head forever.

EVENING

Bless the Lord, O my soul — Psalm 103:22.

THAT IS TO SAY, let your calling be that of the seraphs, saying, *"Holy, holy, holy is Jehovah of hosts; all the earth is full of His glory"* (Isa. 6:3). Let me bless the lord, because no function will be more rich in blessings to my soul than this. The admiring contemplation of His excellence is in reality the appropriation of it. The heart cannot delight in God without becoming like God. Let me do it also because it is the peculiar privilege of man on this earth to bless his Lord. When he would find any to join him in this, he must ascend the skies. Let me bless Him because the earth is fully furnished with the materials of praise. The sands, the seas, the flowers, the birds, the animals, the field, the mountains, the rivers, the trees, the clouds, the sun, the moor, the stars — all these and more wait for me to translate their attributes and distinctions into praise of my Lord. But above all these, so does the new creation.

Let me praise Him because all things that pertain to my existence are of Him, through Him, and to Him — health, comfort, knowledge, dignity, safety, progress, power, and usefulness. A thousand of His ministers in earth, sea and sky are used to provide every mouthful I eat. The breath that I am commanded to modulate in praise neither comes nor goes without a most surprising output of power from Him whom I am to praise (Col. 1:17). Is it not dastardly, then, to be receiving these benefits without even mentioning the name or the goodness of the Giver? Let all candidates for Heaven bless the Lord. It is no place for such as have not learned to praise Him. But how shall I praise Him? Not with fine words. No poetic talent is needed here. Any language that will express heartfelt admiration and thankfulness will be accepted by Him. Praise Him so far as you know Him, and He will make you know more of His glory. (Taken from writings of George Bowen, 1873).

June 23   MORNING

The Lord is merciful and gracious — Psalm 103:8.

THOSE WITH WHOM He deals are sinners. However much He favors them, they are guilty and need mercy at His hands — nor is He slow to pity their lost estate, or reluctant by His grace to lift them out of it. Mercy pardons sin; grace bestows favor. The Lord abounds in both. This is that way of His which He made known to Moses (Ex. 34:6), and in that way He will abide as long as the age of grace shall last, and men are yet in this life. He who *"executes righteousness and judgment,"* yet delights in mercy is *"slow to anger."* He can be angry and can deal out righteous indignation on the guilty, but it is His strange work. He lingers long, with loving pauses, tarrying to give space for repentance and opportunity for accepting His mercy. So He deals with the greatest sinners, and with his own children more so. Toward them His anger is short-lived and never reaches into eternity, and when it is shown in fatherly chastisements he does not afflict willingly. From this we should learn to be ourselves slow to anger. If the Lord is long-suffering under our great provocations, how much more ought we to endure the errors of our brothers and sisters. *"And plenteous in mercy."* He is rich in it, quick in it, overflowing with it. If He were not we would soon be consumed. He is God, and not man, or our sins would soon drown His love; yet above the mountains of our sins the floods of His mercy rise. All the world tastes of His sparing mercy. Those who hear the gospel partake of His inviting mercy and are cheered by His consoling mercy. Those will enter Heaven through His infinite and everlasting mercy. Let grace abounding be our hourly song in the house of our pilgrimage. Let those who feel that they live on it glorify the plenteous fountain from which it so spontaneously flows.

EVENING

Then having these promises, beloved, let us cleanse ourselves from all defilements of flesh and of spirit, perfecting holiness in the fear of God — 2 Corinthians 7:1.

THE CHRISTIAN must maintain the power of holiness in his contest with sin. He must express the power of holiness in the duties of God's worship. He must also do this in his particular calling and worldly employments.

You must not only refuse to commit broad sins, but shun the appearance of sin also; this is to walk in the power of holiness. We are commanded to *"hate even the garment spotted by the flesh"* (Jude 23). The Christian's care should be kept not only his conscience pure, but also his name pure. This is done by avoiding all appearance of evil. Bernard's three questions are worth asking ourselves: (1) Is it lawful? May I do it and not sin? (2) Is it becoming of me as a Christian? May I do it and not wrong my profession of faith in God? (3) Is it expedient? May I do it and still not offend my weak brother? There are some things we must deny ourselves for the sake of others. A man may ride his horse full speed, but should he do so through a town where children are at play? You may do some things not sinful in themselves, but which would bruise the tender consciences and grieve the spirits of weak Christians. Liberty is the goddess of our times. Nakedness is openly condoned, among other things not worthy of a Christian, in the name of liberty. And Christians stand by, stand apart, and do not make known God's condemnation of such things. Such shameful discipleship will bear bitter fruit to all professors who fall into it.
— *The Christian in Complete Armor*, William Gurnall

But she said, True, O Lord. But even the little dogs eat of the crumbs which fall from the table of their masters — Matthew 15:27.

ALTHOUGH you must not cavil with Christ, yet you may plead with Him. *"True, O Lord,"* she says, then she adds, *"but."* Here, then, is a lesson. Set one truth against another. Do not contradict a frowning truth, but bring up a smiling one to meet it. Remember how the Jews were saved out of the hands of their enemies in the days of Haman and Mordecai. The king issued a decree that, on a certain day, the people might rise up against the Jews and slay them, and take their possessions as a spoil. Now, according to the laws of the Medes and Persians, this could not be altered. The decree must stand. What then? How was it to be avoided? Why, by meeting that ordinance by another. Another decree is issued, that although the people might rise against the Jews, yet the Jews might defend themselves. And if anyboy dared to harm them, the Jews might slay them and take their property for a spoil. One decree thus counteracted another.

How often we may use the holy art of looking from one doctrine to another! If a truth looks black on me I will not be wise to be always dwelling on it. But it will be my wisdom to examine the whole range of truth, to see if there is not some other doctrine which will give me hope, Asaph practiced this when he said of himself, *"So foolish was I, and ignorant; I was as a beast before You"* (Psalm 73:22). And then he confidently added, *"Nevertheless I am continually with You; You have taken hold of my right hand."* He does not contradict himself; and yet the second utterance removes all the bitterness which the first sentence left on the palate. The two sentences together set forth the supreme grace of God, who enabled a poor beast-like being to commune with Him. I beg you to learn this holy art of setting one truth side by side with another, that in this way you may have a fair view of the whole situation, and may not despair.

EVENING

But He answered and said, I was not sent to any but the lost sheep of the house of Israel. But she came up, bowing before Him, saying, Lord, help me! — Matt. 15:24.

SOME are stumbled by the sovereignty of God. He will have mercy on whom He will have mercy. He may justly ask, *"Shall I not do as I will with my own?"* Beloved, do not dispute the rights of the eternal God. It is the Lord; let Him do as seems good to Him. Do not quarrel with the King, but come humbly to Him, and plead, *"O Lord, You alone have the right to pardon."* But Your Word declares that if we confess our sins *"You are faithful and just to forgive us our sins."* And You have said that *"whoever believes in the Lord Jesus Christ shall be saved."* This pleading will prevail. Do not kick at the truth, that you not dash your naked foot against iron pricks. Yet, do not dwell on one truth until it distracts you, but look at others until they cheer you. Submit to all truth, but lead on your own behalf that which seems to you to look favorably on you. When you read, *"You must be born again,"* do not be angry. It is true that to be born again is a work beyond your power; it is the work of God the Holy Spirit. This need of a work that is beyond you may well distress you. But the third chapter of John which says, *"You must be born again,"* also says, *"God so loved the world that He gave His only begotten Son, that whoever believes in Him should not perish, but have everlasting life."* So it is clear that the one believing in Jesus is born again. Have an eye to all the land of truth. When you seem to be persecuted in one city of truth, flee to another. For there is a refuge city even for you. Besides, there is a bright side to every truth, if you have but the wit to spy it out. The same key which locks will also unlock — very much depends on the turn of the key, and still more on the turn of your thought.

MORNING

O Ephraim, what shall I do to you? O Judah, what shall I do to you? For your goodness is like a morning cloud, and it goes away like an early dew — Hosea 6:4.

MANY are affected by a strong tendency to immitate those about them. We all imitate one another more or less. But evidently many are not born to set examples, only to follow examples. These easily promise, but easily forget. The love of approval acts on many with great force. Especially will young people follow each other, and follow leaders, if they are praised for it. Converts may easily be made by mutual admiration. If it happens to be a religious time, and it is the fashion to profess conversion, many of all ages go with the rush. Yet these are by no means truly called into the kingdom of God. That religion which lives on companionship is apt to die when the company is changed. Beware of the godliness which is carried off its feet by the crowd. True religion is the personal conviction of one who has repented and believed on his own account. No one can be carried to Heaven by the stream of outside influence. There must be a work within, *"You must be born again."* No doubt we have many who disappoint our hopes. They are moving in the right way, but they are not going there from a force within, but are being compelled to go by an influence from without. One person of great strength of mind may have a vast influence over others. But subjection to the best influence can never take the place of a personal conversion.

We read in the Word of God of a young king who did that which was right in the sight of God all the days of the venerable high priest who had been his rescuer and guardian. But when that gracious man was gone, then the king changed and went his own way; and that way was an evil one (Joash — 2 Chron. 24:18). Many persons are under the holy influence of godly relatives and friends, but they are not gracious themselves; their real character is concealed by the godly ones who overshadow them.

EVENING

O Ephraim, what shall I do to you? O Judah, what shall I do to you? For your goodness is like a morning cloud, and it goes away like the early dew — Hosea 6:4.

IT IS WELL for the preacher to remind men that they are lost by nature, and that in their flesh dwells no good thing. It is well that sin should be made to appear sin, and that self-righteousness should be made to look like filthy rags (Isa. 64:6). Human inability, and the need of the Holy Spirit, must be set forth clearly, and the sovereignty of God must be proclaimed solemnly. The Lord has a right to pass over whom He pleases; but if mercy comes to any one it will be by the sovereign act of God, because God wills to do it — not because anyone deserves it. We must preach the need of cleansing in the precious blood, and the necessity of being born again from above. While the preacher thunders out the doctrine of death by sin, and of life through Christ, and other kindred truths, then it is that God the Spirit hews men by the prophets, and their proud beings fall down, slain by the word of His mouth. "I shall never hope again," says one, "for that sermon drove me to despair." Self-despair is the beginning of true hope in Christ. Go and hear that man again. "Oh, but he hung up all my hopes like so many criminals on the gallows." Go and hear that man again, for more of that hanging needs to be done, until your last carnal hope is executed. "But he hits so hard!" Thank God that he does. There is no hewing stone without hard blows. Oh, it is well to be riddled by the gospel! For God never heals those whom He has not smitten; He never binds up those who have no wounds. Why should the physician come to those who are not sick? It is to you who are bleeding to death that mercy flies on the wings of the Spirit. There will be no delay when you are spiritually at death's door. Look to the Lord and live. He is waiting to heal the wounds He has made.

MORNING

And Your servant is warned by them; in keeping them there is great reward
— Psalm 19:11.

THE WORD OF GOD warns us of our weakness in those duties which it commands, of our tendency to fall into those sins which it forbids. It sets before us a noble example, but it bids us remember that only by Divine power can we follow it. It spreads before us a program of perfect holiness, but it does not flatter us with the notion that by our own strength we can carry it out. It humbles us by showing that we cannot even pray as we ought without the Spirit's intercession. Nor can we so much as think a good thought without His aid (2 Cor. 3:5). Scripture is continually warning us of the deceitfulness of our hearts, of the tendency of sin to advance from one stage of evil to another. Holy Scripture shows us our spiritual inability, apart from the Divine Spirit. And we do greatly need warnings in this way, for we are prone to be self-sufficient. Pride shoots forth from us with very little encouragement.

We buckle on our harness and begin at once to shout as if the battle were won. How soon we think ourselves near perfection, when indeed we are near a fall! We are apt to sit down and imagine that we have won the race, whereas we have not yet traversed on half of the way. The Word of God continually checks our carnal confidence, and it disturbs our self-satisfaction. It bears constant protest against our imagining that we have already attained, when we as yet are only babes in grace. How plainly it tells us, *"He who trusts in his own heart is a fool."* It shows us where our great strength lies; but it calls us off from all trust in our own past experience, or firmness of character, or strength of determination, or depth of sanctification, to lean solely and alone on heavenly grace — grace that we must receive hour by hour. If we give way to price, it is against the admonition of the Divine statutes. For in this what David says here, *"Your servant is warned by them."*

EVENING

And Your servant is warned by them; in keeping them there is great reward
— Psalm 19:11.

THE TEMPTATIONS of the world, and of the flesh, are more on our level than the assaults of Satan. He is the prince of the evil forces, and his attacks are so mysterious, so cunningly adapted to our infirmities, and so ingeniously adjusted to our circumstances, that unless God the Holy Spirit shall daily cover us with His broad shield of grace, we will be in the utmost jeopardy. O Lord, by these words of Yours is Your sevant warned to resist the enemy and escape his wiles! Glory be to Your care.

The teachings of the Lord also warn us to expect trial. The Bible never promises the true believer an easy life. Instead it assures him that he is *"born to trouble as the sparks fly upward"* (Job 5:7). There is no soaring to Heaven on wings of luxurious ease. We must painfully plod along the pilgrim way. We see on the page of inspiration that we cannot be crowned without warfare, nor honored without suffering. Jesus went to Heaven by a rough road, and we must follow Him. Every believer in the cross must bear the cross. If things go easily with you for a long time, do not then say, "My mountain stands firm; I shall never be moved." For God has only to hide His face and you will be troubled. Those happiest of men, of whom it could be said that God had set a hedge about them and all that they had, in due course these had to take their turn at the whipping-post and smart under the scourge. Even Job, that perfect and upright man, was not without his troubles. Beloved, expect to be tried. And when the trial comes, do not count it a strange thing. Your sea will be rough like the sea that tossed our Lord. Your way will be hot and weary, like that which your Master trod. The world is a wilderness to you, as it was to Him.

June 27   MORNING

And Your servant is warned by them; in keeping them there is great reward
— Psalm 19:11.

THE BIBLE WARNS US all of certain great events, especially of the Second Advent of the Lord and the coming judgment. It does not clearly tell us when our Lord will appear, but it warns us that to the unprepared He will come as a thief in the night. It warns us of the general Judgment, and of the Day when all men shall live again and stand before the great white throne. It warns us of that Day when every secret shall be revealed, and when every man shall receive for the things that he has done in his body, according to what he has done, whether it is good or evil. If I live like one of the cattle now, if I have no eye for the future that is hurrying toward me, if my soul never places herself in vision before the judgment seat of Christ — if I never foresee the day when Heaven and earth shall flee away before the presence of the great Judge — then I could be a diligent reader of the Word of God. If I search the Scriptures then I know that I shall be called to walk in the light of the last day and will be made to gird up my loins to face the dread account. Oh, that we might all be warned to be ready, that we may then give in our account with joy! Oh, that we may so take the warnings of Holy Writ as to be ready for death, ready for judgment, and ready for that final sentence which can never be reversed! If we were truly wise, these warnings would put salt into our lives and preserve them from the corruption which is in the world through lust.

Beloved, I trust that every one of us who knows the Lord will use His Holy Book as the constant guard of his life. Let it be like a fog signal to you, going off in warning when the road is hidden by a cloud. Let it be like the red lamp on the railway, suggesting to you to come to a stand, for the road is dangerous.

EVENING

And Your servant is warned by them; in keeping of them there is great reward
— Psalm 19:11.

THERE ARE many rewards to obedient believers. One is great quiet of mind: *Great peace have they who love Your law, and nothing shall offend them."* When a man has done what God bids him to do, his conscience is at peace. And this is a choice blessing. I can bear anybody to be my foe rather than my conscience. We read of David, *"David's heart smote him."* That was a hard knock! When a man's own conscience is his foe, where can he run for shelter? Conscience strikes home, and the wound is deep. But when a man can conscientiously say, "I did the right thing; I held the truth; I honored my God;" then the censures of men go for little. In such a case you have no trouble about the consequences of your action. For if any bad consequences should follow, the responsibility would not lie with you: you did what you were told to do. Having done what God commanded you, the consequences are with your Lord, and not with you. If the heavens were likely to fall, it would not be our duty to shore them up with a lie. If the whole church of God threatened to to to pieces, it would be no business of ours to bind it up by an unhallowed compromise. If you should fail to achieve success in life, as men call success, that is no fault of yours if the case were that your success must be achieved by dishonesty. It will be a greater success to be honest, and to be poor, than to grow rich through trickery. If through grace you have done the will of God, your peace shall be like a river, and your righteousness like the waves of the sea. Can you think of a greater reward than this? A quiet conscience is a little heaven. When we have done right we need no man's pity, however painful the immediate consequence. To do right is infinitely better than merely to prosper.

Having arrived, he much helped those who believed through grace — Acts 18:27.

APOLLOS is not Paul, and Paul is not Apollos. To blend the two in one would be to spoil each one of the two, without producing a good third. It is a great mercy that we have Paul, and Apollos, and Cephas, and other varieties of preachers. For not only is variety charming, but it is necessary. It is not everybody that can be profited by Paul, for it requires a great deal of fixed attention to follow him, and many hearers cannot concentrate their thoughts for long. It is not everybody that can be profited by Apollos, for fine speech is thrown away on simple souls. It is written, *"Then shall the lambs feed according to their pasture."* Each of them has a peculiar manner of feeding. Some of God's people are edified by one minister, and some by another. It is not mere whim, but it arises out of conformation, of character, and of habit of mind. Let Paul be Paul, and he will edify the Pauline class. Let Apollos be Apollos, and he will instruct those of his own sort. I would love to profit by either Paul, Apollos, Cephas, John, or James. But I am happy in hoping that their successors are still with us, each one with his own style of preaching. Let us not try to compare them with each other, but commend each one. And let us thank God for them, by whose grace each one is what he is. It would be a very bad day's work if we could do it, to reduce Paul to Apollos, or to bring Apollos to the style of Paul. In the body there are different members, and all members have not the same office. In the church of God there are different ministries, and all ministries do not work in the same way — though they all work toward the same end. Dear friend, if God gives you grace to bring sinners to Christ, or to plant churches, be thankful that you can imitate Paul. And if you cannot do that, but can help those who are already converted, be thankful for such a gift, and imitate Apollos.

EVENING

Having arrived, he much helped those who believed through grace — Acts 18:27.

LUKE NO DOUBT felt it necessary to insert those words, *"through grace."* Nobody in his day doubted the fact that salvation is worked in men by the grace of God. But the Holy Spirit foresaw that many in later days would conceal or obscure this truth. For this reason He moved the evangelist to note it very plainly. We have it under hand and seal from the Holy Spirit that those who believed in the Lord Jesus believed through grace. Surely, grace is to the front in all good things. And it is grace that gives us the gospel which we believe.

It was grace that chose the people whom God would save, and grace gave them over to the Lord Jesus. It was grace that gave Jesus Christ to stand in their room, and place, and stead, to bear for them that which was due to the justice of God on account of their sin. It was grace which led the Savior to undertake the work of substitution, and to carry it through. Grace wrote the first letter of the gospel and grace will write the last letter of it. Salvation is all of grace from first to last. Oh, that all preachers and all hearers would know the meaning of that word *grace*, that they would not confuse it, mixing it up with human endeavors and supposed creature merits! For in fact, *"it is not of him who wills, nor of him who runs, but of God who shows mercy"* (Rom. 9:16). *"If it be grace, it is no more of works, otherwise grace is no more grace;"* and, *"if it be of works, it is not of grace, otherwise work is no more work — by grace you are saved through faith, and that not of yourselves; it is the gift of God"* (Rom. 11:6; Eph. 2:8). Grace signifies free, undeserved favor. And as it comes from God to us, it is sovereign grace which is moved only by the good pleasure of Jehovah's will. Grace is the active movement of the Divine will to produce the results which He has graciously determined to produce.

June 29   MORNING   181

Having arrived, he much helped those who believed through grace — Acts 18:27.

BY THE PEN OF LUKE you see that the Holy Spirit has been pleased to give to Paul's travels and labors a very large proportion of the Book of the Acts of the Apostles. This part, from the twenty-fourth to the twenty-eighth verse is an episode, a corner marked off to be a record of Apollos. What Apollos did afterwards we do not know. He could well have been a very great evangelist all his life. He certainly was an exceedingly useful brother. But you do not see mentioned in the sacred pages that Apollos complained because he was allotted such a small space in them. He does not sulk because he has only four or five verses, while Paul's acts are described at great length. If you and I work for Christ, if the records of earth never mention us at all, let us not be sorrowful. There is most peace to those who are least talked about. Our sovereign God dispenses according to His will. It may be that one working saint will have all his story told, and it may be his life will make a useful biography, instructing and stimulating many for generations. Let it be so. Another equally earnest and fervent one may never have his life written. There may be one or two anecdotes about him, helpful and good. But let such a one not mind his obscurity. The record of each one is on high. If the chronicles of earth are faulty, the registers of Heaven are perfect. Many a one who has been forgotten here shall be remembered there. In Heaven it will give no saint the least trouble that he was not honored among men. No monument set up? Yea, but all true work is immortal. The diligent workman will be perfectly contented when his Master says to him, *"Well done, good and faithful servant."* The echo of those words shall thrill us in Heaven.

EVENING

Having arrived, he much helped those who believed through grace — Acts 18:27.

THEN KNOW that when grace gives us the gospel to believe, grace also gives us a new heart to believe the gospel. We are personally to believe the gospel, and only so can we be saved. But if nothing more were said than this, "Believe the gospel, and you shall be saved," the message would add to your solemn responsibility; yet it would not save you. For in such a case you would not believe, but would continue in your sins. Man, if left to himself, is an unbeliever; and an unbeliever he will ever be. To meet the deep depravity of our nature, and its settled unbelief, He who gave the gospel to be believed also gives the faith that believes the gospel. This is a wonder of grace. But then in the realm of grace everything is wonderful. We are so set on mischief, so proud, so vainglorious, so unbelieving, that we never do come to receive the gospel, except through the working of the grace of God on our consciences and wills. The faith which causes us to come to God first must come from God.

When I believed in Christ, taking Him to be my trust, and was saved: I believed, and in this way I entered into life and peace. It was not until some time after that I saw the reason why I had believed. I said, "How is it that I have believed in Christ, while others who have attended the same gospel ministry, enjoying the same advantages, have not believed in Him?" The inquiry was not, "Why did they refuse to believe?" Their unbelief was their own fault and folly; the blame must be laid at their door, for they wilfully refused the Savior — but this was not the question. I was not judging them; I was examining myself and inquiring why I had believed in Jesus. I was made to see that if I had believed, it was not to be set down to my personal credit. I could not take any honor because of it, but must give the credit to the grace of God.

Having arrived, he much helped those who believed through grace — Acts 18:27.

APOLLOS HAD BEEN helped, and because of this Apollos was bound to help others. Do not you who are Christians think that you owe something to the church of God as well as to the Christ of God? You were converted. Was it not by the word preached by a pastor, or by a teacher, or by a book citing the word? Will you not repay the church of God that which you owe to her instrumentality? If you have been helped as well as converted, you are especially bound to lay yourself out to help others. When a person who has been very despondent comes out into comfort, he should look out for desponding spirits; he should use his own experience as a cordial to the fainting. You Christians should never feel so much at home in any work as when you are trying to encourage a heart which is on the verge of despair. It is a high honor to nurse the wounded children of our Lord. It is a great gift to have learned by experience how to sympathize. Tell them how you have been where they are. Their eyes may say, "No, surely you have never felt as I do." Then go further and say, "If you feel worse than I did, I pity you indeed; for I could say with Job, *"My soul chooses strangling rather than life"*. In speaking to those who are in such a wretched condition you will find yourself at home. One who has been in a dark dungeon will know the way to the bread and to the water. If you have passed through a deep depression of mind, and the God the Comforter has appeared to your comfort, then lay yourself out to help others who are where you once were. If you were a prisoner, and have gotten out, do not enjoy your own liberty alone, but hasten to set free another captive.

EVENING

Having arrived, he much helped those who believed through grace — Acts 18:27.

SOME HAVE A MEASURE of natural ability to help others. It may be you resemble Apollos. Apollos was an eloquent man. But you say, "Ah, but I am not eloquent." There may be a difference of opinion as to what eloquence is. Eloquence is speaking out of the heart. There is eloquence in a child: it is the whole child working itself up to gain its wish and to have its way. If a child desires a pretty thing, and he is very little, yet tries to speak about it, then will do his best to express his longings. He will point to what he wants; he will clutch at it and cry after it. If he still does not succeed in getting it, then he will work himself up into an agony of desire. He will cry and cry; every bit of him will plead, will strive, will demand. Every hair of his head seems to be pleading for what he wants. He not only cries with his tongue, and with his eyes, but also with his fingers and his hair. He thinks of nothing else but that one thing on which his little heart is set. That is eloquence!

When anyone speaks in earnest, that one is eloquent even though he may be slow of speech. If your whole nature is stirred as you plead with sinners for the Lord Jesus, then you may be sure that will be counted as eloquence. O Christians, you do not know what you can do until you get at it with your whole souls. Like David, *"praise the Lord with your whole heart, in the assembly of the upright, and in the congregation"* — yea, to everyone who comes into your sight (Psalm 111:1).

July 1   MORNING

The Lord is my light and my salvation; whom shall I fear? The Lord is the strength of my life; of whom shall I be afraid? — Psalm 27:1.

SEE HERE personal interest: *"my light; my salvation."* The souls is assured of it, so it declares it boldly, *"my light."* Into the soul at the new birth Divine light is poured as the precursor of salvation. Where there is not enough light to see our own darkness and to long for the Lord Jesus, there is no evidence of salvation. Salvation finds us in the dark, but it does not leave us there. It gives light to those who sit in the valley of the shadow of death. After conversion our God is our joy, our comfort, our guide, our teacher, and in every sense our light. He gives light within, light around, light reflected from us, and light to be revealed to us. No, it is not said merely that the Lord gives light, but that He *is* light; nor that He gives salvation, but that He *is* salvation. Then whoever lays hold on God by faith has all covenant blessings in his possession. Every argument drawn from the darkness of man's nature can be answered with this, *"The Lord is my light and my salvation; whom shall I fear?"* None of the powers of darkness are to be feared, for the Lord, our light, will destroy them. The condemnation of Hell is not to be dreaded by us, for the Lord is our salvation. This is a very different challenge from that of boastful Goliath, for it is based on a different foundation. We do not rest on the conceited vigor of an arm of flesh, but on the real power of the omnipotent I AM.

The Lord is the strength of my life." Here is a third glowing epithet, to show that the writer's hope was fastened with a threefold cord, one that could not be easily broken. We may well accumulate terms of praise where the Lord lavishes deeds of grace. Our life derives all its strength from Him who is the author if it. And if He condescends to make us strong, we cannot be weakened by all the machinations of the adversary: *"of whom shall I be afraid?"* The bold question looks into the future as well as the present: *"If God be for us, who can be against us?"* (Rom. 8:31).

EVENING

Now our salvation is nearer than when we believed — Romans 13:11.

DO YOU REMEMBER — and it will do you good to remember — when you did believe. Oh, that blessed day! Of all days, that one is one of the brightest. It is not to be compared with the day of our natural birth, for that was a day of our first weeping. But in the day of our new birth, there were tears of sacred joy. We had been thrust from death into life, from condemnation to acceptance, from everlasting peril into eternal safety.

That was the day, we may say, when we left the first shore. Those on a journey often look back at the day they left. Remember then how your friends and saintly kinfolk rejoiced over you, how glad they were to hear you tell the tale of saving grace. A new saint is to be prized even above a newborn child in a household. And not only the friends and relatives below, but also the angels looked down from Heaven and rejoiced over you as a repentant sinner. And if it were worth their while to rejoice when you believed, you need not blush to go back and remember that day. Happy have the days since that day when you first became enlisted in the service of your God and Savior, Jesus Christ. When you first left the shores of earth to try and find the new country, the better land, it was a memorable occasion. Dwell on a time a little while and let your soul ring the precious bells of gratitude; bless the Lord that you were not left to perish in your natural unbelief; praise Him that you have been given a new heart to believe in Christ Jesus.

MORNING

Blessed is he whose transgression is forgiven, whose sin is covered — Psalm 32:1.

BLESSED! This Psalm begins with the beatitudes, like the Sermon on the Mount. This is the second Psalm of benediction. The first Psalm describes the result of holy blessedness, the thirty-second details the cause of it. The first pictures the tree in full growth, this depicts it in its first planting and watering. The saint in the first Psalm is a reader of God's Book, here he is a suppliant at God's throne, accepted and heard. He is now blessed — *"Blessed is he whose transgression is forgiven,"* and ever shall be. If he be ever so poor, or sick, or sorrowful, he is yet blessed. Pardoning mercy is of all things in the world the most to be prized, for it is the only sure way to happiness. To hear from God the Spirit the words, "You are absolved" is joy unspeakable. Blessedness is not in this case ascribed to the diligent lawkeeper, for then it would never come to us; but it is to a lawbreaker, one who by grace most rich and free has been forgiven. Self-righteous Pharisees have no portion in this blessedness. Over the returning prodigal the word of welcome is here pronounced; let the music and dancing begin. A full, instantaneous, irreversible pardon of transgression turns the poor sinner's Hell into Heaven; it makes the heir of wrath a partaking of blessing.

The word rendered forgiven is in the original, *'taken off,'* or *'taken away,'* — it is as if a burden has been lifted off, or a barrier removed. What a lift is here! It cost our Savior a sweat of blood to bear our load; yea, it cost Him His life to bear it away. Samson carried the gates of Gaza, but what was that to the weight of sin Jesus bore on our behalf? *"Whose sin is covered:"* covered by God, as the ark was covered by the mercy seat; as Noah was covered from the flood; as the Egyptians were covered by the depths of the sea. What a cover must that be which hides forever all the filthiness of the flesh and the spirit from the sight of an all-seeing God! Anyone who has seen sin in its horrible deformity will appreciate the happiness of seeing it no more forever. Christ's atonement is the propitiation, the covering, the making an end of sin —where this is seen and trusted in, the soul knows itself to be accepted in the Beloved.

EVENING

Make me to hear joy and gladness, that the bones which You have broken may rejoice — Psalm 51:8.

DAVID'S PLIGHT was very painful. He speaks of his bones as being broken. A flesh wound can be painful. But here was a more serious, a more painful injury — as if a bone had been reached and completely crushed. No punishment was more cruelly painful than the breaking of poor wretches alive on the wheel, when a heavy bar of iron smashed the bones of the arms and the legs — surely a most excruciating pain to the last degree. But here David declares that the mental anguish which he endured because of his sin was comparable to such an extreme agony.

The pain of the affliction expressed so feelingly is David's anguish of soul for his sin, accompanied by a glimpse of the consuming fire of God's wrath — the tempest, as Job calls it, of anger. Then there is the pain of setting broken bones again. Though bones are dislocated, they may be set again. Yet this is not done without pain and great extremity to the patient.

Repentance sets all our broken, pained bones. It recovers the soul from the anguish of it. But he that once feels the smart of a true repentance will say that the pleasures of sin are as hard a bargain as ever he made, most dearly bought. They cost tears, the very blood of a wounded heart. They cost sighs and groans which cannot be expressed. They cost watching, fasting, taming of the body, to bring it into subjection; yea, even to the crucifying of the flesh with the lusts of it. For this reason, let no one venture his bones in sin because he has a hope of having them set again by his God" — Samuel Page, from Spurgeon's *Treasury of David*, p. 467.

MORNING

He rebuked the Red Sea also, and it was dried up; so He led them through the depths, as through the wilderness — Psalm 106:9.

THE PANGS after we come out of Egypt are at times even more painful than those we felt in the house of bondage. There usually is a time of trial a little while after the new birth, one which seems more terrible than any previous agony.

The children of Israel had faint hearts at the Red Sea. They no sooner saw the Egyptians than they began to cry out. And when they beheld the Red Sea before them they murmured against God's servants. A faint heart is the worst foe a Christian can have. While his faith is firm, while the anchor is fixed deep in the rock, he need not fear the storm. But when the hand of faith is palsied, or the eye of faith dim, it will go hard with us. We can catch the Egyptian's spear on the shield of faith, not terrified by the weapon. But if we our faith wavers all weapons become deadly darts. While we have strong faith the Red Sea may flow before us as dark and deep as it pleases. But if we have no faith, then the most insignificant stream of trouble causes quivering and crying, though usually faith could take it and drink it all up in a moment. These Israelites were coming out of a downtrodden, faithless state, and confronted with seemingly impossible barriers before and behind, they fell to thinking that slavery was better than this new state of theirs — they wish they had died in Egypt.

When a child of God is first born he has but very little faith because he has had very little experience. He has not tried the promise, and therefore he does not know its faithfulness. He has not used the arm of his faith, and therefore the sinews of it have not yet become strong. Let him live a little longer and he will become confirmed in the faith, as God delivers him again and again. Then he will not fear Red Seas or Egyptians.

EVENING

He rebuked the Red Sea also, and it was dried up; so He led them through the depths, as through the wilderness — Psalm 106:9.

YOUR GREATEST refuge in all your trials, O child of God, is in a Man — not in a Moses, but in Jesus; not in the servant, but in the Master. He is interceding for you, unseen and unheard by you, even as Moses did for the sons of Israel. If you could but catch the sweet syllables of His voice as they distil from His lips; if you could see His heart as He speaks for you, then you would take comfort. For God hears that One when He pleads. He can overcome every difficulty. He does not have a rod, but a cross, which can divide Red Seas. He does not have only a cloudy pillar of forgiving grace, which can dim the eyes of your foes and keep them at a distance; but He has a cross which can open the Red Sea and drown your sins in the very midst. He will not leave you. Look! On yonder rock of Heaven He stands, cross in hand, even as Moses with his rod. Cry to Him, for with His uplifted cross He will make a path for you; He will guide you through all seas. He will make floods of troubles stand apart to allow you to pass through them. Call to Him and He will make a way for you, even paths through pathless seas of afflictions. Cry to Him, and He will sweep all your sins away. Then the king of sin, the Devil, will be overwhelmed beneath the Savior's blood.

Take careful note of God's design in leading the Christian into these exceedingly great trials in the early part of his godly life. This is explained to us by the apostle Paul. Here you will see that a reference Bible is the best commentator in the world, for the most heavenly exposition is the searching out of kindred texts and comparing meanings: *"They were all baptized,"* says the apostle, *"unto Moses in the cloud and in the sea."* God's design in bringing His people into trouble is to give them a thorough baptism into His service, consecrating them forever to Himself.

Now our salvation is nearer than when we believed — Romans 13:11.

WHAT *"salvation"* is this? It is important because we very commonly speak of salvation as that state of grace in which everyone that believes in Jesus is introduced when he passes from spiritual death to life, having been delivered from the power of darkness and translated into the kingdom of God's dear Son.

Salvation, so far as forgiveness of sin, the imputation of righteousness, and the eternal safety of the soul are concerned, is given to us the moment we are brought to trust in Jesus. But here, and in other parts of Scripture, *salvation* signifies that complete deliverance from sin, that glorious perfection which will not be attained by us until the day of the appearing of our Lord and Savior, Jesus Christ. Salvation here signifies entire deliverance from indwelling sin, perfect sanctification. It includes the resurrection of the body and the glorification of the body and soul with Christ Jesus in the world to come. Salvation here means what many think it always implies, namely, eternal glory. At this hour our perfect salvation is nearer than when we first believed.

Observe the date from which the Apostle begins to reckon. He does not say our salvation is nearer than when we were christened. That is a ceremony of which the Apostle never dreamed, a tradition and invention of men which had never crossed his mind. He does not say your salvation is nearer than when you were confirmed. That also was a thing quite unknown to him. He does not reckon even from our baptism; as if he were to say your salvation is nearer than when you put on Christ opening in baptism. No, but he strikes at the vital point; he specifies the true indication for spiritual life, namely, *"belief"* in Christ. What could ever come of all events before believing? It is all death; none of it is worth reckoning.

EVENING

When I kept silence my bones became old through my roaring all the day long. For day and night Your hand was heavy on me — Psalm 32:3,4.

WHEN through neglect I failed to confess, or through despair dared not do so, *my bones became old*, began to decay with weakness, for my grief was so intense as to sap my health and destroy my vital energy. What a killing thing is sin! It is a pestilent disease and a fire in the bones. While we smother sin, it rages within; like a gathering wound it swells horribly and torments terribly. *"Through my roaring all the day long."* He was silent as to confession, but not as to sorrow. Horror at his great guilt drove David to unceasing laments, until his voice was no longer like the articulate speech of man. His sighing and groaning resembled the roaring of a wounded beast. None can know the pangs of conviction like those who have endured them. The rack, the wheel, the flaming fagot are ease compared with the ravages of a guilty conscience. Better suffer all the diseases which the flesh is heir to than to lie under the crushing sense of God's wrath.

"For day and night Your hand was heavy on me." God's finger can crush us. Then what must His be when it presses heavily and continually? Under terrors of conscience men have little rest by night, for the grim thoughts of the day dog them in their bedrooms; their dreams are haunted. Or else they lie awake in a cold sweat of dread. God's hand is very helpful when it uplifts, but it is awful when it presses down. Better a world on your shoulder than God's hand on you heart. David's sap was turned into the drouth of summer. The sap of his soul was dried up, in sympathy his body appeared to be drained of its needful fluids. The oil seems gone from the lamp of his life; its flame flickered as though it would soon expire. Like a fierce poison, unconfessed transgression dries up the fountain of one's strength; it is like a plant withered by scorching heat.

MORNING

A woman of Canaan coming out from those borders cried out to Him, saying, Have mercy on me, O Lord, Son of David! — Matthew 15:22.

JESUS and the seeker have a common attraction. He comes, and she comes. It would have been of no use for her to come from the seacoast of Tyre and Sidon if the Lord Jesus had not also come down to the Israelite border of Phoenicia to meet her. His coming makes her coming a success. What a happy circumstance when Christ meets the sinner, and the sinner meets his Lord!

As the Good Shepherd our Lord Jesus came that way, drawn by the instincts of His heart. He was seeking after lost ones. One was to be found on the borders of Tyre and Sidon. So He must go that way to find that one. It does not appear that He preached, or that He did anything special on the road. He left the ninety and nine by the sea of Galilee to seek that one lost lamb by the Mediterranean shore. Having dealt with her, He went back again to Galilee.

Our Lord was drawn toward this woman, but she was driving toward Him. What made her seek Him? Strange to say, a demon had a hand in it, but not so as to give the demon any of the praise. A gracious God used the demon to drive this woman to Jesus, for her daughter was *"miserably possessed by a demon."* She could not bear to stay at home and see her child in such misery. Oh, how often does a great sorrow drive men and women to Christ, even as a fierce wind compels the mariner to hasten to the harbor! I have known domestic afflictions, a daughter vexed, to influence the heart of a mother to seek the Savior. And no doubt many a father, broken in spirit by the likelihood of losing a darling child, has turned his face toward the Lord Jesus in his distress.

EVENING

But she said, True, O Lord. But even the little dogs eat of the crumbs which fall from the table of their masters. — Matthew 15:27.

IF THE LORD reminds you of your unworthiness and your unfitness, He only tells you what is true. Then it will be your wisdom to say, *"True, O Lord."* Scripture describes you as having a depraved nature, then say, *"True, O Lord."* It describes you as going astray like a lost sheep, and the charge is true. It describes you as having a deceitful heart, and you do have just such a heart. Then say, *"True, O Lord."* It represents you as *"without strength, and without hope."* Let your answer to this be, *"True, O Lord."* The Bible never gives unrenewed human nature a good word, nor does it deserve it (Rom. 1:10). It exposes our corruptions; it lays bare our falseness, pride and unbelief. Do not cavil at the faithfulness of the Word. Take the lowest place and own yourself a sinner that is lost, ruined and undone.

If the Scripture should seem to disgrace you, do not become resentful, but feel that it deals honestly with you. Never let proud nature contradict the Lord, for this is to increase your sin. This woman took the very lowest possible place. She not only admitted that she was like one of the little dogs, but she put herself under the table, and under the children's table, rather than under the master's table. She said, *"The dogs eat of the crumbs which fall from their masters' table."* Most of you have supposed that she referred to the crumbs of the master of the house himself. If you will look at the passage you will see that it is not so. *"Their masters"* refers to several masters. The word is plural; it refers to the children who were the little masters of the little dogs. So she humbled herself to be not only as a dog to the Lord, but as a dog to the house of Israel.

Make me hear joy and gladness, that the bones which You have broken may rejoice
— Psalm 51:8.

WE HEAR persons speak very flippantly of David's sin, boldly offering it as an accusation against godliness, and as an excuse for their own sinful way of living. Let these look also at David's repentance. For if his sin was shameful, his sorrow for it was of the bitterest kind. If the crime was glaring, certainly the afflictions which chastised him were equally remarkable. From that day forward this man, whose ways had been ways of pleasantness, and whose paths had been paths of peace, limped like a cripple along a thorny road. He traversed a pilgrimage of afflictions almost unparalleled. Children of God cannot sin cheaply. Sinners may sin, and this life may seem to prosper — even sometimes seeming to prosper from their sins — but those whom God loves will always find the way of transgression to be exceedingly hard. Their follies will cost them peace of mind, cost them their present comfort; yea, it will cost them all but their souls. David had sinned, and for awhile the sin was pleasurable. All the attendant circumstances appeared to be favorable to his escape from punishment. He had managed adroitly to conceal his crime from the injured Uriah. Then he had with horrible craftiness effected the death of the injured husband. Every circumstance in providence seemed to favor the concealment of the monarch's sin. His conscience was curbed, his passions rioted, his heart was estranged, his grace was at the lowest ebb. He may even have tried to persuade himself that he had an excuse for his behavior. According to Oriental notions he had almost absolute power over the persons of his subjects. It is so easy to persuade ourselves that what custom concedes to us, it is right to take. But because David was a man after God's own heart, his ease in sin did not long continue.

EVENING

Make me hear joy and gladness, that the bones which You have broken may rejoice
— Psalm 51:8.

THE CASE of David was most damaging. Supposing the danger of crippling is past, yet a broken bone is never a gain; it is always a loss. Poor man! While his bone is broken he is quite unable to help himself, much less help others. This drags down the strength of the church of God. Power which might otherwise be employed then has to be turned into the channel of aiding the damaged one. The power of the Christian church ought to be expended mainly in seeking lost souls, and in feeding the sheep. Just one backsliding believer can damage the whole church. Also, while such a one is in that state he can do no good to others. Of what service can he be who does not know his own salvation? How can one point others to the Savior when he cannot see clearly His cross? How shall he comfort another man's faith while his own faith can scarcely touch the hem of Jesus' garment? By what energy and power can he help the weak when he himself is so weak? Even after God in His mercy has healed every broken bone, it is a sad detriment to one to have had his bones weakened by a break. There will never be the same freedom of action and degree of energy in the healed limb as was there before.
It is a great blessing for the cripple to be helped to walk with a crutch, but it is a greater blessing never to have been a cripple. It is an unspeakable blessing to have been able always to run without weariness and to walk without fainting. When one's bone has been broken in childhood, it being ever so well set, yet it will feel starts and shocks unknown before — unpleasant reminders of the break appear, such as feeling them when the weather changes. So it is with us. If we have fallen into a sin, even though we have been recovered from its immediate sorrow, there is a weakness left, a tendency to pain.

July 7   MORNING

Make me hear joy and gladness, that the bones which You have broken may rejoice
— Psalm 51:8.

    Broken bones can end fatally. Around each shattered bone there lingers the evil spirit of gangrene. If that develops, then the healing art is taxed severely — there will be a loss, perhaps of a limb, perhaps of the life. So with the broken bones of the spirit: when a heart is broken with repentance, the gangrene of remorse urgently seeks to enter it. When the spirit is humbled, the gangrene of unbelief covets the opportunity to take possession. When the heart is really emptied, made to feel its own nothingness, then the demon despair beholds a dark cavern in which it may fix its horrible abode. It is a dreadful thing to have the faith broken, the hope broken, the love broken. Then the entire man, as it were, may be reduced to a palpitating mass of pain.
    It is a dreadfully dangerous condition to be in. For, alas! When men have sinned, and have been made to suffer afterwards, how often have they turned to their sins again with greater hardness of heart than ever! With many, the more they are smitten the more they revolt. When the whole head is sick, and the whole heart is faint, and they seem to be nothing but *"wounds and bruises and putrifying sores,"* through the afflictions they have suffered, yet they return to their idols still. Some, the more they are chastened the more they revolt. Think how many professors have backslidden and have been chastened, but have continued in their sins until they have slidden down into Hell. These are not children of God, but professors to be such. My friends, if you are living in known sin at this time, and think yourselves happy in it, then you have great cause to tremble. If you can go on from day to day, from week to week, in neglected prayer and neglected reading of the Word, then you have grave cause to suspect that you are not one of the true children of the living God.

EVENING

Make me hear joy and gladness, that the bones which You have broken may rejoice
— Psalm 51:8.

    THE JOY which the psalmist expected would have much of God in it, for you observe that the Lord appears in this verse twice: *"He breaks the bones, and He makes the ear to hear joy and gladness."* God is appealed to as the breaker, and as the healer. After having been sorely smitten, and having at last found comfort, we always think more of our Lord Jesus than we did before. There may be times when you think that this doctrine or that is the first and most important thing. Then there may be times when you conceive that inward experience is to be the most important thing. But over and above all there must be for the soul a deep sense of God, longing to be in daily personal fellowship witht he Father, and with His Son, Jesus Christ. Surely this being filled with God is a more excellent way. For doctrine may be but food untasted, and experience may turn out to be but fancy. But to live on God by faith, and to serve Christ with the heart, and to feel the Holy Spirit's indwelling — this is reality and truth. When one has such dealings with God as David had, and has received such mercy from Him, then his joy will be fuller of God than it ever was before.
    You will notice in this verse, too, that David sets no end whatever to his joy: *"The bones which you have broken may rejoice,"* but how long? Oh, as long as ever they please. Once let the bone be set, the ground of joy is constant and continuous. A pardoned sinner never need pause in his sacred gratitude; he rejoices always. Let the Lord visit the most brokenhearted among His people, and light their candle, then the Devil cannot blow it out; no, nor can death quench the sacred flame kindled within.

And when they came to Marah, they could not drink of the waters of Marah, because they were bitter. So the name of it was called Marah — Exodus 15:23.

THE PEOPLE murmured against Moses, saying, *"What shall we drink?"* Do not say it was "human nature," or "the tendency of Jewish nature." But rest assured that they were no worse than we are. They are an example to us of what our heart is. Whatever we see in them we shall see it all in ourselves if we watch a little. It was human nature at its best estate that God was testing in the wilderness. Assuredly, the tendency of us all is to murmur. They murmured and complained, finding fault. How simple it is! The very word murmur is made up of two infantile sounds — *mur mur*. There is no sense in it, no wit in it, no thought in it. It is rather the cry of the brute than of a man. It is easy for us to kick against the dispensations of God, to give utterance to our griefs. And what is worse, it is all too easy for us to infer from them that God has forgotten to be gracious. To murmur is our tendency, but will we allow the tendencies of the old nature to rule us? Will we murmur? O that we might have grace rather to say with Job, *"Though He slay me, yet will I trust in Him."* Shall *a living man complain?* Have we not received so much good from the hands of the Lord that we may well receive troubles without rebelling against Him? Will we not rather disappoint Satan by overruling the tendency of the flesh, by saying in the might of God's Spirit, *"The Lord gave, and the Lord has taken away; blessed be the name of the Lord"*? (Job. 1:21). It is not enough to merely say, "human nature;" for saying it is but an attempt to make excuse for our murmuring. But shall we stand still and allow our human nature overrule the Divine nature that is in us?

EVENING

One thing I have desired from the Lord; that I will seek after — that I may dwell in the house of the Lord all the days of my life, to behold the beauty of the Lord, and to pray in His temple — Psalm 27:4.

"ONE THING" — divided aims in us tend to distraction, weakness and disappointment in us. The man of one book is eminent, the man of one pursuit is successful. Let all our affection be bound up in one affection, and that affection set on heavenly things. What we cannot at once attain, it is well to desire. God judges us very much by the desire of our hearts. There is no blame to one for lack of speech if he rides a lame horse; if he makes all the haste he can, and if he would make more if he could. God takes the will for the deed with His children. *"From the Lord* — this is the right target for our desires; this is the well into which we must dip our buckets; this is the door to knock at, the bank to draw from. If we desire of men, then we will lie on the dunghill with Lazarus. If we desire of the Lord, then we will be carried by angels into Abraham's bosom. Our desires of the Lord should be sanctified, humble, constant, submissive, fervent, and with the Psalmist let them be molded into one mass. Under David's painful circumstances we might have expected him to desire repose, safety, and a thousand other things. No, he has set his heart on this: to dwell in the house of the lord all his days.

Holy desires must lead to resolute action. "Wishing never fills a sack" — desires are seeds which must be sown in the good soil of activity, else they will yield no harvest. Unless followed up by practical endeavors we shall find our desires to be like clouds without rain. David longed to dwell always in the house of the Lord for the sake of communion with Him. He desired above all things to be one of the household of God, a home-born child living at home with his Father. This is our dearest wish, extending it to those days of our life of immortality yet to dawn. Let us pine for our Father's house above, our soul's home. If we are to dwell there forever, why desire anything of this life?

July 9 MORNING

And he cried to the Lord. And the Lord showed him a tree. And when he had thrown it into the waters, the waters were made sweet — Exodus 15:25.

AS SOON AS we have a prayer, God has a remedy. The remedy is at hand, but we do not perceive it until it is shown to us. The tree the Lord showed Moses had been growing for years; its purpose to be used here. God has preordained a remedy for all our troubles long before they happen to us. A delightful is to contemplate how long before we meet with a bitter well will there be available a healing tree. All is ready between here and Heaven. He that has gone to prepare a place for us there is the One who has prepared a remedy for us in every case by His providence.

But although there is a remedy for every trouble in this mortal life, you and I do not always discern it. For every lock in Doubting Castle there is a key, but it is in the promises, and there is often great confusion in our minds. If a locksmith should bring you his great bundle of picklocks, you would not know which to use on which lock. You may perhaps go through two-thirds of them before you find the right one. The right one may even be the last one. It is always a blessing to remember that for every affliction there is a promise in the Word of God; it will be a promise which meets the case, one made on purpose for it. But you must find it. You may go fumbling over the Scriptures long before you discover it. But when the Lord shows it to you, when it comes with power to your soul, when your heart can grasp it, then indeed it is such a precious truth as will sweeten your sad discomforts. Oh, what a bliss this is! All glory be to God the Holy Spirit who to this day is ever ready to show to His praying and searching servants the sweetening tree of promise when they come to their bitter streams!

EVENING

They sang His praise — they soon forgot His works — Psalm 106:12, 13.

THE ISRAELITES began with rapturous expression of gratitude to God for their deliverance from Egypt, only to end with murmurs of discontent — both uttered by the same lips. Unhappily, the Israelites are by no means the only persons of whom this may truly be said. Their conduct affords a striking example of that spurious gratitude which often flashes forth when dreaded evils are averted, or unexpected favors given. These expire with the occasion that gave birth to it. Such is like the joy excited in an infant's breast by the gift of some glittering toy — it is received with glee, but it pleases but an hour. When the charm of novelty vanishes, it is thrown aside with indifference. Springing from no higher principle than gratified self-love, it is neither acceptable to God, nor productive of obedience to His laws. Nor does it in any respect resemble that holy, Heaven-born affection whose language it often borrows, and whose name it assumes. It may be called distinctively 'the gratitude of sinners.' Sinners love those that love them, and of course will be grateful to those that are kind to them; even grateful to God when they view Him as being kind to them. But the feeling is usually transient, and the acknowledgement is forgotton almost as soon as it is made.

Alas! How unproductive of salutary effects have all these emotions proved! Appetite and passion, though hushed for a moment, soon renew their importunities. The glitter of wealth and distinction and power soon eclipse the glories of Jehovah in unrenewed hearts. Such sink from the Heaven toward which they seemed to be rising, to plunge afresh into the vortex of earthly pleasures and pursuits. We are all too apt to neglect and disobey Him whom we seemed to adore. Without the inworking of God upon our hearts we will soon again be content to live without Him, without that world which we had just glimpsed as being full of glory. —from a sermon by Edward Payson.

Bless the Lord, O my soul, all that is within me bless His holy name — Psalm 102:1.

O HOW WELL fitted are the soul and blessing. Who so fit for this work as my soul? God knows that my body is gross and heavy, very unfit for so sublime a work. No, my soul is what must do it. And indeed what else has it to do? It is the very work for which it was made. O that my soul were as fit to do the work as the work is fit for it to do! But, alas! It in a manner has become earthy; at least it has lost a great part of its abilities; it will never be able to go through with this great work by itself. If to bless the Lord were no more but to say, *Lord, Lord,* like those who cried, *The temple of the Lord; the temple of the Lord!* — then my tongue along would be sufficient for blessing; then I would not need to trouble any other about it. But to bless the Lord is an eminent work; it requires not only many agents, but very able ones to perform it. For this reason *"all that is within me"* — whether my heart, my spirits, my will, my affections, my understanding, my memory — all must be engaged to bless the lord. (Sir R. Baker).

"All that is within me" — the literal translation of the form here used is *"all my inward parts,"* the strong and comprehensive meaning of the plural being further enhanced by the addition of all, as if to preclude exception and reserve, to comprehend within the scope of the address all the powers and affections. (from the commentary by J. A. Alexander).

"The well is seldom so full that water will at first pumping flow forth. Neither is the heart commonly so spiritual as to pour itself into God's bosom freely, without something to elevate it. Often the springs of grace lie so low that pumping only will not fetch the heart up to a praying frame, but arguments must be poured into the soul before the affections rise. David either found or feared his heart would not be in so good a frame as he desired; consequently he redoubles his charge. He found his heart somewhat drowsy, which made him thus rouse himself. (William Gurnall)

EVENING

Bless the Lord, O my soul — Psalm 103:22.

LET YOUR soul enter on the life of Heaven, where its praise will not cease. Why should I praise Him? Can my praise be any advantage to Him? No, nor that of the heavenly hosts. It is infinite condescension in Him to hear the praises of creatures.

My soul will bless the Lord because no function will be more rich in blessings to it than this. The admiring contemplation of His excellence is in reality the appropriation of it; for the heart cannot delight in God without becoming like God. It is the peculiar privilege of renewed man to bless the Lord. My soul can bless the Lord because it is fully furnished with the materials of praise. Not only the sands, the seas, the flowers, the animals, the fields, the trees, the stars, etc. wait for me to translate their attributes and distinctions into praise, but above all the new creation demands the soul's blessing.

Let my soul bless Him. For because of Him, through Him, and to Him, are all things that pertain to my existence, health, comfort, knowledge, dignity, safety, power and usefulness. The breath that I am commanded and enabled to modulate into praise is mine only because of His condescension, kindness, wisdom, power and presence. Is it not dastardly to be receiving such benefits without even mentioning the name, or describing the goodness of the Giver? Let candidates for Heaven bless the Lord. There is no place in Heaven for such as have not learned the art of praising the Lord.

How shall I praise Him? Not with fine words. No poetic talent is necessary here. Any language that will express heart-felt admiration will be accepted. Praise Him so far as you know Him. Then He will make known to you more of His glory. (George Bowen)

July 11   MORNING

For many in the congregation were not sanctified. Therefore the Levites had the charge of killing the passovers for everyone not clean, to sanctify them to the Lord — 2 Chronicles 30:17.

IT SHOULD BE much to our joy that we do not serve under the ceremonial law, nor live within the legal dispensation. The legal economy exhibited to the people a multitude of types and figures, and consequently it laid down many rules and rituals; and these were enacted with such solemn and terrible penalties that the people were in constant fear of offending, and found obedience irksome by reason of the weakness of their flesh and the unspirituality of their minds. As for our Lord Jesus, His yoke is easy and His burden is light. But concerning the law, even Peter speaks of it as *"a yoke which neither our fathers nor we were able to bear."* We are now brought into the glorious liberty of the children of God, a liberty which those who had been in the bondage could best appreciate. Those who are still under legal restrictions feel the pressure of them when they see the liberty of others. Sitting at dinner with a Samaritan who considered himself under the law of the Pentateuch, I noticed that the worthy man refused first one dish and then another. At length he exclaimed, "Moses, very hard," evidently feeling that the limit on his diet involved a good deal of self-denial. Some of us could cheerfully bear such small matters as abstinence from certain meats and drinks. But if we were surrounded with regulations and prescriptions entering into minute details, our life would be full of care, and we would feel ill at ease.

We have attained the liberty of the gospel, and we are not called on to observe days, and months, and years; nor to border our garments with a certain color, nor to trim our hair by rule; neither are we called to practice various washings and purifyings, or to observe laws and regulations amounting to a continual round of rites.

EVENING

Then stand firm in the freedom with which Christ has made us free. And do not be held again in the yoke of slavery — Galatians 5:1.

THE FREE SPIRIT dwells in us. To us every place is hallowed; our religion is not of the outward, and in the matter of meats we call nothing common or unclean. We have ordinances, it is true, but they are few and simple. They are but two, and each of them is instructive and easy. Baptism and the Supper of the Lord, which are for the Lord's people only, are easy to observe, and are for our help and comfort; they are by no means burdensome. These are not laid on us as yokes, but given to us as privileges. Neither are they enforced by such a sentence as this, *'The soul that forbears to keep the passover shall be cut off from among his people."* Gospel ordinances are choice enjoyments, enjoined on us by the loving rule of Him whom we call Master and Lord. We accept them with joy and delight. In keeping these commandments there is great reward; but they are not presented to us as matters of servitude.

In baptism we are made to see the burial of our Lord, and are helped to enter into spiritual fellowship with Him by it. This is not a burdensome ordinance, but a delight. The Lord's own Supper is a joyful festival, a feast of fat things, of fat things full of marrow, of wines on the lees well refined. All is joy and rest about these two ordinances. In enjoying them we feel that we are not under law, but under grace. I would not have you come to this table with the same trembling with which an Israelite ate the passover, or stand there as the Israelite did, with your loins girded and your staff in your hand, eating in haste and apprehension. No, but you may sit at ease, or even recline, to express the rest which you enjoy at the Lord's table, and the close communion to which your Redeemer invites you. He has called you His friends, and He has honored you to be His table companions, to sit and feast with Him.

Then stand firm in the freedom with which Christ has made us free. And do not be held again in the yoke of slavery — Galatians 5:1.

THAT LIBERTY not degenerate into license, we are not left without command and direction. The law of love is as binding on us as ever the law of works could have been. We are still called to obedience — the obedience of faith. A most strict, but most happy, service grows out of sonship, and no true child of God wishes to disown it. Should not the child honor the father? Does not the Lord Himself say, *"If I am a Father, where is My honor?"* There is a service of which we read, that God spares such a one *"as a man spares his own son that serves him."* We are not under the Law, but yet we are not without law to Christ. Concerning these ordinances which I have described as the privilege of the Lord's free people, there is an order of the Lord's house, and a discipline of His family, which must by no means be set aside by the loving child. We are not slaves fearing the lash, but we are children who have a filial fear of grieving our heavenly Father.

The rules concerning the passover, and the right keeping of that high festival, were plain and definite. To break them would have been a great offense to the God of Israel. These rules required a certain ceremonial cleanness on the part of all who partook of the Paschal lamb, and those who were defiled were kept back, so that they could not present the offering of the Lord in its appointed season. The sacred rite was not to be celebrated in heedless formalism, but with a careful cleansing out of the old leaven, that they might keep the feast correctly. Now, concerning the memorial of the Lord's Supper, we have no rubric as to the bread or the wine, and no prescribed regulation as to posture or manner of procedure. Yet there are certain notes of guidance which we shall do well to follow with loving care.

EVENING

And the Lord listened to Hezekiah and healed the people. And the sons of Israel who were present at Jerusalem kept the feasts of unleavened bread seven days with great gladness — 2 Chronicles 30:20,21.

THERE WAS great gladness in Israel, even among the men of Ephraim who were not ceremonially fit to keep the passover. Following this there was great praise to God. They continued singing to the Lord all the day. The Levites and the priests and the people joined with them, and they brought forth loud instruments to add to the volume of their music. Notice the words, *"singing with loud instruments of the Lord."* They employed everything by which to express their overflowing gratitude, their glowing joy. May the Lord's servants fetch out their loud instruments to sing to Him who loved us and gave Himself for us! Let us lift up the song, *"Worthy is the Lamb, for You were slain, and have redeemed us to God by Your blood. You shall reign forever and ever, King of kings, and Lord of lords. Unto Your name be hallelujahs throughout eternity."* Oh for cymbals, the high-sounding cymbals, that we might express something of the overpowering joy of our spirit with their mighty clash, before the living God!

These were the very people who kept the passover, *"not according as it was written."* They came ill-prepared, unpurified, utterly unfit, but God blessed them and helped them to get ready for the holy feast then and there. He will do so now for those who desire it. How much I long that all of you Christians — even you half-asleep Christians, lukewarm Christians of a doubtful sort, Christians whose right to commune is gravely questioned by yourselves — that you may be quickened suddenly by the Holy Spirit. For He is still in the midst of the church, that you may at once delight yourselves in the Lord, that you may feel a holy nearness to Christ, and a heavenly exhilaration at the mention of His name. So will you, with all of us, eagerly praise the Beloved of your soul, bidding all that is within you to bless His holy name.

MORNING — July 13

But let a man examine himself, then let him eat of the bread and let him drink of the cup in this way — 1 Corinthians 11:28.

FOR MANY reasons the choicest saints at times think themselves disqualified for the Lord's Supper. And that is not altogether an ill feeling; at any rate it is a symptom of many healthy things. If I felt myself worthy in any sense, except the Scriptural one, I would infer from my self-satisfaction that I was unworthy. The Lord's table is no place for Pharisees. Where the Savior presides, there may come none but sinners saved by His grace. If you imagine you have merits of your own of which you can boast, and no sin to confess, you are not the man for whose salvation Christ as Substitute has shed His precious blood. How could He atone for those who have no fault? But if you are a sinner, you are the sort of person whom Jesus came to save. Jesus is the friend of those who see themselves as sinners. He will be yours if you go to Him in that mind. How can we commemorate the shedding of His blood unless we daily feel that we have need to be washed in it? How can we remember Him except as we see how we derive all from Him? Jesus is never seen to be a full Christ except by those who feel their own emptiness apart from Him. He is never prized at true value by those who have a high esteem of themselves. A broken heart knows best His power to comfort. A bleeding heart sees best His power to heal. If you are sensible of your unworthiness, you are not unworthy in the Scriptural sense — you may freely come. The holiest seasons are when the heart lies low before the Lord. No communion is more intensely sweet than that which washes His feet with tears and covers them with kisses of penitential love. When I have been most ashamed, my Lord has been most glorious in my eyes. When I have covered my face in shame, He has in love uncovered His own countenance.

EVENING

Many in the assembly had not sanctified themselves, and the Levites were over the killing of the passover for everyone who was not clean to sanctify to Jehovah — 2 Chronicles 30:17.

WHEN the tribes assembled they removed the idols. They took the altars in Jerusalem and threw them into the brook Kidron. This was a fine beginning for men who did not feel quite up to the mark. Come, let us cast down our altars of creature worship, cut down the groves of carnal confidence, and break up the graven images of unholy love. Now open your heart to Jesus and give to Him all your love. He is worthy of this, and much more.

Young man, do you have any ambitions that are apart from Christ's glory? Break them now, as with a sledge hammer. Christian, do you have any glory apart from the cross of Jesus? At this moment crucify it. Nail your glory to His cross and be done with it. Christian woman, is there any love of yours that is alien to the love of Christ? Do you have any secret delight which you could not expose to His view? Is there any alabaster vial which you would not cheerfully break for Him? Come, cast away all idols. You cannot keep the feast correctly until at least this is done. Doing this you may observe it with gladness. Oh how I love to hear the breaker's hammer going! Can it not be done at once? Unless those idols have been so long set up in your heart that there is a question whether you love the Lord at all, they will readily fall from their pedestals. If you love Jesus your spirit will make your hand quick at this sacred smashing of idols, until you have broken down every image which now defiles the temple of your soul.

Having done that, those who were not all that they desired to be, yet sought to prepare their hearts, and *"Hezekiah prayed for them, saying, O good Jehovah, provide atonement for everyone not clean, to cleanse them to Jehovah."* Do you long to seek God today? Then there is access to Him for you.

MORNING

And the sons of Israel who were present at Jerusalem kept the feast of unleavened bread seven days with great gladness — 2 Chronicles 30:21.

GOD'S ways of acting are the same in all ages. If Hezekiah and his people received the blessing and *"praised the Lord day by day, singing with loud instruments to the Lord,"* then we may look for the same joy and holy exultation. They *"kept the feast of unleavened bread seven days with great gladness."* Beloved, you, too, can enter into that great gladness. If there is any place where we are bound to be glad, it is at the Lord's Supper. Remember, it is no funeral feast. It is no memorial of one who lies rotting in the grave. Here we remember that Jesus died, but we also hear those prophetic words, *"Until I come."* He lives! And He will shortly come with all the glory and majesty of Heaven to claim His own, and to judge the nations in equity. Because of this we have joy as we come to the table. It is a memorial of a death by which life was purchased for myriads. It is the memorial of a great struggle which ended in the most glorious of victories. *"It is finished,"* is the banner which waves over us. Such a victory is a joy forever; let it be gladly commemorated. Here we celebrate the feast of pardoning love delighting itself in being enabled justly to spare the guilty. Here is the feast of redeemed slaves, the jubilee of emancipation from everlasting bondage. We come as those that are alive from the dead, to feast to Him and with Him. In very truth He was slain, but He has risen again and has become our life and our joy. Oh, for a well-tuned harp! **Bring an instrument of ten strings and the psaltery. Let every string be awakened** to ecstasy on behalf of Jesus, to set forth in worthy notes His passion and His triumph.

EVENING

For many in the congregation were not sanctified — 2 Chronicles 30:17.

SOME SUPPOSED disqualifications for coming to the table of the Lord may be removed by an act of faith, or by a fuller knowledge. Do you fear to come because you have such little faith? May not the little children have their supper as well as the grown-up sons? Are not these precisely the members of the family who need to be fed and comforted? The utter absence of faith would shut you out, but not the feebleness of your faith. Come little one; to you I say, *"Come in, blessed of the Lord; why do you stand outside?"*

Do you hesitate because your joy is not now overflowing? Is this a sufficient reason for refusing to obey the command, *"This do in remembrance of Me"*? Were the Twelve full of joy at the first feast? Had they no questioning, saying, *"Lord, is it I?"* May not the feast itself furnish the joy? Is not the Lord of the feast your exceeding joy? If you cannot bring joy with you, then come, that you may find it here.

Do you say, I am spiritually weak in all points? Is that a reason why you should not feed on the best of food? It is rather a chief reason why you should feed often, and heartily. To eat that which is good is a safe prescription for you, and it is a generous invitation from your Lord. Greatly you need it; therefore freely take it. The supply of heavenly bread is intended for those who are faint — *"He has filled the hungry with good things"* — He will fill you who ask it in faith.

Do you complain that you feel so useless? This is a deplorable fact, but what has it to do with the matter in hand? Are you to come to the Lord's table because you are useful to Him? No! It is that the Lord may be useful to you. Surely this is not a wage; it is a provision of free grace. You do not bring the feast; you part is to receive it. So only can you become useful to Christ as Christ is abundantly useful to you.

July 15   MORNING

For the Scripture says, Everyone who believes on Him shall not be ashamed" — Romans 10:11.

WHAT IS believing on Him? It is trusting in Him. The language is not, "Believe Him," — such belief is a part of faith, but not the whole. We believe everything which the Lord Jesus has taught us, but we must go a step further, and trust Him. It is not even enough to believe in Him as being the Son of God, and the anointed of the Lord. But we must believe ON Him, just as in building (for that is the figure used by Isaiah) the builder takes his stone and lays it ON the foundation. There it rests with all its weight. The faith that saves is not the believing of certain truths — not even believing that Jesus is a Savior — but it is to rest ON Him, to depend ON Him, to lie with all your weight on Christ as the foundation of your hope. Believe that He can save you; believe that He WILL save you; in everything leave the whole matter of your salvation with Him in unquestioning confidence. Depend on Him without fear as to your present and eternal salvation. This is the faith which saves the soul.

This faith is believing on a Person:*"He that believes on Him"* — not on *it*, but *Him*. Our Lord Jesus Christ is God; He is also man. He is the appointed and anointed Savior. In His death He is the propitiation for sin; in His resurrection He is the justification of His people; and in His intercession he is the eternal guarantee of their preservation. Believe *on Him*. Our faith fixes on the Person of the Lord Jesus as seen in His sufferings, in His offices, and in His achievements.

The text refers to the truth of those who trust. The Apostle does not say, "Whoever believes on Him with full assurance, or with a high degree of confidence, shall not be ashamed." No, it is not the measure of faith, but the sincerity of our faith.

EVENING

Everyone who believes on Him shall not be ashamed — Romans 10:11.

THE HOLY SPIRIT'S reading of His Word in the Old Testament is, *"He shall not be ashamed."* And this means that he shall not be ashamed at any time by discovering that he has been deluded. Men are ashamed when their hopes fail. If a man has an expectation of eternal life, and suddenly he sees his hope dashed, is he not ashamed? If on his dying bed his confidence should turn out to be based on a falsehood, how ashamed he will be! He will then say, "I am ashamed to think I did not take more care. I am ashamed that I followed my own judgment instead of God's Word." They shall lie down in sorrow who find their hope to be as a spider's web. It will be an awful thing in our last moments when we most need comfort, if we are driven by despair caused by the wreck of our confidence. If any of you are trusting in your gold, it will turn out to be a poor trust when you are called to leave all earthly things.

There was one who, on his deathbed, laid bags of money to his heart. But he was forced to lay them away, and to cry, "These will not do!" It will be a sorry business if we have been trusting our good temper, or our charity, our patriotism, our courage, or our honesty. When we come to die we shall be made to feel that these cannot satisfy the claims of Divine justice, or give us a passport to Heaven. How sad to see supposed robes of righteousness turn to rags, and comeliness into corruption! How wretched to regard one's self as covered with a garment fit for Christ's wedding feast, and then to wake out of that dream and find one's self naked! You will never have this vexation of spirit if you take Christ Jesus to be your confidence. So far from being ashamed, you will glory in the crucified Savior; you will vow with Paul, *"God forbid that I should glory, save in the cross of our Lord Jesus Christ."*

MORNING

But let all who put their trust in You rejoice. Let them always shout for joy, because You defend them. And let those who love Your name be joyful in You — Psalm 5:11.

THIS JOY IS TO BE UNIVERSAL to all who trust. This is not only to the spiritually healthy, but for those who are spiritually sickly. It is not only for the successful, but also for the disappointed. It is not only for those who have the bird in hand, but also for those who only see it in the bush. Let all rejoice! If you have only a little faith, yet you are trusting in the Lord, and you have a right to joy. It may be your joy will not rise so high as it might do if your faith were greater. Still, where faith is true it will give sure ground for joy. O you babes in grace, you little children, you that have been newly converted, you who sadly feel your feebleness, yet you, too, can rejoice. For the Lord will bless those who fear Him, *"both small and great"! "Fear not, worm Jacob" — "Fear not, little flock."* There is joy which is as milk to nourish babies, a joy which is not as meat with bones in it. For the Lord adds no sorrow with it. The little ones of the flock need not yet to know the deep things of God to rejoice, for there is joy in the simple truths where the lambs are safely wading. The joy of the Lord is softened down to feeble constitutions, that it not overpower them. The same great sea which floods vast bays also flows into the tiny creeks.

"Let all who put their trust in You rejoice" — you, Miss Much-afraid, you are to rejoice! You, Mr. Despondency, hardly daring to look up, you must yet learn to sing. As for Mr. Ready-to-halt, he must dance on his crutches, and Mr. Feeble-mind must play the music for him. It is the mind of the Holy Spirit that those who trust in the Lord should rejoice before Him. This joy is to be as constant as to time as it is universal as to persons — *"Let them always shout for joy."*

EVENING

But let all who put their trust in You rejoice. Let them always shout for joy, because You defend them. And let those who love Your name be joyful in You — Psalm 5:11.

LET YOUR JOY be manifested — *"Let them always SHOUT for joy."* Shouting is an enthusiastic utterance. It is a method which men use when they have won a victory, when they divide the spoil, when they beat home the harvest, when they tread the vintage, when they drain the goblet. Believers, you may shout for joy with unreserved delight. Some religionists shout (and we would not wish to stop them), but we do wish that certain ones of them knew better what they are shouting about. Since you know whom you have believed, and what you have believed, and what are the deep sources of your joy, you need not be sobered by your knowledge so as to become dumb. Yea, rather, imitate the children of the temple, who, if they knew little, loved much, and so they shouted in praise of Him they loved. A touch of enthusiam would be the salvation of many a man's religion. Some Christians are good enough people, but they are like wax candles which have not been lighted. Oh, for a touch of flame! Then they would scatter light, and so become of service to their families.

"Let them always shout for joy." Why not? Let not orderly folks object. The shouting need not always be done in a public service, or it might seem to hinder devout hearing. But there are times and places where a glorious outburst of enthusiastic joy would quicken life in all around. The ungodly are not half so restrained in their blasphemy as we are in our praise. How is this? They go home making night hideous with their yells. Are we never to have an outbreak of consecrated delight? Yes, we will have our high days and holidays, and we will sing and shout for joy until the heathen must say, *"The Lord has done great things for them."*

July 17 — MORNING

But let all who put their trust in You rejoice. Let them always shout for joy, because You defend them. And let those who love Your name be joyful in You — Psalm 5:11.

HAPPINESS IS A THING of the heart. For the text says, *"Let those who love Your name be joyful in You."* You who love God, can you not say, *"Lord, You know all things; You know that I love You"* (John 21:17). Is it not a very happy emotion? What is sweeter than to say even with tears in one's eyes, *"My God, I love You."* To sit down and having nothing to ask for, no words to utter, but only for the soul to love — is this not heavenly? Measureless depths of unutterable love are in the soul, and in those depths we find the pearl of joy. When the heart is taken up with so delightful an object as the ever-blessed God, it then feels an intensity of joy which cannot be rivaled. When our whole being is steeped in adoring love, then Heaven comes streaming down and we rejoice *"with joy unspeakable and full of glory"* (1 Peter 1:8). Truly the richest things which are enjoyed by saintly believers is unspeakable. Many of you know of such joy. But my soul even now magnifies the Lord Jesus Christ, and my spirit rejoices in God my Savior. Have a great sympathy for this text, be *"glad in the Lord."* If you sit before the Lord at this time, and if you indulge your souls with an outflow of love to God the Father and God the Son, Jesus Christ, and at the same time if you perceive an inflowing of heavenly joy, it will not much matter how a poor preacher speaks to your ear. For if such is the case with you, the Lord Himself will be heard in your soul; Heaven will flood your being. The believer's joy arises from the God in whom He trusts. When, after many a weary wandering, the dove of your soul has at last come back to the ark, and Noah has put out his hand and pulled her in to him, then the poor, weary creature is bound to be happy.

EVENING

But let all who put their trust in You rejoice. Let them always shout for joy, because You defend them. And let those who love Your name be joyful in You — Psalm 5:11.

OUR JOY ARISES from what the Lord does for us. *"Let them always shout for joy,"* because You, O Lord, defend them. God always guards His people. Whoever may attack them, the Lord is their keeper. Angels are our guardians, providence is our protector, but it is God Himself who is the preserver of His chosen ones. *"You shall not be afraid for the terror by night; nor for the arrow that flies by day; nor for the pestilence that walks in darkness; not for the destruction that wastes at noonday."* No fortress guards the soldier as well as God guards His redeemed ones. The God of our salvation will defend us from all evil. He will defend our souls, *"although a host should encamp against me, my heart shall not fear; although war should rise against me, in this will I be confident"* (Psalm 27:3).

Further, our joy arises out of the love we have toward our God. The more you love God, the more you will delight in Him. It is the profusion of a mother's love to her child which makes her take such delight in it. Her child is her joy because of her love. If we loved Jesus better, we would be happier in Him. Perhaps you do not see the connection between the two things. But there is a connection so intimate, that little love brings little joy in Christ, and that great love to Christ brings great joy in Christ — God grant that we may know this full joy in Christ. Do you see it? When a man comes to God in Christ and says, "This Savior is my Savior; this Father is my Father; this God is my God forever and ever," then that one has everything, and the will be joyful. Such a one has no fear about the past, for God has forgiven him; there is no distress about the present, for the Lord is with him; there is no fear of the future, for the Lord has said, *"I will never leave you nor forsake you."*

MORNING

But let all who put their trust in You rejoice. Let them always shout for joy, because You defend them. And let those who love Your name be joyful in You — Psalm 5:11.

FAITH MAKES joyful discoveries — you who have faith will recognize this. When you first believed in Christ you found that you were saved; you knew that you were forgiven. Some little while after you discovered that your were chosen of God from before the foundation of the world (Eph. 1:4). Oh, the rapture of your soul when the Lord appeared of old to you, saying, *"Yes, I have loved you with an everlasting love; therefore with loving-kindness I have drawn you"* (Jer. 31:3). The glorious doctrine of election is as wines on the lees well refined to those who by faith receive it — it brings with it a new, intense, a refined joy, such as the world can know nothing of. Then, having discovered your election of God, you looked further into your justification, *"For whom He called, them He also justified"* (Rom. 8:29,30). What a pearl is justification! In Christ the believer is as just in the sight of God as if he had never sinned; the believer is covered with a perfect righteousness, and is accepted in the Beloved. What a joy is justification by faith, when it is well understood! What bliss also to learn of our union to Christ! Believers are members of His body, of His flesh, and of His bones. Because He lives, we also live; as He lives always, so shall we. We are one with Jesus — what a wonderful discovery this is! Equally full of joy is our adoption, *"Beloved, we are now the sons of God"* (1 John 3:1). *"And if children, then heirs; heirs of God and joint-heirs with Christ"* (Rom. 8:17). Faith in this way heaps fuel on the fire of our joy, for it keeps on making discoveries out of the Word of the Lord. The more you search the Scriptures, the nearer you live to God, and the more you will enjoy of that great goodness which the Lord has laid up for those who fear Him. Although *"eye has not seen, nor ear heard, nor has it risen into the heart of man the things which God has prepared for those that love Him"* (1 Cor. 2:19), yet *"He has revealed them to us by His Spirit"* (vs. 10). By that He puts gladness into our hearts.

EVENING

But let all who put their trust in You rejoice. Let them always shout for joy, because You defend them. And let those who love Your name be joyful in You — Psalm 5:11.

IF YOU ARE HAPPY in the Lord, then you will be strong: *"the joy of the Lord is your strength"* (Neh. 8:10). If you lose your joy you will be a poor worker. You cannot bear testimony to God, you cannot bear stern trial, you cannot lead a powerful life, without joy in Him. In proportion as you maintain your joy you will be strong in the Lord and for the Lord.

Do you not know that if you are full of joy you will be turning the charming side of Christianity where men can see it? Would you wear your coat with the seamy side out? Some religionists do that. One great professor is said to have looked as if his religion did not agree with him. To be godly is not to be on the rack, or under a thumbscrew. Do not behave as if you felt that you must take your religion as you take medicine. If it takes like nauseous medicine to you then you have the wrong kind; you are poisoning yourself. Do not believe that true godliness is akin to sourness. Cheerfulness is next to godliness: *"When you fast, anoint your head and wash your face, that you not appear to men to fast."* Weed out levity, but still cultivate joy. In this way you will win other hearts to follow Jesus.

Remember that if you are always joyful, then you are rehearsing the music of the skies. We are going to be there soon, so let us not be ignorant of the music of the heavenly choirs. Do not let the choirmaster there say to you, "Do you know your part?" and then have to answer, "Oh, no, I have never sung while I was on earth." Be ready to answer to the heavenly choirmaster, "Yes, I have long been singing with joy Worthy is the lamb.

MORNING

By faith Noah, being warned of God of things not yet seen and moved with fear, prepared an ark for the saving of his house. By this he judged the world guilty and became heir of the righteousness which is by faith — Hebrews 11:7.

NOAH BELIEVED in God in his ordinary life. Before the great test came, before he heard the oracle from the secret place, Noah believed in God. We know that he did, for we read that he walked with God, and in his common conduct he is described as being *"a just man, and perfect in his generations."* To be just in the sight of God is never possible apart from faith, for the *"just shall live by faith."* It is a great thing to have faith in the presence of a terrible trial. But the first essential is to have faith for ordinary everyday living. Have you faith in God as to your daily bread? Have you faith as to your children and your house? Have you faith about your trade or business? Have you faith in the God of providence? — faith in the God who answers prayer? Is it habitual with you to roll your burdens on the Lord? If it is not so with you, what will you do when the flood breaks forth? Faith will not come to you all of a sudden, in the dark night, if you have shut it out through all the bright days. Faith must be a constant tenant, not an occasional guest. I do not think much of the Latter-day Saints (Mormons); I far more admire the Everyday Saints. You need faith on Sunday; have it and come to the communion table with it. But you need faith on Monday, when the shutters are taken down to begin another six days' trading. You will need faith the next day, for who can tell you what will happen? To the end of the week you will need to look to the hills from where your help comes. You need faith anywhere, and everywhere. A man of God alone in his room still needs faith, else solitude may be a nest for temptation. When the servant of Christ is at ease, having no work pressing on him, he has need of faith to keep him; lest he like David fall into temptation and commit folly.

EVENING

By faith Noah, being warned of God of things not yet seen and moved with fear, prepared an ark for the saving of his house. By this he judged the world guilty and became heir of the righteousness which is by faith — Hebrews 11:7.

YOU CANNOT have faith in the promise unless you are prepared to have faith in the threatening also. If you truly believe a man, you believe all he says. He who does not believe that God will punish sin will not believe that God will pardon sin through the atoning blood. He who does not believe that God will cast unbelievers into Hell will not be sure that He will take believers into Heaven. If we doubt God's Word about one thing, we shall have small confidence in it on another thing. Sincere faith in God must treat all God's word alike. For the faith which accepts one word of God and rejects another is evident not faith in God — it is but faith in our own judgment, faith in our own taste. Only that is true faith which believes everything that is revealed by the Holy Spirit, whether it is joyous or distressing.

In this case Noah received a promise. As the dark background to it he had listened to the terrible threatening that God would destroy all living things with a flood. His faith believed both the warning and the promise. If he had not believed the threat, he would not have prepared the ark, and so would not have received the promise. Men do not prepare an ark to escape from a flood unless they believe that there will be a flood. You who profess to be the Lord's, do not be unbelieving with regard to the terrible threatenings of God to the ungodly. Believe the threat, even though it should chill your blood. Believe, even though nature shrinks from the overwhelming doom. For if you do not believe, the very act of disbelieving God about one point will drive you to disbelieve Him on the other parts of revealed truth. Then you will never come to that true, childlike faith which God will accept and honor.

MORNING

By faith Noah, being warned of God of things not yet seen and moved with fear, prepared an ark for the saving of his house. By this he judged the world guilty and became heir of the righteousness which is by faith — Hebrews 11:7.

NOAH believed what seemed highly improbable, if not absolute impossible. There was no sea where Noah laid the keel of the ark; nor even a river there. He was to prepare a seagoing vessel, and construct it on dry land. How could water be brought there to float it? O mad old man! How can you play the fool on so huge a scale as to build a three-decked vessel of vast dimensions where no wataers can ever come? Yet he was bidden of the Lord to do it, and he was persuaded that the Lord's command involved no blunder, that the floods would fill the valley, rise to the hills and prevail above the tops of the mountains. It was an unlikely thing, but he believed this. The faith which believes in what is probable is anybody's faith; publicans and sinners can so believe. The faith which believes what is barely possible is bettter, but it is that faith which cares nothing for probability or possibility which is the faith of God's elect — it rests alone in the Word of the Lord. God deserves such faith, *"for with God all things are possible."* It is not probability, but certainty, that is the groundwork of faith when God has spoken. Noah believed firmly, and because of this he prepared his ship on dry land, quite as cheerfully as he would have built it by the sea.

At times you and I are assailed as to our faith in the Bible. People will say, "How do you make that out? It is in the Scriptures, certainly, but how do you reconcile it with science?" Say this, "We no longer live in the region of argument as to the Word of the Lord; we dwell now in the realm of faith. We are not squabblers, itching to prove our superiority in reasoning. We are children of light, worshiping our God by bowing our whole minds **to the** obedience of faith. We would be humble and learn to believe that which we cannot altogether comprehend, but is in God's word.

EVENING

By faith Noah, being warned of God of things not yet seen and moved with fear, prepared an ark for the saving of his house. By this he judged the world guilty and became heir of the righteousness which is by faith — Hebrews 11:7.

THE LORD had made Noah serenely bear witness against iniquity; yea, even to sit on the throne and condemn the world. Noah never seems to have entered into any dispute with the men of his times. He never argued or cavilled; much less did he wish them ill. He simply believed and told them the truth, kept his faith intact, and went on **building his ark — he practiced what he believed. Doing this he condemned those who** criticized him. Worldlings, you may laugh, but the man of God is your master after all. His preaching condemned them. They knew the way and wickedly refused to run in it. His warning condemned them. They would not regard it and escape. His life condemned them, for he walked with the God whom they despised. Most of all the ark **condemned them. Did none of them ever say, "This is the strangest fabric that ever** was. In all the world there is not another thing like this. Yet Noah is no fool. The man is cool and calm, shrewd and sharp. He has bought as well as any man could. How is that on this matter of this strange structure that he is so strange?" Did not such men at times think that there must be something in what Noah said after all? If they did not think so, at any rate the fact that Noah carried out his principles to the full, and invested all he had in the building of this strange ark, should have forced them to conviction if they had not been hardened through the deceitfulness of sin. Oh how his faith condemned them! When the floods began to rise up, and when the door was shut, how the sight of that floating ark must have condemned them!

MORNING

I will be glad and rejoice in Your mercy, for You have looked on my affliction; You have known my soul in troubles — Psalm 31:7.

FOR MERCY PAST he is grateful. And for mercy future, which he believingly anticipates, he is joyful. In our most importunate intercessions we must find breathing time to bless the Lord. Praise is never a hindrance to prayer, but rather a lively refreshment in it. It is delightful at intervals to hear the notes of the high sounding cymbals, when the dolorous sackbut rules the hour. Those two words, *glad* and *rejoice* are an instructive reduplication. We need not stint ourselves in our holy triumph. This wine we may drink in bowls without fear of excess.

"You have looked on my affliction." You have seen it, weighed it, directed it, fixed a bound to it, and in all ways made it a matter of tender consideration. A man's consideration means the full exercise of his mind. What must God's consideration be? *"You have known my soul in troubles."* God owns His saints when others are ashamed to acknowledge them. He never refuses to know His friends. He does not think the worse of them for their rags. He does not misjudge them and cast them off when their faces are lean with sickness, or their hearts heavy with despondency. More than this, the Lord Jesus knows us in our pangs in a peculiar sense, having deep sympathy toward us in them all. When no others can enter into our griefs, not understanding them experimentally, Jesus dives into the lowest depths with us, comprehending the direst of our woes, because He has felt the same. Jesus is a physician who knows every case; nothing is new to Him. We may be so bewildered as to not know our own state, but He knows. He has known us and will know us. O for grace to know more of Him! 'Man, know yourself' is a good precept, but 'Man, you are known of God,' is a superlative consolation.

EVENING

I was a reproach among all my foes, but especially among my neighbors, and a fear to my friends; those who saw me outside fled from me — Psalm 31:11.

THEY WERE pleased to have something to throw at me. My mournful state was music to them, because they maliciously interpreted it to be a judgment from Heaven on me. Reproach is little thought of by those who are not called to endure it, but the one passing under its lash knows how deep it wounds. The best of men may have the bitterest foes, and may be subjected to the most cruel taunts. *"But especially among my neighbors"* — those who are nearest can stab the sharpest. We fell most the slights of those who should have shown us sympathy. Perhaps David's friends feared to be identified with his declining fortunes, turning against him in order to win the mercy, if not the favor, of his opponents. Self interest rules most men. Ties the most sacred are soon snapped by its influence, and actions of the utmost meanness are perpetrated without scruple. The more intimate men have been before, the more distant they become. Our Lord was denied by Peter, betrayed by Judas, and forsaken by all in the hour of His utmost sorrow. All the herd turn against a wounded deer. The 'milk of human kindness' curdles when a despised believer is the victim of slanderous accusations. Afraid to be seen in the company of a man so thoroughly despised, those who once courted his society will hasten from him as though he had been infected with the plague. How villainous a thing is slander which can thus make an eminent saint, once the admiration of his people, to become the general butt, the universal aversion of mankind! To what extremities of dishonor may innocence be reduced!

All David's youthful prowess was now gone from remembrance. He had been the savior of his country, but his services were buried in oblivion. Men soon forget the deepest obligations. Popularity is evanescent to the last degree. He who is in everyone's mouth today may be fogotten by all tomorrow. But God rmembers His own.

I said, I will take heed to my ways so that I do not sin with my tongue; I will keep my mouth with a bridle while the wicked is before me — Psalm 39:1.

"*I SAID,*" or, I steadily resolved and determined. In his great perplexity his greatest fear was lest he should sin. So he cast about for the most likely method of avoiding it, and he determined to be silent. It is very excellent when a man can strengthen himself in a good course by remembering a well and wisely-formed resolve. "What I have written I have written," or what I have spoken I will perform — such may prove a good strengthener to a man in a fixed course of right. To avoid sin one needs to be very circumspect, to keep one's actions as with a garrison. Unguarded ways are generally unholy ones. Heedless is another word for graceless. In times of troubles we must watch against the sins peculiar to such trials, especially against murmuring and repining.

"*That I do not sin with my tongue*" — tongue sins are great sins. Like sparks of fire ill words spread and do great damage. If believers utter hard words of God in times of depression the ungodly will take them up and use them as justification for their sinful courses. If a man's own children rail at him, no wonder if his enemies' mouths are full of abuse. Our tongue always needs watching, for it is as restive as an ill-broken horse. But especially we must hold it when the sharp cuts of the Lord's rod excite it to rebel. "*I will keep my mouth with a bridle*" (more accurately, *with a muzzle*). The original does not mean a bridle to check, but a muzzle to stop the tongue altogether. David was not so wise. If he had resolved to be very guarded in his speech, it would have been commendable. But when he went so far as to condemn himself to entire silence "*even from good,*" there must have been at least some lack of wisdom. In trying to avoid one fault, he fell into another. To use the tongue against God is a sin of commission, but not to use it at all to serve God involves an evident sin of omission. Commendable virtues may be followed so eagerly that we may fall into vices.

EVENING

Also the helmet of salvation, and the Spirit's sword, which is God's word — Ephesians 6:17.

WE ARE to take this sword with a purpose. We are to use it that we may be able to stand and to withstand. If you want to stand, draw the sword and smite your doubts. How fiercely unbelief assails! Here comes a doubt as to your election. Pierce it through with the Word. Then comes a doubt as to the precious blood. Cleave it from head to foot with the assurance of the Word that the blood of Jesus cleanses us from all sin. Here comes another doubt, and yet another. As quick as arm can move, drive texts of Scripture through every new fallacy, every new denial of truth. Spit the whole of them on the rapier of the Word. It will be for your good to kill these doubts outright. Do not play with them, but fight them in real earnest. You will find that temptations also will come in hordes. Meet them with the precepts of sacred Writ; slay even the desire of evil by the Spirit's application of the Holy Word. The washing of water by the Word is a glorious cleanser. Discouragements arise like morning mists. But God's Word will shine them away with the beams of the promises. Your afflictions multiply, and you will never be able to overcome impatience and distrust except by the infallible Word of God. You can patiently bear trial if you use this weapon to kill anxiety. You will "*stand fast in the evil day,*" and having done all, you will stand if this sword is in your hand.

You have not only to stand fast yourselves, but you have to win souls for Christ. Do not try to conquer sin in others, or capture a heart for Jesus, except with the sword of the Spirit. How the Devil laughs when we try to make converts apart from the Holy Scriptures and the Holy Spirit.

MORNING

Hear my prayer, O Lord, and give ear to my cry. Be not silent to my tears, for I am a stranger with You, a pilgrim, as all my fathers were — Psalm 39:12.

DO NOT drown my pleadings with the sound of Your strokes. You have heard the clamor of my sins, Lord; hear the laments of my prayers and *"give ear to my cry."* Here is advance in intensity. A cry is more vehement, pathetic and impassioned than a prayer. The main thing was to have the Lord's ear and heart. *"Be not silent to my tears"* — this is yet a higher degree of importunate pleading. Who can withstand tears, those irresistible weapons of weakness? How often, women, children, beggars, and sinners have resorted to tears as their last resort, and with that have won the desire of their hearts. Tears speak more eloquently than ten thousand tongues. They act as keys on the wards of tender hearts, and mercy denies them nothing if through them the weeper looks to richer drops, even those of the blood of Jesus. When our sorrows pull up the sluices of our eyes, God will before long interpose and turn our mourning into joy. He may be quiet for long, as though He did not notice, but the hour of deliverance will come. It will come like the morning, when the dewdrops are plentiful.

"For I am a stranger with You" — not TO You, but WITH You. Like You, my Lord, a stranger among the sons of men, an alien from my mother's children. God made the world, sustains it, and owns it. Yet men treat Him as though he were a foreign intruder. And as they treat their Master, so do they deal with His servants. These words may also mean, *"I share the hospitality of God,"* like a stranger entertained by a generous host. Israel was bidden to deal tenderly with the stranger, and the God of Israel has in much compassion treated us poor aliens with unbounded liberality. His fathers knew that this was not their rest. They passed through life in pilgrim guise; they used the world as travelers use an inn. Why should we dream of rest on earth when our fathers' sepulchers are before our eyes?

EVENING

and the Spirit's sword, which is God's word — Ephesians 6:17.

THE SWORD you are to take is *the sword of the Spirit, which is the word of God.* That is our first head. The second is equally on the surface of the text: this sword is to be ours. We are ordered to take the sword of the Spirit and so make it our own sword.

The Word of God which is to be our one weapon is of noble origin, for it is *"the Spirit's sword."* It has the properties of a sword, and those were given it by God the Spirit. Here we note that the Holy Spirit has a sword. He is quiet as the dew, tender as the anointing oil, soft as the zephyr of eventide, and peaceful as a dove. Yet, under another aspect, He wields a deadly weapon. He is the Spirit of judgment and the Spirit of burning, and He does not bear the sword in vain. Of Him it may be said, *"The Lord is a man of war; Jehovah is His name."*

The Word of God in the hand of the Spirit wounds very terribly; it makes the heart of man to bleed. Do you not remember when you used to be gashed with this sword Sunday after Sunday? Were you not cut to the heart by it, even to be angry with it? You almost made up your mind to turn away from hearing the gospel again. That sword pursued you and pierced you in the secrets of your soul; it made you bleed in a thousand places. At last you were *"pricked in the heart,"* which is a far better thin than being *"cut to the heart."* Then execution was done. That wound was deadly to the natural man, and none but He that killed could make you alive. Do you recollect how, after this, your sins were slain one after another? Their necks were laid on the block, and the Spirit acted as an executioner with His sword. After that, blessed be God, your fears, and your doubts, and your despair, and your unbelief were also hacked to pieces by this same sword. The Word gave you life.

And He has put a new song in my mouth, praise to our God; many shall see it and fear and shall trust in the Lord — Psalm 40:3.

AT THE PASSOVER, before His passion, our Lord sang one of the grand old Psalms of praise. But what is the music of His heart now, in the midst of His redeemed? What a song is that in which His glad heart forever leads the chorus of the elect! Neither Miriam's nor Moses' triumphant hymns can for a moment rival that ever new and exulting song. Justice magnified and grace victorious; Hell subdued and Heaven glorified; death destroyed and immortality established; sin overthrown and righteousness resplendent. What a theme for a hymn in that day when our Lord drinks the new red wine with us all in our heavenly Father's kingdom! Even on earth, and before His great passion, he foresaw the joy which was set before Him, and was sustained by the prospect. *"Our God,"* the God of Jesus, the God of Israel, *"my God and your God."* How will we praise Him? He will be the chief player on our stringed instruments. He will lead the solemn hallelujah which shall go up from the sacramental host redeemed by blood. An innumerable number shall see the griefs and triumphs of Jesus, and shall tremble because of their sinful rejection of Him. Through grace others shall receive faith and become trusters of Jehovah. Here is our Lord's reward — here is the assurance which makes preachers bold. Oh make sure you note the way of salvation, a sight, a fear, a trust! Do you know the meaning of these by possessing and practicing them in your own soul? Trust in the Lord is the evidence, the essence of salvation. True believers only are redeemed from the dominion of sin and Satan. A man may be as poor as Lazarus, as hated as Mordecai, as sick as Hezekiah, as lonely as Elijah, but while his hand of faith keeps its hold on God none of his outward afflictions can prevent his being numbered among the blessed. But the wealthiest and most prosperous man who has no faith is accursed, whoever he may be.

EVENING

My times are in Your hand — Psalm 31:15.

THE GREAT truth is this: all that concerns the believer is in the hands of the Almighty God. *"My times"* — these change and shift, but they change only in accordance with unchanging love, and they shift only according to the purpose of One with whom is no variableness nor shadow of a turning. *"My times"* — that is to say, my ups and downs, my health and my sickness, my poverty and my wealth — all these are in the hand of the Lord, who arranges and appoints according to His holy will the length of my days, and the darkness of my nights. Storms and calms vary the seasons at the Divine appointment. Whether times are reviving or depressing remains with Him who is Lord both of time and of eternity. And we are glad that it is so.

We assent to the statement, *"My times are in Your hand,"* as to their result. Whatever is to come out of our life is in our heavenly Father's hand. He guards the vine of life, and He also protects the clusters which shall be produced by it. If life is as a field, the field is under the hand of the great Husbandman. And the harvest of that field is with Him also. The ultimate results of His work of grace on us, and of His education of us in this life, are in the highest hand. We are not in our own hands, nor in the hands of earthly teachers. We are under the skilful operation of hands which make nothing in vain. The close of life is not decided by the sharp knife of fates, but by the hand of love. We shall not die before our time, neither shall we be forgotten and left on the stage too long.

Not only are we ourselves in the hand of the Lord, but all that surrounds us. Our times make up a kind of atmosphere of existence, and all this is under Divine arrangement. We dwell within the palm of God's hand. We are absolutely at His disposal, and all our circumstances are arranged by Him in all their details (Prov. 16:9).

July 25   MORNING

Sacrifice and offering You did not desire; My ears You have opened; burnt offering and sin offering You have not asked — Psalm 40:6.

THIS IS one of the most wonderful passages in the whole of the Old Testament, a passage in which the incarnate Son of God is seen not through a mirror darkly, but as it were face to face. In themselves considered, and for their own sakes, the Lord saw nothing satisfactory in the various offerings of the ceremonial law. Neither the victim pouring forth its blood, nor the fine flour rising in smoke from the altar, could yield content to the mind of Jehovah. He did not care for the flesh of bulls and goats, neither did He have pleasure in corn and wine and oil. As types these offerings had their worth, but when the Antitype, Jesus, came into the world, they ceased to be of value. They were as candles lit before the sunrise — of no importance when it rose.

"My ears You have opened" — our Lord was quick to hear and perform His Father's will. His ears were opened down to His very soul. They were not closed up like Isaac's wells, which the Philistines filled up, but were clear passages down to the fountains of His soul. The prompt obedience of our Lord is here the first idea. However, there is no reason whatever to reject the notion that the digging of the ear here intended may refer to the boring of the ear of the servant (who refused out of love to his master to take his liberty at the year of jubilee). This perforated ear, the token of perpetual service, is a true picture of our blessed Lord's fidelity to His Father's business, and His love to His Father's children. Jesus irrevocably gave Himself up to be the servant of servants for our sake and for God's glory. The Septuagint, from which Paul quoted, has translated this passage, *"A body You have prepared Me."* How this reading arose it is not easy to imagine, but since apostolic authority has sanctioned the variation, we accept it as no mistake. In any case the passage represents the Only Begotten Son as coming into the world equipped for service, and in a real and material body, by actual life and death, putting aside all the shadows of the Mosaic Law.

EVENING

My times are in Your hand — Psalm 31:15.

A CLEAR CONVICTION that our times are in the hand of God will create within us a sense of the nearness of God. If the hand of God is laid on all our surroundings, God Himself is near us. Our Puritanic fathers walked with God the more readily because they believed in God as arranging everything in their daily business and domestic life. And they saw Him in the history of the nation, and in all the events that transpired. The tendency of this age is to get further and further from God. Men will scarcely tolerate a Creator now, but want everything to be evolved. To get God one stage further back is the ambition of modern philosophy. But if they were but wise, they would labor to clear out all obstacles and leave a clear channel for drawing near to God, and for God to draw near to them. When we see that in His hand are all our ways, we feel that God is real and near.

Then there is nothing left to chance or luck. Events happen not to men by a fortune which has no order or purpose in it. *"The lot is cast into the lap, but the whole disposing of it is of the Lord"* (Prov. 16:33). Chance is a heathenish idea which the teaching of the Word of God has cast down, even as the ark threw down Dagon and broke him in pieces. Blessed is that person who has discarded chance, who never speaks of luck. Such a one believes that all things are ordained by the Lord, from the least even to the greatest. we dare not leave out the last event. The creeping of an aphid on a rosebud is as surely arranged by the decree of Providence as the march of a pestilence through a disobedient nation. Believe this, for if the least is omitted from the supreme government, so may the next be, and the next, until nothing is left in the Divine hand. There is no place for chance, since God fills all things.

By faith Abraham obeyed when he was called to go out into a place which he was going to receive for an inheritance. And he went out without knowing where he was going. — Hebrews 11:8.

THE OBEDIENCE which comes of true faith is often bound to be altogether unreckoning and implicit, for it is written: *"He went out without knowing where he was going."* God told Abraham to journey, and he moved at once. Into the unknown land he made his way. Through fertile regions, across a wilderness; among friends, or through the midst of foes, he pursued his journey. He did not know where his way would take him, but he knew that the Lord told him to go. Even bad men will obey God when they think fit. But good men will obey when they do not know what to think of it. It is not ours to judge the Lord's command, but to follow it. Men foolishly say, "Yes, we know that such a course would be right, but the consequences might be painful. Good men would be grieved, the cause would be weakened, and we ourselves would get into a world of trouble." There is not much need to preach caution nowadays, for those who would run any risk for the truth's sake are few enough. Consciences, tender about the Lord's honor, have not been produced in any great number the last few years. Prudent consideration of consequences is superabundant. But the spirit that obeys and dares all things for Christ, where is it? The Abrahams of today will not go out from their kindred. They will put up with anything sooner than risk their livelihoods. If they do go out, they must know where they are going, and how much is to be picked up in the new country. I am not pronouncing any judgment on their conduct; I am merely pointing out how different they are than faithful Abraham. Our Puritan fathers thought little of property or of liberty when these stood in the way of conscience. In faith they defied exile and danger rather than to give up a single grain of truth. Such is scriptural obedience.

EVENING

By faith Abraham obeyed when he was called to go out into a place which he was going to receive for an inheritance. And he went without knowing where he was going — Hebrews 11:8.

THE WAY OF OBEDIENCE is a life of the highest honor. Obedience is the glory of a life — the glory which our Lord has given to His chosen ones, even His own glory, for also *"He learned obedience"* (Heb. 5:8). He never struck out on an original course, but He always did the things which pleased the Father (John 8:29). Be this our glory also. By faith we yield our intelligence to the highest Intelligence. We are led, guided, directed, and in this we follow where our Lord has gone. To us who believe this is honor. To a soldier it is the greatest honor to do what his sovereign commands. They do not debase their humanity who subject it to a honorable command; no, they are even exalted by obeying in the day of danger. The bravest and most honored of Christians are those who implicitly obey the command of the King of kings. Among His children they are best who best know their Father's mind, and who yield to it the gladdest obedience. Should we have any other ambition within the walls of our Father's house than to be perfectly obedient children before Him, and implicitly trustful of Him?

But this is a kind of life which will bring communion with God. God often hides His face behind the clouds of dust which His children make by their self-will. If we transgress against Him, we will soon be in trouble. But a holy walk — the walk described by the text as faith working obedience — is Heaven beneath the stars. God comes down to walk with those who obey Him. If they walk with Him, He walks with them. Obedience is heaven in us, and it is the preface of our being in Heaven. Obedient faith is the way to eternal life — no, it is eternal life revealing itself in us.

MORNING July 27

The helmet of salvation, and the Spirit's sword, which is God's word — Ephes. 6:17.

TO BE A CHRISTIAN is to be a warrior. The good soldier of Jesus Christ must not expect to find ease in this world; it is a battlefield. He must not reckon on the friendship of the world, for that would be enmity against God (James 4:4). His occupation is war. As he puts on his armor piece by piece he may wisely say to himself, "This warns me that there is danger; this prepares me for warfare; this prophesies opposition."

Even when we stand our ground we meet with difficulties, for the Apostle three times bids us to *"stand."* In the rush of the fight men are apt to be carried off their legs. If they can keep their footing they will be victorious. But if they are borne down by their adversaries everything may be lost. You are to put on the heavenly armor in order that you may stand. And you will need it to maintain the position in which your Captain has placed you. If even to stand requires all this care, judge what the warfare must be. The Apostle also speaks of *withstanding* as well as *standing*. We are not merely to defend, but also to assail. It is not enough that you are not conquered; you have to conquer. And from this we find that we are not only to take a helmet to protect the head, but also a sword with which to attack the foe. Then ours is a stern conflict, both standing and withstanding. And we will need all our armor from the Divine armory, all the strength that we can receive from the hand of the mighty God of Jacob.

It is clear that our text teaches that our conquest must be achieved by sheer fighting. Many try compromise, but if you are a true Christian you can never do this well. The language of deceit does not fit a holy tongue. The adversary is the father of lies, and those who are with him understand the art of equivocation, but not the saints.

EVENING

Lord, make me to know my end, and the measure of my days, what it is, that I may know how frail I am — Psalm 39:4.

"I was dumb, I opened not my mouth, because You did it" — Psalm 39:9.

"God is training up His children here. This is the true character of His dealings with them. The education of His saints is the object he has in view. It is training for the Kingdom, education for eternity. . . . It is the discipline of love. Every step of it is kindness. There is no wrath or vengeance in any part of the process. The discipline of this school may be harsh and stern, but that of the family is love. We are sure of this, and the consolation which it affords is unutterable. Love will not wrong us. There will be no needless suffering. If we but kept this in mind there would be fewer hard thoughts of God among men, even when His strokes were most severe. I know not of a better illustration of what the feelings of a saint should be, in the hour of bitterness, than the case of Richard Cameron's father. The aged saint was in prison for the Word of God and for the testimony of Jesus Christ. The bleeding head of his martyred son was brought to him by his unfeeling persecutors, and he was asked derisively if he knew it. 'I know it, I know it,' said the father as he kissed the mangled forehead of his son — 'It is my son's, my own dear son's! It is the will of the Lord! Good is the will of the Lord, who cannot wrong me or mine, but who has made goodness and mercy to follow us all our days.'" — Horatius Bonar, from *The Night of Weeping*.

"Because You did it" — This holy man had a break made both in his body and spirit at this time. He was sick and sad, yet he remembers from whose hand the blow came. You, Lord, did it; You whom I love dearly, and so I can take it kindly; You whom I have offended, and so I take it patiently. Yea, You who might have cast me into a bed of flames instead of my bed of sickness, and so I accept your correction thankfully. So he catches at the blow without retorting it back on God by any quarreling, discontented language" — William Gurnall.

MORNING July 28

and the Spirit's sword, which is God's word — Ephesians 6:17.

DO NOT BURY the Word under other matters, but take it as a sword. This means that we are to believe it, every portion of it. Believe it with a true and real faith, not with a mere creedal faith, saying 'This is the orthodox thing.' Believe it as a matter of fact every day, affecting your life. And when you have believed it, then study it. Oh, for a closer study of the Word of God! Have you truly heard or read all that the Lord has written? Are there not passages of the Bible which you have never seen or heard? If so, it is a melancholy fact. Do read the Bible through and through, from beginning to end. Begin tomorrow — no! Begin today. Then go steadily through the whole of the sacred books with prayer and meditation. Never let it be said of you that God recorded truths in His Word which you have never even read. Study the Word and make out its meaning. Go deep into the spirit of inspiration. The most gold comes to the one digging deepest into this mine — the deeper you go, the richer the ore. The deeper you go under the Spirit's guidance the larger will be the reward for your toil. Take this sword with the grip of sincere faith. Hold it fast by a fuller knowledge, and then exercise yourself daily in its use. The sword of the Lord is to be taken for earnest fight. You will not be long before occasion arises for its use in such a world as this. You will have to parry with it, pierce with it, cut with it, and kill with it. Where shall you begin? Begin at home. For many a day you will have your hands full, and your heart full of joy.

EVENING

Then He said, Lo, I come. In the volume of the Book it is written of Me. I delight to do Your will, O My God; and Your law is within My heart — Psalm 40:7,8.

IT BEING certain that the mere images of atonement, and the bare symbols of propitiation were of no avail, the Lord Jesus intervened in His own person. O blessed Lord, ever give to us to hear and feed on such living words as these, so peculiarly and personally Your own. Behold, O heavens and earth! Here is something worthy of your intense gaze. Sit down and watch with earnestness, for the invisible God comes in the likeness of sinful flesh, even as an infant the Infinite One hangs at a virgin's breast! Immanuel did not send; He came. He came in His own personality, in all that constituted His essential self. He came from the ivory palaces to the abodes of mercy. He came at the destined hour; He came with sacred speed as one freely offering Himself.

"In the volume of the Book it is written of Me" — in the eternal decree it is so recorded. The mystic roll of predestination which providence gradually unfolds contained within it a written covenant, to the Savior's knowledge — that in the fulness of time the divine I AM should descend to earth to accomplish a purpose which multitudes of bulls and rams could not achieve. What a privilege to find our names written in the Book of Life. And what an honor it is, since the name of Jesus heads the page! Our Lord had respect to His ancient covenant agreements, and in this He teaches us to be scrupulously just in keeping our word. Have we so promised, is it so written in the book of remembrance? Then do not let us ever be defaulters.

Our blessed Lord alone could completely do the will of God. The law is too broad for such poor creatures as we to fulfil it to the uttermost. But Jesus not only did the will of the Father, He found a delight in it. From the beginning He desired this work set before Him. In His human life He was troubled until he reached the baptism of agony in which He magnified the law. In agony He yet chose the Father's will, setting aside His own. In this is the essence of obedience, in the soul's cheerful devotion to God.

MORNING

My times are in Your hand — Psalm 31:15.

DAVID was sad. His life was spent with grief, and his years with sighing. His sorrow had wasted his strength, and even his bones were consumed within him. Cruel enemies pursued him with malicious craft, even seeking his life. At such a time he used the best resource of grief, for he says, *"I trusted in You, O Lord."* He had no other refuge but that which he found in faith in the Lord his God. If enemies slandered him, he did not give railing for railing. If they plotted to take away his life, he did not meet violence with violence, but he calmly trusted in his Lord. They ran here and there, using all kinds of nets and traps to make the man of God their victim, but he met all their inventions with the one simple defense of trust in God. Many are the firery darts of the wicked one, but our shield is one. The shield of faith not only quences fiery darts; it breaks arrows of steel. Although the foe's javelins were dipped in the venom of Hell, yet our one shield of faith would hold us harmless, casting them off from us. So David had the grand resource of faith in the hour of danger. Note well that he uttered the most glorious claim a man may make, *"I said, You are my God."* One who can say, "This kingdom is mine," makes a royal claim. One who can say, "This mountain of silver is mine," makes a wealthy claim. But one who can say to the Lord, *"You are my God,"* has said more than all monarchs and millionaires can reach. If this God is your God by His gift of Himself to you, what more could you have? If Jehovah has been made your own by an act of appropriating faith, what more could be conceived of? You have not the world; you have the Maker of the world, and that is far, far more. There is no measuring the greatness of the treasure of one who has God to be his all in all.

EVENING

O Lord my God, many are Your wonderful works which You have done, and Your thoughts which are toward us. They cannot be set in order to You. If I would declare and speak of them, they are more than can be numbered — Psalm 40:5.

CREATION, providence and redemption all teem with wonders. Our special attention is called by this passage to the marvels which cluster around the cross, and flash from it. The accomplished redemption achieves many ends; it compasses a variety of designs. The outgoings of the atonement are not to be reckoned up. The influences of the cross reach further than the beams of the sun. Wonders of grace beyond all enumeration take their rise from the cross. Adoption, pardon, justification, and a long chain of godlike miracles of love proceed from it. Note that our Lord here speaks of Jehovah as *"My God."* The man Christ Jesus claimed for Himself and for us a covenant relationship with Jehovah. Let our interest in our God be ever to us our peculiar treasure.

"And Your thoughts which are toward us" — the Divine thoughts march with the Divine acts, for it is not according to God's wisdom to act without deliberation and counsel. All God's thoughts are good and gracious toward His elect. His thoughts of love are very many, very wonderful and very practical. Think on them, for no sweeter subject ever occupied your mind. If God's thoughts of you are many, let not yours of Him be few. Human minds cannot analyze, enumerate or measure God's ways and thoughts. For He has told us, *"As the heavens are higher than the earth, so are My ways higher than your ways, and My thoughts than your thoughts."* No maze to lose oneself in like the labyrinth of Divine love. How sweet to be outdone, overcome and overwhelmed by the astonishing grace of the Lord our God! Thoughts of eternity, thoughts of my fall, my restoration, my redemption, my conversion, my pardon, my upholding, my perfection, my eternal reward — the value of these mercies is too great for my estimation.

MORNING

My times are in Your hand — Psalm 31:15.

TO HAVE OUR TIMES in God's hands must mean not only that they are at God's disposal, but that they are arranged by the highest wisdom. God's hand never errs, and if our times are in His hand then they are ordered rightly. We need not puzzle our brains to understand the dispensations of Providence. A much easier, wiser course is open to us, to believe the hand of the Lord works all things for the best. Sit still at your great Father's feet and let Him do what seems good. When you cannot comprehend Him, then know that a baby cannot be expected to understand the wisdom of its sire. Your Father comprehends all things, even if you do not. Let His wisdom be enough for you. In the hand of God everything may be left without anxiety; for there it will be carried through to a prosperous result. Things prosper in His hand. If your times are in His hand, then you may be assured that none may disturb, or pervert them. In that Hand we rest as securely as a baby rests on its mother's breast. Where else could our interests be so well secured as in the eternal hand? What a blessing it is to see by the eye of faith all things that concern you being solely in the hand of God. What peace as to every matter which could cause anxiety flows into the soul when we see all our hopes built on so stable a foundation, and preserved by God's supreme power.

"My times are in Your hand" — this does not exclude the whole body of the saints being able to enjoy this safety together. Truth is sweetest when each Christian tastes the flavor of it for himself. Come, let each one of us take this doctrine of the supreme appointment of God, and let us believe that it stands true as to their own case. The Lord Jesus loved me and gave Himself for me, and my times are in His hands, those hands which He allowed to be nailed to the cross in order to obtain my redemption.

EVENING

You have given a banner to them that fear You, that it may be displayed because of the truth — Psalm 60:4.

THE LORD has called back to Himself His servants, and commissioned them for His service, presenting them with a standard to be used in His wars. Their afflictions had led them to exhibit holy fear. Then being fitted for the Lord's favor, He gave them an ensign — this would be a rallying point for their armies, and a proof that He had sent them to fight, also a guarantee of victory. The bravest men are usually entrusted with the banner, and it is certain that those who fear God most have less fear of man than any others. The Lord has given us the standard of the gospel. Then let us live to uphold it; if needful let us die to defend it. Our right to contend for God, and our reason for expecting success, are found in the fact that the faith has been once committed to the saints, and that by the Lord Himself.

"That it may be displayed because of the truth" — banners are for the breeze, the sun, the battle. Israel might well come forth boldly, for a sacred standard was borne aloft before them. To publish the gospel is a sacred duty; to be ashamed of it is a deadly sin. The truth of God was involved in the triumph of David's armies; He had promised them victory. So for us, the proclamation of the gospel is with assurance, for God will give success to His own word. For the truth's sake, then, and because the true God is on our side, let us in these modern days of holy warfare emulate the warriors of Israel. Let us unfurl our banners to the breeze with confident joy. Dark sings of present or coming ill must not dishearten us. If the Lord had meant to destroy us He would not have given us the gospel. The very fact that He has revealed Himself in Christ Jesus involves the certainty of victory.

MORNING

Then David said, My brothers, you shall not do so with that which the Lord has given us. For He has kept us alive and has delivered into our hand the company that came against us — 1 Samuel 30:23.

DAVID PLEADED free grace, for he said to them, *"You shall not do so with that which the Lord has given us."* He did not say, "with that which you have conquered, earning it in battle," but, *"that which the Lord has given us."* Look on every blessing as a gift and you will not think anyone shut out of it, not even yourself. The gift of God is eternal life, so why should you not have it? Do not deny to anyone any comfort of the covenant of grace. Do not think of anyone that they ought not to have so much joy as you. It is all of free grace. And if free grace rules the hour, the least may have it as well as those seeming to be pillars. If it is all of free grace, then though you be but a poor struggling Christian who hardly feels assured of your salvation, yet if you are indeed a believing Christian then you may claim every blessing of the Lord's gracious covenant. God freely gives to you as well as to me, or to any, the provisions of His love. Then let us be glad and not judge ourselves after the manner of the law of condemnation.

Then David pleaded for needfulness, saying, *"These men remained by our possessions."* No army fights well when its camp is unguarded. It is a great thing for a church to know that its stores are well guarded by a praying band. While some of us are teaching in the school or preaching in the street, we have great comfort in knowing that a certain number of our fellow-saints are praying for us. I will not say who does the better service — the man who preaches, or the man who prays. But I do know this, that we can do better without the voice that preaches than without the heart that prays. The petitions of our fellow-Christians are the wealth of the church. The kind of service which seems most commonplace among men is often the most precious to God.

EVENING

Out of weakness they were made strong — Hebrews 11:34.

TRIALS OF CRUEL MOCKINGS are still common today. There are many ways in which the Devil's whip can reach the back of the child of God. Persecution is still abundant, and many a man's foes are from his own household. Many a house is still a place of martyrdom. Gracious sufferers, may the Lord keep you back from anger and unkindness. By faith alone are you able to bear persecution and also turn it to account for the good of others. Do not try to escape by yielding what is right and true, but ask the Lord to help you to stand fast for Him. If it is true that the Lord has His martyrs still, let it be seen that they are as brave as ever. They do not gather now in the great amphitheater, that cruel arena where the emperor and his lords, with all the proud citizens of Rome sitting in the nearer galley, tier on tier, lusting to see Christians torn to pieces by lions. No more do we have to lift up our eyes to the great doors expecting to be the prey of such animals as they came forth roaring and hungry. No more do we see a man and his wife and his children unarmed before such beasts. This is all gone. In His suffering members Christ has conquered the Caesars and pagan Rome — *"for out of weakness they were made strong."* A less barbarian spirit has come over the modern minds, but there is as much enmity against God as there ever was. Now it finds a less public arena, but a meaner mode of torture. Today the tried one suffers alone and misses the encouragement of sympathetic Christian eyes. At times such a one has to feel it would have been better for him to fight with the beasts at Ephesus, as did Paul, than to bear the taunts and threats and slanders of ungodly kinsfolk. My sister, my brother, have faith in God in your hidden sorrow, and out of weakness you will be made strong.

MORNING

Out of weakness they were made strong — Hebrews 11:34.

THERE IS a high and blessed duty and privilege which is to every Christian the necessity of his life. That is to pray. Can you pray? If you know how to pray you can move Heaven and earth. Can you pray? Then you can set almighty forces in operation. Then you will suffer no need, for everlasting supplies await the hand of prayer — *"ask, and it shall be given you."* You cannot miss your way, for you will be guided in answer to prayer. You shall hear a voice behind you, saying, *"This is the way, walk in it"* (Isa. 30:21). But you say that you cannot pray prevailingly. Then you must wrestle, as Jacob did. You cannot seize on the Angel and win the victory? Do you feel in prayer as if the sinew of your strength were shrunken and your knee put out of joint? Well then place this text before your eyes: *"out of weakness"* you will be *"made strong."* Believe in God, in faith pray by His help to be able to wrestle with the Angel. Believe in His promise and plead it. Believe in His Spirit and pray for His help (Rom. 8:27). Believe in Jesus who will make intercession for you. Through Him you may come boldly to the throne of grace. Faith alone can confirm feeble knees: *"According to your faith is it to you."* Seek faith to become a master of the art of prayer. An earnest praying saint has his hand on a leverage that moves the universe. But there is no praying without believing. If you believe, you WILL be heard, for God does not refuse believing prayer. To refuse to keep His promise when it is pleaded would be to falsify His word and change His character — neither of these things can ever be.

EVENING

I waited patiently for the Lord, and He bowed down to me and heard my cry. He brought me up out of a horrible pit, out of the miry clay, and set my feet on a rock and gave sureness to my steps — Psalm 40:1,2.

PATIENT WAITING on God was a special characteristic of our Lord Jesus. Impatience never lingered in His heart, much less escaped His lips. All through His agony in the Garden, His trial of cruel mockings before Herod and Pilate, and His passion on the cross, He waited in omnipotence of patience. No glance of wrath, no word of murmuring, no thought of vengeance came from God's patient Lamb. He waited; He was patient to perfection, far excelling all others who have according to their measure glorified God in the fires. The Christ of God wears the imperial crown among the patient. Did the Only-Begotten Son wait, and shall we be petulant and rebellious? Neither Jesus the Head, nor any of the members of His body, shall ever wait on the Lord in vain. Mark His figure inclining on that cross, as though a suppliant crying out for condescending love to stoop to hear his feeble moans. What a marvel is it that our Lord should have had to cry out, as we do, that He should receive the Father's help after the same process of faith and pleading as we must! The Savior's prayers among the midnight mountains and in Gethsemane expound this verse. The Son of David was brought very low there, but He rose to victory. And here He teaches us how to conduct our conflicts so as to succeed after the same glorious pattern of triumph. Arm yourself with the same mind, the same patience; armed with prayer and girded with faith, you will maintain the Holy War against the flesh, the world, and the Devil.

When our Lord bore in His own person the terrible curse which was due to sin, He was cast down like a prisoner in a deep, dark, fearful dungeon, where the captive hears the tramp of furious foes overhead. Yet the Lord Jehovah made Him to ascend from all His abasement. *"He led captivity captive, and gave gifts to men"* (Eph. 4:8). He will not fail to deliver us from the far lighter griefs we receive from our adversaries today.

MORNING

And after these things God tested Abraham and said to him, Abraham! And he said, Here I am — Genesis 22:1.

GOD DOES DEAL with His people. He is never far away from them. He does not leave them to themselves, but is ever near those who are truly His. God did test Abraham. It is a great thing that God should take any notice of us, poor creatures that we are. *"When I consider Your heavens, the work of Your fingers, the moon and the stars which You have ordained; what is man, that you are mindful of him, and the son of man, that You visit him?"* (Ps. 8:4). Job also wondered that God dealt with him in the way of afflicton, saying, *"Am I a sea, or a whale, that You set a watch over me?"* We are so insignificant that it is indeed a great wonder that God should come to deal with us at all. If you saw some tall angel bending down over an ant's nest, you might wonder that he should so stoop. But this is nothing compared to the condescension of the infinite God, the Maker of all things, to deal with us worms of the earth. Yet He does so. Yea, He says that we are precious in His sight. As the goldsmith assays the metal, as the silversmith refines the silver again and again, so does God test us, trying us and thus purifying us. He sets a high value on us, and for this reason He tests us. O child of God, be glad that God comes near you! Would you not sooner feel His hand heavy on you than to be forgotten by Him? Would you not rather see His face, though wreathed in frowns, than never to see Him at all? Oh, what a dreadful thing it will be for those who will be cast away from Him! To hear Him say, *"Depart from me"* will be at once an infinity of wretchedness. But if He calls us to Him, even to chasten us, His voice has music in it. O Lord, blessed be Your name. For You think on your servants even when you chasten them and when You are purifying them.

EVENING

And after these things God tested Abraham and said to him, Abraham! And he said, Here I am — Genesis 22:1.

IT IS THE TRUE coin that men test. And God, because He loved Abraham, and valued him, and saw His grace in him, He tested him. First of all He tested his fear of God. You will see in the twelfth verse this was the main point: *"Now I know that you fear God."* The Lord delights in those who have a holy reverence for their God. This is a very scarce article nowadays. To hear one say that he has received a "straight tip" from God makes one feel that one capable of speaking in such a manner was never spoken to by the infinite Jehovah. Communicn with God bows a man to the dust, causing him to use lowly and reverent language. God never comes near to us and then leave us in a frame of mind in which we could speak flippantly or irreverently of Him. When I hear professing Christians arraigning God's conduct, foolishly setting up to criticize God's Word, I must doubt them. God's true children tremble at His Word; they never question Him — *"Why do you strive against Him? For He does not give account of any of His matters"* — *"Who are you that replies against God?"* (Job 33:13; Rom. 9:20). The spirit of criticism is alien altogether to the spirit of the child of God. It is not just what they say in their criticism, it is the spirit that dares to say it that is the evil thing. The Lord will try each one of us whether we really fear Him or not. If the test is not so severe as that which Abraham endured, still the test will come. If you object, saying "I cannot do that, for I fear the consequences," that shows you do not fear God enough. The one who fears God fears nothing else. Say, "I must do it, cost what it may, for it would be infinitely more costly not to obey God's leading."

And after these things God tested Abraham and said to him, Abraham! And he said, Here I am — Genesis 22:1.

IN GOD'S dealings with believers He tests them again and again: *"And after these things God tested Abraham."* After all his life of holy obedience he was still not free from trials. God still tested him. He had received great and precious promises, more than any other man of his time; and he believed them, sucking the sweetness out of them. But after these things God again tried Abraham. He had rare enjoyments in his life. Did not angels come and sit at his table? Did not the great Melchizedek himself come out with bread and wine to feast him? But even after these things God tested Abraham. He had been tested before when he left his country — again when he had sent away his son Ishmael, whom he loved. But when the command came, *"Cast out this bondwoman and her son,"* he obeyed. He had been tested many times, but after this he must be tested again. These things are an example to us, the people of God. We are not yet out of the wilderness of this world. We may yet have our greatest testing.

Abraham had reached a very high point of faith. And after a time he had enjoyed a great quiet of spirit. Everything went well with him then. By faith he fought four kings and led them captive. By faith he trampled on the riches of the world, even telling the king of Sodom that he would *"not take from a thread even to a shoelatchet"* from him. By faith he had become great, and God had put part of his own name into Abram's name, making him Abraham, blending the name of God with the name of His servant. Yet God tested Abraham; not Abram only, but even Abraham. Note that God did not try Abraham like this at the beginning. It was *"after these things"* that God tested Abraham so severely. There was a course of education to prepare him for this great testing time.

EVENING

And after these things God tested Abraham and said to him, Abraham! And he said, Here I am — Genesis 22:1.

GOD TESTS His people by actual experience. He did not test Abraham by words only. He did not say to him, "Will you do this?" It is always easy to say that we will do a thing if we do not expect to be compelled to do it. We can make large promises when we think we shall never be called on to fulfill them. We can even think large things today about what we intend to do tomorrow. It is always easy to rise up early overnight. But God does not prove His people in word only, but in deed and in truth. The plain command came to Abraham, and it must be obeyed at once. He must go into the land of Moriah, and he must offer his son there for a burnt offering. It must come to real action. How big you and I are in words! How great some people are in professing obedience. They say, "Oh, we will never fail our Lord." Like Peter they are quick to assert, *"Though all men shall be offended because of You, yet will not I."* They become bold in their boasting, proud in their own conceit — *"professing themselves to be wise, they become as fools."* They may even turn the very grace of God, which enriched them into an occasion of vainglory, saying, "I am perfect, completely dead to the world. There is no fear I shall fall. In time of trial I shall be strong. If martyr times were back how gloriously I would testify for God." But, after all, it is the test of real life, the test of actual experience, that will reveal what a person is. When God comes to real filing and hammering, putting us into the crucible, then it is that He proves how much in us is dross, and how much is true metal.

Some believers are tested more thoroughly than others. In Abraham's case the Lord tried him most severely. What greater test could the Lord have applied to him?

August 4 — MORNING

The grace of our Lord Jesus Christ be with you all — Romans 16:24.

THE CHRISTIAN is a man of generous actions, but his wishes go far beyond his deeds. Where he cannot be beneficient he is benevolent. If he cannot actually accomplish good for all, yet he fervently desires it. If it is not in his power to confer grace on any, yet he prays that God would give His grace to all. His heart entertains thousands, although his house might be overfull with ten. His liberal desires feed nations, though his purse is so scant that he cannot afford more than a penny for a poor child. God, whose providence limits our ability, has set no measure to our willingness. Our wishes may be boundless, even though our powers are contracted. And this will be good for ourselves, and not useless to others.

Christianity never came into the world to make individual professors of it isolated, like the icebergs which float away on the wide sea in solitude. Nor is it intended that we should be so concerned for our own salvation as to be indifferent to the welfare of others. True religion is not a separating and repelling force. Rather it is an attraction; it draws individual atoms into one body and holds them together. It does not shiver to fragments, but welds into one. It is a magnet, not a whirlwind. God in His grace gathers together in one body in Christ Jesus all His scattered ones, and the same Spirit who constrains us to love God also leads us to love our brothers and sisters in Him.

A loving spirit, when it can actually do no more, naturally seizes on the ever open outlet of good wishes, benedictions, and intercessions. In this way the great heart of the apostle relieved itself, although he would have been willing to lay down his life for the brothers, yet he did not think it idle to give them his blessing, nor did they reject it as worthless because it cost him nothing.

EVENING

The grace of our Lord Jesus Christ be with you all — Romans 16:24.

PAUL intends not only grace, but the mercy and love of our Lord Jesus Christ be with you. May that mercy be shown to you by the full pardon of all your sins, and your knowledge that they are pardoned. May your conscience be purged from dead works, and not merely cleansed, but cleansed so that you may know that it is clean. The great mercy is to have no suspicion that sin is left on you, but to be certain that every transgression of evey sort has been forever put away through the precious blood which cleanses from all sin. Alas! There are many Christians who even in their prayers do not appear to understand or distinguish between themselves and the unconverted. It is our duty to ask for pardon every day. Our Lord in the model prayer teaches us to say, *"Forgive us our trespasses as we forgive them that trespass against us."* But we should not confound that petition of a child to its father with the first supplication for pardon which is fitting to us as aliens before we were brought near. As guilty sinners we stood before the Judge, but now we are no longer criminals — for *"there is no condemnation to them that are in Christ Jesus"* (Rom. 8:1). We need not say with Peter, in his enthusiastic folly, *"Do not wash my feet only, but also my hands and my head."* For the Master tells us that we have been washed and are clean, and so we need only to wash our feet, for in Him we are clean every whit. You should not then come before Him with what is too often used as a mere parrot cry, "Lord, have mercy on me, a miserable sinner." If you as a believer are a miserable sinner, you ought not to be. You are sinners, but you ought not to be miserable. You have been forgiven; you are justified by faith in Christ Jesus. Is all this nothing? How can you ignore it and speak of yourself still as you have spoken before you were saved. Ask for pardon as God's child.

The grace of our Lord Jesus Christ be with you all — Romans 16:24.

MAKE THE benediction as large as the apostle did, there is certain a limit to it. For He is speaking to the saints, true believers, and no one else. Have you noticed the form this benediction takes in the epistle to Philemon, and in that to the Galatians? There the apostle puts it this way, *"The grace of our Lord Jesus Christ be with your spirit."* It is only meant, then, for spiritual-minded men, for such as have been born again by God the Holy Spirit. Jesus Christ cannot be with the carnal-minded. He will not give the blessing of His presence to those who mind earthly things: *"For the mind of the flesh is death, but the mind of the Spirit is life and peace; because of this the mind of the flesh is enmity toward God"* (Rom. 8:6,7). When you have been born again you can understand the grace of our Lord Jesus Christ, but not until then. May that gracious work of regeneration be wrought in every soul. The apostle limits it again in his epistle to the Ephesians, uttering a desire that the grace of our Lord Jesus Christ may be with *"all them that love our Lord Jesus Christ in sincerity."* You cannot expect the blessing of Christ to abide with you if you are hypocritical, or formal, or self-deceived. Sincerity is a needful index of the grace of Christ being with you. Do you in sincerity love Jesus Christ? If you do, may His grace be with you.

One other limit the apostle gives. I can never present these words either in public or in private without a conscious shudder. You will find them at the close of the first epistle to the Corinthians, *"The salutation of Paul, with my own hand. If any man does not love the Lord Jesus Christ, let him be Anathema Maranatha (let him be a curse. The Lord comes.) The grace of our Lord Jesus Christ be with you."*

EVENING

If anyone does not love the Lord Jesus Christ, let him be a curse. The Lord comes. — 1 Corinthians 16:22.

THE APOSTLE Paul pronounces a solemn curse on those whom he feels he cannot bless, because they are so base as not to love the infinitely lovely and loving Jesus. Then let such a one be accursed. May God save us all from a curse so well deserved. For not to love such a generous Savior, not to love one so lovely and so gracious, not to love one who loved those who were yet His enemies (Rom. 5:10), when He laid down His life that sinners might live — is that not in itself to be accursed? That spirit is withered already that does not love the Savior. To be able to withhold its affections from so lovely an object is in itself a doom. May God save you from it! May there not be a one who reads this on whom that curse may come, but rather *"may the grace of our Lord Jesus Christ be with you all."*

This will be the result to you if the grace of our Lord Jesus Christ is with you. First, there will be a blessed consequence to you Godward. As you have this grace of Christ in you, you will love God better. You will seek His face more often. You will pray with more confidence and more vehemence. You could not have the grace of Christ without being much in prayer, for we read of Him praying again and again. If you have the grace of Christ you will walk with God, even as He did. Your communion with the Father will be closer than before; it will be less interrupted; it will become thorough. O that I might see a church made up wholly of saints who live in habitual intercourse with God! Let each of your hearts inquire, *"Lord, is it I?"* And if your hearts condemn any of you, may the grace of our Lord Jesus Christ be with you most effectually, that you may amend your ways.

MORNING

The grace of our Lord Jesus Christ be with you all — Romans 16:24.

WOULD NOT PAUL also desire for us that we may exhibit in ourselves the grace which shone so brightly in Christ, and was seen by men and angels to the glory of God the Father? You will never have grace as the Lord Jesus had grace, for His grace was without measure. But you may receive and exhibit the same grace in your measure. Of that you and I may have a high degree of it! Grace displayed itself in the Lord Jesus in a character absolutely perfect, in which not one of the virtues was absent or exaggerated, and in which not a single fault could be found. You can depict the character of John, for a prominent excellence is visible. You can describe the characteristics of Peter; you can give an idea of Paul — for each of these is like a separate gem; each one had its own especial brightness and color — and each one had its own peculiar flaw. But when you come to the altogether lovely One, your descriptive powers will fail you. For in Him all His characteristics met in harmony. The excellences of all the excellent are in Him, and none of the flaws. In Him all perfections meet to make up one perfection. All in Him are divinely compounded, well-balanced as to the proportions. O may that grace be with you which was poured on our glorious Head, and continues to distill to the skirts of His priestly garments. May His sacred unction anoint and perfume us all! Yea, it was poured on Jesus that it might distill and drop onto us. He received this fulness that we might receive out of His fulness grace on top of grace (John 1:16).

EVENING

The grace of our Lord Jesus Christ be with you all — Romans 16:24.

THERE IS NOT ONE who can do without the grace of our Lord Jesus Christ. You experienced Christians are greatly in danger when you think your mountain stands firm and will never be moved. You wise and intelligent believers are in sore peril when you dream that you can battle with error apart from your Master. Conscious weakness is our true strength — *"When I am weak then I am strong"* — *"for My power is perfected in weaknesses"* (2 Cor. 12:10). The boldest, bravest, wisest, most judicious, and most experienced among you need the grace of our Lord Jesus Christ — then surely do the babes in grace, the weaklings of the flock.

More delightful still is it to remember that you all may have it. Having believed in Jesus you all have Him to be your own, and you may then surely have His grace. He who gave you Christ has virtually given you all the grace that is in Christ Jesus. Indeed we know from the best authority that grace was given us in Christ Jesus before the world began (2 Tim. 1:9).

Shall iron break the iron and the brass from the north? — Jeremiah 15:12.

SURELY IF anything can add weight to the prophecy of the judgments of God, it is the trembling love, the urgent fear with which such a messenger as Jeremiah would deliver his warning. The deep sorrow of him who warned them ought to have driven the sinful nation to a speedier repentance. Instead, they rejected his warnings; they despised his person; and they defied his God. As they thus heaped wrath on themselves they also increased his sorrow. He was a delicate, sensitive plant; he felt an inward shudder as he marked the tempest gathering overhead. Although a most loyal servant of his God, he was sometimes very trembling. Although he never like Jonah ventured to flee, yet he cried in the bitterness of his soul, *"O that I had in the wilderness a lodging place of wayfaring men; that I might leave my people and go from them."* The Jews treated him so harshly and unjustly that he feared they would break his heart. They smote him as with an iron rod, and he felt like one crushed beneath their unkindness. To silence his fear the Lord assures him that He will renew his strength: *"Behold, I have made you this day a defensed city, and an iron pillar, and bronze walls against the whole land, against the kings of Judah, against its rulers, against its priests, and against the people of the land. And they shall fight against you, but they shall not prevail against you. For I am with you, says the Lord, to deliver you."* So the Lord promised to His servant the divine support which his trial demanded. He never did and never will place a man in a trying position and then leave him to perish. David dealt treacherously with Uriah, but the Lord does not act so with His servants. If the rebellious seed of Israel were iron, the Lord declared that His prophet would be hardened by sustaining grace into northern iron and steel.

EVENING

Shall iron break the iron and the brass from the north? — Jeremiah 15:12.

WE ARE SENT into the world, if we are believers in Christ, like sheep in the midst of wolves, defenseless, and in danger of being devoured. Yet no power on earth can destroy the chosen disciples of Christ. Weak as they are, they will tread down the strength of their foes. There are more sheep in the world now than wolves. There are parts of the world where wolves once roamed in troops where not a wolf can now be found. One would not be very bold to say that the day will come when the wolf will only be known as an extinct animal, while as long as the world lasts the sheep will continue to multiply. In the animal world the sheep has gained the victory over the wolf in the long run. And it is so with Christ's people. They appear to be weak, but there is a force about them which cannot be put down. They will overcome the ungodly yet; for the day will come when mighty truth shall prevail. May God hasten that blessed day! Until then, when we are persecuted, let us remember that we are not forsaken; when cast down we are not destroyed. Many Christians are placed in positions where they are subject to very great temptations and persecutions; they are mocked, lauged at, ridiculed, called by evil name. Persecuted one, are you tempted to deny the faith? Are you going to put aside your colors and relinquish the cross of Christ? If so, then you are not made of the same stuff as the true disciples of Jesus Christ. For when the grace of God is in them, though the world be iron, they shall be northern iron and steel. They can bear all the blows which the world could possibly choose to lay on them. As the anvil breaks the hammers in the long run, so will they break the force of all persecution and triumph over it, by their patient endurance for the sake of Christ Jesus, their God and Savior.

MORNING

The grace of our Lord Jesus Christ be with you all — Romans 16:24.

SOME OF the greatest works that were ever performed by Christians were not immediate in their results. The farmer waits long for the precious fruits of the earth. Again and again the question has been asked, *"Watchman, what of the night?"* Some have had to labor all their lives and have had to bequeath to their heirs the promise whose fulfilment they had not personally seen. They laid the underground courses of the temple, and others entered into their labors. You know the story of the removal of St. Paul's by Sir Christopher Wren. A very massive piece of masonry had to be broken down, and by pick and shovel the task would have been a very tedious one. So this great architect prepared a battering ram for the job, and a large number of workmen were directed to strike with the ram with force against the wall. After several hours of labor, to all appearances the wall stood fast and firm. Their many strokes had been apparently fruitless, but the architect knew that they were gradually communicating motion to the wall, creating an agitation throughout the whole of it, and that by and by the entire mass would come down beneath a single stroke. No doubt the workmen attributed the result to the one crowning concussion, but their master knew that their previous strokes had only culminated in that one final blow. All the non-resultant work had been necessary to prepare for the stroke which achieved the purpose.

O Christian people, do not expect always to see the full outgrowth of your labors! Go on to serve your God, testify of His truth, tell of Jesus' love, pray for sinners, live a godly life, serve God with might and main. Then if no apparent harvest springs up to your sickle, be assured that others will follow you and will reap what you have sown. And since this will glorify God, it will be enough for you.

EVENING

Shall iron break the iron and the brass from the north? — Jeremiah 15:12.

SEE WHAT the cause of Christ is. It is truth: in this is victory. Who knows not that the truth will and must prevail? There is life in the church of God, and life is a thing you cannot overcome. A dead thing may be cut in pieces and strewn to the winds. But the life in Christ's church is that which has defied and has overcome Satan myriads of times already. In the dark ages the enemy thought he had destroyed the church, but life persisted. And one day it came into the monk in his cell, and Luther shook the world. The church in England fell into a deadly slumber in the days of Whitefield and Wesley, but she was not dead. Therefore a time of awakening came. The flame burned low, but the heavenly fire still lingered among the ashes, only needing the Holy Spirit to blow on it and cause a hallowed conflagation.

Six young men at Oxford University were found guilty of meeting to pray. Their offense was contagious, and soon there sprang up hundreds glorying in the same blessed 'crime.' Earnest servants of the living God were forthcoming, and no one knew from where they came. Like the buds and blossoms which come forth at the bidding of spring, so a people made willing the day of God's power came forward at once. Since there is life in the church of God, you can never calculate what will happen within its bounds tomorrow, for life is an unaccountable thing; it scorns the laws which bind the formal and the inanimate. The statues in St. Paul's Cathedral stand fixed on their pedestals, and the renowned dead in Westminster Abbey never raise a riot — but who can tell what the living may next conceive or attempt? Men have said, "We will put down the troublesome religion of these gospelers. Build prisons enough, forge chains enough, make racks enough, concoct tortures enough, slay enough victims, and we will stamp out this plague." But their designs have never been accomplished.

Shall iron break the iron and the brass from the north? — Jeremiah 15:12.

THOSE WHO SEEK to earn their salvation by their self-righteous efforts should be reminded that the iron will never break the northern iron and the steel. The bonds of guilt are not to be snapped by a merely human power. Here is a man with the fetters of his transgressions binding him, but he says that he can get them off. He imagines that prayer will be his file, that tears shall be the aqua fortis to dissolve the metal; that his own resolution shall dash the links like a hammer. But it cannot be. Habits of sin do not yield to raspings of the unregenerate resolves. Self-righteous one, you are condemned. Only Christ the Son of God can set you free from the fetters which hold you in the condemned cell. All your efforts apart from Jesus are utterly useless. He alone can bring you liberty; you cannot emancipate yourself. You say that you will break off the evil habit. You may break off some habits, but can you alter your evil nature? *"Can the Ethiopian change his skin, or the leopard his spots?"* (Jer. 13:23). That would be an easy task compared with a man renewing his own heart. The imaginations of the thoughts of your heart are only evil, and that continually (Gen. 6:5). And do what you will they will remain so. The dead cannot give themselves life; it needs superior power to deliver the dead from their natural supulcher. Your iron can never break that which binds you to the slavery of Hell. Do you think to force your way into Heaven by ceremony? Do you imagine that baptism can wash away your sin, or that confirmation can convey grace to you? Do you think that the ceremonies of man's devising, or even those of God's instituting, can deliver you from wrath? Do not believe it! There is no power in any or all of those to deliver you from the bonds of guilt which hold you. Your iron cannot ever break the northern iron and the steel.

EVENING

Shall iron break the iron and the brass from the north? — Jeremiah 15:12.

CHRISTIAN, IF YOU cannot break a heart, truly it is no business of yours to do so. Commit that work to Him who is fully equal to the miracle. Keep to your work and do not fear that the Lord will work with you. God bids you to continue prayer, warning, instruction, and invitation. If you knew that every soul you witnessed to would be lost, it would be no less your duty to make the gospel known. For the duty is to tell out the gospel and is not to be influenced by success — it is based on the commission of Christ. Ezekiel's duty is to make the dry bones live. But whether they live or not, it is his duty to prophesy to them. Noah was none the less a preacher of righteousness because none except his own family listened to his appeals and sought shelter in the ark. Go on with your work, but let a sense of your personal inability make you fall back on your God. Let it keep you from one self-reliant word, much more from one self-confident sermon or speech. Every time we try to do good in our own strength, the effort bears the certainty of defeat in its own bowels. To do such is to shoot pointless darts, to wield a blunted sword. Dare not to go to work for God without God. Only God's power can save souls: *"Except the Lord build the house, they labor in vain who build it."* Spiritual children are a heritage of the Lord, and the fruit of our soul's womb is His reward. Feel your weakness, and then you will know your strength. Go to the sinner in God's strength, and then you will see the Divine operation — but certainly not till then. What a blessing it is to be made to lie low in the dust, and to see what unworthy ones we are!

August 10 MORNING 223

For the Lord loves judgment and does not forsake His saints; they are preserved forever — Psalm 37:25.

A DESPONDING SOUL may say, "I shall die for want." But when were the righteous forsaken? If indeed it be so, then your journey here is ended, and you are fully suplied for the hereafter. But one says, "I am not sure of that; were I sure of Heaven it would be another matter." Then you have other matters to trouble yourself about than these. These then should be the least of your cares. Souls perplexed about the want of Christ, pardon of sin, etc. are usually not so solicitous about these temporal things. One that seriously puts such questions as these, "What shall I do to be saved? How shall I know that my sin is pardoned?" will not be troubling himself with, "What shall I eat, what shall I drink, or with what shall I be clothed?"

Does it become the children of such a Father to distrust His all-sufficiency, or to repine at any of His dispensations? Do you well to question His care and love on every new exigency? Say, have you not formerly been ashamed of this? Has not your Father's seasonable provision for you in former difficulties put you to the blush and made you resolve never more to question His love and care? And yet will you again renew your unworthy suspicions of Him? Insincere child! Reason thus with yourself: "If I perish for lack of what is good and needful for me, it must be either because my Father knows not my needs, or He cannot supply them, or He cares not what becomes of me." Which of these will you charge on Him? Not the first, for *My Father knows what I have need of*. Not the second, for *the earth is the Lord's and the fullness of it*; His name is God All-sufficient. Not the last, for *as a Father pities His children, so the Lord pities those that fear Him; the Lord is exceedingly pitiful and full of mercy;* — and will He not hear me? Christ says, *Consider the fowls of the air* — not the fowls at the door that are fed every day by hand, but the fowls of the air that have no one to provide for them. Does He feed and clothe His enemies, and will He forget His children? He even heard the cry of distress from Ishmael. O unbelieving heart, will you still doubt? — John Flavel, from *Keeping the Heart*, pp. 62,63.

EVENING

My eye is also dim because of grief, and all my members are as a shadow — Job 17:7.

JOB'S AFFLICTION was great, yet he follows these words with this: *"But the righteous shall hold firmly on his way"* (verse 8).

"Your poverty is not your sin, but your affliction. If you have not by sinful means brought it on yourself, and if it is but an affliction, it may the more easily be borne. It is hard indeed to bear an affliction coming on us as the fruit and punishment of sin. When men are under trouble on that account, they say, 'O if it were but a single affliction, coming from the hand of God by way of trial, I could bear it. But I have brought it on myself by sin; it comes as the punishment of sin; the marks of God's displeasure are on it. It is the guilt within that troubles and galls more than the want without." But it is not so here; so you have no reason to be cast down under it.

"But though there be no sting of guilt, yet this condition does not lack other stings. For instance, there is discredit of religion. I cannot comply with my engagements in the world, and by this religion is likely to suffer.' It is well that you have a heart to discharge every duty. Yet if God disables you by His providence, it is no discredit to your profession so long as it is your desire and endeavor to do what you can and ought to do. And in this case God's will is that forbearance be exercised toward you.

"But I find such a condition full of temptations, a great hindrance in the way to Heaven." Every condition in the world has its hindrances and attending temptations. If you were in a prosperous condition you might there meet with more temptations and fewer advantages. Here you have an opportunity to discover the sincerity of your love to God, when you can live on Him, find enough in Him, and constantly can follow Him, even when all external inducements and motives fail — John Flavel.

MORNING

I will love You, O Lord, my strength — Psalm 18:1.

"God has, as it were, made Himself over to believers. David does not say, God will give or bestow salvation on me. But he says, *'He is the horn of my salvation.'* It is God Himself who is the salvation and the portion of His people. They would not care much for salvation if God were not their salvation. It pleases the saints that they enjoy God, rather than that they enjoy salvation. False and carnal spirits will express a great deal of desire after salvation, for they like the idea of salvation, Heaven and glory well. But they never express any longing desire after God and Jesus Christ. They love the idea of salvation, but they do not care for a Savior. Now that which faith pitches on most is God Himself; He shall be my salvation — let me have Him, and that is salvation enough. He is my life; He is my comfort; He is my riches; He is my honor; yea, He is my all. So David's heart acted immediately on God: *'I will love You, O Lord, my strength. The Lord is my rock, and my fortress, and my deliverer. My God, my strength, in whom I will trust; my buckler, and the honor of my salvation, and my high tower.'* It pleased holy David more that God was his strength, than that God gave him strength; that God was His deliverer, than that he was delivered — that God was his fortress, his buckler, his horn, his high tower, than that He gave him the effect of all these.

It pleased David, and it pleases all the saints more that God is their salvation, whether temporal or eternal, than that He saves them. The saints look more at God than at all that is God's" — Joseph Caryl.

EVENING

We love Him because He first loved us — 1 John 4:19.

GOD'S LOVE is evidently prior to ours: *"He first loved us."* It is also clear enough from the text that God's love is the cause of our love, for *"We love Him because He first loved us."* Therefore, going back to old time, or rather before all time, when we find God loving us with an everlasting love (Jer. 31:3), we gather that the reason of His choice is not because we loved Him. It was because He willed to love us. His reasons — for He had reasons, for we read of the counsel of His will — are know to Himself, but they are not to be found in any inherent goodness in us, or which was foreseen to be in us. We are chosen simply because He will have mercy on whom He will have mercy (Rom. 9:15). He loved us because He desired to love us. The gift of His dear Son, which was a close consequent on His choice of His people, was too great a sacrifice on God's part to have been drawn from Him by any goodness in the creature. It was not possible for the highest piety to have deserved so vast a boon as the gift of the Only-begotten. It was not possible for anything in man to have merited the incarnation and the passion of the Redeemer. Our redemption, like our election, springs from the spontaneous self-originating love of God. And our regeneration, in which we are made partakers of the Divine blessings in Jesus Christ was not of us, nor by us. We were not converted because we were already inclined that way. Neither were we regenerated because some good thing was in us by nature. But we owe our new birth entirely to His potent love, which dealt with us effectually, turning us from death to life, from darkness to light, and from the alienation of our mind and the enmity of our spirit into the delightful path of love, in which we are now traveling to the skies. As believers in Christ's name we were *"born, not of blood, nor of the will of the flesh, nor of the will of man — but of God"* (John 1:12).

MORNING

We love Him because He first loved us — 1 John 4:19.

LOVE TO GOD does not begin in the heart from any disinterested admiration of the nature of God. After we have loved God (because He first loved us), then we may grow in grace as to love God for what He is. It is possible, perhaps, for us to be the subjects of a state of heart in which our love spends itself on the loveliness of God in His own person. We may come to love Him because He is so wise, so powerful, so good, so patient, so everything that is lovable. This may be produced within us as ripe fruit, the fruit of maturity, in the Divine life. But it is never the first spring and fountain of the grace of love in anyone's heart. Even the apostle John, the man who had looked within the veil and seen the excellent glory beyond any other man, and who had leaned his head on the bosom of the Lord, and had seen the Lord's holiness, and marked the inimitable beauty of the character of the incarnate God — even John does not say, "We love Him because we admire Him." No, but he says, *"We love Him because He first loved us."* For see, if this kind of love which I have mentioned, which is called the love of disinterested admiration, were required of a sinner, how could he readily render it? Take two gentlemen of equal rank in society, and the one is not obliged to the other. Now standing on an equality they can easily feel a disinterested admiration of each other's character, and a consequent disinterested affection. But a poor sinner, by nature sunk in the mire of sin, full of everything that is evil, condemned, guilty of death, his only desert being to be cast into Hell — that one is under such obligations to his Savior and God that it would be idle to talk about a disinterested affection for Him. If you owe your life, your all, to Him, then you cannot be disinterested. Besides, until you catch the gleams of His mercy and His loving-kindness to guilty sinners, His holy, just, and righteous character is not lovable to you — for His purity then condemns your defilement.

EVENING

We love Him because He first loved us — 1 John 4:19.

IT IS CERTAIN, beloved, that faith in the heart always precedes love. We first believe the love of God to us before we love God in return. Oh what an encouraging truth this is, that I, a sinner, do not believe that God loves me because I feel I love Him. No, rather, I first believe that He loves me, sinner though I am, and then having believed this gracious fact, I come to love my Benefactor in return. Perhaps some of you seekers are saying to yourselves, "Oh that we could love God, for then we could hope for mercy." That is not the first step. Your first step is to believe God, and when His truth is fully fixed in your soul by the Holy Spirit, a fervent love to God will spontaneously issue from your soul, even as flowers willingly pour forth their fragrance under the influence of the dew and the sun. Everyone that ever was saved had to come to God not as a lover of God, but as a sinner.

We all wish to take money in our sacks when we go down hungry to Egypt to buy the bread of life. But Heaven's bread is given to us freely, and we must accept it freely, without money and without price (Isa. 55:1). Do you say, "I do not feel one good emotion in my heart, nor appear to possess one good thought; I fear I have no love to God at all"? Do not remain in unbelief until you feel love to God, for if you so remain you will never believe at all. It is true that you ought to love God, but you never will until you believe Him; you must especially believe in His love as revealed in His only begotten Son. If you come to God in Christ, and believe this simple message: *"God was in Christ reconciling the world to Himself, not imputing their trespasses to them,"* (2 Cor. 5:19) then you will find your heart going out after God. For, *"Whoever believes in Jesus Christ shall not perish, but have everlasting life"* (John 3:15). Do you believe this? Can you believe in, trust in Jesus? If you do, Christ died for you.

We love Him because He first loved us — 1 John 4:19.

DAY BY DAY you should see the deeds of God's love to you as He gives you food and clothing, and you receive His mercies in this life — and especially in the covenant blessings which God gives you: the peace He pours out in your heart, the communion which he vouchsafes to you with Himself and His blessed Son, and the answers to prayer which He grants you. Note well these things, and if you consider them carefully and weigh their value, you will be accumulating the fuel on which love feeds its consecrated flame. In proportion as you see in every good gift a new token of your Father's love, in that proportion you will make progress in the sweet school of love. Oh, it is heavenly living to taste God's love in every morsel of bread we eat. It is blessed living to know that we breathe an atmosphere purified and made fragrant with Divine love; that love protects us while we sleep; that love opens the eyelids of the morning to smile on us when we awaken. Ah, even when we are sick, it is love that chastens us. When we are impoverished, love relieves us of a burden. Love gives, and love takes; love cheers, and love smites. We are compassed about with love, above, beneath, around, within, without. If we could but recognize this, we would become as flames of fire, ardent and fervent toward our God. Knowledge and observation are admirable nurses of our infant love.

And, ah, the soul grows rich in love to God when she rests on the bosom of Divine loving-kindness. You, who are tossed about with doubts and fears as to whether you are now accepted, or whether you shall persevere to the end, you can scarcely guess the ardors of heart which inflame those saints who have learned to cast themselves wholly on Jesus. You can hadly know beyond a doubt that His love is unchangeable. Whether I sink or swim, I will have no hope but in Christ; he is my life, my all.

EVENING

We love Him because He first loved us — 1 John 4:19.

GOD'S LOVE to us never changes, but our love to Him too often sinks to a low ebb. Perhaps some of you have become so cold in your affections that it is difficult to be sure that you ever did love God at all. It may be your life has become lax, so much so as to deserve the censure of the church. You who are backsliding, you are in a dangerous condition. Yet if there is indeed spiritual life in you, you will wish to return. You may have gone astray like a lost sheep, but your prayer will be, "seek Your servant, for I do not forget Your commandments." Now note that the cause which originated your love is the same which must restore it. At first you went to Christ as a sinner, and your first act was to believe the love of God to sinners, at a time when there was nothing in you that evidenced it. Go the same way again. Do not stop to pump up love out of the dry well within yourself! Do not think it possible that love will come at your bidding. If one would give all the substance of his house for love, it would be utterly condemned. Think of the Lord's unchanging grace, and you may feel the springtime of love returning to your soul. Still the Lord reserves mercy for the sinful; still He waits to be gracious; still He is willing to receive you now that you have played the prodigal, even as He was to have retained you at home in the bosom of His love. Many considerations ought to aid you, O backslider, to believe more in the love of God than you ever did. For think what love it must be that can invite you still to return. After knowing so much, you have sinned against light and knowledge. After having experienced so much, you have given the lie to your profession of faith. He might justly have cut you down, for you have been cumbering the ground. Yet He yet invites you to return.

August 14   MORNING   227

Though I walk through the valley of death, I will fear no evil — Psalm 23:4.

"WHAT, NOT FEAR THEN? Why, what friend is it that keeps up your spirits, that bears you company in that black and dismal region? The saint will soon tell you that God is with him, and in those slippery ways he leans on His staff, and these were the cordials that keep his heart from fainting. I challenge all the gallants in the world, out of all their merry, jovial clubs, to find such a company of merry, cheerful creatures as the friends of God are. It is not the company of God, but the lack of it, that makes sad. Alas! You do not know what the comforts of God's children are. Strangers to God cannot know their joy. You think that those with so grave a countenance cannot be merry. But they are sure that you cannot truly be merry when you smile, for a curse is on your souls. They know that He spoke that sentence which could not be mistaken, *'even in laughter the heart is sorrowful, and the end of that mirth is heaviness.*' But the calling of your roaring singing, and your laughter mirth, it is what the Spirit of God calls madness (Eccl. 2:2). When a carnal man's heart is ready to die within him, to become like a stone, how cheerfully can they look into the face of God? Which of the valiant ones of the world can outface death, look joyfully into eternity? Which of them can hug a fagot, embrace the flames? This the saint can do, and more too. For he can look infinite justice in the face with a cheerful heart. He can hear of Hell with joy and thankfulness. He can think of the day of judgment with great delight and comfort. Again I challenge the world to produce one out of all their merry companies that can do any or all of this. All you jovial blades, call for your harps and viols; add what you will to make the concert complete. Now, sinner, come away, this night your soul shall appear before God. What do you say now? Where now are your merry companions? Where are your darling pleasures? Have they all come to this? But the saint is different. He is going to his Friend, who will accompany him through *the valley of the shadow of death.* — adapted from James Janeway, on Psalm 144:15.

EVENING

Now You will let Your servant go in peace, Lord, according to Your word. For my eyes have seen Your salvation — Luke 2:29,30.

THERE ARE WORDS to encourage us to the same readiness to depart this life. *According to Your Word, Lord."* Go to the Bible and take from it several choice words all calculated to cheer our hearts in the prospect of departure. And the first is Psalm 23:4: *"Yes, though I walk through the valley of the shadow of death, I will fear no evil, for You are with me; Your rod and Your staff, they comfort me."* We walk — the Christian does not quicken his pace when he dies. He walked with God before, and he is not afraid of death, so he calmly walks on to meet his Lord. It is a walk through a *"shadow"* — there is no substance in death, it is only a shade. Who needs fear a shadow? It is not a lonely walk, either, for *"You are with me."* Neither is it a walk that need cause us terror, for, *"I will fear no evil."* Not only is there no evil, but no fear shall cloud my dying hours. It shall be a departure full of comfort, for, *"Your rod and Your staff, they comfort me"* — it is a fulness of consolation.

Follow the direction of another text, *"According to Your word":* Psalm 37:37, *"Mark the perfect man, and behold the upright; for the end of that man is peace."* If we are perfect, that is sincere; if we are upright, that is honest in heart; then our end shall assuredly be peace.

Psalm 116:15: *"Precious in the sight of the Lord is the death of His saints."* It is not an ordinary thing for a saint to die; it is a spectacle which the eyes of God are delighted with. As kings will delight in their pearls and diamonds, counting them precious, so does God delight in the death beds of His saints; they are precious to Him.

MORNING

> But I am poor and needy. Make haste to me, O God. You are my help and deliverer. O Lord, wait no longer! — Psalm 70:5.

IT IS THE HABIT of faith, when praying, to use pleas. Mere prayer sayers (who really do not pray at all) forget to argue with God. But those who would prevail bring forth their reasons and their strong arguments. They debate the question with the Lord, according to His word. The ones who play at wrestling will catch here and there at random. But wrestlers have a certain way to grasp an opponent, a certain mode of gaining ascendancy, etc.; they work according to order and rule. Faith's art of wrestling is to plead with God, saying with boldness, "Let it be thus and thus, for these reasons." Hosea tells us of Jacob at Jabbok, *"that there he spoke to us,"* by which I understand that Jacob instructed us by example. Now the two pleas which Jacob used were God's precepts and God's promises. First, he said, *"You said to me, Return to your country and to your kindred."* It is as much as if he put it this way, "Lord, I am in difficulty, but I have come here through obedience to You. You told me to do this. Now, since you commanded me to come here into the very teeth of my brother Esau, who is coming to meet me like a lion, then, Lord, You will not bring me into danger and then leave me in it." This was sound reasoning and it prevailed with God. Then Jacob urged a promise also, *"You said, I will surely do you good."* Among men it is a masterly way of reasoning when you challenge your opponent with his own words. You may quote other authorities, and he may say that he denies their force. But when you quote a man against himself, you foil him completely. When you bring a man's promise to his mind, he must either confess himself to be unfaithful and changeable, or if he holds to being the same, and true to his word, you have him. But God is always faithful to His word, and He never changes. Therefore, please learn to use His own words to Him.

EVENING

But I am poor and needy. Make haste to me, O God. You are my help and deliverer. O Lord, wait no longer! — Psalm 70:5.

HERE IS ANOTHER PART of the art and mystery of prayer: the soul grasping God. Faith has pleaded, and has been urgent, but now she comes to close quarters, grasping the covenant Angel with one hand, *"You are my help,"* and with the other, *"You are my deliverer."* Oh, those blessed *my*'s those potent *my*'s! The sweetness of the Bible lies in the possessive pronouns. Any who is taught to use them as the Psalmist did will come off a conqueror with the eternal God. Now you sinners, I pray God you may be helped to say to the blessed Christ of God, *"You are my help and my deliverer."* Perhaps you mourn that you cannot do so, but, poor soul, have you any other help? If you have, you cannot hold two helpers with the same hand. If you say you have no help other than in Christ, then, poor soul, since your hand is empty, that empty hand was made on purpose to grasp your Lord — lay hold on Him. Say to Him today, "Lord I will hang on You as poor lame Jacob did; now I know I cannot help myself, I will cleave to You; I will not let You go except you bless me." But you say that would be too bold. Yea, but the Lord loves boldness in poor sinners, if that one is pleading Christ as the basis for his boldness. It is an unholy bashfulness that dares not trust a Savior God. For Christ died on purpose to save sinners, such as you are. Trust Him. But one says, "I am unworthy." But He came to seek and to save the unworthy. He is not the Savior of the self-righteous. He is the Savior for sinners, a *"friend of sinners."* Unworthy one, lay hold on Him! But you may say that you have no right. Well, but that is the very reason you should grasp Him for your right. He is your right.

August 16   MORNING

But I am poor and needy. Make haste to me, O God. You are my help and deliverer. O Lord, wait no longer! — Psalm 70:5.

YOU SAVED ONES love Christ. So as saints of God you must practice the last part of this prayer. Be sure to lay firm hold on God in prayer, praying, *"You are my help and my deliverer."* Throw yourself on the strength of God. You can do nothing without Him. If you do not mean to be without Him, then hold Him fast. There is a story of a boy at Athens who used to boast that he ruled all Athens. When they asked him how, he said, "Why, I rule my mother, my mother rules my father, and my father rules the city." Anyone who knows how to be a master of prayer will rule the heart of Christ, and Christ can and will do all things for His people; for the Father has committed all things into His hands. You can be full of power if you learn how to pray, powerful in all things which glorify God. What does the Word itself say? *'Let him lay hold on My strength.'* Prayer is designed of God to appeal to the arm that moves the world. Oh that you might have grace to grasp the Almighty through His love. More holdfast prayer is needed, more tugging and gripping and wrestling prayer, prayer that says, "I will not let go until You bless me." So Jacob said, and so Jacob did. And Jacob seemed to be put off at first, and held on, and held on, and strove with the covenant Angel. At last the angel turned from wrestling with Jacob to wounding him in the very seat of his human strength. And Jacob let his thigh go, and all his limbs go, but he will not let the Angel go. And then he was granted the victory. Even so you must hold on. Though your sinew be shrunk, the victory is then near. Never let God go until He has blessed you.

EVENING

But to you who fear My name, the Sun of righteousness shall rise — Malachi 4:2.

DOES YOUR HEART OFTEN SAY, "What shall I do, what shall I say, to give due honor to my Redeemer?" Have you not often felt confounded as to what offering you shall bring to Him? If you had been a possessor of all the worlds, you would have laid them at His feet. If the universe had been your heritage, you would cheerfully have given it to Him. And you would have felt happy to strip yourself of everything you owned in order to give more glory to Him. Since you do not have all this wealth, have you not again and again asked of your soul, "Oh, what shall I do to praise my Savior?" If you could, you would write the best of poems to extol him, but you have not the faculty or skill. You would sing the sweetest songs, compose the most melting music, use all art and wit and music to exalt Him. But you have no such talent, nor have such things any value in themselves to Him. With what then shall you adore Him? His very skirts are bright with brilliant, insufferable light. No flowers of nature will make a fit garland to cast at His feet. The gems or other things precious to men are not fit to crown His head. Of all things visible to you only the sun, that great orb which is the lord of light and the lamp of day is a faint image of your Savior. Here the Lord Himself uses it to speak of His excellent glory, whose countenance shines as the sun it its strength — He is the Sun of righteousness, and He shall arise, and *healing will be in His wings for you. And you shall go forth and frisk like the calf in the stall. And you shall trample the wicked, for they shall be ashes under the soles of your feet in the day which He is preparing, says Jehovah.*

MORNING

August 17

Deep calls to deep — Psalm 42:7.

DO ALLOW YOURSELF to be depressed by the mystery of the doctrine of eternal decrees. For even if these decrees were not in existence, there would still remain the other deep — the mystery of fact. It is a fact that sin is in the world; it is a fact that sorrow is there; it is a fact that death is there. How can you understand these things? Shut your eye to the depth above the firmament if you will, but here below is an amazing depth nearer home. Remember that all men are not saved. It is a dreadful truth that multitudes tread the broad road, and that they reach eternal destruction. Why is this when God is good and omnipotent? Can you understand providence? Is not providence, as we see it, quite as mysterious as predestination? Are not the mysteries rather in the facts themselves than in the purposes which ordained them? Are not both the facts and the decrees mysteries, equal mysteries? But what a wonderful harmony there is between the two depths! Observe how deep has called to deep. Whatever God ordained has been accomplished; His will has been done, and will be done. You may tell me that this is nothing wonderful, since God is omnipotent. Yes, but you must remember that He was pleased to create a race of beings to be free agents, with free choice. Not only the angels were created free in their will, and pure in their persons, but so also were men. Some angels sinned and fell. But all men sinned in their federal head, Adam, wilfully and resolutely choosing their own will above that of their Maker. In doing this they unknowingly fulfilled fore-ordination. Yet they are guilty, disobeying God without compulsion. In this lies the deep marvel, that being voluntary agents they chose themselves as masters instead of God, and at the same time the eternal purpose was fulfilled in every jot and tittle, and is being fulfilled to this moment.

EVENING

Deep calls to deep — Psalm 42:7.

GREAT DEPTHS OF TRIAL bring with them great depths of promise. For you, much afflicted one, there are great and mighty words which are not meant for others of easier experience. You shall drink from deep goblets of truth that are reserved for the giants of faith, men of capacity enough to quaff deep draughts of the well-refined words of God. Trials are mighty enlargers to the soul. We are normally contracted, narrowed, pent up, and can rightly pray, "Lord, enlarge my heart." Yes,but the opening of capacious reservoirs within us can only be effected by the spade of deep, daily tribulation. Then, having been dug out by pain and trouble, room is created in us for the overflowing promises of God. A great adversity will bring great grace to the believer. Whenever the Lord sets His servants to do extraordinary work, then He always gives them extraordinary strength — and He puts them to unusual suffering, giving them unusual patience (as He did with Paul).

"*Deep calls to deep.*" What's that? Why, it is expressed in the verse before, '*O God, my soul is cast down within me*' — '*down,*' that is, *deep* into the jaws of distrust and fear. And, Lord, my soul in this *depth* of sorrow calls for help to Your *depth* of mercy. For though I am sinking, and am going down, yet not so low that Your mercy is yet underneath me. Do, of Your compassions, open those everlasting arms and catch him that has no help or stay in himself. For so it is with one that is falling to a well or a dungeon" — John Bunyan.

If God calls you to common and ordinary trials, He will pay the charges of your warfare by thousands. But if He commands you to an unusual struggle with a tremendous foe, then He will discharge the liabilities of that war by millions, *according to the riches of His grace in which He has abounded toward us through Christ Jesus.* In your better mind, would you want to escape great labors or great trials, since in them are promised to you great graces?

August 18 — MORNING

Deep calls to deep — Psalm 42:7.

HUMAN WRETCHEDNESS is paralleled by Divine grace. See into what an dreadful state our race fell? We were arrainged for high treason through the sin of our father Adam. In this the dignity and honor of our race were forfeited. We were *"conceived in sin and shaped in iniquity"* (Psalm 51:5). With a natural tendency toward evil we came into this world. And ever since we have been in this world we have wickedly and wilfully rebelled against God our Creator. We have rendered ourselves obnoxious to the Divine justice; we deserve to be driven from the glory of His presence by the power of His wrath. Besides all this, we are desperately set on rejecting any offers of mercy on the part of God. Our will has become depraved; our heart is stony. There are no known human means which can bring a soul to God. Man is such an enemy of God that he will not even entertain the thought of being reconciled to Him. Human eloquence and human sympathy are powerless against human depravity. Oh, what a sad case is fallen man! He is lost, utterly, hopelessly, everlastingly lost by nature. Considered in himself, there is no remedy for the awesome disease raging within him. There is no escape from the eternal fire which shall consume him, except that offered through Christ. Do not for a moment make out the abyss of the fall to be less deep than it is — it is bottomless. The miseries of mankind cannot be exaggerated. If our tears could ever flow, if we could be turned each one into a Jeremiah, yet we could never weep enough for the slain of our people. Human misery is deep beyond expression. But what shall I say? How shall I speak? Where shall I find words to express the delight of my soul, that I have such a truth to tell you? There is a deep which answers to the deep of human ruin — it is the deep of Divine grace as revealed in the gospel of Jesus Christ — salvation by faith in Him.

EVENING

Deep calls to deep — Psalm 42:7.

THE DEPTH OF DIVINE LOVE to the saints calls for a depth of consecration in every believing heart. Quietly study for a minute, meditate on the depth of the love of God to you and to all His chosen people. He has loved you without a cause. He has loved you without beginning. Before years, and centuries, and millenniums began to be counted, your name was on His heart. Eternal thoughts of love have been in God's bosom toward you from everlasting (Jer. 31:3). He has loved you without a pause; there has never been a time when He did not love you, if you are His. Your name once engraved in His heart has never been erased, nor has He ever blotted it out of the Book of Life. Since you have been in this world He has loved you most patiently. You have often provoked Him; you have often rebelled against Him, times without number. Yet He has never stayed the outflow of His heart toward you. And, blessed be His name, He never will! You are His; you were always His; and you always will be His. Jesus says to you, *"Because I live, you shall live also."* God's love to you is without boundary. He could not love you any more, for He loves you like God Himself. He will never love you less, because He never changes. All His heart belongs to you — *"As the Father has loved Me, even so I have loved you"* — it is what Jesus says to you (John 15:19).

Contemplate for a moment what you have received as the result of this Divine love. You have received, first of all, the gift of the only-begotten Son. He left the throne of honor for the cross of shame, the brightness of glory for the humiliation of earthly life and the darkness of the tomb. Oh, the depths of the love which is revealed in Calvary! You will never, never, never be able to fathom the depth of the love of God toward you and all others that are His chosen ones, in the gift of His dear Son to be your Redeemer.

MORNING

Bless the Lord, O my soul; and all that is within me, bless His holy name —
Psalm 103:1.

THAT MODE of blessing God to which we are called is very spiritual — a matter of soul and spirit. You are not to bless God with your voice only, nor merely with the help of a fine organ, or a trained choir. But you are to bless Him in a far more difficult manner: *"Bless the Lord, O my soul."* Soul music is the soul of music. The music of the soul is that which pleases the ear of God. The great Spirit is delighted with that which comes from our spirit. Why, surely you do not think that even the music of the best orchestra, majestic though it may be, affords pleasure to God in the sense that such sweet sounds are pleasing to us. As for all human melody, it must be imperfect to the All-glorious One. God's idea of music is framed on a far higher and nobler platform of taste than ever could be reached by mere mortal man. The sons of the cherubs and the seraphs infinitely exceed all that we could ever raise, so far as mere sound is concerned. And mere sound is nothing to God. He could set the winds to music, tune the roaring of the sea and harmonize the crash of tempests. If he wanted music, He would not ask it of human lips and mouths.

A heart that loves God makes music to Him. A heart that praises Him has within itself all the harmonies that He delights in. The sigh of love is to Him a lyric, the sob of repentance is melody, the inward cries of His own children are an oratorio, and their heart-songs are true hallelujahs. The things unheard by man is often best heard by God. Speechless praise: the deep meaning of the heart, this is what God loves. Spiritual worship! Oh, how often this is neglected! Only the conscious presence of the Spirit of God will enable us to worship with the soul — and that is the main thing in prayerful worship.

EVENING

Bless the Lord, O my soul; and all that is within me, bless His holy name —
Psalm 103:1.

"BLESS the Lord, O my soul" — "O how well they are fitted! For what work is so fit for my soul as this? Who is so fit for this work as my soul? God knows that my body is gross and heavy, very unfit for so sublime a work. No, my soul, it is you that must do it. And, indeed, what else have you to do? It is the very work for which you are made, and Oh that you were as fit to do the work as the work is fit for you to do! But, alas! You have become in a manner earthy; at least you have lost a great part of your abilities, and you will never be able to go through with this great work by yourself. If to bless the Lord were no more than to say, Lord, Lord, ... then my tongue alone would be sufficient for it, and I would not need to trouble any other about it. But to bless the Lord is eminent work; it requires not only many but able agents to perform it. Therefore, my soul, when you go about it, go not alone — take with you *"all that is within you;"* all the forces in your whole magazine, whether it be your heart, or your spirits, or your will, or your affections, or you understanding, or your memory — take them all with you, and bless the Lord." (from a sermon by Sir. R. Baker).

"All that is within me" — "Let your *conscience* bless the Lord by unvarying fidelity. Let your *judgment* bless Him by decisions in accordance with His word. Let your *imagination* bless Him by pure and holy musings. Let your *affections* bless Him by loving whatever He loves. Let your *desires* bless Him by seeking only His glory. Let your *memory* bless Him by not forgetting any of His benefits. Let your *thoughts* bless Him by meditating on His excellencies. Let your *hope* bless Him by longing and looking for the glory that is to be revealed. Let every *sense* bless Him by its fealty, your every *word* by its truth, and your every *act* by its integrity." (John Stevenson)

August 20   MORNING

Jesus heard that they threw him out. And finding him He said to him, Do you believe on the Son of God? — John 9:35.

THE EYE OF THE LORD is always on His chosen; He knows every circumstance which occurs to them. *"Jesus heard that they threw him out"* — our Lord had done too much for this man to forget him. Where grace has done a great work, its memory lingers, for it is written, *"You will have a desire to the work of Your hands."* Take comfort in this; if anything is grieving us, Jesus has heard of it and will act on it.

Our Lord sought for the outcast one. Unasked, He had opened his eyes. Unsought, He looks after him in his hour of trouble. He was not easy to find, but our Lord is able to search out all His lost sheep. He persevered until He found him. If at any time we should seem to be cast off by Christ, as well as cast down by proud religionists, be assured that He will find us when we cannot find Him. Bless be His holy name!

Our Lord's object was to do this man real service. He had been cast out of the synagogue, so he needed comfort. The grand thing to comfort him was to lead him onward and upward in the Divine life. Our Lord's way of comforting him was to ask a question which would lead to heart searching, and suggest spiritual advance. It is not the way we might take, but His ways are not our ways, nor are His thoughts our thoughts (Isa. 57:8). Wisdom is justified of her methods. When a man is in soul trouble it is best to make him look to his own condition before God, and specially to his faith. For when he finds that he is right on the main point of faith, this assurance will be to him a well-spring of comfort. We are sure that our Lord took the very best means to bring this man to well-grounded confidence when He said to him, *"Do you believe on the Son of God?"* He helped him by this question to make a considerable advance in faith.

EVENING

Jesus heard that they threw him out. And finding him He said to him, Do you believe on the Son of God? — John 9:35.

DO YOU INQUIRE, 'Do I believe on the Son of God?" — then answer this, Is Christ precious to you? For to you who believe, He is precious. If you love and prize Him as that most precious on earth or in Heaven, you could not have this appreciation of Him if you were not a believer in Him. Tell me, have you undergone the change called the new birth? Have you passed through a process which could be described as being brought out of darkness into marvelous light? If so, your new birth is sure evidence of faith, for these things go together. While faith is a proof of regeneration, regeneration is also a proof that you have faith in the Son of God.   Again, are you obedient to Christ? For faith works by love; it purifies the soul. Is it so with you? Has sin become bitter? Do you loathe it? Has holiness become sweet? Do you follow after it? It is not whether you are perfect, but whether the whole current of your soul yearns toward being perfect? Can you say that if you could live entirely without sin it would be the greatest delight you could have? Would absolute perfection be heavenly to you? Ah! Then it shows which way your mind goes; it shows that there is a change of nature, for no unrenewed heart pines after perfect holiness. Your heart is bending toward Christ's perfect rule and sovereignty; you have believed that He is the Son of God. You are resting on Him with a true and living faith if you take up His cross heartily and follow Him. Again, do you love God? Do you love His people? — *"We know that we have passed from death to life because we love the brothers"* (1 John 3:14). Do you love His Word? Do you delight in His worship? Do you bow in patience before His rod, so that you can take up the bitter cup and say, *"Your will be done"*? These things prove that you have faith in Jesus.

MORNING

And the sons of Israel saw the face of Moses, that the skin of Moses' face shone. And Moses put the veil on his face again, until he went in to speak with Him —
Exodus 34:35.

THIS MAN MOSES not only obtained this brightness by his long communion and his intercessory prayer and self-oblivion, but by his faithfulness among the people. When he went down in the interval between the two fastings, and found the people worshiping the golden calf, he did not spare them. He loved them, but he did not keep back the stern blow of justice. He said, *"Who is on the Lord's side?"* And the tribe of Levi came to him. And he said, *"Go through the camp and each man kill his brother who shall be found rebelling against Jehovah."* At once they cut off the idolaters who were guilty of open treason against the King of Israel. But this was not enough. The whole nation must be chastened for its great sin and humbled by a symbolical punishment. Moses, having broken the tables in his holy wrath, may be supposed to have taken down their idol god, grinding it, pounding it, dissolving it in water, and sternly he made a nauseous, bitter draught of their idol, compelling the tribes to drink of it. By this they would know what it was to turn away from Jehovah their God.

Grand old Moses! Faithful servant of God! Unbending executioner of Divine justice! He was meek, but by no means indifferent to truth and righteousness. For God does not choose milksops who are destitute of backbone to wear His glory on their faces. We have plenty of men nowdays that seem to be made of sugar, who melt into the stream of popular opinion. But such as these shall never ascend into the mount of the Lord, nor stand in His holy place, nor wear the tokens of His glory. O my friend, it is needful that you be true to the Lord in public if you desire to have His fellowship in private.

EVENING

And the sons of Israel saw the face of Moses, that the skin of Moses' face shone. And Moses put the veil on his face again, until he went in to speak with Him —
Exodus 34:35.

MOSES DID NOT SEE the glory of his own face because he had seen the glory of God. When a man gets a clear view of the holiness of God, it is all over with all claims of personal excellence. From that day he abhors himself in dust and ashes. If I once thought myself pure, then realize that He has said that even the heavens are not pure in His sight, that only vain man thinks himself to be wise, that He has even charged His angels with folly — then how can I speak of perfect purity as a thing which I possess. After I have seen the King, the Lord of Hosts, such a notion is shameful. A vision of God is the end of boasting. He who has looked into the face of the sun is blinded to all other light. So it is with the light of the face of God.

It may be profitable to remember that Moses had not seen the shining of his own face because it had never once entered into his thoughts to wish that his face would shine. That is true beauty of character which comes without being south — that unconscious excellence, a character which commands an admiration which it has never desired. Are we not too apt to wish to be bright in the eyes of others? Have we not at times labored to grow in grace so that we might be said to outgrow the grace of others? Is there not a man or two who has prayed for success in his ministry, having a little squint in his eye toward an ambition to be thought eminently useful? Is there no sister who has sought the salvation of her class so that she may be esteemed as a remarkable soul winner? Have you never prayed for holiness, really meaning that you wished to be considered holy? Have you never prayed in public with great fervor, having a half-suppressed wish to be thought a special man with God? Would it not have greatly gratified you to hear men say, "What a prayer that was!" Have you not even labored to be humble so that you might rejoice in your humility? Many have done these things, but not this man Moses. He had looked into the face of God, and it made him meek and humble.

MORNING — August 22

But now in Christ Jesus, you who were at one time far off are made near by the blood of Christ — Ephesians 2:13.

IF AN ANGEL had poised himself in mid-air and had watched Moses gazing down on the people in the wilderness and their surroundings, his eye would have rested on the central spot, the tabernacle. Over it rested the pillar of cloud and fire by day and night, as the outward index of the presence of God. Now, in your mind's eye, observe yonder select persons clad in fair white linen, who come very near to that great center — they are the priests who are engaged from day to day sacrificing bullocks and lambs, serving God according to His commands. They are near to the Lord, engaged in his holy work, but they are not the nearest of all. One man alone comes nearest, the high priest, who once every year enters into the Holy of Holies within the veil. Ah, what condescension is that which gives us, the believers in Christ, the same access to God every day. The priests are servants of God, and very near to Him, but not the nearest. And it would be great grace if God permitted the priests to enter into the most holy place. But our nature today does not compare to that of the priests in those days. We were not devoted to His fear. The grace that has brought us near through the precious blood was much greater than that which admitted a priest within the veil. Every priest that went within the veil entered there with blood to be sprinkled on the mercy-seat. Only blood could make him able to go near the mercy-seat, blood carried and sprinkled by only the High Priest. If the angel continued his gaze he would see lying around the tabernacle the twelve tribes in their tents. These were a people outwardly near to God, for what nation had God so near to them? But they were not as near as the priests. And the priests were not as near as the High Priest. Such a High Priest we have (Heb. 8:1), who *"by His blood has consecrated for us a new and living way through the veil, that is, His flesh"* — then *"let us draw near with a true heart in full assurance of faith, our hearts having been sprinkled from an evil conscience"* (Heb 10:19-23).

EVENING

But now in Christ Jesus, you who were at one time far off are made near by the blood of Christ — Ephesians 2:13.

ISRAEL MAY FITLY REPRESENT the outward church, that is, those members which have not yet received all the spiritual blessing they might have, yet who are blessed and made near. If ever an Israelite advanced into the court of the priests, it must be with blood; he came with sacrifice — there was no access without it. It was a great favor which permitted the Israelite to come into the court of the priests and to partake in Divine worship. But you and I were farther off than Israel, and more grace by far was required to bring us near. By blood alone, and that the most precious blood, are we made near, that blood which displayed all the glory of its power, even the blood of Christ Jesus.

Outside the camp of Israel you would have seen a company of miserable wretches who herded together. These were lepers, unclean, driven outside the camp. This is more like our position. If ever these lepers were brought near enough to come into communion with the camp of Israel, even more to come into communion with the priests, their access must be wholly and alone by blood. The turtle dove, or the young pigeon, must be slain; the lamb must be slaughtered; the scarlet wool and hyssop must be used — there was no purging of the leper to bring him into communion with the tribes of Israel except by blood.

We in our filthiness are so like the leper. We have to praise almighty grace which looked on us when our natural depravity stared us in the face, making it apparent that we continually disobeyed God. We have to praise His mercy which alone has brought us right away from the leper's place to nearness to God, nearer than the accepted high priests of Israel — as near as our present High Priest, Jesus Christ.

MORNING

But now in Christ Jesus, you who were at one time far off are made near by the blood of Christ — Ephesians 2:13.

WE PERCEIVE our nearness to God in the very first hour of our conversion. The father at once fell on the neck of the prodigal son and kissed him. The prodigal is immediately accepted as his true child very near his father's heart. We who sometimes were far off being now His children are near to God. We have a renewed sense of this nearness when we plead the precious blood, saying, *"Purge me with hyssop, and I shall be clean; wash me, and I shall be whiter than snow"* (Ps. 51:7). We come to God and feel that He is near those who are of a broken and contrite heart (Ps. 51:17; Isa. 57:15). Our nearness to God is peculiarly evinced at the mercy-seat. The very term we use for prayer is, *"Let us draw near to God."* But, fellow-believers, we never get to God in prayer unless it is through pleading the precious blood of Christ. We see our nearness to God in the act of praise. In praising Him we often take the wings of seraphs and pass up into the glory of the Lord. But it always is through Him who by His precious blood makes our praise acceptable to the Most High. As believers we came near to God in the act of baptism, for we are baptized in the name of the Father, and of the Son, and of the Holy Spirit. Anyone touching that ordinance is wicked and base unless he sincerely desires fellowship in the Lord's death. The nearness we get to God in baptism by faith depends on whether or not we see the Blood there. If Jesus was buried for us, then we are buried with Him. Also in the Lord's supper we draw near to God. But it all lies in the blood — we get no nearness through the wine, nor through the bread; the elements are nothing in themselves. It is only when we get to feel that our Lord's flesh is food indeed, and His blood drink indeed, that we draw near to Him.

EVENING

But now in Christ Jesus, you who were at one time far off are made near by the blood of Christ — Ephesians 2:13.

LET US LIVE in the power of the nearness which union with Christ and the blood has given us. It is a well-known rule that our minds are sure to be occupied with those things which are most near to us. We may excuse ourselves for being so worldly, because the things of this world are so near us. But we must never venture to repeat that excuse again, since we now know that we are made near to God and heavenly things by the blood. Let your conversation be in Heaven, for *"where your treasure is, there let your heart be."*

Beloved, if we indeed are so near to God through the blood and through union with Christ, let us enjoy those things which this nearness was intended to bring. Those who live near the equator never lack for light or heat. There vegetation is luxuriant and every form of life is well developed. Those who live far away in the frigid zone, where the sun only casts slanting rays, may well be meager and short of stature, and feel the pinch of poverty. We Christians dwelling under the equator of the Lord's love must bring forth luxuriant fruit. Let us *rejoice with joy unspeakable*; let our souls be like those torrid zones, where all the birds of the region have rich and rare plumage, where brilliant flowers abound, where everything is full of vigor. May your Christianity be so.

If we are so near to God, it follows as a very natural exhortation, that we should exercise much faith in Him. If you are brought so near to God, then surely you need not fear He will leave you in poverty. If you were a stranger, and He did not know you, then He might cast you away. But if you are near to Him, as near as Christ is, you know He cannot be unkind, thoughtless, or ungenerous to you. Why, your name is on the palms of Jesus' hands. You live in His heart. If you are in Christ, you are under the very eye of God. He will keep you.

August 24   MORNING

For we do not have a High Priest who cannot be touched with the feeling of our weaknesses, but One who has been tempted in all things like us, but without sin —
Hebrews 4:15.

IT WAS INTENDED that God should commune with men through the high priest. That needs a person of great tenderness. A mind that is capable of listening to God, that understands what He teaches, must be a very tender one, so as to interpret the lofty sense into the lowly language of humanity. If the man is to come from among the infinites down to the ignorance and narrow capacities of mortal men, he must be tender as a nurse to children. For this reason great philosophers have not always been great teachers. Their profundity has prevented their translating their thoughts into the speech of common minds. It is possible to know so much that the knowledge becomes crowded up in human minds; then there is no possible gate for orderly revealing of the multitude of thoughts. The great thoughts of wisdom must be broken to us, even crumbled for the children.

Now the High Priest had to be a man who could commune with God, one hearkening to the sacred oracle. Then he was bound to come out to commonplace men of the wilderness, or men of the farm, and tell them what he had heard in secret from the infinite God — what he had grasped from the Lord he must so put that the people could grasp it and act on it. This is what our Lord has done in the tenderest manner. He reveals the Father. The things of God which He knows are made known to us by His Holy Spirit, as we are able to bear them. We are to learn of Him.

EVENING

For we do not have a High Priest who cannot be touched with the feeling of our weaknesses, but One who has been tempted in all things like us, but without sin —
Hebrews 4:15.

THE HIGH PRIEST was to instruct and to reprove the people. To instruct is delightful, but to reprove is difficult. Only a tender spirit can wisely utter rebuke. Israel's high priest needed to be as meek as Moses in his rebukes of the erring. Our Lord Jesus Christ tells us our faults in tones of love. His rebukes never break the heart. He never upbraids in bitterness, but He does so in faithfulness. Oh, the tenderness of Christ! He has been most gracious in correcting us, in love: *"As many as I love, I rebuke and chasten."* And we can take anything from Jesus. His hands make the bitter sweet. Among men we tend to shun some persons in the hour of our wounding, even if you believe that they would do their best to help you. Yet you do not feel that you could reveal your heart to them. Their kindness is apt to be hard and cold; their counsel is without the sweetening of fellow-feeling. They are as keen as a sword, and as cutting. It may be they are so much above us that we cannot reach up to them, nor expect them to reach down to us. But there are other persons, blessed ones, who seem to be like havens for ships. You rejoice to cast your anchor under their lee. You feel that you could tell them anything, and it would be received with patience and pity, that their heart would go out to you.

Now, beloved, you will be often disappointed if you select a man or a woman to be your confidant. But if you will resort to the Lord Jesus, whom God has commissioned to be a High Priest for you, you will find Him to be just the Friend you need. He loves the troubled, for *"in all their affliction He was afflicted."* He is very careful of the feebleminded, and of the little ones, too. All kinds of men and women will find Him perfectly suited to comfort, instruct, and rebuke them. And He will do it in love.

For we do not have a High Priest who cannot be touched with the feeling of our weaknesses, but One who has been tempted in all things like us, but without sin —
Hebrews 4:15.

WHEN CIRCUMSTANCES are peculiarly trying, Jesus is peculiarly tender. If we are grieved, He is gentle. Did you ever hear any of His people say of their Lord that He is overbearing? In the Song of Songs did His spouse ever say that her Beloved had a rough side to His hand, or a cold place in His heart? He can and does rebuke, for His love is wise. But He is very pitying, and His love knows no limit. His heart is made of tenderness, and His soul melts for love for His chosen ones. We adore our High Priest, not only for His greatness, or for His merit, but for the sweetness of His mercy.

It is beyond us to fitly speak of Him. But this much can be said, Come to Him and rest in Him, for He calls you. He is near at all times, and in all places. You can come to Him anywhere, in the pew, or as you walk by the way. He says, *"Come to Me, all those laboring and being burdened, and I will give you rest"* (Matt. 11:28). Come, you whose souls sink down under a sense of sin; come to Him who as the great High Priest has offered a guilt-removing sacrifice. He sits at the door of the house of mercy, waiting to be gracious to you.

"We do not have a High Priest who cannot be touched with the feeling of our weaknesses." Note that it is not said, "touched BY," but, *"touched with."* Many a man can be touched by the sorrow of another, but he is not touched *with* that sorrow. He has feeling, but not fellow-feeling. He pities the sorrowing, but he does not sorrow with them. Our Lord is touched with a feeling of our weaknesses. You are touched, and He is touched, at the same time. A pang shoots through your heart, and that pang is also felt by your heart, if you are one of His chosen ones.

EVENING

For we do not have a High Priest who cannot be touched with the feeling of our weaknesses, but One who has been tempted in all things like us, but without sin —
Hebrews 4:15.

IT IS NOT MERELY TRUE that He is aware of our weaknesses, since the Lord has said, *"I know their sorrows."* He *"is touched with the feeling of our weaknesses."* Hold that thought! It is a great matter that our God should not forget the trials of His people, that His condescending omniscience should concern itself with their everyday distresses. But this word goes further: He feels with His people, is *"touched with the feeling of our infirmities."* The sense of feeling is more intense, vivid and acute than the sense of sight. It is one thing to see pain, but quite another to be touched with a feeling of it. Treasure up this view of your Lord's sympathy, for it may be a great support in the hour of agony. And it will be a grand restorative in the day of weakness.

Note again, *"the feeling of OUR weaknesses."* Whose weaknesses. Does not *"our"* mean yours and mine? Jesus is touched with the feeling of your infirmities and mine. yes, yours, and yours, and yours, whether you have come from a new-made grave, or if you are being slandered and discredited, or if you are sick and distracted, or if you can scarcely hold up your head for sadness, or if you are afraid. In all these cases, and more, He is *"touched with the feeling of your weaknesses."* Whatever your infirmities or weaknesses, let this text draw you nearer to your great High Priest. Wherever you are, He will meet you there, and there He will be touched with the feeling of your infirmities — of YOUR weaknesses, not just those of some noted or supposed pillars of the church. You may think that you are less than the least of all saints, but He will always be there to comfort and instruct you, touched with the feeling of your weaknesses.

August 26 — MORNING

Order my steps in Your word, and do not let any iniquity rule over me —Psalm 119:133.

DAVID prays to be wholly delivered from the tyranny of sin. Many men are violent against one sin, but the true saint abhors all sin. Are you a teetotaler? That is good, that you will not allow the sin of drunkenness to have dominion over you. But are you selfish and ungenerous? Have you learned habits of strict economy in regard to religious donations, so that you always give a penny where you ought to give a pound? What have you done? You have only changed your idols. You have dethroned one usurper to set up another. If you were once profane, but now are hypocritical, you have only changed iniquities. It is a very curious thing how one sin feeds on another. The death of profligacy may be the resurrection of greed. The flight of pride may be the advent of shameless folly. The man who was lewd, riotous, brawling, and irreligious may have killed those sins and has sown a handful of a more poisonous weed called pride, which will flourish amazingly. It may be London pride, country pride, English pride, or American pride — but it is remarkably adept at growing; it will grow over the rotting carcases of other sins. Unbelief may dethrone superstition, but its own reign may be no real improvement on that of credulity. If you only have thrown down Baal to set up Ashtaroth, what progress have you made toward God? It signifies nothing if you but set up false gods in the temple of Jehovah, for He hates them all.

The right prayer for you is this, *"Do not let any iniquity rule over me."* Some sins are of respectable repute among men, and other sins are disreputable among them. But to a child of God every sin is loathsome. Sins are all what Bunyan calls Diabolonians, and not one of them must be allowed to live in the town of Mansoul.

EVENING

And you shall make a plate of pure gold and carve on it, like the engravings of a signet, Holiness to the Lord — Exodus 28:36.

WHY WAS THE HIGH PRIEST so adorned for glory and beauty? Did we need such a high priest? Paul does not put it so, but says, *"Such a high priest became us"* (Heb. 7:26). It was becoming for us to have this glorious high priest so splendidly arrayed. When I thought over that saying of the Apostle, it seemed to me that even if our High Priest had been covered with ashes, if He had been dressed in rags, He might have seemed such a high priest as would befit us. But God does not think so, for He has written, *"Take away the filthy garments from Him. Let them set a fair miter on His head."* He has covered us with a robe of righteousness, and we are comely with His comeliness which He has put on us. And we are such in God's sight that it is becoming that we should not be represented by a high priest in sordid garments, but by one who is dressed in *"gold, and blue, and purple, and scarlet, and fine linen."*

What great things God thinks of His elect! What a high price He puts on His redeemed! His delight is in His saints. He delights more in those who fear Him than in all creation besides. *"To you who believe Christ is precious"* — but you who believe are also precious to Him. Does He not say, *"Since you were precious in My sight, you have been honorable"?* Therefore, none but an honorable and glorious person shall represent the chosen. Let us humbly rejoice in the beauty and glory of Him who takes our place before the infinitely glorious Jehovah. I thank God that even though I am the meanest and vilest of all His creatures because of my sin, yet He who represents me to God is neither mean in person nor vile in apparel, but He is altogether perfect in Himself, and altogether beauteous in His array.

And it shall be on Aaron's forehead, so that Aaron may bear the iniquity of the holy things which the sons of Israel shall set apart in all their holy gifts — Exodus 28:38.

THEY WERE HOLY THINGS. Despite the iniquity, their offerings were hallowed and holy. This is a precious saving clause. Our prayers, our praises, our service to God — these are holy things, although our iniquity attaches to them. They are holy as to God's ordinance, for He has ordained them for His glory. He has bidden us serve Him. He has bidden us draw near in prayer. He has also said, *"Whoever offers praise glorifies Me."* When we do what God commands us, the act is holy, because it is done in obedience to the Divine ordinance. Such deeds are holy as to the Divine design. For even the sacrifices which the Israelites brought were meant to set forth Christ and His glorious work, and so they were holy. They were meant to be tokens of our gratitude, love, dedication and homage, and so they are holy. The great Father teaches us much precious truth by every institution of the tabernacle and the temple, and the gospel church, and because of this obedience to each ordinance is holy.

These deeds are often holy in the intent of the worshipper. When he brought his turtle doves, or his lamb, or his bullock, if he was not altogether outside of spiritual worship he intended to exercise real reverence, true allegiance, and sincere gratitude to God — and this intent was holy. Our God is so gracious as to call the love, and faith, and labor, and patience of His people *"holy things,"* because He sees how truly their heart's desire is that they should be holy. He knows what is holy, and what is not holy. And although there is a defilement about our holy things, yet they are holy things if they are presented sincerely — for the Lord God Himself calls them so. Blessed is His name!

EVENING

And it shall be on Aaron's forehead, so that Aaron may bear the iniquity of the holy things which the sons of Israel shall set apart in all their holy gifts — Exodus 28:38.

THE HIGH PRIEST bore *"the iniquity of the holy things."* You and I have been guilty of iniquity in our holy things. But here is our joy, that Jesus, our High Priest, bears it all. Putting on His heavenly miter, marked as *"Holiness to Jehovah,"* He bears for us the iniquity. *"The Lord has laid on Him the iniquity of us all."* He was *"made sin for us, who knew no sin"* (Isa. 53:6; 2 Cor. 5:21). It is a wonderful mystery, the transference of sin and of merit. It staggers human reason; faith alone apprehends it. How can the guilty be accounted righteous? How can the perfectly righteous One be made sin? These things are mysterious, but they are true; the Word of God is full of declarations to this effect. In this truth lies the one hope of sinners. All the iniquity of our holy things has been borne by our Lord Jesus, and it is no longer imputed to us.

As He stood before God, even though He bore the iniquity of His people, yet He exhibited to God no iniquity, but on His forehead was written, *"Holinesss to Jehovah."*

Notice that He bore before God a most precious holiness. In token of this, in type, the engraving was incribed on a plate of pure gold. The righteousness of Christ is more precious to God than all the mines of gold in the whole world. His righteousness was absolutely perfect, so there was nothing on that plate of gold but *"Holiness to Jehovah."* There was no iniquity in His holy things. His holiness was conspicuous and undeniable; it shone on the forefront of His miter. That holiness of His was permanent. It was not painted on that sheet of gold, but was engraved like the engraving on a signet. Christ's righteousness shines gloriously; it never loses its virtue; it retains its permanent perfectness before the Lord.

August 28 — MORNING

The Lord will give strength to His people; the Lord will bless His people with peace.
— Psalm 29:11.

PEACE IS A CONDITION of things greatly to be desired. To dread no outward disturbance, and to feel no inward storm — who does not desire such a state? Peace has been called a pearl. And indeed it is precious; it smiles with soft, mild radiance, bedecking the heart that wears it. It is truly a pearl of great price. He who has it has more than riches. If his peace is, in very deed, the true pearl of spiritual peace, anyone wearing it is one of the most favored children of God. There may be some people in the world who do not love peace, but we do not love their spirit. Certain stormy natures delight in tempest, and, like sea birds, ride on the crests of raging billows. Men of the Byron type are restless, and an atmosphere of peace does not suit them. Their spirits, like thunderbolts, rush onward, finding pleasure in the crash with which they force their wilful way. I do not need to go out of my way for such, for in vain we speak to those who will not hear.

Most of us were cast in another mold. We are not ravens, and cannot remain forever on the wing; but, like the dove of Noah, we seek rest for the sole of our foot, and we fly here and there until we find the olive leaf of peace. How often, amid the disturbances of this troubled world, have we cried, *"Oh that I had wings like a dove! For then I would fly away and be at rest."* We were not reared like eaglets on stern crags, among lightnings. We listen to the turtle dove's voice and love the brooks that warble music as they flow. No doubt many of you sigh for rest. You labor that you may enter on it. Peace and rest are two names on earth, but they are only found full blown in Heaven. Yet even the faint perfume of the unopened blossom excites our strong desire.

EVENING

The Lord will give strength to His people; the Lord will bless His people with peace.
— Psalm 29:11.

FALSE PEACE IS A CURSE, but to be soundly at peace with God is an unalloyed blessing; it brings no sorrow with it. To fall back on the Father's bosom and say, "I know that He loves me, and I know that I love Him;" to look up to Jesus and to say, "He loved me and gave Himself for me;" to feel the movings of God the Holy Spirit, and to yield ourselves up to His influences — this is peace unspeakable. To have no quarrel with God; to have no difference between His will and your own — this is a delightful experience. Men may hate you, but if God loves you what does it matter? You may feel the cut of sharp, ungenerous words, but if your God speaks peace to you, who can trouble you? For, *"He will speak peace to His people, and to His saints"* (Psalm 85:8). This is joy indeed!

It is not only a blessing in itself, but it is a blessing in its consequences. There is no one so humble as that one who is at perfect peace with God. He will wonder at the blessing he enjoys. There is no one so grateful; there is no one so courageous; there is no one so little affected by the world; there is no one who bears suffering so patiently; there is no one who is so ready for Heaven as that one who is at perfect peace with God, and knows it. The peace of God, *which passes all understanding*, is a sacred guard to the soul. It will keep our hearts and minds through Jesus Christ. The value of peace as a keeper of the heart and mind is exceeding great. It wards off all sorts of evils; it preserves us to the day of the Lord's appearing. The more you enjoy peace with God, the better. False peace is as stupefying and deadly as opium. Even the smallest drop of this sleeping mixture, false peace, will be mischievous to the spirit.

MORNING

The Lord will give strength to His people; the Lord will bless His people with peace.
— Psalm 29:11.

THIS PEACE ONLY COMES from God: *"Jehovah will bless His people with peace"* — you cannot get that peace apart from Him. It is of no use to work it out of yourself. You may say, "I will get better; I will keep the law; I will do this, or that," but you will never dig peace out of the soil of your own works. You cannot spin peace out of your own bowels, as the spider spins her web. You must go to the Lord for peace, and there is only one way in which you can go to Him; Jesus says, *"I am the way."* Go to the Father through Jesus Christ, by the power of the Holy Spirit. Trust the Father, rest in Christ, yield to the Holy Spirit, and you shall have the peace that God gives. O, if you could come and talk with me, and I would comfort you, it might be of no use to you. If you could go to some full-fledged priest, and he claim to absolve you, it might only be one of the darkest of delusions. But if you go to God and get peace from Him, that peace is solid and abiding. It is founded on eternal truth; it is guaranteed by the God of holiness; it is judged to be sound by the Judge of all the earth. We hear this peace from lips that cannot lie, from a heart which cannot change, through the blood which has made a full atonement. Seek this peace; make sure of it. You see how spiritual it is, for you must come to God for it. And you can only come to Him in spirit and truth. You see how little it depends on externals, on chapel going or church going. It is by a spiritual approach to God that this blessing can be obtained. Come to the Lord, the Giver of peace. Come to Jesus, who IS our peace. Oh, may the Divine Spirit lead you to come to Jesus now, at this moment, for your peace. For in coming to Him you shall receive rest! Please know this promise, *"The Lord will bless His people with peace."*

EVENING

The Lord will give strength to His people; the Lord will bless His people with peace.
— Psalm 29:11.

IS YOUR HOPE based on a false peace? Then overthrow it and leave no stone of it on another one. Refuges of lies must be swept away before refuges of grace will be sought. If you take shelter behind *a bowing wall and a tottering fence* of false peace, you must seek help to over turn it. You need to go to a better shelter, for you will never be on a right foundation until you are off the wrong one. As long as your happiness and peace are false, however fair to look upon, you will never seek true peace. For this reason you must break the idols of false peace to shivers. Do not believe in a security which is at best only a ground of temporary value. Believe the eternal truth of God, and seek eternal life through it. Do not foolishly wrap yourself about with a comfort which you do not dare to prove and test. For if you do not dare to examine it to the very bottom, then do away with it. If it will not bear the closest search, leave it to those who foolishly run such risks. Examine carefully your state; be sure that there is not something wrong with it. Walk in the light of God and then you will have no fellowship with unfruitful hopes, which are works of darkness.

And when you have laid these things to heart, and desire to seek at once to have close dealings with God, do not say, "I will now begin searching the Scriptures." That is a good thing in itself, but you must not rest in Scripture reading alone — you must go to God Himself and beg peace from Him. Do not say, "I will attend more religious services." That also may be well, but if you put them in the place of personal dealings with God, they may be your ruin. No, but your living soul must have personal dealings with God Himself!

August 30   MORNING

Not that we are able of ourselves to judge anything as of ourselves, but our ability to judge is of God —2 Corinthians 3:5.

IN THIS INSTANCE the best of preachers disowns self-sufficiency. Remember who it is that is writing — it is Paul, called to be an apostle, to whom the Lord Jesus had personally appeared, a man of singular zeal and activity, and of remarkable ability in the things of God. He was not a whit behind the chief of the apostles, an expounder of the truth, a founder of churches, a father of myriads of souls. Yet he says, *"Not that we are able of ourselves."* When Paul wrote this epistle he was no beginner in holy oratory, but a well-exercised evangelist. He had been taught of God deeply, had preached the Word fully, and had gained an unrivaled experience. Beginning with a wonderful conversion, going on through sufferings, persecutions, journeys and labors, he had become a man of great weight and influence. After his death his words would be law to us, and yet he confesses, *"Not that we are able of ourselves."* Here was a man who had been inspired by the Holy Spirit; a man to write epistles to churches, a man who spoke with Divine authority, who would not allow that authority to be questioned, for he felt that he was truly sent of God. And yet you see him bowing humbly before the throne of the heavenly grace and admitting his own powerlessness, *"Not that we are able of ourselves."* Here we have a most successful soul-winner making his lowly acknowledgment. Many were already in Heaven, converted under the ministry of the apostle Paul. Many on earth were on the road to glory, led there by his teaching. Many had been inspired with the courage of martyrs, with the holiness of saints. The apostle Paul was a mine of spiritual wealth to the church. What man ever did more for the propagation of the faith than the indefatigable Paul? And yet he writes for the holy education of us all, *"Not that we are able of ourselves."*

EVENING

Not that we are able of ourselves to judge anything as of ourselves, but our ability to judge is of God —2 Corinthians 3:5.

ALL WHO TRUST in the Lord are made *"able ministers of the new covenant."* This is explained to us in the first sentence, *"Our ability to judge is of God."* In God there is all the wisdom, all the thought, all the love, all the power, all the conquering energy which a minister/witness can require — enough to work on the hearts of men lies in the omnipotent grace of God, a fulness of might, so that the stony heart shall be transformed, and on its fleshly tablet shall be written the will of the Lord. That our sufficiency would be of God is infinitely better than if it were of ourselves. For then our sufficiency cannot be questioned, cannot be suspended, cannot be exhausted. If you had to bear your own charges you might soon be bankrupt. But now you are like a child traveling with his father; his father pays for all. Our sufficiency is of God; then let us practically enjoy this truth. We are poor, leaking vessels; the only way for us to keep full is to put our pitcher under the perpetual flow of boundless grace. Then, despite its leakage, the cup will always be full to the brim. One cries, "I do not feel able to win a soul; it is a work too hard for me." Continue to feel that truth, but at the same time let faith balance the feeling by reminding you that our sufficiency is from God. If God sends you, He will go with you. If God gives you a message to deliver, He will prepare the ear and the heart to receive that message. Blessed words are these for every minister and every witness of Christ, for all of you who in any way are working for His dear name.

Not that we are able of ourselves to judge anything as of ourselves, but our ability to judge is of God —2 Corinthians 3:5.

THE APOSTLE evidently means that through grace we are adapted to the work: *"God, who has also made us able ministers of the new covenant."* We are not ministers of the old covenant of command and threatening. For if we were then we might exceedingly fear and quake. But we are sent to be ministers of the spirit of that covenant which says, *"I will also give you a new heart, and I will put a new spirit within you"* (Ezek. 36:26). We are ministers of a covenant of pure grace, in which God, not man, is the worker. We are by the truth spoken in love to convey to men's hearts spiritual help. We are not ministers of the letter of the law which kills, but of the spirit that gives life. One says, "Oh, but that is hard work." On the contrary, it is the easiest of work when Divine power works in us. What is needed to make a man sufficient for this work? He must be able to bear personal witness to the truth of God. Were you ever filled with life by the spirit of the new covenant, the covenant of gracious promise? Then you can tell poor sinners where life is to be had. Were you slain by the law, and are you made alive by the Spirit of God? Then you will witness of the law of God tremblingly, and you will speak of life in Jesus Christ with living certainty. Do you know in your own soul what it is to be enlivened by the Holy Spirit? if not, hands off the ark of God! But if Divine power has come on you and made you live the life of faith in Christ Jesus, then you have one point of ability to be a witness. Beyond this, a living, loving heart is a great necessity. Have tender sympathy with those who have not so learned Christ. Feel an intense desire that they may obtain eternal life. Bring your spiritual life into contact with their spiritual death; as one candle lights another, so may the Lord convey life into other hearts by your testimony.

EVENING

Not that we are able of ourselves to judge anything as of ourselves, but our ability to judge is of God —2 Corinthians 3:5.

DO NOT TRUST your own sufficiency. If we who preach to you, and even those who are far greater than we are bound to say, *"Not that we are able of ourselves to judge anything as of ourselves,"* how little must be your sufficiency. It is very wonderful how fully in Scripture the inability of man is set out. Here we see our inability to think correctly. In another passage we find that a good will is of the Lord: *"Work out your own salvation with fear and trembling. For it is God who works in you both to will and to do of His good pleasure"* (Philip. 2:13). To will correctly is more than to think correctly, but we never make so distinct an advance as to will that which is good until we are made willing by God's power. When we get that far we pull up suddenly to a dead halt, finding with the apostle that, *"to will is present with me, but how to perform that which is good I do not find"* (Rom. 7:18). Then we are driven to God for power to turn our willing into acting. In this going to God we are brought to a standstill again, for we read and feel that, *"we do not know what we should pray for as we ought"* (Rom. 8:26). What can we do, if even in prayer we fail? Suppose we are taught to pray, helped by the Spirit of God. We begin to work, yet we cannot keep on working without fresh grace. For David, when he had worked up the people to a very high degree of consecration, thought it needful to pray that the Lord would *"keep this forever in the imagination of the thoughts of the heart of Your people"* (1 Chr. 29:18). And our Savior prayed, *"Father, keep them;"* for we soon go back to the old deadness and lethargy unless He that first made us alive will still keep us alive.

The centurion answered and said, Lord, I am not worthy that You should come under my roof. But only speak a word and my servant will be healed —Matthew 8:8.

A SENSE OF unworthiness is exceedingly useful in our spiritual lives, for it puts a person where God can bless him. The Lord will only act in conformity with His own attributes. God will always be God, and as He will be God alone in creation, so He will certainly be God alone in the new creation. Our only right position before God is to know that we are undeserving and unworthy, while He is holy and glorious. We must hear Him say, *"I am God, and beside Me there is none else,"* or we shall never look to Him to be saved. If I am somebody, and I stand up with my rights and claims, God cannot bless me without conceding to me that which He will never concede — how dare I claim that which He calls a free gift? *"I will have mercy on whom I will have mercy, and I will have compassion on whom I will have compassion"* (Rom. 9:15). Depend on it: God will be God! And if you will not be saved unless He leaves the throne of His sovereignty, then you will perish without hope. He will be both King and Lord in the work of salvation. You must take it as His free gift, or you will die without it. If it is of grace, it cannot be of right — these things are contradictory. Unutterably great is His pity; immeasurable is His mercy; but still He will have no pity for those whose proud self-will stands out against His sovereign grace. O sinner, if you desire to be pardoned you must confess that the Lord is King. Your touch of Jesus Himself must be like that of Thomas when he put his finger to the wound and cried, *"My Lord and my God!"* You must have Jesus to be Lord and God to you, or He will be nothing to you. Beloved, no one will yield to this until he or she has a thorough conviction of unworthiness. We are not worthy to be saved. If we were, it would be of debt, and not of grace.

EVENING

The centurion answered and said, Lord, I am not worthy that You should come under my roof. But only speak a word and my servant will be healed —Matthew 8:8.

PERSONS UNDER deep distress often doubt the promise of God. They have set aside a great and sure promise, one obviously belonging to them, saying, "It is too good to be true. I cannot believe it because I am unworthy." You may be a liar, but be careful not to make God a liar. You may have made many promises which you have broken, but do not charge God with doing so. You have vowed that you would do this or that, and you have forgotten your pledges and thrown your promises into forgetfulness; but do not dream that God will do so. He is not a man that He should lie. If you feel as if you were on the brink of Hell, be sure you do not doubt God's faithfulness to keep His promises. Do not cast a doubt on His truthfulness. That would be an excess of sinfulness. I feel sometimes that even if I were lost, I must still believe God to be true: *"Though He slay me, yet will I trust in Him"* (Job 13:15). Here, put the killing sword to my neck and let me die the death I deserve; but I will still believe that God is good and true. O Jehovah, You do keep Your word. Such faith is not one jot greater than the Lord deserves of us, for He has never deceived us, and He never will. Dear heart, do take the promise of God to mean what it says, and believe it. Suppose somebody were to trust himself with Christ for salvation, and were to believe God would therefore save him, and yet He should not be saved — what then? I cannot suppose such a case. I will wait until you find me an actual instance, and then I will consider how to answer you. Why, if a soul who trusted in the promise of God, and fled to Christ for refuge, could be sent down to Hell, the legions of the infernal pit would exhibit him as a trophy of their victory over God. Such a thing could never happen. Therefore, do not let such a blasphemous idea be tolerated in your mind for a moment.

And I will put enmity between you and the woman, and between your seed and her seed. He will bruise your head, and you shall bruise His heel — Genesis 3:15.

SOME MASTER in Israel who wanted to help the memories of his hearers has said that the three things to be preached above everything else are the three R's: Ruin, Redemption, and Regeneration. He spoke wisely and well. How will men seek salvation if they do not feel their ruin? Where is there salvation except in the atoning blood? What is salvation but being created anew unto holiness? It is a noteworthy fact that in the Holy Scripture there are three third chapters which deal with these things in the fullest manner. The third of Genesis reveals Ruin; the third of Romans teaches Redemption; the third of John sets forth Regeneration. Read those chapters through with care. Also note carefully that those three chapters not only teach its own R, but it also teaches the other two R's. In this third of Genesis we have not only Ruin, but we have the Redeemer in *"the seed of the woman,"* and we have Regeneration in the expression, *"I will put enmity between you and the woman."* God's regenerating power creates a hatred of evil in the chosen seed. The same you will find in the other chapters. The third of Romans contains a dreadful description of the sin and ruin of mankind. And in the third of John, after you read, *"You must be born again,"* not far from that you find it written, *"And as Moses lifted up the serpent in the wilderness, even so must the Son of man be lifted up, that whoever believes in Him might not perish, but have eternal life."* Believe any of these great truths, and the rest will follow as a necessary consequence.

Never regard that story of the serpent as a fable. Nowadays it is often claimed that it is a mere allegory. Yet there is nothing in the Book of Genesis to mark where history ends and parable begins. It all runs on as actual history, and such it most certainly is.

EVENING

And I will put enmity between you and the woman, and between your seed and her seed. He will bruise your head, and you shall bruise His heel — Genesis 3:15.

IF ANY PART of this narrative is allegorical, no part is naked matter of fact. It seems to me that if there were only an allegorical serpent, there was an allegorical paradise, with allegorical rivers, and allegorical trees; and the men and women were allegorical, and the chapter which speaks of their creation is an allegory. The only thing that exists is an allegorical Heaven and an allegorical earth. If the Book of Genesis is an allegory, it is an allegory all through. Then you have an allegorical Abraham, with allegorical circumcision, and allegorical Jacob and an allegorical Judah. It is not unfair to push the theory onward, to impute to Judah allegorical descendants called Jews. It is idle to call the narrative of the Fall a mere allegory. One had better say at once that he does not believe the Book. There is something sane about that declaration, although it is folly. But to say, "Oh, yes, it is a venerable volume, and worthy to be studied; but it is padded out with many an allegory," is to say something which confutes itself, if you carefully consider it. The Book is intended to be real history. It contains some portions which, by the consent of everybody, are real history. But Moses could not be a historian, and yet set mere fables before us as a part of his story. To write a jumble of allegory and of fact causes a man to lose the character of a reliable historian, and we had better repudiate him at once. There was a real serpent, just as there was a real paradise. There was a real Adam and Eve, who stood at the head of our race. And they really sinned, and our race is really fallen. Believe this!

September 3   MORNING

And I will put enmity between you and the woman, and between your seed and her seed. He will bruise your head, and you shall bruise His heel — Genesis 3:15.

WHEN THE LORD comes to deal with the serpent, He does not question him as to his guilt, and the reason for it; for the guilt of the arch enemy was self-evident. The Lord had no design of mercy for him. He meant to make no covenant of grace for the Devil and his angels. He did not take up the angels, although He took up the seed of Abraham. In the infinite sovereignty of God He passed by the fallen angels, but He chose to raise up fallen mankind. Those who cavil at the doctrine of election should answer this question: Why is it that God has left demon-angels without hope, and yet has sent His Son to redeem mankind? Is not Divine sovereignty manifested here? We can give no answer to the question, What is man that God thus visits him with distinguishing grace? except this: *"He will have mercy on whom He will have mercy, and He will have compassion on whom He will have compassion"* (Rom. 9:15). Therefore, intending no forgiveness to this evil spirit, the Lord put no questions to him. His interrogation of our first parents was a sign of mercy. When God chides with a man's conscience, it is with the view of blessing him. Do I speak to any man whose sense of sin is aroused, who is accused by the Word of God, who feels the Spirit of God working within him as a spirit of bondage? You may be hopeful because it is so. If God had meant to destroy you, He would have left you alone, even as He left the serpent without a word of expostulation. He would have passed sentence on you speedily, too. The very rebukes of God are tokens of His favor toward men. With the serpent, that is, with the evil spirit, God had no upbraidings, but He dealt with him at once by way of doom.

EVENING

And I will put enmity between you and the woman, and between your seed and her seed. He will bruise your head, and you shall bruise His heel — Genesis 3:15.

IN ALL PROBABILITY the reptile called the serpent was a nobler creature before the Fall than now. The words of our text, so far as they literally concern the serpent, threaten that a change would be made in him. It has been a sort of speculative opinion that the creature either had wings, or was able to move without creeping on the earth, as serpents do now. Of that we know nothing. But assuredly the serpent is a hated thing, with which mankind is at war; its form and habit typify all that is mean and cunning. There is nothing noble, nothing brave, nothing true about the idea of a serpent. Satan was among the firstborn of the morning, a swift and shining servant of God. Yet he transgressed against his Sovereign, and he fell. And now he is nothing but a malignant, base, cunning, and untrue Devil. He is fitly figured by *"the wily snake." "He was a murderer from the beginning, and abode not in the truth, because there is no truth in him. When he speaks a lie, he speaks of his own, for he is a liar, and the father of it"* (John 8:44). He goes out to deceive the nations (Rev. 20:8). He works signs and lying wonders (2 Thess. 2:9). He lays snares and takes men captive (2 Tim. 2:26). Keep before your minds the form of a serpent, and remember that after this manner Satan will attack you. Only let me soften your fears with the sight of another serpent, the serpent of brass lifted on a pole brought life to those whom evil serpents had injured. It is a wonder of condescending grace that our Lord Jesus could allow Himself to be symbolized by a form which had been assumed by the great enemy of souls. Yes, there was a brazen serpent lifted high on a pole, and they that looked, though bitten by fiery serpents, lived. Even so is Jesus on the cross the sure remedy for sin of every kind.

MORNING

And I will put enmity between you and the woman, and between your seed and her seed. He will bruise your head, and you shall bruise His heel — Genesis 3:15.

THERE IS A WAR to be waged between Satan and the woman's seed, so long as the world stands. Sometimes it looks as if there was going to be peace. For the world flatters the church, and the church seeks to conform herself to the world. As before Noah's flood the sons of God and the daughters of men were joineed in an unholy alliance, so again and again there have been attempts at truce. But peace there cannot be. Today Satan tempts the ministers of Christ to soften down the gospel, to adapt it to the age, and to make it popular. He also labors to throw down the division between the church and the world, saying, "Cover it over like an old sewer, and forget it ever existed." In this he speaks like the sinner in Proverbs: *"Cast in your lot among us; let us all have one purse."* But mark this, although all the pulpits should be captured by Satan, and although it should seem that the very elect were deceived, yet God will not leave Himself without a witness. Somewhere or other He will find some chosen ones of the seed of the woman to carry on the holy war, even to the end. Jehovah has laid His hand on His throne, and He has sworn to have war with evil, from generation to generation. See how it was in Israel when the high priest of God, even Eli, winked at sin, his own sons committing iniquity at the tabernacle door. Then all Israel was made to do evil. Then would not the lamp of truth go out? Would not the worship of Jehovah be utterly abhorred? Ah, no! A little child was brought by his mother into the tabernacle to be the servant of the Lord. And the Lord made him His champion. In the night God called to Samuel, and he was enabled to answer, *"Here am I."*

EVENING

And I will put enmity between you and the woman, and between your seed and her seed. He will bruise your head, and you shall bruise His heel — Genesis 3:15.

HERE IS THE END of the great conflict. Satan, who heads the powers of evil in the world, is to fight it out with his cunning and strength. And he is so far to succeed as to bruise the heel of the champion with whom he fights. But in the end the seed of the woman is to bruise his head. This was accomplished when the Lord Jesus died, and by dying honored the law, put away sin, slew death, and defeated Hell. When the great Substitute drank the cup of wrath to its utmost dregs for every believing soul, when He unhinged the gate of the sepulcher and carried it away (as Samson carried away the gates of Gaza — post, bar, and all) — when He opened the doorways of Heaven and led captivity captive, then indeed the head of the dragon was broken. What can Satan do now? Is not the accuser of the brothers cast down? He is still doing his best in bitterness and malice, but the Christ has crushed him. Yes, the very Christ who *"was despised and rejected of men,"* (Isa. 53:3) the Man of the thorn crown and the marred visage, the Man of bleeding shoulders and pierced hands and feet, the Man who was born of a virgin, the seed of the woman, has broken the power of the enemy. Hallelujah! Hallelujah! He has cast down the Prince of darkness from his high places! Did He not say, *"I beheld Satan as lightning fall from Heaven?"* (Luke 10:18) — He has bruised the Serpent's head.

This is done in all believers also, and it shall be done yet more effectually. In that day when God the Holy Spirit led us to trust in the Lord Jesus, we bruised the head of the serpent. He had been accustomed to command us, and we to obey him, and so sin had dominion over us. But as soon as we believed in Christ, that dominion was ended, that Dagon fell before the ark of the Lord.

September 5   MORNING

What is the chaff to the wheat? says the Lord — Jeremiah 23:28.

BELOVED, THERE ARE MANY of us who are genuine in our profession of religion, who cannot and who dare not allow the suspicion of hypocrisy to rest on us. It is our feeling that unless we have been awfully deceived, we have put our trust in the Lord Jesus Christ. We are the subjects of a very great change, and we know it. We would be false to our own consciousness if we were to say that we doubted it. Moreover, we are at the present moment in the possession of enjoyments which will not allow us to think ourselves to be in the gall of bitterness. We know what communion with Christ means. We know the power of prayer. We have had such answers to prayer that for us to hesitate in avowing it would be mock-modesty, wicked deception, lying before God. We know Christ, and we are found in Him, not having our own righteousness, but wrapped about with His righteousness. We are without doubt well aware that if we have wheat in us, there must be chaff also. Which predominates? At times it is difficult for us to tell. Some Christians are greatly puzzled when we begin to talk about the experimental riddle which the Christian finds in himself. But if they are perplexed, we cannot help them out of the difficulty except by describing the case. In my own soul I know that I feel myself to be like two distinct men. There is the old man, base as ever. And there is the new man that cannot sin, because he is born of God (see 1 John 3:6). I cannot understand the experience of those Christians who say they do not find a conflict within, for my experience goes to show this, if it shows anything, that there is an incessant contention between the old nature and the new nature. O that we could be rid of the old nature! May God be thanked for the strength of the new nature (see Romans 7:15-25).

EVENING

What is the chaff to the wheat? says the Lord — Jeremiah 23:28.

THERE IS NOT ONLY a great deal of our sin which is chaff, but that a great deal of our religiousness is chaff likewise. Do you never find yourselves borrowing other people's experience? What is that but chaff? Do you never find yourselves at a prayer meeting glowing with somebody else's fervor? What is that but chaff? Does not your faith sometimes depend on companionship with some fellow Christian? Well, your faith may not be chaff, but such growth in faith as is altogether the result of second causes, and not immediately of God, is very much like chaff. How much religion would some of us have if it were all set to cool? There seems to be a great volume of it now while we are living in a warm and genial atmosphere with our friends and comrades in the gospel. But suppose we would be exposed to the trial of a bleak night; suppose we were taken away from the church of which we are members, and made to live in the country where we had no fellow Christians to talk with — how much of the substance and fervor of our religion would we then preserve? It is wonderful how great appearances often diminish and grow small when circumstances change. Remember, Christian, just so much and no more than would abide such an ordeal is the total that you possess now. The rest that only seems to be should be counted for nothing. We sometimes think we grow very fast, when, in fact, our progress is rather like the growth of the mushroom than the growth of an oak. When the Christian does not see his signs, and fears that he does not grow, he often really is growing in grace. He could be growing downwards, being rooted in humility, getting a deeper sense of his own nothingness and unworthiness, and consequently a higher sense of his Lord's fulness and loving-kindness. Then he is growing truly.

Have mercy on me, O God, according to Your loving-kindness. According to the multitude of Your tender mercies, blot out my transgressions. Wash me completely from my iniquity and cleanse me from my sin — Psalm 51:1,2.

DAVID APPEALS at once to the mercy of God, even before he mentions his sin. The sight of mercy is good for eyes that are sore with penitential weeping. Pardon of sin must ever be an act of pure mercy, and so it is to that attribute that the awakened sinner flies, saying, *"O God, according to Your loving-kindness"* act; give mercy like Your mercy. Show mercy such as is congruous with Your grace. What a choice word is that of our English version, a rare compound of precious things: love and kindness sweetly blended in one. Let Your most loving compassion come to me, and make Your pardons such as these would suggest. Reveal all Your gentlest attributes in my case, not only in their essence, but in their abundance. Numberless have been Your acts of goodness, and vast is Your grace. Let me be the object of Your infinite mercy, and repeat it all in me. Make my one case an epitome of all Your tender mercies. By every deed of grace to others I feel encouraged, and I pray You to let me add another and a yet greater one, in my own person, to the long list of Your compassions. My revolts, my excesses, are all recorded against me, but Lord, erase the lines. Draw Your pen through the register. Obliterate the record, although now it seems engraved in the rock forever. Many strokes of Your mercy may be needed to cut out the deep inscription, but then You have a multitude of mercies. Therefore, I beseech You, erase my sins.

It is not enough to blot out the sin. David's person is defiled, and he would willingly be purified. He would have God Himself cleanse him, for none but God could do it effectually. The washing must be thorough; it must be repeated. For this reason he cries, *"Multiply to wash me."* The dye is in itself immoveable, and I, the sinner, have lain long in it until the crimson is ingrained. But, Lord, wash and wash again until the last stain in gone, and not a trace of defilement is left.

EVENING

In whom we have redemption through His blood, the forgiveness of sins, according to the riches of His grace — Ephesians 1:7.

THE FORGIVENESS of sins is bound up with redemption by blood. Take the text: Redemption and forgiveness are so put together as to look as if they were the same thing. Assuredly they are so interlaced and intertwisted that there is no having the one without the other. Do you ask, "How is it that there should always need to be redemption by blood in order for the forgiveness of sin?" Note carefully the expression, *"redemption through His blood."* Observe that it is not redemption through His power — No! It is through His blood. It is not redemption through His love, it is through His blood. This is insisted on emphatically, since forgiveness of sins cannot be given without redemption through His blood. You have it over and over again in Scripture: *"Without shedding of blood is no remission."* But some will say that substitution is not just, that to lay sin on Christ, and to treat Him as guilty, and to let Him die for the unjust — this is unjust. Yet these objectors will go on to say that God forgave men freely without any atonement at all. Is that just? Is it just to pass by breaches of the law of God without penalty? Why then do we have any law at all? And why should men care whether they keep it or break it? If you say that God out of His boundless love treated the guilty man as if he were innocent, then I ask this; if that is right, then where is the wrong of God's treating us as innocent because of the righteousness of Christ? A pardon is needless for a man that is treated as if he were not guilty, even though he is indeed guilty. If all are treated alike, whether guilty or not guilty, why should anyone desire a pardon?

MORNING

Behold, I was brought forth in iniquity, and in sin did my mother conceive me. Behold, You desire truth in the inward parts, and in the hidden part You shall make me to know wisdom — Psalm 51:5,6.

DAVID IS thunderstruck at the discovery of his inbred sin, and he proceeds to set it forth. This was not intended to justify himself, but rather to complete the confession. It is as if he had said, "Not only have I sinned this once, but I am in my very nature a sinner. The fountain of my life is polluted as well as its streams. My birth tendencies are out of the square of equity; I naturally lean to forbidden things. My sin is a constitutional disease rendering my very person obnoxious to Your wrath." He goes back to the earliest moment of his being, not to slander his mother, but to acknowledge the deep taproots of his sin. It is a wicked wresting of Scripture to deny that original sin and natural depravity are taught here. Surely men who cavil at this doctrine have need to be taught by the Holy Spirit what are the first principles of the faith. David's mother was the Lord's handmaid. Outwardly, he was born in chaste wedlock, of a good father. He was himself described by God as *"a man after God's own heart"* (Acts 13:22). Yet his nature was as fallen as that of any other son of Adam; only the occasion for manifesting it needed to occur. In our shaping we were put out of shape, and when we were conceived our nature conceived sin. Alas for poor humanity! That one is most blessed who in his own soul has learned to lament the last estate of mankind.

"Behold!" Here is the great matter of consideration. God desires not merely outward virtue, but inward purity, and the penitent's sense of sin is greatly deepened as with astonishment he discovers this truth, and how far he is from satisfying the Divine demand. The second *"Behold"* is fitly set over against the first. How great the gulf which yawns between them! Reality, sincerity, true holiness, heart fidelity, these are the demands of God. He does not cae for the pretense of purity; He looks to the mind, heart, and soul. Always has the Holy One of Israel estimated men by their inner nature and not by their outward professions. To Him the inward is as visible as the outward.

EVENING

Then was our mouth filled with laughter" — Psalm 126:2.

WE MUST EARNESTLY endeavor to learn this practice, or at the least to attain to some knowledge of it. And we must raise up ourselves with this consideration, that the gospel is nothing else but laughter and joy. This joy properly pertains to captives, that is, to those that feel the captivity of sin and death; to the fleshy and tender hearts that are terrified with the feeling of the wrath and judgment of God. These are the disciples in whose hearts should be planted laughter and joy, and that by the authority of the Holy Spirit, which this verse sets forth. This people was in Zion, and after the outward show of the kingdom and priesthood, they mightily flourished. But if a man considers them according to the spirit, he will see them to be in miserable captivity — their tongue is full of heaviness and mourning because their heart is terrified with the sense of sin and death. This is Moses' tongue or Moses' mouth, full of wormwood and of the bitterness of death, with which he designs to kill none but those who are too lively and full of security. But the ones who feel their captivity will have their mouths filled with laughter and joy — that is, redemption and deliverance from sin and death will be preached to them. This is the sense and meaning of the Holy Spirit here, that the mouth of such shall be filled with laughter — that is, their mouth will show forth nothing else but great gladness through the inestimable consolations of the gospel, with voices of triumph and victory by Christ, overcoming Satan, destroying death, and taking away sins. This was first spoken to the Jews; for this laughter was first offered to that people, who then had the promises. Now He turns to the Gentiles, whom he calls to the partaking of this laughter." — Martin Luther

MORNING

O that I were as in months past, as in the days when God watched over me, when His lamp shone on my head, when I walked through darkness by His light —Job 29:2,3.

IF ANY of you desire now to come into the higher life, and to feel anew your first love, what shall I say to you? Go back to where you started. Do not stay discussing whether you are a Christian or not. Go to Christ as a poor guilty sinner. When the door to Heaven seems shut to me as a saint, I will get through it as a sinner, trusting in the precious blood of Jesus. Come and stand at the foot of the Cross, as though all your sins were on you still, where still may be seen the dropping blood of the infinitely precious atonement, saying, Savior, I trust you again. Guilty, more guilty than I was before, a sinful child of God, I trust You, praying that You will *"wash me thoroughly from my iniquities and purge me from my sin."* You will never have your graces revived unless you go to the Cross. Begin life again. The best air for a man to breathe when he is sickly is said to be that of his birthplace. It was at Calvary that we were born; it is only at Calvary we can be restored when we are declining. Do the first works. As a sinner repair to the Savior and ask to be restored. Then, as a further means of health, search out the cause of your declension. Probably it was a neglect of private prayer. Where the disease began, there must the remedy be applied. Pray more earnestly, more frequently, more importunately. Or was it a neglect of hearing the Word? Were you enticed by novelty or cleverness away from a really searching and instructive ministry? Then go back and feed on wholesome food again; it may cure the disease. Or, have you been too grasping after the world? When you had but one shop, you loved God; now you have two, and you are giving all your time and thoughts to business, and your soul is getting lean. Strike off some of that business, for it is a bad business which makes your soul poor.

EVENING

Let the wicked forsake his way, and the unrighteous man his thoughts. And let him return to the Lord, and He will have mercy on him; and to our God, for He will abundantly pardon — Isaiah 55:7.

GOD'S WAYS of pardon are far above anything you can ever conceive. Look at yourself. Are you slow to forgive? Some find it a long time before they can forget an injury. God forgives rapidly. Through the death of His dear Son He is able to forgive at once, freely, readily, without the violation of His justice. There are no compulsions with Him, *"He delights in mercy."* It is His very self to pardon, for God is love. Do not judge God's heart by that hard heart of yours. He is a God ready to pardon. You can come to an end of your forgiveness very soon. After being offended seven times you do not go on to seventy times seven. If you did, surely you would make a great wonder of it and think that you deserved great praise. But God goes on and on and on; He never comes to the end of pardoning mercy so long as a soul cries for forgiveness.

There are some things you find hard to forgive, and will say, "This is really very provoking; I am of a forgiving spirit, and I have overlooked offenses a great many times, but surely you do not expect me to endure such treatment as this?" No, nobody expects it of you, and if he did he would be disappointed. God does far more in the way of pardon than we ask, or even think. As soon as we cry to Him for pardon, He answers with forgiveness.

But there are many who will claim to forgive, but not to forget. But God promises to forget our iniquities. It is more than omniscience can do to forget, and yet God declares that He does forget: *"I will cast all your sins behind My back,"* He says — and, *"I will cast their iniquities into the depths of the sea. They shall not be remembered against them any more forever."*

September 9   MORNING

He that believes on the Son has everlasting life. But he that refuses to obey the Son shall not see life, but the wrath of God remains on him — John 3:36.

THE UNBELIEVER perpetrates an offense against every person of the blessed Trinity. He may think that his not believing is a small business, but truly it is a barbed shaft shot against Deity. Take the persons of the Trinity, beginning with the Son of God who comes to us most nearly. It is a most surprising thing that *"the Word was made flesh and dwelt among us."* It is no wonder that in Hindustan the missionaries are often met with this remark, "It is too good to be true that God ever took on Himself the nature of such a thing as man!" Yet, it seems much more wonderful when Christ became man, that He took all the sorrows and infirmities of man; yea, in addition, that He was made to bear the sin of many. The most extraordinary of all facts is this, that the infinitely Holy One should be *"numbered with the transgressors,"* and should *"bear their iniquities."* The Lord has made Him, who knew no sin, to be made sin for us (2 Cor. 5:21). O wonder of wonders! it is beyond all degree amazing that He who distributes crowns and thrones should hang on a tree and die, the Just for the unjust, bearing the punishment due to sinners for guilt. Now, knowing this, as most of you do, and yet refusing to believe, in effect you are saying, "I do not believe that the incarnate God can save." If you reply that you sincerely believe that He can save, then it must be that you feel that He will not save you, or that you do not want Him to save you. If you say that you do not say that you will not believe Him. Then I ask, why do you then remain in unbelief? The fact is this, that you do not trust Him; you do not obey Him.

EVENING

He that believes on the Son has everlasting life. But he that refuses to obey the Son shall not see life, but the wrath of God remains on him — John 3:36.

IN MANY persons love of sin rather than any boasted self-righteousness keeps them from the Savior. They do not believe in Jesus, not because they have any doubt about the truths of Christianity, but because they have an enslaving love for their favorite sin. One says, "If I were to believe in Christ, then I must obey Him; to trust and to obey go together. Then I could not be what I am; I could not trade as I do; I could not practice secret licentiousness; I could not frequent the haunts of the ungodly, where laughter is occasioned by sin, and mirth by blasphemy. I do not want to give up these darling sins." Perhaps this sinner hopes that one day, when he can no longer enjoy his sin, he will be able to sneak out of it and try to cheat the Devil of his soul. But in the meantime he prefers the pleasures of sin to obedience to God, unbelief to acceptance of His salvation. O sweet, but bitter sin! How you are murdering the souls of men! As certain serpents before they strike their prey fix their eyes on it and fascinate it, then at last devour it, so does sin fascinate the foolish sons of Adam; they are charmed with it, and they perish for it. It yields but momentary pleasure, and its wage is eternal misery. Yet men are enamored by it. The ways of the strange woman, and the paths of uncleanness lead most plainly to the chambers of death, yet men are attracted to it as moths by the blaze of a candle; and so they are destroyed. Alas! Men recklessly dash against the rocks of dangerous lusts; they perish wilfully beneath the enchantment of sin. It is a sad pity to prefer a harlot to the eternal God, to prefer a few counterfeit coins made by dishonesty to Heaven itself; to prefer the gratification of the belly to the love of the Creator, and the joy of being reconciled and saved. It was a dire insult to God when Israel set up a golden calf and said, *"These are your gods, O Israel."* So do many now.

But they rebelled and troubled His Holy Spirit. Therefore, He was turned to be their enemy, and He fought against them — Isaiah 63:10.

THIS IS A TERRIBLE CASE. When God is turned to be a man's enemy and fights against him, he is in a desperate plight. With other enemies we may contend with some hope of success, but not with the omnipotent God. The enmity of others is an affliction, but the enmity of God is destruction. If He turns to be our enemy, then everything is turned against us. The stars in their courses fight against us, and the stones in the fields are in league for our stumbling. *"If God is for us, who can be against us"* (Rom. 8:31). But if God is against us, who can be for us? The words read like a funeral knell: *"He was turned to be their enemy, and He fought against them."*

This shows us that God is not indifferent to sin. Men may try to persuade themselves that God does not care, that it is nothing to Him how men act, whether they break or keep His laws. Men may plead that He is *kind to the unthankful and to the evil*, and that the same even happens to all, both to the righteous and to the wicked. And so indeed it seems for the present. Our shortsightedness may even assure us that the ungodly prosper and have the best of it. But this is only blindness. God hates sin now and always. He would not be God if He did not. God is stirred with righteous indignation against every kind of evil. It moves His Spirit to anger. Some believe in an impassive God, but certainly the God of the Bible is never so described. He is represented in Scripture after the manner of men; but how else could He be represented to men? If He were represented after the manner of God, we could not understand the description. But as he is represented to us in Scripture, the Lord notes sin, feels sin, grows angry with sin, is provoked, and His Holy Spirit vexed by the rebellion of men.

EVENING

For I confess my transgressions, and my sin is ever before me. Against You, You only, have I sinned and done this evil in Your sight; that You might be justified when You speak and be clear when You judge — Psalm 51:3,4.

HERE DAVID SEES the plurality and immense number of his sins, making open declaration of them. He makes full confession of them, but not as a plea for forgiveness, only as clear evidence that he needs mercy, that he is utterly unable to look to any other quarter for help. Pleading guilty bars him from any appeal against the sentence of justice. He is saying, "O Lord, I cast myself on Your mercy; do not refuse me. You have made me willing to confess. O follow up this work of grace with a full and free remission! My sin as a whole is never out of my mind; it continually oppresses my spirit. I lay it before You because it is ever before me. Lord, put away both from You and me." To an awakened conscience, pain on account of sin is not transient and occasional, but intense and abiding. And this is no sign of Divine wrath, but rather a sure preface of abounding favor.

The virus of sin lies in its opposition to God. The Psalmist's sense of sin toward others rather tended to increase the force of his feeling of sin against God. All his wrongdoing centered, culminated, and climaxed at the foot of the Divine throne. To injure our fellow men is sin, because in doing so we violate the law of God. The penitent's heart was so filled with a sense of the wrong done to the Lord Himself, that all other confession was swallowed up in a brokenhearted acknowledgment of offense against Him. To commit treason before the eye of the king in his very court is impudence indeed. David felt that his sin was in all its filthiness was before Jehovah. No one but a child of God cares for the eye of God, but in a gracious soul it reflects a fearful guilt on every evil act, when we remember that the God whom we offend was present when the trespass was committed. He could not present any argument against Divine justice, if it proceeded at once to condemn him and punish him for his crime.

September 11   MORNING

I dwell in the high and holy place, even with the contrite and humble of spirit, to make live the spirit of the humble and to revive the heart of the contrite ones. For I will not contend forever, nor will I always be angry, — Isaiah 57:15,16.

IS THE LORD contending with you? Is not sin the cause of your sorrow? Do not trifle with this matter. It is a solemn thing to have God fighting against you. Ask Him to show you why He contends with you. Do not despair, for if the Lord meant to destroy you, He would not have promised that He would not be angry forever. If you were hopeless, He would leave you alone. He flogs wanderers back to Him, those He loves. Be wise and see beneath the mask of anger. Understand that He is applying discipline to one of His family. For sin and smart go together to all heirs of Heaven. Seek the Lord; cry to Him and confess your sin. He will dwell in peace with all who are contrite and humble. Repent of your folly, whether it be rebellion, or wasting what He has given you, or failing to obey His commands. Arise, go to Him and ask forgiveness. You know the way. Retrace your steps. Fly to your Father. Put your head on His bosom and sob out your confession, *"Father, I have sinned"* — and before the day is over you will receive your Lord's full absolution. God will soon put away the rod when you put away your sin. If He chooses not to stop the chastisement, you will patiently bear it, and you will bless Him that He has forgiven you. For you will know He has forgiven, that He is not angry any more. As a rule He ceases to fight against the man who ceases from sin.

EVENING

Wash me, and I shall be whiter than snow. Make me to hear joy and gladness, that the bones which You have broken may rejoice — Psalm 51:7,8.

HOLY SCRIPTURE hardly contains a verse more full of faith than this. Considering the nature of the sin, and the deep sense David had of it, it is a glorious faith to be able to see in the the blood all-sufficient merit enough to entirely purge it away. Considering also the deep, natural inbred corruption which David saw and experienced within, it is a miracle of faith that he could rejoice in the hope of perfect purity in his inward parts. Yet, let it be added, the faith is no more than God's word warrants, than the blood of atonement encourages, than the promise of God deserves. O that some reader may take heart, even now while smarting under sin, to do the Lord the honor to rely confidently on the finished sacrifice of Calvary, and the infinite mercy revealed.

"Make me to hear joy and gladness" — he prays about his sorrow late in the Psalm. He began at once with his sin; he asks to hear pardon, and then to hear joy. He seeks comfort at the right time and from the right source. His ear has become heavy with sinning, and so he prays, *"Make me to hear."* No voice could revive his dead joys, but that voice which quickens the dead. Pardon from God would give him double joy. No stinted bliss awaits the forgiven one. He will not only have a double joy, but he will hear it. It will sing with exultation. Some joy is felt, but not heard; for it contends with fears. But the joy of pardon has a voice louder than the voice of sin. God's voice speaking peace is the sweetest music an ear can hear. David was like a poor wretch whose bones are crushed, crushed in his case by Omnipotence itself. He groaned under no mere flesh wounds. His firmest and yet tenderest powers were broken in pieces; his manhood had become a dislocated, mangled, quivering sensibility. Yet if He who crushed would cure, every wound would become a new mouth for song, every bone quivering before with agony would become equally sensible of intense delight. The figure is bold, and so is the supplicant. He is requesting a great thing. He is seeking joy for a sinful heart, music for his crushed bones.

MORNING

September 12

In whom we have redemption through His blood, the forgiveness of sins, according to the riches of His grace — Ephesians 1:7.

WHAT IS THIS *forgiveness of sins*? Too often it is supposed that the chief and main thought to the forgiven sinner is that he has escaped from Hell. Salvation means much more than this. First of all, it means rescue from punishment, for if sin is pardoned, the penalty is extinguished. It would not be possible for God to forgive, yet to punish. That would be a forgiveness quite unworthy of God. It would in fact be no forgiveness at all. The everlasting punishment of sin declared in Scripture will never happen to one who is forgiven. When transgression is removed, the soul stands clear at the bar of God, and there can be no further penalty. One who is forgiven is cleared of the punishment he otherwise would have borne: *"Bless is he whose transgression is forgiven, whose sin is covered."* — *'There is therefore no condemnation to those who are in Christ Jesus"* (Psalm 32:1; Rom. 8:1).

Yet Divine favor restored is still the brightest result of forgiveness to many. Those convicted of sin will feel more the lack of God's approval, than fears of punishment. When the Holy Spirit convinces candidates for salvation of their sin, of their bondage. And with this comes the realization that God is angry, rightly and properly, because of unrepented sin. This under the Spirit's guidance leads to mourning that God is offended with the sinner, that the living God has been grieved, that sin against His righteous will has occurred. Realization that there could be no rejoicing in His favor, no smile from Him whose approval means everything. Then, feeling that it is right for God to be so displeased, the sinner embraces gladly the forgiveness offered. With this forgiveness then comes joy that God has taken away His anger, and double joy that He is now pleased with the repentant sinner, *according to the riches of His grace*.

EVENING

Weeping may endure for a night, but joy comes in the morning — Psalm 30:5.

HOW HEAVILY TROUBLE weighs on us at night. Our wearied nerve and brain seem unable to bear up under the pressure. Our pulse throbs, and the fevered, restless body refuses to help in the work of endurance. We feel miserable and helpless, passionately weeping under the force of events. At last sleep comes. Trouble, temptation, whatever it may be that strives to overcome us, by sheer force drives our poor humanity beyond the present reach of further trial. After such a night of struggle, and the heavy sleep of exhaustion, we awake with a vague sense of trouble. Our thoughts gather, and we wonder over our own actions, as the memory of them returns on us. What was it that seemed so hopeless, so dark? Why were we so helpless and despairing? This morning things do not look so bad — sad indeed, but endurable — hard, but no longer impossible — bad enough, but no cause for despair as we look up to our Father in Heaven in our morning prayers. *"Joy comes in the morning,"* when life with its struggles and toils and sins bring us conflict, but hope with them. For it is our God who *"gives His beloved sleep."* Whether it is the nightly sleep, or the sleep in death, He gives His beloved sleep. In death all believers sleep in Jesus, and they awake to the joy of a morning which will never wane, a true morning of joy. The Sun of Righteousness then beams on them. Light is now on all their ways. Then they can only wonder when they recall the despair, the darkness, the toil, the weeping in their earthly life. Then they can remember the promise of God, that *weeping may endure for the night, but in the morning will come joy*. In that morning when we are seated at Jesus' feet, it will be to us as in that hymn, "When in our Father's happy land, We meet our own once more, Then we shall scarcely understand, Why we have wept before."

MORNING

Be merciful to me, O God, be merciful to me; for my soul trusts in You. Yea, in the shadow of Your wings I will make my hiding-place, until these great troubles pass by — Psalm 57:1.

URGENT NEED suggests the repetition of the cry, for in this way urgency of desire is expressed. If we yearn for quick mercy, then we must be quick to ask mercy, and even ask it twice. For the Psalmist pleads first for mercy; he feels he cannot improve on his plea, and so he repeats it. God is the God of mercy, the Father of mercies. It is most fitting, then, that in distress we should seek mercy from Him in whom it dwells. Faith urges her suit right well. How can the Lord be unmerciful to a trustful soul? Our faith does not deserve mercy, but it always wins it from the sovereign grace of God when it is sincere, as in this case where the soul of the petitioner believed.

Not in the cave alone would he hide, but in the cleft of the Rock of Ages. As the little birds find ample shelter beneath the parental wing, even so would the fugitive believer place himself under the secure protection of the Divine power. The emblem is delightfully familiar and suggestive. When we cannot see the sunshine of God's face, it is a blessing to cower beneath the shadow of His wings. Evil will pass away, and the eternal wings will abide over us until then. Blessed is God, our calamities are matters of time, but our safety is a matter of eternity. When we are under the Divine shadow, the passing over of trouble cannot harm us. The hawk flies across the sky, but this is no evil to the chicks when they are safely nestling beneath the hen. So do we nestle for safety.

"I will cry to God most high." He is quite safe, yet he prays. For faith is never dumb. We pray because we believe. We exercise by faith the spirit of adoption by which we cry, *"Abba! Father!."* He does not say, I do cry, or I have cried, but I will cry. Indeed, this resolution may stand with all of us until we pass through the gates of pearl. For while we are here below we will still have need to cry to Him for mercy.

EVENING

I have loved you with an everlasting love — Jeremiah 31:3.

"BUT GOD, who is rich in mercy, for His great love with which He loves us (even when we were dead in sins) has made us alive together with Christ" (Eph. 2:4-6). God was rich in mercy toward us because of His great love with which He loved us. For love is a desire to communicate good, the greatest possible good. Mercy, however, is the pulling of someone out of a depth. It is mercy that delivers a creature from misery. God's love, then, is toward the creature simply considered. God's mercy is toward him as a created being who has fallen into misery. Parents love their children because they are their children. But when the child falls into misery, then parents are drawn out to show pity and compassion, a love working in a way of pity.

It is love that guides God's mercy. There are vessels of mercy, and there are vessels of wrath (Rom. 9:21,22). Who makes the difference? It is God! Acting in the very beginning, God made the difference. His love singled out certain persons to love and to show His mercy toward, as illustrated in Rom. 9:11-13: *"Jacob have I loved."* And lest we miss the import of this statement, He plainly adds, *"and Esau have I hated."* When? Was it after Jacob had believed and Esau had rejected God? No, but they *"had not yet been born, nor had they done anything good or evil."* Why then did God love the one and hate the other? He answers, *"so that the purpose of God according to election might stand, not of works, but of Him who calls."* Or, as in Eph. 1:5, *"He had marked us out beforehand for adoption through Christ Jesus to Himself, according to the good pleasure of His will."* From everlasting God chose those He would love, to whom He would show mercy, delivering them from the misery of the Fall of man. Praise God for this everlasting love. (From *God's Everlasting Love*, Jay Green).

MORNING

I have loved you with an everlasting love — Jeremiah 31:3.

HOW COULD GOD LOVE US while we were yet sinners? Because Christ was to bear our sin and atone for it. Christ Jesus was made a curse and hung on a tree — the comfort of God's presence was removed from Him. Yet at the same time He suffered all the pain and wrath due for all the sins of those given to Him to save. Yet while the arrows of God's justice pierced Him, and the wrath of God bore down on Him, did not God love His Son with the deepest, the most unspeakable love ever known? Yes, even while He was under wrath, Christ was loved. But did God put the innocent, sinless Son of God under wrath because He loved Him? Yes! Just as surely as Christ willingly offered Himself to be the sacrifice for the elect because He loved them, so God accepted that sacrifice because He loved us and He loves His Son. All these things were done so that the marvelous love of God for His own chosen people could be known. Because He loved Him, He did not leave Christ under wrath. No! Those who are loved by God may be sure that he will not allow anything but His own glory and purpose to separate Him and His loved ones. The instant His purpose is fulfilled, God moves marvelously to triumph and to bring the object of His love back into His embrace. Just as Christ was returned to the bosom of His loving Father, so shall all God's chosen ones find themselves on His warm and comforting breast for all eternity. Without the backdrop of misery experienced on the way to this everlasting happiness, there would not be nearly so much love in our hearts for God. He has wisely decreed that we might see the strength of that love with which He first loved us, that we cannot be completely separated from such a love, that He has both the will and the power to cleanse and restore all those He has loved from the beginning, *from everlasting*, before the world began. (From *God's Everlasting Love*, adapted from Thomas Goodwin by Jay P. Green, Sr.)

EVENING

I have loved you with an everlasting love — Jeremiah 31:3.

THIS LOVE is from the past, *"I have loved you."* We were rebels, and He loved us. We were dead in trespasses and in sins, and yet He loved us. We rejected His grace; we defied His warnings; yet He loved us. We came to His feet trembling and afraid, and He loved us, and washed us, and robed us. He loved us, and because of this He saved us. Since then we have been earthly, sinful, changeful, unbelieving, proud, foolish, yet He has loved us without pause. We have been ill, racked with pain, but He has loved us. We have lost our dearest relatives by His hand, but even in this He loved us. Everything has been in a whirl around us, but He has loved us with fixed affection. Our life has been a strange labyrinth, but He has loved us; yea, that love has been the clue of the maze. How sweet it is, beloved, to roll up the years gone by, to put them away with this label: "Days of the loving-kindness of the Lord"!

The matchless declaration of this text is a voice of love in the present. The Lord loves the believer now. Whatever discomfort you are in, the Lord loves you. Perhaps your heart is failing you with fear; but the Lord still says to you, *"Yes, I have loved you with an everlasting love."* That *everlasting* includes today. Things present are provided for as well as things to come. External circumstances do not change the love of God, nor will your internal condition do so. He has said, *"I am God, I change not."* Everlasting love makes no leaps and jumps so as to leave out this day of trouble, or that hour of temptation. Even at the darkest hour your name is on the heart of your God. This text is a voice of love for the past, for the present, for the future. (Spurgeon).

September 15 — MORNING

Hear me when I call, O God of my righteousness. You have become greater to me in distress. Have mercy on me and hear my prayer — Psalm 4:1.

THIS IS ANOTHER instance of David's common habit of pleading past mercies as a ground for present favor. Here he reviews his Ebenezers and takes comfort from them. It is not to be imagined that He who has helped us in six troubles will leave us in the seventh. God does nothing by halves, and He will never cease to help us until we cease to need. The manna will fall every morning until we cross the heavenly Jordan.

Note that David speaks first to God and then to men. Surely, we should all speak the more boldly to men if we had more constant prior conversation with God. He who dares to face his Maker will not tremble before the sons of men.

The name by which the Lord is here addressed, *"God of my righteousness"* deserves notice, since it is not used in any other part of Scripture. It credits God with being the Author, the Witness, the Maintainer, the Judge, and the Rewarder of my righteousness. To You I appeal from the slander and harsh judgments of men. In this is wisdom; let us imitate it and always take our suit into the superior court of Heaven, and not to the petty courts of human opinion.

"You have become greater to me in distress" — this is a figure taken from an army in straits, hard pressed by the surrounding enemy. God has dashed down the rocks and given me room. He has broken the barriers and set me in a large place. Or, we may understand it this way, that God has enlarged my heart with joy and comfort when I was like a man imprisoned by grief and sorrow. God is a never-failing comforter.

God may justly permit your enemies to destroy your comfort, because of your many sins, yet you must feel to Him for mercy, beseech Him in prayer, to bring you out of all your troubles. The best of men need mercy as truly as the worst of men. All the deliverances of saints, and the pardons of sinners, are the free gifts of heavenly grace.

EVENING

O God, my heart is fixed; I will sing and give praise. Wake up, my soul! Wake up, psaltery and harp! I will awake early; I will praise You, O Lord — Psalm 57:7-9.

HIS HEART is not fluttered. No, but the Psalmist is calm, firm, happy, resolute, established. When the central axle is secure, the whole wheel is right. If our great bower anchor holds, the ship cannot drive. *"O God, my heart is fixed"* — I am resolved to trust You, to serve You, and to praise You. Twice he declares this to the glory of God, who in this way comforts the souls of His servants. Is it well with you? Is your once roving heart now firmly fixed on God and the proclamation of His glory? Vocally and instrumentally will you celebrate God in worship? With lip and with heart will you ascribe honor to Him? Fix your heart on Him, then Satan cannot stop you, nor Saul, nor the Philistines. Make Adullam ring with music, and let all the caverns of it echo with joyous song. Believer, make a firm decree that your soul shall magnify the Lord.

Let the noblest powers of your nature bestir themselves: the intellect which conceives thought, the tongue which expresses it, and the inspired imagination which beautifies it. Let all these be on the alert now that the hour for praise has come. Let all the music with which you are familiar be well attuned for the hallowed service of praise. Awaken the dawn with your joyous notes. Let no sleepy verses or weary notes be heard from you. Thoroughly arouse yourself for this high employment. When you are at your best, you fall short of what the Lord deserves. For this reason make sure that you bring Him your best — if it is marred by your human weaknesses, at least let it not be deteriorated by indolence. Three times the Psalmist calls on himself to awaken. Do we need so much arousing for this glorious work? Then let us not spare it, for the engagement is too honorable, too needful, to be left undone or ill done. Stir yourself.

MORNING

Therefore, with loving-kindness I have drawn you — Jeremiah 31:3.

THE LORD ASSURES us that these are drawings of His loving-kindness. All His drawings are in love. Whenever He draws, it is in love. God knows better about His drawings than we do. It may appear to us that He pulls and snatches in anger, but He knows that He has always drawn in loving-kindness. Because the horse is wilful, it thinks the driver stern. Our waywardness makes us think the Lord is harsh. The forces which he puts forth to work on us are tender, gentle, kind and loving. He has drawn you and me with loving-kindness. Think of it, then bless His holy name. Lord, you have drawn me when I did not desire it, when I did not know it, when I thought I was willingly moving of my own accord, etc. I see it all now, and I bless You for it. Draw me still, that I may say, "Your gentleness has made me great."

What a wonderful word is that *"loving-kindness"* — loving and kindness are two of the choicest diamonds set side by side. Kindness is kinned-ness, and the Lord Jesus treats us as His kith and kin. And He does this in the most loving manner: *"With loving-kindness I have drawn you."* He might have whipped you to Himself. He might have dragged you to the City of Refuge. He might have threatened you into repentance. He might have thundered you into submission. But no, He did it with loving-kindness. You are a specially favored one. Has not the Lord been loving and kind to you? Have you loved Him because He first loved you? Then praise Him for it.

EVENING

Do not let your heart envy sinners, but be in the fear of the Lord all the day long. For surely there is an end; and your hope shall not be cut off — Proverbs 23:17.

TO ABIDE IN THE FEAR of the Lord is to dwell safely. To forsake the Lord would be to invite danger. In the fear of the Lord there is strong confidence, but apart from it there is no security. How honorable is such a state! Men ridicule the religion which is not uniform. One once claimed that he had long been a teetotaler, but some doubted and asked him how long he had been an abstainer. He replied, "off and on for twenty years." You must not believe that you can dare to be a Christian off and on. No one could respect you, and should not. Such seed as this will not grow; there is no vitality in it. Constancy is the best proof of sincerity: *"Be in the fear of the Lord all the day long."* This is the way to happiness. God will trouble the believer who tends to be easy in sin. If you are a Christian you will never find ease or happiness in departing from God. You are spoiled for such pleasure as the world offers. Your joy lies in a closer walk with God; your Heaven while on earth is to be in communion with the Lord.   If you abide in the fear of the Lord, how useful you will be. Your "off and on" people are worth nothing; nobody will be influenced by them. What little good they do, they undo. The abiding man is also the growing man. He that is *"in the fear of the Lord all the day long"* comes to have more of that holy fear; it has more practical power over his life and heart. What a poor life they lead, those who are alternately zealous and lukewarm! Like Penelope, they weave by day, but unravel by night. They blow hot and cold, and so melt and freeze by turns. They build, and then break down, and so are never at rest. Children of God, determine that your conduct will be consistent.

September 17 — MORNING

Do not let your heart envy sinners, but be in the fear of the Lord all the day long. For surely there is an end, and your hope shall not be cut off — Proverbs 23:17,18.

DO NOT HAVE a religion of spasms. You have heard of men and women who have had singularly excellent efforts on one occasion, but never again. They blazed like comets, the wonders of a season, and then disappeared like comets, never to be seen again. Religion produced at high pressure for a supreme occasion is not a healthy growth. We need ordinary, commonplace, everyday godliness, which may be compared to the light of fixed stars which shine evermore. Religion must not be thought of as something apart from daily life. It should be the most vital part of our existence. Our praying should be like our breathing, natural and constant. Our communion with God should be like our taking of food, a happy and natural privilege. Brothers, it is a great pity when people draw a hard and fast line across their life, dividing it into 'sacred' and 'secular.' Do not say, "This is religion, and the other is business," but sanctify all things. Our most common acts should be sanctified by the Word of God and prayer, and thus made into sacred deeds. The best of men have the least of jar or change of tone in their lives. When the great Elijah knew that he was to be taken up, what did he do? If you knew that tonight you would be taken up to Heaven, would you think of something special to do as a farewell to earth? The most fitting thing to do is to continue in your duty, as if nothing had been revealed to you. It was Elijah's business to go to the schools of the prophets and to instruct them. And He went about this business on the way to the place where he would take his seat in the chariot of fire.

EVENING

I will lie down in peace and in sleep. For You alone, O Lord, will make me live in safety — Psalm 4:8.

DAVID WOULD NOT sit up to watch in fear, but lie down in peace and in sleep. He had nothing to fear. For one that has the wings of God above need no other shield. Better than bolts or bars is the protection of the Lord. Armed men kept the bed of Solomon, but it is doubtful that he slept any more soundly than his father David, whose bed was the hard ground, and who was haunted by blood-thirsty foes. Note that he says, *"alone,"* which means that God only was his keeper, without man's help. God alone was his help, and he was alone with God. A quiet conscience is a good bedfellow. How many of our sleepless hours might be traced to our untrusting and disordered minds! They slumber sweetly whom faith rocks to sleep. No pillow is so soft as a promise; no blanket is so warm as an assured interest in Christ. O Lord, give us this calm repose on You. Like David, may we lie down in peace and sleep each night. May we joyfully lie down in the appointed time to sleep in death, to rest in God.

Let us never lose sight of the Lord Jesus while reading this psalm. He is the Lord our righteousness. For this reason, in all our approaches to the mercy seat, let us go there in a language corresponding to this which calls Jesus the Lord our righteousness. While men of the world seek their chief good from the world, let us rather desire His favor which infinitely transcends corn and wine, and all the good things which perish in the using. Lord, Your favor is better than life itself; lovers of You inherit all treasures.

Gracious God and Father, have You in such a wonderful manner set apart one in our nature for Yourself? Have you beheld One in the purity of His nature, as One in every point godly? Have You given Him as the covenant of the people? And have You declared Yourself well pleased with Him? Then may my soul be well pleased in Jesus, Your beloved Son. For then I will know that You will hear me when I call on You in Jesus' name, when I look up to You for acceptance for Jesus' sake.

MORNING

September 18

So let us draw near to the throne of grace with boldness, so that we may receive mercy and find grace to help in time of need — Hebrews 4:16.

ON THE THRONE of grace God is bound to us by His promises. The covenant contains in it many gracious promises, exceeding great and precious. Then, *"Ask, and it shall be given you; seek and you shall find; knock and it shall be opened to you."* Until God had said that word, or a word to that effect, it was at His own option to hear prayer or not. But it is not so now. For now, if it is true prayer offered through Jesus Christ, His truth binds Him to hear it. A man may be perfectly free, but the moment he makes a promise he is no longer free to break it. So also the everlasting God does not break His promises. He delights to fulfil them. He has declared that all His promises are yea and amen in Christ Jesus. But for our consolation when we survey God under the high and terrible aspect of a sovereign, we have this to reflect on, that He is under covenant bonds of promise to be faithful to the souls that seek Him. His throne must be a throne of grace to His people.

And once more, the sweetest thought of all, every covenant promise has been endorsed and sealed with blood. Then far be it from the everlasting God to pour scorn on the blood of His dear Son. When a king has given a charter to a city, he may before have been absolute, and there was nothing to check his prerogatives, but when the city has its charter, then it pleads its rights before the king himself. Even so God has given to His people a charter of untold blessings, bestowing on them the sure mercies of David. The validity of a charter very much depends on the signature and seal. Then how sure is the charter of covenant grace, for the signature is the handwriting of God Himself, and the seal is the blood of His Only-begotten Son. The covenant is ratified with blood, the blood of His own dear Son. Having given His Son, will He not with Him give all good things asked in His name?

EVENING

Be patient until the coming of the Lord. See, the farmer waits for the precious fruit of the earth, having patience for it until it gets the early and late rain — James 5:7.

THE FARMER WAITS with a reasonable hope for the precious fruit of the earth. He has long patience for it until he receives the early and latter rain. He expects the harvest because he has plowed the fields and sown the grain. If he had not, he would not be an example for our imitation. Had he left his fields fallow, never stirred the clods, and never cast in the golden seed, he would be an idiot to expect the soil to produce a harvest. Thorns and thistles would come forth, nothing more. This is the folly of those who flatter their souls with a prospect of good things to come in time, while they neglect the opportunity of sowing good things in the present time. They say they hope it will be well with them at the end, but since it is not well with them now, why should they expect any change? Much less should they expect a change contrary to the entire order of Providence. Is it not written, *"He that sows to the flesh shall of the flesh reap corruption"*? Do you expect to sow to the flesh and reap salvation? That is a blessing reserved for the one who sows to the spirit. For one who sows to the spirit shall of the Spirit reap everlasting life. As for the one who scatters nothing but the wild oats of sin, who simply lives to indulge his own passions, who determinately resolves to neglect the things that make for peace, such a one can but upbraid himself if he expects to reap anything good of God. Such sowers to the wind will reap the whirlwind. Those sowing nothing shall reap nothing but sorrow. It is only those who by God's grace have been enabled to sow abundantly, even though they have gone forth weeping, who shall afterwards come again rejoicing, bringing their sheaves with them.

Be patient until the coming of the Lord. See, the farmer waits for the precious fruit of the earth, having patience for it until it gets the early and late rain — James 5:7.

OUR WAITING, if it is the work of the Holy Spirit, must have this long patience in it. Are you a sufferer? There are sweet fruits that can come from suffering: "Not for the present does it seem to be joyous, but grievous; nevertheless, afterwards it yields the peaceable fruits of righteousness to those who are exercised by it." Have long patience for those peaceable fruits. You shall be brought out of your trouble; deliverance will be found for you out of your affliction when the discipline for which it came has been fulfilled in you. Have long patience, for not the first month does the farmer find a harvest. If he has sown in winter, he does not expect he will reap in early spring. He does not go out with his sickle in May and expect to find golden sheaves. He waits. The moons wax and wane; suns rise and set; but he waits until the appointed time. Wait, O sufferer, until the night is over. Watch after watch you may have passed through. Tarry a little longer, for, *"You shall stand in your lot in the end of the days."* Before long you will have a happy exit out of your present trials. Are you a worker? Then you need as much patience in working as you do in suffering. We must not expect to see immediate results in all cases from the preaching of gospel, from the teaching of Scripture, from distributing religious literature, or from any other kind of effort for God. Immediate results could come; sometimes they do, and they greatly cheer the worker. but it is given to most to wait long, as the farmer waits before the fruit reaches maturity. Truth, like the grain of mustard seed, does not grow into a tree the day after it is sown. It takes its time, but it brings forth fruit manyfold in due season.

EVENING

Be patient until the coming of the Lord. See, the farmer waits for the precious fruit of the earth, having patience for it until it gets the early and late rain — James 5:7.

NOTE THAT the farmer waits with his eye upward. He waits until God shall send him the early and latter rain. He has wit enough for this. Even if he is a worldly man he knows that the harvest depends not only on the seed he sows and on the soil he cultivates, but on the rain that comes only at the bidding of the Almighty. If the skies are brass, the clods will be iron. Unless God shall speak to the clouds, and the clouds shall speak to the earth, the earth will not speak to the grain, and the grain will not make us speak the words of rejoicing. Every farmer is aware of this, and every Christian must remember it. The sufferer says, "I am to wait for God's help and for the graces that come by afflicton. And I must wait with my eye upward, for all the plowing of affliction will not profit me, and all the sowing of meditation will not speed me, unless God shall send His gracious Spirit like showers of heavenly rain. If I am a worker, I must work. When I wait, I must wait, always looking upward."

The keys of the rain-clouds which water the earth bang at the girdle of Jehovah. None but the eternal Father can send the Holy Spirit like showers on the churches. He can send the Comforter, and then our labor will prosper. It will not be in vain in the Lord, then. But if He deny, if He withholds this covenant blessing for now, then our work is useless, our patience worthless, all our cost in vain, until He blesses. In spiritual as in temporal things, *"It is vain to rise up early and sit up late, and eat the bread of carefulness;" "except the Lord build the house, they labor in vain that build it"* (Psalm 127:1,2). We must have the dew, O God, or else our seed shall rot under the clod. We must wait, and wait with our eye upwards, or else our expectation will perish as a stillborn child.

MORNING

Be patient until the coming of the Lord. See, the farmer waits for the precious fruit of the earth, having patience for it until it gets the early and late rain — James 5:7.

THE FARMER waits under changing circumstances and various contingencies. At one time he sees the fair prospect of a good crop. The wheat has come up well. He has never seen more green springing from the ground. But by and by the wheat begins to look yellow. Suddenly he fancies he sees a blight or a black smut on it. Only a farmer knows how his hopes and fear alternate and fluctuate from time to time. It is too hot, too cold, too dry, too wet — it is hardly ever quite right, according to his judgment, or rather according to his unbelief. Yet he waits.

Ah, dear friends, how often this happens when we work for God. There are always changes in the field of Christian labor. At one time we see many conversions, and we bless God that there are so many seals to our testimony. But at times some of the converts disappoint us. There seemed to be blossoms, but no fruit was forthcoming. Also at times there are many that appear to backslide. Their love seems to grow cold. Perhaps we find in the church the black smut of heresy. Some deadly heresy creeps in, and the anxious workers find plenty to do, but no harvest after all. Oh, patience, patience. Many a fretful expression and a murmuring word need to be repented of. O evangelical worker, if you will but wait in faith and with patience, God will give a rich return for all that you have done for Him. Then you will blush that you ever doubted.

EVENING

Oh how great is Your goodness which You have laid up for them that fear You — Psalm 31:29.

"MARK the phrase, *'laid up for them."* It is His mercy and goodness that is intended for them. As a father that lays up a sum of money, writing on the bag, "This is a portion for such a one of my children." But how comes the Christian to have this right to God, and all that vast and untold treasure of happiness which is in Him? This indeed is greatly to be heeded. It is faith that gives us a good title to all this. That which makes a child of one, also makes an heir of him. Now it is faith that makes one a child of God: *'But as many as received Him, to them He gave power to become the sons of God, even to them that believe on His name.'* Therefore, if you would not call your birthright into question, and bring your interest in Christ and those glorious privileges that come along with Him, then look to your faith." (William Gurnall)

"*How great is Your goodness'* — when I reflect on the words of Your prophet, O Lord, it seems to me that he is depicting God as a father who keeps His children under discipline, even subjecting them to the rod. But He, with all His labor and pains, still aims at nothing but to lay up for them a store which may contribute to their comfort when they have grown to maturity and have learned the prudent use of it. My Father, in this world at times You hide Your great goodness from Your children; it is as if it did not pertain to them. But being Your children, we may be well assured that the celestial treasure will be bestowed on no one else. For this reason I will bear my lot with patience. But, oh! From time to time, waft to me a breath of air from the heavenly land, to refresh my sorrowful heart. Then I will wait more calmly for its full fruition." (Christopher Scriver)

September 21   MORNING

Be glad in the Lord, and rejoice, righteous ones, and shout for joy — Psalm 32:11.

    HAPPINESS is not only our privilege, but our duty. Truly we serve a generous God, since He makes it a part of our obedience to be joyful. How sinful are our rebellious murmurings! How natural does it seem that a man blessed with forgiveness should be glad! Shall we who have received the free pardon of the King of kings pine in inexcusable sorrow? *"Be glad in the Lord"* — here is the directory by which gladness is preserved from levity. We are not to be glad in sin, or to find comfort in possessions, but in our God is to be the garden of our soul's delight. That there is a God, and such a God, and that He is ours forever, our Father and our reconciled Lord, is matter enough for a never-ending psalm of rapturous joy. *"And rejoice, righteous ones"* — redouble your rejoicing, peal upon peal. Since God has clothed His choristers in the white garments of holiness, let them not restrain their joyful voices, but sing aloud and shout as those who find great spoil. Our happiness should be demonstrative. Chill lack of love often represses the noble flame of joy. Too often we whisper our praises when a hearty outburst of song would be far more natural. Through an excessive propriety some churches today are too artificial, so that enquiriers' cries and believer's shouts are silenced if they are heard in the assembly. This may be better than boisterous fanaticism, but there is as much danger in this repression of joy.

    Note how the pardoned are represented as upright, righteous, and without guile. A man may have many faults and yet be saved, but a false heart is everywhere the damning mark. A man of twisting, shifty ways, of a crooked and crafty nature, is not saved. Men of double tongues and tricky ways are the least likely of all men to be saved. Certainly where grace has come, it has restored the Christian's mind to its perpendicular, delivering that one from being doubled with vice, twisted with craft, or bent with dishonesty.

EVENING

You forgave the iniquity of my sin — Psalm 32:5.

    THIS SIN seems very probably to have been his adultery with Bathsheba and the murder of Uriah. Now David, to make the pardoning mercy of God more illustrious, says God not only forgave his *sin*, but the *iniquity* of his sin. And what was that? Surely the worst that can be said of his complicated sin is that there was so much hypocrisy in it. He woefully juggled with God and man in it. This, I do not doubt to say, was the iniquity of his sin, and it put a color deeper on it than the blood which he shed. And the rather — I lay the accent here — because God Himself, when He would set out the heinousness of this sin, seems to do it rather from the hypocrisy in the fact than the fact itself. This appears by God's testimony given this holy man, *"David did that which was right in the eyes of the Lord, and turned not aside from anything that He commanded him all the days of his life, except only in the matter of Uriah the Hittite."* Were there not other false steps which David took besides this? Does the Spirit of God, by excepting this, declare His approval of all else that David ever did? No, surely the Spirit of God records other sins that were done by this eminent servant. But all those are drowned here, and this mentioned is the only stain of his life. But why? Surely because there appeared less sincerity; yea, more hypocrisy in this one sin than in all the others. In them David was wrong as to his actions, yet his heart was more right in the way he committed them. But here his sincerity was badly wounded, though not to the total destruction of the habit. And truly the wound went very deep when that grace was stabbed in which was the life blood of all the rest. Though His mercy prompted Him, and His covenant obliged Him, not to let His child die of this wound, yet God had reason to place a mark on this sin, so that we might know how odious hypocrisy is to God. (William Gurnall)

The joy of the Lord is your strength — Nehemiah 8:10.

THE JOY OF THE LORD springs from God, and has God for its object. The believer who is in a spiritually healthy state rejoices mainly in God Himself; he is happy because there is a God, and because God in His person and character is what He is. All the attributes of God become wellsprings of joy to the thoughtful, contemplative believer. Such a man says within his soul, "All these attributes of God are mine. His power is my protection; His wisdom, my guidance; His faithfulness, my foundation; His grace, my salvation." He is a God who cannot lie; His promises are faithful and true. He is all love, and at the same time He is infinitely just, supremely holy. Why, the contemplation of God to one who knows that this God is his or her God forever and ever is enough to make the eyes overflow with tears of joy, because in this is deep, mysterious, unutterable bliss that fills the heart. There was nothing in the character of Jupiter, or any of the pretended gods of the heathen, to make glad a pure and holy spirit. But there is everything in the character of Jehovah both to purify the heart and to make it thrill with delight. How sweet is it to think over all the Lord has done, how He has revealed Himself of old, and especially how He has displayed His glory in the covenant of grace, and in the person of the Lord Jesus Christ. How charming is the thought that He has revealed Himself to me personally, and has made me to see in Him my Father, my Friend, my Helper, my God. Oh, if there is one word out of Heaven that cannot be excelled, even by the brightness of Heaven itself, it is this word, *"My God, my Father,"* and that sweet promise, *"I will be to them a God, and they shall be to Me a people."* There is no richer consolation to be found. Even the Spirit of God can bring nothing home to the heart of a Christian more fraught with delight than that blessed consideration.

EVENING

The joy of the Lord is your strength — Nehemiah 8:10.

A SOURCE OF JOY is found by the Christian who is living near to God in a deep sense of reconciliation to God, of acceptance with God, and yet, beyond that, of adoption and close relationship to God. Does it not make a man glad to know that even though once his sins had provoked the Lord, now they are all blotted out; not one of them remains. Even though once you were estranged from God, and far off from Him by wicked works, yet He is made near by the blood of Christ. The Lord is no longer an angry judge pursuing you with a drawn sword, but a loving Father into whose bosom we pour our sorrows, where we find ease for every pang of heart. Oh, to know that God actually loves us! It is a subject to muse upon in silence, a matter to meditate upon as we sit by the hour. That the Infinite loves an insignificant creature, an ephemera of an hour, a shadow that declines — is this not a marvel? For God to pity is understandable, and for God to condescend to have mercy on you and me is comprehensible; but for Him to love us, for the pure One to love a sinner, for the infinitely great One to love a worm — this is matchless, a miracle of miracles!

Such thoughts must comfort the soul. And then, add to this, that the Divine love has brought us believers into actual relationship with God, so that we are His sons and daughters — this again is a river of sacred pleasure: *"To which of the angels did He say at any time, You are My Son?"* (Heb. 1:5) No minister of flame, although perfect in obedience, has received the honor of adoption. To us, even to us frail creatures of the dust, is given a blessing denied to Gabriel. For through Jesus Christ the Firstborn we are members of the family of God. Oh, the abyss of joy which lies in sonship with God, and join heirship with Christ! (Rom. 8:17) Words are vain here. The joy springing from the spirit of adoption is another portion of the believer's bliss.

September 23 — MORNING

The joy of the Lord is your strength — Nehemiah 8:10.

THE JOY OF THER LORD in the spirit springs also from an assurance that all the future, whatever it may be, is guaranteed by Divine goodness, that being children of God the love of God toward us is not of mutable character, but abides and remains unchangeable. The believer feels an entire satisfaction in leaving himself in the hands of eternal and immutable love. However happy I may be today, if I am in doubt concerning tomorrow, there is a worm at the root of my peace. Although the past may be sweet in retrospect, and the present fair in enjoyment, yet if the future is grim with fear, then my joy is but shallow. If my salvation is still a matter of hazard and jeopardy, unmingled joy is not mine; deep peace is still out of my reach. But when I know that He in whom I have rested has power and grace enough to complete that which He has begun in me, and for me — when I see the work of Christ to be no half-way redemption, but a complete and eternal salvation — when I perceive the promises are established on an unchangeable basis, and are yes and amen in Christ Jesus, ratified by oath and sealed by blood — then my soul has perfect contentment. It is true, that looking forward there may be seen long avenues of tribulation, but the glory is at the end of them. Battles may be foreseen, and woe to the man who does not expect them, but the eye of faith perceives the crown of victory, and is assured. Deep waters are mapped on our journey, but faith can see Jehovah fording these rivers with us, and she anticipates the day when we shall ascend the banks of the other shore and enter into Jehovah's rest. When we have received these priceless truths into our souls, then we are satisfied with favor and full of the goodness of the Lord.

EVENING

The joy of the Lord is your strength — Nehemiah 8:10.

THERE IS GREAT DEPTH of delight for every Christian when he comes into actual fellowship with God. God loves us, and the fact that we are related to Him by ties most near and dear is thrilling to hear. But, oh, when these doctrines become experiences, then are we indeed anointed with the oil of gladness. When we enter into the love of God, and the love of God enters into us; when we walk with God habitually, then our joy is like the Jordan when it overflows all its banks, Do you know what it is to walk with God, to have Enoch's joy; to sit at Jesus' feet, Mary's joy; to lean your head on Jesus' bosom, John's joy? Communion with the Lord is no mere talk with those of us who have experience with Him. We have known it in the chamber of affliction. We have known it in the solitude of many a night of broken rest. We have known it beneath discouragements and under sorrows and defamations, and in suffering all sorts of ills. And we reckon that one dram of fellowship with Christ is enough to sweeten an ocean full of tribulation. Only to know that He is near us, to see the gleaming of His dear eye, would transform even Hell into Heaven, if it were possible for Him to be there. Alas! You do not and cannot know this bliss while you quaff your foaming bowls, listen to your earthy music. You could not dream it, nor could you understand it even though one should tell you of it. As the beast in the meadow does not know the far-reaching of one who reads the stars and threads the spheres, so neither can the carnal man make so much as a guess of what are the joys which God has prepared for them that love Him, which comes to all believers any day and everyday when their hearts seek it. He reveals it to us by His Spirit. This is the *"joy of the Lord,"* and it is our *strength* from fellowship with the Father and with His Son Jesus Christ.

MORNING

The joy of the Lord is your strength — Nehemiah 8:10.

A JOY WORTH WORLDS is the honor of being allowed to serve Him. To teach a little child his letters for Christ will give a true heart some taste of the joy of the Lord, if it is consciously done for the Lord's sake alone. To bear the portion to those for whom nothing is prepared, to visit the sick, to comfort the mourner, to aid the poor, to instruct the ignorant, if done in Jesus' name, are all Christian works. And in their measure these will array us in the joy of the Lord. And we are happy, if when we cannot work we are enabled to lie still and through faith to acquiesce in the providential orderings of the Lord; this, too, brings the joy of the Lord to us. It is sweet even to smart beneath God's correcting rod, to feel that if God would have us suffer, then it is happiness to do so. Though we fall back with the faintness of nature, at the same time we can have the strength of grace, and say, *"Not my will, but Your will be done."* It is joy, though we are crushed between the millstones of life, and yet the oil of thankfulness rises from the ordeal. When bruised beneath the flail of tribulation, it is joy to find that we lose nothing but the chaff within us, and to find that we willingly yield to God the precious grain of entire submissiveness. Why, this is a little Heaven on earth. To glory in tribulation is a high degree of climbing up toward the likeness of our Lord. Perhaps, the usual communions which we have with our Lord, although exceedingly precious, will never equal those which we enjoy when we have to break through thorns and briars to be with Him. When we follow Him into the wilderness, then we feel the love of our espousals to be doubly sweet. It is a joyous thing when in the midst of mournful circumstances we can feel that we cannot mourn because the Bridegroom is with us. Blessed is that one who in the most terrible storm is not driven away from God, but even rides on the crest of the lofty billows nearer toward Heaven.

EVENING

The joy of the Lord is your strength — Nehemiah 8:10.

PREACHING AND PRAYING, and such things, are not the chief end of man, but the glorifying of God. Praising God vocally is just one form. Preaching is sowing; prayer is watering; and praise is the harvest. God aims at His own glory, and so should we: *"whoever offers praise glorifies Me, says the Lord."* Be diligent then to sing His praises with understanding. We have put away harps and trumpets and organs, let us mind that we really rise above the need of them. These are all inferior even in music to the human voice. There is no melody or harmony like those created by living tongues, but let us be careful that we do not put away an atom of the joy of the Lord. Let us be glad when we unite in singing the psalms. It is a wretched thing to hear the praises of God rendered professionally, as if mere music were everything.

"Sing unto the Lord, O ye saints of His." As God requires outward and inward worship, so a spiritual frame for inward worship may be forwarded by the outward composure. Drowsiness hinders the activity of the soul, but active participation furthers it. Singing awakens the soul; it is a lively rousing up of the heart. (John Lightfoot)

"David does not forget the favor which God bestowed on him. My soul, he says, shall rejoice in the salvation of God. He applies all the members of his body to the work of setting forth the praises of God. He shows unfeignedly that his love to God was so strong that he desired to spend his sinews and bones in singing his devotion" (from John Calvin).

September 25 — MORNING

The Lord is the portion of my inheritance — Psalm 16:5.

"*BLESSED are the people whose God is the Lord*" — No greater mercy can be bestowed on any people, family, or person than this, for God to be their portion. If we value this mercy according to its excellence and worth, it is the greatest of all. The greatness of the good will of God in giving Himself to us is evident in the nature of the gift. God gives abundantly to all the works of His hands; He causes the sun to shine on the evil and on the good, and the rain to descend on the just and the unjust. But in giving Himself to be the portion of His saiust in princes." For princes are but men, and not always the truest of men. They are seldom the best of men. At the end of system started with a mistake in the first place, then accumulated and became more colossal by various other mistakes which naturally accrued to it, and at least was perfected by the craft of designing heretics led by the Devil.

Bigotry, ill feeling, and uncharitableness must all be traced, in a large degree, to our failure to read the Bible. Why does a man hate me when I preach what I believe to be right? If what I speak is true, am I responsible for him hating me? Not in the least degree. Some complain that I attack certain parties very hard. I cannot help it. If they are not right, according to the Scriptures, it is not my fault. Suppose two of you should be driving in the road tomorrow, and one of you should be on the right side of the road, but the other runs into you? You would say, "he should pay the damages because he had no business being on the wrong side." It is the same if we preach God's truth. We must go right on the path of Scripture.

EVENING

"*It is better to take refuge in Jehovah than to trust in princes*" — Psalm 118:9.

ZEDEKIAH PROFESSED to be a friend of Jeremiah, yet when the princes sought permission to put the prophet to death, Zedekiah's friendship was not worth much. He said, *"He is in your hand; for the king cannot do anything against you."* Instead of protecting his friend and adviser, he delivered him and left him as a lamb at the mercy of wolves.

It seems very natural to men for them to trust in men. Yet we are warned in the Scriptures that, *"Cursed is the man that trusts in man, and makes flesh his arm."* If you make a mortal man your confidence, you will find your anchor has no grip. Even good men are but broken reeds and cannot bear the strain of the day of trouble. And the bad men are like sharp spears; they stab the man who dares to lean on them. But, if we cannot trust in men, we think that surely we may trust in rulers. If honor were banished from all the rest of ther world, it ought to find a home in the breasts of kings. May we not trust in great men, in noble men, men of high standing? No, for, *"It is better to take refuge in Jehovah than to trust in princes."* Why? It is because princes are but men, and they are not always the truest of men, either. In fact they are seldom the best of men. Certainly they cannot help us one jot in reference to our eternal state. He who puts his confidence in God, the great King, is by this made mentally and spiritually stronger; such a one rises to the highest dignity possible to human beings. The more he trusts, the more he is free.

MORNING

The fool has said in his heart, There is no God. They are rotten and have worked out hateful wickedness; there is none who does good — Psalm 53:1.

BEING A FOOL, khe reflects his nature, saying, *"There is no God."* Being a great fool, he meddles with a great subject and comes to a wild conclusion. Morally, as well as mentally, the atheist is a fool. He is a fool in the heart as well as in the head, a fool in morals as well as in philosophy. With the denial of God as a starting point, we may conclude that the fool's progress is raid, riotous, raving, and ruinous. One beginning at impiety is ready for anything. *"No God"* properly interpreted means no law, no order, no restraint to lust, no limit to evil passion. Who but a fool would be of this mind? What would the world become if such lawless principles came to be universal? One who heartily entertains an irreligious spirit, and follows it out to its legitimate issues, is dangerous to the common welfare; he is not rational. By nature every man is more or less a denier of God. Practical atheism is the religion of humanity. It is idle to compliment them as sincere doubters and amiable thinkers; they are in fact rotten. There is too much dainty dealing nowadays with atheism. It is not a harmless error; it is an offensive, rotten sin. Righteous men should look on it in that light. All men being by nature atheistic, they are also in the same degree corrupt. Their heart is foul; their moral nature is decayed.

"They have worked out hateful wickedness" — bad principles soon lead to bad lives. One does not find virtue promoted by your Voltaires and Tom Paines. Those who talk so abominable as to deny their Maker will act abominable when it serves their turn. It is the denial and forgetfulness of God abounding among men which is the source of the unrighteousness and crime which we see around us. If all men are not outwardly vicious, it is to be accounted for by the power of other and better principles. Left to itself, the *"No God"* spirit would produce nothing but evil acts.

EVENING

The time of my departure is at hand — 2 Timothy 4:6.

MUST YOU DEPART? Christ departed. Some seem pleased to dwell on the idea that they will never die. They think that Christ will come before the time of their decease, for *"we shall not all sleep, but we shall all be changed."* Well, let Him come, and come quickly. But if I had my choice, I would prefer to pass through the portals of the grave. Those that are alive and remain to the coming of the Lord will not go before, or steal a march on, those who are asleep. But surely they will lack one point of conformity to their Lord, for He chose to sojourn a while in the tomb, though it was impossible that He should be held by death. Then let the seal of death be set on this face of mine, that in this matter I might be like Him. Enoch and Elijah were exempt from this privilege. I call it a privilege to be conformed to Christ's death. But it is safe to go by the beaten track, and desirable to travel by the ordinary route to the heavenly city. Jesus died. Through the valley of shadows, the vale of death shades, there are the footprints of Immanuel all the way along. Go down into it without fear. Think, too, that we may well look forward to our departure, and look forward to it comfortably, as Paul did. Is it not expedient by reason of nature? Is it not desirable by reason of grace? Is it not necessary by reason of glory? Is not our departure needful by reason of nature? Men are not, when they come to hoary age, what they were in the prime of their days. The staff is needed for the foot, and the glass for the eye. After a certain number of years even those on whom Time has laid a gentle hand will find that the taste is gone.

September 27   MORNING

Be merciful to me, O God, for man would swallow me up; fighting daily he presses me down. My enemies would daily swallow me up — Psalm 56:1, 2.

IN DEEP distress my soul turns to You, my God. Man has no mercy on me; therefore double Your mercy to me. If Your justice has let loose my enemies, let Your mercy shorten their chain. The tender dovelike spirit of the Psalmist flies to the tenderest attribute of God for aid in the hour of peril. The man who would swallow you is but a creature, a mere man, yet like a monster he is eager for blood. He pants, he gapes for David. He would not merely wound him, or feed on his substance, but he would willingly swallow him altogether, and so make an end of him. The open mouths of sinners, when they rage against us, should open our mouths in urgent prayer. We may plead the cruelty of men as a reason for Divine intervention; for a father is soon aroused when his children are shamefully treated. *"Fighting daily he presses me down"* — he gives me no interval, fighting daily. He is successful in his unrighteous war, oppressing me, crushing me. David has his eye on the leader of his foes, and he lays his plaint against him in the right place. If we may so plead against man, much more against the Devil, that great enemy of souls. We ask in prayer that God be merciful to us, forgiving us our trespasses. Then we pray, *"Lead us not into temptation, but deliver us from evil."* The more violent the attack of Satan, the stronger will be our plea for deliverance from his pressing down on us.

"My enemies would daily swallow me up" — their appetite for blood never fails. With them there is no armistice. They are many, but one mind animates them. Nothing makes them relent. Unless they can devour me, they will never be content. The ogres of nursery tales exist in reality in the enemies of the saints; they would crush the bones of the godly and make a mouthful of them, if they could. Sinners are gregarious creatures; they hunt in packs. These wolves seldom come down on us singly. The number of our foes is a powerful plea of the intervention of the one Defender of the faithful, our God.

EVENING

The Lord bless you and keep you. The Lord make His face shine on you and be gracious to you. The Lord lift up His face to you and give you peace
— Numbers 6:24.

AARON IS NOT told that on such a day, and at such an hour, he shall bless the people. He may do as his heart dictates. On the day of atonement, when the high priest came out from the secret place, he put on his beautiful robes and blessed the people. He was not commanded to do so every day. The Jews say that Aaron always blessed the people after the offering of the morning sacrifice, when the lamb had been slain and consumed on the altar. We know nothing of this, except by tradition. The older divines were accustomed to say that Aaron gave a blessing every morning, but that he could give no blessing in the evening. Now Christ Himself has come in the end of days, and we have no need of a blessing from the Aaronic priesthood, since the great Melchizedek has come. But this is known, that Aaron often blessed the people. And our High Priest, the Lord Jesus, also is ready to bless us. Do you limit your blessings? There is for you a blessing from Him every morning; seek it when you awaken. There is also a blessing for you every evening; do not rest until you seek it. There is a blessing for you at midnight; and a blessing for you at midday, for it is written, *"Your blessing is on Your people"* —that is to say, it is always on them. Our great High Priest does not now and then bless His people, but grace distils as dew from His lips, even as drops of rain, without ceasing.

The Lord is my shepherd, I shall not want — Psalm 23:1.

WHAT CONDESCENSION, that the Infinite Lord assumes the office and character of a Shepherd to His people! It should be the subject of grateful admiration that the great God allows Himself to be compared to anything which will set forth His great love and care for His own people. David had himself been a shepherd; he understood both the needs of the sheep and the many cares of a shepherd. He compares himself to a weak, defenseless, foolish creature, and He takes God to be his Provider, Preserver, Director, even his everything. No one has a right to consider himself the Lord's sheep unless his nature has been renewed. The Scripture describes natural, unconverted men as wolves or goats, not as sheep. A sheep is an object of property, not a wild animal. Its owner sets great store by it, and frequently it is bought with a great price. It is well to know, as did David, that we belong to the Lord our Shepherd. In this there is no if, nor but, nor even an I hope so. David says, *"The Lord IS my shepherd."* Let us cultivate the spirit of assured dependence on our heavenly Father. The sweetest word of the whole is that *"my"* — he does not say, "The Lord is the shepherd of the world at large, leading forth the multitude as His flock." No, *"The Lord is MY shepherd!"* If He is a Shepherd to no one else, He is a Shepherd to me. He cares for me; He watches over me; He preserves me. The words are in the present tense. Every believer is now under His care.   The next words are a sort of inference from the first statement. They are pithy and positive: *"I shall not want."* When the Lord is my Shepherd, He is able to supply all my needs; and He is certainly willing to do so, therefore I shall not want. His heart is full of love, so I shall not lack, not even for temporal things. Does not He feed the ravens? How, then, can He leave His lambs to starve, or to be without needful things?

EVENING

The time of my departure is at hand — 2 Timothy 4:6.

IT IS CERTAIN that we shall not dwell here forever — we shall not live here as long as the first man did, or those antediluvian fathers who tarried some eight or nine hundred years. The length of life then led to greatness of sin. Monstrosities of evil were ripened through the long continuance of physical strength, and the accumulating force of eager passions. All things considered, it is a mercy that life is abridged and not prolonged to nearly a thousand years. Amid the sharp competition of man with man, and class with class, there is a limit to every scheme of personal aggrandizement, to all the spoils of individual despotism; a restraint on the hoardings of anyone's avarice. It is well that it should be so. The narrow span of life clips the wings of ambition and deprives it of its prey. Death comes in to deprive the mighty of his power, to stay the rapacity of the invader, to scatter abroad the possessions of the rich. The most reprobate men must end their career after they have had their three score and ten, or their four score years of wickedness. And as for the good and godly, though we mourn their exit, especially when we think they were premature in death, we must remember how the triumphs of genius have been for the most part achieved in youth. The world has been enriched by the heads and hearts of many who have but sown the seeds of faith, and have left others to reap the fruits. If they have crowded their service into less than the allotted term, then let us save our tears, for our regrets are needless. The summons will reach each one of us before long. We cannot stop here as long as the grey fathers of our race. Rather we expect, and it is fitting, that we be prepared to go.

September 29 — MORNING

The time of my departure is at hand — 2 Timothy 4:6.

IT IS VERY BEAUTIFUL to observe the way in which Paul describes his death in this verse. (*"For I am already being poured out, and the time of my release is here"* — Green's Literal Translation.) Paul felt as one standing like a sacrifice, ready to be laid on the altar. He foresaw that he would die a martyr's death. He knew he could not be crucified, as was his brother apostle Peter, for a Roman citizen was as a rule exempt from that ignominious death. But he expected to die, *"released,"* as he put it. In the original we see that he does not liken himself as an offering on the altar, but as a drink offering. Every Jew would know what that meant. When there was a burnt sacrifice offered, the bullock, or the slain victim, was the main part of the sacrifice. But sometimes there was a little oil and a little wine poured out on the altar, and so a drink offering was said to be added to the burnt sacrifice. Now Christ is, so to speak, the sacrifice on the altar. So Paul here likens himself only to that little wine and oil poured out as a supplement to the sacrifice. It was not necessary to its perfection, but it was tolerated as performing a vow; or it was allowed in connection with a free will offering (See Numbers 15:4-8). The drink offering was a kind of addendum, by which the person who gave it showed his thankfulness. So Paul is saying about himself here.

EVENING

The time of my departure is at hand — 2 Timothy 4:6.

THIS LAND FROM which we go has been a land of mercy to us. There have been sorrows in it, but in bidding it farewell we will do it justice and speak the truth about it. Our sorrows have usually sprung up from our own bosoms, and those that have come from the soil itself would have been very light if it had not been for the plague of our hearts making us vex and fret over them. Oh, the mercy you and I have enjoyed in this life! It has been worthwhile to live, for those of us who are believers. Even if we die like a dog dies, it has been worthwhile to live for the joy and blessedness which God has made to pass before us. That country in which I met my Savior cannot be called evil. It is not an ill life that has seen the Savior, although it is only through a dark mirror. How shall I speak ill of that land where Zion is built, the place of our solemn assemblies, where we have worshiped God? No, cursed as the earth is, to bring forth the thorn and the thistle, the existence of a church of God in that land makes much reparation for the blight of the earth to those of us who know and love the Savior. Have we not gone up the house of God in company, with songs and ecstatic joy? Have we not rejoiced when we gathered around the table of the Lord? Have we not felt it a joyous thing to be found in the assembly of the saints, and in the courts of the Lord, even here? When our cable is loosed, and we bid farewell to earth, it will not be with bitterness. There is sin in it, and we are called to leave it before we can be without sin. There has been trial in it; there has been sorrow in it; and we are glad that we shall go where there will be no more tears, no more sorrow. There we will sit at the feet of Jesus Himself.

MORNING

Give ear to my prayer, O God; and hide not Yourself from my cry. Attend to me and hear me; I mourn in my complaining and make a noise — Psalm 55:1,2.

THE FACT IS so commonly before us, otherwise we would be surprised to observe how universally and constantly the saints resort to prayer in seasons of distress. From the great Elder Brother down to the very least of the Divine family, all of them delight in prayer. They run as naturally to the mercy seat in time of trouble as the little chicks to the hen in the hour of danger. But note well that it is never the bare act of prayer which satisfies the godly. They crave an audience with God, an answer from the throne, and nothing less will content them. *"Hide not Yourself from my cry"* — do not stop Your ear, nor restrain Your hand. When a man sees his neighbor in distress, and he deliberately passes him by, he is said to hide himself from him. The Psalmist begs that the Lord would not so pass him by. Remember that this was one of the most dreadful parts of all the agony suffered by the Son of David, our Lord. Well may each of us deprecate such a calamity as that God should hide Himself from our cries.

"Attend to me and hear me" — this is the third time he prays the same prayer. He is in earnest, in deep and bitter earnest. If his God does not hear, he feels that it is all over with him. He begs for his God to be a listener, and an answerer. He gives sway to his sorrows, permits his mind to rehearse her griefs, and to pour them out in such language as suggests itself at the time, whether it is coherent or not. What a comfort that we may be familiar with our God in this way! We may not complain *of* Him, but we may complain *to* Him. When we are distracted with grief, we may bring our rambling thoughts to Him, even if the utterances are more noise than language. He will attend so carefully that He will understand us, and He will often fulfill desires which we ourselves could not have expressed in intelligible words: *"but the Spirit Himself pleads our case for us with groanings that cannot be uttered"* (Rom. 8:26). Our Lord Himself used strong cryings and tears, and He was heard in that He feared (Heb. 5:7).

EVENING

The mighty God, the Lord, has spoken, and called the earth from the rising of the sun until its going down. Out of Zion, the perfection of beauty, God has shined. Our God shall come and shall not keep silence — Psalm 50:1-3.

EL, ELOHIM, JEHOVAH, three glorious names for the God of Israel. To render the address the more impressive, these august titles are mentioned, just as in royal decrees the names and dignities of monarchs are placed in the forefront. Here the true God is described as Almighty, as the only perfect object of adoration, and as the self-existent One. The dominion of Jehovah extends over the whole earth, and so His decree is directed to all mankind. The east and the west are commanded to hear the God who makes His sun to rise on every quarter of the globe. Shall the summons of the great King be despised? Will we dare provoke Him to anger by slighting His call?

The Lord is represented not only as speaking to the earth, but as coming forth to reveal the glory of His presence to an assembled universe. God of old dwelt in Zion among that chosen nation, but here the beams of His splendor are described as shining forth on all nations. The earthly sun is spoken of in the first verse, but here it is a far brighter Sun. The majesty of God is most conspicuous among His own elect, but it is not confined to them. The church is not a dark lantern, but a lampstand. God shines not only in Zion, but out of her. By His indwelling her perfection in beauty is seen by all when the Lord shines forth from her. Note how with trumpet voice and flaming ensign the infinite Jehovah summons the heavens and the earth to attend to His word.

The Psalmist speaks of himself and his brothers as standing in immediate anticipation of the appearing of the Lord on the scene. *"Our God shall come"* — they can hear His voice from afar; they can perceive the splendor of His attending train. Even so should we wait the long-promised appearing of the Lord from Heaven.

MORNING

The time of my departure is at hand — 2 Timothy 4:6.

THE TIME OF OUR departure, although unknown to us, is fixed by God; it is unalterably fixed. Rightly, wisely, lovingly, it is settled and prepared for. No chance or haphazard can break the spell of destiny. The wisdom of Divine love shall be proven by the carefulness of its provision. You may say, "It is not easy to discern this, since the natural order of things is so often disturbed by casualties of one kind or another." Be reminded that it is through faith, only through faith, that we can understand these things. It is as true now of the providence of God as it was of old of the creation of God, that *"things which are seen were not made of things which do appear."* Because the mode of your departure is beyond your knowledge, it does not follow that the time of your departure is not foreseen by God. You may say, "It seems so shocking for anyone to die suddenly, without warning, and so come to an untimely end." If you take counsel with death, your flesh will find no comfort. But if you trust in God, your faith will cease to parley with these feverish anxieties, and your spirit will enjoy a sweet calm. Dire calamities fell on Job when he was bereaved of his children and his servants, his herds and his flocks. yet he took heed of the different ways in which his troubles were brought about. It mattered little whether it was a Sabean onslaught, or a Chaldean raid, or whether the fire fell from the heavens, or the wind came from the wilderness. Whatever strange facts broke on his ear, one thought penetrated his heart, one expression broke from his lips, *"The Lord gave, and the Lord has taken away; blessed is the name of the Lord."* So when the time of your departure arrives, be it by disease or decay, by accident or assault — rest assured that *"your times are in His hand"* — and know of a surety that *"all His saints are in His hand"* likewise.

EVENING

For now we see in a mirror dimly, but then face to face. Now I know in part, but then I shall know even as I also have been known — 1 Corinthians 13:12

IT IS WRITTEN that the pure in heart shall see God. God is seen now in His works and in His word. Little indeed could these eyes bear the beatific vision, yet we have reason to expect that as far as we can bear the sight of Him, we shall be permitted to see God. In Heaven it is the presence of God that is the light of it. God's more immediate dwelling in the midst of the new Jerusalem is its peerless glory and peculiar bliss. We shall then understand more of God than we do now. We shall come nearer to Him, be more familiar with Him, be more filled with Him. The love of God shall be poured out in our hearts, and we shall know our Father as we cannot yet know Him. Also we shall know the Son to a fuller degree than He has yet revealed Himself to us, and we shall know God the Holy Spirit in His personal love and tenderness toward us, beyond all those influences and operations which have soothed us in our sorrows and guided us in our perplexities here below. Gear up your thoughts and your desires to follow the teaching of the Spirit.

If we have strained our eyes while gazing at certain brilliances in nature, they showing the handiwork of God, how shall we be able to look upon God? I, whose conscience has been awe-stricken as I listened to the voice of God proclaiming His holy law; whose heart has been melted while the tender accents of His blessed gospel broke on my ears; I, who have recognized in the babe of Bethlehem the hope of Israel, the man of Nazareth as the Messiah that should come, in the victim of Calvary, the one Mediator, in the risen Jesus, the well-beloved Son — to me, truly God incarnate has been so plainly revealed that I have almost seen God.

For now we see in a mirror dimly, but then face to face. Now I know in part, but then I shall know even as I also have been known — 1 Corinthians 13:12.

HERE WE SEE Jesus Christ, but we do not see Him as we shall see Him soon. We have seen Him by faith in such a way that we have beheld our burdens laid on Him, and our iniquities carried by Him into the wilderness — where, if they were sought, they would not be found. We have seen enough of Jesus to know that *"He is altogether lovely."* We can say of Him, He *"is all my salvation, and all my desire."* Sometimes, when He shows Himself through the lattice, through windows of agate and gates of carbuncle, in the ordinances of His house, especially at the Lord's Supper, the King's beauty has entranced us, ravished our hearts. Yet all we have ever seen is somewhat like the report which the Queen of Sheba had of Solomon's wisdom. When we get to the court of our great King, we shall declare that the half has not been told. We shall say, *"My eyes shall behold, and not another."* Is not this the very cream of Heaven? Many have speculated on what we shall do in Heaven, and what we shall enjoy, but they all seem to be wide of the mark compared with this one: we shall be with Jesus, be like Him, and shall behold His glory. Oh, to bow before Him, and to kiss His feet! What better can we want than to see God the Son face to face, in His own light, and to speak with Him as a man will speak to his friend? It is pleasant to talk about this, but what will it be there when the pearl gates open to us and we see Him in all His splendid glory? The streets of gold will have small attraction to us then; the harps of angels will but slightly enchant us, for we will be beholding the King of kings in the midst of His throne.

EVENING

When I am afraid, I will trust in You. In God I will praise His word; in God I have put my trust; I will not fear what flesh can do to me — Psalm 56:3,4.

DAVID was no boaster. He does not claim he never was afraid. Nor was he a brutish Stoic free from fear because of lack of tenderness. David's intelligence deprived him of the stupid heedlessness of ignorance. He saw the imminence of his peril, and he was afraid. We are human, so we are liable to overthrow. We are feeble, and so unable to prevent it. We are sinful, and so are deserving of it. For all these reasons we are afraid. But the condition of the Psalmist's mind was complex: he feared, but that fear did not fill the whole area of his mind. For he adds, *"I will trust in You."* It is possible, then, for fear and faith to occupy the mind at the same time. We are strange beings, and our experience in the Divine life is stranger still. We are often in a twilight where light and darkness are both present, and it is hard to tell what predominates. It is a blessed fear which drives us to trust. Unregenerate fear drives from God; gracious fear drives to Him. If I fear man, I need only to trust God and I have the best antidote. To trust when there is no cause for fear is but the name of faith, but to rely on God when occasions for alarm are pressing is the conquering faith of God's elect. This verse is in the form of a resolve, but it became a face in David's life. Let us make it ours also. Whether the fear rises from without or within, from past, present, or future; from temporals or spirituals; from men or devils; let us maintain faith and courage will follow.

Faith brings forth praise. One who can trust will soon sing. God's promise, when fulfilled, is a noble subject for praise, and even before fulfilment it should be the theme of song. It is in or through God that we are able to praise. We praise as well as pray in the Spirit. Or, as we may read it, in extolling the Lord one of the main points for thanksgiving is His revealed will in the Scriptures, and the fidelity with which He keeps His word of promise.

MORNING

Be not like the horse, or like the mule, which have no understanding, whose mouth must be held in with bit and bridle, so that they do not come near you — Psalm 32:9.

WE ARE NOT to imitate creatures devoid of reason. The Psalmist especially lays stress on this, that they are without understanding. What does he mean? Horses and mules have been so trained that they have needed neither bit nor bridle, but have performed marvelous feats at a word. It is possible for these animals to be brought to such high training that they obey a command without the use of force. They come to have an understanding of their owner's intent, and act as if they really entered into their master's design. The horses and mules of David's day were not so, nor those commonly among us. These display little understanding, and we are not to be like them.

You are a reasoning man, so act reasonably. You have understanding, so do not act on mere impulse, blind wilfulness, or ignorant folly. What we need is to come to an understanding with God, and to keep in that condition. The horse understands his driver's wishes by the use of the bit and bridle. Apart from the bit and bridle the horse has no understanding of the human mind. Therefore, the driverr must make him feel a pull at his head and mouth to make him know what to do. It should not be so with us. We need to come to an understanding with God and, *"Be not unwise, but understanding what the will of the Lord is."* Be sensitive to the Spirit of God, and so dwell in God that He dwell in you. His indwelling will cause you to feel at once what He desires you to do. Make your will be so in accord with His will that you will desire what He wills.

EVENING

Be not like the horse, or like the mule, which have no understanding, whose mouth must be held in with bit and bridle, so that they do not come near you — Psalm 32:9.

SURELY YOU would not like to be as the horse or the mule, controlled by bit and bridle. It is unpleasant to think of it. It is not comfortable, even for a mule, to wear bit and bridle; how much more so to a man. Some believers who would seem to be good witnesses have not been useful in converting souls because they could not bear prosperity. The Lord has at times blessed a preacher at first, only to have him grow so great in his own esteem as to become unbearable to others. Then the Lord deems it not useful to use such a man. There are persons who became successful, but grew worldly and purse-proud, forgetful of God, so much so that God found it necessary to take his wealth away. Now he can be devout and lowly and become a good witness. Some persons in health and strength display levity and carelessness, acting as fools. To keep such a one from foolishness, the Lord may give him a sluggish liver, or an aching head, or a sick home, anything that will sober him. If God intends to get you to Heaven, be assured that He will lead you there gently so long as you go freely. But if you are obstinate and hard, He will thrust a bit between your teeth and drive you there. If you are wilful, the more harness is needed; then you will be curbed like a balky mule, for the great Trainer will have the upper hand of you, and He will save you by bit and bridle. There is gladness in going without these curbs, but if you will have them, you shall have them. There are those who are always grumbling; being curbed by the Lord's bit, they find more occasion to grumble. But murmuring flies in the face of understanding. Let us not be as the horse or the mule, which have no understanding.

I will instruct you and teach you in the way you shall go; I will guide you with My eye
— Psalm 32:8.

THE JOY of full forgiveness is described in the first two verses of this Psalm: *"Blessed is he whose transgression is forgiven, whose sin is covered. Blessed is the man to whom the Lord does not charge iniquity, and in whose spirit there is no guile."* Oh, the blessedness of sitting at Jesus' feet, a sinner having been washed in His blood! Outside of Heaven there is no greater joy, and even there they sing of their white robes.

After one is pardoned, anxiety is awakened as to how to keep from sinning in the future. A burned child dreads the fire; even if his burns have healed, he dreads the fire, not less but more. Those who have been scorched by sin tremble even at a distant approach to the flame. You will always know whether you are delivered from the guilt of sin by answering this question: Am I delivered from the love of sin? He who lost his way yesterday feels his need for a guide today. How can the pardoned one endure the thought of sinning against the Lord again? David's anxiety on this score is met by the Lord's gracious answer: *"I will instruct you and teach you in the way you shall go."*

Note another thing: David was now rid of guile as well as guilt. Orientals often pride themselves on their cunning, and David, by nature, had a considerable share of craft about him. He now drives it from his spirit. He will not tolerate himself in deceit in the future. Having thrown away false wisdom, carnal prudence, he felt that he must look elsewhere for guidance. If he is no longer to plot and plan with the cunning he displayed in the matter of Uriah, he will need other direction, and he looks up for it. See here how our gracious God comes in with the promise of guidance.

EVENING

I will instruct you and teach you in the way you shall go; I will guide you with My eye
— Psalm 32:8.

THE NATURE of God's guidane is very full: *"I will instruct you"* — a promise more full of meaning than appears on the surface. God is prepared to give you an inward understanding of spiritual things; His instruction is intensely effectual on the mind. The Lord is prepared to teach you in His truth, to make you wise in heavenly matters. Although saved, you are yet a mere child, unfamiliar with great truths. You know but little of Divine things, little of yourself, little of your danger, little of holiness, and thus little of God. But here He promises to take you as His pupil, to be your Instructor. And His teaching effectually builds up the mind, from which the Psalmist says, *"Through Your precepts I get understanding."* Others can awaken the measure of understanding we already have, but God gives understanding even to the simple. A good understanding is one of the gifts of His grace, and blessed are they who receive it.

"I will teach you" — this teaching is most practical, for the promise is *"in the way which you shall go."* God adds the precept to the doctrine, instructing us in both. Most precious is that practical teaching by which you are made to know what to do, and how to do it. Theoretical teaching is of small importance compared with this practical learning. The Lord will teach us the art and mystery of holiness. He will apprentice us to the Lord Jesus as the master of righteousness. He will make us journeymen one of these days, and will turn us out as full-blown *"workmen that need not be ashamed."*

"I will guide you with My eye" — in this is fellowship as well as instruction. For the guide goes with the traveler, and so will God go with you in the process of instruction, giving us fellowship with Himself. Blessed are those who follow the Lamb wherever He goes. They will have both the privilege of a holy walk, and of heavenly company.

MORNING

October 5

Our fathers did not understand Your wonders in Egypt; they did not remember the multitude of Your mercies, but provoked You at the sea — Psalm 106:7.

IF THE LORD were to take away all that we have, we would only be back where we began. We have nothing but what we have received from Him. He takes nothing from us but what He first gave us. Let us bless a taking as well as a giving God. Oh, for this practical gratitude toward the Lord, that we may in all things either do His will cheerfully or suffer it patiently! If we remember the multitude of His mercies practically we shall be ready to surrender honor, ease, health, estate, yes, life itself for Him who gave Himself for us. Oh, to remember God's mercies practically in everyday life, in thought and word and deed!

The Lord's mercies ought to be remembered progressively, too. We should think more and more of His exceeding kindness. A Christian's life should be like another Bible, another Book of Chronicles. When we come to read through our personal life story we shall say that neither Nehemiah 9 nor Psalm 106 can exceed our experience. The Lord has dealt well with us, according to His word. If some of us had opportunity to write our lives in full, which we would not do because there are private passages between our souls and God which no other should read, how fully could we testify to the faithful love of our covenant God! Sin and weakness and fickleness have been conspicuous in our careers, but on the Lord's part grace and truth and faithfulness and love shine forth as the sun. We must not let go the memory of the Lord's matchless kindness, but we must remember it more and more. The older we are, the more we must trust in Him, for He has not allowed one of His promises to us to fail.

EVENING

O that You would bless me indeed — 1 Chronicles 4:10.

THE BLESSINGS of God's grace are blessings indeed, which in right earnest we ought to seek after. By these marks you shall know them. These blessings come from a pierced hand, from Calvary where blood streamed from the Savior's pierced side: your pardon, your acceptance, your spiritual life, the bread that is meat indeed, the blood that is drink indeed. Even if the harrow goes over and over your soul, and the deep plow cuts into your very heart — even though you are maimed and wounded and left for dead — yet if the Spirit of God do it, truly these are blessings. If He convinces you of sin, of righteousness, and of judgment, even though you have not before been brought to Christ, it is a blessing indeed. Anything that He does, accept it; do not be dubious of it. Pray that He may continue His blessed operations in your soul. Whatever He leads you to do in going to God is a blessing indeed. Riches will not do it. There may be a golden wall between you and God. Health will not do it. Even the strength and marrow of your bones may keep you away from your God. But anything that draws you nearer to Him is a blessing indeed. Even if it is a cross that you must hang on, yet if it raises you to God, it will be a blessing indeed. Anything that reaches into eternity, with a preparation for the world to come; anything that we can carry across the River, the holy joy that is to blossom in those fields beyond the swelling flood, the pure cloudless love of the brotherhood which is to be the atmosphere of truth forever — anything of this kind that has the eternal broad arrow on it, the immutable mark, is a blessing indeed.

Arise, cry out in the night. In the beginning of the watches, pour out your heart like water before the face of the Lord — Lamentations 2:19.

HERE WE SEE that it is never too soon to pray. How many young persons imagine that religion is a thing for older, mature persons. They conceive that while they are in the bloom of their youth they do not need to attend to Christian admonitions. How many have been found counting religion to be a crutch for old age, who reckon it an ornament to gray hairs. They forget that religion is like a chain of gold around the neck of the young, like an ornament set with precious jewels, arraying them with honor. There are many who think it is yet too soon for them to bear the cross of Jesus. They do not want to have their young shoulders galled with an early burden. They think it is untrue that *"it is good for a man to bear the yoke in his youth"* — they forget that Jesus said that His *"yoke is easy,"* His *"burden is light."* For this reason hour after hour, day after day, the malicious demons whisper in their ear: "It is too soon; it is too soon! Postpone! Procrastinate!" Yet it is well known that procrastination is the thief of time; that delays are dangerous; that those are the workings of Satan. For the Holy Spirit, when He strives with anyone, says, *"Today, if you will hear His voice, harden not your heart."* It is never too soon to pray for deliverance from sin, from slavery to Satan.

Are you a child? Your God hears children. Samuel the prophet was called when he was but a child, hearing, *"Samuel! Samuel!"* And he answered, *"Here am I."* We have had our Josiahs, our Timothys; yea, we have seen many in early youth who have been brought to the Savior. Remember, it is not too soon to seek the Savior, before you arrive at maturity. If God in His mercy calls you to Him, I beg you do not think for a moment that He will not hear your answer. Then you, too, can say, *"I know whom I have believed."*

EVENING

Our fathers did not understand Your wonders in Egypt; they did not remember the multitude of Your mercies, but provoked You at the sea — Psalm 106:7.

THIS RED SEA was the place of their consecration, for here they were *"baptized unto Moses in the cloud and in the sea."* Here they promised, *"He is my God, and I will prepare Him a habitation; my father's God, and I will exalt Him."* As they stood by the sea which had swallowed up all their enemies, they sang the praises of God and proposed to do great things in His honor. What wonderful obedience they meant to render! Yet they provoked Him there and then. What! Will you come up from the waters of your baptism and go home and provoke God by unholy behavior and ungovernable temper? Can any of you go from the communion table into sin? This is too gross. Such conduct grieves holy men, how much more it provokes a holy God. To go from prayer to robbery, from reading the Word to fellowship with ungodly ones — this must be terriby provoking to the thrice holy Jehovah. It is as though it were written again, *"They provoked Him at the sea, even the Red Sea."*

It is a high crime to sin in the presence of a great mercy. There is the sea which they have just marched through on dry ground. They have now reached Marah, where the waters are bitter. If they now distrust and complain right after their great deliverance, is that not a crime indeed? O believers, what are you doing? The God who divided the Red Sea, can He not give you all things good for you? O fools and slow of heart to believe that the Almighty can be doubted! Do you doubt in the presence of mercy? Do you doubt while such great favor is before your eyes? This is evil in the deepest dye. Some would read it that they provoked God in the sea, that is while they were still between the walls of water heaped above their heads, they rebelled against their Savior.

MORNING

Yea, though I walk through the valley of the shadow of death, I will fear no evil; for You are with me; Your rod and Your staff, they comfort me — Psalm 23:4.

EVERY WORD in this verse has a wealth of meaning. *"Walk"* — as if the believer did not quicken his pace when he came to die, but still calmly walked with God. To walk indicates a steady advance of a soul that knows the road, knows its end, resolves to follow the path, feels quite safe in it, and is perfectly calm and composed. The dying saint is not in a flurry. He does not run as though alarmed, nor stand still as though he would go no further. He is not confounded nor ashamed, but keeps to his pace. Note that it is not walking IN the valley, but THROUGH the valley. We go through the valley of the shadow of death and emerge into the light of immortality. Saints do not die, but sleep to wake in glory. Death is not the house, but the porch; not the goal, but the passage to it. Mountains have storms breaking on them, but valleys are places of quiet. So often the last days of the Christian are the most peaceful of his life. His valleys are rich in golden sheaves, and many saints reap more joy and knowledge when they come to die than ever was known while they lived.

It is not "the valley of death," but *"the valley of the shadow of death,"* for death in its substance has been removed; only its shadow remains. One said that when there is a shadow there must be light near, and so there is. Death stands by the side of the road we are traveling, but the light of Heaven shines on us, throwing a shadow across our path. Then let us rejoice that there is light beyond. Nobody is afraid of a shadow, for a shadow cannot stop a man even for a moment. The shadow of a dog cannot bite; the shadow of a sword cannot kill; the shadow of death cannot destroy us. Then let us not be afraid, saying, *"I will fear no evil."* The Psalmist does not say that there will be no evil. He had gotten beyond even that high assurance, knowing that Jesus had put all evil away. But he says, *"I will FEAR no evil,"* as if even his fears, those shadows of evil, were gone forever. The worst evils of life are those which do not exist except in our imaginations.

EVENING

Your rod and Your staff, they comfort me. You prepare a table for me before my enemies; You anoint my head with oil; my cup runs over — Psalm 23:4,5.

THE CHRISTIAN that has this preparation of heart never tastes more sweetness in the enjoyments of this life than when he dips these morsels in the meditation of death and eternity. It is no more grief to his heart to think of the removal of these things, which makes way for those far sweeter enjoyments, than it would be to one at a feast to have the first course taken away after he has fed well on it. Then the second course of all rare sweetmeats and banqueting stuff may come in, which it could not until the first course is gone. Holy David brings in this place, as it were, a death's head with his feast. In the same breath almost, he speaks of his dying (verse 4), and of the rich feast he at present sat at through the bounty of God (verse 5), to which he was not so tied by the teeth. But if God, who gave him this cheer, should call him from it, then to look death in the face, he could do it and *fear no evil*, though *in the valley of the shadow of death*. And what do you think of the blessed apostle Peter? Do you not think that he had the true enjoyment of his life as he slept so sweetly in a prison (no desirable place), fast bound between two soldiers (no comfortable position), and this very night expecting to be brought forth before Herod to his execution? One would think it no likely time to get any rest. Yet we find him, even there, sound asleep, so that the angel sent to deliver him from jail must smite him on the side to awaken him (Acts 12:6,7). I question whether Herod himself slept so well as his prisoner did that night. And what was the potion that brought this holy man so quietly to rest? No doubt it was this preparation of the gospel of peace. He was ready to die, and that made him able to sleep. Why should it break his rest in this world, which if it had been effected, would have brought him to his eternal rest in the other? (William Gurnall)

MORNING

I opened my mouth and panted; for I longed for Your commandments
— Psalm 119:131.

THE MAN OF GOD longed for the Lord's commandments. This cannot mean anything else than that he longed to know them, longed to teach them, longed to bring all around him into obedience to them. Many religious people long after the promises, and they do well. But they must not forget to have an equal longing for the commandments. It is a sad sign when a man cannot bear to hear of the precepts, but must always have the preacher touching the string of privileges. To the renewed man it is a privilige to receive a command from the Lord, and a great grace to have the will and power to obey it. To us grace means a power which sways us, as well as a favor which distinguishes us. The greatest privilege in all the world would be perfect holiness. Of all blessings one can conceive, this perfect conformity to the Lord Jesus, or in one word, holiness should be chosen. There is no wisdom above that of moral and spiritual character, and that is holiness. Some will say that it is their greatest desire to be perfect. And that hallowed desire shows which way the heart is going. No unrenewed heart ever sighed and cried after holiness. A mere passing wish is of but little worth. An intense and continual desire of the heart for holiness marks the true saint. We must strive after holiness with an agony of desire. Oh, to be rid of every sin! Oh, to completely escape from every tendency to sin, and from every trace of it! This would be bliss. What more of happiness could we desire than to fulfil that word of our Lord: *"Be perfect, even as your Father who is in Heaven is perfect."*

EVENING

I opened my mouth and panted; for I longed for Your commandments
— Psalm 119:131.

WHEN YOU CRY to God to help you in overcoming your sin, you must consent to do it His way. Now, if it be His will that sanctification involve chastisement, are you willing to take it? "Oh, yes," you say, "Lord, do to me as you usually do to those who love Your name, for it is written, *As many as I love, I rebuke and chasten,* 'Lord, rebuke and chasten me, so long as You but love me." Believers kiss the rod because the Father deigns to kiss us. We assent to the processes of grace so that we may enjoy the results of grace. It may so happen that if God sanctifies you, He may have to grind you very small. Cheerfully yield yourself to His mill. If this is the way in which He deals with those who love His name, do not desire any different treatment. As the result, you may become a butt for the ridicule of ungodly men. But do not complain of this. For this has frequently happened to those who love His name. God sanctifies His people, but not without their own effort in that direction. You must be willing to make the effort, too. Say, "Lord, I will breakfast with Your children; I will dine with Your children; I will sup with Your children; and I will go to bed with Your children, hoping to rise with Your children. Lord take me into Your house and treat me as a child, not a stranger or guest. For I would share the daily bread of Your little ones. If You treat Your children so and so, treat me the same, and I will be grateful. I do not ask to go to Heaven without enduring tribulation, nor to be exempted from that general description, *These are they who came out of the great tribulation, and have washed their robes and made them white in the blood of the Lamb."*

MORNING

Jehovah lives! And blessed be my Rock! And let the God of my salvation be exalted!
— *Psalm 18:46.*

"*THE LORD LIVES*" — "Why do you not oppose one God to all the armies of evils that beset you round? Why do you not take the more content in God when you have the less of the creature to take content in? Why do you not boast in your God? Bear up yourselves big with your hopes in God and expectations from Him. Do you not see young heirs to great estates act and spend accordingly? And shall you, being an heir of the King of kings, be lean and ragged from day to day, as though you were not worth a penny? O live on your portion; chide yourself for not living according to what you have. There are great and precious promises; rich, enriching mercies. You may make use of God's all-sufficiency. Blame none but yourself if you are defective or discouraged. A woman, truly godly for the main, having buried a child, bore up her heart with the expression, *"God lives!"* Having parted with still another child, she redoubled, saying, 'Comforts die, but God lives.'" (Oliver Heywood)

"*The Lord lives, and blessed be my Rock, and let the God of my salvation be exalted*" — Let us unite our hearts in this song for a close of our praises. Honors die; pleasures die; the world dies; but *The Lord lives*. My flesh is as sand; my fleshly life, strength and glory is as a word written on sand; but *blessed be my Rock*. Those are but for a moment; this stands forever. The curse shall devour those; everlasting blessings on the head of this. Let outward salvations vanish; let the saved be crucified; but let the *God of my salvation be exalted*. This Lord is my Rock; this God is my salvation. (Peter Sterry, 1649).

EVENING

Judge me, O God, and plead my cause against an ungodly nation. O deliver me from the deceitful and unjust man — *Psalm 43:1.*

JUDGE ME, O GOD" — Others are unable to understand my motives, and unwilling to give me a just verdict. My heart is clear as to its intent, so I bring my case to You, content that You will impartially weigh my character and right my wrongs. If You will judge, Your acceptance of my conduct will be enough for me. I can laugh at human misrepresentation if my conscience knows that You are on my side. You are the only one I care for. Your verdict will not sleep, but You will see practical justice done to Your slandered servant. *"And plead my cause against an ungodly nation"* — one such advocate as the Lord will more than suffice to answer a nation of brawling accusers. When people are ungodly, it is no wonder they are unjust. Those untrue to God cannot be expected to deal rightly with His people. Hating the King, they will not love His subjects. Popular opinion weighs with many, but Divine opinion is far more weighty with children of grace. One good word from God outweighs ten thousand railing speeches of men. The arrows of calumny fall harmlessly on the shields of faith. *"O deliver me from the deceitful and unjust man"* — Deceit and injustice are boon companions; he who fawns will not fear to slander. From these two devils only God can deliver us. His wisdom can outwit the craft of the Serpent, and His power can overmatch the raging lion. Distilled villains are plentiful, and the only way of dealing with them is to refer the matter to the righteous Judge of all. If we try to fight them with their own weapons, we shall suffer more serious injury from ourselves than from them. O child of God, leave these enemies in better hands, remembering that vengeance does not belong to you, but to the Lord: *"Vengeance is Mine, I will repay."* Turn to Him in prayer, crying, "O deliver me!" And before long you shall be able to publish the remembrance of His salvation.

MORNING

Being persuaded of this very thing, that He who began a good work in you will finish it until the day of Jesus Christ — Philippians 1:6.

PAUL'S CONFIDENCE was that the work in their hearts was a Divine work. The Lord had begun a good work in them. This is a vital matter. Everything turns on the question, "Is this conversion a Divine work, or not?" The man is altered for the better; the woman is certainly improved; a work has surely been done — but is it God's work, or is it the work of the flesh? A moral change may sometimes look so much like a spiritual change that onlookers cannot detect the difference. The child of nature, finely dressed, is not the living child of Divine grace. But how are we to tell the one from the other? *"By their fruits you shall know them."* The apostle found the Philippians to be true in their partnership in the Lord's work. They suffered for their Lord patiently; the faith was bravely defended by them; they spread it zealously; and their lives confirmed it. And so Paul said to himself, *"This is the finger of God; the Lord Himself has begun this work."* How happy we are when we can have this confidence in members of the church, confident that from the beginning God has been at work in their hearts. Do not be satisfied, any of you, with the most promising religiousness, if it is not God's work. If you have undergone a change, take care that it is such a change as only the Creator could have worked in you; that is, a resurrection from the dead, the opening of blind eyes, a turning from darkness to light, a hatred of your sins. If you have not undergone a renewal which shows such heavenly handiwork, be uneasy. Be restless until God makes you anew in Christ Jesus. May the Lord begin this good work in you at once, and may there be signs which give the joy of knowing that truly the Lord has done it.!

EVENING

For I have become like a bottle in the smoke; yet I do not forget Your statutes — Psalm 119:83.

GOD'S PEOPLE have their trials. Trials were in the covenant, and the covenant is as old as the mountains. It was never designed by God when He chose His people that they should be untried people, that they should be chosen to peace and safety, to perpetual happiness here below, and freedom from sickness and the pains of mortality. Rather when He made the covenant He made the rod also. When He drew up the charter of privileges, He also drew up the charter of chastisements. When He gave us the roll of heirship, He put down the rods among the things to which we should inevitably be heirs. Trials are a part of our lot. They were predestinated for us in God's solemn decrees. As surely as He has fashioned the stars, and has fixed their orbits, so surely are our trials weighed in His scales. He has predestinated their season and their place, their intensity and the effect they will have on us. Good men must never expect to escape troubles. If they do, they will be disappointed. None of their predecessors have escaped them.

Mark Job, of whose patience you have heard. Read of Abraham, for he had his trials — it was by his faith under them that he became the *"father of the faithful,"* when he offered up Isaac. Study the biographies of all the patriarchs, of all the prophets, of all the apostles and martyrs, and you will discover that none of them escaped being like bottles in the smoke, though God made them vessels of mercy. It is ordained that the cross of trouble should be engraved on every vessel of mercy, just as earthly kings have marked their vessels of honor. As surely as we are born, we are born to trouble, as the sparks fly upwards (Job 5:17). And when born again, it does seem as if we had a birth to double trouble. Yea, double trouble and toil comes to the one who has double grace and double mercy bestowed on him. Good men and women must have their trials; they must expect to become like a bottle in the smoke.

October 11   MORNING

Being persuaded of this very thing, that He who began a good work in you will finish it until the day of Jesus Christ — Philippians 1:6.

THE CHARACTER of the Philippians confirmed the apostle in his confidence. He adds, *"Both in my bonds and in the defense and confirmation of the gospel, you are all sharers of my grace."* When he was bound, they were not ashamed of his chain. When he was in prison the Philippian jailor washed his stripes and refreshed him at his table. This proved to be a sign of loving liberality throughout life. When Paul was taken away to Rome, the Philippians took care that he should not be left penniless; they sent out of their poverty to his assistance. He felt confidence in a people who would do this. Shame turns many of the weaker sort aside, but the faithful despise it. Those who love holiness, when others despise and ridicule it, are the people to stand fast.

Besides they were partners with Paul in the defense of the gospel. If any Galatian teachers came their way, they gave them the cold shoulder, for they would not give up the grand old gospel to please the 'wise' men of the period. The people who can bear the attacks made on them, and the baits held out to them, can be relied on under God.

They were also with the apostle as to the confirmation of the gospel. Their lives proved the truth of the Word of grace. When Paul was preaching, if he wanted to show that the gospel is the power of God, he pointed to what had been done in Philippi, then none could gainsay the argument. A living argument is invincible. Reason can be overwhelmed by fact. Oh, that every Christian would so live as to prove the power of the gospel! He adds also that they were sharers of his grace. The same grace which had saved him saved them. They ascribed their salvation to sovereign grace, even as he did.

EVENING

This, the beginning of miracles, Jesus did in Cana of Galilee, revealing His glory. And His disciples believed on Him — John 2:11.

CHRIST MANIFESTED His glory. Truly, He glorified the Father, for that was His great end and aim. But yet He showed forth His own glory in that very act. Note that it was His own glory which was revealed. This was never said of any prophet or saint — neither Moses, Samuel, David, nor Elijah had ever manifested their own glory. For, indeed, they had no glory to reveal. Here is One greater than a prophet; here is One greater than the holiest of men. He manifested His own glory; it could not be otherwise. We must adore the Lord Jesus when reading these words. Jesus revealed His own glory as God and as man. During all those former years it had been veiled. He had been an obedient boy, a young, industrious carpenter. Then His glory was a spring shut up, a fountain sealed. But now it began to flow forth in the stream for this great miracle. Think of it! You will see more clearly what glory it was. He appeared to be a man like others, and yet at will He turned water into wine. His mother was there as if to remind us that He was born of a woman. he was a man with a mother, and yet He was so truly *"God over all,"* that He created by His will an abundance of wine. He was but one among many wedding guests, with His six humble followers, but yet He acted the Creator's part. He did not sit arrayed in fine priestly garments, nor did He wear the Pharisee's phylacteries, nor any other form of ornament to show an ecclesiastical office or profession. Yet He did greater wonders than they could attempt. He was simply a man among men, and yet He was God among men. His wish was Law in the world of matter, so that water received the qualities of good wine. Adore Him! Adore Him reverently! Bow low before Him who was a man, a real man, and yet who worked as only Jehovah Himself can work.

MORNING

This, the beginning of miracles, Jesus did in Cana of Galilee, revealing His glory. And His disciples believed on Him — John 2:11.

OUR LORD'S MIRACLES were worked in each case to meet a need. The wine had failed at the wedding feast, and He came in at a time of need, when the bridegroom was fearful of being made ashamed. That need was a great blessing. If there had been sufficient wine for the feast, Jesus would not have worked this miracle, and they would never have tasted this purest and best of wine. It is a blessed need which makes room for Jesus to come in with miracles of love. It is for us to run short, that we may be driven to the Lord by our necessity; for He will more than supply it. If you have no need, Christ will not come to you. But if you are in dire necessity, His hand will be stretched out to you. If your needs stand before you like huge empty waterpots, or if your soul is as full of grief as those pots were filled with water, Jesus can by His sweet will turn all your needs into blessings, all your sighing into singing. Be glad to be weak, that the power of God may rest on you. Be more dependent on the Lord for every particle of strength, and thank God that you can. If you have a failure as to all your natural wine of ability, there may be occasion then for your Lord to come in and supply the wine of strength, of another and more divine quality. You are likely to do your work best when you feel most your insufficiency, when you are driven in on God for help. If you go blundering into service, you shall fail. But if you go trembling, then by confidently looking up to the Lord, you shall be more than a conqueror.

EVENING

This, the beginning of miracles, Jesus did in Cana of Galilee, revealing His glory. And His disciples believed on Him — John 2:11.

WHEN THEY SAW the majestic ease of His working, do you not think it confirmed their faith? He did not call for angels. He did not deliver a long prayer, much less repeat a sacred incantation. He did but will it, and the deed was done. Next time they came into a difficulty, the disciples would believe that the Lord could easily appear for them. They need only to stand still and see the salvation of the Lord. In some way or other the Lord would provide, and he would do wonders without trouble to Himself.

It showed them that from now on they need never be anxious. Will you who read your Greek Testament notice the expression here? Is it said, *"His disciples believed Him,"* or, *"Believed in Him*, or, *Believed on Him"*? It is none of these. The Greek is, *"Believed into Him."* His disciples believed into Him. They so believed that they seemed to submerge themselves in Jesus — *Into Him* — think what that means. John, and Andrew, and Nathanael, and the others, cast their lifelong concerns on Jesus, feeling that they need never have another care. Jesus would see them through to the end. They would leave everything to Him. Mary took the matter a little into her own hands, but she erred in that. The disciples entered into Jesus by the open door of this confirming miracle, and there they rested. May this be your condition, *"casting all your care on Him, for He cares for you."* They believed right into Jesus. It is one thing to believe in Him, another thing to believe Him. It is a restful thing to believe on Him, but best of all to believe right into Him so that your very personality is swallowed up in Christ, and you feel the bliss of living, loving, lasting union with Him.

MORNING — October 13

Being persuaded of this very thing, that He who began a good work in you will finish it until the day of Jesus Christ — Philippians 1:6.

AS TO HIS CONFIDENCE about the future of his converts, it was all in God. It was not confidence in them apart from the work of God in them. He says, God began it, and God will finish it. He does not depend on the strength of their principles, nor the force of their resolutions, nor the excellence of their habits. No, he relies on God, who will perform what he has begun. Did not Paul begin it? No, for if he had begun it, he would have to carry it on, and that he could not do. Did not they begin it in themselves? Certainly not! Does the sinner take the first step? How can he? He is dead in sin. If he does take the first step apart from the Spirit of God, then he can take all the rest without God. It is with the sinner as it was with Romish Saint Denis, who in the fable is said to have had his head cut off, and he picked it up and walked a thousand miles with it in his hand. A scoffer said that the thousand-mile walk was not so remarkable at all; it was only the first step that had any difficulty in it. Just so. When a soul goes to Heaven, if it takes the first step in its own strength, then it can walk all the way, and so have all the glory.

God commences the good work, however faint and feeble the beginning may appear. The tiny brooklet at the riverhead of repentance is of God as much as the broad river of heavenly character. This is a solemn truth. How deeply it should humble us! We cannot even begin; we cannot dig out the foundation; how then can we bring forth the topstone? All is of grace from first to last. While the apostle is so practical, yet see how soundly doctrinal he is. He never quits the grand doctrine of free, sovereign, effectual grace: *"He who began a good work in you will finish it until the day of Jesus Christ."*

EVENING

Being persuaded of this very thing, that He who began a good work in you will finish it until the day of Jesus Christ — Philippians 1:6.

PERFECTION in a modified sense is possible through Divine grace, but not absolute perfection. Old John Trapp very well says that a Christian may be perfect, but not perfectly perfect. Perfection in the scriptural sense is not at all what those make of it who boast of perfection in the flesh. A child is perfect when it is newly born; that is, there is every toe on the tiny foot, and it has eyes, and ears, and nose, and the other organs — it is perfected, complete. But if that child claims to be a perfect man, it is not scriptural. The Christian may be perfect as to all his parts, *"perfect and entire, lacking nothing,"* and yet he may not be perfect as to development by a very long way. One says, "We shall be perfect at death, shall we not?" It is not so written here, but, *"He will finish it until the day of Jesus Christ."* We may be perfect in death, as to the moral and spiritual nature. But a man has a body as well as a soul, and it needs both parts to make a perfect man. While the worms are devouring the body, the man is not yet perfect. He will be perfect as to his whole manhood when the Lord shall come, and the trumpet shall sound, and the dead shall be raised incorruptible. Paul delights to make the Christian leap over that little rivulet called death, and to swallow up the thought of dissolution in the far grander fact of the coming of the Lord. The second advent ought to be much more on our minds than the hour of our death. The Lord will perform the sacrifice which He has begun, until He perfects it in the day when the Lord Jesus Christ shall receive all His own to Himself. Then shall be the general Judgment. Oh, what a blessing will be our perfection in that day of decision! He shall separate the righteous from the wicked, as the shepherd divides his sheep from the goats. When that day is ended, then shall the righteous shine forth as the sun.

MORNING

Will a man rob God? Yet you have robbed Me — Malachi 3:8.

NOT A FEW rob God by rebelling against His sovereignty. I have known men bite their lip and grind their teeth in rage when I have been preaching the sovereignty of God. Yet it is true. God says to these, *"Yes, rather, O man, who are you answering against God? Shall the thing formed say to the One forming it, Why did you make me like this?"* (Rom. 9:20). Above He says, that He will have mercy on whom He desires to have mercy. Men seem to think that God is under obligation to grant salvation to guilty men; that if He saves one, He must save all. They talk about rights, as if any man had any right before the throne of God, except the right to be punished for his sin. Mercy can only be shown to the guilty on the ground of Divine, royal prerogative. It must be the free act of God's grace, done at His own good pleasure, if any guilty man be saved from eternal death. The doctrinaires of today will allow a God, but He must not be King. That is to say, they choose a god who is no god, one rather the servant than the ruler of men. We, however, boldly declare on God's behalf that *"it is not of him who wills, nor of him who runs, but of God who shows mercy"* (Rom. 9:16). At the sound of this Scripture men stamp their foot with rage. They would rob God of His crown, and leave Him neither throne nor will. This will not do for any Bible-believing Christian, whose heart must delight to say, *"It is the Lord; let Him do what seems good to Him."* Whatever is His pleasure shall be my pleasure. Even if the Lord condemn me, I cannot say that He is unjust. But if He has mercy on me, then I must ascribe it wholly to His free and sovereign grace. Oh, do not rob God of His sovereignty, but rejoice that the Lord God Almighty reigns and does His will.

EVENING

Blessed be the Lord my strength, who teaches my hands to war, my fingers to fight —
Psalm 144:1.

DAVID CANNOT DELAY the utterance of his gratitude; he bursts out into a loud note of praise. His best word is given to his best friend, *"Blessed be Jehovah."* When the heart is in a right state it must praise God; it cannot be restrained. Its utterances leap forth as waters forcing their way from a living spring. With all his strength David blesses the God of his strength. Saints ought not to receive so great a boon as strength to resist evil, to defend truth, and to conquer error, without knowing who gave it to us, and rendering to Him the glory of it. Not only does Jehovah give strength to His saints, but He IS their strength. The strength is made theirs because God is theirs. God is full of power, and He becomes the power of those who trust Him. In Him our great strength lies, and to Him be blessings more than we are able to utter.

"Who teaches my hands to war" — If we have strength we are not much the better unless we have skill also. Untrained force is often an injury to the one possessing it, and can even become a danger to those around him. So the Psalmist blesses the Lord as much for teaching as for strength. Let us also bless Jehovah if He has in anything made us efficient. The tuition mentioned was very practical; it was not so much of the brain as of the hands and fingers. For these were the members most needful for conflict. Men with little scholastic education should be grateful for deftness and skill. To a fighting man the education of the hands is of more value than mere book-learning. All wisdom and skill are from the Lord, and for these He deserves to be gratefully extolled. This teaching extends to the smallest members of our frame; the Lord teaches the fingers as well as the hands. Let us be willing pupils of Him, and He shall be our Master, then we will give our Instructor hearty blessing for everything we may be able to accomplish.

October 15 — MORNING

For I am the Lord your God, the Holy One of Israel, your Savior; I gave Egypt for your ransom, Ethiopia and Seba for you — Isaiah 43:3.

IN THIS CHAPTER the Lord comforts His people. By His Divine foresight He perceives that there are great and varied trials ahead. So He prepares them for the ordeal. They are to go through rushing waters and flaming fires; and He kindly bids them not to be afraid. How often in God's Word do we read those tender, gracious words, *"Do not fear"!* Should not the trembling ones listen to the voice of their God and obey it when He says to them, *"Do not fear"?* It is not right for you who fear God to fear anything else. Once brought to know the Lord, what can harm you? Abiding under the shadow of the Almighty, what danger do you dread? Rather, be of good comfort, and press forward with peaceful confidence, even though floods and flames await you.

To encourage His people to rise above their fears, the gracious God goes on to issue matchless promises, *"When you pass through the waters, I will be with you; and through the rivers, they shall not overflow you."* Present good, *"I will be with you"*; absent danger, *"they shall not overflow you."* God stays His people's hearts by His own promises. In proportion to their faith those promises must lift them up. If you do not believe the promise, you shall not be established by it. But if with childlike confidence you accept every word of God as true, then His word shall be to you the joy of your heart, and the delight of your spirit. Then you shall be a stranger to fear.

The Lord proceeds, after giving those promises, to set before them what He Himself is, and what He has done for them, and what they are to Him. Of course He is speaking of Israel, and He says of Israel, His chosen nation, *"I gave Egypt for your ransom, Ethiopia and Seba for you."* What cause for fear now remains?

EVENING

For I am the Lord your God, the Holy One of Israel, your Savior; I gave Egypt for your ransom, Ethiopia and Seba for you — Isaiah 43:3.

THE SEED was not after the flesh, else the children of Ishmael would have been the heirs of the covenant. But the true Seed was born according to promise, and in the power of God. Isaac, from whose loins the true Seed would come, was born when his parents were old, by faith in the power of God. Isaac was born according to promise. And we who are not born of the flesh, nor of the will of man, but of God, by His Spirit, and according to the Divine promise, are the true children of Abraham. We are the spiritual Israel. Although, after the flesh, Abraham is ignorant of us, and Sarah does not acknowledge us, yet we are the true seed of him who was the father of believers. The literal Israel was the type of those chosen and favored ones who by faith are born again according to promise. To these heirs according to promise the Lord says, *"I gave Egypt for your ransom, Ethiopia and Seba for you."* It would not be straining the passage to wholly apply it to the chosen ones of God. Do not be staggered by that term, but be reminded that the chosen of God are made known by their believing in the Lord Jesus Christ. Faith is the sure evidence of election. So if you are a believer in Christ, you are of the true Israel: *"Whoever believes that Jesus is the Christ has been born of God"* (1 John 5:1). And being born of God you are of the family of His love; you are heirs of God, joint-heirs of Jesus Christ (Rom. 8:17). If you are believers in Him, nothing more need be said to comfort you. The unbelieving, those living and dying as such, have no portion in the covenant of grace. If you do not believe, you must perish. The promise is given to obedient faith only: *"He who believes and is baptized shall be saved; but he who does not believe shall be condemned"* (Mark 16:16). If you become a believer this day, you have in that faith the token and mark of this Divine choice, and you assuredly belong to the Israel of God.

Make me hear joy and gladness, that the bones which You have broken may rejoice
— Psalm 51:8.

LET US look at these words more closely: *"that the bones which You have broken may rejoice."* He means that if he is enabled by faith to look to Christ, whose blood is sprinkled by the hyssop on the soul; if he receives perfect pardon through the atoning sacrifice and thus made white as snow — then he will possess a deeper and truer joy than before. Before his tongue rejoiced, but now his very bones will rejoice. Before his flesh rejoiced, but now the marrow of his soul will rejoice. The deep pain which he had felt within the inmost depths of his being would now be exchanged for an equally deep joy, which will gush up from his very bowels like an Artesian well. This joy will rise in a continual flood from his inward being, all fresh with holy exultation. He would now know what sin means as he never knew before. He would know what chastisement for sin was, as he could not have dreamed before. He would know what mercy meant, as he had not before understood. Because of this his inmost nature will praise and bless God in a way in which he had never done until that hour. That deeply experimental, painful, and yet blessed experience of his weakness, and of God's power to deliver, has by now taught him a heart-music which only broken bones could learn. You know that there can be a great deal of flash about many of our spiritual joys. In grosser parts they can be akin to carnal excitement. Especially with young beginners the gladness is too apt to trail off into the mire of mere mental pleasure. Our gladness is frequently far from being deep as we could wish, but after the bone-breaking everything will become more solid, everything is true. What our joy lacks in vividness it will make up in stability and depth. So David means, "the innermost core of my nature, the very essentials of my spiritual being shall rejoice and sing."

EVENING

And the people murmured against Moses, saying, What shall we drink: —
Exodus 15:24.

IT IS worthy to note that the murmuring was not ostensibly against God. They murmured against Moses. Have you ever noticed how the most of us are not honest enough to murmur distinctly against God? Is the child dead? Then we form a conjecture that there was some wrong treatment on the part of the nurse, or the surgeon, or ourselves. We lay our hold on that for which there may not be a shadow of proof, and the murmuring is on that point. Have we lost money and been brought down from opulence to almost poverty? Then some one person was dishonest, a certain party betrayed us in a transaction by failing to fulfill his part. All the murmuring is heaped on a certain person, or persons. Perhaps indignantly we will deny that we are murmuring against God. To prove this we double the zeal with which we murmur against others. To complain of the second cause is about as sensible as the conduct of a dog when he bites the stick with which he is beaten. It owes no anger to the stick, but to the person who uses it. *Is there calamity in the city, and the Lord has not done it?* (Amos 3:6). Whoever is the instrument, the Lord overrules. In our heart of hearts our rebellion is against the Lord Himself. We have not quite honesty enough to rail against God openly and avowedly, and so we hypocritically cover up our repining against Him by murmuring against some person, occasion, or event: "If I had not happened to go out on such an occasion, I might not have had that cold and been laid aside." In this way we blame an accidental circumstance, as if it were not part of the Divine arrangement. Is this complaining of the second cause better than railing against God? No! For in very deed it *is* railing against God. Yea, in addition, it may well be an injustice to the second cause.

MORNING

Who are these who fly like a cloud, and as doves in their windows? — Isaiah 60:8.

YOU WILL MARK, not as clouds, but *"like a cloud";* not as two or three bodies, but as one united and compact mass. Here is the secret of strength. Split us into fractions, and we are conquered; unite us into a compact body and we become invincible. Knit us together as one man, and Satan himself can never tear us apart. Divide us into threads, let our warp and woof be disunited, and we become like rotten fibers that will burn before a single spark of our enemy's fire. But thanks to God, we are as the heart of one man. We have *"one Lord, one faith, one baptism."* Yet the church wonders at it, scarcely understanding, saying, "who are these who fly as one compact and solid cloud?" God grant that we may always continue so! Whatever is said of one of us, let it be said of all of us. Do not let us be stragglers. Those in the rear of an army are always in danger; those hanging about the flanks are subject to insult and injury. Let us march breast to breast, shoulder to shoulder, each of us drawing the sword at one word, doing as the Commander tells us. As surely as truth prevails, unity shall conquer, and our King will honor us and bless us, treading our foes beneath our feet, and making us more than conquerors through Him who has loved us.

Not only is there the idea of unanimity in this verse, but also of power. Who is it that shall bridle a cloud, or stop it in its march? Who by a word can stay the careening clouds and make them still? Who can command them when they are driving northward, turn their course to the south? Who can rein the courses of the wind and forbid them to drag the chariots of darkness toward the west? The clouds yield to none on earth. None can stop the clouds here. They are invincible, uncontrollable by men. In their majesty they move themselves royally, as if kings in the heavens. So will we be.

EVENING

The Lord bless you and keep you. The Lord make His face shine on you and be gracious to you. The Lord lift up His face to you and give you peace —Numbers 6:24

THIS BENEDICTION is of a higher order than intercession. Every man in the camp might have prayed, *"The Lord bless you and keep you, and lift up His face on you."* But no man in all the camp would have dared to speak in the same authoritative style Aaron did. Here is not only faith pleading, but faith receiving and bestowing. Paul said, *"Without doubt the lesser is blessed by the greater;"* and Aaron was greater than the people, having been set apart to a high and honorable office, in which no one else might intrude. He was God's representative, and so he spoke with the authority of his office. Today our Savior's intercession in the heavenly places rises far higher in power and glory than that of any ordinary intercessor. He blesses in fact, while the greatest saints on earth and in Heaven can only bless in desire.

This benediction wears the form of a fiat as well as of a prayer. The priest here speaks the blessing for which he asks. Turning to the Father, our Lord Jesus cried, *"Father, keep through Your name those whom You have given me."* Turning to us He says, *"The Lord bless you and keep you."* What He asks of God He distributes among men, by an authority vested in Him by the Father: *"For it pleased the Father that in Him should all fulness dwell.*"Let your heart delight in thinking of the Lord Jesus Christ at this hour, not as a Gethsemane pleader, with groans and agony and bloody sweat, but as One who has finished His work and now reigns in glory with the Father, having all power in Heaven and in earth. This One sends the blessing to those to whom it comes. This prayer of our great High Priest is so infinitely effectual that He practically gives the blessing Himself, saying, *"If you shall ask anything in My name, I will do it."*

Your people shall be willing in the day of Your power, in the beauty of holiness from the womb of the morning: You have the dew of Your youth — Psalm 110:3.

THIS PSALM is a kind of coronation Psalm. Christ is bidden to take His throne: *"You sit at My right hand."* The scepter is put into His hand, *'The Lord will send the rod of Your strength out of Zion."* And then the question,"Where are His people?" is answered — for a king would be no king without subjects. Where, then, shall Christ find that which shall be the fulness of Him that fills all in all? This we know, that Christ is a King of kings. He is the Lord of creation and of providence. Often we wonderingly ask, Lord, where shall we find Your subjects? Witnessing to hard hearts, and prophesying to dry bones, our unbelief at times suggests that we shall not find children for Christ, that we shall not find those who make up the subjects of His empire. But our fears are put to rest by this and other passages: *"Your people shall be willing in the day of Your power, in the beauty of holiness from the womb in the morning"* — and by that second promise, *"You have the dew of Your youth."* These thoughts are placed here to allay the questionings of God's believing people, and to let them see how Christ will indeed be King of kings, never lacking a multitude of subjects to bow at His feet.

EVENING

They shall put My name on the sons of Israel. And I will bless them — Numbers 6:27.

"I WILL BLESS THEM" — they will have their troubles, but I will bless them through their troubles. When they have earthly goods, I will bless them and make them real comforts. I will bless their basket and their store. If those earthly comforts are taken away, they shall have compensation a thousand-fold in Myself. I gave the mercies, and I will allow no one but Myself to take them away — then it will be done only in love, that I may bless them still more. The world may curse us, but if God blesses us, the curse will be as the whistling wind. Friends may become enemies, or may forget us, but if God blesses us, we can bear the wound. God blessed us when we were young. He kept us from harm in our giddy youth; He blessed us in our manhood, and He helped us when family cares were on us. He will sustain us now that we lean heavily on our staff. He will bless us when sickness lays us low. And when we come to die, Jesus will bless us with dying grace for dying moments. We shall awaken in the likeness of Christ, and then we shall be satisfied with His blessing, being transformed into the image of Him by whom the blessing comes. The Judgment Day will dawn; the earth will pass away, but the Lord will bless us. God's will has an eternal range. When He says, *"I will"* all the demons in Hell cannot turn aside the blessing; all the ages of eternity cannot change the King's word. *"I will bless them"* — how much He will bless them He does not say, but the great I AM who makes the promise blesses like the God He is, directly and personally. Here is absolute certainty based on the faithfulness of the Lord. Here is endless mercy certified by the Divine eternity and immutability.

MORNING

Watch over me, O God, for I put my trust in You — Psalm 16:1.

EVEN AS bodyguards surround their monarch, or as shepherds protect their flocks, God watches over His lambs. Tempted in all points as we are, the manhood of Jesus needed to be preserved from the power of evil. Although His humanity in itself was pure, the Lord Jesus did not confide in that purity of nature, but as an example to His followers He looked to God the Father for preservation. One of God's great names is *"the Preserver of men"* (Job 7:20). The gracious office the Father exercised toward our Mediator was that of preservation. It was promised to Him in express words: *"So says Jehovah, the Redeemer of Israel, and his Holy One, to Him whom man despises, to Him whom the nation hates: I will preserve You and give You for a covenant of the people"* (Isa. 49:7,8). This promise was fulfilled to the letter, both by providential deliverance and sustaining power, to our Lord. Being preserved Himself, He is able to restore the preserved of spiritual Israel, for we are *"preserved in Christ Jesus and called."* Being one with Him, the elect were preserved in His preservation, and we may view this mediatorial supplication as the petition of the great High Priest for all those who are in Him.

Christ's intercession in John 17 is but an amplication of this cry, *"Holy Father, keep through Your own name those whom You have given Me, that they may be one, as We are."* When He says *"preserve Me,"* He means His members, His mystical body, Himself, and all in Him. We may rejoice in this prayer of the Lord Jesus for His members, but let us not forget that He employed it for Himself also. He had so emptied Himself, and so truly taken on Him the form of a servant, that as man He needed Divine keeping, even as we do. He often cried out for strength. Frequently on the mountain He breathed forth this desire. On one occasion He publicly prayed, *"Father, save Me from this hour"* (John 12:27). If Jesus looked for protection for Himself, how much more must we, His erring followers, do so!

EVENING

For we are His workmanship, created in Christ Jesus to good works that God prepared before, that we should walk in them — Ephesians 2:10.

THE OUTCOME of our union with Christ must be holiness: *"What agreement has Christ with Belial?"* What union can He have with men that love sin? How can those who love the world be said to be members of the Head who is in Heaven, in the perfection of His glory? In the power of this text, and in the power of our union with Christ, we must seek to make daily advances in good works, those God has before ordained that we should walk in them. For walking means not only persevering, but advancing. We should go from strength to strength in holiness. We should do more and do better. What are you doing for Jesus? Do twice as much. If you are spreading abroad the knowledge of His name, work with both hands. If you are living uprightly, put away any relics of sin that remain in your character, and glorify the name of God.

This should be our daily exercise: *"that we should walk in them."* Good works are not to be an amusement, but a vocation. We are not to indulge in them occasionally. They are to be the tenor and bent of our lives. You say, "Oh, that is a hard saying"? Well then, this displays and sets in clear light the earlier part of this passage. You see how impossible it is that you should be saved by these good works, do you not? But if you are saved — if you have obtained a present salvation — if you are now a child of God — if you are now assured of your safety — I charge you, by the love you bear to God, by the gratitude you have to Jesus Christ, give yourself wholly to everything that is right and good and pure and just. Help everything that has to do with temperance and righteousness and truth and godliness. *"Let your light so shine before men that they may see your good works, and glorify your Father who is in Heaven."*

MORNING

Then having these promises, beloved, let us cleanse ourselves from all defilements of flesh and of spirit, perfecting holiness in the fear of God — 2 Corinthians 7:1.

"I HAVE had a deep conviction for many years that practical holiness and entire self-consecration to God are not sufficiently attended to by modern Christians. Politics, or controversy, or party-spirit, or worldliness, have eaten out the heart of lively piety in too many of us. The subject of personal godliness has fallen sadly into the background. The standard of living has become painfully low in many quarters. The immense importance of *"adoring the doctrine of God our Savior"* (Titus 2:10), and making it lovely and beautiful by our daily habits and tempers, has been far too much overlooked. Worldly people sometimes complain with reason that 'religious' persons, so-called, are not so amiable and unselfish, and good-natured as others who make no profession of religion. Yet sanctification, in its place and proportion, is quite as important as justification. Sound protestant and evangelical doctrine is useless if it is not accompanied by a holy life. It is worse than useless: it does positive harm. It is despised by keen-sighted and shrewd men of the world, as an unreal and hollow thing; it brings religion into contempt. It is my firm impression that we need a thorough revival about Scriptural holiness" — Bishop J. C. Ryle, from *Holiness*, introduction.

"Would you have your hope strong? Then keep your conscience pure. You cannot defile one without weakening the other. The godly person that is loose and careless in his holy walking will soon find his hope languishing. All sin disposes the soul that tampers with it to trembling fears and shakings of heart" — William Gurnall.

EVENING

Tossed to and fro and carried about with every wind and doctrine —Ephesians 4:14.

THERE IS an amazing ignorance of Scripture among many, and a consequent lack of established, solid religion. In no other way can I account for the ease with which people are, like children, *"tossed to and fro and carried about by every wind of doctrine."* There is an Athenian love of novelty abroad, and a morbid distaste for anything old and regular, and in the beaten path of our forefathers. Thousands will crowd to hear a new voice and a new doctrine, without considering for a moment whether what they hear is true. There is an incessant craving after any teaching which is sensational, and exciting, and rousing to the feelings. There is an unhealthy appetite for a sort of spasmodic and hysterical Christianity. The religious life of many is little better than spiritual dram-drinking. The *"meek and quiet spirit"* which St. Peter commends is clean forgotten. Crowds, and crying, and hot rooms, and high-flown singing, and an unceasing rousing of the emotions, are the only things which many care for. Inability to distinguish differences in doctrine is spreading far and wide, and so long as the preacher is clever and earnest hundreds seem to think it must be all right. They will call you dreadfully narrow and uncharitable if you think that he is unsound. All this is sad, very sad. But if, in addition to this, the true-hearted advocates of increased holiness are going to fall out by the way and misunderstand one another, it will be sadder still. We shall indeed be in evil plight — Bishop J. C. Ryle, *Holiness*, intro.

"None walk so evenly with God as they who are assured of the love of God. Faith is the mother of obedience, and sureness of trust makes way for strictness of life. When men are loose from Christ, they are loose in point of duty, and their floating belief is soon discovered in their inconstancy and unevenness of walking. We do not, with alacrity, engage in that of the success of which we are doubtful. So when we know not whether God will accept us or not, when we are off and on in point of trust, we are just so in the course of our lives, and serve God in fits and starts" — Thomas Manton.

October 21   MORNING

For by grace you are saved, through faith, and this not of yourselves; it is the gift of God; not of works, that not anyone should boast — Ephesians 2:8,9.

IF WE WERE to preach to sinners, dead in trespasses and sins, that salvation would be by their own works, we would be setting aside the way of salvation by grace. There cannot be two ways of salvation for the same people. If we take to the one, we practically deny the other. It cannot be questioned that a guilty man, if saved at all, must be saved through the mercy of God. It cannot be denied, either, that our Savior and His apostles taught that we are saved by faith. One must shut his eyes if he does not see this to be their teaching. If then men are taught that they can be saved by works, then they may conclude from this that salvation by grace is a myth, a mistake, even a mischievous error. Salvation by grace is then set aside. There cannot be more than one way of salvation: *"If by grace, no longer is it of works; also grace no longer becomes grace. But if by works it is no longer grace, else work is no longer work"* (Rom. 11:6). If salvation is of merit, it is not of mercy. But if there is no salvation of men by the pure mercy of God, what an unhappy case we are in. To deny grace is really to deny hope. Where, then, would be the good news? The way of salvation by works is not news. It is the old way of man's devising, the well-known error of all the ages. And certainly it is not good news, for there is nothing good or glad in it. Salvation as a reward for works is that taught by the heathen. Justification by religious performances and meritorious deeds is nothing better than the old Pharisaism with a Christian name stuck on it. Such a doctrine does not need a revelation by the Spirit of God, for it is to be seen by the light of man's own candle. That teaching makes the Lord Jesus a nobody; for if salvation is by works, then salvation through faith in a Savior is needless, even mischievous.

EVENING

For by grace you are saved, through faith, and this not of yourselves; it is the gift of God; not of works, that not anyone should boast — Ephesians 2:8,9.

WHAT ARE the supposed 'good' works that can merit Heaven? What good works will ensure eternal life? Those who imagine such do not realize that their works must be perfectly pure, continuous, and unspotted: *"The law of the Lord is perfect."* It condemns not only acts, but even thoughts, even a glance of the eye. The law of God in the Ten Commandments means much more than the bare words would imply. It deals with the whole range of moral condition, motive and thought. Do not dream that its sweep only includes external acts. Of course it does include externals, but also inward spiritual acts, those that go right through the heart, those that reveal the inward parts of one's spirit. The more one understands the law of God, the more one feels condemned by it, and the less does that one indulge the dream that he, as he is, may ever be able to keep the law. With such foul hands as ours, how can we do clean work? With hearts so polluted, how can we be *"undefiled in the way"*? Nature rises no higher than its source, and that which comes out of the heart will be no better than the heart, and that is *"deceitful above all things, and it is incurable"* (Jer. 17:9).

    The law of God is one. If you break it in any one point, you break it altogether. If in a chain of a hundred links, ninety-nine are perfect; yet if a single link anywhere in the chain should be too weak for the weight placed on it, the load will fall to the ground as surely as if twenty links were snapped. One breakage of the law of God involves transgression against the whole of it: *"For whoever shall keep all the law, but stumbles in one, he has become guilty of all"* (James 2:10). In order to be saved by works, there must be absolutely perfect, continuously perfect obedience to it, in thought, and word, and deed. Furthermore, that obedience must be rendered willingly and cheerfully.

MORNING

For we are His workmanship, created in Christ Jesus to good works that God prepared before that we should walk in them — Ephesians 2:10.

GOD DESIRES that His people should abound in good works. It is His great object to produce a people fit to commune with Himself — a holy people with whom He can have fellowship in time and in eternity. He not only wishes us to produce good works, but to abound in them, and to abound in the highest order of them. He desires and commands us to become imitators of Himself as dear children, possessing the same moral attributes as the Father in Heaven possesses. Is it not written, *"Be perfect, even as your Father who is in Heaven is perfect"*?

A Christian is the noblest work of God. Such a one is the product of the second creation. At first man fell and marred his Creator's work. In the new creation He who makes all things makes us a new creation. Now the object of the new creation is holiness to the glory of God. You are not new-made in the image of the fallen Adam, but in the likeness of the Second Adam. You are not newly created to sin. The new creature does not sin, for it has been born of God (1 John 3:9). The new life is a living and incorruptible seed that lives and abides forever. Man in his old nature sins, and always will sin. But the new life is of God, and it strives daily against the sin of the old nature. It perseveres, pushing forward toward everything that is holy, upright and perfect. Its instincts all run toward perfect holiness. The old nature despises prayer, but the new nature sings and praises God from within. The old nature goes after the flesh, for it is fleshly, carnal; but the new nature seeks the things of the Spirit, for it is spiritual.

EVENING

For we are His workmanship, created in Christ Jesus to good works that God prepared before that we should walk in them — Ephesians 2:10.

THIS IS GOD'S DECREE. Am I ordained to eternal life? Answer the other question: Am I ordained to walk in good works? If I am ordained to good works, then I do walk in them, and the decree of God is clearly carried out in me. But if I make a profession of being a Christian, attend a place of worship, and compliment myself on my safety, yet I am living in sin, then evidently there is no decree that I shall walk in good works. For I am living otherwise than that decree would have caused me to live. It is the eternal purpose of God to make His people holy. Agree with that purpose with the freedom of your renewed will, and with the delight of your regenerated heart. Concur in the will of God. Vehemently desire, heartily pant after, perfect holiness in the fear of God. Then you may in the midst of severe struggles against temptation from without and within fall back on the decree of predestination. Since it is God's decree, that one newly created in Christ should be full of good works, such a one will be so despite the old nature, and despite spiritual weakness. In the new creature of God the decree will be carried out despite surroundings, despite temptations of circumstances, despite the opposition of the Devil. God has before ordained that we should walk in good works, and we shall certainly walk in them, sustained by His Holy Spirit.

So, then, these good works must be in the true Christian. They are not the root, but the fruit of his salvation. They are not the way of the believer's salvation, but his walk in the way of salvation. Where there is healthy life in a tree, the tree will bear fruit according to its kind. So, if God has made our nature good, the fruit will be good.

MORNING

You are my Lord; my goodness is not apart from You. As for the saints who are on the earth, even the excellent, all my delight is in them — Psalm 16:2, 3.

THESE SANCTIFIED ONES, although still on the earth, partake of Jesus' mediatorial work, and by His goodness they are made what they are. The *peculiar* people, zealous of good works, and hallowed to sacred service, are arrayed in the Savior's righteousness and washed in His blood. So they receive of the goodness treasured up in Him. These are the persons who are profited by the work of the man Christ Jesus. But that work added nothing to the nature, virtue or happiness of God. How much more forcibly is this true of us, poor unworthy servants, not fit to be mentioned in comparison with the faithful Son of God. Our hope must ever be that perhaps some child of God may be served by us, for the Father can never need our aid.

Poor believers are God's receivers; they have a warrant from the Crown to receive the revenue of our offerings in the King's name. We cannot bless departed saints. Even prayer for them is of no service. But while they are here we should practically prove our love to them, even as our Master did; for they are the excellent of the earth. Despite their infirmities, their Lord thinks highly of them, reckoning them to be as nobles among men. The title of *"His excellency"* more properly belongs to the meanest saint than to the greatest governor. The true aristocracy are believers in Jesus. They are the only honorable ones. The distinctions of men cannot compare with the graces of the Spirit. God tells us here what He thinks of them, *"My delight is in them."* They are His Hephzibah and His Beulah Land. Before the world began His delights were with these chosen ones. Their own opinion of themselves is far other than their Beloved's opinion of them. They rightly think of themselves as nothing, yet He makes much of them and sets His heart on them. What wonders the eyes of Divine Love can see where the hands of Infinite Power have been graciously at work. It was this quicksighted affection which led Jesus to see in us a recompense for all His agony; this sustained Him under all His sufferings, the joy of redeeming us from going down into the pit.

EVENING

He only is my rock and my salvation — Psalm 62:2.

IF YOU LOOK at anything else, you cannot see Christ so well. You say, "I can see Christ in His mercies" — but you cannot see Him as well there as if you viewed His person. No one can look at two objects at the same time and see both distinctly. You may afford a wink for the work, and a wink for Christ, but you cannot give Christ a whole look and also give the world half an eye. Christian, do not try it. If you look on the world, it will be a speck in your eye. If you trust in anything but Him, between two stools you will come to the ground, and a fearful fall you will have. For this reason, Christian, look only on Him: *"He only is my rock and my salvation."*

Christian, never put anything else with Christ. For as sure as you do you will have the whip for it. There never was a child of God who harbored one of the Lord's traitors in His heart, but He always had a charge against him. God has sent out a search warrant against all of us, and do you know what He has told His officers to search for? He has told them to search for all our lovers, all our treasures, and all our helpers. God cares about our sins as sins, but also counts our sins or even our virtues as usurpers of His throne. There is nothing in the world that you set your heart on that will not be hung on the gallows higher than Haman's. If you love anything except Christ, He will make it do penance. If you love your house better than Christ, He will make it a prison for you. If you love your child better than Christ, He will make it an adder in your breast to bite you. If you love your daily provisions better than Christ, he will make your drink bitter and your food like gravel stones in your mouth, until you come to live wholly on Him. There is nothing which you have, which He cannot turn into a rod, if you love it better than Him. You may rest assured that He will do so if you make it anything to rob Christ of your love.

His breath will go out; he returns to the earth; his thoughts perish in that day —Psalm 146:4.

"*HIS THOUGHTS PERISH*" — The thoughts which the Psalmist here intends are those purposes which are in the minds of great men of doing good to those who are under and depend on them. Those candid, serene, benign, benevolent thoughts which they have of advancing their allies, friends and follows will *perish in that day*. The instability of great men's favor is asserted, those whose smiles are quickly changed into frowns, love into hatred, and so in a moment their mind being changed, their well-wishing thoughts vanish. More rationally, *their thoughts perish in that day* when their persons die, because there is no opportunity of putting their purposes into execution. They perish like the child that comes to the birth, and there is no strength to bring forth; or like the fruit which is plucked off before it is ripe. While they live, we may be deceived in our expectations by the alteration of their minds, yet they are mortal. And when that great change by death comes, their designs, however well-meant, will fail.

It follows that the *thoughts* or *hopes* of any who trust in them will also perish. It is true that the greatest part of men perish by expectation. And for good reason, inasmuch as their expectation, being misplaced, perishes. How strongly this argument serves to press the Psalmist's caution against confidence in man, though never so great, is obvious. Princes and nobles are invested with honor, wealth, and authority, and as such have power in their hands. It may be they have thoughts to do you good. But, alas! The execution of those intentions is uncertain, so only the foolish will depend on them. Rather, *"Trust in the Lord Jehovah, for with Him is everlasting strength."* It is safe to build and trust on God, whose thoughts of mercy are from everlasting to everlasting. Let our resolution be that of David, *"It is better to trust in the Lord than to put confidence in man . . ."* — Psalm 118:8,9 (Nathaniel Hardy).

EVENING

Jehovah takes pleasure in those who fear Him; those who hope in His Mercy — Psalm 147:11.

"WHEN A SINNER is brought on his knees, when as he is laid low by affliction, so he lies low in prayer. The Lord *"takes no pleasure in the legs of a man"* — No man is favored by God because of his outward favor, because he has a beautiful face, or strong, clean limbs. Yea, not only has the Lord no pleasure in any man's legs, but not in any man's brains, how far reachig any man's wit may be; nor in any man's judgment, how deep it may be; nor in any man's tongue, how eloquent it may be. No, *'The Lord takes pleasure in those that fear Him,'* in those that walk humbly with Him and call on Him. All the beauties and rarities of persons or things are dull and flat, even wearisom and loathsome, to God in comparison of a gracious, honest, humble soul. All godly men are God's favorites; He is favorable to them not only above many men in the world, but above all the men of this world who have their portion in this life. He favors the saints because they are the purchase of His Son, and the workmanship of His Spirit, convincing them of sin and humbling them, and creating them after God in righteousness and true holiness. These are His favorites." (Joseph Caryl)

"*'those that fear Him, those that hope in His mercy'* — A sincere Christian is known by both these, a fear of God, constant obedience to His commands, and an affiance, trust and dependence on His mercies. Oh, how sweetly are both these coupled, a uniform sincere obedience to Him, and an unshaken constant reliance on His mercy and goodness! The whole perfection of the Christian life is comprised in these two: believing God, and fearing Him; trusting in His mercy, and fearing His name. The one makes us careful in avoiding sin, and the other diligent to follow after righteousness. The one is a bridle from sin and temptation, the other a spur to our duties. Fear is our curb, and hope is our motive and encouragement. Such as both believe in God and fear to offend Him are the only ones who are acceptable to God and His people. God will take pleasure in them." (Thomas Manton)

MORNING

They that sow in tears shall reap in joy — Psalm 127:5.

"GOSPEL TEARS are not lost; they are seeds of comfort. While the penitent pour out tears, God pours in joy. If you would be cheerful, Chrysostom said, be sad. It was the end of Christ's anointing and coming into the world, that He might comfort those who mourn (Isa. 61:3). Christ had the oil of gladness poured on him, as Chrysostom said, that He might pour it on the mourner. Well then might the apostle call it *'a repentance not to be repented of"* (2 Cor. 7:10). Here is sweet fruit from a bitter stock: Christ caused the earthen vessels to be filled with water, and there He turned the water into wine. So when the eye, that earthen vessel, has been filled with water brim full, then Christ will turn the water of tears into the wine of joy. Holy mourning, said St. Basil, is the seed out of which the flower of eternal joy grows." (Thomas Watson)

"'shall reap in joy' — This spiritual harvest comes not alike soon to all, no more than that which is outward does. But here is the comfort: whoever has a seed-time of grace pass over his soul shall have his harvest-time also of joy. This law God has bound Himself to as strongly as to the harvest, which *'is not to cease while the earth remains'* — yea, more strongly. For that was to the world in general, not to every country, town, or field in particular; for some of these may lack a harvest, and yet God may keep His word. But God cannot perform His promise if any one particular saint should everlastingly go without his reaping time. Therefore, you who think so basely of the gospel and its professors, because at present their peace and comfort have not come, you should know that it is on the way to them, and it will come to stay everlastingly with them. But your peace is going from you every moment, and it is sure to leave you without any hope of returning to you again. Look not how the Christian begins, but how he ends. The Spirit of God by His convictions comes into the soul with some terrors, but it closes with peace and joy. As we say of the month of March: it enters like a lion, but goes out like a lamb; so, *'Mark the perfect man, and behold the upright; for the end of that man is peace'* — Psalm 37:37." (William Gurnall)

EVENING

Will a man rob God? Yet you have robbed Me — Malachi 3:8.

MANY ARE in the habit of robbing God in many ways. When God prospers them, and things go well with them, you may hear them exclaim, "I am a lucky fellow! Bless my lucky stars!" By speeches of this sort they rob God of the thanks they owe Him. It is silly and wicked to talk about a fictitious power called fortune, or luck. Even though the hand of God is distinctly to be seen in the prosperity which men enjoy, they refuse to see it, and talk of chance. God forgive you, for you are robbing Him of His praise. Others, when they prosper in the world, pay homage to themselves, their industry, their prudence, or their business skills. Self-made men, they call themselves. Self-made men are, as a rule, very badly made. It would be a great mercy if they could be broken up and then made anew in Christ Jesus. But when a man begins to brag and boast of what he has gathered by his own genius, he robs God of the honor due to His goodness. Look at Nebuchadnezzar as an example: he walks through his great city; he marks the broad walls of Babylon; he admires the hanging gardens, bearing forests high in the air; then he exalaims, *"Behold this great Babylon which I have built."* A few weeks after, he is a maniac, eating grass with the oxen, having been driven from the dwellings of men. When his hair had grown like eagles' feathers, and his nails like birds' claws, then he was made to know how soon the glorious Lord of Heaven and earth can lay the mighty monarch level with the beasts. Then he wisely humbled himself, and he blessed the Most High, praising and honoring Him who lives forever, *"whose dominion is an everlasting dominion."* It is not that we wish you to be bereft of your wits, but you may be. Perhaps, if your best reason returned, even that which pride has for a while driven away, then it might be that you would remember that it is God that gives you power to get wealth, or to do anything. Then you would quit robbing God.

The Lord bless you and keep you. The Lord make His face shine on you and be gracious to you. The Lord lift up His face to you and give you peace — Numbers 6:24

THIS BENEDICTION may be regarded as the benediction of the Father. It is the preservation of love. It is God who has kept you from falling. We are *"Kept by the power of God through faith unto salvation"* — *"He will keep the feet of His saints"* — *"He that keeps Israel shall neither slumber nor sleep."* To the Father's tender care I would commend each one of you. May He bless you and keep you when you are in great temptation, that you do not yield. May He keep you from your own evil heart of unbelief, that you do not turn aside. Contending with a sinful world, may He keep you from its snares. Marching through a region full of seductions to error, may He keep you from quitting the truth, even as He keeps His own elect. The Lord bless you with all good, and keep you from all evil. The ones who are kept by God are well kept; no one else is kept by Him. There is no keeping like Divine keeping. He says, *"I will be a wall of fire around them"* — *"He kept him as the pupil of His eye"* — *"I the Lord keep it; I will water it every moment; I will keep it night and day that not any hurt it"* — *"The Lord is your keeper"* — *"The Lord will presearve you from all evil. He shall preserve your soul."* We pray, *"Lead us not into temptation, but deliver us from evil,"* and the prayer is directed to our Father in Heaven. You will find a depth of meaning in this first line of the holy hymn of blessing, if you regard it as a benediction of the Father. Do not so regard it exclusively, for there is no clear line of demarcation; each of the three stanzas melt into the other two, and the blessing is still one.

EVENING

Your people shall be willing in the day of Your power, in the beauty of holiness from the womb of the morning: You have the dew of Your youth — Psalm 110:3.

HERE IS A PROMISE concerning time. Christ is not to gather in His people every day, but on one special day, *"the day of His power."* It is not the day when a man feels himself to be the most mighty, that souls are gathered. For God's servants sometimes preach until their self-complacency tells them they have been exceedingly eloquent and that therefore men must be saved. But there is no promise that in the day of OUR power we shall see men gathered to Christ. There are times when the people seem to have a great power of seeking after God, and when they have the power of hearing, but there is no promise that just when an excitement reigns, and when there appears to be power in the creature, that that is the day of God's ingathering. No, but it is *"the day of Your power"* — not of the minister's power, nor of the hearers.

The day of God's power — when is it? It is the day when God pours out His own power on the minister, and the word preached, so that God's children are gathered in. There are times when the ordained servant of the living God will have nothing to do in preaching, but just to open his mouth and allow the words to flow. He will scarcely need to stop and think, but the thoughts will be injected into his mind. And while he preaches he will feel there is a power accompanying the Word preached. Also his hearers will discern it. Some of them will feel as if they were sitting under a sledge hammer beating on their hearts. Others will feel as if truth were stealing into their hearts and slaying all their unbelief, in such a way that they could not resist the blessed Divine power. It will often happen that God's children will find an influence and a might irresistible going with the Word. They have heard that minister before; they were delighted with him and trusted that they had been edified and profited. But on this day there is a special power striking home. Every word is falling on good soil; every blow is hitting the mark. No arrow is shot on this day but that it goes into the center of the soul. Not a syllable is uttered which is not like the word of Jehovah Himself, speaking either from Sinai, or from Calvary.

You are not a God that has pleasure in wickedness . . . . You hate all workers of iniquity — Psalm 5:4, 5.

DAVID is pleading against his cruel and wicked enemies. He uses a most mighty argument. He begs of God to put them away from him, because they were displeasing to God Himself: He says, "When I pray against my tempters, I pray against the very things You hate." You hate evil, Lord. I pray, deliver me from it.

Let us learn here the solemn truth of the hatred which a righteous God must bear toward sin. He has no pleasure in wickedness, however wittily, grandly, or proudly it may array itself. Its glitter has no charm for Him. Men may bow before a successful villain, and forget the wickedness of the battle in the gaudiness of his triumph. But the Lord of Holiness is not such a one as we are. He will not afford evil the least shelter. Neither on earth nor in Heaven shall evil share the mansion of God. Oh, how foolish are we if we attempt to entertain two guests so hostile to one another as Christ Jesus and the Devil. Rest assured, Christ will not live in the parlor of our hearts if we entertain the Devil in the cellar of our thoughts. Sinners are fools written large. A little sin is a great folly, and the greatest of all folly is great sin. All such sinful fools will be banished from the court of Heaven. Earthly kings commonly have fools in their train, but the King of kings will have no fools in His palace above.

"You hate all workers of iniquity" — It is not a little dislike, but a thorough hatred which God bears to workers of iniquity. It is a dreadful thing to be hated by God. Let us faithfully warn the wicked, for it will be a terrible thing for them to fall into the hands of an angry God. And evil speakers will be punished as well as evil workers. All liars shall have their portion in the lake that burns with fire and brimstone. A man may lie without danger of the law of man, but he will not escape the law of God.

EVENING

For there is no faithfulness in their mouth. Their inward part is wickedness. Their throat is an open grave. They flatter with their tongue — Psalm 5:9.

THIS DESCRIPTION of the depravity of mankind is repeated by the apostle Paul, together with some other quotations, and he places them in Romans as being an accurate description of the whole human race — not of David's enemies only, but of all men by nature. Note that remark, *"Their throat is an open grave"* — a sepulcher full of loathsomeness, of poisonous vapors, of pestilence and death. But, worse than that, it is an OPEN grave, with all its evil gases issuing forth, to spread death and destruction all around. So, with the throat of the wicked, it would be a great mercy if it could always be closed. If we could seal the mouth of the wicked in silence, it would be like a grave shut up, no more to produce mischief. If one's throat is an open grave, then all the wickedness of their heart is regurgitated from it.

Take heed of unregenerated man, for there is nothing that He will not say or do to ruin the saints. He will long to destroy your character, and bury you in the grave of his own wicked throat. However, there is one sweet thought here: at the resurrection there will be a resurrection not only of bodies, but characters. This should be a great comfort to a man who has been abused and slandered by evil throats: *"Then shall the righteous shine forth as the sun."* The world may like to think you are vile, and bury your character, but if you have been upright, in that day when the graves shall give up their dead, this open sepulcher of the sinner's throat shall be compelled to give up your heavenly character. Then you will come forth and be honored in the sight of all.

MORNING

In all this Job did not sin, nor charge God foolishly — Job 1:22.

IN ALL HIS TRIAL, and under all this temptation, Job kept right with God. During all the losses of his estate, and the deaths of his children, he did not speak in an unworthy manner. The text speaks admirabley of *"all this,"* and a great *"all"* it was. Some of you are in many troubles, but what are they compared with those of Job? Your afflictions are molehills compared with the Alps of that patriarch's grief. He was suddenly reduced from a peer to a pauper; from a man of great wealth to a person in poverty; from a happy father to a childless mourner. Who can measure or fathom *"all this"*? Yet Job did not sin. Here was the triumph of a gracious spirit. Ah, if God could uphold Job in all this, you may be sure that He can support you. Look to Him for this Divine support.

"all this" — this also alludes to all that Job did and thought and said. He was full to bursting with swelling grief. He shaved his head, tore his garments, and lifted up his voice to the Lord his God. He rose up, for he was a man of action, a man of sensitive and powerful mind, a man of poetic energy, who could not fail to express his emotions in striking symbols. Yet *"in all this Job did not sin."* This is a great deal to say of a man when you see him in the extreme of trial. If in patience he can possess his soul when all the arrows of affliction are wounding him, he is man indeed.

May we ourselves so live that it may be said of us in the end, *"in all this"* we did not sin. He swam through a sea of trouble. The roll of his life story is written with lamentations both within himself and in his outward life. But in all this he did not dishonor the name of his Lord. He did and said many things, but in them all he was patient, resigned, obedient, never uttering a rebellious word.

EVENING

For the oppression of the poor, for the sighing of the needy, I will now rise up, says the Lord. I will set in safety him at whom they puff — Psalm 12:5.

IN DUE SEASON the Lord will hear His elect ones who cry day and night to Him. Even though He may bear long with their oppressors, yet He will avenge them speedily. Note that the mere oppression of saints, however silently they bear it, is in itself a cry to God. Moses was heard at the Red Sea, although he said nothing. Hagar was heard, despite her silence. Jesus feels with His people, and their smarts are mighty orators with Him. And if they sigh and express their misery, then relief comes quickly. Nothing moves a father like the cries of his children. God stirs Himself, overthrows the enemy, and sets His beloved in safety. A puff is too much for the child to bear; the foe is so haughty, laughing one of His little ones to scorn. But the Father comes, and then it is the child's turn to laugh, when he is set above the rage of his tormentor. What virtue there is in a poor man's sighs, that they should move the Almighty God to arise from His throne! The needy did not dare to speak, and could only sigh in secret, but the Lord heard, and could rest no longer; He girds on His sword for the battle. It is a fair day when our soul brings God into her quarrel, for then His arm is bared and the Philistines will regret the day. The darkest hours of the Church are those which precede the break of day. Man's extremity is God's opportunity. Jesus will come to deliver just when His needy ones sigh. O Lord, set Yourself now near at hand; rise up speedily for our help. Should you in your affliction be able to lay hold on the promise of this verse, then you will fetch a fulness of comfort from it. As one may draw out the wine of a whole barrel at one tap, so may a poor soul derive the comfort of the whole covenant to himself through one promise, if he is able to apply it. God promises to set us in safety, and He means by it preservation on earth, and eternal salvation in Heaven.

MORNING

In all this Job did not sin, nor charge God foolishly — Job 1:22.

IN ACTS OF mourning we do not need to sin. You are allowed to weep. You are allowed to show that you suffer by your losses. See what Job did: *"Job arose and tore his mantle, and shaved his head, and fell down on the ground, and worshiped"* and *"in all this Job did not sin."* Job lamented sorely when his beloved children were taken from him. When a dear child is mourned over, tears may not only be perfectly natural, but even holy. Job acted rightly. Much less would have been thought of him if he had not mourned the loss of his children. Weeping is permissible. Did not even Jesus weep?

But there is a measure to be observed in the expression of grief. Job was not wrong in tearing his garment. He might have been wrong if he had torn it into shreds. He was not wrong in shaving his head. He would have erred if he had torn out his hair, as some have done whom despair has turned into maniacs. He deliberately took his razor and shaved his head, and in this he did not sin. It is permissible to wear mourning. Saints have done so in other times. You may weep, for it may perhaps be a relaxing of your strained emotions. Do not restrain the boiling floods of tears. A flood of tears externally may assuage the deluge of grief within. Job's acts of mourning were moderate and seemly, toned down by his faith. It is a shame that Christians so often follow the way of the world at their funerals, not making it clear that they have sorrow for those who do not have hope in Christ. You may wear black so long that it becomes the ensign of rebellion against the will of the Lord. Also, the words of Job were very true, although very strong: *"I came naked out of my mother's womb, and naked I shall return."*

EVENING

In all this Job did not sin, nor charge God foolishly — Job 1:22.

TO COME THROUGH great trial without sin is the honor of the saints. If we are tried, and come forth from it naked as when we were born, we do not need to be ashamed. But if we come out of it without sinning, then the greatness of the affliction increases the honor of our victory. *"In all this Job did not sin"* — the *"all this"* is a part of the glory with which grace covered him. Suppose that your life was all ease — suppose that you were brought up tenderly from a child, well-educated, left with a sufficient fortune to gratify your every wish, happily married, free from sickness, lifted above care and grinding labor and heavy sorrow — what then? Assuredly you could never then be noted for patience. Who would have ever heard of Job if he had not been sorely tried? None would have said of him, *"In all this Job did not sin."* Only by his patience could he be perfected and immortalized. Suppose that your record should be: From birth a sufferer, through life a struggler, at home a wrestler, and abroad a soldier and a cross-bearer — and notwithstanding all this you proved to be full of joy and peace, through strong believing in God; tried to the uttermost, yet found faithful. In such a chronicle there is something worth remembering. There is no glory in being a featherbed soldier, a man bedecked with gorgeous medals, but never beautified by a scar, or enobled by a wound. All that you ever hear of such a soldier is that his spurs jingle on the pavement as he walks. There is no history for this carpet knight. He is just a dandy. He never smelled gunpowder in battle in his life. If he did, he fetched out his cologne to kill the offensive odor. Oh, if we could be wise enough to choose, even were as wise as the Lord Himself, we would choose the troubles which He has appointed to us, and we would not spare ourselves a single pang.

MORNING

In all this Job did not sin, nor charge God foolishly — Job 1:22.

IT IS NOT said that in all this Job was never spoken against. For he was spoken against by Satan to God. And very soon he was falsely accused by men who should have comforted him. You must not expect, dear believer, that you will pass through this world, and have it said at the end of it, "In all this no one ever spoke against him." If you hear it said of a man that he never had an enemy, then you may be sure he never had a friend. He has no friend who never had a foe. Those who secure zealous lovers are pretty sure to call forth intense adversaries. A man who is such a chip in the soup that he never offends anyone, is pretty sure to be equally flavorless in the other direction. The trimmer of his days may dodge through the world without much censure, but he is unlikely to be an out-and-out man of God. A lover of God is not of this world, so the world will hate that one. The blessed and holy Lord Jesus was slandered to the utmost. The ever-blessed God was libeled in Paradise by an old servant who had turned into a backbiting serpent. So you must not wonder if you are abused also. To go through life without slander is not a thing to be expected. But it is worthy of our desire to go through every phase of joy or of sorrow without falling into sin.

Neither is it a chief point for us to seek to go through life without suffering, since the best of the Lord's servants have been matured and mellowed by suffering. Amos, the herdsman, was a bruiser of sycamore figs, a kind of fig that never ripened in Palestine unless it was struck with a rod, and thus was bruised. There are very few of the godly who will fully ripen without affliction. The vine bears but little fruit unless it makes the acquaintance of the knife, and is sternly pruned.

EVENING

Help, Lord, for the godly man ceases; for the faithful fail from among the sons of men — Psalm 12:1.

"HELP, LORD" — A short, but sweet, suggestive, seasonable, and serviceable prayer; a kind of angel's swored, to be turned every way, and to be used on all occasions. The word rendered *"help,"* is largely used for all manner of saving, helping, delivering, preserving, etc. Thus it seems that the prayer is very full and instructive. The Psalmist sees the extreme danger of his position, for a man had better be among lions than among liars. He feels his own inability to deal with such sons of Belial, for "he who shall touch them must be fenced with iron." He therefore turns himself to his all-sufficient Helper, the Lord, whose help is never denied to His servants, and whose aid is enough for all their needs. *"Help, Lord"* is a very useful ejaculative prayer which we may dart up to Heaven on occasions of emergency, whether in labor, learning, suffering, fighting, living, or dying. As small ships can sail into harbors which larger vessels cannot enter, so our brief cries and short petitions may trade with Heaven when our soul is wind-bound, or business-bound (as to longer exercises of devotion) and when the stream of grace seems at too low an ebb to float a more laborious supplication.

"For the godly man ceases." The death, departure, or decline of godly men should be a trumpet call for more prayer. They say that fish smell first at the head, and when godly men decay, the whole commonwealth will soon go rotten. We must not, however, be rash in our judgment on this point, for Elijah erred in counting himself the only servant of God alive, when there were thousands whom the Lord held in reserve. The present times always appear to be peculiarly dangerous, because they are nearest to our anxious gaze, and whatever evils are rife are sure to be observed, while the faults of past ages are further off, and so are more easily overlooked. Yet we expect that in the latter days, *"because iniquity shall abound, the love of many shall wax cold."* Then we must the more thoroughly turn from man, and address ourselves to the Lord of the churches, by whose help the gates of hell shall be kept from prevailing against us.

How long will You forget me, O Lord? Forever? How long will You hide Your face from me? How long shall I meditate in my heart, having sorrow in my heart every day? — Psalm 13:1,2.

TIME FLIES with full-fledged wing in our summer days, but in our winters it flutters painfully. A week in prison is longer than a month at liberty. Long sorrow seems to argue abounding corruption, for the gold which is long in the fire should have been purified. For this reason, the question, *"How long"* may suggest deep searching of heart. Ah, David! Do not be led to talk like a fool. Can God forget? Can Omniscience fail in memory? Above all, can Jehovah's heart forget His own beloved child? Drive away such a thought and hear the voice of our covenant God by the mouth of His prophet, *"But Zion said, The Lord has forsaken me, and my Lord has forgotten me. Can a woman forget her sucking child, that she should not have compassion on the son of her womb? Yes, they may forget, but I will not forget you. Behold, I have engraved you on the palms of My hands. Your walls are continually before Me."* (Isaiah 49:15).

"Forever?" Oh, dark thought! It was bad enough to suspect a temporary forgetfulness, but dare we ask the ungracious question, and imagine that the Lord will forever cast away His people? No, His anger may endure for a night, but His love will abide eternally. *"How long will You hide Your face from me?"* This is a far more rational question, for God may hide His face, and yet He be remembering still. A hidden face is no sign of a forgetful heart. It is in love that His face is turned away. Yet to a real child of God, this hiding of his Father's face is terrible, and he will never be at ease until once more he has his Father's smile. *"How long shall I meditate in my heart, having sorrow in my heart every day?"* In the original there is the idea of setting up counsels in his heart, as if his devices had become many, but unavailing. In this we have often been like David, considering and reconsidering plans day after day, but not discovering the happy device by which to escape from our trouble. Such store is a sad sore. Ruminating on trouble is bitter work. Children fill their mouths with bitterness when they rebelliously chew the pill which they should have obediently taken.

EVENING

Lay hold on eternal life — 1 Timothy 6:12.

THOSE WHO have confessed Christ ought especially to lay hold on eternal life: *"to which you were also called and have confessed a good confession before many witnesses."* Timothy had been baptized, and probably there had been a great number of persons to encourage or watch him as he came forward to confess Christ. This was a double reason why he should hold fast to that of which he had laid hold. O you who have named the name of Christ, having put Him on by that wonderful symbol of death, burial and resurrection, *"Lay hold on eternal life."* Do not play at baptism and the Lord's supper. Let these be stern and sweet realities to you. Lay hold, not only on the symbol alone, but on what the symbol means. Have you been *"buried with Him by baptism into death"*? Then grasp the soul of the symbol. It is not a mere empty form, or only the badge of a sect, but a picture of the end of the old life of the flesh, dying to the world and sin, that we may rise in *"newness of life,"* to walk before God in the land of the living. Of all men, the baptized one should *"lay hold on eternal life."* For, in proportion as his baptism is true, he has no other life to lay hold of, having died and been buried with Christ. Then, also when we come to His table and eat His flesh and drink His blood spiritually, receiving not merely bread and wine as memorials, but Himself by faith, into our hearts. *"Lay hold on eternal life,"* for profession without eternal life is a fearful mockery. Without eternal life, to come to the Lord's supper will be to eat and drink condemnation to yourself, not discerning the Lord's body. You who have professed Him before many witnesses, stand forth and *"lay hold on eternal life."*

Oh you of little faith; why did you doubt? — Matthew 14:31.

WEAK FAITH is too much affected by its surroundings. Peter went on pretty well until he noticed that the stormy wind tossed the waves about furiously, and then he was afraid. Are not many Christians too apt to live by what they feel and see? Do not we often hear a young beginner say, "I know that I am converted, for I feel so happy"? Well, only a new dress is needed to make many a girl happy, or a few pennies will make a youth rejoice. Is this the best evidence that you can bring? Why, if you are very troubled, it may be a better sign of true conversion than feeling happy. It is well to mourn for sin, and to struggle against it, and to try to overcome it. This is a sure mark of grace, a far surer one than overflowing joy. Ah, believer, you will be happy in the highest and best sense if you trust in Jesus. But you will soon lose your happiness if your happiness becomes the ground of your confidence. Happiness is a thing that depends on how things happen. It is often hap-ness, and nothing more. It is a haphazard thing. But faith feasts in Christ, whatever may happen. So it is happy in the happening of sorrow and of grief, because it relies wholly on God. Faith rests on the Lord's faithful word and promise. Another may say, "I feel low and dull; I am heavy even when I try to pray; I cannot pray as I would like." And so you doubt your salvation because of that? Does your salvation depend on the liveliness of your prayers? If you are all up, and then all down, it is a mark of weak faith. If you live by feelings, you will live a wretched life. You will not dwell in the Father's house, but will be a kind of gypsy whose tent is too frail to shut out the weather. Depend on God!

EVENING

Answer me, O Lord, my God! Make my eyes gleam, lest I sleep in death — Psalm 13:3

LIKE THE WATCHMAN who proclaims the daybreak, prayer lifts up her voice. Now the tide will turn and the weeper will dry his eyes. The mercy seat is the life of hope and the death of despair. The gloomy thought that God has hidden from him is still on the Psalmist's soul, and so he cries, *"Answer me, O Lord."* He remembers at once the root of his woe, and cries aloud that it may be removed. The final absence of God is Tophet's fire; even His temporary absence brings His people into the very suburbs of Hell. God is here entreated to see and hear, so that he may be doubly moved to pity. What should we do if we had no God to turn to in the hour of wretchedness?

Note the cry of faith, *"O Lord, my God!"* Is it not a very glorious fact that our interest in our God is not destroyed by all our trials and sorrows? We may lose our gourds, but not our God. The deed to Heaven is not written in the sand, but is eternal.

"Make my eyes gleam" — that is, let the eye of my faith be clear, so that I may see my God in the dark. Let my eye of watchfulness be wide open, that I not be trapped. Let the eye of my understanding be illuminated to see the right way. Perhaps, too, here is an allusion to that cheering of the spirits so frequently called the enlightening of the eyes because it causes the face to brighten, and the eyes to sparkle. Well may we use the prayer, *"Lighten our darkness, we beseech you, O Lord."* For in many respects we need the Holy Spirit's illuminating rays. Darkness engenders sleep, and despondency is not slow in making the eyes heavy. From this faintness and dimness of vision, cause of despair to some, comes slipping forward the iron sleep of death. David feared that his trials would end his life, and he rightly uses his fear as an argument with God in prayer. Deep distress has in it a kind of claim on compassion — not a claim of right, but a plea which has the power of grace.

MORNING

For as I have sworn that the waters of Noah should no more go over the earth, so I have sworn that I would not be angry with you and rebuke you — Isaiah 54:9.

TO BE IN UNION with God is necessary to the happiness of the creature. To have God for its enemy is for the creature to be removed from its foundation and placed where it cannot abide. The whole universe stands because God's power supports it. Only because it is so far in unison with the will of God does it exist in order, peacefulness and joy. Take God away from the world, and the world would become dark, dead, dreary, desolate — no! There would be no world. This great sun, the moon and stars would all subside into their native nothingness, even as the foam melts back into the wave that bears it, and is gone forever. In the same way an intelligent being, a spiritual nature, is lost without its Creator; just as lost as a sheep strayed from the shepherd, lost to all that makes life worth living. It were better for such a creature never to have had an existence, for the wrath of God, when it goes forth in the form of a rebuke on a thoughtful man, is as a seven-fold plague. God's rebuke on any creature is a withering thing, but on an intelligent being it is hellish. Some have felt it to a fearful degree in this life. Remember Cain, who went out from the presence of God a marked man. Who among us would like to have known Cain's dread, living in fear that whoever would find him would kill him; a man accused of the Most High and marked among his fellows. We read of Pashur, in the days of Jeremiah, who had the rebuke of God dwelling on him, so that he became a terror to himself. Remember the word of the Lord in the book of Deuteronomy, where the Lord threatens His erring people: *"And among these nations you will find no ease, nor shall the sole of your foot have rest. But the Lord will give you a trembling heart there, and failing of eyes, and sorrow of mind."*

EVENING

For as I have sworn that the waters of Noah should no more go over the earth, so I have sworn that I would not be angry with you and rebuke you — Isaiah 54:9.

THE WRATH OF GOD does not end with death. This is a truth the preacher cannot mention without trembling, nor without wondering that he does not tremble more. The eternity of punishment is a thought which crushes the heart. You have buried the man, but you have not buried his sins. His sins live, and are immortal. They have gone before him to judgment, or they will follow after him to bear their witness as to the evil of his heart and the rebellion of his life. The Lord God is slow to anger, but when He is once aroused to it, as He will be against those who finally reject His Son, He will put forth all His omnipotence to crush His enemies. He says, *"Consider this, you that forget God, lest I tear you in pieces, and there be none to deliver."* It will be no trifle to fall into the hands of the living God. He will by no means clear the guilty. Forever must His anger burn. We have nothing in Scripture to warrant the hope that God's wrath against evildoers will ever come to an end. Oh, the wrath to come! The wrath which after ages and ages will still be to come, and still to come, and still to come! Well might that mighty preacher, Whitefield, when he preached, lift up his hands and with streaming eyes and breaking heart cry to the crowds, "Oh, the wrath to come, the wrath to come!"

This, then, is what men have most to dread. Did you ever dread it? He that never dreaded it, nor felt in his spirit a trembling and a fear concerning it — alas for him! It is a strong cause for alarm. Well should every believer remember when this awful truth rolled over his or her spirit. It is utterly crushing to realize the lost and hopeless state we are in by nature. But for amazing grace there would be no hope and no future for any.

MORNING

For as I have sworn that the waters of Noah should no more go over the earth, so I have sworn that I would not be angry with you and rebuke you — Isaiah 54:9.

WE OUGHT to believe God's bare word. We are bound to accept His promise as certainty itself, but who will dare to doubt the oath of the Eternal One? You cannot accuse a man of anything worse than perjury. Can you be so profane as to lay this at the door of God? To suspect Him of having sword dishonestly, or dream that He can make a breach of that covenant which He has sealed by an oath — this would be a crime against the thrice-holy God. Shall we tarnish the glory of God by a suspicion that He will break an oath? Yet perhaps we are doing so. Under heavy chastisement do you say, "The Lord is angry with me; He has turned His heart against me"? While you are feeling in your body the smart of fierce disease, or in your estate a gradual decay of your property, or in the person of a dear child or a beloved spouse deceased, do you see the hand of God as being against you? Do you feel like saying, "This cannot be love; the Lord must be so angry with me as to strike me with the blows of a cruel one"? But, dear child of God, you must not allow yourself to think so for a moment. The Lord has sworn that He would not be angry with you, and He cannot break His oath. Nothing but love can guide the hand of His providence. It is not possible that there is even a mixture of motives in His dealings with you. Undiluted affection arranges every step, and perhaps it is because of the greatness of His affection that you are called upon to suffer so grievously. It is well-known that when a father strings up his nerves at last to chastise his darling child, he then gives clearest proof of wise love — for the blow of the rod falls heavier on the father's heart than ever it can on the child's flesh. It is true love of God which whips the erring heir of glory from his sin.

EVENING

For as I have sworn that the waters of Noah should no more go over the earth, so I have sworn that I would not be angry with you and rebuke you — Isaiah 54:9.

THE COVENANT made with Noah was a covenant of pure grace, for Noah found grace in the sight of the Lord. The Lord will deal with us also according to His grace. God destroyed the earth because it was corrupt, and assuredly it is corrupt again. Many times since Noah's day the earth has been polluted with crying sins that might well have provoked God to turn the torrents on our race. Those were horrible days when all men did what seemed good in their own eyes in the days of the Judges. One cannot read the histories of the kings of Israel without feeling sick at heart. The other nations were no better than the Jews, and probably were much worse. But even the favored Jews were as vile as vile can be. Then those horrible days of the Roman emperors, when those who governed the world were monsters in iniquity, and all lands reeked with vice. What cloudy days were those of the Middle Ages, when to be a genuine Christian was to be hunted to death; when every kind of superstition and villainy had sway. The Lord might well have drowned the world in any one of those times quite as justly as He did in Noah's day. It was of His mercy that although He foresaw that the world would be corrupt, and that every imagination of man's heart would still be evil, He yet said that He would not destroy the earth, but that His long-suffering would patiently wait until all His elect should be saved. Now, beloved, this covenant of pure grace is paralleled by the covenant we have been speaking of in your case. He might have been angry with the world a thousand times so as to destroy it with water, but because of His covenant He did not do it. The covenant was not made on account of what men would be, for the Lord knew that they would be evil continually. But He made a covenant because His mercy is great and His tenderness is infinite.

November 4 — MORNING

Christ is all things and in all — Colossians 3:11.

CHRIST IS ALL for us, the surety, the substitute in our stead to bear our guilt: *"For the Lord has laid on Him the iniquity of us all." — "The chastisement of our peace was on Him." — "He has made Him to be sin for us who knew no sin, that we might be made the righteousness of God in Him."* He is also the worker standing in our place to fulfill all righteousness for us. He is the end of the law for righteousness to everyone who believes. All that God requires us to be, Christ is for us. He has not presented to God a part of what was done, but has to the utmost paid all that His people owed. Acting as our forerunner in Heaven, He has taken possession of our inheritance, and as our surety He secures to us our entrance there. For us all, Jesus is all.

And this day He is all TO us. We trust wholly in Him. If you question yourself on many Christian graces, there is one thing you can never doubt, and that is that you know you have no other hope but in the blood and righteousness of Jesus Christ. If a soul can perish relying with all its power on the finished work of the Savior, then I will perish. But if saving faith is an entire reliance on Him whom God has sent forth to be a propitiation for sin, then I can never perish until God's word is broken. Can you not say that? And will it not yield your comfort? Have you anything else you could trust to? Have you one good work that you could rely on? Is there a prayer you have ever offered, an emotion you have ever felt, that you would dare to use to claim salvation for yourself? You must reply that you have nothing; that is, nothing but Christ your Savior; He is all your salvation and all your desire. Putting anything side by side with Him as a ground of your dependence before God is a hateful idea you must reject. Oh, then, assuredly you have the mark of a lamb of Christ, for to all of them "Christ is all things and in all."

EVENING

I will say to the north, Give up; and to the south, Do not keep back — Isaiah 43:6.

AT THIS MOMENT those of us following the footsteps of our King, Jesus, are soldiers of an army which has invaded this world. The land belongs to our great Leader, for He made it. It was right that everywhere, all around the globe, His name should be honored. For He is King among the nations, and their Governor. But our race has revolted and set up another monarch; we have bowed our strength to support another dynasty, the dynasty of darkness and death. We have broken the good and wholesome laws of the great Lord, and have set up new laws and new customs altogether opposed to right and truth. This is a great rebellion, the revolt of mankind, the sedition of sinners. Now, no king will willingly lose His dominions, and therefore the King of kings has sent His Son to conquer this world by force of arms — not by arms of steel, or weapons that cut and kill and wound, yet by arms far more mighty. This earth is yet to be outwardly subdued to the kingdom of the Crown Prince, Jesus Christ, though He has full sovereignty over it. His regenerated people form part of the army of occupation. We have invaded the land allowed to fall into the hands of the Devil. Hard and stern has been the battle to this point. Every inch of ground must be won by sheer force. Effort after effort has been put forth by the church of God under the guidance of her heavenly Leader, and none has been in vain. Previously the Lord has helped us, but there is much yet to be done. Canaanites and Hivites, Jebusites and Philistines must be driven out. Yes, in fact, the whole world seems still to lie in darkness, and under the dominion of the wicked one. Yet we hold here and there a sacred fortress for truth and holiness in the land. These we must retain until the Lord Jesus shall send us more spiritually prosperous times, when the battle shall be turned against the foe, and the kingdom shall be won for our Prince.

For now we see in a mirror dimly, but then face to face. Now I know in part, but then I shall know even as I also have been known — 1 Corinthians 13:12.

ONE OF THE JOYS we are looking for is to come to the general assembly and church of the Firstborn, whose names are written in Heaven, and to have fellowship with those who have fellowship with God through Jesus Christ our Lord.

It is certain that in the next state we shall see and know more of the providence of God than we do now. Here we see the providential acts of God, but it is as in a glass, darkly. There was a glass in the days of the apostles, not a substance such as our windows are now made of, but thick, dull-colored glass, not much more transparent than that used in the manufacture of common bottles. Looking into such a glass would not allow much to be seen. That is like what we now see of Divine providence. We believe all things work together for good to those that love God. We have seen how they work together for good in some cases, and experimentally proved it to be so. But still it is a matter of faith, rather than a matter of sight with us. We cannot tell how every dark and bending line meets in the center of His love. We do not yet perceive how He will make those dark dispensations of trials and afflictions that come on His people really subserve His glory and their good and lasting happiness. But in Heaven we shall see providence as it were face to face. There will be many great surprises to discover how the Lord dealt with us, and how it served His purpose and our good. Some of the circumstances you prayed against may prove to be the best that could have been appointed for us. You may find you have fretted over what was the richest of mercies.

EVENING

For now we see in a mirror dimly but then face to face. Now I know in part, but then I shall know even as I also have been known — 1 Corinthians 13:12.

IT IS SURELY no straining of the text to say that we shall know a great deal more about the doctrines of the gospel, and the mysteries of the faith in the hereafter than we know now. There are some grand doctrines that we love, but even though we love them, our understanding is too feeble to grasp them fully. They are to us mysteries. We reverently acknowledge them, yet we do not dare to explain them. They are matters of faith to us. It may be that even in Heaven there will be counsels of eternal wisdom into which neither saints nor angels can peer. It is the glory of God to conceal some matters. Surely, no creature will ever be able, even when exalted to Heaven, to comprehend all the thoughts of the Creator. We can never be omniscient, as He is. God alone knows everything, and understands everything. But how much more of authentic truth shall we discern when the mists and shadows have been dissolved, none of us can tell — nor how much more we shall understand when raised to that higher sphere and endowed with brighter faculties. Probably, though, things that puzzle us here will be very plain there. Probably we will smile at our ignorance here. I have fancied sometimes that the elucidations of learned doctors of divinity, if they could be submitted to the very least in the kingdom of Heaven, would only cause them to smile at the learned ignorance of the sons of the earth. How little we know, and yet how much we shall know! It is written, *"Then I shall know even as I also have been known"* — we now see things as in a mist, a doctrine here, and a doctrine there. And we are often at a loss to conjecture how one part harmonizes with another part of the same system, or to make out how all these doctrines are consistent. There we shall know and understand. Hallelujah!

November 6 MORNING 311

Even as it has been written, I have made you a father of many nations. This was before God whom he believed, who gives life to the dead and calls the things that are not as if they were — Romans 4:17.

A NOTABLE occasion for faith occurs when a child of God through soul trouble is apprehensive about death. He like Heman cries out, *"My soul is full of troubles, and my life draws near Sheol"* (Psalm 88:3). Although not absolutely dead as to spiritual things, yet the little life which remains seems to be weak, faint, slumbering, and lethargic. Then you may cry, *"I am counted with those who go down into the pit. I am as a man who has no strength; free among the dead, like the slain that lie in the grave, whom You remember no more; and they are cut off from Your hand"* (vss. 4-6). Now is the time to glorify God by believing the promise. You have the sentence of death in yourself, that you may not trust in yourself, but in the Lord Jesus alone. Your old sins rise up and accuse you; your present evil tendencies surround you like a rotting body of death. You find no present comfort or joy in life. Although once you rejoiced before Him, you are forced to sigh as one forsaken by his God, shut up for destruction. Now, even now, you are on a vantage ground for glorifying the Lord by faith. It may be that now you enjoy nothing when you go to Christian services, or while reading or praying at home, the chill of death making every godly exercise a burden. Harassed with fears, worried with cares, tortured by regrets, tried with temptations, you are forced to cry out, *"My God, my God, why have you forsaken me?"* Come now, child of God, look to the strong for strength. You can do nothing, that is clear. Therefore cast yourself on Almighty God, who is able even to quicken the dead. Is there not a foothold here for you? Although you are moaning out, *"O wretched man that I am! Who shall deliver me from the body of this death?"* — grasp this brave hope, *"I thank God through Jesus Christ our Lord."* For, *"The Lord has risen indeed,"* and one that believes in Him, though he were dead, yet shall he live!

EVENING

Even as it has been written, I have made you a father of many nations. This was before God whom he believed, who gives life to the dead and calls the things that are not as if they were — Romans 4:17.

TRUST IN GOD, even though the fig-tree does not blossom, even though there is no herd in the stall, nor flock in the fold, nor corn in the barn. Trust in the promise, *"You shall dwell in the land, and truly you shall be fed."* The Lord who made Heaven and earth can set bread on your table, and put clothes on your back.

Let us trust the Creator concerning His new creation. You bemoan yourself because you are not clothed with power from on high to bring sinners to Jesus. When you get into your class, you may feel yourself to be a dry tree, and not as Aaron's rod which budded and brought forth almonds. If you preach you feel unfit for the hallowed employment. What is worse, the same weakness is almost everywhere. Few seem raised up to preach with power, and to lead on the hosts of God to victory. This is very sad. But suppose death to be everywhere, death in the pew, and death in the pulpit, death among the prophets, and death among the people. Yet the Lord, who calls things that are not as though they were has but to give the word, and great will be the company of those who publish it. Our royal Leader has hidden forces at His command. He can garrison His church in a moment. In her desolation He can people her with such multitudes that she shall ask, "Who has begotten me these?" The Lord can send martyrs if they are wanted, or confessors, preachers, writers, or consecrated men and women of every sort. Let us have no timorous thoughts, but let us glorify God by firm faith. Thus have I set before you the fact that our times of deadness and discontent are grand seasons for believing in Him who quickens the dead, and calls all things into being.

MORNING

Even as it has been written, I have made you a father of many nations. This was before God whom he believed, who gives life to the dead and calls the things that are not as if they were — Romans 4:17.

IF OUR FAITH is to be based on resurrection, what do we know about it? Paul seems to pass over every other resurrection, and to dwell only on the resurrection of our Lord — as in the closing verses of this chapter: *"To those that believe on Him who raised our Lord Jesus from the dead, who was delivered for our sins and was raised for our justification."* You believe that our Lord was crucified, pierced to the heart, dead and buried. A stone was rolled to the mouth of the grave, and it was sealed and guarded that the body not be stolen. Yet He rose from the dead. Realize that resurrection more and more, for your hope lies there. Our Lord *"was delivered for our sins."* God gave Him up to justice, as if He had said, "Take Him away. I have laid on Him the transgressions of My people; take Him to the place of chastisement. Condemn Him, scourge Him, crucify Him; for He is made a curse for My people. I have delivered Him up. I have left Him to suffer, and have hidden My face from Him." See the soldiers leading Him through the streets of Jerusalem. See them fasten His hands and feet with nails to the cruel cross. Behold Him lifted up to die in extreme agony. Then He dies. They take down that precious body, wrap it in white linen, and put it in the sepulcher. He is delivered to the grave for our offenses. There went all my sin, and all your sin, the sins of all believers. He made an end of sin for us in His death. The wrath of God was spent on Him for those sins which were made to meet in the person of the Well-Beloved, and now those sins are gone forever. How do we know? It is so because our Surety is set free. To meet our debt He was put in the prison of death. When He paid the debt, He would be liberated, but not until then. And when He was raised again He *"was raised for our justification"* (Rom. 4:25).

EVENING

Even as it has been written, I have made you a father of many nations. This was before God whom he believed, who gives life to the dead and calls the things that are not as if they were — Romans 4:17.

ABRAHAM looked at the promise, and he could not see how it could be. He had no child, and his wife was old. But God calls him by the name which signified *"Father of a multitude,"* because He viewed him as such. And the Lord talked to him about his household after him, about their number, and about their being aliens in a strange land. To God's foreseeing eye Abraham was what he was to become. He calls the things that *are not as though they were.* Now, faith has the wonderful property of becoming like the God in whom it trusts, and of looking at things as God sees them. O tried one, then you should use your faith to see your troubles as God sees them, that is, as a means to advance you in grace. Look at affliction today as a process that is enriching you. Sinner, when you believe in Jesus, God looks at you as saved, justified, forgiven, and quickened into eternal life. If you believe in Jesus, see yourself as God sees you. It is a great thing for a sinner, dead in himself, to say, *"And yet I live"* — but assuredly he may say it. It is a great thing for one consciously guilty to say, "And yet I am justified" — still, it is true, and it is no presumption to believe it. This is a grand art, to look at things from God's point of view. Faith takes the omnipotence of God, and girds herself with His almighty power. Then faith takes the foresight of God, and although it does not yet appear what we shall be, faith perceives that in Christ the poor, trembling, and guilty soul is made pure, spotless and glorious before God. Believer in Jesus, know yourself to be what the gospel says you are, and hold on to that knowledge. However desperate the tug may be, never let go your conviction that God's view of you in Christ is the true one. God sees the truth of things, and teaches you through faith to see the same.

November 8   MORNING

I will go in the Lord Jehovah's strength; I will speak of Your righteousness, of Yours alone — Psalm 71:16.

THE PSALMIST is confident as to the sufficiency and adaptation of God's strength to every trial or work to which he might be called. The Hebrew is plural, hinting at this, *"I will go in the strengths of the Lord Jehovah."* If I need mental vigor, then God can and will give it to me. If I lack physical strength, then He can and will give it to me. If I need spiritual power, then He can and will give it to me. If the particular demand is for a clear sight, that I may detect and baffle the cunning of the enemy, He can and will give it to me. If I require courage and quick resolve, He can and will give it to me. If it be a patient temper, He can and will give it to me. Nothing is needed by a believer but that strength which God will supply when it is needed. As our days are, so shall our strength be. The supply shall always be equal to the demand of our circumstances.

But you may say, "Oh, but my way is strange. There is a singular difficulty in my case." Friend, do not tell me the particulars, just realize that however strange the case may be, it is not new to God. If you go in the strength of the Lord Jehovah, you have exactly that which is suited for your perplexing path of pilgrimage. It is one of the miracles of God, that to each man He is just such a God as he needs. It is like the Welshwoman who denied that Jesus Christ was not a Jew. She was certain that He was a Welshman. But how was that? How could the Lord Jesus Christ be a Welshman? She answered, "Well, He always speaks to my heart in Welsh." Truly, good woman, He always speaks to my heart in English, and He speaks to the heart of everyone in their mother tongue. The miracle of Pentecost is repeated to all of us when Jesus speaks to us in the language we understand.

EVENING

I will go in the Lord Jehovah's strength; I will speak of Your righteousness, of Yours alone — Psalm 71:16.

THE ONLY TESTIMONY that the Psalmist was going to bear for the rest of his life would be a testimony to the righteousness of the Lord Jehovah. Here was enough work for a lifetime, and here was the one who was at home in the work.

Bear your testimony to the righteousness of God in providence. Stand to it that the Lord never does wrong. He is never mistaken. Whatever He ordains is, and must be, unquestionably right: *"Yes, Lord God Almighty, Your judgments are true and righteous"* (Rev. 16:7). Next, bear witness to His righteousness in salvation. Declare that He does not save without an atonement; that He does not put away sin without being strictly just; that He does not spare the guilty, but has laid on Christ that which was due to the sins of His chosen ones, that He might be *"just and the Justifier of the one who believes."* Go on to tell everybody that the righteousness which saves you is the righteousness of God, not your own righteousness. There is no such thing as human righteousness. The two words make up a contradiction. Any righteousness that you could gain by your own works would be as filthy rags, and filthy rags are not righteousness. We have no personal merit, but we are justified by imputed righteousness. Make mention of the righteousness of Christ which covers you entirely.

Declare the righteousness of God as to a future state. Declare that whatever Scripture speaks of the ungodly is true, and that God is righteous in it. Never mind the cavils and the inventions of this present age. God's character can never be harmed by these dreamers. Stand by your God, and you may rest assured that time will never change the essential truth that He is a holy and a righteous God, and that He will justify His ways to men.

MORNING

The fool has said in his heart, There is no God! They are corrupt. They have done hateful things. There is not one who does good — Psalm 14:1.

THE ATHEIST is a fool pre-eminently, and a fool universally. He would not deny God if he were not a fool by nature. Having denied God, it is no marvel that he becomes a fool in practice. Sin is always folly, and as it is the height of sin to attack the very existence of the Most High, so is it also the greatest imaginable folly. To say there is no God is to lie against the plainest evidence, which is obstinacy. To stifle the consciousness of man is madness. If the sinner could by his atheism destroy the God whom he hates, there would be some sense to it — although there would be much wickedness in his infidelity. It is as if one were to deny the existence of fire when a man is plainly burning in it. Doubting the existence of God will not stop the Judge of all the earth from destroying the rebel who breaks His laws. This atheism is a crime which greatly provokes God, and it will bring down terrible vengeance on the fool who indulges it. The proverb says, *"A fool's tongue cuts his own throat,"* and in this instance it kills both the soul and the body forever. Would to God the mischief stopped there, but one fool makes hundreds. A noisy blasphemer spreads his horrible doctrines as lepers spread the plague. The word used here is *Nabal*, which has the signification of fading, dying, or falling away, as a withered leaf or flower. It is the title given to the foolish man as having lost the juice and sap of wisdom, reason, honesty and godliness. Trapp hits the mark when he calls him "that sapless fellow, that carcase of a man, that walking sepulcher of himself, in whom all religion and right reason is withered and wasted, dried up and decayed." Some translate it the apostate, and others the wretch. With what earnestness should we shun the appearance of doubt as to the presence, activity, power and love of God, for all such mistrust is of the nature of folly. And who among us would wish to be ranked with the fool in the text? Yet let us never foget that all unregenerate men are more or less such fools, practically denying that God is.

EVENING

They have all turned aside. They have together become filthy. There is none doing good; no, not one — Psalm 14:3.

WITHOUT EXCEPTION all men have apostatized from the Lord their Maker, from His laws, and from the eternal principles of right. Like stubborn heifers they have sturdily refused to receive His yoke. Like errant sheep they have found an imagined gap and left the right field. The original speaks of the race as a whole, as a totality. Humanity as a whole has become depraved in heart and defiled in life. *"They have together become filthy"* — as a whole they are spoiled like corrupt leaven; they have become putrid and stinking in their hearts and minds. We do not more clearly see this foulness because we have accustomed ourselves to it. The miller does not note the noise of his own mill. So we are slow to discover our own ruin and depravity. But are all men sinful? The Psalmist says, Yes, they are. He has put it positively. Then he repeats it negatively, *"There is none good, no, not one."* The Hebrew phrase is an utter denial concerning any mere man that he of himself does good, or is good. What can be more sweeping? This is the verdict of the all-seeing Jehovah. As if no hope of finding a solitary specimen of a good man among the unregenerated, the Holy Spirit is not content with saying *all* and *together*, but adds the crushing threefold negative, *"none, no, not one."* What do the opponents to the doctrine of natural depravity say to this? More importantly, what do we feel concerning this? Do we not confess that by nature we are corrupt, and do we not bless the sovereign grace which has renewed us in the spirit of our minds, that sin may no more have dominion over us, but that grace may rule and reign?

MORNING — November 10

O Jehovah, who shall dwell in Your tabernacle? Who shall settle in Your holy mountain? — Psalm 15:1.

O HIGH AND HOLY ONE, who shall be permitted to have fellowship with You? The heavens are not pure in Your sight; You charge Your angels with folly. Who then of mortal mold shall dwell with You? A sense of the glory of the Lord and of the holiness which becomes His house, His service, and His attendants, excites the humble mind to ask this solemn question. Where angels bow with veiled faces, how shall man be able to worship at all? The unthinking may imagine it an easy matter to approach the Most High. In their professed worship they have no questionings of heart as to their fitness. But truly humbled souls often shrink under a sense of utter unworthiness; they dare not to approach the throne of the holy God if it were not for our Lord, our Advocate, who ever lives to make intercession for us, because His righteousness endures forever.

Who will be admitted to be one of God's household, to enjoy communion with Him? Who will be a citizen of Zion, an inhabitant of the heavenly Jerusalem? All men do not have this privilege. Even among professors there are aliens from the commonwealth who have no secret intercourse with God. By law no mere man can dwell with God, for there is not one on earth who answers to the just requirements of His law. These questions are asked of Jehovah, as if none but the Infinite Mind could answer them to the satisfaction of an unquiet conscience. We must hear it from the Lord of the tabernacle what the qualifications for His service are. And having been taught of Him, we will clearly see that only our spotless Lord Jesus, and ones conformed to His image, can ever stand with acceptance before the Majesty on high.

EVENING

He who walks uprightly and works righteousness and speaks truth in his heart — Psalm 15:2.

IN ANSWER to the questions in verse one, Jehovah tells us by His Holy Spirit the character of the man who alone can dwell in His holy hill. In perfection this holiness is found only in the Man of Sorrows, but in a measure it is worked into all His people by God the Spirit. Faith and the graces of the Spirit are not noted here, because this is a description of outward character. But where fruits are found, the root may not be seen, but it is surely there. Note the walk, work, and word of the accepted one: *"He who walks uprightly."* This one keeps himself erect. As one carrying precious but fragile ware in baskets on their heads, they avoid losing their perpendicular. True believers do not cringe as flatterers, wriggle as serpents, bend double as earth-grubbers, or crook on one side as those who have sinister aims. They have the strong backbone of the vital principle of grace within. Being upright themselves, they are able to walk uprightly. Walking is far more important than talking. He only is right who is upright in walk.

"and works righteousness" — His faith shows itself by good works, and so it is not a dead faith. God's house is a hive for workers, not a nest for drones. Those who rejoice that everything is done for them by another, even the Lord Jesus, who hate legality, are the best doers in the world on gospel principles. If we are not positively serving the Lord, and doing His holy will to the best of our power, we may seriously debate our interest in Divine things, for trees which bear no fruit must be hewn down and cast into fire. *"And speaks truth in his heart"* — the fool in Psalm 14 spoke falsely in his heart. Note both here and elsewhere in the two Psalms the striking contrast. Saints not only desire to love and speak truth with their lips, but they seek to be true within. They will not lie even in the closet of their own hearts, for God is there to listen. They scorn double meanings, evasions, equivocations, 'white' lies, flatteries, and deceptions. Truths, like roses, may have thorns about them, but saints wear them in their bosoms.

Maintain my steps in Your tracks, so that my steps may not slip. I have called on You, for You will hear me, O God — Psalm 17:5,6.

UNDER TRIAL it is not easy to behave ourselves correctly. A candle is not easily kept lit when many envious mouths are puffing at it. In evil times prayer is peculiarly needed, and wise men resort to it at once. An old saying says, "When men speak ill of you, live so that no one will believe them." That is good enough advice, but he did not tell us how to carry it out. We have a precept in the text in an example. If we would be preserved we must cry to the Preserver, enlisting Divine support on our side. *"Maintain my steps"* — as a careful driver holds up his horse when going downhill. We have all sorts of paces, both fast and slow, and the road is never long of one sort, but with God to maintain our steps, nothing in the pace or in the road can cast us down. One who has been down once had better redouble his zeal when using this prayer. All of us are weak on our legs through Adam's fall. If our perfect father Adam fell, how shall we, his imperfect offspring, dare to boast?

"in Your tracks" — Forsaking Satan's paths, he prayed to be upheld in God's tracks. We cannot keep from evil without keeping to good. If the bushel is not full of wheat, it may soon be once more full of chaff. In all the appointed ordinances and duties of our most holy faith, may the Lord enable us to run, through His upholding grace. *"that my steps may not slip"* — Slip in God's ways? Yes, the road is good, but our feet are evil, and for this reason they slip, even on the King's highway. Who wonders if carnal men slide and fall in ways of their own choosing, for such ways are full of deadly slimepits? One may trip over an ordinance as well as a temptation. Jesus Christ Himself is a stumbling-block to some, and the doctrines of grace have been the occasion of offense to many. Grace alone can hold up our goings in the paths of truth.

EVENING

Show Your marvelous loving-kindness, O Savior of those who trust in You. By Your right hand save us from those who rise up against us — Psalm 17:7.

HIS LOVING-KINDNESS is marvelous in its antiquity, its distinguishing character, its faithfulness, its immutability, and above all, it is marvelous in the wonders which it works. That marvelous grace which has redeemed us with the precious blood of God's Only-Begotten is here invoked to come to the rescue. That grace is sometimes hidden, so he prays, *"Show"* it. Present enjoyments of Divine love are matchless cordials to support fainting hearts. Believer, what a prayer is this! Consider it well. O Lord, show Your marvelous loving-kindness! Show it to my intellect, and remove my ignorance. Show it to my heart, and revive my gratitude. Show it to my faith, and renew my confidence. Show it to my experience, and deliver me from all my fears. The original word is the same as in Psalm 4:3, *"Set apart Your loving-kindness."* That is, Distinguish Your mercies, set them out, and set apart the choicest to be bestowed on me in this hour of my severest affliction.

"O Savior of those who trust in You — The title here given to our gracious God is eminently consolatory. He is the God of salvation. It is His present and perpetual habit to save believers. He puts forth His best and most glorious strength, using His right hand of wisdom and might to save all those who trust themselves with Him, of whatever rank or class. Happy faith thus to secure the omnipotent protection of Heaven! Blessed God to be so gracious to unworthy mortals, when they have but grace to rely on You! The right hand of God is interposed between the saints and all harm. God is never at a loss for means. His own bare hand is enough. He works without tools as well as with them.

November 12   MORNING

Hide me under the shadow of Your wings, from the wicked who stripped me, even my enemies who go all around me. They are enclosed in their own fat — Psalm 17:8-10.

THE PARENT BIRD completely shields her brood from evil, and cherishes them with the warmth of her own heart, covering them with her wings, even so do with me, most condescending God, for I am Your offspring and You have a perfect parent's love. Confident expectation should keep pace with earnest supplication.

The foes from whom David sought to be rescued were wicked men. It is hopeful for us when our enemies are God's enemies. They are deadly enemies; nothing but our death will satisfy them. The foes of a believer's soul are mortal foes, for they who war against our faith aim at the very life of our life. Deadly sins are deadly enemies, and what sin is there which has not death in its bowels? These foes oppressed David; they laid his spirit waste, as invading armies ravage a country, or as wild beasts desolate a land. He likens himself to a besieged city, and complains that his foes compass him about. It may well quicken our prayers when all around us every road is blockaded by deadly foes. This is our daily position, for all around us dangers and sins are lurking. O God, do protect us from them all.

"They are all enclosed in their own fat" — Luxury and gluttony beget vainglorious fatness of heart. And this shuts up its gates against all compassionate emotions and reasonable judgments. The old proverb says that full bellies make empty skulls, and it is yet more true that they frequently make empty hearts. The rankest weeds grow out of the fattest soil. Riches and self-indulgence are the fuel on which some sins feed their flames. Pride and fulness of bread were Sodom's twin sins (Ezek. 16:49).

EVENING

They now have circled our steps; they set their eyes to cast me to the earth, like a lion who is greedy to tear, and like a young lion sitting in hidden dens — Psalm 17:11,12.

THE FURY of the ungodly is aimed not at one believer alone, but at all the band; they have surrounded us. All the race of the Jews were but a morsel for Haman's hungry revenge, and all because of one Mordecai. The prince of darkness hates all the saints for their Master's sake. The Lord Jesus is the Breaker; He will clear a way for us through the hosts which surround us. The hatred of the powers of evil is continuous and energetic, for they watch every step, hoping that the time may come when they can catch us by surprise. If our spiritual adversaries thus surround every step, how closely should we guard all our movements, lest by any means we should be betrayed into evil! *"They set their eyes to cast me down to the earth"* — John Trapp wittily explains this metaphor by an allusion to a bull when about to run at his victim: he lowers his head, sets his eyes, and then concentrates all his force in the charge. It most probably denotes the malicious jealousy with which the enemy watches the steps of the righteous, as if they studied the ground on which saints tread, looking for some stumbling stone to throw in their way toward Heaven.

Lions are not more greedy, nor their ways more cunning, than are Satan and his helpers when engaged against the children of God. The adversary thirsts after the blood of souls, and all his strength and craft are exercised to the utmost to satisfy his detestable appetite. We are weak and foolish like sheep, but we have a wise and strong Shepherd who knows the wiles of the old lion; he is more than a match for his force. Because of this we will not fear, but will rest in safety in the fold. Let us beware, however, of our lurking foe. For in those parts of the road where we feel most secure, if we do not look about us, our foe may leap on us.

Lay hold on eternal life — 1 Timothy 6:12.

FIGHT, and as you fight, lay hold on the victory. While you are running for Heaven, often anticipate the joys of Heaven. We do not go to Heaven often enough. But you say, "I thought it was when we died we went there." Yes, if you are a believer in Christ, that is sure. But why not go there now? The Christian's position is unique. He is in two worlds at once. Our Lord has made us alive, *"and has raised us up together and made us sit together in the heavenlies in Christ Jesus"* (Eph. 2:6). Do you know that the lower ends of the streets of Heaven are near here? Even now we have heavenly victory when we overcome through the blood of the Lamb. At this moment we have heavenly peace with God, *"being justified by faith, we have peace with God."* Yes, even now we have heavenly holiness, for we are made holy by the work of the Spirit of God in our hearts. Even today we have heavenly communion with God, *"Truly our fellowship is with the Father, and with His Son, Jesus Christ."* Is it not good sometimes to sit down and anticipate the day when you will come into your inheritance? You have heard of a young prince caught by his father putting on the crown. It was awkward in his case, but your Father, the king, will not object to your often putting on your crown. You will then have a new song to sing. Begin to sing it here. You will then have holy work to do, for *"They serve God day and night in His temple."* Serve Him here. Christ is to dwell among us in Heaven; realize that He dwells with us here and now. It was said of an old Puritan that Heaven was in him before he was in Heaven. That is needful for all of us. We must have Heaven in us before we get into Heaven.

EVENING

And now, O Lord God, the word that You have spoken concerning Your servant, and concerning his house; establish it forever, and do as You have said
— 2 Samuel 7:25.

FAITH IN CHRIST never rests in rhapsody. It rests on a *"You have said it."* Ask faith whether it will ever take its standing on anything but a *You have said it*. Faith will answer, "No, I cannot climb to Heaven on a ladder made of dreams; they are too flimsy to bear my feet." Faith, why do you not march on? Why do you not cross the bridge? Faith says, "No, I cannot. It is made up of rhapsodies, and rhapsodies are intoxicating things, and I cannot place my feet on them." Faith will stand on a promise, even if it is no bigger than a grain of mustard seed, but it can never stand on a rhapsody, however large it may be. Faith can build on a *You have said it*, but it cannot build on frames and feelings, on dreams and experiences. Faith only relies on this, *"You have said it."* You must be cautious against superstitions, for some base their salvation on them. Some persons think that the Holy Spirit is a kind of electric shock working in the heart — that there is some mysterious and terrible thing they cannot understand, which they must feel, not only very different from what they ever felt before, but even superior to anything described in God's Word. Now so far from the effectual operation of the Holy Spirit being a dark thing in its manifestation, it is not. It is a thing of simplicity and light when He operates. The way of salvation is no mystery; it is very plain. It is simply, *"believe and live."* And faith needs no mysteries to hang itself on. It catches hold of the bare naked promise of God, and it says, "Lord, do as You have said." Your faith and mine can live on this promise. It can never die on this promise. But faith does not need testimonies of man, nor learning of philosophers, nor eloquence of orators, nor rhapsodies, nor visions, nor direct revelations. It needs nothing else but what God has said applied to the heart. Faith goes to God and says, "Lord, do as You have said."

November 14   MORNING

Then Zedekiah the king said, Behold, he is in your hand. For the king cannot do anything against you — Jeremiah 38:5.

"IT IS better to take refuge in Jehovah than to trust in princes" (Ps.118:9). Zedekiah professed to be a friend of Jeremiah, yet when the princes sought permission to put the prophet to death, Zedekiah's friendship was not worth much. He said, *"He is in your hand; for the king cannot do anything against you."* Instead of protecting his friend and adviser, he delivered him and left him as a lamb at the mercy of wolves. It seems very natural to men for them to trust in men. Yet Scripture warns us that, *"Cursed is the man that trusts in man, and makes flesh his arm."* If you make a mortal man your confidence, you will find your anchor has no grip. Even good men are but broken reeds and cannot bear the strain of the day of trouble. And the bad men are like sharp spears; they stab the man who dares to lean on them. But, if we cannot trust in men, we think that surely we may trust in princes. If honor were banished from all the rest of the world, it ought to find a home in the breasts of kings. May we not trust in great men, in noble men, men of high standing? No, for *"It is better to take refuge in Jehovah than to trust in princes."* For princes are but men, and not always the truest of men. They are seldom the best of men. At the end of his life Wolsey is reported as saying to Sir William Kingston, "Had I but served my God with half the zeal I served my king, He would not in my age have left me naked to my enemies." If "uneasy lies the head that wears the crown," certainly the heart which rests on the crown-wearer should be uneasy. Trust in God, and you will trust the true *"King, immortal, invisible."*

EVENING

Then Zedekiah the king said, Behold, he is in your hand. For the king cannot do anything against you — Jeremiah 38:5.

WHEN A MAN is timid about doing right, and can be easily persuaded to do wrong, there is a lack of the fear of God in him. One that fears God is under no necessity to fear anybody else. True godliness infuses courage into the heart. In this respect also, *"perfect love casts out fear."* If you have learned to tremble before the great, almighty, living God, you have ceased to tremble before any living man; in actuality he is a dying man. For truly life is in God; natural man is a creature that will die and perish like the moth: *"Who are you, that you should be afraid of a man that shall die, and of the son of man that shall be made as grass, and forget the Lord your Maker?"* (Isa. 51:13). If we had a sense of God's presence everywhere we would not dare consent to sin. Then we would be like the three holy ones who stood for God before Nebuchadnezzer, saying, "Yes, we see the burning, fiery furnace, but we also see the living God." The king said, *"It will be heated seven times hotter."* They heard this furious threat of the despot, but they also heard a voice that Nebuchadnezzar could not hear, the voice of God telling them to serve Him. And He strengthened them to do so. John Calvin noted, "All acknowledge that it is better to trust in the Lord, and yet there is scarcely one among a hundred who is fully persuaded that God alone can afford him sufficient help. That man has attained a high rank among the faithful, who resting satisfied in God, never ceases to entertain a lively hope, even when he finds no help on earth." Luther calls it the "art of arts, and that which he had well studied, not to put confidence in man." And of trust in God, he called it the most pleasant and sweetest of all sacrifices, the best of all services we perform to God.

MORNING

I have loved you with an everlasting love — Jeremiah 31:3.

THE TEXT IS FOLLOWED by this: *"Therefore with loving-kindness I have drawn you."* If God loves you with an everlasting love, He has drawn you by His loving-kindness. Is it so, or not? Has He drawn you by His Holy Spirit, so that you have followed on? Are you a believer? Do you carry Christ's cross? You have been drawn to this. Take home these gracious words, then: *"I have loved you with an everlasting love."* If you have not been so drawn, do you not wish you were? Oh, it were worth dying a thousand deaths to be a Christian after that fashion of Christianity which is based on everlasting love! Here is a glorious foundation: love without beginning, love without end — love that is free, sovereign, unchangeable — love not bought by our merit, nor produced by our efforts or entreaties. This love comes to us because God will love, because He has chosen in His divine sovereignty to love us. *Everlasting love;* why the syllables are music to our souls! If you can climb that height, you have climbed where it is worth-while to abide forever. O man, if you cannot claim this, at any rate desire it. Go humbly on your knees to Christ Jesus, and look to Him, and live.

But, child of God, if you know these drawings, and if it is true that God has loved you with an everlasting love, then are you resting? Do you say, "I have a feeble hope"? What? How can you talk so? Anyone who realizes that he is loved with an everlasting love should swim in an ocean of joy. Not a wave of trouble should disturb the glassy sea of such a one's delight. If this will not make one happy, what will? Come, we must have no more hanging of heads. Hallelujah! Hallelujah! If the Lord has loved me with an everlasting love, I will not be cast down, though the earth is removed. His love is better than wealth, better than health, better than honor, better than usefulness. *Everlasting love* is better than all things, and you who believe have it.

EVENING

Remove from me the way of lying, and favor me with Your law — Psalm 119:29.

"THE PROPHET here desires to be confirmed by God against all corruptions in doctrine, and disorder in conversation, which Satan by his witty and wily instruments seeks to set abroad in the world. These are called *"the way of lying,"* 1. Because they are invented by Satan, the father of lies; 2. They are countenanced by man's wit, the storehouse of lies; 3. They seem to be that which they are not, which is the nature of lies; 4. They are contrary to God and His truth, that uncovers the lies" (Richard Greenham).

"He opposes the law of God to the way of lying. First, because it is the only rule of all truth, both in religion and in manners. That which is not agreeable to it is but a lie which will deceive men. Secondly, it destroys and will at length utterly destroy all contrary errors. As the rod of Aaron devoured the rods of the enchanters, so the word, which is the rod of the mouth of God, will in the end eat up and consume all untruths whatsoever. Thirdly, according to the sentence of this word, so shall it be to every man; it deceives none. Men will find by experience that it is true. He who walks in a way condemned by the Word will come to a miserable end. And on the contrary it cannot but be well with those who live according to this rule." (William Cowper)

"David had ever the book of the law. For every king of Israel was to have it always by him, and the Rabbis say, written with his own hand. But, *'Favor me with Your law,'* that is, he desires he might have it not only written by him, but on him — to have it imprinted on his heart, that he might have a heart to observe and keep it. That is the blessing he begs for, *'favor me with Your law,'* on terms of grace, merely according to Your own favor and good pleasure. Here is, 1., The sin deprecated, *'Remove from me the way of lying;'* 2. The good supplicated and asked, *'Favor me with Your law.'* In the first clause you have his malady; David had been enticed into a course of lying. In the second we have his remedy, and that is the law of God." (Thomas Manton)

MORNING — November 16

Judge me, O Jehovah; for I have walked in my integrity. I have trusted also in Jehovah; I shall not slide — Psalm 26:1.

IT IS A SOLEMN appeal to the just tribunal of the heart-searching God, warranted by the circumstances of the writer, regarding the particular offenses with which he was wrongly charged. Worn out by the injustice of men, the innocent spirit flies from its false accusers to the throne of Eternal Right. Anyone who dares to carry his suit to the King of kings needs to have a clear case. Such an appeal as this is not to be rashly made on any occasion. As to the whole of our walk and behavior, it should never be made at all, except we plead our justification by Christ Jesus. A far more fitting prayer for a sinful mortal is the petition, *"Do not enter into judgment with Your servant."*

"I have walked in my integrity" — David held integrity as his principle, and he walked in it as his practice. He had not used any traitorous or unrighteous means to gain the crown, or to keep it. He was conscious of having been guided by the noblest principles of honor in all his actions with regard to Saul and his family. What a comfort it is to have the approval of one's own conscience! If there is peace within the soul, the blustering storms of slander which howl around us are of little consideration. When the little bird of conscience within my bosom sings a merry song, it is no matter if a thousand owls hoot at me from without. Faith is the root and sap of integrity. One leaning on the Lord is sure to walk in righteousness. David knew that God's covenant had given him the crown. So he took no indirect or unlawrful means to secure it. He would not slay his enemy in the cave, nor allow his men to strike him when he slept. Faith will work hard for the Lord, and in the Lord's way. But faith will refuse to lift a finger to fulfill the devices of unrighteous cunning. Rebekah acted out a great falsehood in order to fulfill the Lord's decree in favor of Jacob — this was unbelief; but Abraham trusted the Lord to fulfill His own purposes, and took up the knife to slay his son — this was faith. Faith trusts God to accomplish His own decrees.

EVENING

I have walked in Your truth; I have not sat with lying men — Psalm 26:3,4.

BE AS CAREFUL as you can, that the persons you choose for your companions are those that fear God. The man in the gospel was possessed with demons, dwelling among tombs and conversing with graves and carcases. You are far from walking after the good Spirit if you choose to converse with open sepulchers, with those that are dead in sins and trespasses. David proves the sincerity of his course by his care to avoid such society. There is a twofold *truth:* 1. Truth of doctrine. The law is the truth, free from all dross of corruption and falsehood of error. 2. Truth of affection, or of the inward parts. This is called *"Your truth,"* or, God's truth, though man is the subject of it — partly because it proceeds from Him, partly because it is so pleasing to Him. In this respect a broken heart is called the *"sacrifice of God."* (Psalm 51:6). As if he had said, I could not have walked in the power of religion, and in integrity, if I had associated with vile and vain company. I could never have walked in Your precepts if I had *"sat with lying men."* 1. Sitting is a posture of choice. It is at a man's liberty, whether he will sit or stand. 2. Sitting is a posture of pleasure. Men sit for their ease, and with delight. The glorified are said to *"sit in the heavenlies"* (Eph. 2:6). 3. Sitting is a posture of staying or abiding (2 Kings 5:3). Standing is a posture of going, but sitting of staying. The blessed, who will forever be with the Lord and His chosen ones, are said *"to sit down with Abraham, Isaac, and Jacob, in the kingdom of Heaven"* (Matt. 8:11).

"In neither of these senses does David *"sit with lying men."* He might, as occasions required, use their company, but he dared not knowingly choose such company. They could not be the object of his election who were not the object of his affection. He said, *'I hate the assembly of evildoers.'* To his sorrow he was sometimes among them, but not to his solace. They were to him as the Canaanites, pricks in his eyes, and thorns in his sides. It caused grief, not gladness, that he was forced to be among the profane" — George Swinnock.

MORNING

Blessed is he . . . whose sin is covered; blessed is the man to whom the Lord does not impute iniquity, and in whose spirit is no guile" — Psalm 32:2.

WHERE SINCERITY IS, God approves of that soul, as a holy righteous person, notwithstanding that mixture of sin which is found in him. As God does not like the saint's sin for his sincerity, so he does not unsaint him for that. God will set His hand to Lot's testimonial, that he is a righteous man. And though many sins are recorded in the Scripture which he fell to — and foul ones, too — yet Job is regarded perfect, because the frame of his heart was sincere, the tenure of his holy life holy. He was rather surprised by his sins as temptations, than they entertained by him on choice. Though sincerity does not blind God's eye that He should not see the saint's sin, yet it makes Him see it with a pitiful eye, and not a wrathful one. *'In all this,* God says, *"Job did not sin."* And at the very close of his combat, God brings him out of the field with this honorable testimony to his friends, they who had taken so much pains to bring his godliness into question: they had not spoken right of His servant Job. Truly God said more of Job than Job dared say of himself. He freely confesses his unadvised, even froward speeches, crying out, *'I abhor myself, and repent in dust and ashes."* God saw Job's sin attended with sincerity, and so He judged him perfect and righteous. Job saw his sincerity dashed with many sad failings, and this at the end made him rather confess his sin with shame, than to glory in his grace. God's mercy is larger to His children than their charity is many times to themselves, and to their fellow-saints.

(Abridged from *The Christian in Complete Armor*, William Gurnall.)

EVENING

I have left Myself seven thousand in Israel, all the knees which have not bowed to Baal, and every mouth which has not kissed him" — 1 Kings 19:18.

IT IS AS IF GOD SAID, Comfort yourself, Elijah. Though My number is not great, yet neither is there such a dearth of saints as you fear in this ungodly age. It is true their faith is weak; they dare not justle with the sins of the age as you do. Yet those night-disciples, that for fear carry their light in a dark lantern, have some sincerity, and this keeps them from polluting themselves with these idolatries. They must not, shall not be disowned by Me. Yea, God who bids us to be most tender of His lambs, is much more tender with them Himself. Note how the apostle John describes three ranks of saints: *"fathers," "young men," "little children."* The Spirit of God chiefly shows His tender care of them, mentioning them first (vs. 12). And He leaves the sweet promise of pardoning mercy in their lap and bosom, rather than in that of either of the other: *'I write to you, little children, for your sins are forgiven to you for My name's sake."* But are not the sins of the fathers, and of the young men, also forgiven? Yes, who doubts it? But He does not particularly apply it to them, as to these. It is because these little ones, from the sense of their own failings — out of which the others were more grown — were more prone to dispute against this promise in their own bosoms. Yea, He does not only in plain terms tell them their sins are forgiven, but meets with the secret objection coming forth from their trembling hearts in opposition to this good news, they fretting over their own vileness and unworthiness. He stops its mouth with this: *"forgiven for My name's sake"* — a greater name than the name of their biggest sin, however much it discourages them from believing — William Gurnall.

November 18 — MORNING

He will glorify Me, for He will take that which is Mine and will tell it to you. All things that the Father has are Mine — John 16:14,15.

HERE YOU have the Trinity, and there is no salvation apart from the Trinity. It must be the Father, the Son, and the Holy Spirit. *"All things that the Father has are Mine"* — and the Father has all things. They were always His; they are still His, and they always will be His. They cannot become ours until *all things that the Father has* are in the hands of Christ, by virtue of the representative character of Christ standing as the surety of the covenant that the *all things* of the Father are passed over to the Son, that in turn they may be passed over to us: *"It pleased the Father that in Him should all fulness dwell; and of His fulness we have all received."* But yet we are so dull that we could never get at it, although the conduit pipe is laid to the great fountain. We are lame, but in comes the Third Person of the Divine unity, God the Holy Spirit, and He receives of the things of Christ, and then delivers them to us. So through Jesus Christ we do actually receive what is in the Father, by way of the Holy Spirit.

In the Father — the honey is in the flower, which is at such a distance from us that we could never extract it. In the Son — the honey is in the comb, prepared for us in our Immanuel. But then, next, we have honey in the mouth — the Spirit taking all things, and making application of them, by showing them to us, and working in us to eat and drink with Christ. By Him we share these *all things* — not only the benefits, but Himself. We enjoy the honey of His grace, and we have become sweet to God. His sweetness has been conveyed to us in this manner.

EVENING

For Your loving-kindness is before my eyes — Psalm 26:3.

THE LOVING-KINDNESS of the Lord is an object of memory and a ground of hope. A sense of mercy received sets a fair prospect before the faithful mind in its gloomiest condition, for it yields visions of mercies yet to come, visions not visionary, but real. Dwell on that celestial word, *"loving-kindness."* It has a heavenly savor. Is it not an unmatchable word, unexcelled, unrivaled? The goodness of the Lord to us should be before our eyes as a motive actuating our conduct. We are not under the bondage of the law, but we are under the sweet constraints of grace, which are far more mighty, although far more gentle. Men sin with the law before their eyes, but Divine love when clearly seen sanctifies the conduct. If we were not so forgetful of the way of mercy in which God walks toward us, we would be more careful to walk in the ways of obedience toward Him. The Psalmist was preserved from sin by his assurance of the truthfulness of God's promise, which truth he endeavored to imitate as well as to believe. Note from this verse that an experience of Divine love will show itself in a practical following of Divine truth. Those who neglect either the doctrinal or practical parts of truth must not wonder if they lose the experimental enjoyment of it. Some talk of truth; it is better to walk in it. Some vow to do well in the future, but their resolutions come to nothing. Only the regenerate man can say, *"I have walked in Your truth."*

Not only is the Psalmist not an open offender against God's laws, but he has not even associated with the lovers of evil. He kept aloof from the men of Belial. A man is known by his company. If we keep apart from the wicked, it will always be evidence in our favor if our character is impugned. He who was never in the silo is not likely to have stolen the corn. He who never went to sea is not the man who scuttled the ship.

MORNING

The heavens declare the glory of God — Psalm 19:1.

THE BOOK of nature has three leaves: the heavens, the earth, and the sea. The heavens are the first and most glorious; by this we may see the beauties of the other two. Any book without its first page would be sadly imperfect; and especially the great book of nature, since its first pages, the sun, the moon, and the stars, supply light to the rest of the volume, and are the keys without which the writing which follows would be dark and undiscerned. Man walking erect was evidently made to scan the skies, and he who begins to read creation by studying the heavens begins at the right place.

The heavens are plural for their variety: the watery heavens with their clouds of countless forms; the aerial heavens with their calms and tempests; the solar heavens with all the glories of the day; and the starry heavens with all the marvels of the night. What the Heaven of heavens must be has not entered the heart of man, but there all things are telling the glory of God. Any part of creation has more instruction in it than the human mind will ever exhaust, but the celestial realm is peculiarly rich in spiritual lore. The heavens declare, or are declaring; for the continuance of their testimony is intended by the participles employed. Every moment of God's existence His power, wisdom and goodness are being sounded abroad by the heavenly heralds which shine on us from above. He who would guess at Divine sublimity should gaze upward into the starry vault. He who would imagine infinity must peer into the boundless expanse. He who desires to see Divine wisdom should consider balancing the planets and their orbits. He who would know Divine fidelity must mark the regularity of the planetary motions. He who would attain some conceptions of Divine power, greatness, and majesty, must estimate the forces of attraction, the magnitude of the fixed stars, and the brightness of the whole celestial train. It is not merely glory that the heavens declare, but the *"glory of God,"* for they deliver to us such unanswerable arguments for a conscious, intelligent, planning, controlling and presiding Creator, that no unprejudiced person can remain unconvinced by them.

EVENING

I will awake early — Psalm 57:8.

WE NEED to awaken our souls in praise, or else we shall at times fail altogether in the duty. Only the wakeful are full of praise. Sleeping birds do not sing. The very best praises God receives from earth are from His troubled saints. But then they are awake, for the stokes of the rod have aroused them. When the three holy children sung in the fire, their song was sweet indeed. Yet had they not been thoroughly in earnest, they would not have poured forth a holy hymn. When martyrs have magnified God standing on the burning fagots, they have given God better praise than even the angels can give. It was in an old fable that the nightingale was made to sing by the thorn that pricked her breast. Many a child of God has poured forth his sweetest music when the thorn of affliction has pierced his heart. Wake up your souls, you that are despondent; you that are depressed; you that have a deceased child; you that are expecting soon to go to the grave with those you love; you that have been losing your property; you that are pinched with poverty. Wake up your souls to praise God still, for unless you are well awake you will forget to extol Him. Remember what Job did, when he sat on the dunghill scraping himself with a bit of broken pottery: he praised God and said, *"The Lord gave, and the Lord has taken away; blessed is the name of the Lord."* It was grand of this old patriarch of Uz to be able to extol his Lord in this way, and it was because he was fully awakened by his afflictions. May your innermost parts be so energetic with the power of grace that you may spontaneously and earnestly bless the Lord at all times, in all circumstances.

November 20   MORNING

The voice of the Lord is full of majesty — Psalm 29:4.

ALL GOD'S works praise Him, whether they are magnificent or minute. They all reveal the wisdom, the power, and the benevolence of their Creator. But there are some of His more majestic works which sing the song of praise louder. Some of His doings seem to be engraved in larger letters than usual. Such are the lofty mountains. Such are the rolling seas, too mighty to be managed by man, but held in check by God. Such are the thunders and lightnings, the glances from God's eyes, and the utterings of His voice. The philosophers tell us that the thunders can be accounted for by natural causes. We believe this, but we prefer to look to the first great Cause for their origin, and are content to consider them as the voice of God. It is marvelous what effect the thunder has on all kinds of men. In two verses of Horace he sings like a true Ithurean, despising God and intending to live in merriment. But by and by he hears the thunder and acknowledges that there must be a Jehovah who lives on high, and he trembles before Him. The most wicked of men have been obliged at times to acknowledge that there is a Creator. Men of the stoutest nerve and the boldest blasphemy have become weak when God has manifested Himself in the mighty winds, or in a storm. *"He breaks the cedars of Lebanon."* He brings down the stout hearts; He lays down the mighty; He obliges those who never acknowledged Him, to reverence Him when they hear His voice and see His power in nature. But the Christian hears the voice of God when he hears His thunder, and will look upwards to God and forget the earth as thunder rolls.

EVENING

Praise waits for You, O God of Zion; and to You shall the vow be paid. O prayer-hearing One, to You shall all flesh come — Psalm 65:1,2.

THE PRAISE which God accepts presents itself under a variety of forms. There is praise for God in Zion, and it is often spoken. But there is often praise for God by silence also. There are some who cannot sing vocally, but before God they sing best. Some sing very harshly and inharmoniously to our ears, and yet God may be pleased with them more than the noise of skilfully played music.

"O prayer-hearing One" — "This is one of His titles of honor; he is a God that hears prayer. And it is as truly ascribed to Him as mercy or justice. He hears all prayer, therefore, *"to You shall all flesh come."* He never rejects any that deserve the name of prayer, however weak, however unworthy the petitioner be: *"He is rich to all that call on Him"* — *"You are plenteous in mercy to all that call on You"* — *"He is a reward of them that diligently seek Him"* (Rom. 10:12; Ps. 86:5; Heb. 11:6). This must be believed as certainly as we believe that God is. As sure as God is the true God, so sure is it that none who sought Him diligently departed from Him without a reward. He rewards all seekers, and if all, then why not me? You may well doubt that He is God, as doubt that He will not reward, nor hear prayer: *"If any of you lack wisdom, let him ask of God, who gives to all men liberally, and does not upbraid; and it shall be given to him"* (James 1:5). (David Clarkson)

MORNING

So then we should not sleep as the rest do, but we should watch and be sober
— 1 Thessalonians 5:6.

DO YOU remember in David's life when he went into Saul's camp and found the king and his guards all asleep? Certain men of war ought to have watched Saul, but no one at all was awake. And David and his warrior went all among the sleepers. They came to where the king lay and took a cruse of water and his spear. Little did Saul know as he slept so calmly that Abishai was saying to David, *"Let me stirke him; it shall be but this once."* How easily that strong hand would have pinned the king to the ground with his javelin! Only one stroke, and it would be done, then David's enemy would pursue no more. O sleeping sinners, do you also sleep, lying in imminent danger? At this very moment Satan is saying to God, "Let me strike him; I will strike him but once. Let me prevent his hearing the gospel ever again. Let me thrust the javelin of unbelief into his soul but this once, and then there will not ever be any more light dawn on him, and he will never be saved." Slumbering sinner, wake up! Man, the knife is at your throat, and can you lie there in your sins and sleep? The spear is ready to strike, and will you still dream that all is well with you? The angel of justice hovers above you. Or, as Christ puts it in the parable, there has come one into the vineyard to look at you, and has found you barren, has seen no fruit. These three years he has come and now is saying, "Cut it down! Why does it obstruct the ground?" O mercy, stay the axe, so that this sinner may turn to the living God before it is too late.

EVENING

Come, hear, and let me tell, all you who fear God, what He has done to my soul
— Psalm 66:16.

BEFORE they were told to come and see. Now it is *"Come and hear."* Hearing is faith's seeing. Mercy comes to us by way of ear-gate. *"Hear, and your soul shall live."* They saw how awesome God was, but they heard how gracious He was. *"All you who fear God"* — These are a fit audience when a good man is about to relate his experience. It is well to select our hearers when inward soul matters are our theme. It is forbidden us to throw pearls before swine. We do not want to furnish wanton minds with subjects for their comedies. So it is wise to speak of personal spiritual matters where they can be understood, and not where they will be burlesqued. All God-fearing men may hear us, but be far from the profane. *"And let me tell what He has done for my soul"* — Let me count and recount the mercies of God to me, to my soul, my best part, my most real self. Testimonies ought to be borne by all experienced Christians, that the younger and feebler ones may be encouraged by the recital of God's blessings, and so they more strongly will put their trust in the Lord. To declare man's doings is needless; they are too trivial. Besides, they have enough trumpeters of man's deeds. To declare the gracious acts of God is instructive, consoling, inspiriting, and beneficial in many respects. Let each man speak for himself, for a personal witness is the surest and most forcible of witnesses. Second-hand experience lacks the flavor of first-hand interest. Let no mock modesty restrain the grateful believer from speaking of his dealings with God, or rather of God's dealings with him, for this is justly due to God. And do not let a witness feel forced to shun the use of the first person in telling what God has done for his or her soul — for this is most correct when detailing the ways of love of our Lord. We must not be egotists, but when we bear witness of what the Lord has done for our souls, we cannot but refer to ourselves.

November 22   MORNING

You have let men ride at our head. We went through fire and through water, but You brought us out to plenty — Psalm 66:12.

THERE WAS a great variety of such perils, and of contrary sorts. *"We went through fire and through water"* — either of which singly and alone denotes an extremity of evils. Through water, *"Save me, O God; for the waters have come in to my soul. I sink in deep mire, where there is no standing; I have come into deep waters, where the floods overflow me"* — or through fire, *"And I will set My face against them; they shall go out from one fire, and another fire shall devour them. And you shall know that I am Jehovah, when I set My face against them"* (Ps. 69:1,2; Ezek. 15:7). But when through both successively, one after the other, this denotes an accumulation of miseries, or trials, as we read Isaiah 43:2, with God's promise to His people in such conditions: *"When you pass through the waters I will be with you, and through the rivers, they shall not overflow you; when you walk through fire, you shall not be burned; neither shall the flame kindle on you."* This promise is acknowledged here by the Psalmist to have been performed when God was with the three children when they walked through Nebuchadnezzar's fire; also with the sons of Israel when they went through the water of the Red Sea (Thomas Goodwin).

"You brought us out to plenty" or, *"to saturation, satisfaction"* — "The hand of God led them in that fire and water of affliction through which they went. But who led them out? The Psalmist tells us in these words. They were in fire and water before. Fire is the extremity of heat and dryness; water is the extremity of moistness. A moist place (marginal reading) elegantly shadows that comfortable and contented condition into which the good hand of God had brought them, a place flourishing most in fruitfulness. (Joseph Caryl)

EVENING

If I regard iniquity in my heart, the Lord will not hear me — Psalm 66:18.

THOUGH THE subject-matter of a saint's prayer is founded on the Word, yet if the end he aims at is not leveled right, this is a door at which his prayer will be stopped: *"You ask, and receive not, because you ask amiss, that you may consume it on your lusts"* (James 4:3). Take a Christian in his right temper, and he aims at the glory of God. Yet, as a needle that is touched with a magnet may be removed from its point to which nature espoused it, though trembling until it again recovers it — so a gracious soul may in a particular act vary from aiming at the glory of God, being jogged by Satan; yea, disturbed by an enemy near home, one's own unmortified corruption. Do you not think it possible for a saint, in distress of body and spirit, to pray for health in the one, and comfort in the other, with too selfish a respect to his own ease and quiet? Yes, surely. And to pray for gifts and assistance in some eminent service, with an eye to his own credit and applause; or to pray for a child with too inordinate a desire that the honor of his house may be built up in him — is this not possible? And this may be understood as the sense, in part, of that expression, *"If I regard iniquity in my heart, the Lord will not hear me."* For though to desire our own health, peace, and reputation is not an iniquity in itself, when contained within the limits that God has set. Yet when they overflow at such a height as to overtop the glory of God; yea, to stand but in a level with it; they are an abomination. That which in the first or second degree is wholesome food would be rank poison in the fourth or fifth. So, Christian, catechise yourself before you pray, saying, "O my soul, what sends you on this errand? Know your own mind, what you pray for, and you may soon know God's mind how you shall succeed." Secure to God His glory, and you will soon be heard." (William Gurnall)

Praise waits for You, O God in Zion; and to You shall the vow be paid. O prayer-hearing One, to You shall all flesh come. — Psalm 65:1,2.

SOME TRANSLATORS conceive that the main idea is that of continuance. It remains; it abides, for Zion does not break up when the assembly is gone. We do not leave the holiness in the material house, for it never was in the stone and the timber, but only in the living assembly of the faithful. The people of God, as they never cease to be a church, should maintain the Lord's praise perpetually as a community. Their assemblies should begin with praise and end with praise, and ever be conducted in the spirit of praise. There should be in all our solemn assemblies a spiritual incense altar, always smoking with the incense of unceasing prayer, with thanksgiving which is made up of humility, gratitude, love, consecration, and holy joy in the Lord. And it should be for the Lord alone; it should never go out day or night, for *"His mercy endures forever."* Let our praises endure forever. He makes the outgoings of the morning to rejoice. Let us celebrate the rising of the sun with holy psalm and hymn. He makes the closing in of the evening to be glad. Let Him have our vesper praise. *"One generation shall praise Your works to another, and shall declare Your mighty acts."* If His mercy should cease, then there might be some excuse for staying our praises. But even if it should seem to be so, men who love the Lord would say with Job, *"Shall we receive good at the hand of the Lord and shall we not also receive evil? The Lord gave, and the Lord has taken away; and blessed is the name of the Lord."* Let our praise abide, continue, remain, and be perpetual. To fall asleep blessing God, to rise in the night to meditate on Him, and when we awake in the morning to feel our hearts leap in the prospect of His presence during the day — this is attainable, and each of us should reach it.

EVENING

Praise waits for You, O God in Zion; and to You shall the vow be paid. O prayer-hearing One, to You shall all flesh come. — Psalm 65:1,2.

UPON ZION there was erected an altar dedicated to God for the offering of sacrifices. Except when prophets were commanded by God to break through the rule, burnt offering only was to be offered there. The worship of God on high places was contrary to the Divine command: *"Take heed to yourself that you do not offer your burnt offerings in every place that you see; but in the place which the Lord shall choose in one of your tribes, there you shall offer your burnt offerings, and there you shall do all that I command you."* So the tribes on the other side of Jordan, when they erected a memorial altar, disclaimed all intention of using it for the purpose of sacrifice, saying, *"God forbid that we should rebel against the Lord, and turn this day from following the Lord, to build an altar for burnt offerings, for food offerings, or for sacrifices, beside the altar of the Lord our God that is before His tabernacle."*

In fulfillment of this ancient type, we also *"have an altar by which they have no right to eat that serve the tabernacle"* (Heb. 13:10). Into our spiritual worship allow no observers of materialistic ritualism to intrude. They have no right to eat at our spiritual altar, and there is no other at which they can eat and live forever. There is but one altar: Jesus Christ our Lord. All other altars are impostures and idolatrous inventions. Whether of stone, or wood, or brass, they are the toys with which those amuse themselves who have returned to the beggarly elements of Judaism, or else the apparatus with which clerical jugglers dupe the sons and daughters of men. Holy places made with hands are now abolished. They were once the figures of the true, but now that the substance has come, the type is done away with (Heb. 9:14). The all-glorious person of the Redeemer, God and Man, is the great center of Zion's temple now, and the only real altar of sacrifice.

MORNING

Things of iniquity are mightier than I; as for our transgressions, You atone for them"
— Psalm 65:3.

INFINITE LOVE has made us clean, every whit. Although we were black and filthy with sin, we are washed; washed in the priceless blood of the Lamb! Praise Him for this! Go on and you find, *"Blessed is the man whom You choose and cause to come near."* Is not the blessing of access to God an exceeding choice one? Is it a light thing to feel that even though once far off, we are made near through the blood of Christ — and this because of electing love? You subjects of eternal choice, can you be silent? Has God favored you above others, and can your lips refuse to sing? No, you will magnify the Lord exceedingly, because He has chosen you to Himself for His peculiar treasure. Read on, and praise God that we have an abiding place among His people, *"That he may dwell in Your courts."* Blessed is God that we are not to be cast out and driven out after a while, but we have an entailed inheritance among the sons of God. We praise Him that we have the satisfaction of dwelling in His house as children. *"We shall be satisfied with the goodness of Your house, of Your holy temple."* Clutch this Psalm, as many others, to your breast and let it say to you that there are ten thousand reasons for taking down the harp of your soul and sing God's praises. Yea, there are ten thousand times ten thousand reasons for speaking well of *"Him who loved us, and gave Himself for us."* Truly, *"The Lord has done great things for us, of which we are glad."* If these great things have been done, our souls must be glad; yea, they cannot help but be glad; they must overflow with gratitude to God for all His goodness in providing a Savior as a sacrifice to atone for our sins.

EVENING

So let us draw near the throne of grace with boldness, so that we may receive mercy and find grace to help in time of need — Hebrews 4:16.

TRUE PRAYER is an approach of the soul by the Spirit of God to the throne of God. It is not the utterance of words. It is not alone the feeling of desires, but it is the advance of the desires to God, the spiritual approach of our new nature towards the Lord our God. True prayer is not a mere mental exercise, nor a vocal performance, but it is far, far deeper than that: it is spiritual commerce with the Creator and Ruler of Heaven and earth. God is a Spirit unseen by mortal eye, only to be perceived by the inner man. Our spirit within us, made to live by the Holy Spirit at our regeneration, discerns the Great Spirit, communes with Him, offers requests to Him, and receives answers of peace from Him. It is a spiritual business from beginning to end. Its aim and object do not end with man, but reach to God Himself.

In order for such prayer to occur, the work of the Holy Spirit Himself is needed. If prayer were of the lips alone, we would only need breath in our nostrils to pray. If prayer were of the desires alone, many excellent desires are easily felt, even by natural men. But when it is spiritual desire and spiritual fellowship of the human spirit with the Great Spirit, then the Holy Spirit Himself must be present all through it, to help our infirmities, to give life and power — or else true prayer will never be presented, but the thing offered to God will wear the name and have the form, but the inner life of prayer will be far from it.

Further, it is clear from the connection of our text that the interposition of the Lord Jesus Christ is essential to acceptable prayer. As prayer will not truly be prayer without the Spirit of God, so it will not be prevailing prayer without the Son of God. He, as our great High Priest, must go within the veil for us. Through His crucified person the veil must be entirely taken away. For until then we are shut out from the living God.

So let us draw near to the throne of grace with boldness, so that we may receive mercy and find grace to help in time of need — Hebrews 4:16.

IN PRAYER God is to be viewed as our Father. That is the aspect which is dearest to us, but still we are not to regard Him as though He were such as we are. Our Savior has qualified the expression *"Our Father"* with the words, *"who is in Heaven."* Close at the heels of that condescending name, in order to remind us that our Father is still infinitely greater than ourselves, He has taught us to say, *"Hallowed be Your name; Your kingdom come."* So our Father is still to be regarded as a King, and in prayer we come not only to our Father's feet, but we come also to the throne of the great Monarch of the universe. The mercy seat is a throne, and we must not forget this.

If prayer should be always regarded by us as an entrance into the courts of the royalty of Heaven; if we are to behave ourselves in the presence of an illustrious Majesty; then we are not at a loss to know the right spirit in which to pray. If in prayer we come to a throne, it is clear that our spirit should be one of lowly reverence. It is expected that the subject in approaching to the king will pay him homage and honor. The pride that will not own the king, the treason which rebels against the sovereign will should avoid any near approach to the throne it despises. Let pride bite the curb at a distance; let treason lurk in the corners, for only lowly reverence may come before the King himself when he sits clothed in His robes of majesty. The King before whom we come is the highest of all monarchs, the King of kings, the Lord of lords. Emperors are but the shadows of His imperial power. They call themselves kings by Divine right, but what divine right do they have? Commons sense laughs them to scorn. Our Almighty God alone has divine right, and to Him only does the kingdom belong. He is *"the blessed and only potentate."*

EVENING

So let us draw near to the throne of grace with boldness, so that we may receive mercy and find grace to help in time of need — Hebrews 4:16.

WE ARE CALLED to the throne of grace, not to the throne of law. Rocky Sinai once was the throne of law, when God came to Paran with ten thousand of His holy ones. Who desired to draw near to that throne? Even Israel might not. Bounds were set about the mount; and if but a beast touched the mount, it was stoned or thrust through with a dart. O you self-righteous ones who hope that you can obey the law, and think that you can be saved by it, look to the flames that Moses saw, and shrink, and tremble, and despair. To that throne we do not come now, for through Jesus the case is changed. To a conscience purged by the precious blood there is no anger on the Divine throne.

And, blessed be God, we are not to speak of the throne of ultimate justice. Before that we shall all come, and as many of us as have believed in Jesus, these will find it to be a throne of grace as well as of justice. He who sits on that throne shall pronounce no sentence of condemnation against anyone who is justified by faith. But it is not to the place from which the resurrection trumpet shall ring out that you are called now. Not yet do we see the angels with their vengeful swords come forth to strike the foes of God. Nor are the great doors of the Pit opened to swallow the enemies who would not have the Son of God to reign over them. We are still on praying ground and pleading terms with God. And the throne to which we are bidden to come, and of which we speak at this time, is the throne of grace. It is a throne set up on purpose for the dispensation of grace, a throne from which every utterance is an utterance of grace. The scepter stretched out from it is the scepter of grace. The decrees proclaimed from it are purposes of grace. The gifts scattered down its golden steps are gifts of grace.

November 26   MORNING

So let us draw near to the throne of grace with boldness, so that we may receive mercy and find grace to help in time of need — Hebrews 4:16.

BECAUSE IT IS a throne of grace, all the petitioner's miseries shall be pitied. Suppose you come to the throne of grace with the burden of your sins. There is One on the throne who felt the burden of sin in ages long ago, and He has not forgotten its weight. Suppose you come loaded with sorrow. There is One there who became well-acquainted with sorrow, all to which humanity can be subjected. Are you depressed and distressed? Do you fear that God has forsaken you? There is One on the throne who in His sacrificial agonies said, *"My God! My God! Why have You forsaken Me?"* It is a throne from which grace delights to look on the miseries of mankind with tender eye, to consider them and relieve them. Come, then, you that are not only poor, but wretched, whose miseries make you long for death, and yet you dread it. You captive ones, come in your chains. You slaves, come to have the irons removed from your souls. You who sit in darkness, come blindfolded as your are. The throne of grace will look on you if you cannot look on it. You will receive, although you have nothing to give. You will be delivered, although you cannot raise a finger to deliver yourself.

"The throne of grace" — The word grows as you turn it over in your mind. It is a most delightful reflection that if you come to the throne of God in prayer you may feel a thousand defects, and yet there is hope. But even if your prayers have defects in knowledge, remember that it is a throne of grace, and your Father knows that you have need of these things. Therefore, pray without ceasing, and you will find grace in time of need.

EVENING

So let us draw near to the throne of grace with boldness, so that we may receive mercy and find grace to help in time of need — Hebrews 4:16.

GRACE IS enthroned this day because Christ has finished His work and has gone into Heaven. It is enthroned in power. When we speak of its throne, we mean that it has unlimited might. Grace does not sit on the footstool of God, nor does it stand outside in the courts of God. It sits on the throne. It is the reigning attribute; it is the king today. This is the dispensation of grace, the year of grace. Grace reigns through righteousness to eternal life. We live in the era of reigning grace, for since He ever lives to make intercession for believers, Jesus is able *"to save to the uttermost those that come to God by Him."* Sinner, if you were to meet grace in the byway, like a traveler on his journey, make its acquaintance and ask its influence. If you should meet grace as a merchant on the exchange, with treasure in hand, court its friendship. It will enrich you in the hour of poverty. If you should see grace as one of the peers of Heaven, highly exalted, seek to get its ear. But, oh, when grace sits on the throne of God, then close with it at once. It can be no higher; it can be no greater; for it is written, *"God is love"* — which is an alias for grace. Oh, come and bow before it; come and adore the infinite mercy and grace of God. Do not doubt, or hesitate. Grace is reigning. Since grace is thus enthroned, you must come and receive it. For grace is enthroned by conquest, by right, and by power. And it is enthroned in glory, for God glorifies grace. It is one of His objects now to make His grace illustrious. He delights to pardon penitents. He delights to look on wanderers and restore them, to show His reclaiming grace. He delights to look on the brokenhearted and comfort them, that He may show His consoling grace.

I will bless the Lord at all times; His praise shall always be in my mouth. My soul will make its boast in the Lord — Psalm 34:1,2.

HE IS RESOLVED and fixed, *"I will."* He is personally determined, let others do what they may. He is intelligent in head and inflamed in heart; he knows to whom the praise is due, and what is due, and for what, and when. To Jehovah, and not to second causes our gratitude is to be rendered. The Lord by right has a monopoly in His creature's praise. Even when a mercy may remind us of our sin with regard to it, as in this case David's deliverance from the Philistine king was sure to do, we are not to rob God of His merit of honor because our conscience justly awards a censure to our share in the transaction. Even though the hook was rusty, yet God sent the fish, and we thank Him for it. *"At all times"* — in every situation, under every circumstance; before, in, and after trials; in bright days of glee, and in dark nights of fear. He would never have finished praising, because he was never satisfied that he had done enough. He felt that he always fell short of what the Lord deserved. Happy is the one whose fingers are wedded to his harp. The one who praises God for mercies shall never lack a mercy for which to praise. To bless the Lord is never unseasonable.

Our thankfulness is not to be a dumb thing. It should be one of the daughters of music. Our tongue is our glory and it ought to reveal the glory of God. What a blessed mouthful is God's praise! How sweet, how purifying! If men's mouths were always filled with praises, there would be no repining against God, or slander of neighbors. If we continually rolled this dainty morsel under our tongue, the bitterness of daily affliction would be swallowed in joy. God deserves blessing with the heart, and extolling with the mouth — good thoughts in the closet, and good words in the world.

Boasting is a very natural propensity. If it were used as in this cast, the more it were indulged the better. The exultation of this verse is no mere tongue bragging; David's soul is in it. The boasting is meant and is felt before it is expressed.

EVENING

But I will always hope and will yet praise You more and more — Psalm 71:14.

LET US urge ourselves to this resolution of praising God more and more. It is humbling to remember that we may very well praise God more than we have, for we have praised Him very little as yet. What as believers we have done in glorifying God falls far, far short of His due. Upon consideration, surely each of us will admit this. Think what the Lord has done for you. Some years ago you were in your sin, and death and ruin confronted you. Did you not expect in your first joy of pardon to have done more for Him, to have loved Him more, to have served Him better? What are the returns you have made for the blessings you received? Are they all fitting, or adequate? The farmer looks at his field ripening with precious grain; he has expended so much in rent, so much in plowing, so much in enriching the soil, so much for seed, so much for weeding — there is the harvest, and it yields a good profit; he is contented — but has he given his praise to God? Look at your heart as if it were a field. God has reclaimed it from the wild waste it was, by a power no less than omnipotence. He has hedged it, plowed it, and weeded sin out of it. He has watered it, for the bloody sweat of Christ has bedewed it to remove the primeval curse. God's own Son has given His whole self that this barren waste, your heart, may become a garden. Yet what is the harvest? Is it adequate for the labor expended? What praises have you given back to Him for this wondrous harvest in your heart? Let us all be shamed into a firm resolve, and say it with resolute spirit, "By the good help of infinite grace, I having been so great a laggard, will quicken the pace of my praises, and I will yet praise Him more and more."

November 28   MORNING

But I will always hope and will yet praise You more and more — Psalm 71:14.

BECAUSE OUR HOPES grow brighter and are nearer every day to their fulfilment, therefore the volume of our praise increases. *"But I will always hope, and will yet praise You more and more"* — A dying hope would bring forth declining songs; as the expectations grow more dim, so would the music become more faint. But a hope immortal and eternal, flaming forth each day with more intense brightness, brings forth a song of praise, will gather new force, because it continues to rise. See well to your faith and to your hope, for otherwise God will be robbed of His praise. It will be in proportion as you hope for the good things which He has promised to your faith that you will give to Him the praise which is His royal revenue, acceptable to Him through Jesus Christ, and abundantly due from you.

David had not been slack in praise. Indeed he was the sweet singer of Israel, a choir-master to the Lord. Yet he vowed to praise Him more and more. Those who already do much are usually the people who will do more. He was growing old, but would he praise God more when he was weakened by age, than when he was young and vigorous? If he could not excel with his voice, yet would he with eagerness and earnestness of heart. He was in trouble, too; yet he would not allow the heyday of his prosperity to surpass in its notes of loving adoration the dark hour of his adversity. For him on no account could there be any going back. He had adored the Lord when he was but a youth keeping his father's flock. Harp in hand, standing beneath the spreading tree he had worshiped the Lord his Shepherd, whose rod and staff were his delight.

EVENING

Your righteousness is like the great mountains; Your judgments are a great deep. O Lord, You keep man and beast — Psalm 36:6.

LIKE THE mountains Your righteousness is firm and unmoved, lofty and sublime. As hurricane winds do not shake the Alps, so the righteousness of God is never in any degree affected by circumstances. He is always just. Who can bribe the Judge of all the earth, or by threatening compel Him to pervert judgment? The Lord would not allow His righteousness to be set aside even to save His elect. No awe inspired by mountain scenery can equal that which fills the soul when it beholds the Son of God slain as a victim to vindicate the justice of the Inflexible Lawgiver. Right across the path of every unholy man who dreams of Heaven stand the demands of Divine righteousness, which no unregenerate sinner can ever meet. Against the great day of the Lord's wrath God has laid up in the mountains of His righteousness dreadful ammunition of war with which to overwhelm His adversaries.

God's dealings with men are not to be fathomed by every boaster who demands to see a why for every wherefore. The Lord is not to be questioned by us as to why this and why that. He has His reasons, but He does not choose to submit them to our foolish consideration. Far and wide, terrible and irresistible like the ocean, are the providential dispensations of God. At one time they appear as peaceful as the unrippled sea; at another they are tossed with tempest and whirlwind, buts evermore they are most glorious and full of mystery. Who will uncover the springs of the sea? Then how may anyone hope to comprehend the providence of the Eternal God? As the deep mirrors of the heavens, so the mercy of the Lord is to be seen reflected in all the arrangements of His government on earth, and over the profound depth the covenant rainbow casts its arch of comfort — for the Lord is faithful in all that He does.

Trust not in oppression, and become not vain in robbery; if riches increase, set not your heart on them — Psalm 62:10.

THIS ROBBERY and wrong is done two ways: to God and to man. He who puts his trust for salvation in any other but God loses not only his salvation, but also robs God of His glory, and does God manifest wrong — as did the Jews who said as long as they trusted to the queen of heaven all things prospered with them; but when they listened to the true preachers of God's word, all things came to a worse state, and they were overwhelmed with scarcity and trouble." (John Hooper)

"*'Become not vain in robbery'* — What? Would he have them serious in robbery? No; the meaning is this: Do not trust in a thing of nought. If you rob, oppress, deceive, or wrong others, you trust to a vain thing, in a thing that is not, in a thing that will never do you good. When you think to get riches by wrong dealing, or closely circumventing others, you *'become vain in robbery.' 'If riches increase, set not your heart on them'* — We naturally love riches, and so we naturally spend thoughts on them, both how to get and how to keep them. If a man has riches, or an increase of riches, it is not unlawful for him to think of them. Yet we should be sparing of our thoughts about riches, for the bent of our thoughts should always be on God. What the Psalmist forbids is the settling of our hearts on riches. It is as if he had said, Let not your thoughts stay or dwell there. Riches are transient things, so they should have but our transient thoughts. *'Set not your heart on them'* — for they may quickly be unsettled. Samuel spoke to Saul in the same language about his worldly concern, when he went to seek his father's asses, saying, *'Set not your mind on them.'* It seems Saul was overburdened with thought about them. But Samuel is saying, Do not be solicitous about them, for greater things are coming to you." (Joseph Caryl)

EVENING

All flesh is as grass, and all the beauty of it as the flower of the field! The grass withers, the flower fades, because the Spirit of the Lord blows on it — Isaiah 40:6,7.

LOOK CAREFULLY at this chapter. What is the subject of it? It is the Divine consolation of Zion. Zion has been tossed to and fro with conflicts. She had been smarting under the result of sin. To remove her sorrow, the Lord bids His prophets announce the coming of the long-expected Deliverer, the end and accomplishment of all her warfare and the pardon of all her iniquity. There is no question as to the theme of this prophecy, for the prophet goes on to foretell the coming of John the Baptist as the harbinger of the Messiah: *"Prepare the way of the Lord; make straight a highway in the desert for our God."* The New Testament again and again refers this to the Baptist and his ministry. The object of the coming of the Baptist, and the mission of the Messiah whom he heralded, was the manifestation of Divine glory. Note the fifth verse: *"The glory of the Lord shall be revealed, and all flesh shall see it together; for the mouth of the Lord has spoken it."* Was it needful to mention man's mortality in this connection? No, but there is much more appropriateness in the succeeding verses, if we see their deeper meaning. In order to make room for the display of the Divine glory in Christ Jesus and His salvation there would come a withering of all the glory in which man boasts himself. The flesh would be seen in its true nature as corrupt and dying, and the grace of God alone would be exalted. First this was seen in John the Baptist's ministry, and the preparatory work of the Holy Spirit in men's hearts, in order that the glory of the Lord should be revealed and human pride forever confounded.

November 30   MORNING

I will awake early — Psalm 57:8.

AT ALL TIMES when we are praising God, our minds should be in a state of wakefulness. We ought to always be praising Him, and we ought always to be wakeful when we do so. It is a shame to pray with the mind half asleep. It is an equal shame to attempt to praise God until all the power of the mind are thoroughly aroused. David is a most fitting example, for he sings, *"Wake up, my soul! Wake up, psaltery and harp! I will awake early."*

In private thanksgiving we should be fully awake; the song of our solitude should be full of living joy. There is far too little private singing nowadays. We often hear about private prayer, but very seldom of private praise. Yet there ought to be as much private praise as private prayer. I fear private thanksgiving has grown to be a sleepy affair. Then as to public worship, how earnest it ought to be! Yet how seldom it is hearty and real. How often do we hear half-awake singing! Sometimes we depend on a musical box with its pipes, keys and bellows to do all our adoration for us. The heathens of Tibet turn the wind to account religiously, by making it turn their windmills and pray for them. And we follow their example by an ingenious adjustment of pipes, making the same motive power perform our praise. Where this machinery is not adopted, the Lord is robbed of His praise by other methods. Sometimes a few skilled voices of persons who would be equally at home at the opera, or the theater, as in the house of God, are brought in to perform the singing of psalms for us. And that is supposed to be pleasing to God, these formal notes substituting for the praise of the entire assembly. How far different is the genuine song of gracious men, who lift up their voices to the Lord because their hearts adore Him!

EVENING

Praise waits for You in Zion, O God; and to You shall the vow be paid. O prayer-hearing One, to You shall all flesh come — Psalm 65:1,2.

NOTE THAT it is praise exclusively rendered to God: *"Praise for You, and ALL praise for You"* — NO praise for man, or for any other who may be thought to be, or pretend to be, worthy of praise. There are places called houses of God where the praise is given to 'the Virgin;' where praise has waited for the designated 'saints;' where incense has smoked to the heavens; where songs and prayers are sent up to deceased 'martyrs,' and 'confessors,' who are credited with having power with God. Beloved, this may be so in Rome, but it is NOT so in Zion. To God, and to God alone, the praise of the true church must ascend.

If Protestants and Baptists are free from this deadly error, they often are guilty of another. For in worship they often minister to themselves. This is done when they make the tune and manner of the song to be more important than the matter of the song. Where organs, choirs, and spotlighted singing men and women are left to do the praise of the congregation, men's minds are more occupied with the performance of the music that with the Lord, who alone should be praised. God's house is meant to be sacred to Himself, but too often it is made into an opera house, with Christians forming the audience. This is not an assembly adoring God. Unless great care is taken, the same thing may happen amid the simplest worship, even though everything which does not savor of gospel plainness is excluded. For in that case we may drowsily drawl out the words and notes, with no heart in it whatever. To sing with the soul, this only is to offer acceptable song. Friends, we do not come together to amuse ourselves, or to display our powers of melody, or our aptness in creating harmony. We come to pay our adoration at the footstool of the great King of kings, to whom alone be glory forever and ever. True praise is for God alone!

MORNING

The Lord is my rock and my fortress and my deliverer, my God, my strength — I will trust in Him. He is my shield and the horn of my salvation — Psalm 18:2.

DWELLING AMONG the crags and mountain strongholds of Judea, David had escaped the malice of Saul. Here he compares his God to such a place of concealment and security. Believers are often hidden in their God from the strife of tongues and the fury of the storm of trouble. The clefts of the Rock of Ages are safe abodes. When almost captured, the Lord's people are rescued from the hand of the mighty, for He is mightier than they. This title of *"deliverer"* has many sermons in it, and it is well worthy of the study of all experienced saints. There is a boundless wealth in this expression, *"my God."* It means that He is your perpetual, unchanging, infinite, eternal good. Any who can truly say, *"my God,"* may well add, "my Heaven, my all."

"My strength" — This word is really, *"my rock,"* in the sense of strength and immobility. He is my sure, unchanging, eternal confidence and support. So the word rock occurs twice, but it is no tautology. The first time it is a rock or crag for concealment, for a stronghold — but here it is for firmness and immutability. *"I will trust in Him"* — Faith must be exercised or the preciousness of God is not truly known. God must be the object of faith, or faith is mere presumption. *"My shield"* — God wards off the blows of our the enemies of our faith, shielding us from the fiery darts and venom of the world, the flesh, and the Devil. The Lord furnishes His warriors with weapons both offensive and defensive. Our armory is completely stored so that none need go to battle unarmed. *"The horn of my salvation"* — enables you to push down your spiritual foes, and to triumph over them with holy exultation. God is also *"my high tower"* — a stronghold planted high above and beyond the reach of all enemies. From the heights we can look down on their fury without alarm, and can survey a wide landscape of mercy reaching even to the goodly land beyond Jordan. Here are many titles given to God, that we might profitably examine each one at leisure. Summing up the whole, as Calvin wrote, David here equips the faithful from head to foot.

EVENING

In my distress I called on Jehovah, and I cried to my God. He heard my voice out of His temple, and my cry went before Him, into His ears — Psalm 18:6.

THE SORROW, the cry, the descent of the Divine One, and the rescue of the afflicted, are here set to a holy music worthy of the golden harps of angels. The Messiah, our Savior, is the main and chief subject of this song, over and beyond David or any other believer. While studying it you will become more and more sure that every line here has its deepest and profoundest fulfilment in the Messiah. Death, like a cruel conqueror, seemed to twist the cords of pain round about David, he being a type of the later treatment of the Messiah. He was hemmed in with threats of the most appalling sort. Like a mariner broken by storm and driven on rocks, he found himself in a sad plight, this man after God's own heart. But it is the way Jehovah deals with His sons. Torrents of ungodliness threatened to swamp all true worship, attempting to take away the godly man's hope as a thing to be despised. This threat was so far fulfilled, that even the hero who slew Goliath began to be afraid. The most courageous of men, who for a rule hope for the best, may sometimes fear the worst. Beloved, David knew the depth of the meaning of this verse, and Messiah even more so.

"The sorrows of Hell were all around me" — From all sides the hell-hounds barked furiously. A cordon of demons hunted this man of God, and every way of escape seemed closed up. Satan knows how to blockade our coasts with the warships of sorrow. But blessed be God, the port of prayer is still open. With it grace can run the blockade bearing messages from earth to Heaven, and blessings will return from Heaven to earth to the faithful.

MORNING

Jehovah rewarded me according to my righteousness; according to the cleanness of my hands He has repaid me — Psalm 18:20.

VIEWING this Psalm as prophetical of the Messiah, these strongly expressed claims to righteousness are readily understood, for His garments were white as snow. Considered as the language of David, they have perplexed many. Yet the case is clear, if the words are not strained beyond their original intention. Even though the dispensations of Divine grace are to the fullest degree sovereign and irrespective of human merit, yet in the dealings of Providence there is often discernible a rule of justice by which the injured are at length avenged, and the righteous are ultimately delivered. David's early troubles arose from the wicked malice of envious Saul, who no doubt prosecuted his persecutions under cover of charges brought against the character of this *"man after God's own heart."* These charges were utterly false, and here David asserts that he had a grace-given righteousness which the Lord had given him in defiance of all his slanderers. Before God this man was a humble sinner, but before his slanderers he with unblushing face could speak of the *"cleanness of his hands"* and of the righteousness of his life. If one cannot plead innocence before men, then that one knows little of the sanctifying power of Divine grace. There is no self-righteousness in an honest man who knows that he is honest, not even if he believes that God rewards him in providence because of his honesty; for this is often a most evident matter of fact. It would be self-righteousness indeed if we transferred such thoughts from the region of providential government into the spiritual kingdom. For there grace reigns not only supreme, but sole in the distribution of favors. It is not contrary to the doctrine of salvation by grace, and not evidence of a Pharasaic spirit, when a gracious man stoutly maintains his integrity and vigorously defends his character in the face of slanderers. Is David to deny his own consciousness, and so despise the work of the Holy Spirit, by hypocritically agreeing that he is worse than he is? A godly man prizes his integrity.

EVENING

For Jehovah your God walks in the middle of your camp, to deliver you and to give up your enemies before you. Therefore your camp shall be holy —Deuteronomy 23:14.

WHEREVER YOU ARE, be holy. Do not say, "Now we have one or two friends coming, and we may indulge ourselves somewhat" — be holy. Let the conversation and the entertainment be holy. Do not let only the church meeting be holy, but let the family gathering be holy, whether at Christmas, or on holiday, or at any other time. Let the common meals be holy, no excess or murmuring being tolerated. Let the board and bed be holy. Let the mind and body be holy. Let the commonest act you do be holiness to the Lord. *"Holiness becomes Your house, O God"* — but holiness becomes also all the houses of God's people. Holiness is ordained for every servant of God, and any that does not wear this garment has disgraced himself and his Master. In fact he is wearing the livery of his King's enemies. When Oliver Cromwell was first contending with king Charles, the soldiers who joined him were mostly gentlemen-farmers, and they wore their own buff jerkins. As many on the other side were dressed much the same, mistakes were made. In the rough-and-tumble fighting they did not know cavalier from roundhead. So Cromwell said on a certain occasion that all his soldiers must be dressed in a certain color; not a man in his army came again without such a coat on. Well, holiness is the white clothing of the believer. Be sure you put it on; otherwise how shall we know you to be a believer? Do not wear the colors of the world, and blend in with them; for you will not then be apt to be mistaken for an enemy of God.

For the Lord your God walks in the middle of your camp, to deliver you and to give up your enemies before you. Therefore your camp shall be holy — Deuteronomy 23:14.

THE CHURCH OF GOD is in many respects comparable to a camp. It is a camp for separation. Men who are encamped are separated from the traders, householders, and others outside the camp. They are separated from the adversaries with whom they are at war. When you come near to a camp you will be challenged by the sentry, for you must not come there without warrant. In wartime a picket is sure to be in your path, whichever way you approach the camp. For during a campaign warriors are a separated people and must keep themselves so. So ought the church of God to be. We are crusaders, separated from the mass for the service of the cross which we bear on our hearts. We are in an enemy's country, and we must keep ourselves to ourselves very much, or else we will certainly fail to have the holy military discipline which the Commander of our salvation would have us strictly enforce. An attempt is being made here and there to make the church like the world; it has already been carried out by actual experiment. The most ridiculous and even discreditable things are in such cases done in the name of Christianity, and even under cover of church purposes. O friends, this custom comes from the lowest depths; it is full of the cunning of Satan. It will be our destruction if the attempt should succeed. The great object of a Christian should be to separate the church more and more entirely from the world. Our Lord was not of this world; yea, they crucified Him outside the gate. Therefore, *"Let us go forth to Him outside the camp, bearing His reproach"* (Heb. 13:13). The reproach today, dreaded by feeble minds, is that of being 'narrow-minded,' 'bigoted,' 'strict,' 'precise.' Willingly take it up. It is Christ's reproach. Let us not attempt to escape it.

EVENING

Where is your God? — Psalm 42:10.

"DAVID might rather have said to them, Where are your eyes? For God is not only in Heaven, but also in me. Though David were shut out of the sanctuary, yet David's soul was a sanctuary for God. For God is not tied to a sanctuary made by hands. God has two sanctuaries: in Heaven, and in humble and contrite hearts (Isa. 57:15). God dwelt in David as in His temple (2 Cor. 6:16). God was with David, And He was in him. And He was never more with him, nor never more in him, than when he was in His greatest afflictions. These questioners lacked eyes to see David's God. Sometimes God hides Himself, not only from the world, but from His own children; yet He is there. However much their sorrow may dim their sight so that they cannot see Him, yet He looks on their face, as with Mary in the Garden. She could not see Christ distinctly, thinking Him to be the gardener. There is a kind of concealment managed by heavenly wisdom, yet God is ever present with His children. And they know it by faith, though not always by feeling. So it was an ignorant question they put, *Where is your God?* It showed that they knew nothing of God's dealing with His children, as is true of all atheists, of whom scoffers are chief. God is not only a God of observation, to be observed outwardly. But oftentime He is a God hiding Himself. And He shows Himself in contrary conditions most of all, and most comfortably to His saints. He often works by contraries. But these carnal men were ignorant of the mysteries of true religion, especially of those mysteries of Divine providence working for good to all God's children, those called according to His purpose (Rom. 8:28). — adapted from Richard Sibbes.

December 4   MORNING

O God, You are my God; I earnestly seek You. My soul thirsts for You; my flesh longs for You, as in a dry and weary land without water — Psalm 63:1,2.

"My soul thirsts for You' — "Oh that Christ would come near, and stand still, and give me leave to look on Him! For to look seems the poor man's privilege, since he may behold the sun for nothing. If I had no other thing to do but to behold and eye my fair Lord Jesus, I would have a king's life. If I were held out of Heaven's door, yet I would be happy evermore to look through a hole in the door and see my dearest and fairest Lord's face. O great King! Why do You stand aloof? Why do You remain beyond the mountains? O Well-beloved, why do You pain a poor soul with delays? A long time out of Your glorious presence is two deaths and two Hells to me. We must meet. I must see Him. I am not able to do without Him. Hunger and longing for Christ has brought on such a necessity of enjoying Christ that, cost me as it will, I cannot but assure Christ that I am not able to do without Him. . . ." (Samuel Rutherford)

"O God, You are my God" — "He embraces Him at the first word, as we usually do friends at first meeting. *'Early will I seek You; my soul thirsts for You; my flesh longs for You'* — Surely, David had some extraordinary business now with God to be done for himself, as it follows: *'To see Your power and Your glory, so as I have seen You in the sanctuary,'* where God had met him, and had manifested Himself to him. The very sight of a friend rejoices a man: *'As iron sharpens iron, so does a man the face of his friend'* (Prov. 27:17). It alone whets up joy by a sympathy of spirits. And in answer to this it is characteristically to God's people called the seeking of God's face; that is, seeking Himself, for so His face is taken: *'You shall have no other Gods before My face'* — that is, You shall have Myself, or none but Myself. Personal communion with God is the end of our graces; for as reason and its intercourse makes men sociable with one another, so the Divine nature makes us sociable with God Himself. And the life we live by is but a mirror to bring God down to us" (Thomas Goodwin)

EVENING

For You have been a help to me, and I will rejoice in the shadow of Your wings — Psalm 63:7.

THE LORD has granted us educative mercy. David says, *"Because You have been my Help"* — He does not say that God has worked everything for us, but that He has set us working also. You see, if you do a thing for a man, it is well; but if you help him to do it, it may be better for him. For then he learns the way. It is true that in many deeds of grace, the Lord does help by doing all the work Himself. He chose us before we chose Him, and without our choice He gave us life. We could not help in our own enlivening. He renewed us; and we could not help in our own renewal. By His own power God gave us a new heart and made us new creatures, giving us His Holy Spirit. We could not help in this, for this must be God's unaided work. God made the grass; the grass did not help in its own creation. But God helps the grass to grow, and the grass itself grows by the Divine power. In the same manner, after we have come to spiritual life, then God helps us. Donne wrote, "God has not left me to myself. He has come to my aid. He has been my help. But then, God has not left me out. He has been my help, but He has left something for me to do with Him, and by His help." (John Donne)

We work because God makes us work, and then helps us in it. We bring forth fruit, as do the branches of the vine, but He supplies the sap. He says, *'From Me is your fruit found.* "Lord, You have been my help. If I begin by stammering a few sentences to You, You open my mouth to show forth Your praise. Did you not begin with a faint confession of Christ? And now you dare to stand in the front of the battle! The Lord has helped you, so that you have now been trained to fight His enemies: *"He teaches my hands to war, and my fingers to fight."* Help not only promotes the work, but it blesses you and me by stimulating our powers and developing them.

MORNING

For Your loving-kindness is better than life; my lips give praise to You — Psalm 63:3.

"*MY LIPS give praise to You*" — "Is it possible that anyone should love another and yet not commend him, nor speak of him? If you have but a hawk or a hound you love, you will commend it. And can you stand with love to Christ, yet seldom or never to speak of Him nor of His love; never to commend Him to others, that they may fall in love with Him also? You see the Spouse when she was asked *'what is your Beloved above others?'* She sets Him out in every part of him, concluding: *'He is altogether lovely!' 'I will bless You while I live'* — Can it stand with this life of love, to be always speaking about worldly affairs, or news at the best; both week-day and Sabbath-day; in bed and at board; in good company and in bad; at home and abroad? It will be one main reason why you desire to live, that you may make the Lord Jesus known to your children, friends, acquaintances, that so in the ages to come His name might ring, and His memorial might be of sweet odor from generation to generation. If before your conversation you had poisoned others by your vain and corrupt speeches, after your conversation surely you will seek to season the hearts of others by a gracious, sweet and wise communication of savory and blessed speeches. If you love Him, you will talk of what He has taught you, for His sake and the sake of others (Thomas Sheppard)

"David extols the Lord with his tongue, his hands, his will, his mouth, his memory and his intellect: *'My lips give praise to You;' 'I will bless You while I live;' 'I will lift up my hands in Your name;' 'My soul shall be satisfied as with marrow and fatness;' 'My mouth shall praise You with joyful lips;'* with his memory, *'When I remember You on my bed;'* and with his intellect, *'And meditate on You in the night watches'* (Thomas Le Blanc)

EVENING

The lines have fallen to me in pleasant places; yes, I have a beautiful inheritance — Psalm 16:6.

JESUS FOUND the way of obedience to lead into *"pleasant places."* In spite of all the sorrows which marred His countenance, He exclaimed, *"Lo, I come; in the volume of the Book it is written of Me. I delight to do Your will, O God"* (Heb. 10:7). While no other man was ever so thoroughly acquainted with grief, no other man ever experienced so much joy and delight in service as Jesus did. For no other has served so faithfully, and with such great results in view as His reward. The joy set before Him must have sent some of its splendid beams down the rugged places where He endured the cross, despising the shame. It must have made them in some respects pleasant places to the generous heart of the Redeemer. At any rate we know that Jesus was well content with the blood-bought portion which the lines of electing love marked off as His reward. In that He solaced Himself on earth, and in that He delights Himself in Heaven. He asks no more beautiful inheritance than that His own beloved may be with Him where He is, and there behold His glory. All the saints can use the language of this verse. The more thoroughly they can enter into its contented, grateful, joyful spirit, the better for themselves, and the more glorious to their God. Our Lord had no place to lay His head, as we do. Yet when He mentioned His poverty on earth He never used a word of murmuring. Discontented spirits are as unlike Jesus as the croaking raven is unlike the cooing dove. Martyrs for Christ have been happy in dungeons. Some divines think that discontent was the first sin, the rock which wrecked our race in Paradise. Certainly there can be no paradise where this evil spirit of discontent has power. Its slime will poison all the flowers of our garden.

December 6 — MORNING

Please, O Jehovah, accept the free offering of my mouth, and teach me Your judgments — Psalm 119:108.

IT IS A delightful thing to converse with God. Do you indulge in this habit? If the Lord is your Father, should you not as His child speak with Him day by day? If you are married to Christ, should not you as the spouse speak with your Well-beloved? It would be strange if you do not. Private devotion ought to be a dialogue between the soul and God. The Lord speaks to us by the Bible, and by prayer we speak to Him. At times you will not have much to say while a dear friend talks. You listen. So when prayer is not urgent with you, read your Bible and hear what God the Lord will speak to you, and do listen diligently. But speak to the Lord. Realize His presence, and then speak to Him as a man speaks with his friend. God has no mute children, but he has some who fail to use their tongues when He is with them. Speak with God. This is the noblest use of speech. If half our talk with people were silenced, and our talk with God were multiplied ten times, we would be blessed. Do you allow a day to pass without conversation with God? Can it be right for you to treat the Lord with mute indifference? No, but let us often turn our hearts and our lips heavenward, and say, *'I will bless You while I live. I will lift up my hands in Your name.'*

EVENING

You thought that I was altogether such an one as yourself, but I will rebuke you and set them in order before your eyes — Psalm 50:21.

"SUCH IS the blindness and corruption of our nature that we have very deformed and misshapen thoughts of God, which lasts until the eye of faith sees His face in the mirror of His Word. So Mr. Perkins affirms that all men who ever came of Adam (Christ alone excepted, being begotten by the Holy Spirit) are by nature atheists; because at the same time they acknowledge God they deny His power, presence, and justice, and allow Him to be only what pleases them. Indeed, it is natural for every man to desire to accommodate his lusts with the kind of conception of God that will be most favorable to and suit best with his lusts. God charges some for this: *'You thought that I was altogether such an one as yourself.'* Sinners do with God as the Ethiopians do with angels, whom they picture with black faces so that they may be like themselves" (William Gurnall).

Men picture God to be like themselves "when they plead for sins as 'little,' 'venial,' as that which is below God to take notice of. Because they think themselves so, then God must think it so, too. Men, with a giant-like pride, would climb into the throne of the Almighty and establish a contradiction to the will of God by making his own will the square and rule of his actions, rather than God's will. This principle commenced in Paradise, when Adam would not depend on the revealed will of God, but depended on himself and his own will, by this making himself as God.

'I will set them in order before your eyes' — This is to be understood militarily, when sins shall be set in rank and file, in bloody array against your soul. Or it could be forensic, when they shall be set in order as so many indictments for your rebellion and treason" (Stephen Charnock)

MORNING

With the pure You will show Yourself as pure; and with the froward You will show Yourself froward (perverse) — Psalm 18:26.

DOES THE LORD take color from every one He meets, or change His temper as the company changes? That is the weakness of sinful man; he cannot do so with God, with whom there is no variableness nor shadow of changing. God is pure and upright with the unclean and hypocritical, as well as with the pure and upright; and His actions show Him to be so. God shows Himself froward with the froward when He deals with him as He has said He will deal with the froward; that is, to deny them and reject them. God shows Himself pure with the pure when He deals with them as He has said He will; that is, to hear them and to accept them. Though there is nothing in purity and sincerity which deserves mercy, yet we cannot expect mercy without them. Our comforts are not grounded on our graces, but our comforts are the fruits or consequences of our graces" (Joseph Caryl).

"*'the froward one'* — Here, as in the first promise, the two combatants stand contrasted: the seed of the woman and the serpent — the benignantly bountiful, perfect, pure One, and the froward one who came to destory His works, and who made it his business to circumvent Him whom he feared. The literal meaning of the word is *'tortuous'* or *'crooked,'* and both the ideas of perversity and cunning, which the figure naturally suggests, are very applicable to that *'old serpent, the Devil.'* From the concluding part of the sentence, there is no doubt that it is the latter idea that is intended to be conveyed. God cannot deal perversely with anyone, but He outwits the wise, and takes the cunning in their own craftiness" (John Brown).

EVENING

With the froward You will show Yourself froward — Psalm 18:26.

"THE HEBREW word in the root signifies to wrest or writhe a thing, or to wrest or turn a thing, as wrestlers do their bodies. So, by a trope, it is translated often to wrestle, because a cunning man in wrestling turns and winds his body, and he works himself in and out every way in order to get an advantage of his adversary. So your cunning-headed men, your crafty men, are fitly presented under this word; they are like wrestlers who turn and wind themselves with lies for all advantages; or as we speak, they lie at catch. A man knows not where to place them, or what they mean when they speak plainly, or swear solemnly. When we think we see their faces, we see only their vizards; all their promises and performances are under a disguise. *'You will show Yourself froward'* — that is, if men will be winding and turning, thinking to catch others, or overreach the Lord Himself with tricks and turnings of wit, then the Lord will meet and answer them in their own kind. He can turn as fast as they; He can put Himself in such intricate labyrinths of infinite wisdom and sacred craft as will entangle and ensnare the most cunning of men" (Joseph Caryl).

"It is a similitude taken from wrestlers, and notes a writhing of one's self against an adversary. Compare with Deut. 32:5: *They are a perverse and crooked generation'* — the same two words here. the latter imports that they wriggled and writhed after the manner of wrestlers, winding this way and that when they think to have their adversary here or there. But all will not serve their turn to save them from punishment. God will be sure to meet with them; His Word will lay hold on them; and their sin will surely find them out" (John Trapp)

MORNING

For I am the Lord your God, the Holy One of Israel, your Savior. I gave Egypt for your ransom, Ethiopia and Seba for you — Isaiah 43:3.

THE LORD has a people whom He must and will gather to Himself. He bids the nations to act as His servants in this matter: *"I will say to the north, Give up; and to the south, Do not keep back; bring My sons from afar, and My daughters from the ends of the earth."* Why, they may be up to their necks in the bogs of sin. But they are to be brought home, for the Lord will not allow His sons and daughters to be lost. Perhaps they have wandered far into grievous vices; but if they are called by His name, every one of them must come: *"not being willing for any of us to perish, but all of us to come to repentance"* (2 Peter 3:9). Our almighty Savior can draw a sinner back from the shelving brink of Hell. God will bring back His redeemed, into whatever iniquity they may have fallen. Victorious grace will set free the captives of sin. As to free-will, the Lord will *"make His people willing in the day of His power"* (Psalm 110:3). On the cross, according to Psalm 22, our Lord said, *"A seed shall serve Him; it shall be accounted to the Lord for a generation. They shall come."* He shall make them come; the Lord Jesus will not shed His blood in vain. The Lord gave Egypt for Israel's ransom, Ethiopia and Seba for her, and He will not lose what He has purchased at such a dear price. Whether the exile has been carried west, or east, or north, or south, the Lord will devise means that such a one is not left to perish in the far-off land. Let us say, all you believers, *"There is much people to Me in this city"* (Acts 18:10), we will seek for them. We will find the people You have bought for Yourself at an exceedingly great price." Once one sneeringly said, "If I thought God had a chosen people, I would not preach" — but that is the very reason why we should preach, that these chosen ones should hear the gospel and believe, and become a new creation in Christ Jesus. God has commanded it of us.

EVENING

I tell you truly if anyone keeps My word he will never ever see death — John 8:51.

WHAT DOES this promise mean? It means that our face is turned away from death. Here I am, a poor sinner, convinced of sin, and aroused by my fear of wrath. What is there before my face? What am I compelled to look upon? The Greek word is not fully interpreted by the word 'see' it is a more intense word. It is a long, steady, exhaustive viewing, by which we become slowly acquainted with the nature of the object to which it is directed. The awakened sinner is made to stare at and study eternal death, the threatened punishment for his sin. He stands gazing on the result of sin with terror and dismay. Oh, the wrath to come! the death that never dies! While unforgiven, who can help gazing on death and foreseeing it as doom. When the gospel of the Lord Jesus comes to one, and he keeps His saying by faith, that one is turned completely around. Then his back is on death, and his face is toward eternal life. Death is removed; life is received; and more life is promised. What does a new believer see around and before him? Why, it is life and only life; life in Christ Jesus: *"He is our life."* And in the future, what does he see? A final falling from grace? By no means — never! For Jesus has said, *"I give to My sheep eternal life."* What does the believer see in the eternities? Unending life: *"He who believes in Me has everlasting life"* (John 5:24); *"I am the resurrection; the one believing in Me, although he were dead, yet he shall live."* And again, *"I am the life. He who lives and believes in me shall never die."* The man who has received the saying of the Lord Jesus has passed from death to life; he shall never come into condemnation, and consequently he shall never gaze on spiritual death. All that lies before the believer is life — life more abundantly, life to the full, life eternal. What has become of our death? Our Lord Jesus Christ endured it when He died for us.

MORNING

He comes forth like a bridegroom from his canopy. He rejoices like a hero to run a race — Psalm 19:5.

"IT APPEARS to me very likely that the Holy Spirit in these expressions in verses 4-6, which He most immediately uses about the rising of the sun, has an eye to the rising of the Sun of Righteousness from the grave, and that the expressions that the Holy Spirit uses here are conformed to such a view. The times of the Old Testament are times of night when compared to the gospel day. So the approach of the day of the New Testament dispensation in the birth of Christ is called the Day-spring on high visiting the earth (Luke 1:78). And the commencing of the gospel dispensation as it was introduced by Christ is called the Sun of Righteousness rising (Mal. 4:2). But this gospel dispensation commences with the resurrection of Christ. In this the Sun of Righteousness rises from under the earth, as the sun appears to do in the morning, and comes forth as a bridegroom. He rose as the joyful, glorious bridegroom of His church. For Christ, especially as risen again, is the proper bridegroom, or husband, of His church (Rom. 7:4). Now He comes forth as a bridegroom to bring home His purchased spouse to Him in spiritual marriage, as He soon after did in the conversion of such multitudes, making His people willing in the day of His power. And He has done this many times since, and will do in a yet more glorious degree. As the sun when it rises comes forth like a bridegroom gloriously adorned, so Christ in His resurrection entered on His state of glory. After His state of suffering, He rose to shine forth in unspeakable glory as the King of Heaven and earth, that He might be a glorious bridegroom in whom His church might be unspeakably happy. The Psalmist says that God placed a tabernacle for the sun in the heavens: so God the Father had prepared an abode in Heaven for Jesus Christ. He set a throne for Him there, to which He ascended after He rose. He rose to conquer His enemies, to show forth His glorious power in subduing all things to Himself. The verses following confirm this view. (Jonathan Edwards)

EVENING

I tell you truly if anyone keeps My word, he shall never ever see death — John 8:51.

WHEN THE BELIEVER DIES, he does not gaze on death. He walks through the valley of the shadow of death, but he fears no evil and sees none to fear. A shadow was cast across the road, but the dying believer passed through it, scarcely perceiving that it was there. Why was that? It is because the believer fixes his eye on a strong light beyond. Believers are so rejoiced by the presence of their Lord and Master that they do not observe the shadow of death when they are dying. They rest so sweetly in the embrace of Jesus that they do not hear the voice of wailing. They pass from one world into another. It is all one kingdom, and one Sun shines in both lands. The eternal life that is in the believer glides along from grace to glory without a break. We grow steadily on from the blade to the ear, and from the ear to the full grain, but there is no black line dividing the stages of growth from one to the other. We shall know when we arrive, but the passage may be so rapid that we will hardly see it. From earth to Heaven may seem the greatest of journeys, but it is ended in the twinkling of an eye.

The believer shall never gaze on death. He will pass it by with no more than a glance. He will go through Jordan as though it were dry land, and hardly know that he has passed the River. Like Peter, the departing one will hardly be sure that they have passed through the iron gate; for it will open of its own accord. Then they will know that at last they are free from sin and tears.

December 10 — MORNING

I tell you truly if anyone keeps My word, he shall never ever see death — John 8:51.

THOSE JEWS — what a passion they were in! How unscrupulous their talk! They could not even quote Christ's words correctly, They said, *"You say, If a man keep My saying, he shall never taste of death."* He did not say so. He said, *"shall never see death."* We may be said to taste of death as our Master did, for it is written that "He tasted death for every son" (supplied — see context). And yet in another sense we shall never taste the wormwood and gall of death, for to us it is *"swallowed up in victory."* Its drop of gall is lost in the bowl of victory. But the Lord Jesus did not say that we shall never taste of death; nor did He mean that we shall not die, in the common sense of the word. To the Jews He was using words in that religious sense in which their own prophets used them. The ancient Scriptures so used the word death, and these Jews knew their meaning very well. Death did not always mean the separation of the soul from the body; for the Lord's declaration to Adam was, *"In the day that you eat of it you shall surely die."* Assuredly, Adam and Eve died in the sense intended, but they were not annihilated; nor were their souls separated from their bodies. They still remained on earth to labor. Again, *"the soul that sins, it shall die,"* relates to a death which consists of degradation, misery, inability, ruin. Death does not mean annihilation, but something very different. Overthrow and ruin are the death of a soul, just as perfection and joy are its life forever. The separation of the soul from God is the death penalty, and that is death indeed. The Jews refused to understand our Lord, yet they clearly saw that what Jesus claimed tended to glorify Him above Abraham and the prophets. Hidden away in their abusive words, we find a sense which is instructive. It is not the greatness or the goodness of a believer that secures his eternal life — it is his being linked by faith to the Lord Jesus Christ.

EVENING

May Jehovah answer you in the day of trouble; the name of the God of Jacob set you on high — Psalm 20:1.

"ALL THE DAYS of Christ were *days of trouble*. He was a brother born for adversity, a man of sorrows and acquainted with griefs. But more particularly it was a *'day of trouble'* with Him when He was in the Garden, heavy and sore amazed, when His sweat was, as it were, drops of blood falling on the ground, and His soul was exceedingly sorrowful, even unto death. More especially this was His case when He hung on the cross, when He bore all the sins of His people, endured the wrath of His Father, and was forsaken by Him. Now, in this *day of trouble*, both when in the Garden and on the Cross, He prayed to His Father, as He had usually done in other cases, and at other times. And the church here prays that God would hear and answer — and He did" (John Gill)

"May the Lord answer you in the day of trouble" — "A sweeter wish, or a more consolatory prayer for a child of sorrow was never uttered by man. Who is there of the sons of men to whom a *day of trouble* does not come, whose path is not darkened at times? Or with whom is unclouded sunshine from the cradle to the grave? Old Jacomb said, 'Few plants have both the morning and the evening sun,' and one far older said, *'Man is born to trouble.' (Job 5:7)* A *day of trouble*, then, is the heritage of every child of Adam. How sweet then is this wish. It is the prayer of another in behalf of some troubled one, and yet it implies that the troubled one himself had also prayed. May the Lord hear your prayer in your *day of trouble*." (Barton Bouchier)

In them He has set a tabernacle for the sun, which comes forth like a bridegroom leaving his chamber, and which rejoices as a strong man to run a race — Psalm 19:4.

CHRIST CAME out of His chamber at His ascension, because when He ascended on high, leading captivity captive, He received and gave gifts for men. The gifts were intended for the manifestation of Himself. His church, which is His body, was by His own command sitting still in the chamber, waiting until the power was given. But suddenly the Bridegroom's power was felt. There was heard the sound as of a rushing mighty wind, which filled all the place. Then descending on each favored head came the cloven tongue. And at once you could see that the Bridegroom had come out of His chamber, for the multitude in the street began to hear His voice. It was Peter that spoke, we say; but instead it was Christ, the Bridegroom, who spoke by Peter. It was the Sun of Righteousness bursting through the clouds and beginning to shine on Parthians, and Medes, and Elamites, and the Mesopotamians, and Romans, and Egyptians. Multitudes from these far off lands saw the day which the prophets and kings had waited for, but which had never visited their eyes. Do you hear the joyful motion among the people, the exultation mingled with the sorrows of repentance? This is the singing of the birds, and these dewdrops which hail the rising Sun. The people cry out, *"What must we do to be saved?"* — the shadows are fleeing. They believe in Jesus, and are baptized into His name; the true Light is shining. Three thousand souls are added in one day to the church, for truly the Bridegroom has risen as one out of sleep, and like a mighty man that shouts. Then was the gospel race commenced with a glorious burst of power, such as only our Champion could have displayed.

EVENING

On You do I wait all the day — Psalm 25:5.

"TO *'wait on God'* is, (1) To live a life of desire toward God; to wait on Him as the beggar waits on his benefactor, with earnest desire to receive supplies from Him, as the sick and sore ones at Bethesda's pool waited for the stirring of the water, attending there with desire to be helped and healed. (2) It is to live a life of delight in God, as the lover waits on his beloved. Desire is love in motion, as a bird on the wing; delight is love at rest, as a bird on the nest. Now, though our desire must still be so toward God, as that we must be wishing for more of God, yet our delight must be so in God, as that we must never wish more than God. (3) It is to live a life of dependence on God, as the child waits on his father, whom he has confidence in, and on whom he casts all his care. To wait on God is to expect all good to come to us from Him, as the worker of all good for us and in us, the giver of all good to us, and the protector of us from all evil. So David explains himself, *'My soul, wait only on God'* and continue to do so, for *'my expectation is from Him.'* (4) It is to live a life of devotedness to God, as the servant waits on his master, ready to observe his will, and to do his work, and in everything to consult his honor and interest. To wait on God is entirely and unreservedly to refer ourselves to His wise and holy directions and disposals, and to cheerfully acquiesce in them, and to comply with them. The servant waits on his master, not choosing his own way, but following his master step by step. So must we wait on God, as those that have no will of our own but what is wholly resolved into His. Therefore, we must study to accommodate ourselves to His will" (Matthew Henry, from *Communion with God*).

December 12   MORNING

All the paths of Jehovah are mercy and truth to those who keep His covenant and His testimonies — Psalm 25:10.

"ALL THE PATHS of the Lord" — "Paths, here signifyig tracks or ruts made by the wheels of wagons by often passing over the same ground. Mercy and truth are the paths in which God constantly walks in reference to the children of men. So frequently does He show them mercy, and so frequently does He fulfill His truth, that His paths are easily discerned. How frequent, how deeply indented, and how multiplied are those traces to every family and individual! Wherever we go we see that God's mercy and truth have been there by the deep tracks they have left behind them. But He is more abundantly merciful to those who keep His covenant and His testimonies; that is, those who are conformed, not only to the letter, but to the spirit of His pure religion" (Adam Clarke)

"As His *nature* is love and truth, so all his *ways* are *mercy and truth*. They are mercy in respect of aiming at our good, and truth in respect of fulfilling His promise and faithful carriage to us. So, then, whatever happens to you, though it be clean contrary to your expectation, interpret it in love. Many actions of men are such as a good interpretation cannot be put on them, nor a good construction made of them. For this reason interpreters restrain those sayings of love, that it believes all, etc.; that is, all things believable. But none of God's ways are such, but love and faith may pick a good meaning out of these. From a good God there comes nothing but what is good, and therefore Job says, *Though He kill me, I will trust in Him.'* Endeavor to spy out some end of His for good at the present, and if none arises to your mind, resolve it into faith, and make the best of it" (Thomas Goodwin).

EVENING

Pardon my iniquity, for it is great — Psalm 25:11.

"HE PLEADS the greatness of his sin, not the smallness of it. He enforces his prayer with this consideration, that his sins are very heinous. But how could he make this plea for pardon? Because the greater his iniquity, the more need he had of pardon. It is as if he had said, Pardon my iniquity, for it is so great that I cannot bear the punishment; my sin is so great that I am in grave need of pardon; my case will be exceedingly miserable, unless You be pleased to pardon me. He makes use of the greatness of his sin to enforce his plea for pardon, as a man would make use of the greatness of calamity in begging for relief. In this the glory of grace by the redemption of Christ must consist; namely, in its sufficiency for the pardon of the greatest sinners. The whole contrivance of the way of salvation is for this end, to glorify the free grace of God. God had it on His heart from all eternity to glorify this attribute; and it is for this reason that the device of saving sinners by Christ was conceived. And the greatness of Divine grace appears very much in this, that God by Christ saves the greatest offenders. The greater the guilt of any sinner, the more glorious and wonderful is the grace manifested in his pardon: *'Where sin abounded, grace did much more abound.'* (Rom. 5:20). When telling how great a sinner he had been, the apostle Paul notices the abounding of grace in his pardon: *'Who was a blasphemer, and a persecutor, and injurious; but I obtained mercy'* (1 Tim. 1:13). The Redeemer is glorified in that He proves sufficient to redeem those who are exceedingly sinful; in that His blood proves sufficient to wash away the greatest guilt; in that He is able to save men to the uttermost and in that He redeems even from the greatest misery. It is the honor of Christ to save the greatest sinners when they come to him, as it is the honor of a physician that he cures the most desperate diseases or wounds. Christ will be willing to save the greatest sinners if they come to Him, for he will not be backward to glorify Himself, and to commend the value and virtue of His own blood" (Jonathan Edwards).

MORNING

To appoint to those who mourn in Zion, to give them beauty for ashes, the oil of joy for mourning, the role of praise for the spirit of heaviness — Isaiah 61:3.

"TO APPOINT to those who mourn in Zion" — Mourning souls who mourn in the way described will have comfort appointed for them. It is the prerogative of King Jesus both to appoint and to give. How cheering is the thought that as our griefs are appointed, so also are our consolations. God has allotted a portion to every one of His mourners, even as Joseph allotted a mess to each of his brothers at the feast. You shall have your due share at the table of grace. And if you are a little one, and have double sorrows, you shall have a double portion of comfort. This word *"appoint"* is full of strong consolation. For if it is God that appoints your portion, who can deprive you of it? If He appoints your comfort, who dares to stand in the way? If He appoints it, it is yours by right. But to make the appointment secure, He adds the words *"to give."* The Holy One of Israel in the midst of Zion gives as well as appoints. The rich comforts of the gospel are conferred by the Holy Spirit, at the command of Jesus Christ, on every true mourner in the time when he needs them. They are given to each spiritual mourner in the time when he would faint for lack of them. He can effectually give the comfort appointed for each particular case. All any man can do is to speak of the comfort God gives to mourners. Only He can allot it, or distribute it. My prayer is that He may do so at this moment, that every holy mourner may have a time of sweet rejoicing while sitting at the Master's feet in a waiting posture. Did you never feel, while cast down, suddenly lifted up when some precious promise has come home to your soul? This is the happy experience of all the saints.

EVENING

So that they might be called trees of righteousness, the planting of the Lord, that He might be glorified — Isaiah 61:3.

"THE MARKS of upright, righteous men are not to be taken from an outward hearing of the Word, or receiving of the sacraments, and much less from a formal observation of human traditions in God's tabernacle — for all these things hypocrites usually perform — but from the duties of righteousness, giving every man his due, because the touchstone of piety toward God is charity toward our brother. *'In this are the children of God known, and the children of the Devil: whoever does not righteousness is not of God, nor he that does not love his brother."* (1 John 3:10). Selected from John Boys.

"A man must first be righteous before he can work righteousness of life: *'He that does righteousness is righteous, even as He is righteous'* (1 John 3:7). The tree makes the fruit, not the fruit the tree. So the tree must be good before the fruit can be good (Matt. 7:18). A righteous man may make a righteous work, but no work of an unrighteous man can make him righteous. Now we become righteous only by faith, through the righteousness of Christ imputed to us (Rom. 5:1). Let men work as they will, if they are not true believers in Christ, they are not workers of righteousness; consequently, they will not be dwellers in Heaven. You must then close with Christ in the first place, and by faith receive the gift of imputed righteousness, or you will never truly bear this character of a citizen of Zion. A man shall as soon force fruit out of a branch broken off from the tree, and withered, as to work righteousness without believing in and uniting with Christ, the true Vine. These are two things by which those that hear the gospel are ruined" (Thomas Boston).

December 14 — MORNING

Jehovah is the portion of my inheritance and of my cup. You shall surely uphold my lot — Psalm 16:5.

WITH WHAT confidence and bounding joy the Lord Jesus turns to Jehovah, whom His soul possessed and delighted in! Content beyond measure with His portion in His God, He had not a single desire with which to hunt after other gods. His cup was full, and His heart was full, too. Even in His sorest sorrows He still laid hold with both hands on His Father, crying, *"My God, My God."* He did not have so much as a thought of falling down to worship the Devil when that old serpent tried Him with an *"all these I will give You."*

We, too, can make our boast in the Lord. He is the meat and the drink of our souls. He is our portion, supplying all our necessities, and our cup yielding royal luxuries, our cup in this life, and our inheritance in the life to come. As children of the heavenly Father we inherit, by virtue of our joint heirship with Christ (Rom. 8:17), all the riches of the covenant of grace, and the portion which falls to us sets on our table the bread of Heaven and the new wine of the kingdom. Who would not be satisfied with such a portion? Our shallow cup of sorrow we will drain with resignation, since the deep cup of love stands side by side with it, and it will never be empty. *"You uphold my lot"* — Some tenants have a covenant in their leases that they themselves shall maintain and uphold the leased property. But in our case Jehovah Himself upholds our lot. Our Lord Jesus delighted in this truth, that the Father was on His side, and that He would maintain His right against all the wrongs of men. He knew that the elect of God would be reserved for Him, and that almighty power would preserve them as His lot and reward forever. Let us also be glad because the Judge of all the earth will vindicate our righteous cause, and will uphold the lot of all the saints.

EVENING

Ask of Me, and I will give nations, Your inheritance; and the ends of the earth, Your possession — Psalm 2:8.

"ASK OF ME" — "The priesthood does not appear to be settled on Christ by any other expression than this, *'Ask of Me.'* The Psalm speaks of His investiture in His kingly office; the apostle refers this to His priesthood, His commission for both took date at the same time. Both were bestowed, and both confirmed, by the same authority. The office of asking is grounded on the same authority as the honor of king. Ruling belonged to Him in His royal office; asking belonged to Him in His priestly office. After His resurrection, the Father gives Him a power and command of asking" (Stephen Charnock).

"As the artist looks on the person whose picture he would paint, and draws his lines to answer that person with the nearest similitude that he can — so God looks on Christ as the archetype to which He will conform the saint, in suffering, in grace, in glory. Yet so that Christ will have the pre-eminence in all. Every saint must suffer, because Christ suffered. Christ must not have a delicate body under a crucified head. Yet never any suffered, or could, what He endured. Christ is holy, and therefore so shall every saint be, but in an inferior degree. An image cut in clay cannot be so exact as that engraved on gold. Now, our conformity to Christ appears, that as the promises made to Him were performed on His prayers to His Father, His promises made to His saints are given to them in the same way of prayer: *'Ask of Me,'* God said to His Son, *'and I will give You.'* And the apostle tells us, *'You have not, because you ask not.'* God has promised support to Christ in all His conflicts: *'Behold My Servant, whom I uphold;'* yet He prayed, *'with strong cries and tears,'* when His feet stood within the shadow of death. A seed is promised to Him, and victory over His enemies, yet for both these He prays. Christ acts as a king toward us, but toward His Father as a priest. All He speaks to God is by prayer and intercession. So the saints, the promise makes them kings, rulers over their lusts, conquerors over their enemies. But it makes them priests toward God, by prayer humbly to sue out those great things given in the promise" (William Gurnall)

For I have sworn that the waters of Noah should no more go over the earth, so I have sworn that I would not be angry with you or rebuke you — Isaiah 54:9.

THE FIRST COVENANT with Noah was made after a sacrifice. Noah offered a sacrifice of clean beasts to God. And it is said that the Lord smelled a sweet savor, or a savor of rest, and shortly after that it was that He made the covenant not to destroy the earth by flood. So you see, the flood is kept away from us through a covenant of sacrifice. Now, beloved, the same reason so works with God that He will not be angry with you, or rebuke you. There is a sacrifice in which God always smells a sweet savor of rest, and therefore you are secure. But it is not you that are acceptable to Him in yourselves. Oh, no! But you are *"accepted in the Beloved."* We have no personal sweetness, but because of the savor of our Lord's good ointments all His members smell sweet to God. Christ is as precious incense to God at all times, and this is the reason of our salvation. You recollect how the Israelites were preserved in Egypt on the night of the Passover. It was not said to them, *"When you look at the blood, I will pass over you,"* or, *"When I look at you, I will pass over you."* No, but God said, *"When I see the blood, I will pass over you."* God's eye was fixed on the blood on the lintel; He saw in that the type of the precious blood of Jesus. And for that reason He passed over His people. And so the Lord's eye is fixed on Jesus and His precious sacrifice. God is, for His sake, well-pleased with us, uttering no rebuke or condemning word. When your sins rise in your conscience, and you repent most bitterly of them, and are downcast in your spirit concerning them, yet do not let your sense of sin cause you to question this solemn declaration, sworn to by God's own mouth: *'I will not be angry with you, or rebuke you."*

EVENING

Give to Jehovah the glory due His name — Psalm 96:8.

"IT IS A DEBT, and in equity a debt must be paid. The honor due to God's name is to acknowledge Him to be holy, just, true, powerful: *The Lord, the faithful God,'* good, merciful, long-suffering, etc. Do not defraud His name of the least honor" (Adam Clarke).

"Is all the glory due to God's name, and ought it in strict justice to have been ascribed to Him by men, ever since man began to exist? How immeasurably great, then, is the debt which our world has contracted, and under the burden of which it now groans! During every day which has elapsed since the apostasy of man, this debt has been increasing. For every day and every hour all men ought to have given to Jehovah the glory due to His name. But no man has ever done this fully. And a vast proportion of our race has never done it at all. Now the difference between the tribute which men ought to have paid to God, and that which they have actually paid to Him constitutes the debt of which we are speaking. How vast, then, how incalculable it is!" (Edward Payson).

"Every glory will not serve the turn, but such glory as is proper and peculiar for that God we serve. It is a stated rule in Scripture that, respects to God must be proportioned to the nature of God. God is a spirit, therefore He must be worshiped in spirit and truth. God is a God of peace, therefore lift up pure hands without wrath and doubting. God is a holy God, therefore He will be sanctified. Those who worship the sun among the heathen used a flying horse as a thing most suitable to the swift motion of the sun. Well, then, they that will glorify and honor God with a glory due to His name must sanctify Him as well as honor Him. Why? For *'God is glorious in holiness'* (Exodus 15:11). This is that which God counts to be His chief excellency, and the glory which He will reveal among the sons of men" (Thomas Manton).

December 16   MORNING   351

But now, in the end of the ages, He has appeared to put away sin by the sacrifice of Himself — Hebrews 9:26.

THE TEXT tells us very precisely that in this first coming of our Lord He appeared to put away sin. Notice that fact. By His coming and sacrifice He accomplished many things, but His first end and object was *"to put away sin."* You know what the modern babblers say. They declare that He appeared to reveal to us the goodness and love of God. This is true. But it is only the fringe of the whole truth. The fact is that He revealed God's love in the provision of a sacrifice to put away sin. Then, they say that He appeared to exhibit perfect manhood, and to let us see what our nature ought to be. This also is true, but it is only part of the sacred design. They say, He appeared to manifest self-sacrifice, and to set us an example of love to others. By His self-denial He trampled on the selfish passions of man. We deny none of these things, and yet we are indignant at the way in which the less is made to hide the greater. To put the secondary ends into the place of the grand object is to turn the truth of God into a lie. It is easy to distort truth by exaggerating one portion of it and diminishing another, just as the drawing of the most beautiful face may soon be made a caricature rather than a portrayal by neglect of proportion. You must observe proportion if you would take a true view of things. In reference to the appearing of our Lord, His first and chief purpose was *"to put away sin by the sacrifice of Himself."* The great object of our Lord's coming here was not to live, but to die. He has appeared, not so much to subdue sin by His teaching, as to put it away by the sacrifice of Himself. The master purpose which dominated all that our Lord did was not to manifest goodness, nor to perfect an example, but to put away sin by sacrifice. That which the moderns would thrust into the background, our Lord placed in the forefront.

EVENING

So being once offered to bear the sins of many, Christ shall appear a second time without sin to those expecting Him for salvation — Hebrews 9:28.

WHEN OUR LORD comes to the full in His glory, there will remain no sin on His people. He will present His bride to Himself as a glorious church, not having spot or wrinkle, or any such thing (Eph. 5:27). The day of His appearing will be the revealing of a perfect body, as well as a perfect Head. Then shall the righteous shine forth as the sun, when their Lord's countenance is as the sun shining in His strength. As He will be *"without sin,"* so they will be *"without sin."* What a glorious appearing is this! A true appearing, and yet the very opposite of the first. The text adds *"to salvation."* What does this mean? It means that He will then display the perfect salvation of all those who put their trust in Him. He will come to celebrate the great victory of mercy over sin. At His coming He will set His foot on the dragon's head and bruise Satan under His feet. He will come to have all His enemies put under His feet. Today we fight, and He fights in us. We groan, and He groans in us, for the dread conflict is raging. When He comes again the battle will be ended. He will divide the spoil of vanquished evil and will celebrate the victory of righteousness.

But the resurrection is the salvation principally intended here. Alas, what evil sin has done! When the Lord Jesus shall come and open wide the door of the graves, He will bid us come forth in the entirety of our nature, leaving nothing behind. Salvation shall mean to us the perfection of our humanity in the likeness of our Lord. No aching hands and weary brows then; but we shall be raised in power. Our vile body will be changed and made like His glorious body. Even though sown in corruption, our body shall be raised in incorruption, and this mortal shall put on immortality. What a glorious prospect lies before us in connection with the day of His appearing a second time to salvation!

But now, once in the end of the ages, He has appeared to put away sin by the sacrifice of Himself — Hebrews 9:26.

THE TWO GREAT LINKS between earth and Heaven are the two advents of our Lord; or, rather, He is the great bond of union, by these two appearings. When the world had revolted, and God had been defied by His own creatures, a great gulf was opened between God and man. The first coming of Christ was like a bridge which crossed the chasm and made a way of access from God to man, and then from man to God. Our Lord's second advent will make that bridge far broader, until Heaven shall come down to earth, and ultimately earth will go up to Heaven. At these two points a sinful world is drawn into closest contact with a gracious God. By this Jesus is seen as opening the door which none can shut, by means of which the Lord is beheld as truly Emmanuel, *God with us*.

Here, too, is the place for us to build a grand suspension bridge by which, through faith, we may cross from this side to the other of the stormy river of time. The cross, at whose feet we stand, is the massive column which supports the structure on this side. And as we look forward to the glory, the second advent of our Lord is the solid support on the other side of the deep gulf of time. By faith we first look to Jesus, and then look for Jesus, and in this is the life of our spirits: Christ on the cross of shame, and Christ on the throne of glory — we dwell between these two boundaries. These are our Dan and Beersheba, and all between is holy ground. As for our Lord's first coming, there lies our rest. The once-for-all Sacrifice has put away our sin, and has made our peace with God. As for His second coming, there lies our hope, our joy. For we know that when *"He shall appear, we shall be like Him, for we shall see Him as He is."* The glories of His sacred royalty shall be repeated in all the saints, for He has made us kings and priests to God. And we shall reign with Him forever and ever.

EVENING

But now, once in the end of the ages, He has appeared to put away sin by the sacrifice of Himself — Hebrews 9:26.

OUR LORD JESUS CHRIST has once appeared. And although He will appear again, it will not be for the same purpose. Fix your thoughts on His first appearing, for the like of it will never be seen again. In the bosom of the Father He lay concealed. As the second person of the Godhead, He could not be seen, for *"no man has seen God at any time."* It is true that *"without Him was not anything made that was made;"* and so His hand was seen in His works. But as to Himself, He was still hidden, revealed in type and prophecy, but yet in fact concealed. Jesus was not manifest to the sons of men, until one midnight an angel hastened from the skies and bade the shepherds to know that to them was born a Savior in Bethlehem, that is, Christ the Lord. Then the rest of the angelic host, discovering that one of their number had gone before them on so wonderful an errand, overtook him. And in one mass of glittering glory they filled the midnight skies with heavenly harmony as they sang, *"Glory to God in the highest, and on earth peace, good will toward men."* Well might they sing, for the Son of God now appeared. In the manger He might be seen with the eyes, looked on, and handled, for there the Word was made flesh, and God was incarnate. He whom the ages could not contain, the glorious One who dwelt with the Father unseen from everlasting, now appeared within the bounds of time and space. And humble shepherds saw Him and adored Him. He was seen by Gentiles, for wise men from the east beheld Him as a child obedient to His parents. And eventually He was made manifest to men by the witness of John the Baptist, and the descent of the Holy Spirit at His baptism.

December 18   MORNING

So Christ, having been once offered to bear the sins of many, shall appear a second time without sin to those that look for Him, to salvation — Hebrews 9:28.

WHAT IS IT TO look for that second coming? It is to love the Lord Jesus, to love Him so that you long for Him as a bride longs for her husband. Why are His chariots so long in coming? Come quickly, Lord Jesus! Strong love hates separation; it pines for union. It cries, "Come, Lord! Come, Lord!" Longing follows on the heels of loving. To look for His coming is to prepare for Him. If I were asked to visit you tomorrow, I am sure you would make some preparations for my call. You would prepare because you would welcome me. When we expect our Lord to come, we shall be concerned to have everything ready for Him. Keep the great gates of your soul always open, expecting your Lord to come. It is idle to talk about looking for His coming if we never set our house in order, and never put ourselves in readiness for His reception. Looking for Him means that you stand in a waiting attitude, as a servant who expects His master to be at the door presently. Do not say, "The Lord will not come, and so I will make my plans irrespective of Him for the next twenty or thirty years." You may not be here then; or if you are, your Lord may be here also. He comes. He sent a herald before Him long ago to cry, *"Behold, I come quickly."* He has been coming quickly over the mountains of division ever since, and He must be here soon. If you look for His appearing, you will be found in an attitude of one who waits and watches, that when his Lord comes he may meet Him with joy. Christ is coming; I must not sin. Christ is coming; I must not be rooted in the world.

EVENING

Bless the Lord, O my soul; Bless His holy name — Psalm 103:1.

"GOD'S EYE is chiefly on the soul. Bring a hundred dishes to the table; He will carve of none but this. This is the savory meat He loves. He who is best desires to be served with the best. When we give God the soul in a duty, then we give Him the flower and the cream; by a holy chemistry we distil our spirits for Him. A soul inflamed in service is the cup of *'spiced wine of the juice of the pomegranate'* (S of S 8:2), which the spouse makes Christ to drink of" (Thomas Manton).

"There is nothing that more exalts the glory of Divine grace and of redeeming love toward a soul than the consideration of God's holiness. For if your Maker were not *'of purer eyes than man is'*, yea, if His hatred to sin, and love to righteousness, were not greater than that of the noblest angel, His pardoning of sin, and patience toward transgressors, would not be such a wonderful condescension. But is His name infinitely holy so that *'the heavens are not clean in His sight'*? Is the smallest iniquity the abhorrence of His soul, and what He hates with a perfect hatred? Surely, then, His grace and love must be incomparably greater than our thoughts" (William Dunlop).

"The well is seldom so full that water will at first pumping flow forth. Neither is the heart commonly so spiritual, after our best care in our worldly converse (much less when we somewhat overdo therein) as to pour itself into God's bosom freely, without something to raise and elevate it. Yea, often, the springs of grace lie so low that pumping will not fetch the heart up to a praying frame, but arguments must be poured into the soul before the affections rise. For this reason we find holy men using soliloquies and discourses with their hearts to bring them into a gracious temper, suitable for communion with God in ordinances. It seems by these verses that David either found or feared his heart would not be in so good a frame as he desired. So he redoubles his charge: he found his heart somewhat drowsy, which made him arouse himself in this way" (William Gurnall).

MORNING

For to us a Child is born, to us a Son is given; and the princely power shall be on His shoulder — Isaiah 9:6.

IF CHRIST IS YOUR SAVIOR, He must be your King. The moment we really believe in Jesus as our salvation, we fall before Him and call Him Master and Lord. We serve when He saves. He has redeemed us to Himself, and we acknowledge that we are His. A generous man once bought a slave girl. She was put on the block for auction, and he pitied her and purchased her. When he had bought her, he said to her, "I have bought you to set you free. There are your papers; you are a free woman." The grateful creature fell at his feet and cried, "I will never leave you. If you have made me free, I will be your servant as long as you live, and will serve you better than any slave could do." This is how we feel toward Jesus. He sets us free from the dominion of Satan. And then, as we need a ruler, we say, *"And the princely power shall be on His shoulder."* We are glad to be ruled by *"Immanuel, God with us."* This is also the door of hope to us. That Jesus shall be the monarch of our hearts is an exceeding joy. To us He shall be always *"Wonderful."* When we think of Him, or speak of Him, it shall be with reverent awe. When we need advice and comfort, we will fly to Him, for He shall be our Counselor. When we need strength, we will look to Him as our Mighty God. Born again by His Spirit, we will be His children; and He shall be the Everlasting Father. Full of joy and rest, we will call Him Prince of Peace.

Are you willing to have Christ to rule over you? Will you spend your lives in praising Him? If you say that you are only willing that He pardon you, remember we cannot divide Him. You must also have Him to sanctify you. You must not take the crown from His head, but accept Him as the monarch of your soul. If you have His hand to help you, you must obey the ruling scepter which He holds.

EVENING

Your people shall be willing in the day of Your power — Psalm 110:3.

"YOUR PEOPLE" — "That is, those whom You received from Your Father, and, by setting up the standard and ensign of the gospel, gather to Yourself. *'shall be willing'* — The word is *willingnesses*; that is, a people of great willingness and devotion; or, as the original word is elsewhere used, shall be *free-will offerings* to You (Psalm 119:108). The abstract being put for the concrete, and the plural for the singular, notes how exceedingly forward and free they should be. The Lord, to signify that His people were most rebellious, says that they were *rebellion itself* (Ezek. 2:8). So then the meaning here is *most willing*.

"willing" — "It is power acted and executed with all sweetness, mildness, and gentleness. Here is 'leading, but no force; conduct, but no compulsion' — the will is determined, but not the least violence is done to it so as to infringe its liberty. How spontaneously does the person led follow Him that leads him! This and all other workings of the Spirit are admirably suited to the nature of reasonable and free agents. Efficacious grace does not at all destroy natural liberty. Where the Spirit does not find sinners willing, by His sweet method and power He makes them willing (by giving them life, then a new heart to believe into and to love God the Son — Ed.) *'Your people shall be willing in the day of Your power'* A *'day of power'*, yet *'willing.'* The Spirit's drawing is managed with all consistency to the freedom of the will (by making the sinner a new creature, He gives to him a new will which is then disposed to be willing to believe in the day of His power — Ed.) How traducing and slanderous are those who assert that the Spirit, in this or in any other act, works with compulsion, or in a way destructive to man's essential liberty! (Thomas Jacomb).

December 20   MORNING

The Lord Himself shall give you a sign: Behold! The virgin shall be with child and shall bring forth a son, and she shall call His name Immanuel — Isaiah 7:14.

IN THE WORST times we are to preach Christ and to look to Christ. In Jesus there is a remedy for the direst of diseases, a rescue from the darkest despairs. King Ahaz was in great danger, for he was attacked by two kings, each one stronger than he. But the Lord promised him deliverance and commanded him to choose a sign either in the heights or in the depths. Under a hypocritical pretense he refused to do this. So the Lord chose as His own token the appearance of the heavenly Deliverer who would be God, and yet be born of a woman. He was to eat butter and honey, like other children in that land of milk and honey, and yet He was to be the Mighty God, the Everlasting Father, the Prince of Peace (Isa. 9:6). We see here Godhead in union with manhood. We behold Jesus, a man *"of the substance of His mother,"* and yet, *"God over all, blessed forever."* Surely this God-appointed sign was both in the depth and in the height above — the Man of sorrows, and the Son of the Highest. This vision was the light of the age of Ahaz. It is God's comfort to troubled hearts in all the ages. It is God's sign of grace to us today. The sure hope of sinners and the great joy of saints is the incarnate Lord, Immanuel, God with us. May He be your joy this day. It is He who is the great Light of the people who dwell in the land of the shadow of death. If any of you are in that dreary land, may He be light and life to you! He alone can make the darkness of Zebulun and Naphtali to disappear in a blaze of glory. May He do this for you today.

EVENING

The Lord Himself shall give you a sign: Behold! The virgin shall be with child and shall bring forth a son, and she shall call His name Immanuel — Isaiah 7:14.

THE SIGN of coming light is Jesus. In Judah's trouble the Virgin-born was God's token that He would deliver, and that speedily. For in less time than it would take such a child to reach years when he could *"refuse the evil, and choose the good,"* both of Judah's royal adversaries would be gone. The sign was good for Ahaz, but it is better for us. Behold the incarnate Son of God born of Mary at Bethlehem! What can this intend for us but grace? If the Lord had meant to destroy us, He would not have assumed our nature. If He had not been moved with mighty love to members of a guilty race, He would never have taken on Himself their flesh and blood. It is a miracle of miracles that the Infinite should become an infant; that He who is pure spirit, and who fills all things, should be wrapped in swaddling clothes and cradled in a manger. He did not take on Him the nature of angels, although that would have been a tremendous condescension from Deity. But He descended lower still, for He took on Him the seed of Abraham: *"He was made in all things like His brothers."* And, *"He did not count it robbery to be equal with God."* It is not in the power of human lips to speak all the comfort which this one sign contains. If any troubled soul will look believingly at God in human flesh, he must take heart of hope. If he looks believingly, his comfort will come speedily. The birth of Jesus is the proof of the good will of God to men. What proof could be more sure? He would not have come to be born among men, to live among them, to suffer and to die for them, if He had been slow to pardon, or unwilling to save. Surely, the coming of Immanuel, God with us, among us makes it impossible to doubt the mercy of God toward all who will forsake trust in themselves, and place it in Jesus!

The Lord Himself shall give you a sign: Behold! The virgin shall be with child and shall bring forth a son, and she shall call His name Immanuel — Isaiah 7:14.

JESUS IS OUR STAR of hope as to the destruction of the enemy. The foes of God's people surely will be vanquished and destroyed because of Immanuel. Note well, how it is put twice over, like an exultant taunt: *"Gird yourselves, and you shall be broken in pieces. Gird yourselves, and you shall be broken in pieces. Take counsel together, and it shall come to nothing. Speak the word, and it shall not rise. For Immanuel, God is with us."* (Isa. 8:9,10). In Immanuel, even in our Lord Jesus Christ, dwells all the fulness of the Godhead bodily. And He has brought all that Godhead to bear on the overthrow of the foes of His people. Let the powers of darkness consult and plot as they may, they can never destroy the Lord's redeemed people. Lo! I see councils of evil spirits. They sit down in Pandemonium and conspire to ruin a soul redeemed by Jesus' blood. They use a cunning straight from Hell. They are eager to destroy the soul that rests in Jesus. But praise be to God, their devices are in vain, for the incarnate God is embodied wisdom. Look at them. They rise from the council table; they put on their harness; they did their arrows in malice and make their bows strong. Each foul spirit takes his sword that is fashioned to cut a soul to pieces. But their weapons shall all fail. We only have to fly to Jesus, who is God with us, and all weapons formed against us shall utterly fail. His name is Immanuel; He is the terror of all the demons of Hell. God with us means confusion to our foes. As the death of death, and Hell's destruction, our Immanuel cries to the legions of the pit, *"Gird yourselves, and you shall be broken in pieces!"* Then let us take courage and defy the legions of darkness. Let us charge them with this war cry, *"God is with us, Immanuel."* He has espoused our cause; He is God Himself; He is almighty to save.

EVENING

Kiss the Son, lest He be angry . . . . Blessed are all seeking refuge in Him —Psalm 2:12

"Kiss the Son" — "That is, embrace Him, depend on Him as your kinsman, as your sovereign, at your going, at your coming, at your reconciliation, in the truth of religion.... Kiss Him, and do not be ashamed of kissing Him, as with the spouse, *'I would kiss You, and not be despised'* (S of S 7:1). If you are despised for loving Christ Jesus, the more you are troubled by others for Christ, the more peace you have in Christ. *'Kiss the Son, lest He be angry'* — If He is angry, then kiss His rod, and He will be no longer angry. Love Him, lest He be angry. Fear Him when He is angry. The preservative is easy, and so is the restorative action: your kiss is all that is needed to suck spiritual milk out of His breast, to find mercy in His judgments, reparation in His ruins, feasts in His tents, joy even in His anger" (John Donne).

"To make peace with the Father, kiss the Son. *'Let me kiss Him'* was the prayer of the church (S of S 1:2). For our part, let us kiss Him. Indeed, the Son must first kiss us by His mercy before we can kiss Him by our devotion. Lord, grant in these mutual kisses and interchangeable embraces now that we may come to the wedding supper hereafter, when the choir of Heaven, even the voices of angels, shall sing the nuptial songs at the bridal party of the spouse of the Lamb" (Thomas Adams).

"Blessed are all seeking refuge in Him" — "Have we a share in this blessedness? Do we trust in Him? Our faith may be as slender as a spider's thread, but if it is real, then we are in our measure blessed. The more we trust, the more fully we shall know this blessedness. O Lord, increase our faith!" (C. H. Spurgeon).

December 22   MORNING   357

Jesus Christ, the same yesterday, and today, and forever — Hebrews 13:8.

NOTE OUR LORD'S personal name, Jesus Christ. Jesus stands first. That is our Lord's Hebrew name, *"Jesus"* — *"Joshua"* in the Hebrew. The word signifies a Savior, *"for He shall save His people from their sins."* It was given to Him in His cradle. While He was yet an infant hanging on His mother's breast, He was recognized as Savior. The fact that He, God with us, became incarnate was the sure pledge, guarantee, and commencement of human salvation. At the very thought of His birth the virgin sang, *"My spirit has rejoiced in God my Savior."* There is hope that man shall be lifted up to God, when God condescends to come down to man. Jesus in the manger deserves to be called the Savior, for when it can be said that *"the tabernacle of God is with men, and He dwells among them,"* there is hope that all good things will be given to the fallen race. He was called Jesus in His childhood, *"The Holy Child Jesus."* It was as Jesus that He went up to the temple and sat down with the doctors, hearing them, and asking them questions. Yes, and Jesus as a Teacher in the very first principles of His doctrine is a Savior, by which He emancipates the minds of men from superstition, setting them loose from the traditions of the fathers, scattering even with His infant hand the seeds of truth, the elements of a glorious liberty which emancipates the human mind from the iron bondage of false philosophy and priestcraft. In His active life He was Jesus, and was commonly so called both by His foes and by His friends. It is as Jesus the Savior that He heals the sick, that He raises the dead, that He delivers, as He did Peter when he was sinking, and as He did when the disciples were sinking on the Lake of Galilee. In all the teaching of His middle life, in those laborious three years of diligent service, both in His public ministry, and in His private prayer, He is still Jesus the Savior. For it is by His active obedience, as well as by His passive obedience, that we are saved by having His perfect obedience credited to all believers.

EVENING

And she shall give birth to a Son. And you shall call His name Jesus, for He shall save His people from their sins — Matthew 1:21.

BEARING THE NAME OF JESUS, our Lord rose from the dead. The evangelists delight in calling Him Jesus. In His appearance to Mary Magdalen in the garden, in His manifestation of Himself to the disciples when they met together, He is always Jesus with them as the risen One. Beloved, since we are justified by His resurrection, we may well regard Him as Savior under that aspect. Salvation is still more linked with a risen Christ, because we see Him by His resurrection destroying death, breaking down the prison of the grave, bearing away the gates of the grave. He is a Savior for us since He has vanquished the last enemy that shall be destroyed, that we having been saved from sin by His death should be saved from death through His resurrection. Jesus is the title under which He is called in glory, for *"Him has God exalted with His right hand to be a Prince and a Savior, to give repentance and forgiveness of sins"* (Acts 5:31). He is today *"the Savior of the body."* We adore Him as the only wise God, and our Savior: *"He is able to save to perfection those who come to God through Him, ever living to intercede for them"* (Heb. 7:25). As Jesus He will shortly come, and we are *"Looking for the blessed hope and appearance of the glory of our great God and Savior, Jesus Christ, who gave Himself on our behalf, that He might redeem us from all iniquity, and purify a special people for Himself"* (Titus 2:13,14). Our daily cry is, *"Even so, come, Lord Jesus."* And this is the name by which He is known in Heaven at this hour, where the angels serve Him as Jesus: *"I, Jesus, have sent My angel to testify to these things."* Jesus is coming under that name.

And you, Bethlehem Ephratah, being least among the thousands of Judah, out of you He shall come forth to Me to become the One ruling in Israel, and His goings forth have been from of old, from the days of eternity — Micah 5:2.

THE WORD BETHLEHEM has a double meaning: *"the house of bread,"* and, *"the house of war."* Ought not Jesus Christ to be born in *the house of bread?* He is the Bread of His people, on which they feed. As our fathers ate manna in the wilderness, so do we live on Jesus, our Manna below. Famished by the world, we cannot feed on its shadows. Its husks may gratify the winish taste of worldlings, for they are the pigs before whom we are not to cast our pearls. We need something more substantial. We find a blessed food in the bread of Heaven, made of the bruised body of our Lord Jesus, and baked in the furnace of His agonies. No food is like Jesus to the despondent soul or the strongest saint. The most inferior member of God's family goes to Jesus for bread. From where could our nourishment come except from Him? We have tried Sinai, but her rugged steeps grow no fruits, and her thorny heights yield no grain on which we may feed. We have gone to Tabor, where Christ was transfigured, and there we have not been able to eat His flesh and drink His blood (See John 6:31-34; 49-56).

And it is also called *"the house of war,"* because Christ is food to a righteous man, and war to the wicked men, according to His Word: *Do not think that I came to send peace on the earth; I did not come to bring peace, but a sword. I came to dissever a man from his father, and a daughter from her mother, and a daughter-in-law from her mother-in-law; and a man's enemies shall be those of his house"* (Matt. 10:35,36). Sinner, if you do not know Bethelehem as *the house of bread*, you shall know it as a *house of war*. If you never drink honey from the lips of Jesus, His mouth shall be to you the mouth of destruction and the cause of your calamity.

EVENING

But a mediator is not a mediator of one, but God is one — Galatians 3:20.

A MEDIATOR is not for God alone. A mediator deals with two persons: God and man. A mediator does not come because God desires any kind of mediator for His benefit. He is eternally one. Or, if you view Him as the Trinity, yet He is a Trinity in unity. God is one. Some persons deny the Trinity, calling themselves Unitarians. But All Trinitarians are Unitarians, in that they believe that God the Father, and God the Son, and God the Holy Spirit are one God. So no mediator is needed to reconcile the Divine persons. God is one; and so our God does not need the mediator for Himself.

A mediator! Blessed be God, there is a Mediator. But God does not need Him for His personal purposes. There is another person for whom the Mediator is required. In the very gift of Christ as Mediator, in the sending of Him in His divine and human nature, in Christ's life and death, God had an eye to another party. God was looking out for somebody else, and for that one provided a Mediator. God is looking out for a creature who needs one, and that creature is one of His elect among men. O my soul, may He not be thinking of you, and you, and you. There is a Mediator, and that One cannot be for God alone, for God is one. That Mediator is intended to meet the needs of those sinners He has loved from everlasting, whom He will call according to His original purpose, and through the Mediator, Christ Jesus, He will bring all His elect to justification, sanctification, and finally, to glorification.

December 24   MORNING   359

Glory to God in the highest, and peace on earth, good will toward men — Luke 2:14.

THE COMING OF CHRIST is a joy to all people. It is so, for this verse says, *"peace on earth,"* which is a wide and even unlimited expression. It adds, *"good will toward men"* — not just Jews, but toward *"men"* — all men. The word is the generic term for the entire race. There is no doubt that the coming of Christ brought joy to all sorts of people. And it brought a measure of gladness, if not pure spiritual joy, to all, even those who are not Christians. Christ does not bless them in the highest and truest sense, but the influence of His teaching has imparted benefits such as they are capable of receiving. For wherever the gospel is proclaimed, it is no small blessing to the whole population. There is no land beneath the sun where there is an open Bible and a preached gospel, where a tyrant long can hold his place. It does not matter who he is, whether pope or king; let the pulpit be used properly for preaching of Christ crucified, and the Bible opened to be read by all men, then no tyrant can long rule in peace. England owes her freedom to the Bible. But France will never possess liberty, lasting and well-established, until she comes to reverence the gospel, which for too long she has rejected. There is a joy to all mankind where Christ comes. Christianity makes men think. And to make men think is always dangerous to the power of despots. Christianity sets a man free from superstition. When one believes in Jesus, what does he care for Papal excommunications, or whether priests give or withhold their absolution? The man no longer cringes and bows down. He is not more willing to be led by the nose like a beast. Learning to think for himself, and truly to become a man, he disdains the childish fears by which the Devil and his slaves once held him in slavery.

EVENING

Glory to God in the highest, and peace on earth, good will toward men — Luke 2:14.

THE ANGELS BEGIN with thanksgiving, or with the praises of God. For Scripture everywhere reminds us that we were redeemed from death for this purpose, that we might testify with the tongue, as well as by the actions of life, our gratitude to God. Let us remember the primary reason why God reconciled us to Himself through His Only-begotten Son was that He might glorify His name by revealing the riches of His grace, and of His boundless mercy. Whenever our salvation is mentioned, we should understand that a signal has been given to excite us to thanksgiving and to the praises of God.
   "On earth peace" —What do the angels mean by the word *"peace"*? Not an outward peace cultivated by men with each other; but they say that the earth is at peace when men have been reconciled to God. Then it is that they enjoy an inward tranquillity in their own minds. We know that we are born *"children of wrath"* (Eph. 2:3), and are by nature enemies to God; that we must be distressed by fearful apprehensions so long as we feel that God is angry with us. We obtain peace with God when He begins to be gracious to us, by taking away our guilt, and *"not imputing to us our trespasses"* (2 Cor. 5:19). Then we, relying on His fatherly love address Him with full confidence, and begin to boldly praise Him for the salvation which He has promised to us. Though our life on earth is declared to be a continual *"warfare"* (Job 7:1), yet the angels expressly say that there is *"peace on earth."* This informs us that as long as we trust to the grace of Christ, no troubles will prevent us from enjoying composure and serenity of mind: *"Thou wilt keep him in perfect peace whose mind is stayed on Thee, because he trusts in Thee"* (Isa. 26:3).
   (Abridged from John Calvin's Commentary on Luke 2:14.)

MORNING

Glory to God in the highest, and peace on earth, good will toward men — Luke 2:14.

THE *"GREAT JOY"* which the angels proclaimed is expressly associated with the glory of God by these words, *"Glory to God in the highest,"* so we may be quite clear that it is a pure and holy joy. No other would an angel have proclaimed; and, indeed, no other joy is joy. The wine pressed from the grapes of Sodom may sparkle and foam, but it is bitterness in the end, and the dregs of it are death. Only that which comes from the clusters of Eshcol is the true wine of the Kingdom, making glad the heart of godly men. Holy joy is the joy of Heaven; and that, you can be sure, is the very cream of joy. The joy of sin is a fire fountain, having its source in the burning soil of Hell, maddening and consuming those who drink its fire water. Of such delights believers do not desire to drink. It would be worse than damned to be happy in sin, since it is the beginning of grace to be wretched in sin. And the consummation of grace is to be wholly escaped from sin, and to shudder at the very thought of it. It is Hell to live in sin and misery. It is a deeper Hell when men can fashion an unholy joy in sin. God save us from unholy peace and from unholy joy! The joy announced by the angel of the nativity is as pure as it is lasting, as holy as it is great. Let us then always believe concerning the Christian religion that it has its joy within itself, and holds its feasts within its own pure precincts, a feast whose foods all grow on holy ground. There are those who on this day pretend to exhibit joy in the remembrance of our Savior's birth, but will not in fact seek their pleasure in the Savior. They will need many additions to the feast before they can be satisfied. Joy in Immanuel would be a poor sort of mirth to them. Nowadays one might believe the Christmas festival to be a feast of Bacchus, or of Ceres. It certainly cannot be a commemoration of the birth of Jesus. Yet there is cause enough for us to have holy joy in the Lord Jesus Himself.

EVENING

For today a Savior, who is Christ the Lord, was born to you in the city of David — Luke 2:11.

TO US INDEED a child was born, if we can say that He is our *"Savior, who is Christ the Lord."* Let me ask you a few personal questions: Are your sins forgiven you for His name's sake? Is the head of the serpent bruised in your soul? Does the Seed of the woman reign in sanctifying power over your nature? Oh, then, you have the joy that is to all the people in the truest form of it. And the further you submit yourself to Christ the Lord, the more completely you know Him, and will be like Him; and the fuller will be your happiness. Surface joy is those who live where the Savior is preached. But the great deeps, the great fathomless deeps of solemn joy which glisten and sparkle with exultation and delight, are for such as know the Savior; who obey the Anointed One; who have communion with Him. That one is the most joyful who is the most Christ-like. It is sad that more Christians are not solely Christians. So many are Christians and something else; it would be better if they were altogether, solely Christians. If you could overhear comments being made about you, would it be like this? "Well, he may be somewhat Christian, but he is most at home when he is talking about science, farming, engineering, horses, mining, navigation, racing, or pleasure-taking."

"There is no imagination so pernicious as this: that persons not purified, not sanctified, not made holy in their life, should afterwards be taken into that state of blessedness which consists in the enjoyment of God. Such persons could never enjoy God, nor would God be a reward to them. Holiness indeed is perfected in Heaven. But the beginning of it is invariably confined to this world" (John Owen, *The Holy Spirit*, p 513, Goold's edition).

And the name of the city from that day shall be, THE LORD IS THERE
— Ezekiel 48:35.

THE TRUEST TEMPLE OF GOD is the body of our Lord. The nearest approach of Godhead to our humanity was when there was found lying in a manger, wrapped in swaddling bands, that Child was born to us, that Son who was given to us, whose name to us is *"Wonderful, Counselor, the Mighty God, the Everlasting Father, the Prince of Peace"* (Isa. 9:6). As for you, O Bethlehem, favored above all the towns of the earth, out of you He who is Immanuel came, He who is *"God with us."* Truly your name now is *"THE LORD IS THERE."* All along, through the thirty years and more of His holy labor, and in His shameful death, God was *"in Christ reconciling the world to Himself."* In the gloom of Gethsemane, among those somber olives, when Jesus bowed and prayed, great drops of bloody sweat fell on the ground; there He was *"seen by angels"* as the Son of God bearing human sin. Speak of Gethsemane, and we tell you God was there. Before Herod, and Pilate, and Caiaphas, and on the cross — The Lord was there. Though in a sense there was a hiding of God's face, when Jesus cried out, *"Why have You forsaken Me?"* — yet in the deepest sense Jehovah, God the Father, was there, bruising the great Sacrifice. The thick darkness made a veil for the Lord of glory. And behind it He who had made all things bowed His head and said, *"It is finished."* God was in Christ Jesus on the cross. And we, beholding Him, feel that we have seen the Father when we have seen Christ Jesus the God-Man. O Calvary, we say of you, *"THE LORD IS THERE."*

Oh, do not leave out those other indwellings of God the Holy Spirit, who still by His presence makes holy places even in this unholy world. Be reminded that God is the glory of the most glorious living thing that has been on the earth since our Lord was here. And what is that? It is His *"church of the firstborn, having been enrolled in Heaven"* (Hebrews 12:23).

EVENING

The name of the city from that day shall be, THE LORD IS THERE
— — Ezekiel 48:35

THERE IS a special place where God dwells among men, and that is in His church of the firstborn. All those chosen by eternal election, redeemed by precious blood, called out by the Holy Spirit, recreated into newness of life, are members of this church, and this as a whole is the dwellingplace of the covenant God. Because God is in this church, therefore the gates of Hell shall not prevail against her. *'THE LORD IS THERE"* might be said of the church in all ages. I have seen the crypts and underground chapels of the catacombs, and it made one feel that they were glorious places when we remembered that the Lord God was there, by His Spirit, with those suffering people of His. When holy hymn and psalm and solemn prayer went up from the bowels of the earth there, from men who were hunted to death by their foes, *"the Lord was there."* In those dreary excavations, unvisited by sunlight or wholesome air, God was there. He was not in the palaces of kings, nor in the cathedrals of priests, but He was there. In the past in our land, when a few people met together to hear the gospel and to worship, they had to meet in cottages, in caves, and in hollows in the woods, in order to be *"holiness to the Lord."* Yes, and when those crowds met beneath the oaks, or gathered together by the thousands on a hillside to listen to the pure word of grace (as they did to hear John Bunyan — Ed.), The Lord was there. When the Puritans conversed of the things of God, holding their conventicles for fear of their foes, God was there. On Scotland's bleak moors and mosses, when the covenanters gathered in the darkness and storm, for fear of Claverhouse and his dragoons, God was there. Those who wrote in those days tell us that they never knew such seasons of blessedness as they enjoyed among the hills, amid the heather, or by the brook — not even in days of peace — it was because *"THE LORD WAS THERE."*

But a mediator is not a mediator of one, but God is one — Galatians 3:20.

"A MEDIATOR is not a mediator of one" — but he studies the interests of both parties. Such a Mediator is our Lord Jesus Christ. Coming here on earth, did He come to save men? Yes. Did He come to glorify His Father's name? He came for two purposes, and the two blend together: to glorify God by saving men. He looked after the interests of men, pleading the causes of his soul. He looked after the interests of God, vindicating the honor of God, even to death. He was obedient, that He might magnify the law of God and make it honorable. Yes, and He was the Mediator that He may deliver us from the curse of the law. Beloved, our blessed Mediator is not a mediator for one. A mediator that did not understand more than one side, and was not concerned for anybody but one side, would be unworthy of the name. Our Mediator, the Lord Jesus Christ, has both natures. Is He God? Truly, He is very God of very God. Is He man? Assuredly, of the substance of His mother, as truly man as any man among us. Is He most God, or is He most man? This is a question not to be asked, and therefore not to be answered. He is God's Son. He Himself is God. But He is also the brother of you and me. What better Mediator could we have or desire than this Divine Man, who can lay His hands on both us and God — He who counted it not robbery to be equal with God, yet He who calls man His brother? This Mediator is not a mediator of one, since He wears both natures and espouses both causes. Oh, how dear to the heart of Christ is the glory of God! He lives, He dies, He rises again, to glorify the Father. Oh, how dear to Christ is the salvation of men! He lives, He dies, He rises again, He ever lives to plead for the salvation of sinners. He has the enthusiasm of Divinity, and He has the enthusiasm of humanity. God must be glorified; He will die to do it. Man must be saved; He will die to do it. Hallelujah!

EVENING

To Him who loved us and washed us from our sins in His blood and made us kings and priests to His God and Father — to Him be the glory and the might forever and ever. Amen. — Revelation 1:5,6.

HE LOVES US FREELY. That is clear, if you reflect that He did not love us because we had no sin. If that had been the case, He would not have needed to have washed us in His own blood. He did not love us because we were righteous, because we were obedient, or because we had not omitted any duty nor committed any offense. No! He saw us foul with sin, and yet He loved us. We are described in Scripture sometimes as crimson, and again as scarlet with sin. These are glaring colors, for sin is a glaring, startling thing that must be seen. God has seen it and abhorred it. But even though He saw it on us, He loved us: *"Christ loved the church and gave Himself for it."* What wondrous love it is, that Christ should love a thief! Yet He did, and took one to Paradise the day He died. What amazing condescension that Christ should love an outcast! Yet there was one who loved Him much because He had forgiven her much. How marvelous that Christ should love a swearer! Yet He loved Peter who swore and denied his Master with an oath. It was very strange that Christ should love a persecutor! Yet He loved Saul who persecuted His people, and transformed him into Paul the apostle. Is not this the greatest marvel of all to you, that He should love you and me — that He loved us, even though we have been unworthy of His love; full of sin, and loving it; persevering in sin; refusing to turn from it when bidden to repent; rejecting Christ and all His love; and year after year continuing to rebel against God? Yet He commended His love to us *"in that we yet being sinners, Christ died for us"* (Rom. 5:8). While we were dead in trespasses and sins He loved us out of free, rich, sovereign grace — not because we were lovely, but because He is loving — not because we were gracious, but because *"grace and truth came through Jesus Christ"* (John 1:17).

MORNING

In order that the righteous demand of the law should be fulfilled in us, who do not walk according to the flesh, but according to the Spirit — Romans 8:4.

THE RIGHTEOUSNESS of the law is fulfilled in the Christian by the grace of God. When we believe in Christ, we not only receive pardon, but we also receive new life. Some foolish ones these days teach that a believer only gets pardon at first, and long afterwards he gets a clean heart. On the authority of God's word, no man is pardoned unless and until he has a clean heart, a *"new heart."* God gives this clean, new heart, and then He gives the pardon. You must never divide the renewing of the Holy Spirit from the pardon of sin. They go together; one receiving the new birth is made a new creature in Christ Jesus, and in proper order then receives pardon — it is not a matter of time, but a matter of procession. The work of regeneration, and the act of faith which brings justification to the penitent sinner are simultaneous — but regeneration must needs to come first, then faith, then justification, then pardon, etc. in the proper order of things. There can be no faith except there first be life.

At the present moment the righteousness of the law is fulfilled in the new-born, grace-renewed mind. There is a present obedience actually rendered. We have faults, imperfections and sins still. But we also now strive to be holy, those of you who love Christ. You long to obey Him; yes, and you do obey Him. You have laid aside the works of the flesh. If you are believers, you cannot do those things you used to do. Now you are striving to do things which once would have been irksome to you. You now are honest, true, righteous; you love the Lord and count Him to be your God. You are seeking to do to others as you would have them do to you. You love God, and you love your brother and your neighbor. And although not perfectly, yet in ever increasing measure, by the exercise of the grace of God in you, the law is fulfilled in you in a way that it never could have been fulfilled as a mere law.

EVENING

A Savior was born to you today, who is Christ the Lord — Luke 2:11.

THE WORD LORD used in this verse is tantamount to Jehovah. We cannot doubt that, because it is the same word used twice in the ninth verse. And in the ninth verse none can question that it means Jehovah — *"And, lo, the angel of the Lord came upon them, and the glory of the Lord shone around them."* And if this is not enough, read the 23rd verse, *"As it is written in the law of the Lord, every male that opens the womb shall be called holy to the Lord."* Now the word Lord here assuredly refers to Jehovah, the one God, and so it must do here. Our Savior is Christ, God, and Jehovah. No testimony to His divinity could be plainer; it is indisputable. And what joy there is in this! Suppose an angel had been our Savior; as a creature he would not have been able to bear the load of your sin and mine. If anything less than God had been set up as the ground of our salvation, it would have been found too frail a foundation. But if He who undertakes to save is none other than the Infinite and Almighty God, then the load of our guilt can be carried on such shoulders. The stupendous labor of our salvation can be achieved by such a One, and that with ease: For *"all things are possible with God; He is able to save to the uttermost those that come to God by Him"*(Luke 18:27; Heb. 7:25). You sons of men perceive here the subject of your joy. The God who made you (Col. 1:16), and against whom you have offended, has come down from Heaven and has taken on Himself your nature that He might save you. He has come in the fulness of His glory and the infinity of His mercy that He might redeem you. Will not your hearts be thankful for this? Does such matchless love as this awaken no gratitude in your breast? Were it not for this Savior God, your life here would have been wretchedness, and your life in the future would have been endless woe and pain in Hell.

And next to him was Amasiah the son of Zichri, who willingly offered himself to the Lord — 2 Chronicles 17:16.

AMASIAH is distinguished from the other mighty men of king Jehoshaphat by the fact that he made it his life work to serve the Lord. He *"willingly offered himself to the Lord,"* and he was accepted. He became a lifelong servant of Jehovah, the God of Israel. It should not need much talk to make men feel this is reasonable service. To serve your Maker, who created you for His glory — Surely it is a natural thing for one with spiritual nature to willingly serve the Lord. So when you are asked to serve your Redeemer, who shed His blood that you might be free from sin and might *"yield your members servants to holiness,"* you should willingly do so. Surely, it is a right thing for you to offer yourself to Him who yielded Himself to death for you! This is an argument Amasiah did not have, yet he found reason enough to willingly serve the Lord. How much stronger is His claim on you! And if this plea needs to be strengthened further, think that you are called to serve Him with whom you hope to dwell forever in Heaven. It ought to be an instinct of every reasonable soul to set about such service instantly. Ordinary gratitude should cause every Christian to say to His Lord, "Whom else should I serve? I owe to You my very being, my new life, and all I possess. In You I live; by You I am daily fed. Why should I not serve You?"

Furthermore, this is honorable service. If you like a service that will reflect some kind of approval of you, then do this: serve God willingly, seek His honor and glory. And if this is not done in mere pretense, but in reality, then what a grand life you will lead as a dedicated, approved servant of your God and Savior, Jesus Christ!

EVENING

In order that the righteous demand of the Law should be fulfilled in us, who do not walk according to the flesh but according to the Spirit — Romans 8:4.

THIS RIGHTEOUSNESS is fulfilled through the Lord Jesus Christ. We fulfill the law, but not in any strength which the law gives to us, nor in any power of our own. The obedience to the law is fulfilled in us out of gratitude to Christ for what He has done to us. We flee away from sin out of hatred of the things that nailed Christ to the cross and put Him to death. What the law could not do, the dying Christ has done. His sacrifice makes us hate evil. Naming the name of Christ, we *"depart from iniquity,"* for we realize that it was not Roman soldiers and rabble Jews alone who nailed Him to the tree, but it was our sins that did it. Those 'little' sins of ours were like thorns in His blessed brow. Those sins were like nails in His hands and feet, for as John Flavel once said, "There are no little sins, because there is no little God to sin against."

You who have long toiled in the vain endeavor to give up your sins, come and look at the cross today. See there what your sins have done, and learn to hate them with a perfect hatred. See how sin stooped to the meanness of betrayal, how sin killed the Prince of Life, who had gone among men healing and helping them, doing nothing but good. Your instinct rises against oppressors; will you then seek to throw off the chains of the sin which worked out so cruel a deed that day at Calvary? Sin is your enemy. To you who believe in Christ, remember that on the cross you were crucified; for when Christ died, you died. Say to yourself that if sin that day crucified you, then today you will crucify sin. Paul says, *"I am crucified with Christ; nevertheless I live; yet not I, but Christ lives in me. And the life which I now live in the flesh I live by the faith of the Son of God who loved me and gave Himself for me"* (Gal. 2:20). So, because God sent His Son, and condemned sin in the flesh, we condemn it, too. His death becomes to us the gate of life.

MORNING

Who led them by the right hand of Moses with His glorious arm, dividing the water before them, to make Himself an everlasting name — Isaiah 63:12.

MAN'S CHIEF END is to glorify God. God's greatest and highest object is to make Himself a glorious and everlasting name. Since God is God, it must be so. For He is full of kindness to His creatures, He cannot more fully bless them than by making Himself known to them. Everything that is good, true, holy, excellent, loving is in God. He is not only the giver of *"every good and perfect gift,"* but He is Himself the sum and substance of all blessing. It is for the highest good of all the creatures that they know their God. A frequent exhortation of the earthly philosophers is for man to know himself. Self-knowledge, they say, is the highest form of knowledge. This is not so. A far wiser precept is, "Man, know your God." For the knowledge of God as far excels other knowledge as the heavens are higher than the earth. It is life eternal to know Him as the only true God, and Jesus God whom He has sent for salvation to mankind. Then know your God, for here your hope, your comfort, your holiness, your Heaven will be found.

God may well desire to make a name to Himself; that is, to make Himself known; because He is worthy to be known. There is no name so well worthy of publication. There is no character like His. There is none that can compare to Him. Even if the heathen gods had truly been gods, they would not hold a candle to the glorious, true God. He ought to be known. Therefore, it is a worthy motive in His actions that He should make Himself a great name. This knowledge of God is the Heaven of the perfect. There is no higher joy in the land of light than to know God. The blaze of their glory is the presence of God. The height of their Heaven is that God is near them, and that they are near to Him.

EVENING

The unsearchable riches of Christ — Ephesians 3:8.

SOULS MAY BE RICH in grace and yet not know it, nor perceive it. The child is heir to a crown, but does not know it. Moses' face shone, and others saw it, but he did not. So many a precious soul is rich in grace, and others see it and know it, and bless God for it, and yet the poor soul does not see it. Sometimes this arises from the soul's strong desires of the unsearchable spiritual riches of Christ. The strength of the soul's desires after spiritual riches often takes away the very sense of growing spiritually rich. Man covetous men's desires are so strongly carried after earthly riches that they cannot see it, or even believe it, when they grow rich. It is just so with many a precious Christian: his desires after spiritual riches are so strong that they take away the very sense of his growing rich in spirituals. Many Christians have much worth within them, but they do not see it. Sometimes this arises from men neglecting to cast up their accounts. Many men thrive and grow rich, and yet neglecting their accounts they cannot tell if they go forward or backward. It is so with many precious souls, and this arises sometimes from the soul's too frequent casting up of accounts. If a man casts up his accounts weekly, or monthly, he may not be able to discern that he is growing rich; yet he may be growing rich. Again, this sometimes arises from the soul's mistakes in casting up its accounts, sometimes mistakes and puts down ten for a hundred, and a hundred for a thousand. As hypocrites put down their pence for pounds, prizing themselves above the market, so sincere souls often put down their pounds as pence, their thousands for hundreds, and prize themselves below the true market. Whether because of error of judgment, or more likely, because of humility, Christians often fail to realize how rich they are in the unsearchable riches of Christ (Thomas Brooks).

366   MORNING   December 31

To Him who loved us and washed us from our sins in His blood, and made us kings and priests to His God and Father — to Him be the glory and the might forever and ever. Amen. — Revelation 1:5,6.

THE APOSTLE JOHN was the *"beloved"* disciple, the choicest spirit of the Twelve, the one nearest to the heart of Christ. Not only was He that disciple whom Jesus loved, but he was full of love to his Lord in return, leaning his head on Jesus' bosom at the last supper. All his soul seemed to be aflame with affection toward Christ. *"We love Him, because He first loved us"* are words which come with great power from such a heart, because they were so wonderfully true in John's own experience. Here, when he comes to sing a psalm of praise to his Lord, he does not mention his love to his Master. He does not dwell on that, for his confidence lies deeper than anything in himself, even in the love of the Son of God to him. If you would be like John, then *"keep yourselves in the love of God."* Meditate much on your Master, and on His love. Dwell with Christ and drink daily the sweetness of His wondrous love to you. Live on that, and often let your heart lift up a song of praise because of it. Then shall the blessing of Benjamin be yours: *"The beloved of the Lord shall dwell in safety by Him; and the Lord will cover him all the day long, and He will dwell between his shoulders."*

This verse is fitting to be the song of Heaven. It is indeed the epitome of all those choral symphonies with which the redeemed spirits circle the throne of our great Lord and King. In vision John caught glimpses of the glory land, and he had heard the great multitude which no man can number raise their hallelujahs as they cast their crowns before Him sitting on the throne. As the refrain of a song hums itself over and over again even after the singer has ceased, so when he began to write the Book of Revelation, John seems to have remembered the chorus of those who *"came out of great tribulation and have washed their robes and made them white in the blood of the Lamb."* (Rev. 7:14).

EVENING

Praise Jehovah from the heavens; praise Him in the heights — Psalm 148:1.

WHOEVER YOU MAY BE, you are entreated, invited, commanded by Him to magnify Jehovah. Assuredly He has made you, and if for nothing else, you are bound on the ground of creatureship to adore your Maker. This exhortation can never be out of place, speak it where you may, speak it when you may. *"Praise the Lord from the heavens"* — Since you angels, cherubs and seraphs are nearest the High and Lofty One, praise Jehovah. Do this, then pass it on to other realms. Do not keep your worship to yourselves, but let it fall like a golden shower from the heavens on men beneath. *"Praise Him in the heights"* — This is not a vain repetition of attractive poetry. God is not only to be praised from the heights, but in them. The adoration is to be perfected in the heavens from which it takes its rise. No place is too high for the praises of the Most High. On the summit of creation the glory of the Lord is to be revealed, even as the tops of the highest Alps are tipped with the golden light of the same sun which gladdens the valleys. Heavens and heights become the higher and the more heavenly as they are made to resound with the praises of Jehovah. See how the Psalmist trumpets out this word *"PRAISE."* It sounds forth nine times in the first five verses of this song. Like repeating cannon, exultant exhortations are sounded forth in tremendous force: *Praise! Praise! Praise!* The drum of the great King beats around the world with this one note: *Praise! Praise! Praise!* All this praise is distinctly and personally for Jehovah. Give not praise to His servants nor His works, but to Jehovah personally. Is He not worthy of all possible praise? Pour it forth before Him in full volume, and pour it only there! *"Let them praise the name of Jehovah, for His name alone is exalted; His glory is above the earth and the heavens"* (Psalm 148:13).

9 781878 442505

www.ingramcontent.com/pod-product-compliance
Lightning Source LLC
Chambersburg PA
CBHW070903300426
44113CB00008B/924